CASES AND MATERIALS ON THE LAW OF TORTS

FOURTH EDITION

by
ROBERT M. SOLOMON

Professor of Law,
University of Western Ontario

BRUCE P. FELDTHUSEN

Professor of Law,
University of Western Ontario

and
R.W. KOSTAL

Associate Professor of Law,
University of Western Ontario

CARSWELL
Thomson Professional Publishing

Canadian Cataloguing in Publication Data

Solomon, Robert M., 1946-
Cases and materials on the law of torts

4th ed.
Includes bibliographical references.
ISBN 0-459-56079-4 (bound) ISBN 0-459-56080-8 (pbk.)

1. Torts — Canada — Cases. I. Feldthusen, Bruce, 1949-
II. Kostal, R. W. (Rande W.).   III. Title.

KE1232.A7S64 1996	346.7103	C96-931690-9
KF1249.S64 1996		
(bound)		
KE1232.A7S64 1996a	346.7103	C96-931675-S
KF1249.S64 1996a		
(pbk.)		

Typesetting: Video Text Inc., Barrie, Ontario, Canada

CARSWELL
Thomson Professional Publishing

One Corporate Plaza, 2075 Kennedy Road, Scarborough, Ontario M1T 3V4
Customer Service:
Toronto 1-416-609-3800
Elsewhere in Canada/U.S. 1-800-387-5164
Fax 1-416-298-5094

This book is dedicated to

the memory of

MYER RALPH SOLOMON

Preface

This book was written with three goals in mind. First, we wanted to produce a teaching text that would assist students in understanding the substantive principles of Canadian tort law. Second, through the use of notes, questions and review problems, we have attempted to ensure that students have opportunities to develop their analytical and problem solving skills. These materials are also intended to ensure that students play an active role in the learning process. Third, the book is designed to introduce readers to some of the challenging intellectual issues posed by Canadian tort law, including the forces that have shaped the scope of current tort law, and the relationships between tort law and other branches of law.

This book is intended primarily for use in introductory torts courses, but it should serve equally well in advanced courses. With the exception of defamation, which we could not deal with adequately without significantly expanding the book, we have attempted to provide a detailed discussion of every major area of Canadian tort law. The book was designed to accommodate a wide range of academic interests, teaching styles and philosophies. Each chapter was written to stand alone in order to provide flexibility in the use of the materials. Wherever possible, we used cases and statutory materials from every Canadian common law jurisdiction.

The fourth edition features many new or expanded editorial passages. In some cases, these passages provide summaries of complex areas of tort law that would be difficult or time consuming to teach by the case method. We also used these passages to set out doctrinal, historical or empirical information that we believed was helpful in understanding contemporary developments in Canadian tort law.

Each case or set of cases is followed by notes and questions that will assist the students in class preparation. We have covered a broad range of issues in the notes and questions, realizing full well that it is not possible to address all of these issues in an introductory course. We have included review problems to give students an opportunity to apply the principles to a fact situation. The problems serve to consolidate the students' understanding of the law and to assist in sharpening their analytical and organizational skills.

The fourth edition was prepared by Professors Solomon and Kostal. Although Professor Feldthusen did not participate in the preparation of the fourth edition, his name remains associated with it in recognition of his earlier work from the inception of the text through three editions.

A number of people have assisted in preparing this edition. Professor Brown has provided advice on insurance, no-fault liability and the New Zealand accident compensation system. Professor Feldthusen has kept us abreast of developments in several fields including damages and economic loss. A number of students have assisted us in various research tasks. In particular, we would like to thank Mr. J. Payne, Ms. D. Dudley, Ms. S. Ross, and especially Ms. K. Ewald. We are also indebted to the Ontario Law Foundation and the Faculty of Law for providing research and secretarial support.

Finally, we would like to acknowledge our gratitude to the staff at Thomson Publishing Canada who have made the first four editions of this casebook possible. In particular, we would like to thank Ms. J. Gulej and Mr. J. Morris who have patiently supervised the preparation of this edition.

Table of Contents

PREFACE v

TABLE OF CASES xxv

CHAPTER 1   AN INTRODUCTION TO THE LAW OF TORTS

    1. **The Concept of Torts**................................... **1**
    2. **Torts Distinguished from Other Areas of Law** **2**
        Notes and Questions.................................. 3
        Review Problem....................................... 3
    3. **A Brief History of Tort Law** **4**
        Notes and Questions.................................. 7
    4. **Trespass and Case: A Brief Review of the Case Law** **7**
        Scott v. Shepherd 7
        Notes and Questions.................................. 11
        Leame v. Bray....................................... 11
        Williams v. Holland 12
        Notes and Questions.................................. 13
        Holmes v. Mather 13
        Notes and Questions.................................. 14
        Cook v. Lewis 14
        Notes and Questions.................................. 16
    5. **The Bases for Imposing Liability in Tort**.............. **16**
    6. **The Functions of Tort Law** **18**
        Notes and Questions.................................. 20

CHAPTER 2   THE BASIC CONCEPTS OF REMEDIES IN
                 INTENTIONAL TORTS

    1. **Introduction** **23**
        (a) Judicial and Extrajudicial Remedies................ 23
            Notes and Questions 24
    2. **Classifications of Damages**........................... **24**
        Notes and Questions.................................. 25
    3. **Nominal Damages**................................... **25**
        The Mediana 26
        Notes and Questions.................................. 27
    4. **Compensatory Damages** **27**
        Review Problem....................................... 28
    5. **Punitive Damages** **28**
        Vorvis v. Insurance Corp. of British Columbia 28
        Notes and Questions.................................. 32
        B. (P.) v. B. (W.) 33
        Notes and Questions.................................. 35
        Review Problem....................................... 36

CHAPTER 3   INTENTIONAL INTERFERENCE WITH THE PERSON
    1. **Introduction** **39**
    2. **Basic Principles of Liability** **39**
       (a) Volition 39
          Smith v. Stone 40
          Notes and Questions 40
       (b) Intent 40
          (i) Imputed (Constructive) Intent 41
          (ii) Transferred Intent 41
          Notes and Questions........................... 41
    3. **Related Issues: Motive, Mistake and Accident** **42**
       (a) Motive 42
          Notes and Questions 42
          (i) Duress 42
             Gilbert v. Stone 42
             Notes and Questions........................... 43
          (ii) Provocation.................................. 43
             Miska v. Sivec 43
             Notes and Questions........................... 45
       (b) Mistake 45
          Hodgkinson v. Martin........................... 45
          Ranson v. Kitner 46
          Notes and Questions 47
       (c) Accident 47
          Review Problems 47
       (d) A Note on the Liability of Children and the Mentally
          Ill 47
          Notes and Questions 48
    4. **Battery** **48**
       Bettel v. Yim....................................... 48
       Notes and Questions 51
    5. **Assault** **53**
       Notes and Questions 53
       Holcombe v. Whitaker.............................. 53
       Police v. Greaves................................... 54
       Notes and Questions 56
       Review Problems..................................... 56
    6. **False Imprisonment** **57**
       Bird v. Jones 57
       Notes and Questions 59
       Campbell v. S.S. Kresge Co. 59
       Notes and Questions 61
       Herd v. Weardale Steel, Coal and Coke Co. 62
       Notes and Questions 64
    7. **Malicious Prosecution** **64**
       Nelles v. Ontario 64
       Notes and Questions 69
       (a) A Note on the Tort of Abuse of Process 70

Review Problem 70
8. **Intentional Infliction of Nervous Shock** **70**
   Wilkinson v. Downton 70
   Notes and Questions 72
   Radovskis v. Tomm 73
   Samms v. Eccles 73
   Notes and Questions 76
   (a) A Note on the Innominate Intentional Torts 76
       Notes and Questions 77
       Review Problems 77
9. **Protection of Privacy** **78**
   (a) Introduction 78
       Notes and Questions 78
   (b) Is There a Common Law Tort Action for the
       Invasion of Privacy? 79
       Motherwell v. Motherwell 79
       Notes and Questions 81
   (c) A Note on the Common Law Action for Breach of
       Confidence 82
   (d) The Statutory Protection of Privacy 83
       The Privacy Act (Man.) 84
       Notes and Questions 84
10. **The Common Law Tort of Discrimination** **84**
    *Bhadauria v. Bd. of Gov. of Seneca College of Applied
    Arts and Technology* 85
    *The Bd. of Gov. of the Seneca College of Applied Arts
    and Technology v. Bhadauria* 87
    Notes and Questions 87

CHAPTER 4   INTENTIONAL INTERFERENCE WITH CHATTELS
1. **Introduction** **89**
2. **The Development of the Actions** **89**
   Notes and Questions 91
3. **Trespass to Chattels** **91**
   Fouldes v. Willoughby 91
   Notes and Questions 94
4. **Conversion** **94**
   MacKenzie v. Scotia Lumber Co. 94
   Notes and Questions 96
   Review Problems 98
   Aitken v. Gardiner 98
   Notes and Questions 100
5. **Detinue** **101**
   *Gen. & Finance Facilities Ltd. v. Cooks Cars (Romford)
   Ltd.* 101
   Aitken v. Gardiner 104
   Notes and Questions 105
6. **Replevin** **105**

Notes and Questions 106
Review Problems 106

CHAPTER 5   INTENTIONAL INTERFERENCE WITH REAL
PROPERTY
1. **Trespass to Land** **107**
Entick v. Carrington 107
Turner v. Thorne 108
Notes and Questions 109
Review Problems 110
Harrison v. Carswell 111
Notes and Questions 116
2. **Trespass and Nuisance** **118**
Kerr v. Revelstoke Bldg. Materials Ltd. 118
Notes and Questions 120
3. **Trespass to Airspace and Subsoil** **121**
(a) Trespass to Airspace 121
Bernstein v. Skyviews & Gen. 122
Notes and Questions 124
(b) A Note on Trespass to Subsoil 124
Notes and Questions 125
Review Problems 125

CHAPTER 6   THE DEFENCE OF CONSENT
1. **An Introduction to the Defences** **127**
2. **General Principles of Consent** **127**
(a) Introduction 127
(b) Implied Consent 128
Wright v. McLean 128
Notes and Questions 129
(c) Exceeding Consent 130
Agar v. Canning 130
Notes and Questions 131
(d) Competency to Consent 132
3. **Factors Which Vitiate Consent: Duress, Fraud, Mistake**
and Public Policy **132**
(a) Introduction 132
(b) Duress 133
Latter v. Braddell 133
Notes and Questions 136
(c) Fraud (Deceit) 136
Notes and Questions 137
(d) Mistake 138
Notes and Questions 138
(e) Public Policy 138
Notes and Questions 139
4. **Consent to Criminal or Immoral Acts** **140**
Notes and Questions 140
Review Problems 141

5. **Consent to Treatment and Counselling** **141**
   (a) General Principles 141
       Notes and Questions 142
   (b) Exceptions to the General Principles of Consent 143
       Marshall v. Curry 143
       Malette v. Shulman 145
       Notes and Questions 147
   (c) The Burden of Proof and Consent Forms 148
       Notes and Questions 148
   (d) Competency to Consent 149
       (i) Minors 149
           C. v. Wren 149
           Notes and Questions........................ 151
           Review Problem 152
       (ii) Adults................................. 152
           Notes and Questions........................ 152
   (e) Substitute Consent.............................. 153
       Notes and Questions 153
   (f) Informed Consent: Battery or Negligence?......... 154
       Review Problem 155

CHAPTER 7   DEFENCES RELATED TO THE PROTECTION OF
            PERSON AND PROPERTY
   1. **Self-Defence** **157**
      Wackett v. Calder 157
      Notes and Questions................................ 159
   2. **Defence of Third Parties** **160**
      Gambriell v. Caparelli........................... 160
      Notes and Questions 162
   3. **Discipline**... **163**
      R. v. Dupperon 163
      Notes and Questions............................... 165
   4. **Defence of Real Property** **166**
      MacDonald v. Hees 166
      Notes and Questions............................... 168
      Bird v. Holbrook................................ 169
      Notes and Questions 169
   5. **The Defence and Recapture of Chattels**............... **170**
      Notes and Questions............................... 170
      Review Problem.................................... 171
   6. **Public and Private Necessity** **171**
      (a) Public Necessity 171
          Surocco v. Geary............................ 171
          Notes and Questions 172
      (b) Private Necessity 174
          Vincent v. Lake Erie Tpt. Co. 174
          Notes and Questions 177
   7. **Apportionment of Fault in Intentional Torts** **178**

Notes and Questions 178
Review Problem 179

CHAPTER 8   THE DEFENCE OF LEGAL AUTHORITY
1. **Introduction** **181**
Notes and Questions 181
(a) A Note on the Canadian Charter of Rights and
Freedoms 182
2. **General Powers of Arrest Without a Warrant and
Privilege** **183**
(a) Introduction 183
(b) The Criminal Code's Authorizing Sections — 494
and 495 183
Notes and Questions 184
(c) The Criminal Code's Privileging Section — 25 184
(d) A Peace Officer's Authority and Privilege to Arrest
Without a Warrant 184
R. v. Biron 184
Notes and Questions 190
(e) A Private Citizen's Authority and Privilege to Arrest
Without a Warrant 190
Notes and Questions 191
3. **Rights and Obligations in the Arrest Process** 191
(a) Reasons for the Arrest 191
Koechlin v. Waugh and Hamilton 191
Notes and Questions 194
(b) The Use of Reasonable Force 195
Notes and Questions 196
4. **The Common Law Right to Search Pursuant to a
Lawful Arrest** **197**
Cloutier v. Langlois 197
Notes and Questions 201
5. **A Peace Officer's Common Law Right of Forced
Entry** **203**
Eccles v. Bourque 203
(a) Reasonable and Probable Grounds 205
(b) Announcement 206
Notes and Questions 207
Review Problems 208

CHAPTER 9   INTRODUCTION TO THE LAW OF NEGLIGENCE
1. **The Concept of Negligence** **209**
2. **The Historical Development of Negligence** **209**
Notes and Questions 211
3. **The Elements of a Negligence Action** **212**
(a) Introduction 212
(i) Duty of Care 212
(ii) The Standard of Care and Its Breach 212
(iii) Causation 213

(iv) Remoteness of Damages..................... 213
 (v) Actual Loss................................ 213
(vi) Prejudicial Conduct 212
     Notes and Questions...................... 212
(b) Negligence: A Case Illustration 214
Dunsmore v. Deshield 214
Notes and Questions 216

CHAPTER 10 THE DUTY OF CARE
1. **An Introduction to the Concept of Duty** **219**
(a) The Classical Approach...................... 219
(b) The General Duty of Care Test 220
M'Alister (or Donoghue) v. Stevenson 220
Notes and Questions 224
(c) The Development of the Modern Law of Duty 225
Notes and Questions 226
(d) *Anns* and the Supreme Court of Canada 227
2. **Does Negligence Law Apply? — An Illustration** **228**
Demarco v. Ungaro 228
Notes and Questions................................ 232
3. **Did the Defendant's Conduct Give Rise to a Duty of
   Care? — The Foreseeable Risk of Injury Test** **233**
Moule v. N.B. Elec. Power Comm. 233
Amos v. N.B. Elec. Power Comm...................... 235
Notes and Questions................................ 237
4. **Was the Duty of Care Owed to the Plaintiff? — The
   Foreseeable Plaintiff Test** **238**
Palsgraf v. Long Island Ry. Co......................... 238
Notes and Questions................................ 242
Haley v. London Electricity Bd....................... 243
Notes and Questions................................ 245

CHAPTER 11 SPECIAL CATEGORIES OF NEGLIGENCE: DUTIES OF
           AFFIRMATIVE ACTION
1. **Introduction** **247**
Notes and Questions................................ 247
2. **The Duty to Rescue** **248**
Osterlind v. Hill...................................... 248
Notes and Questions................................ 249
Matthews v. MacLaren; Horsley v. MacLaren 250
Notes and Questions................................ 255
Review Problems.................................... 256
3. **The Duty to Control the Conduct of Others**............ **257**
(a) Liability for the Intoxicated 257
Crocker v. Sundance Northwest Resorts Ltd. 257
Notes and Questions 262
(b) Other Duty to Control Situations 263
Notes and Questions 264
(c) The Duty to Prevent Crime and Protect Others 265

Jane Doe v. Metropolitan Toronto (Municipality) Commissioners of Police 265

Notes and Questions 269

Review Problems 270

4. The Duty to Perform Gratuitous Undertakings **271**

Notes and Questions 272

Smith v. Rae 272

Zelenko v. Gimbel Bros., Inc. 273

Soulsby v. Toronto 273

Notes and Questions 275

Review Problems 276

CHAPTER 12 SPECIAL DUTIES OF CARE

1. Introduction **277**

2. The Duty of Care Owed to Rescuers **277**

Horsley v. MacLaren 277

Notes and Questions 283

Review Problems 285

3. Duties Owed to the Unborn **285**

Notes and Questions 286

4. Nervous Shock **288**

Rhodes v. Canadian National Railway Co. 288

Notes and Questions 294

Review Problem 296

5. A Doctor's Duty to Inform **296**

Haughian v. Paine 297

Notes and Questions 299

Review Problem 300

6. A Manufacturer's and Supplier's Duty to Warn **301**

Hollis v. Dow Corning Corp. 301

Notes and Questions 307

Review Problems 310

CHAPTER 13 THE STANDARD OF CARE

1. Introduction **313**

2. The Common Law Standard of Care: The Reasonable Person Test **314**

Arland v. Taylor 314

Notes and Questions 315

3. Factors Considered in Determining Breach of the Standard of Care **316**

(a) Probability and Severity of the Harm 316

U.S. v. Carroll Towing Co. 316

Notes and Questions 317

Bolton v. Stone 317

Miller v. Jackson 319

Paris v. Stepney Borough Council 322

Notes and Questions 325

(b) Cost of Risk Avoidance 325

Vaughn v. Halifax-Dartmouth Bridge Comm. 325
Law Estate v. Simice............................. 326
Notes and Questions 326
(c) Social Utility 327
Watt v. Hertfordshire County Council 327
Notes and Questions 328
    4. An Economic Analysis of the Standard of Care **329**
Notes and Questions 330
    5. Special Standards of Care **331**
(a) The Standard of Care Expected of the Disabled 331
Buckley and T.T.C. v. Smith Tpt. Ltd. 331
Notes and Questions 333
(b) The Standard of Care Expected of Children 334
Joyal v. Barsby................................. 334
Notes and Questions 337
(c) The Standard of Care Expected of Professionals 337
White v. Turner 337
Notes and Questions 340
  6. Degrees of Negligence **342**
Notes and Questions.............................. 342
  7. Custom... **342**
ter Neuzen v. Korn 342
Notes and Questions.............................. 346
Review Problems................................. 346

CHAPTER 14 CAUSATION
  1. Introduction **349**
  2. Determining the Cause-in-Fact...................... **349**
(a) The But-For Test 349
Cork v. Kirby MacLean Ltd. 349
Kauffman v. Toronto Transit Comm. 351
Notes and Questions 352
(b) Causation and Correlation 353
Snell v. Farrell 353
Notes and Questions 358
  3. Independent Tortfeasors and Multiple Causes **359**
Lambton v. Mellish.............................. 359
Arneil v. Paterson 361
Nowlan v. Brunswick Const. Ltée. 362
Notes and Questions.............................. 362
Review Problems................................. 363
  4. Joint Tortfeasors **363**
Cook v. Lewis 364
Notes and Questions 365
  5. Problems in Assessing the Plaintiff's Loss **366**
(a) Devaluing the Plaintiff's Loss 366
Dillon v. Twin State Gas and Elec. Co. 366
Notes and Questions 368

    (b) Successive Injuries Prior to Trial 368
        Penner v. Mitchell 368
        Notes and Questions 371
        Review Problems 372

CHAPTER 15 REMOTENESS OF DAMAGES
    1. **Introduction** **373**
    2. **Directness Versus Foreseeability** **374**
        (a) The Directness Test 374
        Notes and Questions 374
        (b) The Foreseeability Test 374
        The Wagon Mound (No. 1); Overseas Tankship (U.K.)
        Ltd. v. Morts Dock & Engineering Co. 374
        Notes and Questions 377
        Review Problems 377
    3. **Modifications to the Foreseeability Test** **378**
        (a) The Kind of Injury 378
        Hughes v. Lord Advocate 378
        Notes and Questions 379
        (b) The Thin-Skulled Plaintiff Rule 380
        Smith v. Leech Brain & Co. 380
        Marconato v. Franklin 382
        Notes and Questions 384
        (c) The Possibility of Injury 384
        The Wagon Mound (No. 2); Overseas Tankship (U.K.)
        Ltd. v. Miller Steamship Co. Pty. 384
        Notes and Questions 387
        Assiniboine South School Division, No. 3 v. Greater
        Winnipeg Gas Co. 388
        Notes and Questions 391
    4. **Intervening Causes** **391**
        Bradford v. Kanellos 392
        Notes and Questions 395
        Price v. Milawski 395
        Notes and Questions 398
        Hewson v. Red Deer 399
        Notes and Questions 401
        Review Problem 402

CHAPTER 16 THE ASSESSMENT OF DAMAGES
    1. **Introduction** **403**
        (a) The Purposes of Damage Awards in Negligence 403
        Notes and Questions 404
        (b) Preliminary Issues 405
        Notes and Questions 406
    2. **Damages for Personal Injuries** **408**
        (a) Introduction 408
        Andrews v. Grand & Toy Alta. Ltd. 408
        Notes and Questions 410

(b) Pecuniary Loss: Future Care........................ 411
    Andrews v. Grand & Toy Alta. Ltd. 411
    Notes and Questions 415
(c) Pecuniary Loss: Lost Earning Capacity............ 416
    Andrews v. Grand & Toy Alta. Ltd. 416
    Notes and Questions 418
(d) Considerations Relevant to Both Heads of Non-
    Pecuniary Loss 419
    Andrews v. Grand & Toy Alta. Ltd. 419
    Notes and Questions 421
(e) Non-Pecuniary Loss 422
    Andrews v. Grand & Toy Alta. Ltd. 422
    Notes and Questions 425

**3. Survival Actions and Dependants' Claims for Wrongful
Death or Injury** **426**
(a) Survival Actions 426
    Survival of Actions Act (Alta.)..................... 426
(b) Fatal Accidents Legislation 426
    Fatal Injuries Act (N.S.) 427
    Family Law Act (Ont.) 428
    Notes and Questions 428
    (i) The Death of the Family Provider 429
      Keizer v. Hanna 429
      Notes and Questions......................... 433
    (ii) The Death of a Dependant Spouse and Child... 433
      Alaffe v. Kennedy........................... 433
      Notes and Questions......................... 436

4. Damages for Property Loss **437**
(a) The Assessment of the Damages to the Property
    Itself.. 437
(b) The Assessment of the Economic Losses
    Consequent on the Damage to the Property 438
(c) The Plaintiff's Obligation to Mitigate 438
    Notes and Questions 438

5. Collateral Benefits **440**
(a) The Collateral Source Rule....................... 441
    Cunningham v. Wheeler 441
(b) The Doctrine of Subrogation 445
    Notes and Questions 445
    Review Problems 446

CHAPTER 17 DEFENCES TO NEGLIGENCE LIABILITY
1. Introduction **449**
2. Contributory Negligence............................ **449**
(a) The Development of the Defence 449
    Notes and Questions 450
(b) Conduct Constituting Contributory Negligence 450
    Walls v. Mussens Ltd. 450

Notes and Questions 452
Gagnon v. Beaulieu 453
Notes and Questions 456
(c) Apportionment of Loss 457
Negligence Act (Ont.) 457
Notes and Questions 458
Mortimer v. Cameron 459
Notes and Questions 462
Review Problems 462
3. Voluntary Assumption of Risk **463**
Dube v. Labar 463
Notes and Questions 466
4. Participation in a Criminal or Immoral Act **467**
Hall v. Hebert 467
Notes and Questions 470
5. Inevitable Accident **471**
Rintoul v. X-Ray and Radium Indust. Ltd. 471
Notes and Questions 473
Review Problems 473

CHAPTER 18 PROOF OF NEGLIGENCE
1. The Burden of Proof in a Negligence Action **475**
Wakelin v. London & South Western Ry. Co. 476
Notes and Questions 479
**2. Exceptions to the General Principles Governing the
Burden of Proof** **479**
(a) Statutes and Shifting Burdens of Proof 479
MacDonald v. Woodard 479
Notes and Questions 481
(b) Directly Caused Injury: Unintended Trespass 482
Dahlberg v. Naydiuk 482
Notes and Questions 483
(c) Multiple Negligent Defendants 483
Cook v. Lewis 483
Notes and Questions 486
3. Res Ipsa Loquitur **487**
(a) Introduction 487
(b) When Does *Res Ipsa Loquitur* Apply? 488
Kirk v. McLaughlin Coal & Supplies Ltd. 488
Clayton v. J.N.Z. Invt. Ltd. 489
Tataryn v. Co-Op. Trust Co. 490
Notes and Questions 493
(c) The Procedural Effects of *Res Ipsa Loquitur* 494
McHugh v. Reynolds Extrusion Co. 494
Holmes v. Bd. of Hosp. Trustees of London 498
Notes and Questions 499
Review Problem 499

CHAPTER 19 STATUTORY PROVISIONS AND TORT LIABILITY
1. **Introduction** **501**
   Notes and Questions.................................... 501
2. **Express Statutory Causes of Action** **502**
   Trespass to Property Act (Ont.)....................... 502
   Competition Act (Can.).............................. 502
   Notes and Questions.................................. 503
   Trachsler v. Halton................................. 503
   Notes and Questions.................................. 504
   Review Problem....................................... 505
3. **The Use of Statutes in Common Law Negligence** **505**
   R. in Right of Can. v. Sask. Wheat Pool 505
   Notes and Questions................................. 512
   Horsley v. MacLaren 512
   Notes and Questions................................. 513
   Rintoul v. X-Ray and Radium Indust. 513
   Notes and Questions................................. 514
4. **The Relationship Between Common Law and Statutory**
   Causes of Action **514**
   Bux v. Slough Metals Ltd. 514
   Notes and Questions................................. 516
5. **A Note on the Canadian Charter of Rights and**
   Freedoms.. **516**
   The Canadian Charter of Rights and Freedoms,
   Constitution Act, 1982............................... 516
   Notes and Questions................................. 518
   Review Problems..................................... 519

CHAPTER 20 TORT LAW: THEORIES, CRITICISMS AND
           ALTERNATIVES
1. **Introduction** **521**
2. **Theoretical Criticism of Tort Law**..................... **521**
   (a) Introduction...................................... 521
       Notes and Questions 522
   (b) Deterrence....................................... 522
       Notes and Questions 523
   (c) Compensation.................................... 524
       Notes and Questions 525
   (d) Theories of Tort Law Based on Concepts of
       Justice 526
       Notes and Questions 527
   (e) Democratic Radical Views 528
       Notes and Questions 528
3. **The No-Fault Alternatives** **529**
   (a) Introduction..................................... 529
   (b) No-Fault Accident Compensation in New Zealand .. 530
       Notes and Questions 531
   (c) Workers' Compensation........................... 532

Notes and Questions 532
(d) No-Fault Automobile Insurance in Canada 533
Notes and Questions 534
Review Problem 535

CHAPTER 21 INTENTIONAL INTERFERENCE WITH ECONOMIC
            INTERESTS
1. Introduction 537
2. Deceit (Fraud) 537
   Derry v. Peek 537
   Notes and Questions 540
3. Passing Off 541
   Ciba-Geigy Canada Ltd. v. Apotex Inc. 541
   Notes and Questions 545
4. Interference with Contractual Relations 545
   Posluns v. Toronto Stock Exchange 545
   Notes and Questions 549
5. Intimidation 550
   Central Can. Potash v. Govt. of Sask. 550
   Notes and Questions 552
6. Conspiracy 553
   Posluns v. Toronto Stock Exchange 553
   Roman Corp. v. Hudson's Bay Oil & Gas Co. 555
   Notes and Questions 556
7. The Innominate Action 557
   Gershman v. Man. Vegetable Producers' Marketing Bd. ... 557
   Notes and Questions 562
   Review Problem 563

CHAPTER 22 NEGLIGENT MISREPRESENTATION
1. Introduction 565
2. Negligent Misrepresentation Causing Pure Economic
   Loss 565
   (a) When Does a Duty of Care Arise? 565
       Hedley Byrne & Co. v. Heller & Partners Ltd. 565
       Queen v. Cognos Inc. 571
       Notes and Questions 573
   (b) The Problem of Potentially Indeterminate Liability.. 575
       Haig v. Bamford 575
       Notes and Questions 579
3. Negligent Misrepresentation and Contract 580
   (a) Pre-Contractual Misrepresentations 580
       Queen v. Cognos Inc. 580
       Notes and Questions 582
   (b) Concurrent Liability in Tort and Contract 583
       BG Checo International Ltd. v. B.C. Hydro & Power
       Authority 583
       Notes and Questions 594
       Review Problem 594

CHAPTER 23 RECOVERY OF PURE ECONOMIC LOSS IN
NEGLIGENCE
1. Introduction **597**
2. Product Quality Claims **598**
   Rivtow Marine Ltd. v. Washington Iron Works 598
   Notes and Questions 604
   Review Problems 605
3. Relational Economic Loss **606**
   *Canadian National Railway v. Norsk Pacific Steamship
   Co.* 606
   Notes and Questions 612

CHAPTER 24 OCCUPIERS' LIABILITY
1. Introduction **615**
2. The Common Law Principles of Occupiers' Liability ... **616**
   (a) Who is an Occupier? 616
       Palmer v. St. John 616
       Notes and Questions 617
   (b) The Categories of Entrants and the Corresponding
       Duties 618
       (i) Contractual Entrants 618
           Finigan v. Calgary 618
           Notes and Questions 620
       (ii) Invitees and Licensees 621
           McErlean v. Sarel 621
           Notes and Questions 624
       (iii) Trespassers 625
           Veinot v. Kerr-Addison Mines Ltd. 625
           Notes and Questions 630
3. The Provincial Occupiers' Liability Acts **631**
   (a) Introduction 631
   (b) The British Columbia Occupiers Liability Act,
       R.S.B.C. 1979, c. 303, as amended 1989, c. 64,
       s. 31 632
       Notes and Questions 634
       Review Problem 634

CHAPTER 25 STRICT AND VICARIOUS LIABILITY
1. Introduction **635**
2. Liability for Animals **635**
   (a) Cattle Trespass 635
       Acker v. Kerr 635
       Notes and Questions 638
   (b) Dangerous Animals 638
       Richard v. Hoban 638
       Notes and Questions 641
3. Escape of Dangerous Substances — *Rylands v. Fletcher* **642**
   (a) Introduction 642
       Rylands v. Fletcher 642

Notes and Questions 644
(b) Escape. 645
  Read v. J. Lyons & Co. 645
  Notes and Questions 649
(c) Non-Natural Use 649
  Gertsen v. Metro. Toronto 649
  Notes and Questions 651
(d) Defences to the Rule in *Rylands v. Fletcher* 652
  (i) Consent 652
  (ii) Common Benefit. 653
  (iii) Default of the Plaintiff 653
  (iv) Act of God 653
  (v) Act of a Stranger 653
  (vi) Statutory Authority 654
    Review Problems. 654
4. A Note on *Rylands v. Fletcher* **654**
5. Products' Liability — The American Approach **656**
  Notes and Questions 656
  Henningsen v. Bloomfield Motors Inc. 657
  Greenman v. Yuba Power Products Inc. 661
  Notes and Questions 663
5. Vicarious Liability **664**
(a) The Rationale for Vicarious Liability. 664
  T.G. Bright & Co. v. Kerr 664
(b) Master-Servant Relationships 665
  Armstrong v. Mac's Milk Ltd. 665
(c) In the Course of Employment 666
  C.P.R. v. Lockhart 666
  Griggs v. Southside Hotel Co. 668
  Notes and Questions 669

CHAPTER 26 NUISANCE
1. Introduction **671**
2. Private Nuisance **672**
  340909 Ont. Ltd. v. Huron Steel Products (Windsor) Ltd. . 672
  Notes and Questions 676
  Hollywood Silver Fox Farm Ltd. v. Emmett 677
  Notes and Questions 680
  Tock v. St. John's Metropolitan Area Bd. 680
  Notes and Questions 685
3. Public Nuisance **686**
  A.-G. Ont. v. Orange Productions Ltd. 686
  Hickey v. Elec. Reduction Co. 688
  Notes and Questions 690
4. Remedies **691**
  Mendez v. Palazzi 691
  Notes and Questions 693
  Miller v. Jackson 693

Spur Indust. Inc. v. Del. E. Webb Dev. Co. 698
Notes and Questions 700
Review Problem 702

CHAPTER 27 THE TORT LIABILITY OF PUBLIC AUTHORITIES
1. Introduction **703**
2. Judicial Review **704**
3. Special Immunity Rules **704**
   (a) Members of Parliament and the Legislatures 704
   (b) Judicial Officers 705
      Bradley v. Fisher 705
      Notes and Questions 706
4. The Tort Liability of Administrative Authorities **708**
   (a) Preliminary Issues 708
      Notes and Questions 708
   (b) Intentional Torts and Nuisance 708
      Roncarelli v. Duplessis 709
      Notes and Questions 712
   (c) Negligence Liability 712
      Just v. B.C. 713
      Notes and Questions 720
      Review Problem 721

Table of Cases

A.

A. & B. Sound Ltd. v. Future Shop Ltd. 550
A.G. v. Nissan 173
A.-G. v. P.Y.A. Quarries Ltd. 686
A.G. B.C. v. Astaforoff 148
A.G. B.C. v. Couillard 690
A.G. Can. v. Diamond Waterproofing Ltd.; Pillar
 Const. v. Defence Const. (1951) Ltd. 652
A.G. Can. v. Notre Dame Hospital 148
A.G. Can. v. Vantour 117
A.G. Man. v. Adventure Flights Centre
 Ltd. 698
A.G. Man. v. Campbell 124, 680
A.G. N.S. v. Beaver 690, 693
A.G. N.S. v. Christian 557
A.G. Ont. v. Fatehi 439
A.G. Ont. v. Keller 452, 481
A.-G. Ont. v. Orange Productions Ltd. 686
A.G. Sask. v. Pritchard 185, 186, 190
Abel v. McDonald 540
Abramzik v. Brenner 294
Acker v. Kerr 635
Agar v. Canning 130
"Agent Orange" Product Liability Litigation,
 Re 358
Airedale N.H.S. Trust v. Bland 148
Aitken v. Gardiner 98, 104
Aitkin Agencies Ltd. v. Richardson 98
Alaffe v. Kennedy 433
Alaica v. City of Toronto 622
Albert v. Lavin 159, 195
Alcock v. Chief Constable of the South
 Yorkshire Police 295
Aldridge and O'Brien v. Van Patten 645
Allan v. Saskatoon 504
Allard v. Manahan 309
Allarie v. Victoria (City) 190, 196, 353
Allen v. C.F.P.L. Broadcasting Ltd. 88
Allen v. Flood 547, 556, 559, 560, 562, 678
Allen v. Head C. Ltd. 61
Allen v. Lucas 466
Allen v. Wright 191
Alliance & Leicester Building Society v.
 Edgestop Ltd. 453
Allis-Chalmers, Rumely Ltd. v. Forbes
 Equipment Ltd. 106
Allison v. Rank City Wall Can. Ltd. 269, 618
Allsop v. Allsop 72
Almeroth v. Chivers & Sons, Ltd. 243
Alphacell Ltd. v. Woodward 356

Amalgamated Food Employees' Union, Local
 590 v. Logan Valley Plaza Inc. 113
Amin (Litigation Guardian of) v.
 Klironomos 308
Amos v. N.B. Elec. Power Comm. 235
Anderson v. Stevens 458
Andrews v. Grand & Toy Alberta Ltd. 27, 369,
 370, 407, **408, 411, 416, 419, 422,** 432
Andrews v. R.A. Douglas 677
Angelopoulos v. Machen 481
Annand v. The Merchant's Bank 98
Anns v. Merton London Borough Council 6,
 226, 227, 228, 232, 248, 258, 266, 269, 291,
 467, 605, 611, 715, 718, 719, 720, 721
Antell v. Simons 379
Archer v. Brown 540
Argyll v. Argyll 82
Arkwright v. Newbould 538
Arland v. Taylor 314
Armak Chemicals Ltd. v. Canadian National
 Railway Co. 439
Armstrong v. Mac's Milk Ltd. 665
Arndt v. Smith 288, 300
Arneil v. Paterson 361, 363
Arnold v. Teno 408, 418, 432, 525
Arsenault v. Charlottetown (City) 721
Asamera Oil Corp. v. Sea Oil & Gen.
 Corp. 101, 105
Ashby v. White 86, 87, 88, 513
Ashland Dry Goods Co. v. Wages 62
**Assiniboine South School Division, No. 3 v.
 Greater Winnipeg Gas Co. 388**
Athans v. Can. Adventure Camps Ltd. 81
Atkinson v. Newcastle & Gateshead Waterworks
 Co. 507
Atlantic Aviation Ltd. v. N.S. Light & Power
 Ltd. 121
Augustus v. Gosset 405
Austin v. 3M Canada Ltd. 308, 310
Austin v. Dowling 61
Austin v. Rescon Construction (1984) Ltd. 110,
 124, 125
Auto Concrete Curb Ltd. v. South Nation River
 Conservation Authority 574
Aziz v. Adamson 88

B.

B. (a minor), Re 153, 154
B. (N.) v. Hôtel-Dieu du Québec 148
B. (P.) v. B. (W.) 33, 52
B. (P.A.) v. Curry 670

B. (R.) v. Children's Aid Society of Metropolitan Toronto 154
BBMB Finance (Hong Kong) Ltd. v. Eda Holdings Ltd. 101
B.C. Elec. Ry. Co. v. Loach 450
B.C. Electric Ry. Co. v. Clarke 406
B.C. Lightweight Aggregate Ltd. v. Can. Cement LaFarge Ltd. See Can. Cement LaFarge Ltd. v. B.C. Lightweight Aggregate Ltd.
B.D.C. Ltd. v. Hofstrand Farms Ltd. 598
BG Checo International Ltd. v. B.C. Hydro & Power Authority 572, 580, 581, 582, **583**
Babcock v. Archibald. See Babcock v. Carr.
Babcock v. Carr 549
Bahlman v. Hudson Motor Car Co. 659
Bain v. Calgary Board of Education 264
Baird v. Williamson 643
Bajkov v. Canil 337, 453
Baker v. Bolton 426
Baker v. Willoughby 368, 369, 370, 371
Balkos v. Cook 428
Ball v. Manthorpe 168
Balmain New Ferry v. Robertson 59
Banerjee v. K-Mart Can. Ltd. 191
Banfai v. Formula Fun Centre Inc. 693
Bank of Montreal v. Young 574
Bank of N.S. v. Gaudreau 549
Banks v. Bliefernich 69
Banks v. Goodfellow 332
Banyasz v. K-Mart Can. Ltd. 191
Barnett v. Chelsea & Kensington Hosp. Mgmt. Committee 275
Barnett v. Collection Service Co. 75
Barratt v. North Vancouver (District of) 714, 719, 720
Barrette v. Fox 669
Bartlett v. Weiche Apartments Ltd. 622
Barton v. Weaver 487
Basra v. Gill 473
Bateman v. Doiron 327
Batty v. Metro. Property Realizations Ltd. 593, 605
Baud Corp. v. Brook 105
Bauder v. Wilson 182
Bauman v. Stein 493
Baumeister v. Drake 263
Baurose v. Hart 407
Baxter v. Ford Motor Co. 659
Baxter & Co. v. Jones 272, 275
Bayley v. Manchester, Sheffield & Lincolnshire R. Co. 668, 669
Beals v. Hayward 482
Beaudesert Shire Council v. Smith 77, 562
Beaudry v. Hackett 34
Beaudry v. Tollman 652
Beaulieu v. Sutherland 295
Beaulne v. Ricketts 540

Beausoleil v. Soeurs de la Charite 152
Bechard v. Haliburton Estate 242, 243, 295, 384
Becker v. Schwartz 287
Beckford v. R. 159
Beebe v. Robb 580
Beecham v. Henderson 366
Beecham v. Hughes 289, 293, 295
Behrens v. Bertram Mills Circus 641
Beim v. Goyer 196
Belknap v. Meakes 358
Bell v. Great Northern Ry. Co. of Ireland 72
Bell Canada v. Cope (Sarnia) Ltd. 178, 458, 483
Bell-Ginsburg v. Ginsburg 76, 137
Bell Telephone Co. v. The Mar-Tirenno 174
Belzile v. Dumais 380
Benning v. Wong 654
Benstead v. Murphy 419
Berezowski v. Edmonton 505
Bernstein v. Skyviews & Gen. 122, 124
Bettel v. Yim 48
Betts v. Sanderson Estate 263, 466
Bhadauria v. Bd. of Governors of Seneca College of Applied Arts and Technology 85, 87, 515, 519
Bhatti v. Insurance Corp. of British Columbia 493
Bielitski v. Obadiak 41, 73
Big Point Club v. Lozon 124
Bigcharles v. Merkel 168
Bingo Enterprises Ltd. v. Plaxton 84
Birchard v. Alta. Securities Commission 233
Bird v. Holbrook 169
Bird v. Jones 57, 77
Bisson v. District of Powell River 418
Bitton v. Jakovljevic 540
Black v. New York, New Haven & Hartford Railroad 248
Blackwood v. Butler 473
Blades v. Higgs 170
Blair's Plumbing & Heating Ltd. v. McGraw 439
Blake v. Barnard 55
Blake v. Kensche 618
Blakely v. 513953 Ont. Ltd. 141
Blatch v. Archer 356
Blessing v. United States 715
Block v. Martin 398
Blyth v. Birmingham Waterworks Co. 314, 315, 318, 376
Boase v. Paul 138
Bodley v. Reynolds 99
Body v. Murdoch 549
Boehringer v. Montalto 125

Bolduc v. R.   137
Bolton v. Forest Pest Management
   Institute   690, 693
Bolton v. Stone   **317**, 321, 325, 385, 386, 387,
   396
Bond v. Chief Constable of Kent   76
Bond v. Loutit (Noonen)   140
Bonsor v. Musicians' Union   549
Boomer v. Atlantic Cement Co.   698, 701
Boomer v. Penn   40, 334
Booth v. St. Catharines   400
Boothman v. R.   670
Boss v. Robert Simpson Eastern Ltd.   398
Bottom v. Ont. Leaf Tobacco Co.   701
Boulay v. Charbonneau   341
Boulay v. Rousselle   450
Boulet c. Enterprises M. Canada (Abitibi)
   Ltée   168
Bourden v. Alloway   9
Boutcher v. Stewart   473
Boutin v. Boutin   110
Bow Valley Husky (Bermuda) Ltd. v. Saint John
   Shipbuilding Ltd.   309
Bowen v. Paramount Bldrs. (Hamilton)
   Ltd.   605
Boyle v. Rogers   119
Bradford Corpn. v. Pickles   678, 680
Bradford v. Kanellos   **392**, 397, 398
Bradley v. Fisher   **705**
Bradley v. Wingnut Films   81
Brady v. Schatzel   53
Brandner v. Brandner   34
Brauer v. New York Cent. H.R.R. Co.   401
Bray v. Palmer   487, 494
Breen v. Saunders   182
Bresatz v. Przibilla   417
Brian v. Mador   407
Bridlington Relay Ltd. v. Yorkshire Electricity
   Bd.   677
Briggs v. Laviolette   191
Brimelow v. Casson   548
Bristol & West of England Bk. v. Midland R.
   Co.   104
British Celanese Ltd. v. A.H. Hunt (Capacitors)
   Ltd.   602
British Railways Board v. Herrington   625, 626,
   629, 630, 631
Bronson v. Evans and Evans   481
Brown v. Boorman   586
Brown v. British Columbia (Minister of
   Transportation & Highways)   721
Brown v. Dunsmuir   471
Brown v. Wilson   159
Brown and Brown v. B. & F. Theatres Ltd.   619
Brownlie v. Campbell   538
Bruce v. Dyer   53, 160
Brumer v. Gunn   341

Brushett v. Cowan   148, 398
Buchan v. Ortho Pharmaceutical (Can.)
   Ltd.   299, 305, 306, 309, 310
Buckland v. Guildford Gas Light & Coke
   Co.   235
Buckley and T.T.C. v. Smith TPT Ltd.   **331**
Buckley v. John Allen & Ford (Oxford)
   Ltd.   430
Buehl v. Polar Star Enterprises Inc.   263
Burdett v. Abbott   206
Burmah Oil Co. v. Lord Advocate   173
Burman's Beauty Supplies Ltd. v.
   Kempster   574
Burnett v. Canada   81, 82
Burnie Port Authority v. General Jones
   Ltd.   655, 656
Burrowes v. Lock   538
Burrows v. Burke   540
Bushell v. Hamilton   366
Buteikis v. Adams   384
Buthmann v. Balzer   605
Butler v. Egg Bd.   101
Butler v. Standard Telephones & Cables,
   Ltd.   692
Butterfield v. Forrester   450
Bux v. Slough Metals Ltd.   **514**
Byrne v. Boadle   488

C.

C. v. Wren   **149**
C.N.R. v. Bakty   284
C.N.R. Co. v. Norsk Pacific Steamship Co. (The
   "Jervis Crown")   620, 621
C.N.R. Co. v. Sask. Wheat Pool   380
C.P.R. v. Lockhart   **666**, 669
C.R.F. Holdings Ltd. v. Fundy Chemical Int.
   Ltd.   540
Cachay v. Nemeth   52, 159, 162
Caltex Oil Australian Property Ltd. v. The
   Dredge "Willemstad"   612
Calvert v. Law Soc. of Upper Can.   233, 707
Cambridge Water Co. v. Eastern Counties
   Leather plc   655, 677
Camden Nominees, Ltd. v. Forcey   547, 548
Cameron v. Morang   94
Campbell v. Calgary Power Ltd.   238
Campbell v. Dominion Breweries Ltd.   101
Campbell-Fowler v. Royal Trust Co.   88
Campbell v. Hudyma   195
Campbell v. Royal Bank of Canada   623
Campbell v. S.S. Kresge Co.   **59**
Can. Cement LaFarge Ltd. v. B.C. Lightweight
   Aggregate Ltd.   140, 556
Can. Gen. Elec. Co. v. Pickford & Black
   Ltd.   242
Can. Pac. Ltd. v. Gill   446

Can. Pacific Ltd. v. Paul   117
Can. Safeway Ltd. v. Man. Food & Commercial Wkrs. Loc.   77, 563
Can. Western Natural Gas Co. v. Pathfinders Surveys Ltd.   440, 458
Canada v. Lukasik   69
Canada (Attorney General) v. Ottawa-Carleton (Regional Municipality)   685, 712
Canadian Aero Service Ltd. v. O'Malley   82
Canadian Assn. of Regulated Importers v. Canada (A.G.)   519
Canadian Commercial Bank v. Crawford, Smith & Swallow   580
Canadian Indemnity Co. v. Andrews & George C.   592
Canadian National Railway v. Norsk Pacific Steamship Co.   606
Candler v. Crane, Christmas & Co.   568, 576, 579
Canson Enterprises Ltd. v. Boughton & Co.   540
Cant v. Cant   76, 77
Canterbury v. Spence   298
Capan v. Capan   81
Caparo Industries Plc. v. Dickman   291, 573, 579
Car & General Ins. Corp. Ltd. v. Seymour   464
Cardy   629, 630
Carr v. Edmonton (City) Police   62
Carriere v. Bd. of Gravelbourg School Dist. No. 2244 of Sask.   620
Carriss v. Buxton   619
Carroll v. Chicken Palace Ltd.   245, 333
Carson v. Thunder Bay   466
Carstairs v. Taylor   653
Carter v. Higashi   494
Casey v. Auto. Renault Can. Ltd.   69
Castle v. Stockton Waterworks   646
Cataford v. Moreau   288
Catre Industries Ltd. v. Brown   584
Cattle v. Stockton Waterworks Co.   597, 601, 606
Caxton Publishing Co. v. Sutherland Publishing Co.   99
Central B.C. Planers Ltd. v. Hocker   573, 574
Central Can. Potash v. Govt. of Sask.   550
Central & Eastern Trust Co. v. Rafuse   341, 581, 582, 583, 584, 585, 586, 587, 588, 592, 593
Chaisson v. Hebert   337
Chamberland v. Fleming   462
Champigny v. Ste-Marie   341
Chand v. Sabo Bros. Realty Ltd.   574
Chapman v. Hearse   284
Chapman v. 3M Canada Inc.   88
Chappell v. Baratti   439

Charing Cross Electric Co. v. Hydraulic Power Co.   646
Charrington v. Simons & Co. Ltd.   121
Chartier v. A.G.-Que.   190
Check v. Andrews Hotel Co.   45
Cheevers v. Van Nordern   342
Chernesky v. Armadale Publishers Ltd.   458
Cherrey v. Steinke   466
Cherry v. Ivey   69
Cherry (Guardian ad litem of) v. Borsman   288, 341
Chessie v. J.D. Irvine Ltd.   691
Cheticamp Fisheries Co-operative Ltd. v. Canada   550
Child v. Vancouver General Hospital   396
Children's Aid Society of Western Man. and Danick, Re   207
Chilton v. Carrington   103
Chin v. Venning   16
Chipchase v. British Titan Products Co. Ltd.   515
Christie v. Davey   679
Christie v. Leachinsky   193
Christopherson v. Saanich (District)   196
Chu v. Dawson   652, 677
Ciba-Geigy Canada Ltd. v. Apotex Inc.   541
City of Brandon v. Farley   623
City of Ft. Smith v. Western Hide & Fur Co.   700
City of Phoenix v. Johnson   698, 699
Claiborne Industries Ltd. v. National Bank of Canada   36, 557
Clark v. Canada   76, 88
Clark v. Naqvi   584
Clark v. Orr   104
Clarke v. Penny   408
Claxton v. Grandy   472
Clayton v. J.N.Z. Invt. Ltd.   489, 493
Clayton v. Woodman & Son (Builders) Ltd.   574
Cleary v. Hansen   284
Clegg, Parkinson & Co. v. Earby Gas Co.   617
Clement v. Leslies Storage Ltd.   436
Clissold v. Cratchley   69
Cloutier v. Langlois   197
Cluett v. R.   196
Clyke v. Clyke   284
Coco v. A.N. Clark (Engineers) Ltd.   82
Coe Estate v. Tennant   436
Cogar Estate v. Central Mountain Air Services Ltd.   494
Coggs v. Bernard   272
Cohen v. Lion Products Co.   74
Colangelo v. Mississauga (City of)   519, 708
Colby v. Schmidt   131
Colet v. R.   110, 190
Collin v. Lussier   36
Collins v. Renison   167

Com'r for Railways (N.S.W.) v. Cardy 625
Com'r for Railways v. Quinlan 625, 629
Comeau v. Laliberte 453
Comeau's Sea Foods Ltd. v. Canada (Minister of Fisheries & Oceans) 720
Cominco Ltd. v. Westinghouse Can. Ltd. 308
Conklin v. Smith 406
Conn v. David Spencer Ltd. 61
Connery v. Gov't of Man. 378
Connors v. Doak 35
Conrad v. Crawford 466
Constantine v. Imperial London Hotels Ltd. 85
Consumers Distributing Co. v. Seiko Time Can. Ltd. 542, 543
Cook v. Lewis 5, 14, 49, 364, 482, 483
Cook v. Swinfen 295
Cooper v. Wandsworth Bd. of Works 712
Cope v. Sharpe 172
Cork v. Kirby Maclean Ltd.. 255, 349
Corothers v. Slobodian 284
Cormack v. Mara (Township) 631
Cormier v. St. John (City) 195
Corrie v. Gilbert 406
Costello v. Blakeson 384
Costello v. Calgary (City) 110
Couch v. McCann 617
Couch v. Steel 507
Coughlin v. Kuntz 142, 299, 405
Couillard v. Waschulewski Estate 398
County of Parkland No. 31 v. Stetar 275
County of Parkland No. 31 v. Woodrow. See County of Parkland No. 31 v. Stetar.
Cousins v. Wilson 109
Couture-Jacquet v. Montreal Children's Hospital 154
Coward v. Baddeley 52
Cox v. Fleming 291, 395
Crawford v. Halifax 245, 333
Cresswell v. Sirl 170
Crew v. Nicholson 481
Crocker v. Sundance Northwest Resorts Ltd. 238, 258, 466
Crofter Hand Woven Harris Tweed Co., Ltd. v. Veitch 555, 557, 559, 560, 561
Cronk v. F.W. Woolworth 191
Crosby v. Curry 638
Crossman v. R. 36
Crowe v. Noon 184
Cryderman v. Ringrose 142, 288
Cudney v. Clements Motor Sales Ltd. 496
Cummings (or McWilliams) v. Sir William Arrol & Co. Ltd. 515
Cunningham v. Wheeler 440, 441
Curll v. Robin Hood Multi-foods Ltd. 295
Curran v. Northern Ireland Co-ownership Housing Assoc. Ltd. 227
Currie v. Blundell 299

Curtis, Re 206

D.

D & F Estates Ltd. v. Church Commissioners for England 605
D.C. Thomson & Co. Ltd. v. Deakin 546
Dabous v. Zuliani 341
Dahlberg v. Naydiuk 49, 124, 482
Dahler v. Bruvold 652
Daigle v. Theo Couturier Ltd. 670
Dale v. Munthali 341
Dalgliesh v. Green 534
Dallison v. Caffery 196, 202
D'Amato v. Badger 380
Daniels v. Ford Motor Co. Ltd. 514
Danku v. Town of Fort Frances 653
Darbishire v. Warren 438, 439
Davenport v. Miller 76
Davey v. Harrow Corp. 692
Davey v. Victoria General Hospital 288
David v. Abdul Cader 712
David v. Toronto Transit Comm. 398
Davidson v. Chief Constable of North Wales 61
Davidson v. Connaught Laboratories 309
Davies v. Gabel Estate 341
Davies v. Mann 450
Davies v. Powell Duffryn Associated Collieries, Ltd. 435
Davies v. Taylor 406
Davis v. Anderson 456
Davis v. Lisle 205
Davis v. McArthur 81
Day v. Chaleur Developments Ltd. 618
De Gurse v. Henry 481
De Jetley Marks v. Greenwood (Lord) 554
Deakins v. Aarsen 670
Decker & Sons, Inc. v. Capps 662
Dehghani v. Canada (Minister of Employment & Immigration) 195
Dehn v. A.G. 117
Delancey v. Dale and Co. 69
Delaney v. Cascade River Holidays Ltd. 466
Dellwo v. Pearson 337
Demarco v. Ungaro 228
Dendaas v. Yackel 288
Dendekker v. F.W. Woolworth Co. 191
Dennis v. Charnwood Borough Council 720
Dennison v. Sanderson 27
Dept. of the Environment v. Thomas Bates and Son 227
Depue v. Flateau 168, 175, 177
Dering v. Uris 27
Derry v. Peek 537, 568, 570
Deshana v. Deere & Co. 310
Devoe v. Long 170
Devon Lumber Co. v. MacNeill 120, 121, 680

Deyo v. Kingston Speedway Ltd.   649

Deziel v. Deziel   287

Dhalla v. Jodrey   340

Dickey v. McCaul   98

Didow v. Alta. Power Ltd.   124

Dietelbach v. Pub. Trustee   295

Dill v. Excel Packing Company   699

Dillon v. LeRoux   340

Dillon v. O'Brien   199, 201, 202

Dillon v. Twin State Gas and Elec. Co.   366

District of North Vancouver v. McKenzie Barge
   & Marine Ways Ltd.   683

Dixon v. R. in Right of B.C.   366

Dobbs v. Mayer   40, 334, 473

Dodd Properties (Kent) Ltd. v. Canterbury City
   Council   27, 28, 380

Doe d. Rochester v. Bridges   506, 507

Doern v. Phillips Estate   353, 481

Doiron v. Brideau   466

Doiron v. Caisse Populaire d'Inkerman
   Ltée   179

Dokuchia v. Domansch   649

Dom. Chain Co. v. Eastern Const. Co.   178,
   587, 592

Dom. Securities Ames Ltd. v. Deep   341

Dom. Securities Ltd. v. Glazerman   101

Donnelly v. Jackman   52

Donoghue v. Stevenson. See M'Alister (or
   Donoghue) v. Stevenson.

Dooley v. C.N. Weber Ltd.   70

Dorschell v. Cambridge   342

Dorset Yacht Co. Ltd. v. Home Office   720

Doughty v. Turner Mfg. Co.   379

Douglas College v. Douglas/Kwantlen Faculty
   Assoc.   519

Downey v. 502377 Ont. Ltd.   669

Dredger Liesbosch v. Steamship Edison   438,
   439

Dube v. Labar   463

Dube (Litigation guardian of) v. Penlon
   Ltd.   295, 425

Duce v. Rourke; Pearce v. Rourke   374, 401

Ducharme v. Davies   453

Duchman v. Oakland Dairy Co. Ltd.   691

Dudeck v. Brown   652

Dudley v. Victor Lynn Lines Inc.   275

Dulieu v. White & Sons   290, 381

Dumbell v. Roberts   190

Duncan v. Braaten   624

Duncan v. Cammell Laird & Co. Ltd.   617

Dunn v. Birmingham Canal Co.   650, 653

Dunn v. Dominion Atlantic Railway Co.   168,
   260

Dunne v. Clinton   191

Dunsmore v. Deshield   214

Dupuis v. New Regina Trading Co. Ltd.   280

Dutton v. Bognor Regis United Building Co.
   Ltd.   574

Dutton v. Bognor Regis Urban District
   Council   605

Duval v. Seguin   285, 286

Duwyn v. Kaprielian   294

Dwyer v. Staunton   173, 177

Dyck v. Man. Snowmobile Assn.   466, 589

E.

Eady v. Tenderenda   341, 494

East St. Johns Shingle Co. v. City of
   Portland   699

East Suffolk Rivers Catchment Board v.
   Kent   281, 284

Eastern & South African Telegraph Co. v. Cape
   Town Tramways Cos.   678, 679

Eccles v. Bourque   182, 190, 198, **203**

Edgar v. Richmond (Township)   315

Edgeworth Construction Ltd. v. N.D. Lea &
   Associates Ltd.   580

Edwards v. Railway Executive   625

Edwards v. Lee's Adm'r   125

Eid v. Dumas; Hatherly v. Dumas   464, 466

Elder, Dempster & Co., Ltd. v. Paterson
   Zochonis & Co., Ltd.   590

Elderkin v. Merrill Lynch, Royal Securites
   Ltd.   573, 574

Elfsy v. Sylben Invts. Ltd.   652

Elliot and Elliot v. Amphitheatre Ltd.   129

Ellis v. Stenning   102

Elloway v. Boomars   383

Elston v. Dore   77

Emerald Const. Co. v. Lowthian   550

Engel v. Kam-Ppelle Holdings Ltd.   398, 407,
   419

Engemoen Holdings Ltd. v. 100 Mile
   House   125

Engle v. Clark   699

Engler v. Rossignol   342

Entick v. Carrington   107, 110

Epstein v. Cressey Development Corp.   36, 110,
   125

Erie Ry. Co. v. Stewart   275

Erven Warnink B.V. v. J. Townend & Sons (Hull)
   Ltd.   541

Escola v. Coca-Cola Bottling Co.   662

Esso Petroleum Co. v. Mardon   580, 582, 585,
   594

"Eve" v. "Mrs. E"   153, 154

Everett v. Griffiths   707

Eyers v. Gillis & Warren Ltd.   315

F.

F. (P.) v. Ontario   81

Falkenham v. Zwicker   378
Fanjoy v. Gaston   620
Fardon v. Harcourt-Rivington   386
Farish v. Nat. Trust Co.   574
Farrington v. Thomson   712
Farro v. Nutone Electrical Ltd.   494
Federic v. Perpetual Invt. Ltd.   652
Feener v. McKenzie   481
Feist v. Gordon   299
Fellowes v. Rother District Council   720
Fender v. St. John-Mildmay   80
Fenn v. Peterborough   419, 425
Ferguson v. Hamilton Civic Hospitals   152, 494
Ferguson v. McBee Technographics Inc.   84
Ferguson v. McCann. See Couch v. McCann.
Ferland v. Keith   272
Fillier v. Whittom   458
Fillion v. New Brunswick International Paper
   Co.   689
Fillipowich v. Nahachewsky   131
Findlay v. Driver   453
Fine's Flowers Ltd. v. Gen. Accident Assur. Co.
   of Can.   272, 574
Finigan v. Calgary   618
Finlay v. Auld   499
Finnigan v. Sandford   207
Fisher v. Knibbe   404
Fivey v. Pennsylvania R.R. Co.   659
Flame Bar-B-Q Ltd. v. Hoar   69
Fleeming v. Orr   640
Fleming v. Atkinson   638, 642
Fletcher v. Autocare & Transporters Ltd.   414
Fletcher v. Bealey   692
Fletcher v. Collins   182, 184
Fletcher v. Manitoba Public Insurance
   Corp.   272, 584
Floyd and Barker   705
Fobel v. Dean   419
Fogden v. Wade   56
Fogg v. McKnight   31
Fontin v. Katapodis   45
Foran v. Tatangello   707
Foster v. Morton   141
Foster v. Registrar of Motor Vehicles for Province
   of Ontario   396, 481
Fouldes v. Willoughby   91, 96
Fowler v. Lanning   482
Frame v. Smith   76
France v. Gaudet   99
Francis v. Cockrell   619, 620
Francis v. Dingman   540
Franklin v. Gramophone Co. Ltd.   515
Franks v. Sanderson   493
Fraser v. Bd. of School Trustees of School
   District No. 72 (Campbell River)   341
Fraser v. Berkeley   44
Fraser v. Vancouver General Hospital   341

Frawley v. Asseltine   436
Frey v. Fedoruk   188, 190
Frome v. Dennis   96
Froom v. Butcher   455, 456
Funk Estate v. Clapp   264, 268, 395
Funnell v. C.P.R.   178

G.

G.(A.) v. Supt. of Fam. and Child Services   270
G. (K.) v. T. (J.)   34
Gagne v. St. Regis Paper Co.   238
Gagnon v. Beaulieu   453
Gala v. Preston   471
Galantiuk v. Regina   440
Galaske v. O'Donnell   453, 456
Gallant v. Central Credit Union Ltd.   573
Gambriell v. Caparelli   49, 160
Gamracy v. R.   195
Garland v. Rowsell   428
Garratt v. Dailey   41, 48
Garry v. Sherritt Gordon Mines Ltd.   549, 550,
   556
Gaunt v. Fynney   679
Gehrmann v. Lavoie   429
Geld v. Dehavilland Aircraft of Can. Ltd.   439
**Gen. & Finance Facilities Ltd. v. Cooks Cars
   (Romford) Ltd.   101**
Gen. Motors Accept. Corp. v. Fulton Ins.
   Agencies Ltd.   574
Gen. Motors Products of Can. Ltd. v.
   Kravitz   663
General Baking Co. v. Gorman   544
General Motors Corp. v. Dodson   662
Genik v. Ewanylo   457
George v. Skivington   224
Gerigs v. Rose   48
German v. Major   232
Gerrard v. Manitoba   549
**Gershman v. Man. Vegetable Producers'
   Marketing Bd.   557, 712**
Gertsen v. Metro. Toronto   645, 649, 654
Gervais v. Richard   428, 429
Giannone v. Weinberg   416
Giffels Associates Ltd. v. Eastern Const.
   Co.   458
Gifford v. Dent   122
Gilbert v. Showerman   699
Gilbert v. Stone   42
Gill v. Humberstone & Co. Ltd.   515
Gillick v. West Norfolk & Wisbech Area Health
   Authority   150
Gilson v. Kerierr District Council   653
Glamorgan Coal Co. Ltd. v. South Wales Miners'
   Federation   547
Glanville v. Sutton   641
Glanzer v. Shepard   578, 579

Glasgow Corpn. v. Taylor   245
Glasgow Corporation v. Muir   314
Glivar v. Noble   346
Gloster v. Toronto Electric Light Co.   325
Godbolt v. Fittock   460
Godin v. Wilson Laboratories Inc.   310
Goguen v. Crowe   493, 494
Goh Choon Seng v. Lee Kim Soo   667
Goldhawke v. Harder   398
Goldman v. Hargrave   653, 693
Goldsworthy v. Catalina Agencies Ltd.   494
Good-Wear Treaders v. D. & B. Holdings
   Ltd.   310
Goodwin v. McCully   346
Goodwin v. Pine Point Park   691
Goodwyn v. Cheveley   638
Gootson v. R.   40, 334
Gordelli Management Ltd. v. Turk   574
Gordon v. Moen   580
Gordon v. Wallace   40, 334
Governors of the Peabody Donation Fund v. Sir
   Lindsay Parkinson & Co.   227, 291
Graham v. Bottenfield's Inc.   662
Graham v. Hodgkinson   473
Graham v. K.D. Morris and Sons Pty. Ltd.   121
Graham v. Persyko   315
Graham v. Picot Gorman and A.E.S. Consultants
   Ltd.   341
Graham v. Rourke   384, 419
Graham v. Saville   77, 137, 540
Granby Const. and Equipment Ltd. v.
   Milley   106
Grand Restaurants of Can. Ltd. v. Toronto   574
Grant v. Australian Knitting Mills, Ltd.   495
Gray v. Cotic   384, 398
Gray v. Gill   407
Great Atlantic & Pacific Tea Co. v. Roch   74
Green v. Goddard   167
Greening v. Wilkinson   99
Greenman v. Yuba Power Products Inc.   661
Greenock Corp. v. Caledonia Ry. Co.   653
Greeven v. Blackcomb Skiing Enterprises
   Ltd.   466
Griffiths v. C.P.R.   293
Griggs v. Southside Hotel Co.   668
Grise v. Rankin   472
Griswold v. Boston & Maine Railroad   249
Gross v. Wright   117, 132
Grosvenor Park Shopping Centre Ltd. v.
   Waloshin   112
Grove Services Ltd. v. Lenhart Agencies
   Ltd.   276
Guay v. Sun Publishing Co.   73, 295
Guilford Industries Ltd. v. Hankinson
   Management Services Ltd.   70
Guimond v. Laberge   138
Guy v. Trizec Equities Ltd.   446

H.

H. (M.) v. Bederman   269
Haag v. Marshall   358
Hackshaw v. Shaw   168
Hague v. Billings   263, 366
Hague v. Deputy Gogernor of Parkhurst Prison;
   Weldon v. Home Office   59
Haig v. Bamford   341, 574, **575**
Hajgato v. London Health Assn.   494, 499
Hale v. Jennings Brothers   654
Haley v. London Electric Board   243, 333
Haley v. Richardson; McCrae v.
   Richardson   456
Hall v. Hebert   140, 141, 263, 462, **467**
Hall v. Smith   664
Halushka v. University of Saskatchewan   142
Hambourg v. T. Eaton Co. Ltd.   622
Hambrook v. Stokes Brothers   290
Hamel v. Prather   424
Hamlyn v. Houston & Co.   664
Handcock v. Baker   191, 207
Hanson v. City of St. John   622
Hanson v. St. John Horticultural Assn.   466
Harbutt's "Plasticine" v. Wayne Tank & Pump
   Co.   439
Harder v. Brown   34, 83, 139
Harker v. Birkbeck   8
Harland v. Fancsali   540
Harpe v. Lefebvre   366
Harris v. Wong   168
Harrison v. Carswell   27, 111, 117, 173, 519
Harrison v. University of British Columbia   117
Hartlen v. Chaddock   131, 140
Hartman v. Fisette   458
Hasenclever v. Hoskins   76, 81
Hashem and Hashem v. N.S. Power
   Corporation   124
Haskett v. Univ. of Western Ont.   618
Hatherly v. Dumas. See Eid v. Dumas.
Hatton v. Webb   51
Haughian v. Paine   297
Haverkate v. Toronto Harbour
   Commissioners   494, 499
Haward v. Bankes   8
Hawkins v. McGee   28
Hay or Bourhill v. Young   242, 291, 294, 295,
   388
Hayduk v. Pidoborozny   670
Hayes v. Harwood   400
Haynes v. Nfld. Telephone Co.   109, 125
**Heard v. Weardale Steel, Coal and Coke
   Co.   62**
Hearndon v. Rondeau   406
Heath v. Weist-Barron School of Television Can.
   Ltd.   81
Heaven v. Pender   221, 222, 224

Hedley Byrne & Co. Ltd. v. Heller & Partners Ltd.   225, 226, 271, 540, 541, **565**, 571, 572, 573, 574, 576, 577, 580, 581, 597, 600, 602, 603, 608, 609, 612

Heeney v. Best   346, 452, 453

Hefferman v. Elizabeth Irving Service Centre   439

Heffron v. Imperial Parking Co.   97

Hegarty v. Shine   137, 140

Heighington v. Ont.   76, 295, 405

Heintzman & Co. v. Hashman Const. Ltd.   652

Heinz v. Berry   295

Hempler v. Todd   263

Henderson v. Volk   110

Hendrick v. De Marsh   395, 574

Hendricks v. R.   275

Henningsen v. Bloomfield Motors Inc.   541, **657**, 662, 663

Henry Thorne & Co. v. Sandow   545

Henwood v. Municipal Tramways Trust (S.A.)   469

Hern v. Nichols   664

Hercules Management Ltd. v. Ernst & Young   573

Hersees Ltd. v. Goldstein   557

Hewitt v. Bonvin   665

Hewson v. Red Deer   399

Hickey v. Faulkner   65

Hilderman v. Rattray   481

Hill v. Chief Constable of West Yorkshire   266, 269

Hill v. Church of Scientology of Canada   36, 425, 519

Himmelman v. Nova Const. Co.   654

Hinde v. Skibinski   69

Hoare v. McAlpine   653

Hobson v. Munkley   499

Hodgkinson v. Martin   45, 47

Hofstrand Farms Ltd. v. B.D.C. Ltd.   341, 608

Holcombe v. Whitaker   53, 56

Holderness v. Goslin   654

Holinaty v. Hawkins   652, 654

Hollebone v. Barnard   178

Hollett v. Coca-Cola Ltd.   401

Hollins v. Fowles   97

Hollis v. Dow Corning Corp.   300, **301**, 353

Hollis v. Richardson   249

Hollywood Silver Fox Farm Ltd. v. Emmett   677

Holmes v. Bd. of Hosp. Trustees of London   498

Holmes v. Mather   5, 13

Holt v. Verbruggen   45

Home Office v. Dorset Yacht Co. Ltd.   225, 226, 264

Honan v. Gerhold   670

Hongkong Bank of Canada v. Richardson Greenshields of Canada Ltd.   407

Hooey v. Mancini   269

Hooiveld v. Van Biert   384

Hook v. Cunard SS. Co.   166

Hooper v. Rogers   693

Hopp v. Lepp   143, 146, 155, 297, 298, 299

Horner v. Comeau   481

Horseshoe Bay Retirement Society v. S.I.F. Development Corp.   36, 110

Horsley v. Maclaren   88, 255, **277, 512**, 514

Host v. Bassett   487

Houle v. S.S. Kresge Co.   624

Howard v. Furness Houlder Argentine Lines, Ltd.   646

Howarth v. The Queen   707

Howes v. Crosby   407

Hudson v. Riverdale Colony of Hutterrian Brethern   652

Hughes v. Lord Advocate   378, 384, 389, 396

Hunt v. Burgess   494

Hunt v. T & N plc.   309, 359

Hunter v. Briere   377, 450, 458

Hunter v. Manning   384

Hurley v. Eddingfield   275

Hurley v. Moore   45

Hutchings v. Nevin   333, 453

Hutscal v. I.A.C. Ltd.   100

Hutterly v. Imperial Oil Ltd.   284

Hymas v. Ogden   103

Hynes v. Hynes   693

I.

ITO — International Terminal Operators Ltd. v. Miida Electronics Inc.   466

Indermaur v. Dames   619, 620, 622

Indian Towing Co.   716

Indust. Teletype Electronics Corp. v. Montreal   439

Ingram v. Lowe   264

Innes v. Wylie   53

Ins. Corp. of B.C. v. Mandzuk   416

Int. Brotherhood of Teamsters v. Therien   553, 562

International Union, U.A.W. v. Johnson Controls, Inc.   287

Irvington Holdings Ltd. v. Black   97

Irwin v. Ware (Town)   269

Isreal James Hussey   168

J.

J. (a minor), Re   154

J. (J.L.) v. L. (A.M.)   34

J. (L.A.) v. J. (H.)   270

J. Nunes Diamonds v. Dom. Elec. Protection Co. 586, 600

J.C. Kerhoff & Sons Contracting Ltd. v. XL Ironworks Co. 553

J.T. Stratford & Son Ltd. v. Lindley 553, 561, 562

Jack Crewe Ltd. v. Jorgenson 446

Jacks v. Davis 341

Jackson v. Harrison 140

Jackson v. Millar 424, 494

Jacobson v. Kinsmen Club of Nanaimo 263

James Street Hardware and Furniture Co. v. Spizziri 439

Jane Doe v. Metropolitan Toronto (Municipality) Commissioners of Police 265

Janiak v. Ippolito 398, 406, 407

Jarvis v. Moy, Davies, Smith, Vandervell & Co. 593

Jarvis v. Williams 97, 105

Jens v. Mannix Co. Ltd. 439

Jerabek c. Accueil Verte-Pré d'Huberdeau 264

Jinks v. Cardwell 264

Jobling v. Associated Dairies Ltd. 372

John Lewis & Co. v. Tims 191, 196

John Maryon Int. Ltd. v. N.B. Telephone Co. 440, 586

Johnson v. B.C. Hydro and Power Authority 109, 117

Johnson v. Leigh 205

Johnson v. Royal Can. Legion Grandview Branch No. 179 139

Johnston v. Burton 366

Jones v. Dowle 102, 104

Jones v. Livox Quarries 350

Jones v. Wabigwan 377, 378

Jones v. Wright 295

Jordan House Ltd. v. Menow 88, 168, 258, 259, 260, 261, 262, 263, 466, 513

Joseph Brant Memorial Hospital v. Koziol 341, 486

Joule Ltd. v. Poole 97

Joyal v. Barsby 334

Juelle v. Trudeau 98

Junior Books Ltd. v. Veitchi Co. 605

Just v. B.C. 713

K.

K and Public Trustee, Re 154

Kahler v. Midland Bank 97

Kamloops (City) v. Nielsen 266, 268, 597, 598, 607, 608, 609, 610, 715, 718, 719, 720, 721

Karogiannis v. Poulus 191

Karpenko v. Paroian 232

Katzman v. Yaeck 398

Kauffman v. Toronto Transit Comm. 351

Keeble v. Hickeringill 562, 678

Keep v. Quallman 47

Keith v. Guar. Trust Co. of Can. 363

Keizer v. Hanna 421, 429

Kelsen v. Imperial Tobacco Co. (of Great Britian and Ireland) Ltd. 122, 124

Kendall v. Gambles Can. Ltd. 191

Kenlin v. Gardiner 159, 195

Kennaway v. Thompson 700

Kennedy v. Hughes Drug 377

Kent v. Dom. Steel & Coal Corp. Ltd. 676

Kent v. East Suffolk Rivers Catchment Board 718

Kent v. Ellis 97

Kerlenmar Holdings Ltd. v. Matsqui (District) 677

Kerr v. Revelstoke Bldg. Materials Ltd. 118

Ketterer v. Armour & Co. 663

Khan v. El Al Israel Airlines 64

Khorasandjian v. Bush 81, 677

King v. Fanklin 166

King v. Phillips 242, 294, 388

Kingsbridge Development Inc. v. Hanson Needler Corp. 121, 124

Kingu v. Walmar Ventures Ltd. 580

Kirk v. McLaughlin Coal & Supplies Ltd. 488, 493

Kirkham v. Boughey 616

Kirkham v. Chief Constable of Greater Manchester Police 140

Klein v. Duchess Sandwich Co. 663

Knutson v. Farr 425

Koechlin v. Waugh and Hamilton 191

Kohn v. Globerman 62

Kopka et ux. v. Bell Telephone Co. of Pennsylvania 109

Kozak v. Gruza 380

Kraft v. Oshawa General Hospital 404

Kralj v. Murray 314

Kroeker v. Jansen 419

Krouse v. Chrysler Can. Ltd. 81, 82

Kubby v. Hammond 698

L.

L.D.K.; Children's Aid Society of Metro. Toronto v. K. and K., Re 151

LAC Minerals Ltd. v. International Corona Resources Ltd. 83

La Societe Anonyme de Remorquage a Helice v. Bennetts 601

Labrecque v. Sask. Wheat Pool 308

Lacroix v. R. 124

Laferrière v. Lawson 353

Lafleur v. Maryniuk 269

Lai v. Gill 436

Lajeunesse v. Janssens 670

Lamb v. London Borough of Camden 401

Lambert v. Bessey   644

Lambert v. Lastoplex Chemicals Co.   301, 302, 303, 308

Lambton v. Mellish   359, 363

Lampert v. Simpson Sears Ltd.   624

Lan v. Wu   419

Landry v. Patterson   45

Lane v. Holloway   45, 131, 138, 139, 140

Lang v. Burch   62, 195

Langridge v. Levy   71

Lankenau v. Dutton   372

LaPlante (Guardian ad litem of) v. LaPlante   264, 337

Lapensee v. Ottawa Day Nursery Inc.   264

Lapierre v. A.G. Que.   173, 309

Laporte and R., Re   202

Larche v. Ontario   264

LaSalle Extension University v. Fogarty   74

Latham v. R. Johnson & Nephew Ltd.   400

Latter v. Braddell   133

Lauritzan v. Barstead   379

Lavallee v. R.   160

Lavigne v. O.P.S.E.U.   518

Laviolette v. C.N.R.   337, 453, 466

Law Estate v. Simice   326

Lawson v. Wellesley Hospital   48

Layden v. Cope   340

Le Lievre v. Gould   221, 222, 224, 580

Leaman v. Rea   487

Leame v. Bray   5, 11

LeBar v. Canada   59, 62

Lebrun v. High-Low Foods   61

Lee v. O'Farrell   341, 453

Lee (Guardian ad litem of) v. Barker   453

Lehnert v. Nelson   263

Lehnert v. Stein   464, 465

Leigh v. Cole   200, 201

Leigh & Sillavan Ltd. v. Aliakmon Shipping Co.   227, 607

Leininger v. Stearns-Rogers Mfg.   605

Lem v. Borotto Sports Ltd.   309

Leslie v. Ball   228, 231

Leszczynski v. Clark   534

Letang v. Cooper   482

Letnick v. Metro. Toronto (Mun.)   358

Levesque v. Day & Ross Ltd.   473

Levesque v. Wedge   342

Lewis v. Oeming   642

Lewis v. Todd   422, 452

Lewis (Guardian ad litem of) v. British Columbia   721

Lewvest Ltd. v. Scotia Towers Ltd.   121

Lian v. Money   436

Lickoch v. Madu; Oscar v. Lickoch   652, 691

Lindal v. Lindal   425

Line v. Taylor   640

Linn v. Radio Center Delicatessen   662

Lister v. Romford Ice & Cold Storage Co.   592, 669

Little v. Peers   184

Littleford v. Loanex Financial Services   106

Lloyd Corp. Ltd. v. Tanner   113

London Borough of Southwark v. Williams   173

London Drugs Ltd. v. Kuehne   466

London Graving Dock Co. Ltd. v. Horton   622

London Passenger Transport Board v. Upson   506, 516

Long v. Gardner   45, 458

Long v. R.   97

Long v. Registrar of Motor Vehicles   481

Long v. Toronto Ry. Co.   450

Lonrho plc v. Fayed   557

Lonrho plc v. Fayed (No. 5)   557

Lonrho plc v. Tebbit   707

Lord v. Allison   36, 182, 183

Lorenz v. Winnipeg (City)   238

Lothrop Publishing Co. v. Lothrop, Lee & Shepard Co.   249

Lowry v. Cdn. Mountain Holidays Ltd.   346

Lucas v. Antoniak   456

Ludlow v Burgess   195

Lumley v. Gye   559

Lynch v. Knight   72

Lyon v. Village of Shelburne   654

Lyth v. Dagg   139, 270

M.

M. (J.) v. Toronto Board of Education   152

M. (K.) v. M. (H.)   52, 270

M.(M.) v. K.(K.)   138, 139, 152

MacAlpine v. H. (T.)   707

MacDonald v. Alderson   415

Macdonald v. Hees   166

MacDonald v. Mitchell   670

MacDonald v. Sebastian   52, 405

Macdonald v. Woodard   479

Macdonald (Guardian ad litem of) v. Neufeld   416, 425

MacKay v. Buelow   76, 81

MacKay v. MacLellan   458

MacKeigan v. Hickman   707

MacKenzie v. MacLachlin   712

MacKenzie v. Scotia Lumber Co.   94, 96, 97

MacKinnon v. Ellis   638

MacLachlan & Mitchell Homes Ltd. v. Frank's Rentals & Sales Ltd.   494

MacLean v. Liquor Licence Bd. of Ont.   708

Maclenan v. Segar   620

MacPherson v. Buick Motor   603

Mader v. MacPhee   670

Madouros v. Kansas City Coca-Cola Bottling Co.   658

Magnusson v. Bd. of Nipawin School Unit No. 51 of Sask. 264
Maguire v. Calgary 557
Mahal v. Young 51, 53, 77
Mainville v. Ottawa Board of Education 264
Malette v. Shulman 145
M'Alister (or Donoghue) v. Stevenson 6, 79, 210, 211, **220**, 225, 289, 303, 376, 468, 495, 567, 573, 601, 603, 606, 631, 648, 656
Mallett v. McMonagle 419
Mallet v. Province of N.B. 88
Malone v. Metropolitan Police Commissioner 82
Manitoba Sausage Mfg. Co. v. Winnipeg 574
Mann v. Balaban 159
Mann v. Hilton 480
Mann v. Saulnier 120
Mannsz v. Macwhyte Co. 659
Marconato v. Franklin 382, 384
Marks v. Campbell 481
Marshall v. Babcock & Wilcox Ltd. 514
Marshall v. Curry 143
Martin v. Benson 27
Martin v. McNamara Construction Ltd. 397
Martin v. Reynolds Metal Co. 120
Martin v. Watson 69
Marynowsksky v. Stuartburn (District) 27
Mason v. Morrow's Moving & Storage Ltd. 272
Mason v. Peters 428, 436
Matheson v. Governors of Dalhousie College and University 129
Mathews v. Dwan 205
Mathison v. Hofer 295
Matthews v. Maclaren; Horsley v. Maclaren 250
Matuszczyk v. National Coal Board 515
Maxey v. Can. Permanent Trust Co. 272
Mayfair Ltd. v. Pears 110
Maynes v. Galicz 642
Mazetti v. Armour & Co. 658
McAlister (or Donoghue) v. Stevenson. See M'Alister (or Donoghue) v. Stevenson.
McBain v. Laurentian Hospital 148
McC v. Mullan 707
McCann v. Sheppard 417
McCombe v. Read 692
McCrae v. Richardson. See Haley v. Richardson.
McCutcheon v. Lightfoot 97
McDermott v. Ramadanovic Estate 436
McDowall v. Great Western Railway Co. 400
McEllistrum v. Etches 335, 337
McElroy v. Cowper-Smith 31
McErlean v. Sarel 337, **621**
McEvoy v. Capital Motors 453
McGeough v. Don Enterprises Ltd. 624
McGhee v. Nat. Coal Bd. 353, 354, 355, 356, 358, 486, 487

McGillivray v. Kimber 710
McGinlay v. British Railway Bd. 466
McGinty v. Cook 620
McGivney v. Rustico Summer Haven 620
McGrath v. MacLean 605
McHale v. Watson 16
McHugh v. Reynolds Extrusion Co. 494, 499
McIntosh v. Bell 472
McIntyre v. Sawatsky 342
McKay v. Board of Govan School Unit No. 29 of Saskatchewan 417
McKay v. Essex Area Health Authority 287
McKay v. Gilchrist 493
McKenna v. Greco (No. 2) 624
McKew v. Holland 398
McKinney v. University of Guelph 518
McLaren v. B.C. Institute of Technology 550
McLeod v. Palardy 446
McLorie v. Oxford 202
McLoughlin v. O'Brian 291, 292, 294, 295
McMullin v. F.W. Woolworth Co. 295
McNamara v. Duncan 131
McNeill v. Frankenfield 641, 642
McRae v. British Norwegian Whaling Co. Ltd. 688
Mears v. London & South Western Ry. Co. 97
Mee v. Gardiner 110
Melnychuck v. Moore 481
Mendelssöhn v. Normand Ltd. 582
Mendez v. Palazzi 691
Menna v. Gugglietti 272
Mennie v. Blake 105
Mercer v. Gray 397, 398
Mercer v. South Eastern & Chatham Ry. Co.'s Managing Committee 275, 398
Mero v. Waterloo (Regional Municipality) 721
Mete v. Mississauga 342
Metropolitan Asylum District v. Hill 684
Meyer v. Bright 534
Meyer v. Packard Cleveland Motor Co. 659
Meyer Estate v. Rogers 143, 299
Michalak v. Governors of Dalhousie College and University 264
Michaud v. Dupuis 264
Middleton v. Humphries 692
Middleton v. Whitridge 273
Migliore v. Gerard 264
Mile v. Club Med Inc. 255
Milgaard v. Kujawa 233, 707
Miller v. Decker 141, 464
Miller v. Jackson 121, 319, 325, **693**
Miller v. Wolbaum 328, 452
Miller Dredging Ltd. v. "Dorothy Mackenzie" (The) 440
Millette v. Kalogeropoulos. See R. v. Cote.
Milton v. Savinkoff 82
Minister of Pensions v. Chennell 350

Min. of Housing and Local Govt. v. Sharp 601
Mintuck v. Valley River Band No. 63A 553
Miradizadeh v. Ont. 708
Mirhadizadeh v. Ontario 519
Miska v. Sivec 43
Mitchell v. C.N.R. Co. 662, 623, 624
Mitchell v. McDonald 152
Mitchell v. John Heine & Son Ltd. 66
Moffett v. Downing; Downing v. Moffett 642
Mogul S.S. Co. v. McGregor, Gow & Co. 556
Molnar v. Coates 264
Montaron v. Wagner 148
Monteith v. N.B. Command, Royal Can.
  Legion 624
Moore v. Fanning 269, 328, 401, 452, 481
Moore v. R. 195
Moorgate Mercantile Co. Ltd. v. Finch 98
Moran v. Pyle National (Canada) Ltd. 396
Morash v. Lockhart & Ritchie Ltd. 276
Morgan v. Khyatt 692
Morgan v. Loyacomo 52
Morier v. Rivard 707
Morris v. Baily 642
Morris v. Beardmore 207
Morrisey v. Gammon 494
Morrish v. Murrey 205
Morrison v. Fishwick 98
Morrison v. Thomas 170
Morrow v. Hôpital Royal Victoria 139, 142
Mortimer v. Cameron 459
Morton v. William Dixon 325
Moss v. Ferguson 346, 401
Mostyn v. Fabrigas 711
Motherwell v. Motherwell 79, 82, 677
Moule v. N.B. Elec. Power Comm. 233, 237
Moxley v. The Canada Atlantic Railway
  Company 364
Muir v. Alberta 154
Muirhead v. Industrial Tank Specialties
  Ltd. 605
Muirhead v. Timber Brothers Sand and Gravel
  Ltd. 120, 677
Mullen v. Barr & Co. 224
Municipal Spraying & Contracting Ltd. v. J.
  Harris & Sons Ltd. 439
Munn & Co. v. The Motor Vessel Sir John
  Crosbie 177
Munro v. Willmott 104
Munshaw Colour Service Ltd. v.
  Vancouver 238
Murphy v Brentwood District Council 6, 226,
  294, 605, 608, 721
Murphy v. Culhane 45, 141
Murphy v. St. Catharines Gen. Hosp. 308
Murray v. Bitango 618
Murray v. McMurchy 147
Murray v. Minister of Defence 59

Mustafic v. Smith 264
Mutual Life And Citizens' Assur. Co. v.
  Evatt 574
Myers v. Haroldson 35
Myers v. Peel County Bd. of Ed. 264, 337, 453
Myran, Meeches v. R. 117

N.

N.B. Telephone Co. v. Wright 439
Nader v. General Motors Corp. 81
Nan v. Black Pine Manufacturing Ltd. 439
Nance v. B.C. Electric R. Co. 409
Nantel v. Parisien 110
Nat. Trust Co. v. Wong Aviation Ltd. 494
National Coal Board v. England 515
National Hockey League v. Pepsi Cola Ltd. 545
National Trust Co. v. Wong Aviation Ltd. 355
Nelles v. Ontario 64, 233
Nelson v. Welsh and Snow 404
Nelson v. Whetmore 96
Neufeld v. Landry 452
New Brunswick Broadcasting Co. v. New
  Brunswick (Speaker of the House of
  Assembly) 518
New Brunswick Telephone Co. v. John Maryon
  International Ltd. *See* John Maryon Int. Ltd. v.
  N.B. Telephone Co.
Newcastle (Town) v. Mattatall 366
Nicholls v. Township of Richmond 550
Nichols v. Marsland 653
Nicholson v. John Deere Ltd. 308
Nielsen v. Kamloops (City) 467
Nielsen v. Kaufmann 429, 436
Nightingale v. Mazerall 437
Nilsson Bros. Inc. v. McNamara Estate 97
Nippa v. C.H. Lewis (Lucan) Ltd. 693
Nocton v. Lord Ashburton 567
Nolan v. Dental Manufacturing Co. Ltd. 515
Nor-Video Services Ltd. v. Ont. Hydro 677, 680
Norberg v. Wynrib 139
Norman v. Soule 69
Norris v. Syndic Manufacturing Co. Ltd. 514
Northern Territory of Australia v. Mengel 77
Northwestern Mut. Ins. Co. v. J.T. O'Bryan &
  Co. 272
Northwestern Utilities Ltd. v. London Guarantee
  & Accident Co. 646, 654
Norwich City Council v. Harvey 291
Nowlan v. Brunswick Const. Ltee. 362, 363
Nowsco Well Service Ltd. v. Can. Propane Gas &
  Oil Ltd. 358

O.

Oakley v. Webb 672
Ocsko v. Cypress Bowl Recreations Ltd. 466

O'Fallan v. Inecto Rapid (Can.) Ltd. 309
Ogg-Moss v. The Queen 164, 165
O'Grady v. Brown 288
Ogwo v. Taylor 378
O'Hara v. Belanger 418, 433
Oke v. Weide Tpt. Ltd. 395
Oleschak Estate v. Wilganowski 433
Oliver v. Ashman 417
Oliver v. Miles 485
O'Neill v. Esquire Hotels Ltd. 652
O'Rourke v. Schacht 504, 513
Oscar v. Lickoch. *See* Lickoch v. Madu.
Osterlind v. Hill 248, 255
Ott v. Fleishman 82
Otto v. Bolton 226
Otto v. J. Grant Wallace 191
Ottosen v. Kasper 337
**Overseas Tankship (U.K.) Ltd. v. Miller
Steamship Co. Pty. 384,** 389, 396, 685, 693,
694
**Overseas Tankship (U.K.) Ltd. v. Morts Dock &
Engineering Co. 374,** 380, 381, 384, 385,
387, 388, 389, 390, 396, 397, 398
Oxford Pendaflex Canada Ltd. v. Korr Marketing
Ltd. 541

P.

P Perl (Exporters) Ltd. v. Camden London
Borough Council 401
Pabon v. Hackensack Auto Sales Inc. 662
Pac. Blasting Ltd. v. D.J. Byrne Const. Ltd. 439
Pac. Elevators Ltd. v. C.P.R. Co. 439
Pacific Associates Inc. v. Baxter 291
Page v. Smith 295
Pajot v. Commonwealth Holiday Inns of Can.
Ltd. 624
Palma v. Stora Kopparbergs Berslags
Aktiebolag 652
Palmer v. N.S. Forest Industries 667, 693
Palmer v. St. John 616, 621
Palsgraf v. Long Island Ry. Co. 238, 245, 273
Pannett v. McGuinness & Co. Ltd. 626, 631
Papadimitropoulus v. R. 137
Papp v. Leclerc 398
Paragon Properties Ltd. v. Magna Investments
Ltd. 31
Paramount Pictures Corp. v. Howley 545
Parasiuk v. Can. Newspapers Co. 81, 84
Paris v. Stepney Borough Council 322
Parkhurst v. Forster 8
Parkland No. 31 v. Stetar 505
Parmley v. Parmley and Yule 138, 147
Parry v. Cleaver 443
Pasley v. Freeman 71, 540
Pasternack v. Poulton 456
Patenaude c. Roy 329

Patten v. Silberschein 401
Pattison v. Prince Edward Region Conservation
Authority 653
Pauluik v. Paraiso 353, 398
Pawlak v. Doucette 670
Payne v. Maple Leaf Gardens Ltd. 466
Payton v. New York; Riddick v. New York 207
Paziuk v. Ewbank 372
Pearce v. Rourke. *See* Duce v. Rourke.
Pearl v. Pac. Enercon Inc. 550
Penfolds Wines Proprietary Ltd. v. Elliott 94,
96
Penn v. Singbeil 196
Penn West Petroleum Ltd. v. Koch Oil Co. 493
Penner v. Mitchell 368
Penney v. Gosse 110
Percy v. Glasgow Corp. 664
Perka v. R. 174
Perron v. R.J.R. Macdonald Inc. 310
Perry v. Fried 195
Perry v. Kendricks Transport Ltd. 645
Perry v. Truefitt 541
Pesonen v. Melnyk 384
Peters v. Prince of Wales Theatre (Birmingham)
Ltd. 652
Pett v. Sims Paving & Road Construction Co.
Pty. Ltd. 650
Pettis v. McNeil 131
Phillips v. Brittania Hygienic Laundry Co. 472
Phillips v. Calif. Standard Co. 120
Phillips v. Ford Motor Co. of Can. 663
Phillips v. Soloway 48
Picka v. Porter 263
Pickering v. Rudd 123
Pierce (Next Friend of) v. Marshall 341
Pilieri v. Lockett 165
Pinard v. Coderre 543
Pittman v. Manufacturers Life Insurance
Co. 584
Pittman Estate v. Bain 143, 299, 341
Pitts v. Hunt 467, 471
Pizzolon v. Pedrosa 263, 366
Ploof v. Putnam 175, 177
Plumb v. Cobden Flour Mills Co. 667
Pohoretsky v. R. 202
Poirier v. Canada (Minister of Veterans
Affairs) 519
Poitras v. Goulet 458
Polemis and Furness Wilthy & Co. Ltd.,
Re 374, 375, 376, 377, 380, 381, 389, 396
Police v. Greaves 54
Pollard v. Makarchuk 294
Polnicky v. Queen's Motel 622
Ponting v. Noakes 653
Polsinelli v. Marzilli 545
Poole v. Ragen 81

Posluns v. Toronto Stock Exchange   545, 553,
    556
Poulos v. Matovic   70
Pound v. Nakonechny   341
Poupart v. Lafortune   190
Pratt v. British Medical Ass'n   547
Pratt & Goldsmith v. Pratt   295
Prescott v. Connell   284
Preston v. Canadian Legion of British Empire
    Service League, Kingsway Branch No.
    175   624
Prete v. Ontario   707, 708
Price v. Garcha   384
Price v. Milawski   395
Price v. Seeley   191
Pridham v. Nash   148
Priestman v. Colangelo   190, 196, 328, 329,
    452
Prinse v. Fraser Valley Foods Ltd.   479
Prior v. Hanna   494
Pugh v. London, Brighton and South Coast Ry.
    Co.   72
Pugliese v. Taxiarchis   140
Purdy v. Woznesensky   41, 72, 73

Q.

Q. v. Minto Management Ltd.   269
Qualcast (Wolverhampton) Ltd. v. Haynes   352,
    515
Quartz Hill Consol. Gold Mining v. Eyre   69
Queen v. Cognos Inc.   571, 580
Queensway Tank Lines Ltd. v. Moise   510
Quondam v. Francis Belliveau Excavations
    Ltd.   652

R.

R. in Right of Can. v. Sask. Wheat Pool   501,
505
R. in Right of Ont. v. Schenck; R. in Right of
    Ont. v. Rokeby   721
R. v. Anderson   195
R. v. Baptiste   165
R. v. Baugh   196
R. v. Beare   196
R. v. Big M Drug Mart Ltd.   199
R. v. Biron   183, 184, 191
R. v. Blair   159, 168
R. v. Bogue   159
R. v. Brennan   190, 329
R. v. Brezack   200, 202
R. v. Brydges   195
R. v. Burko   117
R. v. Carroll   195
R. v. Cey   131
R. v. Charles   196

R. v. Ciccarelli   131
R. v. Clarence   137
R. v. Cohen   202
R. v. Colet   207
R. v. Collins   199, 202
R. v. Cote   395, 396
R. v. Cote; Millette v. Kalogeropoulos   504
R. v. Curvan   189
R. v. Custer   207
R. v. Debot   199, 202
R. v. Dedman   198
R. v. Delong   207
R. v. Dudley and Stephens   173
R. v. Duffy   161, 162
R. v. Dupperon   163
R. v. Dyment   202
R. v. Elshaw   195
R. v. Erickson and Hathaway   195
R. v. Fennell   160, 161
R. v. G. (J.M.)   165
R. v. Green   131
R. v. Greffe   201
R. v. Halcrow   165
R. v. Harms   137
R. v. Hastings   194
R. v. Haverstock   168
R. v. Huggins   8
R. v. Ironstand   201
R. v. Jennings   504
R. v. Jobidon   131, 132, 138, 139, 141
R. v. Klimchuk   190
R. v. Koszulap   196
R. v. Landry   198, 207
R. v. Larlham   159
R. v. Leclair   195
R. v. Lee   137
R. v. Leitch   195
R. v. Lyons   168
R. v. M. (S.)   131, 132
R. v. Macooh   207
R. v. Macquarie   59
R. v. Maki   131
R. v. Manninen   195
R. v. Meikle   202
R. v. Mellenthin   202
R. v. Miller   200
R. v. Morrison   200
R. (L.) v. Nyp   81, 341
R. v. Nord-Deutsche Versicherungs-
    Gesellschat   275
R. v. Ogal   158
R. v. Peters   111, 112, 116
R. v. Proulx   190
R. v. Rao   202
R. v. Roberge   196
R. v. Rousseau   202
R. v. Ryan   160

R. v. Sask. Wheat Pool   88
R. v. Scopelliti   160
R. v. Simmons   201
R. v. St. George   53
R. v. Ssenyonga   137
R. v. Storrey   190, 196
R. v. Sullivan   288
R. v. Sweet   165
R. v. Therens   195
R. v. Tooley   189
R. v. Tremblay   195
R. v. Truchanek   202
R. v. W. (J.J.)   165
R. v. Wetmore   165
R. v. Whitfield   182
R. v. Whynot (Stafford)   160
R. v. Williams   137
R. v. Wilson   189
R. v. Wong   202
R. v. Wood   195
R.F. Fry & Associates (Pacific) Ltd. v.
   Reimer   101
R.H. Willis and Son v. Br. Car Auctions Ltd.   97
R.W.D.S.U., Local 580 v. Dolphin Delivery
   Ltd.   199, 518
Rabideau v. Maddocks   462
Radovskis v. Tomm   **73**, 76
Rahemtulla v. Vanfed Credit Union   76
Rainbow Industrial Caterers Ltd. v. C.N.R.   540,
   580, 587
Rainham Chemical Works, Ltd. (in Liquidation)
   v. Belvedere Fish Guano Co., Ltd.   651
Ralston Purina of Can. Ltd. v. Whittaker   100
Randy Knitwear Inc. v. Amer. Cyanamid
   Co.   541, 605
Ranson v. Kitner   **46**
Ratko v. Woodstock (City) Pacific Public Utility
   Commission   685
Rattray v. Daniels   680
Ratych v. Bloomer   440, 441, 442, 443, 444,
   445
Ravenscroft v. Rederiaktiebolaget
   Transatlantic   295
Rayner v. Knickle   415
Read v. Coker   55
Read v. Friendly Society of Operative
   Stonemasons of England, Ireland &
   Wales   548
Read v. J. Lyons & Co.   644, **645**, 649, 650,
   651
Reckitt & Colman Products Ltd. v. Borden
   Inc.   541
Reed v. Maley   75
Reese v. Coleman (No. 1)   242
Reeve v. Palmer   102
Reibl v. Hughes   143, 155, 296, 297, 298, 305
Reid v. Webster   61, 69

Reidy v. McLeod   428
Reilly v. R.   160
Rendall v. Ewert   269, 624
Renken v. Harvey Aluminum Inc.   677
Reynen v. Antonenko   201
Reynolds v. Clarke   8, 10
Rhode Island Hospital Trust National Bank v.
   Swartz, Bresenoff, Yavner & Jacobs   578
Rhodes v. Canadian National Railway Co.   **288**
Rice v. Connolly   195
Richard v. Hoban   **638**
Richard v. C.N.R.   352, 377
Rickards v. Lothian   650, 651, 654
Riddick v. New York. *See* Payton v. New York.
Rigby v. Chief Constable of
   Northamptonshire   173, 174, 207
Rinas v. Regina (City)   516
Rintoul v. X-Ray and Radium Indust.   **471, 513**
Rioux v. Smith   35
Rivtow Marine v. Washington Iron Works   303,
   308, **598**, 607, 608, 609, 656
Roberge v. R.   452
Robert Addie & Sons (Collieries), Ltd. v.
   Dumbreck   625
Robert Simpson Co. v. Foundation Co.   605
Roberts v. Ramsbottom   333
Robertson v. Joyce   196
Robinson v. Kilvert   678
Robinson v. National Bank of Scotland   568
Robinson v. Post Office   398
Robitaille v. Vancouver Hockey Club Ltd.   36,
   404
Robson v. Ashworth   264
Rocky Mountain Rail Society v. H & D Hobby
   Distributing Ltd.   70
Roe v. Min. of Health   343, 486, 494
Roehl v. Houlahan   553
Rogers v. Toni Home Permanent Co.   659, 662
Rollinson v. R.   101, 183, 438
Rolof v. Morris   299
**Roman Corp. v. Hudson's Bay Oil & Gas
   Co.**   **555**, 556, 562, 706, 707
Roncarelli v. Duplessis   556, **709**
Roncato v. Coverly   574
Rondel v. Worsley   228, 229, 230, 231, 232
Rookes v. Barnard   **30**, 31, 32, 36, 43, 551,
   552, 553
Roper v. Harper   138
Rose v. Miles   690
Rosenburg v. Grand River Conservation
   Authority   690
Rosenthal v. Alderton & Sons, Ltd.   102, 103
Rosewell v. Prior   8
Roth v. Roth   81, 553
Rothwell v. Raes   309, 346
Rowland's Transport Ltd. v. Nasby Sales &
   Services Ltd.   405

Royal Bank v. W. Got & Associates Electric Ltd.   101
Royal Bank of Can. v. Aleman   574
Royal Can. Legion Branch 177, Re   707
Rozon v. Patenaude   638
Ruckheim v. Robinson   638
Rumsey v. R.   45, 196, 404
Rusch Factors, Inc. v. Levin   578
Rushmer v. Polsue & Afieri Ltd.   675
Russell Tpt. Ltd. v. Ont. Malleable Iron Co.   685
Russell v. Esson (M.F.) & Sons Ltd.   398
Rutter v. Palmer   569
Ryan v. Auclair   195
Ryan v. Hickson   337
Rydzik v. Edwards   504
Rylands v. Fletcher   319, **642**, 646, 647, 649, 651, 652, 653, 654, 655, 656, 681, 721

S.

S. (J.) v. Clement   264
SCM (U.K.) Ltd. v. W.J. Whittall & Son Ltd.   601, 602
Saccardo v. Hamilton   398, 654
Saccone v. Orr   81, 82
Sachs v. Miklos   99, 101, 102
Said (Husain) v. Said   137
Saif Ali v. Sidney Mitchell & Co. (a firm)   230, 232
Saint-Jacques v. Canada (Solicitor General)   59
Samms v. Eccles   73
Sandberg v. Steer Holdings Ltd.   624
Santor v. A & M Karagheusian Inc.   541, 605
Saltman Engineering Co. v. Campbell Engineering Co.   82
Saunders v. Smith   123
Sauve v. Provost   624
Savage v. Boies   74
Savard v. Urbano   466
Savoie v. Bouchard   494
Sayers v. Harlow Urban Dist. Council   284
Scandinavia Belting Co. v. Asbestos & Rubber Works of America, Inc.   544
Scarff v. Wilson   416
Scarmar Const. Ltd. v. Geddes Contracting Co.   366
Scarth, Re   102
Sceptre Resources Ltd. v. Deloitte Haskins & Sells   341
Schacht v. R.   267
Schell v. Truba   195
Schenck v. R.; Rokeby v. R.   121, 652, 654, 685
Schentag v. Gauthier   105
Schlink v. Blackburn   243
Schmidt v. Sharpe   263
School Div. of Assiniboine South v. Hoffer (No. 3)   516

Schroth v. Innes   670
Schrump v. Koot   406
Schubert v. Sterling Trusts Corp.   645, 654
Schulz v. Leeside Dev. Ltd.   264, 310
Schwartz-Torrance Investment Corp. v. Bakery and Confectionery Workers' Union, Local 31   113
Schweizer v. Central Hospital   138
Scott v. McAlpine   98
Scott v. R.   196, 202
Scott v. Shepherd   5, 7, 42, 400
Scurfield v. Cariboo Helicopter Skiing Ltd.   466
Sczebel v. Silverston   372
Sealand of the Pacific v. Robert McHaffie Ltd.   574
Searle v. Walbank   638
Sears Can. Inc. v. Smart   190, 191
Seaway Hotels Ltd. v. Cragg (Canada) Ltd. and Consumers Gas Co.   603
Sedleigh-Denfield v. O'Callaghan   694
Seede v. Camco Inc.   429
Seeley v. White Motor Co.   541, 605
Segal v. Derrick Golf and Winter Club   121
Seigelman v. Cunard White Star   660
Selig v. Mansfield   553
Semayne's Case   204, 206
Seymour v. Greenwood   668
Shanklin Pier Ltd. v. Detel Products Ltd.   582
Shaw v. Gorter   45
Shaw v. Roemer   456
Shaw v. Trudel   712
Shelfer v. London Electric Lighting Co.   691
Sherrin and Sherrin v. Haggerty   110, 177
Shiffman v. Order of St. John   645
Shilson v. Northern Ont. Light & Power Co.   325
Siametis v. Trojan Horse (Burlington) Inc.   540
Sidaway v. Bethlem Royal Hospital Governors   298
Sigouin (Guardian ad litem of) v. Wong   340
Simms v. Butt   374
Simpson v. Geswein   52
Simpson v. Monture   494
Sinclair v. Woodward's Store Ltd.   61
Sinclaire v. Boulton   299
Sindell v. Abbott Laboratories   286, 358, 487
Singer Manufacturing Co. v. Loog   541
Singh v. Ali   105
Singleton v. Williamson   638
Sirros v. Moore   707, 712
Sisters of Charity of the Immaculate Conception v. Fudge (Robert J.) Ltd.   499
Skelding (Guardian ad litem of) v. Skelding   436
Skelton v. Collins   417, 423
Skelton v. London and North Western R.W. Co.   274

Slater v. Baker   8
Slattery v. Haley   331
Smart v. Simpson Sears Ltd.   61
Smith v. B.C. (A.G.)   264, 315, 341, 395
Smith v. Chadwick   538
Smith v. East Elloe Rural Dist. Council   712
Smith v. Eric S. Bush (a firm)   341
Smith v. Gray   494
Smith v. Jenkins   140
Smith v. Kendrick   643
Smith v. Leech Brain & Co.   **380**, 382, 384
Smith v. Littlewoods Organisation Ltd.   380
Smith v. London & South Western Ry. Co.   381
Smith v. Ont. & Minnesota Power Co.   653
Smith v. Rae   256, **272**, 275
Smith v. Scott   654
Smith v. Stone   **40**, 43
Smith v. Widdicombe   652
Smithies v. National Ass'n of Operative
   Plasterers   548
Smythe v. Reardon   137
Snell v. Farrell   **353**, 486
Sodd Corp. v. Tessis   573, 580
Solloway v. McLaughlin   99
Sorensen v. Kaye Holdings Ltd.   540
Sorrell v. Smith   556
Soulsby v. Toronto   **273**, 275
South Wales Miners' Federation v. Glamorgan
   Coal Co. Ltd.   547
Southam v. Smout   205
Southern Pacific Co. v. Jensen   113
Southern Portland Cement Ltd. v. Cooper   626,
   629, 630, 631
Spagnolo v. Margesson's Sports Ltd.   269, 401
Sparks v. Thompson   462
Spartan Steel & Alloys Ltd. v. Martin & Co.
   (Contractors)   601, 603, 604, 607
Spence v. Three Rivers Bldrs. & Masonry Supply
   Inc.   605
Spiewak v. 251268 Ont. Ltd.   341
Spracklin v. O'Flaherty's Estate   363
Spring v. Guardian Assurance plc   574
Spur Indust. Inc. v. Del E. Webb Dev. Co.   **698**
Squittieri v. De Santis   48
St. Lawrence & Ottawa R. Co. v. Lett   434
St. Pierre v. Ont.   677
Stamp v. R. in Right of Ontario   487
Stanley v. Powell   14, 15
Stansbie v. Troman   401
Stapley v. London, Brighton, and South Coast
   R.W. Co.   274
State Farm Mut. Auto. Ins. Co. v. Anderson-
   Weber, Inc.   662
State v. Johnson   159
Steadman v. Erickson Gold Mining Corp.   121
Steagald v. U.S.   207
Steenblok v. Funk   406

Steiman v. Steiman   101
Stein v. Gonzales   690
Stephens v. Corcoran   132
Stephens v. Myers   53, 56
Stephenson v. Waite Tileman   391
Sterling Trusts Corp. v. Postma   506, 510
Stevens v. Rockport Granite Co.   700
Stevenson v. Basham   73
Stevenson Jordan and Harrison, Ltd. v.
   Macdonald and Evans   665
Stewart v. Ottawa Electric R. Co. and
   Hollis   480
Stewart v. Pettie   238, 263
Stewart v. Stonehouse   52
Stewart v. Traders Trust Co.   138
Stoffman v. Ont. Veterinary Assoc.   69
Stott v. Gamble   548
Stratford (J.T.) & Son Ltd. v. Lindley   550
Strickland v. St. John's   333
Stringer v. Ashley   624
Strom (Litigation Guardian of) v. White   642
Strong v. Moon   295
Stuart v. R. in Right of Can.   618
Sturges v. Bridgman   685, 696
Sulisz v. Flin Flon   712
Summers v. Tice   364, 485
Suite c. Cooke   288
Sunrise Co. v. The Ship "Lake Winnipeg"   372
Superintendent of Belchertown State School v.
   Saikewicz   154
Superintendent of Family and Child Services and
   Dawson, Re   154
Surocco v. Geary   **171**
Surrey (District) v. Marall Homes Ltd.   557
Surrey v. Carroll-Hatch & Associates Ltd.   605
Sutherland Shire Council v. Heyman   226, 717
Swaile v. Zurdayk   110
Swales v. Cox   207
Swami v. Lo   384, 398
Swansburg v. Smith   190
Sweeney v. Old Colony & Newport
   Railroad   248
Sweeney v. Starrat   170
Swinamer v. Nova Scotia (Attorney
   General)   721
Swinimer v. R.   196
Sylvester v. Crits   338
Szarfer v. Shodos   82
Szeliga Estate v. Vanderheide   295

T.

T. (a minor) v. Surrey County Council   270,
   574
T.G. Bright & Co. v. Kerr   **664**, 669
Taaffe v. Downes   705
Taft v. Bridgeton Worsted Co.   249

Taller (Guardian ad litem of) v.
Goldenshtein 642
Tallow v. Tailfeathers 140
Tanner v. Norys 63
Tarasoff v. Regents of the Univ. of
California 270
Tataryn v. Co-Op. Trust Co. 490, 499
Taylor v. Ashton 539, 540
Taylor v. Asody 462
Taylor v. King 264
Taylor v. Weston Bakeries Ltd. 295
Taylor v. Whitehead 173
Teece v. Honeybourn 140
Temilini v. Commissioner of the Ont. Prov.
Police 69
Temperton v. Russell 559
Temple v. Hallem 129, 466
Tenning v. Gov't of Manitoba 88
Teno v. Arnold 424
Teolis v. Moscatelli 131
ter Neuzen v. Korn 340, **342**, 425
The Arpad 381
The Case of the King's Prerogative in
Saltpetre 173
The Koursk 365, 366
The Lancashire Wagon Co. Ltd. v. Fitzhugh 98
The Mediana 26, 404
The Queen in Right of Man. v. Air Can. 124
The Queen v. Jennings 418, 420
The Schwan 472, 473
The Winkfield 97
Theakston v. Bowley 407
Thermo King Corp. v. Prov. Bank of Can. 549
Thiele v. Rod Service (Ottawa) Ltd. 401
Thomas v. Hamilton (City) Board of
Education 337
Thomas v. Sawkins 205
Thomas v. Whitehorse 604
Thompson v. London County Council 362
Thompson v. Toorenburgh 398
Thorne v. Deas 271, 272, 275
Thornton v. Board of School Trustees of School
District No. 57 (Prince George) 408, 424,
432
Thorson v. A.G. Can. 690
Tillander v. Gosselin 48
Timmerman v. Buelow 73, 76, 77
Timothy v. Simpson 191
**Tock v. St. John's Metropolitan Area
Board** 652, **680**, 712
Tomizza v. Fraser 398
Tompkins Hardware Ltd. v. North West Flying
Services Ltd. 458
Toneguzzo-Norvell (Guardian ad litem of) v.
Burnaby Hospital 419
Toronto Ry. Co. v. Grinstead 374
Torquay Hotel Co. v. Cousins 550

Toy v. Argenti 284
Tracy v. Atkins 574
Trachsler v. Halton 503
Trans World Airlines Inc. v. Curtiss-Wright
Corp. 605
Tronrud v. French 416
Trueman v. The King; Dewan v. The King 504
Tubervell v. Savadge 55, 56
Tucker (Public Trustee of) v. Asleson 366
Turenne v. Chung 406
Turner v. Delta Shelf Co. 677
Turner v. Thorne 47, **108**, 110, 138
Tutton v. A.D. Walter Ltd. 242

U.

U.S. v. Caltex (Philippines) Inc. 173
U.S. v. Carroll Towing Co. 316
U.S. v. Holmes 173
Ultramares Corp. v. Touche 576, 578, 579,
597, 606
Unident v. DeLong 550
United Motors Service Inc. v. Hutson 496
United Service Funds (Trustees of) v. Richardson
Greenshields of Can. Ltd. 458
United States v. S.A. Empresa De Viacao Aerea
Rio Grandense (Varig Airlines) 716
Univ. Hospital Bd. v. Lepine; Monckton v.
Lepine 264
Universite Laval v. Carriere 276
University of Regina v. Pettick 407, 584
Unruh (Guardian ad litem of) v. Webber 466
Urbanski v. Patel 242, 284
Uren v. John Fairfax & Sons Pty. Ltd. 31

V.

V.K. Mason Const. Ltd. v. Bank of N.S. 573,
580
Vale v. R.J. Yohn Construction Co. Ltd. 436
Valleyview Hotel Ltd. v. Montreal Trust
Co. 494
Valiquette c. Gazette (The) 81
Vana v. Tosta 435, 436
Vancouver Gen. Hosp. v. McDaniel 346
Vancouver General Hospital v. Stoffman 519
Vancouver-Fraser Park District v.
Olmstead 343
Vanvalkenburg v. Northern Navigation
Co. 252, 255, 277, 281
Varcoe v. Sterling 516
**Vaughn v. Halifax-Dartmouth Bridge
Comm. 325**, 327
Veinot v. Kerr-Addison Mines Ltd. 625
Veinot v. Veinot 45, 159, 168
Victorian Railways Commissioners v.
Coultas 71, 72, 290

Videan v. British Transport Commission   278, 280, 282, 283, 625
Videto v. Kennedy   148, 297
Vincent v. Lake Erie Tpt. Co.   174
Vlchek v. Koshel   36, 308, 404
Volkswagen Can. Ltd. v. Spicer   562
Vorvis v. Insurance Corp. of British Columbia   28, 36, 404
Vykysaly v. Jablowski   624

W.

Wackett v. Calder   157
Wade v. Ball   228, 231
Wade v. C.N.R.   525, 631
Wade v. Hoyt   231
Wade v. Martin   131, 139, 140
Wagner v. International R. Co.   282, 283
Wakelin v. London & South Western Ry. Co.   476
Waldick v. Malcolm   624
Waldman's Fish Co. v. Anderson Ins. Ltd.   341
Walker (Litigation Guardian of) v. Region 2 Hospital Corp.   151
Walker v. Pioneer Construction Co.   691
Wallace v. Berrigan   457
Walls v. Mussens Ltd.   450
Walmsley v. Humenick   48, 482
Walt Disney Productions v. Triple Five Corp.   545
Walters v. W.H. Smith & Son   191
Wandsworth Board of Works v. United Telephone Co. Ltd.   123
Ward v. Blaine Lake (School Board)   165
Ward v. Cannock Chase Dist. Council   401
Ward v. James   423
Ward v. Magna International Inc.   680, 693
Ward v. T.E. Hopkins & Son, Ltd; Baker v. T.E. Hopkins & Son, Ltd.   281
Warren v. King   417, 423
Waskul v. Cardinal   494
Waterloo Warehousing & Storage Ltd. v. Swenco Mfg. Ltd.   439
Watkins v. Olafson   411, 416
Watt v. Hertfordshire County Council   327
Weatherall v. A.G. Can.   201
Webb v. Attewell   117
Webber v. Crawford   457
Wechsel v. Stutz   232
Weiner v. Zoratti   377
Weiss v. Solomon   142
Welbridge Holdings Ltd. v. Greater Winnipeg   720
Wells v. Parsons   453
Wenden v. Trikha   264, 270, 333
Wentzell v. Veinot   170
Werbeniuk v. Maynard   269, 401

Wessell v. Kinsmen Club of Sault Ste. Marie Ont. Inc.   428
West Coast Finance Ltd. v. Gunderson, Stokes, Walton & Co.   540
Western Stevedoring Co. v. Pulp, Paper & Woodworkers of Can.   557
Whaley v. Cartusiano   48
Whaling v. Ravenhorst   622
White, Re   166
White v. Blackmore   466
White v. Sheaves   473
White v. Turner   337
Whitehorse (City) v. Domingue   642
Whiteley Ltd. v. Hilt   103
Wieland v. Cyril Lord Carpets Ltd.   398
Wilcox v. Cavan   494
Wilcox v. Police   117, 173
Wiley v. Tymar Management Inc.   618
Wilkinson v. Downtown   7, **70**, 73, 76, 88
Williams v. Holland   5, 12
Williams v. New Brunswick   264
Williams v. Polgar   580
Williams v. Saint John (City)   380
Willington v. Marshall   35
Wills v. Doe   398
Wills v. Saunders   341
Wilmington Gen. Hosp. v. Manlove   275
Wilsher v. Essex Area Health Authority   353, 354, 355, 356, 357, 486
Wilson v. Lind   404
Wilson v. Martinello   411
Wilson v. New Brighton Panelbeaters Ltd.   97
Wilson v. Pringle   52
Wilson v. Swanson   338
Wilson v. Tyneside Window Cleaning Co.   515
Wiltshire v. Barrett   186, 188
Windrem v. Hamill   638
Winnipeg Condominium Corp. No. 36 v. Bird Construction Co.   227, 380, 605, 612
Winnipeg Elec. Ry. Co. v. Can. Nor. Ry.   374
Winnipeg Electric Co. v. Geel   480
Wipfli v. Britten   76, 446
Witman v. Johnson   642
Woods v. Duncan   376
Woollerton v. Richard Costain   121
Wormald v. Cole   638
Wotta v. Haliburton Oil Well Cementing Co. Ltd.   487, 494
Wright v. Davidson   399
Wright v. McCrea   401
Wright v. McLean   128
Wright v. Wilson   59
Wright Estate v. Davidson   384
Wyant v. Crouse   110

Y.

Y. (A.), Re   151
Yates v. Lansing   705
Ybarra v. Spangard   486
Yelic v. Gimli (Town)   624
Yoner, Re   707
Yuan v. Farstad   454
Yuen Kun-yeu v. A.G. of Hong Kong   227

Z.

Zapf v. Muckalt   466

Zbarsky v. Lukashuk   677
Zelenko v. Gimbel Bros., Inc.   273, 275
Zervobeakos v. Zervobeakos   284, 452
Zinck v. Strickland and Blake   139

270233 Ontario Ltd. v. Weall & Cullen Nurseries
    Ltd.   680
281856 B.C. Ltd. v. Kamloops Revelstoke
    Okanagan Building Traders Union   117
**340909 Ont. Ltd. v. Huron Steel Products
    (Windsor) Ltd.   672**
384238 Ont. Ltd. v. The Queen in Right of
    Can.   94

1

AN INTRODUCTION
TO THE LAW OF TORTS

1. The Concept of Torts
2. Torts Distinguished from Other Areas of Law
3. A Brief History of Tort Law
4. Trespass and Case: A Brief Review of the Case Law
5. The Bases for Imposing Liability in Tort
6. The Functions of Tort Law

1. The Concept of Torts

At the beginning of any course, students want to know what they will be studying. The reply that they will study the law of torts is likely to be unsatisfying, but to go beyond this and provide a comprehensive definition is difficult. The word "tort" is derived from the Latin word "tortus" which means twisted or crooked and has come to be used in English to mean a wrong. In legal terminology, torts are commonly referred to as a type of civil wrong. Since there are a number of civil wrongs that are not torts, this definition does not greatly advance our understanding. Nevertheless, several basic distinctions can be drawn between torts and other branches of the law, and this is where we begin our inquiry.

The absence of a comprehensive definition or theory of torts can be best understood in an historical context. This lack of a general theory is not surprising, considering that tort was not recognized as a distinct branch of law until the second half of the last century. Prior to this, tort law was a residual category of civil wrongs that was dominated by the procedural formalities of the writ system. Much can be learned about modern tort law by examining its historical development, and this is the perspective adopted in the third section of the chapter.

The law of torts may also be examined by dividing it into broad areas of study based on the rule of liability that is applied. For example, in the intentional torts, liability is predicated on intentional wrongdoing, whereas in negligence, liability is imposed for conduct that is careless. Moreover, in certain tort actions, liability will be imposed in the absence of either intentional wrongdoing or carelessness. We will examine a range of liability rules in the fifth section of this chapter.

An alternative method of examining tort law is to consider the functions that it can and should serve. In recent years, considerable attention has been focused on the effectiveness of tort law in meeting certain goals. This development has sparked calls for the abolition of much of the existing tort law in favour of legislative alternatives, such as comprehensive compensation schemes. Moreover, legislators and judges have become increasingly explicit in identifying the goals that their legal policies are intended to serve. In the sixth section of this chapter, we will briefly discuss some of the goals of tort law.

In summary, this chapter does not provide a precise answer to the question of what tort law is, but instead examines various approaches that students may use to resolve this issue for themselves. It should become apparent that these approaches are not mutually exclusive.

2. Torts Distinguished from Other Areas of Law

The boundaries of tort law were not fixed by grand design, but rather emerged as other branches of law became established. Although space does not permit a detailed historical account of this process, it is important to understand how tort differs from criminal law and other civil actions.

Tort and criminal law share a common heritage that predates the Norman Conquest, but they gradually diverged in the 11th century as the distinction between public and private wrongs became more sharply defined. A crime is an offence against society at large, for which the state will bring proceedings in the form of criminal prosecution. The primary purpose of the criminal law is to protect and vindicate the interest of the public by punishing the offender and deterring others. While tort law may indirectly protect the public by punishing wrongdoers and deterring others, it involves civil proceedings commenced and maintained by the injured party. Regardless of the other functions tort law may serve, the plaintiff is usually motivated by the prospect of obtaining compensation from the wrongdoer.

Both tort and contract give rise to civil actions initiated by an aggrieved party for the purpose of obtaining damages. The interests protected in these actions, however, are different. Traditionally, liability in contract stemmed from a breach of an agreement made by the contracting parties. The parties themselves determined their mutual obligations, and only they could sue when the contract was not honoured. In contrast, obligations in tort are imposed by the operation of general principles of law, rather than by agreement. Generally, anyone who is injured by the defendant's tortious behavior may sue for damages.

Equity was a body of legal principles and procedures developed by the King's Chancellor and later administered by the Court of Chancery. Its origins lay in the petitions which were brought to the Chancellor, when redress was unavailable in the common law courts. As the common law became increasingly formalized and developed substantive doctrines, equity gradually emerged as a separate body of law. Its function became one of overcoming the rigidity of the common law, serving as a parallel legal system to provide remedies where the common law was considered unfair. Tort law was a product of the common law and, therefore, was independent of the civil wrongs associated with equity. Although the administration of common law and equity were merged by the Judicature Acts in the late 19th century, the legal mould had been cast. Consequently, the modern law of torts does not encompass the specialized civil wrongs traditionally adjudicated by equity, such as breach of trust and unjust enrichment.

In addition to contract law and equity, there are other civil wrongs that are not part of tort law. For example, although the law of torts retains some connection with property law through the tort of trespass to land, there are also separate civil actions for the recovery of real property.

Thus, we have isolated the residual category of civil wrongs that collectively define modern tort law. Torts are not crimes, breaches of contract or infringements of equitable rights. A tort is a civil wrong, separate from these wrongs, for which the individual may seek a common law remedy in damages. Nevertheless, it is important to emphasize that these categories of law are not mutually exclusive. One fact situation may give rise to a tort action for deceit, an equitable remedy for breach of trust, a criminal charge for theft, and an action for breach of contract.

NOTES AND QUESTIONS

1. The boundary between tort and contract law has been blurred by recent developments in both areas. Many contractual obligations are now imposed by law once the parties enter into a contract. Moreover, several authors suggest that reliance, rather than the parties' intentions, is the basis of contractual obligations. Similarly, some tort obligations will only be imposed if the defendant voluntarily undertakes to perform certain acts. See generally, Blom, "The Interface Between Contract and Tort", in Burns (ed.), *Donoghue v. Stevenson and the Modern Law of Negligence* (1991), 139-90.

2. See generally, Keeton *et al., Prosser and Keeton on the Law of Torts*, 5th ed. (1984), 1-15; Heuston and Buckley, *Salmond and Heuston on the Law of Torts*, 20th ed. (1992), 9-17; and Rogers, *Winfield and Jolowicz on Tort*, 14th ed. (1994), 1-16.

REVIEW PROBLEM

Angus, a consumer advocate, was conducting a speaking tour criticizing the safety standards of a new Canadian subcompact automobile. The car, which had been hailed as the key to the future of the Canadian automobile industry, was supposed to reverse the trend of falling sales and high unemployment. Several days before his appearance in Windsor, Angus received threatening phone calls. As a precaution he hired Joseph, a local private detective, who agreed to serve as his bodyguard during his speech.

Just before the end of the speech, a man jumped onto the stage shouting "Canadian jobs first!" and flailed at Angus. Joseph ran off to call the police, but offered no direct assistance. Angus' secretary, Doris, who was an expert in the martial arts, also failed to come to his assistance. The assailant, an unemployed auto worker named Victor, was eventually restrained by two members of the audience, but not before he had severely beaten Angus.

1. As you are probably aware, Victor's attack on Angus is a violation of Canadian criminal law. Who is responsible for bringing charges against Victor, gathering the evidence, and conducting and paying for the prosecution? What role will Angus play at the criminal trial? What private and social benefits result from the criminal prosecution?

2. Victor's attack on Angus also constitutes the intentional tort of battery. Contrast the events involved in bringing a tort suit against Victor with the criminal process. What general distinctions between criminal and tort law emerge?

3. Angus and Joseph are in a contractual relationship. What legal wrong has Joseph done to Angus? What is the public interest in enforcing contractual obligations?

4. Angus also wants to sue Doris, whose legal wrong, if any, was a failure to come to Angus' aid. Distinguish Angus' legal relationship with Doris, from his legal relationship with Joseph.

5. A failure to act is referred to as a nonfeasance. In tort law, it has always been more difficult to establish liability for a nonfeasance than for a misfeasance, which is a wrongful positive act. Can you explain why? Provided that the defendant has agreed to act, he will generally be held liable in contract for his failure to do so. Why should nonfeasance be more readily actionable in contract than in tort?

6. Should Doris be held liable in tort if she knew of the threats against Angus and promised to protect him? Would your answer be different if: (a) Angus had relied on her assurances and told Doris that he had dismissed Joseph; or (b) Doris was unaware that Angus had dismissed Joseph?

3. A Brief History of Tort Law

The history of the law of torts is not the evolution of a single idea, but rather the history of how a residual category of civil wrongs came to be formed. Initially, this involved the separation of the notions of public and private wrongs. Subsequently, the scope of tort law emerged as contracts and other areas of the law grew apart from the general body of civil wrongs.

In Anglo-Saxon England, the primary object of the law was to prevent blood feuds among the clans. There were few divisions in the law, and no distinction was drawn between crimes and torts. The appeasement of the clan's pride and the symbolism of public adjudication were the law's main goals. The wrongdoer paid a *bot* to the other clan for appeasement and a *wite* to the King for having breached the peace. Gradually, as political power became centralized in the King, the distinction between public and private wrongs developed. By the 11th century the appeal of felony, a criminal action that could not be amended by private payment, was recognized. Parallelling this development was a breakdown in the agreed scale of the *bot* among the clans. As a result, there was no legal mechanism for making a private claim for damages.

After the Norman Conquest, there were further attempts to centralize and unify legal authority. In order to consolidate his power and to avoid the inconvenience that the diverse local laws caused his tax collectors and judicial officers, William the Conqueror sought to impose a uniform set of laws throughout England. This set of laws came to be known as the common law. A central feature of the common law was the writ system — a system that became dominated by an intense concern with procedural formality.

The writs themselves were standardized pleadings issued by the Chancery clerks on behalf of the King, stating that a defendant had committed certain unlawful acts. In order to commence an action in the King's common law courts, a plaintiff had to allege facts that would bring his case within the standard form of the writ. No matter how obviously wrongful the defendant's conduct, no action would lie if it was not governed by an existing writ.

At first, access to the King's courts was limited to suits concerning violent acts; those done with force of arms and against the King's peace (*vi et armis et contra pacem regis*). Causes of action which are now recognized as torts were grouped into a family of writs called trespass. It included actions for assault, battery, trespass to land, and the taking of goods.

The most important factor in the history of tort law after 1200 was jurisdiction, not policy. To meet the demand for access to the King's courts and to expand the King's jurisdiction, it was necessary to broaden the types of wrongs that could be heard. However, this had to be accomplished without increasing the limited number of writs. Thus, plaintiffs would plead trespass *vi et armis et contra pacem regis* even if no force or breach of the peace was involved, and the clerks would honour this fiction to assume jurisdiction. For example, if the defendant refused to return goods in storage, the plaintiff would plead that the defendant took them *vi et armis et contra pacem regis* in order to have the case tried in the King's courts.

Although the King's courts eventually assumed jurisdiction over most civil wrongs and the *vi et armis* allegation became unnecessary in the 1300s, the writ system remained. A second writ, called trespass on the case, emerged. Its origins are a matter of dispute. The pleadings in an action on the case raised special circumstances which made the act wrongful, whereas in the original trespass action a general plea would suffice.

For centuries, virtually nothing of significance turned on the distinction between the actions in trespass *vi et armis* and trespass on the case. Yet, by the 18th century, the distinction became crucial. Once the plaintiff obtained a writ, he still had to prove to the court that the facts of the case satisfied the chosen writ. If the plaintiff failed to do so he was non-suited, even if the facts of his case satisfied the terms of a different writ.

During the 18th and 19th centuries, the courts attempted to draw a distinction between trespass and case, based initially on whether the plaintiff's injuries were directly or indirectly caused. It was in *Scott v. Shepherd, infra,* that the courts first clearly held that trespass was limited to direct harms and that case governed indirect harms. Much of tort law was governed by this formalistic exercise of defining the scope of the writs. This development was perplexing given that this distinction had not previously existed and was difficult to apply. Nevertheless, it was this type of procedural consideration and not policy or principle that dominated the evolution of modern tort law.

It is a matter of debate whether proof of direct harm was sufficient to give rise to liability, in the absence of fault. Some authors suggest that direct causation was regarded as fault before more complex theories of morality developed. Others argue that the records are too sketchy to resolve the issue. In *Leame v. Bray, infra,* it was held that liability for direct harm arose without proof of fault. However, that conclusion, like so many others, may have been based on procedural considerations rather than any concern with fault.

Thereafter, fault began to assume more significance in the law of torts. In *Williams v. Holland, infra,* the court held that an allegation based on negligence could be brought in case, even if the harm was directly caused. In *Holmes v. Mather, infra,* it was established that a defendant could not be held liable for direct harm unless the act was either intentional or negligent.

After 50 years of debate, the writ system in England was abolished by the Judicature Acts in the 1870s. Similar legislation soon followed in other common law jurisdictions, including Canada. It was no longer necessary for a litigant to fit his claim within an existing writ. Instead, the plaintiff pleaded the facts of his case and if these facts justified relief under any recognized cause of action, the courts would grant that relief. Nevertheless, the break with the old forms of actions was neither sharp nor complete. While the Judicature Acts had freed the law from the old forms of actions, they continued to influence the categorization of tort law and the substantive elements of the specific actions. For example, the intentional torts derived from trespass *vi et armis* have remained strictly defined, typically require proof of direct injury and have developed little over the years. As *Cook v. Lewis, infra,* illustrates, a plaintiff still benefits if he can prove that he was directly injured.

It was not until the end of the last century that academics and lawyers began to speak of torts as a distinct branch of law. Initially, the search for a theoretical basis for tort law centred on the issue of whether there was a general principle of tortious liability. Sir John Salmond argued that tort law was merely a patchwork of distinct causes of action, each protecting different interests and each based on separate principles of liability. Essentially, the law of torts was a finite set of independent rules, and the courts were not free to recognize new heads of liability. In contrast, writers such as Pollock contended that the law of torts was based upon the single unifying principle that all harms were tortious unless they could be justified. The courts were thus free to recognize new torts.

The debate over the existence of a general theory of tort liability was not limited to academics. The courts, confronted with new claims in the growing area of negligence, also had to decide whether to expand tort liability and, if so, upon what principles. In *Donoghue v. Stevenson*, [1932] A.C. 562 at 580 (H.L.), Lord Atkin suggested that, at least in the tort of negligence, the courts were prepared to expand the scope of recovery and recognize a general theory of liability:

> At present I content myself with pointing out that in English law there must be, and is, some general conception of relations giving rise to a duty of care, of which the particular cases found in the books are but instances. The liability for negligence, whether you style it such or treat it as in other systems as a species of "culpa," is no doubt based upon a general public sentiment of moral wrongdoing for which the offender must pay.

The increased role of government in all facets of society, the growth of social welfare and social services, continued urbanization, and rapid technological change have all influenced the expansion of tort liability in the last 50 years. New approaches to defining the scope of liability have been provided by the courts. In *Anns v. London Borough of Merton*, [1977] 2 All E.R. 492 at 498 (H.L.), Lord Wilberforce stated:

> [T]he position has now been reached that in order to establish that a duty of care arises in a particular situation, it is not necessary to bring the facts of that situation within those of previous situations in which a duty of care has been held to exist. Rather the question has to be approached in two stages. First one has to ask whether, as between the alleged wrongdoer and the person who has suffered damage there is a sufficient relationship of proximity or neighbourhood such that, in the reasonable contemplation of the former, carelessness on his part may be likely to cause damage to the latter, in which case a prima facie duty of care arises. Secondly, if the first question is answered affirmatively, it is necessary to consider whether there are any considerations which ought to negative, or to reduce or limit the scope of the duty or the class of person to whom it is owed or the damages to which a breach of it may give rise.

The two-step duty approach in *Anns* was initially followed in England, Canada and New Zealand. However, the English courts began to question, limit and criticize *Anns* by the mid-1980s. The House of Lords finally over-ruled *Anns* in *Murphy v. Brentwood District Council*, [1990] 2 All E.R. 908. The general theory of negligence in *Anns* was too open-ended, and led to capricious results. The House of Lords indicated that new duties should be based on logical extensions of existing precedents and should evolve on a category-by-category basis. Only Parliament could create new duties based on policy goals. Despite its demise in England, the Supreme Court of Canada continues to apply *Anns* as a general test of new duties of care. It seems reasonable to expect judicial attitudes to swing between the extremes of *Anns* and *Murphy* for the foreseeable future.

In the early days of the writ system, the challenge was to break down the rigid boundaries of tort law to facilitate its expansion. However, the challenge now appears to be in deciding whether to restrain the outward thrust of liability and, if so, on what bases. If anything, the search for general theories and the debate over the nature of tort law has intensified as economists, historians and philosophers have joined the discussion.

NOTES AND QUESTIONS

1. Anglo-Saxon law was characterized by very strict ideas of causation. The issue of fault was largely ignored and an actor was held liable for even the most remote consequences of his actions. It was common, in fact, for offending animals and even inanimate objects which had been the instruments of harm to be destroyed merely because they were part of the causal chain. On the history of Anglo-Saxon law see Winfield, "The Myth of Absolute Liability" (1926), 42 L.Q.R. 37; Baker, *An Introduction to English Legal History*, 3rd ed. (1990), 1-43; and Pollock and Maitland, *History of English Law Before the Time of Edward I*, 2nd ed. (1898), vol. 1, 1-63. See also Arnold, "Accident, Mistake, and Rules of Liability in the Fourteenth Century Law of Torts" (1979), 128 U. Pa. L. Rev. 361.

2. On the origins of the writ of trespass *vi et armis* see Ames, *Lectures On Legal History* (1886-7), 41-60; Maitland, *Forms of Actions* (1904), 48-50; Woodbine, "The Origin of the Action of Trespass" (1924), 33 Yale L.J. 799 and (1925), 34 Yale L.J. 343; and Milsom, *Historical Foundations of the Common Law*, 2nd ed. (1981), 283-313. See also Fifoot, *History And Sources of the Common Law* (1952), 44-65.

3. For a history of the writ of trespass on the case see Landon, "The Action on the Case and the Statute of Westminster II" (1936), 52 L.Q.R. 68; Dix, "The Origins of the Action of Trespass on the Case" (1937), 46 Yale L.J. 1142; Kiralfy, *The Action on the Case* (1951); and Milsom, *supra*.

4. It is debatable whether fault first assumed significance in the 19th century or whether the absence of fault had long provided a valid defence that was simply not apparent from the writ system. See Malone, "Ruminations on the Role of Fault in the History of the Common Law of Torts" (1970), 31 La.L.Rev. 1.

5. Largely as a result of frequent usage, most of the actions in trespass and some of the actions in trespass on the case acquired specific names. As a category, these are known as the nominate actions. There are other torts, innominate actions, that have not been named.

6. With the enactment of the Judicature Acts, the plaintiff no longer had to fit his claim into an existing writ. However, the Acts did not address whether the courts could create new tort actions to deal with situations that had not been covered by the writs. In *Wilkinson v. Downton*, [1897] 2 Q.B. 57, the court created a new innominate action for intentional, indirectly caused physical injury. This filled some of the gaps left by the established nominate torts. Although it is now generally accepted that courts may recognize new causes of action, plaintiffs have had considerable difficulty establishing new intentional tort claims. In contrast, the scope of liability in negligence has increased dramatically.

4. Trespass and Case: A Brief Review of the Case Law

SCOTT v. SHEPHERD

[1558-1774] All E.R. 296

Action of trespass and assault for throwing, casting and tossing a lighted squib at and against the plaintiff and striking him therewith on the face and so burning one of his eyes that he lost the sight of it. The defendant denied liability.

At the trial before Nares, J., the jury found a verdict for the plaintiff with £100 damages, subject to the opinion of the court on a case.

On the evening of the fair day at Milborne Port, Oct. 28, 1770, the defendant threw a lighted squib made of gunpowder, etc., from the street into the market-house which was a covered building supported by arches and enclosed at one end, but open at the other and both the sides, where a large concourse of people were assembled. The lighted squib fell on the stall of one William Yates, who sold ginger-bread, etc. One James Willis instantly, and to prevent injury to himself and the wares of Yates, took up the lighted squib from off the stall and then threw it across the market-house where it fell on another stall there of one Ryal, who sold the same sort of wares. He instantly and to save his own goods from being injured took up the lighted squib from off the stall and then threw it to another part of the market-house and, in so throwing it, struck the plaintiff then in the market-house in the face therewith, and the combustible matter then bursting, put out one of the plaintiff's eyes. The question for the opinion of the court was whether this action was maintainable.

NARES, J.: — I am of opinion that trespass would well lie in the present case. The natural and probable consequence of the act done by the defendant was injury to somebody, and, therefore, the act was illegal at common law. The throwing of squibs has by 9 Will. 3, c. 7 [Fireworks Act, 1697: repealed], been since made a nuisance. Being, therefore, unlawful, the defendant was liable to answer for the consequences, be the injury mediate or immediate. YEAR BOOK 21 Hen. 7, 28, is express that malus animus is not necessary to constitute a trespass. . . . The principle I go on is what is laid down in *Reynolds v. Clarke* [(1725), 93 E.R. 747], that if the act in the first instance be unlawful, trespass will lie. Wherever, therefore, an act is unlawful at first, trespass will lie for the consequences of it. So, in Y.B. 12 Hen. 4, fo. 3, pl. 4, trespass lay for stopping a sewer with earth so as to overflow the plaintiff's land. In Y.B. 26 Hen. 8, 8, for going on the plaintiff's land to take the boughs off which had fallen thereon in lopping. . . . I do not think it necessary, to maintain trespass, that the defendant should personally touch the plaintiff; if he does it by a mean it is sufficient. Qui facit per aliud facit per se. He is the person who, in the present case, gave the mischievous faculty to the squib. That mischievous faculty remained in it until the explosion. No new power of doing mischief was communicated to it by Willis or Ryal. It is like the case of a mad ox turned loose in a crowd. The person who turns him loose is answerable in trespass for whatever mischief he may do. The intermediate acts of Willis and Ryal will not purge the original tort in the defendant. But he who does the first wrong is answerable for all the consequential damages: so held in *R. v. Huggins* [(1730), 92 E.R. 518]; *Parkhurst v. Forster* [(1698), 87 E.R. 746]; *Rosewell v. Prior* [(1701) 90 E.R. 1175]. And it was declared by this court, in *Slater v. Baker* (1767), 2 Wils. K.B. 359, that they would not look with eagle's eyes to see whether the evidence applies exactly or not to the case; but if the plaintiff has obtained a verdict for such damages as he deserves, they will establish it if possible.

BLACKSTONE, J. (dissenting): — I am of opinion that an action of trespass does not lie for the plaintiff against the defendant on this Case. I take the settled distinction to be that, where the injury is immediate, an action of trespass will lie; where it is only consequential, it must be an action on the Case: *Reynolds v. Clarke* [above]; *Haward v. Bankes* [(1760), 97 E.R. 740]; *Harker v. Birkbeck* [(1764), 97 E.R. 978]. The lawfulness or unlawfulness of the original act is not the criterion, although something of that sort is put into Lord Raymond's mouth in *Reynolds v. Clarke* [above], where it can only mean that if the act then in question, of erecting a spout, had been in itself unlawful, trespass might have lain; but as it was a lawful act (on the defendant's own ground) and the injury to the plaintiff only consequential, it must be an action on the case. But this cannot be the general rule, for it is held by the court in the same case that if I throw a log of timber into the highway (which is an unlawful act) and another man tumbles over it and is hurt, an action on the case only lies, it being a consequential damage; but if in throwing it I hit another man, he may bring trespass because it is an immediate wrong. Trespass may sometimes lie for the consequences of a lawful act. If in lopping my own trees a bough accidentally falls on my neighbour's ground and I go thereon to fetch it, trespass lies. This is the case cited from Y.B. 6 Edw. 4, fo. 7, pl. 18. But then the entry is of itself an immediate wrong. And case will sometimes lie for the consequence of an unlawful act. If by false imprisonment I have a special damage, as if I forfeit my recognisance thereby, I shall have an action on the case: per Powell, J., in *Bourden v. Alloway* [(1708), 88 E.R. 975]. Yet here the original act was unlawful, and in the nature of trespass. So that lawful or unlawful is quite out of the case.

The solid distinction is between direct or immediate injuries on the one hand and mediate or consequential on the other, and trespass never lay for the latter. If this be so, the only question will be whether the injury which the plaintiff suffered was immediate, or consequential only; and I hold it to be the latter. The original act was, as against Yates, a trespass; not as against Ryal or the plaintiff. The tortious act was complete when the squib lay at rest on Yates's stall. He, or any bystander, had, I allow, a right to protect themselves by removing the squib, but should have taken care to do it in such a manner as not to endanger others. But the defendant, I think, is not answerable in an action of trespass and assault for the mischief done by the squib in the new motion impressed on it, and the new direction given it, by either Willis or Ryal, who both were free agents and acted on their own judgment. This distinguishes it from the cases put of turning loose a wild beast or a madman. They are only instruments in the hand of the first agent. Nor is it like diverting the course of an enraged ox, or of a stone thrown, or an arrow glancing against a tree; because there the original motion, the vis impressa, is continued, though diverted. Here the instrument of mischief was at rest until a new impetus and a new direction are given it, not once only, but by two successive rational agents. But it is said that the act is not complete, nor the squib at rest, until after it is spent or exploded. It certainly has a power of doing fresh mischief, and so has a stone that has been thrown against my windows and now lies still. Yet if any person gives that stone a new motion and does further mischief with it, trespass will not lie for that against the original thrower. No doubt but Yates may maintain trespass against the defendant. And, according to the doctrine contended for, so may Ryal and the plaintiff. Three actions for one single act! nay, it may be extended in infinitum. If a man tosses a football into the street and, after being kicked about by one hundred people, it at last breaks a trades-man's windows, shall he have trespass against the man who first produced it? Surely only against the man who gave it that mischievous direction. But it is said, if the plaintiff has no action against the defendant, against whom must be seek his remedy? I give no opinion whether case would lie against the defendant for the consequential damage; though, as at present advised, I think that on the circum-stances, it would. But I think that, in strictness of law, trespass would lie against Ryal, the immediate actor in this unhappy business. Both he and Willis have exceeded the bounds of self-defence and not used sufficient circumspection in removing the danger from themselves. The throwing it across the market-house instead of brushing it down, or throwing it out of the open sides into the street (if it was not meant to continue the sport, as it is called), was at least an unneces-sary and incautious act. Not even menaces from others are sufficient to justify a trespass against a third person, much less a fear of danger to either his goods or his person; nothing but inevitable necessity ...

It is said by Lord Raymond, and very justly, in *Reynolds v. Clarke* [above]: "We must keep up the boundaries of actions, otherwise we shall introduce the utmost confusion." As I, therefore, think no immediate injury passed from the defendant to the plaintiff (and without such immediate injury no action of trespass can be maintained), I am of opinion that in this action judgment ought to be for the defendant.

GOULD, J.: — I am of the same opinion with Nares, J., that this action is well maintainable. The whole difficulty lies in the form of the action and not in the substance of the remedy. The line is very nice between case and trespass on these occasions. I am persuaded that there are many instances wherein both or either will lie. I agree with Nares, J., that, wherever a man does an unlawful act, he is answerable for all the consequences; and trespass will lie against him, if the consequence be in nature of trespass. But, exclusive of this, I think that the defendant may be considered in the same view as if he himself had personally thrown the squib in the plaintiff's face. The terror impressed on Willis and Ryal excited self-defence and deprived them of the power of recollection. What they did was, therefore, the inevitable consequence of the defendant's unlawful act. Had the squib been thrown into a coach full of company, the person throwing it out again would not have been answerable for the consequences. What Willis and Ryal did was by necessity, and the defendant imposed that necessity on them.

DE GREY, C.J.: — This case is one of those wherein the line drawn by the law between actions on the case and actions of trespass is very nice and delicate. Trespass is an injury accompanied with force, for which an action of trespass vi et armis lies against the person from whom it is received. The question here is whether the injury received by the plaintiff arises from the force of the original act of the defendant, or from a new force by a third person. I agree with Blackstone, J., as to the principles he has laid down but not in his application of those principles to the present case. The real question certainly does not turn on the lawfulness or unlawfulness of the original act; for actions of trespass will lie for legal acts when they become trespasses by accident, as in the cases cited of cutting thorns, lopping of a tree, shooting at a mark, defending oneself by a stick which strikes another behind, etc. They may also not lie for the consequences even of illegal acts, as that of casting a log in the highway, etc. But the true question is whether the injury is the direct and immediate act of the defendant; and I am of opinion that in this case it is.

. . .

I look on all that was done subsequent to the original throwing as a continuation of the first force and first act which will continue until the squib was spent by bursting. I think that any innocent person removing the danger from himself to another is justifiable; the blame lights on the first thrower. The new direction and new force flow out of the first force, and are not a new trespass. The writ in the REGISTER, 95 a, for trespass in maliciously cutting down a head of water which thereupon flowed down to and overwhelmed another's pond shows that the immediate act need not be instantaneous, but that a chain of effects connected together will be sufficient. It has been urged that the intervention of a free agent will make a difference; but I do not consider Willis and Ryal as free agents in the present case, but acting under a compulsive necessity for their own safety and self-preservation. On these reasons I concur with Gould and Nares, JJ., that the present action is maintainable.

Judgment for plaintiff.

NOTES AND QUESTIONS

1. In reference to Blackstone J. and his judgment in *Scott*, Lord Denning has stated in *What's Next in the Law* (1982), 18: "like many learned men, he was not a great judge. He was too technical. He was one of four judges in an important case of those days called Scott v. Shepherd. . . . He had a technical point about the difference in ancient learning between an action of trespass and an action on the case." Do you agree with Lord Denning that Blackstone J. was simply arguing a technical point?

2. In *Scott*, did the court require that intent or negligence be established? If not, on what issue was liability based?

3. Could the court have concluded that the action should have been framed in trespass on the case and nonsuited the plaintiff? As we have already seen, the plaintiff had to predict in advance whether the action properly lay in trespass *vi et armis* or trespass on the case. As *Scott* illustrates, it was not always possible to make such predictions with any assurance.

4. It is ironic that in the case establishing the importance of direct harm, the judges could not agree on whether the plaintiff's injuries were directly caused.

LEAME v. BRAY

(1803), 3 East. 573, 102 E.R. 724 (K.B.)

This was an action of trespass, in which the plaintiff declared that the defendant with force and arms drove and struck a single-horse chaise which the defendant was then driving along the King's highway with such great force and violence upon and against the plaintiff's curricle drawn by two horses, and upon and against the said horses so drawing, &c., and in which said curricle the plaintiff was then and there riding with his servant, which servant was then driving the said curricle and horses along the King's highway aforesaid, that by means thereof the plaintiff's servant was thrown out of the curricle upon the ground, and the horses ran away with the curricle, and while the horses were so running away with the curricle the plaintiff, for the preservation of life, jumped and fell from the curricle upon the ground and fractured his collar bone, &c. Plea, not guilty.

It appeared in evidence at the trial before Lord Ellenborough C.J. at the last sittings at Westminster, that the accident described in the declaration happened in a dark night, owing to the defendant driving his carriage on the wrong side of the road, and the parties not being able to see each other; and that if the defendant had kept his right side there was ample room for the carriages to have passed without injury. But it did not appear that blame was imputable to the defendant in any other respect as to the manner of his driving. It was therefore objected for the defendant, that the injury having happened from negligence, and not wilfully, the proper remedy was by an action on the case and not of trespass vi et armis; and the plaintiff was thereupon nonsuited.

LORD ELLENBOROUGH C.J.: — The true criterion seems to be whether the plaintiff received an injury by force from the defendant. If the injurious act be the immediate result of the force originally applied by the defendant, and the plaintiff be injured by it, it is the subject of an action of trespass vi et armis by all the cases both ancient and modern. It is immaterial whether the injury be wilful or not.

. . . here the defendant himself was present, and used the ordinary means of impelling the horse forward, and from that the injury happened. And therefore there being an immediate injury from an immediate act of force by the defendant, the proper remedy is trespass; and wilfulness is not necessary to constitute trespass.

[Grose, Lawrence and LeBlanc JJ. concurred.]

WILLIAMS v. HOLLAND

(1833), 10 Bing. 112, 131 E.R. 848 (C.P.)

The declaration stated that Plaintiff . . . was lawfully possessed of a certain cart, and of a certain horse drawing the same; in which said cart certain persons, to wit, John Williams, being the son and servant, and Mary Ann Williams, being the infant daughter of the Plaintiff, were then riding in and along a certain public and common highway: and the Defendant was then and there possessed of a certain gig, and of a certain other horse drawing the same, which said gig and horse were then and there under the care, government, and direction of the Defendant, in and along the said highway, to wit, at, &c. Nevertheless the Defendant so carelessly, unskilfully, and improperly drove, governed, and directed his said gig and horse, that, by and through the carelessness, negligence, unskilfulness, and improper conduct of the Defendant, the said gig and horse of the Defendant then and there ran and struck with great violence upon and against the cart and horse of the Plaintiff, and thereby then and there crushed, broke to pieces, and damaged the same; and the said cart of the Plaintiff thereby then and there became and was rendered of little or no value to the Plaintiff: and thereby the said John Williams and Mary Ann Williams were then and there cast and thrown with great force and violence from and out of the said cart to and upon the ground there, and by means of the several premises aforesaid, the Plaintiff was deprived of the service of his son, and put to expense for doctor's bills, &c. Plea, not guilty.

. . .

TINDAL C.J.: — . . . The declaration, in this case, states the ground of action to be an injury occasioned by the carelessness and negligence of the Defendant in driving his own gig; and that such carelessness and negligence is, strictly and properly in itself, the subject of an action on the case, would appear, if any authority were wanting, from Com. Dig. tit. Action upon the Case for Negligence; and the jury have found in the very terms of the declaration, that the jury was so occasioned. Under such a form of action, therefore, and with such a finding by the jury, the present objection ought not to prevail, unless some positive and inflexible rule of law, or some authority too strong to be overcome, is brought forward in its support. If such are to be found, they must, undoubtedly, be adhered to; for settled forms of action, adapted to different grievances, contribute much to the certain administration of justice.

But upon examining the cases cited in argument, both in support of, and in answer to, the objection, we cannot find one in which it is distinctly held, that the present form of action is not maintainable under the circumstances of this case.

. . .

Where the injury is occasioned by the carelessness and negligence of the Defendant, the Plaintiff is at liberty to bring an action on the case, notwithstanding the act is immediate, so long as it is not a wilful act; and, upon the authority of that case, we think the present form of action maintainable to recover damages for the injury.

NOTES AND QUESTIONS

1. Why was the plaintiff nonsuited at trial in *Leame*? Why did Lord Ellenborough disagree? What is the *ratio* of the case, and what distinction is made between trespass and case?

2. The great significance of *Williams* was that it gave a plaintiff a choice between trespass and case, when there was a direct, negligent act. For a detailed consideration of this case see Prichard, "Trespass, Case and the Rule in *Williams v. Holland*", [1964] Cambridge L.J. 234.

3. The immediate result of *Williams* was a marked increase in the number of actions brought in case. Nevertheless, it was still necessary for the plaintiff to frame the action in either trespass or case. It was not until the Common Law Procedure Act, 1852 (15 & 16 Vict.), c. 76, that a plaintiff was able to join the two actions. See generally Winfield, "Trespass and Negligence" (1933), 49 L.Q.R. 359.

HOLMES v. MATHER

(1875), L.R. 10 Exch. 261

[The defendant and his servant were driving a horse cart on the highway when the horses became unmanageable. The servant attempted to guide the runaway horses, but with limited success. While turning a corner, the servant led the horses into the plaintiff's path, knocking him down and injuring him. The plaintiff sued in negligence and trespass. The jury found that there was no negligence.]

BRAMWELL B.: — . . . The driver is absolutely free from all blame in the matter; not only does he not do anything wrong, but he endeavours to do what is the best to be done under the circumstances. The misfortune happens through the horses being so startled by the barking of a dog that they run away with the groom and the defendant, who is sitting beside him. Now, if the plaintiff under such circumstances can bring an action, I really cannot see why she could not bring an action because a splash of mud, in the ordinary course of driving, was thrown upon her dress or got into her eye and so injured it. It seems manifest that, under such circumstances, she could not maintain an action. For the convenience of mankind in carrying on the affairs of life, people as they go along roads must expect, or put up with, such mischief as reasonable care on the part of others cannot avoid. I think the present action not to be maintainable.

That is the general view of the case. Now I will put it a little more specifically, and address myself to the argument of Mr. Herschell. Here, he says, if the driver had done nothing, there is no reason to suppose this mischief would have happened to the woman, but he did give the horses a pull, or inclination, in the direction of the plaintiff — he drove them there. It is true that he endeavoured to drive them further away from the place by getting them to turn to the right, but he did not succeed in doing that. The argument, therefore, is, if he had not given that impulse or direction to them, they would not have come where the plaintiff was. Now, it seems to me that argument is not tenable, and I think one can deal with it in this way. Here, as in almost all cases, you must look at the immediate act that did the mischief, at what the driver was doing before the mischief happened, and not to what he was doing next before what he was then doing. If you looked to the last act but one, you might as well argue that if the driver had not started on that morning, or had not turned down that particular street, this mischief would not have happened.

I think the proper answer is, You cannot complain of me unless I was immediately doing the act which did the mischief to you. Now the driver was not doing that. What I take to be the case is this: he did not guide the horses upon the plaintiff; he guided them away from her, in another direction; but they ran away with him, upon her, in spite of his effort to take them away from where she was. It is not the case where a person has to make a choice of two evils, and singles the plaintiff out, and drives to the spot where she is standing. That is not the case at all. The driver was endeavouring to guide them indeed, but he was taken there in spite of himself. I think the observation made by my Brother Pollock during the argument is irresistible, that if Mr. Herschell's contention is right, it would come to this: if I am being run away with, and I sit quiet and let the horses run wherever they think fit, clearly I am not liable, because it is they, and not I, who guide them; but if I unfortunately do my best to avoid injury to myself and other persons, then it may be said that it is my act of guiding them that brings them to the place where the accident happens. Surely it is impossible.

As to the cases cited, most of them are really decisions on the form of action, whether case or trespass. The result of them is this, and it is intelligible enough: if the act that does an injury is an act of direct force vi et armis, trespass is the proper remedy (if there is any remedy) where the act is wrongful, either as being wilful or as being the result of negligence. Where the act is not wrongful for either of these reasons, no action is maintainable, though trespass would be the proper form of action if it were wrongful. That is the effect of the decisions.

[Cleasby and Pollock BB. concurred.]

NOTES AND QUESTIONS

1. How does Bramwell B. distinguish this case from one in which the defendant has to choose between two evils, and singles out the plaintiff to suffer harm? Is the distinction meaningful?

2. What is the *ratio*? What is the impact of *Holmes* on the elements of a trespass action?

3. The principle in *Holmes* was reaffirmed and extended to accidents other than those that occurred on the highway in *Stanley v. Powell*, [1891] 1 Q.B. 86.

COOK v. LEWIS

[1951] S.C.R. 830, [1952] 1 D.L.R. 1

CARTWRIGHT J.: — . . . On the 11th of September, 1948, the plaintiff was hunting with his brother John Lewis and one Dennis Fitzgerald in the vicinity of Quinsam Lake on Vancouver Island. It was the opening day of the hunting season for blue grouse and deer and it was said that the country in which they were hunting was full of hunters. The defendants, accompanied by John Wagstaff, then sixteen years of age, were hunting grouse together. They were using a dog which belonged to Akenhead. They had agreed to divide their bag evenly.

It is said that Cook, Akenhead and Wagstaff were proceeding approximately in line, Cook being on the left, Akenhead in the centre and Wagstaff to the right. The dog, which was some little distance ahead of them, came to a point and at about that moment Fitzgerald, who had come into view on Cook's left, called out a warning and pointed towards a clump of trees which was ahead of Cook and Akenhead and in which at that moment the plaintiff was. Cook heard Fitzgerald's call but did not hear what he said. He thought that Fitzgerald was pointing at the dog and was calling attention to the fact that the dog was on point. Akenhead states that he did not hear Fitzgerald's call. Momentarily after this, a covey of some four or five grouse flew up a short distance in front of the dog. Akenhead says that he fired at the bird which was farthest to the right, leaving the other birds to Cook. Cook says that he fired at a bird straight ahead of him. They appear to have fired almost simultaneously. Immediately afterwards there was a scream from the clump of trees, mentioned above, and the plaintiff appeared. He had received several shot in his face, one of which caused the loss of an eye.

. . .

It was the theory of the plaintiff that either Cook or Akenhead or both of them had shot him and that each was liable even if only one of them had fired the shot which struck him. The theory of the defendant Cook was that he had fired only one shot and had fired in such a direction that it was quite impossible that any shot from his gun could have struck the plaintiff. He also stated that there had been a third shot fired almost simultaneously with those fired by himself and Akenhead and suggested that an unidentified third person had fired the shot which injured the plaintiff. His counsel disclaimed before the jury any suggestion that Akenhead had shot the plaintiff.

Akenhead's position at the trial was that he had fired to the right, that he could not have shot the plaintiff and that if it was either of them it was Cook and not he who had done so.

. . .

With the greatest respect, I think that the learned trial judge did not charge the jury correctly in regard to the onus of proof of negligence. While it is true that the plaintiff expressly pleaded negligence on the part of the defendants he also pleaded that he was shot by them and in my opinion the action under the old form of pleading would properly have been one of trespass and not of case. In my view, the cases collected and discussed by Denman J. in *Stanley v. Powell* established the rule (which is subject to an exception in the case of highway accidents with which we are not concerned in the case at bar) that where a plaintiff is injured by force applied directly to him by the defendant his case is made by proving this fact and the onus falls upon the defendant to prove "that such trespass was utterly without his fault." In my opinion *Stanley v. Powell* rightly decides that the defendant in such an action is entitled to judgment if he satisfies the onus of establishing the absence of both intention and negligence on his part.

[The judgment of Estey, Cartwright and Fauteux JJ. was delivered by Mr. Justice Cartwright. Mr. Justice Rand gave a separate concurring judgment, and Locke J. dissented on a different issue.]

NOTES AND QUESTIONS

1. According to *Cook*, why is this an action in trespass and not case? What are the advantages of suing in trespass? What is the practical significance of this advantage in cases such as *Cook*? Does the distinction between directly and indirectly caused harms warrant maintaining these advantages?

2. In *Letang v. Cooper*, [1965] 1 Q.B. 232, the Court of Appeal rejected the approach in *Cook*. Rather, it required a plaintiff to bring his action in negligence even if he was directly injured, unless the defendant had acted intentionally. For a discussion of the Australian position see *McHale v. Watson* (1964), 111 C.L.R. (Aust. H.C.); and *Chin v. Venning* (1975), 49 A.L.J.R. 378 (H.C.).

3. Even in Canada, the rule in *Cook* has been widely criticized. See Wright, "Res Ipsa Loquitur", in Linden (ed.), *Studies in Canadian Tort Law* (1968), 41 at 42-45; and Sharp, "Negligent Trespass in Canada: A Persistent Source of Embarrassment" (1978), 1 Advocates' Q. 311. But see Sullivan, "Trespass to the Person in Canada: A Defence of the Traditional Approach" (1987), 19 Ottawa L. Rev. 533. See also Fridman, "Trespass or Negligence?" (1971), 9 Alta. L. Rev. 250; and Tindale, "The Burden of Proof in Actions for Negligent Trespass in Canada" (1971), 49 Can. Bar Rev. 612.

5. The Bases for Imposing Liability in Tort

As we have seen, early tort law was dominated by the procedural formalities of the writ system and its focus on directly and indirectly caused injury. It was only in the last half of the 19th century that fault in the form of intent or negligence was established as a prerequisite of liability in most areas of tort law. With the Judicature Acts and the abolition of the writ system, fault in various forms emerged as a central organizing principle of tort law. Generally, modern tort law is divided into four categories of actions: intentional torts, negligence, strict liability, and a residual group of actions, such as defamation and nuisance, which are based on unique principles of liability.

We have used these four categories of actions to structure our text. Nevertheless, in this section we will briefly examine the full range of liability rules, the relationships among them and how they may be used to serve specific functions of tort law. Students should have a broad perspective at the outset of the course, before they begin the detailed study of any one category of tort law. The following diagram illustrates the bases or rules for imposing liability in tort.

The Bases of Liability in Tort Law

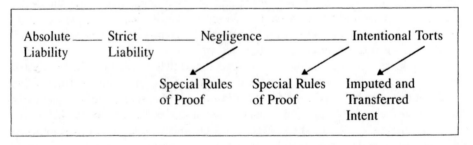

Under a rule of absolute liability, the defendant is held liable if his conduct causes the plaintiff's loss. The plaintiff need not prove that the defendant's conduct was intentional, negligent or otherwise blameworthy, and no defences are available. The essential issue is causation, not fault. Although no modern tort actions are predicated on absolute liability, the concept is relevant for the purposes of comparison.

It is important to distinguish between absolute and strict liability. While strict liability involves liability without intent or negligence, there are other preconditions to liability and certain defences may be recognized. For example, in many jurisdictions in the United States manufacturers are held strictly liable for injuries caused by defective products. As a condition precedent to recovery, the plaintiff must prove that the product that injured him was defective when it left the manufacturer. This can be contrasted with a theory of absolute liability in which liability would be imposed even if there was no defect in the product.

There are also several principles of vicarious liability in tort law that impose strict liability on one party for harm caused by the tortious conduct of another. The most important common law example of vicarious liability is the principle of *respondeat superior*. Under this doctrine, an employer is held strictly liable for torts committed by his employees. The plaintiff must first establish that the employee committed a tort while he was acting within "the course of his employment". In addition, he must show that the employer and the employee were in a "master/servant" relationship. In these circumstances, the employer will be held strictly liable for the employee's torts, notwithstanding the absence of any fault on the employer's part.

Negligence is the failure to take reasonable care to prevent foreseeable harm to others. The difference between negligence and strict liability may also be illustrated using a products liability example. In negligence, the plaintiff must prove that the defendant failed to take reasonable care to prevent the defect that caused the harm. However, in strict liability, proof of the defect and the causal connection will suffice. It should be noted that in some situations the law will aid the plaintiff in a negligence action by shifting the burden of proof to the defendant. This may provide the plaintiff with some of the advantages of strict liability.

Liability for intentionally inflicted harm is, like negligence, based on fault. In most cases, the plaintiff must prove actual subjective intent on the defendant's part. There are several legal principles that assist the plaintiff in proving intent. For example, under the doctrine of imputed intent, the law imputes intent to the defendant if the plaintiff's loss was certain or substantially certain to follow from the defendant's act. Moreover, in Canada, if the plaintiff proves that he was directly injured, the burden of proof shifts to the defendant to disprove intent and negligence. Although this rule arises in some negligence cases, it is more relevant in intentional torts.

There are harms which are simply not recognized under any rule of tort liability, even if the person causing the harm did so intentionally or negligently. Although there is a causal connection between the defendant's conduct and the plaintiff's loss, either the type of conduct or the type of harm lies outside the ambit of tort law. For example, parents whose child has been killed by the defendant's negligence will not be awarded redress for the grief they have suffered as a result of the child's death.

6. The Functions of Tort Law

In discussing the functions of tort law, we are not suggesting that it developed from a co-ordinated attempt to achieve specific social goals. The common law process is highly decentralized, and modern tort law is a patchwork of judicial decisions and statutory provisions. As the history section illustrates, much of tort law has been shaped by procedural concerns rather than policy. Today, legislators and judges do attempt to shape the law to achieve particular social goals. Nevertheless, there is no governing principle that dictates the proper goals of tort law.

Every judicial decision, legal principle or set of legal rules favours certain interests over others. The law is not objective or value free. It is a social institution which serves social functions. Therefore, it is appropriate to debate what are and what ought to be the goals of a particular legal principle or branch of law, to assess the extent to which these goals are being met, to examine alternative legal and non-legal means of accomplishing these ends, and to recommend changes in the law or other social institutions. In essence, this is what is involved in a functional approach to the study of law. Obviously, we cannot resolve the controversies over what ought to be the social functions of tort law. It is enough at this point that students are aware of what is entailed in a functional analysis and are familiar with the major social goals that tort law may serve.

Some of the debate about the functions of tort law stems from a failure to identify the perspective used in addressing the issue. If one focuses on the litigants' objectives, the goals of tort law will be defined narrowly in reference to the expectations of those with a financial stake in the process. It is legitimate to be concerned about the parties' motivations, because such considerations determine which issues are brought to court, and thus shape substantive principles. However, this narrow focus does not necessarily assist us in defining the broader social functions of tort law, which are the primary concerns of this section.

Even if we adopt a broad focus, the debate about the functions of tort law is largely speculative. There is little empirical evidence on the impact of tort law. This is hardly surprising, given the serious methodological difficulties of isolating the effects of tort law from those of other legal and social forces.

There are two additional reasons for approaching the debate with caution. First, several inherent features of tort law limit its impact. With few exceptions, tort law operates indirectly on behaviour. Although the prospect of litigation may influence some people, the primary vehicle through which tort law operates is an award of damages. If the defendant is impecunious, insured or otherwise able to pass on the cost of liability, the impact of tort law may be minimal. Moreover, many valid tort claims are not pursued for reasons other than the merits of the case. Many wrongdoers are never identified. Some potential plaintiffs may not realize that they have a remedy and others may choose not to pursue their legal rights.

Second, tort law is simply one of many legal and non-legal mechanisms of social control in society. The role that tort law plays or should play in any given society will reflect a broad range of factors, such as the crime rate, the effectiveness of the criminal justice system, the regulation of health and safety standards and their enforcement, the scope of the social welfare system, and the availability of state-funded universal health care. Debates about the functions of tort law often mask unstated views about these other issues.

We have attempted to summarize the acknowledged functions of tort law in the following material. You should read this material critically, assess the empirical assumptions upon which it is based and consider its relevance in our society.

Compensation, in the sense of reparation for loss is, from the plaintiff's point of view, the most important function of tort law. Society also has a legitimate interest in minimizing the disruptions accompanying an injury by ensuring that the aggrieved party is compensated. Nevertheless, the present system of tort law cannot be explained or justified as a mechanism of accident compensation. First, tort law provides compensation to a relatively small number of accident victims and then only in very limited circumstances. Second, the accident victim must make a substantial financial investment to initiate the process. Third, the plaintiff must prove fault, not need, and will only recover if he is fortunate enough to be injured by a tortfeasor with assets. Finally, it is generally accepted and clearly documented that tort law is an extremely inefficient mechanism for providing compensation. Thus, from society's point of view, compensation is merely one of several functions that tort law may serve.

A tort action may also provide the plaintiff with a means of having the defendant's conduct condemned and his own rights publicly vindicated. This appeasement function was an important aspect of Anglo-Saxon and early common law. Today, nominal damages are awarded to redress a violation of the plaintiff's rights for certain intentional torts where the plaintiff has suffered no actual harm. Given the cost and inconvenience of litigation, few plaintiffs are likely to pursue a tort action solely for this purpose.

As already noted, criminal and tort law share a common heritage. Although criminal law is most often associated with punishing wrongdoers, tort law has retained traces of its early punitive elements. For example, punitive damages are awarded to sanction a defendant for high-handed, vicious or otherwise outrageous conduct. As tort law has become increasingly dominated by negligence, the importance of punishment has declined. As well, most of the morally blameworthy conduct that warrants punishment in tort law constitutes a federal or provincial offence. It might be argued that in such circumstances the issue of punishment should be left to the criminal justice system.

Punishment must be distinguished from deterrence. Punishment looks backward at the wrongful act and attempts to mete out the punishment to reflect the wrong. Generally, only advertent wrongdoing is considered worthy of punishment. Deterrence is concerned with discouraging the defendant (specific deterrence) and others (general deterrence) from repeating the wrong. It may be intended to discourage inadvertent carelessness, as well as deliberate wrongdoing. Deterrence and punishment are closely related, in that any punishment may also have a deterrent effect. However, the penalty necessary to achieve optimum deterrence may be quite different from that necessary to achieve just punishment.

In order to be an effective deterrent, tort law must clearly define the undesirable conduct and then provide sufficient inducements for discouraging it. Deterrence works best when the defendant is aware of both the required legal standard and the sanctions for its breach. Thus, tort law will have a greater deterrent impact on premeditated conduct than on spontaneous careless behaviour. Even when the conduct is planned, the potential damage award must be sufficient to change the defendant's behaviour. The law will have a limited impact if it is cheaper for the tortfeasor to pay damages and weather adverse publicity, than to alter his conduct. If the criminal justice system is any indication, there is little reason for optimism about the deterrent impact of tort law.

Some academics, particularly economists, analyze tort law as a system for allocating accident losses. "Market deterrence" is an important loss allocation goal. The basic idea is to incorporate the costs of accidents into the price of the activity that generates them. A good example is the rule in most American states that holds manufacturers strictly liable for injuries caused by their defective products. Manufacturers increase their prices to cover their potential liability costs. As prices rise, fewer products are sold and fewer product-related injuries occur. To the extent that a product continues to be purchased at the higher price, economists would say that consumers have demonstrated that they believe that the benefits of the product exceed the cost of the accidents it generates. According to economists, this allocation of accident costs through the market enables society to experience the "optimum" number of accidents.

The term "loss allocation" has also been used to describe several other possibly inconsistent schemes. Posner explains that an actor should be held liable in negligence, whenever the cost of harm exceeds what it would have cost to prevent it. The defendant's fault lies in squandering scarce social resources. Thus, Posner's loss allocation system furthers the goal of efficiency. The term "loss allocation" is also used to describe a "loss spreading" function, whereby the loss is imposed on the party who is best able to distribute it over time and among a large number of people. Others speak of the "deep pocket" approach to loss distribution, whereby tort law is used to allocate the loss to the party who is best able to bear it. Even if one assumed that the courts had sufficient information and expertise to make the correct allocative decision, many argue that it is inappropriate to use tort law as a system to redistribute wealth.

In recent years, legal philosophers have begun to study tort law. Having found the traditional explanations unsatisfactory, they have focused on the theories of justice underlying tort law. Some tort doctrines can be explained in terms of retributive justice. Other tort principles are apparently designed to achieve distributive justice, that is, to ensure that wealth is properly distributed within society. However, most legal philosophers view corrective justice as central to tort law. Corrective justice accepts the existing distribution of wealth and is concerned with correcting deviations in this pattern by annulling "wrongful" gains and compensating "wrongful" losses. The classification of a gain or loss as "wrongful" is made with reference to several different principles. Depending upon the particular principle, what constitutes a "wrong" may be defined in terms of the actor's conduct, the victim's loss or a combination of these factors.

NOTES AND QUESTIONS

1. On the aims of tort law, see generally Wright, "The Province and Function of the Law of Torts", in Linden (ed.), *Studies in Canadian Tort Law* (1968), 1; Cane, *Atiyah's Accidents, Compensation and the Law*, 5th ed. (1993), 348-94; Linden, *Canadian Tort Law*, 5th ed. (1993), 1-29; and Englard, "The System Builders: A Critical Appraisal of Modern Tort Theory" (1980), 10 J. Leg. Studies 27.

See also Saks, "Do We Really Know Anything About the Behavior of the Tort Litigation System — And Why Not? (1992), 140 U. Pa. L. Rev. 1147, who casts doubt on our ability to accurately analyze the tort system.

2. Even assuming that compensation is an appropriate social goal, the relative effectiveness of tort law in achieving this goal is questionable. The Ontario Law Reform Commission, in its Report on Motor Vehicle Accident Compensation (1973), commented:

> All the studies demonstrate that the tort system pays only about one-third of the total pecuniary losses ... and further that the money paid out is distributed very unevenly among the victims. Less than half the people who suffer losses receive compensation through the tort regime. More important, perhaps, is the consistent finding in all studies that the more serious the accident, and therefore, generally speaking, the greater the loss, the lower the recovery percentage. Even with non-tort sources added, a large fraction of pecuniary losses remain uncompensated, and the pattern of maldistribution does not improve.

See also *Inquiry into Motor Vehicle Accident Compensation in Ontario* (Osborne J., Commissioner), 1988, Queen's Printer, Ontario.

3. The importance of appeasement in Anglo-Saxon law is illustrated by Malone, in "Ruminations on the Role of Fault in the History of the Common Law of Torts" (1970), 31 La. L.R. 1, at 2:

> This same demand for appeasement of the sense of honor was manifested in non-fatal injuries. Here the amount of the tariff to be paid was determined to a large extent by the public shame that attended the wound. According to the laws of Ethelbert: "If the bruise be black in a part not covered by the clothes, let bot be made with thirty scaetts. If it be covered by the clothes, let bot be made for each with twenty scaetts." Pound refers to a provision of Howell the Good, King of the Welsh, to the effect that a scar on the face is worth six score pence, whereas the permanent loss of both joints of the thumb (an injury that would virtually disable the hand) brought only seventy-six pence and a half-penny.

4. Linden has suggested that tort law can act as an ombudsman. A private law suit may focus public attention on systemic wrongdoing that might otherwise go undetected or unprosecuted by the state. The adverse publicity generated by such suits may provide a powerful deterrent and motivate the government to take corrective action. Can you suggest a situation in which tort law has, or might, serve this function? See Linden, "Reconsidering Tort Law as Ombudsman" in Steel and Rogers-Magnet (eds.), *Issues in Tort Law* (1983), 1.

5. Assume that just punishment for a wrong is a fine of $100 and that the perceived conviction rate is one in one hundred. How large should the penalty be to deter the wrong? Would the imposition of that penalty be unjust? Explain.

6. What do economists mean by the "optimum" number of accidents? Why is the optimum number of accidents not zero? See England, "Law and Economics in American Tort Cases: A Critical Assessment of the Theory's Impact on Courts" (1991), 41 U.T.L.J. 359.

7. For a discussion of the deterrent function of tort law, see Calabresi, *The Cost of Accidents* (1970); Posner, "A Theory of Negligence" (1972), 1 J. Leg. Studies 29; Brown, "Deterrence in Tort and No-Fault; The New Zealand Experience" (1985), 73 Cal. L. Rev. 796; Viscusi, "Toward a Diminished Role for Tort Liability: Social Insurance, Government Regulation, and Contemporary Risks to Health and Safety" (1989), 6 Yale J. on Regulation 65; and Komesar "Injuries and Institutions: Tort Reform, Tort Theory, and Beyond" (1990), 65 N.Y.U.L. Rev. 23.

8. For a discussion of the loss allocation function of tort law, see Coase, "The Problem of Social Costs" (1960), 3 J. Law and Ecom. 1; Calabresi; "Some Thoughts on Risk Distribution and the Law of Torts" (1961), 70 Yale L.J. 449; and Posner, *supra*.

9. For a philosophical analysis of the functions of tort law see Fletcher, "Fairness and Utility in Tort Theory" (1972), 85 Harv. L.J. 537; Epstein, "A Theory of Strict Liability" (1973), 2 J. Leg. Studies 151; Steiner, "Economics, Morality and the Law of Torts" (1976), 26 U.T.L.J. 227; Weinrib, "Understanding Tort Law" (1989), Valparaiso U.L. Rev. 1; Dewees and Trebilcock, "The Efficacy of the Tort System And Its Alternatives: A Review of Empirical Evidence" (1992), 30 Osgoode Hall L.J. 57; and Coleman, *Risks and Wrongs* (1992).

2

THE BASIC CONCEPTS OF REMEDIES
IN INTENTIONAL TORTS

1. Introduction
2. Classifications of Damages
3. Nominal Damages
4. Compensatory Damages
5. Punitive Damages

1. Introduction

In a tort action, the plaintiff must first establish the elements of the specific tort in issue. Even after the plaintiff has proven the requisite elements of the tort, the defendant will not necessarily be held liable. If the defendant can establish a valid defence, she will be absolved of liability. Thus, it is only after the plaintiff has proven the commission of the tort and the defendant has failed to establish a valid defence that the issue of an appropriate remedy arises. In a tort action, therefore, issues relating to remedies are usually addressed last.

There are, however, two reasons for introducing the general concepts of remedies before examining the torts and defences. First, it is important to emphasize that establishing liability is merely a means to an end. The plaintiff is ultimately seeking a remedy for the wrong caused by the defendant. The nature of the available remedy will influence the plaintiff's decision to bring an action. On a more practical level, many of the cases in the following chapters raise issues which cannot be appreciated without some understanding of remedies, particularly damages.

(a) JUDICIAL AND EXTRAJUDICIAL REMEDIES

There are two broad categories of remedies: judicial and extrajudicial. Judicial remedies fall into four sub-categories, the first and most important being the award of damages. An award of damages is available across a range of tort actions. Contrary to popular belief, an award of damages does not result in the immediate transfer of money from defendant to the plaintiff. Rather, it merely grants the plaintiff a legal right to a specific sum. In order to collect the award, the plaintiff may have to pursue creditors' remedies that are entirely independent of tort law.

The second sub-category of judicial remedy is the injunction. An injunction is an order made by a court to a party to control her conduct. A court may direct a defendant to refrain from (prohibitive injunction) or undertake (mandatory injunction) a particular act. A person who ignores the terms of an injunction may be held in contempt of court. Unlike damage awards, injunctions were only granted by courts of equity. An important element of a plaintiff's claim for an injunction, or any other form of equitable relief, was the assertion that the common law remedies were inadequate. Even in such cases, the granting of an injunction was discretionary. Although courts have had the power to grant both common law and equitable remedies since the Judicature Acts were passed, historical factors remain important. As a general rule, a court will only issue an injunction if an award of damages would be an inadequate remedy in all of the circumstances of the case.

The other two judicial remedies are a declaration and an order of specific restitution. A declaration is a formal statement or decision of a court and is usually issued to settle a dispute or an issue of legal rights. An order of specific restitution directs a party to restore a pre-existing condition or return an object. Like injunctions, these remedies are granted in limited circumstances and are sought in relatively few tort actions.

The extrajudicial or self-help remedies, such as recapture of chattels, re-entry onto land and abatement of nuisance, are also applicable in a small number of cases. We will discuss these remedies when they arise in relation to individual torts.

NOTES AND QUESTIONS

1. For a comprehensive review of the Canadian law of damages see Waddams, *The Law of Damages*, 2nd ed. (1991); and Klar *et al.*, *Damages and Remedies in Tort* (1995).

2. Although frequent reference is made to the general rule that an injunction will only be granted when a damage award would be inadequate, the Canadian courts appear to be adopting a more flexible approach. For a comprehensive analysis of injunctions see Sharpe, *Injunctions and Specific Performance*, 2nd ed. (1992). See also Berryman (ed.), *International Symposium on The Law of Remedies*, (1990).

3. For a discussion of the extrajudicial remedies, see Heuston and Buckley, *Salmond and Heuston on the Law of Torts*, 20th ed. (1992), 583-89; and Keeton *et al.*, *Prosser and Keeton on the Law of Torts*, 5th ed. (1984), 137-43 and 641-43.

2. Classifications of Damages

Academics, practitioners and judges have classified damage awards according to various criteria, such as the nature of the plaintiff's loss, the way in which the loss is calculated and proven, and the purpose for which the award is given. Since the criteria are unrelated, the corresponding classification systems are not mutually exclusive. The task of mastering the terminology of damages is further complicated by disagreements on the definition of at least some of the terms.

Perhaps the simplest way to analyze damages is to divide the plaintiff's claims into pecuniary (monetary) and non-pecuniary (non-monetary) losses. A pecuniary loss is one which can be calculated in dollars and cents, such as lost earnings, medical bills or repair costs. Pain, humiliation, disfigurement, and other non-pecuniary losses have no monetary equivalent and thus cannot be subject to exact calculation.

A classification used in pleading a cause of action is that of special and general damages. Special damages are those capable of exact quantification at the time of trial, whereas general damages are those incapable of such quantification. The plaintiff is required to strictly plead and prove the former, but not the latter because of their speculative nature.

Although both classification systems can be applied to damages arising from any tort, they are most frequently associated with complex damage claims. Such claims arise more commonly in negligence than in intentional torts. Further discussion of these classification systems will be deferred until the chapter on damages in the negligence materials.

In intentional torts, damages are most frequently classified according to the purpose for which they are awarded or the function which they are intended to serve. There are three basic categories of damages in this functional classification system — nominal (token), compensatory and punitive (exemplary or vindictive) damages.

NOTES AND QUESTIONS

1. Although the terms special and general damages have several distinct meanings, we have used the definitions which are most relevant to the issue of pleadings. See Cooper-Stephenson and Saunders, *Personal Injury Damages in Canada*, 2nd ed. (1996), 91-94. For a discussion of pecuniary and non-pecuniary losses see Cooper-Stephenson and Saunders, *supra*, 89-90, 481-530.

3. Nominal Damages

Nominal damages are awarded to redress a violation of a legal right that the law deems worthy of protection, even in the absence of actual harm. For example, a defendant who steps onto the plaintiff's property causing no harm to the land will be held liable in trespass for nominal damages. The award of nominal damages vindicates the plaintiff's legal right to exclusive possession. Had the defendant crushed several flowers, the plaintiff would have been awarded compensatory damages to redress her for her actual losses. Although the award of nominal damages in the first case would not be much smaller than the award of compensatory damages in the second, it is important to emphasize that the distinction between these awards is based upon the purposes for which they are given, not their amounts. Unfortunately, the term nominal damages is not always used consistently, and some judges have used it to refer to a small award of compensatory damages.

According to the traditional view, nominal damages are only awarded in tort actions that are actionable *per se*, that is, actionable without proof of loss. The intentional torts derived from the writ of trespass *vi et armis*, such as battery and trespass to land, are actionable *per se*. However, the intentional torts derived from trespass on the case, such as malicious prosecution, and torts based on negligence are not actionable *per se*. Rather, the plaintiff must establish actual damages in these cases as an essential element of her cause of action. If the plaintiff fails to establish loss, she has no legal cause of action, and consequently the issue of damages will not arise.

THE MEDIANA

[1900] A.C. 113 (H.L.)

. . .

EARL OF HALSBURY: — And, my Lords, here I wish, with reference to what has been suggested at the bar, to remark upon the difference between damages and nominal damages. "Nominal damages" is a technical phrase which means that you have negatived anything like real damage, but that you are affirming by your nominal damages that there is an infraction of a legal right which, though it gives you no right to any real damages at all, yet gives you a right to the verdict or judgment because your legal right has been infringed. But the term "nominal damages" does not mean small damages. The extent to which a person has a right to recover what is called by the compendious phrase damages, but may be also represented as compensation for the use of something that belongs to him, depends upon a variety of circumstances, and it certainly does not in the smallest degree suggest that because they are small they are necessarily nominal damages.

. . .

Supposing a person took away a chair out of my room and kept it for twelve months, could anybody say you had a right to diminish the damages by shewing that I did not usually sit in that chair, or that there were plenty of other chairs in the room? The proposition so nakedly stated appears to me to be absurd; but a jury have very often a very difficult task to perform in ascertaining what should be the amount of damages of that sort. I know very well that as a matter of common sense what an arbitrator or a jury very often do is to take a perfectly artificial hypothesis and say, "Well, if you wanted to hire a chair, what would you have to give for it for the period"; and in that way they come to a rough sort of conclusion as to what damages ought to be paid for the unjust and unlawful withdrawal of it from the owner. Here, as I say, the broad principle seems to me to be quite independent of the particular use the plaintiffs were going to make of the thing that was taken, except — and this I think has been the fallacy running through the arguments at the bar — when you are endeavouring to establish the specific loss of profit, or of something that you otherwise would have got which the law recognises as special damage. In that case you must shew it, and by precise evidence, so much so that in the old system of pleading you could not recover damages unless you had made a specific allegation in your pleading so as to give the persons responsible for making good the loss an opportunity of inquiring into it before they came into court. But when we are speaking of general damages no such principle applies at all, and the jury might give whatever they thought would be the proper equivalent for the unlawful withdrawal of the subject-matter then in question. It seems to me that that broad principle comprehends within it many other things. There is no doubt in many cases a jury would say there really has been no damage at all: "We will give the plaintiffs a trifling amount" — not nominal damages, be it observed, but a trifling amount; in other cases it would be more serious.

NOTES AND QUESTIONS

1. In contrast to the traditional view, Klar *et al.* have stated that nominal damages may be awarded in tort actions that require proof of loss. See *Damages and Remedies in Tort* (1995), 27-45 to 27-47. See also *Marynowsky v. Stuartburn (District)*, [1994] 10 W.W.R. 602 (Man. C.A.). What purpose would such an award serve? Should nominal damages be awarded in such cases?

2. In the example of the appropriated chair cited in *The Mediana*, damages are said to be "at large" because the jury has considerable latitude in quantifying them. The award is not limited to the pecuniary losses that the plaintiff has specifically pleaded and proven. The Earl of Halsbury indicated that, depending on the facts of the case, the jury could award a trifling sum as compensatory damages. Distinguish such an award from an award of nominal damages.

3. The court may also award a trifling sum where damages are at large if it feels that the plaintiff should not have brought the action, despite its technical validity. Such awards, referred to as contemptuous (derisory) damages, are given to express the court's disapproval of the plaintiff's suit. See *Martin v. Benson*, [1927] 1 K.B. 771; *Dennison v. Sanderson*, [1946] 4 D.L.R. 314 (Ont. C.A.); and *Dering v. Uris*, [1964] 2 All E.R. 660. Explain the difference between nominal and contemptuous damages.

4. Another mechanism the courts may use to show their disapproval of a plaintiff's claim is an award of costs. Costs are generally awarded to the successful party. However, the court has discretion to deny costs to a successful plaintiff, or perhaps even award costs against her, if it feels that her claim was a frivolous attempt at "empty vindication". See *Harrison v. Carswell* (1976), 62 D.L.R. (3d) 68 at 73 (S.C.C.), per Laskin C.J.C., in dissent.

5. Given the current social and private costs of civil litigation, does an action for nominal damages serve a worthwhile purpose for society or the plaintiff? Does your answer depend on whether the case involves personal security, real property or personal property?

6. For a detailed discussion of nominal damages see Cooper-Stephenson and Saunders, *Personal Injury Damages in Canada*, 2nd ed. (1996), 99-101; and Waddams, *The Law of Damages*, 2nd ed. (1991), 10-1 to 10-5.

4. Compensatory Damages

Most tort actions are brought to obtain financial redress for actual loss. The general principle for assessing compensatory damages was stated by Donaldson L.J. in *Dodd Properties (Kent) Ltd. v. Canterbury City Council*, [1980] 1 All E.R. 928 at 938 (C.A.):

> The general object underlying the rules for the assessment of damages is, so far as is possible by means of a monetary award, to place the plaintiff in the position which he would have occupied if he had not suffered the wrong complained of, be that wrong a tort or a breach of contract.

Despite its apparent simplicity, this principle may be extremely difficult to apply. What is the monetary value of a unique work of art or a prized family heirloom? How do you calculate the damages that should be awarded to a young person who is rendered a quadriplegic by the defendant's conduct? Equally difficult questions arise in attempting to compensate an individual for non-pecuniary losses. As Dickson J. stated in *Andrews v. Grand and Toy (Alta.) Ltd.* (1978), 83 D.L.R. (3d) 452 at 475 (S.C.C.):

> Andrews used to be a healthy young man, athletically active and socially congenial. Now he is a cripple, deprived of many of life's pleasures and subjected to pain and disability. For this, he is entitled to compensation. But the problem here is qualitatively different from that of pecuniary losses. There is no medium of exchange for happiness. There is no market for expectation of life. The monetary evaluation of non-pecuniary losses is a philosophical and policy exercise more than a legal or logical one. The award must be fair and reasonable, fairness being gauged by earlier decisions; but the award must also of necessity be arbitrary or conventional.

Although such issues can arise in intentional torts cases, they are far more common in negligence actions. Consequently, a detailed examination of the case law governing the assessment of compensatory damages will be left to the damage chapter in the negligence material.

REVIEW PROBLEM

The palm of the plaintiff's hand was severely disfigured by scar tissue. The defendant doctor had a special interest in experimental skin grafting and induced the plaintiff to undergo an operation by stating that he would guarantee to make the hand 100 percent perfect. The plaintiff agreed and the doctor grafted skin from the plaintiff's chest to his hand. Unfortunately, the operation was unsuccessful. Not only did considerable scar tissue remain, but hair began to grow on the plaintiff's palm.

This fact situation is based on the case of *Hawkins v. McGee* (1929), 146 A. 641 (N.H. S.C.). The court held that the doctor's statement constituted a binding contractual promise to give the plaintiff a perfect hand and that the doctor was strictly liable in contract for breaching this warranty. Assume that a parallel situation arose in tort. For example, if the doctor had made the statement knowing it to be false and there was no contractual relationship between the parties, the plaintiff could have brought an action for the tort of deceit. The following questions are designed to illustrate some basic principles in the quantification of compensatory damages in tort, as well as several differences between tort and contract law.

(a) What damages would you award in tort to compensate the plaintiff for having to live the rest of his life with a scarred and hairy hand? Should this calculation be based on the judge's objective assessment of this disability or on the plaintiff's subjective self-perception?

(b) Applying the principles stated in *Dodd Properties*, calculate the plaintiff's compensatory damages in deceit. For the purpose of this calculation, assume that the hand had been worth $50 before the operation, $25 after the operation and that it would have been worth $100 had the operation succeeded.

As stated above, the court in *Hawkins* considered the doctor's statement about making the hand perfect to be a contractual warranty. Based on the values of the hand, what should be the plaintiff's compensatory damage award in contract? If you had calculated correctly, you would have concluded that the plaintiff's compensatory damages were not the same in tort and contract. Can you reconcile this result with the statement in *Dodd Properties*?

(c) Assume that the plaintiff had lost $100 in wages when he missed work to undergo the operation. Based on the values of the hand stated above, recalculate the plaintiff's compensatory damages in tort and contract.

5. Punitive Damages

VORVIS v. INSURANCE CORP. OF BRITISH COLUMBIA

(1989), 58 D.L.R. (4th) 193 (S.C.C.)

[The plaintiff sued the defendant for wrongful dismissal and claimed that he had been subject to harsh, humiliating and distressing conduct before his dismissal. The plaintiff sought recovery for mental distress and punitive damages. The trial judge concluded that mental distress could only be recovered if actual damage was established and that punitive damages could not be awarded for wrongful dismissal. Consequently, the judge dismissed the plaintiff's claim and the Court of Appeal upheld the trial judgment. The plaintiff appealed to the Supreme Court.]

McIntyre J.: — . . .

Aggravated damages

In his statement of claim, the appellant advanced a claim for mental distress as the result of the termination of his contract of employment in these terms:

> The plaintiff makes a claim for mental distress, anxiety, vexation and frustration suffered by the plaintiff as a result of the termination of his contract of employment by the defendant.

Later, in the prayer for relief, in addition to asserting claims for general and special damages for breach of contract, he claimed punitive damages. In pursuit of his claim for mental distress, the appellant argued at trial that the offensive and unjustifiable conduct of Reid, a superior in his employment, was such that it caused great mental distress, anxiety, vexation and frustration as alleged in the pleadings, and in support of his claim he cited several cases.

. . .

Before dealing with the question of punitive damages, it will be well to make clear the distinction between punitive and aggravated damages, for in the argument before us and in some of the materials filed there appeared some confusion as to the distinction. Punitive damages, as the name would indicate, are designed to punish. In this, they constitute an exception to the general common law rule that damages are designed to compensate the injured, not to punish the wrongdoer. Aggravated damages will frequently cover conduct which could also be the subject of punitive damages, but the role of aggravated damages remains compensatory. The distinction is clearly set out in Waddams, *The Law of Damages*, 2nd ed. (1983), at p. 562, para. 979, in these words:

> An exception exists to the general rule that damages are compensatory. This is the case of an award made for the purpose, not of compensating the plaintiff, but punishing the defendant. Such awards have been called exemplary, vindictive, penal, punitive, aggravated and retributory, but the expressions in common modern use to describe damages going beyond compensatory are exemplary and punitive damages. "Exemplary" was preferred by the House of Lords in *Cassell & Co. Ltd. v. Broome*, but "punitive" has also been used in many Canadian courts including the Supreme Court of Canada in *H.L. Weiss Forwarding Ltd. v. Omnus*. The expression "aggravated damages", though it has sometimes been used interchangeably with punitive or exemplary damages, has more frequently in recent times been contrasted with exemplary damages. In this contrasting sense, aggravated damages describes an award that aims at compensation, but takes full account of the intangible injuries, such as distress and humiliation, that may have been caused by the defendant's insulting behaviour. The expressions vindictive, penal and retributory have dropped out of common use.

Aggravated damages are awarded to compensate for aggravated damage. As explained by Waddams, they take account of intangible injuries and by definition will generally augment damages assessed under the general rules relating to the assessment of damages. Aggravated damages are compensatory in nature and may only be awarded for that purpose. Punitive damages, on the other hand, are punitive in nature and may only be employed in circumstances where the conduct giving the cause for complaint is of such nature that it merits punishment.

The issue which is faced by this court is whether punitive damages may be awarded by the court in an action for breach of contract, based on wrongful dismissal of an employee, and, if so, whether the circumstances of this case would merit such an award. Also, before the court is a similar question with respect to aggravated damages. This question was not shown in the appellant's factum as a question in issue but much of the argument and many of the cases cited concerned the question, presumably on the theory that aggravated damages were included in the concept of punitive damages, and for that reason this issue will be addressed first.

. . .

[McIntyre J. then discussed the leading cases.]

From the foregoing authorities, I would conclude that while aggravated damages may be awarded in actions for breach of contract in appropriate cases, this is not a case where they should be given. The rule long established in the *Addis* and *Peso Silver Mines* cases has generally been applied to deny such damages, and the employer/employee relationship (in absence of collective agreements which involve consideration of the modern labour law régime) has always been one where either party could terminate the contract of employment by due notice, and therefore the only damage which could arise would result from a failure to give such notice.

I would not wish to be taken as saying that aggravated damages could never be awarded in a case of wrongful dismissal, particularly where the acts complained of were also independently actionable, a factor not present here.

. . .

[While] the conduct complained of, that of Reid, was offensive and unjustified, any injury it may have caused the appellant cannot be said to have arisen out of the dismissal itself. The conduct complained of preceded the wrongful dismissal and therefore cannot be said to have aggravated the damage incurred as a result of the dismissal. Accordingly, I would refuse any claim for aggravated damages in respect of the wrongful dismissal.

Punitive damages

Problems arise for the common law wherever the concept of punitive damages is posed. The award of punitive damages requires that:

> . . . a civil court . . . impose what is in effect a fine for conduct it finds worthy of punishment, and then to remit the fine, not to the State Treasury, but to the individual plaintiff who will, by definition, be over-compensated.

(Waddams, *The Law of Damages, supra*, at 563.) This will be accomplished in the absence of the procedural protections for the defendant — always present in criminal trials where punishment is ordinarily awarded — and upon proof on a balance of probabilities instead of the criminal standard of proof beyond a reasonable doubt. Nevertheless, despite the peculiar nature of punitive damages, it is well settled in law that in appropriate cases they may be awarded: see *Rookes v. Barnard*, [1964] A.C. 1129. But all authorities accept the proposition that an award of punitive damages should always receive the most careful consideration and the discretion to award them should be most cautiously exercised. As has been mentioned earlier, punitive damages are not compensatory in nature. The scope of punitive damages was restricted in *Rookes v. Barnard*, and, as noted by Waddams, Lord Devlin in that case retained two categories for their application, namely, abuse of power by government, and torts committed for profit. In Canada, however, Spence J. stated in *McElroy v. Cowper-Smith* (1967), 62 D.L.R. (2d) 65, [1967] S.C.R. 425, 60 W.W.R. 85, a defamation case, that the jurisdiction in this country to award punitive damages is not so limited. Though this was said in dissent, the majority did not deal with the point and did not comment on the statement: see, as well, *Paragon Properties Ltd. v. Magna Investments Ltd.* (1972), 24 D.L.R. (3d) 156, [1972] 3 W.W.R. 106 (Alta. C.A.), *per* Clement J.A. The courts of Australia and New Zealand have also dealt with *Rookes v. Barnard,* and in general have rejected its approach in this connection: see *Uren v. John Fairfax & Sons Pty. Ltd.* (1966), 117 C.L.R. 118, in the High Court of Australia, and *Fogg v. McKnight,* [1968] N.Z.L.R. 330, in the Supreme Court of New Zealand. It is fair to say that the courts of the Commonwealth, outside of the United Kingdom, have not, in general, accepted the limitations on the power of the courts to award punitive damages: see Waddams, p. 570, para. 996. I would conclude that the *Rookes v. Barnard* limitation should not apply in Canada. The law of British Columbia, then, accords wider scope for the application of punitive damages than that envisaged in *Rookes v. Barnard.*

When then can punitive damages be awarded? It must never be forgotten that when awarded by a judge or a jury, a punishment is imposed upon a person by a court by the operation of the judicial process. What is it that is punished? It surely cannot be merely conduct of which the court disapproves, however strongly the judge may feel. Punishment may not be imposed in a civilized community without justification in law. The only basis for the imposition of such punishment must be a finding of the commission of an actionable wrong which caused the injury complained of by the plaintiff.

. . .

Turning to the case at bar, it is clear from the judgments below that the appellant's superior, Reid, treated him in a most offensive manner. As has been noted, the trial judge would have awarded punitive damages had he been of the view that it was open to him to do so. The question before us now is whether the trial judge was right in concluding that it was not open to him to award the punitive damages. In my view, while it may be very unusual to do so, punitive damages may be awarded in cases of breach of contract. It would seem to me, however, that it will be rare to find a contractual breach which would be appropriate for such an award. In tort cases, claims where a plaintiff asserts injury and damage caused by the defendant, the situation is different. The defendant in such a case is under a legal duty to use care not to injure his neighbour, and the neighbour has in law a right not to be so injured and an additional right to compensation where injury occurs. The injured party is entitled to be made whole. The compensation he is entitled to receive depends upon the nature and extent of his injuries and not upon any private arrangement made with the tortfeasor. In an action based on a breach of contract, the only link between the parties for the purpose of defining their rights and obligations is the contract. Where the defendant has breached the contract, the remedies open to the plaintiff must arise from that contractual relationship, that "private law", which the parties agreed to accept. The injured plaintiff then is not entitled to be made whole; he is entitled to have that which the contract provided for him or compensation for its loss. This distinction will not completely eliminate the award of punitive damages but it will make it very rare in contract cases.

Moreover, punitive damages may only be awarded in respect of conduct which is of such nature as to be deserving of punishment because of its harsh, vindictive, reprehensible and malicious nature. I do not suggest that I have exhausted the adjectives which could describe the conduct capable of characterizing a punitive award, but in any case where such an award is made the conduct must be extreme in its nature and such that by any reasonable standard it is deserving of full condemnation and punishment.

. . .

In the case at bar, the plaintiff was entitled to have the salary and benefits agreed upon under the contract of employment while he continued in such employment. Each party had the right to terminate the contract without the consent of the other, and where the employment contract was terminated by the employer, the appellant was entitled to reasonable notice of such termination or payment of salary and benefits for the period of reasonable notice. The termination of the contract on this basis by the employer is not a wrong in law and, where the reasonable notice is given or payment in lieu thereof is made, the plaintiff — subject to a consideration of aggravated damages which have been allowed in some cases but which were denied in this case — is entitled to no further remedy: see *Addis, supra*, and *Peso Silver Mines* case, *supra*.

It is argued that the conduct of the defendant, that is, the supervisor Reid, prior to the dismissal was such that it caused mental distress and frustration to the appellant. This conduct, however, was not considered sufficiently offensive, standing alone, to constitute actionable wrong; see Hinkson J.A., *supra*, and in my view was not of such nature as to justify the imposition of an award of punitive damages. I would, accordingly, dismiss the appeal with costs.

[Beetz and Lamer JJ. concurred with McIntyre J. Wilson J., with L'Heureux-Dubé J. concurring, dissented. Wilson J. held that aggravated damages for mental distress caused by wrongful dismissal should be recoverable if such distress was foreseeable when the contract was entered. On the particular facts, she concluded that mental distress was not foreseeable. However, she held that punitive damages could be awarded for breach of contract and were justified in this case.]

NOTES AND QUESTIONS

1. Based on *Vorvis*, what is the purpose of aggravated damages and in what circumstances will they be awarded? The Supreme Court accepted the House of Lords' analysis of aggravated damages in *Rookes v. Barnard*, [1964] A.C. 1129. Aggravated damages were defined in *Rookes* as a form of compensatory damages that were awarded to compensate the plaintiff for injury to proper feelings of dignity or pride stemming from the defendant's motive or the manner in which the tort was committed.

2. Why did the majority refuse to award aggravated damages in *Vorvis*? Why did the minority refuse? Do you agree with their analyses?

3. Unlike the House of Lords in *Rookes*, the Supreme Court refused to limit punitive damages to specific categories of cases. Based on *Vorvis*, what is the purpose of punitive damages and in what circumstances will they be awarded?

However, the Supreme Court was concerned with limiting punitive damages. What was the Supreme Court's rationale for this restraint, and what principle did it indicate should be used for this purpose?

4. Why did the majority refuse to award punitive damages in *Vorvis*? Do you agree with its analysis?

5. The Canadian courts often define the purposes of punitive damages as punishment and deterrence, apparently without recognizing that these goals may be incompatible. Can you suggest a fact situation in which the punishment rationale would lead to a larger award than the deterrence rationale? Can you suggest a situation in which the deterrence rationale would result in a larger award?

It is generally accepted in Canada that the main purpose of punitive damages is and should be punishment. This point is underscored by the Supreme Court's preference for the term "punitive damages" in *Vorvis*, rather than the term "exemplary damages", which was used in *Rookes*. The deterrence rationale is more prominent in the United States, a fact that may account for the American courts' tendency to award much larger punitive damages awards than their Canadian counterparts.

6. Since *Vorvis* requires the plaintiff to establish that the defendant's conduct was reprehensible in order to recover either aggravated or punitive damages, is there any need for both kinds of awards? Why should compensation for injuries to dignity and pride depend on proof of socially unacceptable behaviour?

B. (P.) v. B. (W.)

(1992), 11 O.R. (3d) 161 (Gen. Div.)

[The plaintiff had been repeatedly sexually assaulted by her father from the age of 5 until 18. There were other incidents of violence and threatened violence, and her father raped her when she was 20. Her father pleaded guilty to having committed incest, but two additional charges related to the rape were stayed. The father was sentenced to 5½ years imprisonment on the incest conviction.

The plaintiff sued her father for assault and battery. He did not defend the action. The case proceeded on the issue of damages. The plaintiff's doctor testified that she was the most traumatized sexual assault victim he had ever seen. He stated that she was left emotionally and socially dysfunctional, and it was highly unlikely that she would ever be able to function in normal relationships.]

CUNNINGHAM J.: —

. . .

Non-pecuniary general damages

There can be no doubt that the repugnant and reprehensible conduct of the defendant towards his daughter has severely affected her life. Abuse by fathers has to have a far more negative impact upon children than any other form of abuse. More particularly, a very special relationship exists between fathers and daughters and when that trusting, loving relationship is violated, the results can be catastrophic. They certainly were here. This plaintiff has been, in the words of Dr. Bartashunas, as severely psychologically damaged as anyone he has seen, not only in his practice but in the literature. Not only was there a total breach of trust involved here but also a very significant element of fear. Violence permeated this entire family unit and during her tender years, while being subjected to regular sexual abuse by her father, she often witnessed her mother being beaten by the defendant and indeed had been subjected to his physical violence herself. By the time the plaintiff reached her mid-teens, she began to experience great difficulty coping with her life. She suffered blackouts and before she was brought to the attention of Dr. Bartashunas, she had been through neurological and CAT scan examinations, all of which proved negative.

This case is clearly the most serious I have seen in my review of Canadian authorities. As the plaintiff described in her evidence, it is worse than being murdered. It is something that she has had to live with for a very long time and probably will have to live with every day for the rest of her life. Her great fear, because she recognizes her difficulty in forming meaningful relationships, is that she will grow old alone.

Accordingly, for her non-pecuniary general damages the plaintiff will have the sum of $100,000. In arriving at this amount, I have carefully considered the following cases: *J. (J.L.) v. L. (A.M.)* (1988), 47 C.C.L.T. 65, [1989] 1 W.W.R. 438 (Man. Q.B.); *Harder v. Brown* (1989), 50 C.C.L.T. 85 (B.C.S.C.); *B. (A.) v. J. (I.)*, [1991] 5 W.W.R. 748, 81 Alta. L.R. (2d) 84 (Q.B.); *Brandner v. Brandner* (1991), 71 Man. R. (2d) 265 (Q.B.); *Beaudry v. Hackett* (June 28, 1991), Thackray J. (B.C.S.C.) (unreported); and *G. (K.) v. T. (J.)* (1992), 12 L.W. 1216-027, Parrett J. (B.C.S.C.) (unreported). In my view, the closest to our case is *Brandner v. Brandner*, where a father sexually abused his daughter, almost continuously from six to fifteen leaving her severely traumatized. In that case, the professional witnesses described it as being one of the worst cases of a sexually damaged person ever encountered, a person who would need continual psychotherapy. In fact, most of the difficulties suffered by the plaintiff in that case are very similar to the difficulties being experienced by this plaintiff. Feelings of vulnerability, victimization and profound shame with the attendant lack of self-esteem and self-worth are the results in both cases. In *Brandner*, De Graves J. awarded the sum of $100,000 for psychological trauma and $50,000 for aggravated damages. I intend to deal with aggravated damages separately.

Aggravated damages

Aggravated damages are awarded in cases where, because of the defendant's conduct, the measure of damages is increased. In my view, aggravated damages are not punitive damages which I will deal with later in these reasons. Aggravated damages may be taken into account in the overall assessment of non-pecuniary general damages but in certain circumstances, may be dealt with separately and in addition to general damages where the facts so warrant. This, in my view, is one of those situations. The assaults in this case occurred over a period of many years on a little girl who loved and trusted her father. It was not until she was about 10 years of age that she realized, through interaction with her peers at school, something was wrong with her relationship with her father. This defendant, even during periods of access while the plaintiff was living with her mother, continued his predatory and disgraceful conduct on a young girl approaching adolescence. Even worse, after obtaining custody of the plaintiff in her early teens, he continued his disgusting conduct. Never have I seen a situation where a person in authority has taken such advantage of another and accordingly, I assess aggravated damages at $75,000 for this gross breach of trust. Had it not been for this pattern of abuse, I have no doubt this young woman would today be functioning at a much higher level. I adopt entirely the comments of Veit J. in *B. (A.) v. J. (I.), supra*, at p. 755 W.W.R., pp. 91-92 Alta. L.R.:

. . .

In this case, the emotional and psychological injuries suffered by each of the plaintiffs has undoubtedly been aggravated, not only by the seriousness of the assaults, the repetition of the assaults and the length of time during which the assaults occurred, but by the defendant's abuse of his relationship of trust with them. This is a situation in which aggravated damages is both called for and allowed.

Punitive damages

In my view, it is clear law that where tortious acts are also crimes and the conduct has already been sanctioned, to award punitive damages in a civil lawsuit would amount of [*sic*] double jeopardy: *B. (A.) v. J. (I.), supra; Rioux v. Smith* (1983), 48 B.C.L.R. 126 (C.A.).

In the present case, as I indicated early on, only part of the defendant's conduct was criminally sanctioned. The defendant pleaded guilty to having committed incest upon his daughter between the years 1976 and 1987. From my reading of the proceedings in the criminal court, although there was some brief mention of the 1989 occurrence, the full details of that sexual assault were not documented. The plaintiff has testified that on that occasion she was raped by her father at a time when she was in a particularly vulnerable state. The recitation of the facts in the criminal court indicated that the defendant fondled the plaintiff's breasts and rubbed his penis against her vagina suggesting to her that, despite the fact she was having her menstrual period, it would be a good time to have sex. What the recitation of the facts did not disclose, however, was the fact of the rape. I am satisfied that this conduct in 1989, was not sanctioned. Accordingly, the plaintiff will have punitive damages against the defendant in the amount of $50,000.

NOTES AND QUESTIONS

1. Could the judge have simply awarded $150,000 general damages and not made an award of aggravated damages? Do you think that the total award of $150,000 provides adequate compensation. See Feldthusen, "Discriminatory Damage Quantification in Civil Actions for Sexual Battery" (1994), 44 U.T.L.J. 133.

2. It is generally accepted in Canada that an award of punitive damages cannot be made if the defendant has been punished criminally for the same act. The sentence imposed by the criminal courts is viewed as providing appropriate punishment. Can you suggest factors in the criminal justice system that would call into question this rationale? Would this rule discourage victims from contacting the police when doing so might preclude recovery of punitive damages? Do you think that the judge's analysis of punitive damages in *B. (P.)* was influenced by this rule?

Some courts appear to be relaxing this rule, particularly if the defendant has not been sentenced to imprisonment in the criminal case. See for example, *Connors v. Doak* (1978), 24 N.B.R. (2d) 85 (C.A.); and *Willington v. Marshall* (1994), 21 C.C.L.T. (2d) 198 (B.C. S.C.).

It should be noted that a defendant's criminal conviction and sentence has no impact on a plaintiff's claim for aggravated damages.

3. Does the fact that the criminal justice system is overburdened justify expanding the role of punitive damages in torts, particularly in cases of deliberate and repeated wrongdoing? Although some commentators adopt this position, others are concerned about imposing severe penalties in a civil system in the absence of the procedural safeguards available in criminal law. See respectively England, "The System Builders: A Critical Appraisal of Modern American Tort Theory" (1980), 9 J. Leg. Studies 27; and Jefferies, Jr., "A Comment on the Constitutionality of Punitive Damages" (1986), 22 Va. L. Rev. 139.

4. Do aggravated and punitive damages have an important role to play in the public condemnation of socially unacceptable behaviour and the acknowledgment of the plaintiff's losses and injuries? Do you think that these considerations influenced the court's analysis in *B. (P.)*? See also *Myers v. Haroldson*, [1989] 3 W.W.R. 604 (Sask. Q.B.), where the plaintiff sought aggravated and punitive damages from the man who had raped her, after the police failed to charge him. The plaintiff did so knowing that the man was unlikely to be able to pay the judgment.

5. There is concern about the lack of principles governing the quantification of punitive damage awards, especially in the United States where million dollar awards are not uncommon. In contrast, punitive damage awards in Canada have traditionally been modest in size and relatively uncommon. An Ontario Law Reform Commission study found that punitive and aggravated damages were awarded in less than 2% of civil cases excluding matrimonial cases, or in roughly 10% of civil cases if contract and negligence cases are also excluded. The largest reported punitive damage award before 1988 was $50,000, but most were far smaller. Most lawyers surveyed at that time believed that punitive damage awards were seldom large enough to justify making an argument for them. See Vidmar and Feldthusen, "Exemplary Damage Claims in Ontario: An Empirical Profile" (1990), 16 Can. Bus. L.J. 262. By far the largest punitive damage award in Canada was the $4.8 million award in *Claiborne Industries v. National Bank of Canada* (1989), 69 O.R. (2d) 65 (C.A.). This award was premised on the court's finding that the defendant had made a profit of $4.8 million from its tortious conduct.

There appear to have been increases in the frequency and size of punitive damage awards in Canada, particularly in cases of defamation, sexual assault and deliberate corporate wrongdoing. For example, in *Hill v. Church of Scientology of Toronto* (1994), 18 O.R. (3d) 385 (C.A.), aff'd. [1995] 2 S.C.R. 1130, a Crown counsel was awarded $300,000 in general damages, $500,000 in aggravated damages and $800,000 in punitive damages in a libel and slander action. See also Barnes, "$1 Million Jury Award over Arson Accusation" (Jan. 19, 1996), *The Toronto Star*, A10. In *Horseshoe Bay Retirement Society v. S.I.F. Development Corp.* (1990), 3 C.C.L.T. (2d) 75 (B.C. S.C.), the plaintiffs were awarded $33,000 in compensatory and $100,000 in punitive damages against a corporate developer who had cut down a number of their trees to increase the sale value of its lots. See also *Epstein v. Cressey Development Corp.*, [1992] 3 W.W.R. 556 (B.C. C.A.).

6. With few exceptions, negligence involves conduct which is careless, but not otherwise morally blameworthy. Consequently, it is very unlikely that the defendant's conduct in a negligence suit will meet the criteria for imposing punitive damages. In *Robitaille v. Vancouver Hockey Club Ltd.* (1981), 16 C.C.L.T. 225, the British Columbia Court of Appeal held that punitive damages could be awarded in a negligence suit provided the defendant's conduct was sufficiently arrogant and high-handed. *Robitaille* was approved by the Supreme Court of Canada in *Vorvis*. See also *Vlchek v. Koshel* (1988), 52 D.L.R. (4th) 371 (B.C. S.C.), leave to appeal ref'd. by B.C. C.A. (1988), 52 D.L.R. (4th) 371n, allowing a claim for punitive damages in a products liability suit. Would you favour awarding punitive damages against drunken drivers in negligence cases? See Whitehall, "Taylor v. Superior Court: Punitive Damages for Nondeliberate Torts — The Drunk Driving Context" (1980), 68 Cal. L. Rev. 911.

7. Section 24(1) of the Canadian Charter of Rights and Freedoms provides that a person whose rights under the Charter have been denied or infringed "may apply to a court of competent juris-diction to obtain such remedy as the court considers appropriate and just in the circumstances." In *Collin v. Lussier* (1983), 6 C.R.R. 89 (Fed. Ct. T.D.), aff'd. (1984), 20 C.R.R. 29 (Fed. C.A.), the court held that prison officials had violated the plaintiff's right to security of the person under s. 7 of the Charter by arbitrarily transferring him to an institution that could not adequately deal with his heart condition. The judge voided the transfer, ordered a new placement and awarded $18,000 in damages, of which $7,500 was for punitive damages. Is this decision to award punitive damages and the size of the award consistent with the other punitive damages cases? Should the courts develop special principles to govern punitive damages in Charter cases? See also *Crossman v. R.* (1984), 9 D.L.R. (4th) 588 (Fed. Ct. T.D.); *Lord v. Allison* (1986), 3 B.C.L.R. (2d) 300 (S.C.); and *Patenaude v. Roy* (1994), 26 C.C.L.T. (2d) 237 (Que. C.A.).

8. For a discussion of punitive damages see Waddams, *The Law of Damages*, 2nd ed. (1991), 11-1 to 11-29; Klar *et al,* *Damages and Remedies in Tort* (1995), 27-47 to 27-63; and Feldthusen, "Punitive Damages in Canada: Can the Coffee Ever Be Too Hot?" (1995), 17 Loy. L.A. Int'l & Comp. L.J. 793.

REVIEW PROBLEM

What damages would be awarded in the following fact situations under the principles established in *Rookes* and *Vorvis*?

(a) The defendant strikes John and breaks his jaw. The defendant is a renowned bully with previous criminal convictions for assault. No criminal charge is pending in this case.

(b) The same bully strikes John and breaks his jaw at an office party, attended by the plaintiff's wife, friends and co-workers. The defendant ridicules the plaintiff while administering the beating.

(c) The bully strikes John and breaks his jaw at the office party, but is unaware that John is in the company of family and friends. The defendant remains silent and bears the plaintiff no personal malice.

(d) The bully is hired for $5,000 to beat the plaintiff. Compensatory damages, other than aggravated damages, are $2,000.

3

INTENTIONAL INTERFERENCE
WITH THE PERSON

1. Introduction
2. Basic Principles of Liability
3. Related Issues: Motive, Mistake and Accident
4. Battery
5. Assault
6. False Imprisonment
7. Malicious Prosecution
8. Intentional Infliction of Nervous Shock
9. Protection of Privacy
10. The Common Law Tort of Discrimination

1. Introduction

This chapter begins with the intentional torts which protect an individual's physical integrity. Most of these actions — battery, assault and false imprisonment — were derived from the writ of trespass *vi et armis* and thus were characterized by direct and forceful interference with the person. These actions have remained largely unchanged over the years. The chapter also includes the torts of malicious prosecution and the intentional infliction of nervous shock, actions derived from the writ of trespass on the case. While intent is an essential element of both torts, the interference with the person is indirect. Privacy and discrimination, the remaining intentional tort actions discussed in this chapter, focus on personal interests other than physical integrity. Although these two actions have been recognized in some American jurisdictions, their existence is a matter of debate in Canada.

2. Basic Principles of Liability

Generally, a defendant will only be held liable in intentional torts if his conduct is both voluntary and intentional. Before turning to the specific elements of the individual intentional torts, it is important to carefully define the concepts of volition and intent, and clearly distinguish them from the related concepts of motive, mistake and accident. This task is complicated because many of the terms have a unique legal meaning which may be confused with their meaning in common usage.

(a) VOLITION

The first issue to address in an intentional tort suit is whether the defendant's act was voluntary. Basically, the issue of volition refers to whether the individual has control over his physical actions. To be liable in intentional torts the defendant's conduct must be voluntary, in that it must be directed by a conscious mind.

SMITH v. STONE

(1647), 82 E.R. 533 (K.B.)

Special justification in trespasse pedibus ambulando. Trespasse.

Smith brought an action of trespasse against Stone pedibus ambulando, the defendant pleads this speciall plea in justification, viz. that he was carried upon the land of the plaintiff by force, and violence of others, and was not there voluntarily, which is the same trespasse, for which the plaintiff brings his action. The plaintiff demurs to this plea: in this case Roll Iustice said, that it is the trespasse of the party that carried the defendant upon the land, and not the trespasse of the defendant: as he that drives my cattel into another mans land is the trespassor against him, and not I who am owner of the cattell.

NOTES AND QUESTIONS

1. Would the defendant's act have been voluntary if: (a) he had been chased onto the plaintiff's land by a swarm of bees; or (b) he had entered the plaintiff's land to prevent a child from drowning? Would an individual who reached out instinctively and grasped another's arm to avoid falling have acted voluntarily?

2. The issue of volition is rarely contentious and consequently there is little reference to it in the case law. In intentional torts, this issue will most likely arise in relation to children and the mentally ill. The most comprehensive discussion of the question is provided in negligence cases involving drivers who are rendered unconscious by sudden illness. See, for example, *Gootson v. R.*, [1948] 4 D.L.R. 33 (S.C.C.) (epileptic seizure); *Boomer v. Penn* (1965), 52 D.L.R. (2d) 673 (Ont. H.C.) (insulin reaction); and *Gordon v. Wallace* (1973), 42 D.L.R. (3d) 342 (Ont. H.C.) and *Dobbs v. Mayer* (1985), 32 C.C.L.T. 191 (Ont. Div. Ct.) (heart attack). See also Blalock, "Liability of the Unconscious Defendant" (1970), 6 Trial 29; and Smith, "Automatism — A Defence to Negligence?" (1980), 130 New L.J. 1111.

(b) INTENT

In tort law, the term intent is used to refer to an actor's desire to bring about the results or consequences of his act, rather than his desire to do the physical act itself. If the defendant fires at a crow but the bullet misses and hits a cow, his shooting of the cow is unintentional because he did not desire this result. The fact that he desired to do the physical act of pulling the trigger is not relevant to this issue. A single act may bring about several consequences, only some of which may be intentional and only one of which may be relevant to the tort suit in question. For example, assume that the defendant, believing that he is alone in a secluded forest, shoots at a tin can and hits it, but the bullet ricochets and strikes the plaintiff. The consequence of hitting the tin can is intentional, because the defendant desired to shoot that object. However, if the plaintiff sues the defendant for the intentional tort of battery, the relevant issue is whether the defendant desired to cause an offensive or harmful physical contact with the plaintiff. Since the shooting of the plaintiff was unintentional, this action would fail.

The essential issue is whether the defendant desired to bring about the specific consequence giving rise to the tort action in question. The defendant's intent need not be hostile or otherwise blameworthy. For example, a defendant who at great personal risk saves a child's life by pushing her out of the path of a car, has the requisite intent to be held liable in battery. The fact that the defendant had intent does not mean that he will be held liable — intent is only one element of an intentional tort suit. One must then analyze the substantive elements of the action.

However, the fact that the defendant did not desire to bring about the consequence giving rise to the tort may not necessarily resolve the intent issue. As we discuss below, the plaintiff may establish intent under the doctrines of imputed and transferred intent.

(i) Imputed (Constructive) Intent

The concept of intent includes not only the desired consequences of an act, but also those unintended consequences that are certain or substantially certain to result from it. Thus, a defendant who plants a powerful bomb in the outer office of his former boss will be held liable to the staff injured in the ensuing explosion. Although the defendant may not have wished to injure the staff, such an intent will be imputed to him if this consequence was certain or substantially certain to follow from his act.

(ii) Transferred Intent

The doctrine of transferred intent provides another basis for imposing liability on a defendant for the unintended consequences of his act. It is invoked when a defendant has the intent to commit an intentional tort against one party, but unintentionally commits an intentional tort against the plaintiff. The doctrine also applies if the defendant intends to commit one type of intentional tort against the plaintiff, but unintentionally commits another. In essence, the defendant's wrongful intent regarding the first tort is transferred to the second claim to permit recovery. Traditionally, transferred intent was restricted to directly caused injuries involving hurling, casting and shooting. It was also limited to the intentional torts derived from the writ of trespass *vi et armis*, namely battery, assault, false imprisonment, trespass to chattels, and trespass to land. The Canadian courts have not addressed whether these historical limits on the doctrine should be maintained.

NOTES AND QUESTIONS

1. What is the rationale for the doctrine of imputed intent? American authorities have defined imputed intent in terms of the actor's own belief in the certainty or substantial certainty of the consequences. See the American Law Institute, *Restatement of the Law, Second, Torts* (1965), para. 8A; and *Garratt v. Dailey* (1955), 279 P. (2d) 1091 (Wash. S.C.). What problems, if any, arise from adopting this subjective definition of imputed intent?

2. In *Bielitski v. Obadiak* (1922), 65 D.L.R. 627 (Sask. C.A.) and *Purdy v. Woznesensky*, [1937] 2 W.W.R. 116 (Sask. C.A.), the court applied an extremely broad test of imputed intent, based in part on the criminal law presumption that an individual is deemed to intend the natural and probable consequences of his acts. What is the practical effect of this presumption? For a critique of its use in intentional torts, see Atrens, "Intentional Interference with The Person", in Linden (ed.), *Studies in Cana-*

dian Tort Law (1968), 378 at 381-82. But see Epstein, "Intentional Harm" (1975), 4 J. of Leg. Studies 391.

3. What is the rationale for the doctrine of transferred intent? Historical factors aside, should it still be limited to torts derived from trespass *vi et armis* and situations involving hurling, casting and shooting? See generally Prosser, "Transferred Intent" (1967), 45 Tex. L. Rev. 650.

4. Give an example in which: (a) both transferred and imputed intent would apply; (b) only transferred intent would apply; and (c) only imputed intent would apply. See *Scott v. Shepherd* (1773), 96 E.R. 525.

3. Related Issues: Motive, Mistake and Accident

(a) MOTIVE

The concept of intent refers to the actor's desire to bring about a particular result, not his motive or reason for wanting that result to occur. A friend who moves your car to prevent it from being impounded, a practical joker who moves it on April Fool's Day, and a thief who steals it all have intent to commit trespass to chattels, but obviously their motives differ. The plaintiff must prove that the defendant's conduct was intentional, but he does not have to establish that the defendant had a blameworthy motive. Unlike intent, motive is not generally an element of the cause of action. Thus, in the example above, all three defendants have committed the tort of trespass to chattels, even though their motives ranged from greed to altruism. The concept of motive is extremely broad, encompassing the complete range of factors which induce human behaviour. The following discussions of duress and provocation should be viewed as illustrations of the courts' response to motive.

NOTES AND QUESTIONS

1. Motive is an essential element of some of the intentional torts derived from the writ of trespass on the case. For example, in order to establish the tort of malicious prosecution the plaintiff must prove, among other things, that the defendant acted maliciously or for some other improper purpose.

2. A praiseworthy motive is not a defence *per se*, although the defendant's motive may be relevant in establishing a valid defence. For example, to invoke the defence of public necessity, a defendant must establish that he was acting to protect the public interest from an impending harm.

3. There are several ways in which the parties' motives may be taken into account in assessing damages. Depending on the jurisdiction, the defendant's motive may provide grounds for awarding aggravated or punitive damages. It may also influence the size of the general damage award, because the trier of fact has considerable discretion in setting this figure. In some jurisdictions, the fact that the plaintiff provoked the defendant may result in reducing the compensatory damages. Similarly, the court may express its disapproval of a vexatious plaintiff by awarding only contemptuous damages.

(i) *Duress*

GILBERT v. STONE

(1648), 82 E.R. 539 (K.B.)

Demurrer upon a plea in trespasse.

Gilbert brought an action of trespasse quare clausum fregit, and taking of a gelding, against Stone. The defendant pleads that he for fear of his life, and wounding of twelve armed men, who threatened to kill him if he did not the fact, went into the house of the plaintiff, and took the gelding. The plaintiff demurred to this plea; Roll Iustice, This is no plea to justifie the defendant; for I may not do a trespasse to one for fear of threatnings of another, for by this means the party injured shall have no satisfaction, for he cannot have it of the party that threatened. Therefore let the plaintiff have his judgement.

NOTES AND QUESTIONS

1. Analyze the issues of volition, intent and motive in the *Gilbert* case. Distinguish this case from *Smith v. Stone, supra*. Is the defendant's conduct in *Gilbert* any more morally blameworthy than that in *Smith*? Can you suggest another rationale for the different results in these two cases?

2. Duress will neither negate volition and intent, nor serve as a defence. Rather, it is simply a factor that the courts may consider in assessing damages. Fleming has argued that duress ought to be recognized as a defence, in keeping with the principle of no liability without fault. See *The Law of Torts*, 8th ed. (1992), 98. Outline the competing interests at stake in resolving this issue.

3. Although he has no defence in reference to Gilbert, Stone would have a valid claim in assault against the armed men. As well, their conduct would now give rise to an action for intimidation. In *Rookes v. Barnard*, [1964] A.C. 1129, the House of Lords defined intimidation as coercing a person, by unlawful threats, into doing or refraining from doing that which he has a right to do.

4. Is it appropriate that compulsion (duress) is a defence in criminal law, but not tort law? See Criminal Code, R.S.C. 1985, c. C-46, s. 17 (hereafter referred to as the Criminal Code).

5. Under s. 17 of the Criminal Code, the defence of compulsion is limited to threats of immediate physical injury and cannot be raised by an accused who is charged with treason, murder or other serious crimes of violence. If duress were recognized as a defence in tort law, how would you define it? Should it be limited to: (a) threats of immediate physical harm; (b) threats involving any federal criminal offence; or (c) threats involving any illegal act?

(ii) *Provocation*

MISKA v. SIVEC

[1959] O.R. 144, 18 D.L.R. (2d) 363 (Ont. C.A.)

. . .

The plaintiff's claim was for damages for injuries sustained by him when the defendant intentionally shot him with a shotgun. The defence was self-defence. The defendant's appeal was based on two points, first that the trial Judge had instructed the jury that the onus was on the defendant to show that the force used by him in self-defence was not excessive, and secondly that he had failed to instruct the jury that they ought to take provocation into account in assessing the damages.

The defendant's evidence, which was denied by the plaintiff was that the plaintiff had blocked his car with his, the plaintiff's, car on the road, that the plaintiff had then got out of his car and threatened him with a knife and an iron bar, that the defendant had then fled from his car some 200 yds. to his house with the plaintiff in pursuit; that he had then fired two warning shots from his house and the plaintiff had moved into the line of fire. Evidence was also given of bad blood between the parties for a considerable time.

. . .

MORDEN J.A., [delivering the judgment of the court]

. . .

In my opinion, Wells, J., properly directed the jury on the burden of proof, and the first ground of appeal fails.

The defendant's second ground of appeal was that the learned trial Judge failed and when requested by counsel for the defendant refused to charge the jury on the effect of provocation in mitigation of damages. There is no doubt that where there is evidence of provocation the jury should be instructed to consider it in assessing damages for assault. In this connection, Mr. Goodman submitted that the bad feeling and other incidents between the parties, going back over a period of eight or nine months, should be considered evidence of provocation.

The conduct of the plaintiff to be capable of being considered provocation must have been such as to cause the defendant to lose his power of self-control and must have occurred at the time of or shortly before the assault. In *Fraser v. Berkeley* (1836), 7 C. & P. 621, three days after the plaintiff published a libel on the defendant and his family, the defendant beat the plaintiff with a heavy whip and his fists and in the action for damages for assault evidence of this libel was given. Lord Abinger in charging the jury said at p. 624: —

> The law I think would be an unwise law, if it did not make allowance for human infirmities; and if a person commit violence at a time when he is smarting under immediate provocation, that is a matter of mitigation.

. . .

In deciding in this case whether there was evidence of provocation, incidents occurring between the parties prior to the night of the assault are not to be considered. They were not immediate and by the night in question, if available at all to the defendant, could only be available to show provocation if it were asserted that the effect of the immediate provocative acts upon the defendant's mind was enhanced by those previous incidents being recalled to him and thereby inflaming his passion. There is no such evidence directly or by way of inference to be drawn from the defendant's testimony. A careful perusal of the defendant's evidence of the occurrences on the fateful evening does not disclose any insulting or abusive conduct or language on the part of the plaintiff, nor any sudden passion, lack of self-control or even any annoyance on the defendant's part. His evidence was that the plaintiff had blocked his car and approached him armed with an iron bar and a knife. The defendant then beat a successful retreat back to his house which was about 200 yds. away. After he entered the house his wife locked the door and he loaded his shotgun and went upstairs. At this point his wife went to the telephone to notify the police. The defendant took up his position at an open window on the second story from which he fired without any warning at the plaintiff. He did not say that at that time he was annoyed or provoked. His conduct was careful and deliberate and belied the existence of any sudden and uncontrolled passion. In my opinion, there was no evidence of provocation to be left to the jury and the learned trial Judge was correct in refusing to do so.

On both grounds the appeal fails and must be dismissed with costs.

NOTES AND QUESTIONS

1. How did Morden J.A. define provocation? Did you find his application of this definition to the facts convincing? Why did Morden J.A. not consider the previous incidents between the parties as evidence of provocation?

2. In *Miska*, the court appears to use a subjective test which focuses on whether the defendant lost his power of self-control. Nevertheless, the test is usually phrased in more objective terms: did the plaintiff's conduct cause the defendant, as a reasonable person, to lose his power of self-control? Should the defendant's claim of provocation be denied if his loss of self-control was reasonable, but his retaliatory behaviour was out of proportion to the plaintiff's provocative behaviour?

3. One of the most confusing issues is the impact of provocation on the assessment of damages. Initially, the Canadian courts considered provocation a factor in reducing the plaintiff's claim for both compensatory and punitive damages. In *Check v. Andrews Hotel Co.* (1974), 56 D.L.R. (3d) 364 (Man. C.A.), the majority rejected these authorities in favour of *Fontin v. Katapodis* (1962), 108 C.L.R. 177 (Aust. H.C.) and *Lane v. Holloway*, [1968] 1 Q.B. 379 (C.A.). In both of these cases, the court held that provocation was only relevant in determining whether to award punitive damages. In *Murphy v. Culhane*, [1976] 3 All E.R. 533 (C.A.), Denning M.R. distinguished both *Fontin* and *Lane* as cases in which the plaintiff's conduct was trivial relative to the defendant's savage behaviour. Thus, Lord Denning concluded in *Culhane* that provocation could reduce compensatory damages.

In *Shaw v. Gorter* (1977), 77 D.L.R. (3d) 50, the Ontario Court of Appeal held that provocation was only relevant in determining whether to award punitive damages. However, in reaching this decision, the Court stated that there were no Canadian cases directly on point. *Gorter* was followed with considerable reservations by MacKinnon A.C.J.O. in *Landry v. Patterson* (1978), 93 D.L.R. (3d) 345 (Ont. C.A.). He indicated that this issue should be resolved by the Supreme Court of Canada. What arguments would you make if you were appealing *Landry* to the Supreme Court?

Courts in some other provinces have continued to rely upon provocation as a factor that may reduce compensatory damages. See, for example, *Veinot v. Veinot* (1977), 81 D.L.R. (3d) 549 (N.S. C.A.); *Holt v. Verbruggen* (1981), 20 C.C.L.T. 29 (B.C. S.C.); and *Hurley v. Moore* (1993), 18 C.C.L.T. (2d) 78 (Nfld. C.A.). For a discussion of this issue see Osborne, "Annotation" (1981), 20 C.C.L.T. 29.

4. It has been argued that a plaintiff's provocative act may constitute contributory negligence and thus give rise to apportionment of damages under the provincial negligence acts. If this argument is accepted, the plaintiff's damages would be reduced by a specified percentage to reflect his contributory negligence. See *Long v. Gardner* (1983), 144 D.L.R. (3d) 73 (Ont. H.C.); and *Rumsey v. R.*, [1984] 5 W.W.R. 585 (Fed. Ct. T.D.).

5. Unlike duress, provocation is not a defence in criminal law. Rather, provocation operates to reduce a murder charge to manslaughter. Criminal Code, s. 232.

(b) MISTAKE

In tort law, a mistake occurs when the defendant intends the consequences of his act, but those consequences have a different factual or legal significance than that contemplated. Since mistake, by definition, has no effect on the issue of intent, it is not relevant in establishing the elements of a cause of action. Moreover, neither a mistake of fact nor a mistake of law is recognized *per se* as a defence to intentional tort liability.

HODGKINSON v. MARTIN

[1928] 3 W.W.R. 763, [1929] 1 D.L.R. 367 (C.A.)

MARTIN J.A.: — This is an action for trespass to the person and in view of certain unusual incidents I have carefully read the whole appeal book in addition to those portions cited by counsel with the result that it was, in my opinion, open to the Judge below, upon the sharply conflicting evidence to take the view that the defendant, being the deputy minister of industries and industrial commissioner, laid his hands upon the plaintiff and wrongfully put him out of the office premises in question without using any more force than was necessary to effect that object, and that the act was unlawful and therefore a trespass, and that it was done in the sincerely mistaken belief that the defendant was justified in the protection of the interests of the Crown in doing so in order to retain access to the premises which had been in his possession through his servants for 10 days beforehand, and also that his intention in preserving such right of access was not to exclude the custodian in bankruptcy from the premises but to insure their common access thereto.

. . .

It then becomes a question of the amount of damages to be awarded, upon said facts and the appellant submits that the sum of $500 assessed below is excessive and can only be supported on the basis of exemplary damages which are foreign to the case. This, in my opinion, is the proper view to take of the matter which has been made too much of because while the sincere yet mistaken belief of the defendant in the propriety of his illegal action is not excuse therefor yet it is a mitigation of his liability which must be taken into consideration where not the slightest injury has been occasioned to the plaintiff's person, clothing or reputation. It is truly said in that high authority Salmond on the Law of Torts, 7th ed., p. 145, that: — "Exemplary damages. . . . are given only in cases of conscious wrongdoing in contumelious disregard of another's rights." See Clerk & Lindsell on Torts, 7th ed. p. 140.

It is with reluctance that I feel compelled to interfere in the assessment of damages but having no doubt that nominal damages will amply compensate the plaintiff for the trespass it is my duty to give effect to my opinion by awarding the sum of $10.

RANSON v. KITNER

(1888), 31 Ill. App. 241 (Ill. C.A.)

CONGER J.: — This was an action brought by appellee against appellants to recover the value of a dog killed by appellants, and a judgment rendered for $50.

The defense was that appellants were hunting for wolves, that appellee's dog had a striking resemblance to a wolf, that they in good faith believed it to be one, and killed it as such.

Many points are made, and a lengthy argument filed to show that error in the trial below was committed, but we are inclined to think that no material error occurred to the prejudice of appellants.

The jury held them liable for the value of the dog, and we do not see how they could have done otherwise under the evidence. Appellants are clearly liable for the damages caused by their mistake, notwithstanding they were acting in good faith.

We see no reason for interfering with the conclusion reached by the jury and the judgment will be affirmed.

NOTES AND QUESTIONS

1. Are *Hodgkinson* and *Ranson* cases of mistake of fact or mistake of law? Outline an additional fact situation involving each type of mistake.

2. What impact did the defendants' mistakes have in *Hodgkinson* and *Ranson*? What did the judge mean in *Hodgkinson* when he said that the defendant's sincere but mistaken belief "is a mitigation of his liability"? Do you agree with the judge's use of the term nominal damages in *Hodgkinson*?

3. Would an individual be liable in intentional torts if he shot at a wolf, but the bullet ricocheted and hit a neighbour's dog? Distinguish this situation from that in *Ranson*.

4. What arguments would you make for recognizing a general defence of mistake? Would your answer depend on: (a) the interest invaded by the mistaken defendant; and (b) whether it was a mistake of law or fact?

5. The impact of a mistake of fact on the validity of the defences varies. Thus, a defendant who strikes the plaintiff in a reasonable but mistaken belief that the latter is about to attack him may successfully plead self-defence. See *Keep v. Quallman* (1887), 32 N.W. 233 (Wisc. S.C.). However, the defendant cannot raise as a defence his honest but mistaken belief that the plaintiff consented, if in fact he had not. See *Turner v. Thorne* (1960), 21 D.L.R. (2d) 29 (Ont. H.C.). See Keeton *et al., Prosser and Keeton on the Law of Torts*, 5th ed. (1984), 110-12 for a general explanation of why mistake invalidates some defences but not others. See also Forbes, "Mistake of Fact with Regard to Defences in Tort Law" (1970), 4 Ottawa L. Rev. 304; and Hertz, "Volenti Non Fit Injuria: A Guide", in Klar (ed.), *Studies in Canadian Tort Law* (1977), 101 at 105-108.

(c) ACCIDENT

In early English common law, the concept of inevitable accident was limited to cases in which the defendant could prove that the tort occurred utterly without fault on his part. As the principle of no liability without fault became increasingly entrenched in intentional torts, the definition of accident was broadened. The term accident is now used to refer to any situation in which the defendant unintentionally and without negligence injured the plaintiff. By definition, a defendant cannot be held liable in intentional torts or negligence for injuries caused by accident. It is the absence of intent that distinguishes accident from mistake.

REVIEW PROBLEMS

Analyze Mr. Smith's conduct in the following situations:

1. John shouted insults at Mr. Smith through an open window. In response, Mr. Smith threw a rock at John which missed, smashing a neighbour's window. The neighbour sues Mr. Smith.

2. John insulted Mr. Smith for several days. Later that week Smith spotted John standing at the window and threw a rock at him. Unknown to Smith, John's window was closed. The rock broke the window, but missed John. John sues Mr. Smith for the broken window.

3. Mr. Smith attempted to get Bill's attention by gently throwing a few small pebbles at his window. Unfortunately, one of the pebbles cracked the window. Bill sues Mr. Smith for the cracked window.

4. As Mr. Smith was leaving the locker room he picked up what he thought was his wallet. In fact, it belonged to Ralph. On his way home Smith was grabbed by a mugger armed with a gun, who ordered Smith to hand over his wallet. Mr. Smith turned over Ralph's wallet, believing it to be his own. Analyze Smith's conduct at the point he picked up Ralph's wallet and then when he handed it to the mugger.

(d) A NOTE ON THE LIABILITY OF CHILDREN AND THE MENTALLY ILL

Children and the mentally ill are governed by the same principles of liability in intentional torts as others. Thus, it should be determined whether the child's or mentally ill person's act was voluntary and intentional. Nevertheless, rather than applying the accepted tests of volition and intent, the Canadian courts have tended to apply different principles, based on what is now part of the Criminal Code defence of mental disorder in section 16(1). The issue is often framed in terms of whether the specific defendant was capable of "appreciating the nature and quality" of his acts. The courts have not explained why they have adopted this test or how it relates to the concepts of volition and intent.

It should be noted that parents and guardians are not held vicariously liable for the torts of their children or wards. Rather, parents and guardians can only be held liable if they were negligent in supervising or controlling the child or ward.

NOTES AND QUESTIONS

1. In *Tillander v. Gosselin*, [1967] 1 O.R. 203 (C.A.), the court held that the defendant, a child just under three, could not be held liable in battery because he did not have "the mental ability to appreciate or know the real nature of the act he was performing." The defendant child had pulled an infant out of her carriage and dragged her 100 feet across the property. Would the result have been the same if the standard tests of volition and intent had been applied? Is the test used in *Tillander* easier to apply than the standard tests?

2. In *Tillander*, it was also held that the child could not be held liable in negligence because he lacked sufficient judgment to exercise reasonable care. How does this test differ from the one that was used to determine liability in intentional torts?

3. See *Walmsley v. Humenick*, [1954] 2 D.L.R. 232 (B.C. S.C.); *Garratt v. Dailey* (1955), 279 P. (2d) 1091 (Wash. S.C.); Bohlen, "Liability in Tort of Infants and Insane Persons" (1924), 23 Mich. Law Rev. 9; and Alexander, "Tort Liability of Children and Their Parents" in Mendes da Costa (ed.), *Studies in Canadian Family Law* (1972), 845 at 852.

4. The Criminal Code, s. 13 provides that no child under 12 can be convicted of a criminal offence. Would you favour a statutory provision to govern a child's liability in torts? If so, what should be the age requirement?

5. The defendant in *Squittieri v. De Santis* (1976), 15 O.R. (2d) 416 (H.C.) had been found not guilty by reason of insanity at his criminal trial. Even though he appreciated the nature and quality of his act in stabbing Squittieri, he did not know that it was wrong. In holding the defendant liable in battery, the court stated that the issue in a civil action was whether the defendant was capable of understanding the nature and quality of his actions.

Does this test relate to volition, intent or both issues? Why is the issue of whether the defendant knew that his conduct was wrong relevant in criminal, but not tort law?

6. Is tort law consistent in the way it deals with motive, mistake, duress, and insanity?

7. See *Phillips v. Soloway* (1956), 6 D.L.R. (2d) 570 (Man. Q.B.); *Lawson v. Wellesley Hospital* (1975), 61 D.L.R. (3d) 445 (Ont. C.A.), aff'd. [1978] 1 S.C.R. 893; *Gerigs v. Rose* (1979), 9 C.C.L.T. 222 (Ont. H.C.); and *Whaley v. Cartusiano* (1990), 72 O.R. (2d) 523 (C.A.). See also Picher, "The Tortious Liability of the Insane in Canada ..." (1975), 13 Osgoode Hall L.J. 193; and Coleman, "Mental Abnormality, Personal Responsibility, and Tort Liability" in Brody and Engelhardt (eds.), *Mental Illness: Law and Public Policy* (1980), 107.

4. Battery

BETTEL v. YIM

(1978), 20 O.R. (2d) 617, 88 D.L.R. (3d) 543 (Ont. Co. Ct.)

BORINS CO. CT. J.: — In this action the infant plaintiff, Howard Bettel, seeks damages for assault. His father, Murray Bettel, seeks special damages in the amount of $1,113. . . .

The facts

The events giving rise to this action took place on May 22, 1976, in a variety store owned and operated by the defendant, Ki Yim, situated in a small commercial plaza located in Metropolitan Toronto.

. . .

The defendant testified that the plaintiff, together with six or seven other boys, entered the store and went to the area of the pinball machines. Some of the boys were playing with a toy football and toy guns and the defendant told them to leave his store. Half of the boys, including the plaintiff, left and went outside. The defendant saw the plaintiff lighting matches and throwing them into the store. On the first occasion the plaintiff entered the store and retrieved a burning match. The second match that was thrown into the store burned itself out. Then the plaintiff re-entered the store, proceeded toward the pinball machines and said "What's the smell?" The defendant smelled nothing, but after 20 or 30 seconds he saw flames coming from the bag of charcoal and proceeded to remove the bag from the store unassisted by the plaintiff who remained inside. The defendant did not see who had thrown the match which started the fire.

As the defendant returned to the store he saw the plaintiff walking toward the door. He grabbed the plaintiff by the arm as he did not want the plaintiff to leave. The plaintiff denied that he set the fire. The plaintiff did not try to leave. He stood where he was. Because the plaintiff denied setting the fire the defendant grabbed him firmly by the collar with both hands and began shaking him. His purpose in doing so was to obtain a confession from the plaintiff before he called the police. The plaintiff's constant denials had made the defendant unhappy. He shook the plaintiff two or three times and then his head came down and struck the plaintiff's nose. He relaxed his hold on the plaintiff who fell to the ground. The defendant obtained some kleenex for the plaintiff, who was bleeding from the nose, and helped him to his feet. The defendant then telephoned the police.

In explaining the incident the defendant said: "I shook him maybe three times and my head and his nose accidentally hit; I didn't intend to hit him." In cross-examination he stated that he did not mean to hit the plaintiff with his head and that is why he said it was an accident. . . .

The law

The plaintiff has framed his action in assault. Properly speaking the action should have been framed in battery which is the intentional infliction upon the body of another of a harmful or offensive contact. However, in Canada it would appear that the distinction between assault and battery has been blurred and when one speaks of an assault, it may include a battery: *Gambriell v. Caparelli* (1974), 7 O.R. (2d) 205, 54 D.L.R. (3d) 661. It is on the basis that this is an action framed in battery that I approach the facts in this case.

It would appear to be well established in this country (although not necessarily warmly received), following the dictum of Cartwright, J. (as he then was), in *Cook v. Lewis*, [1951] S.C.R. 830 at p. 839, [1952] 1 D.L.R. 1 at p. 15, that once the plaintiff proves that he was injured by the direct act of the defendant, the defendant is entitled to judgment only "if he satisfies the onus of establishing the absence of both intention and negligence on his part": *Dahlberg v. Naydiuk*

(1969), 10 D.L.R. (3d) 319, 72 W.W.R. 210 (Man. C.A.), *per* Dickson, J.A. (as he then was), at pp. 328-9. On the defendant's evidence, his act in grabbing the plaintiff with both his hands and shaking him constituted the intentional tort of battery. It is obvious that he desired to bring about an offensive or harmful contact with the plaintiff for the purpose of extracting a confession from him. Viewed as such, the defendant's own evidence proves, rather than disproves, the element of intent in so far as this aspect of his physical contact with the plaintiff is concerned. Indeed, the defendant's admitted purpose in grabbing and shaking the plaintiff does not fit into any of the accepted defences to the tort of battery — consent, self-defence, defence of property, necessity and legal authority: Fleming, *Law of Torts*, 5th ed. (1977), p. 74 *et seq.*

. . .

That there is no liability for accidental harm is central to the submission of defence counsel who argues that the shaking of the plaintiff by the defendant and the striking of the plaintiff by the defendant's head must be regarded as separate and distinct incidents. While he concedes that the defendant intentionally grabbed and shook the plaintiff, he submits that the contact with the head was unintentional. I have, of course, accepted the defendant's evidence in this regard. This, in my view, gives rise to the important question: Can an intentional wrongdoer be held liable for consequences which he did not intend? Another way of stating the problem is to ask whether the doctrine of foreseeability as found in the law of negligence is applicable to the law of intentional torts? Should an intentional wrongdoer be liable only for the reasonably foreseeable consequences of his intentional application of force or should he bear responsibility for all the consequences which flow from his intentional act?

To approach this issue one must first examine what interests the law seeks to protect. A thorough discussion of the history of old actions of trespass and case is found in Prosser, *Law of Torts*, 4th ed. (1971), p. 28 *et seq.* Terms such as battery, assault and false imprisonment, which were varieties of trespass, have come to be associated with intent. The old action on the case has emerged as the separate tort of negligence. Today it is recognized that there should be no liability for pure accident, and that for there to be liability the defendant must be found at fault, in the sense of being chargeable with a wrongful intent, or with negligence. Thus, "with rare exceptions, actions for injuries to the person or to tangible property, now require proof of an intent to inflict them, or of failure to exercise proper care": Prosser, *supra*, p. 30.

In discussing battery Fleming writes, *supra*, pp. 23-4:

> Of the various forms of trespass to the person the most common is the tort known as battery, which is committed by intentionally bringing about a harmful or offensive contact with the person of another. The action, therefore, serves the dual purpose of affording protection to the individual not only against bodily harm but also against any interference with his person which is offensive to a reasonable sense of honour and dignity. The insult involved in being touched without consent has been traditionally regarded as sufficient to warrant redress, even though the interference is only trivial and not attended with actual physical harm. "The least touching of another in anger is a battery", and so is such offensive and insulting behaviour as spitting in another man's face, cutting his hair or kissing a woman. The element of personal indignity is given additional recognition in the award of aggravated damages to compensate for any outrage to the plaintiff's feelings ....

Battery is an intentional wrong: the offensive contact must have been intended or known to be substantially certain to result. On the other hand, it is not necessary that the actor intended to inflict bodily harm, since we have seen that the legal injury is complete without it. Indeed it may be sufficient that he intended only to frighten but in a manner fraught with serious risk of bodily contact or harm. [Footnotes omitted]

. . .

It is my respectful view that the weight of opinion is that the concept of foreseeability as defined by the law of negligence is a concept that ought not to be imported into the field of intentional torts. While strong policy reasons favour determining the other limits of liability where conduct falls below an acceptable standard, the same reasons do not apply to deliberate conduct, even though the ultimate result in terms of harm caused to plaintiff is not what was intended by the defendant. In the law of intentional torts, it is the dignitary interest, the right of the plaintiff to insist that the defendant keep his hands to himself, that the law has for centuries sought to protect. In doing so, the morality of the defendant's conduct, characterized as "unlawful", has predominated the thinking of the Courts and is reflected in academic discussion. The logical test is whether the defendant was guilty of deliberate, intentional and unlawful violence or threats of violence. If he was, and a more serious harm befalls the plaintiff than was intended by the defendant, the defendant, and not the innocent plaintiff, must bear the responsibility for the unintended result. If physical contact was intended, the fact that its magnitude exceeded all reasonable or intended expectations should make no difference. To hold otherwise, in my opinion, would unduly narrow recovery where one deliberately invades the bodily interest of another with the result that the totally innocent plaintiff would be deprived of full recovery for the totality of the injuries suffered as a result of the deliberate invasion of his bodily interests. To import negligence concepts into the field of intentional torts would be to ignore the essential difference between the intentional infliction of harm and the unintentional infliction of harm resulting from a failure to adhere to a reasonable standard of care and would result in bonusing the deliberate wrongdoer who strikes the plaintiff more forcefully than intended.

. . .

NOTES AND QUESTIONS

1. How did Borins Co. Ct. J. define battery? Identify the act of the defendant that gave rise to this tort. Why was the burden of disproving intent and negligence imposed on the defendant? Would the result have been the same if the burden of proving these issues had been on the plaintiff? See *Hatton v. Webb* (1977), 81 D.L.R. (3d) 377 (Alta. Dist. Ct.).

2. Are Borins Co. Ct. J.'s reasons for holding individuals liable for all the consequences of their intentional acts compelling? Would it have made a difference if he had limited recovery to foreseeable losses? See Klar, "Annotation" (1978), 5 C.C.L.T. 66; and *Mahal v. Young* (1986), 36 C.C.L.T. 143 (B.C. S.C.), a case in which the defendant was held liable for the plaintiff's unforeseeable depressive reaction to the defendant's assault.

3. Could the defendant have successfully argued provocation? If so, what effect would it have had on the damage award? Given the facts of *Bettel*, would you advocate that provocation be taken into account to reduce compensatory damages?

4. Borins J. quotes Fleming to the effect that the contact necessary for battery must be harmful or offensive. Given the increased emphasis on individual autonomy, it is best to assume that any contact will be considered harmful or offensive, unless the defendant can establish otherwise. It is generally

agreed that accepted social practices, such as gently tapping a person on the shoulder to get his attention, will not give rise to a battery action. Are such socially accepted practices excused because they do not constitute batteries or because they are viewed as being justified by implied consent? Is this choice of approach to socially accepted practices of any practical importance? See *Coward v. Baddeley* (1859), 157 E.R. 927 (Ex. Ct.); and *Donnelly v. Jackman*, [1970] 1 All E.R. 987 (Q.B.). See also *Wilson v. Pringle*, [1987] Q.B. 237 (C.A.), where the court suggested that ordinary school horseplay might constitute an accepted social practice.

5. Should the plaintiff's, defendant's or society's perspective be adopted in defining acceptable social practices? Should the test be objective or subjective? Would the practice of a hostess, who greeted guests at her party with a kiss, subject her to liability in battery? Would it make any difference if one of the guests considered such conduct to be immoral, unsanitary and extremely offensive? How would you resolve the issue of liability in a case where a female interpreted a male associate's affectionate greeting as a sexual assault and struck him in self-defence? See *Cachay v. Nemeth* (1972), 28 D.L.R. (3d) 603 (Sask. Q.B.).

6. The tort of battery is very much concerned with protecting an individual's dignity. Consequently, a plaintiff who is publicly slapped in the face, spit on or touched in a sexually inappropriate manner may be awarded far greater damages than a plaintiff who is punched and suffers much greater physical pain and injury.

7. Aside from socially acceptable practices, the tort of battery prohibits a broad range of physical interferences with the person. The plaintiff need not suffer any physical injury or be conscious of the physical contact at the time it occurred. See *Stewart v. Stonehouse* (1926), 20 Sask. L.R. 459 (C.A.).

8. A defendant may also be held liable in battery for intentionally interfering with anything that the plaintiff is carrying, wearing or riding upon. See *Morgan v. Loyacomo* (1941), 1 So. (2d) 510 (Miss. S.C.).

9. In keeping with its historical origins, a battery can only be committed when the defendant undertakes a positive act which causes a physical contact. For example, blocking another's path will not constitute a battery, although it may give rise to liability in false imprisonment. See *Innes v. Wylie* (1844), 174 E.R. 800 (Q.B.). But see *MacDonald v. Sebastian* (1987), 43 D.L.R. (4th) 636 (N.S. S.C.), where the defendant landlord was held liable in battery for failing to inform the plaintiff that the water supply was contaminated with arsenic.

10. Battery was traditionally confined to cases of directly caused injury. Consequently, if the plaintiff was indirectly injured by having his food poisoned or a trap set in his path, he could not claim in battery. American authorities have redefined battery to include such indirect physical interferences, and some Canadian authors have followed suit. Most Commonwealth authors, however, have maintained the requirement of direct injury. See the American Law Institute, *Restatement of the Law, Second, Torts* (1965), para. 13(b); Linden, *Canadian Tort Law*, 5th ed. (1993), 40-41; and Sullivan, "Trespass to the Person in Canada: A Defence of the Traditional Approach" (1987), 19 Ottawa L. Rev. 533. What position did the court adopt in *Bettel*?

11. A defendant's conduct will often give rise to both a criminal charge of assault and a civil suit in battery. In *Simpson v. Geswein* (1995), 25 C.C.L.T. (2d) 49 (Man. Q.B.), it was held that the certificate of conviction and the judge's reasons in the criminal trial were admissible as evidence in a subsequent civil suit arising from the same event. The certificate and reasons were not to be regarded as conclusive proof, but as strong *prima facie* evidence. Should a defendant be allowed to introduce into evidence the fact that the police did not lay criminal charges or dropped the criminal charges against him? Should a defendant's acquittal be admissible as "strong *prima facie* proof" in a subsequent civil suit?

12. As illustrated by *B. (P.) v. B. (W.)* (1992), 11 O.R. (3d) 161 (Gen. Div.), which was included in the last chapter, there has been an extremely dramatic rise in the number of civil suits brought by the victims of childhood sexual abuse. Many of these cases involve conduct that has occurred 10, 15 or even 20 years ago — long after the limitations period has expired. The courts are increasingly willing to postpone the running of the limitation period until such time as the plaintiff becomes aware of the wrongful conduct and is psychologically capable of dealing with it and its harmful consequences. See, for example, *M. (K.) v. M. (H.)* (1992), 14 C.C.L.T. (2d) 1 (S.C.C.).

13. Outline the principles of law governing the tort of battery.

5. Assault

The tort of assault may be defined as the intentional creation in the mind of another of a reasonable apprehension of immediate physical contact. It has been stated that conditional threats, future threats, and words alone, without some overt act, cannot constitute assault. However, the courts have begun to reconsider these limitations and focus instead on the impression created in the plaintiff's mind.

NOTES AND QUESTIONS

1. The defendant threw a chair at B who ducked, as did C, D and E, the three people standing behind B. The chair hit F and G who were standing nearby. F saw the chair coming but could not get out of the way, and G had his back turned. Which parties have been assaulted by the defendant?

2. Can a police officer who stands passively in a doorway blocking the plaintiff's path be held liable in assault? If the plaintiff continues walking towards the motionless officer, making a collision inevitable, would the officer have a cause of action in assault? See *Innes v. Wylie* (1844), 174 E.R. 800 (Q.B.).

3. Would a 50-kilogram unarmed man be held liable in assault for threatening to hit a 120-kilogram professional boxer who viewed the threat with disdain?

4. It has been held that once the defendant has the apparent intent and ability to cause physical contact, whether he actually intends or has the ability to do so is irrelevant. For example, as a practical joke, the staff of the Club Med in Cancun staged a very realistic bus hijacking. Two guests, who were held at gun point for 30 minutes, sued, claiming $1,000,000 each in assault and false imprisonment. "Practical joke victims seek their last laughs in court", Ont. Lawyers Weekly, April 5, 1985, 14. See also *R. v. St. George* (1840), 173 E.R. 921 (N.P.); and *Brady v. Schatzel*, [1911] Q.S.R. 206 (Nor. Ct.).

5. Damage awards for assault unaccompanied by battery are often small. See *Stephens v. Myers* (1830), 172 E.R. 735 (C.P.), where the plaintiff was awarded one shilling. However, in *Mahal v. Young* (1986), 36 C.C.L.T. 143 (B.C. S.C.), the plaintiff was awarded $6,000 damages in assault arising from the defendant's unprovoked threat to kill him. The defendant had previously assaulted the plaintiff and they worked together under circumstances in which the defendant could readily carry out the threat. The plaintiff suffered a severe depression following the threat and missed several months of work.

6. If the assault is a prelude to battery, the assault may be discussed superficially and not considered in assessing damages. Nevertheless, the occurrence of an assault may colour the court's interpretation of subsequent events. The fact that the defendant was assaulted may provide the basis for a defence of consent or self-defence, or for raising the issue of provocation. See *Bruce v. Dyer* (1966), 58 D.L.R. (2d) 211 (Ont. H.C.); aff'd. (1967), 8 D.L.R. (3d) 592 (Ont. C.A.).

HOLCOMBE v. WHITAKER

(1975), 318 So. (2d) 289 (Ala. S.C.)

SHORES JUSTICE: — The next issue argued by defendant [doctor] concerns the assault count. The plaintiff claimed that the defendant committed an assault when in June of 1971, she went to see him and tried to get him to get an annulment, he said "If you take me to court, I will kill you."; and again in October, 1971, after she filed the instant suit on September 29, 1971, when he went to her apartment and beat on the door, tried to pry it open, and said again, "If you take me to court, I will kill you." (The complaint was amended to include this act.) The defendant claims this in no way can constitute an assault, because it was merely a conditional threat of violence and because no overt act was involved.

In order to safeguard freedom from apprehension of harm or offensive conduct, the law provides an individual with a remedy at law.

. . .

While words standing alone cannot constitute an assault, they may give meaning to an act and both, taken together, may constitute an assault. Prosser, supra (2nd Ed. 1955). In addition, words may negative an act in a manner that apprehension in such a case would be unreasonable. "On the other hand, a show of force accompanied by an unlawful or unjustifiable demand, compliance with which will avert the threatened battery, is an assault." 1 Harper & James, The Law of Torts, page 223 (1956). " . . . the defendant is not free to compel the plaintiff to buy his safety by compliance with a condition which there is no legal right to impose". Prosser, supra, page 40 (4th Ed. 1971). It is obvious that the defendant in the instant case had no right to impose the condition he did on the plaintiff; and we cannot say that this condition explained away his threat to harm her.

The defendant says his conduct cannot constitute an assault because there was no overt action taken by him. The evidence from the plaintiff was that the defendant was pounding on her door making every effort to get into the apartment, and threatening to kill her if she persisted in "taking him to court." We cannot say as a matter of law, that this was not sufficient to arouse an apprehension of harm or offensive conduct. We think it was a jury question, as was the question of whether the defendant had the apparent ability to effectuate the threatened act.

. . .

According to the testimony offered on behalf of the plaintiff, the doctor succeeded in his efforts to frighten the plaintiff. She was fearful enough to ask friends to stay with her at night; never left the apartment alone after the threats on her life; had her brother-in-law nail the windows closed after the break-in of her apartment; and told one of her friends that she was afraid there might be poison in her coffee. We believe this testimony was relevant under the circumstances of this case. The defendant threatened to kill the plaintiff if she did something she had a legal right to do. We think the evidence of what occurred subsequent to his threats and emanating from them was relevant to the issues being tried.

We find no error to reverse, and turn now to the plaintiff's cross-appeal.

. . .

HEFLIN, C.J., and MERRILL, MADDOX, and JONES, JJ., concur.

POLICE v. GREAVES

[1964] N.Z.L.R. 295 (C.A.)

The facts were these — a Mrs. Tolley who occupied with her children a State house situated in Kowhai Street, Naenae, called on the police for help after she had been attacked by the respondent who also resided in the house. It appears that he was somewhat inebriated. When two policemen arrived, the respondent came to the door with a carving knife in his right hand poised at waist height and pointed towards the leading constable, and said, "Don't you bloody move.

You come a step closer and you will get this straight through your ——— guts."
The leading constable continued, "The defendant was in a maniacal mood and
was not prepared to listen to any reasoning at all. He said, 'Get off this ———
property before you get this in your guts.' "

The constables, faced with this threat, withdrew to obtain further assistance.

The appellant was convicted of assault in the Magistrate's Court but the conviction was quashed in the Supreme Court on the ground that the threat made by
the appellant was a conditional one and did not constitute an assault.

The prosecutor appealed by special leave to the Court of Appeal.

. . .

The judgment of the Court was delivered by NORTH P. [after stating the facts
as above]:

. . .

In our opinion, if the other conditions of the definition were met — as they
undoubtedly were — there is no reason why a conditional threat should not constitute an assault. A threat in its very nature usually provides the person threatened with an alternative, unpleasant though it may often be. It is only necessary
to recall the oft repeated threat of the highwayman, "Your money or your life"
to see that if a pistol be pointed at the victim it would be idle to say that there
was not a threat to apply force to the person of another in circumstances in which
the person making the threat had, or at least caused the other to believe on reasonable
grounds that he had, present ability to effect his purpose, and therefore that an
assault had been committed. On the facts of the present case it was enough that
the menacing attitude of the respondent caused the police officers to retire. . . .
The present case is to be distinguished from such cases as *Tubervell v. Savadge*
(1669) 1 Mod. 3; 86 E.R. 684, where the person from whom the threat came made
it clear that he had no present intention of carrying out his threat. In that case
the words used were, "Were it not assize time" he would tell more of his mind.

With all respect for the view of the learned Judge, we do not think that *Read
v. Coker* (1853) 13 C.B. 850; 138 E.R. 1437 which was relied on by the prosecution is distinguishable from the present case. There the plaintiff, being in the
defendant's workshop and refusing to quit when desired, was surrounded by the
defendant's servants, who tucked up their sleeves and aprons and threatened to
break his neck if he did not go out. It was argued that this did not constitute an
assault, but the Court was clearly of opinion that it did, Jervis C.J. saying, "If
anything short of actual striking will in law constitute an assault, the facts here
clearly show that the defendant was guilty of an assault. There was threat of violence exhibiting an intention to assault and a present ability to carry the threat
into execution" (*ibid.*, 860; 1441). There is not the slightest suggestion in the argument or in the judgment that the fact that the plaintiff was offered an alternative prevented the threat from constituting an assault. Again, in *Blake v. Barnard*
(1840) 9 Car. & P. 626; 173 E.R. 985, the report of Lord Abinger's summing
up to the jury makes no point of the fact that the cocked pistol presented at the
defendant's head was accompanied by the statement that "if Blake was not quiet
he would blow his brains out." We can see no difference in principle between
a demand that the person threatened should retire and a demand that he should
not proceed further on his lawful occasions. The policemen were present here on

their lawful occasions and their entry was barred; that in our opinion was sufficient. But in any event — though nothing was made of this either in the Court below or before us — it would appear that in fact both kinds of threats were made.

Accordingly, we are of the opinion that the appeal must be allowed and the conviction and sentence entered by the Magistrate restored.

NOTES AND QUESTIONS

1. In *Holcombe*, the judge indicated that words alone, without some overt act, cannot give rise to assault. Although this principle has been accepted in cases of insulting or abusive language, it has been criticized where the words were intended to cause, and in fact caused, reasonable apprehension of imminent physical contact. As indicated by Keeton *et al.* in *Prosser and Keeton on the Law of Torts*, 5th ed. (1984), 45: "It is the immediate physical threat that is important, rather than the manner in which it is conveyed". Had the defendant in *Holcombe* merely threatened to kill the plaintiff and not engaged in any other aggressive conduct, would he have been held liable in assault? See Handford, "Tort Liability For Threatening or Insulting Words" (1976), 54 Can. Bar Rev. 563.

2. In *Fogden v. Wade*, [1945] N.Z.L.R. 724 (S.C.), the accused was convicted of assault when he approached a woman and, while he was close enough to touch her, stated: "Don't go in yet, you've got time for a quick one". The woman screamed and the accused ran off without touching her. Would the accused's conduct have constituted an assault in tort law?

3. How did the judge in *Greaves* distinguish the case of *Tubervell*? Given that the essence of assault is the impression created in the plaintiff's mind, is this distinction valid? How would you distinguish *Tubervell* and *Holcombe*?

In *Greaves*, the court also distinguished between conditional threats that require the plaintiff to take immediate action to avoid the threat and conditional threats that do not. Is this distinction justifiable?

4. To what extent was the decision in *Greaves* influenced by the fact that the officers were under a legal duty to apprehend the defendant? Had the defendant made the same threat to a door-to-door saleswoman, would she have had an action in assault? See the American Law Institute, *Restatement of the Law, Second, Torts* (1965), para. 30.

5. Generally, future threats will not constitute assault because of the requirement of immediacy. The early cases suggest that the threat must be capable of being carried out at once. See, for example, *Stephens v. Myers* (1830), 172 E.R. 735 (C.P.). It is likely that the immediacy requirement will be relaxed, in keeping with the focus on the impact of the defendant's threat on the plaintiff. At what point in the following scenarios would the immediacy requirement be met? (a) The defendant, who lives 30 minutes away, calls and threatens to come over and beat up the plaintiff; (b) the defendant calls en route and repeats the threat; (c) the defendant calls from a pay phone across from the plaintiff's apartment; and (d) the defendant knocks on the plaintiff's door.

6. Even if the defendant's conduct falls short of assault it may give rise to liability for other torts, such as intentional infliction of nervous shock, defamation or intimidation. The criminal law also prohibits a broad range of offensive, obscene and racist conduct. See for example, the Criminal Code: s. 264 (criminal harassment); s. 264.1 (uttering threats); s. 296 (libel); ss. 318-320 (hate propaganda); s. 346 (extortion); and s. 372 (indecent or harassing telephone calls and letters).

7. Summarize the legal principles governing the tort of assault.

REVIEW PROBLEMS

1. George drove into a gas station and asked Ralph, the attendant, to fill up his car. Ralph was distracted by some other customers and did not return for 10 minutes. George, furious at the delay, called him an incompetent fool. Ralph, who was 10 meters away, threatened to beat George's brains in if he did not apologize immediately. George approached Ralph, punched him in the head once and walked away. Ralph picked up a wrench and threw it at George, who ducked. The wrench struck Mr. Smith, who was walking on the sidewalk 15 meters in front of the station.

Ralph has sought your advice as to the legal actions he may bring, and the liability he may have incurred in assault and battery.

2. The defendant attempted to rob a bank with an unloaded shotgun. When a police officer rushed

in, the defendant threatened to shoot Mr. Marple, a teller, if the officer came any closer. Mr. Marple, who was standing three meters from the defendant, fainted when the threat was made and fell to the floor fracturing his skull. In the confusion, the defendant was apprehended. Mr. Marple and the officer wish to know whether they would succeed in an assault action.

6. False Imprisonment

Originally designed to provide a remedy for wrongful incarceration, the tort of false imprisonment now encompasses most situations in which an individual's movement is intentionally restrained. The restraint of movement must be total, even if only momentarily. The restraint may be imposed by barriers, other physical means, an implicit or explicit threat of force, or an assertion of legal authority. Although often defined as an element of the tort, the issue of lawful justification is treated by the courts as a defence which the defendant must raise and prove.

BIRD v. JONES

(1845), 7 Q.B. 742, 115 E.R. 668 (Q.B.)

COLERIDGE J. . . . . [T]he plaintiff, being in a public highway and desirous of passing along it, in a particular direction, is prevented from doing so by the orders of the defendant, and that the defendant's agents for the purpose are policemen, from whom, indeed, no unnecessary violence was to be anticipated, or such as they believed unlawful, yet who might be expected to execute such commands as they deemed lawful with all necessary force, however resisted. But, although thus obstructed, the plaintiff was at liberty to move his person and go in any other direction, at his free will and pleasure: and no actual force or restraint on his person was used, unless the obstruction before mentioned amounts to so much.

I lay out of consideration the question of right or wrong between these parties. The acts will amount to imprisonment neither more nor less from their being wrongful or capable of justification.

And I am of opinion that there was no imprisonment. To call it so appears to me to confound partial obstruction and disturbance with total obstruction and detention. A prison may have its boundary large or narrow, visible and tangible, or, though real, still in the conception only; it may itself be moveable or fixed: but a boundary it must have; and that boundary the party imprisoned must be prevented from passing; he must be prevented from leaving that place, within the ambit of which the party imprisoning would confine him, except by prison-breach. Some confusion seems to me to arise from confounding imprisonment of the body with mere loss of freedom: it is one part of the definition of freedom to be able to go whithersoever one pleases; but imprisonment is something more than the mere loss of this power; it includes the notion of restraint within some limits defined by a will or power exterior to our own.

. . .

PATTESON J. . . . . I have no doubt that, in general if one man compels another to stay in any given place against his will, he imprisons that other just as much as if he locked him up in a room: and I agree that it is not necessary, in order to constitute an imprisonment, that a man's person should be touched. I agree, also, that the compelling a man to go in a given direction against his will may amount to imprisonment. But I cannot bring my mind to the conclusion that, if one man merely obstructs the passage of another in a particular direction, whether by threat of personal violence or otherwise, leaving him at liberty to stay where he is or to go in any other direction if he pleases, he can be said thereby to imprison him. He does him wrong, undoubtedly, if there was a right to pass in that direction, and would be liable to an action on the case for obstructing the passage, or of assault, if, on the party persisting in going in that direction, he touched his person, or so threatened him as to amount to an assault. But imprisonment is, as I apprehend, a total restraint of liberty of the person, for however short a time, and not a partial obstruction of his will, whatever inconvenience it may bring on him. The quality of the act cannot, however, depend on the right of the opposite party. If it be an imprisonment to prevent a man passing along the public highway, it must be equally so to prevent him passing further along a field into which he has broken by a clear act of trespass. . . .

LORD DENMAN C.J. [dissenting]. . . . A company unlawfully obstructed a public way for their own profit, extorting money from passengers, and hiring policemen to effect this purpose. The plaintiff, wishing to exercise his right of way, is stopped by force, and ordered to move in a direction which he wished not to take. He is told at the same time that a force is at hand ready to compel his submission. That proceeding appears to me equivalent to being pulled by the collar out of the one line and into the other.

I had no idea that any person in these times supposed any particular boundary to be necessary to constitute imprisonment, or that the restraint of a man's person from doing what he desires ceases to be an imprisonment because he may find some means of escape.

It is said that the party here was at liberty to go in another direction. I am not sure that in fact he was, because the same unlawful power which prevented him from taking one course might, in case of acquiescence, have refused him any other. But this liberty to do something else does not appear to me to affect the question of imprisonment. As long as I am prevented from doing what I have a right to do, of what importance is it that I am permitted to do something else? How does the imposition of an unlawful condition shew that I am not restrained? If I am locked in a room, am I not imprisoned because I might effect my escape through a window, or because I might find an exit dangerous or inconvenient to myself, as by wading through water or by taking a route so circuitous that my necessary affairs would suffer by delay?

. . .

It is said that, if any damage arises from such obstruction, a special action on the case may be brought. Must I then sue out a new writ stating that the defendant employed direct force to prevent my going where my business called me, whereby I sustained loss? And, if I do, is it certain that I shall not be told that I have misconceived my remedy, for all flows from the false imprisonment, and that should have been subject of an action of trespass and assault? For the jury properly found that the whole of the defendant's conduct was continuous: it commenced in illegality; and the plaintiff did right to resist it as an outrageous violation of the liberty of the subject from the very first.

NOTES AND QUESTIONS

1. Although the law is settled, do you prefer the majority or minority view of false imprisonment? What problems, if any, would arise from adopting the minority definition?

2. Would it have made any difference to the majority if the plaintiff had been on an urgent business trip that could not have been delayed without serious financial loss? Should it make any difference if the defendant's purpose in obstructing the bridge was praiseworthy?

3. Since false imprisonment will not lie in the absence of total restraint, the court may have to determine if there was a reasonable means of escape known to the plaintiff. Clearly, the plaintiff need not risk physical injury in attempting to escape. Less certain, however, is the exact amount of inconvenience that the plaintiff will be expected to endure in attempting to free himself. See *R. v. Macquarie* (1875), 13 N.S.W. S.C.R. 264; and *Balmain New Ferry v. Robertson* (1906), 4 C.L.R. 379 (H.C.). But see *Wright v. Wilson* (1699), 91 E.R. 1394, in which the defendant was held not liable in false imprisonment, even though the plaintiff could only escape by trespassing on a third party's property.

4. Alan, Barb and Carol were about to leave the 115th-floor observation deck of the C.N. Tower, when they were informed that the elevator service was being discontinued for 30 minutes to permit publicity photos to be taken. All three refused to use the stairs, the only other exit. They now wish to know whether they can maintain false imprisonment actions against C.N. Alan is 30, Barb is 23 and 5 months pregnant, and Carol is 68.

5. Initially, in both England and the United States, the plaintiff had to establish that he was conscious of the imprisonment at the time it occurred. This requirement has been dropped in England and, presumably, in Canada, American authorities have modified their position; the plaintiff may succeed if he was aware of the imprisonment when it occurred or was harmed by it. See *Murray v. Ministry of Defence*, [1988] 1 W.L.R. 692 (H.L.); Prosser, "False Imprisonment: Consciousness of Confinement" (1955), 55 Columbia L. Rev. 847; and the American Law Institute, *Restatement of the Law, Second, Torts* (1965), para. 42.

6. A prisoner who is detained after he should have been released may sue in false imprisonment. See, for example, *LeBar v. Canada* (1989), 46 C.C.C. (3d) 103 (Fed. C.A.). More controversial, however, is the issue of whether a false imprisonment action can be brought if a lawfully detained prisoner is improperly held in segregation, improperly transferred to another institution, or held in intolerable conditions. In *Hague v. Deputy Governor of Parkhurst Prison; Weldon v. Home Office*, [1991] 3 All E.R. 733, the House of Lords held that such prisoners may have a public remedy and a private action in negligence, but not a false imprisonment action. The court viewed the conduct in issue as affecting the conditions of confinement and not the prisoners' liberty. The result in Canada may well be different. See *Saint-Jacques v. Canada (Solicitor General)* (1991), 45 F.T.R. 1, where a prisoner was awarded damages in false imprisonment for being wrongfully put in solitary confinement.

7. The terms false imprisonment and false arrest are often used interchangeably. However, false arrest refers to only one category of false imprisonment actions — namely those in which the restraint is imposed by an assertion of legal authority. It is not essential in a false arrest action that the defendant be a peace officer or have a warrant.

CAMPBELL v. S.S. KRESGE CO.

(1976), 21 N.S.R. (2d) 236, 74 D.L.R. (3d) 717 (N.S. T.D.)

HART J.: — On December 14, 1974, about 6 p.m., the plaintiff went to the K-Mart store of the corporate defendant at Dartmouth to do some pre-Christmas shopping. She took a cart and placed a hockey stick and one or two other articles in the cart and then tried to get the attention of one of the clerks at a counter at the back of the store to make a further purchase. She says that she waited about five minutes while the two clerks discussed their own personal affairs, and decided to wait no longer. She left the cart with the several items in it and proceeded out the main door of the shop.

The defendant, Gary Williamson, was a full-time member of the Dartmouth Police Force with the rank of corporal, who was employed by S.S. Kresge Company

Limited as a security officer during his off-duty hours. His chief responsibility for the defendant was the protection of the defendant's property and the catching of shoplifters.

In the early evening of December 14th, while Corporal Williamson was on floor duty in the store, a lady asked him if he was a police officer. He confirmed that he was, and she advised him that she thought she had seen the plaintiff put something in her coat pocket. Corporal Williamson then observed the plaintiff and noticed that she had abandoned her shopping cart and was leaving the store. He followed her outside and confronted her in the parking lot. He showed her his police badge and said that he had reason to believe that she had something that did not belong to her and asked that she come into the store to his office to avoid embarrassment to them both. The plaintiff was upset but went into the store and started towards the back of the store with Corporal Williamson following behind. When she reached the location of the jewellery counter she stopped and demanded to know what it was all about before she went any further. She offered her purse to Corporal Williamson claiming that there was nothing in it that belonged to the store and offered to be searched. At this point Corporal Williamson, not now being able to see the woman who had given him the information, told the plaintiff that he was merely trying to get the facts and that she was free to go. Mrs. Campbell then left the store.

The plaintiff says that she was very upset by this encounter and drove to her mother-in-law's house where she told what had happened. She then returned to the store and spoke to the manager. From this office she proceeded to Mr. Williamson's office to speak with him. They met in the store and she asked if there was a private place where they could talk. He indicated that the security office would be suitable and they went there. The plaintiff then asked why Corporal Williamson had stopped her, and he advised that a woman, who he was not able to identify, had told him that she had put something on her person. He said that he felt this combined with her leaving of the articles in the store cart made him suspicious and that he wanted to get the facts.

In his evidence Corporal Williamson says that he followed the same procedure with Mrs. Campbell that he would have followed if he were certain that a shopper had something on her person taken from the store. He indicates that he probably would have let her go if she had refused to come inside with him, but I am satisfied that the plaintiff being confronted by a member of the police force and being invited inside to avoid embarrassment would have felt that she was obligated to follow the request. It was only when the plaintiff rebelled inside the store and the police officer realized that his source of information was no longer there, and the plaintiff had offered her purse to be searched, that he told her she was free to go.

I am satisfied from the evidence as a whole that the plaintiff was imprisoned by Corporal Williamson, acting in his capacity as agent for the corporate defendant, from the time she was confronted outside the store until the time she was told that she was free to go. In the mind of Corporal Williamson he was not arresting her but merely taking her in in order to get a statement of the facts, but he was using the force of his position as a police officer to take her in a direction that she did not wish to go. She was not consenting to accompany Corporal Williamson, but was going with him out of fear of the consequences should she refuse.

If, as Corporal Williamson said, he was not going to arrest her and there was no one present to observe what was going on, then there could have been no "embarrassment" to be avoided and they could easily have had their discussion in the parking lot. The impression he was giving, however, was that she should accompany him or else there might be a scene which would be embarrassing to her. It was the practice of Corporal Williamson to physically detain those suspects whom he believed to have stolen goods on their person, and there is nothing to indicate that he would not have followed the usual procedure had the plaintiff refused to accompany him. He did not know when he was outside the store that his informant would not be present when he returned with the suspect.

[The court proceeded to discuss and then reject the defence of legal authority. Assessing the damages, the court continued:]

The plaintiff alleges that she was greatly upset by this experience and suggests that she was additionally embarrassed that it took place in the presence of many members of the public. I am satisfied from the evidence, however, that the matter was handled discreetly by Corporal Williamson and, although there were shoppers in the vicinity, that no scene was created which would have brought her in disrepute. The damages which she suffered therefore are limited to her personal inconvenience and upset arising from the incident, and I assess these damages in the amount of $500.

The plaintiff will also be entitled to her costs of action to be taxed.

NOTES AND QUESTIONS

1. At what point did the officer imprison the plaintiff? In terms of the criminal law, did the officer intend to or, in fact, arrest the plaintiff? Why did the plaintiff submit to the defendant's assertion of authority? Can you distinguish between a situation in which a suspect reluctantly cooperates and one in which a suspect is submitting against his will? See *Conn v. David Spencer Ltd.*, [1930] 1 D.L.R. 805 (B.C. S.C.); *Sinclair v. Woodward's Store Ltd.*, [1942] 2 D.L.R. 395 (B.C. S.C.); and *Allen v. Head C. Ltd.* (1985), 160 A.P.R. 108 (Nfld. S.C.). Even if the plaintiff willingly goes with the security staff, the staff can be held liable in false imprisonment if they subsequently detain him. See *Smart v. Simpson Sears Ltd.* (1984), 150 A.P.R. 215 (Nfld. Dist. Ct.), aff'd. (1987), 36 D.L.R. (4th) 756 (Nfld. C.A.).

2. An individual may be liable in false imprisonment not only for restraining the plaintiff, but also for ordering another person to do so. For example, if a store manager shouts "Stop that man, he's a thief!" and a police officer does so, then both are responsible for the imprisonment. However, if the manager merely provides information to the officer who, after assessing it, decides to make an arrest, then the officer alone is responsible. It may be difficult to distinguish between these situations. If an individual makes the statement "I think that man has my wallet", is he giving an implicit order to arrest or merely providing information? Had the informant in *Campbell* been identified, could she have been held liable in false imprisonment? See *Reid v. Webster* (1966), 59 D.L.R. (2d) 189 (P.E.I. S.C.); *Lebrun v. High-Low Foods* (1968), 69 D.L.R. (2d) 433 (B.C. S.C.); and *Davidson v. Chief Constable of North Wales*, [1994] 2 All E.R. 597 (C.A.).

3. A defendant who swears out an information before a judicial officer cannot be held liable in false imprisonment when the plaintiff is arrested on the charge. While a police officer may serve as a defendant's agent, a judge is seen as exercising independent, judicial decision-making authority. The judge is the source of the detention. Nevertheless, in certain limited circumstances the plaintiff may sue the defendant for the tort of malicious prosecution, which provides redress for the wrongful initiation of criminal charges. See *Austin v. Dowling* (1870), L.R. 5 C.P. 534 at 540, where the court explained: "The party making the charge is not liable to an action for false imprisonment, because he does not set a ministerial officer in motion, but a judicial officer. The opinion and judgment of a judicial officer are interposed between the charge and the imprisonment."

4. Why was the store held vicariously liable for the officer's conduct in *Campbell*? Should the police department have been held vicariously liable?

5. Do you think that the damage award was appropriate in this case? Punitive damages are often awarded in false imprisonment actions. See *Lang v. Burch* (1982), 140 D.L.R. (3d) 325 (Sask. C.A.); and *LeBar v. Canada* (1989), 46 C.C.C. (3d) 103 (Fed. C.A.).

6. In *Ashland Dry Goods Co. v. Wages* (1946), 195 S.W. (2d) 312 (Ky. C.A.), the judge held that the seizure of the plaintiff's purse and the statement that she could not leave with the goods until they were wrapped amounted to an imprisonment. Would a parent be able to recover in false imprisonment if he remained with his child who had been detained? What factors would be relevant in resolving this issue? See *Carr v. Edmonton (City) Police*, [1993] 2 W.W.R. 111 (Alta. C.A.).

7. Even a shoplifter apprehended in the act may easily establish the elements of a false imprisonment action — volition, intent and a total restraint of movement. Once the plaintiff has proven that the tort has been committed, the defendant will be held liable unless he can establish a defence. The plaintiff's guilt or innocence may be relevant to, but not necessarily determinative of, the validity of the defence. The exact impact of a suspect's guilt on the defence of legal authority will be discussed in chapter 8.

8. Advise a store detective on how to approach a suspected thief without committing false imprisonment.

9. Although most false imprisonment claims involve the police and store detectives, the issue can arise under the civil commitment provisions of the provincial mental health legislation. See *Tanner v. Norys*, [1980] 4 W.W.R. 33 (Alta. C.A.); and *Kohn v. Globerman*, [1986] 4 W.W.R. 1 (Man. C.A.).

HERD v. WEARDALE STEEL, COAL AND COKE CO.

[1915] A.C. 67 (H.L.)

Appeal from an order of the Court of Appeal reversing a judgment of Pickford J.

The appellant was employed as a hewer at the Thornley Colliery in the county of Durham. The respondents the Weardale Steel, Coal and Coke Company were the proprietors of the colliery, the respondent Curry was the manager, and the respondent Turner was an overman employed at the colliery.

The appellant brought an action against the respondents for damages for false imprisonment. By his statement of claim he alleged that on May 30, 1911, the respondents wrongfully prevented him from using the cage, which was the only means of egress from the mine, whereby he was imprisoned in the mine till 1:30 p.m. The respondents denied the alleged false imprisonment and justified their refusal to raise the appellant on the ground that he had been guilty of a breach of contract in refusing to do some work which he was ordered to do.

. . .

VISCOUNT HALDANE L.C.: — My Lords, by the law of this country no man can be restrained of his liberty without authority in law. That is a proposition the maintenance of which is of great importance; but at the same time it is a proposition which must be read in relation to other propositions which are equally important. If a man chooses to go into a dangerous place at the bottom of a quarry or the bottom of a mine, from which by the nature of physical circumstances he cannot escape, it does not follow from the proposition I have enunciated about liberty that he can compel the owner to bring him up out of it. The owner may or may not be under a duty arising from circumstances, on broad grounds the neglect of which may possibly involve him in a criminal charge or a civil liability. It is unnecessary to discuss the conditions and circumstances which might bring about such a result, because they have, in the view I take, nothing to do with false imprisonment.

My Lords, there is another proposition which has to be borne in mind, and that is the application of the maxim volenti non fit injuria. If a man gets into an express train and the doors are locked pending its arrival at its destination, he is not entitled, merely because the train has stopped by signal, to call for the doors to be opened to let him out. He has entered the train on the terms that he is to be conveyed to a certain station without the opportunity of getting out before that, and he must abide by the terms on which he has entered the train. So when a man goes down a mine, from which access to the surface does not exist in the absence of special facilities given on the part of the owner of the mine, he is only entitled to the use of these facilities (subject possibly to the exceptional circumstances to which I have alluded) on the terms on which he has entered.

. . .

So, my Lords, it is not false imprisonment to hold a man to the conditions he has accepted when he goes down a mine.

. . .

Now, my Lords, in the present case what happened was this. The usage of the mine — a usage which I think must be taken to have been notified — was that the workman was to be brought up at the end of his shift. In this case the workman refused to work; it may have been for good reasons or it may have been for bad, — I do not think that question concerns us. He said that the work he had been ordered to do was of a kind that was dangerous, and he threw down his tools and claimed to come up to the surface. The manager, or at any rate the person responsible for the control of the cage, said: "No, you have chosen to come at a time which is not your proper time, and although there is the cage standing empty we will not bring you up in it," and the workman was in consequence under the necessity of remaining at the bottom of the shaft for about twenty minutes. There was no refusal to bring him up at the ordinary time which was in his bargain; but there was a refusal, — and I am quite ready to assume that the motive of it was to punish him, I will assume it for the sake of argument, for having refused to go on with his work — by refusing to bring him up at the moment when he claimed to come. Did that amount to false imprisonment? In my opinion it did not. No statutory right under the Coal Mines Regulation Act, 1887, avails him, for the reason which I have already spoken of. Nor had he any right in contract. His right in contract was to come up at the end of his shift. Was he then falsely imprisoned? There were facilities, but they were facilities which, in accordance with the conditions that he had accepted by going down, were not available to him until the end of his shift, at any rate as of right.

. . .

My Lords, I am aware that this question is one which will probably give rise to great general interest; but, whatever may be the feeling about questions of this kind, it is still more important that in deciding matters arising out of them strict adherence is maintained to intelligible and well-defined principles of our law so long as they stand part of it. The law of England seems to me, as it stand today, to be perfectly defined as regards cases of the kind, and, if it is to be altered, it must be altered by statute. It may obviously be very difficult to make any provision in relation to coal mines which requires that a workman should be entitled to come up at any moment he pleases. The nature of the employment will probably always require reasonable restrictions. But what we are concerned with at the moment is this and this simply: that no conditions existed which enabled the miner in this case to claim the right which he asserted, and that there was nothing which comes within the definition well known in the law of England which amounts to false imprisonment.

Under these circumstances, my Lords, I am unable to come to any other conclusion than that Pickford J. was wrong and that the majority of the Court of Appeal were right, and that this appeal ought to be dismissed with costs. I move your Lordships accordingly.

[Lords Shaw of Dunfermline and Moulton gave concurring speeches.]

NOTES AND QUESTIONS

1. Did the plaintiff consent unconditionally to go down the mine shaft and remain there until the shift ended? See Ames, "A Note On Contractual Restraint of Liberty" (1928), 44 L.Q.R. 464; and *Khan v. El Al Israel Airlines* (1991), 4 O.R. (3d) 502 (Gen. Div.).

2. To what extent was this decision affected by the then prevailing views of labour and management relations? Would the case be decided differently today?

3. Comprehensive occupational safety standards are now imposed by both federal and provincial legislation. For example, the Occupational Health and Safety Act, R.S.O. 1990, c. O.1, s. 43(3) allows employees to refuse to work in unsafe conditions.

4. Outside the entrance of his store, the defendant posted a large sign which read: "The management reserves the right to inspect all unsealed packages and shopping bags". The plaintiff, who is blind, entered the store with her seeing-eye dog. After learning that the store did not carry what she wanted, the plaintiff attempted to leave. The defendant politely explained that she could not leave until her shopping bag was inspected. The plaintiff refused to permit the search and was detained until the police arrived and resolved the issue. Will the plaintiff succeed in false imprisonment? Would the outcome be different if the plaintiff were illiterate, rather than blind? Which party has the burden of proving consent?

5. Summarize the principles of law governing false imprisonment.

7. Malicious Prosecution

Both false imprisonment and malicious prosecution provide redress for unjustified interference with individual freedom and the embarrassment, injury to reputation and other losses that flow from it. Malicious prosecution, however, is derived from trespass on the case. Consequently, it is concerned with indirect interferences, namely those that result from the improper institution of criminal proceedings against an individual.

NELLES v. ONTARIO

(1989), 49 C.C.L.T. 217 (S.C.C.)

[The plaintiff was charged with first degree murder in the deaths of four babies at the Hospital for Sick Children in Toronto. After a lengthy and extremely well-publicized preliminary hearing, all charges were dropped against her because of a lack of evidence. She sued a number of police officers, the Ontario Attorney General and the Crown for false imprisonment, malicious prosecution, negligence and violation of her Charter rights.

The following excerpt from the Supreme Court decision addresses the issue of malicious prosecution and whether the Attorney General and Crown are immune to such criminal suits.]

LAMER J. (DICKSON C.J.C. and WILSON J. concurring):—

. . .

2. The Tort of Malicious Prosecution

There are four necessary elements which must be proved for a plaintiff to succeed in an action for malicious prosecution:

a) the proceedings must have been initiated by the defendant;

b) the proceedings must have terminated in favour of the plaintiff;

c) the absence of reasonable and probable cause;

d) malice, or a primary purpose other than that of carrying the law into effect.

(See Fleming, J.G., *The Law of Torts*, 5th ed. (London: Sweet & Maxwell, 1977) at 598.)

The first two elements are straightforward and largely speak for themselves. The latter two elements require explicit discussion. Reasonable and probable cause has been defined as "an honest belief in the guilt of the accused based upon a full conviction, founded on reasonable grounds, of the existence of a state of circumstances, which, assuming them to be true, would reasonably lead any ordinarily prudent and cautious man, placed in the position of the accuser, to the conclusion that the person charged was probably guilty of the crime imputed" (*Hicks v. Faulkner* (1881), 8 Q.B.D. 167 at 171, Hawkins J., aff'd 46 L.T. 130 (C.A.)).

This test contains both a subjective and objective element. There must be both actual belief on the part of the prosecutor and that belief must be reasonable in the circumstances. The existence of reasonable and probable cause is a matter for the Judge to decide as opposed to the jury.

The required element of malice is, for all intents, the equivalent of "improper purpose". It has according to Fleming, a "wider meaning than spite, ill-will or a spirit of vengeance, and includes any other improper purpose, such as to gain a private collateral advantage" (Fleming, op. cit., at p. 609). To succeed in an action for malicious prosecution against the Attorney General or Crown Attorney, the plaintiff would have to prove both the absence of reasonable and probable cause in commencing the prosecution, *and* malice in the form of a deliberate and improper use of the office of the Attorney General or Crown Attorney, a use inconsistent with the status of "minister of justice". In my view this burden on the plaintiff amounts to a requirement that the Attorney General or Crown Attorney perpetrated a fraud on the process of criminal justice and in doing so has perverted or abused his office and the process of criminal justice. In fact, in some cases this would seem to amount to criminal conduct. (See for example breach of trust, s. 122, conspiracy re: false prosecution s. 465(1)(b), obstructing justice s. 139(2) and (3) of the *Criminal Code*, R.S.C. 1985, c. C-46.

Further, it should be noted that in many, if not all cases of malicious prosecution by an Attorney General or Crown Attorney, there will have been an infringement of an accused's rights as guaranteed by ss. 7 and 11 of the *Canadian Charter of Rights and Freedoms.*

By way of summary then, a plaintiff bringing a claim for malicious prosecution has no easy task. Not only does the plaintiff have the notoriously difficult task of establishing a negative, that is the absence of reasonable and probable cause, but he is held to a very high standard of proof to avoid a non-suit or directed verdict (see Fleming, op. cit., at p. 606, and *Mitchell v. John Heine & Son Ltd.* (1983), 38 S.R. (N.S.W.) 466, at pp. 469-471). Professor Fleming has gone so far as to conclude that there are built-in devices particular to the tort of malicious prosecution to dissuade civil suits (at p. 606):

> "The disfavour with which the law has traditionally viewed the action for malicious prosecution is most clearly revealed by the hedging devices with which it has been surrounded in order to deter this kind of litigation and protect private citizens who discharge their public duty of prosecuting those reasonably suspected of crime."

3. Policy Considerations

In light of what I have said regarding the role of the prosecutor in Canada, and the tort of malicious prosecution, it now is necessary to assess the policy rationales. I would begin by noting that even those decisions that have come out firmly in favour of absolute immunity have described the role as "troubling", a "startling proposition", "strained and difficult to sustain".

. . .

It is said by those in favour of absolute immunity that the rule encourages public trust and confidence in the impartiality of prosecutors. However, it seems to me that public confidence in the office of a public prosecutor suffers greatly when the person who is in a position of knowledge in respect of the constitutional and legal impact of his conduct is shielded from civil liability when he abuses the process through a malicious prosecution. The existence of an absolute immunity strikes at the very principle of equality under the law and is especially alarming when the wrong has been committed by a person who should be held to the highest standards of conduct in exercising a public trust. (See Filosa, op. cit., at p. 982, and Marilyn L. Pilkington, "Damages as a Remedy for Infringement of the Canadian Charter of Rights and Freedoms" (1984) 62 Can. Bar Rev. 517 at 560-561.)

Regard must also be had for the victim of the malicious prosecution. The fundamental flaw with an absolute immunity for prosecutors is that the wrongdoer cannot be held accountable by the victim through the legal process. As I have stated earlier, the plaintiff in a malicious prosecution suit bears a formidable burden of proof and in those cases where a case can be made out, the plaintiff's *Charter* rights may have been infringed as well. Granting an absolute immunity to prosecutors is akin to granting a licence to subvert individual rights. Not only does absolute immunity negate a private right of action, but in addition, it seems to me, it may be that it would effectively bar the seeking of a remedy pursuant to s. 24(1) of the *Charter.* It seems clear that in using his office to maliciously prosecute an accused, the prosecutor would be depriving an individual of the right to liberty and security of the person in a manner that does not accord with the principles of fundamental justice. Such an individual would normally have the right under

s. 24(1) of the *Charter* to apply to a Court of competent jurisdiction to obtain a remedy that the Court considers appropriate and just if he can establish that one of his *Charter* rights has been infringed. The question arises then, whether s. 24(1) of the *Charter* confers a right to an individual to seek a remedy from a competent Court. In my view it does. When a person can demonstrate that one of his *Charter* rights has been infringed, access to a Court of competent jurisdiction to seek a remedy is essential for the vindication of a constitutional wrong. To create a right without a remedy is antithetical to one of the purposes of the *Charter* which surely is to allow Courts to fashion remedies when constitutional infringements occur. Whether or not a common law or statutory rule can constitutionally have the effect of excluding the Courts from granting the just and appropriate remedy, their most meaningful function under the *Charter*, does not have to be decided in this appeal. It is, in any case, clear that such a result is undesirable and provides a compelling underlying reason for finding that the common law itself does not mandate absolute immunity.

It is also said in favour of absolute immunity that anything less would act as a "chilling effect" on the Crown Attorney's exercise of discretion. It should be noted that what is at issue here is not the exercise of a prosecutor's discretion within the proper sphere of prosecutorial activity as defined by his role as a "minister of justice". Rather, in cases of malicious prosecution we are dealing with allegations of misuse and abuse of the criminal process and of the office of the Crown Attorney. We are not dealing with merely second-guessing a Crown Attorney's judgment in the prosecution of a case but rather with the deliberate and malicious use of the office for ends that are improper and inconsistent with the traditional prosecutorial function.

Therefore it seems to me that the "chilling effect" argument is largely speculative and assumes that many suits for malicious prosecution will arise from disgruntled persons who have been prosecuted but not convicted of an offence. I am of the view that this "flood-gates" argument ignores the fact that one element of the tort of malicious prosecution requires a demonstration of improper motive or purpose; errors in the exercise of discretion and judgment are not actionable. Furthermore, there exist built-in deterrents on bringing a claim for malicious prosecution. As I have noted, the burden on the plaintiff is onerous and strict. . . .

Finally, the potential that costs will be awarded to the defendant if an unmeritorious claim is brought acts as financial deterrent to meritless claims. Therefore, ample mechanisms exist within the system to ensure that frivolous claims are not brought. In fact, the difficulty in proving a claim for malicious prosecution itself acts as a deterrent. This high threshold of liability is evidenced by the small number of malicious prosecution suits brought against police officers each year. In addition, since 1966, the Province of Quebec permits suits against the Attorney General and Crown prosecutors without any evidence of a flood of claims. Therefore, I find unpersuasive the claim that absolute immunity is necessary to prevent a flood of litigation.

As for alternative remedies available to persons who have been maliciously prosecuted, none seem to adequately redress the wrong done to the plaintiff. The use of the criminal process against a prosecutor who in the course of a malicious prosecution has committed an offence under the *Criminal Code*, addresses itself mainly to the vindication of a public wrong not the affirmation of a private right of action.

. . .

I do however pause to note that many cases of genuine malicious prosecution will also be offences under the *Criminal Code*, and it seems rather odd if not incongruous for reparation to be possible through a probation order but not through a private right of action.

Further, the use of professional disciplinary proceedings, while serving to some extent as punishment and deterrence, do not address the central issue of making the victim whole again. And as has already been noted, it is quite discomforting to realize that the existence of absolute immunity may bar a person whose *Charter* rights have been infringed from applying to a competent Court for a just and appropriate remedy in the form of damages.

III. CONCLUSION

A review of the authorities on the issue of prosecutorial immunity reveals that the matter ultimately boils down to a question of policy. For the reasons I have stated above I am of the view that absolute immunity for the Attorney General and his agents, the Crown Attorneys, is not justified in the interests of public policy. We must be mindful that an absolute immunity has the effect of negating a private right of action and in some cases may bar a remedy under the *Charter*. As such, the existence of absolute immunity is a threat to the individual rights of citizens who have been wrongly and maliciously prosecuted. Further, it is important to note that what we are dealing with here is an immunity from suit for malicious prosecution; we are not dealing with errors in judgment or discretion or even professional negligence. By contrast the tort of malicious prosecution requires proof of an improper purpose or motive, a motive that involves an abuse or perversion of the system of criminal justice for ends it was not designed to serve and as such incorporates an abuse of the office of the Attorney General and his agents the Crown Attorneys.

There is no doubt that the policy considerations in favour of absolute immunity have some merit. But in my view those considerations must give way to the right of a private citizen to seek a remedy when the prosecutor acts maliciously in fraud of his duties with the result that he causes damage to the victim. In my view the inherent difficulty in proving a case of malicious prosecution combined with the mechanisms available within the system of civil procedure to weed out meritless claims is sufficient to ensure that the Attorney General and Crown Attorneys will not be hindered in the proper execution of their important public duties. Attempts to qualify prosecutorial immunity in the United States by the so-called functional approach and its many variations have proven to be unsuccessful and unprincipled as I have previously noted. As a result I conclude that the Attorney General and Crown Attorneys do not enjoy an absolute immunity in respect of suits for malicious prosecution. I would therefore dismiss the appeal as against the Crown, there being no order as to costs. I would allow the appeal as against the Attorney General with costs and direct that the matter be returned to the Supreme Court of Ontario for trial of the claim against the Attorney General.

NOTES AND QUESTIONS

1. Based on *Nelles*, define the elements of a malicious prosecution action. Although not discussed by the court, the plaintiff must also prove that he has suffered loss or damage. Since malicious prosecution is derived from the writ of trespass on the case, it is not actionable without proof of loss.

2. Explain the objective and subjective elements of "reasonable and probable cause". Would a prosecutor meet this test if there were grounds to believe that the accused committed the offence, but the prosecutor did not personally believe that the accused did it?

3. How did the court define the element of malice or improper purpose? Would it be improper to charge a suspect with 12 similar break and entries, if there was only evidence linking the suspect to 4 of these offences?

4. What arguments were made in support of the immunity rule? On what basis did the court reject these arguments? What additional policy issues did the court raise in favour of a no-immunity rule?

5. In *Reid v. Webster* (1966), 59 D.L.R. (2d) 189 (P.E.I. S.C.), the court defined criminal proceedings broadly. It held that a municipal by-law prosecution can give rise to a malicious prosecution action if the by-law provides imprisonment in default of payment, the prosecution affects the plaintiff's trade, and the publicity creates an aura of scandal. See *Delancey v. Dale and Co.* (1959), 20 D.L.R. (2d) 12 (N.S. S.C.) — arrest as a potential absconding debtor; and *Stoffman v. Ont. Veterinary Assoc.* (1990), 73 O.R. (2d) 737 (Div. Ct.) — charge of professional misconduct.

6. A defendant cannot be held liable in malicious prosecution for merely providing information to the police or testifying in court. Rather, a defendant must be the driving force in the initiation or prosecution of the action. In most cases, this requirement is met by laying the criminal charge. However, a defendant may also be responsible for initiating the proceedings if he has lied to the police or wrongfully pressured them to lay the charges. See *Casey v. Auto. Renault Can. Ltd.*, [1965] S.C.R. 607; *Canada v. Lukasik* (1985), 18 D.L.R. (4th) 245 (Alta. Q.B.); *Temilini v. Commissioner of the Ont. Prov. Police* (1990), 73 O.R. (2d) 664 (C.A.), leave to appeal refused (1991), 1 O.R. (3d) xii (note) (S.C.C.); and *Hinde v. Skibinski* (1994), 21 C.C.L.T. (2d) 314 (Ont. Gen. Div.).

7. In *Casey*, the majority held that the defendant had initiated criminal proceedings by laying a criminal charge before a magistrate who was competent to deal with the matter, even though the defendant withdrew the charge before the magistrate took any action. The court further held that the subsequent withdrawal of the charge amounted to a termination of the proceedings in the plaintiff's favour.

8. A defendant can be held liable in malicious prosecution not only for the wrongful initiation of the charge, but also for its wrongful continuation. What impact would this principle have on a police officer who laid four charges of theft, but learned prior to trial that the accused could not have been responsible for two of the thefts?

9. In *Banks v. Bliefernich* (1988), 44 C.C.L.T. 144 (B.C. S.C.), it was held that even though the plaintiff pleaded guilty to one charge, the stay of proceedings on the other charges constituted a termination in the plaintiff's favour. What impact will this case have on plea-bargaining?

10. In *Martin v. Watson*, [1994] 2 All E.R. 606, the English Court of Appeal decided that a person who made a false allegation to the police in order to cause the arrest of the plaintiff had not "set the law in motion", and was not therefore liable in malicious prosecution. This decision represents a controversial departure from the previous position of the English common law. Should it be followed in Canada?

11. Given that in the past, many criminal cases were prosecuted by private citizens and that there were no mechanisms for efficiently coordinating the criminal justice system, it is not surprising that malicious prosecution was narrowly defined. Has the establishment of an elaborate, publicly-funded system of criminal justice undercut the rationale for restricting this tort?

12. Although malicious prosecution initially provided redress for the wrongful initiation of certain civil actions, it is now limited almost exclusively to penal matters. The wrongful institution of bankruptcy and winding-up proceedings are the most notable exceptions: See *Quartz Hill Consol. Gold Mining v. Eyre* (1883), 11 Q.B.D. 674 (C.A.); *Clissold v. Cratchley*, [1910] 2 K.B. 244 (C.A.); *Flame Bar-B-Q Ltd. v. Hoar* (1980), 106 D.L.R. (3d) 438 (N.B. C.A.); and *Cherry v. Ivey* (1982), 37 O.R. (2d) 361 (H.C.). See also *Norman v. Soule* (1991), 7 C.C.L.T. (2d) 16 (B.C. S.C.), which suggests that these limited exceptions are not likely to be extended to any other types of civil litigation.

13. Summarize the principles governing malicious prosecution.

(a) A NOTE ON THE TORT OF ABUSE OF PROCESS

Until recently, it was widely accepted that no remedy existed for the misuse of civil proceedings. However, courts in Alberta, Ontario and British Columbia have recently recognized a common law tort action for abuse of process. Unlike malicious prosecution, abuse of process is not primarily concerned with the wrongful initiation of proceedings. Rather, it focuses on the misuse of civil proceedings for some collateral or illicit purpose other than the resolution of the claim. In order to recover, the plaintiff must prove that the defendant used the proceedings for an extrinsic purpose and undertook a specific act in furtherance of that purpose. The plaintiff must also establish damages. See *Guilford Industries Ltd. v. Hankinson Management Services Ltd.*, [1974] 1 W.W.R. 141 (B.C. S.C.); *Poulos v. Matovic* (1989), 47 C.C.L.T. 207 (Ont. H.C.); *Dooley v. C.N. Weber Ltd.* (1994), 19 O.R. (3d) 779 (Gen Div.); *Rocky Mountain Rail Society v. H & D Hobby Distributing Ltd.* (1995), 24 C.C.L.T. (2d) 97 (Alta. Q.B.); and Irvine, "The Resurrection of Tortious Abuse of Process" (1989), 47 C.C.L.T. 217.

REVIEW PROBLEM

Vincent was browsing in the Super Mart. The store detective, Joe Stevens, became suspicious because Vincent spent 10 minutes at the cosmetic counter and had a bottle of deodorant sticking out of his shopping bag. When Vincent left without paying for the deodorant, Stevens ran after him and tapped him on the shoulder. When Vincent turned around, Stevens politely asked him to come to the manager's office. Vincent, who neither spoke nor understood English, smiled and accompanied Stevens. John, the store manager, listened to Stevens' explanation and called the police. After several minutes, Vincent became nervous and stated in Italian that he was leaving. John told him in Italian that he had to remain, and Stevens pushed him towards a chair. Vincent finally realized that he was being arrested, but he had no idea why.

John explained the situation in English to the officers and told them that he was going to press charges. The officers took Vincent into custody and seized his shopping bag as evidence. Once at the station, the desk sergeant explained to Vincent in Italian the reason for his arrest. Vincent replied that there was a receipt in his shopping bag to prove that the deodorant had been purchased at another store. The desk sergeant said that he would look into the matter. The sergeant thought Vincent might be an illegal immigrant and decided to lay the theft charge as a means of holding him until his immigration status could be determined. Vincent was charged with theft, brought before a judge and released on a promise to appear. When the desk sergeant learned later in the day that Vincent was a lawful visitor he looked into the shopping bag for the first time. Upon finding the receipt, he called the prosecutor to withdraw the charge.

Vincent has sought your legal advice. He wishes to know what tort actions he can bring against the various parties, the bases for such actions and their likelihood of success.

8. Intentional Infliction of Nervous Shock

WILKINSON v. DOWNTON

[1897] 2 Q.B. 57

WRIGHT J.: — In this case the defendant, in the execution of what he seems to have regarded as a practical joke, represented to the plaintiff that he was charged by her husband with a message to her to the effect that her husband was smashed up in an accident, and was lying at The Elms at Leytonstone with both legs broken, and that she was to go at once in a cab with two pillows to fetch him home.

All this was false. The effect of the statement on the plaintiff was a violent shock to her nervous system, producing vomiting and other more serious and permanent physical consequences at one time threatening her reason, and entailing weeks of suffering and incapacity to her as well as expense to her husband for medical attendance. These consequences were not in any way the result of previous ill-health or weakness of constitution, nor was there any evidence of predisposition to nervous shock or any other idiosyncrasy.

In addition to these matters of substance there is a small claim for 1s. 10½d. for the cost of railway fares of persons sent by the plaintiff to Leytonstone in obedience to the pretended message. As to this 1s. 10½d. expended in railway fares on the faith of the defendant's statement, I think the case is clearly within the decision in *Pasley v. Freeman* [(1789), 100 E.R. 450]. The statement was a misrepresentation intended to be acted on to the damage of the plaintiff.

The real question is as to the £100, the greatest part of which is given as compensation for the female plaintiff's illness and suffering. It was argued for her that she is entitled to recover this as being damage caused by fraud, and therefore within the doctrine established by *Pasley v. Freeman* [*supra*] and *Langridge v. Levy* [(1837), 2 M. & W. 519]. I am not sure that this would not be an extension of that doctrine, the real ground of which appears to be that a person who makes a false statement intended to be acted on must make good the damage naturally resulting from its being acted on. Here there is no injuria of that kind. I think, however, that the verdict may be supported upon another ground. The defendant has, as I assume for the moment, wilfully done an act calculated to cause physical harm to the plaintiff — that is to say, to infringe her legal right to personal safety, and has in fact thereby caused physical harm to her. That proposition without more appears to me to state a good cause of action, there being no justification alleged for the act. This wilful injuria is in law malicious, although no malicious purpose to cause the harm which was caused nor any motive of spite is imputed to the defendant.

It remains to consider whether the assumptions involved in the proposition are made out. One question is whether the defendant's act was so plainly calculated to produce some effect of the kind which was produced that an intention to produce it ought to be imputed to the defendant, regard being had to the fact that the effect was produced on a person proved to be in an ordinary state of health and mind. I think that it was. It is difficult to imagine that such a statement, made suddenly and with apparent seriousness, could fail to produce grave effects under the circumstances upon any but an exceptionally indifferent person, and therefore an intention to produce such an effect must be imputed, and it is no answer in law to say that more harm was done than was anticipated, for that is commonly the case with all wrongs. The other question is whether the effect was, to use the ordinary phrase, too remote to be in law regarded as a consequence for which the defendant is answerable ... It is, however, necessary to consider two authorities which are supposed to have laid down that illness through mental shock is a too remote or unnatural consequence of an injuria to entitle the plaintiff to recover in a case where damage is a necessary part of the cause of action. One is the case of *Victorian Railways Commissioners v. Coultas* [(1888), 13 App. Cas. 222], where it was held in the Privy Council that illness which was the effect of shock caused by fright was too remote a consequence of a negligent act which caused the fright, there being no physical harm immediately caused. That decision was treated in the Court of Appeal in *Pugh v. London, Brighton and South Coast Ry. Co.* [[1896] 2 Q.B. 248] as open to question. It is inconsistent with a decision in the Court of Appeal in Ireland: see *Bell v. Great Northern Ry. Co. of Ireland* [(1890), 26 L.R. Ir. 428]), where the Irish Exchequer Division refused to follow it; and it has been disapproved in the Supreme Court of New York: see Pollock on Torts, 4th ed. p. 47(*n*). Nor is it altogether in point, for there was not in that case any element of wilful wrong; nor perhaps was the illness so direct and natural a consequence of the defendant's conduct as in this case. On these grounds it seems to me that the case of *Victorian Railways Commissioners v. Coultas [supra]* is not an authority on which this case ought to be decided.

A more serious difficulty is the decision in *Allsop v. Allsop* [(1860), 157 E.R. 1292], which was approved by the House of Lords in *Lynch v. Knight* [(1861), 11 E.R. 854]]. In that case it was held by Pollock C.B., Martin, Bramwell, and Wilde BB., that illness caused by a slanderous imputation of unchastity in the case of a married woman did not constitute such special damage as would sustain an action for such a slander. That case, however, appears to have been decided on the ground that in all the innumerable actions for slander there were no precedents for alleging illness to be sufficient special damage, and that it would be of evil consequence to treat it as sufficient, because such a rule might lead to an infinity of trumpery or groundless action. Neither of these reasons is applicable to the present case. Nor could such a rule be adopted as of general application without results which it would be difficult or impossible to defend. Suppose that a person is in a precarious and dangerous condition, and another person tells him that his physician has said that he has but a day to live. In such a case, if death ensued from the shock caused by the false statement, I cannot doubt that at this day the case might be one of criminal homicide, or that if a serious aggravation of illness ensued damages might be recovered. I think, however, that it must be admitted that the present case is without precedent. . . .

There must be judgment for the plaintiff for £100-1*s.*-10½.

NOTES AND QUESTIONS

1. What was the basis upon which the plaintiff was permitted to recover the cost of her railway ticket? Why was she denied damages for nervous shock on this basis?

2. How did Wright J. define the principles governing the intentional infliction of nervous shock? Do you agree with the way he applied these principles to the facts? Why was he not bound by *Victorian Railways Commrs. v. Coultas* and *Allsop v. Allsop*?

3. Prior to *Wilkinson*, a plaintiff could not recover for nervous shock unless he also suffered some physical injury. The courts' attitude to nervous shock was summarized by Lord Wensleydale in *Lynch v. Knight* (1861), 11 E.R. 854 at 863 (H.L.): "Mental pain or anxiety the law cannot value, and does not pretend to redress, when the unlawful act complained of causes that alone; though where a material damage occurs, and is connected with it, it is impossible a jury, in estimating it, should altogether overlook the feelings of the party interested." Why else might the courts have been hesitant to recognize an action for nervous shock? How did Wright J. address these concerns?

4. Did Wright J. consider nervous shock to be an independent action or merely an indirect means of causing physical injury? What is the practical significance of such a distinction?

5. In *Purdy v. Woznesensky*, [1937] 2 W.W.R. 116 (Sask. C.A.), the female plaintiff suffered nervous shock when the defendant punched her husband in the head, knocking him unconscious. The judge held that the defendant should have foreseen that by causing the plaintiff to witness the attack,

he would probably upset her nervous system. Consequently, the judge imputed this intent to the defendant. In *Bielitski v. Obadiak* (1922), 65 D.L.R. 627 (Sask. C.A.), the defendant started a rumour that the plaintiff's son had hanged himself. After being retold several times, the rumour reached the plaintiff, who suffered a serious nervous shock and became physically ill. Noting the defendant's failure to explain his conduct, the majority imputed intent to him. Haultain C.J.S. dissented, holding that the plaintiff's injury was not intentionally inflicted, nor the natural, probable or necessary consequence of the defendant's act. Was the doctrine of imputed intent applied correctly in *Wilkinson, Purdy* and *Bielitski*? See also *Timmerman v. Buelow* (1984), 38 C.C.L.T. 136 (Ont. H.C.). Why did the court not apply the doctrine of transferred intent?

Contrast the approach taken in these cases with that in *Bunyan v. Jordan* (1937), 57 C.L.R. 1 (Aust. H.C.); and *Stevenson v. Basham*, [1922] N.Z.L.R. 225 (S.C.). See also the American Law Institute, *Restatement of the Law, Second, Torts* (1965), paras. 46 and 47.

RADOVSKIS v. TOMM

(1957), 65 Man. R. 61, 9 D.L.R. (2d) 751 (Man. Q.B.)

WILLIAMS C.J.Q.B.: — On August 28, 1956, the infant plaintiff, 5½ years old Anda Radovskis, was raped by the defendant who was convicted of the offence and is presently serving a lengthy sentence in the Penitentiary.

This action is brought by the child suing by her father Robert Radovskis as next friend to recover damages for the trespass to her person; by the father to recover hospital and medical expenses, loss of wages, and for "worry and inconvenience"; and by the child's mother to recover damages for nervous shock alleged to have been sustained by the mother.

. . .

No medical evidence was offered and the mother did not give evidence. Her husband did say that his wife had not good nerves before and that since they had been bad.

But that is not sufficient to support a claim for damages. In *Guay v. Sun Publishing Co., supra*, Estey J., after discussing the medical evidence before the Court, said (p. 589 D.L.R., p. 238 S.C.R.):

> Moreover, it is important to keep in mind what must be proved in order that damages may be recovered, as stated in Pollock on Torts, 15th ed., pp. 37-8, as follows: "A state of mind such as fear or acute grief is not in itself capable of assessment as measurable temporal damage. But visible and provable illness may be the natural consequence of violent emotion, and may furnish a ground of action against a person whose wrongful act or want of due care produced that emotion . . . In every case the question is whether the shock and the illness were in fact natural or direct consequences of the wrongful act or default; if they were, the illness, not shock, furnishes the measurable damage, and there is no more difficulty in assessing it than in assessing damages for bodily injuries of any kind."

In this case there was no visible and provable illness within the meaning of this quotation. The mother's action is dismissed without costs.

SAMMS v. ECCLES

(1961), 358 P. (2d) 344 (Utah S.C.)

CROCKETT JUSTICE: — Plaintiff Marcia G. Samms sought to recover damages from David Eccles for injury resulting from severe emotional distress she claims to have suffered because he persistently annoyed her with indecent proposals.

. . .

Plaintiff alleged that she is a respectable married woman; that she has never encouraged the defendant's attentions in any way but has repulsed them; that all during the time from May to December, 1957, the defendant repeatedly and persistently called her by phone at various hours including late at night, soliciting her to have illicit sexual relations with him; and that on one occasion came to her residence in connection with such a solicitation and made an indecent exposure of his person. She charges that she regarded his proposals as insulting, indecent and obscene; that her feelings were deeply wounded; and that as a result thereof she suffered great anxiety and fear for her personal safety and severe emotional distress for which she asks $1,500 as actual, and a like amount as punitive, damages.

. . .

Due to the highly subjective and volatile nature of emotional distress and the variability of its causations, the courts have historically been wary of dangers in opening the door to recovery therefor. This is partly because such claims may easily be fabricated: or as sometimes stated, are easy to assert and hard to defend against. They have, therefore, been reluctant to allow such a right of action unless the emotional distress was suffered as a result of some other overt tort. Nevertheless, recognizing the reality of such injuries and the injustice of permitting them to go unrequited, in many cases courts have strained to find the other tort as a peg upon which to hang the right of recovery.

Some of these have been unrealistic, or even flimsy. For instance, a technical battery was found where an insurance adjuster derisively tossed a coin on the bed of a woman who was in a hospital with a heart condition, and because of this tort she was allowed to recover for distress caused by his other attempts at intimidation in accusing her of gold-bricking and attempting to defraud his company; courts have also dealt with trespass where hotel employees have invaded rooms occupied by married couples and imputed to them immoral conduct; and other similar torts have been used as a basis for such recovery. But a realistic analysis of many of these cases will show that the recognized tort is but incidental and that the real basis of recovery is the outraged feelings and emotional distress resulting from some aggravated conduct of the defendant. The lengths to which courts have gone to find a basis for allowing such recoveries serves to emphasize their realization that justice demands that grossly wrong conduct which causes such an injury to another should be held accountable.

In recent years courts have shown an increasing awareness of the necessity and justice of forthrightly recognizing the true basis for allowing recovery for such wrongs and of getting rid of the shibboleth that another tort peg is necessary to that purpose. Examples are: Great Atlantic & Pacific Tea Co. v. Roch, injuries caused by shock where a grocery man included a dead rat in a package as a joke; Savage v. Boies, distress caused by false representation that plaintiff's child had been injured in an automobile accident; Cohen v. Lion Products Co., distress to plaintiff's husband resulted from mandatory orders and charges of failure made to him as an employee by defendant's officers.

In LaSalle Extension University v. Fogarty, upon defendant's refusal to pay plaintiff's demand, plaintiff sent threatening letters to the defendant, and to his neighbors and employer, for the purpose of harassing him into paying their claim, against which it ultimately proved he had a good defense. Recovery was allowed on his counterclaim for emotional distress thus wrongfully caused him. The court cited the Iowa case of Barnett v. Collection Service Co. and quoted the rule which has come to be widely recognized that: "where the act is willful or malicious, as distinguished from being merely negligent, that recovery may be had for mental pain, though no physical injury results."

A case closely analogous to the instant one where such recovery was allowed is the recently decided one of Mitran v. Williamson. It holds that a complaint alleging that the defendant had repeatedly solicited plaintiff to have illicit intercourse and had sent obscene photographs of himself to her stated a cause of action . . .

Our study of authorities, and of the arguments advanced, convinces us that, conceding such a cause of action may not be based upon mere negligence, the best considered view recognizes an action for severe emotional distress, though not accompanied by bodily impact or physical injury, where the defendant intentionally engaged in some conduct toward the plaintiff, (a) with the purpose of inflicting emotional distress, or, (b) where any reasonable person would have known that such would result; and his actions are of such a nature as to be considered outrageous and intolerable in that they offend against the generally accepted standards of decency and morality. This test seems to be a more realistic safeguard against some false claims than to insist upon finding some other attendant tort, which may be of minor character, or fictional.

It is further to be observed that the argument against allowing such an action because groundless charges may be made is not a good reason for denying recovery. If the right to recover for injury resulting from the wrongful conduct could be defeated whenever such dangers exist, many of the grievances the law deals with would be eliminated. That some claims may be spurious should not compel those who administer justice to shut their eyes to serious wrongs and let them go without being brought to account. It is the function of courts and juries to determine whether claims are valid or false. This responsibility should not be shunned merely because the task may be difficult to perform.

We quite agree with the idea that under usual circumstances the solicitation to sexual intercourse would not be actionable even though it may be offensive to the offeree. It seems to be a custom of long standing and one which in all likelihood will continue. The assumption is usually indulged that most solicitations occur under such conditions as to fall within the well-known phrase of Chief Justice Magruder that, "there is no harm in asking." The Supreme Court of Kentucky in Reed v. Maley pertinently observed that an action will not lie in favor of a woman against a man who, without trespass or assault, makes such a request; and that the reverse is also true: that a man would have no right of action against a woman for such a solicitation.

But the situations just described, where tolerance for the conduct referred to is indulged, are clearly distinguishable from the aggravated circumstances the plaintiff claims existed here. Even though her complaint may not flawlessly state such a cause of action, the facts were sufficiently disclosed that the case she proposes to prove could be found to fall within the requirements herein above discussed. Therefore, the trial court erred in dismissing the action.

WADE, C.J., and MCDONOUGH, J., concur.

NOTES AND QUESTIONS

1. Why did the mother's claim fail in *Radovskis*? Is the judge suggesting that grief and mental distress are not worthy of compensation or that they are incapable of assessment in the absence of physical injury?

2. The Canadian and English courts have required the plaintiff to prove either actual physical harm or some serious psychological illness to recover for nervous shock. For example, in *Heighington v. The Queen in right of Ont.* (1987), 60 O.R. (2d) 641 (H.C.), the court stated that damages were recoverable in nervous shock for recognizable psychiatric disorders, but not for stress, strain, upset, or anxiety, aff'd. (1989), 69 O.R. (2d) 484 (C.A.). See also *Wipfli v. Britten* (1982), 22 C.C.L.T. 104 (B.C. S.C.); *Timmerman v. Buelow* (1984), 38 C.C.L.T. 136 (Ont. H.C.); and *Hasenclever v. Hoskins* (1988), 47 C.C.L.T. 225 (Ont. S.C.). But see *Bond v. Chief Constable of Kent*, [1983] 1 All E.R. 456 (Q.B.); *Rahemtulla v. Vanfed Credit Union* (1984), 29 C.C.L.T. 78 (B.C. S.C.); *Bell-Ginsburg v. Ginsburg* (1993), 14 O.R. (3d) 217 (Gen. Div.); and *MacKay v. Buelow* (1995), 24 C.C.L.T. (2d) 184 (Ont. Gen. Div.), where less rigorous criteria were applied.

3. According to the judge in *Samms*, what must the plaintiff establish to succeed in an action for intentional infliction of nervous shock? Based on these principles, would the mother in *Radovskis* have recovered?

4. The courts have identified three difficulties with claims for nervous shock — concern with false, trivial and numerous actions; concern that socially-acceptable conduct might cause some sensitive individuals mental distress; and difficulty in assessing damages for mental distress in the absence of physical injury. How have the courts in *Radovskis* and *Samms* addressed these issues and which approach is preferable?

5. In *Clark v. Canada* (1994), 20 C.C.L.T. (2d) 241 (Fed. Ct.), a female RCMP officer, who was driven to resign by the harassing conduct of her male colleagues over a protracted period, recovered damages for the intentional infliction of nervous shock. The court also found her superiors liable in negligence for failing to intervene to protect her.

6. In *Cant v. Cant* (1984), 49 O.R. (2d) 25 (Co. Ct.), the court entertained a claim for intentional infliction of nervous shock arising out of a custody battle over a child. However, in *Frame v. Smith* (1987), 42 C.C.L.T. 1 (S.C.C.), Wilson J. stated that this tort action should not be available in family law cases because it provides arbitrary coverage and would encourage vindictive litigation. See also *Davenport v. Miller* (1990), 70 D.L.R. (4th) 181 (N.B. Q.B.). It should be noted that Wilson J. was dissenting and that the majority did not address this issue. Do you prefer the approach of Wilson J. to that in *Cant*? See Cole, "Intentional Infliction of Emotional Distress Among Family Members" (1984), 61 Denver L. Rev. 533.

7. For a more detailed discussion of intentional infliction of nervous shock see Keeton *et al.*, *Prosser and Keeton on the Law of Torts*, 5th ed. (1984), 54-66; and Trindale, "The Intentional Infliction of Purely Mental Distress" (1986), 6 Oxford J. Legal Stud. 219.

8. Summarize the legal principles governing intentional infliction of nervous shock.

(a) A NOTE ON THE INNOMINATE INTENTIONAL TORTS

Several Commonwealth authors have viewed *Wilkinson v. Downton* as establishing an innominate intentional tort action for all unjustified, intentionally-inflicted bodily injuries — nervous shock being but one example. The other illustrations cited include intentionally infecting someone with a disease, setting a trap in someone's path, poisoning someone's food, and removing essential medicine from an incapacitated patient. Although such intentional conduct is morally blameworthy and likely to cause serious injury, it does not come within the traditional definitions of the nominate intentional torts. Thus, the innominate action provides a convenient mechanism for redressing such claims without disturbing accepted principles.

NOTES AND QUESTIONS

1. It is difficult to determine the exact scope of this action. For example, does it apply solely to bodily injury or does it also include other interferences with physical autonomy? If accepted, would the innominate intentional tort action have provided a remedy in *Bird v. Jones* (1845), 7 Q.B. 742? Could it be invoked in cases of sexual harassment, which did not involve assault, battery or nervous shock? See Fleming, *The Law of Torts*, 8th ed. (1992), 34-5.

2. In the United States, the courts have tended to deal with indirect injury cases by relaxing the requirements of directness in the nominate actions. This approach eliminates the need for an innominate intentional tort action for indirect battery and permits the intentional infliction of nervous shock to be recognized as an independent tort that is not tied to proof of physical injury.

Nevertheless, there is support in the American case law for a *"prima facie* tort doctrine" — a principle that appears to be broader, but otherwise comparable to the innominate intentional tort action. In the words of one author:

> The *prima facie* tort is generally defined as the "infliction of intentional harm, resulting in damages, without excuse or justification, by an act or series of acts which would otherwise be lawful". The specific applications of this definition vary greatly based on the manner in which courts interpret these elements. These divergencies in interpretation lead courts to apply the *prima facie* tort in inconsistent ways.

Shapiro, "The Prima Facie Tort Doctrine: Acknowledging the Need for Judicial Scrutiny of Malice" (1983), 63 Boston U.L. Rev. 1101.

3. The High Court of Australia recognized a related cause of action in *Beaudesert Shire Council v. Smith* (1966), 40 A.L.J.R. 211. The court stated at p. 215 "... independently of trespass, negligence or nuisance but by an action for damages upon the case, a person who suffers harm or loss as the inevitable consequence of the unlawful, intentional and positive acts of another is entitled to damages from that other." This decision has generated academic criticism and has been largely ignored by other courts. See *Elston v. Dore* (1982), 43 A.L.R. 577 (H.C.); *Northern Territory of Australia v. Mengel* (1994), 95 N.T.R. 8 (C.A. N.T.); Dworkin and Harari, "The Beaudesert Decision — Raising the Ghost of the Action upon the Case" (1967), 40 Aust. L.J. 296, 347; and Sadler, "Whither Beaudesert Shire Council v. Smith?" (1984), 58 Aust. L.J. 38.

4. The Canadian position is difficult to assess because of the dearth of academic and judicial discussion. See Atrens, "Intentional Interference with the Person", in Linden (ed.), *Studies in Canadian Tort Law* (1968), 378 at 397-401; *Graham v. Saville*, [1945] O.R. 301 at 310-11 (C.A.); *Can. Safeway Ltd. v. Man. Food & Commercial Wkrs. Loc. 832* (1983), 25 C.C.L.T. 1 (Man. C.A.); and *Cant v. Cant* (1984), 49 O.R. (2d) 25 (Co. Ct.).

5. Although the innominate intentional tort action, the *prima facie* tort action and the *Beaudesert* decision create distinct causes of action, they all reflect a concern with the inflexibility of intentional torts. Based on the intentional tort actions we have studied, is this a legitimate concern? Can you suggest alternative mechanisms for dealing with this concern? As we shall see, at least some Canadian courts have responded to this situation by attempting to create new nominate intentional tort actions.

REVIEW PROBLEMS

1. The torts of assault and the intentional infliction of nervous shock both involve the apprehension created in the mind of the plaintiff. Provide an example of conduct that would give rise to both actions. See *Timmerman v. Buelow* (1984), 38 C.C.L.T. 136 (Ont. H.C.); and *Mahal v. Young* (1986), 36 C.C.L.T. 143 (B.C. S.C.).

2. Jones, a professional boxer, was incensed by a story that had been written about him by a local sports writer, Mr. Smith. Jones called and told Smith to retract the story or expect a beating within the next few days. While Jones was not a particularly good boxer, he was widely known for his vicious temper and long criminal record for unprovoked assaults. Smith was terrified and began to tremble. When he explained to his wife what had happened, she fainted and hit her head on the floor, suffering a concussion. As Smith was preparing to take his wife to the hospital, Jones called again and indicated that he was coming over to "discuss these matters." Smith, who had a weak heart, suffered a minor heart attack brought on by both the severe emotional strain of his wife's injuries

and Jones' threats. Mr. and Mrs. Smith survived the incident and now wish to sue Jones. Your initial investigation has revealed that Jones was aware of Smith's weak heart.

9. Protection of Privacy

(a) INTRODUCTION

In Canada, privacy is protected in a piecemeal fashion by a myriad of civil actions and statutory provisions. The nominate intentional torts were not designed to redress invasions of privacy and only incidentally protect these interests. For example, a plaintiff will succeed in trespass to land against someone who has planted a listening device on his property, but not against an individual who intercepts his conversations without entering his land. Similar illustrations can be cited involving assault, intentional infliction of nervous shock, defamation, and intimidation. Shortcomings in the existing remedies have prompted consideration of both a common law tort for invasion of privacy and the enactment of privacy legislation.

Perhaps the most challenging problem is defining the concept of privacy. The broader the definition of privacy, the more it will conflict with other interests, such as freedom of speech, movement and association. These problems have led some authors to seriously question the value of privacy as a legal concept.

NOTES AND QUESTIONS

1. For a discussion of the protection provided by the existing nominate torts see Gibson, "Common Law Protection of Privacy: What to do Until the Legislators Arrive", in Klar (ed.), *Studies in Canadian Tort Law* (1977), 343; Burns, "Privacy and the Common Law: A Tangled Skein Unravelling?", in Gibson (ed.), *Aspects of Privacy Law* (1980), 21; and Irvine, "The Invasion of Privacy in Ontario: A 1983 Survey", [1983] Special Lectures L.S.U.C. 25.

2. Most jurisdictions in the United States recognize a common law tort action for the invasion of privacy. These actions typically reflect the position of the American Law Institute, *Restatement of the Law, Second, Torts* (1977), para. 652A, which provides that the right of privacy is violated by: unreasonable intrusion of the seclusion of another; appropriation of another person's name or likeness; unreasonable publicity given to another's private life; and publicity that unreasonably places another in a false light before the public. The Institute states that other privacy interests may be recognized as justifying protection. Can you suggest some additional privacy interests that warrant recognition?

3. For a review of the American authorities, see Prosser, "Privacy" (1960), 48 Cal. L. Rev. 383; Westin, "Science, Privacy, and Freedom: Issues and Proposals for the 1970's" (1966), 66 Columbia L. Rev. 1003, 1207; Gavison, "Privacy and the Limits of Law" (1980), 89 Yale L. Rev. 421; and Post, "The Social Foundations of Privacy: Community and Self in the Common Law Tort" (1989), 77 Cal. L. Rev. 957.

4. For a searing criticism of the concept of privacy see Wacks, "The Poverty of 'Privacy' " (1980), 96 L.Q.R. 73. In his conclusion, at p. 88 he states:

"Privacy" has grown into a large and unwieldy concept. Synonymous with autonomy, it has colonised traditional liberties, become entangled with confidentiality, secrecy, defamation, property, and the storage of information. It would be unreasonable to expect a notion so complex as "privacy" not to spill into regions with which it is closely related, but this process has resulted in the dilution of "privacy" itself, diminishing the prospect of its own protection as well as the protection of the related interests.

By locating, as the core of the issue, the regulation of "personal information," the subject is liberated from a tendentiously predetermined general theory, and specific answers may more easily be sought to specific, and frequently disparate, questions. Such progress is possible only if the law eschews the ambiguity, the abstractions and the poverty of "privacy."

Is Wacks opposed to protecting the specific interests that have fallen within the rubric of privacy or opposed to the lumping of all of these matters into privacy? See also Bezanson, "The Right to Privacy Revisited: Privacy, News, and Social Change, 1890-1990" (1992), 80 Cal. L. Rev. 1133.

(b) IS THERE A COMMON LAW TORT ACTION FOR THE INVASION OF PRIVACY?

MOTHERWELL v. MOTHERWELL

[1976] 6 W.W.R. 550, 73 D.L.R. (3d) 62 (Alta. C.A.)

CLEMENT J.A.: . . . the appellant had on numerous occasions "contacted the plaintiffs by telephone, making false accusations and statements against the plaintiffs and refuses to cease making such allegations and false statements", and "written letters to the plaintiffs making unfounded statements and accusations concerning the affairs of the plaintiffs." The appellant persisted in this conduct despite demands that she cease, which the plaintiffs assert to be an invasion of their privacy, and a nuisance, and pray for nominal damages and

> . . . an interim and a permanent injunction against the Defendant or anyone acting on her behalf enjoining her or anyone else acting on her behalf from contacting, telephoning, writing, visiting or in any other way communicating with the Plaintiffs or their children.

The defence of the appellant with which we are concerned is that "no action lies by the plaintiffs or either of them to restrain her lawful communications with the plaintiffs."

. . .

The arguments in appeal advanced by the appellant draw a distinction between nuisance and invasion of privacy. It is said that invasion of privacy does not come within the principle of private nuisance, and that it is a species of activity not recognized as remedial by the common law. It is urged that the common law does not have within itself the resources to recognize invasion of privacy as either included in an existing category or as a new category of nuisance, and that it has lost its original power, by which indeed it created itself, to note new ills arising in a growing and changing society and pragmatically to establish a principle to meet the need for control and remedy; and then by categories to develop the principle as the interests of justice make themselves sufficiently apparent.

. . .

Let me observe here that I do not wish to be entrapped in semantics or nomenclature. For the present purposes I will employ the term *principle* as a general concept of legal rights and duties in an aspect of human activities in which some common element is to be found: Lord Atkin in *Donoghue v. Stevenson* at p. 580; and I will employ the term *categories* as the application of the principle to particular circumstances, discernible in precedents, which have been found to come within the principle. The scope of principle of private nuisance, as well as its established categories, requires consideration in the issues in appeal.

The rule of *stare decisis* operates, as it seems to me, to regulate the application of precedents to cases which can be said to fall within a category. When the circumstances of a case do not appear to bring it fairly within an established category, they may lie sufficiently within the concept of a principle that consideration of a new category is warranted. The scope of a category may in time be broadened by a trend in precedents which reflect judicial considerations going beyond the disciplines of *stare decisis*. Those same considerations, arising from adequately demonstrated social need of a continuing nature, may lead, when necessary to maintain social justice, to a new category or the review of a principle. The considerations I refer to were termed public policy by Lord Wright in *Fender v. St. John-Mildmay*, [1938] A.C. 1. At p. 38 he said:

> In one sense every rule of law, either common law or equity, which has been laid down by the Courts, in that course of judicial legislation which has evolved the law of this country, has been based on . . . public . . . policy.

[The court discussed the law of private nuisance at length and made particular reference to the three categories of nuisance recognized in Clerk & Lindsell on Torts, 13th ed. (1969), p. 781. The third category — the undue interference with a neighbour in the comfortable and convenient enjoyment of his land — was the most germane to the case at bar.]

I think that the interests of our developing jurisprudence would be better served by approaching invasion of privacy by abuse of the telephone system as a new category, rather than seeking by rationalization to enlarge the third category recognized by *Clerk & Lindsell*. We are dealing with a new factor. Heretofore the matters of complaint have reached the plaintiff's premises by natural means; sound through the air waves, pollution in many forms carried by air currents, vibrations through the earth, and the like. Here, the matters complained of arise within the premises through the use by the appellant of communication agencies in the nature of public utilities available to everyone, which the plaintiffs have caused to serve their premises. They are non-selective in the sense that so long as they are employed by the plaintiffs they have no control over the incoming communications. Nevertheless there are differences between the two agencies of telephone and mail and it does not necessarily follow from their similarities that both should be accepted into a new category.

The telephone system is so much the part of the daily life of society that many look on it as a necessity. Its use is certainly taken as a right at least in a social sense. It virtually makes neighbours not only of the persons close at hand, but those in distant places, other cities, other countries. It is a system provided for rational and reasonable communication between people, and its abuse by invasion of privacy is a matter of general interest within the meaning given the phrase by Lord Atkin in *Fender v. St. John-Mildmay*, [1938] A.C. 1. It is essential to the operation of such a system that a call from someone be signalled to the intended receiver by sound such as the ringing of a bell. The receiver cannot know who is calling until he answers. Calls must be answered if the system is to work. There are not many who would assert that protection against invasion of privacy by telephone would be a judicial idiosyncrasy. Further than that, the people of this Province through the Legislature have expressed a public interest in the proper use of the system in enacting s. 31 of the *Alberta Government Telephones Act*.

In *Clerk & Lindsell*, p. 785, para. 1396, this is said: "A nuisance of this kind, to be actionable, must be such as to be a real interference with the comfort or convenience of living according to the standards of the average man." This statement is amply supported by authority and I take it to be applicable to invasion of privacy.

. . .

[Mr. Justice Clement concluded that the respondents had valid claims in nuisance for the invasion of their privacy through abuse of the telephone system. He upheld the trial judge's award of nominal damages and granting of an injunction against further calls.]

NOTES AND QUESTIONS

1. What was the basis of the decision in *Motherwell*? What factors did Clement J.A. consider in deciding to extend common law protection?

2. What remedies did the plaintiffs seek in *Motherwell*? Why did they not claim compensatory damages? Should that have been fatal to their claim? See *Hasenclever v. Hoskins* (1988), 47 C.C.L.T. 225 (Ont. Div. Ct.), a case in which the inadequacies in pleading damages resulted in the dismissal of a claim that was similar to that in *Motherwell*.

3. There has been an increase in the number of "harassment" claims. Some, like *Motherwell*, involve offensive calls and mail, but others include direct verbal confrontations, threats and stalking. In these latter situations, the courts have recognized the conduct as giving rise to a common law tort action for the invasion of privacy, independent of whatever other tort action that may be brought. See *Capan v. Capan* (1980), 14 C.C.L.T. 191 (Ont. H.C.); *Roth v. Roth* (1991), 4 O.R. (3d) 740 (Gen. Div.); and *MacKay v. Buelow* (1995), 24 C.C.L.T. (2d) 184 (Ont. Gen. Div.).

In *Khorasandjian v. Bush*, [1993] 3 All E.R. 669 (C.A.), the court appeared to recognize an action for harassment, independent of private nuisance. See Brazier, "Personal Injury by Molestation—An Emergent or Established Tort" (1992), 22 Fam. L. 346; and Bridgeman and Jones, "Harassing Conduct and Outrageous Acts: A Cause of Action for Intentionally Inflicted Mental Distress?" (1994), 14 Legal Studies 180.

4. The courts have not yet resolved whether watching and following a person in public or questioning the person's friends or neighbours constitutes an actionable wrong. Should there be any limits on such behaviour? See *Poole v. Ragen*, [1958] O.W.N. 77 (H.C.); *Nader v. General Motors Corp.*, 25 N.Y. (2d) 560 (C.A. 1970); and *Davis v. McArthur* (1971), 17 D.L.R. (3d) 760 (B.C. C.A.).

5. The Canadian courts have recognized a common law tort action for the appropriation of personality — the unauthorized use of a person's name or likeness. However, as the following references illustrate, it is not clear if this is to be treated as a form of invasion of privacy or as an intentional economic tort. See *Krouse v. Chrysler Can. Ltd.* (1973), 1 O.R. (2d) 225 (C.A.); *Athans v. Can. Adventure Camps Ltd.* (1977), 4 C.C.L.T. 20 (Ont. H.C.); *Heath v. Weist-Barron School of Television Can. Ltd.* (1981), 34 O.R. (2d) 126 (H.C.); Irvine, "The Appropriation of Personality" in Gibson (ed.), *Aspects of Privacy Law* (1980), 163; and Howell, "The Common Law Appropriation of Personality Tort" (1986), 2 I.P.J. 149.

6. Increasingly, the Canadian courts are recognizing that unwanted media attention may constitute an invasion of privacy in certain circumstances. In *Burnett v. Canada* (1979), 94 D.L.R. (3d) 281 (Ont. H.C.) and *F. (P.) v. Ontario* (1989), 47 C.C.L.T. 231 (Ont. Dist. Ct.), the court refused to strike out the plaintiff's statements of claim that were based on this issue.

In *Valiquette c. The Gazette* (1991), 8 C.C.L.T. (2d) 302 (Que. Sup. Ct.) — media disclosing that a teacher had AIDS, and *R. (L.) v. Nyp* (1995), 25 C.C.L.T. (2d) 309 (Ont. Gen. Div.) — media disclosing that an undercover police officer was sexually assaulted, the courts awarded damages. But see *Parasiuk v. Cdn. Newspapers Co.*, [1988] 2 W.W.R. 737 (Man. Q.B.).

In what circumstances should the media's public disclosure of private facts give rise to liability for the invasion of privacy? In *Bradley v. Wingnut Films*, [1993] 1 N.Z.L.R. 415 (H.C.), the action was limited to public disclosures that would be "highly offensive and objectionable to a reasonable person of ordinary sensibility".

7. In *Saccone v. Orr* (1981), 19 C.C.L.T. 37 (Ont. Co. Ct.), the defendant, without the plaintiff's knowledge, tape-recorded their telephone conversation. When the plaintiff learned of the tape, he warned the defendant not to use it, but the defendant denied that there was any tape. The defendant subse-

quently played the tape at a municipal council meeting in an effort to clear himself of certain allegations. The local newspaper then printed the tape's contents to the embarassment of the plaintiff.

After briefly referring to *Krouse, Motherwell* and *Burnett, supra,* the judge summarized the facts and stated without further explanation, at 46:

> . . . it's my opinion that certainly a person must have the right to make such a claim as a result of a taping of a private conversation without his knowledge, and also as against the publication of the conversation against his will or without his consent.
>
> Certainly, for want of a better description as to what happened, this is an invasion of privacy, and despite the very able argument of defendant's counsel that no such action exists, I have come to the conclusion that the plaintiff must be given some right of recovery for what the defendant has in this case done.

Has the judge provided a sufficient argument to support his decision? What other arguments would you have made in support of the plaintiff's privacy claim? What arguments would you have made if you had represented the defendant?

8. Based on *Saccone*, is it the unauthorized recording and/or the unauthorized playing of the tape that constitutes an invasion of privacy? Unless the plaintiff in *Saccone* had demanded and received assurances of confidentiality, why should he assume that the defendant would keep their conversation private? Should different considerations apply when a person who is not a party to the conversation secretly tapes the call?

In contrast to *Saccone*, the court in *Malone v. Metropolitan Police Commissioner,* [1979] 1 All E.R. 256 (C.A.) held that the plaintiff had no right of privacy protecting him from police wiretapping of his telephone calls. Assuming the approach in *Saccone* is adopted, should the common law protection apply equally to mail, telegrams, fax, and other forms of communication?

9. If a common law tort action for invasion of privacy is recognized, what interests should it protect and how would you define it?

(c) A NOTE ON THE COMMON LAW ACTION FOR BREACH OF CONFIDENCE

The Canadian action for breach of confidence is still evolving. The action derives from the equitable principle that a trustee or other fiduciary may not profit from his relationship with his principal. Fiduciary duties may arise in employment or commercial dealings, or in professional relationships, such as those between solicitors and clients, or physicians and patients. It is well-established that the use of confidential information obtained in a fiduciary relationship will lead to an action for breach of fiduciary duty. For examples of misuse of confidential information in commercial and professional settings, see *Canadian Aero Service Ltd. v. O'Malley*, [1974] S.C.R. 592; *Ott v. Fleishman*, [1983] 5 W.W.R. 721 (B.C. S.C.); and *Szarfer v. Chodos* (1986), 36 C.C.L.T. 181 (Ont. H.C.).

Although a breach of confidence action can now arise outside of a fiduciary relationship, the situations that give rise to liabilty remain uncertain. The first such actions arose from business dealings involving the misuse of trade secrets and similar confidential information. In *Saltman Engineering Co. v. Campbell Engineering Co.* (1948), 65 R.P.C. 203, the English Court of Appeal held that a confidentiality obligation may exist in a business relationship independent of any contractual term. Lord Greene M.R. stated that any person who uses non-public information obtained from another person, without express or implied consent, violates that person's rights. The English courts refined this principle in a series of trade secret cases, culminating in *Coco v. A.N. Clark (Engineers) Ltd.*, [1969] R.P.C. 41 (Ch. D.). In an influential judgment, Megarry J. outlined the essential elements of a breach of confidence action: the information itself must have a quality of confidence; the information must have been imparted in circumstances creating an obligation of confidence; and the unauthorized use of the information must have been detrimental to the confider.

The Supreme Court of Canada referred to this analysis in *LAC Minerals Ltd. v. International Corona Resources Ltd.*, [1989] 2 S.C.R. 574. The majority of the Court found the defendant liable for breach of confidence, even though there was no fiduciary relationship between the parties and the disclosed information was partly public. The majority held that an action would lie if the information was given with an expectation of confidence, the information was confidential and the defendant misused the information. In *LAC*, the defendant used the confidential information to purchase a lucrative property that the plaintiff would have otherwise acquired.

LAC Minerals demonstrates the Canadian courts' increasing recognition of confidentiality obligations in a variety of relationships. It appears that liability may now arise in personal relationships. In *Argyll v. Argyll*, [1967] 1 Ch. 302 (Ch. D.), the court stated that disclosure by a spouse of personal communications made during marriage may be actionable. In *Harder v. Brown* (1989), 50 C.C.L.T. 85 (B.C. S.C.), the court ordered a sexual abuser to return indecent photographs of his young female victim. However, in *Milton v. Savinkoff* (1993), 18 C.C.L.T. (2d) 288, the same court rejected the plaintiff's action under the provincial privacy act, where the defendant circulated topless pictures of the plaintiff that she had inadvertently left in his possession.

As we have discussed, both equity and the common law protect confidentiality interests in certain limited circumstances. While liability for breach of confidence will likely continue to expand, it remains to be seen how far the Canadian courts will extend this liability beyond fiduciary and business relationships.

(d) THE STATUTORY PROTECTION OF PRIVACY

The Canadian Charter of Rights and Freedoms contains various guaranteed rights and freedoms, and provides remedies for their infringement. Although the term privacy is not used in the Charter, this interest is an integral part of many of the fundamental freedoms in section 2 and the legal rights in sections 7 to 15. The Supreme Court of Canada has stated that the Charter will be interpreted broadly and purposefully to protect the rights and freedoms it guarantees. If an individual's Charter rights have been violated and that violation cannot be justified, the individual may apply to a court of competent jurisdiction under section 24(1) for a remedy. The court has broad discretion to grant whatever remedy it deems appropriate in the circumstances. However, it should be noted that the Charter is limited by section 32 to federal and provincial laws and the actions of governments and government officials.

Existing federal and provincial legislation may also serve to protect an individual's right to privacy. For example, Parliament has made the unauthorized electronic interception of private communications an indictable offence punishable by imprisonment for up to five years. The Criminal Code also prohibits obscene, racist, threatening, harassing, and other behaviour which may infringe upon an individual's privacy. Similarly, the provincial governments have enacted legislation regulating land use, trespass, noise levels, and the collection and dissemination of academic, medical, legal, and other kinds of personal information. However, the most specific statutory protection of the right to privacy is provided by the British Columbia, Manitoba, and Saskatchewan Privacy Acts. The following sections of the Manitoba Act illustrate a legislative definition of privacy.

THE PRIVACY ACT

R.S.M. 1987, c. P125

Violation of privacy.
2 (1) A person who substantially, unreasonably, and without claim of right, violates the privacy of another person, commits a tort against that other person.

Action without proof of damage.
2 (2) An action for violation of privacy may be brought without proof of damage.

Examples of violation of privacy.
3   Without limiting the generality of section 2, privacy of a person may be violated
(a) by surveillance, auditory or visual, whether or not accomplished by trespass, of that person, his home or other place of residence, or of any vehicle, by any means including eavesdropping, watching, spying, besetting or following; or
(b) by the listening to or recording of a conversation in which that person participates, or messages to or from that person, passing along, over or through any telephone lines, otherwise than as a lawful party thereto or under lawful authority conferred to that end; or
(c) by the unauthorized use of the name or likeness or voice of that person for the purposes of advertising or promoting the sale of, or any other trading in, any property or services, or for any other purposes of gain to the user if, in the course of the use, that person is identified or identifiable and the user intended to exploit the name or likeness or voice of that person; or
(d) by the use of his letters, diaries and other personal documents without his consent or without the consent of any other person who is in possession of them with his consent.

NOTES AND QUESTIONS

1. It is not possible in this text to discuss all of the Charter provisions which may be relevant to the protection of privacy. Nor is there one article or book which deals directly with this issue. In order to understand the Charter's impact on privacy interests, it is necessary to analyze each of the relevant rights and freedoms. See generally Beaudoin and Mendes (eds.), *The Canadian Charter of Rights and Freedoms*, 3rd ed. (1996); and Laskin *et al.* (eds.), *The Canadian Charter Annotated* (1990).

2. The American courts have interpreted their constitution as containing a right to privacy. See, for example, Tribe, *American Constitutional Law*, 2nd ed. (1988), 889-990.

3. In certain cases, individuals convicted of violating the federal wiretap legislation may be ordered to pay the aggrieved party up to $5,000 in punitive damages. See the Criminal Code, ss. 183-196. For a comprehensive review of the legislation see Watt, *Law of Electronic Surveillance in Canada* (1979), and *Law of Electronic Surveillance in Canada, First Supplement* (1983); and Cohen, *Invasion of Privacy, Police and Electronic Surveillance in Canada* (1983).

4. In recent years, Parliament has enacted legislation regulating the collection of information and its dissemination from federal data banks. See The Privacy Act, R.S.C. 1985, c. P-21; Rankin, "Privacy and Technology: A Canadian Perspective" (1984), 22 Alta. L. Rev. 323; and Kyer, "The Federal Privacy Act" (1985), 2 Can. Comp. L. Rep. 189. There is similar legislation in several provinces. See for example, the Freedom of Information and Protection of Privacy Act, R.S.O. 1990, c. F.31.

5. There is provincial legislation controlling credit reporting agencies and other commercial data banks. See Gibson, "Regulating the Personal Information Industry", in Gibson (ed.), *Aspects of Privacy Law* (1980), 111.

6. Has the Manitoba Act overcome the problem of defining the tort of privacy? See *Bingo Enterprises Ltd. v. Paxton* (1986), 26 D.L.R. (4th) 604 (Man. C.A.); *Parasiuk v. Can. Newspapers Co.*, [1988] 2 W.W.R. 737 (Man. Q.B.); and *Ferguson v. McBee Technographics Inc.*, [1989] 2 W.W.R. 499 (Man. Q.B.). Is the Manitoba approach to this issue preferable to that of the American Law Institute?

7. For a review of the provincial privacy legislation, see Osborne, "The Privacy Acts of British Columbia, Manitoba and Saskatchewan", in Gibson (ed.), *supra*, p. 73.

8. Regardless of whether it is based on common law or statute, how useful will tort law be in controlling invasions of privacy? What role should activity-specific regulation and criminal law play in protecting privacy?

10. The Common Law Tort of Discrimination

BHADAURIA v. BD. OF GOV. OF SENECA COLLEGE OF APPLIED ARTS AND TECHNOLOGY

(1979), 27 O.R. (2d) 142, 105 D.L.R. (3d) 707 (Ont. C.A.)

WILSON J.A.: — The plaintiff in this case complains that she has been discriminated against by the defendant on the ground of her ethnic origin. She makes the following allegations in her statement of claim. She is a highly educated East Indian woman holding a Bachelor of Arts, Master of Arts, and Doctorate of Philosophy in Mathematics. She is also qualified to teach in the Province of Ontario and has seven years' teaching experience. From June of 1974 to May of 1978, she applied for 10 openings on the teaching staff of the defendant college. All of these openings were advertised in the Toronto press. The plaintiff was not granted an interview for any of them although she had the requisite qualifications. She alleges that this was because of her ethnic origin.

The plaintiff, instead of filing a complaint under the *Ontario Human Rights Code*, R.S.O. 1970, c. 318, as amended, issued a writ claiming damages for discrimination and for breach of s. 4 [re-enacted 1972, c. 119, s. 5; am. 1974, c. 73, s. 2] of the Code. In her statement of claim she identifies the nature of her damages. She alleges that she has been deprived of the opportunity to join the defendant's teaching staff and to earn her livelihood as a teacher and that she has suffered mental distress, frustration and loss of dignity and self-esteem.

Section 4(1) of the Code reads as follows:

4(1) No person shall,

(a) refuse to refer or to recruit any person for employment;
(b) dismiss or refuse to employ or to continue to employ any person;
(c) refuse to train, promote or transfer an employee;
(d) subject an employee to probation or apprenticeship or enlarge a period of probation or apprenticeship;
(e) establish or maintain any employment classification or category that by its description or operation excludes any person from employment or continued employment;
(f) maintain separate lines of progression for advancement in employment or separate seniority lists where the maintenance will adversely affect any employee; or
(g) discriminate against any employee with regard to any term or condition of employment,

because of race, creed, colour, age, sex, marital status, nationality, ancestry, or place of origin of such person or employee.

Counsel for the defendant concedes that the conduct alleged against it in the statement of claim falls within cls. (*a*) and (*b*) above.

The judgment of Mr. Justice Birkett in *Constantine v. Imperial London Hotels, Ltd.*, [1944] 2 All E.R. 171, is also instructive in this area. In that case the manageress of the defendant hotel, in what was alleged to be a contemptuous and insulting manner, had refused the plaintiff a room because of his colour. He was, however, able to obtain accommodation quite readily at another hotel owned by the defendant. Accordingly, he suffered no special damage. No claim for defamation or slander was made and the learned trial Judge held on the pleadings that the plaintiff's action was an action on the case for the defendant's refusal to accommodate him in a hotel of his choice without any just cause or excuse. The gist of the action on the case, however, is special damage and in this case the plaintiff was unable to prove special damage.

The judgment is a significant one because the learned Judge applied the celebrated principle of *Ashby v. White et al.* (1703), 2 Ld. Raym. 938, 92 E.R. 126, enunciated by Chief Justice Holt at p. 953, as follows:

> If the plaintiff has a right, he must of necessity have a means to vindicate and maintain it, and a remedy if he is injured in the exercise or enjoyment of it; and indeed it is a vain thing to imagine a right without a remedy; for want of right and want of remedy are reciprocal.

Mr. Justice Birkett found that a common law right of the plaintiff was violated in this case. The defendant was an innkeeper under a duty to receive and house the plaintiff. The action was maintainable without proof of special damage because, as Chief Justice Holt had made plain, the injury itself imported damage. He awarded the plaintiff nominal damages in the amount of five guineas.

. . .

Against this background of authorities, we are called on to decide the matter now on appeal before us, namely, assuming that the plaintiff can prove the allegations set forth in her statement of claim, do they give rise to a cause of action at common law and, if they do not, do they give rise to a civil cause of action under the *Ontario Human Rights Code*?

In my view, they give rise to a cause of action at common law. While no authority cited to us has recognized a tort of discrimination, none has repudiated such a tort. The matter is accordingly *res integra* before us.

Prosser in his text, *Handbook of the Law of Torts*, 4th ed. (1971), at pp. 3-4, states:

> The law of torts is anything but static, and the limits of its development are never set. When it becomes clear that the plaintiff's interests are entitled to legal protection against the conduct of the defendant, the mere fact that the claim is novel will not of itself operate as a bar to remedy.

I think there can be no doubt that the interests of persons of different ethnic origins are entitled to the protection of the law. The preamble to the *Ontario Human Rights Code* reads as follows:

> WHEREAS recognition of the inherent dignity and the equal and inalienable rights of all members of the human family is the foundation of freedom, justice and peace in the world and is in accord with the Universal Declaration of Human Rights as proclaimed by the United Nations;
>
> AND WHEREAS it is public policy in Ontario that every person is free and equal in dignity and rights without regard to race, creed, colour, sex, marital status, nationality, ancestry or place of origin;
>
> AND WHEREAS these principles have been confirmed in Ontario by a number of enactments of the Legislature;
>
> AND WHEREAS it is desirable to enact a measure to codify and extend such enactments and to simplify their administration;

> *Therefore, Her Majesty, by and with the advice and consent of the Legislative Assembly of the Province of Ontario, enacts as follows:*

I regard the preamble to the Code as evidencing what is now, and probably has been for some considerable time, the public policy of this Province respecting fundamental human rights. If we accept that "every person is free and equal in dignity and rights without regard to race, creed, colour, sex, marital status, nationality, ancestry or place of origin", as we do, then it is appropriate that these rights receive the full protection of the common law. The plaintiff has a right not to be discriminated against because of her ethnic origin and alleges that she has been injured in the exercise or enjoyment of it. If she can establish that, then the common law must, on the principle of *Ashby v. White et al., supra*, afford her a remedy.

I do not regard the Code as in any way impeding the appropriate development of the common law in this important area. While the fundamental human right we are concerned with is recognized by the Code, it was not created by it. Nor does the Code, in my view, contain any expression of legislative intention to exclude the common law remedy. Rather the reverse since s. 14*a* [enacted 1974, c. 73, s. 5] appears to make the appointment of a board of inquiry to look into a complaint made under the Code a matter of ministerial discretion.

It is unnecessary, in view of the finding that a cause of action exists at common law, to determine whether or not the Code gives rise to a civil cause of action.

I would allow the appeal and set aside the order of Callaghan, J. The defendant shall have 20 days from the date of the order herein to file its statement of defence. The appellant shall have her costs both here and below in the cause.

THE BD. OF GOV. OF THE SENECA COLLEGE OF APPLIED ARTS AND TECHNOLOGY v. BHADAURIA

(1981), 17 C.C.L.T. 106 (S.C.C.)

LASKIN C.J.C. : — . . . The view taken by the Ontario Court of Appeal is a bold one and may be commended as an attempt to advance the common law. In my opinion, however, this is foreclosed by the legislative initiative which overtook the existing common law in Ontario and established a different regime which does not exclude the Courts but rather makes them part of the enforcement machinery under the Code.

For the foregoing reasons, I would hold that not only does the Code foreclose any civil action based directly upon a breach thereof but it also excludes any common law action based on an invocation of the public policy expressed in the Code. The Code itself has laid out the procedures for vindication of that public policy, procedures which the plaintiff respondent did not see fit to use.

NOTES AND QUESTIONS

1. What factors did Wilson J.A. consider in deciding to recognize a new common law tort of discrimination? How did she use: (a) the remarks of Holt C.J., dissenting in *Ashby v. White* (1703), 2 L.D. Raym. 938, rev'd. without reference to this point 1 Bro. Parl. Cas. 62 (H.L.); and (b) the Ontario Human Rights Code?

2. Laskin C.J.C. distinguished *Ashby* as a case in which the plaintiff was granted a remedy for an independent pre-existing right and suggested that Wilson J.A. had relied on *Ashby* to create the right. Do you agree with Laskin C.J.C.?

3. The Commission responsible for enforcing the Human Rights Code has broad discretion in deciding whether to initiate an investigation, convene a hearing or take a matter to court. Given the Commission's control over the proceedings and the complainant's subordinate role, is there any reason why the Code proceedings and a common law tort action for discrimination should not co-exist?

4. Laskin C.J.C.'s judgment is difficult to reconcile with the Canadian courts' approach to the relationship between common law causes of action and statutes. There is ample support for Wilson J.A.'s use of a statute in deciding to recognize a common law tort action. Laskin C.J.C. himself did the same thing in the landmark cases of *Horsley v. MacLaren* (1971), 22 D.L.R. (3d) 545 (S.C.C.), and *Jordan House Ltd. v. Menow* (1973), 38 D.L.R. (3d) 105 (S.C.C.). See also *R. v. Sask. Wheat Pool*, [1983] 3 W.W.R. 97 (S.C.C.). Is there something unique about a common law tort action for discrimination that would justify departing from the general trend?

5. Would Bhadauria have a cause of action against the College based on *Wilkinson v. Downton*, [1897] 2 Q.B. 57?

6. The Ontario Court of Appeal decision in *Bhadauria* was followed in *Aziz v. Adamson* (1979), 11 C.C.L.T. 134 (Ont. H.C.), and endorsed by at least one Canadian author. See Gibson, "The New Tort of Discrimination: A Blessed Event for the Great-Grandmother of Torts" (1980), 11 C.C.L.T. 141. See also Hunter, "Civil Actions for Discrimination" (1977), 55 Can. Bar Rev. 106.

The Supreme Court decision in *Bhadauria* has been applied in cases involving the Manitoba and New Brunswick Human Rights Codes. See *Tenning v. Gov't. of Manitoba* (1983), 4 D.L.R. (4th) 418 (Man. C.A.); and *Mallet v. Province of N.B.* (1982), 142 D.L.R. (3d) 161 (N.B. Q.B.), aff'd. (1983), 47 N.B.R. (2d) 234 (C.A.).

7. Would *Bhadauria* prevent a plaintiff from recovering damages based on a common law tort for sexual harassment? Two cases have permitted recovery and two have reached the opposite conclusion. See *Campbell-Fowler v. Royal Trust Co.*, [1994] 1 W.W.R. 193 (Alta. Q.B.); *Clark v. Canada* (1994), 20 C.C.L.T. 241 (Fed. Ct.); *Allen v. C.F.P.L. Broadcasting Ltd.* (1995), 24 C.C.L.T. (2d) 297 (Ont. Gen. Div.); and *Chapman v. 3M Canada Inc.* (1995), 24 C.C.L.T. (2d) 304 (Ont. Gen. Div.).

8. Section 15 of the Charter grants every individual the right to equal protection and benefit of the law without discrimination, and in particular discrimination based on race, national or ethnic origin, colour, religion, sex, age, or mental or physical disability. Provided the Charter applies, the combined impact of ss. 15 and 24(1) is to create a constitutional tort action for discrimination.

9. For a general discussion of s. 15, see Hogg, *Constitutional Law of Canada*, 3rd ed. (1992), 163-92; Gibson, *The Law of the Charter: Equality Rights* (1990); and Knopff, "On Proving Discrimination: Statistical Methods and Unfolding Policy Logics" (1986), 12 Canadian Public Policy 573.

10. Should the courts, rather than legislatures, extend protection against discrimination, invasions of privacy and other similar intentional interferences with the person?

11. For a discussion of the civil remedies for discrimination in the United States, see the American Law Institute, *Restatement of the Law, Second, Torts* (1979), paras. 865-66. and comments.

4

INTENTIONAL INTERFERENCE WITH CHATTELS

1. Introduction
2. The Development of the Actions
3. Trespass to Chattels
4. Conversion
5. Detinue
6. Replevin

1. Introduction

The modern law governing the intentional interference with chattels is the product of a tangled history, one in which pleadings and procedure preceded the development of substantive principles. Moreover, the origins of this body of law do not lie exclusively within the realm of torts, but within the interplay of tort, property and contract principles. As we shall discuss, trespass to chattels was characteristic of tort actions. It was predicated on blameworthy conduct for which the plaintiff was entitled to damages for actual losses. In contrast, the action for detinue was proprietary in nature. It focused on the vindication of the plaintiff's rights of possession and ownership, not on the nature of the defendant's conduct. The traditional remedy was the return of the chattel, rather than damages. In many detinue cases, the relationship between the parties was further complicated by a contract or bailment.

This chapter begins with a short history of the tort actions governing the intentional interference with chattels. We then discuss the three major modern actions — trespass to chattels, conversion and detinue — which are followed by a brief examination of replevin. The complexity of this body of law, a legacy of its evolution, may provide the impetus for change. There is a growing sentiment that this branch of law requires comprehensive legislative reform. Consequently, in proceeding through the chapter, you should consider whether these actions meet the needs of modern tort law.

2. The Development of the Actions

The common law recognized that a person could be deprived of her chattels by wrongful taking, detention or disposal, and created a distinct remedy for each situation — namely, the actions of trespass, detinue and trover. These actions now overlap. Conversion, the modern equivalent of trover, has emerged as the dominant cause of action. As the most recent of the three actions, conversion evolved in response to the perceived procedural defects of the other two.

The predecessor of the modern action for trespass to chattels, trespass *de bonis asportatis*, emerged in the 13th century, apparently as a response to difficulties in recovering property in the criminal actions of theft and larceny. Initially, the plaintiff could only invoke trespass *de bonis asportatis* for the taking or destroying of a chattel in her possession. Only later did trespass extend to cases of mere interference or damage. In order to succeed, the plaintiff had to establish that she had possession at the time the trespass occurred and that the defendant's conduct was direct and forceful. Consequently, trespass could not be used against bailees because they acquired possession lawfully. With the abolition of the writ system, intent became a prerequisite of liability. Trespass now provides a remedy for any direct and intentional interference with chattels in the possession of another. However, as we shall later explain, a plaintiff will often sue in conversion instead of in trespass, if the chattel has been seriously damaged or destroyed.

The actions for detinue and debt have a common origin in the *praecipe* writs. These writs instructed the sheriff to command (*praecipe*) the defendant to do right or else explain her conduct before the King's justices. In detinue and debt, the command was to return the plaintiff's chattel or to pay the debt that was being unjustly withheld. Unlike trespass, the *praecipe* writs sought to vindicate proprietary interests.

The central issue in detinue was the plaintiff's claim that she had an immediate right to possess a chattel which the defendant was wrongfully withholding. The law recognized two distinct situations in which detinue could arise. Detinue *sur bailment* governed those cases in which the defendant had originally come into possession of the chattel as a result of a bailment. Detinue *sur trover* dealt with cases in which the defendant had found the chattel or had come into possession in some way other than by bailment.

Detinue *sur bailment* evolved into a strict action. Once the plaintiff established that there was a bailment and that she had an immediate right to possession, the defendant was required to return the chattel or, if unable to do so, pay its full market value. The fact that the bailee was no longer in possession generally provided no defence. However, detinue *sur bailment* could not be invoked once the bailee returned the chattel, even if it was damaged. The bailee could only claim these damages by bringing a second action in trespass on the case.

Detinue *sur trover* could be brought against a finder, thief or even an innocent 'purchaser' who had lawfully come into possession of the chattel. However, the action was subject to several major limitations. First, the plaintiff had to be able to trace possession of the chattel from herself to the defendant, and each transaction could be challenged. Second, detinue *sur trover* could only be brought against a defendant who was in actual possession of the chattel at the time the action was brought. Thus, the plaintiff had no redress if the defendant had carelessly lost the chattel, wrongfully sold it and pocketed the proceeds, or had intentionally destroyed it. Third, once the defendant returned the chattel, regardless of its condition, no further remedy was available in detinue. Finally, the defendant could rely upon wager of law, a procedure that has been likened to licensed perjury. The defendant denied the plaintiff's allegation, swore to the denial in court and found 12 people who were willing to swear to her integrity.

Although the history is complex, it is clear that the shortcomings of detinue led to the emergence of an action in trespass on the case *sur trover*, or simply the action in trover. The essential feature of trover was the defendant's wrongful appropriation of the chattel for her own use. Typical of the old forms of action, the plaintiff alleged that she was in lawful possession of a chattel, lost it and that the defendant found and converted it. By the end of the 16th century, the court refused to permit any challenge to the allegations of the loss or finding. The essential issue was whether the defendant by some positive act had converted the chattel, thereby infringing the plaintiff's right to possession. The defendant could not defeat the action by wager of law, by returning the chattel in a damaged condition, or by proving that she was no longer in possession. Thus, everyone who dealt with the chattel did so at their peril, even if they honestly believed that they were acting lawfully. Since trover was derived from trespass on the case, the plaintiff was only entitled to monetary damages, which were based on the market value of the chattel at the time of the conversion.

Trover, or conversion as it is now called, substantially displaced both detinue and trespass. However, detinue remains the sole remedy where a bailee loses the chattel or carelessly allows it to be stolen, because conversion requires some positive and intentional exercise of ownership rights over a chattel. A plaintiff could also bring a detinue action if she wanted the return of the chattel or its market value at the time of trial.

Trespass to chattels remains the only remedy for a mere interference with a chattel that falls short of an intentional exercise of ownership rights. If the chattel is destroyed or seriously damaged, a plaintiff will often elect to proceed in conversion because it entitles her to the market value of the chattel and not just damages for the actual loss.

NOTES AND QUESTIONS

1. The concept of possession is central to all the intentional property torts. Trespass, conversion and, arguably, detinue directly protect the plaintiff's possessory interests. Ownership and title *per se* are not the primary concerns of this branch of law. The essence of possession appears to be physical custody or control, coupled with the intent to possess. See Terry, *Principles of Anglo-Canadian Law* (1884), 268; and Pollock and Wright, *An Essay on Possession in the Common Law* (1888).

2. For a more detailed account of the history of the intentional property torts see Holmes, *The Common Law* (1881), 77-129, 165-205; Ames, "The History of Trover" (1897), 11 Harv. L. Rev. 277-89, 374-86; Fifoot, *History and Sources of the Common Law: Tort and Contract* (1949), 24-65, 102-5; Baker, *An Introduction to English Legal History*, 3rd ed. (1990), 439-53; and Milsom, *Historical Foundations of the Common Law*, 2nd ed. (1981), 262-75, 366-79.

3. Trespass to Chattels

FOULDES v. WILLOUGHBY

(1841), 8 M. & W. 540, 151 E.R. 1153 (Ex. Ct.)

. . .

On the 15th October 1840, the plaintiff had embarked on board the defendant's ferry-boat at Birkenhead, having with him two horses, for the carriage of which he had paid the usual fare. It was alleged that the plaintiff misconducted himself and behaved improperly after he came on board the steam-boat, and when the defendant came on board he told the plaintiff that he would not carry the horses over, and that he must take them on shore. The plaintiff refused to do so, and the defendant took the horses from the plaintiff, who was holding one of them by the bridle, and put them on shore on the landing slip. They were driven to the top of the slip, which was separated by gates from the high road, and turned loose on the road. They were shortly afterwards seen in the stables of an hotel at Birkenhead, kept by the defendant's brother. The plaintiff remained on board the steam-boat, and was conveyed over the river to Liverpool. On the following day the plaintiff sent to the hotel for the horses, but the parties in whose possession they were refused to deliver them up. A message, however, was afterwards sent to him by the hotel-keeper, to the effect that he might have the horses on sending for them and paying for their keep; and that if he did not send for them and pay for their keep, they would be sold to pay the expense of it. The plaintiff then brought the present action. The horses were subsequently sold by auction. The defence set up at the trial was, that the plaintiff had misconducted himself and behaved improperly on board, and that the horses were sent on shore in order to get rid of the plaintiff, by inducing him to follow them. The learned Judge told the jury, that the defendant by taking the horses from the plaintiff and turning them out of the vessel, had been guilty of a conversion, unless they thought the plaintiff's conduct had justified his removal from the steam-boat, and he had refused to go without his horses; and that if they thought the conversion was proved, they might give the plaintiff damages for the full value of the horses. The jury found a verdict for the plaintiff with £40 damages, the value of the horses.

In Easter Term last, a rule was obtained calling upon the plaintiff to shew cause why the verdict should not be set aside on the ground of misdirection.

. . .

LORD ABINGER C.B.: — This is a motion to set aside the verdict on the ground of an alleged misdirection; and I cannot help thinking that if the learned Judge who tried the cause had referred to the long and frequent distinctions which have been taken between such a simple asportation as will support an action of trespass, and those circumstances which are requisite to establish a conversion, he would not have so directed the jury. It is a proposition familiar to all lawyers, that a simple asportation of a chattel, without any intention of making any further use of it, although it may be sufficient foundation for an action of trespass, is not sufficient to establish a conversion. I had thought that the matter had been fully discussed and this distinction established, by the numerous cases which have occurred on this subject; but, according to the argument put forward by the plaintiff's counsel to-day, a bare asportavit is sufficient foundation to support an action of trover. I entirely dissent from this argument; and therefore I think that the learned Judge was wrong, in telling the jury that the simple fact of putting these horses on shore by the defendant, amounted to a conversion of them to his own use. In my opinion, he should have added to his direction, that it was for them to consider what was the intention of the defendant in so doing. If the object, and whether rightly or wrongfully entertained is immaterial, simply was to induce the plaintiff to go on shore himself, and the defendant, in furtherance of that object, did the act in question, it was not exercising over the horses any right inconsistent with, or adverse to, the rights which the plaintiff had in them. Suppose, instead of the horses, the defendant had put the plaintiff himself on shore, and on being put on shore, the plaintiff had refused to take his horses with him, and the defendant had said he would take them to the other side of the water, and had done so, would that be a conversion? That would be a much more colourable case of a conversion than the present, because, by separating the man from his property, it might, with some appearance of fairness, be said the party was carrying away the horses without any justifiable reason for so doing. Then, having conveyed them across the water, and finding neither the owner nor any one else to receive them, what is he to do with them? Suppose, under those circumstances, the defendant lands them, and leaves them on shore, would that amount to a conversion? The argument of the plaintiff's counsel in this case must go the length of saying that it would. Then, suppose the reply to be, that those circumstances would amount to a conversion, I ask, at what period of time did the conversion take place? Suppose the plaintiff had immediately followed his horses when they were put on shore, and resumed possession of them, would there be a conversion of them in that case? I apprehend, clearly not. It has been argued that, the mere touching and taking them by the bridle would constitute a conversion, but surely that cannot be: if the plaintiff had immediately gone on shore and taken possession of them, there could be no conversion. Then the question, whether this were a conversion or not, cannot depend on the subsequent conduct of the plaintiff in following the horses on shore. Would any man say, that if the facts of this case were, that the plaintiff and defendant had had a controversy as to whether the horses should remain in the boat, and the defendant had said, "If you will not put them on shore, I will do it for you," and in pursuance of that threat, he had taken hold of one of the horses to go ashore with it, an action of trover could be sustained against him? There might, perhaps, in such a case, be ground for maintaining an action of trespass, because the defendant may have had no right to meddle with the horses at all: but it is clear that he did not do so for the purpose of taking them away from the plaintiff, or of exercising any right over them, either for himself or for any other person.

. . .

In order to constitute a conversion, it is necessary either that the party taking the goods should intend some use to be made of them, by himself or by those for whom he acts, or that, owing to his act, the goods are destroyed or consumed, to the prejudice of the lawful owner. As an instance of the latter branch of this definition, suppose, in the present case, the defendant had thrown the horses into the water, whereby they were drowned, that would have amounted to an actual conversion; or as in the case cited in the course of the argument, of a person throwing a piece of paper into the water; for, in these cases, the chattel is changed in quality, or destroyed altogether. But it has never yet been held, that the single act of removal of a chattel, independent of any claim over it, either in favour of the party himself or any one else, amounts to a conversion of the chattel. In the present case, therefore, the simple removal of these horses by the defendant, for a purpose wholly unconnected with any the least denial of the right of the plaintiff to the possession and enjoyment of them, is no conversion of the horses, and consequently the rule for a new trial ought to be made absolute.

NOTES AND QUESTIONS

1. Did the defendant's act of removing the horses from the barge constitute a trespass? If so, what would have been the appropriate measure of damages? Why did this act not amount to a conversion? If the defendant had pushed the horses off the barge in the middle of the crossing and they drowned, what damages would have the plaintiff have been entitled to in trespass and conversion?

2. The authorities disagree on whether trespass to chattels is actionable without proof of loss. Given that trespass to land and trespass to the person are actionable *per se*, how would you justify adopting a different rule for trespass to chattels?

English authors generally take the view that trespass to chattels is actionable without proof of loss. However, in the United States, a distinction is drawn between dispossession and mere interference. Dispossession is considered sufficient damage in itself, whereas interference is not actionable without proof of loss. Do you favour the English or American position? See Heuston and Buckley, *Salmond and Heuston on the Law of Torts*, 20th ed. (1992), 98; Rogers, *Winfield and Jolowicz on Tort*, 14th ed. (1994), 487; and the American Law Institute, *Restatement of the Law, Second, Torts* (1965), para. 218.

3. It is a well-established principle that a defendant's honest but mistaken belief that she is entitled to possession of the plaintiff's chattels provides no defence. See, for example, *Cameron v. Morang* (1978), 32 N.B.R. (2d) 22 (Co. Ct.); and *384238 Ont. Ltd. v. The Queen in Right of Can.* (1983), 8 D.L.R. (4th) 676 (Fed. C.A.), leave to appeal to S.C.C. ref'd. (1983), 8 D.L.R. (4th) 476n. Should a reasonable and honest mistake be recognized as a defence to trespass to chattels?

4. The central importance of possession in trespass is illustrated by *Penfolds Wines Proprietary Ltd. v. Elliott* (1946), 74 C.L.R. 204 (Aust. H.C.). The proceedings were brought in connection with two Penfolds wine bottles that were delivered to the defendant by his brother. The defendant filled the bottles with a different brand of wine and returned them to his brother. The plaintiff sued in trespass, conversion and detinue. In addressing the trespass issue, Dixon J. said at 224-25:

> I think that it is quite clear that trespass would not lie for anything which the foregoing facts disclose. Trespass is a wrong to possession. But, on the part of the respondent, there was never any invasion of possession. At the time he filled the two bottles his brother left with him, he himself was in possession of them. If the bottles had been out of his own possession and in the possession of some other person, then to lift the bottles up against the will of that person and to fill them with wine would have amounted to trespasses. The reason is that the movement of the bottles and the use of them as receptacles are invasions of the possession of the second person. But they are things which the man possessed of the bottles may do without committing trespass. The respondent came into possession of the bottles without trespass.

5. Fleming, *The Law of Torts*, 8th ed. (1992), 53-54, lists trustees, personal representatives and owners of a franchise as exceptions to the principle that only the person in actual possession is protected in trespass. He also states that a person with a mere right to possession can sue in trespass if his servant, agent or bailee at will had actual possession at the time of the wrong. These exceptions are considered by Rogers, *Winfield and Jolowicz on Tort*, 14th ed. (1994), 489. The author, while acknowledging that these parties can sue in trespass, doubts whether they really are exceptions. What is the significance of this controversy?

4. Conversion

MACKENZIE v. SCOTIA LUMBER CO.

(1913), 47 N.S.R. 115, 11 D.L.R. 729 (N.S. S.C.)

RUSSELL J.: — I base my judgment in this case on the learned Judge's findings, as to the facts. The plaintiff was the owner of a raft which had drifted away from its proper, or perhaps improper, moorings, and had become, without any interference of the defendants, attached to two rafts belonging to the defendants, which had also gone adrift, all three rafts being stranded on a ledge called "Stopper Rock," in St. Mary's river, Guysborough.

The defendants sent their servants for their own rafts, not for the rafts of anybody else. The servants, finding all three rafts together, and supposing that all three belonged to the defendants, brought them all to the defendants' mill. I take it that the defendants did not know that the raft was at their mill. It is certain that they did not know that the plaintiff's raft was at their mill, but the statement in this form would be equivocal, for although they did not know that the plaintiff's raft was at their mill, they may have known that this particular raft, which was in fact the plaintiff's raft, was at their mill. And it is upon this *équivoque* that the plaintiff bases his claim, contending that if the defendants, under the mistaken idea that the raft was their own, detained it for ever so short a period, treating it as their own, and exercising a dominion over it as their own property, they are liable for a conversion of the raft, even though the moment they discovered the mistake, they returned it to the proper owner.

. . .

The only evidence I can find of a conversion in this case is that of a possible conversion by the servants of the defendants, who, acting without authority from the defendants, did certainly exercise acts of ownership on behalf of the defendants over the raft, under the mistaken idea that the raft belonged to the defendants. Although this proceeding on the part of the servants was not authorized or acquiesced in by any responsible official of the defendant company, I assume that it was so far within the scope of the servants' duty that the company must answer for the act of their servants if that act was a tort.

We are, therefore, I think, obliged to answer the question whether one who takes the property of another person, mistaking it for his own, but returns it to the owner immediately upon discovery of the mistake, can be held liable for conversion of the property. The case must have occurred a thousand times, but the reason why counsel, who argued the appeal, were unable to cite any authority directly bearing upon the question, is probably that, until this case arose, there never was anybody wrongheaded enough to make such an accident the subject of an action at law.

I have examined all the cases collected by Ames and also the selection of cases on torts made by Mr. Wigmore, and I can find none to answer the simple question whether one who, by mistake, takes up the defendant's umbrella in place of his own, but who discovers his mistake before he has reached the street, and immediately returns it to the owner, is, or is not, liable for a conversion of the umbrella. I suspect that he would, strictly speaking, be legally liable, but if upon tender of the umbrella to the owner, the latter were to accept and resume the ownership, I am quite certain it would be a mistake to give damages for the full value of the umbrella and adjudge the property to the defendant. And that is what has been done, in this case. The defendant returned the raft, in the present case, to the plaintiff immediately upon the discovery of the mistake and the plaintiff resumed the ownership, when he asked for the use of a boat to take the raft up the river. From that moment until the action was brought, the plaintiff and defendant were both treating the property as the property of the plaintiff. I suppose that the right of action, having once arisen, the plaintiff must recover nominal damages, but why he should have the full value of the property which was returned to him and which he accepted back from the defendants, I cannot understand, and I think that the judgment of the learned trial Judge is erroneous in this respect.

The question of law is interesting, but there would be no utility in an examination of the authorities. The New Jersey case of *Frome v. Dennis*, 45 N.J. 515, 1 Ames' Cases on Torts 294, comes the nearest to the one before us, but it unfortunately does not decide the question because the act of the defendant was not, in that case, such as to be inconsistent with a recognition of the plaintiff's ownership and there was, therefore, no conversion. He had merely borrowed a plough for temporary use from another, whom he mistakenly supposed to be the owner.

The case of *Nelson v. Whetmore*, from South Carolina, 1 Rich. L. 318 (1 Ames' Cases on Torts 349), is also closely in point, but it was decided in favour of the defendant because he did not know that the plaintiff's slave, whom he engaged as a servant, was property at all, and could not therefore have had the intention of converting the defendant's property: "His treatment of Frank as a servant did not indicate an assertion of property." He did not exercise any act of ownership over the defendant's property, because he did not treat the slave as property at all. In this dearth of authority and absence of any clear answer to the question, I think we must hold that the defendants' servants did convert the plaintiff's property, and as they did it in the course of the employment by the defendant company, the latter must be held liable for conversion. But the plaintiff cannot have the property and the full damages for its conversion at the same time. Whether the defendants would have been liable for the full value of the property if the plaintiff had not accepted it, the defendants being ready and willing and offering to return it, may be an open question, but there can be no such question here, because the property was taken back by the plaintiff when the mistake was discovered.

The appeal should therefore be allowed with costs, and there should be judgment for the plaintiff for nominal damages only.

. . .

[Drysdale and Ritchie JJ. concurred.]

NOTES AND QUESTIONS

1. Fleming defines a conversion as "an intentional exercise of control over a chattel which so seriously interferes with the right of another to control it that the intermeddler may justly be required to pay its full value." *The Law of Torts*, 8th ed. (1992), 54. See also the American Law Institute, *Restatement of the Law, Second, Torts* (1965), para. 222A; and Prosser, "The Nature of Conversion" (1957), 42 Cornell L.Q. 168 at 173-74. Based on Fleming's approach, deliberate wrongdoing will likely result in a finding of conversion even if the chattel can be returned undamaged. However, innocent intermeddling will not give rise to conversion unless the plaintiff suffers considerable damages. Is Fleming's view consistent with either *Fouldes* or *MacKenzie*? If not, would you favour the adoption of Fleming's approach?

Even if the defendant is held liable in conversion, the court may permit her to return the chattel and reduce the damages accordingly, if it considers a forced judicial sale to be unwarranted. Given this discretionary power, how significant is the difference between Fleming's approach and that in *Fouldes* and *MacKenzie*?

2. The precise nature of the chattel may be critical in determining whether there has been an act of conversion. See *Penfolds Wines Proprietary Ltd. v. Elliott* (1946), 74 C.L.R. 204 at 243 (Aust. H.C.), *per* Williams J.

3. As *MacKenzie* illustrates, a defendant who makes an innocent and reasonable mistake in handling the plaintiff's chattels may be held liable in conversion. Should such mistakes be recognized as providing

a defence? If so, how could you justify recognizing mistake as a defence in conversion, but not the other intentional torts? In addition to *MacKenzie*, see *R.H. Willis and Son v. Br. Car Auctions Ltd.*, [1978] 2 All E.R. 392 (C.A.); *Irvington Holdings Ltd. v. Black* (1987), 58 O.R. (2d) 449 (C.A.); *Wilson v. New Brighton Panelbeaters Ltd.*, [1989] 1 N.Z.L.R. 74 (H.C.); and *Nilsson Bros. Inc. v. McNamara Estate*, [1992] 3 W.W.R. 761 (Alta. C.A.).

4. There are several exceptions to the rule that an innocent mistake provides no defence to conversion. Two of the more important common law exceptions are the rule governing involuntary bailees and the rule in *Hollins v. Fowler* (1875), L.R. 7 H.L. 757. There are now also several statutory exceptions created by the provincial sale of goods legislation. See Fridman, *Sale of Goods in Canada*, 4th ed. (1995), 107.

An involuntary bailee will not be held liable in conversion for misdelivering a chattel, provided she acted with reasonable care and solely for the purpose of returning it to the rightful owner. The scope of this doctrine remains uncertain and is subject to several complex restrictions. See *Long v. R.* (1922), 63 D.L.R. 134 (Ex. Ct.); Burnett, "Conversion by an Involuntary Bailee" (1976), 76 L.Q.R. 364; and Palmer, *Bailment*, 2nd ed. (1991), 689-97.

In *Hollins v. Fowler*, Blackburn J. stated at 767:

> ... one who deals with goods at the request of the person who has the actual custody of them, in the *bona fide* belief that the custodier is the true owner, should be excused for what he does if the act is of such a nature as would be excused if done by the authority of the person in possession, if he was a finder of the goods, or intrusted with their custody. ... A warehouseman with whom goods have been deposited is guilty of no conversion by keeping them, or restoring them to the person who deposited them with him, though that person turns out to have had no authority from the true owner.

For a discussion of this principle, see Palmer, *Bailment*, 2nd ed. (1991), 219-23; and Rogers, *Winfield and Jolowicz on Tort*, 14th ed. (1994), 506-8.

5. Since conversion is an intentional tort, a carrier or custodian can be held liable in conversion for innocently delivering the plaintiff's chattels to a third party, but not for carelessly losing them. Is this result justified? See *Joule Ltd. v. Poole* (1924), 24 S.R. 387 (N.S.W.); and *Heffron v. Imperial Parking Co.* (1974), 46 D.L.R. (3d) 642 (Ont. C.A.). It should be noted, however, that the careless defendant in these cases may be held liable in detinue and negligence.

6. The majority of cases and authors hold that a conversion action may be brought by a party who was either in actual possession or had an immediate right to possession at the time the defendant converted the chattel. There are, however, some cases which appear to require that the plaintiff have a right of property in addition to a possessory interest. See *Kent v. Ellis* (1900), 31 S.C.R. 110; *McCutcheon v. Lightfoot*, [1929] 1 D.L.R. 971 (Man. C.A.); *Kahler v. Midland Bank*, [1950] A.C. 241 (H.L.); *Jarvis v. Williams*, [1955] 1 All E.R. 108 (C.A.); and Warren, "Qualifying as a Plaintiff in Conversion" (1936), 49 Harv. L. Rev. 1084.

7. When reliance is placed on an immediate right to possession, rather than actual possession, the defendant is entitled to raise the *jus tertii* defence; that is, to allege that she is not liable because a third party who has a better right to the chattel, has authorized her actions. See Fleming, *supra*, 66-68.

8. A bailee asserting nothing more than a possessory interest is entitled to recover in full from the defendant in conversion, even though she may have no obligation to account to the bailor for any sum recovered. See *The Winkfield*, [1902] P. 42 (C.A.). What is the rationale for this principle? How does this relate to the issue of who should be permitted to sue in conversion? For a criticism of *The Winkfield*, see Warren, *supra*.

9. The common law also recognized an innominate action on the case which governed certain limited situations in which trespass, conversion and detinue were inapplicable. For example, if Allen permanently damaged Mary's car while it was on lease to Bill, Mary could not succeed in trespass because she was not in possession. Nor could she succeed in conversion, because she had no immediate right to possession. Detinue would not arise because Allen never possessed or withheld the car. However, provided the damage to the car would effect her reversionary interest, Mary may recover her losses in an innominate action on the case against Allen. In essence, this action protects the reversionary interests of owners who are out of possession when their chattels are damaged. See *Mears v. London & South Western Ry. Co.* (1862), 142 E.R. 1029. Is this action redundant in light of modern negligence law?

REVIEW PROBLEMS

It is now well established that conversion can be committed in several different ways. However, the essential issue remains the same, namely has the defendant intentionally acted in a way that interferes with the plaintiff's right to possess the goods. As the following fact situations illustrate, this principle is often difficult to apply.

(a) *Taking Possession*: If Barry takes Allen's car without his consent, Barry will be liable in conversion. Would Barry be liable in conversion if, in an effort to make room for his own vehicle, he pushed Allen's car three meters without damaging it? See *Aitkin Agencies Ltd. v. Richardson*, [1967] N.Z.L.R. 65 (S.C.).

(b) *Withholding Possession*: If Mary asks Barry to return her chattels in accordance with their storage contract and Barry refuses, he will be held liable in conversion. If she demands that the chattels be delivered at midnight and he refuses, but promises to deliver them the next morning, he will not be liable in conversion. Can you explain these two holdings? Would Barry be held liable in conversion if he refused to deliver the chattels without receiving proof that Mary was the true owner? See *Scott v. McAlpine* (1887), 6 U.C.C.P. 302 (U.C.C.P); *Annand v. The Merchant's Bank* (1878), 12 N.S.R. 329 (S.C.); and *Morrison v. Fishwick* (1879), 13 N.S.R. 59 (S.C.).

(c) *Transferring Possession*: Assume that Allen, acting as an agent for Barry, negotiates to purchase goods from Carol, which have been stolen from Diane. Assume as well that Allen delivers them to Barry. In this situation, both Allen and Carol will be liable in conversion. If Barry had negotiated the purchase himself and Allen had only picked up the goods from Carol and delivered them to Barry, then Allen would not be liable in conversion. Can you explain these results? If Allen receives goods from Barry which he had not ordered and he mistakenly returned them to Carol instead of Barry, would Allen be liable in conversion? See *The Lancashire Wagon Co. Ltd. v. Fitzhugh* (1861), 158 E.R. 206 (Ex. Ct.); *Dickey v. McCaul* (1887), 14 O.A.R. 166 (C.A.); *Juelle v. Trudeau* (1968), 7 D.L.R. (3d) 82 (Que. S.C.); and Lawson, "The Passing of Property and Risk in Sale of Goods" (1949), 65 L.Q.R. 35.

(d) *Destruction, Damage and Use*: If Allen stores ice in a freezer and Barry intentionally opens the freezer door causing some of the ice to melt, Barry will be liable for conversion of the melted ice. Would he also be liable in conversion for the remaining ice? See *Moorgate Mercantile Co. Ltd. v. Finch*, [1962] 2 All E.R. 467 (C.A.).

(e) *Asserting Ownership*: Assume Allen has stored some chattels on property which Barry subsequently purchased. If Barry refuses to permit Allen to recover the chattels and Barry then removes some of them, he will be liable in conversion. Would Barry have been liable if he had simply refused to permit Allen to recover the chattels? See *Dickey v. McCaul* (1887), 14 O.A.R. 166 (C.A.).

AITKEN v. GARDINER

[1956] O.R. 589, 4 D.L.R. (2d) 119 (Ont. H.C.)

[The defendants purchased share certificates without knowing that they had been stolen from the plaintiff. By the time the action came to trial, the defendants had already sold some of the certificates. Spence J. concluded that the defendants were liable in either conversion or the old action of detinue *sur trover*. He ordered the defendants to return the remaining certificates they possessed, and then considered the proper measure of damages for the shares they had sold. The defendants argued that they were liable only in conversion for the sold certificates and that the proper measure of damages was the value of the certificates when they were converted, rather than their much higher value at the time of the trial. Only the portion of Spence J.'s judgment dealing with the measure of damages in conversion is reproduced below.]

SPENCE J.: . . . Even if I am in error in concluding that the plaintiff is entitled to assert her claim in an action like the old action of *detinue sur trover*, and is limited to an action for conversion, it is not at all certain that the result of such limitation would be to confine her damages to the small sum of money realized by the defendants upon the sale of these shares. It is true, and it has been stated time after time, that the measure of damages in actions in conversion is *generally* the value of the chattel converted at the time of the conversion.

In 4 C.E.D. (Ont.), 2nd ed., p. 168, it is said: "In an action for conversion the general principle of law, although not an inflexible one, is that the jury can give no more damages than the value of the goods at the time of the conversion."

In *Caxton Publishing Co. v. Sutherland Publishing Co.*, [1939] A.C. 178 at p. 203, Lord Porter said:

> There is no dispute as to the principle on which in general the measure of damages of conversion is calculated. It is the value of the thing converted at the date of the conversion, and this principle was accepted by both sides in the present case.

In *Solloway v. McLaughlin*, [1937] 4 D.L.R. 593 at p. 596, [1938] A.C. 247, Lord Atkin said:

> Their disposal of the deposited shares amounted to nothing short of conversion: and the client on each occasion on which the shares were sold had vested in him a right to damages for conversion which would be measured by the value of the shares at the date of the conversion.

Mayne on Damages, 11th ed., p. 417, explains the latter case further. The defendant stockbroker had converted the plaintiff's shares, but on the closing of the plaintiff's account with him he bought the same number of shares in the same company at a substantially lower price than at the conversion, and tendered these to the plaintiff, who took them without knowledge of the conversion. On discovering this the plaintiff sued for damages and the Court held that the defendants were liable for damages for the conversion and that the measure of damages was the value at the date of the conversion, less the value of the shares bought in replacement at the time when the plaintiff accepted such shares.

In Salmond on Torts, *op. cit.*, p. 348, it is said:

> If, on the other hand, the property increases in value after the date of the conversion, a distinction has to be drawn. If the increase is due to the act of the defendant, the plaintiff has no title to it, and his claim is limited to the original value of the chattel . . .
>
> If, however, the subsequent increase in value is not due to the act of the defendant, but would have occurred in any case, even had no conversion been committed, the plaintiff is entitled to recover it as special damage resulting from the conversion, in addition to the original value of the property converted: as when goods taken or detained have risen in value by reason of the fluctuation of the market.

The author cites *Greening v. Wilkinson* (1825), 1 Car. & P. 625, 171 E.R. 1344, but adds in a footnote that it is different "if the plaintiff knew or ought to have known of the conversion" for in such case "he cannot claim the benefit of the subsequent rise in value: *Sachs v. Miklos*, [1948] 2 K.B. 23."

Salmond continues at p. 349: "In all actions for a conversion the plaintiff may recover, in addition to the value of the property . . . any additional damage which he may have sustained by reason of the conversion which is not too remote." He cites *Bodley v. Reynolds* (1846), 8 Q.B. 779, 115 E.R. 1066, and *France v. Gaudet* (1871), L.R. 6 Q.B. 199.

It would seem that the damage which a plaintiff suffers due to the defendants' inability to deliver certificates which have increased in value from a few cents to $17.50 per share are not damages which are too remote to enter into the calculation of her loss. Mayne is not so definite as is Salmond, and at p. 416 the author remarks: "Where the article has fluctuated in price, it is by no means settled in England whether it is to be estimated at its value at the time of conversion, or at any later time." And at p. 417 he expresses the opinion that an increase in value of goods from a rise in price is a gratuitous and accidental bonus, obtained by the holder of the goods, and that, consequently, if, in trover for goods, damages were fixed at the time of their conversion, it might deprive the rightful owner of a profit, but that profit might be one which he never would have acquired, and for which he gave no consideration. Nevertheless, I am of the opinion that a person who owns shares and holds them for subsequent sale is a person who intends to acquire a profit if and when those shares increase in value, and that the conversion of those shares has deprived the plaintiff of an opportunity to obtain the profit which the plaintiff planned to obtain should the shares increase in value, and that the deprivation of the opportunity to obtain that profit is a proper element in considering the loss which the plaintiff suffered by the conversion.

. . .

[Spence J. concluded by giving the defendants the opportunity to return share certificates of the same kind to the plaintiff, or pay $35,000 damages, the value of the share certificates at the date of trial. He also indicated, in *obiter*, that the proper date for assessing damages was the trial date and not the judgment date if the values on these dates differed.]

NOTES AND QUESTIONS

1. *Aitken* raises the measure of damages issue in conversion and detinue. Traditionally, a plaintiff suing in conversion is entitled to the market value of the chattel at the time of the conversion, and a plaintiff suing in detinue is entitled to the market value of the chattel at the time of trial. Consequently, it is said that if the plaintiff has an option, she should sue in detinue in a rising market and sue in conversion in a falling market. This apparently simple principle is not helpful in fluctuating markets, as is often the case with stocks and other investments. Similar problems arise in cases in which the plaintiff has an obligation to mitigate her loss, once she becomes aware of the defendant's wrongdoing.

2. As *Aitken* illustrates, a plaintiff in a conversion action may be entitled to recover not only the market value of the chattel at the time of the conversion, but also the consequential economic losses that result from the conversion. Spence J. appears to adopt Salmond's analysis of the circumstances in which the plaintiff can recover consequential economic losses. What limitations does Salmond impose on such awards? Are they compatible with a plaintiff's obligation to mitigate her losses?

3. In *Ralston Purina of Can. Ltd. v. Whittaker* (1973), 6 N.B.R. (2d) 443 (C.A.), the defendant seized the plaintiff's pigs and sold them. Had the pigs not been converted, the plaintiff would have kept them until they were heavier and sold them at a higher price. The court awarded the plaintiff the value of the pigs at the date of conversion, plus an additional amount to compensate him for what the pigs would have been worth had they been marketed in due course.

In *Hutscal v. I.A.C. Ltd.* (1974), 48 D.L.R. (3d) 638 (Y.T. C.A.), the defendant unlawfully repossessed the plaintiff's house trailer. The plaintiff was awarded the value of the trailer at the date of the conversion, but denied damages for the loss of use of the trailer while it was in the defendant's possession. The court held that to do so would, in effect, compensate the plaintiff twice for the same loss. Do you agree?

Can you reconcile *Hutscal* and *Ralston*? Are these cases consistent with Salmond's analysis of damage awards in conversion?

4. In *Sachs v. Miklos*, [1948] 1 All E.R. 67 (C.A.), the court suggested that there was no practical difference between the measure of damages in detinue and conversion, because the plaintiff could recover any increase in the chattel's value after it had been converted by means of a claim for consequential economic loss.

As we shall discuss, the court in *Gen. & Finance Facilities Ltd. v. Cooks Cars (Romford) Ltd.*, [1963] 2 All E.R. 314 (C.A.) specifically rejected this view, while reaffirming that consequential economic loss was available in certain situations involving conversion. This view was also rejected in *Steiman v. Steiman* (1982), 143 D.L.R. (3d) 396. The Manitoba Court of Appeal held that if a plaintiff sues in conversion the damages must be calculated on the basis that she replaced the chattel at the earliest date it was reasonably possible to do so. A plaintiff who has replaced the converted chattel would not lose any appreciation in a rising market. If the plaintiff were permitted to recover consequential economic loss, she would recover appreciation twice — once on the converted chattel and again on the replacement chattel. Do you agree with this analysis? Is *Steiman*, in effect, merely trying to ensure that a plaintiff who is aware of the conversion at the time it occurs makes a reasonable effort to mitigate her loss? Can you reconcile *Steiman*, *General Finance* and *Aitken*? See *Dom. Securities Ltd. v. Glazerman* (1984), 29 C.C.L.T. 194 (Man. C.A.); and Irvine's extremely helpful "Annotation" (1984), 29 C.C.L.T. 195. See also *Asamera Oil Corp. v. Sea Oil & Gen. Corp.*, [1979] 1 S.C.R. 633; *R.F. Fry & Associates (Pacific) Ltd. v. Reimer*, [1993] 8 W.W.R. 663 (B.C. C.A.); and Waddams, "Damages for Failure to Return Shares" (1979), 3 Can. Bus. L.J. 398.

5. As a general principle of damages, the plaintiff is not entitled to be put in a better position than she would have been in had the tort not been committed. Does the result in *Solloway*, which is discussed in *Aitken*, violate this principle? Can you suggest a countervailing principle that justifies the result in *Solloway*? See *Butler v. Egg Bd.* (1966), 114 C.L.R. 185 at 189 (Aust. H.C.), *BBMB Finance (Hong Kong) Ltd. v. Eda Holdings Ltd.*, [1991] 2 All E.R. 129 (P.C.); *Campbell v. Dominion Breweries Ltd.*, [1994] 3 N.Z.L.R. 559 (C.A.); and Tettenborn, "Loss, Damage and Wrongful Detention" (1982), 132 New L.J. 154.

6. See generally Sutton, "Damages for Conversion of Goods Sold" (1969), 43 A.L.J. 95; Peden, "Measure of Damages in Conversion and Detinue" (1970), 44 A.L.J. 65; and Tettenborn, "Damages in Conversion — The Exception or the Anomaly?" (1993), 52 Cambridge L.J. 128.

7. In *Royal Bank v. W. Got & Associates Electric Ltd.*, [1994] 5 W.W.R. 337 (Alta. Q.B.), the bank was held liable for $100,000 in punitive damages for its high-handed trespass and conversion of the plaintiff's business assets. See also *Rollinson v. R.* (1994), 20 C.C.L.T. (2d) 92 (Fed. Ct.), where Customs and RCMP officers were held liable in conversion for compensatory, aggravated and punitive damages for repeatedly seizing the plaintiff's boat and "escalating their eight-year malicious, rotten mistreatment of the Rollinsons, from a very bad, stupid beginning." The court awarded the plaintiffs an additional $8,000 under s. 24(1) of the Charter for the defendants' violation of their ss. 7, 8, 12 and 15 rights.

8. Summarize the principles of law governing conversion. To what extent has the impact of the action been ameliorated by the courts' discretion in awarding damages and in allowing the return of the chattel.

5. Detinue

GEN. & FINANCE FACILITIES LTD. v. COOKS CARS (ROMFORD) LTD.

[1963] 1 W.L.R. 644, [1963] 2 All E.R. 314 (C.A.)

DIPLOCK L.J.: — This appeal raises a neat point as to the remedies available to a plaintiff who sues for the wrongful detention of goods. The plaintiffs by a specially endorsed writ claimed "the return of a mobile crane index No. OMF 347 or its value and damages for detaining the same." They pleaded their title to the crane and relied on a demand for its delivery updated May 8, 1961. The prayer included an alternative claim for damages for conversion.

There are important distinctions between a cause of action in conversion and a cause of action in detinue. The former is a single wrongful act and the cause of action accrues at the date of the conversion; the latter is a continuing cause of action which accrues at the date of the wrongful refusal to deliver up the goods and continues until delivery up of the goods or judgment in the action for detinue. It is important to keep this distinction clear, for confusion sometimes arises from the historical derivation of the action of conversion from detinue sur bailment and detinue sur trover; of which one result is that the same facts may constitute both detinue and conversion. Demand for delivery up of the chattel was an essential requirement of an action in detinue and detinue lay only when at the time of the demand for delivery up of the chattel made by the person entitled to possession the defendant was either in actual possession of it or was estopped from denying that he was still in possession. Thus, if there had been an actual bailment of the chattel by the plaintiff to the defendant the latter was estopped from asserting that he had wrongfully delivered the chattel to a third person or had negligently lost it before demand for delivery up and the plaintiff could sue in detinue notwithstanding that the defendant was not in actual possession of the chattel at the time of the demand (see *Jones v. Dowle* [(1841), 152 E.R. 9]; *Reeve v. Palmer* [(1858), 141 E.R. 9]). Alternatively the plaintiff could sue in conversion for the actual wrongful delivery of the chattel to the third person, though not for its loss. On the other hand an unqualified refusal to comply with a demand for delivery up of a chattel made by the person entitled to possession may also amount to conversion, but only if the defendant at the time of the refusal was in actual possession of the chattel. If he has wrongfully delivered it to a third person before the date of the demand the prior wrongful delivery constitutes the conversion, not the subsequent refusal to comply with the demand (see *Sachs v. Miklos* [[1948] 1 All E.R. 67]). But even where, as in the present case, the chattel is in the actual possession of the defendant at the time of the demand to deliver up possession, so that the plaintiff has alternative causes of action in detinue or conversion based on the refusal to comply with that demand, he has a right to elect which cause of action he will pursue (see *Rosenthal v. Alderton & Sons, Ltd.* [[1946] 1 All E.R. 583]) and the remedies available to him will differ according to his election.

The action in conversion is a purely personal action and results in a judgment for pecuniary damages only. The judgment is for a single sum of which the measure is generally the value of the chattel at the date of the conversion together with any consequential damage flowing from the conversion and not too remote to be recoverable in law. With great respect to the dictum of Lord Goddard, C.J., in *Sachs v. Miklos* [*supra*], this is not necessarily the same as the measure of damages for detinue, where the same act constitutes detinue as well as conversion, although in many cases this will be so. This dictum was based on the headnote to *Rosenthal v. Alderton* [*supra*], which, in my view, misrepresents the effect of the last paragraph of the actual judgment. The law is in my view correctly stated in the current edition of *Salmond on Torts* at pp. 287 and 288. A judgment for damages for conversion does not, it is true, divest the plaintiff of his property in the chattel (see the analysis of the cases in *Ellis v. Stenning* [[1932] All E.R. Rep. 597]). The judgment, however, does not entitle the plaintiff to the assistance of the court or the executive, videlicet the sheriff, in recovering possession of the chattel.

On the other hand the action in detinue partakes of the nature of an action in rem in which the plaintiff seeks specific restitution of his chattel. At common law it resulted in a judgment for delivery up of the chattel or payment of its value as assessed, and for payment of damages for its detention. This, in effect, gave the defendant an option whether to return the chattel or to pay its value, and if the plaintiff wished to insist on specific restitution of the chattel he had to have recourse to Chancery (see *Re Scarth* [(1874), 10 Ch. App. 234], per Mellish, L.J.). The Common Law Procedure Act, 1854, s. 78, gave the court power to order delivery up of the chattel by the defendant without giving him the option to pay its value as assessed. Such an order was enforceable by execution and if the chattel could not be found distraint could be had on the defendant's lands and goods until he delivered up the specific chattel, or at the option of the plaintiff, distraint could be had of the defendant's goods for the assessed value of the chattel. This, in effect, where the court thought fit to make such an order, gave the plaintiff an option to insist on specific restitution of his chattel if the defendant did not deliver it up voluntarily; but this remedy was not available unless and until the value of the chattel had been assessed (see *Chilton v. Carrington* [(1855), 139 E.R. 735]). This remedy continues to exist under the modern law, but if the plaintiff does not wish to exercise his option to recover the assessed value of the chattel the assessment of its value is no longer a condition precedent to an order for specific restitution (see *Hymas v. Ogden* [[1950] 1 K.B. 246]; R.S.C., Ord. 48, r. 1). In addition to an order for specific restitution of the chattel or for payment of its value as assessed the plaintiff was always entitled to damages for wrongful detention of the chattel.

In the result an action in detinue today may result in a judgment in one of three different forms: (i) for the value of the chattel as assessed and damages for its detention; or (ii) for return of the chattel or recovery of its value as assessed and damages for its detention; or (iii) for return of the chattel and damages for its detention. A judgment in the first form is appropriate where the chattel is an ordinary article in commerce, for the court will not normally order specific restitution in such a case, where damages are an adequate remedy (see *Whiteley Ltd. v. Hilt* [[1918] 2 K.B. 808]). A judgment in this form deprives the defendant of the option which he had under the old common law form of judgment of returning the chattel; but if he has failed to do so by the time of the judgment the plaintiff, if he so elects, is entitled to a judgment in this form as of right (cf. R.S.C., Ord. 13, r. 6). In substance this is the same as the remedy in conversion although the sum recoverable, as I have indicated, may not be the same as damages for conversion, for the cause of action in detinue is a continuing one up to the date of judgment and the value of the chattel is assessed as at that date (see *Rosenthal v. Alderton & Sons, Ltd.* [*supra*]). A final judgment in such a form is for a single sum of money. A judgment in the second form gives to the defendant the option of returning the chattel, but it also gives to the plaintiff the right to apply to the court to enforce specific restitution of the chattel by writ of delivery, or attachment or sequestration as well as recovering damages for its detention by writ of fieri facias (R.S.C., Ord. 42, r. 6). This is an important right and it is essential to its exercise that the judgment should specify separate amounts for the assessed value of the chattel and for the damages for its detention, for if the plaintiff wishes to proceed by writ of delivery for which he can apply ex parte (Ord. 48, r. 1) he has the option of distraining for the assessed value of the chattel if the chattel itself is not recovered by the sheriff. He would be deprived of this option if the value of the chattel were not separately assessed. A judgment in the third form is unusual but can be given (see *Hymas v. Ogden* [*supra*]). Under it the only pecuniary sum recoverable is damages for detention of the chattel. Its value need not be assessed and the plaintiff can obtain specific restitution of the chattel only by writ of delivery, attachment, or sequestration. He has no option under the writ of delivery to distrain for the value of the chattel.

. . .

[Pearson L.J. delivered a separate concurring judgment.]

AITKEN v. GARDINER

[1956] O.R. 589, 4 D.L.R. (2d) 119 (H.C.)

SPENCE J.: . . . Also, the plaintiff alleges that in order to succeed in an action for detinue he need only prove (1) that the chattel was in the possession of the defendant who refuses to deliver the same, and (2) that, if the defendant on the issuance of the writ no longer had possession of the chattel, he parted with it wrongfully. Counsel for the defendants on the other hand submitted that the action of detinue is restricted to actions based on a bailment by the plaintiff to the defendants.

Clerk & Lindsell on Torts, 11th ed., pp. 441 *et seq.*, points out that the two types of action in detinue are (1) an action in *detinue sur trover*, and the other, an action in *detinue sur bailment*, and the same matter is dealt with in much the same fashion in Potter. Historical Introduction to English Law, 2nd ed., pp. 353 *et seq.* At p. 355 the latter author says: "During the fifteenth century this plea gave rise to a special form of action of Detinue known as *detinue sur trover*, which must be distinguished from the action of Trespass on the Case *sur trover* (shortly called *Trover*), which ultimately took its place . . . This distinction [between *detinue sur trover* and *detinue sur bailment*] represented the recognition of the two forms of wrongful detention: one based upon a purely tortious wrong and the other connected with agreement between the parties."

Salmond on Torts, 11th ed. pp. 317-8, quotes Parke B. in *Jones v. Dowle* (1841), 9 M. & W. 19, 152 E.R. 9, as follows: "'Detinue does not lie against him who never had possession of the chattel, but does lie against him who once had but has improperly parted with the possession of it.'" The author continues: "This being so, it is clear that detinue was available as a remedy for wrongful conversion as well as for wrongful detainer."

The action of detinue declined in popularity because of certain defects — defects which have been largely cured now that, since 1852, the Court has had the option of ordering the actual return of the chattel rather than merely granting damages for it. The fact that the defendants had not possession of the certificate at the time the writ was issued is no answer to an action in detinue so long as they got rid of the possession of the chattel improperly: *Jones v. Dowle, supra*, and *Bristol & West of England Bk. v. Midland R. Co.*, [1891] 2 Q.B. 653.

In *Clark v. Orr* (1854), 11 U.C.Q.B. 436 at p. 437, Robinson C.J. says: "It seems clear, we think, on numerous authorities, that it is not indispensable to shew that the defendant in the action of *detinue* had possession of the goods when the action was brought; if he had possession of them before, that may suffice."

In *Jones v. Dowle, supra*, the Court said: "Detinue does not lie against him who never had possession of the chattel, but it does against him who once had, but has improperly parted with the possession of it."

See also *Munro v. Willmott*, [1948] 2 All E.R. 983.

Was, then, the defendants' parting with the certificates in question in this action an improper parting? I have found that the certificates were stolen and I have come to the opinion that no principle of negotiability gave to the defendants any right which they could assert as against the true owner of the certificates. In these circumstances I am of the opinion that the sale by the defendants of the shares represented by those certificates was, in law, a conversion, and was therefore an improper parting with possession and was a sufficient basis for the present action in detinue.

. . .

[Spence J. held that the plaintiff had an option of suing in either detinue or conversion, and went on to assess damages.]

NOTES AND QUESTIONS

1. Do Diplock L.J. and Spence J. agree on when a detinue action will lie against a defendant who is no longer in possession? If not, which view is correct?

2. Under what circumstances will the plaintiff have the option of suing in conversion or detinue? When will the plaintiff be limited to either conversion or detinue?

3. Aside from the differences in remedies, what are the relative advantages and disadvantages of conversion and detinue? See Great Britain, *Law Reform Committee, Eighteenth Report: Conversion and Detinue* (1971); and Palmer, *Bailment*, 2nd ed. (1991), 241-48. It should be noted that the United Kingdom abolished detinue in 1978. For a discussion of the impact of the legislation see Palmer, "The Abolition of Detinue" (1981), 45 Conv. & Prop. Law 62.

4. In *Baud Corp. v. Brook* (1973), 40 D.L.R. (3d) 418 (Alta. C.A.), varied without reference to this point [1979] 1 S.C.R. 633, (*sub nom. Asamera Oil Corp. Ltd. v. Sea Oil & Gen. Corp.*), the court held that a formal demand and refusal is not required if the plaintiff clearly shows that the demand would have been refused. But see Palmer, "Comment" (1975), 53 Can. Bar Rev. 121.

5. Although there is disagreement, it appears that where a detinue action is based on an immediate right to possession, a right of property must be established. Unfortunately, it is not clear what the courts mean by "a right of property" in these cases. See, for example, *Jarvis v. Williams*, [1955] 1 All E.R. 108 (C.A.); and *Singh v. Ali*, [1960] A.C. 167 (P.C.). But see *Schentag v. Gauthier* (1972), 27 D.L.R. (3d) 710 (Sask. Dist. Ct.).

6. According to *Gen. & Finance Facilities Ltd.*, in what circumstances is a plaintiff entitled to specific restitution of her chattel in detinue? But see *Schentag v. Gauthier* (1972), 27 D.L.R. (3d) 710 (Sask. Dist. Ct.).

6. Replevin

Replevin is an interlocutory remedy which enables a dispossessed plaintiff to recover possession of a chattel pending a judicial resolution of the case. The function of replevin was stated in *Mennie v. Blake* (1856), 119 E.R. 1078 at 1080 (Q.B.):

> . . . as a general rule it is just that a party in the peaceable possession of land or goods should remain undisturbed . . . until the right be determined and the possession shewn to be unlawful. But, where, either by distress or merely by a strong hand, the peaceable possession has been disturbed, an exceptional case arises; and it may be just that, even before any determination of the right, the law should interpose to replace the parties in the condition in which they were before the act done, security being taken that the right shall be tried, and the goods be forthcoming to abide the decision.

NOTES AND QUESTIONS

1. In *Allis-Chalmers, Rumely Ltd. v. Forbes Equipment Ltd.* (1969), 8 D.L.R. (3d) 105 (B.C. S.C.), the plaintiff agreed to supply machinery to the defendant on consignment. After the defendant's alleged default, the plaintiff terminated the agreement and sought recovery of the property under the provincial Replevin Act. The court in granting recovery held that it is not necessary to determine the merits of the case before an order of replevin may be granted. The plaintiff need only show substantial grounds for the allegations. See also *Granby Const. and Equipment Ltd. v. Milley* (1974), 47 D.L.R. (3d) 427, rev'd. [1974] C.T.C. 701 (B.C. C.A.); and *Littleford v. Loanex Financial Services* (1986), 28 D.L.R. (4th) 613 (Man. C.A.).

REVIEW PROBLEMS

1. The defendant wrongfully refused to respond to the plaintiff's demand for the return of his shares at a time when they were worth five dollars each. The shares then rose in value to ten dollars, but fell to seven dollars at the date of trial. Can the plaintiff recover ten dollars a share in detinue and in conversion?

2. The defendant took the plaintiff's taxi. Ten days later, the plaintiff demanded its return, while it was still in the defendant's possession. The taxi's value did not change from the date it was taken until the date of trial. Would you suggest suing in conversion or detinue, given that the plaintiff prefers damages to specific restitution?

3. Smith lent his car to Jones to make a return trip to New York City. While in New York, Brown intentionally scratched the car. What action can Smith maintain against Brown? Must Smith wait until Jones returns the scratched car before bringing an action?

4. Assume in the above situation that Smith had agreed with Jones to assume all responsibility for damages while Jones had the car and that Brown stole and destroyed the car in New York. What actions could Jones maintain against Brown? Can Brown raise the agreement between Smith and Jones as a defence? If Brown is held liable to Jones, would Jones be required to compensate Smith?

5. Allan was the owner of an expensive portable TV, but his need to meet pressing debts forced him to sell it. His friend Judy told him that she was interested in buying it, but would like to have it for a week on trial to help her decide. Allan agreed and on Sunday evening Judy took the TV, promising either to return it or purchase it by the following Monday.

On Wednesday, Judy took the TV to the beach to watch her favourite programs while tanning. During the late afternoon Judy met a group of friends and went for a walk, carelessly leaving the TV and some clothing behind. While Judy was away, Justin appeared on the scene. Finding the beach deserted and the TV and clothing in danger of being swept away by the advancing tide, Justin took them home for safekeeping. He immediately placed an advertisement in the "lost and found" column of the local newspaper.

Meanwhile, Judy informed Allan of the loss of the TV. On Thursday, Allan spotted Justin's advertisement. Justin refused to return the TV to Allan, explaining that the TV's owner must also be the owner of the clothing which obviously did not belong to Allan. Judy also noticed Justin's advertisement and visited him on Saturday of the same week. Confronted with proof that Judy was the owner of the clothing, Justin was convinced that the TV also belonged to her and agreed to return it. Justin had lent the TV to Sarah on Friday night so he phoned her and told her Judy would be coming to pick it up. Judy collected the TV from Sarah, but instead of returning it to Allan, she absconded.

One month later, after failing to find Judy, Allan sued Justin. Allan's TV is now worth 40 per cent more than it was two weeks earlier, due to a shortage of portable television parts. Advise Allan.

5

INTENTIONAL INTERFERENCE WITH REAL PROPERTY

1. Trespass to Land
2. Trespass and Nuisance
3. Trespass to Airspace and Subsoil

1. Trespass to Land

The tort of trespass to land may be defined as the direct and intentional physical intrusion onto the land in the possession of another. Given the central role of land in society, the elements of this action were broadly defined under the writ system. Despite the fundamental changes brought about by urbanization and industrialization in the last 200 years, the courts have only recently begun to re-examine the elements of this tort.

ENTICK v. CARRINGTON

(1765), 19 State Tr. 1029 (C.P.)

[The defendants, claiming authority under a warrant from the Secretary of State, broke into the plaintiff's house and carried away some papers. The plaintiff sued the defendants in trespass.]

The great end, for which men entered into society, was to secure their property. That right is preserved sacred and incommunicable in all instances, where it has not been taken away or abridged by some public law for the good of the whole. The cases where this right of property is set aside by positive law, are various. Distresses, executions, forfeitures, taxes, &c. are all of this description; wherein every man by common consent gives up that right, for the sake of justice and the general good. By the laws of England, every invasion of private property, be it ever so minute, is a trespass. No man can set his foot upon my ground without my licence, but he is liable to an action, though the damage be nothing; which is proved by every declaration in trespass, where the defendant is called upon to answer for bruising the grass and even treading upon the soil. If he admits the fact, he is bound to shew by way of justification, that some positive law has empowered or excused him. The justification is submitted to the judges, who are to look into the books; and if such a justification can be maintained by the text of the statute law, or by the principles of common law. If no such excuse can be found or produced, the silence of the books is an authority against the defendant, and the plaintiff must have judgment.

TURNER v. THORNE

[1960] O.W.N. 20, 21 D.L.R. (2d) 29 (Ont. H.C.)

McRUER C.J.H.C.: — This is an action brought to recover damages sustained by the plaintiff on September 5, 1958. The facts are simple. The defendant Robert N. Thorne operates a business known as the Speedit Delivery Service, and the defendant George Thorne was a driver employed by his co-defendant.

The business of the Speedit Delivery Service is to pick up parcels on request for delivery to designated persons. On the day in question a call was received from a customer of the defendant to pick up 14 cartons of material for delivery to the Gas Machinery Co. (Canada) Ltd., Lime Ridge Rd., on the outskirts of the City of Hamilton.

. . .

The Gas Machinery Co. (Canada) Ltd. had done business before in a garage in the rear of some private property and the defendant George Thorne had made deliveries to that garage. On the day in question, on arriving at Lime Ridge Rd., Mr. Thorne without further information assumed that the Gas Machinery Co. was located on the plaintiff's property. He went to the plaintiff's house and rapped on the door but got no answer. In fact, both the plaintiff and his wife were at work. Without making further inquiries Mr. Thorne went to the plaintiff's double garage, which is shown in ex. 14 and found it unlocked. The garage has two sets of doors; to open the doors, the west door is pulled east and the east door is pulled west. On leaving the premises in the morning the plaintiff had taken his automobile from the west section of the garage, leaving a half-ton truck in the east section. There was a space of about 3 ft. between the rear of the half-ton truck and the door. The plaintiff closed the west door and went out of the garage by way of the east door and closed it after him. It is said in evidence that the west door was left a few inches open but, be that as it may, I do not think that has any real bearing on the result of the case.

Finding no one at home on the plaintiff's property, Mr. Thorne backed his truck into the driveway and opened the west door and unloaded the cartons which were about 24 ins. long and 9 ins. square, and piled them in the centre of the garage where they would be between the truck and the automobile if the automobile was in the west section of the garage. There is some dispute as to whether the cartons were piled so as to project southerly past the end of the truck. I am satisfied that they were. When the plaintiff came home that evening he and his wife went shopping and returned after dark. The garage was not equipped with any artificial light. For the purpose of opening the west door the plaintiff entered the east door of the garage and walked past the rear of the truck and fell over the cartons which had been deposited in the garage, sustaining serious injuries which were assessed by the jury at $9,626, including out-of-pocket expenses.

. . .

I think the defendant George Thorne is undoubtedly liable in damages. He was a trespasser on the plaintiff's property and it was a trespass to leave the packages in the garage.

"Trespass to land consists in any unjustifiable intrusion by one person upon land in the possession of another . . .

It is also trespass to place anything on or in land in the possession of another": Clerk & Lindsell on Torts, 11th ed. p. 516. . . .

Liability for incidental damage resulting from trespass is most concisely dealt with in the Restatement of the Law of Torts, vol. I, commencing at p. 359. At pp. 375-6 it is stated: "A trespass, actionable under the rule stated in s. 158, may be committed by the continued presence on the land of a structure, chattel or other thing which the actor has tortiously placed thereon, whether or not the actor has the ability to remove it."

A most useful discussion of the relevant law is contained in *Kopka et ux. v. Bell Telephone Co. of Pennsylvania* (1952), 91 Atl. (2d) 232. Although this is a case in the United States Courts I think it accurately states the common law applicable in Ontario. The case arose out of injuries sustained by the owner of land when he fell into a hole dug on his land by servants of the defendant. At p. 235 Mr. Justice Stern, giving the judgment of the Court of Appeal of the State of Pennsylvania, stated:

> Before considering the question of the liability of a trespasser for personal injuries suffered by the possessor of land as an indirect result of the trespass, there are two relevant legal principles to be borne in mind. The first is that the fact that a trespass results from an innocent mistake and, in that sense, is not deliberate or wilful, does not relieve the trespasser of liability therefor or for any of the results thereof.

And on the same page:

> The liability of defendant Company for the trespass involved in the digging of the hole on plaintiff's land without his knowledge or consent being thus established, does such liability extend to the personal injuries sustained by him as the result of his falling into the hole? The authorities are clear to the effect that where the complaint is for trespass to land the trespasser becomes liable not only for personal injuries resulting directly and proximately from the trespass but also for those which are indirect and consequential.

At p. 236 the learned Judge quoted from s. 163 of the Restatement of the Law of Torts as follows: "'So too, he [a trespasser] is liable for any harm to the possessor . . . if such harm is caused by the actor's presence on the land, irrespective of whether it was caused by conduct which, were the actor not a trespasser, would have subjected him to liability.'"

. . .

The plaintiff is therefore entitled to judgment in the sum of $9,626, the damages as assessed by the jury.

NOTES AND QUESTIONS

1. A trespass may be committed by entering the plaintiff's land in person, propelling an object or third person onto the property, or by failing to leave after permission to enter has been terminated. A trespass may also be committed by bringing an object onto the plaintiff's land and wrongfully failing to remove it. The doctrine of continuing trespass applies in such situations, allowing the plaintiff to maintain successive actions until the object is removed. Damages are assessed at the date of each action. For a discussion of continuing trespass see *Johnson v. B.C. Hydro and Power Authority* (1981), 16 C.C.L.T. 10 (B.C. S.C.); *Haynes v. Nfld. Telephone Co.* (1985), 168 A.P.R. 162 (Nfld. Dist. Ct.); and *Cousins v. Wilson*, [1994] 1 N.Z.L.R. 463 (H.C.).

2. In order to maintain a trespass action, the plaintiff is generally required to be in possession of the land at the time of the intrusion. Even a squatter without title who has possession of the land

can maintain a trespass action against a subsequent trespasser. *Swaile v. Zurdayk*, [1924] 2 W.W.R. 555 (Sask. C.A.). However, a person who is merely using the land without any possessory interest cannot maintain a trespass action. As indicated in *Penney v. Gosse* (1974), 6 Nfld. & P.E.I.R. 344 at 346 (Nfld. S.C.): "Any form of possession, so long as it is clear and exclusive and exercised with the intention to possess, is sufficient to support an action for trespass against a wrongdoer. Actual possession is good against all except those who can show a better right of possession in themselves." Why does trespass protect possession, rather than ownership? See also *Boutin v. Boutin* (1985), 23 D.L.R. (4th) 286 (Sask. Q.B.).

3. The doctrine of trespass by relation provides an exception to the possession requirement. The doctrine permits a plaintiff, who only had an immediate right to possession when the trespass occurred, to sue in trespass for that intrusion once he subsequently acquires possession. This result is achieved through a legal fiction which deems the plaintiff to have been in possession from the moment his right of entry accrued. Trespass by relation is most frequently invoked in cases involving vacant land.

4. As illustrated by *Entick* and *Turner*, the action for trespass to land is strictly defined and applied. What are the rationales for treating a defendant's motive as irrelevant to liability and for refusing to recognize mistake as a defence? See *Sherrin and Sherrin v. Haggerty*, [1953] O.W.N. 962 (Co. Ct.); *Colet v. R.* (1981), 119 D.L.R. (3d) 521 (S.C.C.); and *Costello v. Calgary (City)* (1995), 23 C.C.L.T. (2d) 125 (Alta. Q.B.). But see *Henderson v. Volk* (1982), 35 O.R. (2d) 378 (C.A.).

5. Once it is established that the defendant is a trespasser, he is liable for all the consequences of the trespass, whether or not they are foreseeable. In addition to *Turner*, see *Wyant v. Crouse* (1901), 86 N.W. 528 (Mich. S.C.) — spread of fire; and *Mee v. Gardiner*, [1949] 3 D.L.R. 852 (B.C. C.A.) — tramp spreading skin disease. But, see *Mayfair Ltd. v. Pears*, [1987] 1 N.Z.L.R. 459 (C.A.) where the defendant was absolved of liability for the unforeseeable consequences of his trespass. Which position is preferable?

6. A defendant in a trespass action cannot raise the defence of *jus tertii* claiming that a third party has a better right to possession than the plaintiff, unless that third party authorized the defendant's entry.

7. Trespass to land must be distinguished from ejectment which is not a tort action, but a proprietary action for the recovery of land. Unlike trespass, ejectment does not depend on the plaintiff's possession of, or entry onto, the land. The plaintiff may succeed in ejectment by establishing that he has a better right to possession than the defendant. However, the defendant may raise the *jus tertii* defence in an ejectment action.

8. The Canadian courts have awarded substantial punitive damages in cases in which the defendant has trespassed in a high-handed or arrogant fashion. In *Nantel v. Parisien* (1981), 18 C.C.L.T. 79 (Ont. H.C.), a corporate defendant was required to pay $35,000 in punitive damages and $11,200 in general damages for its "tyrannical and arrogant trespass". The defendant's employees broke into the plaintiff's business without warning in order to demolish the building, despite the fact that the plaintiff had a valid lease and was in lawful possession. In *Horseshoe Bay Retirement Society v. S.I.F. Development Corp.* (1990), 66 D.L.R. (4th) 42 (B.C. S.C.), the court awarded $100,000 in punitive damages against the defendant, who had cut down the plaintiff's trees to enhance the price of the lots it was developing. See also *Austin v. Rescon Construction (1984) Ltd.* (1989), 57 D.L.R. (4th) 591 (B.C. C.A.); and *Epstein v. Cressey Development Corp.*, [1992] 3 W.W.R. 566 (B.C. C.A.).

9. For a detailed discussion of trespass to land see Magnet, "Intentional Interference with Land" in Klar (ed.), *Studies in Canadian Tort Law* (1977), 287; Heuston and Buckley, *Salmond and Heuston on Tort*, 20th ed. (1992), 44-49; and Keeton *et al.*, *Prosser and Keeton on the Law of Torts*, 5th ed. (1984), 67-84.

REVIEW PROBLEMS

1. Arthur lives in a mansion in one corner of his 500-acre estate. Unknown to him, Bill erected a small home on the opposite corner of the estate and lived there for two years. While Bill was away for several days, Carl moved into his house. What actions may Bill bring against Carl? What actions may Arthur bring against Carl and Bill?

2. Ned rented his house to Tom for a year. After six months, Ned went to see how Tom was faring, only to find that Tom was on holidays and that a squatter had moved in with some old furniture.

The squatter left, but refused to take his furniture with him until he could get resettled. Advise Ned on the actions that he may bring against the squatter.

HARRISON v. CARSWELL

[1976] 2 S.C.R. 200, 62 D.L.R. (3d) 68 (S.C.C.)

. . .

DICKSON J.: — The respondent, Sophie Carswell, was charged under the *Petty Trespasses Act*, R.S.M. 1970, c. P50, with four offences (one on each of four days) of unlawfully trespassing upon the premises of the Fairview Corporation Limited, trading under the firm name and style of Polo Park Shopping Centre, located in the City of Winnipeg, after having been requested by the owner not to enter on or come upon the premises. The appellant, Peter Harrison, manager of Polo Park Shopping Centre swore the informations. The charges were dismissed by the Provincial Judge, but on a trial *de novo* in the County Court, Mrs. Carswell was convicted and fined $10 on each of the charges. The convictions were set aside by the Manitoba Court of Appeal (Freedman, C.J.M., and Matas, J.A., with Guy, J.A., dissenting) [17 C.C.C. (2d) 521, 48 D.L.R. (3d) 137, [1974] 4 W.W.R. 394] and the present appeal followed, by leave of this Court.

. . .

With great respect, I am unable to agree with the majority reasons, delivered in the Court of Appeal by Chief Justice Freedman, for I find it difficult, indeed impossible, to make any well-founded distinction between this case and *R. v. Peters* (1971), 17 D.L.R. (3d) 128*n*, decided by this Court four years ago in a unanimous decision of the full Bench. The constitutional issue raised in *Peters* no longer concerns us; the only other issue was whether the owner of a shopping plaza had sufficient control or possession of the common areas, having regard to the unrestricted invitation to the public to enter upon the premises, as to enable it to invoke the remedy of trespass. The Court decided it did. That case and the present case came to us on much the same facts, picketing within a shopping centre in connection with a labour dispute. . . .

The judgment of the Ontario Court of Appeal in *R. v. Peters* (1970), 2 C.C.C. (2d) 336, 16 D.L.R. (3d) 143, [1971] 1 O.R. 597, was delivered by Chief Justice Gale who said, at p. 338 C.C.C., p. 146 D.L.R.:

> With respect to the first ground of appeal, it is our opinion that an owner who has granted a right of entry to a particular class of the public has not thereby relinquished his or its right to withdraw its invitation to the general public or any particular member thereof, and that if a member of the public whose invitation to enter has been withdrawn refuses to leave, he thereby becomes a trespasser and may be prosecuted under the *Petty Trespass Act*. Here, the invitation extended by the owner was of a general nature and included tenants, employees, agents and all persons having or seeking business relations with the tenants. However, notwithstanding the general nature of the invitation, the owner did not thereby lose its right to withdraw the invitation from the general public or any particular member thereof. In addition, it is also our view with respect to trepass that possession does not cease to be exclusive so long as there is the right to control entry of the general public, and here the owner had not relinquished that right of control.

The brief judgment in this Court . . . neither adopted nor repudiated the reasons delivered in the Court of Appeal, but it should not be overlooked that when the

Peters case was before the Ontario Court of Appeal, counsel for Peters relied upon the decision of the Court of Appeal for Saskatchewan in *Grosvenor Park Shopping Centre Ltd. v. Waloshin et al.* (1964), 46 D.L.R. (2d) 750, 49 W.W.R. 237. That case arose out of injunction proceedings during a strike of employees of Loblaw Groceterias Co. Ltd., in Saskatoon, who were picketing with placards on the sidewalk adjacent to store premises located in a shopping centre. The pertinent part of the judgment of the Saskatchewan Court of Appeal reads [at p. 755]:

> Learned counsel for the appellant argued that the respondent did not have that degree of possession essential to an action in trespass.
>
> The area upon which it is alleged the appellants have trespassed is part of what is well known as a shopping centre. While legal title to the area is in the respondent, it admits in its pleadings that it has granted easements to the many tenants. The evidence also establishes that the respondent has extended an unrestricted invitation to the public to enter upon the premises. The very nature of the operation is one in which the respondent, both in its own interests and in the interests of its tenants, could not do otherwise. Under the circumstances, it cannot be said that the respondent is in actual possession. The most that can be said is that the respondent exercises control over the premises but does not exercise that control to the exclusion of other persons. For that reason, therefore, the respondent cannot maintain an action in trespass against the appellants: *vide* 38 Hals., 3rd ed., p. 743, para. 1212. Support, too, for this view may be found in *Zeller's (Western) Ltd. v. Retail Food & Drug Clerks Union, Local 1518* (1963), 42 D.L.R. (2d) 582, 45 W.W.R. 337.
>
> . . .

So when the *Peters* case came to this Court for consideration, the Court had before it the reasoning of the Court of Appeal for Ontario in that case and the reasoning, difficult to reconcile, of the Court of Appeal for Saskatchewan in *Grosvenor Park*; the reasoning of the Ontario Court prevailed. There has been no suggestion that *Peters* was wrongly decided; therefore, I would think it must be regarded as controlling unless it can properly be distinguished from the case at bar. No distinction can be made on the ground of contract; there is a copy of the lease from Fairview to Dominion Stores, among the papers, but it would not appear, nor has it been argued, that any distinction can rest on that document. As to a possible statutory distinction, the petty trespass acts of Manitoba and Ontario do not differ in any material respect and indeed s. 24 of the *Labour Relations Act*, 1972 (Man.), c. 75 (continuing consolidation, c. L10), specifically preserves rights against trespassers. Therefore it would seem the appeal must succeed unless a valid distinction can be drawn on the ground that the president of the Brampton Labour Council, in *Peters*, was a mere member of the general public from whom permission to remain on the premises could be withdrawn at will, whereas Mrs. Carswell was an employee of one of the tenants of the shopping centre on strike in support of a current labour dispute, from whom permission to remain on the premises could not, as a matter of law, be withdrawn. I find myself unable to accept that any ground in law supports such a distinction.

The evidence discloses that distribution of pamphlets or leaflets in the mall of Polo Park Shopping Centre or on the parking lot, has never been permitted by the management of the centre and that this prohibition has extended to tenants of the centre. The centre as a matter of policy has not permitted any person to walk in the mall carrying placards. There is nothing in the evidence supporting the view that in the present case the owner of the centre was acting out of caprice or whimsy or *mala fides*. In a comment entitled *Labour Law — Picketing in Shopping*

Centres, 43 *Can. Bar Rev.* 357 at p. 362 (1965), H.W. Arthurs referred to the following as one of the legitimate concerns of the landlord of a shopping centre:

> ... while public authorities may, on behalf of the community, strike a reasonable balance between
> traffic and picketing on public sidewalks and streets, the shopping centre owner can hardly be
> expected to make such a choice: he has no authority to speak for the community; to grant picketing
> or parading privileges to all would invite chaos, while to do so selectively would invite com-
> mercial reprisals. He is thus driven to adopt a highly restrictive approach to granting permission
> to groups who wish to parade or picket in the shopping centre.

It is urged on behalf of Mrs. Carswell that the right of a person to picket
peacefully in support of a lawful strike is of greater social significance than the
proprietary rights of an owner of a shopping centre, and that the rights of the
owner must yield to those of the picketer. The American example has been cited,
but I cannot say that I find the American cases to which we have been referred
of great help. The facts in *Schwartz-Torrance Investment Corp. v. Bakery and Confectionery Workers' Union, Local 31* (1964), 394 P. 2d 921, decided by the Supreme
Court of California are almost identical with those in *Grosvenor Park*, but I think
it not unimportant to note that in *Schwartz-Torrance*, Justice Tobriner, early in his
judgment, drew attention to the fact that the Legislature of the State of California
had expressly declared that the public policy of the State favoured concerted
activities of employees for the purpose of collective bargaining and had enacted
the policy into an exception to the criminal trespass law. Construing that exception,
the California Supreme Court in a case antedating *Schwartz-Torrance* had concluded
that the Legislature, in dealing with trespasses, had specifically subordinated the
rights of the property owner to those of persons engaged in lawful labour activities.
Schwartz-Torrance is, therefore, of small aid in this case and indeed can be said
to support, in a negative sense, a position inimical to that of Mrs. Carswell. And
one need only read *Amalgamated Food Employees' Union, Local 590 v. Logan Valley
Plaza Inc.* (1968), 391 U.S. 308, and then read *Lloyd Corp. Ltd. v. Tanner* (1972),
407 U.S. 551, to apprehend the uncertainties and very real difficulties which emerge
when a Court essays to legislate as to what is and what is not a permissible activity
within a shopping centre.

The submission that this Court should weigh and determine the respective
values to society of the right to property and the right to picket raises important
and difficult political and socio-economic issues, the resolution of which must,
by their very nature, be arbitrary and embody personal economic and social beliefs.
It raises also fundamental questions as to the role of this Court under the Canadian
Constitution. The duty of the Court, as I envisage it, is to proceed in the discharge
of its adjudicative function in a reasoned way from principled decision and established concepts. I do not for a moment doubt the power of the Court to act creatively
— it has done so on countless occasions; but manifestly one must ask — what
are the limits of the judicial function? There are many and varied answers to this
question. Holmes, J., said in *Southern Pacific Co. v. Jensen* (1917), 244 U.S. 205
at p. 221: "I recognize without hesitation that judges do and must legislate, but
they can do it only interstitially; they are confined from molar to molecular actions".
Cardozo, *The Nature of the Judicial Process* (1921), p. 141, recognized that the
freedom of the Judge is not absolute in this expression of his view:

> This judge, even when he is free, is still not wholly free. He is not to innovate at pleasure. He

is not a knight-errant, roaming at will in pursuit of his own ideal of beauty or of goodness. He is to draw his inspiration from consecrated principles.

The former Chief Justice of the Australian High Court, Sir Owen Dixon, in an address delivered at Yale University in September, 1955, "Concerning Judicial Method", had this to say:

> But in our Australian High Court we have had as yet no deliberate innovators bent on express change of acknowledged doctrine. It is one thing for a court to seek to extend the application of accepted principles to new cases or to reason from the more fundamental of settled legal principles to new conclusions or to decide that a category is not closed against unforeseen instances which in reason might be subsumed thereunder. It is an entirely different thing for a judge, who is discontented with a result held to flow from a long accepted legal principle, deliberately to abandon the principle in the name of justice or of social necessity or of social convenience. The former accords with the technique of the common law and amounts to no more than an enlightened application of modes of reasoning traditionally respected in the courts. It is a process by the repeated use of which the law is developed, is adapted to new conditions, and is improved in content. The latter means an abrupt and almost arbitrary change.
>
> . . .

Society has long since acknowledged that a public interest is served by permitting union members to bring economic pressure to bear upon their respective employers through peaceful picketing, but the right has been exercisable in some locations and not in others and to the extent that picketing has been permitted on private property the right hitherto has been accorded by statute. For example, s. 87 [since rep. & sub. 1975, c. 33, s. 21] of the *Labour Code of British Columbia Act*, 1973 (B.C.) (2nd Sess.), c. 122, provides that no action lies in respect of picketing permitted under the Act for trespass to real property to which a member of the public ordinarily has access.

Anglo-Canadian jurisprudence has transitionally recognized, as a fundamental freedom, the right of the individual to the enjoyment of property and the right not to be deprived thereof, or any interest therein, save by due process of law. The Legislature of Manitoba has declared in the *Petty Trespasses Act* that any person who trespasses upon land, the property of another, upon or through which he has been requested by the owner not to enter, is guilty of an offence. If there is to be any change in this statute law, if A is to be given the right to enter and remain on the land of B against the will of B, it would seem to me that such a change must be made by the enacting institution, the Legislature, which is representative of the people and designed to manifest the political will, and not by this Court.

I would allow the appeal, set aside the judgment of the Court of Appeal for Manitoba and restore the judgment of the County Court Judge.

LASKIN C.J.C. (dissenting): — An ancient legal concept, trespass, is urged here in all its pristine force by a shopping centre owner in respect of areas of the shopping centre which have been opened by him to public use, and necessarily so because of the commercial character of the enterprise based on tenancies by operators of a variety of businesses. To say in such circumstances that the shopping centre owner may, at his whim, order any member of the public out of the shopping centre on penalty or liability for trespass if he refuses to leave, does not make sense if there is no proper reason in that member's conduct or activity to justify the order to leave.

Trespass in its civil law sense, and in its penal sense too, connotes unjustified invasion of another's possession. Where a dwelling-house is concerned, the privacy associated with that kind of land-holding makes any unjustified or unprivileged entry a trespass, technically so even if no damage occurs. A Court, however, would be likely to award only nominal damages for mere unprivileged entry upon another's private premises where no injury occurs, and it is probable that the plaintiff would be ordered to pay costs for seeking empty vindication. If the trespasser refuses to leave when ordered, he could be forcibly removed, but, more likely, the police would be called and the issue would be resolved at that point, or a basis for an action, or for a penal charge would arise. In short, apart from privileged entry, a matter to which I will return in these reasons, there is a significant element of protection of privacy in resort to trespass to exclude or remove persons from private dwellings.

The considerations which underlie the protection of private residences cannot apply to the same degree to a shopping centre in respect of its parking areas, roads and sidewalks. Those amenities are closer in character to public roads and sidewalks than to a private dwelling. All that can be urged from a theoretical point of view to assimilate them to private dwellings is to urge that if property is privately owned, no matter the use to which it is put, trespass is as appropriate in the one case as in the other and it does not matter that possession, the invasion of which is basic to trespass, is recognizable in the one case but not in the other. There is here, on this assimilation, a legal injury albeit no actual injury. This is a use of theory which does not square with economic or social fact under the circumstances of the present case.

What does a shopping centre owner protect, for what invaded interest of his does he seek vindication in ousting members of the public from sidewalks and roadways and parking areas in the shopping centre? There is no challenge to his title and none to his possession nor to his privacy when members of the public use those amenities. Should he be allowed to choose what members of the public come into those areas when they have been opened to all without discrimination? Human rights legislation would prevent him from discriminating on account of race, colour or creed or national origin, but counsel for the appellant would have it that members of the public can otherwise be excluded or ordered to leave by mere whim. It is contended that it is unnecessary that there be a reason that can stand rational assessment. Disapproval of the owner, in assertion of a remote control over the "public" areas of the shopping centre, whether it be disapproval of picketing or disapproval of the wearing of hats or anything equally innocent, may be converted (so it is argued) into a basis of ouster of members of the public. Can the common law be so devoid of reason as to tolerate this kind of whimsy where public areas of a shopping centre are concerned?

. . .

It seems to me that the present case involves a search for an appropriate legal framework for new social facts which show up the inaptness of an old doctrine developed upon a completely different social foundation. The history of trespass indicates that its introduction as a private means of redress was directed to breaches of the peace or to acts likely to provoke such breaches. Its subsequent enlargement beyond these concerns does not mean it must be taken as incapable of further adaptation, but must be applied on what I can only characterize as a level of abstraction which ignores the facts. Neither logic nor experience (to borrow from Holmes' opening sentence in his classic *The Common Law*) supports such a conclusion.

Recognition of the need for balancing the interests of the shopping centre owner with competing interests of members of the public when in or on the public areas of the shopping centre, engaged Courts in the United States a little earlier than it did the Courts in this country. Making every allowance for any constitutional basis upon which Courts there grappled with this problem, their analyses are helpful because they arise out of the same economic and social setting in which the problem arises here. Thus, there is emphasis on unrestricted access to shopping centres from public streets, and on the fact that access by the public is the very reason for the existence of shopping centres; there is the comparison drawn between the public markets of long ago and the shopping centre as a modern market place; there is the appreciation that in the light of the interests involved there can be no solution to their reconciliation by positing a flat all or nothing approach. The cases in the United States, and I cite a few of them here without further elaboration appear to me to reject the appellant's proposition that (as his counsel put it) "the issue is trespass, not picketing" because that, in my opinion, involves a predetermination without regard to the issues of fact.

. . .

A more appropriate approach, to which I adverted earlier, is to recognize a continuing privilege in using the areas of the shopping centre provided for public passage subject to limitations arising out of the nature of the activity thereon and to the object pursued thereby, and subject as well to a limitation against material damage. There is analogy in existing conceptions of privilege as an answer to intentional torts, such as trespass.

. . .

I would agree that it does not follow that because unrestricted access is given to members of the public to certain areas of the shopping centre during business hours, those areas are available at all times during those hours and in all circumstances to any kind of peaceful activity by members of the public, regardless of the interest being prompted by that activity and regardless of the numbers of members of the public who are involved. The Court will draw lines here as it does in other branches of the law as may be appropriate in the light of the legal principle and particular facts. In the present case it is the respondent who has been injured rather than the shopping centre owner.

I would dismiss the appeal.

[Martland, Judson, Ritchie, Pigeon, and De Grandpré JJ. concurred with Dickson J., and Spence and Beetz JJ. concurred with Laskin C.J.C. Note that the order of the reasons for judgment has been reversed.]

NOTES AND QUESTIONS

1. Do you agree with Dickson J. that *Peters* and the statute resolve the issue? Can Laskin C.J.C.'s judgment be reconciled with *Peters* and the statute?

2. Would Dickson J.'s analysis and conclusion have been the same if the case had been a common law action for trespass, rather than a prosecution under the Petty Trespasses Act?

3. How did Dickson J. and Laskin C.J.C. deal with the American cases? Whose analysis is more pursuasive?

4. Does Dickson J.'s judgment reflect an inherent bias in the common law process? Would you agree with Colangelo's statement in "Labour Law: *Harrison v. Carswell*" (1976), 34 U. of T. Fac. L.R. 236, that Dickson J.'s judgment lacks creativity? What values underlie the judgments of Laskin C.J.C. and Dickson J.?

5. Is Laskin C.J.C.'s rationale for modifying the traditional definition of trespass compelling? What impact would Laskin C.J.C.'s approach have on the provincial offence of trespass and on the common law tort? How was Laskin C.J.C. suggesting that the conflicting interests of plaza owners and picketers be resolved? Can meaningful distinctions be drawn between different types of landowners and picketers?

In *Wilcox v. Police*, [1994] 1 N.Z.L.R. 243 (H.C.), 10 anti-abortionists were convicted of trespass for continuing to block entry to a hospital after they had been told to leave. The defendants sought to justify the trespass on the need to protect the unborn from unlawful abortions. Although the court accepted the honesty of the defendants' beliefs, it still convicted them in any event. How would Laskin C.J.C. have resolved this case? See also *Webb v. Attewell* (1993), 18 C.C.L.T. 299 (B.C. C.A.), where the court emphasized that a landowner has an unqualified right to refuse and control entry.

6. Manitoba amended its trespass legislation shortly after the decision in *Harrison*. In general terms, the amendment provided that individuals who peacefully protest outside of premises which are normally open to the public are not guilty of an offence under the Act. See Petty Trespasses Act, R.S.M. 1987, c. P-50, s. 4.

7. Is it appropriate for courts to resolve the value conflicts in cases such as *Harrison*? Are such decisions better left to the legislature?

8. Section 2 of the Charter guarantees a broad range of fundamental freedoms, including freedom of expression, peaceful assembly and association. However, by virtue of s. 32, the Charter does not apply to private persons and associations in a common law tort action. See *281856 B.C. Ltd. v. Kamloops Revelstoke Okanagan Building Traders Union* (1986), 37 C.C.L.T. 262 (B.C. C.A.). See generally, *Harrison v. University of British Columbia* (1990), 77 D.L.R. (4th) 55 (S.C.C.); and Domes, "The Courts, the Common Law, and the Constitutional Imperative: Beyond Dolphin Delivery" (1989), 27 Alta. L. Rev. 430. Nevertheless, since the Charter does apply to both federal and provincial legislation, trespass legislation which limits or infringes the rights guaranteed by the Charter may be struck down. If the legislation is struck down, there can be no prosecution or statutory cause of action based on such provisions. See *R. v. Layton* (1986), 38 C.C.C. (3d) 550 (Ont. Prov. Ct.), a case that is similar to *Harrison*.

9. *Harrison* raises the issue of the revocability of a licence to enter private property. See also *Gross v. Wright*, [1923] S.C.R. 214; *R. v. Burko* (1969), 3 D.L.R. (3d) 330 (Ont. Mag. Ct.); and *Dehn v. A.G.*, [1988] 2 N.Z.L.R. 564 (H.C.).

10. Increasingly, trespass actions have been brought in native land claim disputes. See, for example, *Can. Pacific Ltd. v. Paul*, [1988] 2 S.C.R. 654, where the Supreme Court of Canada granted a permanent injunction to restrain members of an Indian band from blocking a railway line which was located on land claimed by the band. See also *Myran, Meeches v. R.*, [1976] 1 W.W.R. 196 (S.C.C.); *A.G. Can. v. Vantour* (1979), 63 A.P.R. 434 (N.B. C.A.); and *Johnson v. B.C. Hydro and Power Authority* (1981), 16 C.C.L.T. 10 (B.C. S.C.). While a trespass action may resolve a specific legal dispute, it cannot address the native communities' longstanding grievances concerning land claims and treaty rights.

11. The plaintiff may have the option of bringing the action under the trespass legislation, rather than the common law. For example, the Trespass to Property Act, R.S.O. 1990, c. T.21, provides:

12.—(1) Where a person is convicted of an offence under section 2, and a person has suffered damage caused by the person convicted during the commission of the offence, the court shall, on the request of the prosecutor and with the consent of the person who suffered the damage, determine the damages and shall make a judgment for damages against the person convicted in favour of the person who suffered the damage, but no judgment shall be for an amount in excess of $1,000.

(2) Where a prosecution under section 2 is conducted by a private prosecutor, and the defendant is convicted, unless the court is of the opinion that the prosecution was not necessary for the protection of the occupier or his interests, the court shall determine the actual costs reasonably incurred in conducting the prosecution and, despite section 60 of the *Provincial Offences Act*, shall order those costs to be paid by the defendant to the prosecutor.

(3) A judgment for damages under subsection 1, or an award of costs under subsection 2, shall be in addition to any fine that is imposed under this Act.

(4) A judgment for damages under subsection 1 extinguishes the right of the person in whose favour the judgment is made to bring a civil action for damages against the person convicted arising out of the same facts.

(5) The failure to request or refusal to grant a judgment for damages under subsection 1 does not affect a right to bring a civil action for damages arising out of the same facts.

The British Columbia and Prince Edward Island Acts contain similar provisions requiring trespassers to provide damages. However, unlike the Ontario and B.C. statutes, the P.E.I. statute does not extinguish the right to bring a civil action once damages have been awarded under the statute. See also the Criminal Code, s. 430.

12. Note that the Alberta, Manitoba, Ontario, New Brunswick, and Newfoundland trespass legislation authorizes an occupant to arrest trespassers without a warrant. See also the Criminal Code, ss. 40, 41 and 177.

2. Trespass and Nuisance

We discuss the law of private nuisance in detail later in the text; it is only introduced at this stage to distinguish it from trespass. A private nuisance may be defined as a substantial and unreasonable interference with the use and enjoyment of land in the possession of another. Unlike in trespass to land, a plaintiff must establish damages to recover in nuisance. The major functional distinction between the two actions is that trespass protects possession, whereas nuisance protects the quality of that possession. The law of nuisance is concerned with the effect of the defendant's conduct on the plaintiff's use and enjoyment of the land, and not with the nature of that conduct. Liability may be imposed in nuisance even if the defendant's conduct was neither intentional nor negligent.

KERR v. REVELSTOKE BLDG. MATERIALS LTD.

[1976] W.W.D. 139, 71 D.L.R. (3d) 134 (Alta. S.C.)

SHANNON J.: — In this action the plaintiffs allege trespass, nuisance and negligence. They seek an injunction and damages . . .

During his youth Mr. Kerr worked in a general store and later, in 1935, operated a service station and garage at Coleman, Alberta. He and his wife decided that they wanted to build and operate a motel business . . .

The site selected was chosen for its tranquility and scenic beauty. Looking to the south from the site they had a magnificent view of a river valley in a natural state, except for a railway line, and beyond that foothills and a range of rocky mountains dominated by the Crowsnest Mountain peak.

They used approximately two acres of that parcel for the motel site. The remainder was used for agricultural purposes. On the motel site they built a residence and six motel units which were opened for business in 1951. The business was known as "Chinook Motel". In the summer of 1953 two more units were constructed and opened for business. Two additional units were constructed and opened in the summer of 1955. Mr. Kerr was in charge of construction operations and was assisted by his wife and sons. Some outside assistance was obtained but it was primarily a family project as was the motel operation thereafter . . .

The defendant is an Alberta lumber company that has carried on an active business in this Province for many years.

It commenced business across the highway from the Chinook Motel in 1958. A planing mill and small teepee burner went into operation that year. The defendant's loading ramp was approximately 800 ft. from the office door of the motel. A sawmill was moved to the same site and commenced operating in 1968. Chipper and debarker operations were added to the sawmill complex in 1971. Also, other industries, such as Phillips Cables Ltd., Sartoga Processing Co. Ltd. and Petro-Chemicals Ltd. were established in the valley. The operation of the defendant's planing mill and teepee burner in 1958 caused the plaintiffs some concern and disturbance but the situation worsened when the sawmill, chipper and debarker operations were introduced later.

It should be noted that the defendant's decision to bring the chipper and debarker operations to the site in 1971 was influenced to some extent by the fact that it received financial inducements from the federal Government to do so. The Crowsnest Pass area was then designated as a depressed economic area and the Government provided incentives to encourage industry to locate there.

From time to time the plaintiffs complained about smoke, sawdust, dust, fly ash and objectionable noises emanating from the defendant's operations. The defendant tried to ameliorate the situation by enclosing a conveyor belt in 1971, lubricating the conveyer belt with rock-drill oil in 1972, enclosing the planer in 1972-73, enclosing the chipper in 1973, enlarging the garage for warm-up of machinery in 1972 and adding an under-fire to the teepee burners to improve their efficiency.

Notwithstanding the foregoing efforts on the part of the defendant the plaintiffs continued to complain and in the fall of 1971 they closed their motel operation and it has never been reopened.

I am satisfied on the evidence that they have established a cause of action founded in trespass. The evidence establishes that their premises were invaded from time to time by smoke, sawdust, fly ash and objectionable sounds. The physical invasion of their premises by sawdust and fly ash was so severe on occasion that it interfered with their use and enjoyment of their property. Actual samples of fly ash were collected and placed in vials by the plaintiff James Runciman Kerr, and were entered in evidence as exhibits.

"Every invasion of property, be it ever so minute, is a trespass": *Entick v. Carrington* (1765), 19 St. Tr. 1030 at p. 1066; *Salmond on the Law of Torts*, 15th ed. (1969), at p. 49; *Boyle v. Rogers*, [1921] 2 W.W.R. 704, 31 Man. R. 263; affirmed [1922] 1 W.W.R. 206, 31 Man. R. 421 (Man. C.A.).

"It is a trespass to place any chattel upon the plaintiff's land, or to cause any physical object or noxious substance to cross the boundary of the plaintiff's land ...": *Salmond on the Law of Torts*, 15th ed. (1969), at p. 53.

I am also convinced by the preponderance of evidence that the plaintiffs are entitled to succeed in nuisance. The fly ash, smoke and dust which assaulted the plaintiff's premises from time to time was serious enough in itself, but the objectionable sounds which emanated from the sawmill operations were such that they constituted a nuisance which was so serious it substantially interfered with the operation of the plaintiff's motel business and with their use and enjoyment of their premises. Also the concern, anxiety and discomfort generated by the situation had a harmful effect on the health of Mrs. Kerr. She became nervous, preoccupied, humourless and irritable and that in turn had a negative effect on her husband

and his enjoyment of life. The offensive noises were not constant. They came and went depending upon the state of the lumber market and the resultant activities across the highway at the sawmill.

The intensity and frequency of the objectionable noises increased substantially after the sawmill commenced operating in 1968 and again later in 1971 when the chipper and debarker were added. It is difficult to provide a comprehensive description of the objectionable noises because they were many and varied. Various witnesses, who were guests at the motel, used such adjectives as "squealing, clanking, whining, ear piercing, etc.", to describe them. Another witness referred to the noise as "a high pitched squeal that seemed to go on all night", while another likened the sound to that which is given off by a jet engine. In any event it was so intense at times that it interfered with ordinary conversation in the plaintiff's yard. It also seriously interfered with their rest and sleep and with that of their motel guests because the sawmill carried on its operations at night and during the early morning hours.

On the facts of this case I am unable to find that the defendant was negligent in its operations. The simple fact is that the two business operations were not compatible.

In these circumstances an injunction would not be an appropriate remedy and that form of relief will not be granted. However, the plaintiffs are entitled to succeed in trespass and nuisance and the appropriate remedy is damages ...

The plaintiffs are awarded judgment against the defendant in the amount of $30,000.

The parties may speak to the matter of costs.

NOTES AND QUESTIONS

1. In *Mann v. Saulnier* (1959), 19 D.L.R. (2d) 130 (N.B. C.A.), snow and frost caused the top of the defendant's fence to encroach on the plaintiff's land by several inches. The court held that this was neither a trespass because the injury was indirectly caused, nor a nuisance because no special damages were proven. Can you suggest additional reasons why the trespass and nuisance claims should be dismissed?

2. A substantial and unreasonable interference is one that is offensive and inconvenient to a reasonable person. The unreasonableness of the interference is assessed in terms of the plaintiff's use of his property and the relative interests of the defendant and plaintiff. See *Devon Lumber Co. v. MacNeill* (1987), 42 C.C.L.T. 192 (N.B. C.A.).

3. In *Kerr*, which interferences were held to be trespasses and which were held to be nuisances? Do you agree with Shannon J.'s analysis? See also *Muirhead v. Timber Brothers Sand and Gravel Ltd.* (1977), 3 C.C.L.T. 1 (Ont. H.C.).

4. Traditionally, the tort of trespass to land has been limited to the direct, intentional intrusion of objects that are visible to the naked eye. However, in *Martin v. Reynolds Metal Co.* (1959), 342 P. (2d) 790 (Oregon S.C.), the defendant manufacturer was held liable in trespass because its operations caused invisible fluoride particles to settle on the plaintiff's land making it unfit for cattle. The judge rejected the argument that the size of the invading object should be a criterion for distinguishing between trespass and nuisance, preferring instead to emphasize the issue of energy and force. As in *Harrison*, the court in *Martin* was faced with the task of applying established legal principles to new situations. Did the court in *Martin* make a compelling argument in favour of altering the traditional principles of trespass to land? What impact would the principles in *Martin* have on the distinction between trespass and nuisance? What would be the result of applying these principles in *Kerr*? Apparently, the Canadian courts have not considered the approach used in *Martin*. See "Deposit of Gaseous and Invisible Solid Industrial Wastes Held to Constitute Trespass" (1960), 60 Columbia L.R. 877; and Keeton, "Trespass, Nuisance, and Strict Liability" (1959), Columbia L.R. 457.

5. Explain what action or actions you would bring in the following situations:

(a) The defendant's seismographic explosions cause vibrations which damage the plaintiff's well. *Phillips v. Calif. Standard Co.* (1960), 31 W.W.R. 331 (Alta. S.C.).

(b) Golf balls from the defendant's golf course are hit so frequently onto the plaintiff's land that he is unable to use his backyard. *Segal v. Derrick Golf and Winter Club* (1977), 76 D.L.R. (3d) 746 (Alta. T.D.). See also *Miller v. Jackson*, [1977] Q.B. 966 (C.A.).

(c) The Ministry of Transport's use of salt on the highway results in a salt spray being deposited on the plaintiff's fruit orchards causing substantial damages. *Schenck v. R.; Rokeby v. R.* (1981), 20 C.C.L.T. 128 (Ont. H.C.); aff'd. (1988), 50 D.L.R. (4th) 384 (S.C.C.).

(d) The defendant's construction causes silt to be carried into the plaintiff's reservoir that contains his domestic water supply. *Steadman v. Erickson Gold Mining Corp.* (1987), 43 D.L.R. (4th) 712 (B.C. S.C.), aff'd. (1989), 56 D.L.R. (4th) 577 (B.C. C.A.).

(e) The defendant's lumber mill produces a very fine dust that enters the plaintiff's home causing serious inconvenience and annoyance. See *Devon Lumber Co. v. MacNeill* (1987), 42 C.C.L.T. 192 (N.B. C.A.).

6. The courts almost always exercise their discretion to grant injunctions in trespass cases, whereas in nuisance they are much more reluctant to do so. Why do the principles for granting injunctions vary in trespass and nuisance? See Sharpe, *Injunctions and Specific Performance*, 2nd ed. (1992), 4-1 to 4-37.

In *Woollerton v. Richard Costain*, [1970] 1 All E.R. 483 (Ch. D.), the defendant's crane periodically swung over the plaintiff's building, causing no damage and little interference with the plaintiff's use and enjoyment of his land. The judge felt compelled by authority to grant an injunction to restrain the defendant's trespass, but suspended its operation until the project was completed. The judge noted that the defendant offered to settle but the plaintiff stubbornly refused. He suggested that such disputes should be negotiated between the parties outside of the courts. What is the impact of this approach on the distinction between trespass and nuisance? The decision to suspend the injunction in *Woollerton* has been seriously questioned. See *Charrington v. Simons & Co. Ltd.*, [1971] 2 All E.R. 588 at 592 (C.A.); *Graham v. K.D. Morris and Sons Pty. Ltd.*, [1974] Qd. R. 1; and *Lewvest Ltd. v. Scotia Towers Ltd.* (1981), 126 D.L.R. (3d) 239 (Nfld. S.C.), aff'd. (1983), 149 D.L.R. (3d) 371 (Nfld. C.A.). But see *Kingsbridge Dev. Inc. v. Hanson Needler Corp.* (1990), 71 O.R. (2d) 636 (H.C.).

3. Trespass to Airspace and Subsoil

(a) TRESPASS TO AIRSPACE

The elements of this action are essentially the same as those of trespass to land. A defendant may be held liable for trespass to airspace for any direct and intentional physical intrusion into the airspace above the plaintiff's land. However, the need for unfettered air traffic has resulted in a distinction being drawn between overflights and other types of intrusions. Although the theories concerning overflights vary, they all tend to limit the landowner's rights in order to facilitate air traffic.

In *Atlantic Aviation Ltd. v. N.S. Light & Power Co.* (1965), 55 D.L.R. (2d) 554 (N.S. S.C.), the court stated in *obiter* that an overflight at any altitude constitutes a trespass, but the overflight will be privileged if it is done for a legitimate purpose, in a reasonable manner, and at a height that does not unreasonably interfere with the possessor's use of his land. On the central issue of the case, the court ruled that aviators have no common law right to prevent landowners from putting up buildings or transmission wires that might impede flights in and out of nearby airports.

BERNSTEIN v. SKYVIEWS & GEN.

[1978] Q.B. 479, [1977] 2 All E.R. 902

GRIFFITHS J. . . . By the statement of claim it is alleged that the defendants wrongfully entered the air space above Lord Bernstein's premises in order to take an aerial photograph of his house and were thus guilty of trespass and an actionable invasion of his right to privacy. The defendants admit that they took the aerial photograph but deny that they entered the air space above the premises to do so; they say that the photograph was taken when the aircraft was flying over adjoining land not owned by Lord Bernstein. Alternatively they say that if they did fly over Lord Bernstein's land to take the photograph they had his implied permission to do so . . .

I turn now to the law. The plaintiff claims that as owner of the land he is also owner of the air space above the land, or at least has the right to exclude any entry into the air space above his land. He relies upon the old Latin maxim, cujus est solum ejus est usque ad coelum et ad inferos, a colourful phrase often upon the lips of lawyers since it was first coined by Accursius in Bologna in the 13th century. There are a number of cases in which the maxim has been used by English judges, but an examination of those cases shows that they have all been concerned with structures attached to the adjoining land, such as overhanging buildings, signs or telegraph wires, and for their solution it has not been necessary for the judge to cast his eyes towards the heavens; he has been concerned with the rights of the owner in the air space immediately adjacent to the surface of the land . . .

In *Gifford v. Dent*, [1926] W.N. 336, Romer J. held that it was a trespass to erect a sign that projected 4 ft. 8 ins. over the plaintiff's forecourt and ordered it to be removed. He invoked the old maxim in his judgment; the report reads:

> . . . the plaintiffs were tenants of the forecourt and were accordingly tenants of the space above the forecourt usque ad coelum, it seemed to him that the projection was clearly a trespass upon the property of the plaintiffs.

That decision was followed by McNair J. in *Kelsen v. Imperial Tobacco Co. (of Great Britain and Ireland) Ltd.*, [1957] 2 Q.B. 334, in which he granted a mandatory injunction ordering the defendants to remove a sign which projected only 8 ins. over the plaintiff's property. The plaintiff relies strongly upon this case, and in particular upon the following passage when, after citing the judgment of Romer J. to which I have already referred, McNair J. continued, at p. 345:

> That decision, I think, has been recognised by the textbook writers, and in particular by the late Professor Winfield, as stating the true law. It is not without significance that the legislature in the Air Navigation Act 1920, section 9 (replaced by section 40(1) of the Civil Aviation Act 1949), found it necessary expressly to negative the action of trespass or nuisance arising from the mere fact of an aeroplane passing through the air above the land. It seems to me clearly to indicate that the legislature at least were not taking the same view of the matter as Lord Ellenborough in *Pickering v. Rudd*, but rather taking the view accepted in the later cases, such as the *Wandsworth District* case, subsequently followed by Romer J. in *Gifford v. Dent*. Accordingly, I reach the conclusion that a trespass and not a mere nuisance was created by the invasion of the plaintiff's air-space by this sign.

I very much doubt if in that passage McNair J. was intending to hold that the plaintiff's rights in the air space continued to an unlimited height or "ad coelum" as Mr. Gray submits. The point that the judge was considering was whether the sign was a trespass or a nuisance at the very low level at which it projected. This to my mind is clearly indicated by his reference to *Winfield on Tort*, 6th ed. (1954) in which the text reads, at p. 380: "it is submitted that trespass will be committed by [aircraft] to the air space if they fly so low as to come within the area of ordinary user." The author in that passage is careful to limit the trespass to the height at which it is contemplated an owner might be expected to make use of the air space as a natural incident of the user of his land. If, however, the judge was by his reference to the Civil Aviation Act 1949 and his disapproval of the views of Lord Ellenborough in *Pickering v. Rudd* (1815) 4 Camp. 219, indicating the opinion that the flight of an aircraft at whatever height constituted a trespass at common law, I must respectfully disagree.

I do not wish to cast any doubts upon the correctness of the decision upon its own particular facts. It may be a sound and practical rule to regard any incursion into the air space at a height which may interfere with the ordinary user of the land as a trespass rather than a nuisance. Adjoining owners then know where they stand; they have no right to erect structures overhanging or passing over their neighbours' land and there is no room for argument whether they are thereby causing damage or annoyance to their neighbours about which there may be much room for argument and uncertainty. But wholly different considerations arise when considering the passage of aircraft at a height which in no way affects the user of the land.

There is no direct authority on this question, but as long ago as 1815 Lord Ellenborough in *Pickering v. Rudd* expressed the view that it would not be a trespass to pass over a man's land in a balloon; and in *Saunders v. Smith* (1838) 2 Jur. 491, Shadwell V.-C. said, at p. 492:

> Thus, upon the maxim of law, 'Cujus est solum ejus est usque ad coelum' an injunction might be granted for cutting timber and severing crops; but, suppose a person should apply to restrain an aerial wrong, as by sailing over a person's freehold in a balloon; this surely would be too contemptible to be taken notice of . . .

I can find no support in authority for the view that a landowner's rights in the air space above his property extend to an unlimited height. In *Wandsworth Board of Works v. United Telephone Co. Ltd.*, 13 Q.B.D. 904 Bowen L.J. described the maxim, usque ad coelum, as a fanciful phrase, to which I would add that if applied literally it is a fanciful notion leading to the absurdity of a trespass at common law being committed by a satellite every time it passes over a suburban garden. The academic writers speak with one voice in rejecting the uncritical and literal application of the maxim: see by way of example only *Winfield and Jolowicz on Tort*, 10th ed. (1975), p. 305, *Salmond on Torts*, 16th ed. (1973), p. 44, *Shawcross & Beaumont on Air Law*, 3rd ed. (1966), p. 536, *McNair, The Law of the Air*, 3rd ed. (1964), p. 97 and *Halsbury's Laws of England*, 4th ed., vol. 7 (1974), p. 684. I accept their collective approach as correct. The problem is to balance the rights of an owner to enjoy the use of his land against the rights of the general public to take advantage of all that science now offers in the use of air space. This balance is in my judgment best struck in our present society by restricting the rights of an owner in the air space above his land to such height as is necessary for the ordinary use and enjoyment of his land and the structures upon it, and declaring that above that height he has no greater rights in the air space than any other member of the public.

Applying this test to the facts of this case, I find that the defendants' aircraft did not infringe any rights in the plaintiff's air space, and thus no trespass was committed. It was on any view of the evidence flying many hundreds of feet above the ground and it is not suggested that by its mere presence in the air space it caused any interference with any use to which the plaintiff put or might wish to put his land. The plaintiff's complaint is not that the aircraft interfered with the use of his land but that a photograph was taken from it. There is, however, no law against taking a photograph, and the mere taking of a photograph cannot turn an act which is not a trespass into the plaintiff's air space into one that is a trespass ...

NOTES AND QUESTIONS

1. How does the court's approach to overflights in *Atlantic Aviation* differ from liability based on private nuisance?

2. In *A.G. Man. v. Campbell* (1985), 32 C.C.L.T. 57 (Man. C.A.), the defendant built a 70-foot tower on his land to obstruct the adjacent airport and to prevent its further development. The plaintiff's claim in nuisance was successful and an injunction was granted ordering the defendant to dismantle the tower. How would you reconcile this case with *Atlantic Aviation*? See also *Hashem and Hashem v. N.S. Power Corp.* (1980), 43 N.S.R. (2d) 150 (S.C.), where the defendant's tower and lines, although an unwelcome annoyance to pilots, did not interfere with the safe use of the plaintiff's aerodrome, and thus did not constitute an actionable nuisance.

3. Summarize the principles governing tort liability for overflights based on *Bernstein*. What is the basic difference between *Bernstein* and *Atlantic Aviation*, and what is its significance? Which position do you favour?

4. Although the Canadian courts have clearly rejected the *usque ad coelum* maxim, they have not addressed whether *Atlantic* or *Bernstein* should govern overflights. Nevertheless, the Canadian authorities appear to be more consistent with *Bernstein*. See *Lacroix v. R.*, [1954] 4 D.L.R. 470 (Ex. Ct.); *The Queen in Right of Man. v. Air Can.* (1980), 111 D.L.R. (3d) 513 (S.C.C.); *Didow v. Alta. Power Ltd.*, [1988] 5 W.W.R. 606 (Alta. C.A.); and *Kingsbridge Development Inc. v. Hanson Needler Corp.* (1990), 71 O.R. (2d) 636 (H.C.). See, generally, Wherry and Condon, "Aerial Trespass Under the Restatement of the Law of Torts" (1935), 6 Air Law R. 113; Richardson, "Private Property Rights in the Air Space at Common Law" (1953), 31 Can. Bar Rev. 117; and Silverman and Evans, "Aeronautical Noise in Canada" (1972), 10 Osgoode Hall L.J. 607.

5. As indicated by *Bernstein*, it was generally accepted that any direct and intentional intrusion into the airspace within the plaintiff's zone of use constitutes a trespass. This proposition appeared to establish the defendant's liability in trespass for shooting across, swinging a crane over, or building a sign that encroached on the plaintiff's land. See *Big Point Club v. Lozon*, [1943] 4 D.L.R. 136 (Ont. H.C.); *Kelsen v. Imperial Tobacco Co.*, [1957] 2 All E.R. 343; and *Dahlberg v. Naydiuk* (1969), 10 D.L.R. (3d) 319 (Man. C.A.).

However, it has been suggested that temporary intrusions, such as those involving a crane, should be treated as nuisances rather than trespasses to encourage the parties to resolve the conflict. See *Woollerton v. Richard Costain*, [1970] 1 All E.R. 483 (Ch. D.). For a searing criticism of the view that landowners have any obligation to accommodate their neighbours, entrepreneurial or otherwise, see *Austin v. Rescon Construction (1984) Ltd.* (1989), 48 C.C.L.T. 64 (B.C. C.A.). See also Irvine, "Some Thoughts on Trespass to Airspace" (1986), 37 C.C.L.T. 99.

(b) A NOTE ON TRESPASS TO SUBSOIL

Subterranean intrusions raise the same issue as intrusions into airspace; namely, which interferences should be governed by trespass and which by nuisance. In *Austin v. Rescon Construction (1984) Ltd.* (1989), 48 C.C.L.T. 64 (B.C. C.A.), the defendant was held liable in trespass for inserting steel anchor rods beneath the plaintiff's land at three different unidentified depths. Aside from causing temporary vibrations, the insertion of the rods caused no damage to the plaintiff's land, did not interfere with the foundations of the house or limit the plaintiffs use of his property. In increasing the punitive damage award to $30,000, the Court of Appeal emphasized that landowners may deny entry for any reason they choose and have no obligation to accomodate a contractor or anyone else wishing to enter. In *Epstein v. Cressey Development Corp.*, [1992] 3 W.W.R. 566 (B.C. C.A.), the defendant was held liable for $45,000 in punitive damages for temporarily inserting anchor rods into the plaintiff's subsoil.

The court in *Austin* did not address the issue of whether the depth of the intrusion would affect the cause of action. However, in *Boehringer v. Montalto* (1931), 254 N.Y.S. 276 (S.C.), the court held that the existence of a sewer 150 feet underground was not a trespass. The court concluded that a landowner's title to the subsoil extends only to the depth which he can reasonably use.

NOTES AND QUESTIONS

1. Can you reconcile *Austin* and *Epstein* with the cases that suggest that temporary intrusions into airspace ought to be treated as nuisances?

2. Can you reconcile *Austin* and *Epstein* with *Boehringer*? See also *Haynes v. Nfld. Telephone Co.* (1985), 168 A.P.R. 162 (Nfld. Dist. Ct.); and *Engemoen Holdings Ltd. v. 100 Mile House*, [1985] 3 W.W.R. 47 (B.C. S.C.).

3. In *Edwards v. Lee's Adm'r.* (1936), 96 S.W. (2d) 1028 (Ky. C.A.), the defendant operated a very profitable cave touring business from an entrance located on his own property. The plaintiff discovered that one-third of the cave was under his property, but there was no entrance from his land to the cave which was 360 feet below. The court concluded that the defendant was a trespasser and granted an injunction and an accounting. Pursuant to the accounting, which is an equitable remedy, the plaintiff was awarded a share of the defendant's net proceeds from the cave tours. Do you agree that the defendant was a trespasser? If so, how would you reconcile *Edwards* and *Boehringer*? Could the plaintiff have recovered in nuisance? Had the plaintiff not sought an accounting, what damages would you have awarded for the trespass?

REVIEW PROBLEMS

1. Amy and Bruce own adjoining rural properties. Amy has an orchard, and Bruce produces organically grown vegetables for health food stores. On a day when a strong wind was blowing directly onto Bruce's property, Amy sprayed chemicals on her fruit trees. A large quantity of the chemicals drifted onto Bruce's mature vegetables. No apparent damage was done, but Bruce's usual customers refused to purchase the crop because it came in contact with the spray. As a result, Bruce was forced to sell the vegetables as pig food. The spray also killed the bees on Bruce's property, interfering with the pollination and the production of the new crop. Amy knew that Bruce grew vegetables, but she was unaware that they were sold as organically grown crops. Bruce now seeks your advice on suing Amy for his losses.

2. Albert is an experienced private pilot. Early one Sunday morning in February, he and his son rented a plane from his flying club to do some stunts. Although the officer at the club had directed Albert to a particular plane, Albert misunderstood and took a plane of the same model that belonged to Bob, an instructor at the club. The key fit Bob's plane and Albert did not realize his mistake. The plane intended for Albert's use had been cleared for stunt flying, but Bob's had not. The clearance involved a careful check of the plane to ensure that nothing would come loose.

Once Albert got over open country, he decided that it was safe to begin. As the plane somer-saulted a tool box came loose and burst through the door of the plane. The box crashed onto a farm-house some 1,000 meters below, severely damaging a greenhouse. The cold winter air ruined the valuable orchids that were growing inside. While Albert's son struggled to close the door, Albert rapidly reduced his altitude to bring down the air pressure. He swooped so low over a barn that he frightened a horse, causing it to kick its stall, breaking a back leg. As soon as he could, Albert returned to the airport.

You have now been asked to advise Albert on his potential liability.

6

THE DEFENCE OF CONSENT

1. An Introduction to the Defences
2. General Principles of Consent
3. Factors Which Vitiate Consent: Duress, Fraud, Mistake, and Public Policy
4. Consent to Criminal or Immoral Acts
5. Consent to Treatment and Counselling

1. An Introduction to the Defences

Once the plaintiff establishes that the defendant has committed an intentional tort, it must then be determined whether liability will be imposed. Both the common law and statutes recognize a number of defences that the defendant may raise to privilege her tortious conduct. For analytical purposes, we have divided these defences into three categories — consent; defences related to the protection of person and property; and defences arising from the assertion of legal authority. The latter two will be discussed in the following chapters. The defences are not mutually exclusive and a defendant may plead two or more defences in a single tort action.

2. General Principles of Consent

(a) INTRODUCTION

There is considerable older authority for the view that consent is not a defence. Rather, it is argued that the lack of consent is a substantive element of the intentional torts. Thus, the plaintiff must assert and prove the absence of consent to establish the tort.

Some authors accept this proposition in reference to certain intentional torts, but not others. Although the Canadian courts have not squarely addressed this issue, they have in recent years treated consent as a defence that the defendant must argue and prove.

The issue of consent must be framed specifically in terms of the tort action in issue. In other words, did the plaintiff consent to the act giving rise to the tort action? The consent may be given explicitly either verbally or in writing, or implicitly by participation, demeanour or other behaviour. It is generally accepted that consent to an act extends to the normal risks inherent in that act. Thus, a hockey player in a full contact league will be viewed as consenting to being body-checked. Although this principle is easy to apply in some cases, it is extremely difficult to apply in others. For example, is the hockey player also consenting to the various infractions of the rules that typically or may foreseeably occur in a game?

(b) IMPLIED CONSENT

WRIGHT v. McLEAN

(1956), 7 D.L.R. (2d) 253 (B.C. S.C.)

MacFarlane J.: — . . . Four boys were playing near a mound of earth thrown up in an excavation incident to the construction of a house on a city lot. They were tossing mud balls or lumps of clay found on the pile of earth there at each other. The infant defendant was passing on his bicycle delivering the afternoon paper around 4:30 p.m. One of these mud balls or lumps came up around the infant defendant and another he says went through the spokes of the wheel of the bicycle he was riding. He was not in a hurry, so he dismounted, pushing his bicycle up against a tree and went over toward a mound of this material which he calls the embankment and said "want a fight?" They continued throwing at each other. There is no exact evidence as to how many of these missiles were thrown or how long. One boy said it continued for probably 5 minutes but he says he quit because he was being pelted too much. It would appear that one boy Ross who admits he threw the lumps at McLean while he was on his bicycle, when asked if he was inviting him to play the game, said "In a way I guess so". He appears to have been the leader of the 3 or 4 boys, originally engaged in this play and he and the infant plaintiff and McLean were throwing at each other when the lump or whatever it was which hit the infant plaintiff was thrown by McLean.

. . .

. . . He put his hand to his temple, cried out and fell or sat down. The play stopped immediately. It is agreed by all the boys that the fighting was not carried on in anger and that there was no malice. The infant plaintiff was then 12 years of age; Ross, a little older, and the other two boys on their side a little younger. McLean was 14. It was not the thought of any of them that the injury was serious as it then appeared as no more than a slight scratch and the infant plaintiff went to a party with the two younger boys and both Ross and McLean went about their ways, after having talked and after McLean had expressed his regrets.

It was not contended that there was any evidence that it was a stone that hit the boy who was injured unless that is to be inferred from the nature of the injuries. McLean quite frankly says that he did not look when he reached down to pick up something to throw, his attention obviously and of necessity being directed to dodging the missiles coming at him, and did not notice just what it was he picked up but threw it in the direction in which they (his opponents) were. He said he would not deliberately pick up a rock or stone and did not intend to do so.

I think the boys were old enough to have a finding of negligence made if such is warranted in the circumstances. Negligence is a breach of a duty to take that care which a reasonable person would take in all the circumstances.

. . .

[The judge then considered the issue of consent and quoted *Pollock on Torts*, 15th ed., p. 112]

"Harm suffered by consent is, within limits to be mentioned, not a cause of civil action." Very briefly, the purport of that paragraph is that in sport where there is no malice, no anger and no mutual ill will, that combatants consent to take the ordinary risks of the sport in which they are engaged. In a note given at the foot of p. 114 in Pollock, there is a reference to an article in the Law Quarterly Review, vol. 6, pp. 111-12. In that article, the author uses this language: "The reasonable view is that the combatants consent to take the ordinary risks of the sport in which they engage, the risks of being struck, kicked, or cuffed, as the case may be, and the pain resulting therefrom; but only while the play is fair, and according to rules, and the blows are given in sport and not maliciously. . . . If these tacit conditions of fair play and good temper are not kept the consent is at an end, and the parties are remitted to their rights."

In all the circumstances where it is agreed that there was no ill will and where the evidence shows that the infant defendant was invited to join the game by the others, then I think that no liability arises apart from culpable carelessness. I think it is quite clear that there is no evidence of that in this case.

. . .

I therefore dismiss the action.

Action dismissed.

NOTES AND QUESTIONS

1. To what acts did the plaintiff consent? What were the risks inherent in those acts? Would it have made any difference if it was established that: (a) the plaintiff's injuries were caused by a stone; (b) the defendant had been completely indifferent as to whether he was throwing a mudball or a stone; or (c) the defendant realized he had a stone in his hand but threw it anyway?

2. The judge indicated that he would have held the defendant liable if the defendant had been motivated by anger or spite. Is this element relevant to the issue of the plaintiff's consent? Can you suggest a situation in which such motives would not affect the outcome?

3. For other cases in which implied consent has been raised to defeat a claim for a sports injury, see *Matheson v. Governors of Dalhousie College and University* (1983), 25 C.C.L.T. 91 (N.S. T.D.); and *Temple v. Hallem*, [1989] 5 W.W.R. 669 (Man. C.A.), leave to appeal ref'd. (1990), 65 Man. R. (2d) 80 (note) (S.C.C.).

4. Do spectators implicitly consent to injuries incidental to attending at sporting events? In *Elliott and Elliott v. Amphitheatre Ltd.*, [1934] 3 W.W.R. 225 (Man. K.B.), the defendant was absolved of liability for the injuries the plaintiff suffered when hit by a puck that went into the seats. The court held that as an amateur hockey player, the plaintiff was aware of the risks and the protections customarily provided. Would it have made any difference if: (a) this had been the plaintiff's first visit to the arena and the protective screens were substantially lower than those provided at other arenas; or (b) the plaintiff had been visiting from another country and was completely unaware of the possibility of being hit by a puck?

5. For a discussion of whether the lack of consent is an element of the intentional torts or whether consent is a defence, see Hertz, "Volenti Non Fit Injuria: A Guide" in Klar (ed.), *Studies in Canadian Tort Law* (1977), 101 at 103-04; Linden, *Canadian Tort Law*, 5th ed. (1993), 63-64; Rogers, *Winfield and Jolowicz on Tort*, 14th ed. (1994), 724-25; Keeton *et al.*, *Prosser and Keeton on the Law of Torts*, 5th ed. (1984), 112-14; and Blay, "Onus of Proof of Consent in an Action for Trespass to the Person" (1987), 61 Aust. L.J. 25.

(c) EXCEEDING CONSENT

AGAR v. CANNING

(1965), 54 W.W.R. 302 (Man. Q.B.) [Aff'd. (1996), 55 W.W.R. 384 (Man. C.A.)]

BASTIN J.: — This is an action by a member of a hockey team against a member of an opposing team, for damages arising out of injuries sustained during the course of a hockey match.

. . . The plaintiff and defendant followed the puck into the south-west corner at the Hartney end of the rink. Defendant body-checked plaintiff, took possession of the puck and started to skate with it, or after it, in the direction of the Killarney goal. Plaintiff attempted to delay defendant by hooking him with his stick and in so doing hit defendant a painful blow on the back of the neck. Defendant thereupon stopped, turned, and holding his stick with both hands, brought it down on plaintiff's face, hitting him with the blade between the nose and right eye. I find that he did this in retaliation for the blow he had received. Plaintiff fell to the ice unconscious and the game terminated at that point.

. . .

Neither counsel has been able to find a reported case in which a claim was made by one player against another for injuries suffered during a hockey game. Since it is common knowledge that such injuries are not infrequent, this supports the conclusion that in the past those engaged in this sport have accepted the risk of injury as a condition of participating. Hockey necessarily involves violent bodily contact and blows from the puck and hockey sticks. A person who engages in this sport must be assumed to accept the risk of accidental harm and to waive any claim he would have apart from the game for trespass to his person in return for enjoying a corresponding immunity with respect to other players. It would be inconsistent with this implied consent to impose a duty on a player to take care for the safety of other players corresponding to the duty which, in the normal situation, gives rise to a claim for negligence. Similarly, the leave and licence will include an unintentional injury resulting from one of the frequent infractions of the rules of the game.

The conduct of a player in the heat of the game is instinctive and unpremeditated and should not be judged by standards suited to polite social intercourse.

But a little reflection will establish that some limit must be placed on a player's immunity from liability. Each case must be decided on its own facts so it is difficult, if not impossible, to decide how the line is to be drawn in every circumstance. But injuries inflicted in circumstances which show a definite resolve to cause serious injury to another, even when there is provocation and in the heat of the game, should not fall within the scope of the implied consent. I have come to the conclusion that the act of the defendant in striking plaintiff in the face with a hockey stick, in retaliation for the blow he received, goes beyond the limit marking exemption from liability.

. . .

Even though provocation was not pleaded, and defendant denied acting on provocation, I have made a finding that defendant acted on provocation so I should take this into account in my assessment of damages.

Special damages amount to $115, consisting of doctor's accounts of $30 and hospital accounts of $85. The medical evidence is that the plaintiff has lost all useful vision of his right eye and has injuries to his nose which will affect his breathing and may require to be corrected by an operation. I allow damages of $250 for pain and suffering and for the injuries to the nose, and $5,500 for the loss of the sight of the right eye. I am reducing these damages by one-third, on the ground that there was great provocation, and, therefore, plaintiff will have judgment for $3,910, together with costs, to be taxed, and fiat for discovery.

NOTES AND QUESTIONS

1. Would any conduct in violation of the rules have exceeded the plaintiff's consent? By breaching the rules himself, did the plaintiff implicitly consent to the risks inherent in other players violating the rules? Had the defendant only retaliated by tripping the plaintiff, could he have availed himself of the defence of consent? See *McNamara v. Duncan* (1979), 26 A.L.R. 584 (A.C.T. S.C.); *Pettis v. McNeil* (1979), 32 N.S.R. (2d) 146 (T.D.); and *Colby v. Schmidt* (1986), 37 C.C.L.T. 1 (B.C. S.C.), aff'd. (1966), 55 W.W.R. 384 (Man. C.A.).

2. Traditionally, the Canadian courts were reluctant to convict hockey players of assault when they intentionally injured each other in fights. See, for example, *R. v. Green* (1970), 16 D.L.R. (3d) 137 (Ont. Prov. Ct.); and *R. v. Maki* (1970), 14 D.L.R. (3d) 164 (Ont. Prov. Ct.).

However, the Canadian courts have become less tolerant of hockey violence. In *R. v. Cey*, [1989] 5 W.W.R. 169 (Sask. C.A.), the court stated that it cannot be assumed that a player implicitly consents to a specific type of assault simply because it occurs with some frequency in the sport. The court also indicated that the defendant's action may not have been one to which the plaintiff could, in law, consent for the purposes of criminal liability. See also *R. v. Ciccarelli* (1989), 54 C.C.C. (3d) 121 (Ont. Dist. Ct.).

3. In a mutually agreed-to fist fight, one party's resorting to a knife or other weapon would exceed the other party's consent. See *Teolis v. Moscatelli* (1923), 119 A. 161 (R.I. S.C.); and *Fillipowich v. Nahachewsky* (1969), 3 D.L.R. (3d) 544 (Sask. Q.B.).

4. Even if both parties use only their fists, is there a point at which the loser's consent would no longer protect the victor? For example, in a mutually agreed-to fist fight would the plaintiff's initial consent be exceeded if the defendant punched him while: (a) he was lying on the ground; or (b) he was struggling to get to his feet?

5. How would you analyze the issue of consent in a mutually agreed-to fight if it was obvious from the outset that the plaintiff had been no match for the defendant? Although the courts have provided redress in these kinds of situations, they have predicated recovery on the defendant's use of excessive or unnecessary force. Is this rationale compatible with the principles governing consent? See *Wade v. Martin*, [1955] 3 D.L.R. 635 (Nfld. S.C.); *Hartlen v. Chaddock* (1957), 11 D.L.R. (2d) 705 (N.S. S.C.); and *Lane v. Holloway*, [1968] Q.B. 379 (C.A.).

6. In *R. v. Jobidon* (1991), 7 C.R. (4th) 233 (S.C.C.), the accused was charged with manslaughter when the other combatant died following their consensual fight. The trial judge acquitted the accused because it was a fair fight and the victim's consent had not been exceeded. The Court of Appeal held that the common law concept of consent applies to the Criminal Code's assault provisions and limits consent to cases where bodily harm is neither intended nor caused. The Court reasoned that this interpretation was consistent with the goal of protecting the public and keeping the peace. Consequently, the Court of Appeal overturned the acquittal and entered a manslaughter conviction. The Supreme Court of Canada affirmed the Court of Appeal decision.

The reasoning in *Jobidon* has been roundly criticized on various grounds. For example, the common law concept of consent was not limited to situations in which harm was neither intended nor caused. In any event, why did the court incorporate a "common law" concept into the clear statutory language of section 265(1) of the Criminal Code? It states that the offence of assault is limited to situations where force is applied to another without consent. The lack of consent is a substantive element of the offence which the prosecutor must prove. In effect, the Supreme Court of Canada has created a new criminal offence of assault. See Usprich, "Annotation" (1991), 7 C.R. (4th) 235. See also *R.*

v. M. (S.) (1995), 22 O.R. (3d) 605 (C.A.), where the court appears to have discreetly distanced itself from *Jobidon*.

7. Is the decision in *Jobidon* consistent with the common law's preference for autonomy? Our law does not prevent individuals from engaging in a wide array of high-risk behaviour, from sky-diving to high-speed automobile racing. As we shall discuss, an individual has an almost unfettered right to consent or refuse consent to medical treatment, regardless of the imprudence or consequences of the decision. In *Jobidon*, is there a compelling public policy basis for invalidating consent?

Do you think the court would have reached the same decision on the consent issue if the combatant had not died? How can you reconcile *Jobidon* with the thousands of bar room fights and scores of televised hockey brawls that routinely occur without any criminal charges being brought?

8. *Jobidon* is a criminal case. What impact, if any, should it have on the defence of consent in tort law?

9. For a discussion of exceeding consent in trespass to land see *Gross v. Wright*, [1923] S.C.R. 214; and *Stephens v. Corcoran* (1965), 65 D.L.R. (2d) 407 (Ont. H.C.).

(d) COMPETENCY TO CONSENT

In order for consent to be valid, the person giving it must be capable of appreciating the nature and consequences of the act to which it applies. If the person cannot make such a determination due to age, physical or mental illness, intoxication, or other incapacitating condition, the consent will be invalid. The issue of competency to consent addresses a person's ability to understand the act in issue. The fact that the courts or others view the decision itself as unreasonable is not necessarily relevant to the issue of competency. This broad test of competency is consistent with the common law's concern with safeguarding autonomy. If a person is competent, the law must uphold her right to make both wise and unwise decisions.

It should be noted that some statutes may deem certain individuals to be incapable of giving a valid consent in specific circumstances. For example, section 150.1 of the Criminal Code provides that the consent of a person under the age of 14 is not generally a defence to the charge of sexual assault. The issue of competency to consent will be examined in greater detail in the materials on consent to medical procedures.

3. Factors Which Vitiate Consent: Duress, Fraud, Mistake, and Public Policy

(a) INTRODUCTION

Once the defendant has established that the plaintiff consented to the act giving rise to the tort action, the plaintiff may raise factors that would negate or vitiate an otherwise valid consent. If the consent is vitiated, the defendant will be held liable as if there had been no consent. As we shall discuss, the Canadian courts have tended to rely on criminal law concepts and narrowly defined these factors. While these narrow definitions may be appropriate in criminal law, which focuses on moral blameworthiness, it is questionable whether they are appropriate in tort law, which deals with compensation.

(b) DURESS

LATTER v. BRADDELL

(1880), 50 L.J. Q.B. 166 (C.P.)

LOPES J.: — This was an action of assault which was tried before my brother Lindley, at the last Manchester Assizes, and resulted in a verdict for the defendant Sutcliffe. The learned Judge at the end of the plaintiff's evidence withdrew the case against Captain and Mrs. Braddell from the jury, holding that there was no evidence against them upon which a jury could reasonably act.

A rule was obtained calling upon the defendant to shew cause why the verdict should not be set aside and a new trial had on the ground that the Judge ought not to have withdrawn the case as against Captain and Mrs. Braddell, and that the verdict was against the weight of evidence. The Court is now asked to make that rule absolute. I think the rule should be made absolute. The case, in my opinion, is a very important one, and I regret that I am not able to come to the same conclusion as my brother Lindley. I need not say that I have felt compelled to differ from him after mature and careful consideration. I think the case against Captain and Mrs. Braddell ought to have been left to the jury. I do not think it was correct to tell the jury that to maintain this action the plaintiff's will must have been overpowered by force or the fear of violence. This I understand was the direction given by the learned Judge to the jury in summing up the case against the defendant Sutcliffe, and I presume this view of the law induced him to withdraw from the jury the case against Captain and Mrs. Braddell.

I will now call attention to the facts. The plaintiff was a housemaid in the service of Captain and Mrs. Braddell. Captain and Mrs. Braddell had been absent from home, and returned on the 23rd of December. From some information given by a charwoman, Mrs. Braddell came to the conclusion that the plaintiff was in the family way. On the 27th of December Mrs. Braddell told the plaintiff to pack up and leave before twelve o'clock, as she was in the family way. This the plaintiff denied. Mrs. Braddell replied, "The doctor will be here directly". (The doctor had been previously sent for unknown to the plaintiff.) Mrs. Braddell told the plaintiff to go to her room. The plaintiff cried. Mrs. Braddell forbade her to speak. The plaintiff went to her bedroom. The doctor came and went to the plaintiff's bedroom. The plaintiff cried and said she never had such treatment before. She asked the doctor what he was going to do, and said she did not wish to be examined. The doctor said he was a professional man, and told the plaintiff to take off her dress. The plaintiff said she did not like to do so. The doctor said, "Never mind, it would satisfy Mrs. Braddell and him". The doctor told the plaintiff to take off her petticoat. The plaintiff cried and said she did not like to take off her other things. The doctor said, "You must". The plaintiff took off her stays. The doctor said she must take off her chemise. The plaintiff said she did not like to do so. The doctor said she must, and told her to slip her arms through. The doctor then told her to lie on her back on the bed and to loosen the strings of her drawers. He then pinched her breasts and stomach and sounded it. The plaintiff cried all the time. The doctor, after examining her, said she was all right, and he must speak seriously to Mrs. Braddell about it. The plaintiff then dressed.

. . .

If the plaintiff voluntarily consented, or if, in other words, the assault was committed with her leave and licence, the action is not maintainable; and to justify the ruling of the learned Judge, what was done must have been so unmistakably with the plaintiff's consent that there was no evidence of non-consent upon which a jury could reasonably act. It seems to me there was abundant evidence of non-consent to be left to the jury.

The sending for a doctor by a master or mistress and directing him to examine a female servant, without first apprising her, is, in any circumstances, an arbitrary and high-handed proceeding, and cannot, in my opinion, be justified unless the servant's consent is voluntarily given. A submission to what is done, obtained through a belief that she is bound to obey her master and mistress; or a consent obtained through a fear of evil consequences to arise to herself, induced by her master's or mistress's words or conduct, is not sufficient. In neither case would the consent be voluntarily given: it would be consent in one sense, but a consent to which the will was not a party. The plaintiff's case is stronger. She swears she did not consent. I know not what more a person in the plaintiff's position could do unless she used physical force. She is discharged without a hearing, forbidden to speak, sent to her room, examined by her mistress's doctor alone, no other female being in the room, made to take off all her clothes and lie naked on the bed. She complains of the treatment, cries continuously, objects to the removal of each garment and swears the examination was without her consent. Could it be said, in these circumstances, that her consent was so unmistakably given that her state of mind was not a question for a jury to consider? I cannot adopt the view that the plaintiff consented because she yielded without her will having been over-powered by force or fear of violence. That, as I have said, is not, in my opinion, an accurate definition of consent in a case like this.

I do not understand why, if there was a case against the doctor there was none against Captain and Mrs. Braddell. The doctor was employed to see if the plaintiff was in the family way. The plaintiff does not suggest in her evidence that he did more than was necessary for ascertaining that fact. If this is so, the Braddells are responsible for what was done by the doctor.

It is said there ought to be no new trial as against the doctor. I cannot agree with the definition of consent given by the learned Judge, and I think the withdrawing the case against the Braddells influenced the jury in finding for the doctor. They would naturally think the doctor only did what he was told. The Braddells put him in motion, and it would be hard, when the principals are acquitted, to find the agent guilty.

There should be a rule absolute for a new trial.

LINDLEY J.: — I am of opinion that, assuming everything said by the plaintiff in this case to be true, a verdict in her favour against the master and mistress could not be supported in point of law, and that as to them she was properly nonsuited.

The plaintiff was in service with the defendants Braddell, who on their return after an absence from home received information from the charwoman which caused Mrs. Braddell to bid the plaintiff leave her service by twelve o'clock on the day that order was given, as she was in the family way. The plaintiff denied this, and Mrs. Braddell then said, "Well, the doctor will be here directly, and we shall then see." The plaintiff was then told to go to her bedroom, and she went, whither the doctor on his arrival followed her. He told her to take off her garments, which she did, saying, however, "Must I take off this?" or that she "did not like to take off that", as each article of clothing had to be removed by her under the doctor's directions. She also said that she cried and protested, and that it was all done without her consent. The examination was, however, submitted to by her, and the doctor found that the plaintiff was not in the family way. This is the assault complained of.

The plaintiff's case cannot be put higher than this, namely, that without consulting her wishes, her mistress ordered her to submit to be examined by a doctor, in order that he might ascertain whether she (the plaintiff) was in the family way, and that she (the plaintiff) complied with that order reluctantly — that is, sobbing and protesting — and because she was told she must, and she did not know what else to do. There was, however, no evidence of any force or violence, nor of any threat of force or violence, nor of any illegal act done or threatened by the mistress beyond what I have stated; nor did the plaintiff in her evidence say that she was in fear of the mistress or of the doctor, or that she was in any way overcome by fear. She said she did not consent to what was done; but the sense in which she used this expression was not explained, and to appreciate it regard must be had to the other facts of the case. The plaintiff had it entirely in her own power physically to comply or not to comply with her mistress's orders, and there was no evidence whatever to shew that anything improper or illegal was threatened to be done if she had not complied. It was suggested that her mistress ordered the examination with a view to see whether she could dismiss her without paying a month's wages. But there was no evidence of any threat to withhold wages, nor of any conversation on the subject of wages, until the plaintiff was paid them on leaving. The question, therefore, is reduced to this: Can the plaintiff, having complied with the orders of her mistress, although reluctantly, maintain this action upon the ground that what was done to her by the doctor was against her will, or might properly be so regarded by a jury? I think not. It is said that the jury ought to have been asked whether the plaintiff in effect gave her mistress leave to have her examined, or whether the plaintiff's will or mind went with what she did. But, in my opinion, such questions inadequately express the grounds on which alone the defendants can be held liable. The plaintiff was not a child; she knew perfectly well what she did and what was being done to her by the doctor. She knew the object with which he examined her, and upon the evidence there is no reason whatever for supposing that any examination would have been made or attempted if she had told the doctor she would not allow herself to be examined. Under these circumstances I am of opinion that there was no evidence of want of consent as distinguished from reluctant obedience or submission to her mistress's orders, and that in the absence of all evidence of coercion, as distinguished from an order which the plaintiff could comply with or not as she chose, the action cannot be maintained.

. . .

In the present case there was no evidence of any threat at all, in the event of non-compliance with the orders of the mistress; and it appears to me that there was no evidence to shew that Mrs. Braddell did anything illegal, or, in other words, to shew that what she ordered to be done was done against the plaintiff's will in any accurate sense of that expression. This, however, is what has to be established — see *Christopherson v. Bare* [(1848), 116 E.R. 554].

I do not, however, wish to be understood as being of opinion that the plaintiff had no cause of complaint against her mistress; but, in my opinion, the real substantial grievance was that the plaintiff accused of being in the family way was ordered to be examined, and when the accusation proved to be unfounded was summarily dismissed without any apology. Whether the mistress could or could not have justified such harsh conduct I cannot say, not having heard her evidence. But, harsh as such conduct apparently was, it does not affect the question on which this action turns. I cannot, however, help thinking that if the conduct of the mistress as regards the manner of dismissal had been more considerate, the impossibility of maintaining this action would be more plainly apparent.

As regards the doctor, who is made a defendant, I am of opinion, for the reasons already given, that there was no misdirection in point of law, and that the verdict in his favour was perfectly correct. His conduct throughout was kind and considerate; and whatever grievance the plaintiff may have against her mistress, she has none whatever against the doctor. This action has been tried twice, and although I am extremely reluctant to adhere to my own opinion when other persons who are more likely than I am to be right think I am wrong, I cannot give my voice for further litigation in a case in which I feel convinced no injustice has been done.

I am of opinion that this rule ought to be discharged.

Rule Discharged.

[The Court of Appeal affirmed Lindley J.'s judgment discharging the rule. *Latter v. Braddell* (1881), 50 L.J.Q.B. 448 (C.A.).]

NOTES AND QUESTIONS

1. Did Lindley J. adequately address the issue of consent before focusing on duress? Did the plaintiff in *Latter* consent to the medical examination?

2. How did Lindley J. define duress? What economic threats, if any, would be included in his definition? Do you agree with how he applied this definition to the facts of the case? Answer these questions in reference to Lopes J.'s judgment. Which judgment do you prefer?

3. Under s. 17 of the Criminal Code, the concept of compulsion (duress) is defined narrowly in terms of a credible threat of immediate death or bodily injury. Although the American Law Institute rejects such a restrictive definition of duress, it does not attempt to provide its own definition. *Restatement of the Law, Second, Torts* (1979), para. 892 B, comment on subsection (3). See also Keeton *et al., Prosser and Keeton on the Law of Torts*, 5th ed. (1984), 121. Should the definition of duress be the same in tort law as in criminal law? How would you define duress for the purposes of tort law?

4. Should an employee who submitted to her employer's sexual demands in order to keep her job succeed in a battery action based on the argument that her consent was vitiated by duress? Would your answer be different if the employer's threat of dismissal contravened the provincial labour and human rights legislation?

(c) FRAUD (DECEIT)

The fact that the plaintiff's consent was based on a fraudulently induced belief will not necessarily vitiate the consent. First, it must be established that the defendant was aware of, or responsible for, the plaintiff's misapprehension. Second, the fraud will only negate consent if it relates to the nature of the act, as opposed to a "collateral matter." In keeping with the approach in criminal law, the courts in tort cases have adopted a broad view of what they consider to be collateral matters and have rarely negated the plaintiff's consent. Consequently, a man who lied about his marital status to induce a woman to have sex could not be held liable in battery.

Most cases involving the issue of fraud deal with written or verbal statements. However, the defendant's conduct or even failure to reveal information may amount to fraud in some situations. Fraud includes situations in which the defendant either knowingly deceives the plaintiff or acts in total disregard as to the truth of her statements.

NOTES AND QUESTIONS

1. This distinction between fraud as to the nature of the act and fraud as to collateral matters is clearly established in criminal law. In *R. v. Williams*, [1923] 1 K.B. 340 (C.A.) a singing teacher, who induced a 16-year old student to have intercourse under the pretense that it was a therapeutic procedure to improve her voice, was convicted of rape. The court emphasized that the girl did not know that she was engaging in a sexual act. In *Papadimitropoulos v. R.* (1957), 98 C.L.R. 249 (Aust. H.C.), the accused was acquitted of rape for having intercourse with an illiterate woman after he had fraudulently convinced her that they had been married. In this case, the woman was aware that she was participating in a sexual act and consented to it. The court held that the fraud went to a collateral matter and thus did not vitiate her consent. See also *R. v. Harms*, [1944] 2 D.L.R. 61 (Sask. C.A.); *Bolduc v. R.* (1967), 63 D.L.R. (2d) 82 (S.C.C.); and Hooper, "Fraud in Assault and Rape" (1967-68), 3 U.B.C. L.R. 117.

2. Similar reasoning has been adopted in civil cases. In *Graham v. Saville*, [1945] 2 D.L.R. 489 (Ont. C.A.) and *Smythe v. Reardon* (1949), 23 A.L.J. 409 (Circ. Ct.), the defendant fraudulently claimed to be a bachelor and induced the plaintiff to marry him. In both cases the plaintiff recovered damages based on the tort of deceit, but presumably could not have recovered in battery. What arguments would you make for treating fraud as to collateral matters differently in tort than in criminal law? See Fischer, "Fraudulently Induced Consent to Intentional Torts" (1977), 46 Cinn. L. Rev. 71.

3. Whose perspective should be adopted in determining which matters are collateral? Since the defendant has the burden of proving that the plaintiff consented, should the plaintiff's views predominate? See *Said (Husain) v. Said* (1986), 38 C.C.L.T. 260 (B.C. C.A.).

4. Should the plaintiff's consent be valid if she is aware of the nature of the act, but is deceived as to its harmful consequences? In *Hegarty v. Shine* (1878), 4 L.R. Ir. 288 (C.A.), the plaintiff contracted venereal disease from her lover who knew he was infected, but did not inform her. The court concluded that the defendant's failure to disclose his infection did not vitiate her consent, but the judges appeared primarily concerned with denying her redress for the consequences of her illicit sexual relationship. See also *R. v. Clarence* (1888), 22 Q.B.D. 23; *R. v. Lee* (1991), 3 O.R. (3d) 726 (Gen. Div.); and *R.v. Ssenyonga* (1992), 73 C.C.C. (3d) 216 (Ont. Prov. Div.), which have failed to negate the victim's consent. In *Lee* the accused suspected that he might be infected, whereas in *Ssenyonga* the accused knew he was infected.

The decision in *Hegarty* has been widely criticized and most authors now indicate that deceit as to the harmful consequences of an act vitiates consent. See Hertz, "Volenti Non Fit Injuria: A Guide" in Klar (ed.), *Studies in Canadian Tort Law* (1977), 101 at 104; American Law Institute, *Restatement of the Law, Second, Torts* (1979), para. 892 B (2); Fleming, *The Law of Torts*, 8th ed. (1992), 80-81; and Keeton *et al., Prosser and Keeton on the Law of Torts*, 5th ed. (1984), 119-20.

The dramatic increases in sexually transmitted diseases, such as herpes and AIDS, have focused attention on the issue of fraud as to the harmful consequences of one's acts. See, for example, *Bell-Ginsburg v. Ginsburg* (1993), 14 O.R. (3d) 217 (Gen. Div.); Prentice and Murray, "Liability for Transmission of Herpes: Using Traditional Tort Principles to Encourage Honesty in Sexual Relationships" (1984), 11 J. Contemp. L. 67; and Murray and Winslett, "The Constitutional Right to Privacy and Emerging Tort Liability for Deceit in Interpersonal Relationships", [1986] Ill. L. Rev. 779.

5. It should be noted that polygamy and feigning a marriage ceremony are offences under ss. 292 and 293 of the Criminal Code. In 1985, the offence of communicating a veneral disease, unless one was unaware of the infection, was repealed.

(d) MISTAKE

The fact that the plaintiff gave consent under a mistaken belief will only vitiate the consent if the defendant was responsible for creating the plaintiff's misapprehension. The American authorities support a broader rule. In *Restatement of the Law, Second, Torts* (1979), para. 892 B (2), the American Law Institute indicates that the defendant's mere knowledge that the plaintiff consented under a mistaken belief vitiates the consent.

These types of situations must be distinguished from those in which the defendant mistakenly believes that the plaintiff has consented, when in fact, she has not. In this latter case, the plaintiff has not consented to the act giving rise to the tort claim and thus, the defence of consent will fail.

NOTES AND QUESTIONS

1. There are surprisingly few cases on the impact of the plaintiff's mistaken belief on the validity of her consent. See *Roper v. Harper* (1837), 132 E.R. 696; *Stewart v. Traders Trust Co.*, [1936] 4 D.L.R. 139 (Man. C.A.); and *Guimond v. Laberge* (1956), 4 D.L.R. (2d) 559 (Ont. C.A.).

2. Keeton *et al.* state that the plaintiff's consent will be vitiated if the defendant knew or ought to have known that the plaintiff's consent was based on a mistaken belief. *Prosser and Keeton on the Law of Torts*, 5th ed. (1984), 119. Their position is even broader than that of the American Law Institute. See also Hertz, "Volenti Non Fit Injuria: A Guide" in Klar (ed.), *Studies in Canadian Tort Law* (1977), 101 at 113-14, who adopts the Institute's position without comment. See generally, Forbes, "Mistake of Fact With Regard to Defences in Tort Law" (1970), 4 Ottawa L. Rev. 304. Which rule should the courts adopt to govern these situations?

3. Several cases clearly establish that the defendant's mistaken belief that the plaintiff consented provides no defence. See *Boase v. Paul*, [1931] 4 D.L.R. 435 (Ont. C.A.); *Parmley v. Parmley*, [1945] 4 D.L.R. 81 (S.C.C.); *Turner v. Thorne*, [1960] O.W.N. 20 (H.C.); and *Schweizer v. Central Hospital* (1974), 6 O.R. (2d) 606 (H.C.).

(e) PUBLIC POLICY

The courts have increasingly recognized public policy considerations in negating what would otherwise have been a valid defence of consent. For example, in *Lane v. Holloway*, [1968] 1 Q.B. 379 (C.A.), the court refused to accept the defence of consent because it was obvious from the outset of the fight that the plaintiff was no match for the defendant. As indicated, in *R. v. Jobidon* (1991), 7 C.R. (4th) 233, the Supreme Court of Canada held that even in a fair fight, the defence of consent, albeit for the purposes of criminal law, is limited to cases where bodily harm is neither intended nor caused.

Some courts may also negate the defence of consent if the defendant exploited her position of trust or authority. In *M.(M.) v. K.(K.)* (1989), 38 B.C.L.R. (2d) 273 (C.A.), the defendant was convicted under section 153(1)(a) of the Criminal Code for having sex with his 15-year-old foster daughter. The foster daughter also brought a civil suit, but it was dismissed at trial on the basis that she had initiated and consented to the sexual contact. However, the Court of Appeal reversed the trial judgment and found for the foster daughter. The court rejected the defence of consent because it was dependant on the defendant's wrongdoing, which included criminal misconduct, breach of trust and breach of his duty to act in the plaintiff's best interests. [Affirmed on different grounds (1992), 14 C.C.L.T. (2d) 1 (S.C.C.).]

In *Norberg v. Wynrib* (1992), 12 C.C.L.T. (2d) 1, the defendant doctor offered to continue an addicted patient's prescription for narcotics if she submitted to his sexual advances. She only reluctantly agreed after she failed to secure another source. After recovering from her drug addiction, the patient sued the defendant for battery, negligence and breach of fiduciary duty, and was awarded $20,000 in general damages and $10,000 in punitive damages. The majority held the doctor liable in battery, stating that the parties' unequal power and the exploitive relationship made it impossible for the plaintiff to "meaningfully consent". Two justices held that the doctor was liable for breaching his fiduciary duty, which they viewed as being independent of tort and contract law. The remaining justice stated that the doctor could not be held liable in battery because of the plaintiff's consent. Rather, the justice held that the doctor was liable in negligence for breaching the accepted standards of medical practice.

NOTES AND QUESTIONS

1. Can you identify an underlying principle to explain *Lane, Jobidon, M.(M.)* and *Norberg*? Do you agree with these decisions?

2. Would the result have been the same in *M.(M.)* if the defendant's conduct had not been illegal, but merely violated his position of trust? For example, assume that the defendant had been a private music teacher or volunteer basketball coach. See also *Lyth v. Dagg* (1988), 46 C.C.L.T. 25 (B.C. S.C.); and *Harder v. Brown* (1989), 50 C.C.L.T. 85 (B.C. S.C.).

3. What do you think the majority meant by the term "meaningfully consent" in *Norberg*? Would a person who consents to counselling only because it is a term of her probation be able to "meaningfully consent"? Which of the three approaches in *Norberg* is preferable and why?

Norberg raises the issue of doctors' and counsellors' sexual exploitation of their patients. See Coleman, "Sex in Power Dependency Relationships: Taking Unfair Advantage of the Fair Sex" (1988), 53 Albany L. Rev. 95; Jorgenson *et al.*, "The Furor Over Psychotherapist-Patient Sexual Contact: New Solutions to an Old Problem" (1991), 32 Wm. and Mary L. Rev. 645; and The Task Force on Sexual Abuse of Patients (Ontario), *The Final Report of the Task Force on Sexual Abuse of Patients* (Toronto: College of Physicians and Surgeons of Ontario, 1991).

4. Can you suggest other types of situations in which it would be appropriate to deny the defendant's right to raise the plaintiff's consent as a defence?

5. The courts have not reconciled the public policy analysis with the conflicting concept of individual autonomy. Nor have the courts considered the implications of negating a person's consent on policy grounds in other areas, such as a consent or refusal to consent to medical treatment. There is considerable caselaw that accepts the plaintiff's consent at face value and does not address these concerns. In reference to consensual fights, see *Wade v. Martin*, [1955] 3 D.L.R. 635 (Nfld. S.C.); *Zinck v. Strickland and Blake* (1981), 86 A.P.R. 451 (N.S. S.C.); and *Johnson v. Royal Can. Legion Grandview Branch No. 179*, [1988] 5 W.W.R. 267 (B.C. C.A.). In contrast to *Norberg*, see *Morrow v. Hôpital Royal Victoria* (1989), 3 C.C.L.T. (2d) 87 (Que. C.A.), leave to appeal ref'd. (1990), 111 N.R. 239n (S.C.C.), where the schizophrenic patient's consent to electroshock therapy was upheld, even though she had not been informed that the defendant doctor was being paid by the CIA to conduct brain-washing experiments. The court held that because the patient was herself a doctor who was aware of the risks, her consent was valid.

6. Can you reconcile the Canadian courts' upholding of the validity of the plaintiff's consent when she is deceived as to the harmful consequences of the act, but their negating of consent on public policy grounds in *Norberg, M. (M.)* and *Jobidon*?

4. Consent to Criminal or Immoral Acts

In *Hegarty v. Shine* (1878), 14 Cox. C.C. 145 (Ir. C.A.), the female plaintiff sued her lover in battery for infecting her with a venereal disease. One of the bases upon which the court denied her claim was the principle that a person cannot recover in tort law for the consequences of her own illegal or immoral conduct. This concept, which is often referred to by the Latin maxim *ex turpi causa non oritur actio*, was first applied in contract law. The principle was gradually extended to torts, serving as a complete defence to both intentional torts and negligence.

The principle has generated considerable controversy, in large part because the courts failed to clarify the underlying purpose of the doctrine. Consequently, the principle was applied on a case-by-case basis, making the ensuing decisions difficult to reconcile or explain. Nevertheless, the general trend in Canada has been to narrow the doctrine in various ways. For example, some courts have held that it only applies to illegal but not immoral acts; others have limited it to federal criminal offences but not provincial and municipal offences. Some courts have concluded that it does not apply to some federal criminal offences.

Finally, in *Hall v. Hebert* (1993), 15 C.C.L.T. 93, the Supreme Court of Canada identified the purpose of the doctrine and clarified the circumstances in which it applies. The court stated that the goal of the doctrine is to protect the integrity of the legal system. A classic example is a case in which awarding damages would result in the plaintiff profiting financially from his or her illegal or immoral behaviour. The court then stated that the defence would rarely apply to plaintiffs seeking compensation for an actual physical loss.

NOTES AND QUESTIONS

1. In *Tallow v. Tailfeathers* (1973), 44 D.L.R. (3d) 55 (Alta. C.A.), the *ex turpi* defence was limited to truly criminal behaviour, namely violations of federal criminal law, and not provincial or municipal enactments. In the court's words, "anti-social behaviour" and an "aura of criminality" will not do. However, in *Can. Cement LaFarge Ltd. v. B.C. Lightweight Aggregate Ltd.* (1983), 24 C.C.L.T. 111, the Supreme Court held that the doctrine applies to both criminal and immoral conduct, including involvement in illegal agreements.

2. One concern has been that the concept of immorality is too open-ended, and will vary both over time and among jurisdictions. For example, would *Hegarty* be decided the same way now? In *Kirkham v. Chief Constable of Greater Manchester Police*, [1990] 3 All E.R. 246 (C.A.), the plaintiff's husband committed suicide while in police custody. The court rejected the police department's defence of *ex turpi causa* because suicide was no longer viewed as a "moral affront".

3. The doctrine is limited to cases in which the plaintiff's injuries are a direct result of her participation in immoral or illegal conduct. However, some courts apply the concept of directness more narrowly than others. For example, should the defence apply to a plaintiff, who is injured in a car accident caused by the defendant's negligent driving while they are joy-riding together in a stolen car? Contrast *Smith v. Jenkins* (1970), 119 C.L.R. 397 (Aust. H.C.) and *Tallow v. Tailfeathers, supra,* with *Jackson v. Harrison* (1978), 19 A.L.R. 129 (Aust. H.C.), and *Bond v. Loutit (Noonen)*, [1979] 2 W.W.R. 154 (Man. Q.B.). See also *Pugliese v. Taxiarchis* (1988), 67 O.R. (2d) 641 (H.C.).

4. In *Teece v. Honeybourn* (1974), 54 D.L.R. (3d) 549 (B.C. S.C.), the Court held that the defendant police officer could not raise the defence against the deceased, an escaping car thief whom he had negligently shot, because the officer was not one of the deceased's criminal accomplices. This controversial limitation was specifically rejected by the Supreme Court in *Hall, supra,* at 110.

5. Several courts have simply refused to apply the defence if the loser of a consensual fight was badly injured. The fact that the plaintiff was no match for the defendant and that excessive force was used appears to have influenced these decisions. See *Hartlen v. Chaddock* (1957), 11 D.L.R. (2d) 705

(N.S. S.C.); and *Lane v. Holloway*, [1967] 3 All E.R. 129 (C.A.). But see *Wade v. Martin*, [1955] 3 D.L.R. 635 (Nfld. S.C.); and *Murphy v. Culhane*, [1976] 3 All E.R. 533 (C.A.). Has *Jobidon* rendered these cases moot?

Some courts have refused to apply the doctrine to certain Criminal Code offences, such as impaired driving. In *Foster v. Morton* (1956), 4 D.L.R. (2d) 269 at 273 (N.S. S.C.), the judge stated without any explanation that there were weighty reasons why the doctrine should not apply in drinking and driving cases. This statement was accepted by both the majority and dissent in *Miller v. Decker*, [1957] S.C.R. 624. See also *Blakely v. 513953 Ont. Ltd.* (1985), 49 O.R. (2d) 651 (S.C.). What impact will *Hall* have on this line of cases?

6. Do you agree with *Hall* that the doctrine should be limited to preserving the "integrity of the legal system"? What other purposes could the doctrine serve? Assuming that the doctrine should be limited to preserving the integrity of the legal system, does it follow that the doctrine would rarely apply to wrongdoing plaintiffs who are seeking compensation for actual injuries?

7. The defence has generated considerable academic attention. See, for example, McDougall, "*Ex Turpi Causa*: Should a Defence Arise from a Base Cause?" (1991), 55 Sask. L. Rev. 1; Klar, "Negligence — Defences . . ." (1993), 72 Can. Bar Rev. 553; and Kostal, "Currents in the Counter-Reformation: Illegality and Duty of Care in Canada and Australia" (1995), 3 Tort L. Rev. 100.

REVIEW PROBLEMS

1. George, a 110-kilogram college football player, rudely pushed his way to the bar. When Bill, a slight, middle-aged man complained, George challenged him to a fist fight outside. After 10 minutes of verbal abuse, Bill reluctantly agreed. As Bill approached, George held the door open and bowed, stating: "after you, coward." Seizing this opportunity, Bill kicked George in the head once, knocking him unconscious and ending the fight. What tort liability, if any, has Bill incurred as a result of this altercation?

2. Steve suffered a broken arm when brought down by a well-executed tackle on the first play of a football game at the local playground. He was caught off guard because he thought they were playing touch football. Although he missed the preliminary discussions, he simply assumed it was touch football — no one was wearing football equipment, his friends rarely played tackle and he had not been told that it was tackle. Advise Steve on the possible tort actions that he may pursue.

3. Martha left some hashish-laden brownies in her school locker to take to a party that evening. Janet, her locker partner, spotted the brownies and asked if she might have one. Thoroughly annoyed by Janet's endless requests for favours, Martha graciously told her to help herself but decided not to inform her of the brownies' contents. Several hours after eating a brownie, Janet became disoriented while riding home on her bicycle. Having had no previous experience with drugs, she panicked and crashed into a parked car. Advise Janet on the tort actions that she may bring against Martha.

5. Consent to Treatment and Counselling

(a) GENERAL PRINCIPLES

As a general rule, a health care professional must obtain consent to initiate any physical examination, test, procedure, surgery, or counselling. The consent should be obtained in advance and cover not only the intervention, but also any related issues regarding record-keeping, reporting and other disclosures of information. The consent must relate to the specific procedure or treatment that is undertaken. If the patient is competent to give a valid consent, then it is her consent alone that is required. As we shall discuss, the consent of the next-of-kin is only relevant if the patient is incapable of consenting. Even in these circumstances, there are limits on the validity of substitute consent.

To be valid, a consent must be given "voluntarily", in the sense that the patient's decision is the product of her conscious mind. The legal definition of volition is extremely broad. For example, patients who reluctantly consent to treatment because it is a term of probation or because they have been threatened with being fired from a job or expelled from school will still be held to have "voluntarily" consented.

The consent must be based on a full and frank disclosure of the nature of the intervention and its risks. The patient need not understand the technical details or the underlying theory. A patient may consent implicitly, by participation, other behaviour or demeanour, or explicitly, either orally or in writing. The fact that a patient comes for treatment provides some measure of implicit consent.

Patients may seek treatment, and yet expressly limit the scope of their consent. A health care professional may refuse to treat a patient if these limitations are unreasonable. However, a health care professional cannot ignore a patient's express prohibitions or override them.

NOTES AND QUESTIONS

1. For a review of the general principles of consent see Sharpe, *The Law and Medicine in Canada*, 2nd ed. (1987), 29-93; Picard, *Legal Liability of Doctors and Hospitals in Canada*, 2nd ed. (1984), 41-147; and Rozovsky and Rozovsky, *The Canadian Law of the Consent to Treatment* (1990).

2. The common law principles of consent had been largely supplanted by the Consent to Treatment Act, 1992, S.O. 1992, c. 31. Although the government indicated that the Act merely codified the common law principles of consent, this was simply not the case. The Act greatly increased the information that health professionals must provide to patients and altered the principles governing emergency treatment and substitute consent. However, the Act only applied to regulated health professionals, such as doctors, nurses and psychologists. The common law continued to govern social workers, addiction counsellors, employment assistance workers, and a broad range of other therapists. This Act has recently been replaced by the Health Care Consent Act, 1996, S.O. 1996, c. 2, Sch. A. If nothing else, this legislative flurry has succeeded in baffling many health professionals and care providers.

3. Hall J.A. summarized the principles governing consent to research procedures in *Halushka v. University of Saskatchewan* (1965), 53 D.L.R. (2d) 436 at 443-444 (Sask. C.A.). He indicated that a doctor's obligation to potential subjects in research was greater than that owed to patients. Research subjects were entitled to a full and frank disclosure of all the facts, probabilities and opinions that a reasonable person would want before giving consent. See also *Cryderman v. Ringrose* (1978), 89 D.L.R. (3d) 32 (Alta. C.A.); *Weiss v. Solomon* (1989), 48 C.C.L.T. 280 (C.S. Que.); and *Morrow v. Hôpital Royal Victoria* (1989), 3 C.C.L.T. (2d) 87 (Que. C.A.), leave to appeal ref'd. (1990), 111 N.R. 239n (S.C.C.).

4. Should a health professional have an affirmative duty to inform patients that a proposed treatment is experimental, novel or not the standard therapy? In *Coughlin v. Kuntz* (1989), 2 C.C.L.T. (2d) 42 (B.C. C.A.), the defendant surgeon, who had strong and unique views, performed experimental surgery of his own design on the patient. The operation failed, prolonging the plaintiff's suffering and necessitating additional surgery. The doctor was held negligent in diagnosing the problem, in proceeding with drastic, unsupported, experimental surgery, and in failing to adequately inform the patient. In addition to compensatory damages, the plaintiff was awarded $25,000 in exemplary damages to punish and deter the doctor for his arrogance and disregard for his patient.

5. See generally Delgado, "Informed Consent in Human Experimentation: Bridging the Gap Between Ethical Thought and Current Practice" (1986), 34 U.C.L.A. L. Rev. 67; Roth, "Informed Consent in Psychiatric Research" (1987), 39 Rutgers L. Rev. 425; Medical Research Council of Canada, *Guidelines on Research Involving Human Subjects* (Ottawa: Medical Research Council, 1987); and Law Reform Commission of Canada, *Biomedical Experimentation Involving Human Subjects* (Ottawa: Law Reform Commission, 1989).

(b) EXCEPTIONS TO THE GENERAL PRINCIPLES OF CONSENT

Traditionally, the courts have relaxed the strict requirements of consent in three situations. First, in an unforeseen medical emergency, where it is impossible to obtain the patient's consent, a health care professional is allowed to intervene without consent to preserve the patient's health or life. It is on this basis that emergency room staff, and lay people, for that matter, are permitted to provide treatment or first aid to unconscious accident victims. Although the next-of-kin may be consulted, their consent is irrelevant. This right to proceed without consent is narrowly defined.

The second exception to the principles of consent involves patients who have given a general consent to a course of counselling, a treatment program or an operation. In such situations, a patient will be viewed as implicitly consenting to any subsequent counselling sessions or subordinate tests and procedures that are necessarily incidental to the agreed treatment. However, this implied consent will be negated if the patient objects.

Third, at one time the Canadian courts held that health care professionals had a right to withhold information if its disclosure would undermine the patient's morale and discourage her from having needed medical treatment. In two somewhat conflicting cases, the Supreme Court of Canada cast some doubt on the continued existence of the privilege. *Hopp v. Lepp* (1980), 112 D.L.R. (3d) 67 at 79; and *Reibl v. Hughes* (1980), 114 D.L.R. (3d) 1 at 13. In keeping with the rise in patients' rights, the subsequent cases have either rejected the privilege altogether (*Meyer Estate v. Rogers* (1991), 2 O.R. (3d) 356 (Gen. Div.)) or significantly narrowed its scope and application (*Pittman Estate v. Bain* (1994), 112 D.L.R. (4th) 257 (Ont. Gen. Div.)).

MARSHALL v. CURRY

60 C.C.C. 136, [1933] 3 D.L.R. 260 (N.S. S.C.)

CHISHOLM C.J.: — The plaintiff, a master mariner residing at Clifton in the County of Colchester, brings this action in which he claims $10,000 damages against the defendant who is a surgeon of high standing, practising his profession in the City of Halifax.

The plaintiff in his statement of claim alleges: —

(1) That after being employed to perform and while performing an operation on the plaintiff for the cure of a hernia and while plaintiff was under the influence of an anaesthetic, the defendant without the knowledge or consent of the plaintiff removed the plaintiff's left testicle;

(2) In the alternative, that the defendant was negligent in diagnosing the case and in not informing the plaintiff that it might be necessary in treating the hernia to remove the testicle; and

(3) In the further alternative, that in removing the testicle in the above mentioned circumstances, the defendant committed an assault upon the plaintiff.

The defence, in addition to general denials, is, that the removal of the testicle was a necessary part of the operation for the cure of the hernia; that the necessity for removing the testicle could not have been reasonably ascertained by diagnosis before any operation was begun; that consent to the further operation was implied by plaintiff's request to cure the hernia and that the plaintiff's claim is barred by the Statute of Limitations . . .

The defendant states that plaintiff had asked him in July, 1929, what he thought of this hernia. The defendant replied that there was a reasonable chance of curing it; that he thought it was a case suitable for the ordinary hernia operation: the abdominal muscles were in a reasonably good condition. In the operation the defendant found the muscles very much weaker than he had anticipated. In opening the inguinal canal the testicle appeared and was found grossly diseased; it was enlarged, nodular and softened. In order to cure the hernia it was necessary in the defendant's opinion to obliterate the canal completely so as not to leave any space. The defendant deemed it necessary to remove the testicle in order to cure the hernia, and also because it would be a menace to the health and life of the plaintiff to leave it. That, he says, was his best judgment in the circumstances. After the operation the defendant cut the testicle in two and found multiple abscesses in it. The defendant gave as his opinion that if the testicle had not been removed, it might have become gangrenous, and the pus might be absorbed into the circulation, and a condition of blood-poisoning have set up . . .

[The Court then considered various authorities which supported the following legal principles.]

1. That in the ordinary case where there is opportunity to obtain the consent of the patient it must be had. A person's body must be held inviolate and immune from invasion by the surgeon's knife, if an operation is not consented to. The rule applies not only to an operation but also to the case of mere examination, and it is pointed out in Taylor's Medical Jurisprudence, p. 59, that although the fact that a visit paid by a private patient to a practitioner implies consent to a certain amount of examination it must not be concluded that such a visit entitles the practitioner to compel an examination more intimate than the patient desires. Such an examination can only be made with the patient's consent; if made without such consent, it is technically an assault.

2. That such consent by the patient may be express or implied. If an operation is forbidden by the patient, consent is not to be implied; and Taylor again says: — "It must be constantly remembered that in this connection silence does not give consent, nor is compliance to be taken as consent."

3. That consent may be implied from the conversation preceding an operation or from the antecedent circumstances. It is said that if a soldier goes into battle with a knowledge beforehand that surgeons attached to the army are charged with the care of the wounded, the consent of the patient may be implied therefrom for such operations as the surgeon performs in good faith upon the soldier.

I am unable to see the force of the opinion, that in cases of emergency, where the patient agrees to a particular operation, and in the prosecution of the operation, a condition is found calling in the patient's interest for a different operation, the patient is said to have made the surgeon his representative to give consent. There is unreality about that view. The idea of appointing such a representation, the necessity for it, the existence of a condition calling for a different operation, are entirely absent from the minds of both patient and surgeon. The will of the patient is not exercised on the point. There is, in reality, no such appointment. I think it is better, instead of resorting to a fiction, to put consent altogether out of the case, where a great emergency which could not be anticipated arises, and to rule that it is the surgeon's duty to act in order to save the life or preserve the health of the patient; and that in the honest execution of that duty he should not be exposed to legal liability. It is, I think, more in conformity with the facts and with reason, to put a surgeon's justification in such cases on the higher ground of duty.

. . .

In the case at bar, I find that the defendant after making the incisions on plaintiff's body, discovered conditions which neither party had anticipated, and which the defendant could not reasonably have foreseen, and that in removing the testicle he acted in the interest of his patient and for the protection of his health and possibly his life. The removal I find was in that sense necessary, and it would be unreasonable to postpone the removal to a later date. I come to this conclusion despite the absence of express and possibly of implied assent on the part of the plaintiff.

[*Action dismissed*]

MALETTE v. SHULMAN

(1987), 63 O.R. (2d) 243 (Ont. H.C.)

[The plaintiff was seriously injured in a car accident and taken to the hospital where she was treated by Dr. Shulman. A nurse found a card in Mrs. Malette's wallet indicating the she was a Jehovah's Witness and was not to be given blood under any circumstances. Dr. Shulman was told of the card. However, when her condition deteriorated, Dr. Shulman, believing that she would otherwise die, started the first of several blood transfusions. When the plaintiff's daughter arrived four hours later, she confirmed that her mother was a practicing Jehovah's Witness and ordered the blood transfusions to be stopped. Dr. Shulman only stopped the transfusions after the plaintiff's condition was stabilized. She was transferred to the Toronto General Hospital and made a good recovery. She then sued Dr. Shulman in negligence and assault.]

DONNELLY J.: — Dr. Shulman, on being confronted by an unconscious patient in a life-threatening situation in whose possession was found a card refusing blood as a Jehovah's Witness, faced a dilemma of dreadful finality. An immediate decision was required, either to follow the instruction given by the card or to administer the blood transfusion which he regarded as medically essential. He squarely faced the fundamental issue of the conflict between the patient's right over her own body and society's interest in preserving life.

Dr. Shulman acknowledged an awareness of the patient's right to make a decision against a certain treatment in favour of alternative treatment and of his ethical obligation to abide by that decision. However, upon considering the validity of the card, he was not reasonably satisfied that it constituted an adequate instruction because there was no evidence that: (1) it represented the plaintiff's current intent; (2) the instruction applied to the present life-threatening circumstances; (3) at the time the plaintiff made the decision and signed the card she was fully informed of risks of refusal of treatment and accordingly that this was a rational and informed decision.

The "card" was subject to attack by the defence on the basis of its inherent frailties — that it may have been signed because of religious peer pressure, under medical misinformation, not in contemplation of life-threatening circumstances, or that it may not represent current instructions.

It was further argued, on behalf of Dr. Shulman, that the relatives' participation compounds the problem by adding further uncertainties, such as: is the relative the closest relative in blood; speaking for an unanimous consensus amongst the relatives; competent to give lawful consent; capable of understanding the risks; and devoid of self-interest.

Mrs. Bisson's participation has the effect of rendering unlikely these speculative frailties. It confirms the card and signature as her mother's, her mother's current status as a Jehovah's Witness and her mother's wish not to have blood. It raises nothing inconsistent with the card representing the mother's current intent applying to life-threatening situations. The card itself presents a clear, concise statement, essentially stating, "As a Jehovah's Witness, I refuse blood". That message is unqualified. It does not exempt life-threatening perils. On the face of the card, its message is seen to be rooted in religious conviction. Its obvious purpose, as a card, is as protection to speak in circumstances where the card carrier cannot (presumably because of illness or injury). There is no basis in evidence to indicate that the card may not represent the current intention and instruction of the card holder.

I therefore find that the card is a written declaration of a valid position which the card carrier may legitimately take in imposing a written restriction on her contract with the doctor. Dr. Shulman's doubt about the validity of the card, although honest, was not rationally founded on the evidence before him. Accordingly, but for the issue of informed refusal, there was no rationally founded basis for the doctor to ignore that restriction.

. . .

The defence contended that the doctrine of informed consent should be extended to informed refusal on the following analysis. Since there is an obligation on the doctor recommending treatment to advise as to the risks, it must logically follow there is a higher duty where the patient proposes a course of action that the doctor believes to be prejudicial. Thus, Dr. Shulman was obliged in law to advise the refusing patient of the attendant risks. Only then could he be satisfied that the refusal was based on a proper understanding of risks. There was no opportunity to fulfill his obligation to ensure there was an opportunity for an informed choice and so he was not bound by the refusal of treatment.

No case has been cited supporting this concept of informed refusal of treatment. Accordingly, I proceed without the benefit of authority and rely upon the following analysis. The principle underlying the doctrine of informed consent finds its roots in the patient's well-recognized right to self-determination of his body. The patient has the right to decide what, if anything, will be done to his body: *Hopp v. Lepp*, [1980] 2 S.C.R. 192, 13 C.C.L.T. 66, [1980] 4 W.W.R. 645, 22 A.R. 361, 112 D.L.R. (3d) 67, 4 L. Med. Q. 202, 32 N.R. 145 (S.C.C.). The treating doctor avoids liability for battery only with a valid consent. To be valid, that consent must be informed. Hence the need for the doctor to explain risks. The doctor is legally and ethically obliged to treat within the confines of that consent. The same liability considerations do not apply to a patient's refusal to accept treatment. In that instance the doctor is not exposed to a claim in battery. The right to refuse treatment is an inherent component of the supremacy of the patient's right over his own body. That right to refuse treatment is not premised on an understanding of the risks of refusal.

However sacred life may be, fair social comment admits that certain aspects of life are properly held to be more important than life itself. Such proud and honourable motivations are long entrenched in society, whether it be for patriotism in war, duty by law enforcement officers, protection of the life of a spouse, son or daughter, death before dishonour, death before loss of liberty, or religious martyrdom. Refusal of medical treatment on religious grounds is such a value.

. . .

The doctrine of informed consent does not extend to informed refusal. The written direction contained in the card was not properly disregarded on the basis that circumstances prohibited verification of that decision as an informed choice. The card constituted a valid restriction of Dr. Shulman's right to treat the patient and the administration of blood by Dr. Shulman did constitute battery.

[The judge awarded the plaintiff $20,000 in general damages for her mental distress. The Court of Appeal affirmed the trial judgment, but decided that it was unnecessary to address the issue of informed refusal. The court concluded that Dr. Shulman had no reason to doubt the validity of the instructions on the card. (1990), 2 C.C.L.T. (2d) 1.]

NOTES AND QUESTIONS

1. Based on *Marshall*, what must a doctor establish in order to operate without the plaintiff's consent? Do you agree with the application of these principles to the facts?

In *Murray v. McMurchy*, [1949] 2 D.L.R. 442 (B.C. S.C.), the defendant surgeon tied the plaintiff's fallopian tubes during a Caesarian section when he discovered tumours in the wall of her uterus. The court held that the health hazards posed by the tumours in the event of a subsequent pregnancy did not warrant this drastic action and awarded the plaintiff $3,000 damages. How would you reconcile *Marshall* and *Murray*? See also *Parmley v. Parmley and Yule*, [1945] 4 D.L.R. 81 (S.C.C.).

2. Could *Malette* have been argued as an unforeseen medical emergency? Do you agree with the trial judge that a patient's refusal is valid even if it is not premised on an understanding of the risks? Do you think the decision would have been the same if the plaintiff's daughter had not been a Jehovah's Witness and had urged Dr. Shulman to start the blood transfusions? See Siebrasse, "*Malette v. Shulman*: The Requirement of Consent in Medical Emergencies" (1989), 34 McGill L.J. 1080.

3. How sure must a health professional be that the patient prefers death to treatment? What should a health professional do if there is reason to believe that the patient who is refusing treatment is drunk, has a concussion or is in shock?

4. What are the implications of *Malette* for cases of attempted suicide? Would you advise a doctor to pump the stomach of an unconscious patient who had taken a potentially lethal overdose of drugs and left a clear note explaining why she preferred death to going on with life? Would her reasons for wanting to die be relevant? Should it make a difference if the doctor was convinced that the patient would change her mind about wanting to die if she could be kept alive for several days?

5. In light of *Malette*, can a competent patient give a binding advanced directive not to be resuscitated? See Silberfield, Madigan and Dickens, "Liability Concerns about the Implementation of Advanced Directives" (1995), 14 Estates & Trusts J. 241. For a discussion of do not resuscitate orders see Rabin, Gillerman and Rice, "Orders Not to Resuscitate" (1976), 295 New England J. Med. 364; Hashimoto, "A Structural Analysis of the Physician-Patient Relationship in No-Code Decisionmaking" (1983), 93 Yale L.J. 362; and Griener, "Stopping Futile Treatment and the Slide Toward Non-Voluntary Euthanasia" (1994), 2 Health L.J. 67.

6. For a discussion of an individual's right to refuse lifesaving treatment or care, see *A.G. B.C. v. Astaforoff* (1983), 6 C.C.C. (3d) 498 (B.C. C.A.); *A.G. Can. v. Notre Dame Hospital* (1984), 8 C.R.R. 382 (Que. S.C.); Cassell, "Autonomy in the Intensive Care Unit: The Refusal of Treatment" (1986), 13 Primary Care 395; and Gochnauer, "Refusal of Medical Treatment: Taking Respect for the Person Seriously" (1987), 2 Can. L.J. & Society 121.

7. Should a distinction be drawn between a patient refusing and withdrawing from lifesaving equipment? It must be noted that section 14 of the Criminal Code prohibits anyone from consenting to having death inflicted upon them, and section 241 makes it a federal criminal offence to aid, assist or counsel another to commit suicide. See *B. (N.) v. Hôtel-Dieu de Québec* (1992), 86 D.L.R. (4th) 385 (Que. S.C.); *Airedale N.H.S. Trust v. Bland*, [1993] A.C. 789 (H.L.); Gilmour, "Withholding and Withdrawing Life Support from Adults at Common Law" (1993), 31 Osgoode Hall L.J. 473; and Canada, *Of Life and Death: Report of the Special Senate Committee on Euthanasia and Assisted Suicide* (Ottawa: Minister of Supply and Services Canada, 1995).

(c) THE BURDEN OF PROOF AND CONSENT FORMS

Although the issue has generated academic debate, the courts have held that health professionals have the burden of proving consent on the balance of probabilities. In the absence of a statute to the contrary, the consent may be given orally or in writing. However, there has been a tendency for health professionals to be lulled into a false sense of security by having a signed consent form. A signed consent form provides only some evidence, not conclusive proof, of consent. The key issue is whether the patient understood the basic nature of the procedures and their risks, and consented to them, not whether she signed a piece of paper.

A signed consent form is only as good as the information it contains and the circumstances in which it is signed. A consent form will be of little value if it is written in general terms that do not identify the proposed procedure and explain its risks, is too technical for the patient to understand, or is presented to the patient as a mere formality or in circumstances in which there is no opportunity to read it. Similar problems will arise if the patient signs a consent form while intoxicated, drugged or in severe pain.

NOTES AND QUESTIONS

1. A significant percentage of the Canadian population cannot read English. In *Montaron v. Wagner* (1988), 43 C.C.L.T. 233 (Alta. Q.B.), aff'd. (1989), 70 Alta. L.R. (2d) 86 (C.A.), the plaintiff, who had obvious difficulties in understanding English, signed a consent form for far more radical surgery than he had verbally agreed to. Since no attempt had been made to ensure that he understood the procedure, the court held that the consent form was invalid. Would the result have been the same if the plaintiff's inability to read English had not been obvious? In other words, should health professionals assume that patients are functionally literate?

2. In *Brushett v. Cowan* (1990), 69 D.L.R. (4th) 743 (Nfld. C.A.), the plaintiff consented to a muscle biopsy and signed a form that stated, "I also consent to such further or alternative measures as may be found to be necessary during the course of the operation". In performing the muscle biopsy, the defendant observed an abnormal area of bone and did a bone biopsy. The court held that the consent form should be interpreted broadly, consistent with the goal of determining the cause of the plaintiff's medical problem. Consequently, it held that the form provided consent for the bone biopsy. In contrast, the trial court held that the open-ended wording of the consent form was too general to provide consent for the bone biopsy. Which judgment is preferable? See also *Pridham v. Nash* (1986), 57 O.R. (2d) 347 (H.C.).

3. For a discussion of the burden of proof and its relation to consent, see *Videto v. Kennedy* (1980), 107 D.L.R. (3d) 612 (Ont. H.C.), rev'd. on other grounds (1981), 125 D.L.R. (3d) 127; *McBain v. Laurentian Hospital* (1982), 35 C.P.C. 292 (Ont. H.C.); Blay, "Onus of Proof of Consent in an Action for Trespass

to the Person" (1987), 61 Australian L.J. 25; and Rhoden, "Litigating Life and Death" (1988), 102 Harvard L. Rev. 375.

(d) COMPETENCY TO CONSENT

To be valid, consent must be given by a patient who is legally competent. The common law test of competency focuses on the patient's ability to understand the nature of the proposed treatment and its risks, not her ability to make a reasoned or prudent decision. By defining competency broadly, the common law safeguards the autonomy of the individual. This very low threshold test must be applied on a case-by-case basis. If the patient is competent, it is her consent alone that is relevant. Indeed, it would be inappropriate to even discuss a patient's treatment with the next-of-kin without a patient's consent as that would involve a breach of confidence.

(i) *Minors*

There is no single recognized age of consent for medical treatment. The test for competency is the same, whether the patient is a minor or an adult. Generally, the courts will assess whether the patient is capable of understanding the nature of the proposed procedure and its risks. If the minor meets this test, then her consent is valid and parental consent is not required or relevant. In some cases, the courts have relied upon indicia of independence as a guide to the minor's competency.

In contrast to the common law's flexible test of competency, there are several provincial statutes, such as public hospital, mental health, human tissue gift and child welfare legislation, that may impose a minimum age requirement for consent to specified procedures in certain situations.

C. v. WREN

(1986), 35 D.L.R. (4th) 419 (Alta. C.A.)

KERANS J.A.: — Perhaps at the outset we should say what this case is *not* about. We agree with the learned chambers judge when he said:

> The only real issue in the case is the capacity of the expectant mother to consent to the proposed procedure. Other than the issue as to the capacity of the mother to consent, the conduct and authority of the therapeutic abortion committee had not been challenged [in these proceedings]. The issue is not whether or not abortions are legal, let alone morally right or wrong; the issue is simply one of the capacity to consent.

Perhaps I should add that the issue also is not whether the law recognizes any rights held by, to use a neutral term, foetal existence. None has been asserted in this case.

A 16-year-old girl became pregnant by her boyfriend while she was living at home. Several weeks later, she abruptly left home and went elsewhere and has since avoided contact with her parents. She also attended on a physician and surgeon with a view to an abortion and has received approval for it by the statutory committee provided under the *Criminal Code*. The urgency of the matter is that a statutory deadline looms.

The suit is by the parents against the doctor, and not the child. The doctor is not represented but the child has retained counsel and she intervenes.

The ground of appeal is that the learned chambers judge erred in finding that the expectant mother had given informed consent to the proposed surgical procedure.

The law in Alberta is that a surgeon may proceed with a surgical procedure immune from suits for assault if she or he has informed consent from the patient. That test was applied by the learned trial judge, and he found on the evidence before him that this child was capable of giving informed consent and had done so. Without more, that is an end to the matter.

It is argued before us today that informed consent means consent after consideration of issues like the ethics of abortion and the ethics of obligation by children to parents. It may be, as Lord Fraser has said in *Gillick v. West Norfolk & Wisbech Area Health Authority et al.*, [1985] 3 All E.R. 402, that doctors have an ethical obligation in circumstances like this to discuss issues of that sort with young patients. If so, the doctor would account to the College of Physicians and Surgeons for the performance of that obligation. That is not the issue before us today. Rather, the issue is whether these issues relate to the defence of consent to assault. In our view, they do not.

We agree with the learned chambers judge that no serious suggestion exists on the evidence here of a lack of informed consent. Accordingly, there are no grounds to enjoin the doctor from proceeding because there is no suggestion that there will be an illegal assault.

The real issue here relates to an obvious and painful dispute between parent and child about the appropriateness in non-medical terms of the proposed abortion. We express in that respect our sympathy both to the parents and the child for this unfortunate confrontation.

The real thrust of argument before us was that children should obey their parents and the courts should intervene to prevent others from interfering with parental control of those children who are committed to their custody and control. That is not quite the suit that has been brought here today, but we will deal with the issue. Parental rights (and obligations) clearly do exist and they do not wholly disappear until the age of majority. The modern law, however, is that the courts will exercise increasing restraint in that regard as a child grows to and through adolescence. The law and the development of the law in this respect was analyzed in detail by Lord Scarman in the *Gillick* case. He analyzes the law back to Blackstone and extracts this principle [at p. 421]:

> The principle is that parental right or power of control of the person and property of his child exists primarily to enable the parent to discharge his duty of maintenance, protection and education until he reaches such an age as to be able to look after himself and make his own decisions.

He then reviews the application of that principle in cases over the past century, especially in the "age of discretion" cases. He says [at p. 422]:

> The "age of discretion" cases are cases in which a parent or guardian (usually the father) has applied for habeas corpus to secure the return of his child who has left home without his consent. The courts would refuse an order if the child had attained the age of discretion, which came to be regarded as 14 for boys and 16 for girls, and did not wish to return. The principle underlying

them was plainly that an order would be refused if the child had sufficient intelligence and understanding to make up his own mind.

He then concludes that the governing rule is [at p. 423]:

> In the light of the foregoing I would hold that as a matter of law the parental right to determine whether or not their minor child below the age of 16 will have medical treatment terminates if and when the child achieves a sufficient understanding and intelligence to enable him or her to understand fully what is proposed.

We accept that in that context he says that "understand fully" means understand things like obligation to parents as well as medical matters.

What is the application of the principle in this case? We infer from the circumstances detailed in argument here that this expectant mother and her parents had fully discussed the ethical issues involved and, most regrettably, disagreed. We cannot infer from that disagreement that this expectant mother did not have sufficient intelligence and understanding to make up her own mind. Meanwhile, it is conceded that she is a "normal intelligent 16 year old". We infer that she did have sufficient intelligence and understanding to make up her own mind and did so. At her age and level of understanding, the law is that she is to be permitted to do so.

Accordingly, we dismiss the appeal.

Appeal dismissed.

NOTES AND QUESTIONS

1. What was the basis of the decision in *C. v. Wren*? Would the court have reached the same decision if C. had been 13 years old and living at home? What impact would these factors have had on C.'s competency?

2. The Criminal Code, s. 215 requires parents and guardians to provide the "necessaries of life" for a child under the age of 16. The failure to do so without a lawful excuse constitutes a federal criminal offence. The provincial child welfare legislation typically imposes a similar legal duty on parents and guardians. See, for example, the Child and Family Services Act, R.S.O. 1990, c. C.11, s. 79.

What impact does this penal legislation have on the common law principles which permit competent children to make their own treatment decisions regardless of their parents' wishes?

3. In *Re L.D.K.; Children's Aid Society of Metro. Toronto v. K. and K.* (1985), 48 R.F.L. (2d) 164 (Ont. Prov. Ct.), the court held that a 12-year-old girl, who was suffering from leukemia, had the Charter right to refuse chemotherapy. Would the decision have been different if L.D.K.'s parents had urged the court to order a blood transfusion? The girl was a Jehovah's Witness and refused to undertake the treatment which included blood transfusions. The court stated at 168:

> L's position is now and has been from the day she saw a documentary on this disease that she does not want any part of chemotherapy and blood transfusions. She takes this position not only because it offends her religious beliefs, and I am satisfied that it does, but also because she does not want to experience the pain and anguish associated with the treatment process.

By considering L.D.K.'s wishes, did the court imply that she was competent to consent or withhold consent to medical treatment? The Children's Aid Society was making the application because the girl's parents also refused consent. Would the court have upheld the validity of L.D.K.'s refusal if she had not been terminally ill? See also *Re Y. (A.)* (1993), 111 Nfld. & P.E.I.R. 91 (Nfld. U.F.C.); and *Walker (Litigation Guardian of) v. Region 2 Hospital Corp.* (1994), 116 D.L.R. (4th) 477 (N.B. C.A.).

4. As discussed earlier, some courts have been willing to negate the plaintiff's otherwise valid consent on "public policy" grounds. Should the courts apply this principle to cases in which young, competent patients make medical decisions that threaten their physical or mental well-being? What

is the justification for negating a competent minor's medical decisions, but not the equally threatening decisions of competent adults?

5. Can you rationalize negating the consent of the foster daughter to sex in *M.(M.) v. K.(K.)* (1989), 38 B.C.L.R. (2d) 273 (C.A.), but not negating the consent of a competent minor who makes a medical decision that threatens her well-being?

REVIEW PROBLEM

The Children's Aid Society received information that Sara, a 13-year-old girl, has been sexually abused by her father. When confronted, Sara denied the allegations and appeared very upset. She was concerned about the impact such a charge would have on her father and family. Sara's school friends said that Sara was afraid of her father. The Society has requested that Sara undergo a medical examination at the local Children's Hospital. Both Sara and her parents have vehemently refused consent to the examination. Advise the Society as to its potential tort liability if it proceeds with the examination. See *M. (J.) v. Toronto Bd. of Education* (1987), 38 D.L.R. (4th) 627 (Ont. H.C.).

(ii) *Adults*

The issue of an adult's competency arises most often in cases involving mentally ill or senile patients. However, the mere fact that a patient is mentally ill or senile does not mean that he or she is incapable of giving a valid consent. Health professionals must assess the capacity of each patient in relation to the specific procedure or treatment. This principle may be extremely difficult to apply in many situations. For example, one need only consider the case of an occasionally disoriented alcoholic, a sedated patient or a patient in shock.

These general principles apply equally to those in custody or under other legal restraints, unless there is express statutory authority to the contrary. The fact that a patient's refusal to consent or accept treatment may constitute a violation of her probation does not alter the healthcare professional's obligation to abide by the decision.

NOTES AND QUESTIONS

1. The Canadian courts have held that a consent given while a patient is sedated or in pain may be invalid. See *Beausoleil v. Soeurs de la Charite* (1964), 53 D.L.R. (2d) 65 (Que. C.A.); *Ferguson v. Hamilton Civic Hospitals* (1983), 23 C.C.L.T. 254 (Ont. H.C.), aff'd. (1985), 33 C.C.L.T. 56 (Ont. C.A.). In *Mitchell v. McDonald* (1987), 40 C.C.L.T. 266 (Alta. Q.B.), the court held that the plaintiff's agonized plea, "For God's sake, stop", in the middle of an injection did not constitute an express withdrawal of consent. The court viewed the plaintiff's cry as a plea to stop the pain. See also *Ciarlariello v. Schacter* (1991), 5 C.C.L.T. (2d) 221 (Ont. C.A.), aff'd. [1993] 2 S.C.R. 119.

2. Healthcare professionals must refuse police requests to take blood samples or conduct other tests on unwilling or unconscious suspects. This situation must be distinguished from an unforeseen medical emergency in which it is impossible to obtain the suspect's consent. In these situations, the staff may intervene in an effort to save the life or preserve the health of the suspect. Nevertheless, the sample or test results should not be given to the police. Rather, the police would have to obtain a search warrant authorizing the seizure of the data. In 1985, Parliament introduced a special warrant which authorizes police to have health professionals take blood samples from unconscious drinking and driving suspects in limited circumstances. See Criminal Code, s. 256.

In July 1995, Parliament amended the Criminal Code (ss. 487.04-487.09) and the Young Offenders Act, R.S.C. 1985, c. Y-1 (s. 44.1) to authorize the collection of hair, saliva and blood samples for DNA testing for certain offences.

3. In the absence of a statute to the contrary, can health professionals force feed prisoners, the

elderly or those suffering from anorexia nervosa? See Dresser, "Feeding the Hunger Artists: Legal Issues in Treating Anorexia Nervosa" [1984] Wis. L. Rev. 297; and Zellick, "The Forced Feeding of Prisoners: An Examination of the Legality of Enforced Therapy", [1976] Pub. L. 153.

4. For a discussion of consent to treatment for prisoners and the mentally ill, see Somerville, "Refusal of Medical Treatment in 'Captive' Circumstances" (1985), 63 Can. Bar Rev. 59; and Miller, "The U.S. Supreme Court Looks at Voluntariness and Consent" (1994), 17 Int'l J. L. & Psych. 293.

5. For a discussion of consent and competency issues involving the elderly, see Sadavoy, "Psychiatric Aspects of Mental Competence and Protection Issues in the Elderly" (1983), 4 Health Law in Can. 1; Schafer, "Restraints and the Elderly: When Safety and Autonomy Conflict" (1985), 132 Can. Med. Assoc. J. 1257; and Alzheimer Society of Metropolitan Toronto Inc., *Alzheimer's Disease: Legal and Financial Concerns*, 2nd rev. ed. (Nov. 1989).

(e) SUBSTITUTE CONSENT

Certain patients such as young children and the severely mentally ill are clearly incapable of giving a valid consent to treatment. The practice in such cases has been for health professionals to obtain substitute consent from the patient's next-of-kin. The courts have upheld these consents provided the patient was incompetent, the next-of-kin acted in good faith and the procedure was in the patient's best interest. While relatively easy to state, these principles may be extremely difficult to apply.

The legal issues concerning substitute consent are even more complex when the procedure is performed solely for research purposes. Since these procedures cannot be justified as being in the patient's best interest, the substitute consent may be invalid and the doctor may be held civilly and criminally liable. Members of the medical profession have argued that research based on substitute consent is essential to the development of effective treatment for childhood diseases, degenerative mental illnesses and other medical conditions. To date these issues have been discussed in the medical and legal communities, but have not been squarely addressed by either the legislatures or the courts.

NOTES AND QUESTIONS

1. In *"Eve" v. "Mrs. E."*, [1986] 2 S.C.R. 388, the court unanimously held that the non-therapeutic sterilization of an incompetent mentally handicapped adult could never be justified as being in the patient's interests pursuant to a substitute consent. La Forest J., writing for the court, strongly stated that the interests of the parents, the institution or others could not be considered in defining the patient's best interests.

But see *Re B. (a minor)*, [1987] 2 All E.R. 206 (H.L.), where Lord Hailsham states at 213:

... I find, with great respect, his conclusion (at 32) that the procedure of sterilisation "should *never* be authorised for non-therapeutic purposes" (my emphasis) totally unconvincing and in startling contradiction to the welfare principle which should be the first and paramount consideration in wardship cases. Moreover ... the distinction he purports to draw between "therapeutic" and "non-therapeutic" purposes of this operation ... [is] totally meaningless. ... To talk of the "basic right" to reproduce of an individual who is not capable of knowing the causal connection between intercourse and childbirth, the nature of pregnancy, what is involved in delivery, unable to form maternal instincts or to care for a child appears to me wholly to part company with reality.

2. Which of these judgments do you prefer? See Keyserlingk, "The Eve Decision — A Common Law Perspective" (1987), 18 R.G.D. 657; Grubb and Pearl, "Sterilization and the Courts" (1987), 46(3) Cambridge L.J. 439; and Olesen, "Eve and the Forbidden Fruit: Reflections on a Feminist Methodology" (1994), 3 Dalhousie J. Leg. Stud. 231.

3. In *Re K. and Public Trustee* (1985), 19 D.L.R. (4th) 255 (B.C. C.A.), the court authorized performing a hysterectomy on a severely mentally handicapped girl who had a phobic aversion to blood and would otherwise begin menstruation soon. Leave to appeal ref'd. [1985] 4 W.W.R. 757n (S.C.C.). The Supreme Court of Canada in *Eve* questioned the decision in *Re K.*, but ultimately distinguished the case on the grounds that it raised an issue quite different from that of sterilization for contraceptive purposes. Do you agree?

4. The issue of sterilizing the apparently handicapped has been highlighted by *Muir v. Alberta* (1996), 36 Alta. L.R. (3d) 305 (Q.B.). In 1996, Ms. Muir was awarded $740,780 against the Alberta government, which had authorized her sterilization in 1959 under the province's sterilization act. This legislation was enacted in 1928, but not repealed until 1972, well after the eugenics movement had been discredited by the Nazi regime and new research had established that "feeble mindedness" was not inherited. The legislation permitted the sterilization of "mental defectives", "psychotics" and those with Huntington's Chorea. Over 2,900 people were sterilized under the act. British Columbia and at least 15 American states had similar legislation.

5. What are the implications of *Re Eve* for the validity of substitute consent to participation in research, donations of regenerative tissue and the circumcision of males for religious purposes? See Schollenberg, "Medical Care Disputes and the Best Interests of the Child: Integrating the Medical Evidence" (1989), 18 Man. L.J. 308; and Baylis and Downie, "An Ethical and Criminal Law Framework for Research Involving Children in Canada" (1993), 1 Health L.J. 39.

6. What principles should govern parents' refusal to authorize life-saving treatment for their children? As indicated, such conduct may render the parents criminally liable and result in the child being a ward of the Crown. See *Re Superintendent of Family & Child Services and Dawson* (1983), 145 D.L.R. (3d) 210 (B.C. S.C.); *Couture-Jacquet v. Montreal Children's Hospital* (1986), 28 D.L.R. (4th) 22 (Que. C.A.); and *B. (R.) v. Children's Aid Society of Metropolitan Toronto* (1992), 10 O.R. (3d) 321 (C.A.). See also *Re B. (a minor)*, [1990] 3 All E.R. 927 (C.A.); *Re J. (a minor)*, [1990] 3 All E.R. 930 (C.A.); and *Re J. (a minor)*, [1992] 4 All E.R. 614 (C.A.).

This issue has generated considerable academic debate. See, for example, Keyserlink, "Non-Treatment in the Best Interests of the Child . . ." (1987), 32 McGill L.J. 413; Magnet and Kluge, *Withholding Treatment from Defective Newborn Children* (1985); Neal, "Ethical Aspects in the Case of Very Low Birth Weight Infants" (1990), 17 Paediatrician 92; and Griffith, "The Best Interests Standard: A Comparison . . ." (1991), 7 Issues in L. & Med. 283.

7. In *Superintendent of Belchertown State School v. Saikewicz*, 370 N.E. 2d 417 (Mass. S.C., 1977), the court considered whether a 67-year-old mentally retarded man who was dying of leukaemia should undergo the painful chemotherapy needed to prolong his life. The chemotherapy would not provide a cure, but rather a 30% to 40% chance of a temporary remission. On average, the remission prolonged the patient's life by one year. Saikewicz had an IQ of 10 and because of this extremely limited mental capacity, could not cooperate with chemotherapy. He was not in any pain and was expected to die relatively painlessly within weeks or months if he was not given chemotherapy. The trial court held that the chemotherapy was not in Saikewicz's best interest and ordered that no treatment be administered. The appeal court affirmed the decision.

Was it in Saikewicz's best interests to be allowed to die without treatment? Do you think the decision would have, or should have, been the same if: (a) Saikewicz had been incompetent, but not mentally retarded; or (b) the therapy had a 30% to 40% chance of prolonging his life by five years? What are the implications of *Saikewicz* for patients with Alzheimer's disease or who are in a coma? See generally "Symposium — Mental Incompetents and the Right to Die" (1977), 11 Suffolk U. L. Rev.; and Annas, "Reconciling *Quinlan* and *Saikewicz*: Decision Making for the Terminally Ill Incompetent" [1979] Am. J. L. & Med. 367.

(f) INFORMED CONSENT: BATTERY OR NEGLIGENCE?

Traditionally, a doctor's failure to obtain a valid consent was viewed as a basis for a battery action, whether the lack of consent was due to a failure to disclose the risks or misrepresentation. In the late 1950s, the American courts began to analyze some medical consent cases in terms of negligence — has the doctor failed to exercise a reasonable standard of care in advising the patient of the nature of the procedure and its risks? The Canadian courts adopted a similar approach. As in the United States, this development created uncertainty as to the boundary between medical battery and medical negligence.

The Supreme Court of Canada had an opportunity to specifically address this issue in *Reibl v. Hughes* (1980), 114 D.L.R. (3d) 1, and *Hopp v. Lepp* (1980), 112 D.L.R. (3d) 67. It held that once a plaintiff is aware of the general nature of the treatment, she cannot bring a battery action because she has not been informed of the risks. Rather, battery actions are limited to cases in which the patient did not consent at all, the consent was exceeded or the consent was obtained fraudulently. In all other cases, the plaintiff must bring a negligence action for failure to disclose the risks. By requiring a plaintiff to frame these actions in negligence, the Supreme Court has significantly limited the scope of healthcare professionals' potential liability.

However, in Ontario the Health Care Consent Act stipulates that a consent is not valid unless it is informed. Therefore, under the Act, if a patient is not informed of the risks of her treatment her consent will be invalid and she will be able to bring a battery action.

REVIEW PROBLEM

A physician has contacted you about a 62-year-old alcoholic patient in the emergency room. The patient, who lives alone, fell down his stairs and lay there for several hours before his daughter found him. The patient has a bad gash that requires stitches, but the physician is more concerned about the patient's alcoholism which has repeatedly brought him into hospital since his wife died two years ago. The physician wants to admit the patient to hospital for about a week in order to "dry him out", conduct medical tests and procedures related to his alcoholism, stabilize his deteriorating physical condition, and encourage him to enter an alcohol treatment program.

The patient is still somewhat intoxicated, but fully aware of his surroundings. At his daughter's urging, he has reluctantly agreed to have the gash sutured, sleep over in the hospital, and have "any stupid tests you want". However, the patient vehemently denies that he is an alcoholic or that his drinking has caused any problems in his life. If his past behaviour is any indication, the patient will leave the next day, as soon as he feels well enough to get a cab and go home.

The patient's daughter has pleaded with the physician to keep her father in hospital long enough to get him back on his feet and break the cycle of his self-destructive behaviour. In the daughter's view, her father's denial of his alcoholism and rapidly deteriorating physical and mental health provide overwhelming proof of his incompetency. She is willing to sign whatever documents are necessary to give substitute consent for her father's hospitalization and treatment.

The physician has sought your advice on two issues: (1) Is the patient competent to consent to his admission to hospital and treatment that night?; and (2) Would the patient be competent to refuse treatment and leave the hospital the next day?

DEFENCES RELATED TO THE PROTECTION OF PERSON AND PROPERTY

1. Self-Defence
2. Defence of Third Parties
3. Discipline
4. Defence of Real Property
5. The Defence and Recapture of Chattels
6. Public and Private Necessity
7. Apportionment of Fault in Intentional Torts

1. Self-Defence

In order to invoke the defence of self-defence, the defendant must establish on the balance of probabilities that he reasonably believed he was about to be assaulted and that the amount of force he used was reasonable in the circumstances. The defendant's right to invoke the defence ceases once the danger has passed. Self-defence is a complete defence.

WACKETT v. CALDER

(1965), 51 D.L.R. (2d) 598 (B.C. C.A.)

DAVEY J.A.: — I would allow the appeal and dismiss the action for the reasons given by my brother Bull.

MACLEAN J.A. (dissenting): — The defendant appeals a judgment for damages for an assault following an encounter between the plaintiff and defendant in a beer parlour at Dawson Creek, B.C.

The facts have been found by the learned trial Judge as follows:

> The most accurate account of what occurred outside the hotel is to be found in the evidence of the defendant and of his brother, Raymond Calder, both of whom were truthful witnesses. The plaintiff testified untruthfully on so many occasions as to the events that occurred earlier that afternoon and during the evening in question that it is impossible to give any credence to his evidence except where it is corroborated by other credible evidence. Having arrived outside, the plaintiff reiterated his insulting remarks and invited the defendant to engage in a fight. He endeavoured, without much success, to strike both the defendant and his brother. He lurched at them and with his fists pounded them in a rather futile way upon their chests, doing no harm whatever. On one occasion when the plaintiff struck at the defendant, the defendant hit the plaintiff in the face with his fist, knocking the plaintiff to the ground. The plaintiff got up and went for the defendant again. The defendant hit him again and that time the plaintiff "didn't get up so fast." The defendant then returned to the beer parlour, leaving the plaintiff still wanting to fight.

The learned Judge then went on to find that the force used by the defendant was excessive under the circumstances, and finally he concluded:

> The anger of the defendant is easily understood, but it is the policy of the law to discourage violence. Challenges to fight are accepted at some considerable peril, at law. It must have been apparent to the defendant soon after he went outside that the plaintiff's challenge to fight was alcoholic-induced bravado and that, by reason of his intoxication, he was incapable of anything but talk and wild swinging. The defendant could and should have terminated the whole unpleasant episode by returning into the hotel, leaving the authorities to deal with the plaintiff. Instead he delivered two blows to the face of the plaintiff with considerable force — sufficient to knock him down and break a well-protected bone in the cheek. While it is not clear how the plaintiff's wrist got broken, I think it is probable that he must have fallen upon it during the fight.

In my view there is implicit in this judgment a finding that the defendant was not entitled to rely on self-defence — he could have walked away and avoided "the unpleasant episode by returning to the hotel," and secondly, that even if he was entitled to use force to defend himself, he used "excessive force under the circumstances."

I take it that in coming to the latter conclusion the learned Judge was aware of the long line of cases which enunciate the principle that a defendant or accused person when attacked is not required to "measure with complete nicety" the force necessary to repel the attack or apprehended attack: *R. v. Ogal*, [1928] 3 D.L.R. 676, 50 C.C.C. 71, 23 A.L.R. 511, [1928] 2 W.W.R. 465.

In my view the learned Judge's conclusions are supported by the evidence and I would not venture to disturb his judgment.

I would dismiss the appeal.

BULL J.A.: — It is clear that what constitutes excessive force beyond what was reasonably necessary under all circumstances depends in each case upon its own facts, and is a matter for the trial Judge, the findings of whom an appellate Court should not lightly question. However, with the greatest deference, it seems apparent that the finding of excessive force was based on conclusions and inferences from evidence which did not wholly support them. Although there was evidence that the respondent was clearly intoxicated, there was no evidence that he was physically incapacitated or unduly unco-ordinated, or in any way incapable of doing serious physical damage to others. He was a man of middle age weighing some 192 pounds and the evidence was clear that he was not staggering, but was in a belligerent and obviously dangerous mood. Again, the learned trial Judge, in giving his views as to what the appellant might have done to end the dispute, seems to have overlooked the evidence of both the appellant and his brother, both of whom he found truthful witnesses, that they were turning away to re-enter the hotel when the respondent attacked and struck the appellant the second time and, received, in turn, the appellant's second blow. It seemed clear that it was this second blow which was the most serious and caused the injury to the defendant's face.

As the learned trial Judge weighed the force used on conclusions which were, in part at least, unsupported by the evidence, an appellate Court is justified in reassessing the evidence directed to this issue and is, I submit with deference, in as good a position as the trial Judge to do so.

The only question here was whether the two blows by the appellant were more than reasonably necessary under all the attendant circumstances, and no question of the use of disproportionate force is involved. The appellant was entitled to reject force with force and, under the authorities, not being bound to take a passive defence, is entitled to return blow for blow. He could act in the light of the apparent urgency of the situation, but he could not trespass beyond the reasonable limits thereof. However, it has been long held that an attacked person defending himself and confronted with a provoking situation is not held down to measure with exactitude or nicety the weight or power of his blows.

In this case there is no evidence whatsoever that the two blows given by appellant were vicious. That one at least was forceful is obvious, but the combined effect of both were not sufficient to render the intoxicated respondent "hors de combat". The first blow was insufficient to stop the respondent's attack on the appellant, and, in my respectful opinion, the second more forceful blow was well justified to put an end to the episode.

Accordingly, on the facts as found by the learned trial Judge, excluding only his conclusions as to the quantum or measure of force used, I would allow the appeal and order the action dismissed.

NOTES AND QUESTIONS

1. Was the defendant in danger of physical injury? Must the defendant prove that the plaintiff posed a threat of physical injury or merely a threat of any socially offensive or physically harmful contact? See *Cachay v. Nemeth* (1972), 28 D.L.R. (3d) 603 (Sask. Q.B.).

2. Is Maclean J.A. suggesting that self-defence cannot be used by a defendant who ignored an opportunity to walk away from a fight? Would you favour the adoption of this principle? What impact, if any, should the fact that the defendant did not walk away from the threat have on the issue of excessive force?

3. Did the defendant use excessive force in the circumstances? How do you reconcile the principle that the force used must be reasonable with the concept that a person who is attacked is not required to measure with "nicety the weight of his blows"? The burden of proof is on the defendant to establish that he was in danger and that he used only reasonable force. See *Mann v. Balaban*, [1970] S.C.R. 74.

In determining whether the force used was excessive, the court should consider the nature of the force used and the circumstances, but not the resultant injuries. For example in *Brown v. Wilson* (1975), 66 D.L.R. (3d) 295 (B.C. S.C.), the defendant picked up Brown, who was about to hit him, in a bear hug. In attempting to carry Brown out of the bar, the defendant slipped and Brown fell, hitting his head on the concrete. Although Brown died, the court held that the use of a bear hug was reasonable in the circumstances even though it led to a tragic result.

4. The criminal courts now use a subjective/objective test in determining whether the defendant used excessive force in the circumstances. The Privy Council in *Beckford v. R.*, [1987] 3 All E.R. 425, stated that the defendant is expected to react to the threat he subjectively perceives as would a reasonable person in the circumstances as the defendant believed them to be. See also *R. v. Blair*, [1987] B.C.J. No. 581 (Q.L.) (Co. Ct.).

5. The right to use deadly force in self-defence is limited to situations in which it is necessary to protect oneself from death or serious physical injury. See the Criminal Code, ss. 34-35; *R. v. Smith* (1837), 173 E.R. 441 (N.P.); and *R. v. Bogue* (1976), 30 C.C.C. (2d) 403 (Ont. C.A.).

Contrary to some American authorities, the Canadian courts will not permit a person to use deadly force in self-defence, merely because the altercation took place in his home. Contrast *State v. Johnson* (1964), 136 S.E. (2d) 84 (N.C. S.C.) and *Veinot v. Veinot* (1977), 81 D.L.R. (3d) 549 (N.S. C.A.).

6. For a discussion of self-defence in the context of resisting arrest and search, see *Kenlin v. Gardiner*, [1966] 3 All E.R. 931 (Q.B.); *R. v. Larlham*, [1971] 4 W.W.R. 304 (B.C. C.A.); and *Albert v. Lavin*, [1981] 3 All E.R. 878 (H.L.).

7. Although a defendant must usually establish that he was in danger at the time he acted, he does not have to wait for the other party to strike the first blow. A defendant who attempts to pre-

empt an assault by becoming the aggressor may still invoke self-defence. The plaintiff's reputation for violence or prior violent behaviour can be raised to justify the defendant's decision to strike first. See *R. v. Scopelliti* (1981), 63 C.C.C. (2d) 481 (Ont. C.A.); *R. v. Ryan* (1989), 49 C.C.C. (3d) 490 (Nfld. C.A.); and *Bruce v. Dyer*, [1966] 2 O.R. (H.C.), aff'd. [1970] 1 O.R. 482n (C.A.).

A more troubling situation arises where the defendant kills a person to end an ongoing relationship of violence. In *Lavallee v. R.*, [1990] 1 S.C.R. 852, a battered woman shot her partner in the back of the head as he was leaving the room. He had beaten her frequently, and on that night had physically abused her and taunted her that if she did not kill him, he would kill her. The court relied on the psychiatric testimony about the difficulty battered women have in escaping abusive relationships and their ongoing terror. The psychiatrist also testified that the accused sincerely believed that shooting the deceased was the only way to avoid being killed that night. The Supreme Court restored her acquittal on the basis of self-defence.

However, it is unclear how immediate the threat has to be before the defence can be raised. In *R. v. Whynot (Stafford)* (1983), 61 N.S.R. (2d) 33 (C.A.), a woman shot and killed her common law spouse, who had become drunk and passed out. Although the deceased had a history of violence and had beaten the accused from time to time, the Court of Appeal held that self-defence was not available, because "no person has the right in anticipation of an assault that may or may not happen, to apply force to prevent the imaginary assault." Can you reconcile *Whynot* and *Lavallee*? What non-legal factors might explain the different results in these cases?

8. A person who makes a reasonable and *bona fide* mistake of fact in acting in self-defence will be privileged. See *R. v. Fennell*, [1970] 2 All E.R. 215 (C.A.); *Reilly v. R.* (1984), 15 C.C.C. (3d) 1 (S.C.C.); Forbes, "Mistake of Fact with Regard to Defences to Tort Law" (1970), 4 Ottawa L. Rev. 304; and Giles, "Self-Defence and Mistake: A Way Forward" (1990), 53 Mod. L. Rev. 187.

2. Defence of Third Parties

GAMBRIELL v. CAPARELLI

(1974), 7 O.R. (2d) 205, 54 D.L.R. (3d) 661 (Ont. Co. Ct.)

CARTER, CO. CT. J.: — At about 5:30 in the afternoon of July 17, 1970, Fred Caparelli, then 21 years of age, and the son of the defendant, decided to wash his automobile which he had parked in the said laneway at the rear of the back-yard of his residence. While he was getting the garden hose, the plaintiff (then aged 50), whose car was parked at the rear of his lot, decided to go shopping. In backing out of his lot onto the laneway, the rear of his vehicle came into contact with the rear of young Caparelli's vehicle.

Attracted by the noise of the impact, the Caparelli lad came running out and saw a little dent in the bumper of his car. He and the plaintiff began screaming at each other. Caparelli said he was going to call the police, there was further argument, the plaintiff started to get back in his car, Caparelli grabbed the plaintiff, who then hit Caparelli on the face with his fist. The blow was returned, other blows exchanged. The Caparelli boy, in the course of the fight, was backing up towards the rear of the plaintiff's car and fell back against the car. The plaintiff says that the Caparelli boy kicked him in the chest, leaving a heel mark on the skin, but this is not concurred in by the plaintiff's wife, nor did the plaintiff show this alleged mark to the police.

The Caparelli boy states that the plaintiff then put both hands around his neck and held him down and was choking him and that he was having trouble breathing. The plaintiff said that he never touched the boy's throat.

At this juncture, the defendant, a woman of 57 years at the time, the mother of young Caparelli, appeared on the scene, attracted by the screaming. She said she saw the plaintiff holding her son by the neck, that her son was under the plaintiff and that she thought her son was being choked. She said that she yelled — "stop! stop! stop!" She then ran into her garden and got a metal three-pronged garden cultivator tool with a five-foot-long wooden handle. She said she struck the plaintiff with this three times on the shoulder and then on the head. As soon as the plaintiff saw the blood flowing from his head he released the defendant's son.

. . .

In *R. v. Duffy*, [1967] 1 Q.B. 63, one Kathleen Duffy hit a man named Mohammed Akbar in a tavern. Elizabeth Duffy, sister of Kathleen, appeared from the wash-room and saw Kathleen on her knees on the floor fighting with Akbar, who was holding her by the hair. Elizabeth pulled Akbar's hair to pull him off her sister but did not succeed, and when he kicked her on the leg she hit him on the head with a bottle, as a result of which Akbar received severe lacerations to his face, forehead and head. Elizabeth was convicted of unlawful wounding. On appeal to the Court of Criminal Appeal, the Court quashed her conviction, and at p. 67, Edmund Davies, J. (as he then was), reading the judgment of the Court, said:

> Quite apart from any special relations between the person attacked and his rescuer, there is a general liberty even as between strangers to prevent a felony.

. . .

Again in *R. v. Fennell*, [1971] 1 Q.B. 428 at p. 431, Lord Justice Widgery, delivering the judgment of the Court said:

> Where a person honestly and reasonably believes that he or his child is in imminent danger of injury it would be unjust if he were deprived of the right to use reasonable force by way of defence merely because he had made some genuine mistake of fact.

While the cases I have cited all deal with criminal matters, the principles outlined therein are of equal weight in a civil case of this nature.

It would appear therefore that, where a person in intervening to rescue another holds an honest (though mistaken) belief that the other person is in imminent danger of injury, he is justified in using force, provided that such force is reasonable; and the necessity for intervention and the reasonableness of the force employed are questions to be decided by the trier of fact.

Having regard, therefore, to the facts as I have found them and to the law as I understand it, in my opinion, when the defendant appeared on the scene and saw her son at the mercy of the plaintiff, and being of the belief that her son was in imminent danger of injury, she was justified in using force to prevent that injury from occurring.

. . .

The next question is — Was the force she used reasonable in the circumstances? In the witness-box, the defendant impressed me as a woman who, under normal circumstances, would be quite cool and collected. She is a woman of average build, and as I have indicated, of mature years. As her knowledge of English was slight, her evidence was given in Italian and translated by an interpreter. When she saw her son with the plaintiff's hand about his neck, she shouted for the plaintiff to stop, to no avail. Then she ran and seized the nearest implement she could find, which happened to be a cultivator fork. She struck the plaintiff three times on the shoulder, again to no avail, and finally struck him on the head. I think the fact that the plaintiff sustained only lacerations to his head rather than a fractured skull is indicative of the fact that the force she used in striking the plaintiff was not, in the circumstances, excessive.

In my opinion she had little other choice. If the plaintiff could overpower her son, the empty-handed aid of a woman some seven years older than the plaintiff would have availed little. On the evidence, she was alone in the laneway with the exception of the combatants and Mrs. Gambriell, who did nothing to assist. Had she run for aid, her son might well have been beyond recovery before she returned, especially as, speaking Italian, she may have encountered difficulty in summoning aid. While I am loath to excuse violence, there are times, and I think this is one of them, when the violence inflicted by the defendant on the plaintiff and the degree of such violence was justified and not unreasonable in the circumstances. I would therefore dismiss the plaintiff's case.

I should, in the event that I am in error in my disposition of the plaintiff's claim, assess the plaintiff's damages. No special damages were claimed. The doctor's report indicated that there were no resulting effects from the head injury and that the plaintiff had fully recovered. I am not satisfied that the plaintiff received an injury to his chest. Further, in cross-examination, he indicated that, although he had headaches for two months, it did not interfere with his work at all.

I am of the opinion that the plaintiff was the author of his own misfortune. On the evidence, the plaintiff struck the first blow, and in the course of the fight, the Caparelli boy was backing away from the plaintiff, and the plaintiff could well have desisted. Under all these circumstances, even had I found for the plaintiff, I would not have awarded damages in excess of $1.

I do not, however, think that this is a proper case for costs, and I therefore, as I have said above, dismiss the plaintiff's case, but without costs.

NOTES AND QUESTIONS

1. If the only weapon available to the defendant had been a knife, would she have been privileged to stab the plaintiff in defence of her son?

2. The judge indicated that he would have awarded the plaintiff only one dollar had his action succeeded. Could such an award have been justified based on the principles of damages in intentional torts?

3. In *Cachay v. Nemeth* (1972), 28 D.L.R. (3d) 603 (Sask. Q.B.), the plaintiff, while at a party, attempted to kiss the defendant's wife on the cheek. The defendant, who was trained in karate, reacted by striking the plaintiff, fracturing his lower jaw and breaking two teeth. The court rejected the defendant's argument that he acted in defence of his wife, because the force used was excessive in the circumstances. Nevertheless, the plaintiff's provocative act was taken into account to reduce damages. Would the result have been the same if: (a) the defendant had not been trained in karate, but had merely struck a lucky blow; or (b) the defendant's wife, untrained in karate, had punched the plaintiff causing the same injury?

4. As stated in *R. v. Duffy* (1973), 11 C.C.C. (2d) 519 (Ont. C.A.), the defence of third parties is not limited to relatives or others in some special relationship with the person in need of protection. Rather, the defence may be raised by anyone who appears on the scene.

5. There is some conflict concerning when an individual will be privileged to intervene to help a third party. The majority of American cases suggest that an intervenor should only be privileged if the person he sought to protect had a right of self-defence. Thus, if the third party was an addict who was unlawfully resisting arrest by an undercover officer, the unwitting intervenor could not raise the defence of a third party. However, the majority of authors have rejected this proposition. See Keeton

et al., Prosser and Keeton on the Law of Torts, 5th ed. (1984), 129-30; and Fleming, *The Law of Torts*, 8th ed. (1992), 86.

In Canada, it appears that an intervenor's right to raise the defence is independent of the legal rights or position of the person being defended. See the Criminal Code, ss. 27 and 37.

3. Discipline

Although attitudes and values have changed dramatically, the common law still recognizes a defence of discipline that parents and guardians can invoke to privilege the use of force in dealing with children. A similar defence to criminal liability exists for parents, guardians and educators in s. 43 of the Criminal Code. The Canadian courts have largely assumed that s. 43 governs both the criminal and civil defences of discipline.

R. v. DUPPERON

(1984), 16 C.C.C. (3d) 453 (Sask. C.A.)

BY THE COURT: — The appellant was charged that on or about November 19, 1983, at the City of Saskatoon, in the Province of Saskatchewan, he did in committing an assault on Michael James Dupperon cause harm to him contrary to s. 245.1(1)(*b*) of the *Criminal Code* of Canada.

After a trial before a judge of the provincial court he was convicted, fined $400 and placed on probation for 18 months. He appeals against his conviction.

The evidence is that he strapped his 13-year-old son on the bare buttocks with a leather belt approximately 10 times leaving four or five bruises on the boy's left buttock which were blue and in a linear pattern. Each bruise was approximately four inches long and of a width of one-quarter to one-half an inch.

. . .

. . . In the morning on the day of the assault, Michael had been caught smoking out behind the house and for this he was "grounded". Later that morning the father, Linda Dupperon (his present wife and step-mother to Michael) and Michael were working at the Bingo Palace where the appellant had a janitorial contract. There, Michael admitted, he was "slacking off and doing things I shouldn't have"; and he also used foul language against his father. For this he was grounded for a whole week. When the appellant, Linda Dupperon and Michael returned home from work both the appellant and his wife later left the house and Michael was alone. It was then that he decided to leave home. He left a note to his father which was not produced but concerning which Michael testified: "I think I told him off. I said I wasn't going to come back to home and shit like that." He packed his clothes, radio and some food and left the house. A short time later, Linda Dupperon arrived home, saw the note and telephoned her husband. The appellant came home and about 15 minutes later the telephone rang. It was a call from Michael, who had been at a friend's home down the street, saying he was coming home.

. . .

From the uncontradicted evidence given by Michael there were ample grounds upon which the appellant could conclude that Michael was deserving of a more severe punishment than he had already meted out to him and I am satisfied that he honestly believed that a strapping was required by way of correction. Given the weight of the evidence adduced in this respect, it was unreasonable for the learned trial judge not to have held that the strapping was for correction:

. . .

... It is quite clear from both the evidence of Michael and Linda Dupperon that the first strapping consisted of only three or four strokes and that would have been the end of the strapping but for the foul language Michael then employed against his father. This resulted in a further five or six strokes. There is no dispute that the total strapping did not exceed 10 strokes.

. . .

Here the learned trial judge in the course of his judgment said:

> Secondly, I do not view it at all appropriate in the circumstances to pull down a 13-year-old boy's pants and flail him with a strap on his bare buttocks to the extent of this case. It is an unnatural manner of dealing out punishment and is not justified in these circumstances and in the manner in which it was administered.

. . .

While it appears from the above exchange and from other passages in the transcript that the learned trial judge may be opposed, in principle, to corporal punishment, that is his privilege and unless he allowed such views to interfere with his determination of whether the force applied was reasonable under the circumstances, it was not an error to express his personal view.

Put in another way, I think most people would be shocked if corporal punishment were employed in an institution such as Kilburn Hall or in any agency of government designed for the protection of abused children.

. . .

There is some anomaly in the fact that corporal punishment of criminals is now prohibited while corporal punishment of children is still permitted. The *rationale* of s. 43 of the *Criminal Code* has been explained by Dickson J. (as he then was) in the recent judgment of the Supreme Court rendered September 17, 1984, in *Ogg-Moss v. The Queen* [(1984), 11 D.L.R. (4th) 549] ...

> Section 43 authorizes the use of force "by way of correction". As Blackstone noted, such "correction" of a child is countenanced by the law because it is "for the benefit of his education". Section 43 is, in other words, a *justification*. It exculpates a parent, schoolteacher or person standing in the place of a parent who uses force in the correction of a child, because it considers such an action not a wrongful, but a *rightful* one. It follows that unless the force is "by way of correction", that is, for the benefit of the education of the child, the use of force will not be justified.

In this case I have said that, in my opinion, all of the evidence supports the view that the force used was by way of correction and that the learned trial judge ought to have so found. However, when we come to the second question, namely, whether the force used exceeded what was reasonable under the circumstances, I think the evidence fully supports the finding of the trial judge.

. . .

The only matter with which I am concerned here, therefore, is whether the force used exceeded what was reasonable under the circumstances so as to deprive the appellant of the protection afforded by s. 43 of the *Criminal Code*. In determining that question the court will consider, both from an objective and subjective standpoint, such matters as the nature of the offence calling for correction, the age and character of the child and the likely effect of the punishment on this particular child, the degree of gravity of the punishment, the circumstances under which it was inflicted, and the injuries, if any, suffered. If the child suffers injuries which may endanger life, limbs or health or is disfigured that alone would be sufficient to find that the punishment administered was unreasonable under the circumstances.

. . .

In my opinion, the evidence in this case amply supports the finding of the trial judge. Ten strokes of a leather belt on the bare buttocks is a severe beating, particularly under the circumstances in which it was inflicted here on an emotionally disturbed boy. There is, therefore, no basis upon which this court would be justified in reversing that finding.

[The court accepted the appellant's argument that he should only be convicted of assault and not assault causing bodily harm. However, it held that the sentence imposed at trial was still appropriate.]

NOTES AND QUESTIONS

1. What must the defendant establish to invoke the defence of discipline under s. 43?

2. Do you agree that the force used in *Dupperon* was used for the purpose of correction? What was the intended benefit? Can a parent who hits a child solely to punish him for misbehaviour raise the defence of discipline? See *R. v. Wetmore*, [1996] N.B.J. No. 15 (Q.L.), in which the Queen's Bench held that using force to teach a child respect served a legitimate correctional purpose. Can you reconcile this case with *Ogg-Moss*, which is referred to in *Dupperon*?

3. It has been held that s. 43 should be interpreted in light of prevailing social standards and customs, rather than those of the accused. See *R. v. Baptiste* (1980), 61 C.C.C. (2d) 438 (Ont. Prov. Ct.); and *R. v. Halcrow* (1993), 80 C.C.C. (3d) 320 (B.C. C.A.), aff'd. [1995] 1 S.C.R. 440. In *Halcrow*, the court also indicated that the accused's religious beliefs were not relevant.

Although the courts' position is clear, do you think it is necessary to rely on Canadian customs in order to interpret s. 43?

4. In addition to s. 43 of the Criminal Code, educators are granted broad authority under the provincial education acts to maintain order and discipline in school, on school grounds and at school-related events. The courts have held that these provisions can be used to justify detaining and questioning students, taking physical control of students, and enforcing rigorous behavioural, dress and appearance codes. See *R. v. Sweet*, [1986] O.J. No. 2083 (Q.L.) (Dist. Ct.); *Pilieci v. Lockett* (May 16, 1989), unreported (Ont. Dist. Ct.); and *Ward v. Blaine Lake (School Board)*, [1971] 4 W.W.R. 161 (Sask. Q.B.).

In *R. v. G. (J.M.)* (1986), 56 O.R. (2d) 705 (C.A.), leave to appeal ref'd. (1987), 59 O.R. (2d) 286n (S.C.C.), the court held that the obligation to maintain order and discipline required principals to investigate any allegation of illicit drug use or other serious violation of the school rules. This power was defined broadly to include authority to search the student, the student's belongings and his locker, and to use force if necessary for these purposes. See also *R. v. W. (J.J.)* (1990), 83 Nfld. & P.E.I.R. 13 (Nfld. S.C.).

5. In *Ogg-Moss v. R.* (1984), 11 D.L.R. (4th) 549, the Supreme Court held that s. 43 could not be invoked by mental health staff to privilege the use of force in disciplining mentally handicapped adults. The court also stressed that even in regard to children, the defence would be strictly interpreted and applied. The decision in *Ogg-Moss* reflects the growing concern about child abuse, the recognition of the independent legal rights of children and the hardening of attitudes toward the use of violence. Given these changes in society, should s. 43 be repealed? Can it be challenged under the Charter?

6. Ship captains, pilots and others in similar positions of authority also have a common law right

to use physical force to maintain order and discipline. Although this power could be used to punish rebellious crews and passengers at one time, it will now probably be limited to maintaining safety and order. See *King v. Fanklin* (1858), 175 E.R. 764; *Hook v. Cunard SS. Co.*, [1953] 1 All E.R. 1021 (Q.B.); *Re White* (1954), 12 W.W.R. 315 (B.C. C.A.), rev'd. [1956] S.C.R. 154; and the Criminal Code, s. 44.

4. Defence of Real Property

MACDONALD v. HEES

(1974), 46 D.L.R. (3d) 720 (N.S. S.C.)

COWAN C.J.T.D.: — In this action, the plaintiff claims against the defendant for injury, loss and damage said to have been suffered by the plaintiff as a result of an assault alleged to have been committed on the plaintiff by the defendant.

The injuries suffered by the plaintiff were sustained during the early morning of September 23, 1972, when the defendant forcibly ejected the plaintiff from a motel room at the Peter Pan Motel, New Glasgow, Nova Scotia. The defendant, in his defence, in addition to denying any assault, set up the additional defence that, if he used any force upon the person of the plaintiff, he was justified in law and the application of force was due to the unlawful entry of the plaintiff and invasion of the defendant's privacy:

. . .

It is clear that the defendant was in lawful occupation of the motel unit No. 54. That unit had been reserved for his use on the night in question . . . I find that the defendant had not expressly invited the plaintiff or Boyd to visit him, nor was there any implied invitation to anyone to visit him at the motel unit. However, in my opinion, this is not quite the case of a stranger walking in a motel room without any apparent right. The plaintiff was an officer of the local political party in whose interests the defendant was active that day. The plaintiff wished to introduce Glen Boyd to the defendant, and the circumstances to which I have referred above give some excuse to the plaintiff for his entry to the motel unit occupied by the defendant. The plaintiff was told that there were two units set aside for the defendant's use and, when he went to the area so set aside, it was apparent that the light was on in one of the units, while the other was in darkness. The plaintiff cannot be criticized for his action in knocking on the door of the unit which had the light showing. He then heard someone call from the adjoining unit and assumed, erroneously, that he was being invited to enter that unit.

. . .

With regard to the other defence, *i.e.*, that the defendant was justified in law and that the application of force was due to the unlawful entry of the plaintiff and invasion of the defendant's privacy, it is clear that, as stated in Salmond, *op. cit.*, p. 131:

> It is lawful for any occupier of land, or for any other person with the authority of the occupier, to use a reasonable degree of force in order to prevent a trespasser from entering or to control his movements or to eject him after entry.

It is clear, however, that a trespasser cannot be forcibly repelled or ejected until he has been requested to leave the premises and a reasonable opportunity of doing so peaceably has been afforded him. It is otherwise in the case of a person who enters or seeks to enter by force. In *Green v. Goddard* (1702), 2 Salkeld 641, 91 E.R. 540, it was said that, in such a case:

> . . . I need not request him to be gone, but may lay hands on him immediately, for it is but returning violence with violence; so if one comes forcibly and takes away my goods, I may oppose him without any more ado, for there is no time to make a request.

Even in such a case, however, the amount of force that may be used must not exceed that which is indicated in the old forms of pleading by the phrase *molliter manus imposuit*. It must amount to nothing more than forcible removal and must not include beating, wounding, or other physical injury: Salmond, *op. cit.*, p. 131, and the case of *Collins v. Renison* (1754), Sayer 138, 96 E.R. 830, there cited. In that case, the plaintiff sued for the assault of throwing him off a ladder. It was held a bad plea that the plaintiff was trespassing and refused, after request, to leave the premises, and that the defendant thereupon [at p. 139] "gently shook the ladder, which was a low ladder, and gently overturned it, and gently threw the plaintiff from it upon the ground, thereby doing as little damage as possible to the plaintiff." It was held that such force was not justifiable in defence of the possession of land.

In the present case, I find that there was no forcible entry by the plaintiff of the motel unit occupied by the defendant. I accept the evidence of the plaintiff and of Glen Boyd, to the effect that the plaintiff, thinking that he had been invited to enter the motel unit occupied by the defendant, opened the unlocked, outside combination screen and storm door and merely touched the door-knob of the inside door when it opened. It was obviously unlocked. The plaintiff then entered the motel unit, at the same time telling the defendant who he was. The plaintiff said that he was about to apologize for the intrusion when he realized that the defendant was in bed. Even if there had been forcible entry, the defendant did not request the plaintiff and his companion to leave and give them any reasonable opportunity of doing so, peaceably. As indicated above, where the evidence of the defendant conflicts with that of the plaintiff and Glen Boyd, I do not accept his evidence but that of the plaintiff and Glen Boyd.

The evidence of Glen Boyd was to the effect that the plaintiff had merely stepped into the room and made the statement referred to above, and that the time which elapsed from the time when he opened the door to the time when he was thrown back out through the inner door and into the storm door, was very short. Glen Boyd said that it was only long enough for the plaintiff to walk in and be thrown back out. He said that the defendant had not asked the plaintiff to leave before he threw him out.

I find that the use of force by the defendant to eject the plaintiff was not justified, in the circumstances, and that, in any event, the force used was excessive. I find that the defendant threw the plaintiff bodily through the inside motel door which was open, and against the closed combination screen and storm door, in such a way that the plaintiff's head hit the lower portion of the glass in the door, causing it to break and causing severe lacerations to the plaintiff's head.

I therefore find that the defence that the application of force was justified in law, in that it was due to the unlawful entry of the plaintiff and invasion of the defendant's privacy, has not been established. It follows, therefore, that the plaintiff is entitled to recovery against the defendant of damages for the injury, loss and damage which he suffered by the reason of the action of the defendant in assaulting him, and throwing him against the closed combination door.

NOTES AND QUESTIONS

1. As indicated in *Hees*, the defence of real property is based on the legal status of the entrant. According to *Hees*, what are the principles governing the defence as it relates to trespassers and violent intruders?

2. Why did the court reject Hees' argument that he was acting in defence of property? Assume that Hees had been startled out of a heavy sleep by the plaintiff and had awakened knowing only that there was an intruder in his room. Would Hees have been privileged to use the element of surprise to overpower the plaintiff without first asking him to leave? If so, what would be the basis of his defence? See *Boulet c. Entreprises M. Canada (Abitibi) Ltée* (1986), 38 C.C.L.T. 271 (Que. S.C.), aff'd. [1989] R.R.A. 795 (Que. C.A.).

3. The Canadian courts have held that an occupier may be required to tolerate the presence of a trespasser if ejecting him would pose a foreseeable risk of physical injury. See, for example, *Depue v. Flateau* (1907), 111 N.W. 1 (Minn. S.C.); *Dunn v. Dom. Atlantic Ry. Co.*, [1920] 2 W.W.R. 705 (S.C.C.); and *Jordan House Ltd. v. Menow*, [1974] S.C.R. 239.

4. The Canadian courts will not permit an occupier to use force likely to cause death or serious bodily injury solely for the purpose of ejecting a trespasser, who cannot be induced to leave by less violent means. See *Harris v. Wong* (1971), 19 D.L.R. (3d) 589 (Sask. Q.B.); and *Veinot v. Veinot* (1977), 31 A.P.R. 630 (N.S. C.A.). While an occupier cannot shoot trespassers, it may be permissible to threaten them with a loaded gun. See *R. v. Haverstock* (1979), 32 N.S.R. (2d) 595 (Co. Ct.); and *R. v. Blair*, [1987] B.C.J. No. 581 (Q.L.) (Co. Ct.).

The older cases indicate that deadly force could be used to repel a violent intruder, prevent being dispossessed or prevent a crime from being committed. See *R. v. Lyons* (1892), 2 C.C.C. 218 (Ont. Co. Ct.); and *Isreal James Hussey* (1924), 18 Cr. App. R. 160 (Ct. of Crim. App.). However, the more recent cases prohibit the use of deadly force simply to protect property. See *Bigcharles v. Merkel*, [1973] 1 W.W.R. 324 (B.C. S.C.); and *Hackshaw v. Shaw* (1984), 56 A.L.R. 417 (H.C. Aust.).

5. The American courts have held that a reasonable and *bona fide* mistake of fact will not negate the defence of real property, unless the intruder is entering as of legal right. See Keeton *et al.*, *Prosser and Keeton on the Law of Torts*, 5th ed. (1984), 131-32; and The American Law Institute, *Restatement of the Law, Second, Torts* (1965), para. 77. This issue has not yet been addressed in Canada. Would you support the adoption of the American position?

6. The right to eject a trespasser does not necessarily include the right to imprison. See *Ball v. Manthorpe* (1970), 15 D.L.R. (3d) 99 (B.C. Co. Ct.). However, some of the provincial trespass acts authorize an occupant to arrest trespassers without a warrant. See, for example, the Trespass to Property Act, R.S.O. 1990, c. T.21, s. 9.

7. The use of reasonable force in defending real property and ejecting trespassers is also privileged in criminal law. See the Criminal Code, ss. 40 and 41. See also s. 177, which prohibits trespassing at night, without lawful excuse, on the property of another near a dwelling house; and s. 494(2), which permits an occupant to arrest without warrant anyone he finds committing a criminal offence on, or in relation to, his property.

8. At common law, an occupier was entitled to damage or even destroy the property of another if it was necessary to protect his own property and the damage done was reasonable in relation to the interest protected. Thus, a farmer would be privileged to kill a trespassing dog that was attacking his sheep, but not to kill a cow that had merely entered his field. In addition, under the principle of "distress damage feasant", an occupier could seize any chattel that was unlawfully on his land and had caused damage, and detain it until he had been compensated. For a discussion of the common law, see Fleming, *The Law of Torts*, 8th ed. (1992), 87-88; and Keeton *et al.*, *supra*, 136-37.

BIRD v. HOLBROOK

(1828), 4 Bing. 628, 130 E.R. 911 (C.P.)

[The defendant possessed a walled garden in which he grew valuable tulips. Because of previous acts of vandalism, the defendant set up a spring gun with trip wires across the garden. No notice of the spring gun was posted. Indeed, the defendant sought to keep its existence a secret "lest the villain should not be detected."

A peahen escaped from a neighbouring house and landed in the garden. The plaintiff, seeing that a servant girl was upset at not being able to recover the bird, offered to help. He climbed the garden wall and called several times for the occupant. After receiving no answer he jumped into the garden to retrieve the hen. The gun discharged, seriously wounding him.]

BEST C.J.: . . .

I am reported to have said, expressly, "Humanity requires that the fullest notice possible should be given, and the law of England will not sanction what is inconsistent with humanity."

It has been argued that the law does not compel every line of conduct which humanity or religion may require; but there is no act which Christianity forbids, that the law will not reach: if it were otherwise, Christianity would not be, as it has always been held to be, part of the law of England. I am, therefore, clearly of opinion that he who sets spring guns, without giving notice, is guilty of an inhuman act, and that, if injurious consequences ensue, he is liable to yield to redress to the sufferer. But this case stands on grounds distinct from any that have preceded it. In general, spring guns have been set for the purpose of deterring; the Defendant placed his for the express purpose of doing injury; for, when called on to give notice, he said, "If I give notice, I shall not catch him." He intended, therefore, that the gun should be discharged and that the contents should be lodged in the body of his victim, for he could not be caught in any other way. On these principles the action is clearly maintainable, and particularly on the latter ground.

. . .

BURROUGH J.: — . . . the present case is of a worse complexion than those which have preceded it; for if the Defendant had proposed merely to protect his property from thieves, he would have set the spring guns only by night. The Plaintiff was only a trespasser: if the Defendant had been present, he would not have been authorised even in taking him into custody, and no man can do indirectly that which he is forbidden to do directly.

NOTES AND QUESTIONS

1. In *Bird*, what impact did the defendant's intent have on the defence of real property? The court also discussed the absence of a warning sign. What impact should the presence or absence of a warning sign have on the defence of real property? What other impact would a warning sign have on the defendant's case?

2. Would the defendant have been held liable if his trained dog had attacked the plaintiff causing equally serious injuries? Would the defendant have been held liable if the plaintiff had been an armed and dangerous felon who was planning to break into the house?

3. See generally Bohlen and Burns, "The Privilege to Protect Property by Dangerous Barriers

and Mechanical Devices" (1926), 35 Yale L.J. 525; Hart, "Injuries to Trespassers" (1931), 47 L.Q.R. 92; and Palmer, "The Iowa Spring Gun Case: A Study in American Gothic" (1970-71), 56 Iowa L. Rev. 1219. See also s. 247 of the Criminal Code, which prohibits the use of traps, devices or other mechanisms for the purpose of causing death or bodily harm to others.

5. The Defence and Recapture of Chattels

The legal principles governing the defence of real property generally apply to the defence of chattels. If a person innocently picks up the defendant's book, the defendant must request its return before using any force. However, if the person grabbed the book out of the defendant's hand, the defendant could use force to prevent being dispossessed without first making a request for its return. The specific facts of the case will dictate whether the possessor was privileged to use force and whether the force used was reasonable. For example, in *Cresswell v. Sirl*, [1948] 1 K.B. 241 (C.A.), the court held that the defendant would be privileged in shooting a dog if he had no other practical means of protecting his livestock from attack. Except in cases of hot pursuit, an individual cannot invoke the defence of chattels once dispossessed of them. He may seek to regain possession by court action or may be entitled to resort to the self-help remedy of recapture.

The remedy of recapture places the owner of a chattel in the role of a potential aggressor who is attempting to regain possession of the goods from another. As a result, the remedy has been narrowly defined. It may only be invoked by an individual who has an immediate right to possession, and then only after a request has been made for the chattel's return. Although the authorities are divided, it appears that only peaceful means can be used to recapture a chattel from a person who came into possession lawfully. Thus, an individual could not use force to recapture a chattel from a bailee who refused to return it. The right to use force is limited to circumstances in which an individual who wrongfully gained possession refuses to hand over the chattel after being requested to do so.

There is a common law privilege to enter another's land to recapture chattels in limited circumstances. If the chattel came onto the land accidentally or was left there by a wrongdoer, the owner could enter the property to retake his chattel, provided he did not use force or cause a breach of the peace. If the occupier of the land came into possession of the chattel unlawfully, its owner could make a forced entry, but only if his request for its return had been denied.

NOTES AND QUESTIONS

1. Although the issue is not completely resolved, it appears that a reasonable and *bona fide* mistake of fact will not negate the defence of chattels, but will negate the remedy of recapture of chattels. Do you favour this position? See Keeton *et al.*, *Prosser and Keeton on the Law of Torts*, 5th ed. (1984), 137-38.

2. For a discussion of the defence of chattels, see in addition to Keeton *et al.*, the American Law Institute, *Restatement of the Law, Second, Torts* (1965), paras. 77-87. See also the Criminal Code, ss. 38, 39 and 494 which create broad authority to use force and make arrests without a warrant to protect chattels.

3. For a review of the law of recapture, see *Blades v. Higgs* (1861), 142 E.R. 634 (H.L.); *Morrison v. Thomas* (1922), 65 D.L.R. 364 (Sask. C.A.); *Sweeney v. Starrat*, [1931] 2 D.L.R. 473 (N.S. C.A.); *Wentzell v. Veinot*, [1940] 1 D.L.R. 536 (N.S. S.C.); and *Devoe v. Long*, [1951] 1 D.L.R. 203 (N.B. C.A.).

4. Given the potential for violence, should the remedy of recapture of chattels be abolished?

REVIEW PROBLEM

Al and Bob obtained permission to camp and hunt on the waterfront property of one of their friends. They misunderstood his directions, and beached their canoe and pitched their tent on the wrong property. Al built a fire to keep warm and Bob went for a walk. The owner of the property, Mr. Stevens, was hunting nearby when he came across Al and the campsite. Stevens told him to pack up and leave immediately. Al paid little heed. Stevens yelled, "I'm not joking, get off my land or else!" Al poured himself a cup of coffee and replied, "What's your hurry old man?" Infuriated, Stevens blasted the tent to bits and then pointed his shotgun at Al.

Bob heard the shot and came running back as Stevens screamed, "Is there any reason why I shouldn't blow your head off?" Stevens had no intention of shooting Al, he just wanted to scare him. Fearing the worst, Bob picked up a rock and tried to knock the shotgun out of Stevens' grasp. Unfortunately, the rock hit Stevens in the head. He fell to the ground unconscious. The shotgun fell beside him, discharging and several pellets grazed Al's shoulder. Both Al and Bob became alarmed when Stevens showed no signs of regaining consciousness. They placed Stevens in their canoe and rushed him to the hospital.

Al and Bob have contacted you from the hospital, wishing to know whether they may return to Stevens' land and retrieve their camping equipment. They also wish your advice about the civil actions that they could bring against Stevens, and the actions that he might bring against them.

6. Public and Private Necessity

(a) PUBLIC NECESSITY

The defence of public necessity allows an individual to intentionally invade the property rights of another in order to save lives or to protect the public interest from external threats of nature, such as fires, floods or storms. Public necessity provides a complete defence, privileging both the interference with the plaintiff's legal rights to the property and any damages to it.

SUROCCO v. GEARY

(1853), 3 Cal. 69 (Cal. S.C.)

MURRAY, Chief Justice, delivered the opinion of the Court. HEYDENFELDT, Justice, concurred.

This was an action, commenced in the court below, to recover damages for blowing up and destroying the plaintiff's house and property, during the fire of the 24th of December, 1849 . . .

The only question for our consideration is, whether the person who tears down or destroys the house of another, in good faith, and under apparent necessity, during the time of a conflagration, for the purpose of saving the buildings adjacent, and stopping its progress, can be held personally liable in an action by the owner of the property destroyed.

The right to destroy property, to prevent the spread of conflagration, has been traced to the highest law of necessity, and the natural rights of man, independent of society or civil government. "It is referred by moralists and jurists to the same great principle which justifies the exclusive appropriation of a plank in a ship-wreck, though the life of another be sacrificed; with the throwing overboard goods in a tempest, for the safety of a vessel; with the trespassing upon the lands of another, to escape death by an enemy. It rests upon the maxim, *Necessitas inducit privilegium quod jura privata.*"

The common law adopts the principles of the natural law, and places the justification of an act otherwise tortious precisely on the same ground of necessity. (See 1st Zabriskie, American Print Works v. Lawrence, and the cases there cited.)

This principle has been familiarly recognized by the books from the time of the saltpetre case, and the instances of tearing down houses to prevent conflagration, or to raise bulwarks for the defence of a city, are made use of as illustrations, rather than as abstract cases, in which its exercise is permitted. At such times, the individual rights of property give way to the higher laws of impending necessity.

A house on fire, or those in its immediate vicinity, which serve to communicate the flames, becomes a nuisance, which it is lawful to abate, and the private rights of the individual yield to the considerations of general convenience, and the interests of society. Were it otherwise, one stubborn person might involve a whole city in ruin, by refusing to allow the destruction of a building which would cut off the flames and check the progress of the fire, and that, too, when it was perfectly evident that his building must be consumed ...

The counsel for the respondent has asked, who is to judge of the necessity of the destruction of property?

This must, in some instances, be a difficult matter to determine. The necessity of blowing up a house may not exist, or be as apparent to the owner, whose judgment is clouded by interest, and the hope of saving his property, as to others. In all such cases the conduct of the individual must be regulated by his own judgment as to the exigencies of the case. If a building should be torn down without apparent or actual necessity, the parties concerned would undoubtedly be liable in an action of trespass. But in every case the necessity must be clearly shown. It is true, many cases of hardship may grow out of this rule, and property may often in such cases be destroyed, without necessity, by irresponsible persons, but this difficulty would not be obviated by making the parties responsible in every case, whether the necessity existed or not.

The evidence in this case clearly establishes the fact, that the blowing up of the house was necessary, as it would have been consumed had it been left standing. The plaintiffs cannot recover for the value of the goods which they might have saved; they were as much subject to the necessities of the occasion as the house in which they were situate; and if in such cases a party was held liable, it would too frequently happen, that the delay caused by the removal of the goods would render the destruction of the house useless.

The court below clearly erred as to the law applicable to the facts of this case. The testimony will not warrant a verdict against the defendant.

NOTES AND QUESTIONS

1. As *Surocco* suggests, a reasonable and *bona fide* mistake of fact as to the apparent necessity will not negate the defence. See also *Cope v. Sharpe*, [1912] 1 K.B. 496 (C.A.).

What damages would the plaintiff have been entitled to if the defence of public necessity had failed? See generally, Finan and Ritson, "Tortious Necessity: The Privileged Defense" (1992), 26 Akron L. Rev. 1.

2. In order to invoke the defence, the defendant must have acted reasonably in terms of the damages caused relative to the likely public benefit. What limits, if any, should be imposed on the exercise of public necessity in cases where only property is threatened?

3. The defence of public necessity has been limited to cases in which the defendant has interfered with the plaintiff's property interests. Should a defendant be privileged to intentionally inflict minor physical injury on the plaintiff to protect another party from serious personal injury or death? Should the law privilege the intentional sacrifice of one innocent person in order to save many other innocent people? In *R. v. Dudley and Stephens* (1884), 14 Q.B.D. 273, the defendants, while adrift in a lifeboat, killed and ate a fellow passenger to save their own lives. The defendants were found guilty of murder, but were subsequently pardoned. Contrast *Dudley* with *U.S. v. Holmes* (1842), 26 Fed. Cas. 360 (Cir. Ct. Penn.). See also Fuller, "The Case of the Speluncean Explorers" (1949), 62 Harv. L. Rev. 616.

Surocco suggests that an individual would not be held liable for using force to acquire exclusive possession of a plank that can only keep one person afloat. How does this differ from *Dudley* and *Holmes*? What defence would apply in the example with the plank?

4. Both the House of Lords and the United States Supreme Court have indicated that the government need not compensate people for losses inflicted during wartime operations, presumably because the military is acting under a special kind of public necessity. See *Burmah Oil Co. v. Lord Advocate*, [1965] A.C. 75 (H.L.); *U.S. v. Caltex (Philippines) Inc.* (1952), 73 S. Ct. 200; and "The Burmah Oil Affair" (1966), 79 Harv. L. Rev. 614. However, the courts differed on whether the intentional destruction of private property to prevent it from falling into enemy hands comes within this principle. The House of Lords held that the plaintiffs were entitled to damages in such circumstances. However, the plaintiffs' victory was short-lived as Parliament immediately enacted legislation which negated the decision. For a discussion of the Crown's right to seize property for purposes of war, see *The Case of the King's Prerogative in Saltpetre* (1606), 77 E.R. 1294; and *A.G. v. Nissan*, [1970] A.C. 179 (H.L.).

5. In *Rigby v. Chief Constable of Northamptonshire*, [1985] 2 All E.R. 985 (Q.B.), the police burned down the plaintiff's shop by firing tear gas cannisters into the building in an effort to force out a dangerous psychopath. The police were absolved of liability in trespass on the basis of public necessity, although they were held liable in negligence for not having any firefighting equipment available. Should the defence of public necessity extend to law enforcement? This issue has not been addressed by the Canadian courts.

6. The defence of public necessity appears to apply to travellers who are forced to cross adjoining land when the public highway is blocked. See *Taylor v. Whitehead* (1781), 99 E.R. 475 (K.B.); and *Dwyer v. Staunton*, [1947] 4 D.L.R. 393 (Alta. Dist. Ct.).

7. Traditionally, the defence of necessity has been limited to situations in which the imminent threat is posed by some external force of nature. Thus, in *London Borough of Southwark v. Williams*, [1971] 2 All E.R. 175 (C.A.), it was held that homeless squatters could not invoke the defence of public necessity to privilege their entry into vacant houses owned by the Council. Lord Denning M.R. explained at 179:

> If homelessness were once admitted as a defence to trespass, no one's house could be safe. Necessity would open a door which no man could shut. It would not only be those in extreme need who would enter. There would be others who would imagine that they were in need, or would invent a need, so as to gain entry. Each man would say his need was greater than the next man's. The plea would be an excuse for all sorts of wrongdoing. So the courts must, for the sake of law and order, take a firm stand. They must refuse to admit the plea of necessity to the hungry and homeless; and trust their distress will be relieved by the charitable and the good.

Contrast Denning M.R.'s comments with those of Laskin C.J.C. in *Harrison v. Carswell* (1975), 62 D.L.R. (3d) 68 at 76-77 (S.C.C.). See also *Wilcox v. Police*, [1994] 1 N.Z.L.R. 243 (H.C.), where the court rejected the defence of public necessity asserted by anti-abortion protestors who had blocked the entrance to a hospital.

8. The rationale for absolving an individual of liability when acting under public necessity is clear. However, since the public as a whole benefits, why is the state not required to compensate the party whose property has been sacrificed? What is the justification for imposing the entire burden of public necessity on a single innocent property owner? In maritime law, if part of a cargo is jettisoned to prevent a ship from sinking, the loss is apportioned among all the ship and cargo owners. Should a similar concept be adopted in public necessity cases?

9. In *Lapierre v. A.G. Que.* (1985), 16 D.L.R. (4th) 554 (S.C.C.), a five-year-old girl was left totally

incapacitated after suffering an idiosyncratic reaction to an injection that she received as part of a provincial immunization program. Although such reactions are known to occur, the program as a whole saves lives and reduces illness caused by infectious diseases. There was no negligence on the part of either the manufacturer of the serum or those who administered the program. The Supreme Court dismissed the girl's action, stating that there is no general legal principle that damages suffered by individuals for the public benefit must be borne by the community based on the theory of necessity. See Capriolo and Turcot, "Strict Liability for Acts of the State: Liability for Non-Negligent Vaccination" (1985), 13 C.C.L.T. 37.

10. An individual who negligently caused or contributed to the emergency situation will not be allowed to benefit from the defence of public necessity. See *Bell Telephone Co. v. The Mar-Tirenno* (1974), 52 D.L.R. (3d) 702, aff'd. (1976), 71 D.L.R. (3d) 608 (Fed. C.A.); and *Rigby v. Chief Constable of Northamptonshire*, [1985] 2 All E.R. 985 (Q.B.).

11. Various statutes grant public officials broad powers to invade private property in emergency situations. For example, the fire department may be empowered to invade private dwellings to extinguish a fire or to prevent it from spreading.

12. In *Perka v. R.* (1984), 14 C.C.C. (3d) 385, the Supreme Court of Canada held that necessity could be raised as a defence to criminal charges. Perka was smuggling over 33 tons of marijuana from Columbia to the international waters off Alaska, when mechanical problems and bad weather forced him to take refuge in a deserted cove on the British Columbia coast. The accused argued that he had never intended to enter Canadian waters and that he was entitled to raise the defence of necessity. The majority of the Supreme Court agreed and ordered a new trial. See Wells, "Necessity and the Common Law" (1985), 5 Oxford J. Legal Stud. 471.

(b) PRIVATE NECESSITY

VINCENT v. LAKE ERIE TPT. CO.

(1910), 124 N.W. 221 (Minn. S.C.)

O'BRIEN J.: — The steamship Reynolds, owned by the defendant, was for the purpose of discharging her cargo on November 27, 1905, moored to plaintiff's dock in Duluth. While the unloading of the boat was taking place a storm from the northeast developed, which at about 10 o'clock p.m., when the unloading was completed, had so grown in violence that the wind was then moving at 50 miles per hour and continued to increase during the night. There is some evidence that one, and perhaps two, boats were able to enter the harbor that night, but it is plain that navigation was practically suspended from the hour mentioned until the morning of the 29th, when the storm abated, and during that time no master would have been justified in attempting to navigate his vessel, if he could avoid doing so. After the discharge of the cargo the Reynolds signaled for a tug to tow her from the dock, but none could be obtained because of the severity of the storm. If the lines holding the ship to the dock had been cast off, she would doubtless have drifted away; but, instead, the lines were kept fast, and as soon as one parted or chafed it was replaced, sometimes with a larger one. The vessel lay upon the outside of the dock, her bow to the east, the wind and waves striking her starboard quarter with such force that she was constantly being lifted and thrown against the dock, resulting in its damage, as found by the jury, to the amount of $500.

We are satisfied that the character of the storm was such that it would have been highly imprudent for the master of the Reynolds to have attempted to leave the dock or to have permitted the vessel to drift away from it. One witness testified upon the trial that the vessel could have been warped into a slip, and that, if the attempt to bring the ship into the slip had failed, the worst that could have happened would be that the vessel would have been blown ashore upon a soft and muddy bank. The witness was not present in Duluth at the time of the storm, and while he may have been right in his conclusions, those in charge of the dock and the vessel at the time of the storm were not required to use the highest human intelligence, nor were they required to resort to every possible experiment which could be suggested for the preservation of their property. Nothing more was demanded of them than ordinary prudence and care, and the record in this case fully sustains the contention of the appellant that, in holding the vessel fast to the dock, those in charge of her exercised good judgment and prudent seamanship.

It is claimed by the respondent that it was negligence to moor the boat to an exposed part of the wharf, and to continue in that position after it became apparent that the storm was to be more than usually severe. We do not agree with this position. The part of the wharf where the vessel was moored appears to have been commonly used for that purpose. It was situated within the harbor at Duluth, and must, we think, be considered a proper and safe place, and would undoubtedly have been such during what would be considered a very severe storm. The storm which made it unsafe was one which surpassed in violence any which might have reasonably been anticipated.

The appellant contends by ample assignments of error that, because its conduct during the storm was rendered necessary by prudence and good seamanship under conditions over which it had no control, it cannot be held liable for any injury resulting to the property of others, and claims that the jury should have been so instructed. An analysis of the charge given by the trial court is not necessary, as in our opinion the only question for the jury was the amount of damages which the plaintiffs were entitled to recover, and no complaint is made upon that score.

The situation was one in which the ordinary rules regulating property rights were suspended by forces beyond human control, and if, without the direct intervention of some act by the one sought to be held liable, the property of another was injured, such injury must be attributed to the act of God, and not to the wrongful act of the person sought to be charged. If during the storm the Reynolds had entered the harbor, and while there had become disabled and been thrown against the plaintiff's dock, the plaintiff would not have recovered. Again, if while attempting to hold fast to the dock the lines had parted, without any negligence, and the vessel carried against some other boat or dock in the harbor, there would be no liability upon her owner. But here those in charge of the vessel deliberately and by their direct efforts held her in such a position that the damage to the dock resulted, and, having thus preserved the ship at the expense of the dock, it seems to us that her owners are responsible to the dock owners to the extent of the injury inflicted.

In Depue v. Flatau, 100 Minn. 299, 111 N.W. 1, 8 L.R.A. (N.S.) 485, this court held that where the plaintiff, while lawfully in the defendant's house, became so ill that he was incapable of traveling with safety, the defendants were responsible to him in damages for compelling him to leave the premises. If, however, the owner of the premises had furnished the traveller with proper accommodations and medical attendance, would he have been able to defeat an action brought against him for their reasonable worth?

In Ploof v. Putnam, 71 Atl. 188, 20 L.R.A. (N.S.) 152, the Supreme Court of Vermont held that where, under stress of weather, a vessel was without permission moored to a private dock at an island in Lake Champlain owned by the defendant, the plaintiff was not guilty of trespass, and that the defendant was responsible in damages because his representative upon the island unmoored the vessel, permitting it to drift upon the shore, with resultant injuries to it. If, in that case, the vessel had been permitted to remain, and the dock had suffered injury, we believe the shipowner would have been held liable for the injury done.

Theologians hold that a starving man may, without moral guilt, take what is necessary to sustain life; but it could hardly be said that the obligation would not be upon such person to pay the value of the property so taken when he became able to do so. And so public necessity, in times of war or peace, may require the taking of private property for public purposes; but under our system of jurisprudence compensation must be made.

Let us imagine in this case that for the better mooring of the vessel those in charge of her had appropriated a valuable cable lying upon the dock. No matter how justifiable such appropriation might have been, it would not be claimed that, because of the overwhelming necessity of the situation, the owner of the cable could not recover its value.

This is not a case where life or property was menaced by any object or thing belonging to the plaintiff, the destruction of which became necessary to prevent the threatened disaster. Nor is it a case where, because of the act of God, or unavoidable accident, the infliction of the injury was beyond the control of the defendant, but is one where the defendant prudently and advisedly availed itself of the plaintiff's property for the purpose of preserving its own more valuable property, and the plaintiffs are entitled to compensation for the injury done.

LEWIS J.: — I dissent. It was assumed on the trial before the lower court that appellant's liability depended on whether the master of the ship might, in the exercise of reasonable care, have sought a place of safety before the storm made it impossible to leave the dock. The majority opinion assumed that the evidence is conclusive that appellant moored its boat at respondent's dock pursuant to contract, and that the vessel was lawfully in position at the time the additional cables were fastened to the dock, and the reasoning of the opinion is that, because appellant made use of the stronger cables to hold the boat in position, it became liable under the rule that it had voluntarily made use of the property of another for the purpose of saving its own.

In my judgment, if the boat was lawfully in position at the time the storm broke, and the master could not, in the exercise of due care, have left that position without subjecting his vessel to the hazards of the storm, then the damage to the dock, caused by the pounding of the boat, was the result of an inevitable accident. If the master was in the exercise of due care, he was not at fault. The reasoning of the opinion admits that if the ropes, or cables, first attached to the dock had not parted, or if, in the first instance, the master had used the stronger cables, there would be no liability. If the master could not, in the exercise of reasonable care have anticipated the severity of the storm and sought a place of safety before it became impossible, why should he be required to anticipate the severity of the storm, and, in the first instance, use the stronger cables?

I am of the opinion that one who constructs a dock to the navigable line of waters, and enters into contractual relations with the owner of a vessel to moor at the same, takes the risk of damage to his dock by a boat caught there by a storm, which event could not have been avoided in the exercise of due care, and further, that the legal status of the parties in such a case is not changed by renewal of cables to keep the boat from being cast adrift at the mercy of the tempest.

JAGGARD J., concurs herein.

NOTES AND QUESTIONS

1. What were the bases upon which O'Brien J. concluded that: (a) inevitable accident; and (b) public necessity did not apply? What was the basis of Lewis J.'s dissent?

2. The first issue that arises in private necessity, as in public necessity, is whether the defendant is privileged to invade the plaintiff's proprietary interests. As Fleming states in *The Law of Torts*, 8th ed. (1992), at 96, "If the emergency is sufficiently great and the good it is intended to do is not disproportionate to the harm likely to result, one may trespass upon the land of another to save himself or his property." This balancing of interests is often expressed in terms of requiring the defendant to act reasonably both in terms of his decision to enter and his subsequent conduct. See Keeton *et al., Prosser and Keeton on the Law of Torts*, 5th ed. (1984), 145-48; and *Rogers, Winfield and Jolowicz on Tort*, 14th ed. (1994), 751-53.

3. Should public or private necessity apply if the defendant is attempting: (a) to save his own life; (b) to protect his own interests but in doing so advances the public interest — *Dwyer v. Staunton*, [1947] 4 D.L.R. 393 (Alta. Dist. Ct.); and (c) to protect the plaintiff's property — *Sherrin v. Haggerty*, [1953] O.W.N. 962 (Co. Ct.).

4. As with other self-help remedies, such as recapture of chattels, there is a potential for violence inherent in the assertion of private necessity. How is this factor to be taken into account in assessing the appropriateness of the defence? Can you justify granting broader powers of entry in private necessity than in recapture of chattels?

5. What is the significance of the imminent peril requirement? How would you distinguish *Vincent* from a case in which a landowner found it impossible to complete a construction project without trespassing on the adjoining property?

6. Once a court decides that the defendant was privileged to enter, it must then determine who should pay for whatever actual losses ensue. As indicated in *Vincent*, private necessity is generally considered to be a partial or incomplete defence in the United States. See Bohlen, "Incomplete Privilege to Inflict Intentional Invasions of Interests of Property and Personalty" (1926), 39 Harv. L. Rev. 307; The American Law Institute, *Restatement of the Law, Second, Torts* (1965), paras. 196, 197, 262 and 263; and Keeton, "Conditional Fault in the Law of Torts" (1959), 72 Harv. L. Rev. 401.

7. Is it inconsistent to grant the defendant a right to trespass, but hold him liable for the damages that result? Why would a defendant plead private necessity if he still has to pay for the damage he causes? See *Ploof v. Putnam* (1908), 71 A. 188 (Vt. S.C.); and Epstein, "Defenses and Subsequent Pleas in a System of Strict Liability" (1974), 3 J. of Leg. Studies 165 at 165-70.

8. It is not clear whether private necessity is a complete or partial defence in England and Canada. What arguments would you make in favour of each position? See Williams, "The Defence of Necessity" (1953), 6 Current Legal Problems 216 at 219-23; Sussman, "The Defence of Private Necessity and the Problem of Compensation" (1967), 2 Ottawa L. Rev. 184; and Finan and Ritson, "Tortious Necessity: The Privileged Defense" (1992), 26 Akron L. Rev. 1.

9. The facts in *Munn & Co. v. The Motor Vessel Sir John Crosbie*, [1967] 1 Ex. C.R. 94 were similar to those in *Vincent*, but it was pleaded and decided in negligence. Although the statement was made in *obiter*, the court expressed a preference for the dissent in *Vincent*. See Sussman, *supra*.

10. Although there is no right to intentionally injure another person in the assertion of either public or private necessity, physical force can be used to overcome resistance to the exercise of necessity. Given the potential for violence inherent in this principle, should it be limited to public necessity? See the American Law Institute, *Restatement of the Law, Second, Torts* (1965), paras. 196, comment (b) and 197, comment (g). An individual who causes harm or injury in resisting the exercise of public or private necessity can be held civilly liable. See *Depue v. Flateau* (1907), 111 N.W. 1 (Minn. S.C.); and *Ploof v. Putnam, supra*.

11. Can you justify the fact that the common law recognizes a defence for public and private necessity but not for duress?

7. Apportionment of Fault in Intentional Torts

At common law, the fact that the plaintiff had negligently contributed to his own injuries provided the defendant with a complete defence to negligence liability. The all-or-nothing approach came to be viewed as inappropriate, for it imposed the entire loss on only one of the two negligent parties. Consequently, legislation was introduced in most common law jurisdictions to apportion losses in negligence actions between the defendant and the plaintiff, according to their respective degrees of fault. Generally, the legislation in Canada's common law provinces applies in any case where the damages have been caused by "fault or neglect". Depending on the courts' interpretation of the word "fault", the legislation may apply beyond the bounds of negligence. The question has arisen whether a defendant in an intentional tort action can invoke the apportionment legislation, and use the plaintiff's contributory negligence as a partial defence.

Although a trend appears to be emerging in Ontario, the picture in the remaining provinces is unclear. Nevertheless, the Ontario experience may prove to be prophetic. In *Hollebone v. Barnard*, [1954] 2 D.L.R. 278, the Ontario High Court held that the terms "fault" and "negligence" were used as synonyms and therefore the Ontario legislation applied solely to negligence cases. This decision was followed in *Funnell v. C.P.R.*, [1964] 2 O.R. 325 (H.C.), where it was held that the apportionment legislation did not apply in a nuisance case. Jessup J.A. expressed a contrary view in *Dom. Chain Co. v. Eastern Const. Co.* (1976), 12 O.R. (2d) 201 at 206, affirmed [1978] 2 S.C.R. 1346. He stated: "no doubt 'fault' includes a breach of statute or other act or omission giving rise to liability in tort whether negligent or not." The statement was made in *obiter* and no analysis or authority was provided.

In *Bell Can. v. Cope (Sarnia) Ltd.* (1980), 11 C.C.L.T. 170 (Ont. H.C.), Linden J. concluded that the term fault was broader than negligence, including all intentional wrongdoing and other types of wrongful conduct. Even though the defendant was liable in trespass to land, he was able to raise the plaintiff's contributory negligence to reduce his liability by one-third. The Ontario Court of Appeal, at 119 D.L.R. (3d) 254, subsequently affirmed the judgment and appeared to overturn *Hollebone*. It is difficult to tell from the Appeal Court's short judgment whether the Ontario apportionment legislation will be applied to all intentional torts or only those derived from the writ of trespass *vi et armis*.

NOTES AND QUESTIONS

1. In order to establish the defence of contributory negligence, the defendant must prove on the balance of probabilities that the plaintiff acted negligently or in an intentionally wrongful manner, and that this behaviour caused or contributed to the plaintiff's injuries or losses.

2. The debate over the scope of the term fault involves branches of law other than torts. See generally Weinrib, "Contribution in a Contractual Setting" (1976), 54 Can. Bar Rev. 338; University of Alberta, Institute of Law Research and Reform, *Contributory Negligence and Concurrent Wrongdoers*

(1979), 11-25; and Klar, "Developments in Tort Law: The 1979-80 Term", [1981] 2 Sup. Ct. L. Rev. 325 at 340-54. See also *Doiron v. Caisse Populaire d'Inkerman Ltée.* (1985), 32 C.C.L.T. 73 (N.B. C.A.).

3. Some courts have attempted to avoid the impact of applying the traditional defences in cases in which both parties were to blame. For example, the limitations that the courts have imposed on the *ex turpi causa* doctrine appear to reflect concern about denying a wrongdoing plaintiff any redress. The complex case law governing consensual fights, factors vitiating consent, and the impact of provocation on damages appears to be based on related concerns. In what other areas of intentional torts would the apportionment legislation be relevant? See generally Crocker, "Apportionment of Liability and the Intentional Torts: The Time is Right for Change" (1982-83), 7 Dalhousie L.J. 172; and Manchester, "Trespass and Contributory Negligence in Ontario" (1982), 31 Int. and Comp. L.Q. 203.

Although the apportionment legislation would be applicable in many intentional torts cases, it is infrequently raised.

REVIEW PROBLEM

Despite a storm warning, Fred and Mike set out for their cottage late one evening in a small boat, carrying their hunting and camping equipment. Unfortunately, the storm hit sooner and with greater intensity than anticipated. Realizing that they would not make it to their own cottage, they headed for the nearest landfall. They docked their boat at a private wharf and headed up the steep wooded hill looking for shelter. As lightning felled trees around them, they ran as fast as they could, carrying their shotguns and other valuables.

As a result of some recent threats on his life, the owner of the land had hired a private security company to patrol his grounds. From his vantage point at the top of the hill, the guard spotted Fred and Mike running through the underbrush carrying shotguns. The guard screamed for them to stop and identify themselves, but to no avail. He even fired three warning shots, yet they appeared to duck into the bush and kept approaching. Fearing the worst, the guard released his two trained dogs. Once the dogs had disarmed and immobilized Fred and Mike, the guard cautiously approached to arrest them. Fred eventually convinced the guard that they were only seeking shelter and that they had not seen the no trespassing sign near the wharf, or heard either his screams or his warning shots. The guard allowed Mike and Fred to use the phone in the guardhouse to call a friend to pick them up.

Mr. Green, the owner of the land, was also caught in the storm. When he swung his large boat around to moor it, he saw that his way was blocked by the trespassing boat. Faced with the prospect of running aground, Green attempted to nudge the smaller boat forward and moor behind it. Although he was extremely careful, Mr. Green still did $800 damage to Mike's boat and over $1,000 damage to his own. Nevertheless, this was only a fraction of the damage that could have occurred if his boat had run aground on the nearby rocks.

You have been consulted by Fred and Mike, who wish to know what civil actions they may pursue and what actions may be brought against them as a result of this incident.

8

THE DEFENCE OF LEGAL AUTHORITY

1. Introduction
2. General Powers of Arrest Without a Warrant and Privilege
3. Rights and Obligations in the Arrest Process
4. The Common Law Right to Search Pursuant to a Lawful Arrest
5. A Peace Officer's Common Law Right of Forced Entry

1. Introduction

This chapter deals with the assertion of legal authority as a defence to false imprisonment and the other intentional torts that may be committed during an arrest, search, seizure, or entry. The defence evolved from a body of common law civil and criminal cases that narrowly defined the enforcement powers of police and private citizens. The enactment of the Criminal Code, other federal criminal statutes and provincial penal legislation has largely supplanted the common law, and greatly expanded enforcement powers and police officers' immunity to criminal liability. It is often difficult to determine whether the courts will interpret a criminal or penal statute as governing civil as well as criminal liability.

Regardless of whether the defence is based upon legislation or the common law, a single framework of analysis may be adopted. The defence of legal authority can be divided into three issues. First, was the defendant's act that gave rise to the tort specifically authorized by statute or common law? Second, was the defendant privileged from criminal and civil liability? Third, did the defendant fulfil the other obligations that were imposed upon her in this process? For example, even if the defendant is authorized and privileged to make an arrest, she will incur civil liability if she used excessive force.

Given the multitude of federal and provincial statutes that authorize arrest, search, seizure, and entry, it is not possible to review comprehensively the operation of the defence in these materials. Rather, we will examine three common situations in which the defence arises: arrest without a warrant, the common law right to search pursuant to a lawful arrest and a peace officer's common law right of entry in search of a wanted person.

NOTES AND QUESTIONS

1. For a discussion of the English common law enforcement powers, see Harris, *Principles of the Criminal Law*, 1st ed. (1877), 303-12; Stephen, *A History of the Criminal Law of England* (1883), vol. 1, 184-206; and Hall, "Legal and Social Aspects of Arrest Without a Warrant" (1936), 49 Harv. L. Rev. 566.

2. The Canadian courts' reliance on the Criminal Code and other federal criminal statutes to define civil liability raises complex constitutional issues regarding the division of powers between the

federal and provincial governments. Although it has been stated that the criminal and civil defences of legal authority ought to be treated as distinct issues, the constitutional question has not been squarely addressed. See, for example, *Fletcher v. Collins* (1968), 70 D.L.R. (2d) 183 at 188 (Ont. H.C.); and *Eccles v. Bourque* (1974), 50 D.L.R. (3d) 753 at 755 (S.C.C.) per Dickson J. What constitutional argument would you make in support of the courts' reliance on the Criminal Code in civil cases? Would your argument vary depending on whether the defendant was a peace officer or a private citizen?

3. Another complicating factor in relying on criminal statutes and case law in torts cases is that the criminal law concept of arrest does not correspond to the tort concept of imprisonment. In *R. v. Whitfield* (1969), 7 D.L.R. (3d) 97 at 98 (S.C.C.), Judson J. quoting 10 Hals. (3d) 342, stated: "Arrest consists of the actual seizure or touching of a person's body with a view to his detention. The mere pronouncing of words of arrest is not an arrest, unless the person sought to be arrested submits to the process and goes with the arresting officer." How do the concepts of arrest and imprisonment differ?

4. Most of the early case law is English, but it is difficult to apply in Canada because of the different ways in which crimes are categorized in the two jurisdictions. The English common law distinction between felonies and misdemeanors was abandoned in Canada with the enactment of our first Criminal Code in 1892. Instead, offences are divided into those tried by indictment and those tried by summary conviction. There is a third category, hybrid offences, in which the prosecutor is given discretion to proceed by either indictment or summary conviction.

(a) A NOTE ON THE CANADIAN CHARTER OF RIGHTS AND FREEDOMS

The Charter has added another dimension to the analysis of the defence of legal authority. Since it is designed to protect individuals against improper use of state power, the Charter applies to federal and provincial laws, and to the conduct of government departments, agencies and officials. Certain sections of the Charter are specifically designed to protect persons subject to criminal charges or other state-imposed detention, while other sections have a more general application. Sections 7 to 15 of the Charter guarantee a broad range of legal rights and freedoms, including the right to be secure against unreasonable search or seizure (section 8), and the right not to be arbitrarily detained or imprisoned (section 9).

Once an individual establishes that her Charter rights have been violated, the burden falls to the government to try to justify or excuse that violation under section 1. If the government cannot satisfy the requirements of section 1, the individual may pursue one or more remedies under the Charter. Section 24(1) gives a judge discretion to grant the aggrieved individual whatever remedy the judge considers "appropriate and just in the circumstances". Section 24(2), which is primarily relevant in criminal cases, requires the judge to exclude evidence obtained in violation of the accused's Charter rights, if its admission would "bring the administration of justice into disrepute". Moreover, section 52 provides that the Charter is the supreme law of Canada, and renders any law that is inconsistent with it of no force or effect to the extent of the inconsistency. These provisions can affect civil liability actions in two distinct ways.

First, if a suspect's Charter rights are violated, the suspect may seek a remedy under section 24(1). Since this may include damages, the section creates a constitutional statutory cause of action. Canadian courts have so far been reluctant to award damages for the Charter violation itself, and have usually required the plaintiff to prove actual loss. For example, in *Bauder v. Wilson* (1989), 43 C.R.R. 149 (B.C. S.C.), the court held that damages for the Charter violation *per se* were neither appropriate nor just. This restrictive approach was also adopted in *Breen v. Saunders* (1986), 71 N.B.R. (2d) 404 (Q.B.), and other cases. However, in *Lord v. Allison* (1986), 3 B.C.L.R. (2d) 300 (S.C.), the court held the R.C.M.P. and the province of British Columbia liable for several Charter violations, and awarded $500 for each violation in addition to compensatory and punitive damages. In *Rollinson v. R.* (1994), 20 C.C.L.T. (2d) 92 (F.C. T.D.), the plaintiffs were awarded $8,000 for violation of their Charter rights, in addition to substantial pecuniary and punitive damages.

Second, assume that a statute authorizes and privileges an officer to arrest a suspect. If the suspect establishes that the statute violates the Charter, it will be struck down under section 52, to the extent of the inconsistency. Consequently, the arrest may not be authorized and privileged by statute, and the officer may be unable to establish the defence of legal authority in any subsequent tort action.

2. General Powers of Arrest Without a Warrant and Privilege

(a) INTRODUCTION

Peace officers and private citizens will often raise the defence of legal authority in false imprisonment and battery actions brought by those they have arrested or detained. In such cases, the defendant must prove that the specific act that gave rise to the tort action was authorized by the common law or statute. The most important sources of legal authority to arrest are sections 494 and 495 of the Criminal Code. Section 494 outlines the situations in which individuals are authorized to arrest another person without a warrant. Section 495 defines a number of additional circumstances in which peace officers are authorized to arrest without a warrant. As we shall see in *R. v. Biron*, [1976] 2 S.C.R. 56, the Canadian courts interpreted these sections to give peace officers broad discretion in performing their duties. However, with the advent of the Charter and increasing emphasis on individual rights, the courts have begun to read these sections more strictly.

Once an officer or other defendant has established that her conduct was authorized, she must then prove that her actions were legally privileged. The Criminal Code and other statutes contain sections privileging the actions of peace officers and private citizens. The most important of these is section 25, the general privileging provision of the Criminal Code. This section has been interpreted as protecting peace officers and others from liability, if their conduct was authorized by law, if they acted reasonably and if they used no more force than was reasonably necessary. As with the authorizing provisions, the Canadian courts had interpreted section 25 broadly, thereby insulating police from criminal or civil liability.

(b) THE CRIMINAL CODE'S AUTHORIZING SECTIONS — 494 and 495

494. (1) Any one may arrest without warrant
    (*a*) a person whom he finds committing an indictable offence, or
    (*b*) a person who, on reasonable grounds, he believes
        (i) has committed a criminal offence, and
        (ii) is escaping from and freshly pursued by persons who have lawful authority to arrest that person.
    (2) Any one who is
    (*a*) the owner or a person in lawful possession of property, or
    (*b*) a person authorized by the owner or by a person in lawful possession of property,

may arrest without warrant a person whom he finds committing a criminal offence on or in relation to that property.

(3) Any one other than a peace officer who arrests a person without warrant shall forthwith deliver the person to a peace officer.

495. (1) A peace officer may arrest without warrant
(*a*) a person who has committed an indictable offence or who, on reasonable grounds, he believes has committed or is about to commit an indictable offence,
(*b*) a person whom he finds committing a criminal offence, or
(*c*) a person in respect of whom he has reasonable grounds to believe that a warrant of arrest or committal, in any form set out in Part XXVIII in relation thereto, is in force within the territorial jurisdiction in which the person is found.

NOTES AND QUESTIONS

1. As indicated, a peace officer may invoke the powers in s. 494, in addition to those specifically granted to her in s. 495 by virtue of her special status. It should also be noted that s. 2 of the Code defines the term peace officer to include not only police, but also sheriffs, mayors, commercial pilots, fishery officers, and others.

2. Other sections of the Code and various federal statutes authorize arrest without a warrant for specific offences. See, for example, the Criminal Code, s. 31 (breach of the peace); and the Immigration Act, R.S.C. 1985, c. I-2, s. 20(1). The provincial liquor, hunting, fishing, trespass to property, and highway traffic statutes may also contain broad powers of arrest without a warrant.

3. For a discussion of a peace officer's power to arrest with a warrant see *Fletcher v. Collins* (1968), 70 D.L.R. (2d) 183 (Ont. H.C.); *Crowe v. Noon* (1970), 16 D.L.R. (3d) 22 (Ont. H.C.); and *Little v. Peers*, [1988] 3 W.W.R. 107 (B.C. C.A.). See also ss. 28 and 29 of the Code.

4. In the 1985 revisions to the Criminal Code, the term "reasonable grounds" was inserted in place of the term "reasonable and probable grounds". It has been argued that the terms have the same meaning. As a matter of statutory interpretation, do you agree that the terms mean the same thing? Can you suggest a situation in which the police would have reasonable grounds to arrest, but not reasonable and probable grounds?

(c) THE CRIMINAL CODE'S PRIVILEGING SECTION — 25

25. (1) Every one who is required or authorized by law to do anything in the administration or enforcement of the law
(*a*) as a private person,
(*b*) as a peace officer or public officer,
(*c*) in aid of a peace officer or public officer, or
(*d*) by virtue of his office,
is, if he acts on reasonable grounds, justified in doing what he is required or authorized to do and in using as much force as is necessary for that purpose.

(d) A PEACE OFFICER'S AUTHORITY AND PRIVILEGE TO ARREST WITHOUT A WARRANT

R. v. BIRON

[1976] 2 S.C.R. 56, 59 D.L.R. (3d) 409 (S.C.C.)

[Biron was arrested by Constable Maisonneuve for the summary conviction offence of creating a disturbance contrary to s. 171(*a*)(i) of the Criminal Code. While being led to the police wagon, he struggled with Constable Dorion and was charged with resisting a peace officer in the execution of his duty contrary to s. 118(*a*) of the Code. Following his acquittal on the first charge, the Quebec Court of Appeal acquitted him on the second. The Court reasoned that since Biron had not been found committing the offence of creating a disturbance as required by s. 450(1)(*b*), Constable Maisonneuve had no authority to arrest him for this summary conviction offence. Thus, Constable Dorion had not acted lawfully in attempting to detain Biron, and the conviction for resisting arrest could not stand.

The Crown's appeal of Biron's acquittal on the charge of resisting arrest raised issues concerning the interpretation of the Code's authorizing and privileging sections.]

MARTLAND J.: — On the appeal to this Court, the Crown relied upon the provisions of s. 31(2) of the *Code*, the effect of which had not been argued in the Court of Appeal. Section 31 provides as follows:

> 31(1) Every peace officer who witnesses a breach of the peace and every one who lawfully assists him is justified in arresting any person whom he finds committing the breach of the peace, or who, on reasonable and probable grounds, he believes is about to join in or renew the breach of the peace.
>
> (2) Every peace officer is justified in receiving into custody any person who is given into his charge as having been a party to a breach of the peace by one who has, or who on reasonable and probable grounds he believes has, witnessed the breach of the peace.

The question in issue is as to whether the charge against Biron of resisting Dorion in the execution of his duty must fail because of his successful appeal from his conviction under s. 171(*a*)(i) for causing a disturbance.

It is contended on behalf of Biron that he could not be so convicted because he was not under lawful arrest, and so was entitled to resist Dorion's efforts to take him to the patrol wagon. It is argued that he had not been lawfully arrested because Maisonneuve's right to arrest him for a summary conviction offence had to be based on s. 450(1)(*b*) [rep. & sub. R.S.C. 1970, c. 2 (2nd Supp.), s. 5] of the *Code* which provides that:

> 450(1) A peace officer may arrest without warrant
>
>   . . .
>
> (*b*) a person whom he finds committing a criminal offence.

It is submitted by the respondent that Maisonneuve did not find him committing a criminal offence because he was acquitted on the charge laid against him. Reliance is placed on the judgment of the Court of Appeal for Saskatchewan in *A.-G. Sask. v. Pritchard* (1961), 130 C.C.C. 61, 35 C.R. 150, 34 W.W.R. 458.

Paragraph (*a*) of s. 450(1) permits a peace officer to arrest without a warrant:

> (*a*) a person who has committed an indictable offence or who, on reasonable and probable grounds, he believes has committed or is about to commit an indictable offence,

This paragraph, limited in its application to indictable offences, deals with the situation in which an offence has already been committed or is expected to be committed. The peace officer is not present at its commission. He may have to rely upon information received from others. The paragraph therefore enables him to act on his belief, if based on reasonable and probable grounds.

Paragraph (*b*) applies in relation to any criminal offence and it deals with the situation in which the peace officer himself finds an offence being committed.

His power to arrest is based upon his own observation. Because it is based on his own discovery of an offence actually being committed there is no reason to refer to a belief based upon reasonable and probable grounds.

If the reasoning in the *Pritchard* case is sound, the validity of an arrest under s. 450(1)(*b*) can only be determined after the trial of the person arrested and after the determination of any subsequent appeals. My view is that the validity of an arrest under this paragraph must be determined in relation to the circumstances which were apparent to the peace officer at the time the arrest was made.

This was the view of the Court of Appeal in England in *Wiltshire v. Barrett*, [1965] 2 All E.R. 271, when interpreting a provision of the *Road Traffic Act*, 1960 (U.K.) c. 16.

. . .

In the *Wiltshire* case the statutory provision involved the power to arrest without a warrant a person unfit to drive because of drink or drugs and the Court referred to the public importance of an arrest being promptly made in such circumstances. Paragraph (*b*) of s. 450(1) deals with the power to arrest without a warrant a person found committing any criminal offence. It is certainly of public importance that the peace officer should be able to exercise this power promptly.

If the words "committing a criminal offence" are to be construed in the manner indicated in the *Pritchard* case, para. (*b*) becomes impossible to apply. The power of arrest which that paragraph gives has to be exercised promptly, yet, strictly speaking, it is impossible to say that an offence is committed until the party arrested has been found guilty by the Courts. If this is the way in which this provision is to be construed, no peace officer can ever decide, when making an arrest without a warrant, that the person is "committing a criminal offence". In my opinion the wording used in para. (*b*), which is over simplified, means that the power to arrest without a warrant is given where the peace officer himself finds a situation in which a person is apparently committing an offence.

In the present case, Constable Maisonneuve observed an apparent offence being committed by Biron. That he was justified in so thinking is shown by the fact that, at trial, Biron was convicted of the offence of causing a disturbance, and that his appeal from conviction resulted from the fact that the information charged only causing a disturbance "by shouting", which "shouting" the Judge on appeal found was not established by the evidence.

In my opinion, the arrest of Biron by Maisonneuve was lawful, and, consequently, the resistance offered by Biron to Dorion constituted an offence.

Even if the arrest by Maisonneuve was not lawful, it is my view that Biron was guilty of the offence charged. It was Maisonneuve who made the arrest, not Dorion. Following the arrest, Biron was placed in the custody of Gauthier, who then placed him in the custody of Dorion. The resistance with which Biron was charged was resistance to Dorion and the question in issue is as to whether Dorion was resisted in the execution of his duty.

His duty is defined in s. 54 [am. 1968, c. 18, s. 2] of the *Police Act*, 1968 (Que.), c. 17:

> 54. It shall be the duty of every municipal police force and each member thereof to maintain peace, order and public safety in its territory and in any other territory under its jurisdiction, to prevent crime and infringements of its by-laws and to seek out the offenders.

On the night in question Dorion was one of a group of police who conducted a raid upon a bar in Montreal. It was a part of his duty, in connection with that raid, to take custody of persons who might be arrested by police officers in the building, and that is what happened in the case of Biron. In taking him into custody he was carrying out the duty which had been given to him as a police officer.

Section 31(2) of the *Code* provides that Dorion was justified in receiving Biron into custody. The arrest made by Maisonneuve was because he considered Biron to be committing a disturbance, in a public place, which would be a breach of the peace. It is evident that Dorion, who was a part of the police force conducting the raid, reasonably believed that Gauthier, who turned Biron over to him, had witnessed a breach of the peace.

I interpret the word "justified" in s. 31(2) as meaning that Dorion had lawful sanction to receive Biron into his custody. He received him into his custody in the course of performance of his duties as a peace officer at the scene of the raid. Biron offered resistance to him in the execution of that duty. In my opinion that is sufficient to make Biron guilty of the offence with which he was charged under s. 118(*a*).

I would allow the appeal and restore the conviction.

LASKIN C.J.C. (dissenting): — Whether the accused was guilty of an offence under s. 118(*a*) depends in this case on whether he was under lawful arrest. I do not question, despite the contentions of counsel for the respondent accused, that the accused offered resistance to Dorion; it was not, however, suggested that it was of such a character as to amount in itself to the use of excessive force. There was, however, but one arrest, that effected by Maisonneuve in the restaurant; there was no suggestion of any release and rearrest. The issue turns therefore on its lawfulness. We are not concerned in this case with a constable's own responsibility or liability for effecting an allegedly unlawful arrest. It is to that that provisions such as s. 25 of the *Criminal Code* are addressed. I would find it astonishing that a provision concerned with a constable's criminal or other responsibility, and which immunizes him in specified circumstances in respect of an arrest that he has made, should become the vehicle for providing a basis upon which an accused may himself be convicted of resisting the arrest. To do that is to turn a protective provision, a shield, for the constable into a sword against an accused by treating the protection as an expansion of the powers of arrest given by what is now s. 450 [rep. & sub. R.S.C. 1970, c. 2 (2nd Supp.), s. 5], of the *Criminal Code.*

The particular provision of s. 450, which is of relevance here is s-s. (1)(*b*), authorizing a peace officer to arrest without a warrant "a person whom he finds committing a criminal offence." Maisonneuve arrested the accused without a warrant and the charge laid in respect of that arrest was causing a disturbance by shouting under the now s. 171(*a*). It turns out that no such offence was committed at the time and place, and the arrest therefor was, *qua* the accused, unlawful. So far as the constable was concerned, his unlawful conduct was protected under s. 25. I repeat that the protection of the constable did not make the arrest lawful *qua* the accused.

. . . I am of the opinion that Culliton, C.J.S., stated the law correctly, as it applies here, in the last paragraph of his reasons as follows (at pp. 65-6 C.C.C., p. 154 C.R.):

> While a Peace Officer has no right to arrest without a warrant a person he finds committing an offence unless an offence was in fact committed, nevertheless, even if the officer was in error in so arresting, if he acted on reasonable and probable grounds, he is given protection under s. 25 of the *Code.*

In short, the position of a person accused of an offence founded upon an allegedly lawful arrest which turns out to have been unlawful is one thing; the position of the arresting officer as a possible accused in a criminal prosecution or as a defendant in a civil suit arising out of the arrest is an entirely different thing: see *Frey v. Fedoruk* (1950), 97 C.C.C. 1, [1950] 3 D.L.R. 513, [1950] S.C.R. 517.

The reasoning and judgment of the English Court of Appeal in *Wiltshire v. Barrett*, [1965] 2 All E.R. 271, have no application to this case. It was a civil action for damages against a constable for assault and wrongful arrest, not a criminal prosecution, as here, against an accused person for resisting a peace officer in the execution of his duty. The *Wiltshire* case involved a provision of the English *Road Traffic Act, 1960*, which prohibited a person, on pain of fine or imprisonment, from driving or attempting to drive a motor vehicle on a road or other public place when he was unfit to drive through drink or drugs. This prohibition, in s. 6(1), was fortified by s. 6(4) which empowered a police constable to arrest without warrant a person committing the aforesaid offence. There was no such provision in the *Road Traffic Act, 1960* as s. 25 of the *Criminal Code*, which provides justification for a police constable when acting on reasonable and probable grounds. Hence, when the issue arose in *Wiltshire* as to protection of the constable from civil suit if he overstepped the literal command of s. 6(4), the Court there looked to statutory purpose and context and interpreted "committing" in s. 6(4) to mean "apparently committing", so as to make it immaterial whether the arrested person be found not guilty of the offence for which he was arrested without warrant.

. . .

There is a further point that merits emphasis. If the word "apparently" is to be read into s. 450(1)(b), logical consistency, if not also ordinary canons of construction, demand that the word be read into s. 449(1)(a) [s. 449 rep. & sub. *idem.*] which empowers any person to arrest without warrant a person whom he "finds committing" an indictable offence. Moreover, it is plain to me, on grounds of context in aid of construction, that when s. 449(1)(a) is read with s. 449(1)(b), the former could not possibly embrace arrest without warrant on apparency or on reasonable and probable grounds. Further, reasonable and probable grounds for an arrest without warrant govern s. 450(1)(a) and s. 450(1)(c) but the words are excluded from s. 450(1)(b), and I see no textual or policy justification for reading them or the equivalent term "apparently" into s. 450(1)(b).

Of course, as Kaufman, J.A., points out in his reasons, a constable's lot is a heavy and even unenviable one when he has to make an on-the-spot decision as to an arrest. But he may be overzealous as well as mistaken, and it may be too that when a charge or charges come to be laid, the Crown attorney or other advising counsel may mistake the grounds and thus lay a charge which does not support the arrest. We cannot go on a guessing expedition out of regret for an innocent mistake or a wrong-headed assessment. Far more important, however, is the social and legal, and indeed political, principle upon which our criminal law is based, namely, the right of an individual to be left alone, to be free of private or public restraint, save as the law provides otherwise. Only to the extent to which it so provides can a person be detained or his freedom of movement arrested.

The position as it relates to resistance to unlawful arrest was established at common law as early as 1709 in *R. v. Tooley et al.* (1709), 2 Ld. Raym. 1296, 92 E.R. 349, and has been reaffirmed time and again; see, for example, *R. v. Curvan* (1826), 1 Mood. 131, 168 E.R. 1213; *R. v. Wilson,* [1955] 1 All E.R. 744, at p. 745, referring also to the qualification of the use of excessive force in resisting. It has been part of our criminal law from the beginning and is reflected in the provisions of the *Criminal Code,* which has sought to balance the competing interests in freedom and order by giving the peace officer protection in specified circumstances where he has exceeded his authority to make an arrest. Our law has not, as I understand it, deprived the citizen of his right to resist unlawful arrest. His resistance may be at his own risk if the arrest proves to be lawful, but so too must the police officer accept the risk of having effected a lawful arrest. Of course, even if the resisted arrest is unlawful, the person resisting may still become culpable if he uses excessive force.

Where does s. 31(2) of the *Criminal Code* stand in this assessment? It reads as follows:

> 31(2) Every peace officer is justified in receiving into custody any person who is given into his charge as having been a party to a breach of the peace by one who has, or who on reasonable and probable grounds he believes has, witnessed the breach of the peace.

Section 31 is not an arrest power, but a protection for the person or persons making an arrest, just as is s. 25. Moreover, it is limited to protection in respect of an arrest for breach of the peace, and in that respect has a connection with s. 30, which does speak expressly of detention of a person committing a breach of the peace. By no stretch of the imagination can either s. 30 or s. 31 be turned into a general power of either arrest or justification in respect of any criminal offence on the theory that all offences under the *Criminal Code* constitute breaches of the peace. This would eliminate at one swoop, and by a side wind at that, any protection that an accused would have against any consequential charges if he was illegally arrested under ss. 449 and 450, the provisions of the *Criminal Code* which define powers of arrest.

But there is more to be said on s. 31(2) to show its inapplicability here. It is patent on its face that any resort to it can only be to give Dorion protection for receiving the accused into his custody, albeit the latter was unlawfully arrested by Maisonneuve. Even so, this may be taking the matter too far because it is arguable, in the context of ss. 30 and 31, that s. 31(2) is limited to a peace officer taking in charge a person detained by an ordinary citizen. Be that as it may, it is simply a "bootstrap" argument to contend that resistance to Dorion became unlawful because he, Dorion, was justified in taking custody of the accused following his arrest by Maisonneuve.

I would dismiss the appeal.

[Judson, Ritchie, Pigeon, and De Grandpré JJ. concurred with Martland J., and Spence and Dickson JJ. concurred with Laskin C.J.C. Note that the order of Martland J.'s and Laskin C.J.C.'s judgments has been reversed.]

NOTES AND QUESTIONS

1. Explain in detail the bases upon which Martland J. concluded that Biron's arrest and subsequent detention were authorized by law. What were the bases upon which Laskin C.J.C. held that Biron's arrest and subsequent detention were not authorized? Which line of reasoning is more compelling?

2. How does the issue of whether the officers were authorized relate to Biron's criminal liability?

3. One issue dividing the court was whether s. 31(2) authorized the officer to arrest Biron. As a matter of statutory interpretation is Martland J.'s or Laskin C.J.C.'s position preferable? This issue previously caused the courts difficulty in regard to s. 25. See *Frey v. Fedoruk*, [1950] S.C.R. 517; *Eccles v. Bourque* (1974), 50 D.L.R. (3d) 753 (S.C.C.); and *Colet v. R.* (1981), 119 D.L.R. (3d) 521 (S.C.C.).

4. As indicated by Laskin C.J.C., the term "justified" in s. 25 has been interpreted to mean protected from both criminal and civil liability. See also *Priestman v. Colangelo*, [1959] S.C.R. 615; *Poupart v. Lafortune* (1973), 41 D.L.R. (3d) 720 (S.C.C.); *Eccles v. Bourque, supra; Allarie v. Victoria (City)*, [1995] 1 W.W.R. 655 (B.C. S.C.); and *Swansburg v. Smith*, [1995] 1 W.W.R. 324 (B.C. S.C). Can Laskin C.J.C.'s view be justified based on the constitutional division of power, statutory interpretation or policy?

5. The courts have also held that an individual who is not authorized will be privileged under s. 25 if she made a mistake of fact and acted on reasonable grounds. This interpretation casts the hardship involved in any reasonable mistake of fact on the innocent suspect, rather than on the officer. Does the wording of s. 25 support this interpretation? Is there another basis upon which this result could be justified? See *Frey v. Fedoruk, supra; A.G. Sask. v. Pritchard* (1961), 130 C.C.C. 61 (Sask. C.A.); *Poupart v. Lafortune, supra; Sears Can. Inc. v. Smart* (1987), 36 D.L.R. (4th) 756 (Nfld. C.A.).

6. Contrary to *Biron*, the Ontario Court of Appeal in *R. v. Brennan* (1989), 75 C.R. (3d) 38, interpreted the Code's authorizing and privileging sections narrowly. The accused police officer was attempting to stop the driver of a suspected stolen vehicle. A high speed chase ensued during which the police officer drove through a stop sign without stopping. The court upheld the police officer's conviction for failure to stop at a stop sign. While the officer was authorized to arrest the suspect, he was not authorized to run a stop sign. Since his conduct was not specifically authorized, he was not privileged under s. 25.

7. The legality of an arrest under the Code, and various federal and provincial statutes often turns on whether there were reasonable grounds to suspect the accused. The test of what constitutes reasonable grounds is often defined in terms of whether the facts would create in the mind of a reasonable person a strong and honest belief that the suspect had committed the offence in question. Mere suspicion is not enough. Although there is broad agreement on the test of reasonable grounds, considerable litigation arises concerning its application in specific fact situations. See *Dumbell v. Roberts*, [1944] 1 All E.R. 326 (C.A.); *Chartier v. A.G.-Que.* (1979), 48 C.C.C. (2d) 34 (S.C.C.); *R. v. Storrey* (1990), 53 C.C.C. (3d) 316 (S.C.C.); *R. v. Klimchuk* (1991), 8 C.R. (4th) 327 (B.C. C.A.); *R. v. Proulx* (1993), 81 C.C.C. (3d) 48 (Que. C.A.); and *Swansburg v. Smith, supra*.

8. For a discussion of arrest powers see Martin, "Police Detention and Arrest Privileges in Canada" (1961-62), 4 Cr. L.Q. 54; Archibald, "The Law of Arrest", in Del Buono (ed.), *Criminal Procedure in Canada* (1982), 125; and Salhany, *Canadian Criminal Procedure*, 6th ed. (1996), 3-8 to 3-17.

(e) A PRIVATE CITIZEN'S AUTHORITY AND PRIVILEGE TO ARREST WITHOUT A WARRANT

The early common law did not distinguish between the powers and privileges of citizens and law enforcement officials, because the apprehension of criminals was considered a community responsibility. It was only in the last century that the common law began to make such distinctions. In terms of civil liability, a peace officer was privileged to arrest without a warrant, provided she had reasonable and probable grounds to believe that the suspect had committed a felony. However, a private citizen had to prove not only that she had reasonable and probable grounds to believe the suspect had committed a felony, but also that the felony had been committed.

In Canada, the powers of private citizens and police to arrest are now defined by federal and provincial statutes. For private citizens, the most important provision is section 494 of the Criminal Code, because it contains the general powers to arrest without a warrant. There is now some question as to whether a private citizen's protection from civil liability is governed by the old common law principles or by section 25 of the Code. The recent case law is divided on this issue.

NOTES AND QUESTIONS

1. For a discussion of a private citizen's common law powers, privileges and obligations in the arrest process, see *Handcock v. Baker* (1800), 126 E.R. 1270 (H.L.); *Timothy v. Simpson* (1835), 149 E.R. 1285 (Exch.); *Allen v. Wright* (1838), 173 E.R. 602 (C.P.); *Price v. Seeley* (1843), 8 E.R. 651 (H.L.); *Walters v. W.H. Smith & Son, Ltd.*, [1914] 1 K.B. 595; *Dunne v. Clinton*, [1930] Ir. R. 366 (H.C.); and *John Lewis & Co. v. Tims*, [1952] A.C. 676 (H.L.). See also Hall, "Legal and Social Aspects of Arrest Without a Warrant" (1936), 49 Harv. L.R. 566; and Spencer, "Citizens Arrest — At Their Peril" (1992), 51 Cambridge L.J. 405.

2. While the Canadian courts have broadly defined peace officers' statutory powers under the Code, they have been inconsistent in applying these provisions to cases involving private citizens. For example, *Biron* was applied in interpreting the term "finds committing" in s. 494(1)(*a*) in *Dendekker v. F.W. Woolworth Co.*, [1975] 3 W.W.R. 429 (Alta. S.C.); *Karogiannis v. Poulus*, [1976] 6 W.W.R. 197 (B.C. S.C.); and *Banerjee v. K-Mart Can. Ltd.* (1983), 127 A.P.R. 252 (Nfld. Dist. Ct.), but rejected in *Kendall v. Gambles Can. Ltd.*, [1981] 4 W.W.R. 718 (Sask. Q.B.); *Banyasz v. K-Mart Can. Ltd.* (1986), 57 O.R. (2d) 445 (H.C.); and *Sears Can. Inc. v. Smart* (1987), 36 D.L.R. (4th) 756 (Nfld. C.A.).

3. These same cases are also divided on whether a private citizen's defence of legal authority in torts is based on the common law or on s. 25 of the Code. See also *Cronk v. F.W. Woolworth Co.*, [1986] 3 W.W.R. 139 (Sask. Q.B.); *Otto v. J. Grant Wallace* (1988), 47 D.L.R. (4th) 439 (Alta. Q.B.); and *Briggs v. Laviolette* (1994), 21 C.C.L.T. (2d) 105 (B.C. S.C.).

4. As indicated, the Supreme Court of Canada has held that s. 25 of the Code provides peace officers with a defence to both civil and criminal liability. Would the Court be bound to conclude that s. 25, rather than the common law, governs a private citizen's defence to tort liability?

3. Rights and Obligations in the Arrest Process

(a) REASONS FOR THE ARREST

KOECHLIN v. WAUGH and HAMILTON

[1957] O.W.N 245, 11 D.L.R. (2d) 447 (Ont. C.A.)

LAIDLAW J.A. (orally): — This is an appeal by the plaintiffs from a judgment pronounced by His Honour Judge Shea, in the County Court of the County of York, on May 21, 1956, dismissing with costs an action brought by the plaintiffs for damages alleged for unlawful arrest and imprisonment ...

On the evening of October 11, 1955, the infant plaintiff, aged about 20 years, and his friend Victor Wassilgew, attended a picture show in the Township of Scarborough. The show ended about midnight. They went to a restaurant for coffee and, afterwards, started to walk on the sidewalk on Kingston Road in the direction of the home of Wassilgew. They were stopped by the defendants, who are police officers of the Township of Scarborough. The police officers were in plain clothes and were in a police cruiser car. The police called the infant plaintiff and his companion to their car and asked for their identification. Wassilgew gave his identification at once and told the police officers that they were on their way home after the show. The infant plaintiff objected to giving his identification unless the police officer, Hamilton, who spoke to him, first identified himself. The defendant Hamilton produced a badge and said he was a police officer, but the infant plaintiff was not satisfied with that identification and requested the name and number of the officer. The officer did not give his name, but his number was on the badge. The infant plaintiff continued to refuse to identify himself, and a scuffle ensued during which the infant plaintiff fell into a deep ditch. Subsequently, force was used by the police officer and other officers who were called to the scene to put the infant plaintiff into a police car. He was not told any reason for his arrest. He was taken to the police station and told that he would be charged with assault of a police officer.

The adult plaintiff stated in evidence that he was informed about 2 o'clock in the morning that his son was in custody; he went to the police station; he asked the Sergeant of Police the reason his son was there in custody; the sergeant told him it was for assaulting a police officer. The adult plaintiff asked the sergeant how it happened and, according to the evidence of the adult plaintiff, the sergeant said "he would not tell me, that I would hear about it the next day in Court about 10 o'clock in the morning." He says he asked the sergeant if he could see his son and was refused permission. It was 9 or 10 o'clock the following evening before the infant plaintiff was released on bail. On November 18th, the charge against the infant plaintiff was heard and was dismissed.

The learned Judge stated in reasons given by him that the police officers stopped the infant plaintiff and his companion because they were sauntering along the street, and because of "their dress". There was in fact nothing distinctive about the dress of the infant plaintiff, but his companion was wearing rubber-soled shoes and a jacket. The learned Judge referred also to the fact that there had been a number of "break-ins" in the neighbourhood a few nights before and that the police had reported that a person wearing rubber-soled shoes was involved in one or more of those break-ins. After referring to the reasons for stopping the infant plaintiff and his companion and asking for identification, the learned Judge said: "Then, from then on, the actions of Koechlin, and his words, would in my opinion justify the officers in believing that this man had or was about to commit a crime." Later, he said, referring to Koechlin — "his refusal to cooperate — made the officers still more suspicious and firm in the belief, as I said, that something was wrong."

. . .

A police officer has not in law an unlimited power to arrest a law-abiding citizen. The power given expressly to him by the Criminal Code to arrest without warrant is contained in s. 435, but we direct careful attention of the public to the fact that the law empowers a police officer in many cases and under certain circumstances to require a person to account for his presence and to identify himself and to furnish other information, and any person who wrongfully fails to comply with such lawful requirements does so at the risk of arrest and imprisonment. None of these circumstances exists in this case. No unnecessary restriction on his power which results in increased difficulty to a police officer to perform his duties of office should be imposed by the Court. At the same time, the rights and freedom under law from unlawful arrest and imprisonment of an innocent critizen must be fully guarded by the Courts. In this case, the fact that the companion of the infant plaintiff was wearing rubber-soled shoes and a windbreaker and that his dress attracted the attention of the police officers, falls far short of reasonable and probable grounds for believing that the infant plaintiff had committed an indictable offence or was about to commit such an offence. We do not criticize the police officers in any way for asking the infant plaintiff and his companion to identify themselves, but we are satisfied that when the infant plaintiff, who was entirely innocent of any wrongdoing, refused to do so, the police officer has no right to use force to compel him to identify himself. It would have been wise and, indeed, a duty as a good citizen, for the infant plaintiff to have identified himself when asked to do so by the police officers. It is altogether likely that if the infant plaintiff had been courteous and cooperative, the incident giving rise to this action would not have occurred, but that does not in law excuse the defendants for acting as they did in the particular circumstances.

We direct attention to an important fact. The infant plaintiff was not told by either of the police officers any reason for his arrest. The infant plaintiff was entitled to know on what charge or on suspicion of what crime he was seized. He was not required in law to submit to restraint on his freedom unless he knew the reason why that restraint should be imposed. In *Christie v. Leachinsky*, [1947] 1 All E.R. 567, a decision of the House of Lords, Lord Simon, after referring to many authorities, said at pp. 572-3:

> These citations . . . seem to me to establish the following propositions:
>
> 1. If a policeman arrests without warrant on reasonable suspicion of felony, or of other crime of a sort which does not require a warrant, he must in ordinary circumstances inform the person arrested of the true ground of arrest. He is not entitled to keep the reason to himself or to give a reason which is not the true reason. In other words, a citizen is entitled to know on what charge or on suspicion of what crime he is seized.
>
> 2. If the citizen is not so informed, but is nevertheless seized, the policeman, apart from certain exceptions, is liable for false imprisonment.
>
> 3. The requirement that the person arrested should be informed of the reason why he is seized naturally does not exist if the circumstances are such that he must know the general nature of the alleged offence for which he is detained.
>
> 4. The requirement that he should be so informed does not mean that technical or precise language need be used. The matter is a matter of substance, and turns on the elementary proposition that in this country a person is, *prima facie*, entitled to his freedom and is only required to submit to restraint on his freedom if he knows in substance the reason why it is claimed that this restraint should be imposed.
>
> 5. The person arrested cannot complain that he has not been supplied with the above information as and when he should be, if he himself produces the situation which makes it practically impossible to inform him, *e.g.*, by immediate counter-attack or by running away.
>
> There may well be other exceptions to the general rule in addition to those I have indicated, and the above propositions are not intended to constitute a formal or complete code, but to indicate the general principles of our law on a very important matter. These principles equally apply to a private person who arrests on suspicion. If a policeman who entertained a reasonable suspicion that X had committed a felony were at liberty to arrest him and march him off to a police station without giving any explanation of why he was doing this, the *prima facie* right of personal liberty would be gravely infringed. No one, I think, would approve a situation in which, when the person arrested asked for the reason, the policeman replied: "That has nothing to do with you. Come along with me." Such a situation may be tolerated under other systems of law, as for instance, in the time of *lettres de cachet* in the eighteenth century in France, or in more recent days when the Gestapo swept people off to confinement under an overriding authority which the executive in this country happily does not in ordinary times possess. This would be quite contrary to our conceptions of individual liberty.

In this case it was held that although the police officers *bona fide* and on reasonable grounds believed the plaintiff had committed an offence, they had not informed him as to why he was being arrested and were, therefore, liable in damages for false imprisonment. In *R. v. Hastings*, 90 Can. C.C. 150, [1947] 4 D.L.R. 748, 21 M.P.R. 23, it was held by the New Brunswick Court of Appeal that a person being unlawfully arrested without a warrant is entitled to resist such unlawful arrest.

There is one further matter that deserves comment. A person who has been arrested should not be held *incommunicado*. We do not find it necessary to find as a fact that the infant plaintiff was denied his right to communicate with his father at the first reasonable opportunity. If, however, the father of the infant plaintiff was refused permission by the Sergeant of Police to see his son at any time before the charge came on for hearing in Court, such practice cannot be justified in this or in any other case. A person in custody should never be denied his right to communicate with his relatives at the earliest reasonable opportunity so that he may avail himself of their advice and assistance. That right ought to be recognized and given effect in all cases and care should be exercised by police authorities to see that it is not wholly disregarded.

Finally, we are not in accord with the view expressed by the learned trial Judge that the actions of the infant plaintiff in resisting the efforts of the police officers can be regarded as justification for their belief that he "either had or was about to commit a crime." In the particular circumstances he was entitled in law to resist the efforts of the police officers, and they have failed in this case to justify their actions.

It was stated in the course of giving oral reasons for judgment that the Courts would strive diligently to avoid putting any unnecessary obstacle in the way of the detection of crime or the lawful arrest of persons in the proper performance of the duties of a police officer. We repeat an expression of that policy of the Courts. Nothing in these reasons for judgment should be taken as encouragement to any person to resist a police officer in the performance of his duties; on the contrary, it is not only highly desirable, but vitally important, that every person should co-operate to the utmost with police officers for the good of the public and to ensure the preservation of law and order in his community.

In this case the police officers exceeded their powers and infringed the rights of the infant plaintiff without justification. Therefore, the appeal will be allowed with costs. The judgment of the Court below will be set aside and in place thereof there will be judgment for the plaintiffs in the amounts assessed, respectively, for damages suffered by the infant plaintiff and by the adult plaintiff. The amount of judgment in favour of the infant plaintiff will be paid into Court in accordance with the usual practice. The plaintiffs are also entitled to the costs of the action.

NOTES AND QUESTIONS

1. At what point was the plaintiff arrested and on what charge? What authority did the police have prior to the arrest to stop and question the plaintiff? Did the police have any legal authority to use force prior to the arrest?

2. Were the defendants authorized and privileged to arrest the plaintiff in the circumstances? Would they have been held liable even if they had properly informed him of the reasons? What arguments would you have made on behalf of Koechlin for punitive damages?

3. What impact does the failure to inform a suspect of the reasons for the arrest have on the

validity of the arrest? Can the suspect simply leave or use physical force to prevent her detention? See *Campbell v. Hudyma*, [1986] 2 W.W.R. 444 (Alta. C.A.); *Schell v. Truba* (1989), 79 Sask. R. 27 (Q.B.), aff'd. (1990), 89 Sask. R. 137 (C.A.); and *Cormier v. St. John (City)* (1994), 153 N.B.R. (2d) 293 (C.A.).

4. Laidlaw J.A. was very critical of the defendants for holding the plaintiff incommunicado. Should such conduct result in liability even if the arrest was lawful and the suspect was informed of the reasons for her arrest? See *Perry v. Fried* (1972), 32 D.L.R. (3d) 589 (N.S. T.D.); and *Lang v. Burch* (1982), 140 D.L.R. (3d) 325 (Sask. C.A.).

5. Section 29 of the Criminal Code also imposes disclosure requirements on an individual making an arrest. However, these provisions have been interpreted as being less stringent than those imposed by civil law. See *Gamracy v. R.*, [1974] S.C.R. 640; and *R. v. Erickson and Hathaway*, [1977] 4 W.W.R. 374 (Alta. S.C.).

6. In addition to bringing a common law tort action, an individual who is not informed of the reasons for her arrest may seek redress under the Charter. Section 10 of the Charter provides that "everyone has the right on arrest or detention (a) to be informed promptly of the reasons therefor; [and] (b) to retain and instruct counsel without delay and to be informed of that right."

Section 10 has generated a great deal of litigation and academic debate. For a discussion of what constitutes a "detention", see *R. v. Therens*, [1985] 1 S.C.R. 613; *R. v. Tremblay*, [1987] 2 S.C.R. 435; *R. v. Elshaw*, [1991] 3 S.C.R. 24; and *Dehghani v. Canada (Minister of Employment & Immigration)*, [1993] 1 S.C.R. 1053. The right to counsel under s. 10(b) has two components: the right to retain counsel without delay, and the right to be informed of that right. An unjustified violation of either of these rights will give rise to a s. 24 Charter remedy. For a discussion of police obligations under s. 10(b), see *R. v. Anderson* (1984), 45 O.R. (2d) 225 (C.A.); *R. v. Brydges*, [1990] 1 S.C.R. 190; *R. v. Manninen*, [1987] 1 S.C.R. 1233; and *R. v. Leclair*, [1989] 1 S.C.R. 3.

7. As suggested in *Koechlin*, an individual is generally under no obligation to identify herself, account for her presence, answer questions, remain on the scene, accompany an officer, or submit to a search. See *R. v. Carroll* (1959), 126 C.C.C. 19 (Ont. C.A.); *Rice v. Connolly*, [1966] 2 Q.B. 414; *Kenlin v. Gardiner*, [1967] 2 Q.B. 510; *Ludlow v. Burgess*, [1971] Cr. L.R. 238 (Q.B.); *Albert v. Lavin*, [1981] 3 All E.R. 878 (H.L.); *R. v. Wood* (1984), 52 A.R. 356 (Q.B.); and *Campbell v. Hudyma*, [1986] 2 W.W.R. 444 (Alta. C.A.). There are, however, many statutory exceptions to this rule. See, for example, the provincial highway traffic statutes which may require a driver to identify herself.

8. The issue has been further complicated by the Supreme Court's decision in *Moore v. R.*, [1979] 1 S.C.R. 195. The majority of the Court held that a person who violates a provincial statute may, in effect, have a positive duty to cooperate with the police. Moore had refused to identify himself to an officer who was attempting to ticket him for riding his bicycle through a red light. The officer then arrested Moore under s. 129 of the Code for obstructing a peace officer in the execution of his duty. The Supreme Court reasoned that the officer had a legal duty to enforce the provincial highway traffic act and that Moore's refusal to identify himself prevented the officer from performing this duty. The Court concluded that the officer was justified in arresting Moore pursuant to s. 129 and that, therefore, Moore was properly convicted of this offence. The decision in *Moore* has been widely criticized. See, for example, Cohen, "The Investigation of Offences and Police Powers" (1981), 13 Ottawa L. Rev. 549 at 551-56; and *R. v. Leitch* (1992), 18 C.R. (4th) 224 (Alta. Prov. Ct.), rev'd. on other grounds (1993), 13 Alta. L.R. (3d) 97 (Q.B.).

In *Ryan v. Auclair* (1989), 60 D.L.R. (4th) 212 (Que. C.A.), the police arrested two nuns, who were violating a municipal by-law by distributing religious pamphlets, after they refused to identify themselves beyond giving their religious names. When the nuns resisted, the officers used force to overpower them. The Court of Appeal upheld the trial judge's dismissal of the nuns' claim for false imprisonment. Should the police have the right to arrest those who refuse to identify themselves in cases involving municipal by-laws and provincial offences?

(b) THE USE OF REASONABLE FORCE

Both the common law and Criminal Code give those acting pursuant to legal authority broad powers to use force. Nevertheless, as a general rule, suspects must be given an opportunity to submit peacefully before any force is used. If a suspect resists, then as much force as is reasonably necessary may be used to subdue the suspect. In assessing whether the force used was reasonable, the courts examine the nature of force used in the specific circumstances and not the resultant injuries. A reasonable and *bona fide* mistake of fact as to the need to use force will not defeat the assertion of the right to use force. Provided an individual is acting lawfully, she will not be held liable for using force simply because the suspect is innocent.

The right to use deadly force is limited to circumstances in which an individual reasonably believes it is necessary to protect herself or a third person from death or grievous bodily harm. Moreover, section 25(4) of the Criminal Code gives peace officers the right to use deadly force to prevent the escape of a suspect who cannot be stopped in any less violent manner. An individual may incur both civil and criminal liability for using excessive or unnecessary force, or for using any force when acting unlawfully.

NOTES AND QUESTIONS

1. Can you suggest a situation in which self-defence and the right to use force in the assertion of legal authority would overlap?

2. For cases involving the issue of reasonable force, see *Scott v. R.* (1975), 61 D.L.R. (3d) 130 (Fed. C.A.); *Rumsey v. R.*, [1984] 5 W.W.R. 585 (Fed. Ct.); *Cluett v. R.* (1985), 21 D.L.R. (4th) 306 (S.C.C.); *Swinimer v. R.* (1986), 71 N.S.R. (2d) 173 (S.C.); *Penn v. Singbeil* (1986), 44 Sask. R. 312 (Q.B.), aff'd. (1987), 56 Sask. R. 314 (C.A.); and *Christopherson v. Saanich (District)*, [1995] 4 W.W.R. 381 (B.C. S.C.).

3. The right to use deadly force to prevent the escape of a fleeing suspect is a controversial issue. See *Robertson v. Joyce*, [1948] 4 D.L.R. (2d) 436 (Ont. C.A.); *Priestman v. Colangelo*, [1959] S.C.R. 615; *Beim v. Goyer*, [1965] S.C.R. 638; *R. v. Roberge* (1983), 147 D.L.R. (3d) 493 (S.C.C.); *Allarie v. Victoria (City)*, [1995] 1 W.W.R. 655 (B.C. S.C.); and Abraham *et al.*, "Police Use of Lethal Force: A Toronto Perspective" (1981), 19 Osgoode Hall L.J. 199. What arguments would you make in favour of abolishing the right to use deadly force to apprehend fleeing suspects?

4. In addition to s. 25, the Criminal Code authorizes the use of force to prevent the commission of certain offences (s. 27), to prevent breaches of peace (s. 30), to suppress riots (s. 32), in self-defence (s. 34), to prevent assaults (s. 37), to defend personal property (s. 38), and to defend real property (ss. 40-41). The Canadian courts appear to assume that these sections govern both criminal and civil liability.

5. It should be noted that there are additional rights and obligations in the arrest process which have not been raised in these materials. For example, at common law once a private citizen made an arrest she had to hand over the suspect to the police or a justice as soon as possible. This obligation is now codified in s. 494(3) of the Criminal Code. Although granted somewhat more leeway to investigate the incident, a peace officer was under a similar obligation to bring a suspect before a justice without unreasonable delay. See *John Lewis & Co. v. Tims*, [1952] A.C. 676 (H.L.); and *Dallison v. Caffery*, [1964] 2 All E.R. 610 (C.A.). See also the Criminal Code, s. 503; and *R. v. Koszulap* (1974), 20 C.C.C. (2d) 193 (Ont. C.A.).

This issue has also arisen under s. 9 of the Charter which guarantees everyone protection from arbitrary detention or imprisonment. In *R. v. Charles* (1987), 36 C.C.C. (3d) 286 (Sask. C.A.), the court held that a 36-hour detention before being brought before a justice violated s. 9. However, in *R. v. Storrey* (1990), 53 C.C.C. (3d) 316 (S.C.C.), the court held that an 18-hour delay to arrange a line-up did not violate s. 9.

6. For a discussion of the complex pre-trial provisions of the Code, see ss. 493-515; and Salhany, *Canadian Criminal Procedure*, 6th ed. (1996), 3-19 to 3-21 and 4-3 to 4-16. See also the police powers of fingerprinting and photographing contained in the Identification of Criminals Act, R.S.C. 1985, c. I-1. See also *B. v. Baugh*, [1984] 3 W.W.R. 577 (S.C.C.); and *R. v. Beare* (1988), 45 C.C.C. (3d) 57 (S.C.C.). Parliament enacted legislation in 1995 creating a judicial warrant to authorize the taking

of hair, saliva and blood samples for DNA testing from those suspected of certain serious criminal offences. Criminal Code, ss. 487.05-487.09.

4. The Common Law Right to Search Pursuant to a Lawful Arrest

CLOUTIER v. LANGLOIS

[1990] 1 S.C.R. 158

L'HEUREUX-DUBÉ J.:

. . .

The facts out of which this issue arose are not in dispute and may be summarized as follows. The appellants Langlois and Bédard are constables employed by the police department of the Montréal Urban Community. The respondent Cloutier is a lawyer practising in that city. On November 3, 1983, early in the evening, the respondent made a right turn from the centre lane of St-Denis St. in Montréal. In so doing, the respondent's vehicle passed directly in front of a police vehicle parked at the street corner. The constables decided that the respondent's turn was in breach of a municipal by-law, stopped him and asked for his driver's licence and other documents for identification purposes. As conceded by the respondent in this court, "the tone became somewhat heated" during this exchange.

While Constable Langlois was writing up a notice of violation, Officer Bédard learned by radio contact with police headquarters that a warrant of committal had been issued against the respondent in the municipal court for unpaid traffic fines. The constables informed the respondent and asked him to accompany them to the police station. When they asked the respondent to get into the patrol car, the constables carried out a "frisk" search: the hands of the accused were placed on the hood of the car, his legs spread and the constables patted him down. The respondent was then taken to the police station.

Subsequent to these events the respondent, relying on the provision of the *Criminal Code*, R.S.C. 1970, c. C-34, dealing with summary convictions, filed an information against each of the police officers for common assault, contrary to s. 245(*b*) of the *Criminal Code*.

The primary allegation made by the respondent in his pleading was that the arrest was illegal, since the police officers had no power to arrest him unless they had actual possession of the arrest warrant issued by the municipal court. The respondent also argued incidentally that the police officers were not authorized to search him. He contended that the arrest and the search constituted assaults within the meaning of the *Criminal Code*. However, in the course of events, the respondent's incidental submission became his principal argument.

. . . .

[L'Heureux-Dubé J. accepted the trial judge's and Quebec Court of Appeal's finding that Cloutier's arrest was lawful. She then reviewed the British, American and Canadian authorities on the common law power of search pursuant to a lawful arrest.]

In general, despite certain comments in scholarly discussion, it seems beyond question that the common law as recognized and developed in Canada holds that the police have a power to search a lawfully arrested person and to seize anything in his or her possession or immediate surroundings to guarantee the safety of the police and the accused, prevent the prisoner's escape or provide evidence against him. The common thread in this line of authority is the objective of guaranteeing safety and applying the law effectively. While the existence of the power is accepted, there seems to be some uncertainty as to its scope. While at common law the British courts did not impose reasonable grounds as a prerequisite to the power to search a person lawfully arrested, neither have they gone so far as to recognize a power to search as a simple corollary of arrest. The Canadian courts on the other hand do not seem to have hesitated in adopting this latter approach.

Analysis

In determining the exact scope of a police power derived from the common law, this court often had recourse to considerations of principle, and the weighing of the competing interests involved: *Eccles v. Bourque* (1974), 19 C.C.C. (2d) 129, 50 D.L.R. (3d) 753, [1975] 2 S.C.R. 739; *R. v. Dedman* (1985), 20 C.C.C. (3d) 97, 20 D.L.R. (4th) 321, [1985] 2 S.C.R. 2, and *R. v. Landry* (1986), 25 C.C.C. (3d) 1, 26 D.L.R. (4th) 638, [1986] 1 S.C.R. 145. Competing interests are important factors in determining the limits of a common-law power. When the power in question comes into conflict with individual freedoms, it is first necessary to decide whether the power falls within the general scope of the duty of peace officers. This duty, clearly identified, must historically have been recognized by the courts as tending to promote the effective application of the law. Secondly, the court must determine whether an invasion of individual rights is justified. In this regard, Le Dain J. in *Dedman* defined what he meant by "justifiable use of the power" in question (at p. 122):

> The interference with liberty must be *necessary* for the carrying out of the particular police duty and it must be *reasonable*, having regard to the nature of the liberty interfered with and the importance of the public purpose served by the interference.

(Emphasis added.) It is therefore necessary in this second stage to determine whether an invasion of individual rights is necessary in order for the peace officers to perform their duty, and whether such an invasion is reasonable in light of the public purposes served by effective control of criminal acts on the one hand and on the other respect for the liberty and fundamental dignity of individuals.

Having stated these premises, I now turn to considering the power of search at the time of a lawful arrest.

As we have seen, the power to search a lawfully arrested person has its roots deep in the common law. In fact, at common law the police power of search extended to encompass a search of the surroundings of the arrest location and the seizure of anything they found there. The precedents I have referred to make it unnecessary to consider this aspect at greater length. What must be determined, rather, is the extent to which the competing interests in the context of a lawful arrest justify a search as an incident of the arrest.

In terms of applying the law, the ultimate purpose of criminal proceedings is to convict those found guilty beyond a reasonable doubt. Our system of criminal justice is based on the punishment of conduct that is contrary to the fundamental values of society, as statutorily enshrined in the *Criminal Code* and similar statutes. That is its primary purpose. The system depends for its legitimacy on the safe and effective performance of this function by the police. In the context of an arrest, these requirements entail at least two primary considerations. First, the process of arrest must be capable of ensuring that those arrested will come before the court. An individual who is arrested should not be able to evade the police before he is released in accordance with the rules of criminal procedure, otherwise the administration of justice will be brought into disrepute. In light of this consideration, a search of the accused for weapons or other dangerous articles is necessary as an elementary precaution to preclude the possibility of their use against the police, the nearby public or the accused himself. Incidents of this kind are not unknown. Further, the process of arrest must ensure that evidence found on the accused and in his immediate surroundings is preserved. The effectiveness of the system depends in part on the ability of peace officers to collect evidence that can be used in establishing the guilt of a suspect beyond a reasonable doubt. The legitimacy of the justice system would be but a mere illusion if the person arrested were allowed to destroy evidence in his possession at the time of the arrest. These interests have been recognized since the courts first considered the power to search; in *Dillon v. O'Brien, supra,* at p. 250, Palles C.B. wrote:

> . . . the interest of the State in the person charged being brought to trial in due course necessarily extends, as well to the preservation of material evidence of his guilt or innocence, as to his custody for the purpose of trial. His custody is of no value if the law is powerless to prevent the abstraction or destruction of this evidence, without which a trial would be no more than an empty form.

However, while the common law gives the police the powers necessary for the effective and safe application of the law, it does not allow them to place themselves above the law and use their powers to intimidate citizens. This is where the protection of privacy and of individual freedoms becomes very important.

. . .

Though the parties have not relied on the Charter, and have simply referred to the common-law sources in examining the scope of the power to search, I feel that the courts should "apply and develop the principles of the common law in a manner consistent with the fundamental values enshrined in the Constitution": *RWDSU, Local 580 v. Dolphin Delivery Ltd.* (1986), 33 D.L.R. (4th) 174 at p. 198, [1986] 2 S.C.R. 573, [1987] 1 W.W.R. 577. In this regard this court has held that, consistent with the values contained in the Charter, a search will not be wrongful if it is authorized by law, if the law is itself reasonable and if the search is conducted in a reasonable manner: *R. v. Collins* (1987), 33 C.C.C. (3d) 1 at pp. 14-5, 38 D.L.R. (4th) 508, [1987] 1 S.C.R. 265; and *R. v. Debot, supra,* at p. 4 [p. 200 C.C.C.], *per* Lamer J., and at p. 15 [p. 209 C.C.C.], *per* Wilson J. The concept of freedom as traditionally safeguarded by the courts has been re-examined since the Charter and now generally means the absence of constraint and coercion. As Dickson J. (now C.J.C.) noted in *R. v. Big M Drug Mart Ltd.* (1985), 18 C.C.C. (3d) 385 at pp. 417-8, 18 D.L.R. (4th) 321, [1985] 1 S.C.R. 295:

> Freedom can primarily be characterized by the absence of coercion or constraint. If a person is compelled by the State or the will of another to a course of action or inaction which he would

not otherwise have chosen, he is not acting of his own volition and he cannot be said to be truly free. One of the major purposes of the Charter is to protect, within reason, from compulsion or restraint.

As important and fundamental as these values may be, they are not absolute. As the Law Reform Commission of Canada notes, "Our Criminal Procedure" (1988), Report 32, at p. 14:

> In order to safeguard freedom it is sometimes necessary to limit it, through prohibitions. However, if human dignity, freedom and justice are among the major values which the criminal law enshrines, we must carefully assess the way in which the law is enforced in order to ensure that our law and practices respect and do not undermine these values.

As we have seen, the common law gave the police only such powers as were consistent with the protection of individual rights. The courts have always held that a proper balance between these two fundamental components is vital, as illustrated by the observations of Williams J. in 1853 in *Leigh v. Cole, supra* (at pp. 330-1):

> On one hand, it is clear the police ought to be fully protected in the discharge of an onerous, arduous, and difficult duty — a duty necessary for the comfort and security of the community. On the other hand, it is equally incumbent on every one engaged in the administration of justice, to take care that the powers necessarily entrusted to the police are not made an instrument of oppression of or tyranny towards even the meanest, most depraved, and basest subjects of the realm.

In this regard a "frisk" search is a relatively non-intrusive procedure: outside clothing is patted down to determine whether there is anything on the person of the arrested individual. Pockets may be examined but the clothing is not removed and no physical force is applied. The duration of the search is only a few seconds. Though the search, if conducted, is in addition to the arrest, which generally entails a considerably longer and more sustained loss of freedom and dignity, a brief search does not constitute, in view of the objectives sought, a disproportionate interference with the freedom of persons lawfully arrested. There exists no less intrusive means of attaining these objectives.

A "frisk" search incidental to a lawful arrest reconciles the public's interest in the effective and safe enforcement of the law on the one hand, and on the other its interest in ensuring the freedom and dignity of individuals. The minimal intrusion involved in the search is necessary to ensure that criminal justice is properly administered. I agree with the opinion of the Ontario Court of Appeal as stated in *R. v. Brezack, R. v. Morrison* and *R. v. Miller, supra*, that the existence of reasonable and probable grounds is not a prerequisite to the existence of a police power to search. The exercise of this power is not, however, unlimited. Three propositions can be derived from the authorities and a consideration of the underlying interests.

1. This power does not impose a duty. The police have some discretion in conducting the search. Where they are satisfied that the law can be effectively and safely applied without a search, the police may see fit not to conduct a search. They must be in a position to assess the circumstances of each case so as to determine whether a search meets the underlying objectives.

2. The search must be for a valid objective in pursuit of the ends of criminal justice, such as the discovery of an object that may be a threat to the safety of the

police, the accused or the public, or that may facilitate escape or act as evidence against the accused. The purpose of the search must not be unrelated to the objectives of the proper administration of justice, which would be the case, for example, if the purpose of the search was to intimidate, ridicule or pressure the accused in order to obtain admissions.

3. The search must not be conducted in an abusive fashion and, in particular, the use of physical or psychological constraint should be proportionate to the objectives sought and the other circumstances of the situation.

A search which does not meet these objectives could be characterized as unreasonable and unjustified at common law.

. . .

I accordingly consider that, as incident to the lawful arrest of the respondent, the frisk search was justified and, accordingly, Judge Choquette made no error in dismissing the informations for assault brought against the appellants. This is sufficient to dispose of the appeal.

NOTES AND QUESTIONS

1. Contrary to what *Cloutier* suggests, the common law right to search pursuant to a lawful arrest was very narrowly defined. Although the police had the right to safeguard themselves from potentially violent suspects that they took into custody, the right to search for evidence and weapons does not appear automatic. See, for example, *Dillon v. O'Brien* (1887), 16 Cox. C.C. 245 (Exch.); and *Leigh v. Cole* (1853), 6 Cox. C.C. 329. See also Wade, "Police Search" (1934), 50 L.Q.R. 354; and Leigh, "Recent Developments in the Law of Search and Seizure" (1970), 33 Mod. L. Rev. 268.

2. Based on *Cloutier*, outline the common law power to search pursuant to an arrest. Should *Cloutier* be limited to cases in which the police are taking the suspect into physical custody?

L'Heureux-Dubé J. discusses the common law "considerations of principles", "the ultimate purpose of criminal proceedings", and "fundamental values enshrined in the Constitution" in formulating the common law principles. How does she use these factors and should they be relevant? For a critique of *Cloutier*, see Stuart, "Annotation, *Cloutier v. Langlois*" (1980), 74 C.R. (3d) 318.

3. Section 8 of the Charter guarantees everyone protection from unreasonable search and seizure. As indicated, L'Heureux-Dubé J. states that the common law should be applied in a manner consistent with Charter values. Is an automatic right to search pursuant to lawful arrest consistent with s. 8?

4. The common law power to search did not extend to intimate physical searches. Nevertheless, the Canadian courts permitted such searches in drug cases. See, for example, *Reynen v. Antonenko* (1975), 54 D.L.R. (3d) 124 (Alta. S.C.). Intimate physical searches have generated considerable controversy. See Ontario, *Report of the Royal Commission on the Conduct of Police Forces at Fort Erie on the 11th of May, 1974* (1975); and MacDonald, "Intimate Search in Police Raid Angers Women", *The Ottawa Citizen*, May 8, 1978, at 1.

5. In *R. v. Greffe* (1990), 55 C.C.C. (3d) 161 (S.C.C.), customs officers at an airport received a tip that the accused was carrying heroin. However, no heroin was found when he was strip-searched. The RCMP then arrested the accused for unpaid traffic tickets, and arranged for him to be given a rectal search using a sigmoidoscope. Two bags of heroin were recovered. The Crown admitted that the search violated s. 8, but argued that the evidence should not be excluded under s. 24(2). The majority of the Court held that a rectal search pursuant to an arrest for traffic tickets, without any reasonable grounds that the accused was carrying drugs, was a serious violation of s. 8 that required exclusion of the evidence.

This lukewarm disapproval of unfounded, intimate physical searches is not inconsistent with earlier Charter decisions which have upheld invasive drug searches. See *R. v. Simmons* (1988), 45 C.C.C. (3d) 296 (S.C.C.); *Weatherall v. A.G. Can.*, [1989] 1 F.C. 18 (C.A.), aff'd. (1993), 23 C.R. (4th) 1 (S.C.C.); and *R. v. Ironstand* (1989), 8 W.C.B. (2d) 691 (Man. Prov. Ct.).

Unfortunately, with the advent of the Charter, the courts have tended to ignore the issue of whether the search was specifically authorized by statute or common law. Rather, the courts have focused almost exclusively on whether the search was "reasonable".

6. The common law power to search did not extend to performing surgical or other medical procedures on suspects. The Canadian Committee on Corrections stated at page 62 that, "the right to search the person and clothing of a person under arrest to obtain evidence of the offence does not authorize the withdrawal of blood, the use of stomach pumps or other quasi-surgical measures to obtain evidence." Can., *Report of the Canadian Committee on Corrections* (1968). See also *Re Laporte and R.* (1972), 8 C.C.C. (2d) 343 (Que. Q.B.); and *R. v. Truchanek* (1984), 39 C.R. (3d) 137 (B.C. Co. Ct.).

The Canadian courts have consistently held that the taking of blood samples solely for evidentiary purposes in drinking and driving cases violates s. 8 of the Charter. See, for example, *Pohoretsky v. R.* (1987), 33 C.C.C. (3d) 398 (S.C.C.); and *R. v. Dyment* (1988), 45 C.C.C. (3d) 244 (S.C.C.). However, the courts have upheld giving drug suspects laxatives and drugs to induce vomiting in order to recover drugs. See *R. v. Meikle* (1983), 9 C.C.C. (3d) 91 (Ont. H.C.); and *R. v. Rousseau*, [1985] R.L. 108 (Que. Cour Des Sessions De La Paix). Can these drug cases be justified under the common law, the Charter or public policy considerations?

7. In the absence of specific statutory authority, there is generally no right to search a suspect until after she has been lawfully arrested. However, the Canadian courts have created exceptions to this and other principles for officers engaged in drug enforcement. See *R. v. Brezack* (1949), 96 C.C.C. 97 (Ont. C.A.) and *Scott v. R.* (1975), 61 D.L.R. (3d) 130 (Fed. C.A.), in which the courts upheld the use of "throat holds". Typically, the suspect is grabbed by the throat without any warning to prevent her from swallowing any drugs that she may be carrying in her mouth. Is it appropriate for the courts to limit the traditional rights and freedoms of drug suspects? How would you resolve the potential conflict between an individual's right to use reasonable force in self-defence against unidentified assailants and the officer's right to use extraordinary search procedures without warning? See also *R. v. Debot* (1986), 30 C.C.C. (3d) 207 (Ont. C.A.), aff'd. (1989), 52 C.C.C. (3d) 193 (S.C.C.).

There have been several post-Charter cases on the use of throat-holds, but the courts have largely ignored the violence and dangers inherent in their use. See *R. v. Cohen* (1983), 33 C.R. (3d) 151 (B.C. C.A.); and *R. v. Collins* (1987), 33 C.C.C. (4th) 1 (S.C.C.). In *Collins*, the Supreme Court held that the use of a throat-hold would not constitute an unreasonable search if the officer reasonably believed the suspect was a "drug handler". Does this test adequately balance the physical integrity of drug suspects and the interests of the state? See the Law Reform Commission of Canada, *Police Powers — Search and Seizure in Criminal Law Enforcement* (1983), 227-38.

8. Following a lawful arrest, an officer had a common law right to search not only the suspect, but also her personal effects and the immediate scene, provided the arrest took place in public or in the suspect's premises. It is doubtful whether this search power provides authority for a wholesale search of the suspect's house or a third party's home simply because the suspect was apprehended there. See *R. v. Rao* (1984), 12 C.C.C. (3d) 97 (Ont. C.A.), leave to appeal ref'd. [1984] 2 S.C.R. ix; *R. v. Wong* (1987), 34 C.C.C. (3d) 51 (Ont. C.A.), aff'd. (1990), 1 C.R. (4th) 1 (S.C.C.); and Hutchinson *et al., Search and Seizure Law in Canada* (1993), 3-20 to 3-29. Similar doubts have been raised about an officer's right to take a suspect home to search her residence. See *Dillon v. O'Brien* (1887), 16 Cox C.C. 245 (Exch.); *McLorie v. Oxford*, [1982] 3 All E.R. 480 (Q.B.); and Wade, "Police Search" (1934), 50 L.Q.R. 354. But see *Dallison v. Caffery*, [1964] 2 All E.R. 610 (C.A.).

9. Various federal and provincial statutes contain broad powers to search suspects which may be invoked independently of the common law power. See, for example, the Criminal Code, ss. 101-103 (search and seizure of weapons); the Narcotic Control Act, R.S.C. 1985, c. N-1, ss. 10-14 (search and seizure of illicit drugs); and the provincial liquor, parks, highway traffic, hunting, and fishing statutes. However, the post-Charter cases have limited these powers. See *R. v. Mellenthin*, [1993] 1 W.W.R. 193 (S.C.C.).

5. A Peace Officer's Common Law Right of Forced Entry

ECCLES v. BOURQUE

[1975] 2 S.C.R. 739, 50 D.L.R. (3d) 753 (S.C.C.)

. . .

MARTLAND J.: — I do not wish to express any view with respect to the application of s. 25(1) of the *Criminal Code* to the circumstances of this case. Subject to this, I agree with the reasons of my brother Dickson and I would dispose of this appeal in the manner which he proposes.

JUDSON J., concurs with DICKSON J.

RITCHIE J., concurs with MARTLAND J.

SPENCE J., concurs with DICKSON J.

PIGEON J., concurs with MARTLAND J.

DICKSON J.: — The claim of the appellant, Mr. Eccles, is against the respondents, three constables on the Vancouver Police Force, for damages for trespass alleged to have been committed when the police officers entered the apartment occupied by Mr. Eccles in the City of Vancouver at about 4:00 p.m. on August 12, 1971. The constables were in plain clothes but were armed. The purpose of the entry was to apprehend one Edmund Cheese, also known as Billy Deans, for whom there were three outstanding Montreal warrants. Cheese was not found in the apartment. The trial Judge, Wootton J., concluded he had not been there or had successfully made his escape, by climbing to the roof of the building from one of the two balconies adjoining the apartment, at the moment when or immediately after the police officers entered. Mr. Eccles was successful at trial. Mr. Justice Wootton awarded him $300 damages and costs. The Court of Appeal for British Columbia by a majority (Robertson and Taggart, JJ.A., with Nemetz, J.A., dissenting) reversed. Leave to appeal to this Court was granted by the Court of Appeal for British Columbia.

There are two issues: (1) Were the respondents authorized by s. 25 of the *Criminal Code* forcibly to enter and search the appellant's apartment pursuant to their right of arrest without warrant under s. 450 [rep. & sub. R.S.C. 1970, c. 2 (2nd Supp.), s. 5] (then s. 449) of the *Code*? (2) If not, were their actions justified on common law principles? On the first issue, s. 450(1)(a) of the *Code* provides that any one may arrest without warrant a person who, on reasonable and probable grounds, he believes has committed a criminal offence. There were reasonable and probable grounds for believing that Cheese had committed a criminal offence and had the respondents found him in the apartment or elsewhere there is no doubt they would have been authorized by s. 450(1)(a) to arrest him. Section 25(1) of the *Code* then provides that:

> 25(1) Every one who is required or authorized by law to do anything in the administration or enforcement of the law
>> (a) as a private person,
>> (b) as a peace officer or public officer,
>> (c) in aid of a peace officer or public officer, or
>> (d) by virtue of his office,
>
> is, if he acts on reasonable and probable grounds, justified in doing what he is required or authorized to do and in using as much force as is necessary for that purpose.

It is the submission of counsel for the respondents that a person who is by s. 450 authorized to make an arrest is, by s. 25, authorized by law to commit a trespass with or without force in the accomplishment of that arrest, provided he acts on reasonable and probable grounds. I cannot agree with this submission. Section 25 does not have such amplitude. The section merely affords justification to a person for doing what he is required or authorized by law to do in the administration or enforcement of the law, if he acts on reasonable and probable grounds, and for using necessary force for that purpose. The question which must be answered in this case, then, is whether the respondents were required or authorized by law to commit a trespass; and not, as their counsel contends, whether they were required or authorized to make an arrest. If they were authorized by law to commit a trespass, the authority for it must be found in the common law for there is nothing in the *Criminal Code*. The first issue, therefore, depends upon the second issue, *videlicet*, can the trespass be justified on common law principles? For these principles, we go back to vintage common law, to 1604, and *Semayne's Case*, 5 Co. Rep. 91a, 77 E.R. 194, in which the principle, so firmly entrenched in our jurisprudence, that every man's house is his castle, was expressed in these words [at p. 91b]: "That the house of every one is to him as his castle and fortress, as well for his defence against injury and violence, as for his repose . . .". That, then, is the basic principle, as important today as in Biblical times (Deuteronomy 24:10) or in the 17th century. But there are occasions when the interest of a private individual in the security of his house must yield to the public interest, when the public at large has an interest in the process to be executed. The criminal is not immune from arrest in his own home nor in the home of one of his friends. So it is that in *Semayne's Case* a limitation was put on the "castle" concept and the Court resolved that:

> In all cases when the King is party, the Sheriff (if the doors be not open) may break the party's house, either to arrest him, or to do other execution of the K.'s process, if otherwise he cannot enter. But before he breaks in, he ought to signify the cause of his coming, and to make request to open doors . . .

See also a century later, to the same effect, Hale, *Pleas of the Crown* (1736), 582; Foster, Crown Law (1762), 320. Thus it will be seen that the broad basic principle of sanctity of the home is subject to the exception that upon proper demand the officials of the King may break down doors to arrest. The incidental point was made in *Semayne's Case* that [at p. 93a] "the house of any one is not a castle or privilege but for himself, and shall not extend to protect any person who flies to his house . . ."

The *Criminal Code* empowers a Justice, on proper grounds being shown, to issue a warrant authorizing a search for things but there is no power to issue a warrant to search for persons. Counsel for Mr. Eccles advanced the argument that if a fugitive was in the home of a friend a police officer could not enter to arrest him unless the homeowner gave consent. I cannot agree that this properly expresses the position in law. If that be right, a fugitive could obtain permanent sanctuary merely by residing with a friend. I know of no place that gives a criminal fugitive sanctuary from arrest.

In some of the American jurisdictions a distinction is drawn between entering to arrest a fugitive in his own home and entering the home of another person to arrest the fugitive. I am unable to find any Anglo-Canadian authority supporting a distinction of this nature and in principle it seems to me to be wrong. The fact that the premises to be entered are those of a third person may have a bearing in the determination of reasonable and probable cause. There may be less likelihood of a fugitive being in the home of another than in his own home, but otherwise I can see no good reason for distinguishing between the two types of case.

I would wish to make it clear, however, that there is no question of an unrestricted right to enter in search of a fugitive. Entry can be made against the will of the householder only if (a) there are reasonable and probable grounds for the belief that the person sought is within the premises and (b) proper announcement is made prior to entry.

(a) REASONABLE AND PROBABLE GROUNDS

In the case of civil process the rule is that if a Sheriff's officer enters the house of A to execute process against the goods of B or to arrest B he enters at his peril and if the goods or B, as the case may be, are not present, he is guilty of trespass. It is said the entry can be justified only by the event: *Johnson v. Leigh* (1815), 6 Taunt. 246, 128 E.R. 1029; *Morrish v. Murrey* (1844), 13 M. & W. 52, 153 E.R. 22; *Southam v. Smout*, [1964] 1 Q.B. 308. But in the execution of criminal process the test is whether there are reasonable and probable grounds for acting. If so, the entry does not become unlawful if the fugitive is not found on the premises. The entry of the police is legal or illegal from the moment of entry and does not change character from the result. The only case which would seem to run counter to this principle is *Mathews v. Dwan*, [1949] N.Z.L.R. 1037, in which Gresson, J., concluded that the justification for entry and arrest is the presence on the premises of the individual sought and there is no authority to the police forcibly to enter premises to effect the arrest of a named person upon a "mere suspicion, however well based" that the person is upon the premises. The learned Judge referred to *Davis v. Lisle*, [1936] 2 K.B. 434, and *Thomas v. Sawkins*, [1935] 2 K.B. 249. In the *Davis* case police officers had entered a garage to make inquiries and were told by the proprietor to "get out" and it was held they thereafter were trespassers. The case did not involve entry to make an arrest. The *Thomas* case concerned the right of a police officer to remain on premises in which a public meeting was being held, contrary to the wishes of the convenors, to prevent a possible breach of peace. I find little support in these cases for the proposition that entry against the will of the owner will always be a trespass unless the person sought is apprehended on the premises. In my opinion that is not the principle which emerges from the earlier cases. If the police officer has reasonable and probable cause to believe that the person named in the warrant for arrest is in the home of a stranger he has the right, after proper demand, to enter the home forcibly, to search and to arrest. In the present case there can be no doubt the police officers believed and, in my view, had reasonable and probable grounds for believing that Cheese, or Deans as he was known to Mr. Eccles, was in the Eccles apartment. Constable Simmonds had been told by one of his superiors that Eccles was the closest known associate of Cheese. That this information was hearsay does not exclude it from establishing a probable cause. Additionally, both Eccles and Cheese had informed Constable Simmonds prior to the entry that Cheese had been staying in the Eccles apartment. On August 12, 1971, the day of the alleged trespass, Cheese had been in the apartment, he had been seen entering and leaving the building and just prior to the impugned entry had been seen to enter the building. Constable Bourque had seen police department bulletins pertaining to both Eccles and to Cheese.

(b) ANNOUNCEMENT

Except in exigent circumstances, the police officers must make an announcement prior to entry. There are compelling considerations for this. An unexpected intrusion of a man's property can give rise to violent incidents. It is in the interests of the personal safety of the householder and the police as well as respect for the privacy of the individual that the law requires, prior to entrance for search or arrest, that a police officer identify himself and request admittance. No precise form of words is necessary. In *Semayne's Case* it was said he should "signify the cause of his coming, and to make request to open doors." In *Re Curtis* (1756), Fost. 135, 168 E.R. 67, nine of the Judges were of opinion that it was sufficient that the householder have notice that the officer came not as a mere trespasser but claiming to act under a proper authority, the other two Judges being of opinion that the officers ought to have declared in an explicit manner what sort of warrant they had. In *Burdett v. Abbott* (1811), 14 East. 1, 104 E.R. 501, Bayley J., was content that the right to break the outer door should be preceded simply by a request for admission and a denial. The traditional demand was "Open in the name of the King". In the ordinary case police officers, before forcing entry, should give (i) notice of presence by knocking or ringing the doorbell, (ii) notice of authority, by identifying themselves as law enforcement officers and (iii) notice of purpose, by stating a lawful reason for entry. Minimally they should request admission and have admission denied although it is recognized there will be occasions on which, for example, to save someone within the premises from death or injury or to prevent destruction of evidence or if in hot pursuit notice may not be required. Was proper notice given in this case? The police officers gave notice of presence by knocking on the door of the apartment. After a pause it was opened and an officer gave notice of identity by production of his badge and the words "Vancouver City Police". On August 10th, two days before the alleged trespass, Mr. Eccles had been stopped and searched by two of the respondents. One of the respondents had stopped him on two earlier occasions, so the identity of two of the three persons who appeared at the door of the apartment on August 12th could hardly have been a matter of which Mr. Eccles was ignorant. Whether notice of purpose was given is more difficult. Mr. Eccles testified that when the door was opened one man stood there while the other two ran into different rooms without identifying themselves or their purpose. In his evidence-in-chief, Constable Simmonds, after referring to the opening of the door, said:

> I don't recall if Mr. Eccles answered, I don't recall if he said: "What do you want", or something like that, he probably did and Constable Bourque said: "We're looking for a wanted man and we want to search the premises", so forth —

Constable Wise testified, "Constable Bourque told Mr. Eccles that we were looking for a man wanted on a warrant." Constable Bourque said that when the door opened he observed Mr. Eccles standing in the doorway and he, Bourque, entered the apartment. In reply to the question by Mr. Eccles, "What do you want?" Constable Bourque replied, according to his evidence: "I told him that I had reason to believe a man wanted by our department had just entered this apartment." In my view, the police officers, on the facts of this case, discharged the duty which rested upon them to give notice before forcing entry.

I would, accordingly, dismiss the appeal with costs.

[Laskin C.J.C. and Judson and Spence JJ. concurred with Dickson J. Ritchie, Pigeon, Beetz and De Grandpré JJ. concurred with Martland J.]

NOTES AND QUESTIONS

1. According to Dickson J., what is the source of an officer's authority and privilege to make a forced entry without a search warrant to arrest a wanted person? What is the effect of *Eccles* on the issue of whether s. 25 can be used as an authorizing provision?

2. Did Dickson J. limit this power of forced entry to cases involving suspects named in an outstanding warrant? Is it limited to suspects wanted for indictable, rather than summary conviction offences? What is the practical significance of these restrictions?

3. What is required in making a proper announcement? Do you agree with Dickson J.'s application of these requirements to the facts in *Eccles*? See Foster and Magnet, "The Law of Forcible Entry" (1977), 15 Alta. L. Rev. 271.

4. The general principles in *Eccles* were affirmed by the Supreme Court of Canada in *R. v. Landry* (1986), 25 C.C.C. (3d) 1. While the court limited the entry power to persons wanted for indictable offences, it held that the police could also enter if they reasonably believed an indictable offence was about to be committed. But see LaForest J.'s dissent in *Landry*.

Although not well defined, there was a common law right of forced entry to prevent the commission of murder and other felonies, but it was distinct from the right of entry to search for wanted suspects. Aside from the nature of the impending harm, this right appears similar to that granted in cases of public necessity. See *Handcock v. Baker* (1800), 126 E.R. 1270 (C.P.); and *R. v. Custer* (1984), 32 Sask. R. 287 (C.A.). See also *Re Children's Aid Society of Western Man. and Daniels* (1981), 128 D.L.R. (3d) 751 (Man. C.A.); and *Rigby v. Chief Constable of Northamptonshire*, [1985] 2 All E.R. 985 (Q.B.).

5. In *R. v. Delong* (1989), 31 O.A.C. 339, the Court of Appeal held that the requirements for entry established in *Landry* apply equally to cases in which the door is open.

6. Both the House of Lords and the United States Supreme Court have defined this common right of entry far more narrowly than the Canadian Supreme Court. See *Payton v. New York; Riddick v. New York* (1980), 100 S. Ct. 1371; *Steagald v. U.S.* (1981), 101 S. Ct. 1642; *Morris v. Beardmore*, [1980] 2 All E.R. 753 (H.L.); and *Finnigan v. Sandiford*, [1981] 2 All E.R. 267 (H.L.). See also Watson, "Fourth Amendment — Balancing the Interests in Third Party Home Arrests" (1981), 72 J. Crim. Law and Criminology 1263; Leigh, *Police Powers in England and Wales*, 2nd ed. (1985), 203-11; and La Fave, *Search and Seizure*, 3d ed. (1996), v. 3 at 223-95 and 335-410.

7. The common law authorized the police to enter a private dwelling in hot pursuit of a person who had committed an arrestable offence. The crime, pursuit and arrest had to be continuous, forming a single transaction. See *Swales v. Cox*, [1981] 1 All E.R. 1115 (Q.B.). In *R. v. Macooh* (1993), 22 C.R. (4th) 70, the Supreme Court of Canada extended this doctrine to provincial offences. What are the justifications for allowing forced entry in hot pursuit situations? Do you agree with the Supreme Court that there is no logical reason to distinguish between indictable and provincial offences in analyzing hot pursuit?

8. The common law did not authorize entry without a warrant to seize evidence of an offence or to carry out general investigations. This common law principle has recently been affirmed in several cases. See *Morris v. Beardmore, supra; Finnigan v. Sandiford, supra; R. v. Colet* (1981), 119 D.L.R. (3d) 521 (S.C.C.); *and R. v. Custer, supra.*

9. The police may also be granted powers of forced entry without a warrant by statute. See, for example, the Narcotic Control Act, R.S.C. 1985, c. N-1, s. 10.

REVIEW PROBLEMS

1. Fifteen members of a local motorcycle gang pulled into John's Service Station and Restaurant. The owner, aware of the gang's reputation for violent crime, called the police. The gang went to the service centre where one of the cyclists politely asked to borrow a wrench, which the attendant retrieved from the back of the station. Upon her return, the attendant noticed that two small cans of lubricating oil were missing from the display, but she did not see who took them. Nevertheless, she assumed that one of the cyclists had stolen the oil in her brief absence.

When six police officers and their trained dog arrived, the attendant explained that one of the cyclists had stolen some oil, but she had no idea which one it was. Officer Jones approached the gang leader, Steve, and asked him to open his pack. Steve ignored Jones until the dog, on Jones' command, bared its teeth and backed him into a corner. In the interim, Jones was informed that no oil had been found in the possession of the other cyclists. He ordered Steve to open his pack. Steve, who was unaware of the attendant's allegation, refused and walked to his motorcycle.

Jones signalled the dog to subdue Steve. It jumped on Steve's back, knocking him to the ground. Just before the dog struck, Jones shouted, "You are under arrest for theft!" Steve was handcuffed and led away to a police car. Although the search of his pack revealed that it was empty, Steve was told that he was under arrest for obstructing a peace officer in the execution of his duty.

The charge against Steve was dropped and he now wishes to sue Jones and the attendant in tort.

2. Mrs. Smith spotted a person prowling around her neighbour's backyard at 3:00 a.m. and called the police. Upon their arrival, the plainclothes officers observed a person forcing open a back window. Believing that they had finally trapped the burglar, who had been victimizing the neighbourhood, the officers quietly approached the house. In fact, the supposed prowler was the homeowner's son, Tom, who had just returned from a night at the local tavern where he had lost his house keys. Awakened by his son's entry, Tom's father came downstairs to investigate the noise. At that point, the two officers kicked in the door. Instinctively, Tom's father struck out at the two burly figures as they crashed into his hall, and knocked both to the ground. The struggle ended as soon as the officers identified themselves. You have been retained by Tom's father to advise him of the potential tort consequences of this unfortunate incident.

3. Ralph, a former professional football player, ran a small cigar store. Late one night he heard someone yell "Help! Thief! Help!" As he stepped outside, he saw Gaston approaching him on the run carrying an expensive camera. In hot pursuit, about 30 metres behind, was George. Both were strangers to Ralph, and were unexceptional in size or manner of dress. Gaston turned into a dead-end alley and Ralph, still well ahead of George, joined in the chase. Just as Gaston slowed down at the end of the alley, Ralph brought him to the ground with a tackle. Gaston attempted to struggle free, but Ralph hauled him to his feet with ease and threw him into a fence with such force that it knocked down an overhanging neon sign. Breathless and badly shaken, Gaston was finally able to scream at Ralph, "I'm not the thief, he is getting away!" When Ralph turned around he saw that George had disappeared, and realized his mistake. Ralph has sought your legal advice regarding his potential tort liability.

INTRODUCTION TO THE
LAW OF NEGLIGENCE

1. The Concept of Negligence
2. The Historical Development of Negligence
3. The Elements of a Negligence Action

1. The Concept of Negligence

The term "negligence" is used in two distinct ways. In its broadest sense, negligence refers to the branch of tort law that is concerned with liability for inadvertent conduct. Initially, the boundaries of negligence may be more difficult to grasp than those of the intentional torts. The intentional torts consist of a limited number of distinct actions, each of which is based on a specific kind of conduct. In contrast, negligence law encompasses a multitude of situations in which the law imposes a legal duty on an individual to conform to an objective standard of reasonable care. In its narrower meaning, negligence refers to conduct which falls below this standard of care. Thus, when the courts state that the defendant acted negligently, they are referring to this single aspect of a negligence suit. Just as intent is a necessary element of intentional torts, negligence, in the sense of carelessness, is an essential element of a negligence action.

2. The Historical Development of Negligence

The modern law of negligence, like that of intentional torts, has its origins in the writ system. Trespass *vi et armis*, the first writ of a tortious nature, provided strict liability for direct, forceful interferences with person or property. If the plaintiff established that he was directly injured, the defendant would be held liable unless he could prove that the injury occurred utterly without fault on his part. It was not until well into the last century that a defendant could escape liability by disproving intent and negligence. The defendant's direct and forceful intrusion was considered a sufficient wrong to warrant redress, even in the absence of actual loss.

The writ of trespass on the case developed after trespass *vi et armis*, providing a remedy for losses that were not directly and forcefully inflicted. Such incidents were less likely to cause violent confrontations. Consequently, the action for trespass on the case was never as strict as that for trespass *vi et armis*. The plaintiff was required to prove that he had suffered actual loss and that the defendant's conduct was wrongful, in that it was either intentional or negligent. A variety of actions on the case were eventually established, including defamation, nuisance, deceit, and negligence.

The first negligence actions involved those in public callings, such as apothecaries, surgeons, common carriers, and innkeepers, who were alleged to have breached the standards of customary practice. Outside of these types of relationships, an individual was not generally held accountable simply because he indirectly injured another through carelessness.

While the scope of negligence liability expanded, it remained a relatively insignificant action in England until the growth of cities and industries greatly increased the number and severity of inadvertently caused injuries. These claims bore little resemblance to the existing categories of negligence recognized in the action on the case. If the principles characteristic of trespass *vi et armis* had been applied, factory owners, railroad companies and cartage firms would have been held liable for virtually every injury that was directly and causally related to their activities.

Although the factors shaping these developments are subject to historical debate, it is clear that the courts in the Victorian era began to adopt the principle of "no liability without fault" as a middle ground between imposing strict liability and providing no redress at all.

Despite widespread acceptance of the principle of no liability without fault in negligence, no common rationale was found to explain when the courts would impose a legal duty on the defendant to take care. As Baker noted in *An Introduction to English Legal History*, 3rd ed. (1990), 468-69:

> . . . the problem for the substantive law was to settle the cases in which the law imposed a duty to take care in the absence of an undertaking or custom. We have seen that the law sometimes imposed duties independently of any prior relationship between the parties. Yet duties of care cannot be imposed on everyone in every situation. At the beginning of the eighteenth century no one, it seems, could see any pattern emerging; the kinds of cases were "almost infinite, daily increasing, and continually receiving new forms". By the middle of the century, however, a general answer had been formulated in an influential treatise, printed in 1768 from a manuscript supposedly written by Lord Bathurst (1714-94) in the 1750s, which became a standard practitioners' manual in its subsequent editions by Buller and Onslow. The author suggested for the first time a principle which is now familiar to every English law student: "Every man ought to take reasonable care that he does not injure his neighbhour; therefore, wherever a man receives hurt through the default of another, though the same were not wilful, yet if it be occasioned by negligence or folly the law gives him an action to recover damages for the injury so sustained . . . However, it is proper in such cases to prove that the injury was such as would probably follow from the act done."

The attempts made during the late 19th century to refine this proposition were largely unsuccessful. The concept of negligence as an independent cause of action, rather than merely a means of committing recognized torts, was still in its infancy. Indeed, this issue remained a subject of debate among English academics until the mid-1920s. Even those who accepted negligence as a distinct branch of tort law usually did little more than classify the growing volume of negligence cases. It was not until 1932 that the House of Lords articulated a generally accepted theory of negligence. In what is now regarded as a classic speech, Lord Atkin stated in *M'Alister (or Donoghue) v. Stevenson*, [1932] A.C. 562 at 580 (H.L.):

> At present I content myself with pointing out that in English law there must be, and is, some general conception of relations giving rise to a duty of care, of which the particular cases found in the books are but instances. The liability for negligence, whether you style it such or

treat it as in other systems as a species of "culpa," is no doubt based upon a general public sentiment of moral wrongdoing for which the offender must pay. But acts or omissions which any moral code would censure cannot in a practical world be treated so as to give a right to every person injured by them to demand relief. In this way rules of law arise which limit the range of complainants and the extent of their remedy. The rule that you are to love your neighbour becomes in law, you must not injure your neighbour; and the lawyer's question, Who is my neighbour? receives a restricted reply. You must take reasonable care to avoid acts or omissions which you can reasonably foresee would be likely to injure your neighbour. Who, then, in law is my neighbour? The answer seems to be persons who are so closely and directly affected by my act that I ought reasonably to have them in contemplation as being so affected when I am directing my mind to the acts or omissions which are called in question.

The case was of fundamental importance because it established a basic framework that could be used for determining when to recognize a duty of care. Despite difficulties in interpretation, Lord Atkin's test of duty became widely accepted as governing liability for negligent acts causing physical injury to the plaintiff or his property. There was far greater reluctance, however, to apply the test to those well-established categories of negligence that had been subject to restrictive liability rules. These special categories of negligence included cases involving a defendant's failure to act for the plaintiff's benefit, negligent statements, nervous shock, pure economic loss, and occupiers' liability. During the past 60 years, the courts have gradually rejected much of this pre-1932 case law in favour of broader principles more akin to those in *Donoghue*, but this process has occurred in a piecemeal fashion on a category-by-category basis.

NOTES AND QUESTIONS

1. Winfield identified four areas of the early common law from which the modern negligence action evolved: liability in nuisance; liability based on the control of dangerous things; duties voluntarily undertaken in assumpsit; and the duty cast upon bailees and persons pursuing a common calling. See "The Myth of Absolute Liability" (1926), 42 L.Q.R. 37 and 184. See also Wigmore, "Responsibility for Tortious Acts: Its History" (1894), 7 Harv. L. Rev. 315 and 383; Ames, "Law and Morals" (1908), 22 Harv. L. Rev. 97; and Arterburn, "The Origin and First Test of Public Callings" (1926-27), 75 U. of Pa. L. Rev. 411.

2. There has been considerable debate over the impact of the Industrial Revolution and the concept of fault on the emergence of negligence as an independent tort action. The orthodox view is perhaps best reflected by Fifoot in *History and Sources of the Common Law* (1949), 164:

The prime factor in the ultimate transformation of negligence from a principle of liability in Case to an independent tort was the luxuriant crop of "running down" actions reaped from the commercial prosperity of the late eighteenth and early nineteenth century. Their significance lay rather in their number than in their nature. So long as they could be indulged as the occasional accidents of litigation, they called for no special attention; but when they became a daily occurrence, the judges were forced to recognize a formidable phenomenon which could not be confined, without too gross an artificiality, within the conventional categories.

White contends that the evolution of negligence in the United States was more complex than the orthodox view suggests. He maintains that the development of negligence was fostered by three 19th century trends: the impulse towards conceptualization among American intellectuals; the collapse of common law writ pleading; and a gradual change in tort cases from those involving parties in "closely defined relations to those involving strangers". Only the last factor is directly related to industrialization and urbanization. See White, *Tort Law In America: An Intellectual History* (1980). See also Melamed and Westin, "Anti-Intellectual History" (1981), 90 Yale L.J. 1497.

3. Legal historians continue to debate the question of the social and economic impact of the rise of the negligence tort. In his influential book, *The Transformation of American Law, 1780-1860* (1970), Horwitz argued that the judicial development and application of fault-based negligence principles

delivered crucial subsidies to American industry, especially in the area of work-related accidents. This view has been substantially revised by more recent scholarship emphasizing the diversity — doctrinal, regional, and temporal — of negligence law and its consequences for American history. See generally, Schwartz, "Tort Law and the Economy in Nineteenth Century America: A Reinterpretation" (1981), 90 Yale L.J. 1717; Kaczorowski, "The Common Law Background of Nineteenth Century Tort Law" (1990), 51 Ohio State L.J. 1127; and Bergstrom, *Courting Danger* (1994).

For a recent study of the relationship between negligence law and the rise of industry in England, see Kostal, *Law and English Railway Capitalism 1825-1875* (1995), 254-321.

4. As late as 1926, Salmond argued that negligence was not an independent branch of tort law. Salmond, *Law of Torts*, 6th ed. (1924). Contrast his position with that of Winfield, "The History of Negligence in the Law of Torts" (1926), 46 L.Q.R. 184.

5. Relatively little has been published on the historical development of tort law in Canada. But see Risk, "The Last Golden Age: Property and the Allocation of Losses in Ontario in the Nineteenth Century" (1977), 27 U. of T. L.J. 199; and Kostal, "Legal Justice, Social Justice: The Social History of Work-Related Accident Law in Ontario, 1880-86" (1988), 6 Law and Hist. Rev. 1.

6. It should be noted that several academics had formulated theories of negligence which were very similar to that eventually articulated by Lord Atkin. See, for example, Pollock, *The Law of Torts*, 13th ed. (1929), 451.

3. The Elements of a Negligence Action

(a) INTRODUCTION

Unlike the nominate intentional torts, each negligence case may be analyzed within a single conceptual framework, regardless of the activity in question or the interest invaded. This is not to say that the principles governing the different types of negligence cases are exactly the same. For example, the liability rules applicable to nervous shock are far more restrictive than those for personal injury. Yet both kinds of claims are subject to the same framework of analysis. Unfortunately, there is no consensus among judges, academics and practitioners on the terminology that should be used to describe the component elements of this common framework. Nevertheless, it is important for students to approach negligence law in an orderly fashion, and for this purpose we have adopted the following framework consisting of six distinct elements. The plaintiff usually has the burden of proving the first five elements, and the defendant has the burden of proving the sixth.

(i) *Duty of Care*

The court must decide, as a matter of law, whether the defendant is under any legal obligation to exercise care for the plaintiff's interests in the type of case under consideration and, if necessary, determine the nature of the obligation. As illustrated by the historical development of negligence, the duty of care issue has been the major battleground of legal policy, for it defines the scope of liability.

(ii) *The Standard of Care and Its Breach*

Having defined the duty, the court must establish the standard of care that is required of the defendant. Ordinarily, the defendant is expected to conform to the standard of care that would have been exercised by a reasonable person. The court will then assess the defendant's conduct and decide if he has breached the requisite standard. As previously indicated, this issue is often phrased in terms of whether the defendant has been negligent.

(iii) *Causation*

Even if the defendant is under a duty of care and breaches the required standard, he will not be held liable unless his negligent conduct is a cause of the plaintiff's loss. The courts and legal authors often refer to this element of a negligence suit as the cause-in-fact issue.

(iv) *Remoteness of Damages*

Once it has been established that the defendant negligently caused the plaintiff's loss, the court must then decide if the causal relationship between the defendant's negligent act and the plaintiff's loss is too tenuous or remote to warrant recovery. In intentional torts, a defendant is liable for all the consequences of his tortious acts. However, in negligence, liability is usually limited to injuries or losses that are a foreseeable result of the defendant's negligent act.

(v) *Actual Loss*

The plaintiff must establish that he has suffered legally recognized damages as an element of his cause of action. Unlike most intentional torts, negligence is not actionable *per se*.

(vi) *Prejudicial Conduct*

Finally, the court must consider whether the plaintiff's own conduct should be taken into account to reduce or eliminate his claim. The four defences are contributory negligence, voluntary assumption of risk, *ex turpi causa non oritur actio*, and inevitable accident.

NOTES AND QUESTIONS

1. The English authors divide negligence into three main issues: duty, breach, and damages. See, for example, Heuston and Buckley, *Salmond and Heuston on the Law of Torts*, 20th ed. (1992), 201-4; and Rogers, *Winfield and Jolowicz on Torts*, 14th ed. (1994), 78. This framework may prove difficult for students because it tends to fuse, rather than isolate, the issues that must be resolved in a negligence case.

2. For alternative formulations of the elements of negligence see The American Law Institute, *Restatement of the Law, Second, Torts* (1965), para. 281; Fleming, *The Law of Torts*, 8th ed. (1992), 103-4; and Linden, *Canadian Tort Law*, 5th ed. (1993), 92. See also Gibson, "A New Alphabet of Negligence", in Linden (ed.), *Studies in Canadian Tort Law* (1968), 189; and Smith, *Liability in Negligence* (1984). The major differences arise primarily in the authors' approaches to the elements of duty and remoteness.

3. Our analysis begins with the duty of care issue, although many judges and authors start with the standard of care. See, for example, Linden, *Canadian Tort Law*, 5th ed. (1993), 107. Consequently, you may wish to read the introductory materials on the standard of care in chapter 13 before beginning chapter 10.

(b) NEGLIGENCE: A CASE ILLUSTRATION

The following case is typical of many negligence decisions, particularly at the trial level. The facts dominate the court's attention, while legal principles are only briefly discussed. Some issues may be analyzed at length, while others are not mentioned. In many cases, judges appear to decide whether the plaintiff has a meritorius claim and then set about the task of legally justifying their initial conclusion. This pragmatic, result-oriented approach makes it difficult to identify the legal basis of the decision.

DUNSMORE v. DESHIELD

(1977), 80 D.L.R. (3d) 386 (Sask. Q.B.)

MACPHERSON J.: — The plaintiff was playing touch football when he collided with another player and one lens of his glasses broke and injured his right eye. The defendant Deshield is the optometrist who supplied the glasses, the defendant Imperial Optical (Imperial) manufactured the lenses.

The plaintiff ordered from Deshield a type of lens known as Hardex which is specially treated by Imperial in a hot and cold process to make it more impact-resistant than ordinary glass lenses. The glasses were supplied as Hardex by Imperial to Deshield and in turn to the plaintiff about February 26, 1973, who wore them off and on until the accident on September 7, 1974.

I am satisfied on the balance of probabilities that the lenses were not Hardex.

The plaintiff sues both defendants for damages alleging that if they were Hardex they would not have broken and he would not have been injured. The action against Deshield is in breach of contract or, alternatively, negligence. Against Imperial he claims in negligence.

The plaintiff is now 34 (then 31). He is a highly educated man who occupies a responsible position in the civil service.

Both defendants plead contributory negligence. The burden of establishing this plea is upon them. They must satisfy me that the plaintiff caused or contributed to his loss and injury by playing touch football with his glasses on. If they were to succeed on this point, the defendants had to show that it was, like football, a game of violence and this they failed to do. The plaintiff said it was a non-contact game but on this occasion he collided with another player. It is a running game in which, he admitted, there has been the odd broken wrist or sprained ankle. There was no evidence that the game involved bodily contact except on this occasion.

I cannot take judicial notice of the rules of the game or how it was played on this occasion. I was not told how many were playing.

I cannot find contributory negligence even on the balance of probabilities.

Imperial was negligent in failing to supply Hardex lenses. Its system of supply and manufacture is not flawless as Mr. Most, its manufacturing optician for 35 years, admitted. Sometimes ordinary lenses are delivered as Hardex. The percentage is small, but is impossible to estimate because it is not known how many are tested by the ophthalmologists or optometrists through whose hands they pass to the consumer. Imperial and many of the optical practitioners possess a small machine called a colmiscope (I think) through which a lens is examined and if it is Hardex a characteristic Maltese cross pattern appears in it. The test is easily done. In addition to its failure to temper the lenses, Imperial failed to test them before delivery to Deshield.

Deshield, likewise, did not test them. He now has a colmiscope but probably did not have one at the time of delivery. In my view he had a duty to the plaintiff to test them but instead relied on Imperial, thus accepting or adopting Imperial's negligence.

But negligence is only part of the plaintiff's cause of action. His more difficult hurdle is causation, the causal relationship between the negligence and the injury. The plea of *res ipsa loquitur* does not help the plaintiff. That involves an inference of negligence not causation. The defendant's wrong cannot be the cause of the injury if it would have happened without the wrong. Therefore, the defendants argue quite rightly that the plaintiff must prove that the impact he received, although sufficient to break the ordinary and untempered lens he wore, would probably not have been sufficient to break a Hardex lens.

Imperial is possessed of another machine, one designed to test the hardness of Hardex lenses. It drops a steel ball having a diameter of $\frac{5}{8}$ of an inch onto a lens from a height of 50 ins. Any properly tempered Hardex lens is expected to withstand this blow. Only about one such lens is so tested each month in Imperial's laboratory in Regina, probably enough.

I cannot with certainty conclude that the blow of the steel ball on the lens was lighter or harder than the impact which caused the plaintiff's lens to shatter. I had no expert evidence. But the plaintiff's burden is not to show certainty. He has only to show that more probably than not the one which caused the injury was less violent or of less force than the steel ball test.

I feel the plaintiff has met this burden. The steel ball test shows the strength of Hardex lenses and their ability to withstand a direct blow of considerable force. The momentum of the collision between the plaintiff and the other player would be greater but much diffused, I would think, not as concentrated as the steel ball. All of the force of the bodies in collision at the time of the injury would not be on the lens which broke.

There was evidence suggesting that the Hardex lens breaks in a manner different from an ordinary lens. If acceptable, this evidence would be useful to the plaintiff because the injury might have been less severe or trifling, if, in fact, a Hardex lens had broken in the circumstances. But the evidence on the point is not good enough for me to draw that conclusion. Mr. Most broke an ordinary lens and a Hardex lens of identical prescription in the identical manner and brought the pieces to the trial. My unskilled eye could see nothing but similarity in the glass fragments of the two, but Drs. Griffith and Deshield who have considerable experience seemed to expect smaller fragments. Whether this would cause less injury is too speculative for me to judge.

The plaintiff is not the type of young man who might take unnecessary risks. There seems nothing frivolous about him. If he had known that the lenses were not Hardex, he would not have worn them on this occasion. The defendants by their error failed in their duty to protect the plaintiff against the risk of breakage of ordinary lenses. The risk was foreseeable whether or not they knew that he had athletic pastimes.

The defendants are therefore liable.

In the accident, part of the fractured lens entered the plaintiff's right eye. He was taken to hospital where he saw his family doctor who in turn called Dr. Griffith, an ophthalmologist. He found an irregular laceration of the cornea which healed after removal of a number of small fragments of clear glass from the eye.

Over the next year to 18 months the vision in the right eye improved until it stabilized at 20/25. Before the accident it was 20/20 as was (and is) the left eye. The references are to corrected vision because the plaintiff has been near-sighted all his life.

He was just a few days in hospital and six days off work.

Previously he was able to wear soft contact lenses but now because of the irregularity of the corneal surface he finds them uncomfortable, and wears them only when playing hockey or football. His vision in the right eye is now not as good with contacts as with glasses.

Even with glasses the right eye tires earlier which is a material considera-tion to a man who plans a career in government requiring much reading and other close work. This factor makes the assessment of damages difficult.

I award the plaintiff $7,500 in general damages and special damages in the agreed amount of $646.50.

Each of the defendants has made a claim over against the other for indemnity.

As I view the facts each of the defendants had a duty to the plaintiff to ensure that he got Hardex lenses and avoided the risk consequent upon the breakage of ordinary lenses. I cannot say that the manufacturer had a greater duty than the optometrist or *vice versa*, but the duty is to the plaintiff. What is their duty to one another? Imperial had no promise or undertaking or contract with Deshield that Deshield would test lenses for hardness before delivery to the plaintiff or any other consumer. Mr. Most does not know today which optometrists have colmiscopes and which do not. How, then, can Imperial say that Deshield had a duty to Imperial to apply the Hardex test? Optical practitioners have colmiscopes to protect their patients not Imperial, I would think. Deshield was entitled to rely on Imperial's duty to supply Hardex lenses notwithstanding Deshield's own duty to his patient, the plaintiff.

Therefore I award judgment against the defendants jointly and severally for the sum of $8,146.50 and costs to be taxed.

The defendant Deshield shall have indemnification from Imperial for the entire judgment plus his own costs.

NOTES AND QUESTIONS

1. As is often the case, the judge did not discuss the basis upon which he concluded that the defendants owed the plaintiff a duty of care. Why do you think the judge imposed a duty on the defen-dants in this situation?

2. Did the judge specifically address the question of the standard of care that the defendants are expected to meet? How did Deshield and Imperial Optical breach the standard of care? If, as the judge suggests, Deshield did not have a colmiscope, why was he held negligent for not testing the lenses? Considering that Imperial Optical is a large company, should it be found negligent every time it delivers the wrong lenses to one of its clients?

3. What did the plaintiff have to prove in order to establish that Deshield and Imperial Optical caused his injury? If the collision between the plaintiff and the other player was violent enough to

shatter a normal glass lens, is it not likely that it would have shattered a Hardex lens? How did the judge decide this issue without expert testimony?

4. How did the judge resolve the issue of remoteness of damages?

5. Summarize the plaintiff's material losses. What was the basis upon which the judge determined that $7,500 was an appropriate award of general damages?

6. Why did the judge conclude that the plaintiff was not contributorily negligent? Do you think that this conclusion would have been different if the game were tackle football?

7. What is the legal effect of finding the defendants jointly and severally liable? Why did Imperial Optical have to indemnify Deshield for the entire judgment? Would the result have been the same if the judge had relieved Deshield of liability and simply found Imperial Optical liable?

10

THE DUTY OF CARE

1. An Introduction to the Concept of Duty
2. Does Negligence Law Apply? — An Illustration
3. Did the Defendant's Conduct Give Rise to a Duty of Care? — The Foreseeable Risk of Injury Test
4. Was the Duty of Care Owed to the Plaintiff? — The Foreseeable Plaintiff Test

1. An Introduction to the Concept of Duty

As we discussed in the last chapter, the core concept of the tort of negligence is the legal duty to take care. In order to sustain a negligence action, the plaintiff must establish that the defendant had a legal obligation to take care not to cause harm. The following material outlines the evolution of the duty concept. It is designed to assist students in understanding the ongoing debates about the scope of liability.

(a) THE CLASSICAL APPROACH

In the 19th and early 20th centuries, the duty of care was confined to a narrow set of actors and conduct. While the ambit of the duty was expanded in isolated cases, the expansion was cautious and piecemeal. Most common law lawyers and judges operated within a fairly rigid set of legal, social and political assumptions about the nature and purpose of negligence law. This set of assumptions may be viewed as the "classical" approach to the duty of care.

The first premise of the classical approach was that legal responsibility for negligence did not flow inexorably from moral responsibility. The classical lawyers respected precedent and the absence of precedent. If the common law had not established a particular legal duty of care, that was reason enough to doubt its desirability. The conservatism of Victorian judges was driven in part by trust in the wisdom of the common law and by a particular vision of social responsibility. In a society committed to individual liberty and self-reliance, legal rights and obligations were seen to be a consequence of voluntary agreements between consenting parties. Legal duties of care imposed by courts, irrespective of individual agreements, did not square with these convictions.

The second premise of the classical view was political in nature. As unelected bodies within representative democracies, courts were seen as having a limited role in imposing liability outside the confines of common law precedent. Even if a broader duty of care was required, it was for legislators to enact it.

The third premise concerned the theory of legal obligations. Positive acts and omissions in the course of conduct were more culpable than mere failures to act. Misfeasances, that is, acts that are harmful, were actionable; whereas nonfeasances, that is, failures to act for the plaintiff's benefit, were not. For example, a captain who negligently ran his ship aground might be liable to injured passengers, but would have no obligation to assist drowning strangers. Whatever morality might dictate, there was no legal obligation to be one's "brother's keeper".

Fourth, the classical view rested on assumptions about the value of various interests. Physical injuries to individuals and property were broadly compensable, but emotional harms and loss of commercial profits were not. Physical injuries were seen as more tangible and measurable. The common law also more readily compensated harms caused by deeds than those caused by words. While a banker had a legal duty to prevent his customers' entrusted valuables from being stolen, he had no legal obligation to ensure that his gratuitous financial advice was accurate or sound. Again, the common law focused on what was perceived as a more concrete and cautious basis for imposing negligence liability.

As we shall see, some of the classical currents are reflected in *Donoghue v. Stevenson*, particularly in the dissent of Lord Buckmaster. Even though *Donoghue* marks the beginning of the modern law of negligence, the classical approach to duty — albeit in an altered form — has continued to shape the evolution of the duty of care.

(b) THE GENERAL DUTY OF CARE TEST

M'ALISTER (or DONOGHUE) v. STEVENSON

[1932] A.C. 562 (H.L.)

[The plaintiff's friend purchased a dark, opaque bottle of ginger-beer and gave it to the plaintiff. She drank some before her friend discovered a decomposed snail in the bottle. The plaintiff sued the manufacturer, alleging shock and severe gastro-enteritis.]

LORD ATKIN: — My Lords, the sole question for determination in this case is legal: Do the averments made by the pursuer in her pleading, if true, disclose a cause of action? I need not restate the particular facts. The question is whether the manufacturer of an article of drink sold by him to a distributor, in circumstances which prevent the distributor or the ultimate purchaser or consumer from discovering by inspection any defect, is under any legal duty to the ultimate purchaser or consumer to take reasonable care that the article is free from defect likely to cause injury to health. I do not think a more important problem has occupied your Lordships in your judicial capacity: important both because of its bearing on public health and because of the practical test which it applies to the system under which it arises. The case has to be determined in accordance with Scots law; but it has been a matter of agreement between the experienced counsel who argue this case, and it appears to be the basis of the judgments of the learned judges of the Court of Session, that for the purposes of determining this problem the laws of Scotland and England are the same. I speak with little authority on this point, but my research, such as it is, satisfies me that the principles of the law of Scotland on such a question as the present are identical with those of English law; and I discuss the issue on that footing. The law of both countries appears to be that in order to support an action for damages for negligence the complainant has to show that he has been injured by the breach of a duty owed to him in the circumstances by the defendant to take reasonable care to avoid such injury. In the present case we are not concerned with the breach of the duty; if a duty exists, that would be a question of fact which is sufficiently averred and for present purposes must be assumed. We are solely concerned with the question whether, as a matter of law in the circumstances alleged, the defender owed any duty to the pursuer to take care.

It is remarkable how difficult it is to find in the English authorities statements of general application defining the relations between parties that give rise to the duty. The Courts are concerned with the particular relations which come before them in actual litigation, and it is sufficient to say whether the duty exists in those circumstances. The result is that the Courts have been engaged upon an elaborate classification of duties, as they exist in respect of property, whether real or personal, with further divisions as to ownership, occupation or control, and distinctions based on the particular relations of one side or the other, whether manufacturer, salesman or landlord, customer, tenant, stranger, and so on. In this way it can be ascertained at any time whether the law recognizes a duty, but only where the case can be referred to some particular species which has been examined and classified. And yet the duty which is common to all the cases where liability is established must logically be based upon some element common to the cases where it is found to exist. To seek a complete logical definition of the general principle is probably to go beyond the function of the judge, for the more general the definition the more likely it is to omit essentials or to introduce non-essentials. The attempt was made by Brett M.R. in *Heaven v. Pender*, in a definition to which I will later refer. As framed, it was demonstrably too wide, though it appears to me, if properly limited, to be capable of affording a valuable practical guide.

At present I content myself with pointing out that in English law there must be, and is, some general conception of relations giving rise to a duty of care, of which the particular cases found in the books are but instances. The liability for negligence, whether you style it such or treat it as in other systems as a species of "culpa," is no doubt based upon a general public sentiment of moral wrongdoing for which the offender must pay. But acts or omissions which any moral code would censure cannot in a practical world be treated so as to give a right to every person injured by them to demand relief. In this way rules of law arise which limit the range of complainants and the extent of their remedy. The rule that you are to love your neighbour becomes in law, you must not injure your neighbour; and the lawyer's question, Who is my neighbour? receives a restricted reply. You must take reasonable care to avoid acts or omissions which you can reasonably foresee would be likely to injure your neighbour. Who, then, in law is my neighbour? The answer seems to be — persons who are so closely and directly affected by my act that I ought reasonably to have them in contemplation as being so affected when I am directing my mind to the acts or omissions which are called in question. This appears to me to be the doctrine of *Heaven v. Pender* as laid down by Lord Esher (then Brett M.R.) when it is limited by the notion of proximity introduced by Lord Esher himself and A.L. Smith L.J. in *Le Lievre v. Gould.* Lord Esher says:

> That case established that, under certain circumstances, one may owe a duty to another, even though there is no contract between them. If one man is near to another, or is near to the property of another, a duty lies upon him not to do that which may cause a personal injury to that other, or may injure his property.

And A.L. Smith L.J.:

> The decision of *Heaven v. Pender* was founded upon the principle, that a duty to take due care did arise when the person or property of one was in such proximity to the person or property of another that, if due care was not taken, damage might be done by the one to the other.

I think that this sufficiently states the truth if proximity be not confined to mere physical proximity, but be used, as I think it was intended, to extend to such close and direct relations that the act complained of directly affects a person whom the person alleged to be bound to take care would know would be directly affected by his careless act. That this is the sense in which nearness or "proximity" was intended by Lord Esher is obvious from his own illustration in *Heaven v. Pender* of the application of his doctrine to the sale of goods.

> This (i.e., the rule he just formulated) includes the case of goods, etc., supplied to be used immediately by a particular person or persons, or one of a class of persons, where it would be obvious to the person supplying, if he thought, that the goods would in all probability be used at once by such persons before a reasonable opportunity for discovering any defect which might exist, and where the thing supplied would be of such a nature that a neglect of ordinary care or skill as to its condition or the manner of supplying it would probably cause danger to the person or property of the person for whose use it was supplied, and who was about to use it. It would exclude a case in which the goods are supplied under circumstances in which it would be a chance by whom they would be used or whether they would be used or not, or whether they would be used before there would probably be means of observing any defect, or where the goods would be of such nature that a want of care or skill as to their condition or the manner of supplying them would not probably produce danger of injury to person or property.

I draw particular attention to the fact that Lord Esher emphasizes the necessity of goods having to be "used immediately" and "used at once before a reasonable opportunity of inspection." This is obviously to exclude the possibility of goods having their condition altered by lapse of time, and to call attention to the proximate relationship, which may be too remote where inspection even of the person using, certainly of an intermediate person, may reasonably be interposed. With this necessary qualification of proximate relationship as explained in *Le Lievre v. Gould*, I think the judgment of Lord Esher expresses the law of England; without the qualification, I think the majority of the Court in *Heaven v. Pender* were justified in thinking the principle was expressed in too general terms. There will no doubt arise cases where it will be difficult to determine whether the contemplated relationship is so close that the duty arises. But in the class of cases now before the Court I cannot conceive any difficulty to arise. A manufacturer puts up an article of food in a container which he knows will be opened by the actual consumer. There can be no inspection by any purchaser and no reasonable preliminary inspection by the consumer. Negligently, in the course of preparation, he allows the contents to be mixed with poison. It is said that the law of England and Scotland is that the poisoned consumer has no remedy against the negligent manufacturer. If this were the result of the authorities, I should consider the result a grave defect in the law, and so contrary to principle that I should hesitate long before following any decision to that effect which had not the authority of this

House. I would point out that, in the assumed state of the authorities, not only would the consumer have no remedy against the manufacturer, he would have none against any one else, for in the circumstances alleged there would be no evidence of negligence against any one other than the manufacturer; and, except in the case of a consumer who was also a purchaser, no contract and no warranty of fitness, and in the case of the purchase of a specific article under its patent or trade name, which might well be the case in the purchase of some articles of food or drink, no warranty protecting even the purchaser-consumer. There are other instances than of articles of food and drink where goods are sold intended to be used immediately by the consumer, such as many forms of goods sold for cleaning purposes, where the same liability must exist. The doctrine supported by the decision below would not only deny a remedy to the consumer who was injured by consuming bottled beer or chocolates poisoned by the negligence of the manufacturer, but also to the user of what should be a harmless proprietary medicine, an ointment, a soap, a cleaning fluid or cleaning powder. I confine myself to articles of common household use, where every one, including the manufacturer, knows that the articles will be used by other persons than the actual ultimate purchaser — namely, by members of his family and his servants, and in some cases his guests. I do not think so ill of our jurisprudence as to suppose that its principles are so remote from the ordinary needs of civilized society and the ordinary claims it makes upon its members as to deny a legal remedy where there is so obviously a social wrong.

It will be found, I think, on examination that there is no case in which the circumstances have been such as I have just suggested where the liability has been negatived. There are numerous cases, where the relations were much more remote, where the duty has been held not to exist.

. . .

My Lords, if your Lordships accept the view that this pleading discloses a relevant cause of action you will be affirming the proposition that by Scots and English law alike a manufacturer of products, which he sells in such a form as to show that he intends them to reach the ultimate consumer in the form in which they left him with no reasonable possibility of intermediate examination, and with the knowledge that the absence of reasonable care in the preparation or putting up of the products will result in an injury to the consumer's life or property, owes a duty to the consumer to take that reasonable care.

It is a proposition which I venture to say no one in Scotland or England who was not a lawyer would for one moment doubt. It will be an advantage to make it clear that the law in this matter, as in most others, is in accordance with sound common sense. I think that this appeal should be allowed.

LORD BUCKMASTER (dissenting): — . . . . The authorities are against the appellant's contention, and, apart from authority, it is difficult to see how any common law proposition can be formulated to support her claim.

The principle contended for must be this: that the manufacturer, or indeed the repairer, of any article, apart entirely from contract, owes a duty to any person by whom the article is lawfully used to see that it has been carefully constructed. All rights in contract must be excluded from consideration of this principle; such contractual rights as may exist in successive steps from the original manufacturer down to the ultimate purchaser are ex hypothesi immaterial. Nor can the doctrine be confined to cases where inspection is difficult or impossible to introduce. This conception is simply to misapply tort doctrine applicable to sale and purchase.

The principle of tort lies completely outside the region where such considerations apply, and the duty, if it exists, must extend to every person who, in lawful circumstances, uses the article made. There can be no special duty attaching to the manufacture of food apart from that implied by contract or imposed by statute. If such a duty exists, it seems to me it must cover the construction of every article, and I cannot see any reason why it should not apply to the construction of a house. If one step, why not fifty? Yet if a house be, as it sometimes is, negligently built, and in consequence of that negligence the ceiling falls and injures the occupier or any one else, no action against the builder exists according to English law, although I believe such a right did exist according to the laws of Babylon. Were such a principle known and recognized, it seems to me impossible, having regard to the numerous cases that must have arisen to persons injured by its disregard, that, with the exception of *George v. Skivington*, no case directly involving the principle has ever succeeded in the Courts, and, were it well known and accepted, much of the discussion of the earlier cases would have been waste of time, and the distinction as to articles dangerous in themselves or known to be dangerous to the vendor would be meaningless.

In *Mullen v. Barr & Co.*, a case indistinguishable from the present excepting upon the ground that a mouse is not a snail, and necessarily adopted by the Second Division in their judgment, Lord Anderson says this:

> In a case like the present, where the goods of the defenders are widely distributed throughout Scotland, it would seem little short of outrageous to make them responsible to members of the public for the condition of the contents of every bottle which issues from their works. It is obvious that, if such responsibility attached to the defenders, they might be called on to meet claims of damages which they could not possibly investigate or answer.

In agreeing, as I do, with the judgment of Lord Anderson, I desire to add that I find it hard to dissent from the emphatic nature of the language with which this judgment is clothed. I am of opinion that this appeal should be dismissed, and I beg to move your Lordships accordingly.

[Lords Macmillan and Thankerton gave concurring speeches and Lord Tomlin gave a dissenting speech. Note that the order of Lord Atkin's and Lord Buckmaster's speeches has been reversed.]

NOTES AND QUESTIONS

1. What role did *Heaven v. Pender* (1883), 11 Q.B.D. 503 and *Le Lievre v. Gould*, [1893] 1 Q.B. 491 play in Lord Atkin's analysis? What factors did he consider justified applying negligence law to products liability?

2. What was the legal basis of Lord Buckmaster's dissent? What considerations did he raise against extending negligence to products' liability? Were his concerns about extending negligence to other areas of tort liability justified? Did Lord Atkin adequately address these issues?

3. How did Lord Atkin define the test for determining when a duty of care would be imposed in a products' liability case? Based on his analysis, would negligence law extend to cases in which: (a) the retailer or consumer had an opportunity to inspect the bottle's contents before consumption;

(b) the product was simply unpalatable, rather than harmful; or (c) the product was a dangerously defective machine intended solely for industrial use?

4. How did Lord Atkin determine if the duty of care was owed to the plaintiff? Explain what this test means in your own words. If a thirsty waiter drank the ginger beer that M'Alister had left in the bottle, would he have been owed a duty of care?

5. What standard of care did Lord Atkin suggest ought to apply? How would the plaintiff prove that the defendant breached the standard in a products liability case?

6. One major problem in interpreting the case is that it deals with many of the most important issues in negligence law. This is compounded by the fact that Lord Atkin discusses several of these issues together in the space of about 10 lines. Although Lord Atkin's duty principles have been used for nearly 60 years, little progress has been made in reaching a consensus on analyzing their component elements.

7. Despite the absence of a consensus, it may be helpful for analytical purposes to view the duty of care issue as comprised of three subissues. First, as a matter of legal policy, does the law of negligence apply to this type of claim or situation? Second, if negligence law applies, has the defendant's conduct in this case given rise to a duty of care? Third, does the defendant owe this duty of care to the plaintiff?

8. Smith attributes much of the conceptual confusion in negligence to the ambiguity of the duty concept and the misuse of duty language. In his view, the duty concept is used as a convenient, but misleading, label that masks the real issues. If the duty concept has to be preserved, he would limit it to two basic questions. First, as a matter of public policy, should negligence law extend to this area? Second, did the defendant's conduct create a foreseeable risk of injury? He argues that the question of whether the defendant owed the duty to the plaintiff should be dealt with in remoteness, not duty. For definitional purposes, he refers to these three issues as questions of extension, foreseeability and proximity. See Smith, "The Mystery of Duty", in Klar (ed.), *Studies in Canadian Tort Law* (1977), 1; and generally Smith, *Liability In Negligence* (1984).

8. For alternative analyses of the duty concept see Fleming, "Remoteness and Duty: The Control Devices in Liability for Negligence" (1953), 31 Can. Bar Rev. 471; Heuston, "*Donoghue v. Stevenson* in Retrospect" (1957), 20 Mod. L. Rev. 1; Gibson, "A New Alphabet of Negligence", in Linden (ed.), *Studies in Canadian Tort Law* (1968), 189; and Symmons, "The Duty of Care in Negligence: Recently Expressed Policy Elements — Part I and Part II" (1971), 34 Mod. L. Rev. 394 and 509. For an interesting historical review of duty see Winfield, "Duty in Tortious Negligence" (1934), 34 Colum. L. Rev. 41.

(c) THE DEVELOPMENT OF THE MODERN LAW OF DUTY

Lord Atkin's formulation of duty has been applied well beyond the confines of products' liability. The case has been used to support the proposition that negligence law extends, with some limited exceptions, to any act or omission which causes physical injury. This principle is so deeply entrenched in the law that the courts will often simply assume that negligence law applies. For example, a judge will rarely make more than passing reference to the fact that a driver owes a duty of care to other users of the road or that a surgeon owes a duty of care to her patients.

As indicated in chapter 9, the courts were far more reluctant to extend this general test of duty to those special categories of cases in which they had previously refused to recognize any duty or had imposed a limited duty. While the courts rejected much of this pre-1932 case law in favour of broader principles that were more akin to *Donoghue*, they did so on a category-by-category basis. This incremental expansion of the duty of care within specific categories of precedents did not represent a wholesale break with the classical approach.

Not until the 1960s did appellate courts begin to use *Donoghue* to overturn traditional assumptions about the duty of care. In *Hedley Byrne & Co. v. Heller & Partners Ltd.*, [1964] A.C. 465, the House of Lords held that in certain situations a duty of care could be imposed for negligent financial advice. In *Home Office v. Dorset Yacht Co.*, [1970] A.C. 1004, the House of Lords held that public authorities could be held liable in negligence with respect to their statutory functions and operations. These cases are important not only as leading cases in the special categories of negligence, but also as examples of the evolving and expanding scope of the duty of care. The search for a general approach to the duty of care culminated in Lord Wilberforce's now-famous speech in *Anns v. London Borough of Merton*, [1977] 2 All E.R. 492 at 498 (H.L.):

> Through the trilogy of cases in this House, *Donoghue v. Stevenson, Hedley Byrne & Co. Ltd. v. Heller & Partners Ltd.* and *Home Office v. Dorset Yacht Co. Ltd.*, the position has now been reached that in order to establish that a duty of care arises in a particular situation, it is not necessary to bring the facts of that situation within those previous situations in which a duty of care has been held to exist. Rather the question has to be approached in two stages. First one has to ask whether, as between the alleged wrongdoer and the person who has suffered damage there is a sufficient relationship of proximity or neighbourhood such that, in the reasonable contemplation of the former, carelessness on his part may be likely to cause damage to the latter, in which case a prima facie duty of care arises. Secondly, if the first question is answered affirmatively, it is necessary to consider whether there are any considerations which ought to negative, or to reduce or limit the scope of the duty or the class of person to whom it is owed or the damages to which a breach of it may give rise.

Unlike Lord Atkin's speech, this passage does not provide a specific test for determining whether to recognize a duty of care. Rather, it sets out an approach for analyzing the existing categories of negligence and novel negligence claims. Adoption of Lord Wilberforce's approach will not necessarily result in the general duty principles in *Donoghue* being applied to all the special categories of negligence. For example, in *Anns, Hedley Byrne* and *Home Office*, the House of Lords recognized special considerations that justified the adoption of restricted duty principles.

Although the English courts initially adopted the *Anns* approach in a broad range of cases, they began to distance themselves from it by the mid-1980s. After narrowly interpreting *Anns* or ignoring it, the House of Lords decisively overruled it in *Murphy v. Brentwood District Council*, [1990] 2 All E.R. 908. The *Anns* approach was criticized as leading to capricious results, providing unworkable tests of liability, unduly expanding the scope of liability and lacking any foundation in established principle. The demise of *Anns* reflects a dramatic retreat from the rapid expansion of the duty of care and thus the spiralling growth in the scope of liability. In rejecting *Anns*, the High Court of Australia in *Sutherland Shire Council v. Heyman* (1985), 157 C.L.R. 424, appeared to harken back to the classical approach when it stated at 428 that the law should evolve "incrementally and by analogy with established categories".

NOTES AND QUESTIONS

1. The court's initial reluctance to apply *Donoghue* to the special categories of negligence cases is illustrated by *Otto v. Bolton*, [1936] 2 K.B. 46. About a year after the first plaintiff purchased a new home from the defendants, a large part of the ceiling fell on the second plaintiff, seriously injuring her. The judge found that the defendants had been negligent in constructing the house, but concluded that they could not be held liable because it was a well-established principle of law that a vendor, even if he is the builder, owes no duty of care to a purchaser. The defendant's liability, if any, arose solely in contract. The judge indicated that *Donoghue* did not alter the principles governing a vendor's liability, since it dealt with defective chattels.

2. It was not until *Anns* that the House of Lords finally rejected the earlier authorities and held

that a builder/vendor owed a duty of care to a subsequent purchaser of the premises. In *Dept. of the Environment v. Thomas Bates and Son*, [1990] 2 All E.R. 943, the House of Lords clarified the scope of a builder's duty. Builders could only be held liable for the cost of repairing defects that resulted in physical damage to the property or injury to the occupants or posed an imminent danger to personal safety and health. However, there is no liability for repairs simply to make a building safe or useable for its intended purpose. This case resolved much of the confusion that arose after *Anns* regarding a builder's liability. See Grubb, "A Case for Recognizing Economic Loss in Defective Building Cases" (1984), 43 Cambridge L.J. 111; and Wallace, "Negligence and Defective Buildings: Confusion Compounded?" (1989), 105 L.Q.R. 46.

3. In Canada, a builder is liable for defects that result in personal injuries or physical damage to the plaintiff's property. In *Winnipeg Condominium Corp. No. 36 v. Bird Construction Co.* (1995), 23 C.C.L.T. (2d) 1, the Supreme Court of Canada extended a builder's or contractor's liability to include the repair costs for defects that pose a real and substantial danger to the building's occupants.

4. There were dramatic increases in the scope of negligence liability as the "neighbour principle" in *Donoghue* was applied to new relationships and to many of the special duty of care situations that had previously been governed by more restrictive principles. This led to concern about the adequacy of these principles for resolving modern torts problems. See Linden, "The Good Neighbour on Trial: A Fountain of Sparkling Wisdom" (1983), 17 U.B.C. L.R. 67; and Smith and Burns, "The Good Neighbour on Trial: Good Neighbours Make Bad Law" (1983), 17 U.B.C. L.R. 93. See also Little, "Erosion of Non-Duty Rules in England, the United States, and Common Law Commonwealth Nations" (1983), 20 Hous. L. Rev. 959.

5. The English and Australian courts' growing disenchantment with *Anns* can be traced through a series of cases. See, for example, *Governors of the Peabody Donation Fund v. Sir Lindsay Parkinson & Co.*, [1985] A.C. 210 (H.L.); *Leigh and Sillavan Ltd. v. Aliakmon Shipping Co.*, [1986] A.C. 785 (H.L.); *Curran v. Northern Ireland Co-ownership Housing Assoc. Ltd.*, [1987] 2 All E.R. 13 (H.L.); and *Yuen Kun-yeu v. A.G. of Hong Kong*, [1987] 2 All E.R. 705 (P.C.).

6. For commentaries on the rise and fall of *Anns*, see Smillie, "The Foundation of the Duty of Care in Negligence" (1989), 15 Monash Univ. L. Rev. 302; Howarth, "Negligence After *Murphy*: Time to Rethink" (1991), 50 Camb. L.J. 58; Wallace, "Anns Beyond Repair" (1991), 107 L.Q.R. 228; and Markensis & Deakin, "The Random Element . . ." (1992), 50 Mod. L. Rev. 619.

(d) *ANNS* AND THE SUPREME COURT OF CANADA

Anns established a new, but not necessarily radical, approach to the duty of care issue. Lord Wilberforce stated that the duty principle was no longer confined to situations governed by precedent. Every new negligence case was to be decided on its merits. The plaintiff only had to establish that a relationship of "proximity" existed with the defendant. Such a relationship would arise if the defendant's conduct created a foreseeable risk of harm to the plaintiff. At this point, the defendant would owe a *prima facie* duty of care to the plaintiff. The onus then shifted to the defendant to demonstrate why, as a matter of law or policy, the duty ought to be negated or limited.

While this two-step approach was a major departure from the category-by-category evolution of duty, it was not a blank cheque for plaintiffs. Lord Wilberforce appears to have anticipated that many defendants would be able to justify negating or limiting the duty of care, especially in the special category of cases in which the plaintiff's claim was unsupported by precedent. Many of the factors that initially led to limiting the duty of care in the special categories of negligence cases remained relevant to the second part of Lord Wilberforce's analysis. Thus, *Anns* is more a reformulation of the elements of duty, rather than a wholesale rejection of the pre-existing principles.

The Supreme Court of Canada has adopted a pro-plaintiff interpretation of

Anns. This approach has had three general features. First, the Court has adopted a very flexible concept of "proximity". As a result, few plaintiffs have had difficulty establishing a *prima facie* duty of care. Second, the court has consistently failed to consider the second stage of the *Anns* test, namely, the legal and policy reasons for negating or limiting the duty of care. Lastly, the Supreme Court has been reluctant to provide explicit analyses of the social and legal choices underlying its duty decisions. Opportunities to consider the empirical evidence concerning such issues as risk, foreseeability and social costs have been shunned in favour of what frequently appear to be *ad hoc* policy preferences. The classical approach, with its commitment to judicial caution, deference to legislatures, distinctions between misfeasance and nonfeasance, words and deeds, physical and emotional harms, and physical harms and financial losses, has been largely jettisoned.

While the classical approach was too inflexible and outmoded to warrant retention, the category-by-category evolution of duty provided an ordered and principled mechanism for modernizing the duty of care concept. Thus, it was not surprising that the English and Australian courts returned to this approach when they concluded that *Anns* was unworkable.

Even though the Supreme Court is unlikely to do an about-face on *Anns* in the immediate future, the pre-existing special categories of negligence remain important for two reasons. First, the Supreme Court has not adopted *Anns* as a universal approach to duty. Rather, *Anns* has been used in addressing new or emerging claims that are not governed by the existing common law precedents. The extensive case law in many, if not most, of the special categories of negligence cases may remain relevant in resolving routine claims in that area. Second, while the Supreme Court may never flatly reject *Anns*, we believe that it will eventually have to consider the special categories of negligence cases in applying the second stage of Lord Wilberforce's analysis.

In order to ensure that students are equipped to analyze the duty of care issue, it is necessary to present both the special categories of negligence cases and the *Anns*-based cases. In Canada, *Anns* has been most prominent in the analysis of economic loss and the liability of public authorities — special categories of negligence that are discussed later in this book.

2. Does Negligence Law Apply? — An Illustration

DEMARCO v. UNGARO

(1979), 8 C.C.L.T. 1, 95 D.L.R. (3d) 385 (Ont. H.C.)

KREVER J.: — In Ontario is a lawyer immune from action at the suit of a client for negligence in the conduct of the client's civil case in Court? That is the important question of substantive law that, to paraphrase Maine weakly, is secreted interstitially by this procedural motion relating to the adequacy of pleadings. The defendants' motion, on its face, is for an order under Rule 126 striking out certain paragraphs of the statement of claim on the ground that they disclose no cause of action and are frivolous and vexatious . . . *Rondel v. Worsley*, [1969] 1 A.C. 191, [1967] 3 All E.R. 993, the decision of the House of Lords which reaffirmed, by providing a fresh *rationale* for, the historical immunity enjoyed by an

English barrister from an action for negligence in the conduct of a trial, was, Mr. Epstein submitted, good law in Ontario.

Much more must be said later about *Rondel v. Worsley*, but, in the meantime, one matter of significance should be mentioned and that is the different potential consequence of the reconsideration by the House of Lords of the English doctrine of immunity of the barrister for England (and Scotland), on the one hand, and Ontario, on the other. In England, which has a divided profession, and in which, except for the practice of the "dock brief" (now, I understand superseded by a legal aid-system) the barrister enters into no contract with the client and is not entitled to sue for his or her fee, to reconsider the doctrine of immunity on the basis of public policy, posed the possibility of changing the law by sweeping the immunity away. In placing the doctrine on a modern footing the House of Lords elected to maintain immunity. In Ontario, in which lawyers are both barristers and solicitors, and in which the lawyer conducting litigation contracts directly with the client and is entitled to sue for his or her fee, to reconsider the law respecting the right of a client to sue his or her barrister for negligence, on the basis of the view of the House of Lords as to public policy, posed the possibility of changing the law by introducing the immunity of the lawyer, for, as I shall show, before *Rondel v. Worsley*, an Ontario lawyer, in his or her role as advocate, was not immune from action at the suit of the client.

[Krever J. went on to discuss *Leslie v. Ball* (1863), 22 U.C.Q.B. 512, and *Wade v. Ball* (1870), 20 U.C.C.P. 302 (C.A.), two cases in which it was held that barristers were not immune to civil liability.]

The question of a lawyer's liability to action at the suit of a client for negligence in Court in the conduct of litigation does not seem to have arisen again in Ontario between the date of the decision in *Wade v. Ball* and *Rondel v. Worsley*. It is reasonable, it seems to me, to believe that, until the latter case was decided, it had been assumed that no immunity from action attached to a lawyer in the conduct of litigation in Ontario. As long as the doctrine of barristers' immunity rested on the inability of the barrister to sue for his fees in England, a disability which did not exist in Ontario, that assumption was not only understandable but also logically unassailable. With the decision in *Rondel v. Worsley* to base the immunity on the ground of public policy, it was reasonable to expect that the question would be re-examined in Ontario . . .

It would, in my view, be tedious and of little utility, to examine in minute detail every speech that was delivered by the Members of the House who sat on the case. . . . For my purposes it will be sufficient to summarize the grounds on which it was held in *Rondel v. Worsley* that public policy requires immunity of the barrister. I shall limit myself to four of these grounds.

The first ground related to the duty, which, in interest of proper administration of justice, every counsel must discharge to the Court, a duty which was said to be higher than and, in some cases, in conflict with, the duty owed to the client . . .

Clearly related to the duty owed by a barrister to the Court was the expressed risk that, in the absence of the barrister's immunity, counsel, out of fear of a potential action for negligence by his or her client, would prolong proceedings, contrary to his or her best judgment, in effect, to prevent the client from complaining.

The second ground was the harm to the public interest that would result for relitigating the original issue in the negligence against the client's counsel . . .

The third consideration related to the obligation of a barrister to accept any client, however difficult, who sought his or her services, an obligation on which the very freedom of the subject was said to depend . . .

The final consideration to which I intend to refer is the anomaly that would result from the absence of barristers' immunity in the light of the absolute privilege all participants in a proceeding in Court enjoy with respect to what is said by them in Court. . . .

In 1978, the House of Lords again had occasion to consider the doctrine of a barrister's immunity, this time, however, in the context of a civil action. In *Saif Ali v. Sidney Mitchell & Co. (a firm) et al.*, [1978] 3 W.L.R. 849, the House of Lords reversed the decision of the Court of Appeal and held that the immunity of the barrister did not extend to the barrister's pre-trial performance of his duties connected with a civil action for damages arising out of an automobile accident. My reading of the speeches of the majority demonstrates a desire to restrict the doctrine as much as possible in recognition of the countervailing interest of a person who has suffered damage by reason of another's negligence. The *Saif Ali* case dealt with the propriety of third party proceedings against a barrister brought by a firm of solicitors being sued by their client . . .

I have come to the conclusion that the public interest (another phrase used in the speeches of *Rondel v. Worsley*) in Ontario does not require that our Courts recognize an immunity of a lawyer from action for negligence at the suit of his or her former client by reason of the conduct of a civil case in Court. It has not been, is not now, and should not be, public policy in Ontario to confer exclusively on lawyers engaged in Court work an immunity possessed by no other professional person. Public policy and the public interest do not exist in a vacuum. They must be examined against the background of a host of sociological facts of the society concerned. Nor are they lawyers' values as opposed to the values shared by the rest of the community. In the light of recent developments in the law of professional negligence and the rising incidence of "malpractice" actions against physicians (and especially surgeons who may be thought to be to physicians what barristers are to solicitors), I do not believe that enlightened, non-legally trained members of the community would agree with me if I were to hold that the public interest requires that litigation lawyers be immune from actions for negligence. I emphasize again that I am not concerned with the question whether the conduct complained about amounts to negligence. Indeed, I find it difficult to believe that a decision made by a lawyer in the conduct of a case will be held to be negligence as opposed to a mere error of judgment. But there may be cases in which the error is so egregious that a Court will conclude that it is negligence. The only issue I am addressing is whether the client is entitled to ask a Court to rule upon the matter.

Many of the sociological facts that are related to public policy and the public interest may be judicially noticed. The population of Ontario is approximately eight and a quarter million people. In 1978 there were approximately 12,300 lawyers licensed by the Law Society of Upper Canada to practise law in Ontario. All of them have a right of audience in any Court in Ontario as well as in the Federal Court of Canada and the Supreme Court of Canada. The vast majority of these lawyers are in private practice and, as such, are required to carry liability insurance in respect of negligence in the conduct of their clients' affairs. No distinction is made in this respect between those exclusively involved in litigation and all other lawyers. The current rate of increase in the size of the profession is approximately 1,000 lawyers annually. It is widely recognized that a graduating class of that size places such an enormous strain on the resources of the profession that the articling experience of students-at-law is extremely variable. Only a small percentage of lawyers newly called to the Bar can be expected to have had the advantage of working with or observing experienced and competent counsel. Yet very many of those recently qualified lawyers will be appearing in Court on behalf of clients. To deprive these clients of recourse if their cases are negligently dealt with will not, to most residents of this Province, appear to be consistent with the public interest.

It is with a great sense of deference that I offer a few brief remarks on the grounds and consideration which formed the basis of the public policy as expressed by the House of Lords in *Rondel v. Worsley*. I am only concerned with the applicability of those considerations to Ontario conditions and have no hesitation in accepting them as entirely valid for England. With respect to the duty of counsel to the Court and the risk that, in the absence of immunity, counsel will be tempted to prefer the interest of the client to the duty to the Court and will thereby prolong trials, it is my respectful view that there is no empirical evidence that the risk is so serious that an aggrieved client should be rendered remediless. Between the dates of the decisions in *Leslie v. Ball*, 1863, and *Rondel v. Worsley*, 1967, immunity of counsel was not recognized in Ontario and negligence actions against lawyers respecting their conduct of Court cases did not attain serious proportions. Indeed, apart from the cases I have cited, I know of no case in which a lawyer was sued for negligence by his or her client in the conduct of a case in Court. A very similar argument is advanced in many discussions of the law of professional negligence as it applies to surgeons. Surgeons, it is claimed, are deterred from using their best judgment out of fear that the consequence will be an action by the patient in the event of an unfavourable result. This claim has not given rise to an immunity for surgeons. As to the second ground — the prospect of relitigating an issue already tried, it is my view that the undesirability of that event does not justify the recognition of lawyers' immunity in Ontario. It is not a contingency that does not already exist in our law and seems to me to be inherently involved in the concept of *res judicata* in the recognition that a party, in an action *in personam*, is only precluded from relitigating the same matter against a person who was a party to the earlier action. I can find no fault with the way in which Hagarty, C.J., dealt with this consideration in *Wade v. Ball et al.* (1870), 20 U.C.C.P. 302 at p. 304: "Practically, such a suit as the present may involve the trying over again of *Wade v. Hoyt*. This cannot be avoided." Better that than that the client should be without recourse.

The third consideration related to the obligation of a lawyer to accept any client. Whether that has ever been the universally accepted understanding of a lawyer's duty in Ontario is doubtful. In any event, I do not believe that such a duty exists in the practice of civil litigation and that is the kind of litigation with which I am now concerned. Indeed, as I understand the speech of Lord Diplock in *Saif Ali v. Sidney Mitchell & Co. (a firm) et al.*, [1978] 3 W.L.R. 849, that learned Law Lord was not persuaded of the validity of this ground . . .

The last consideration to be dealt with is the perceived anomaly related to the absolute privilege enjoyed in respect of anything said in Court by a lawyer. I confess that I am unable to appreciate why it should follow from the existence of that privilege that a lawyer may not be sued by his or her client for the negligent performance of the conduct of the client's case in court. The privilege, a fundamental aspect of the law of slander, is not concerned with relationships among persons. It relates to legal proceedings in open Court. The special relationship of lawyer and client is not involved as it is, of course, when one is considering the law of negligence.

. . .

It may, in conclusion, be of interest, from a comparative point of view that, in the United States, the Courts have not granted immunity to an attorney in the conduct of litigation: "an attorney must exercise reasonable care, skill and knowledge in the conduct of litigation . . . and must be properly diligent in the prosecution of the case" (see 7 C.J.S. pp. 982-4, § 146).

To sum up, for the reasons I have given, in Ontario, a lawyer is not immune from action at the suit of a client for negligence in the conduct of the client's civil case in Court. The defendants' motion, in effect, for a determination that a lawyer does enjoy such immunity is, therefore, dismissed with costs to the plaintiff in the cause.

NOTES AND QUESTIONS

1. Compare Krever J.'s approach in *Demarco* to the approach in *Anns*. Would the factors considered under the *Anns* approach have been different to those addressed by Krever J.? Would the result under *Anns* have been different?

2. What role did the early case law play in Krever J.'s analysis?

3. What were the bases upon which Krever J. rejected the House of Lords' policy considerations in *Rondel v. Worsley*, [1969] 1 A.C. 191? What considerations did he rely on in concluding that lawyers engaged in litigation ought to owe their clients a duty of care? On balance, do the differences in the legal profession and practice in England and Ontario warrant imposing a duty in one jurisdiction, but not in the other?

4. Krever J. makes only passing reference to the issues that courts will have to resolve in imposing liability on lawyers engaged in litigation. For example, what effect should a successful action have on the original case? Would it make a difference if the original case were criminal or civil?

5. Given the nature of litigation, it may be very difficult for the plaintiff to establish that her lawyer was negligent. In *Karpenko v. Paroian* (1980), 117 D.L.R. (3d) 383 (Ont. H.C.), the court held that a lawyer could only be found negligent for recommending a settlement of a civil suit prior to trial, if she made some "egregious error". The judge noted that it was in the public interest to discourage litigation, that lawyers should not be unduly inhibited in encouraging settlements and that the lawyer's decision to recommend acceptance or rejection of a settlement involved various factors. In *Wechsel v. Stutz* (1980), 15 C.C.L.T. 132 (Ont. Co. Ct.), the court rejected the plaintiff's claim that his former lawyer had been negligent in conducting the cross-examination at trial. The judge stated that the method of cross-examination had to be left to the judgment of counsel.

6. In *German v. Major* (1985), 20 D.L.R. (4th) 703 (Alta. C.A.), the defendant had been the prosecuting attorney in a tax evasion case against the plaintiff. After the acquittal, the plaintiff sued the defendant in negligence for "failure to investigate" and "take care". The court held that a prosecutor does not owe an accused any duty of care in negligence, except possibly in cases of bad faith. In dismissing the action, the court stated at 718, "If this suit were permitted, every convict could have

his case retried in a civil case." Should prosecutors be subject to different liability principles than other counsel in litigation? Did the judge's concern about relitigation warrant limiting prosecutors' potential liability in negligence?

In *Milgaard v. Kujawa*, [1994] 9 W.W.R. 305 (Sask. C.A.), the plaintiff had served 22 years of a life sentence for murder when it was revealed that the prosecutor had failed to disclose information that had been received during the original appeal period that tended to incriminate another person. The Saskatchewan Court of Appeal refused to strike out Milgaard's statement of claim against the prosecutor. The court stated that the allegations, if true, constituted a form of abuse that should not be protected by prosecutorial immunity. See also *Nelles v. Ontario* (1989), 49 C.C.L.T. 217 (S.C.C.), for a discussion of the limits of prosecutorial immunity.

7. In *Calvert v. Law Society of Upper Canada* (1981), 121 D.L.R. (3d) 169 (Ont. H.C.), it was held that the Law Society could not be held liable for negligently admitting or failing to disbar a lawyer. The court stated that such decisions were quasi-judicial in nature and that they could not be reviewed by a court unless it was shown that the Society acted maliciously. Is the result in *Calvert* consistent with the policy underlying *Demarco*? See also *Birchard v. Alta. Securities Commission* (1987), 42 D.L.R. (4th) 300 (Alta. Q.B.).

8. For a discussion of a barrister's liability see Hutchinson, "Negligence — Barrister ..." (1979), 57 Can. Bar Rev. 339; Bogart, "Immunity of Advocates From Suit: The Unresolved Issue" (1980), 29 U.N.B. L.J. 27; and Baynham and Baldwin, "Barristers' Immunity" (1985), 43 The Advocate 611.

9. The barristers' cases are simply one example of the ongoing debates over the scope of negligence liability that have preoccupied the Canadian, English and American courts for the last 20 years.

3. Did the Defendant's Conduct Give Rise to a Duty of Care? — The Foreseeable Risk of Injury Test

MOULE v. N.B. ELEC. POWER COMM.

(1960), 44 M.P.R. 317, 24 D.L.R. (2d) 305 (S.C.C.)

RITCHIE J.: — This is an appeal from a judgment of the Appeal Division of the Supreme Court of New Brunswick [22 D.L.R. (2d) 253], setting aside the judgment rendered at the trial of this action by Anglin J. whereby he awarded the infant appellant damages in the amount of $8,021.95 in respect of injuries sustained by him when he came in contact with live high voltage wires erected by the respondent some 33ft. 6 ins. above the ground.

. . .

At the place where this accident occurred, there was a maple tree which at ground level was some 5 ft. from the pole. This tree really consisted of two intertwined trees and at the height of 33 ft. 6 ins. its trunk was only 3 ft. 2 ins. from the wires; it was cleared of all branches on the side nearest to the wires to a height of about 40 ft. but on the side furthest from the wires there were some branches from about 25 ft. up and there was a crotch in the tree at very nearly the same level as the wires themselves.

A few feet further away from the pole and the wires was a spruce tree which had been cleared of limbs to a height of approximately 13 ft. from the ground but to which some person other than the infant appellant had attached boards which formed a species of ladder so that it was possible for a child to climb up to the lowest remaining branches above which a platform had been constructed going across to the maple tree and just above the platform on the maple tree a board and some straps had been nailed which made it possible to climb up to the lowest remaining branch on the side of that tree which was furthest away from the wires.

About noon on Sunday, September 15, 1957 the infant appellant, who at that time was 10½ years old, had climbed up the spruce tree, crossed on the platform to the maple tree and thence to the crotch of that tree, when he called out to his little friend, Joan Rogers, who came over and who herself climbed up on the platform at which time she says that the appellant "must have been standing in the curve of the tree" and "a little above the wires". The little girl says that she hollered to the boy but got no answer and then saw some smoke coming from where the boy was and she ran for his mother. She and Richard Stewart were the only children who gave evidence except for the appellant himself. They had both been living in the area for 2 or 3 months and neither of them had ever seen any boys climbing the maple tree. The appellant himself says that he had never seen anybody climb as high as he was on the day in question.

The appellant himself does not remember how he got up the tree and in fact says that all he can remember is stepping on a rotten branch. He does, however, admit on cross-examination that he recognized the wires to be dangerous and would not have touched them if he could have avoided them.

. . .

In finding that the respondent "should be held liable for the accident and its consequences" the learned trial Judge said:

> But a tree is much more of an allurement for small boys than a power line pole, and I think it fair to say that it might well be anticipated that they would nail cleats to the tree for climbing purposes. I also think it reasonably foreseeable that a child might slip or fall in his climb and come in contact with a conductor only about 3 feet from the top part of the tree. All of which is not highly probable, but likely enough that where the conductor was such a dangerous source of harm a commensurate degree of care called for removing the tree altogether.

The nature of the boy's injuries make it clear that in falling he not only came "in contact with a conductor about 3 feet from the top part of the tree" but that he did so in such a manner as to bring his body in contact with the tree and the wires at the same time. With the greatest respect for the views of the learned trial Judge, I am nonetheless of the opinion that when this circumstance is considered in conjunction with the presence of the cleats on both trees, the platform between them, the unusual height to which the boy climbed and the fact that he had the misfortune to put his weight on a rotten branch, it discloses a sequence of events which was so fortuitous as to be beyond the range of the foreseeable results which a reasonable man would anticipate as a probable consequence of the presence of the high tension wires, isolated as they were from normal human contact, in the area in question.

Having regard to the proximity of this wooded area to houses occupied by the families of military personnel, it was to be expected that children would play there, and although the respondent was not the owner or the occupier of the land and the pole had been installed by the New Brunswick Telephone Co., the wires were nonetheless a dangerous agency which had been brought into the area by the respondent and it was, therefore, under a duty to take precautions but only against any foreseeable consequence of the presence of that danger which could be said to involve a reasonable probability of causing harm.

That high voltage wires are dangerous goes without saying, and the fact that children are likely to climb trees is certainly a foreseeable circumstance and that it is one to which power companies should give heed in placing their wires so that young climbers will not come unexpectedly on a live wire concealed by the branches of a tree is shown by the case of *Buckland v. Guildford Gas Light & Coke Co.*, [1949] 1 K.B. 410. This does not mean, however, that such a company is necessarily responsible for every accidental contact with its wires by climbing children or that it is deemed to be endowed with prevision of every harmful contingency to which the curiosity, agility and daring of active children may expose them.

In placing the wires 33 ft. 6 ins. from the ground and causing the adjacent trees to be limbed as they were at the place of this accident, I am of opinion that the respondent had taken adequate precautions against such dangers inherent in the presence of the wires as could be reasonably foreseen, and I agree with the learned Judge who, in rendering the decision from which this appeal is taken, has said: "The defendant should not be held guilty of negligence for not having foreseen the possibility of the occurrence of such an unlikely event as happened in this case and provided against it by the removal of the maple tree."

. . .

In view of all the above, I would dismiss this appeal with costs if demanded.

AMOS v. N.B. ELEC. POWER COMM.

[1977] 1 S.C.R. 500, 70 D.L.R. (3d) 741 (S.C.C.)

SPENCE J.: — This is an appeal by leave from the judgment of the Appeal Division of the Supreme Court of New Brunswick pronounced on March 21, 1975. By that judgment, the Appeal Division allowed an appeal from the judgment of Leger, J., given after trial whereby he had allowed the appellants' claim and awarded damages of $36,275.45 and costs.

The infant plaintiff, on July 1, 1970, then nine years old, was visiting his uncle at Kedgwick, New Brunswick, and that afternoon was engaged in play with two other boys Gilbert Le Bourque, age 13, and Leopold Simon, age 10. The uncle's home is located on the edge of a highway and about 25 to 30 ft. therefrom. Along the edge of this highway and within the limits of the highway, the respondent had erected a row of wooden poles carrying various wires, which shall be more particularly described hereafter.

Directly in front of the uncle's house and also on the highway right-of-way, grew a poplar tree. Of course, in July, the tree was in full leaf and made a perfect screen for the series of wires which ran through it. The lowest of those wires was a telephone cable and that cable was 21 ft. above the ground. Some 40 inches farther up was one low voltage line carrying only 110 volts and then some 9 inches to a foot above that two more similar low voltage lines. Above that again, a neutral ground wire and uppermost and 48 inches higher than the neutral ground wire were wires carrying very heavy charges said to be of 7,200 volts. These last three wires were attached to the cross-bar at the top of the pole.

In their play, the three boys devised a contest to determine which one of the three could climb the tree the farthest and the fastest. The plaintiff, although only nine, appears to have been the most agile of the three and he climbed the highest on the tree. He climbed high enough in the tree so that his weight would cause the tree to sway or bend and either the trunk of the tree itself or one of the branches of the tree brushed against these high tension wires. The boy was immediately struck by severe electric shock, knocked unconscious and was actually burning in the tree. A neighbour, at what both Courts below noted was great personal risk, took a chain saw and cut the tree down, so that it fell on the road and the badly injured plaintiff was then taken first to a hospital in nearby St. Quentin and thereafter transferred to a hospital in Montreal.

No issue as to the quantum of damage arose in either the Appeal Division or in this Court, and we are simply concerned with the issue of liability.

In the first place, it may be noted that the power lines and tree were on a public highway and the question of trespass does not arise.

This Court and other Courts have, from time to time, stressed the duty of those who erect electric lines carrying heavy charges to take proper precautions against injury resulting therefrom . . .

In the present case, the learned trial Judge said [9 N.B.R. (2d) 358 at p. 361]:

> After having considered all of the evidence I have concluded that the tree in combination with the wires constituted an invitation and an allurement for small boys imbued with the natural instinct to climb as high as their strength and energy would permit; that in permitting the power lines to remain without insulation and in failing to maintain the particular tree properly trimmed in proximity to the power lines where the branches or the infant plaintiff could come in contact with them constituted a concealed danger in the nature of a trap for such small infants. The defendant ought reasonably to have foreseen the danger and they must be deemed to have had knowledge of it and ought to have taken the necessary steps to obviate it. Their failure to accomplish this constituted negligence on their part.

With respect, apart from the learned trial Judge's reference to lack of insulation, I agree with him.

Bugold, J.A., giving judgment for the Appeal Division was, in my opinion, ready to accept the law as outlined by the learned trial Judge but was of the opinion that the particular facts in the present case could not result in liability for the respondent because the respondent could not have reasonably foreseen the accident which did occur, and, again, in my opinion, felt that the matter was foreclosed by the decision of this court in *Moule v. N.B. Electric Power Com'n, supra* . . .

Let us contrast those circumstances and the conduct of the power company in that case with the circumstances of the present case and the conduct of the power company in the present appeal.

The poplar, as noted by the learned trial Judge, is a fast growing tree. The fast growing tree stood directly beneath lines running along the top of the poles and carrying up to 7,200 volts. Yet, the only evidence as to an attempt to keep the tree away from those heavily charged wires was almost casual the inspector of the power company saying it was the practice to trim such trees every four to seven years and so far as he knew the practice had been kept up in reference to this poplar tree. That such practice was indeed insufficient is illustrated by the fact that the accident occurred because it did occur when the tree swayed sufficiently to have the trunk or a branch touch the high tension wires. Those wires were at least 30 ft. above the ground and any contact with those high tension wires could have been avoided by the simple expedient of cutting off the top of the poplar tree. It was left uncut and this heavily leafed tree in mid-summer adequately concealed the presence of the wires from a boy carrying out the perfectly normal play of an active little fellow in climbing the tree.

In *Moule*, in order to get himself injured, the boy had to climb one tree and then cross from it to the maple which had been protected in the fashion I have outlined and then only came in contact with the wire when he stepped on a dead branch and fell. In this appeal, the boy, by climbing what seemed to be a normal poplar tree, caused the tree to bend so that it contacted high tension wires which it should not even have been near. As Ritchie, J., pointed out in *Moule*, that children are likely to climb trees is certainly a foreseeable circumstance. Morris J., said in *Buckland v. Guildford Gas Light & Coke Co.*, [1949] 1 K.B. 410 at p. 419:

> It required no vivid imagination on the part of anyone traversing the route of the wires to appreciate the great peril of having the wires above a tree that could be easily climbed, and whose foliage, being dense in the month of June, would obscure the wires. If anyone did climb the tree he would with every step approach a hidden peril of the direst kind. The facts of the present case show all too dramatically the nature of the peril. It was, in my judgment, easily foreseeable that someone might climb the tree and so might become in close proximity to an unseen deadly peril.

I am of the opinion that those words are particularly applicable to the present appeal.

Although the long series of circumstances which, added together, resulted in the accident in the *Moule* case, could not have been foreseen, I am of the opinion that the accident in the present case was one which could be foreseen and which was almost inevitable when given active boys and a poplar tree running up through and hiding high tension wires, especially when that tree was directly in front of their home.

For these reasons, I am of the opinion that *Moule v. N.B. Electric Power Com'n* does not apply in the present circumstances and that the respondent was liable for the damage caused to the infant plaintiff.

I would allow the appeal, set aside the judgment of the Appeal Division and restore the judgment at trial. The appellants are entitled to costs throughout.

[Ritchie J. wrote a short concurring judgment, and the remaining Justices concurred with Spence J.]

NOTES AND QUESTIONS

1. The issue of foreseeability of harm is relevant to three elements of a negligence action — duty, standard of care and remoteness of damages. Even if negligence law applies in the situation, the courts will only impose a duty of care if the defendant's conduct created a foreseeable risk of injury. Second, the probability of injury is one of four factors considered in determining whether the defendant breached the requisite standard of care. Finally, the plaintiff's losses will be held to be too remote if they are not a foreseeable result of the defendant's breach of the standard of care. The courts do not always clearly distinguish among these three foreseeability tests or explain their significance.

Identify the foreseeability of harm tests used in *Moule* and *Amos*. What was the legal significance of the courts' findings on these issues? Since the foreseeability issue arises at three different times, is there any reason for the defendant to argue it primarily at the duty stage, rather than at the standard of care or remoteness stage?

2. Do you agree that *Moule* can be distinguished from *Amos*? Specifically, what facts prompted the court to dismiss the claim in *Moule*, but award damages in *Amos*? Would the result in *Amos* have

been the same if the tree had swayed into the wires as a result of the combined effects of the child's weight and an unusually strong gust of wind?

3. In the duty of care analysis, the test for the foreseeability of injury is generally viewed as being broad in scope. It is not necessary to foresee the exact injury that occurred or the way in which it came about. Since the issue is framed as a hypothetical question — did the defendants' act create a foreseeable risk of injury? — the fact that injury resulted should not colour the resolution of the issue.

4. For additional cases discussing the foreseeability of risk test in duty, see *Munshaw Colour Service Ltd. v. Vancouver* (1962), 33 D.L.R. (2d) 719 (S.C.C.); *Gagne v. St. Regis Paper Co.* (1973), 36 D.L.R. (3d) 301 (S.C.C.); *Crocker v. Sundance Northwest Resorts Ltd.* (1988), 44 C.C.L.T. 225 (S.C.C.); *Campbell v. Calgary Power Ltd.* (1988), 62 Alta. L.R. (2d) 253 (C.A.); *Lorenz v. Winnipeg (City)*, [1994] 1 W.W.R. 558 (Man. C.A.); and *Stewart v. Pettie* (1995), 23 C.C.L.T. (2d) 89 (S.C.C.).

4.   Was the Duty of Care Owed to the Plaintiff? — The Foreseeable Plaintiff Test

PALSGRAF v. LONG ISLAND RY. CO.

(1928), 248 N.Y. 339 (N.Y. C.A.)

CARDOZO C.J.: — Plaintiff was standing on a platform of defendant's railroad after buying a ticket to go to Rockaway Beach. A train stopped at the station, bound for another place. Two men ran forward to catch it. One of the men reached the platform of the car without mishap, though the train was already moving. The other man, carrying a package, jumped aboard the car, but seemed unsteady as if about to fall. A guard on the car, who had held the door open, reached forward to help him in, and another guard on the platform pushed him from behind. In this act, the package was dislodged, and fell upon the rails. It was a package of small size, about fifteen inches long, and was covered by a newspaper. In fact it contained fireworks, but there was nothing in its appearance to give notice of its contents. The fireworks when they fell exploded. The shock of the explosion threw down some scales at the other end of the platform many feet away. The scales struck the plaintiff, causing injuries for which she sues.

The conduct of the defendant's guard, if a wrong in its relation to the holder of the package, was not a wrong in its relation to the plaintiff, standing far away. Relatively to her it was not negligence at all. Nothing in the situation gave notice that the falling package had in it the potency of peril to persons thus removed. Negligence is not actionable unless it involves the invasion of a legally protected interest, the violation of a right. "Proof of negligence in the air, so to speak, will not do."

. . .

The plaintiff, as she stood upon the platform of the station, might claim to be protected against intentional invasion of her bodily security. Such invasion is not charged. She might claim to be protected against unintentional invasion by conduct involving in the thought of reasonable men an unreasonable hazard that such invasion would ensue. These, from the point of view of the law, were the bounds of her immunity, with perhaps some rare exceptions, survivals for the most part of ancient forms of liability, where conduct is held to be at the peril of the actor.

. . .

If no hazard was apparent to the eye of ordinary vigilance, an act innocent and harmless, at least to outward seeming, with reference to her, did not take to itself the quality of a tort because it happened to be a wrong, though apparently not one involving the risk of bodily insecurity, with reference to someone else. "In every instance, before negligence can be predicated of a given act, back of the act must be sought and found a duty to the individual complaining, the observance of which would have averted or avoided the injury."

. . .

The argument for the plaintiff is built upon the shifting meanings of such words as "wrong" and "wrongful," and shares their instability. What the plaintiff must show is "a wrong" to herself; i.e., a violation of her own right, and not merely a wrong to someone else, nor conduct "wrongful" because unsocial, but not "a wrong" to any one. We are told that one who drives at reckless speed through a crowded city street is guilty of a negligent act and therefore of a wrongful one, irrespective of the consequences. Negligent the act is, and wrongful in the sense that it is unsocial, but wrongful and unsocial in relation to other travelers, only because the eye of vigilance perceives the risk of damage. If the same act were to be committed on a speedway or race course, it would lose its wrongful quality. The risk reasonably to be perceived defines the duty to be obeyed, and risk imports relation; it is risk to another or to others within the range of apprehension.

. . .

This does not mean, of course, that one who launches a destructive force is always relieved of liability, if the force, though known to be destructive, pursues an unexpected path. "It was not necessary that the defendant should have had notice of the particular method in which an accident would occur, if the possibility of an accident was clear to the ordinarily prudent eye."

. . .

Some acts, such as shooting are so imminently dangerous to any one who may come within reach of the missile however unexpectedly, as to impose a duty of prevision not far from that of an insurer. Even to-day, and much oftener in earlier stages of the law, one acts sometimes at one's peril.

. . .

The range of reasonable apprehension is at times a question for the court, and at times, if varying inferences are possible, a question for the jury. Here, by concession, there was nothing in the situation to suggest to the most cautious mind that the parcel wrapped in newspaper would spread wreckage through the station. If the guard had thrown it down knowingly and willfully, he would not have threatened the plaintiff's safety, so far as appearances could warn him. His conduct would not have involved, even then, an unreasonable probability of invasion of her bodily security. Liability can be no greater where the act is inadvertent.

Negligence, like risk, is thus a term of relation. Negligence in the abstract, apart from things related, is surely not a tort, if indeed it is understandable at all.

. . .

Negligence is not a tort unless it results in the commission of a wrong, and the commission of a wrong imports the violation of a right, in this case, we are told, the right to be protected against interference with one's bodily security. But bodily security is protected, not against all forms of interference or aggression, but only against some. One who seeks redress at law does not make out a cause of action by showing without more that there has been damage to his person. If the harm was not willful, he must show that the act as to him had possibilities of danger so many and apparent as to entitle him to be protected against the doing of it though the harm was unintended. Affront to personalty is still the keynote of the wrong.

. . .

The victim does not sue derivatively, or by right of subrogation, to vindicate an interest invaded in the person of another. Thus to view his cause of action is to ignore the fundamental difference between tort and crime. Holland, Jurisprudence (12th Ed.) p. 328. He sues for breach of a duty owing to himself.

The law of causation, remote or proximate, is thus foreign to the case before us. The question of liability is always anterior to the question of the measure of the consequences that go with liability. If there is no tort to be redressed, there is no occasion to consider what damage might be recovered if there were a finding of a tort. We may assume, without deciding, that negligence, not at large or in the abstract, but in relation to the plaintiff, would entail liability for any and all consequences, however novel or extraordinary.

. . .

The judgment of the Appellate Division and that of the Trial Term should be reversed, and the complaint dismissed, with costs in all courts.

. . .

ANDREWS J. (dissenting).: — The result we shall reach depends upon our theory as to the nature of negligence. Is it a relative concept — the breach of some duty owing to a particular person or to particular persons? Or, where there is an act which unreasonably threatens the safety of others, is the doer liable for all its proximate consequences, even where they result in injury to one who would generally be thought to be outside the radius of danger? This is not a mere dispute as to words. We might not believe that to the average mind the dropping of the bundle would seem to involve the probability of harm to the plaintiff standing many feet away whatever might be the case as to the owner or to one so near as to be likely to be struck by its fall. If, however, we adopt the second hypothesis, we have to inquire only as to the relation between cause and effect. We deal in terms of proximate cause, not of negligence.

. . .

But we are told that "there is no negligence unless there is in the particular case a legal duty to take care, and this duty must be one which is owed to the plaintiff himself and not merely to others." Salmond, Torts (6th Ed.) 24. This I think too narrow a conception. Where there is the unreasonable act, and some right that may be affected there is negligence whether damage does or does not result. That is immaterial. Should we drive down Broadway at a reckless speed, we are negligent whether we strike an approaching car or miss it by an inch. The act itself is wrongful. It is wrong not only to those who happen to be within the radius of danger, but to all who might have been there — a wrong to the public at large. Such is the language of the street. Such the language of the courts when speaking of contributory negligence. Such again and again their language in speaking of the duty of some defendant and discussing proximate cause in cases where such a discussion is wholly irrelevant on any other theory.

. . .

The proposition is this: Every one owes to the world at large the duty of refraining from those acts that may unreasonably threaten the safety of others. Such an act occurs. Not only is he wronged to whom harm might reasonably be expected to result, but he also who is in fact injured, even if he be outside what would generally be thought the danger zone. There needs be duty due the one complaining, but this is not a duty to a particular individual because as to him harm might be expected. Harm to some one being the natural result of the act, not only that one alone, but all those in fact injured may complain. We have never, I think, held otherwise. Indeed in the Di Caprio Case we said that a breach of a general ordinance defining the degree of care to be exercised in one's calling is evidence of negligence as to every one. We did not limit this statement to those who might be expected to be exposed to danger. Unreasonable risk being taken, its consequences are not confined to those who might probably be hurt.

If this be so, we do not have a plaintiff suing by "derivation or succession." Her action is original and primary. Her claim is for a breach of duty to herself — not that she is subrogated to any right of action of the owner of the parcel or of a passenger standing at the scene of the explosion.

. . .

The act upon which defendant's liability rests is knocking an apparently harmless package onto the platform. The act was negligent. For its proximate consequences the defendant is liable. If its contents were broken, to the owner; if it fell upon and crushed a passenger's foot, then to him; if it exploded and injured one in the immediate vicinity, to him also as to A in the illustration. Mrs. Palsgraf was standing some distance away. How far cannot be told from the record — apparently 25 or 30 feet, perhaps less. Except for the explosion, she would not have been injured. We are told by the appellant in his brief, "It cannot be denied that the explosion was the direct cause of the plaintiff's injuries." So it was a substantial factor in producing the result — there was here a natural and continuous sequence — direct connection. The only intervening cause was that, instead of blowing her to the ground, the concussion smashed the weighing machine which in turn fell upon her. There was no remoteness in time, little in space. And surely, given such an explosion as here, it needed no great foresight to predict that the natural result would be to injure one on the platform at no greater distance from its scene than was the plaintiff. Just how no one might be able to predict. Whether by flying fragments, by broken glass, by wreckage of machines or structures no one could say. But injury in some form was most probable.

Under these circumstances I cannot say as a matter of law that the plaintiff's injuries were not the proximate result of the negligence. That is all we have before us. The court refused to so charge. No request was made to submit the matter to the jury as a question of fact, even would that have been proper upon the record before us.

The judgment appealed from should be affirmed, with costs.

POUND, LEHMAN, and KELLOGG, JJ., concur with CARDOZO, C.J.

ANDREWS, J., dissents in opinion in which CRANE and O'BRIEN, JJ., concur.

NOTES AND QUESTIONS

1. How did the majority's analysis of duty differ from that of the dissent? What is the practical significance of this difference?

2. Since the majority dismissed the plaintiff's action at the duty stage, only the dissent dealt with the other elements of a negligence action. It should be noted that at the time *Palsgraf* was decided, the courts in both the United States and England used a directness test of remoteness. Thus, Andrews J. framed the remoteness question in terms of whether the plaintiff's losses were a direct result of the defendant's negligence. Given that directness was the test of remoteness, would Andrews J.'s approach have significantly broadened the scope of recovery? Now that foreseeability is the accepted test of remoteness, is there any practical difference between the majority and dissenting judgments?

3. *Palsgraf* generated volumes of academic comment. In an article entitled, "Palsgraf Revisited" (1953-54), 52 Mich. L. Rev. 1, Prosser lists about 20 references, stating that almost everyone who writes in the negligence field has something to say about *Palsgraf*. His own conclusions on the case were tentative.

4. Smith has provided one of the more scathing criticisms of the foreseeable plaintiff test in "The Mystery of Duty," in Klar (ed.), *Studies in Canadian Tort Law* (1977), 1 at 24:

the courts have created a doctrine of privity in the law of negligence. It is a privity of fault rather than of contract. The doctrine of privity has raised problems and difficulties in the law of contract. It is a freak, an abortion, in the law of torts. The doctrine of privity confuses questions of risk of harm with problems of remoteness, and the language of duty of care is the vehicle of this confusion.

Judges have said that there is no such thing as negligence in the abstract or in the air, and this is, of course, true. A risk of harm must be a risk to someone in order for it to be a risk of harm or negligence. It is often the case, however, that as a result of negligence persons who are not the prime subjects of the risk are harmed as well. It could be someone whose presence could not be anticipated. It might be a person who suffers a nervous shock as the result of witnessing the main or initial harm, or it might be a rescuer who is injured in trying to prevent the harm. These examples all raise questions of remoteness of damage because the legal issue is whether or not the defendant's liability extends to these persons as well as the persons who were the prime subjects of the risk, or, to rephrase the issue another way, whether the damage suffered by these persons is too remote from the original risk which is the foundation of the finding of negligence. We know that injuries to one person will often result in, or bear a causal connection to, other people. No event stands in a causal isolation. We have to place some limits, however, on just how much of this we are going to require the defendant to compensate.

Smith seems to agree with Andrews J. in viewing the foreseeable plaintiff issue as a practical problem of controlling the extent of the defendant's liability, an issue generally considered under remoteness of damages. However, Cardozo C.J. appears to have had an additional concern; namely, that there be a pre-existing relationship between the parties in order to justify a duty of care. For him, this was a theoretical concern as much as a practical one. Is Cardozo C.J.'s concern justified?

5. Despite the criticisms of Cardozo C.J.'s approach, it has been accepted by the English and Canadian courts. Therefore, the plaintiff must prove both that the defendant's conduct gave rise to a duty of care and that the duty was owed to her. This does not mean that the individual plaintiff must be foreseeable, but rather that the plaintiff must belong to a class of persons foreseeably at risk. For additional discussions of the foreseeable plaintiff test see *Hay (or Bourhill) v. Young*, [1942] 2 All E.R. 396 (H.L.); *Can. Gen. Elec. Co. v. Pickford & Black Ltd.*, [1971] S.C.R. 41; *Reese v. Coleman (No. 1)*, [1979] 4 W.W.R. 58 (Sask. C.A.); and *Tutton v. A.D. Walter Ltd.*, [1985] 3 All E.R. 757 (Q.B.D.).

6. The breadth of the foreseeable plaintiff test varies considerably with the type of interest at stake. For example, a very broad test is applied in cases of rescuers, whereas a narrow test is applied in nervous shock cases. Contrast *King v. Phillips*, [1953] 1 Q.B. 429 (C.A.), with *Urbanski v. Patel; Firman v. Patel* (1978), 84 D.L.R. (3d) 650 (Man. Q.B.). By manipulating the foreseeable plaintiff test, the courts have been able to control the ambit of recovery in negligence. See also *Bechard v. Haliburton*

Estate (1991), 10 C.C.L.T. (2d) 156 (Ont. C.A.); and *Schlink v. Blackburn* (1993), 18 C.C.L.T. (2d) 173 (B.C. C.A.).

HALEY v. LONDON ELECTRICITY BD.

[1965] A.C. 778, [1964] 3 All E.R. 185 (H.L.)

. . .

LORD REID: — My Lords, the appellant became blind many years ago as a result of an accident. He conquered his disability to such an extent that for some years before 1956 he was employed as a telephonist by the London County Council. He lived in a street in south-east London and it was his habit to walk unaccompanied from his home for about one hundred yards along the pavement and then to get someone to help him to cross the main road where he boarded a bus. With the aid of his white stick he had learned to avoid all ordinary obstacles. On the morning of Oct. 29, 1956, he had walked some fifty yards from his house. On that morning unknown to him the respondents' workmen had begun excavating a trench in the pavement, and they had placed an obstacle, which I shall describe in a moment, near the end of the trench. The appellant tripped over it and fell heavily. As a result of his head striking the pavement he has become deaf. He now sues the respondents on the grounds of negligence. The case was decided against him by the trial judge and by the Court of Appeal and he now appeals to this House.

. . .

The trial judge held that what the respondents' men did gave adequate warning to ordinary people with good sight, and I am not disposed to disagree with that. The excavation was shallow and was to be filled before nightfall, and the punner (or pick and shovel) together with the notice boards and heap of soil on the pavement beside the trench were, I think, sufficient warning to ordinary people that they should not try to pass along the pavement past the trench. I agree with SOMERVELL, L.J., in saying that a person walking along a pavement does not have "to keep his eyes on the ground to see whether or not there is any obstacle in his path" (*Almeroth v. Chivers & Sons, Ltd.*); but even allowing for that degree of inadvertence of which most people are often guilty when walking along a pavement, I think that what the respondents' men did was just sufficient to attract the attention of ordinary people with good sight exercising ordinary care.

On the other hand, if it was the duty of the respondents to have in mind the needs of blind or infirm pedestrians, I think that what they did was quite insufficient. Indeed the evidence shows that an obstacle attached to a heavy weight and only nine inches above the ground may well escape detection by a blind man's stick and is for him a trap rather than a warning. So the question for your lordships' decision is the nature and extent of the duty owed to pedestrians by persons who carry out operations on city pavement. The respondents argue that they were only bound to have in mind or to safeguard ordinary able-bodied people and were under no obligation to give particular consideration to the blind or infirm. If that is right, it means that a blind or infirm person who goes out alone goes at his peril. He may meet obstacles which are a danger to him, but not to those with good sight, because no one is under any obligation to remove or protect them; and if such an obstacle causes him injury he must suffer the damage in silence.

I could understand the respondents' contention if it was based on an argument that it was not reasonably foreseeable that a blind person might pass along that pavement on that day; or that, although foreseeable, the chance of a blind man coming there was so small and the difficulty of affording protection to him so great that it would have been in the circumstances unreasonable to afford that protection. Those are well recognized grounds of defence; but in my judgment neither is open to the respondents in this case.

In deciding what is reasonably foreseeable one must have regard to common knowledge. We are all accustomed to meeting blind people walking alone with their white sticks on city pavements. No doubt there are many places open to the public where for one reason or another one would be surprised to see a blind person walking alone, but a city pavement is not one of them; and a residential street cannot be different from any other. The blind people whom we meet must live somewhere, and most of them probably left their homes unaccompanied. It may seem surprising that blind people can avoid ordinary obstacles so well as they do, but we must take account of the facts. There is evidence in this case about the number of blind people in London and it appears from government publications that the proportion in the whole country is near one in five hundred. By no means all are sufficiently skilled or confident to venture out alone, but the number who habitually do so must be very large. I find it quite impossible to say that it is not reasonably foreseeable that a blind person may pass along a particular pavement on a particular day.

No question can arise in this case of any great difficulty in affording adequate protection for the blind. In considering what is adequate protection again one must have regard to common knowledge. One is entitled to expect of a blind person a high degree of skill and care because none but the most foolhardy would venture to go out alone without having that skill and exercising that care. We know that in fact blind people do safely avoid all ordinary obstacles on pavements; there can be no question of padding lamp posts as was suggested in one case. A moment's reflection, however, shows that a low obstacle in an unusual place is a grave danger; on the other hand it is clear from the evidence in this case and also I think from common knowledge that quite a light fence some two feet high is an adequate warning. There would have been no difficulty in providing a fence here. The evidence is that the Post Office always provide one, and that the respondents have similar fences which are often used. Indeed the evidence suggests that the only reason why there was no fence here was that the accident occurred before the necessary fences had arrived. So, if the respondents are to succeed, it can only be on the ground that there was no duty to do more than safeguard ordinary able-bodied people.

. . .

I can see no justification for laying down any hard and fast rule limiting the classes of persons for whom those interfering with a pavement must make provision. It is said that it is impossible to tell what precautions will be adequate to protect all kinds of infirm pedestrians or that taking such precautions would be unreasonably difficult or expensive. I think that such fears are exaggerated, and it is worth recollecting that when the courts sought to lay down specific rules as to the duties of occupiers the law became so unsatisfactory that Parliament had to step in and pass the Occupiers Liability Act, 1957. It appears to me that the ordinary principles of the common law must apply in streets as well as elsewhere, and that fundamentally they depend on what a reasonable man, careful of his neighbour's safety, would do having the knowledge which a reasonable man in the position of the defendant must be deemed to have. I agree with the statement of law at the end of the speech of Lord Sumner in *Glasgow Corpn. v. Taylor* —

> ... a measure of care appropriate to the inability or disability of those who are immature or feeble in mind or body is due from others who know of, or ought to anticipate, the presence of such persons within the scope and hazard of their own operations.

I would therefore allow this appeal. The assessment of damages has been deferred and the case must be remitted for such assessment.

[Lords Morton Of Henryton, Evershed, Hodson, and Guest gave concurring speeches.]

NOTES AND QUESTIONS

1. Would the court have concluded that Haley was a foreseeable plaintiff if: (a) only one in 10,000 people in the general population were blind; (b) the barrier was located on a lightly travelled sidewalk that was extremely steep and winding; or (c) this barrier was going to be used for only 20 minutes until a more suitable barrier was delivered?

2. Given that the Canadian Charter of Rights and Freedoms and both the federal and provincial human rights legislation prohibit discrimination on the basis of disability, what assumptions should be made about the foreseeability of disabled people being present in public? What are the implications of holding that a disabled person is not a foreseeable plaintiff?

3. How would you reconcile the result in *Haley* with the result in *Palsgraf*?

4. What factors did Lord Reid consider in determining whether the defendant had breached the standard of care? See also *Carroll v. Chicken Palace Ltd.*, [1955] 3 D.L.R. 681 (Ont. C.A.); and *Crawford v. Halifax* (1977), 81 D.L.R. (3d) 316 (N.S. T.D.).

SPECIAL CATEGORIES OF NEGLIGENCE: DUTIES OF AFFIRMATIVE ACTION

1. Introduction
2. The Duty to Rescue
3. The Duty to Control the Conduct of Others
4. The Duty to Perform Gratuitous Undertakings

1. Introduction

The common law has traditionally distinguished between injuries caused by misfeasance or positive acts and those caused by nonfeasance or failures to act. While liability was once imposed for misfeasance even in the absence of fault, there was no general duty to take affirmative action to benefit others. Some limited duties of affirmative action were recognized in cases where the parties were in a special relationship or the defendant had a statutory or contractual obligation to intervene. In most cases, however, the law merely required an individual to refrain from interfering with the legal interests of others. Thus, a trespasser who innocently entered his neighbour's land, believing it to be his own, was held liable. In contrast, an individual, who sat idly by and watched a young child drown or a blind man walk into a dangerous machine, was immune from liability.

As the next two chapters illustrate, the courts clung to the general principle that there was no liability in negligence for nonfeasance. Nevertheless, in the late 20th century, the scope of liability increased dramatically as the courts recognized various exceptions to this rule. The end result was a complex patchwork of specialized principles governing individual categories of cases. The general principle was preserved, but it applied to fewer and fewer cases. Increasingly, the Canadian courts have abandoned these lines of specialized cases in favour of the two-step approach in *Anns v. London Borough of Merton,* [1977] 2 All E.R. 492 (H.L.). It is not yet clear whether *Anns* will be limited to emerging issues that do not fall within the existing principles or whether it is intended to replace these principles altogether.

In this chapter, we examine the expansion of liability in three duties of affirmative action — the duty to rescue, the duty to control the conduct of others and the duty to fulfill gratuitous undertakings.

NOTES AND QUESTIONS

1. The distinction between misfeasance and nonfeasance is often difficult to draw. Bohlen suggested that the essential difference is that misfeasance involves worsening the plaintiff's position, whereas

nonfeasance involves failing to improve it. "The Moral Duty to Aid Others as a Basis of Tort Liability" (1908), 56 U. Pa. L. Rev. 217 at 220. Although Bohlen's distinction is widely cited and accepted, both courts and academics have continued to find the issue troublesome. See, for example, Weinrib, who describes Bohlen's distinction as "skeletal" and states that its incompleteness undermines its possible usefulness. "The Case for a Duty to Rescue" (1980), 90 Yale L.J. 247 at 251-58. See also Wright, "Negligent 'Acts or Omissions'" (1941), 19 Can. Bar Rev. 465; McNiece and Thornton, "Affirmative Duties in Tort" (1948), 58 Yale L.J. 1272; and Smith, *Liability in Negligence* (1984), 29-47.

2. For a review of liability for nonfeasance, see Little, "Erosion of No-Duty Negligence Rules in England, the United States, and Common Law Commonwealth Nations" (1983), 20 Hous. L. Rev. 959; and Markensinis, "Negligence, Nuisance and Affirmative Duties of Action" (1989), 105 L.Q.R. 104.

2. The Duty to Rescue

OSTERLIND v. HILL

(1928), 160 N.E. 301 (Mass. S.C.)

. . .

BRALEY J.: — This is an action of tort, brought by the plaintiff as administrator of the estate of Albert T. Osterlind to recover damages for the conscious suffering and death of his intestate. There are four counts in the original declaration and five counts in the amended declaration, to each of which the defendant demurred. The first count of the original declaration alleges that, on or about July 4, 1925, the defendant was engaged in the business of letting for hire pleasure boats and canoes to be used on Lake Quannapowitt in the town of Wakefield; that it was the duty of the defendant to have a reasonable regard for the safety of the persons to whom he let boats and canoes; that the defendant, in the early morning of July 4, 1925, in willful, wanton, or reckless disregard of the natural and probable consequences, let for hire, to the intestate and one Ryan, a frail and dangerous canoe, well knowing that the intestate and Ryan were then intoxicated, and were then manifestly unfit to go upon the lake in the canoe; that, in consequence of the defendant's willful, wanton, or reckless disregard of his duties, the intestate and Ryan went out in the canoe, which shortly afterwards was overturned and the intestate, after hanging to it for approximately one-half hour, and making loud calls for assistance, which calls the defendant heard and utterly ignored, was obliged to release his hold, and was drowned; that in consequence of the defendant's willful, wanton, or reckless conduct the intestate endured great conscious mental anguish and great conscious physical suffering from suffocation and drowning.

. . .

The declaration must set forth facts which, if proved, establish the breach of a legal duty owed by the defendant to the intestate. Sweeney v. Old Colony & Newport Railroad, 10 Allen, 368, 372, 87 Am. Dec. 644. The plaintiff relies on Black v. New York, New Haven & Hartford Railroad, 193 Mass. 448, 79 N.E. 797, 7 L.R.A. (N.S.) 148, 9 Ann. Cas. 485, as establishing such a duty on the part of the defendant. In that case the jury would have been justified in finding that the plaintiff was "so intoxicated as to be incapable of standing or walking or caring for himself in any way." There was testimony to the effect that, "when he fell, he did not seize hold of anything, his arms were at his side." The defendant's employees placed a helpless man, a man impotent to protect himself, in a dangerous position.

In the case at bar, however, it is alleged in every count of the original and amended declaration that after the canoe was overturned the intestate hung to the canoe for approximately one-half hour and made loud calls for assistance. On the facts stated in the delaration the intestate was not in a helpless condition. He was able to take steps to protect himself. The defendant violated no legal duty in renting the canoe to a man in the condition of the intestate. The allegation appearing in each count of the amended declaration that the intestate was incapacitated to enter into any valid contract states merely a legal conclusion. Hollis v. Richardson, 13 Gray, 392, 394; Lothrop Publishing Co. v. Lothrop, Lee & Shepard Co., 191 Mass. 353, 356, 77 N.E. 841, 5 L.R.A. (N.S.) 1077. The allegations, therefore, in the counts of the amended declaration to the effect that the intestate was incapable of exercising any care for his own safety is controlled by the allegations in the same counts that he hung to the side of the canoe for approximately one-half hour, calling for assistance.

In view of the absence of any duty to refrain from renting a canoe to a person in the condition of the intestate, the allegations of involuntary intoxication relating as they do to the issues of contributory negligence become immaterial. The allegations of willful, wanton or reckless conduct also add nothing to the plaintiff's case. The failure of the defendant to respond to the intestate's outcries is immaterial. No legal right of the intestate was infringed. Griswold v. Boston & Maine Railroad, 183 Mass. 434, 67 N.E. 354, Taft v. Bridgeton Worsted Co., 237 Mass. 385, 387, 388, 130 N.E. 48, and cases cited. The allegation common to both declarations that the canoe was "frail and dangerous" appears to be a general characterization of canoes. It is not alleged that the canoe was out of repair and unsafe.

It follows that the order sustaining each demurrer is affirmed.

NOTES AND QUESTIONS

1. The plaintiff's action was based on two allegations of negligence, each of which arises from a distinct duty of affirmative action. How would you characterize these duties?

2. The judge suggested that Hill would have been under a duty of care if the deceased had been helpless when he rented the canoe. Why did the fact that the deceased was helpless once the canoe overturned not give rise to a duty to rescue?

3. Would the case have been decided differently if: (a) the deceased were a young child; (b) the deceased had drowned within arm's length of the dock because Hill refused to throw him a nearby rope; or (c) Hill had canoed out to rescue the deceased but changed his mind when he arrived at the scene?

4. Assuming that a duty to rescue had been imposed on Hill, how would you define the standard of care? Should the defendant be required to take action which might involve: (a) a risk of personal injury; (b) a risk of property damage; or (c) considerable inconvenience?

5. There are several situations in which the common law now imposes a duty to rescue. The defendant has a duty to rescue if he innocently or negligently created the plaintiff's perilous situation, physically worsened the plaintiff's position, denied the plaintiff other opportunities for aid, or induced the plaintiff to rely upon him to the plaintiff's detriment. How do these situations differ from that in *Osterlind*?

6. For a general discussion of the common law duty to rescue and render aid, see The American Law Institute, *Restatement of the Law, Second, Torts*, (1965), paras. 314, 314A, 314B; Gregory, "The Good Samaritan and the Bad: The Anglo-American Law", and Waller, "Rescue and the Common Law:

England and Australia", in Ratcliffe (ed.), *The Good Samaritan and the Law* (1966), at 23 and 141 respectively; Fleming, *The Law of Torts*, 8th ed. (1992), 148-49; and Keeton *et al.*, *Prosser and Keeton on the Law of Torts*, 5th ed. (1984), 375-82.

MATTHEWS v. MACLAREN; HORSLEY v. MACLAREN

[1969] 2 O.R. 137, 4 D.L.R. (3d) 557 (Ont. H.C.)

LACOURCIERE J.: — These two actions under the *Fatal Accidents Act*, R.S.O. 1960, c. 138, were tried together, and involve the claim of the widows and children respectively of the late Roland Edgar Matthews and the late John Albert Horsley, both of whom lost their lives in a tragedy on Lake Ontario on May 7, 1966. The defendant Kenneth MacLaren was at the material time the owner and operator of an Owens, Empress 30-foot six inch cabin cruiser known as the "Ogopogo" powered by two inboard 100 h.p. engines driving two propellors or twin screws. . . .

On the day of the fatal accident, the late Roland Edgar Matthews and the late John Albert Horsley were gratuitous passengers, or invited guests, of the defendant on this boat, which left Port Credit Yacht Club at approximately 6:30 p.m. for the return voyage to Oakville. The weather at that time was starting to cool and a wind, blowing from the north-west created a light chop on Lake Ontario. The "Ogopogo" with the defendant at the helm was proceeding at a speed of 10 to 12 knots; at that time Matthews, who had looked after the bowline on leaving Port Credit, was still sitting on the port side of the foredeck: another passenger, . . . Richard J. Jones, was in the pilot's cockpit and the other four passengers, *i.e.*, Horsley, one Donald Marck, and the two ladies — Mrs. MacLaren and Mrs. Jones — were in the cabin below. Jones observed Matthews get up and proceed towards the stern along the narrow catwalk on the port side of the boat, holding on to the rail, with his back to the water, and topple over backwards at the level of the windscreen. Jones immediately hollered "Roly's overboard" and the rescue operation began.

The defendant threw the boat controls in the neutral position and on leaning back could see Matthews, floating, with head and shoulders out of the water, some 40 or 50 ft. astern to starboard: he reversed the motors and backed towards Matthews, having pinned the control wheel with his stomach and looking over his shoulder using the throttle to manoeuvre and, according to Jones, swerving a bit, until the man in the water disappeared from his view behind the transom. The defendant then shut the engines down completely to drift towards Matthews: meanwhile, Jones had gone to the stern and thrown a life ring which landed some 10 ft. in front of Matthews, and as the boat got closer Donald Marck, also at the stern, was attempting to hook Matthews with a six-foot pikepole. Matthews was still floating — arms outward with his eyes open and staring, apparently unconscious. The motors had been shut down when the stern of the boat got to within four or five feet of Matthews, who could not be hooked when the boat was blown or drifted away a distance of 10 to 20 ft. The defendant MacLaren started the engines and reversed again towards Matthews. Meanwhile, Jones had thrown a second life-jacket which had fallen on top of Matthews or under his nose.

By then some three or four minutes had elapsed since Matthews had fallen overboard and the situation was getting desperate. Horsley from the stern took off his shoes and trousers and yelling "my friend, my friend!" dived in while the boat was moving, and surfaced some 10 ft. away from Matthews. Mrs. Jones then noticed Matthews' body fall forward — face and head in the water: she then courageously jumped in, one foot away, to hold his head up but Matthews had gone under the starboard quarter and could not be helped. Jones, seeing his wife in the water ran up to the defendant and took over the controls without argument, swung the boat around and approached his wife "bow on", getting her on the starboard side. MacLaren and Marck grabbed her arms and pulled her out of the water. MacLaren reassumed the controls and shortly thereafter Horsley was picked up, but could not be resuscitated and was pronounced dead later at Port Credit.

Although the outside temperature had been warm and pleasant in the afternoon, with a temperature of approximately 65°, the water was extremely cold: the only person who survived the immersion, Jean Jones, described how she felt paralysed, as if in a vat of ice cubes. The witness Burtershaw, chief operator of the Waterworks Department of the Oakville Public Utilities, gave evidence that the recorded water temperature at the intake pipe some 2,400 ft. from shore was a constant 39° on that day, with surface temperature probably five degrees higher.

The pathologist, Dr. D. F. Brunsdon, who examined Horsley's body, ascribed the cause of death to cardiac failure resulting from either sudden shock on immersion or from prolonged immersion in cold water. In the latter case, unconsciousness would precede death. It was his opinion after conducting the autopsy that death was probably due to sudden shock as a result of immersion, in which case death would be immediate or extremely quick; the deceased had been perfectly healthy before and there was no evidence of heart or any other disease. The body of Matthews was never recovered and the cause of his death remains undetermined.

Because of the allegation made in both actions (among other items of negligence) that the defendant was operating his motor boat while his ability to do so was impaired by alcohol, I will summarize the events leading up to the tragic occurrence.

The defendant, then a 51-year-old steel salesman, had earlier in the morning one pint of beer with a sandwich at the Oakville Club, later a hamburger and one beer at the Oakville Powerboat Club with Mr. and Mrs. Jones; the outing was improvised, and a case of 24 pints of beer put on board: the defendant and each passenger had one pint of beer on the trip to Port Credit. The arrival of the "Ogopogo" at the Port Credit Club, and the docking process there was described in great detail by various witnesses because of the incident of damage to the stanchion, a vertical member of the stainless steel pulpit, on the stern of the "Stormalong" which was slightly damaged when hit by the bow of the "Ogopogo". I am satisfied that this was a mere mishap caused by the temporary failure of one engine of the "Ogopogo", which can in no way reflect on the ability of the defendant who was at the helm.

The defendant, as captain of the first boat — so he claimed — to dock at the Port Credit Yacht Club that season, arrived in jovial and exuberant mood and ordered champagne for all present. The steward of the yacht club relates that approximately forty people in the club shared four large (32 oz.) bottles of champagne. The MacLaren party was in the club between 3:30 and 6:30. The defendant admits having consumed two glasses of champagne during that period, intermingling freely with the Port Credit members, many of whom were friends. There is no evidence that the defendant had any of the other drinks being ordered and served that afternoon. After the accident, a glass of amber coloured liquid, presumably containing whisky, was found in a glass-holder near the controls of the cockpit. The defendant disclaims any knowledge of its contents and says that it must have been pressed upon him by friends upon leaving the dock of the Port Credit Yacht Club and forgotten and untouched by him.

Liability:

1. *Re Matthews' Claim*

Notwithstanding the allegations pleaded that the defendant failed to ensure the safety of his passengers and particularly of the deceased Matthews by having them wear life-preservers on board, I am satisfied that in the circumstances this does not constitute actionable negligence. The only negligence argued here relates to the defendant's condition and to his conduct following Matthews' fall into the water. The first question therefore is whether there existed a legal duty on the part of the defendant to come to the rescue of a passenger who fell overboard by reason of his own misfortune or carelessness, and without any negligence on the part of the defendant or any person for whom the defendant would be vicariously responsible. This question, strictly a determination of law for the Court and not a question of fact for the jury, was repeatedly answered in the negative in the 19th century decisions (based on the distinction between "misfeasance" and "nonfeasance") illustrated in Ontario by the 1913 decision of the Ontario Court of Appeal in *Vanvalkenburg v. Northern Navigation Co.* (1913), 30 O.L.R. 142, 19 D.L.R. 649. In that case, a seaman employed on a steamboat had fallen overboard by his own carelessness, and drowned: Mulock C.J.Ex., speaking for the Appellate Division said at p. 146 O.L.R., p. 652 D.L.R.:

> The question then arises whether the defendants were guilty of any actionable negligence in not using all reasonable means in order to rescue the drowning man. Undoubtedly such is one's moral duty, but what legal duty did the defendants owe to the deceased to rescue him, if possible, from his position of danger, brought about, not by their, but his own, negligence?

And at p. 148 O.L.R., p. 653 D.L.R.:

> His voluntary act in thus putting himself in a position of danger, from the fatal consequences of which, unfortunately, there was no escape except through the defendants' intervention, could not create a legal obligation on the defendants' part to stop the ship or adopt other means to save the deceased.

This decision was followed by an amendment to the *Canada Shipping Act*, R.S.C. 1927, c. 186, enacting [1934, c. 44, s. 519] what is now s. 526 [R.S.C. 1952, c. 29]:

> 526(1) The master or person in charge of a vessel shall, so far as he can do so without serious danger to his own vessel, her crew and passengers, if any, render assistance to every person, even if that person be a subject of a foreign state at war with her Majesty, who is found at sea and in danger of being lost, and if he fails to do so he is liable to a fine not exceeding one thousand dollars.

The section may not be applicable to or refer to the assistance to a passenger who falls overboard, but the shocking reluctance of the common law to recognize as a legal duty the moral obligation to assist a fellow human being in this predicament has been overcome in cases where a special relation exists, such as that of a carrier to a passenger in peril overboard, by thinly disguising the moral obligation as an "implied contract": See *Prosser on Torts*, 3rd ed., c. 10, p. 336 under the heading "Duty to Aid One in Peril"; *Fleming on Torts*, 2nd ed., p. 166; *Salmond on Torts*, 14th ed., p. 57.

. . .

It is still in the modern law of negligence that, there is no general duty to come to the rescue of a person who finds himself in peril from a source completely unrelated to the defendant, even where little risk or effort would be involved in assisting: thus a person on a dock can with legal impunity ignore the call for help of a drowning person, even refusing to throw a life ring. The law leaves the remedy to a person's conscience.

There is, however, in the words of Fleming, *ibid.*, at p. 148, ". . . strong support for a duty of affirmative care, including aid and rescue, incidental to certain special relations, like that of employer and employee, carrier and passenger, and occupier and his lawful visitors."

Extending the *quasi*-contractual duty of a carrier to his passenger in peril, it seems to me that the relation between the master of a pleasure boat and his invited guest should also require a legal duty to aid and rescue: Parliament reflecting the conscience of the community has seen fit to impose on the master a duty to render assistance to any stranger, including an enemy alien "found at sea and in danger of being lost" (s. 526, *Canada Shipping Act*); the common law can be no less solicitous for the safety of an invited guest and must impose upon the master the duty to attempt a rescue, when this can be done without imperilling the safety of the vessel, her crew and passengers. The common law must keep pace with the demands and expectations of a civilized community, the sense of social obligation, and brand as tortious negligence the failure to help a man overboard in accordance with the universal custom of the sea.

In any event, if the defendant, as he did here, affirmatively undertakes the rescue operation, he is by law regarded as assuming a duty to act, and will thereafter be liable for his negligence: *Prosser on Torts* (1941), pp. 194-5, puts it this way:

> But further, if the defendant attempts to aid him, and takes control of the situation, he is regarded as entering voluntarily into a relation of responsibility, and hence assuming a duty. Thereafter he will be liable for any failure to use reasonable care in dealing with him, until the emergency has ended, and particularly if he abandons him in a position of danger.

Having found a legal duty to rescue, or a voluntary assumption of duty, the next question is, what is the standard of conduct applicable in the performance of such duty? Bearing in mind that the man in the street would not have any knowledge of a sea rescue operation, the test here is: what would the reasonable boat operator do in the circumstances, attributing to such person the reasonable skill and experience required of the master of a cabin cruiser who is responsible for the safety and rescue of his passengers? [reasonable persons test]

Expert witnesses were called on behalf of the plaintiffs to assist the Court in setting out what such ordinary, prudent, reasonable boat operator would have done in the circumstances. The first was Captain Livingstone, Chairman of the Marine Department at George Brown Community College, Toronto, a qualified sea captain under a British certificate who recently acted as Education Vice-Commander to the Toronto Power Squadron, with considerable experience since 1925 on all ships including yachts of the "Ogopogo" type. The other expert was Captain John Kenneth Mumford, Communications Officer for the Toronto Harbour Commission, British Master's Certificate 1957, and the author of a boating course covering all safety aspects of operating a power cruiser, and winner of every major navigation contest on Lake Ontario. These two highly qualified seamen agree that there are no statutory regulations or guidelines covering the rescue procedure in a "man overboard" situation, and that none is mentioned in the well-known Canadian booklet "Safety Afloat". This situation, according to them, is a common emergency calling for the common sense of every prudent seaman who should be prepared to react quickly and instinctively, so to speak automatically.

The following should be the procedure followed: having ascertained on which side the man fell, the master first turns his boat towards the same side to clear the propellers and leaves the engine in neutral unless the man overboard is astern and in no danger from them. A life ring is cast, and the master then turns around to approach the man against the wind, allowing him to come on the leeward side where passengers or crewmen can grasp him and haul him in at the lowest point of the boat. The maximum time involved would be one to two minutes or slightly more. Both experts emphasized many reasons why the procedure of reversing the engines and backing should never be adopted, unless in a confined area where the boat cannot be turned around: in addition to loss of control and manoeuvrability, there is the impossibility of keeping sight of the man astern when approaching, the danger of the propellers, and complete loss of control, at the mercy of wind and wave, on shutting down the engines. In the opinion of Captain Mumford, the bearing down stern first here adopted by the defendant was the sign of an incompetent operator: the average prudent owner of a 30-foot boat according to both experts should be competent in the rescue procedure described, and if not should not undertake to operate his boat. It is the procedure taught to students, and one in fact known by the defendant and practised by him on many previous occasions.

I can only conclude that the defendant's adoption of the wrong procedure in the circumstances was negligent, being a failure to exercise the reasonable care that the ordinary, prudent, reasonable operator would have shown in effecting the "man overboard" rescue. The defendant in his evidence admitted that he made what he described as an error of judgment and did not attempt to justify the rescue procedure adopted.

Detective Sergeant John Brooks of the Town of Port Credit Police, who had ample opportunity to observe the defendant at the yacht club, and at the Police Station after the accident, formed the opinion that MacLaren's ability to drive an automobile or operate a vessel was impaired by alcohol, and he would have recommended the laying of criminal charges to the Crown Attorney. The admitted consumption by the defendant and the necessary inferences from surrounding circumstances, plus the extraordinary conduct of the defendant during the rescue attempt, force me to the conclusion that the defendant was unable to exercise proper judgment in the emergency created because of his excessive consumption of alcohol.

It is trite law that liability does not follow a finding of negligence, even where there exists a legally recognized duty, unless the defendant's conduct is the effective cause of the loss: *Cork v. Kirby MacLean, Ltd.*, [1952] 2 All E.R. 402 at p. 407.

. . .

In the present case the burden is on the plaintiff to prove by a preponderance of evidence that the defendant's negligence was the effective cause of Matthews' death. Obviously the defendant is not responsible for Matthews' fall overboard. There is no evidence in the present case that Matthews was ever alive after falling in the water: all witnesses agree that he was motionless and staring. Bearing in mind that Horsley, a younger man than Matthews, in the opinion of the pathologist probably died of shock immediately or shortly after his immersion, it is reasonable to think that Matthews, 16 years older, did not survive longer, and after he hit the water there never was a sign of life or consciousness. It was impossible in the present case to discharge this burden by a pathologist's report; in the case of a missing body, witnesses' evidence of some struggle or sign of life on the part of the deceased during rescue operations would be required. I am reluctantly forced to the conclusion that, on the balance of probabilities, it has not been shown that Matthews' life could have been saved. The defendant's negligence therefore was not the cause of Matthews' death and there can be no liability.

[Lacourcière J.'s discussion of the action arising from Horsley's death is omitted. It was ultimately resolved by the Supreme Court of Canada on different grounds than Matthews' claim. That decision is reproduced in the next chapter.]

NOTES AND QUESTIONS

1. What was the basis on which Lacourcière J. found that MacLaren was under a duty to rescue Matthews? How would you reconcile this result with the decision in *Vanvalkenburg v. Nor. Navigation Co.* (1913), 19 D.L.R. 649 (Ont. C.A.)?

2. Why did Lacourcière J. refer to the Canada Shipping Act, R.S.C. 1952, c. 29, s. 526(1)?

3. What standard of care was MacLaren required to meet in rescuing Matthews? What factual evidence did Lacourcière J. rely upon in concluding that MacLaren breached this standard?

4. Would the result have been different if the burden had been on MacLaren to prove that his negligence did not cause Matthews' death? For a critical analysis of causation in rescue cases see Benditt, "Liability for Failing to Rescue" (1982), 1 Law and Phil. 391, at 396-400.

5. What is the *ratio decidendi* of Lacourcière J.'s judgment?

6. In the *Horsley* appeal, both the majority and dissent in the Supreme Court of Canada held that *Vanvalkenburg* was no longer good law and that a special relationship giving rise to a common law duty to rescue exists between a boat captain and his gratuitous passengers. The majority held that the trial judge erred in finding that MacLaren had breached the standard of care, whereas the dissent agreed with Lacourcière J. on this issue. See *Horsley v. MacLaren* (1971), 22 D.L.R. (3d) 545 (S.C.C.). For a review of this case, see Binchy, "The Good Samaritan at the Crossroads: A Canadian Signpost" (1974), 25 N.I.L.Q. 147.

7. As illustrated by the Supreme Court's decision, the courts have greatly expanded the common law duty to rescue in recent years by recognizing new special relationships in which they will impose an affirmative duty to act. What characteristics should the courts consider in determining whether to recognize a special relationship — control, reliance, expertise, or some other factor? Should the relationship that existed between the deceased and the defendant in *Osterlind v. Hill* (1928), 160 N.E. 301 (Mass. S.C.) have been considered a special relationship? In *Mile v. Club Med Inc.* (1988), 88 D.R.S. 48,837 (Ont. S.C.), the court appeared to simply assume that the defendant resort owed the plaintiff, a guest who nearly drowned in the pool, a duty to rescue.

8. Should a physician, other health professional, or off-duty police officer or firefighter have any special duty to rescue and render aid at the scene of an accident? See Stiepel, "Good Samaritans and Hospital Emergencies" (1981), 54 Cal. L. Rev. 385; McCabe, "Police Officers' Duty to Rescue or Aid: Are They Only Good Samaritans?" (1984), 72 Cal. L. Rev. 661; and Sharpe, *The Law and Medicine in Canada*, 2nd ed. (1987), 271-89.

Should a physician have a special duty to respond to a request for urgent medical assistance from one of his regular patients? The early cases suggest not, but the courts have now recognized that health professionals cannot "abandon a patient." Under this concept, a doctor cannot discontinue care without making adequate arrangements for the patient's ongoing medical treatment. Does this principle address the issue of responding to an urgent request for assistance? See generally, *Smith v. Rae* (1919), 51 D.L.R. 323 (Ont. C.A.); and Rozovsky and Rozovsky, "Saying NO With Legal Grace", [October 1985] Canadian Doctor 60.

9. Several countries have enacted broad criminal legislation which imposes a general duty on members of the public to stop and render aid in emergency situations. See Tunc, "The Volunteer and the Good Samaritan"; Dawson, "Rewards for the Rescue of Human Life?"; and Rudzinski, "The Duty to Rescue: A Comparative Analysis"; in Ratcliffe (ed.), *The Good Samaritan and the Law* (1966), at 43, 63 and 91 respectively. See also McInnes, "The Question of a Duty to Rescue in Canadian Tort Law: An Answer from France" (1990), 13 Dalhousie L.J. 85.

In contrast, the Canadian Criminal Code contains only two narrow provisions which require an individual to stop and render aid. Section 129(b) requires an individual, unless he has a reasonable excuse, to comply with an officer's request for assistance in making an arrest or preserving the peace. Except in unusual circumstances, s. 252 requires a driver who is involved in an accident causing personal injury to stop, give his name and offer assistance. Some of the provincial highway traffic acts contain comparable provisions. See the Law Reform Commission of Canada, *Omissions, Negligence and Endangering (Working Paper 46)* (1985).

10. There are several alternative means of encouraging rescue. Legislation has been enacted in some jurisdictions to provide rescuers with partial immunity to civil suit or a statutory right to compensation. See, for example, the Emergency Medical Aid Act, R.S.A. 1980, c. E-9; The Volunteer Services Act, R.S.N.S. 1989, c. 497; and the Compensation for Victims of Crime Act, R.S.O. 1990, c. C.24, s. 5. See also Miller and Zimmerman, "The Good Samaritan Act of 1966: A Proposal", in *The Good Samaritan and the Law* (1966), 279; and McInnes, "Good Samaritan Statutes: A Summary and Analysis" (1992), 26 U.B.C. L. Rev. 239. In "Waiting for Rescue: An Essay on the Evolution and Incentive Structure of the Law of Affirmative Obligations" (1986), 72 Virg. L. Rev. 879, Levmore criticizes the existing common law principles because they do not reward those who rescue or punish those who fail to rescue.

11. Most commentators have supported the expansion of an individual's duty to rescue. See Weinrib, "The Case for a Duty to Rescue" (1980), 90 Yale L.J. 247; Lipkin, "Beyond Good Samaritans and Moral Monsters: An Individualistic Justification of the General Legal Duty to Rescue" (1983), 31 U.C.L.A. Rev. 352; Rodriguez, "I am My Brother's Keeper: A Trend Towards Imposing a General Duty Upon a Bystander to Assist a Person in Danger" (1985), 26 Boston College L. Rev. 49; and Prentice, "Expanding the Duty to Rescue" (1985), 19 Suffolk U. L. Rev. 15. However, Epstein has argued that recognition of such an affirmative duty results in an unacceptable interference with individual liberty. "A Theory of Strict Liability" (1973), 2 J. Legal Stud. 151 at 193-204. See also Denton, "The Case Against a Duty to Rescue" (1991), 4 Can. J.L. & Juris. 101.

12. Would you favour or oppose the expansion of criminal and/or civil liability for failure to rescue? What arguments would you make in support of granting rescuers: (a) some form of civil immunity; and (b) a statutory right of compensation? Do you think that the law plays a significant role in encouraging individuals to stop and render aid? Can you suggest additional means of encouraging rescue?

REVIEW PROBLEMS

1. Analyze whether a duty to rescue will be imposed in the following fact situations:

(a) Mike hired a local guide to take him fishing in a canoe. Mike hooked a large carp and stood up in an attempt to land it. The canoe began to rock and Mike, who could not swim, fell into the water.

(b) The guide was paddling while Mike fished from the bow. While daydreaming, the guide paddled into a rock, throwing Mike into the water.

(c) Mike was clinging to a floating log in the water when the guide paddled to his side and urged him to grab his hand and climb back into the canoe. Releasing his hold on the log, Mike lunged for the guide's hand, but missed and fell back into the water.

(d) Luke and John were hunting ducks from a row boat in the vicinity when they heard Mike's screams for help. They rowed close to the log and told Mike to stop yelling, because he was scaring away their game.

(e) When the guide realized that he could not rescue Mike with the canoe, he approached some other hunters for help. They agreed and rowed up to Mike as he was slowly slipping from the log. When they came within five feet of Mike, they changed their minds and rowed off in the opposite direction.

2. Would the result be different if these situations were analyzed under the duty of care principle established in *Anns v. London Borough of Merton*, [1977] 2 All E.R. 492 (H.L.)?

3. The Duty to Control the Conduct of Others

This has been one of the most rapidly expanding areas of negligence law during the last 25 years. While the rule that there is no general duty to control the conduct of another remains well entrenched, the courts have recognized a growing number of special relationships in which they will impose such a duty. The duty to control the conduct of the intoxicated, discussed in *Crocker*, is simply one of the many new "special relationship" situations.

(a) LIABILITY FOR THE INTOXICATED

CROCKER v. SUNDANCE NORTHWEST RESORTS LTD.

(1988), 44 C.C.L.T. 225 (S.C.C.)

WILSON J.: — The principal issue in this appeal is whether the ski resort had a positive duty at law to take certain steps to prevent a visibly intoxicated person from competing in the resort's dangerous "tubing" competition. The resort contends that it had no such duty but, if it did, it adequately discharged it. The appellant Crocker contends that it had such a duty and failed to discharge it.

I The Facts

The respondent, Sundance Northwest Resorts Ltd. ("Sundance") operates a ski resort. Sundance held a tubing competition in order to promote its resort. This competition involved teams of two people sliding down a mogulled portion of a steep hill in oversized inner tubes. One evening Crocker went skiing at Sundance with a friend. After their skiing they went to a bar at the resort to drink. At the bar a video of the previous year's race was shown. The video showed people being thrown from their inner tubes. Crocker and his friend did not, however, watch much of this video.

Crocker and his friend decided to enter the competition and attempt to win the $200 in prize money. They signed an entry and waiver form and paid the $15 entry fee. The trial Judge found as a fact, however, that Crocker did not read the form and did not appreciate that it was a waiver.

The race was held 2 days later. On the morning of the race Crocker and his friend drank large quantities of their own alcoholic beverages. They also bought alcoholic drinks from the bar at the resort. They were wearing bibs that identified them as "tubing" competitors when they did so.

Crocker and his friend were the winners of their first heat. During the race the two were thrown from their tube and Crocker suffered a cut above his eye. Between the first and second heats Crocker drank two large swallows of brandy offered to him by the driver of a Molson beer van and was sold two more drinks at the bar.

The owner of Sundance, Beals, saw Crocker between the first and second heats. Noting Crocker's condition Beals asked him whether he was in any condition to compete in another heat. Crocker responded that he was. Beals did nothing more to dissuade him.

At the top of the hill Crocker fell down and his inner tube slid down the hill. The competition organizers obtained a new inner tube for him and his friend. Crocker was visibly drunk and Durno, the manager of Sundance, suggested that it would be a good idea if he did not continue in the competition. But Crocker insisted on competing and Durno took no further steps to restrain him.

Crocker and his friend hit a mogul on the way down the hill. The two were flipped out of their inner tube. Crocker injured his neck in the fall and was rendered a quadriplegic. Earlier that afternoon another competitor had been hospitalized for neck injuries sustained during another heat of the race.

Crocker sued Sundance in tort. At trial Sundance was held to be liable for 75 per cent of the damages suffered by Crocker. Crocker was found contributorily negligent.

II The Courts Below

Supreme Court of Ontario: Trial Division

Fitzpatrick J. held that Sundance was under a duty to warn Crocker that there was a risk of serious injury in tube racing and that it had failed to discharge that duty: see (1983), 43 O.R. (2d) 145, 25 C.C.L.T. 201, 150 D.L.R. (3d) 478. He found also that under the principle laid down in *Jordan House Ltd. v. Menow*, [1974] S.C.R. 239, 38 D.L.R. (3d) 105 (S.C.C.), the defendant resort was under an affirmative duty to prevent the plaintiff from putting himself at risk. The defendant "ought not to have permitted the fateful heat to commence until the plaintiff had been removed from it, by calling the provincial police, if necessary."

Fitzpatrick J. rejected the argument that the plaintiff had waived his right to sue the defendant in tort. The defendant could not rely on the general exclusion of liability clause in the plaintiff's ski pass. It did not constitute a waiver because: (a) the words did not exclude liability for negligence, and (b) the injury occurred outside the operations contemplated by the contract of which those clauses formed a part. Nor did the entry and waiver form signed by the plaintiff constitute a waiver of his legal rights because the provision was not drawn to his attention, he had not read it, and he did not know of its existence. Finally, Fitzpatrick J. rejected the argument that the plaintiff voluntarily assumed the risk of the activity. While he may have assumed the physical risk, he did not assume the legal risk. The plaintiff did, however, contribute to his injuries by his own want of care in deliberately getting drunk and participating in the races.

Ontario Court of Appeal

Finlayson J.A. (Arnup J.A. concurring) overturned the trial Judge's finding that the defendant was liable: see (1985), 51 O.R. (2d) 608, 33 C.C.L.T. 73, 20 D.L.R. (4th) 552, 9 O.A.C. 286 (Ont. C.A.). He concluded that the plaintiff could not establish that the resort breached its duty to warn him of the risks involved.

Further, he held that the defendant did not bear any affirmative duty to rescue the plaintiff that extended beyond the duty to warn him of the risks involved.

Dubin J.A. in dissent would have upheld the trial Judge's diposition of the liability issue. He noted that the resort had organized this risky event in order to make a profit. It was well aware of the plaintiff's intoxicated condition and, indeed, had supplied him with alcohol. It was therefore under a duty to take preventive measures to avoid the risk of grave injury to the plaintiff. It was not enough simply to "warn" him not to continue when such a warning would obviously be of no avail because of his inebriated state.

III The Issue

People engage in dangerous sports every day.

In general, when someone is injured in a sporting accident the law does not hold anyone else responsible. The injured person must rely on private insurance and on the public health care system. The broad issue in the present appeal is whether there is something to distinguish the situation here from the run of the mill sports accident. In order to answer this question the Court must address six sub-issues. . . .

1. Duty of Care

The common law has generally distinguished between negligent conduct (misfeasance) and failure to take positive steps to protect others from harm (nonfeasance). The early common law was reluctant to recognize affirmative duties to act. Limited exceptions were carved out where the parties were in a special relationship (e.g., parent and child) or where the defendant had a statutory or contractual obligation to intervene. . . .

Canadian Courts have become increasingly willing to expand the number and kind of special relationships to which a positive duty to act attaches.

. . .

The *Jordan House* case, supra, is the leading Supreme Court authority on the imposition of a duty to take positive action to protect another. In this case the Court held that a tavern owed a duty of care to its intoxicated patron. . . .

[Laskin J. writing for the majority in *Jordan House*]

. . . considered the relationship between the hotel and Menow and concluded that there was a close enough nexus to require the imposition of a duty of care on the hotel. He stated at pp. 248-49:

"The hotel, however, was not in the position of persons in general who see an intoxicated person who appears to be unable to control his steps. It was in an invitor-invitee relationship with Menow as one of its patrons, and it was aware, through its employees, of his intoxicated condition, a condition which, on the findings of the trial judge, it fed in violation of applicable liquor licence and liquor control legislation. There was a probable risk of personal injury to Menow if he was turned out of the hotel to proceed on foot on a much-travelled highway passing in front of the hotel.

. . .

Given the relationship between Menow and the hotel, the hotel operator's knowledge of Menow's propensity to drink and his instruction to his employees not to serve him unless he was accompanied by a responsible person, the fact that Menow was served not only in breach of this instruction but as well in breach of statutory injunctions against serving a patron who was apparently in an intoxicated condition, and the fact that the hotel operator was aware that Menow was intoxicated, the proper conclusion is that the hotel came under a duty to Menow to see that he got home safely by taking him under its charge or putting him under the charge of a responsible person, or to see that he was not turned out alone until he was in a reasonably fit condition to look after himself. There was, in this case, a breach of this duty for which the hotel must respond according to the degree of fault found against it. The harm that ensued was that which was reasonably foreseeable by reason of what the hotel did (in turning Menow out) and failed to do (in not taking preventive measures)."

Thus the relationship between the hotel operator and the patron in this case was close enough to justify the imposition of a duty of care. This duty of care required the defendant to take certain positive steps to avert potential calamity.

The general approach taken in *Jordan House* has been applied in a number of cases. Car owners who have permitted or instructed impaired persons to drive their cars have been found liable ... The common thread running through these cases is that one is under a duty not to place another person in a position where it is foreseeable that that person could suffer injury. The plaintiff's inability to handle the situation in which he or she has been placed — either through youth, intoxication or other incapacity — is an element in determining how foreseeable the injury is. The issue in the present appeal is whether the relationship between Sundance and Crocker gave rise to this kind of duty.

. . .

Sundance set up an inherently dangerous competition in order to promote its resort and improve its financial future. Sundance employees were in charge of the way in which the event was to be conducted. Sundance provided liquor to Crocker during the event and knew of Crocker's inebriated and injured condition before the start of the second heat. Sundance officials were well aware that Crocker's condition heightened the chance of injury. Both Beals and Durno questioned Crocker's ability to continue. It is clearly not open to Sundance to characterize itself as a stranger to Crocker's misfortune. The nexus between Sundance and Crocker is much too close for that. Sundance must accept the responsibility as the promoter of a dangerous sport for taking all reasonable steps to prevent a visibly incapacitated person from participating.

The jurisprudence in this area seems to me to make this conclusion inevitable. When a railway company removes a drunken passenger from one of its trains it owes a duty of care to this passenger to take reasonable steps to see that the passenger does not come to harm: *Dunn v. Dominion Atlantic Railway Co.*, 60 S.C.R. 310, [1920] 2 W.W.R. 705, 28 C.R.C. 214, 52 D.L.R. 149 (S.C.C.). Likewise, when a hotel ejects a drunken patron, it owes a duty of care to the patron to take certain steps to ensure that the patron arrives home safely (*Jordan House*). It would seem a fortiori that when a ski resort establishes a competition in a highly dangerous sport and runs the competition for profit, it owes a duty of care towards visibly intoxicated participants. The risk of calamity in the latter case is even more obvious than in the two preceding cases. I would conclude, therefore, that Sundance was subject to a duty to Crocker to take all reasonable steps to prevent him from entering such a competition. The question that must now be decided is whether Sundance took sufficient steps to discharge that duty.

2. *Standard of Care*

. . .

Numerous steps were open to Sundance to dissuade Crocker from competing. It could, for instance, have disqualified him when it realized he was drunk. This would have been the easiest course to follow. Or it could have tried to prevent him from competing. It certainly did not have to supply him with a fresh tube when he fell down on the slope before the second heat and his tube rolled down to the bottom of the hill! Sundance could have attempted to bring home to Crocker the risk of serious injury in competing while drunk. None of these preventive measures imposed a serious burden on the resort. And yet Sundance did none of them. Sundance officials made mild suggestions that Crocker might not be in any condition to race but this was as far as it went. I agree with the learned trial Judge and with Dubin J.A. dissenting on the Court of Appeal that Sundance failed to meet its standard of care. . . . While it may be acceptable for a ski resort to allow or encourage sober able-bodied individuals to participate in dangerous recreational activities, it is not acceptable for the resort to open its dangerous competitions to persons who are obviously incapacitated. This is, however, what Sundance did when it allowed Crocker to compete. I conclude, therefore, that it failed to meet its standard of care in the circumstances.

3. *Causation*

Sundance strongly urged that, even if it was negligent, its negligence did not cause the injury suffered by Crocker. The argument here is that tubing is inherently dangerous and demands no skill whatsoever. It is thus no more risky to participate in this sport when inebriated than it is to participate in it when sober. Sundance submits, therefore, that Crocker's injury cannot be attributed to his drunkenness. The failure of Sundance to take reasonable steps to prevent Crocker from competing because he was drunk did not cause his injury.

This submission is completely at odds with a finding of fact made at trial.

. . .

4. *Voluntary Assumption of Risk*

The defence of voluntary assumption of risk is based on the moral supposition that no wrong is done to one who consents. By agreeing to assume the risk the plaintiff absolves the defendant of all responsibility for it. . . . Since the volenti defence is a complete bar to recovery and therefore anomalous in an age of apportionment, the Courts have tightly circumscribed its scope. It only applies in situations where the plaintiff has assumed both the physical and the legal risk involved in the activity.

. . .

In the present appeal an attempt could be made to found a volenti defence either on (a) Crocker's voluntary participation in a sport that was obviously dangerous or (b) the fact that Crocker signed a waiver form 2 days before the competition. I will examine each of these bases in turn.

The first basis can be disposed of in short order. Crocker's participation in the tubing competition could be viewed as an assumption of the physical risks involved. Even this, however, is dubious because of the fact that his mind was clouded by alcohol at the time. It is well-nigh impossible to conclude, however, that he assumed the legal risk involved. Sliding down a hill in an oversized inner tube cannot be viewed as constituting per se a waiver of Crocker's legal rights against Sundance.

The argument that Crocker voluntarily assumed the legal risk of his conduct by signing a combined entry and waiver form is not particularly convincing either. The trial Judge, having heard all the evidence, drew the following conclusion on the issue of the waiver at pp. 158-59:

> "I find that no attempt was made to draw the release provision to Mr. Crocker's attention, that he did not read it, nor in fact, did he know of its existence. Therefore, Sundance had no reasonable grounds for believing that the release truly expressed Mr. Crocker's intention. In fact, in so far as he was signing anything other than an application form, his signing was not his act."

Given this finding of fact, it is difficult to conclude that Crocker voluntarily absolved the resort of legal liability for negligent conduct in permitting him, while intoxicated, to participate in its tubing competition. I would conclude, therefore, that Crocker did not, either by word or conduct, voluntarily assume the legal risk involved in competing. The volenti defence is inapplicable in the present case.

[Wilson J. applied the same analysis to reject the waiver as a contractual defence. She accepted the trial judge's finding that Crocker should be held only 25% contributorily negligent.]

*Appeal allowed; trial judgment
restored, and new trial ordered
as to quantum of damages.*

NOTES AND QUESTIONS

1. What two distinct bases of liability did the trial judge recognize? Did Wilson J. base her duty analysis on the same issues? Would the Resort have owed Crocker a duty to control his conduct if: (a) he was equally intoxicated, but the Resort had not provided him with any alcohol; or (b) he was sober when allowed to participate in the race? What impact would these factors have on whether the standard of care had been breached?

2. Do you agree with Wilson J.'s analysis of voluntary assumption of risk and contributory negligence? What other steps could the Resort have taken to alert Crocker to the dangers? Would this have changed Wilson J.'s analysis of these issues?

3. *Jordan House*, which is referred to in *Crocker*, generated considerable criticism. See Binchy, "Comment" (1975), 53 Can. Bar Rev. 344. In particular, the author was critical of the apportionment

of fault, dismissal of the *volenti* defence and the failure to consider the *ex turpi* defence. See also Scott, "Negligence: Duty of Care..." (1974), 6 Ottawa L. Rev. 622. For more recent reviews, see Klar, "Negligence — Reactions Against Alleged Excessive Imposition of Liability — A Turning Point?" (1987), 66 Can. Bar Rev. 159; and Solomon, Usprich and Waldock, "Drink, Drive and Sue: Liability for the Intoxicated" (1993), 4 J.M.V.L. 239.

4. The common law duty to control the conduct of the intoxicated person was broadened in a series of cases. In both *Picka v. Porter* (1983), unreported (Ont. C.A.) and *Schmidt v. Sharpe* (1983), 27 C.C.L.T. 1 (Ont. H.C.), the court held the alcohol provider liable even though it did not have actual knowledge of the patron's intoxication. In *Hague v. Billings* (1989), 48 C.C.L.T. 192, the Ontario High Court stated that once the staff realized that Billings was intoxicated and intended to drive, they had a legal duty to take all reasonable steps to stop him. If they failed, they then had a legal duty to call the police. This court also stated that Billings' drinking buddies were equally liable with him for the accident because all three had agreed in advance to go drinking and driving. Affirmed (1993), 15 C.C.L.T. (2d) 264 (Ont. C.A.). But see *Pizzolon v. Pedrosa* (1988), 46 C.C.L.T. 243 (B.C. S.C.).

In *Baumeister v. Drake* (1986), 5 B.C.L.R. (2d) 382 (S.C.), the court applied the liability principles from *Jordan House* to a private social host. The claim against the defendant homeowners was dismissed but only because they had not provided any alcohol to the intoxicated driver.

5. The broadening of alcohol-related liability was reversed by *Stewart v. Pettie* (1995), 23 C.C.L.T. 89 (S.C.C.). While an alcohol provider's duty to prevent foreseeable risks of injury posed by intoxicated patrons was reaffirmed, the Supreme Court held that serving patrons past the point of intoxication did not, in itself, pose a foreseeable risk. Rather, the court held that the overservice had to be supplemented by some additional risk factor. Since the intoxicated defendant in this case was accompanied by three sober adults, the court held that it was not foreseeable that he would drive. Consequently, the defendant dinner theatre, which had served the intoxicated driver between five and seven double rum and colas, was held not to have negligently breached the standard of care. Given the convoluted analysis, the unique facts, and the fact that the case could have been resolved on the basis of causation, the decision's long-term impact is unclear. Kostal, "Liability for the Sale of Alcohol: *Stewart v. Pettie*" (1996), 75 Can. Bar Rev. 169.

6. The liquor licence legislation in Manitoba, Nova Scotia, Ontario, and the Northwest Territories creates a statutory cause of action against those who sell alcohol to a patron past the point of intoxication. Although these provisions differ in scope, they all create a narrower cause of action than that created at common law. See, for example, the Liquor Licence Act, R.S.O. 1990, c. L.19, s. 39.

7. Members of the hospitality industry and private social hosts have long been held liable under principles of occupiers' liability for alcohol-related injuries that occur on their property. See *Lehnert v. Nelson*, [1947] 4 D.L.R. 473 (B.C. S.C.); *Jacobson v. Kinsmen Club of Nanaimo* (1976), 71 D.L.R. (3d) 227 (B.C. S.C.); *Buehl v. Polar Star Enterprises Inc.* (1989), 72 O.R. (2d) 573 (H.C.); and Tyler, "Guest Who Ignored Warning Wins $2 Million for Injury", *The Toronto Star*, Feb. 1, 1994, A2.

8. The courts have also held that the owner of a vehicle has a common law duty not to permit an intoxicated person to drive. See *Hempler v. Todd* (1970), 14 D.L.R. (3d) 637 (Man. Q.B.); *Betts v. Sanderson Estate* (1988), 53 D.L.R. (4th) 674 (B.C. C.A.); and *Hall v. Hebert*, [1993] 2 S.C.R. 159. Should a common law duty of care also be imposed on an owner if he lends his car to a friend for a week, knowing that his friend has a tendency to drink and drive?

9. Given that approximately 50 per cent of all fatal car accidents involve at least one intoxicated driver, and that alcohol is a significant factor in many murders, suicides, drownings, falls, fires, and other serious crimes and accidents, would you favour creating broader common law and statutory duties for those who provide alcohol to others? See Working Group on Alcohol Statistics, National Health and Welfare, *Alcohol in Canada: A National Perspective*, 2nd ed. (1984), 32-53; and Addiction Research Foundation, *Drugs in Ontario* (1990), 8-15.

(b) OTHER DUTY TO CONTROL SITUATIONS

Generally, the law does not impose a duty to control another in the absence of some legal power or authority to control. The relationships that typically give rise to the duty include: master and servant; employer and employee; occupier and entrant; police/guards and prisoners; and coaches/instructors/supervisors and students. However, the most common duty to control situation involves parents, teachers and others who are responsible for supervising children. The courts will often discuss the duty issue only in passing. Usually, the contentious issue is whether the standard of care has been breached in the circumstances.

NOTES AND QUESTIONS

1. For a general discussion of the duty to control see Harper and Kime, "The Duty to Control the Conduct of Another" (1934), 43 Yale L.J. 886, and Fleming, *The Law of Torts*, 8th ed. (1992), 151-55.

2. A duty of care is imposed on those supervising prisoners to ensure that they do not injure themselves, each other or members of the public. See *Williams v. New Brunswick* (1985), 34 C.C.L.T. 299 (N.B. C.A.), where a prisoner set a fire that killed 21 inmates in jail; *Funk Estate v. Clapp* (1988), 54 D.L.R. (4th) 512 (B.C. C.A.), where a prisoner committed suicide; *Smith v. B.C. (A.G.)* (1988), 30 B.C.L.R. (2d) 356 (C.A.), where one prisoner was beaten by other prisoners in a drunk tank; and *Home Office v. Dorset Yacht Co.*, [1970] A.C. 1004 (H.L.), where prisoners escaped and damaged the plaintiff's property. See also *S. (J.) v. Clement* (1995), 22 O.R. (3d) 495 (Gen. Div.); and *Jerabek c. Accueil Vert-Pré d'Huberdeau* (1995), 26 C.C.L.T. (2d) 208 (C.S. Qué.).

3. Similar principles apply to those responsible for supervising institutionalized mental health patients. See *Univ. Hospital Bd. v. Lepine; Monckton v. Lepine*, [1966] S.C.R. 561; and *Jinks v. Cardwell* (1989), 39 C.P.C. (2d) 147 (Ont. H.C.), rev'd. on issue of doctor's liability (September 8, 1989), unreported (Ont. C.A.).

See also *Robson v. Ashworth* (1987), 40 C.C.L.T. 164 (Ont. C.A.); *Mustafic v. Smith* (1988), 55 Man. R. (2d) 188 (C.A.), leave to appeal ref'd. (1989), 60 Man. R. (2d) 80n (S.C.C.); *Larche v. Ontario* (1990), 75 D.L.R. (4th) 377 (Ont. C.A.), leave to appeal to S.C.C. ref'd. [1991] 1 S.C.R. xi; and *Wenden v. Trikha* (1991), 8 C.C.L.T. (2d) 138 (Alta. Q.B.), aff'd. (1993), 14 C.C.L.T. (2d) 225 (Alta. C.A.), leave to appeal ref'd. (1993), 17 C.C.L.T. (2d) 285n (S.C.C.), where health professionals were absolved of liability when non-custodial mentally ill patients were injured, or committed suicide or acts of violence against third parties. But see *Molnar v. Coates* (1991), 5 C.C.L.T. (2d) 236 (B.C. C.A.).

4. Coaches, instructors and supervisors may be sued on several grounds, including failure to control the participants and failure to provide adequate warnings, instruction and equipment. See *Schulz v. Leeside Dev. Ltd.*, [1978] 5 W.W.R. 620 (B.C. C.A.); *Michalak v. Governors of Dalhousie College and University* (1983), 133 A.P.R. 374 (N.S. C.A.); *Bain v. Calgary Board of Education* (1993), 18 C.C.L.T. (3d) 249 (Alta. Q.B.); Kelly, "Prospective Liabilities of Sports Supervisors" (1989), 63 Aust. L.J. 669; and Davis, "Sports Liability of Coaches and School Districts", [1989] FICQ 307.

5. The courts readily acknowledge that children cannot be supervised at all times or prevented from getting into mischief. Nevertheless, if parents, teachers or other supervisors are aware of a child's hazardous activities or permit a child to have unsupervised access to snowmobiles, guns and similar objects, the court will impose a rigorous standard of care.

For a discussion of the parental duty to control, see *Ingram v. Lowe* (1974), 55 D.L.R. (3d) 292 (Alta. C.A.), where a 9-year-old was allowed to have a pellet gun; *Michaud v. Dupuis* (1977), 20 N.B.R. (2d) 305 (Q.B.), where an 11-year-old had a propensity to throw rocks; *Migliore v. Gerard* (1987), 61 O.R. (2d) 438 (H.C.), where children were injured, in part because they were not required to wear seat-belts; and *LaPlante (Guardian ad litem of) v. LaPlante* (1992), 93 D.L.R. (4th) 249 (B.C. S.C.), aff'd. (1995), 125 D.L.R. (4th) 596 (B.C. C.A.), where a 16-year-old with physical and mental impairments was permitted to drive. But see *Taylor v. King*, [1993] 8 W.W.R. 92 (B.C. C.A.).

6. For a discussion of the liability of school authorities see: *Magnusson v. Bd. of Nipawin School Unit No. 61 of Sask.* (1975), 60 D.L.R. (3d) 572 (Sask. C.A.) and *Mainville v. Ottawa Board of Education* (1990), 75 O.R. (2d) 315 (Prov. Div.), which dealt with supervision on school grounds; *Myers v. Peel County Board of Education* (1981), 123 D.L.R. (3d) 1 (S.C.C.), which dealt with supervision during gymnastics; and *Lapensee v. Ottawa Day Nursery Inc.* (1986), 35 C.C.L.T. 129 (Ont. H.C.), which dealt with supervision in home care.

See also Barnes, "Tort Liability of School Boards to Pupils", in Klar (ed.), *Studies in Canadian Tort Law* (1977), 189; MacKay, *Education Law in Canada* (1984), 107-71; and Hoyano, "The Prudent Parent: The Elusive Standard of Care" (1984), 18 U.B.C. L. Rev. 1.

7. Should parents, teachers and others supervising children be held vicariously liable for the torts

committed by children under their authority? Are there any reasons for distinguishing this relationship from that of an employer/employee?

(c) THE DUTY TO PREVENT CRIME AND PROTECT OTHERS

The duty to control typically involves situations in which the defendant has direct control over, or direct supervision of, another. Related issues arise when the defendant has only indirect control or authority, such as the situation with probationers and parolees who are living in the community. In other cases, the defendant will simply have an opportunity to prevent or reduce the likelihood of a crime or accident occurring. Several different lines of cases have emerged in this rapidly expanding area of Canadian tort law. The following case illustrates the complex legal and policy issues that must be addressed in these types of cases.

JANE DOE v. METROPOLITAN TORONTO (MUNICIPALITY) COMMISSIONERS OF POLICE

(1990), 5 C.C.L.T. (2d) 77 (Ont. Div. Ct.)

MOLDAVER J. (orally): —

BRIEF SUMMARY OF CASE

On August 24, 1986, Jane Doe was confronted by an intruder. He had gained access to her second-floor apartment by forceable entry through a locked balcony door. Ms. Doe was raped. The attacker fled. The police were called immediately.

Several months later, the attacker was captured. He ultimately pleaded guilty to a number of sexual assaults. These included the attack upon Ms. Doe and assaults upon several other women who had been previously violated in a manner similar to Ms. Doe. The accused was sentenced to 20 years' imprisonment.

All of the prior attacks had occurred within a 1-year period in the vicinity of Church and Wellesley Streets, Toronto. They involved white, single women, living in second or third-floor apartments. In each case, the attacker had gained entry through a balcony door.

Ms. Doe has now started a civil action against:

(1) Kim Derry and William Cameron, the investigating officers in charge of the case;

(2) Jack Marks, Chief of the Metropolitan Toronto Police Force at that time; and

(3) the Board of Commissioners of Police for the Municipality of Metropolitan Toronto.

She seeks damages for pain and suffering, inconvenience and loss of enjoyment of life. In addition, she has incurred expenses and lost income. She suffers from serious and prolonged bouts of depression and anxiety. This has led to psychiatric counselling and therapy.

Ms. Doe has raised two causes of action against each of the defendants. The first of these is framed in tort.

[The second action involved the Charter and has been omitted.]

. . .

ISSUE ONE

Do The Pleadings Support A Legal Cause of Action Against The Defendants, Or Any Of Them, In Tort

Under what circumstances will the police owe a private law duty of care to a member of the public?

Section 57 of the *Police Act*, R.S.O. 1980, c. 381 reads as follows:

> "The members of the police forces appointed under Part II, except assistants and civilian employees, *are charged with the duty of preserving the peace, preventing robberies and other crimes and offences, including offences against the by-laws of the municipality, and apprehending offenders*, and commencing proceedings before the proper tribunal, and prosecuting and aiding in the prosecuting of offenders, and having generally all the powers and privileges and are liable to all the duties and responsibilities that belong to constables." [Emphasis added.]

This section imposes certain duties upon the police. They include (1) preserving the peace, (2) preventing crimes, and (3) apprehending offenders. The police are charged with the duty of preserving law and order within our society, including the protection of the public from those who would commit or have committed crimes.

When a crime has been committed, society is best protected by the ultimate detection and apprehension of the offender. This holds especially true when the criminal is at large and likely to commit further offences.

For the most part, the police are free to go about their task of detecting and apprehending criminals without fear of being sued by individual members of society who have been victimized. The reason for this is simple. While the police owe certain duties to the public at large, they cannot be expected to owe a private law duty of care to every member of society who might be at risk.

Foreseeability of risk alone is not sufficient to impose a private law duty of care. See *Hill v. Chief Constable of West Yorkshire*, [1988] 2 All E.R. 238 (H.L.).

To establish a private law duty of care, foreseeability of risk must co-exist with a special relationship of proximity. In the leading case of *Anns v. Merton London Borough Council*, [1978] A.C. 728, [1977] 2 W.L.R. 1024, [1977] 2 All E.R. 492 (H.L.), Lord Wilberforce defined the requirements of this special relationship as follows at p. 751 (A.C.):

> "First one has to ask whether, as between the alleged wrongdoer and the person who has suffered damage there is a sufficient relationship of proximity or neighbourhood such that, in the reasonable contemplation of the former, carelessness on his part may be likely to cause damage to the latter — in which case a prima facie duty of care arises."

This principle has been approved by the Supreme Court of Canada in *Kamloops (City) v. Nielsen*, [1984] 2 S.C.R. 2, 29 C.C.L.T. 97, [1984] 5 W.W.R. 1, 66 B.C.L.R. 273, 11 Admin. L.R. 1, 8 C.L.R. 1, 26 M.P.L.R. 81, 10 D.L.R. (4th) 641, 54 N.R. 1.

Do the pleadings support a private law duty of care by the defendants in this case?

The plaintiff alleges that the defendants knew of the existence of a serial rapist.

It was eminently foreseeable that he would strike again and cause harm to yet another victim. The allegations, therefore, support foreseeability of risk.

The plaintiff further alleges that, by the time she was raped, the defendants knew or ought to have known that she had become part of a narrow and distinct group of potential victims, sufficient to support a special relationship of proximity. According to the allegations, the defendants knew:

(1) that the rapist confined his attacks to the Church-Wellesley area of Toronto;

(2) that the victims all resided in second or third-floor apartments;

(3) that entry in each case was gained through a balcony door; and

(4) that the victims were all white, single and female.

Accepting as I must the facts as pleaded, I agree with Henry J. that they do support the requisite knowledge on the part of the police sufficient to establish a private law duty of care. The harm was foreseeable and a special relationship of proximity existed.

Do the pleadings support a breach of the private law duty of care?

The law is clear that, in certain circumstances, the police have a duty to warn citizens of foreseeable harm. See *Schacht v. R.*, [1973] 1 O.R. 221, 30 D.L.R. (3d) 641 (C.A.), aff'd (1974), (sub nom. *O'Rourke v. Schacht*) [1976] 1 S.C.R. 53, 55 D.L.R. (3d) 96, (sub nom. *Schacht v. O'Rourke*) 3 N.R. 453, and *Beutler v. Beutler* (1983), 26 C.C.L.T. 229 (Ont. H.C.). The obvious purpose of the warning is to protect the citizens.

I would add to this by saying that, in some circumstances, where foreseeable harm and a special relationship of proximity exist, the police might reasonably conclude that a warning ought not to be given. For example, it might be decided that a warning would cause general and unnecessary panic on the part of the public which could lead to greater harm.

It would, however, be improper to suggest that a legitimate decision not to warn would excuse a failure to protect. The duty of protect would still remain. It would simply have to be accomplished by other means.

In this case, the plaintiff claims, inter alia, that the duty owed to her by the defendants required (1) that she be warned of the impending danger; or (2) in the absence of such a warning, that she be adequately protected. It is alleged that the police did neither.

Instead, she claims they made a conscious decision to sacrifice her in order to apprehend the suspect. They decided to use her as "bait". They chose not to warn her due to a stereotypical belief that, because she was a woman, she and others like her would become hysterical. This would have "scared off" the attacker, making his capture more difficult.

. . .

Basis upon which the police chose not to warn

The defendants submitted that the decision not to warn was obviously one of policy. As such, it could not form the basis of a cause of action in tort so long as it was reasonably and responsibly made. Mere error in judgment, if such were the case here, would not support the claim.

This principle is well established. It has been recognized and approved by the Supreme Court of Canada. See *Kamloops (City) v. Nielsen, supra.* In that case, Madam Justice Wilson, speaking for the majority of the Court, stated that, even if a private law duty of care exists, policy decisions made by public officials will not attract liability in tort so long as they are reasonably and responsibly made. On the other hand, when it comes to the implementation of policy decisions, i.e., the operational area, public officials who owe a private law duty of care will be exposed to the same liability as others if they fail to take reasonable care in discharging their duties.

While this distinction will undoubtedly be important at trial, in my opinion it does not affect the validity of these pleadings. Whether the decision not to warn was one of policy made in the operational context or an operational decision made in the context of some broader policy, the facts pleaded support a claim in either case.

If the decision not to warn was based on policy, the plaintiff implicity alleges that it was made arbitrarily, unreasonably and irresponsibly. It stemmed from a conscious decision to use the plaintiff as "bait", combined with an unwarranted stereotypical belief that such warning would cause hysteria.

I would go further and suggest that, even if the decision not to warn was one of policy and was responsibly made, it may have carried with it an enhanced duty to provide the necessary resources and personnel to protect the plaintiff and others like her. As already indicated, the plaintiff has alleged that the defendants failed to do this.

Causation

This leaves the question of causation. How can it be proved that, if the police had discharged their private law duty of care to the plaintiff, she would not have been assaulted?

In my opinion, it is open to the plaintiff to show that had she been warned, she could have taken steps to prevent the attacker from entering her apartment. Alternatively, she could have moved; stayed with a friend or had someone stay with her. Many options would have been available to her, all of which she was denied as a result of the failure to warn.

Furthermore, the plaintiff pleads that, in the absence of warning, if the police had properly protected her, she would not have been assaulted.

Where the negligent conduct alleged is the failure to take reasonable care to guard against the very happening which was foreseeable, the claim should not be dismissed for want of causal connection. See *Funk v. Clapp* (1986), 35 B.C.L.R. (2d) 222, 68 D.L.R. (4th) 229 (C.A.).

For all of these reasons, the claim in tort against all defendants must be allowed to proceed.

. . .

CONCLUSIONS

The plaintiff is entitled to proceed with both causes of action against each of the defendants. Furthermore, the pleadings need not be amended.

I wish to make it perfectly clear that this decision merely entitles the plaintiff to continue her action. It should not be taken as an indication that the allegations or any of them against the defendants are true or that the defendants are liable to the plaintiff. These are matters for trial.

Costs of this appeal to the plaintiff (respondent).

Appeal dismissed.

NOTES AND QUESTIONS

1. The defendants in *Doe* settled with the plaintiff before the matter went to trial. Therefore, even though the Court indicated that a duty to protect or warn might arise in certain circumstances, the scope of that duty remains unresolved.

2. The court in *Doe* purported to apply the *Anns* test. Explain, in your words, the factors that the Court of Appeal considered at each step in the *Anns* test. Do you agree with the court's analysis? How would *Doe* have been resolved under the special duty of care principles that generally apply to controlling the conduct of others?

How directly must potential victims be warned? In *Doe*, would it have been sufficient for the police to hold a press conference concerning the serial rapist? Was the court's analysis of the causation issue in *Doe* compelling?

3. What are the implications of *Doe* for prison and police officials who learn that a convicted rapist, arsonist, pedophile, or bank robber will be released from prison into a community? What policy considerations do these cases pose that were not relevant to *Doe*?

4. In *Hill v. Chief Constable of West Yorkshire*, [1988] 2 All E.R. 238 (H.L.), the deceased's family sued claiming that, had the police acted reasonably, they would have been able to arrest the serial killer before he killed their daughter. The court struck out the statement of claim, stating that the police owe no duty to the victims of crime, unless the offender commits the offence while in police custody or after escaping police custody. Is the narrow scope of the police duty in *Hill* preferable to the broad duty in *Doe*?

5. Should the police be held liable if they stop but do not arrest a drunk driver who subsequently causes a car accident? See *Irwin v. Ware (Town)* (1984), 467 N.E. (2d) 1292 (Mass. S.C.); *Hooey v. Mancini*, [1988] 4 W.W.R. 149 (Man. Q.B.); and *Lafleur v. Maryniuk* (1990), 4 C.C.L.T. (2d) 78 (B.C. S.C.).

6. See generally, "Police Liability for Negligent Failure to Prevent Crime" (1981), 94 Harv. L. Rev. 820; Krause, "Municipal Liability: The Failure to Provide Adequate Police Protection . . .", [1984] Wis. L. Rev. 499; and Moroz, "*Jane Doe* and Police Liability for Failure to Apprehend: The Role of the *Anns* Public Policy Principle in Canada and England" (1995), 17 Advoc. Q. 261.

7. The courts have begun to impose affirmative duties on private citizens to prevent crime. Landlords have been held liable to their tenants for injuries caused by attackers who gained access because of inadequate security. See *Allison v. Rank City Wall Can. Ltd.* (1984), 29 C.C.L.T. 50 (Ont. H.C.); *Q. v. Minto Management Ltd.* (1985), 49 O.R. (2d) 531 (H.C.), aff'd. (1986), 57 O.R. (2d) 781 (C.A.); Merril, "Landlord Liability for Crimes Committed By Third Parties Against Tenants on the Premises" (1985), 38(2) Vand. L. Rev. 431; and Glesner, "Landlords as Cops: Tort, Nuisance and Forfeiture Standards Imposing Liability on Landlords for Crime on the Premises" (1992), 42 C.W.R.L. Rev. 679.

See also *Rendall v. Ewart* (1989), 60 D.L.R. (4th) 513 (B.C. C.A.), leave to appeal ref'd. (1990), 65 D.L.R. (4th) viii (S.C.C.); and *H. (M.) v. Bederman* (1995), 27 C.C.L.T. (2d) 152 (Ont. Gen. Div.).

8. Should drivers who leave their keys in their car be held liable if the vehicle is stolen and involved in a car accident? See *Spagnolo v. Margesson's Sports Ltd.* (1983), 41 O.R. (2d) 65 (C.A.); *Moore v. Fanning* (1987), 41 C.C.L.T. 67 (Ont. H.C.); and *Werbeniuk v. Maynard*, [1994] 7 W.W.R. 704 (Man. Q.B.).

9. The duty to protect children from physical and sexual abuse has generated a great deal of controversy and litigation. See *Lyth v. Dagg* (1988), 46 C.C.L.T. 25 (B.C. S.C.); *G. (A.) v. Supt. of Fam. & Child Services*, [1990] 1 W.W.R. 61 (B.C. C.A.); *M. (K.) v. M. (H.)* (1992), 96 D.L.R. (4th) 289 (S.C.C.); *J. (L.A.) v. J. (H.)* (1993), 13 O.R. (3d) 306 (Gen. Div.); and *T. (a minor) v. Surrey County Council*, [1994] 4 All E.R. 577 (Q.B.). See also Kearney, "Breaking the Silence: Tort Liability for Failing to Protect Children from Abuse" (1994), 42 Buff. L. Rev. 405.

10. What obligations do counsellors, therapists and health professionals have to protect their patients and those endangered by their patients? What impact should the fact that the information was obtained in confidence have on these duties?

In *Tarasoff v. Regents of the University of California*, 17 Cal. Rptr. 3d (U.S. 1976), a patient told his psychologist at the University Hospital that he intended to kill his former girlfriend when she returned from her vacation. The psychologist concluded the patient was dangerous, and contacted the campus police. The patient was picked up, briefly detained and then released. Neither the woman nor her family were warned of the potential danger. When the woman returned, the patient killed her. The family sued the psychologist for failing to warn. The court acknowledged the psychologist's arguments about the difficulty of predicting dangerousness, but indicated that this was not the issue. The psychologist was not being sued because he had negligently assessed his patient. Rather, he was being sued because he had concluded that the patient was dangerous and yet failed to warn the intended victim. The psychologist argued that there should be no duty to warn because it would necessitate breaching confidentiality. In rejecting this argument, the court emphasized that the confidentiality obligation to the patient ends when the public peril begins. Consequently, the judge rejected the psychologist's request to dismiss the family's claim and sent the case to trial. The psychologist and the University settled out of court before the trial.

The dilemma posed by *Tarasoff* is not limited to violent crime. What should a therapist do if an extremely intoxicated patient attempts to leave a treatment session with her car keys in hand? Even if the therapist is willing to breach confidence by calling the police, will this do any good? Should the therapist attempt or threaten to physically restrain the patient? What if a patient poses only a risk to herself?

11. The *Tarasoff* case has generated substantial academic interest in both the legal and treatment communities. See for example, Givelber, Bowers and Blitch, "*Tarasoff*, Myth and Reality: An Empirical Study of Private Law in Action", [1984] Wisc. L. Rev. 433; Salter, "The Duty to Warn Third Parties: A Retrospective on *Tarasoff*" (1986), 18 Rutgers L.J. 145; Egley, "Defining the *Tarasoff* Duty" (1991), 19 J. Psych & Law 19; and Lake, "Revisiting *Tarasoff*" (1994), 58 Albany L. Rev. 97.

The Canadian courts have not yet squarely addressed the *Tarasoff* issue. But see *Wenden v. Trikha* (1992), 8 C.C.L.T. (2d) 138 (Alta. Q.B.), aff'd. (1993), 14 C.C.L.T. (2d) 225 (Alta. C.A.), leave to appeal ref'd. (1993), 17 C.C.L.T. (2d) 285n (S.C.C.).

REVIEW PROBLEMS

Answer the following questions based on: (a) the special duty of care principles and (b) *Anns*.

1. John, the owner of a local variety store, sold one dollar's worth of firecrackers and three packages of matches to Billy, a 10-year-old child. Billy was severely burned while he was playing alone with the firecrackers. Would John owe Billy a common law duty of care in these circumstances? How would your analysis differ if: (a) Billy's mother had told John not to sell Billy any firecrackers; (b) Billy had told John that he was taking the firecrackers home to light with his 17-year-old brother; (c) Billy had always appeared to be a polite, well-behaved child; or (d) John had received complaints from some parents about selling their children matches, cigarettes and firecrackers?

2. Mr. Green pulled into a plaza and ran into a store, leaving the engine of the car running and the door unlocked. As he emerged a minute later, he saw a teenager pulling away in his car. He had noticed some teenagers milling about in front of the store, but had thought nothing of it. An hour later Green was contacted by the police, who informed him that the driver had lost control of the car and slammed into a bus. The driver of his car and several passengers in the bus were severely injured. Would Mr. Green owe a common law duty of care to the thief or the passengers?

3. Maureen, a drug addict who is HIV-positive, told her doctor that she had no intention of practicing safe sex or informing her partner. The doctor contacted the medical officer of health but did not inform Maureen's partner. Fourteen months later, Maureen's partner tested HIV-positive and now wants to

sue the doctor for not warning him of the risk. Did the doctor owe the partner a duty of care? Would it make a difference if: (a) the local medical officer of health had adopted a policy of not contacting sexual partners; (b) Maureen had many sexual partners; or (c) the partner was also one of the doctor's patients?

4. The Duty to Perform Gratuitous Undertakings

In keeping with the distinction between misfeasance and nonfeasance, the common law did not generally require an individual to honour a gratuitous promise. The failure to fulfil such a promise was characterized as a nonfeasance and the remedy, if any, lay in contract and not tort. However, once an individual began to act on a promise or perform a service, his action would be characterized as a misfeasance and subject to whatever tort liability principles governed that kind of conduct. In the classic case of *Thorne v. Deas* (1809), 4 Johns. 84 (N.Y.), the defendant twice assured the plaintiffs that he would obtain insurance on a boat they jointly owned. Relying on these promises, the plaintiffs did nothing further on the matter. When the boat was wrecked and the plaintiffs learned that it had not been insured, they sued the defendant in tort for their loss. In dismissing their action, the court stated that "by the common law ... one who undertakes to do an act for another without reward, is not answerable for omitting to do the act, and is only responsible when he attempts to do it, and does it amiss."

Once the defendant begins performance of a gratuitous undertaking, he may be held liable for negligently injuring the plaintiff. However, he is under no general common law duty to complete the task itself or otherwise act for the plaintiff's benefit, unless he has somehow worsened the plaintiff's original position. Thus, having begun performance, the defendant may incur liability for injuring the plaintiff as a result of lulling him into a false sense of security, denying him other opportunities for aid or putting him in a more precarious physical position. These principles have been applied to situations in which the defendant has withdrawn a gratuitous service that he has customarily provided.

Although the rule in *Thorne* has been criticized, it has rarely been rejected — no doubt in part because its impact can now be avoided in many cases. First, the courts may skirt the issue in *Thorne* by classifying the defendant's conduct as a misfeasance, rather than as a nonfeasance. Second, subsequent developments in contract and tort law have greatly expanded recovery for failure to honour gratuitous undertakings by creating specific remedies in many situations in which *Thorne* provides no redress. For example, if the parties are in a contractual relationship the courts may now invoke the concept of promissory estoppel to enforce some gratuitous promises. Furthermore, liability is imposed in tort for pure economic losses caused by fraudulent misrepresentations, negligent or innocent misrepresentations made in fiduciary relationships, and negligent misrepresentations made in the special circumstances defined in *Hedley Byrne & Co. v. Heller & Partners Ltd.*, [1964] A.C. 465 (H.L.). A defendant may also be held liable in tort for making a negligent statement which creates a foreseeable risk of physical injury. Recent changes in the common law governing the duties of builders, occupiers, manufacturers, suppliers, and public authorities have further increased the numbers and kinds of cases in which the failure to fulfill a gratuitous undertaking may give rise to tort liability. In the end result, while the principle in *Thorne* has not been directly rejected, it has been very significantly eroded by the growing number of exceptions to it.

NOTES AND QUESTIONS

1. The principles governing the performance of gratuitous promises appear to have been established in *Coggs v. Bernard* (1703), 92 E.R. 107 (Q.B.), but they were more clearly stated in *Thorne*. One of the first Canadian cases in which these issues were addressed, *Baxter & Co. v. Jones* (1903), 6 O.L.R. 360 (C.A.), cited both *Coggs* and *Thorne* as authority. Thereafter, the Canadian courts have cited *Baxter*, rather than either *Coggs* or *Thorne* in support of these principles.

2. What is the rationale for refusing to impose liability in tort for injuries resulting from a defendant's failure to fulfil a gratuitous promise?

3. It is interesting to contrast *Thorne* with the subsequent cases in which individuals have been held liable for failing to honour a gratuitous promise to obtain insurance. In *Baxter & Co. v. Jones* (1903), 6 O.L.R. 360 (C.A.) and *Menna v. Guglietti* (1969), 10 D.L.R. (3d) 132 (Ont. H.C.), the courts characterized the agent's conduct in filling out the application form and taking down information as misfeasance and imposed liability in negligence. See also *Ferland v. Keith* (1958), 15 D.L.R. (2d) 472 (Ont. C.A.) (liability for breach of an independent or collateral contract); *Northwestern Mut. Ins. Co. v. J.T. O'Bryan & Co.* (1974), 51 D.L.R. (3d) 693 (B.C. C.A.) (liability in tort for negligent misrepresentation); and *Fine's Flowers Ltd. v. Gen. Accident Assur. Co. of Can.* (1977), 81 D.L.R. (3d) 139 (Ont. C.A.) (liability for breach of contract, and liability in tort for negligent misrepresentation and breach of a fiduciary duty). But see *Mason v. Morrow's Moving & Storage Ltd.* (1978), 5 C.C.L.T. 59 (B.C. C.A.); *Maxey v. Can. Perm. Trust Co.*, [1984] 2 W.W.R. 469 (Man. C.A.); and *Fletcher v. Man. Public Insurance Co.* (1989), 58 D.L.R. (4th) 23 (Ont. C.A.).

4. The rule in *Thorne* also conflicts with a growing body of case law in which defendants have been held liable for economic losses resulting from the negligent performance of, or failure to perform, a gratuitous business or professional service. What makes these cases unique is that a duty is imposed even though there is no contractual relationship between the parties and the defendant made no representation to the plaintiff. A typical case of this kind involves a beneficiary who loses his inheritance, due to the negligence of the deceased's lawyer in drafting the will.

5. The American Law Institute has identified a number of situations in which it favours imposing tort liability for the negligent performance of a gratuitous undertaking. However, the Institute has not expressed an opinion on the more troubling issue of whether the defendant's mere failure to honour a gratuitous promise, in the absence of actual performance of some kind, should be actionable. *Restatement of the Law, Second, Torts* (1965), para. 323, comment on caveat:

> There is no essential reason why the breach of a promise which has induced reliance and so caused harm should not be actionable in tort. This is true particularly where the harm is physical harm, to the person, land, or chattels of the plaintiff. The technicalities to which the courts have resorted in finding some commencement of performance indicate a development of the law toward such liability. In the absence of sufficient decisions, however, the question is left open.

SMITH v. RAE

(1919), 46 O.L.R. 518, 51 D.L.R. 323 (Ont. C.A.)

MIDDLETON J.A.: — The action was brought by a married woman against a practising physician and surgeon residing in the city of Toronto. The plaintiff, expecting confinement, called, with her husband, upon the defendant, who undertook and agreed to attend her.

Upon the facts there can be no doubt that the contract was made with the plaintiff's husband. The confinement, which was expected to take place about the middle of November, did not take place until the 2nd December, 1918. The defendant did not attend the plaintiff, and the child died during delivery. The action is against the defendant for his alleged breach of duty in failing to attend at the time of the confinement.

[The court held that the appellant doctor had not been negligent in failing to attend the birth, given the information that he had received and his other responsibilities.]

Quite apart from this, there is, I think, a serious difficulty in the plaintiff's way. The contract was with the husband. The action is by the wife. She cannot sue on the contract, and her claim must, therefore, be based upon tort. Had there been actual misfeasance in anything done to the plaintiff, she could undoubtedly recover for the tort, but where the action is for damages for failure to attend, then it must be based on a breach of a contract to attend.

ZELENKO v. GIMBEL BROS., INC.

(1936), 287 N.Y.S. 134 (S.C.)

LAUER JUSTICE.: — The general proposition of the law is that if a defendant owes a plaintiff no duty, then refusal to act is not negligence. Palsgraf v. Long Island R. Co., 248 N.Y. 339, 162 N.E. 99, 59 A.L.R. 1253. But there are many ways that a defendant's duty to act may arise. Plaintiff's intestate was taken ill in defendant's store. We will assume the defendant owed her no duty at all; the defendant could have let her be and die. [But if a defendant undertakes a task, even if under no duty to undertake it, the defendant must not omit to do what an ordinary man would do in performing the task.]

Here the defendant undertook to render medical aid to the plaintiff's intestate. Plaintiff says that defendant kept his intestate for six hours in an infirmary without any medical care. If the defendant had left plaintiff's intestate alone, beyond doubt some bystander, who would be influenced more by charity than by legalistic duty, would have summoned an ambulance. Defendant segregated this plaintiff's intestate where such aid could not be given and then left her alone.

The plaintiff is wrong in thinking that the duty of a common carrier of passengers is the same as the duty of this defendant. The common carrier assumes its duty by its contract of carriage. This defendant assumed its duty by meddling in matters with which legalistically it had no concern. The plaintiff is right in arguing that when the duty arose, the same type of neglect is actionable in both cases. See Middleton v. Whitridge, 213 N.Y. 499, 108 N.E. 192, Ann. Cas. 1916C, 856.

The motion is denied.

[Affirmed without reasons (1936), 287 N.Y.S. 136 (C.A.).]

SOULSBY v. TORONTO

(1907), 15 O.L.R. 13 (Ont. H.C.)

BRITTON J.: — On the 30th October, 1906, the plaintiff was employed as the driver of a baker's delivery wagon, and was delivering bread to customers in the western part of the city. On that day the plaintiff entered High Park, and drove along the road through the park, which leads out of the park, across the tracks of the Grand Trunk Railway and to the Lake Shore road. Within the park and near the railway crossing, the city has erected gates, and during the season when the park is most frequented, the city keeps a watchman at the gate nearest the crossing, keeping it open for users of the road when there is no danger from passing trains, and closing it when trains are approaching this crossing. The statement of claim alleges that the plaintiff on the day mentioned was approaching the crossing along the road in High Park, intending to proceed to the Lake Shore road. When he arrived at the crossing, he found the gate open, and, relying upon that fact as notice to him that no train was approaching, he proceeded to cross the tracks, and while so crossing was struck by a train and seriously injured.

At the close of the evidence, counsel for the defendants asked that the action be dismissed, on the grounds that no actionable negligence had been shewn, and that the plaintiff was guilty of contributory negligence. It was then agreed that the only thing to be left to the jury was the assessment of damages, and that I should dispose of all other questions, subject to the rights of parties to appeal . . .

The case of *Stapley v. London, Brighton, and South Coast R.W. Co.* (1865), L.R. 1 Ex. 21, was relied upon by the plaintiff. That case is clearly distinguishable. "At the time of the accident, *contrary to the provisions*, by *statute* and by the *defendants' rules*, for the safety of carriage-traffic, the gates on one side of the line were partially open, and there was no gatekeeper." It was held that there was evidence of negligence, inasmuch as by neglecting the required precautions "the defendants might be considered to have intimated that their line might safely be traversed by foot passengers."

It was argued that even if the defendants were not compelled to establish the gate and employ the watchman, having undertaken it, the plaintiff was entitled to rely upon its continuance, at least until notice, actual or constructive, to the contrary.

Skelton v. London and North Western R.W. Co. (1867), L.R. 2 C.P. 631, is against the plaintiff's contention. In that case a railway, consisting of several lines, crossed a public footpath on a level, at a point near a station. On each side of the railway was a gate, as required by statute. The railway company, by way of extra precaution, usually, but not invariably, fastened the gates when a train was approaching. S., wishing to cross the railway, found the gate unfastened, and a coal train standing immediately in front of it. He waited until the coal train had moved off, and then, without looking up or down the line, commenced crossing the railway, and was killed by a passing train. If he had looked up the line, he would have seen the train in time to stop and avoid the accident. It was held that S. contributed to the accident by his negligence, and could not recover. And it was also held by Willes, J., "that the mere failure to perform a self-imposed duty is not actionable negligence; that the omission to fasten the gate did not amount to an invitation to S. to come on the line; and that, therefore, even if S. was not guilty of contributory negligence, the company were not liable."

Here the plaintiff found the gate open, but did not see the watchman. That in itself should have suggested to the plaintiff the possibility at least that the gate was open, not as an intimation that there was no danger, but that the watchman had been withdrawn — that there was no watchman in fact. No inquiry was made. The plaintiff thought the watchman was in his cabin — if so, he was not attending to the gate. The plaintiff knew of the railway, that this road led across it, and he knew of the ordinary danger at any railway crossing, and had these all in mind, so there was nothing to relieve the plaintiff of the duty of taking care and using caution when the crossing was reached, unless that care and caution were unnecessary by the fact of the gate being open.

The plaintiff relied upon *Baxter v. Jones* (1903), 6 O.L.R. 360, and upon cases cited in Anson on Contracts, 10th ed., p. 98. One case is where a person undertook gratuitously to effect insurance upon another person's house, and, having failed to do so, was held liable. These cases, which are cases of mandate, and nothing of the kind exists here, are said to rest upon this broad ground, as stated by Willes, J., in the *Skelton* case, that if a person undertake to perform a voluntary act, he is liable if he performs it improperly, but not if he neglects to perform it. The charge here is that a watchman employed did not do his duty properly. He was not at the gate at all. He was, as to the plaintiff and the public, when this accident happened, the same as during the night time — or during the rest of the year after October — when withdrawn from the gate.

I do not think the defendants are liable for merely leaving the gate open, as there is not, in my opinion, any duty to keep the gate closed at the time of approaching or passing trains.

NOTES AND QUESTIONS

1. What was the basis upon which the judge resolved the duty issue in *Smith*? Did the doctor deny the plaintiff an opportunity to obtain another doctor by agreeing to attend the birth? Assuming that he had, would this have given rise to a duty to fulfill his promise to attend? See also *Hurley v. Eddingfield* (1901), 59 N.E. 1058 (Ind. S.C.). How would the courts resolve this issue now?

2. What was the basis upon which the judge resolved the duty issue in *Zelenko*? If the store's employees had attended to the plaintiff without moving him, but after a few minutes discontinued their efforts, would they have been liable in negligence? Can you reconcile the decision in *Smith* with that in *Zelenko*? Is the decision in *Zelenko* compatible with the principles in *Thorne*? See *Dudley v. Victor Lynn Lines Inc.* (1958), 138 A. (2d) 53 (N.J. C.A.); and *Barnett v. Chelsea & Kensington Hosp. Mgmt. Committee*, [1969] 1 Q.B. 428.

3. What was the basis of the plaintiff's argument in *Soulsby*? Is Britton J. suggesting that an individual can never be held liable for discontinuing a gratuitous service? Do you think that the case would have been decided the same way if the watchman had been present and knew of the train's imminent arrival, but chose not to lower the gate or otherwise warn the plaintiff? Can you distinguish *Soulsby* from *Zelenko*?

4. In *Mercer v. South Eastern & Chatham Ry. Co.'s Managing Committee*, [1922] 2 K.B. 549, the court held that the defendant's regular practice of closing the gate when a train approached constituted a tacit invitation to cross the tracks when the gate was up. The defendant was held liable for the injuries sustained by the plaintiff when he acted upon this invitation and was struck by a train. Can you reconcile *Soulsby* and *Mercer*? See also *Erie Ry. Co. v. Stewart* (1930), 40 F. (2d) 855 (Sixth Cir. C.A.).

5. What must an individual do to notify the public that he is withdrawing a gratuitous service? Would it be sufficient for a railroad company to post a sign at the crossing a month before it withdraws its gatekeeper? In such a case, would the company owe a duty of care to an illiterate pedestrian who still expected a gatekeeper to be present at the crossing to warn him? Would the company have to post a notice prior to changing a gatekeeper's hours? Do the same principles apply to a municipality that wishes to withdraw a lifeguard from a public beach, a supervisor from a playground or a crossing guard from a school crossing? See generally *Wilmington Gen. Hosp. v. Manlove* (1961), 174 A (2d) 135 (Delaware S.C.); *Hendricks v. R.*, [1970] S.C.R. 237; *R. v. Nord-Deutsche Versicherungs-Gesellschaft*, [1971] S.C.R. 849; and *County of Parkland No. 31 v. Stetar; County of Parkland No. 31 v. Woodrow*, [1975] 2 S.C.R. 884.

6. An insurance company, which has in the past sent renewal reminders to its clients prior to the expiry of their policies, may be under a duty of care in tort to continue this practice until it notifies

the policyholders of its contrary intentions. See *Morash v. Lockhart & Ritchie Ltd.* (1978), 48 A.P.R. 180 (N.B. C.A.); and *Grove Services Ltd. v. Lenhart Agencies Ltd.* (1979), 10 C.C.L.T. 101 (B.C. S.C.).

7. The Criminal Code, s. 217, imposes a criminal law duty on an individual who "undertakes to do an act" to complete it, if an omission to do so is or may be dangerous to life. Although the section's origins can be traced to Canada's first Criminal Code in 1892, these provisions have generated little comment. Nevertheless, it is interesting to note that one's criminal liability for discontinuing a gratuitous undertaking appears to be far broader than one's civil liability.

8. There have not been any recent reviews of this area of the law. See Seavey, "Reliance Upon Gratuitous Promises or Other Conduct" (1950-51), 64 Harv. L. Rev. 913; and Gregory, "Gratuitous Undertakings and the Duty of Care" (1951-52), 1 De Paul L. Rev. 30.

REVIEW PROBLEMS

1. Bill had told John that he would give him a lift to the university to write the L.S.A.T. On the morning of the examination, Bill drove halfway to John's house before he realized that he had left his identification card at home. In his rush and nervousness, Bill forgot about his promise to John. As a result, John missed the last sitting of the L.S.A.T. for the next academic year. Discuss whether Bill owed John a duty of care to perform his promise. See *Universite Laval v. Carriere* (1987), 38 D.L.R. (4th) 503 (Que. C.A.).

2. The Vista Credit Card Company had widely advertised that it would provide $100,000 flight insurance free of charge to any cardholder who purchased an airline ticket with the card. The plan was quietly dropped six months after it was initated, because Vista's market researchers indicated that the free insurance offer was having little impact on sales. Under what circumstances, if any, would Vista owe a duty of care to notify a cardholder that it was withdrawing this service?

3. The Marvel Bleach Company marketed its highly toxic household bleach in a childproof jug for 10 years. In an attempt to reduce costs, the Company planned to replace the expensive child-proof top with an identical looking, but easy-to-open spout. Since it had never advertised that the jug was childproof, the Company decided to switch tops without advertising this change. You have been asked to advise the Marvel Company on the potential tort consequences, if any, of this decision.

SPECIAL DUTIES OF CARE
(collection of unrelated issues)

1. Introduction
2. The Duty of Care Owed to Rescuers
3. Duties Owed to the Unborn
4. Nervous Shock (psychiatric harm) looked @ already
5. A Health Professional's Duty to Inform - looked @ already
6. A Manufacturer's and Supplier's Duty to Warn (of inherent risk of product) - will look @ later

1. Introduction

Unlike the duties of affirmative action, each of the special duties in this chapter evolved independently based on separate rationales, and each is governed by distinct principles. In the first part of the chapter, we examine some of the special duties relating to particular classes of plaintiffs including rescuers, the unborn, and those who have suffered nervous shock. In the second part, we discuss two of the special duties of care that arise from a defendant's professional or business relationships — namely, a health professional's duty to inform patients of the risk of treatment or care, and a manufacturer's or supplier's duty to warn customers of risks inherent in the use of its products. It should be noted that the special duties relating to negligent misrepresentation, pure economic loss, the liability of public authorities, and occupiers' liability will be examined in later chapters, following consideration of the other elements of a negligence action. Each of these subjects raises complex issues which warrant more detailed analysis than can be provided in this chapter.

2. The Duty of Care Owed to Rescuers

❧ HORSLEY v. MACLAREN

[1972] S.C.R. 441, 22 D.L.R. (3d) 545 (S.C.C.)

RITCHIE J.: — I have had the opportunity of reading the reasons for judgment of my brother Laskin and I agree with him that the case of *Vanvalkenburg v. Northern Navigation Co.* (1913), 19 D.L.R. 649, 30 O.L.R. 142, should no longer be considered as good law and that a duty rested upon the respondent MacLaren in his capacity as a host and as the owner and operator of the "Ogopogo", to do the best he could to effect the rescue of one of his guests who had accidentally fallen overboard.

The learned trial Judge recognized the existence of such a duty, but Schroeder, J.A., made no finding in this regard since he found that the duty owed by MacLaren in the present case was born of his having already embarked on the rescue of Matthews and being therefore bound to carry it through without negligence. I agree with the learned trial Judge and Laskin, J., that the duty was a pre-existing one arising out of Matthews' position as a guest and passenger.

Whatever the origins of this duty may be, the finding of the learned trial Judge that no breach of such duty either caused or contributed to the death of Matthews has not been questioned.

The duty, if any, owing to the late Mr. Horsley stands on an entirely different footing. If, upon Matthews falling overboard, Horsley had immediately dived to his rescue and lost his life, as he ultimately did upon contact with the icy water, then I can see no conceivable basis on which the respondent could have been held responsible for his death.

There is, however, no suggestion that there was any negligence in the rescue of Horsley and if the respondent is to be held liable to the appellants, such liability must in my view stem from a finding that the situation of peril brought about by Matthews falling into the water was thereafter, within the next three or four minutes, so aggravated by the negligence of MacLaren in attempting his rescue as to induce Horsley to risk his life by diving in after him.

I think that the best description of the circumstances giving rise to the liability to a second rescuer such as Horsley is contained in the reasons for judgment of Lord Denning, M.R., in *Videan v. British Transport Commission*, [1963] 2 Q.B. 650, where he said, at p. 669:

> It seems to me that, if a person *by his fault* creates a situation of peril, he must answer for it to any person who attempts to rescue the person who is in danger. He owes a duty to such a person above all others. The rescuer may act instinctively out of humanity or deliberately out of courage. But whichever it is, so long as it is not wanton interference, if the rescuer is killed or injured in the attempt, he can recover damages *from the one whose fault has been the cause of it.*

The italics are my own.

In the present case a situation of peril was created when Matthews fell overboard, but it was not created by any fault on the part of MacLaren, and before MacLaren can be found to have been in any way responsible for Horsley's death, it must be found that there was such negligence in his method of rescue as to place Matthews in an apparent position of increased danger subsequent to and distinct from the danger to which he had been initially exposed by his accidental fall. In other words, any duty owing to Horsley must stem from the fact that a new situation of peril was created by MacLaren's negligence which induced Horsley to act as he did . . .

In assessing MacLaren's conduct in attempting to rescue Matthews, I think it should be recognized that he was not under a duty to do more than take all reasonable steps which would have been likely to effect the rescue of a man who was alive and could take some action to assist himself . . .

Reconstructing the events from the evidence of those who were actually at the scene, it appears to me that MacLaren was first alerted to Matthews' fall when the body was only about a boat-length and a half behind him. He put the engines momentarily in neutral and as soon as he saw the body he reversed, almost immediately after which Jones threw a life-ring within 10 ft. of the man in the water . . .

Just before the gust of wind carried the boat to port, Marck had the pike pole within Matthews' reach if he had been able to grab it . . .

I am satisfied that Matthews' body had been in the water for a little less than two minutes when Marck first had the pike pole within his grasp and a life-jacket thrown by Jones was within six inches of him.

The finding of the learned trial Judge that MacLaren was negligent in the rescue of Matthews is really twofold. On the one hand he finds that there was a failure to comply with the "man overboard" rescue procedure recommended by two experts called for the plaintiff, and on the other hand he concludes that MacLaren "was unable to exercise proper judgment in the emergency created because of his excessive consumption of alcohol." In the course of his reasons for judgment in the Court of Appeal, Mr. Justice Schroeder expressly found that there was nothing in the evidence to support the view that MacLaren was incapable of proper management and control owing to the consumption of liquor, the question was not seriously argued in this Court, and like my brother Laskin, I do not think there is any ground for saying that intoxicants had anything to do with the fatal occurrences . . .

The procedure recommended by the experts in such circumstances was to bring the boat bow on towards the body and the witness Mumford, who had written a "boating course" for the Canadian Boating Federation and had considerable experience in small boats, testified that "it would take about two minutes to turn the boat around and come back on him and have him along side, and possibly another twenty-five, thirty seconds to get him on the boat". The other expert, Livingstone, took the view that by using the bow-on procedure it would take a maximum of two minutes to effect the rescue . . .

As I have indicated, the evidence discloses that the boat was first brought to a stop in a maximum of two minutes after the body was sighted and at that time there was not only a life-jacket but a pike pole within Matthews' grasp had he been conscious.

In the present case, however, although the procedure followed by MacLaren was not the most highly recommended one, I do not think that the evidence justifies the finding that any fault of his induced Horsley to risk his life by diving as he did. In this regard I adopt the conclusion reached by Mr. Justice Schroeder in the penultimate paragraph of his reasons for judgment where he says [at p. 287]:

> . . . if the appellant erred in backing instead of turning the cruiser and proceeding towards Matthews "bow on", the error was one of judgment and not negligence, and in the existing circumstances of emergency ought fairly to be excused.

I think it should be made clear that, in my opinion, the duty to rescue a man who has fallen accidentally overboard is a common law duty, the existence of which is in no way dependent upon the provisions of s. 526(1) of the *Canada Shipping Act*, R.S.C. 1952, c. 29 [now s. 516(1), R.S.C. 1970, c. S-9].

I should also say that, unlike Jessup, J.A., the failure of Horsley to heed Mac-Laren's warning to remain in the cockpit or cabin plays no part in my reasoning.

For all these reasons I would dismiss this appeal with costs.

LASKIN J. (dissenting): — ... In this Court, counsel for the appellants relied on three alternative bases of liability. There was, first, the submission that in going to the aid of Matthews, as he did, MacLaren came under a duty to carry out the rescue with due care in the circumstances, and his failure to employ standard rescue procedures foreseeably brought Horsley into the picture with the ensuing fatal result. The second basis of liability was doubly found as resting (a) on the common law duty of care of a private carrier to his passengers, involving a duty to come to the aid of a passenger who has accidentally fallen overboard, or (b) on a statutory duty under s. 526(1) of the *Canada Shipping Act*, R.S.C. 1952, c. 29 [now s. 516(1), R.S.C. 1970, c. S-9], to come to the aid of a passenger who has fallen overboard. There was failure, so the allegation was, to act reasonably in carrying out these duties or either of them, with the foreseeable consequence of Horsley's encounter of danger. The third contention was the broadest, to the effect that where a situation of peril, albeit not brought about originally by the defendant's negligence, arises by reason of the defendant's attempt at rescue, he is liable to a second rescuer for ensuing damage on the ground that the latter's intervention is reasonably foreseeable.

None of the bases of liability advanced by the appellants is strictly within the original principle on which the "rescue" cases were founded. That was the recognition of a duty by a negligent defendant to a rescuer coming to the aid of the person imperilled by the defendant's negligence. The evolution of the law on this subject, originating in the moral approbation of assistance to a person in peril, involved a break with the "mind your own business" philosophy. Legal protection is now afforded to one who risks injury to himself in going to the rescue of another who has been foreseeably exposed to danger by the unreasonable conduct of a third person. The latter is now subject to liability at the suit of the rescuer as well as at the suit of the imperilled person, provided, in the case of the rescuer, that his intervention was not so utterly foolhardy as to be outside of any accountable risk and thus beyond even contributory negligence.

Moreover, the liability to the rescuer, although founded on the concept of duty, is now seen as stemming from an independent and not a derivative duty of the negligent person. As *Fleming on Torts*, 3rd ed. (1965), has put it (at p. 166), the cause of action of the rescuer in arising out of the defendant's negligence, is based "not in its tendency to imperil the person rescued, but in its tendency to induce the rescuer to encounter the danger. Thus viewed, the duty to the rescuer is clearly independent...". This explanation of principle was put forward as early as 1924 by Professor Bohlen (see his *Studies in the Law of Torts*, at p. 569) in recognition of the difficulty of straining the notion of foreseeability to embrace a rescuer of a person imperilled by another's negligence. Under this explanation of the basis of liability, it is immaterial that the imperilled person does not in fact suffer any injury or that, as it turns out, the negligent person was under no liability to him either because the injury was not caused by the negligence or the damage was outside the foreseeable risk of harm to him: *cf. Videan v. British Transport Commission*, [1963] 2 Q.B. 650. It is a further consequence of the recognition of an independent duty that a person who imperils himself by his carelessness may be as fully liable to a rescuer as a third person would be who imperils another. In my opinion, therefore, *Dupuis v. New Regina Trading Co. Ltd.*, [1943] 4 D.L.R. 275, [1943] 2 W.W.R. 593, ought no longer to be taken as a statement of the common law in Canada in so far as it denies recovery because the rescuer was injured in going to the aid of a person who imperilled himself. The doctrinal issues are sufficiently canvassed by the late Dean Wright in 21 *Can. Bar Rev.* 758 (1943); and see also *Ward v. T.E. Hopkins & Son, Ltd.; Baker v. T.E. Hopkins & Son, Ltd.,* [1959] 3 All E.R. 225.

I realize that this statement of the law invites the conclusion that Horsley's estate might succeed against that of Matthews if it was proved that Matthews acted without proper care for his own safety so that Horsley was prompted to come to his rescue. This issue does not, however, have to be canvassed in these proceedings since the estate of Matthews was not joined as a co-defendant ...

MacLaren was not a random rescuer. As owner and operator of a boat on which he was carrying invited guests, he was under a legal duty to take reasonable care for their safety. This was a duty which did not depend on the existence of a contract of carriage, nor on whether he was a common carrier or private carrier of passengers. Having brought his guests into a relationship with him as passengers on his boat, albeit as social or gratuitous passengers, he was obliged to exercise reasonable care for their safety. That obligation extends, in my opinion, to rescue from perils of the sea where this is consistent with his duty to see to the safety of his other passengers and with concern for his own safety. The duty exists whether the passenger falls overboard accidentally or by reason of his own carelessness.

I would hold that *Vanvalkenburg v. Northern Navigation Co.* (1913), 19 D.L.R. 649, 30 O.L.R. 142, should no longer be considered as good law in so far as it declared that operators of a ship were not under any legal duty to a seaman in their employ to go to his rescue when he fell overboard through his own carelessness ...

There is an independent basis for a common law duty of care in the relationship of carrier to passenger, but the legislative declaration of policy in s. 526(1) is a fortifying element in the recognition of that duty, being in harmony with it in a comparable situation.

It follows from this assessment that MacLaren cannot be regarded as simply a good Samaritan. Rather it is Horsley who was in that role, exposing himself to danger upon the alleged failure of MacLaren properly to carry out his duty to effect Matthews' rescue. The present case is, therefore, not one to which the principles propounded in *East Suffolk Rivers Catchment Board v. Kent*, [1941] A.C. 74, are applicable. In the Court of Appeal, both Schroeder, J.A., and Jessup, J.A., referred to this case with approval. The former relied on it to support his rejection of the trial Judge's holding that MacLaren was liable when, having undertaken to rescue Matthews, he failed to use reasonable care in the rescue operation. In the opinion of Schroeder, J.A., as noted earlier in these reasons, there was no basis for holding that MacLaren's rescue efforts, even if improperly carried out, worsened Matthews' condition and thus induced Horsley to come to his rescue. Jessup, J.A., would have applied this test of liability if the case, for him, had turned on the voluntary undertaking by MacLaren of rescue operations. Since, on the view taken by Jessup, J.A., MacLaren had an antecedent or original duty to render assistance, the *East Suffolk Rivers Catchment Board* case did not apply.

Whether a case involving the exercise of statutory powers (but not duties) by a public authority should govern the issue of liability or non-liability to an injured rescuer is a question that need not be answered here. . .

On the view that I take of the issues in this case and, having regard to the facts, the appellants cannot succeed on the first of the alternative submissions on liability if they cannot succeed on the second ground of an existing common law duty of care. Their third contention was not clearly anchored in any original or supervening duty of care and breach of that duty; and, if that be so, I do not see how their counsel's submission on the foreseeability of a second rescuer, even if accepted, can saddle a non-negligent first rescuer with liability either to the rescuee or to a second rescuer. Encouragement by the common law of the rescue of persons in danger would, in my opinion, go beyond reasonable bounds if it involved liability of one rescuer to a succeeding one where the former has not been guilty of any fault which could be said to have induced a second rescue attempt . . .

The present case is thus reduced to the question of liability on the basis of (1) an alleged breach of a duty of care originating in the relationship of carrier and passenger; (2) whether the breach, if there was one, could be said to have prompted Horsley to go to Matthews' rescue; and (3) whether Horsley's conduct, if not so rash in the circumstances as to be unforeseeable, none the less exhibited want of care so as to make him guilty of contributory negligence.

Whether MacLaren was in breach of his duty of care to Matthews was a question of fact on which the trial Judge's affirmative finding is entitled to consider-able weight. That finding was, of course, essential to the further question of a consequential duty to Horsley. Lacourciere, J., came to his conclusion of fact on the evidence, after putting to himself the following question: "What would the reasonable boat operator do in the circumstances, attributing to such person the reasonable skill and experience required of the master of a cabin cruiser who is responsible for the safety and rescue of his passengers?" (see 4 D.L.R. (3d) 557 at p. 564, [1969] 2 O.R. 137). It was the trial Judge's finding that MacLaren, as he himself admitted, had adopted the wrong procedure for rescuing a passenger who had fallen overboard. He knew the proper procedure and had practised it. Coming bow on to effect a rescue was the standard procedure and was taught as such . . .

I do not see how it can be said that the trial Judge's finding against Mac-Laren on the issue of breach of duty is untenable. In relation to Horsley's inter-vention, the finding stands unembarrassed by any question of causation in relation to Matthews . . .

I turn to the question whether the breach of duty to Matthews could properly be regarded in this case as prompting Horsley to attempt a rescue. Like the trial Judge, I am content to adopt and apply analogically on this point the reasoning of Cardozo, J., as he then was, in *Wagner v. International R. Co.* (1921), 133 N.E. 437, and of Lord Denning, M.R., in *Videan v. British Transport Commission, supra.* To use Judge Cardozo's phrase, Horsley's conduct in the circumstances was "within the range of the natural and probable." The fact, moreover, that Horsley's sacrifice was futile is no more a disabling ground here than it was in the *Wagner* case, where the passenger thrown off the train was dead when the plaintiff went to help him, unless it be the case that the rescuer acted wantonly . . .

In responding as he did, and in circumstances where only hindsight made it doubtful that Matthews could be saved, Horsley was not wanton or foolhardy.

Like the trial Judge, I do not think that his action passed the point of brave acceptance of a serious risk and became a futile exhibition of recklessness for which there can be no recourse. There is, however, the question whether Horsley was guilty of contributory negligence. This was an alternative plea of the respondent based *inter alia*, on Horsley's failure to put on a life-jacket or secure himself to the boat by a rope or call on the other passengers to stand by, especially in the light of the difficulties of Matthews in the cold water. The trial Judge rejected the contentions of contributory negligence, holding that although "Wearing a life-jacket or securing himself to a lifeline would have been more prudent ... Horsley's impulsive act without such precautions was the result of the excitement, haste and confusion of the moment, and cannot be said to constitute contributory negligence" (see 4 D.L.R. (3d) at p. 569). In view of its conclusions on the main issue of MacLaren's liability, the Ontario Court of Appeal did not canvass the question of contributory negligence.

The matter is not free from difficulty. About two minutes passed after Matthews had fallen overboard and MacLaren made his first abortive attempt at rescue by proceeding astern. Two life-jackets had been successively thrown towards Matthews without any visible effort on his part to seize them. Then came the second attempt at rescue by backing the boat, and it was in progress when Horsley dived in. Horsley had come on deck at the shout of "Roly's overboard" and was at the stern during MacLaren's first attempt at rescue, and must have been there when the life-jackets were thrown towards Matthews. However, in the concern of the occasion, and having regard to MacLaren's breach of duty, I do not think that Horsley can be charged with contributory negligence in diving to the rescue of Matthews as he did. I point out as well that the evidence does not indicate that the failure to put on a life-jacket or secure himself to a lifeline played any part in Horsley's death.

. . .

[Judson J. and Spence J. concurred with Ritchie J.; and Hall J. concurred with Laskin J.]

NOTES AND QUESTIONS

1. Both the majority and dissent in *Horsley* refer to Denning M.R.'s judgment in *Videan v. British Transport Comm.*, [1963] 2 All E.R. 860 (C.A.). In *Videan*, the stationmaster's young son wandered onto the tracks and the stationmaster attempted to rescue him from an approaching trolley. The driver, who was not keeping a proper look-out, could not stop. The stationmaster was killed and his son was badly injured. The infant's claim was dismissed because, as a trespasser, his presence was unforeseeable. Nevertheless, Denning M.R. held that the driver ought to have foreseen that his conduct might create an emergency of some kind. Consequently, the stationmaster's presence as a rescuer was foreseeable and he was owed a duty of care. Is Denning M.R.'s analysis compelling?

2. Cardozo J. had adopted a similar position in *Wagner v. Int. Ry. Co.* (1921), 133 N.E. 437 at 437 (N.Y. C.A.). His statement that "Danger invites rescue" is now generally accepted. Given this broad test of foreseeability, under what circumstances would a rescuer be denied recovery as an unforeseeable plaintiff? How is the foreseeable plaintiff test applied differently in rescue cases than in other negligence cases? Is this appropriate? See Linden, "Down with Foreseeability! Of Thin Skulls and Rescuers" (1969), 47 Can. Bar Rev. 545 at 558-70; and Smith, "The Mystery of Duty", in Klar (ed.), *Studies in Canadian Tort Law* (1977), 1 at 30-32.

3. In *Horsley*, Ritchie J. also quotes Denning M.R.'s statement "if a man by his fault creates a situation of peril, he must answer for it to any person who attempts to rescue the person who is in danger." What does this mean?

According to Ritchie J., what had to be established to prove that MacLaren owed Horsley a duty of care? What is the test for breaching the standard of care? Based on the expert evidence, was MacLaren's use of the reverse, rather than the bow-on method, a causal factor in inducing Horsley's rescue attempt? Why did Ritchie J. dismiss Horsley's claim?

4. What was the basis upon which Laskin J. held that MacLaren owed Horsley a duty of care? How did Laskin J.'s analysis relate to the appellant's three alternative bases of liability? What was the basis upon which Laskin J. concluded that MacLaren breached the standard of care? Do you agree with Laskin J.'s analysis of the causation or contributory negligence issue? Assuming Horsley realized that Matthews was dead, would he have been contributorily negligent in jumping overboard to recover the body?

5. Although the courts have occasionally held rescuers to be contributorily negligent, their sympathies clearly lie with the rescuer. See *Sayers v. Harlow Urban Dist. Council*, [1958] 2 All E.R. 342 (C.A.); *Corothers v. Slobodian*, [1975] 2 S.C.R. 633; *Toy v. Argenti*, [1980] 3 W.W.R. 276 (B.C. S.C.); and *Cleary v. Hansen* (1981), 18 C.C.L.T. 147 (Ont. H.C.). See also Binchy, "Torts — Rescuers . . ." (1974), 52 Can. Bar Rev. 292.

6. The defence of voluntary assumption of risk has been all but eliminated in rescue cases. In *Urbanski v. Patel* (1978), 84 D.L.R. (3d) 650 (Man. Q.B.), the plaintiff donated a kidney to his daughter after the defendant surgeon had negligently removed her only kidney. The plaintiff claimed that the loss of his donated kidney had been caused by the defendant's negligence in injuring his daughter. The court found for the plaintiff, concluding that his act was a reasonably foreseeable result of the defendant's negligence. The defence of voluntary assumption of risk was dismissed with a statement to the effect that the defence is inapplicable where the plaintiff consciously faces a risk in an attempt to rescue another who has been imperilled by the defendant's negligence. In light of *Urbanski*, can you suggest a situation in which a rescuer might be denied recovery on the basis of voluntary assumption of risk? See Robertson, "A New Application of the Rescue Principle" (1980), 96 L.Q.R. 19.

In many jurisdictions in the United States, police officers, firefighters and other professional rescuers are denied recovery from the original tortfeasors for injuries sustained in their rescue efforts. The "fireman's rule", as it is called, is based in part on voluntary assumption of risk. However, in *Ogwo v. Taylor*, [1987] 3 All E.R. 961, the House of Lords stated that the rule had no place in English law. In Canada, it also appears that firefighters and other professional rescuers can recover for the injuries that they sustain in rescue attempts. What argument would you make in favour of the "fireman's rule"?

7. Since the rescuer's claim is independent of that of the person being rescued, a rescuer may recover for injuries sustained in assisting a person who has negligently imperilled herself. See *Chapman v. Hearse* (1961), 106 C.L.R. 112 (Aust. H.C.); *Corothers v. Slobodian*, [1975] 2 S.C.R. 633; and *C.N.R. v. Bakty* (1977), 18 O.R. (2d) 481 (Co. Ct.). But see *Clyke v. Clyke* (1987), 80 N.S.R. (2d) 149 (T.D.), aff'd. (1988), 83 N.S.R. (2d) 79 (C.A.), leave to appeal ref'd. (1988), 86 N.S.R. (2d) 179n (S.C.C.).

8. The general principles governing rescuers also apply to cases in which the plaintiff is injured in attempting to save herself or her own property. See *Sayers v. Harlow Urban Dist. Council*, [1958] 2 All E.R. 342 (C.A.); *Zervobeakos v. Zervobeakos* (1969), 8 D.L.R. (3d) 377 (N.S. C.A.); *Prescott v. Connell* (1893), 22 S.C.R. 147; *Hutterly v. Imperial Oil Ltd.* (1956), 3 D.L.R. (2d) 719 (Ont. H.C.); and *Toy v. Argenti*, [1980] 3 W.W.R. 276 (B.C. S.C.).

9. One unresolved issue in *Horsley* is whether the general principles governing the discontinuance of a gratuitous undertaking apply to rescue cases. The majority of the Court of Appeal indicated that an individual who has voluntarily begun a rescue attempt is under no duty to continue it unless she has worsened the victim's original position. The Court of Appeal cited *East Suffolk Rivers Catchment Bd. v. Kent*, [1941] A.C. 74 (H.L.) as authority, even though that case concerned the liability of public authorities for negligence in exercising their statutory powers. Why did the Supreme Court of Canada not find it necessary to address the gratuitous rescue issue? What was Laskin J.'s response to the Court of Appeal's argument?

10. As indicated in the last chapter, section 217 of the Criminal Code requires an individual who undertakes an act to complete it if an omission to do so is, or may be, dangerous to life. Although there are no reported cases involving rescue attempts, the section should apply to an individual who, having undertaken a voluntary rescue attempt, abandoned the victim in a life-threatening situation. Based on this criminal law provision, what argument would you make for recognizing a parallel common law duty in negligence?

REVIEW PROBLEMS

1. The Apex Corporation was shooting a gangster film in downtown Toronto. One of the scenes depicted two thugs beating a police officer just outside of the Toronto Art Gallery. Apex had obtained permission to film the scene on the Gallery's property, cordoned off the outside area and staged the scene behind the Gallery away from possible intermeddlers. During the middle of the scene, a patron in the Art Gallery burst through a firedoor and lunged at the two thugs. He had lost his way in the basement of the Gallery. All he could see through the small window beside the firedoor was the officer on the ground being kicked. Believing the officer was in danger, he opened the firedoor hoping to set off the alarm and scare off the thugs. Unfortunately, in lunging at the thugs, he slipped and broke his leg. You have been asked to advise the patron on his prospects of recovering from the Apex Corporation.

2. Several weeks after he was informed that he had terminal cancer, Mr. Smith decided to commit suicide. However, when he stepped out on the ledge of his fourth floor apartment window, he began to have second thoughts. While he was deliberating, a passerby called the police and fire departments. Within minutes, two emergency rescue teams arrived on the scene. By this time Smith had changed his mind and re-entered his apartment. Smith died of natural causes shortly thereafter. The rescue teams wish to sue Smith's estate for their expenses in coming to the scene.

3. Duties Owed to the Unborn

Initially, the key issue in this area was whether a fetus injured during pregnancy could recover damages after birth. It was argued that a fetus was not a foreseeable plaintiff and thus could not be owed a duty of care. In *Duval v. Seguin* (1972), 26 D.L.R. (3d) 418 (Ont. H.C.), aff'd. (1973), 40 D.L.R. (3d) 666 (Ont. C.A.), the High Court held that if a child is born alive, she can recover for injuries she sustained during pregnancy. Although this is now an established principle, the courts are being asked to resolve far more complex issues concerning preconception torts, negligent genetic counselling and prenatal diagnosis, wrongful sterilizations, and the measure of damages for having to raise an unwanted child. Unfortunately, there is little consensus in some of these areas and confusion over terms such as wrongful life and wrongful birth.

For analytical purposes, it is helpful to divide the duties to the unborn into three categories: prenatal injuries; preconception injuries; and wrongful life. It is also important to clearly separate the mother's claim for physical injury, the parents' claim for the financial costs of raising the child, and the child's claim for injuries and loss of potential earnings. We will also discuss a fourth category of cases, wrongful birth control, sterilization or abortion. While some of these wrongful birth control, sterilization and abortion cases involve a single claim from an adult patient, others may include claims from both an adult patient and a child.

The first category, prenatal injury cases, arises when the defendant negligently injures the fetus and, as a result, the child is born injured or handicapped. A common example of this action occurs when a pregnant woman is involved in a car accident that results in injury to the fetus. One of the more controversial issues in this area is whether the injured child can sue her own parents if they negligently caused or contributed to her injuries.

The second category, preconception torts, involves negligent injury to one of the parents, usually the mother, prior to the child's conception. For example, the mother or father may have been exposed to hazardous chemicals that caused injury to her ova or his sperm. As a result of these genetic defects, the child that is subsequently conceived and born suffers serious injuries. Aside from very complex problems of causation, these cases often pose policy issues concerning the scope of a defendant's potential liability. Should the parents' knowledge of the potential genetic problems have any bearing on the defendant's liability?

The third category, wrongful life claims, poses perhaps the most difficult legal and policy issues. A typical claim might involve a doctor who has negligently failed to inform a woman that she has a much greater than normal risk of giving birth to a handicapped child. Relying on the doctor's advice, the woman continues a pregnancy that she would have otherwise terminated. Unlike prenatal and preconception torts, the defendant in wrongful life cases has not caused the injury to the child. Rather, the defendant has failed to put the woman in a position to avoid the pregnancy or to end the pregnancy. These cases usually involve the mother's claim for breach of duty to inform and the disabled child's claim for wrongful life.

The mother's claim is based on fairly straightforward principles governing a health professional's duty to inform patients — an issue that is discussed at length later in the chapter. The child's claim for wrongful life is more problematic. The child is asserting that but for the defendant's negligence, she would not have been born and would not have had to live as a disabled individual. This claim is premised on the assertion that the child would be better off not having been born, rather than being born disabled. The courts have struggled with questions concerning the sanctity of life, the need to value the disabled and the assessment of damages.

The fourth category, wrongful birth control, sterilization and abortion claims, is based on general principles of medical negligence. For example, a woman who has had to undergo a second abortion procedure may sue her original doctor who negligently failed to terminate the pregnancy. The woman may claim economic losses, pain and suffering, and emotional harm from having to undergo a second abortion. If the woman does not have a second abortion and a child is born, the woman may still claim for her pain and suffering, and financial losses attributable to the unwanted pregnancy, labour and delivery. Generally, if a healthy child is born, the courts have not awarded damages for the costs of rearing the child. However, if the child is born handicapped, some courts have awarded the parents damages for the additional costs of addressing the child's disability. If the doctor also injured the fetus during the initial procedure, the child would have a claim for her prenatal injuries.

NOTES AND QUESTIONS

1. The principle in *Duval* has been codified in s. 66 of the Ontario Family Law Act, R.S.O. 1990, c. F.3, which provides that no person is disentitled from recovering damages simply because the injuries were incurred before birth.

2. Much of the concern with prenatal injuries stemmed from the birth defects caused by thalidomide in the 1960s. Recent advances in the medical sciences have made it easier to prove that drugs, chemicals, radiation, and other substances can cause birth defects. For example, in *Sindell v. Abbott Laboratories* (1980), 607 P. (2d) 924 (Cal. S.C.), a mother's use of a prescription drug, DES, during pregnancy was proven to cause a particular form of deadly cancer in female children a minimum of 10 to 12 years after birth.

For a general discussion of prenatal injuries see Winfield, "The Unborn Child" (1942-44), 8

Cambridge L.J. 76; Weiler and Catton, "The Unborn Child in Canadian Law" (1976), 14 Osgoode Hall L.J. 643; and Pace, "Civil Liability For Pre-Natal Injuries" (1977), 40 Mod. L. Rev. 141.

3. It has been generally accepted that a child can recover from her own parents for prenatal injuries caused by negligent driving. More controversial issues arise, however, if the child claims damages based on the mother's careless eating habits, drug use, alcohol consumption, or failure to obtain prenatal medical care. These situations raise questions concerning a child's right to be born free of injuries versus a woman's right to control her own body. There is little Canadian law on point, but see *Deziel v. Deziel*, [1953] 1 D.L.R. 651 (Ont. H.C.). See also Beal, "Can I Sue Mommy? An Analysis of a Woman's Tort Liability for Prenatal Injuries to Her Child Born Alive" (1984), 21 San Diego L. Rev. 325; Johnsen, "The Creation of Fetal Rights: Conflicts with Women's Constitutional Rights to Liberty, Privacy, and Equal Protection" (1986), 95 Yale L.J. 599; and Bambrick, "Developing Maternal Liability Standards for Prenatal Injury" (1987), 61 St. John's L. Rev. 592.

4. Are such civil suits likely to have any beneficial effect on fetal health? Can you suggest other means of addressing this issue? Should the state have the power to intervene to protect fetal health? Would such legislation be any more effective than civil liability? What constitutional arguments would be raised in challenging such laws? How would these challenges be resolved? For a review of the ongoing debate see Fortin, "Legal Protection for the Unborn Child" (1988), 51 Mod. L. Rev. 54; Hanigsberg, "Power and Procreation: State Interference in Pregnancy" (1991), 23 Ottawa L. Rev. 35; and Kirman, "Four Dialogues on Fetal Protection" (1993), 2(2) Health L. Rev. 31.

5. What limits should be placed on recovery for preconception torts? Assume that a child suffers injuries during delivery because of her mother's misshapen pelvis. Assume as well that the mother's pelvis was misshapen because she was run over by a negligent driver 15 years ago. What claim, if any, should the child have against the driver?

Should different considerations apply in preconception cases involving workplace exposures to hazardous products? Should the employer's obligation be limited to: (a) fully informing all potential employees; (b) complying with workplace health and safety legislation; (c) complying with industry safety norms; or (d) obtaining a waiver of liability from the employees? Should employers be free to deny jobs or limit placements to women of child-bearing age?

In *International Union, U.A.W. v. Johnson Controls, Inc.* (1991), 111 S. Ct. 1196, the American Supreme Court struck down a fetal protection policy that excluded all fertile women from working in a battery manufacturing plant. Even though airborne lead in the plant posed a fetal hazard, the court held that Johnson Controls' policy discriminated against women in violation of federal law. The court voted unanimously to permit women to decide for themselves whether to risk the fetal hazards present in the plant. This decision left employers in a quandary, choosing between enacting fetal protection plans which contravene federal legislation, or exposing themselves to liability under state tort law for fetal harm. One author has suggested that employers may be able to argue that a discriminatory plan is warranted given the potential for ruinous fetal tort liability. See Grover, "The Employer's Fetal Injury Quandary After *Johnson Controls*" (1992-93), 81 Kentucky L.J. 639. Do you agree with the decision? Advise Johnson Controls on how they should proceed?

6. In *Becker v. Schwartz* (1978), 386 N.E. (2d) 807 (N.Y. C.A.), a 37-year-old woman gave birth to a retarded infant suffering from Down's Syndrome. The woman contended that her obstetricians were negligent in failing to advise her of the increased risk of Down's Syndrome in children born to women over 35. Nor was she informed of the availability of a test that could have determined before birth whether the child would be afflicted. An action for "wrongful life" was brought on behalf of the child. Essentially, it was argued that, but for the physician's inadequate advice, the infant would not have been born to experience the pain and suffering caused by her disabilities. The trial court dismissed the suit for failure to disclose a cause of action. On appeal, it was held that the child had not sustained any injury recognized at law. However, the parents were allowed to recover the additional financial burdens of caring for a disabled child. They could not, however, recover damages for any accompanying emotional harm.

This issue has sparked heated debate in the United States. See Capron, "Tort Liability in Genetic Counseling" (1979), 79 Colum. L. Rev. 618; Sonnenburg, "A Preference for Nonexistence: Wrongful Life and a Proposed Tort of Genetic Malpractice" (1982), 55 S. Cal. L. Rev. 477; and Jankowski, "Wrongful Birth and Wrongful Life Actions Arising from Negligent Counselling: The Need for Legislation Supporting Reproductive Choice" (1989), 17 Fordham Urb. L.J. 27.

7. In *McKay v. Essex Area Health Authority*, [1982] 2 All E.R. 771 (C.A.), the plaintiff contracted German measles early in her pregnancy, but the infection was not diagnosed in the blood tests that

were done. As a result of the disease, the child was born severely disabled. The mother and child sued the doctor and health authority for failing to treat the infection and to advise the mother of the desirability of an abortion. The court struck out the child's claim as not showing any reasonable cause of action. The only basis on which the child's claim could succeed is if one accepts that the child had a right not to be born. The court stated that such a claim for wrongful life is contrary to public policy as a violation of the sanctity of human life. Do you agree? Moreover, the court stated that it was impossible to assess damages by comparing the value of nonexistence to the value of existence in a disabled state. Is this an appropriate test for assessing the child's losses? The court did not address the mother's damage claim. See Simmons, "Policy Factors in Actions For Wrongful Birth" (1987), 50 Mod. L. Rev. 269.

8. The issue of "wrongful life" is unresolved in Canada. In *Arndt v. Smith* (1994), 21 C.C.L.T. (2d) 66 (B.C. S.C.), a mother gave birth to a severely handicapped child as a result of contracting chicken pox during pregnancy. Although such disabilities rarely result from chicken pox, the physician was found to be negligent for failing to inform the mother of these risks and offer her the option of an abortion. The court commented favourably on the dropping of the child's claim for wrongful life, stating that no viable suit could be brought on that basis in British Columbia. The father's claim to recover the costs of supporting the child was dismissed. The court accepted that the mother could claim for the additional expenses of rearing a handicapped child, but held that this action failed on causation. The plaintiff could not prove that a reasonable woman in her position would have had an abortion if informed of the very small risks of serious birth defects. The British Columbia Court of Appeal reversed the trial judgment on this causation issue and ordered a new trial: (1995), 25 C.C.L.T. (2d) 262 (B.C. C.A.), leave to appeal granted (May 6, 1996), Doc. 24943 (S.C.C.).

9. Women have been awarded substantial damages following failed sterilizations and abortions. See *Cryderman v. Ringrose* (1978), 89 D.L.R. (3d) 32 (Alta. C.A.); *Dendaas v. Yackel* (1980), 109 D.L.R. (3d) 455 (B.C. S.C.); and *Cherry (Guardian) v. Borsman* (1990), 75 D.L.R. (4th) 668 (B.C. S.C.), varied on damages (1992), 94 D.L.R. (4th) 487 (B.C. C.A.), leave to appeal ref'd. (1993), 99 D.L.R. (4th) vii (note) (S.C.C.).

In *Cataford v. Moreau* (1978), 114 D.L.R. (3d) 585 (Que. S.C.), the court held that the mother was entitled to any losses that flowed from the unwanted pregnancy, and the cost and inconvenience of undergoing a second sterilization operation. In denying recovery for the cost of raising the unwanted child, the court noted that this burden was offset by the benefits of having the child in the family. In *Doiron v. Orr* (1978), 86 D.L.R. (3d) 719 (Ont. H.C.), the court stated that it would be contrary to public policy to award damages for rearing an unwanted child. But see *Suite v. Cooke* (1993), 15 C.C.L.T. (2d) 15 (Que. S.C.), aff'd. [1995] R.J.Q. 2765 (C.A.), where damages were awarded to help defray the costs of raising an unplanned, healthy child.

10. In Canada, damages are not awarded for the death of a fetus; rather the child must be born alive. *Davey v. Victoria General Hospital* (1995), 27 C.C.L.T. (2d) 303 (Man. Q.B.). This position is consistent with the Supreme Court of Canada's position concerning criminal liability. See *R. v. Sullivan*, [1991] 1 S.C.R. 489; and McCourt, "Foetus Status After *R. v. Sullivan and LeMay*" (1991), 29 Alta. L. Rev. 916.

Some American jurisdictions have modified the "born alive" rule in tort actions, allowing the parents to claim for the loss of companionship and comfort of a fetus that would have, but for the defendant's negligence, been born alive. These jurisdictions recognize the anomaly that a defendant who negligently kills a fetus escapes liability, while a negligent defendant who inflicts less serious injury is held accountable. See *O'Grady v. Brown* (1983), 654 S.W. 904 (Mo. S.C.). Should the "born alive" rule be retained in negligence?

11. What impact, if any, would the *Anns* approach have on these four categories of cases?

12. What recommendations would you make to a provincial law reform commission on improving and rationalizing this branch of negligence law?

4. Nervous Shock

RHODES v. CANADIAN NATIONAL RAILWAY CO.
(1990), 75 D.L.R. (4th) 248 (B.C. C.A.)

MACFARLANE J.A.: — The question raised by this appeal is whether a mother, whose loved one has died as a result of the negligent act of a third party, has a cause of action in damages against the third party for a psychiatric illness resulting from the impact upon her of the death of her son.

The circumstances are detailed in the reasons of Mr. Justice Taylor, and a summary will suffice.

The plaintiff's son was killed in a railway crash in Alberta. The defendant admits that the death was caused by the negligence of its servants. The plaintiff was on Vancouver Island in British Columbia when the accident occurred. She heard of her son's death from other persons. She did not see her son's body.

The trial judge acknowledged that recovery has never been granted in any case where the plaintiff has merely heard about the accident from a third party, but concluded that the court in *Beecham v. Hughes* (1988), 52 D.L.R. (4th) 625, 45 C.C.L.T. 1, [1988] 6 W.W.R. 33 (B.C.C.A.), had expressly left the door open to such a claim. In his opinion, "it is for the trier of fact to determine on a case-by-case basis just how wide that opening should be" [49 C.C.L.T. 64 at p. 78, 36 B.C.L.R. (2d) 1, 15 A.C.W.S. (3d) 203].

With respect I do not agree that the court in *Beecham* expressly or impliedly suggested that such a claim might succeed. I adopt the reasons of Mr. Justice Taylor in that respect. Secondly, it is my opinion that the question whether such a cause of action may be sustained is not a question for the jury, but is a question of law. It is for a judge to decide whether, accepting as true the allegations of the plaintiff, a duty of care arises. Only if there is a duty of care at law can the jury be asked if the duty was breached, and whether the alleged injury was caused by the breach.

In my opinion *Beecham* affirms that the test upon which liability for nervous shock is based is not foreseeability alone, but foreseeability limited by proximity considerations: *per* Taggart J.A. at p. 664.

I agree with Mr. Justice Wallace when he says [*post*, pp. 265-6]:

> The requisite proximity relationship is made up of a combination of various relational elements or factors. These include, *inter alia*, relational proximity (the closeness of the relationship between the claimant and the victim of the defendant's conduct); locational proximity (being at the scene and observing the shocking event); temporal proximity (the relation between the time of the event and the onset of the psychiatric illness).
>
> . . . . .
>
> It has been clearly recognized that no one proximity relationship is by itself, or in a combination with others, decisive in establishing reasonable foreseeability of psychiatric injury. However, the closeness of the relationship between the claimant and the victim is generally regarded as a predominant factor. All such factors, which together constitute the requisite degree of relational proximity between the complainant and the defendant's conduct are material in considering whether the risk of direct psychiatric injury was reasonably foreseeable "in the sense of points on a continuum on which, as distance increases, foreseeability recedes": J.G. Fleming, *Law of Torts*, 5th ed. (Sydney: The Law Book Co. Ltd. 1977), at p. 156.

I also agree with his view that considerations of policy must enter into the determination of the foreseeability issue.

I think that there is general agreement in the authorities that the basis for that limitation is to be found in the famous dictum of Lord Atkin in *Donoghue v. Stevenson*, [1932] A.C. 562 at p. 580, [1932] All E.R. Rep. 1 (H.L.). (I need not refer to the authorities in detail because I adopt the analysis of those cases which is to be found in the reasons of Wallace J.A. and Taylor J.A.) As I understand the authorities someone "closely and directly affected" by the negligent act is, in "nervous shock" cases, a person who is able to establish the requisite proximity relationship.

Mr. Justice Wallace has traced the experience of the courts in dealing with mental shock. None of them support the proposition that a tortfeasor is liable for injury to someone who hears about the death of a loved one from a third party, and who does not experience the shock of the event which caused the death.

It is not surprising that there is no support in the authorities for such a proposition. The liability is not for causing the death of a person. That claim is to be dealt with under the appropriate fatal accidents legislation. The liability in question arises from the impact of the tortious act upon the claimant, who does not herself suffer any personal injury. The impact must be direct in the sense that the claimant is frightened, terrified or horrified and that fright, terror or horror causes a permanent impact on the claimant's mind (the language of Madam Justice Southin [*post*, p. 272]). Mr. Justice Taylor puts it in this way [*post*, p. 298]: "[T]here must, in my view, be proof that the injury was caused by some experience of an alarming, startling, or frightening nature . . .".

. . .

I would allow the appeal . . . and dismiss the plaintiff's claim for damages arising out of her psychological illness. I would order that there be no costs with respect to this application in this court or in the court below.

WALLACE J.A.: —

. . .

We are here concerned with the question of whether as a matter of law, in the agreed circumstances, the defendants owed a duty of care to the plaintiff and, if so, did the defendants' conduct cause the psychiatric illness of which the complainant suffers.

. . .

The following case trace the experience of the English courts dealing with mental shock. In *Victorian Railways Com'rs v. Coultas* (1888), 13 App. Cas. 222 (P.C.), a pregnant lady crossing the train tracks in a carriage was narrowly missed by an oncoming train. Her claim for the mental shock she sustained was dismissed on the ground that she had ot been physically injured.

In *Dulieu v. White & Sons*, [1901] 2 K.B. 669, the plaintiff, a pregnant lady who worked behind a public bar, suffered nervous shock when the defendant's horse-drawn carriage was driven into the public-house while she was behind the bar and consequently she feared for her safety. The claim for nervous shock was allowed although she was not physically injured and had sustained the shock solely from a reasonable fear of injury.

In *Hambrook v. Stokes Brothers*, [1925] 1 K.B. 141 (C.A.), the plaintiff's wife, who had been walking up the street with her children, had just parted with them a little below the point where the street made a bend, when she saw a runaway lorry rushing around the bend towards her. She became very frightened for the safety of her children, who by that time were out of sight and who she knew must have met the lorry in its course. She became very agitated. She found that her daughter, who had been knocked down by the lorry, had suffered considerable injuries. At the time the mother was three or four months advanced in pregnancy and, in consequence of her fright and anxiety, suffered nervous shock which eventually caused her death. The court held, on the assumption that the shock was caused by what the woman saw with her own eyes as distinguished from what she was told by bystanders, that the plaintiff was entitled to recover notwithstanding that the shock was brought about by the fear for her children's safety and not by fear for her own. Sargant L.J. dissented, expressing the view that nervous shock caused to a plaintiff by fear of injury occasioned by a near miss was indistinguishable, as far as the defendant's duty is concerned, from injury by direct impact whereas nervous shock caused by the fear or sight of injury to another is beyond the defendant's anticipation and hence beyond the range of his duty.

In *Hay or Bourhill v. Young*, [1942] 2 All E.R. 396 (H.L.), the plaintiff, descending from a tram, suffered nervous shock as a result of having heard the noise caused by the impact of a motor cycle and a motor car, and having seen blood on the roadway after the body of the motor-cyclist had been removed. The question arose whether the motor-cyclist owed any duty to the plaintiff in that he ought to have contemplated the likelihood of her sustaining injury in the circumstances. The claim was rejected on the ground that the driver of the motor cycle, even though careless, was entitled to assume that the ordinary frequenter of the streets had sufficient fortitude to endure such incidents as may from time to time be expected to occur in them, including the noise of a collision and the sight of injury to others, and is not to be considered negligent towards one who does not possess the "customary phlegm".

The parameters of the duty of care in tort law generally were further developed by the House of Lords in *Anns v. Merton London Borough Council*, [1978] A.C. 728, [1977] 2 All E.R. 492, where Lord Wilberforce expressed his oft-quoted two-stage test at pp. 751-2:

> Rather the question has to be approached in two stages. First one has to ask whether, as between the alleged wrongdoer and the person who has suffered damage there is a sufficient relationship of proximity or neighbourhood such that, in the reasonable contemplation of the former, carelessness on his part may be likely to cause damage to the latter, in which case a prima facie duty of care arises. Secondly, if the first question is answered affirmatively, it is necessary to consider whether there are any considerations which ought to negative, or to reduce or limit the scope of the duty or the class of person to whom it is owed or the damages to which a breach of it may give rise.

This test has been construed in subsequent cases to place an undue emphasis on "foreseeability" as establishing whether a duty of care arises (see *Governors of Peabody Donation Fund v. Sir Lindsay Parkinson & Co. Ltd.*, [1985] A.C. 210, [1984] 3 W.L.R. 953 (H.L.); *Norwich City Council v. Harvey*, [1989] 1 W.L.R. 828, [1989] 1 All E.R. 1180 (C.A.); *Pacific Associates Inc. v. Baxter*, [1989] 3 W.L.R. 1150, [1989] 2 All E.R. 159 (C.A.); *Caparo Industries plc v. Dickman*, [1990] 2 W.L.R. 358, [1990] 1 All E.R. 568 (H.L.)) when in fact the required proximity relationship necessitates the presence of other relational factors before the negligent actor is under a duty of care to the injured party. Indeed, Lord Wilberforce evidently was of this view as appears from his reasoning in *McLoughlin v. O'Brian*, [1983] 1 A.C. 410 at pp. 420-1, [1982] 2 All E.R. 298 (H.L.):

. . .

The *McLoughlin* case dealt with a road accident in which the plaintiff's husband and three children were involved. One of the plaintiff's children was killed and her husband and the other two children were severely injured. The plaintiff was told of the accident by a motorist who had been at the scene, and she was taken to the hospital where she saw the injured members of her family and the extent of their injuries and shock, and heard that her daughter had been killed. As a result of hearing and seeing the results of the accident, the plaintiff suffered severe and persisting nervous shock.

Lord Wilberforce upheld the plaintiff's claim finding that the plaintiff came within the required proximity by applying the following factors: the class of person advancing the claim (relational proximity); the proximity in distance and time of such persons to the accident (locational and temporal proximity); and the nature of the event which caused the shock.

On the question of locational and temporal proximity, Lord Wilberforce stated that the shock must come through sight or hearing of the event or its immediate aftermath (p. 423). He had previously noted (p. 422) that:

> It is, after all, the fact and consequence of the defendant's negligence that must be proved to have caused the "nervous shock". Experience has shown that to insist on direct and immediate sight or hearing would be impractical and unjust and that under what may be called the "aftermath" doctrine one who, from close proximity, comes very soon upon the scene should not be excluded.

Accordingly, he found the plaintiff to be within the required proximity relationship to the defendant to give rise to a duty of care, on the part of the defendant, not to cause her injury.

With respect to the nature of the conduct which created the "shock", Lord Wilberforce observed, at pp. 422-3:

> . . . as regards communication, there is no case in which the law has compensated shock brought about by communication by a third party . . . The shock must come through sight or hearing of the event or its immediate aftermath. Whether some equivalent of sight or hearing, e.g. through simultaneous television, would suffice may have to be considered.

Lord Edmund-Davies also rejected, as the sole test of the duty of care and consequent liability, the reasonable foreseeability of injury to the plaintiff through nervous shock resulting from the defendant's wrongful conduct. Rather, he concluded that the court should properly take into account considerations of public policy which in his view supported the plaintiff's claim in the circumstances of the case.

Lord Russell of Killowen expressed his opinion that foreseeability was sufficient to establish liability. He stated, at p. 429:

> . . . if the effect on his wife and mother of the results of the negligence is considered to have been reasonably foreseeable, I do not see the justification for not finding the defendants liable in damages therefor.

Lord Scarman also adopted "foreseeability" as the appropriate principle to apply — leaving policy curtailment to the judgment of Parliament.

Lord Bridge treated the causal connection between the defendant's negligence and the "psychiatric illness" as a question of fact and the "foreseeability" of such consequence resulting from the defendant's negligent act as a question of law (p. 432).

. . .

In summary, it would appear that Lord Wilberforce and Lord Edmund-Davies found that reasonable foreseeability, by itself, was not sufficient to create liability for damages for nervous shock, whereas Lord Russell, Lord Scarman and Lord Bridge considered reasonable foreseeability, *simpliciter*, sufficient to create a duty of care.

. . .

British Columbia authorities

In *Griffiths v. C.P.R.* (1978), 6 B.C.L.R. 115 (C.A.), Taggart J.A. upheld a trial decision which refused to award damages where a husband's emotional condition was found to arise, not from seeing his wife die, but from the grief he experienced because of her death and from his inability to manage the situation in which he then found himself.

In *Beecham v. Hughes* (1988), 52 D.L.R. (4th) 625, [1988] 6 W.W.R. 33, 27 B.C.L.R. (2d) 1 (C.A.), the court considered a factual situation where the claimant sustained relatively minor damages in a car accident in which his common-law wife suffered brain damage. The claimant suffered from "reactive depression". The trial judge held that the condition arose, not from the husband seeing his wife injured or from the shock of the accident, but from his sorrow and his inability to accept the fact that his wife would never again be the person she was before the accident.

. . .

This review of the authorities has led me to reach the following conclusions:

Nervous shock cases, unaccompanied by physical injury, differ significantly from the traditional case of tortious conduct inflicting direct physical injury and they necessitate a different approach in fixing liability. The difference arises from the fact that generally the plaintiff's psychiatric injury is alleged to have been caused by observing, experiencing, or being informed of the injury or death to a third party (usually a close relative). In this sense, the injury is the indirect result of a direct physical injury to a third party. When one appreciates that grief, sorrow or reactive depression are not compensable, the problems of determining foreseeability and causation of such psychiatric illness are clearly apparent. Accordingly, to resolve the issues of foreseeability and causation, some factors beyond the psychiatric illness sustained by the plaintiff and the foreseeability of injury must be established.

. . .

The claimant, Mrs. Rhodes, in my view, must first establish that the defendants were under a duty of care to her — as distinct from that which it owed her son. That duty of care turns on whether her psychiatric illness was a reasonable foreseeable consequence of the defendants' negligent conduct.

In the present case, Mrs. Rhodes was not at the scene of the accident and did not observe the conduct of the defendants. She heard of the train crash on the radio; was uncertain for some period of time as to whether her son was indeed a victim of that crash. She did not arrive at the scene until some eight days after the accident. There were other post-accident incidents which regrettably contributed to Mrs. Rhodes's distress but they were not acts attributable to the defendants. It is clear that the relationship between Mrs. Rhodes and her son was an exceptionally strong one, but this factor by itself is not, in my view, sufficient to establish the required proximity relationship necessary to conclude that Mrs. Rhodes's psychiatric injury was a reasonably foreseeable, direct consequence of the defendants' conduct. Accordingly, I do not consider in the circumstances that prevailed that the defendants were under a duty of care to Mrs. Rhodes to avoid causing the injury she sustained.

. . .

I would allow the appeal and answer the questions in the negative.

SOUTHIN J.A.: —

. . .

It is understandable that a person present at the time of a negligently-caused accident who suffers psychological illness as a result of what he or she sees or hears at the scene may be said to have done so as a foreseeable close and direct consequence of the negligence concerned. But someone who suffers psychological injury as a result of being informed of the death of a relative, or of ruminating on the circumstances of the relative's death, or of visiting the scene some days later cannot, in the absence of any unexpected alarming or horrifying experience caused by the circumstances of the accident, be said to have been closely and directly affected by the negligence which caused it.

For exposure to the "aftermath" of an accident to be the basis of recovery for psychological injury there must, in my view, be proof that the injury was caused by some experience of an alarming, startling or frightening nature, and that it was foreseeable that such injury might ensue.

I would allow the appeal.

[Leave to appeal ref'd. [1991] 1 S.C.R. xiii.]

NOTES AND QUESTIONS

1. In *Hay or Bourhill v. Young*, [1943] A.C. 92, the House of Lords held that a duty of care to avoid nervous shock would arise in any case in which the defendant's conduct created a foreseeable risk of nervous shock to the plaintiff. Despite the lipservice paid to the foreseeability test, the courts continued to limit the duty to specific categories of cases. Basically, the plaintiff would be considered a foreseeable plaintiff if her nervous shock resulted from: (a) physical injury or fear for personal safety; (b) witnessing some aspect of a serious accident involving a relative; or (c) the trauma of rescuing victims of a serious accident. Redress was consistently denied to: (a) innocent bystanders who suffered nervous shock from witnessing accidents; and (b) relatives of accident victims who did not see or hear the accident or its aftermath with their own unaided senses. The courts' attempts to explain these limitations in terms of foreseeability further confused the issues. See for example *King v. Phillips*, [1953] 1 Q.B. 429 (C.A.); *Pollard v. Makarchuk* (1958), 16 D.L.R. (2d) 225 (Alta. C.A.); *Abramzik v. Brenner* (1967), 65 D.L.R. (2d) 651 (Sask. C.A.); and *Duwyn v. Kaprielian* (1978), 94 D.L.R. (3d) 424 (Ont. C.A.).

2. However, with the expansion of negligence law and the decision in *Anns*, the courts began to question and remove some of these limits. In *McLoughlin v. O'Brian*, [1982] 2 All E.R. 298, the majority in the House of Lords held that the sole test of whether a duty existed is reasonable foreseeability of nervous shock without any limitation in terms of space, time, distance, the nature of the injuries sustained, or the relationship of the plaintiff to the victim.

After *Anns* was rejected in *Murphy v. Brentwood District Council*, [1990] 2 All E.R. 908 (H.L.), the English courts began to re-impose limits on nervous shock claims. In *Alcock v. Chief Constable of the South Yorkshire Police*, [1991] 4 All E.R. 907, the House of Lords stated that damages for nervous shock would not be awarded unless: the plaintiff's relationship with the victim was sufficiently close in terms of love and affection so that it was reasonably foreseeable that she might suffer nervous shock if she apprehended that the victim had been or might be injured; the plaintiff was sufficiently proximate to the accident or its aftermath in space or time; and the plaintiff suffered nervous shock from seeing or hearing the accident or its immediate aftermath.

3. What test of duty did the judges adopt in *Rhodes*? Was their analysis consistent with *Hay* or *McLoughlin*?

4. For recent decisions that are consistent with *Rhodes* and *Alcock*, see *Strong v. Moon* (1992), 13 C.C.L.T. (2d) 296 (B.C. S.C.); *Ravenscroft v. Rederiaktiebolaget Transatlantic*, [1991] 3 All E.R. 73 (Q.B.); and *Dube (Litigation Guardian of) v. Penlon Ltd.* (1994), 21 C.C.L.T. (2d) 268 (Ont. Gen. Div.). But see *Bechard v. Haliburton Estate* (1991), 5 O.R. (3d) 512 (C.A.); and *Page v. Smith*, [1995] 2 W.L.R. 644 (H.L.).

5. Should the added horror of seeing a loved one's mangled body in the hospital or morgue be deemed as part of the "aftermath"? The courts have been divided on this issue. See *Cox v. Fleming* (1993), 13 C.C.L.T. (2d) 305 (B.C. S.C.), varied on other grounds (1995), 15 B.C.L.R. (3d) 201 (C.A.); *Szeliga Estate v. Vanderheide*, [1992] O.J. No. 2856; and *Jones v. Wright*, [1991] 3 All E.R. 88 (C.A.), aff'd. (*sub nom. Alcock v. Chief Constable of the South Yorkshire Police*) [1991] 4 All E.R. 907 (H.L.).

6. As in intentional torts, the English and Canadian courts have defined nervous shock narrowly in an attempt to exclude claims for minor emotional upsets. In effect, the plaintiff is required to prove that the nervous shock manifested itself in some form of physical or psychiatric disorder. See *Beaulieu v. Sutherland* (1986), 35 C.C.L.T. 237 (B.C. S.C.); and *Heighington v. Ontario* (1987), 41 C.C.L.T. 230 (Ont. H.C.), aff'd. (1989), 69 O.R. (2d) 484 (C.A.).

7. The courts also draw a distinction between illness caused by nervous shock which is recoverable and illness caused by grief or sorrow which is not recoverable. Is this a meaningful distinction and can it be applied consistently? Should the courts continue to deny recovery for grief? See *Heinz v. Berry*, [1970] 2 Q.B. 40 (C.A.); *Mathison v. Hofer*, [1984] 3 W.W.R. 343 (Man. Q.B.); *Beecham v. Hughes* (1988), 45 C.C.L.T. 1 (B.C. C.A.); *Cox v. Fleming* (1993), 13 C.C.L.T. (2d) 305 (B.C. S.C.), varied on other grounds (1995), 15 B.C.L.R. (3d) 201 (C.A.); and *Dube (Litigation Guardian of) v. Penlon Ltd.* (1994), 21 C.C.L.T. (2d) 268 (Ont. Gen. Div.).

8. Although most cases involve serious automobile, industrial and household accidents, nervous shock claims have arisen in a broad range of fact situations. See, for example, *Curll v. Robin Hood Multi-foods Ltd.* (1974), 56 D.L.R. (3d) 129 (N.S. S.C.) and *Taylor v. Weston Bakeries Ltd.* (1976), 1 C.C.L.T. 158 (Sask. Dist. Ct.) (contaminated food products); *Guay v. Sun Publishing Co.*, [1953] 2 S.C.R. 216 (false newspaper report of husband's and children's deaths); *Cook v. Swinfen*, [1967] 1 All E.R. 299 (C.A.) (solicitor's negligence in divorce proceedings); *Dietelbach v. British Columbia (Public Trustee)* (1973), 37 D.L.R. (3d) 621 (B.C. S.C.); *Pratt & Goldsmith v. Pratt*, [1975] V.R. 378 (Vict. S.C.) (trauma of adjusting to the injuries of close relatives); and *McMullin v. F.W. Woolworth Co.* (1974), 9 N.B.R. (2d) 214 (Q.B.) (diseased turtle infecting plaintiff's children). Except in the food products cases, the courts held that the plaintiffs were not owed a duty of care because nervous shock was unforeseeable.

9. Can the distinction between recovery for nervous shock and physical injuries still be justified? Do nervous shock claims pose any unique concerns about false or trivial claims, problems of proof, or indeterminate liability? Do these concerns simply obscure a gender bias in the law? See Chamallas and Kerber, "Women, Mothers, and the Law of Fright: A History" (1990), 88 Mich. L. Rev. 814.

10. The development of the law of nervous shock may be traced through a series of articles. See Magruder, "Mental and Emotional Disturbance in the Law of Torts" (1936), 49 Harv. L. Rev. 1033; Goodhart, "The Shock Cases and Area of Risk" (1953), 16 Mod. L. Rev. 14; Trindale, "The Principles Governing the Recovery of Damages for Negligently Caused Nervous Shock" (1986), 45 Cambridge L.J. 476; Teff, "Liability for Psychiatric Illness after *Hillsborough*" (1992), 12 Oxford J. of Legal Studies 440; and Robertson, "Liability in Negligence for Nervous Shock" (1994), 57 Mod. L. Rev. 649.

REVIEW PROBLEM

John Smith fell asleep at the wheel of his truck, crashed through a barrier and struck an oncoming car. The driver of the car, Mike Berry, was killed and his wife Helen was injured. Although Helen's physical injuries healed quickly, she was unable to cope with the shock of the accident and her husband's death. It was only after 15 months of intensive psychiatric care that Helen was able to return to work and a relatively normal lifestyle. Steven Finch, the other passenger in the Berry car, was uninjured. Unfortunately David Finch, his father, had been following the Berry car and suffered severe shock on witnessing the collision, as did Mrs. Pewter, an old friend who was travelling in the Finch car. As a result of his attempts to assist the accident victims, Melvin, a bystander, suffered recurring nightmares. The gruesome scene triggered Melvin's memories of a childhood accident in which his younger brother had been killed. As Sarah Berry drove past the scene she recognized the demolished car of her brother, Mike Berry. By the time she stopped and ran back to the scene, all of the accident victims had been taken to the hospital. She fought back her tears long enough to ask one of the officers what had happened. All he was able to tell her was that the accident had been a serious one involving several members of the Berry family. Sarah was overwhelmed and passed out. She was informed of her brother's death when she regained consciousness in the hospital. Lastly, Mike Berry's mother suffered a heart attack when she heard of her son's death in a radio broadcast.

You have been consulted by John Smith for advice concerning his possible liability for the negligent infliction of nervous shock.

5. A Health Professional's Duty to Inform

As indicated in chapter 6, the Supreme Court of Canada decided in *Reibl v. Hughes* (1980), 114 D.L.R. (3d) 1, to limit a doctor's liability in battery to cases in which the patient did not consent at all, the consent was exceeded, or the consent was obtained fraudulently. Once the patient is aware of the general nature of the proposed treatment and consents to it, the doctor's failure to inform will not vitiate the consent and give rise to liability in battery. Rather, the Supreme Court indicated that doctors may be held liable in negligence for breaching their affirmative duty to disclose the risks of the proposed treatment. This duty is a special duty of care that arises independently of the doctor's general duty to exercise reasonable care in treating patients.

The court focused on the information that a reasonable patient in the plaintiff's position would want. More specifically, the court stated that doctors must disclose all material risks of the proposed treatment. A "material risk" includes a low percentage risk of a serious consequence. In *Reibl*, it was held that a 4 per cent chance of death and a 10 per cent chance of paralysis constituted material risks. A relatively minor consequence of high probability may also constitute a material risk. As well, doctors have an obligation to disclose non-material risks that they know, or ought to know, would be of particular concern to the patient. For example, a doctor may not have to disclose a 5 per cent risk of minor residual stiffness in the shoulder to a patient who is a school teacher, but would have to disclose this risk to a patient who is a professional tennis player.

Patients may choose to rely on their doctor's judgment and decide that they do not wish to be informed of the risks. However, the decision not to be fully informed is the patient's and she must expressly communicate this to the doctor. All questions must be answered honestly and fully, even if they relate to minor matters or if the answers might be upsetting.

Doctors who do not meet these disclosure requirements will be held to have breached the requisite standard of care. However, a patient must also establish that this failure to be informed was a cause of her loss. In effect, the patient must prove that had she been adequately informed, she would not have proceeded with the treatment. In *Reibl*, the Supreme Court of Canada rejected the general common law test of causation and adopted a special objective/subjective test of causation. The plaintiff must prove that a reasonable person in the plaintiff's position would have refused the procedure if properly informed.

As the following case and the accompanying notes and questions illustrate, the courts have broadened the duty to inform considerably since it was first established in *Reibl*. The duty is no longer limited to warning patients of the risks of the specific procedure; rather, the doctor is required to provide the patient with sufficient information to make an informed decision. The definition of what constitutes a material risk has been broadened to include very remote risks of death or serious injury. The courts are far less willing to give doctors discretion to withhold information because the doctor believes it will be disconcerting to the patient. Finally, these principles governing the duty to inform now appear to apply to all health professionals and care givers.

HAUGHIAN v. PAINE
(1987), 40 C.C.L.T. 13 (Sask. C.A.)

[The plaintiff underwent disc surgery which left him paralyzed. A second operation partially alleviated the paralysis. The plaintiff's action against the defendant surgeon for failing to obtain an informed consent was dismissed at trial and the plaintiff appealed.]

SHERSTOBITOFF J.A.: — [The judge quoted from *Videto v. Kennedy* (1981), 33 O.R. (2d) 497 (C.A.), a summary of the Supreme Court of Canada's conclusions from *Reibl* and *Hopp*.]

I would add to the principles outlined above a matter which was not under direct consideration in the foregoing cases: In order to enable a patient to give informed consent, a surgeon must also, where the circumstances require it, explain to the patient the consequences of leaving the ailment untreated, and alternative means of treatment and their risks. In *Reibl v. Hughes*, supra, the Court said at p. 895:

> "A useful summary of issues on which medical evidence in non-disclosure cases remains significant is found in a comment, 'New Trends in Informed Consent?' (1975), 54 Neb. L. Rev. 66, at pp. 90-91, where, after noting that medical evidence should not control determination of the breach of the standard of care, it continued, as follows (referring to *Canterbury v. Spence, infra*):
>
> 'Even *Canterbury* specifically notes that expert testimony will be required, in all but the clearest instances, to establish (1) risks inherent in a given procedure or treatment, (2) *the consequences of leaving the ailment untreated*, (3) *alternative means of treatment and their risks*, and (4) the cause of the injury suffered by the plaintiff-patient. Finally, if the defendant-physician claims a privilege, expert testimony is needed to show the existence of (1) an emergency which would eliminate the need for obtaining consent, and (2) the impact upon the patient of risk disclosure where a full disclosure appears medically unwarranted." (italics added)

. . .

In my respectful view, the trial Judge erred in failing to give any weight, under the aspect of informed consent, to the duty of the respondent in this case to advise the appellant of the consequences of leaving the ailment untreated and the duty to advise of alternate means of treatment. A careful examination of the evidence (most of it quoted above) under the head of negligence indicates that there was no adequate discussion, if any at all, of the consequences of leaving the ailment untreated or of undergoing conservative management, and that the consequences were, at worst, a continuation of pain and discomfort and possible need for surgery in the future. The appellant was not told that the prospect was that the condition might, in a matter of months, very well improve, albeit with the prospect of recurrence from time to time. If the condition deteriorated, surgery was always an option in the future. In the absence of such information having been given to the appellant, he was not in a position to give informed consent.

It makes no difference that the respondent may have been under a misconception that the appellant had had conservative management. If that was the case it was due to the respondent's negligence in failure to take an adequate history, or to consider it.

The other aspect of the informed consent is the failure of the respondent to warn the appellant of the possibility of total paralysis, the risk which in fact materialized. Although no exact statistics were given, a consensus seems to have arisen amongst the neurosurgeons giving evidence that the risk of paralysis in surgery such as under consideration here is not more than one in five hundred. The respondent's practice was not to give any warning if the risk was less then one in one hundred.

. . .

The trial Judge made reference to the similarity of facts in *Hopp v. Lepp* and this case: both involve disc surgery. He commented that the doctor was found not liable in *Hopp v. Lepp* and he told the patient less of the risks than the respondent did in this case. However, a careful reading of *Hopp v. Lepp* does not disclose that any alternative such as conservative management was available in that case. It was certainly not an issue. That is sufficient to distinguish it, on the facts, from this case.

Finally, I touch upon an argument advanced by the respondent. His position is that statistically the risk of paralysis is less than one in five hundred, a risk so insignificant that it could not be considered material. In my respectful view, the issue of materiality cannot be reduced to numbers for all cases. Statistics are but one factor to be taken into account.

In my respectful view, the disclosure made by the respondent was not adequate to enable the appellant to give informed consent. On the principles laid down above which I have quoted from *Hopp v. Lepp*, *Reibl v. Hughes*, *Canterbury v. Spence*, and the dissenting opinion of Lord Scarman in *Sidaway v. Bethlem Royal Hospital Governors*, the following deficiencies in disclosure are apparent in this case:

1. A failure to advise adequately, or at all, of the available options of no treatment, or conservative management. While it may have been open to the respondent not to recommend these options by way of treatment, the patient was entitled to be advised that these alternatives were open to him.

2. A failure to advise of the risk of paralysis. Admittedly, the risk was small, but given that alternative non-surgical treatment was available, with lack of risk,

a significant chance of success, and the paucity of evidence that the condition disabled the appellant significantly, disclosure should have been made.

A significant factor is that the trial Judge considered failure to warn of risk of paralysis, and failure to advise of alternatives to surgery, independently of, and in isolation from, each other. These two elements of informed consent have, on the facts of this case, a strong bearing on each other. One cannot make an informed decision to undertake a risk without knowing the alternatives to undergoing the risk.

There is no suggestion here that the respondent withheld the information because of "therapeutic privilege". There was no suggestion that disclosure would have unduly frightened the appellant, caused him psychological harm or deterred him from taking treatment essential to his health. The respondent's position was simply that it was not his practice to warn of this risk.

. . .

[Appeal allowed; judgment for plaintiff.]

NOTES AND QUESTIONS

1. How does *Haughian* expand the principles in *Reibl*? What role did the alternative treatments play in the judge's conclusion in *Haughian* that a 1 in 500 chance of paralysis was a material risk? See also *Coughlin v. Kuntz* (1989), 2 C.C.L.T. (2d) 42 (B.C. C.A.).

2. In *Reibl* and *Haughian*, the courts suggest that a health professional has a limited "therapeutic privilege" to withhold information if its disclosure would unduly frighten or deter the patient. However, in *Hopp v. Lepp* (1980), 112 D.L.R. (3d) 67 (S.C.C.), the court suggested that the privilege no longer existed. In *Meyer Estate v. Rogers* (1991), 2 O.R. (3d) 356 (Gen. Div.), the judge stated that the doctrine was no longer part of the law. In *Pittman Estate v. Bain* (1994), 112 D.L.R. (4th) 257 (Ont. Gen. Div.), the court acknowledged that the privilege existed, but defined it narrowly. In what circumstances, if any, should the courts recognize a privilege to withhold information?

3. The scope of what constitutes a material risk has been progressively broadened since *Reibl*. See, for example, *Buchan v. Ortho Pharmaceutical (Canada) Ltd.* (1986), 25 D.L.R. (4th) 658 (Ont. C.A.) (very rare chance of a stroke as a result of taking oral contraceptives); *Feist v. Gordon* (1989), 67 Alta. L.R. (2d) 283 (Q.B.), aff'd. (1990), 76 Alta. L.R. (2d) 234 (C.A.) (1 in 40,000 risk of puncturing eyeball with cortisone treatment); *Rolof v. Morris* (1990), 109 A.R. 128 (Alta. Q.B.) (1 in 1,000 risk of an intra-uterine contraceptive device leaving the uterus and requiring surgical removal); and *Meyer Estate v. Rogers* (1991), 2 O.R. (3d) 356 (Gen. Div.) (1 in 40,000 to 1 in 100,000 chance of death as a result of a severe reaction to a diagnostic dye).

4. Failing to inform the patient that a resident, as opposed to a fully-qualified specialist, would be performing the cardiac catherization was held to be a material risk that had to be disclosed. See *Currie v. Blundell* (1992), 10 C.C.L.T. (2d) 288 at 290 (Que. S.C.). But see *Hopp v. Lepp* (1980), 112 D.L.R. (3d) 67 (S.C.C.).

5. Must a health practitioner inform patients that his or her success rate is lower than average? Is the seriousness of the procedure a factor which should be considered in resolving this issue? Is the fact that a health professional is being sued for malpractice or investigated by the governing professional body a material risk?

6. Is the fact that a doctor or dentist is HIV-positive a material risk that must be disclosed? One difficulty in resolving this issue is the divergent estimates of the risks of infection from doctor to patient. Nevertheless, aside from one unresolved incident in Florida, there has not been one proven case of a health professional transmitting HIV to a patient. See also Flanagan, "AIDS-Related Risks in the Health Care Setting: HIV Testing of Health Care Workers and Patients" (1993), 18 Queen's L.J. 71.

7. Even if the risks discussed in notes 5 and 6 are held not to be material, should they be viewed as special risks if the patient has expressed concern about them?

8. It has been held that a health professional must answer a patient's questions fully, even if they relate to minor aspects of the procedure. See *Sinclaire v. Boulton* (1985), 33 C.C.L.T. 125 (B.C. S.C.).

However, the courts have not defined the range of questions that a health professional must answer. Should doctors be required to answer questions about whether they are HIV-positive or have any communicable disease? Similarly, must doctors answer direct questions about their success rates and past malpractice claims?

The preceding questions involve issues that are at least potentially relevant to treatment. Does a health professional have to answer questions that are unrelated to the patient's treatment? For example, are doctors required to answer questions about their religion, position on abortion, or ethnic background?

9. There are numerous situations in which the plaintiff's claim turns on proving that she relied upon the defendant's advice — yet in these cases no special causation test is adopted. Are there any unique factors that warrant adopting a special causation test in cases involving a doctor's duty to inform? Given the test of causation, can a patient ever succeed on the issue of causation in cases of non-elective surgery? See Robertson, "Overcoming the Causation Hurdle in Informed Consent Cases: The Principle in *McGhee v. N.C.B.*" (1984), 22 U.W.O. L. Rev. 75; and Osborne, "Causation and the Emerging Canadian Doctrine of Informed Consent to Medical Treatment" (1985), 33 C.C.L.T. 131.

This special test of causation has recently been questioned, but not specifically rejected. See *Arndt v. Smith* (1995), 25 C.C.L.T. (2d) 262 (B.C. C.A.); Osborne, "Annotation" (1995), 25 C.C.L.T. (2d) 264; and *Hollis v. Dow Corning Corp.* (1995), 129 D.L.R. (4th) 609 (S.C.C.).

10. The Health Care Consent Act, 1996, S.O. 1996, c. 2, s. 11, makes obtaining an informed consent a requirement of consent. Consent which is not "informed" is not valid. However, the Act is silent on the civil liability consequences of providing treatment without an informed consent. Will a health professional's failure to obtain an informed consent now give rise to a battery action in any case involving a physical contact? What legal implications flow from framing the action in battery? Are there any circumstances in which a patient would want to proceed in negligence? See Robertson, "Ontario's New Informed Consent Law: Codification or Radical Change?" (1994), 2 Health L.J. 88.

11. For a general discussion of informed consent see Robertson, "Informed Consent Ten Years Later: The Impact of Reibl v. Hughes" (1991), 70 Can. Bar Rev. 423.

REVIEW PROBLEM

Andrew distrusts all doctors and has a morbid fear of hospitals and operations. He was understandably upset when informed that he required an operation to repair a weak blood vessel in his brain. He was told that it was a serious operation and that without it he would live only 8 to 10 years. The general mortality rate for this procedure was 10 per cent, although one surgeon in London, Ontario had a mortality rate of less than 5 per cent. Dr. Baker, Andrew's surgeon, had lost 15 per cent of her patients, but this was due in part to the large number of high-risk patients in her practice. Dr. Baker informed Andrew of the general mortality rate of 10 per cent, but did not mention her own record or that of the very successful surgeon. In addition to the risk of mortality, there was a 5 per cent risk of partial paralysis, and a 1 per cent risk of infection which is common to all operations. Because of Andrew's general anxiety and the effect that this information might have on his condition, Dr. Baker thought it best not to trouble him with this additional information.

Andrew consented to the operation. Regrettably, the operation left him partially paralyzed, and an infection set in hindering his recovery. It had been Andrew's lifelong dream to fly a balloon across the Atlantic solo, but this was now impossible. Dr. Baker knew nothing of the planned flight, which she now dismisses as the unreasonable desire of an eccentric personality. Nonetheless, prior to the operation Andrew had acquired the sponsorship of a major brewery, for what Dr. Baker calls "his flight of fantasy." Andrew is in the depths of depression. He now says that had he known about these other risks, Dr. Baker's personal record and that of the London surgeon, he would have postponed the operation, made his flight and then gone to the surgeon in London. Advise Andrew on suing Dr. Baker for breaching her duty to inform.

6. A Manufacturer's and Supplier's Duty to Warn

HOLLIS v. DOW CORNING CORP.

(1995), 129 D.L.R. (4th) 609 (S.C.C.)

[In 1983, the plaintiff had surgery for the implantation of two silicone breast implants manufactured by the defendant corporation. One of the implants ruptured after 17 months and the plaintiff required several operations to remove the gel and implant covering. The literature accompanying the product warned of the risk of rupture during surgery, but not of any risks of post-surgical rupturing "from ordinary, non-traumatic, human activities". The plaintiff sued both the surgeon and Dow. At trial, the claim against the surgeon was dismissed because this risk was not well-known among surgeons at the time or extensively discussed in the literature. However, Dow was held liable on the basis that the implant had been negligently manufactured.

The British Columbia Court of Appeal granted the plaintiff's appeal and ordered a new trial on the surgeon's liability. The court held Dow liable, but not on the basis that the implant had been negligently manufactured. Rather, Dow was held liable because it had failed to warn of the risks of post-surgery rupture, even though it had received about 50 reports of ruptures by 1983. Dow appealed to the Supreme Court.]

LA FOREST J. (L'HEUREUX-DUBÉ, GONTHIER, CORY and IACOBUCCI JJ. concurring): —

. . .

The sole issue raised in this appeal is whether the Court of Appeal erred in finding Dow liable to the respondent Ms Hollis for failing adequately to warn the implanting surgeon, Dr. Birch, of the risk of a post-surgical implant rupture inside Ms Hollis' body. The appellant Dow does not contest Bouck J.'s factual finding that Ms Hollis' seven-year surgical ordeal caused her great physical and psychological pain, residual scarring on her breasts, and a loss of past and future income. However, Dow submits that it was not responsible for Ms Hollis' injuries. In support of this submission, Dow argues, first, that the warning it gave Dr. Birch was adequate and sufficient to satisfy its duty to Ms Hollis, and second, that even if it did breach its duty to warn Ms Hollis, this breach was not the proximate cause of her injuries.

For the reasons that follow, it is my view that the Court of Appeal reached the correct conclusion and that the appeal should be dismissed.

. . .

It is well-established in Canadian law that a manufacturer of a product has a duty in tort to warn consumers of dangers inherent in the use of its product of which it has knowledge or ought to have knowledge. This principle was enunciated by Laskin J. (as he then was), for the court, in *Lambert v. Lastoplex Chemicals Co.* (1971), 25 D.L.R. (3d) 121 at pp. 124-5, [1972] S.C.R. 569.

. . .

The duty to warn is a continuing duty, requiring manufacturers to warn not only of dangers known at the time of sale, but also of dangers discovered after the product has been sold and delivered: see *Rivtow Marine Ltd. v. Washington Iron Works* (1973), 40 D.L.R. (3d) 530 at pp. 536-7, [1974] S.C.R. 1189, [1973] 6 W.W.R. 692, *per* Ritchie J. All warnings must be reasonably communicated, and must clearly describe any specific dangers that arise from the ordinary use of the product:

. . .

The rationale for the manufacturer's duty to warn can be traced to the "neighbour principle", which lies at the heart of the law of negligence, and was set down in its classic form by Lord Atkin in *Donoghue v. Stevenson*, [1932] A.C. 562 (H.L.). When manufacturers place products into the flow of commerce, they create a relationship of reliance with consumers, who have far less knowledge than the manufacturers concerning the dangers inherent in the use of the products, and are therefore put at risk if the product is not safe. The duty to warn serves to correct the knowledge imbalance between manufacturers and consumers by alerting consumers to any dangers and allowing them to make informed decisions concerning the safe use of the product.

The nature and scope of the manufacturer's duty to warn varies with the level of danger entailed by the ordinary use of the product. Where significant dangers are entailed by the ordinary use of the product, it will rarely be sufficient for manufacturers to give general warnings concerning those dangers; the warnings must be sufficiently detailed to give the consumer a full indication of each of the specific dangers arising from the use of the product. This was made clear by Laskin J. in *Lambert, supra*, where this court imposed liability on the manufacturer of a fast-drying lacquer sealer who failed to warn of the danger of using the highly explosive product in the vicinity of a furnace pilot light. The manufacturer in *Lambert* had placed three different labels on its containers warning of the danger of inflammability. The plaintiff, an engineer, had read the warnings before he began to lacquer his basement floor and, in accordance with the warnings, had turned down the thermostat to prevent the furnace from turning on. However, he did not turn off the pilot light, which caused the resulting fire and explosion. Laskin J. found the manufacturer liable for failing to provide an adequate warning, deciding that none of the three warnings was sufficient in that none of them warned specifically against leaving pilot lights on near the working area. . . .

In the case of medical products such as the breast implants at issue in this appeal, the standard of care to be met by manufacturers in ensuring that consumers are properly warned is necessarily high. Medical products are often designed for bodily ingestion or implantation, and the risks created by their improper use are obviously substantial. The courts in this country have long recognized that manufacturers of products that are ingested, consumed or otherwise placed in the body, and thereby have a great capacity to cause injury to consumers, are subject to a correspondingly high standard of care under the law of negligence:

. . .

Given the intimate relationship between medical products and the consumer's body, and the resulting risk created to the consumer, there will almost always be a heavy onus on manufacturers of medical products to provide clear, complete and current information concerning the dangers inherent in the ordinary use of their product.

. . .

As a general rule, the duty to warn is owed directly by the manufacturer to the ultimate consumer. However, in exceptional circumstances, a manufacturer may satisfy its informational duty to the consumer by providing a warning to what the American courts have, in recent years, termed a "learned intermediary".

. . .

Generally, the rule is applicable either where a product is highly technical in nature and is intended to be used only under the supervision of experts, or where the nature of the product is such that the consumer will not realistically receive a direct warning from the manufacturer before using the product. In such cases, where an intermediate inspection of the product is anticipated or where a consumer is placing primary reliance on the judgment of a "learned intermediary" and not the manufacturer, a warning to the ultimate consumer may not be necessary and the manufacturer may satisfy its duty to warn the ultimate consumer by warning the learned intermediary of the risks inherent in the use of the product.

However, it is important to keep in mind that the "learned intermediary" rule is merely an exception to the general manufacturer's duty to warn the consumer. The rule operates to discharge the manufacturer's duty not to the learned intermediary, but to the ultimate consumer, who has a right to full and current information about any risks inherent in the ordinary use of the product. Thus, the rule presumes that the intermediary is "learned", that is to say, fully apprised of the risks associated with the use of the product. Accordingly, the manufacturer can only be said to have discharged its duty to the consumer when the intermediary's knowledge approximates that of the manufacturer. To allow manufacturers to claim the benefit of the rule where they have not fully warned the physician would undermine the policy rationale for the duty to warn, which is to ensure that the consumer is fully informed of all risks.

. . . [I]t is my view that the "learned intermediary" rule is applicable in this context, and that Dow was entitled to warn Dr. Birch concerning the risk of rupture without warning Ms Hollis directly. A breast implant is distinct from most manufactured goods in that neither the implant nor its packaging are placed directly into the hands of the ultimate consumer. It is the surgeon, not the consumer, who obtains the implant from the manufacturer and who is therefore in the best position to read any warnings contained in the product packaging.

. . .

Although Bouck J. declined to rule on this issue, a majority of the Court of Appeal found that Dow's warning to Dr. Birch was inadequate. In my view, the Court of Appeal was correct in reaching this conclusion. . . .

It is significant that the only reference in the 1976 and 1979 warnings to a risk of post-surgical rupture was the statement that "abnormal squeezing or trauma" might rupture the implants. There is no reference in these warnings to the possibility of rupture arising from normal squeezing or non-traumatic, everyday activity. This is significant because, in 1985, Dow began warning physicians of the possibility of rupture due to normal, non-traumatic activity in the product insert for the Silastic II implant, a new breast implant developed in the early 1980s with a thicker envelope and greater durability than the earlier Silastic I model. . . .

It is clear from a comparison of the 1985 warning with the earlier warnings that the 1985 warning is far more explicit, both with respect to the potential causes of post-surgical implant rupture and the potential effects. Of particular significance, in my view, is the statement in the 1985 warning that rupture can be caused by "excessive stresses or manipulation as may be experienced during normal living experiences" such as "vigorous exercise, athletics, and intimate physical contact". There is, without question, a substantial difference between "trauma", on the one hand, and the "stresses" and "manipulation" of "everyday living experiences", on the other hand. The difference is that, while the earlier warnings implied that rupture would occur only in extreme cases of violent impact, the 1985 warning made it clear that a patient who received an implant would have to consider altering her lifestyle to avoid rupture. The difference between the 1985 warning and the earlier warnings was significant to a woman in Ms Hollis' position because, subsequent to her surgery, she decided to enrol in a baker's course, which involved regular and heavy upper body movements. While a baker's course may not cause "trauma" to an implant, it would certainly create a risk of "excessive stresses or manipulation". Thus, a more accurate warning could quite reasonably have affected her choice of profession and her resulting exposure to unnecessary risk.

This is not to say, of course, that the standard of care to which Dow must be held for its warning practices in 1983 should be measured according to its knowledge of the risks of implant rupture in 1985. In light of the significant differences between the 1985 warning and the earlier warnings, the crucial next question is whether Dow knew or should have known of the risks referred to in the 1985 warning when Ms Hollis had her implantation surgery in 1983. In my view, there was sufficient evidence adduced at trial to establish that Dow did have such knowledge.

. . .

. . . [I]t is apparent that, by late 1983, Dow had already received between 48 and 61 of the 78 unexplained rupture reports it received before issuing its revised 1985 warning. Counsel for Dow conceded that the nature and quantity of the information available to Dow did not change significantly between late 1983 and early 1985. Thus, although the reports were admitted into evidence at trial for the purpose of establishing their existence and not as to the truth of their contents, the mere fact that Dow had these reports in their possession demonstrates that, in 1983, Dow had notice that ruptures were occurring that were not directly attributable to abnormal squeezing or trauma. Counsel for Dow was unable to explain why it took Dow more than two years to convey the information concerning the unexplained ruptures to either the medical community or the consumers.

A similar lag time can be discerned with respect to Dow's warnings concerning the effects of implant ruptures on the body. The evidence indicates that, prior to 1983, and even as early as 1979, Dow was aware that implant ruptures could cause adverse reactions in the body arising from loose gel. . . .

In my view, Dow had a duty to convey its findings concerning both the "unexplained" rupture phenomenon and the possible harm caused by loose gel inside the body to the medical community much sooner than it did. In light of the fact that implants are surgically placed inside the human body, and that any defects in these products will obviously have a highly injurious effect on the user, the onus on Dow to be forthcoming with information was extremely high throughout the relevant period. Despite this fact, for over six years Dow took no action to express its concerns to the medical community. Given Dow's knowledge of the potential harm caused by loose gel in the body, this lag time is simply unacceptable. The duty to warn is a continuing one and manufacturers of potentially hazardous products have an obligation to keep doctors abreast of developments even if they do not consider those developments to be conclusive. As Robins J.A. noted in *Buchan*, supra, at p. 678:

> . . . where medical evidence exists which tends to show a serious danger inherent in the use of a drug, the manufacturer is not entitled to ignore or discount that information in its warning because it finds it to be unconvincing; the manufacturer is obliged to be forthright and to tell the whole story.
>
> . . .

I conclude, therefore, that the Court of Appeal made no error in ruling that Dow did not discharge its duty to Ms Hollis by properly warning Dr. Birch concerning the risk of post-surgical implant rupture.

2. *Did Dow's breach of the duty to warn cause Ms Hollis' injury?*

Dow raises two distinct causation issues in this appeal. The first is whether Ms Hollis would have elected to have the operation if she had been properly warned of the risk by Dr. Birch. Dow submits that a reasonable woman in Ms Hollis' position would have consented to the surgery despite the risk and, on this basis, argues that its failure to warn was not the proximate cause of Ms Hollis' injury. The second issue Dow raises is whether Dr. Birch would have warned Ms Hollis if he had been properly warned by Dow of the risk. Dow submits that Ms Hollis had the onus of establishing that Dr. Birch would not have warned Ms Hollis even if fully apprised by Dow of the risk and, once again, argues that its failure to warn cannot be the proximate cause of her injuries. Counsel for Ms Hollis sought to meet the first issue on a factual basis alone. As to the second issue, however, he contested as well the underpinnings of Dow's argument, which as will appear raises more substantial legal issues. I shall accordingly approach the issues on that basis.

(a) *Would Ms Hollis have consented to the operation if properly warned of the risk?*

(i) *The appropriate test*

In determining whether Ms Hollis would have consented to the operation had she been properly warned by Dr. Birch of the risk of rupture, Prowse J.A. applied the modified objective test developed by this court in *Reibl, supra*, which involved a negligence action by a patient against a surgeon for failing to warn him of the risk of paralysis entailed in elective surgery performed by that surgeon. The test applied by Prowse J.A. was as follows: would a reasonable woman in Ms Hollis' particular circumstances have consented to the surgery if she had known all the material risks? I note, however, that in *Buchan, supra*, at pp. 685-7, Robins J.A. found the *Reibl* test to be inapplicable to products liability cases, and instead applied a subjective test. . . .

As Robins J.A. intimated in *Buchan*, the duty of the doctor is to give the best medical advice and service he or she can give to a particular patient in a specific context. It is by no means coterminous with that of the manufacturer of products used in rendering that service. The manufacturer, on the other hand, can be expected to act in a more self-interested manner. In the case of a manufacturer, therefore, there is a greater likelihood that the value of a product will be overemphasized and the risk underemphasized. It is, therefore, highly desirable from a policy perspective to hold the manufacturer to a strict standard of warning consumers of dangerous side-effects to these products. There is no reason, as in the case of a doctor, to modify the usual approach to causation followed in other tortious actions. Indeed the imbalance of resources and information between the manufacturer and the patient, and even the doctor, weighs in the opposite direction. Moreover, it is important to remember that many product liability cases of this nature will arise in a context where no negligence can be attributed to a doctor. It would appear ill-advised, then, to distort the rule that is appropriate for claims against a manufacturer simply because of an apparent anomaly that results in cases where a doctor is also alleged to have been negligent.

(ii) *The application of the test to the facts of the case at bar*

In my view, there was sufficient evidence adduced at trial to satisfy the subjective *Buchan* test. Ms Hollis testifies quite clearly at trial that, had she been properly warned by Dr. Birch of the risk of rupture, she would not have had the surgery.

. . .

The second causation issue *raised by Dow* is whether Dr. Birch would have warned Ms Hollis of the risk of rupture if Dow had properly warned Dr. Birch about that risk. Dow argues that there is no direct causal link between its breach of the duty to warn and Ms Hollis' injury because, in 1983, Dr. Birch was aware of the risk of implant rupture but did not make a habit of warning his patients about that risk. In support of this argument, Dow relies on Dr. Birch's testimony at trial that, in 1983, he was warning only 20% to 30% of his patients of implant rupture, and that, in determining the nature and scope of his warnings to patients, he relied more on the articles he read in medical journals than on manufacturers' warnings.

It is right to say, however, that the trial judge found that in 1983 the average plastic surgeon in British Columbia did not in fact know about the possibility that rupture of Silastic implants could be a factor of any significance. This finding is supported and amplified by the fact that after Dow began circulating its more extensive 1985 warning and knowledge of the risk of rupture in the medical community became more prevalent, Dr. Birch adapted his practice accordingly, and by 1989 he was warning all his patients of the risk of rupture.

I do not propose to enter further into or assess these factors. I say this because, while Dow is correct in submitting that there was some ambiguity at trial concerning Dr. Birch's warning practices in 1983, Dow's argument is based upon the assumption that to succeed in her claim against Dow Ms Hollis must prove that Dr. Birch would have warned her if Dow had properly warned Dr. Birch. I do not think this assumption is well founded. Ms Hollis, it will be remembered, demonstrated that Dow had breached its duty to warn her of the risk of rupture, that she would not have undergone the medical procedure if she had been fully informed of the risks, and that she suffered injury from the rupture. Had Dr. Birch been adequately warned but had not passed on the information to Ms Hollis, Dow would, it is true, have been absolved of liability by virtue of the learned intermediary doctrine. But I fail to see how one can reason from this that, for Dow to be liable, Ms Hollis must now establish that Dr. Birch would have informed her if he had known. To require her to do so would be to ask her to prove a hypothetical situation relating to her doctor's conduct, one, moreover, brought about by Dow's failure to perform its duty. While the legal and persuasive onus in a negligence case generally falls on the plaintiff, I do not see how this can require the plaintiff to prove a hypothetical situation of this kind.

. . .

Simply put, I do not think a manufacturer should be able to escape liability for failing to give a warning it was under a duty to give, by simply presenting evidence tending to establish that even if the doctor had been given the warning, he or she would not have passed it on to the patient, let alone putting an onus on the plaintiff to do so. Adopting such a rule would, in some cases, run the risk of leaving the plaintiff with no compensation for her injuries. She would not be able to recover against a doctor who had not been negligent with respect to the information that he or she *did* have; yet she also would not be able to recover against a manufacturer who, despite having failed in its duty to warn, could escape liability on the basis that, had the doctor been appropriately warned, he or she still would not have passed the information on to the plaintiff. Our tort law should not be held to contemplate such an anomalous result.

. . .

Conclusion

On the basis of the foregoing, it is my view that Dow breached its duty to warn Dr. Birch concerning the risks of post-surgical rupture in the Silastic implant and because of this failure to warn is liable to Ms Hollis for her injuries. Accordingly, I would dismiss the appeal.

[Sopinka J., with McLachlin J. concurring, dissented. Sopinka J. held that the plaintiff was not entitled to succeed unless she could establish that a reasonable person would have refused the implant if properly warned and that her surgeon would have passed the warning on to her if he had been properly informed.]

NOTES AND QUESTIONS

1. Based on *Hollis*, define a manufacturer's duty to inform consumers of the risks inherent in the use of its products. Did the court impose a different standard of care on manufacturers of pharmaceuticals and medical products?

2. In what circumstances can a manufacturer rely on the learned intermediary rule? According to *Hollis*, what information must a manufacturer disclose to a learned intermediary to meet its duty to warn? What obligation, if any, does a manufacturer have after it had adequately informed a learned intermediary to ensure that the information is passed on to the consumer?

3. Given Dow's knowledge of the unexplained ruptures and the accompanying risks, was Dow negligent in continuing to market the implant in 1983? Had the plaintiff's case proceeded on this basis, would the adequacy of the warning have been relevant?

4. What was La Forest J.'s rationale for adopting the subjective test of causation in *Hollis*? Was

it compelling? If it was, is there any justification for continuing to use the special objective/subjective test in cases involving health professionals' duty to inform?

Sopinka J., in dissent, stated that the subjective approach fails to address the inherent unreliability of the plaintiff's "self-serving assertions" or the fact that the plaintiff's opinion is likely to be coloured by the injury she has suffered. Is there anything unique about the credibility issues in this area that would warrant special rules of causation?

5. What assumptions can a manufacturer make about the people who are likely to use its products? What impact should such considerations have on the standard of care and its breach? In *Austin v. 3M Canada Ltd.* (1974), 54 D.L.R. (3d) 656 (Ont. Co. Ct.) the plaintiff, who professed to be an auto-body repairman, was injured by the defendant's grinding disc which disintegrated while being used at 9,200 r.p.m. No warnings were provided about the speeds at which the discs should be used. However, the court found that any reasonably competent repairman would have known that it was hazardous to use the discs at more than 8,000 r.p.m. The court held that the defendant was not negligent in failing to warn the plaintiff of this danger. Would the result have been the same if a neighbour, inexperienced in auto-body repair, borrowed an unopened package of discs and suffered injury while using them at an excessive speed? See *Murphy v. St. Catharines Gen. Hosp.* (1963), 41 D.L.R. (2d) 697 (Ont. H.C.).

The duty to warn is specific to the primary user of the product. Therefore, a manufacturer must be careful not to assume that a risk is obvious in circumstances where a child or young person is likely to be the primary consumer. See *Amin (Litigation Guardian of) v. Klironomos*, [1996] O.J. No. 826.

6. Given that the plaintiff in *Lambert v. Lastoplex Chemicals Co.* (1971), 25 D.L.R. (3d) 121 (S.C.C.), cited in *Hollis*, was aware of the danger of working with the product near an open flame, should he have been held contributorily negligent for not turning off the pilot light? In *Labrecque v. Saskatchewan Wheat Pool* (1980), 110 D.L.R. (3d) 686 (Sask. C.A.), an experienced farmer was held contributorily negligent because he should have been aware of certain dangers, despite the defendant manufacturer's inadequate warning. Can you reconcile *Lastoplex* and *Saskatchewan Wheat Pool*?

7. In *Cominco Ltd. v. Westinghouse Can. Ltd.* (1981), 127 D.L.R. (3d) 544 (B.C. S.C.), varied on other grounds (1983), 147 D.L.R. (3d) 279 (B.C. C.A.), it was held that a manufacturer who hears of a new risk after its product is distributed has a duty to warn users as soon as possible. The plaintiff did not have to prove that the manufacturer had actual knowledge, provided the manufacturer ought to have been aware of the new risk. See also *Rivtow Marine v. Washington Iron Works*, [1974] S.C.R. 1189; *Nicholson v. John Deere Ltd.* (1986), 58 O.R. (2d) 53 (H.C.), varied on costs (1989), 68 O.R. (2d) 191 (C.A.); and *Vlchek v. Koshel* (1988), 44 C.C.L.T. 314 (B.C. S.C.), leave to appeal ref'd. (1988), 52 D.L.R. (4th) 371 (note) (B.C. C.A.).

8. In *Hollis*, the Supreme Court indicated that manufacturers have a broad obligation to inform learned intermediaries of new research findings of adverse consequences, even if those findings are speculative or inconclusive. Does this principle create potential problems? At what point would a manufacturer be required to inform learned intermediaries? Would that obligation have arisen after Dow received 20, 10 or 5 reports of unexplained ruptures? Are such isolated, adverse findings of practical use to the learned intermediary? Is there a risk of overloading the intermediaries and consumers with reports of isolated, unanalyzed adverse findings?

9. In *Beshada v. Johns-Manville Products Corp.* (1982), 447 A. 2d 539 (N.J. S.C.), the defendant was held liable for failing to warn of asbestos-related illness, despite the medical community's "presumed unawareness" of such risks at the time. The court stated at 549:

> The burden of illness from dangerous products such as asbestos should be placed upon those who profit from its production and, more generally, upon society at large, which reaps the benefits of the various products our economy manufactures. That burden should not be imposed exclusively on the innocent victim. Although victims must in any case suffer the pain involved, they should be spared the burdensome financial consequences of unfit products. At the same time, we believe this position will serve the salutary goals of increasing product safety research and simplifying tort trials.

> Defendants have argued that it is unreasonable to impose a duty on them to warn of the unknowable. Failure to warn of a risk which one could not have known existed is not unreasonable conduct. But this argument is based on negligence principles. We are not saying what defendants should have done. That is negligence. We are saying that defendants' products were not reasonably safe because they did not have a warning. Without a warning, users of the product were

unaware of its hazards and could not protect themselves from injury. We impose strict liability because it is unfair for the distributors of a defective product not to compensate its victims. As between those innocent victims and the distributors, it is the distributors — and the public which consumes their products — which should bear the unforeseen costs of the product.

Is this an appropriate solution to the allocation of losses arising from hazardous products? Is there something unique about manufacturers as opposed to other defendants, that justifies imposing liability on them in the absence of negligence? Are the courts an appropriate institution for deciding how to allocate such losses? See Berry, "*Beshada v. Johns-Manville Products Corp.*: Revolution — Or Aberration — in Products' Liability Law" (1984), 52 Fordham L. Rev. 786; Boivin, "Negligence, Strict Liability, and Manufacturer Failure to Warn: On Fitting Round Pegs in a Square Hole" (1993), 16 Dalhousie L.J. 299; and *Hunt v. T&N plc.* (1990), 4 C.C.L.T. (2d) 1 (S.C.C.).

It is interesting to contrast the approach in *Beshada* with that adopted by the Supreme Court of Canada in *Lapierre v. A.G. Que.* (1985), 16 D.L.R. (4th) 554. In *Lapierre*, the Court refused to impose strict liability on the government for its measles vaccine which caused the infant plaintiff to suffer a severe attack of encephalitis. See also *Davidson v. Connaught Laboratories* (1980), 14 C.C.L.T. 251 (Ont. H.C.); and *Rothwell v. Raes* (1988), 66 O.R. (2d) 449 (H.C.), aff'd. (1990), 2 O.R. (3d) 332 (C.A.), leave to appeal ref'd. [1991] 1 S.C.R. xiii.

10. A supplier's duty to warn of risks in the use of its products is basically the same as that of a manufacturer. Suppliers are required to warn of risks of which they know or ought to know. See *Allard v. Manahan* (1974), 46 D.L.R. (3d) 614 (B.C. S.C.); and *Lem v. Borotto Sports Ltd.* (1976), 69 D.L.R. (3d) 276 (Alta. C.A.).

Although the courts increasingly require manufacturers to be experts in their field and undertake research or at least keep current with the scientific, academic and industry literature, suppliers would not be expected to have the same level of expertise. Can you suggest a situation in which the manufacturer would be held liable for failing to warn, but the supplier would not be? See also *Buchan v. Ortho Pharmaceutical (Can.) Ltd.* (1986), 35 C.C.L.T. 1 (Ont. C.A.). The courts have extended the duty to warn to installers and repairers. See *Bow Valley Husky (Bermuda) Ltd. v. Saint John Shipbuilding Ltd.* (1995), 126 D.L.R. (4th) 1 (Nfld. C.A.).

11. Should the way in which a supplier markets a product affect its duty or standard of care? Should a greater obligation be imposed on a specialty store that waits on customers than on a department store, self-service shop or mail-order house?

12. To what extent can a manufacuturer or supplier discharge its obligation to warn by providing instructions and cautions in printed material accompanying the product? In *Lem v. Borotto Sports Ltd., supra*, the court denied the plaintiff's claim on the assumption that the plaintiff was aware of the warnings in the instruction booklet, even though he had not read it. The product in question, a shotgun shell reloader, did not appear to be particularly difficult to use, provided the step-by-step instructions were followed. However, in *O'Fallan v. Inecto Rapid (Can.) Ltd.*, [1939] 1 D.L.R. 805 (B.C. S.C.), aff'd. [1940] 4 D.L.R. 276 (B.C. C.A.), it was held that the manufacturer should have put a warning on the container of its hair dye because the warning provided in the separate accompanying literature might not come to the user's attention. Can you reconcile these two cases?

13. In determining if consumers have been adequately informed, the courts will examine the totality of the manufacturer's marketing and promotional activities. In addition to the actual warnings provided, the court may consider any countervailing messages, or advertising, marketing or promotional activities. A manufacturer may be held liable despite providing an adequate warning, if that warning has been obscured or undermined. See *Buchan v. Ortho Pharmaceutical (Can.) Ltd., supra*; Klar, "Recent Developments in Canadian Law: Tort Law" (1991), 23 Ottawa L. Rev. 177; and G. Howells, *Comparative Product Liability* (1993), 262.

14. Another important issue raised by *Lem v. Borotto Sports Ltd.* (1976), 69 D.L.R. (3d) 276 at 287 (Alta. C.A.) is the manufacturer's and supplier's duty to warn of risks arising from the misuse of a product:

In respect of such dangers the duty . . . is to give adequate warning, that is to say explicit warning, not only as to such that would arise out of the contemplated proper use of the product, but also as to such that might arise out of reasonably foreseeable fault on the part of the purchaser in its contemplated use . . . The duty . . . grows more exacting with the degree of danger . . . arising from its misuse, and accordingly the reach of foreseeability is extended further as the circumstances may reasonably require . . . On the other side of the scale, the dangers of use or misuse may be sufficiently apparent or well known to the ordinary prudent person that a warning in respect of them should be taken to be unnecessary in law. An example would be a sharp knife; another, the effect of electricity at high voltage on the human body.

The issue of what constitutes an obvious risk has generated considerable litigation. In addition to *Austin v. 3M Canada Ltd.* (1974), 54 D.L.R. (3d) 656 (Ont. Co. Ct.), see *Schulz v. Leaside Devs.* (1978), 6 C.C.L.T. 248 (B.C. C.A.), leave to appeal ref'd. (1979), 90 D.L.R. (3d) 98n (S.C.C.); *Deshane v. Deere & Co.* (1993), 15 O.R. (3d) 225 (C.A.), leave to appeal ref'd. (1994), 20 C.C.L.T. (2d) 318n (S.C.C.); and *Godin v. Wilson Laboratories Inc.* (1994), 145 N.B.R. (2d) 29 (Q.B.).

15. What obligations should tobacco companies have to warn consumers of the dangers of smoking? How should the following facts influence the manufacturer's duty to warn: (a) smoking is by far the largest preventable cause of death and illness in Canada (estimated at 40,000 deaths per year); (b) smoking is addictive; (c) most smokers become addicted before the age of 18; and (d) the sale of cigarettes to minors is a federal and provincial offence. For a review see Ashley, *The Health Effects of Tobacco Use*, The National Clearinghouse on Tobacco and Health (1995).

For a case involving tobacco manufacturers' duty to warn, see *Perron v. R.J.R. Macdonald Inc.*, [1995] B.C.J. No. 613 (S.C.). See also Linden, "The Potential for a Tort Action Against Tobacco Manufacturers in Canada" [June 1987] The Advocates' Society Journal 25; Cunningham, "Tobacco Products Liability in Common Law Canada" (1990), 11 Health Law in Canada 43; Nolan, "Passive Smoking Litigation in Australia And America: . . ." (1993), 9 J. of Contemporary Health Law and Policy 563; and Cashman and Kellam (eds.), (1993), 4 Australian Product Liability Reporter.

16. It should be noted that a manufacturer who complies with federal or provincial warning legislation, may still be held liable for failing to adequately inform. See *Buchan, supra*; and Waddams, *Products Liability*, 3rd ed. (1993), 50-53.

17. In *Good-Wear Treaders v. D. & B. Holdings Ltd.* (1979), 98 D.L.R. (3d) 59 (N.S. C.A.), the appellant supplier warned a purchaser that the retreaded tires he wanted were unsuitable for the front wheels of a heavy gravel truck. Although the appellant knew that the purchaser was going to ignore the warning, he completed the sale. One of these tires failed and the truck crossed the centre line, demolishing an oncoming car. The driver of the car and his two children were killed, and his widow sued both the purchaser and supplier. She succeeded at trial. The supplier appealed, claiming that he had not breached his duty. The court indicated that the warnings absolved the supplier of liability to the purchaser, but not to third parties. The supplier should not have sold the tires to someone he knew would misuse them and thereby endanger other users of the road.

Should this obligation extend to cases in which a supplier merely suspects that a purchaser will misuse a product? Must the misuse of a product pose an obvious risk of injury to third parties? Is the *Good-Wear* case based on a supplier's and manufacturer's duty to warn or on an individual's obligation to control the conduct of others?

18. For additional academic commentary, see Logie, "Affirmative Action in the Law of Tort: The Case of the Duty to Warn" (1989), 48 Camb. L.J. 115; Peppin, "Drug/Vaccine Risks: Patient Decision-Making and Harm Reduction in the Pharmaceutical Company Duty to Warn Action" (1991), 70 Can. Bar Rev. 473; and Roccamo, "Medical Implants and Other Health Care Products: Theories of Liability and Modern Trends" (1994), 16 Adv. Q. 421.

REVIEW PROBLEMS

1. Acme Company manufactures special gauges and valves with built-in warning devices for use in the chemical industry. Acme sells gauges to distributors, who in turn resell them to chemical companies. In June 1996, Acme discovered that about one-tenth of its K12 valves were defective in that they were prone to emit false warning signals. Acme had stopped making K12 valves in 1990. To the best of Acme's knowledge, its distributors had sold only four valves in 1990 and none in the years since then. Acme was in the midst of a major advertising campaign, focusing on the reliability of its new valves and gauges. Consequently, it was most reluctant to issue a general recall of its K12 valves. It has sought your advice concerning its potential liability if it were to simply ignore this defect in its K12 valves.

2. Mark, an avid amateur repairman, enjoyed fixing his car. When Mark realized that his brakes were becoming worn he decided to replace them. He went to the local Apex Auto Store and purchased a set of very complicated brake drums. The salesman asked Mark if he was having the job done by the Apex service department or whether he was going to take it to another garage. Mark replied that

he would install the brakes himself. The salesman asked Mark if he was a certified automobile mechanic. Mark responded that he was not, but that he enjoyed maintaining his own car. This struck the salesman as being odd because these brakes were extremely difficult to install. The salesman knew that it was highly unlikely that anyone other than a certified mechanic could properly install these brakes. Indeed, he knew that many mechanics refused such work and that they referred it to mechanics who specialized in brake work. Nevertheless, the salesman handed the brakes to Mark without another word or providing any warning as to the difficulty of installing them.

Mark went home and installed the brakes. Unfortunately, he had not installed them properly. While driving in busy traffic, the brakes failed and he ran over Mrs. Winter. Mrs. Winter has sought your advice about suing the Apex Auto Store in negligence for the injuries that she has suffered.

13

THE STANDARD OF CARE

1. Introduction
2. The Common Law Standard of Care: The Reasonable Person Test
3. Factors Considered in Determining Breach of the Standard of Care
4. An Economic Analysis of the Standard of Care
5. Special Standards of Care
6. Degrees of Negligence
7. Custom

1. Introduction

Although there is disagreement concerning the elements of a negligence action and their correct analysis, most common law judges recognize a distinction between the concepts of duty and standard of care. The duty of care analysis is generally understood to be an inquiry into the existence, nature and scope of any legal relationship between the plaintiff and the defendant. As we have seen, the duty of care concept is the legal foundation of torts of negligence. It involves a combination of legal and public policy analysis regarding the boundaries of legal responsibility in the particular factual circumstances of a case. The duty of care is a legal issue which lies within the exclusive control of judges.

Once it has been established that the defendant owed the plaintiff a legal duty of care, the next issue is whether the defendant was "negligent" — that is, whether the defendant met community expectations of reasonable conduct in the circumstances. The questions of standard of care and its breach are often referred to as the "negligence issues" of the negligence action. These issues have both legal and factual elements, and are analyzed in two stages. First, as a question of law, what standard of care was the defendant required to meet, and what factors are to be considered in determining whether it was breached? These legal questions are resolved by judges. Second, based on the specific facts of the case, has the plaintiff proven that the defendant breached the required standard of care? The second stage of the inquiry is a factual issue which lies within the exclusive control of the trier-of-fact.

As the cases and notes below illustrate, making consistent and fair judgments about the reasonableness of conduct is a difficult matter both for judges and juries. Attempts to harness the evaluation of conduct to more systematic mathematical or economic formulae have been resisted by the courts. It is probable that the analysis of the standard of care and its breach will remain the element of a negligence action that is most dependent upon the vagaries of human judgment.

2. The Common Law Standard of Care: The Reasonable Person Test

ARLAND v. TAYLOR

[1955] O.R. 131, [1955] 3 D.L.R. 358 (Ont. C.A.)

[The plaintiff was injured in a motor vehicle accident. At trial, the jury held that the defendant had not breached the requisite standard of care and held for the defendant. The plaintiff appealed, objecting to the trial judge's charge to the jury.]

LAIDLAW J.A.: — ... The second ground of appeal arises from the following passage, in particular, in the charge to the jury:

> First of all you will consider his [the respondent's] negligence. I suggest that you put yourself in the driver's seat of his car. After you have determined the weather and the conditions that existed, ask yourself — "Would I have done that? Was that reasonable for him to do? What precautions would I have taken that he did not? Would I have gone over that hill at the same speed that he did? Would I have reduced my speed?", especially if you decide that as he approached he could not have seen over that hill.

I extract another passage of the charge in which the learned judge said: "... having put yourself in the driver's seat and asked yourself whether he satisfied you under the circumstances, then we go on to the next question ..." The learned trial judge told the jury in more than one part of his charge that ten of them "set the standard of what is reasonable under a given set of circumstances."

The learned trial judge was in error in those instructions to the jury, and this manner of leaving the case to the jury was the subject of disapproval in *Kralj v. Murray, supra.* The standard of care by which a jury is to judge the conduct of parties in a case of the kind under consideration is the care that would have been taken in the circumstances by "a reasonable and prudent man". I shall not attempt to formulate a comprehensive definition of "a reasonable man" of whom we speak so frequently in negligence cases. I simply say he is a mythical creature of the law whose conduct is the standard by which the Courts measure the conduct of all other persons and find it to be proper or improper in particular circumstances as they may exist from time to time. He is not an extraordinary or unusual creature; he is not superhuman; he is not required to display the highest skill of which anyone is capable; he is not a genius who can perform uncommon feats, nor is he possessed of unusual powers of foresight. He is a person of normal intelligence who makes prudence a guide to his conduct. He does nothing that a prudent man would not do and does not omit to do anything a prudent man would do. He acts in accord with general and approved practice. His conduct is guided by considerations which ordinarily regulate the conduct of human affairs. His conduct is the standard "adopted in the community by persons of ordinary intelligence and prudence." See *Blyth v. Birmingham Waterworks Co.* (1856), 11 Exch. 781, 156 E.R. 1047, and Mazengarb, *Negligence on the Highway,* 2nd ed. 1952, p. 15.

In *Glasgow Corporation v. Muir et al.,* [1943] A.C. 448, [1943] 2 All E.R. 414, Lord Macmillan at p. 457 said:

> The standard of foresight of the reasonable man is, in one sense, an impersonal test. It eliminates the personal equation and is independent of the idiosyncracies of the particular person

whose conduct is in question. Some persons are by nature unduly timorous and imagine every path beset with lions. Others, of more robust temperament, fail to foresee or nonchalantly disregard even the most obvious dangers. The reasonable man is presumed to be free both from over-apprehension and from over-confidence, but there is a sense in which the standard of care of the reasonable man involves in its application a subjective element. It is still left to the judge to decide what, in the circumstances of the particular case, the reasonable man would have had in contemplation, and what, accordingly, the party sought to be made liable ought to have foreseen. Here there is room for diversity of view ... What to one judge may seem far-fetched may seem to another both natural and probable.

In Mazengarb, *op. cit.*, p. 18, the learned author says:

In fixing responsibility, the law has adopted an external standard of care. It realizes that care is a matter of degree, and therefore it has set a standard which is neither too high nor too low. It seeks safety without at the same time unduly hampering transport and transit. It does not require the highest degree of care of which mankind is capable.

And I quote further from p. 20:

The legal standard of care always remains the same in the sense that it is what a reasonably prudent man would have done in like circumstances. But although this legal standard is fixed and immutable, the factual standard changes from time to time and from place to place.

It will be plain from the statements I have quoted that it is improper for a juryman to judge the conduct of a person in given circumstances by considering, after the event, what he would or would not have done in the circumstances.

In *Eyres v. Gillis & Warren Ltd.*, 48 Man. R. 164 at 170, [1940] 3 W.W.R. 390, [1940] 4 D.L.R. 747, Trueman J.A., delivering the unanimous judgment of the Court of Appeal of Manitoba, referred to the definition of negligence as given by Baron Alderson in *Blyth v. Birmingham Waterworks Co., supra*, and then said:

In determining the standard of duty so defined a Judge must not interpose himself, for, the accident having happened, his point of view may be warped by extraneous or subjective considerations, however much he may think he is free from bias. It is for this reason that a jury must not be instructed by the Judge or counsel to put themselves in the place of a defendant in a negligence action when called upon to pronounce upon his conduct.

. . .

[Although Laidlaw J.A. felt that there had been a misdirection, he held that there was no substantial wrong caused by the misdirection in this case and dismissed the appeal.]

NOTES AND QUESTIONS

1. State the common law standard of care. Is the reasonable person test objective, subjective or a combination of both?

2. The degree to which the perception of "reasonable" conduct is influenced by factors such as the trier-of-fact's sex, race, social class, and ethnic background, is a subject of debate among legal academics and trial lawyers. For an introduction to a feminist analysis of the standard of care, see generally Bender, "An Overview of Feminist Torts Scholarship" (1993), 78 Cornell L. Rev. 575.

3. As *Arland* indicates, the reasonable person test is not a standard of perfection. Thus, the courts have distinguished between non-negligent mistakes, referred to as errors of judgment, and negligence. For recent cases involving errors of judgment see *Graham v. Persyko* (1986), 55 O.R. (2d) 10 (C.A.), leave to appeal ref'd. (1986), 57 O.R. (2d) 512 (S.C.C.); *Smith v. B.C. (A.G.)* (1988), 30 B.C.L.R. (2d) 356 (C.A.); and *Edgar v. Richmond (Township)* (1991), 6 C.C.L.T. (2d) 241 (B.C. S.C.).

4. If the prospect of the plaintiff suffering injury is virtually unforeseeable to the reasonable person, should the plaintiff's claim be resolved at the duty or standard of care stage?

5. Why did the Court of Appeal conclude that the trial judge's charge to the jury constituted a misdirection? Why did the judge not order a new trial?

6. Although most negligence cases are governed by the reasonable person test, specific jurisprudence has developed concerning many commonly litigated activities. In a motor vehicle negligence case, for example, it may be helpful to consult the case law to determine whether the conduct in issue has previously been held to have breached the standard of care.

7. For a discussion of the common law standard of care see Seavey, "Negligence — Subjective or Objective" (1927), 41 Harv. L. Rev. 1; James, "The Qualities of the Reasonable Man in Negligence Cases" (1951), 16 Mod. L. Rev. 1; Green, "The Reasonable Man — Legal Fiction or Psychological Reality?" (1968), 2 Law & Society Rev. 241; and Linden, *Canadian Tort Law*, 5th ed. (1993), 106-21.

3. Factors Considered in Determining Breach of the Standard of Care

Although there is no consensus, most judges consider, or ask the jury to consider, four factors in determining if the defendant's conduct breached the standard of care. The probability and likely severity of the risks posed by the defendant's act are weighed against the private and social costs of avoiding the risks and the social utility, if any, of the conduct.

(a) PROBABILITY AND SEVERITY OF THE HARM

U.S. v. CARROLL TOWING CO.

(1947), 159 F. (2d) 169 (2nd Circ.)

. . .

L. HAND, Circuit Judge: — . . . It appears from the foregoing review that there is no general rule to determine when the absence of a bargee or other attendant will make the owner of the barge liable for injuries to other vessels if she breaks away from her mooring. However, in any cases where he would be so liable for injuries to others, obviously he must reduce his damages proportionately, if the injury is to his own barge. It becomes apparent why there can be no such general rule, when we consider the grounds for such a liability. Since there are occasions when every vessel will break from her moorings, and since, if she does, she becomes a menace to those about her; the owner's duty, as in other similar situations, to provide against resulting injuries is a function of three variables: (1) the probability that she will break away; (2) the gravity of the resulting injury, if she does; (3) the burden of adequate precautions. Possibly it serves to bring this notion into relief to state it in algebraic terms: if the probability be called P; the injury, L; and the burden, B; liability depends upon whether B is less than L multiplied by P: i.e., whether B is less than PL. Applied to the situation at bar, the likelihood that a barge will break from her fasts and the damage she will do, vary with the place and time; for example, if a storm threatens, the danger is greater; so it is, if she is in a crowded harbor where moored barges are constantly being shifted about. On the other hand, the barge must not be the bargee's prison, even though he lives aboard; he must go ashore at times. We need not say whether, even in such crowded waters as New York Harbor a bargee must be aboard at night at all; it may be that the custom is otherwise, as Ward, J., supposed in "The Kathryn B. Guinan," supra; and that, if so, the situation is one where custom should control. We leave that question open; but we hold that it is not in all cases a sufficient answer to a bargee's absence without excuse, during working hours, that he has properly made fast his barge to the pier, when he leaves her. In the case at bar the bargee left at five o'clock in the afternoon of January 3rd, and the flotilla broke away at about two o'clock in the afternoon of the following day, twenty-one hours afterwards. The bargee had been away all the time, and we hold that his fabricated story was affirmative evidence that he had no excuse for his absence. At the locus in quo — especially during the short January days and in the full tide of war activity — barges were being constantly "drilled" in and out. Certainly it was not beyond reasonable expectation that, with the inevitable haste and bustle, the work might not be done with adequate care. In such circumstances we hold — and it is all that we do hold — that it was a fair requirement that the Connors Company should have a bargee aboard (unless he had some excuse for his absence), during the working hours of daylight.

NOTES AND QUESTIONS

1. What factors did Hand J. consider in determining whether the defendant breached the standard of care? What did he mean by the phrase "the burden of adequate precautions"?

2. Justice Hand's judgment in *Carroll Towing* was an innovative attempt to reduce the question of breach to a matter of mathematical calculation. What are the strengths and weaknesses of this approach? See generally White, "Risk-Utility Analysis and the Learned Hand Formula: A Hand that Helps or a Hand that Hides?" (1990), 32 Ariz. L. Rev. 77.

☀BOLTON v. STONE

[1951] A.C. 850, [1951] 1 All E.R. 1078 (H.L.)

. . .

LORD REID: — My Lords, it was readily foreseeable that an accident such as befell the respondent might possibly occur during one of the appellants' cricket matches. Balls had been driven into the public road from time to time, and it was obvious that if a person happened to be where a ball fell that person would receive injuries which might or might not be serious. On the other hand, it was plain that the chance of that happening was small. The exact number of times a ball has been driven into the road is not known, but it is not proved that this has happened more than about six times in about thirty years. If I assume that it has happened on the average once in three seasons I shall be doing no injustice to the respondent's case. Then there has to be considered the chance of a person being hit by a ball falling in the road. The road appears to be an ordinary side road giving access to a number of private houses, and there is no evidence to suggest that the traffic on this road is other than what one might expect on such a road. On the whole of that part of the road where a ball could fall there would often be nobody and seldom any great number of people. It follows that the chance of a person ever being struck even in a long period of years was very small.

This case, therefore, raises sharply the question what is the nature and extent of the duty of a person who promotes on his land operations which may cause damage to persons on an adjoining highway. Is it that he must not carry out or permit an operation which he knows or ought to know clearly can cause such damage, however improbable that result may be, or is it that he is only bound to take into account the possibility of such damage if such damage is a likely or probable consequence of what he does or permits, or if the risk of damage is such that a reasonable man, careful of the safety of his neighbour, would regard that risk as material? I do not know of any case where this question has had to be decided or even where it has been fully discussed. Of course there are many cases in which somewhat similar questions have arisen, but, generally speaking, if injury to another person from the defendants' acts is reasonably foreseeable the chance that injury will result is substantial and it does not matter in which way the duty is stated. In such cases I do not think that much assistance is to be got from analysing the language which a judge has used. More assistance is to be got from cases where judges have clearly chosen their language with care in setting out a principle, but even so, statements of the law must be read in light of the facts of the particular case. Nevertheless, making all allowances for this, I do find at least a tendency to base duty rather on the likelihood of damage to others than on its foreseeability alone.

The definition of negligence which has, perhaps, been most often quoted is that of Alderson, B., in *Blyth v. Birmingham Waterworks Co.* [(1856), 11 Exch. 781 at 784]:

> Negligence is the omission to do something which a reasonable man, guided upon those considerations which ordinarily regulate the conduct of human affairs, would do, or doing something which a prudent and reasonable man would not do.

I think that reasonable men do, in fact, take into account the degree of risk and do not act on a bare possibility as they would if the risk were more substantial.

. . .

Counsel for the respondent in the present case had to put his case so high as to say that, at least as soon as one ball had been driven into the road in the ordinary course of a match, the appellants could and should have realised that that might happen again, and that, if it did, someone might be injured, and that that was enough to put on the appellants a duty to take steps to prevent such an occurrence. If the true test is foreseeability alone I think that must be so. Once a ball has been driven on to a road without there being anything extraordinary to account for the fact, there is clearly a risk that another will follow and if it does there is clearly a chance, small though it may be, that somebody may be injured. On the theory that it is foreseeability alone that matters it would be irrelevant to consider how often a ball might be expected to land in the road and it would not matter whether the road was the busiest street or the quietest country lane. The only difference between these cases is in the degree of risk. It would take a good deal to make me believe that the law has departed so far from the standards which guide ordinary careful people in ordinary life. In the crowded conditions of modern life even the most careful person cannot avoid creating some risks and accepting others. What a man must not do, and what I think a careful man tries not to do, is to create a risk which is substantial. Of course, there are numerous cases where special circumstances require that a higher standard shall be observed and where that is recognized by the law, but I do not think that this case comes within any such special category. It was argued that this case comes within the principle in *Rylands v. Fletcher* [(1868), L.R. 3 H.L. 330], but I agree with your Lordships that there is no substance in this argument. In my judgment, the test to be applied here is whether the risk of damage to a person on the road was so small that a reasonable man in the position of the appellants, considering the matter from the point of view of safety, would have thought it right to refrain from taking steps to prevent the danger. In considering that matter I think that it would be right to take into account, not only how remote is the chance that a person might be struck, but also how serious the consequences are likely to be *in this case,* if a person is struck, but I do not think that it would be right to take into account *nothing could be* the difficulty of remedial measures. If cricket cannot be played on a ground without *done here* creating a substantial risk, then it should not be played there at all. I think that this is in substance the test which Oliver, J., applied in this case. He considered whether the appellants' ground was large enough to be safe for all practical purposes and held that it was. This is a question, not of law, but of fact and degree. It is not an easy question, and it is one on which opinions may well differ. I can only say that, having given the whole matter repeated and anxious consideration, I find myself unable to decide this question in favour of the respondent. I think, however, that this case is not far from the border-line. If this appeal is allowed, that does not, in my judgment, mean that in every case where cricket has been played on a ground for a number of years without accident or complaint those who organise matches there are safe to go on in reliance on past immunity. I would have reached a different conclusion if I had thought that the risk here had been other than extremely small because I do not think that a reasonable man, considering the matter from the point of view of safety, would or should disregard any risk unless it is extremely small.

. . .

In my judgment, the appeal should be allowed.

. . .

[Lords Porter, Normand, Oaksey, and Radcliffe delivered separate concurring speeches.]

MILLER v. JACKSON

[1977] Q.B. 966, [1977] 3 All E.R. 338 (C.A.)

[The plaintiffs bought a house in a new subdivision which was adjacent to a small well-established cricket club. They sued the club in negligence and nuisance after a number of balls had been hit onto their property, causing minor damage to the house. The defendant club admitted that it would be impossible to prevent balls from occasionally being hit onto the plaintiffs' property, but argued that they had taken all reasonable steps to protect the plaintiffs and had not unreasonably interfered with the use and enjoyment of their property. At trial, the plaintiffs succeeded in both nuisance and negligence and were awarded damages and granted an injunction. The defendants appealed.]

LORD DENNING M.R.: — In summer time village cricket is the delight of everyone. Nearly every village has its own cricket field where the young men play and the old men watch. In the village of Lintz in County Durham they have their own ground, where they have played these last 70 years. They tend it well. The wicket area is well rolled and mown. The outfield is kept short. It has a good club-house for the players and seats for the onlookers. The village team plays there on Saturdays and Sundays. They belong to a league, competing with the neighbouring villages. On other evenings after work they practise while the light lasts. Yet now after these 70 years a judge of the High Court has ordered that they must not play there any more. He has issued an injunction to stop them. He has done it at the instance of a newcomer who is no lover of cricket. This newcomer has built, or has had built for him, a house on the edge of the cricket ground which four years ago was a field where cattle grazed. The animals did not mind the cricket. But now this adjoining field has been turned into a housing estate. The newcomer bought one of the houses on the edge of the cricket ground. No doubt the open space was a selling point. Now he complains that, when a batsman hits a six, the ball has been known to land in his garden or near his house. His wife has got so upset about it that they always go out at weekends. They do not go into the garden when cricket is being played. They say that this is intolerable. So they asked the judge to stop the cricket being played. And the judge, much against his will, has felt that he must order the cricket to be stopped; with the consequences, I suppose, that the Lintz Cricket Club will disappear. The cricket ground will be turned to some other use. I expect for more houses or a factory. The young men will turn to other things instead of cricket. The whole village will be much the poorer. And all this because of a newcomer who has just bought a house there next to the cricket ground.

I must say that I am surprised that the developers of the housing estate were allowed to build the houses so close to the cricket ground. No doubt they wanted to make the most of their site and put up as many houses as they could for their own profit. The planning authorities ought not to have allowed it. The houses ought to have been so sited as not to interfere with the cricket. But the houses have been built and we have to reckon with the consequences.

. . .

It must be admitted, however, that on a few occasions before 1974 a tile was broken or a window smashed. The householders made the most of this and got their rates reduced. The cricket club then did everything possible to see that no balls went over. In 1975, before the cricket season opened, they put up a very high protective fence. The existing concrete fence was only six feet high. They raised it to nearly 15 feet high by a galvanised chain-link fence. It cost £700. They could not raise it any higher because of the wind. The cricket ground is 570 feet above sea level. During the winter even this high fence was blown down on one occasion and had to be repaired at a cost of £400. Not only did the club put up this high protective fence. They told the batsmen to try to drive the balls low for four and not hit them up for six. This greatly reduced the number of balls that got into the gardens. So much so that the rating authority no longer allowed any reduction in rates.

Despite these measures, a few balls did get over. The club made a tally of all the sixes hit during the seasons of 1975 and 1976. In 1975 there were 2,221 overs, that is, 13,326 balls bowled. Of them there were 120 six hits on all sides of the ground. Of these only six went over the high protective fence and into this housing estate. In 1976 there were 2,616 overs, that is 15,696 balls. Of them there were 160 six hits. Of these only nine went over the high protective fence and into this housing estate.

No one has been hurt at all by any of these balls, either before or after the high fence was erected. There has, however, been some damage to property, even since the high fence was erected. The cricket club has offered to remedy all the damage and pay all expenses. They have offered to supply and fit unbreakable glass in the windows, and shutters or safeguards for them. They have offered to supply and fit a safety net over the garden whenever cricket is being played. In short, they have done everything possible short of stopping playing cricket on the ground at all. But Mrs. Miller and her husband have remained unmoved. Every offer by the club has been rejected. They demand the closing down of the cricket club. Nothing else will satisfy them. They have obtained legal aid to sue the cricket club.

In support of the case, the plaintiff relies on the dictum of Lord Reid in *Bolton v. Stone* [[1951] 1 All E.R. 1078 (H.L.)]: 'If cricket cannot be played on a ground without creating a substantial risk, then it should not be played there at all.' I would agree with that saying if the houses or road were there first, and the cricket ground came there second. We would not allow the garden of Lincoln's Inn to be turned into a cricket ground. It would be too dangerous for windows and people. But I do not agree with Lord Reid's dictum [*supra*, at p. 1086] when the cricket ground has been there for 70 years and the houses are newly built at the very edge of it. I recognize that the cricket club is under a duty to use all reasonable care consistently with the playing of the game of cricket, but I do not think the cricket club can be expected to give up the game of cricket altogether. After all they have their rights in their cricket ground. They have spent money, labour and love in the making of it; and they have the right to play on it as they have done for 70 years. Is this all to be rendered useless to them by the thoughtless and selfish act of an estate developer in building right up to the edge of it? Can the developer or purchaser of a house say to the cricket club: 'Stop playing. Clear out.' I do not think so. And I will give my reasons.

. . .

This case is new. It should be approached on principles applicable to modern conditions. There is a contest here between the interest of the public at large and the interest of a private individual. The *public* interest lies in protecting the environment by preserving our playing fields in the face of mounting development, and by enabling our youth to enjoy all the benefits of outdoor games, such as cricket and football. The *private* interest lies in securing the privacy of his home and garden without intrusion or interference by anyone. In deciding between these two conflicting interests, it must be remembered that it is not a question of damages. If by a million-to-one chance a cricket ball does go out of the ground and cause damage, the cricket club will pay. There is no difficulty on that score. No, it is a question of an injunction. And in our law you will find it repeatedly affirmed that an injunction is a discretionary remedy. In a new situation like this, we have to think afresh as to how discretion should be exercised. On the one hand, Mrs. Miller is a very sensitive lady who has worked herself up into such a state that she exclaimed to the judge:

> I just want to be allowed to live in peace. Have we got to wait until someone is killed before anything can be done?

If she feels like that about it, it is quite plain that, for peace in the future, one or other has to move. Either the cricket club has to move, but goodness knows where. I do not suppose for a moment there is any field in Lintz to which they could move. Or Mrs. Miller must move elsewhere. As between their conflicting interests, I am of opinion that the public interest should prevail over the private interest. The cricket club should not be driven out. In my opinion the right exercise of discretion is to refuse an injunction; and, of course, to refuse damages in lieu of an injunction. Likewise as to the claim for past damages. The club was entitled to use this ground for cricket in the accustomed way. It was not a nuisance, nor was it negligence of them so to run it. Nor was the batsman negligent when he hit the ball for six. All were doing simply what they were entitled to do. So if the club had put it to the test, I would have dismissed the claim for damages also. But as the club very fairly says that they are willing to pay for any damage, I am content that there should be an award of £400 to cover any past or future damage.

I would allow the appeal, accordingly.

. . .

[In the majority judgment, Geoffrey Lane L.J. agreed with Cumming-Bruce L.J. that the risk of property damage was both foreseeable and foreseen by the defendants. Geoffrey Lane L.J. further decided that the plaintiffs had "no obligation . . . to protect themselves in their own home" from the threat presented by the defendants' activities. While both judges agreed that the defendants were liable in nuisance and negligence, only Geoffrey Lane L.J. was prepared to grant an injunction.]

PARIS v. STEPNEY BOROUGH COUNCIL

[1951] A.C. 367, [1951] 1 All E.R. 42 (H.L.)

LORD OAKSEY: — My Lords, I agree entirely with the opinion just delivered by my noble and learned friend Lord Normand.

The duty of an employer towards his servant is to take reasonable care for the servant's safety in all the circumstances of the case. The fact that the servant has only one eye, if that fact is known to the employer, and that if he loses it he will be blind, is one of the circumstances which must be considered by the employer in determining what precautions if any shall be taken for the servant's safety. The standard of care which the law demands is the care which an ordinarily prudent employer would take in all the circumstances. As the circumstances may vary infinitely it is often impossible to adduce evidence of what care an ordinarily prudent employer would take. In some cases, of course, it is possible to prove that it is the ordinary practice for employers to take or not to take a certain precaution, but in such a case as the present, where a one-eyed man has been injured, it is unlikely that such evidence can be adduced. The court has, therefore, to form its own opinion of what precautions the notional ordinarily prudent employer would take. In the present case the question is whether an ordinarily prudent employer would supply goggles to a one-eyed workman whose job was to knock bolts out of a chassis with a steel hammer while the chassis was elevated on a ramp so that the workman's eye was close to and under the bolt. In my opinion Lynskey, J., was entitled to hold that an ordinarily prudent employer would take that precaution. The question was not whether the precaution ought to have been taken with ordinary two-eyed workmen and it was not necessary, in my opinion, that Lynskey, J., should decide that question — nor did he purport to decide it, although it is true that he stated the question in one sentence too broadly as "whether the employers in adopting this system and not providing or requiring the use of goggles for the workers on this system were taking reasonable care to provide a suitable system of work and to provide a suitable plant."

The risk of splinters of steel breaking off a bolt and injuring a workman's eye or eyes may be and, I think, is slight and it is true that the damage to a two-eyed workman if struck by a splinter in the eye or eyes may be serious, but it is for the judge at the trial to weigh up the risk of injury and the extent of the damage and to decide whether, in all the circumstances, including the fact that the workman was known to be one-eyed and might become a blind man if his eye was struck, an ordinarily prudent employer would supply such a workman with goggles. It is a simple and inexpensive precaution to take to supply goggles, and a one-eyed man would not be likely, as a two-eyed man might be, to refuse to wear the goggles. Lynskey, J., appears to me to have weighed the extent of the risk and of the damage to a one-eyed man and I am of opinion that his judgment should be restored.

. . .

LORD MORTON OF HENRYTON (dissenting): — My Lords, it cannot be doubted that there are occupations in which the possibility of an accident occurring to any workman is extremely remote, while there are other occupations in which there is constant risk of accident to the workmen. Similarly, there are occupations in which, if an accident occurs, it is likely to be of a trivial nature, while there are other occupations in which, if an accident occurs, the results to the workman may well be fatal. Whether one is considering the likelihood of an accident occurring, or the gravity of the consequences if an accident happens, there is in each case a gradually ascending scale between the two extremes which I have already mentioned.

In considering generally the precautions which an employer ought to take for the protection of his workmen it must, in my view, be right to take into account both elements, the likelihood of an accident happening and the gravity of the consequences. I take as an example two occupations in which the risk of an accident taking place is exactly equal; if an accident does occur in the one occupation, the consequences to the workman will be comparatively trivial; if an accident occurs in the other occupation the consequences to the workman will be death or mutilation. Can it be said that the precautions which it is the duty of an employer to take for the safety of his workmen are exactly the same in each of these occupations? My Lords, that is not my view. I think that the more serious the damage which will happen if an accident occurs, the more thorough are the precautions which an employer must take.

If I am right as to this general principle, I think it follows logically that if A and B, who are engaged on the same work, run precisely the same risk of an accident happening, but if the results of an accident will be more serious to A than to B, precautions which are adequate in the case of B may not be adequate in the case of A, and it is a duty of the employer to take such additional precautions for the safety of A as may be reasonable. The duty to take reasonable precautions against injury is one which is owed by the employer to every individual workman.

In the present case it is submitted by counsel for the appellant that although the appellant ran no greater risk of injury than the other workmen engaged in the maintenance work, he ran a risk of greater injury. Counsel points out that an accident to one eye might transform the appellant into a blind man, and this event in fact happened. A similar accident to one of his comrades would transform that comrade into a one-eyed man, a serious consequence indeed but not so serious as the results have been to the appellant.

My Lords, the Court of Appeal thought that the one-eyed condition of the appellant, known to his employers, was wholly irrelevant in determining the question whether the employer did or did not take reasonable precautions to avoid an accident of this kind. I do not agree. Applying the general principle which I have endeavoured to state, I agree with your Lordships and with Lynskey, J., that the condition of the appellant was a relevant fact to be taken into account.

There still remains, however, the question whether the judge rightly came to the conclusion that there was, "so far as this particular plaintiff was concerned, a duty upon the employers to provide goggles and require the use of goggles as part of their system." He thought, as I read his judgment, and as the Court of Appeal read it, that there was no duty upon the employers to provide goggles for two-eyed men who were employed on the same work as the appellant. With this latter view the Court of Appeal agreed, and I take the same view. The evidence given at the trial has already been analysed by my noble and learned friend on the woolsack, and I shall only add that, although Captain Paterson had knowledge of about half-a-dozen eye injuries in the course of thirty-two years' experience, he did not say whether any of them was of a serious nature. The only other eye injury deposed to was that of Mr. Seeley. He was asked by the judge "Were you off work at all with your eye?", and he answered "Oh no". "Just that something got into your eye?" said the judge. "Yes, and I got it out," replied the witness.

My Lords, is it really possible to draw a distinction, on the facts of the present case, between a two-eyed man and a one-eyed man? If the employers were not negligent in failing to provide goggles for two-eyed men doing this work, during all the years prior to this accident, did they become negligent, so far as regards the appellant alone, as from July 22, 1946, when Mr. Boden, their public cleansing officer, became aware for the first time that the appellant had practically no vision in his left eye? The loss of an eye is a most serious injury to any man, and I can only see two alternatives in this case: (a) that the employers were negligent throughout in failing to provide goggles and insist on their use by all men employed in this type of work; or (b) that the risk of an eye injury to any man was so remote that no employer could be found negligent in failing to take these precautions.

My Lords, I think the first alternative must be rejected. Applying the test laid down by Lord Dunedin in *Morton v. William Dixon* [[1909] S.C. 807] already quoted by my noble and learned friend Lord Normand, I cannot find that the provision of goggles "was a thing which was commonly done by other persons in like circumstances." The evidence is conclusive to the contrary. Nor does the evidence support the view that it was "a thing which was so obviously wanted that it would be folly in anyone to neglect to provide it." Although I recognize that the one-eyed condition of the appellant was a factor to be taken into account, I think alternative (b) is correct. I cannot reach the conclusion that a one-eyed man, but not a two-eyed man, has a remedy against the employer for so serious an injury. I think it must be both or neither, and on the facts of the present case I agree with the conclusion of the Court of Appeal, that the evidence does not establish any negligence on the part of the respondents.

I would dismiss the appeal.

[Lords Normand and MacDermott delivered separate concurring speeches. Lord Simonds dissented for reasons similar to those of Lord Morton of Henryton.]

NOTES AND QUESTIONS

1. In *Bolton*, what factors did Lord Reid consider in determining whether the defendant breached the standard of care? Do you think the defendant would have been absolved of liability if: (a) balls were hit out of the club an average of two times a year; (b) the club was surrounded by busy roadways; or (c) the risk factors were the same but the last time a ball was hit out it seriously injured a pedestrian walking on the quiet street?

2. In *Miller*, what life-experiences and personal preferences appear to have influenced Lord Denning's analysis of the breach issue? Having read a brief summary of the judgments of Geoffrey Lane L.J. and Cumming-Bruce L.J., what preferences appear to have influenced their analyses of the same issue? Is there any principled means of resolving disagreements of this kind?

3. Explain the difference between Lord Oaksey's and Lord Morton's assessment of the risk factors in *Paris*. Would Lord Oaksey have reached the same decision if the plaintiff had possessed normal vision? Would Lord Morton have reached the same conclusion if there had been a previous accident involving a two-eyed worker? See also *Shilson v. Northern Ont. Light & Power Co.* (1919), 59 S.C.R. 433; and *Gloster v. Toronto Electric Light Co.* (1906), 38 S.C.R. 27, where the court considered the probability of children coming into contact with exposed electric wires.

(b) COST OF RISK AVOIDANCE

VAUGHN v. HALIFAX-DARTMOUTH BRIDGE COMM.

(1961), 46 M.P.R. 14, 29 D.L.R. (2d) 523 (N.S. S.C.)

MACDONALD J.: — . . . We must take it that no amount of ordinary care would prevent the dripping paint nor the likelihood of its being carried by the wind varying distances up to some hundreds of feet, to various parts of the dockyard (including the parking lot in question) when the painting operations were carried on in the general area of the bridge adjacent thereto. Thus we may conclude that it was inevitable that paint should fall on the cars in the parking lot in question and during the painting operations in early July. The duty of the defendant was to take all reasonable measures to prevent that result or to minimize damage from falling paint.

The usual horrific argument was made as to the impracticability of any effective steps to do so except at prohibitive cost, particularly because of the large area of affection, say 300-400 ft. of the dockyard north of the bridge to which paint might come from an extent of the bridge 500 ft. long. The answer is that the season of such painting did not exceed a month; and that we are only concerned with precautions in respect of one parking lot relatively close to the bridge. More-over, no policy was established of warning car owners or the dockyard author-ities in advance of painting operations, though the defendant well knew of the danger to them implicit in such operations. On occasion, however, when complaints did come, as they did from time to time, the defendant did bestir itself by advising the Security Officer of the dockyard of painting operations, with the result that certain cars were moved to safer parts of the dockyard. These instances suggest the feasibility of such a practice which if adopted would have obviated damage in this case. Nor can it be said that the defendant could not have asked for permission to post warning signs at the parking lot (or other parts of the dockyard) or communicated *via* press or radio similar warnings of danger from painting expected to be done in the neighbourhood of that lot. If it be said that neglect in this regard was overcome by the provision of a man in the dockyard charged with the duty of wiping fallen paint from the parked cars, the answer is that this method depended upon the wiping operation being done promptly; and that during such a painting season as that in question such provision was clearly inadequate in point of number of men, as is illustrated by the employment of four or more on other occasions. It is notable that precautions in either of these regards would have entailed relatively little expense in view of the shortness of the painting season and would in all probability have prevented or at least minimized the plaintiff's damage.

[Currie J. and Patterson J. also concluded that the defendant was negligent; Ilsley C.J. did not address this issue.]

LAW ESTATE v. SIMICE

(1994), 21 C.C.L.T. (2d) 288 (B.C. S.C.)

[The plaintiff sued the defendant doctors, claiming that her husband died because of their negligent failure to provide timely, appropriate and skillful emergency care. Among other things, they had not initially taken a CT scan of the patient. The case dramatically raised the issue of the allocation of limited and costly medical resources.]

· · ·

SPENCER J.: —

I must observe that throughout this case there were a number of times when doctors testified that they feel constrained by the British Columbia Medical Insurance Plan and by the British Columbia Medical Association standards to restrict their requests for CT scans as diagnostic tools. No doubt such sophisticated equipment is limited and costly to use. No doubt there are budgetary restraints on them. But this is a case where, in my opinion, those constraints worked against the patient's interest by inhibiting the doctors in their judgment of what should be done for him. That is to be deplored. I understand that there are budgetary problems confronting the health care system. I raise it in passing only to point out that there were a number of references to the effect of financial restraint on the treatment of this patient. I respectfully say it is something to be carefully considered by those who are responsible for financing it. I also say that if it comes to a choice between a physician's responsibility to his or her individual patient and his or her responsibility to the medicare system overall, the former must take precedence in a case such as this. The severity of the harm that may occur to the patient who is permitted to go undiagnosed is far greater than the financial harm that will occur to the medicare system if one more CT scan procedure only shows the patient is not suffering from a serious medical condition.

[Several of the doctors who had treated the patient were held liable in negligence.]

NOTES AND QUESTIONS

1. In *Vaughn*, what factors did the court consider in determining if the defendant breached the standard of care? Would the result have been the same if it had been proven that the accident prevention costs exceeded the total damages?

2. Is a patient entitled to the best available or the most affordable medical care? Did the court in *Law Estate* apply an appropriate perspective in assessing the physician's reluctance to order a CT scan? If health professionals have no role to play as financial gatekeepers or allocators of scarce resources, who should play these roles? Has the court adequately considered that ordering a CT scan or booking an operation in one case may result in delays or denials of treatment in other cases?

3. In *Bateman v. Doiron* (1991), 8 C.C.L.T. (2d) 284 (N.B. Q.B.), aff'd. (1993), 18 C.C.L.T. (2d) 1 (N.B. C.A.), leave to appeal ref'd. (1994), 20 C.C.L.T. (2d) 320n (S.C.C.), the court accepted that a Moncton hospital had no choice but to grant privileges to general practitioners in order to staff its emergency department. The court acknowledged that this practice resulted in physicians with limited skill and experience staffing the emergency room. However, the court stated at 292 that:

> to suggest that the defendant Moncton Hospital might be reasonably expected by the community to staff its emergency department with physicians qualified as expert in the management of critically ill patients does not meet the test of reality, nor is it a reasonably expected community standard. The non-availability of trained and experienced personnel, to say nothing of the problems of collateral resource allocation, simply makes this standard unrealistic, albeit desirable.

The majority of the Court of Appeal did not address this issue, but Mr. Justice Rice wrote a scathing dissent, criticizing the staffing and administrative practices of the emergency department.

Should hospitals be held liable in negligence because they cannot afford to adequately staff emergency rooms? Are inadequately staffed emergency rooms preferable to no emergency rooms? Can or should a hospital be held liable in negligence for not allocating sufficient resources to its emergency department? What role, if any, should courts play in reviewing resource allocation and other hospital management decisions?

4. How should courts assess cost of avoidance issues in dealing with limited health resources? Should the same approach be adopted in analyzing public agencies, such as the police and child welfare departments, which do not have adequate resources to respond to all the demands for service?

(c) SOCIAL UTILITY

WATT v. HERTFORDSHIRE COUNTY COUNCIL

[1954] 1 W.L.R. 835, [1954] 2 All E.R. 368 (C.A.)

[The plaintiff, a fireman, responded to an emergency call requiring the use of a special jack. The jack had been used only once in the last 15 years. The truck which was fitted for carrying the jack was unavailable and consequently the jack was loaded in the rear of another vehicle. When the driver braked suddenly, the jack became dislodged and seriously injured the plaintiff.]

. . .

The plaintiff claimed that the defendants, his employers, were negligent in that they (a) failed to load or secure the jack in such a way that it could not become dislodged; (b) loaded the jack in such a way that they knew or ought to have known it was likely that if the lorry pulled up suddenly the jack would become dislodged and cause injuries to any person riding on the back of the lorry; (c) permitted and/or caused the plaintiff to ride on the back of the lorry on to which the jack had been loaded; (d) caused or permitted the jack to be transported on the lorry which, as the defendants knew or ought to have known, was not provided with clips, straps, or other suitable means to secure it; (e) failed to provide any or any adequate supervision of the loading of the jack on to the lorry; and it was claimed that the plaintiff's accident was due to negligence and that he was entitled to recover damages against the defendants.

. . .

DENNING L.J.: — It is well settled that in measuring due care you must balance the risk against the measures necessary to eliminate the risk. To that proposition there ought to be added this: you must balance the risk against the end to be achieved. If this accident had occurred in a commercial enterprise without any emergency there could be no doubt that the servant would succeed. But the commercial end to make profit is very different from the human end to save life or limb. The saving of life or limb justifies taking considerable risk, and I am glad to say that there have never been wanting in this country men of courage ready to take those risks, notably in the fire service.

In this case the risk involved in sending out the lorry was not so great as to prohibit the attempt to save life. I quite agree that fire engines, ambulances and doctors' cars should not shoot past the traffic lights when they show a red light. That is because the risk is too great to warrant the incurring of the danger. It is always a question of balancing the risk against the end. I agree that this appeal should be dismissed.

[Singleton and Morris L.JJ., gave separate concurring judgments, dismissing the fireman's claim.]

NOTES AND QUESTIONS

1. In *Watt*, would the defendant have been found negligent if the emergency call had involved only property damage? Would the case have been decided differently if the plaintiff had been a volunteer?

2. Police high-speed chases pose other controversial social utility issues. Should the police be subject to a reduced standard of care because they are attempting to apprehend a fleeing suspect? What effect, if any, should the alleged offence have on assessing the officer's conduct?

As *Priestman* illustrates, the courts were very supportive of police. In *Priestman v. Colangelo*, [1959] S.C.R. 615, the defendant police officers had attempted several times to stop a suspected car thief. While travelling at high speeds, the officer in the front passenger seat leaned out the window and fired at the rear tire of the suspect's car in an attempt to stop it as it approached a busy intersection. The bullet hit the car frame, ricocheted and struck the driver, rendering him unconscious. The car went out of control, mounted the curb, hit a hydro pole, and struck and killed two pedestrians. The court reasoned that the officers were under an affirmative duty to apprehend suspects and were justified by s. 25(4) of the Criminal Code in using as much force as was necessary to prevent their escape. Do you think that the officer was negligent in shooting at the vehicle? What impact should the fact that the officer was under a statutory duty to apprehend the suspect have on the issue of negligence? See also *Miller v. Wolbaum* (1986), 47 M.V.R. 162 (Sask. Q.B.); and *Moore v. Fanning* (1987), 41 C.C.L.T. 67 (Ont. H.C.).

3. Would a suit based on the facts in *Priestman* be decided differently now? How have public and judicial attitudes toward policing and police changed in the past 25 years? See *Patenaude c. Roy* (1994), 26 C.C.L.T. (2d) 237 (Que. C.A.), leave to appeal ref'd. (1995), 187 N.R. 239n (S.C.C.). In the 1980s, most police departments in Canada adopted strict rules to govern both high-speed chases and the use of firearms. For example, a directive of the Ontario Solicitor General limits police pursuits to a "measure of last resort". The directive lists 11 factors to be considered by police, including the seriousness of the offence, the presence of bystanders and traffic and the age of the fleeing driver. See "Woman Killed as Truck Rams Bus" *The Globe and Mail* (28 June 1996). Within the past decade, a number of negligence suits against police for injuries to innocent bystanders have been settled out of court. See "Police Settle with Victims of Crash", *Toronto Star* (22 October 1993). See also *R. v. Brennan* (1989), 52 C.C.C. (3d) 366 (Ont. C.A.).

4. Generally, the courts only consider the social utility of the defendant's conduct if he is a public officer or is employed by a public authority. Should the social utility of a private citizen's conduct also be considered in determining whether he acted negligently? What problems would arise from this approach? See Griffiths, "The Standard of Care Expected of a First-aid Volunteer" (1990), 53 Mod. L. Rev. 255.

4. An Economic Analysis of the Standard of Care

✻ Posner states in "A Theory of Negligence" in Manne (ed.), *The Economics of Legal Relationships* (1975), 213 at 216:

It is time to take a fresh look at the social function of liability for negligent acts. The essential clue, I believe, is provided by Judge Learned Hand's famous formulation of the negligence standard — one of the few attempts to give content to the deceptively simple concept of ordinary care. Although the formulation postdates the period of our primary interest, it never purported to be original but was an attempt to make explicit the standard that the courts had long applied. In a negligence case, Hand said, the judge (or jury) should attempt to measure three things: the magnitude of the loss if an accident occurs, the probability of the accident's occurring, and the burden of taking precautions that would avert it. If the product of the first two terms exceeds the burden of precautions, the failure to take those precautions is negligence. Hand was adumbrating, perhaps unwittingly, an economic meaning of negligence. Discounting (multiplying) the cost of an accident if it occurs by the probability of occurrence yields a measure of economic benefit to be anticipated from incurring the costs necessary to prevent the accident. The cost of prevention is what Hand meant by the burden of taking precautions against the accident. It may be the cost of installing safety equipment or otherwise making the activity safer, or the benefit foregone by curtailing or eliminating the activity. If the cost of safety measures or of curtailment — whichever cost is lower — exceeds the benefit in accident avoidance to be gained by incurring that cost, society would be better off, in economic terms, to forego accident prevention. A rule making the enterprise liable for the accidents that occur in such cases cannot be justified on the grounds that it will induce the enterprise to increase the safety of its operations. When the cost of accidents is less than the cost of prevention, a rational profit-maximizing enterprise will pay tort judgments to the accident victims rather than incur the larger cost of avoiding liability. Furthermore, overall economic value or welfare would be diminished rather than increased by incurring a higher accident-prevention cost in order to avoid a lower accident cost. If, on the other hand, the benefits in accident avoidance exceed the costs of prevention, society is better off if those costs are incurred and the accident averted, and so in this case the enterprise is made liable, in the expectation that self-interest will lead it to adopt the precautions in order to avoid a greater cost in tort judgments.

One misses any reference to accident avoidance by the victim. If the accident could be prevented by the installation of safety equipment or the curtailment or discontinuance of the underlying activity by the victim at lower cost than any measure taken by the injurer would involve, it would be uneconomical to adopt a rule of liability that placed the burden of accident prevention on the injurer. Although not an explicit part of the Hand formula this qualification, as we shall see, is implicit in the administration of the negligence standard.

Perhaps, then, the dominant function of the fault system is to generate rules of liability that if followed will bring about, at least approximately, the efficient — the cost-justified — level of accidents and safety. Under this view, damages are assessed against the defendant as a way of measuring the costs of accidents, and the damages so assessed are paid over to the plaintiff (to be divided with his lawyer) as the price of enlisting their participation in the operation of the system. Because we do not like to see resources squandered, a judgment of negligence has inescapable overtones of moral disapproval, for it implies that there was a cheaper alternative to the accident. Conversely, there is no moral indignation in the case in which the cost of prevention would have exceeded the cost of the accident. Where the measures necessary to avert the accident would have consumed excessive resources, there is no occasion to condemn the defendant for not having taken them.

If indignation has its roots in inefficiency, we do not have to decide whether regulation, or compensation, or retribution, or some mixture of these best describes the dominant purpose of negligence law. In any case, the judgment of liability depends ultimately on a weighing of costs and benefits.

*Fleming states in *The Law of Torts*, 8th ed. (1992), 118-19:

The negligence concept, with its complex balance just described, has a decidedly utilitarian flavour. Indeed, it has been forcibly argued that the negligence matrix reflects norms of economic efficiency, tending to maximise wealth and minimise costs, by encouraging cost justified accident prevention while discouraging excessive investment in safety. If the loss caused by a given activity to the actor and his victim is greater than its benefit, the activity should be (and is) discouraged by being labelled negligent and requiring the actor to compensate the victim; if the balance is the other way, the actor may go ahead scot-free.

But negligence cannot be reduced to a purely economic equation. True, economic factors are given weight, especially regarding the value of the defendant's activity and the cost of eliminating the risk. In a few situations, allowance for the defendant's limited financial resources has been expressly sanctioned. But in general, judicial opinions do not make much of the cost factor, and for good reasons. For one thing, our legal tradition in torts has strong roots in an individualistic morality with its focus primarily on interpersonal equity rather than broader social policy. The infusion of economic criteria like insurability, loss distribution and efficient resource allocation has so far remained largely unsystematic, interstitial and controversial. Secondly, the calculus of negligence includes some important non-economic values, like health and life, freedom and privacy, which defy comparison with competing economic values. Negligence is not just a matter of calculating the point at which the cost of injury to victims (that is the damages payable) exceeds that of providing safety precautions. The reasonable man is by no means a caricature cold blooded, calculating Economic Man. Lastly, courts remain sceptical as to their ability, let alone that of juries, to pursue economic analyses.

NOTES AND QUESTIONS

1. How would Posner determine whether a defendant breached the standard of care? According to Posner what is the purpose of tort law? Would you agree with Posner's assumption that most actors are rational profit-maximizers who are amenable to deterrence?

2. As pointed out by England in "The System Builders: A Critical Appraisal of Modern American Tort Theory" (1980), 9 J. Legal Stud. 27 at 54, and noted by Hand J. himself in *Moisan v. Loftus* (1949), 178 F. 2d 148 (2d. Cir.), the cost of avoiding the risk may be very difficult to calculate. What impact would this have on the certainty of Posner's cost-benefit approach?

3. Are Fleming's concerns about the economic analysis of tort law warranted? More specifically, does an economic approach exclude "non-economic values, like health and life, freedom and privacy"? Do such values "defy comparison with competing economic values"? See Veljanovski, "Economic Theorizing About Tort" [1985] Current Legal Prob. 117; England, "Law and Economics in American Tort Cases: A Critical Assessment of the Theory's Impact on Courts" (1991), 41 U.T.L.J. 359; and Saks, "Do We Really Know Anything About the Behavior of the Tort Litigation System — And Why Not" (1992), 140 U. Penn. L. Rev. 1147.

4. Many otherwise valid tort claims fail on technical grounds and others are settled for far less than the full loss. Moreover, the law of damages does not permit the plaintiff to recover for certain

losses such as grief and has limited recovery for other types of injuries, such as nervous shock. Consequently, a tortfeasor's accident liability costs may be far less than the actual social costs of his conduct. Does Posner's approach adequately address these features of the tort system? See Epstein, "A Theory of Strict Liability" (1973), 2 J. Legal Stud. 151; Grady, "A New Positive Economic Theory of Negligence" (1983), 92 Yale L.J. 799; and Williams, "Second Best: The Soft Underbelly of Deterrence Theory in Tort" (1993), 106 Harv. L. Rev. 932.

5. Weinrib has indicated that the Hand formulation may be adopted on moral rather than economic grounds. One must first assume that this test provides a standard that a rational actor would use in deciding whether to take a risk of personal injury or loss. An actor who breaches the standard and injures another is held liable in negligence for imposing upon others a risk which he would not himself have taken. Thus, the Hand test is used to impose liability on those who have acted in a morally impermissible manner in failing to extend equal consideration to others. "Toward a Moral Theory of Negligence Law" (1983), 2 Law and Phil. 37, at 49-52. See also Abel, "A Critique of Torts" (1994), 2 Tort L. Rev. 99.

[handwritten margin note: Beck on tort, Law - moral theory]

5. Special Standards of Care

(a) THE STANDARD OF CARE EXPECTED OF THE DISABLED

BUCKLEY and T.T.C. v. SMITH TPT. LTD.
[1946] O.R. 798, [1946] 4 D.L.R. 721 (Ont. C.A.)

[handwritten margin note: (leading case on standard of care) + ment dis]

ROACH J.A.: — This is an appeal by the defendant from the judgment pronounced by the Honourable Mr. Justice Urquhart on June 16, 1945, awarding damages to the plaintiff Buckley in the sum of $475 and to the plaintiff Commission in the sum of $963.13 and costs.

. . .

There is no doubt that the collision was caused solely by the manner in which the transport unit was operated.

The defence, as pleaded and developed in evidence, is that the driver, Taylor, suddenly and without warning, had become insane and was labouring under an insane delusion that the transport unit was under some sort of remote electrical control manipulated from the head office of his employer in the City of Toronto, as a result of which he was unable to control the speed of the vehicle or stop it. Under these alleged circumstances, the defendant pleaded that the collision was an unavoidable accident. Taylor was taken into custody immediately after the collision, and in due course was medically examined and it was found that he was suffering from syphilis of the brain. He died in the Ontario Mental Hospital at Toronto on November 3, 1944, from general paresis.

. . .

In *Slattery v. Haley*, [1923] 3 D.L.R. 156 at p. 160, 52 O.L.R. 95 at p. 99, Middleton J. whose judgment was later sustained by this Court, said:

> I think that it may now be regarded as settled law that to create liability for an act which is not wilful and intentional but merely negligent it must be shewn to have been the conscious act of the defendant's volition. He must have done that which he ought not to have done, or omitted that which he ought to have done, as a conscious being.

He continues in the next paragraph, as follows:

> When a tort is committed by a lunatic, he is unquestionably liable in many circumstances,

but under other circumstances the lunacy may shew that the essential *mens rea* is absent; but, when "the lunacy of the defendant is of so extreme a type as to preclude any genuine intention to do the act complained of, there is no voluntary act at all, and therefore no liability": Salmond, 5th ed., pp. 74 and 75.

Although the latter statement is only *obiter* in that case, it is supported by English decisions and texts to which that learned Judge refers, and I subscribe to it. In my opinion the question of liability must in every case depend upon the degree of insanity.

Supposing a man who was labouring under the insane delusion that his wife was unfaithful to him, but who was otherwise mentally normal, due to the manner in which he operated a motor vehicle on the highway injured some other person on the highway, no one would suggest that he would not be liable in damages simply because of the fact that he had that one particular insane delusion. Then, add to that one delusion the further delusion that his next-door neighbour was conspiring against him to burn down his house, would he still be liable? I entertain no doubt that he might be liable. He might still be a man who, to use the language of Cockburn C.J. in *Banks v. Goodfellow, supra*, would be "in all other respects rational, and capable of transacting the ordinary affairs and fulfilling the duties and obligations incidental to the various relations of life." In particular, notwithstanding those delusions, he might still understand and appreciate the duty which rested upon him to take care. That surely must be the test in all cases where negligence is the basis of the action. If that understanding and appreciation exist in the mind of the individual, and delusions do not otherwise interfere with his ability to take care, he is liable for the breach of that duty. It is always a question of fact to be determined on the evidence, and the burden of proving that a person was without that appreciation and understanding and/or ability is always on those who allege it. Therefore, the question here, to my mind, is not limited to the bare inquiry whether or not Taylor at the time of the collision was labouring under this particular delusion, but whether or not he understood and appreciated the duty upon him to take care, and whether he was disabled, as a result of any delusion, from discharging that duty.

The delusion or delusions may manifest the fact that due to mental disease the individual's mind has become so deteriorated or dilapidated or disorganized that he has neither the ability to understand the duty nor the power to discharge it. If I have correctly stated the law, as I think I have, then the question is: What was the extent of Taylor's insanity? Did he understand the duty to take care, and was he, by reason of mental disease, unable to discharge that duty?

To the police constable, within 20 minutes after the collision, he told the story of this remote electrical control. Later that same evening at the police station, he told another officer who interrogated him, "that electricity had pushed him down the hill and he could not stop with this electricity." He said: "It turned me around some loop away out the highway somewhere, and that was where the electricity did the damage."

The day following the collision he was examined by the physician at the Toronto Jail. To that physician he told the story of this remote electrical control having caused the truck to turn off the road at or near Whitby, which is many miles east of the Hunt Club, but did not refer to the fact that he had been, as he thought, stalled at the Hunt Club. That physician found great difficulty in getting facts from him. He did not get a clear story, but as the physician testified, "a few facts could be picked up here and there but he would quite quickly forget the facts and tell us something else, but nothing was reliable." He said further: "I was able to get some scattered details but I could not make a continued story of it. His answers were slow and poor."

He was seen at the police station the night of the collision by an official of the defendant company, to whom he said: "That machine was under remote control and when you people put the power on I could not do anything." Taylor had a vacant look in his eyes, and his appearance, and the nature of his conversation, were such that the official was frightened.

Having regard to all the evidence, I have reached the conclusion that at the time of the collision Taylor's mind was so ravaged by disease that it should be held, as a matter of reasonable inference, that he did not understand the duty which rested upon him to take care, and further that if it could be said that he did understand and appreciate the duty, the particular delusion prevented him from discharging it. Therefore, no liability for the damages which he caused could attach to him.

. . .

In my opinion, no liability could attach to the defendant. I would therefore allow the appeal with costs and direct that judgment be entered dismissing the action, with costs.

NOTES AND QUESTIONS

1. Did the court apply a special standard of care in *Taylor* or conclude that he did not have the capacity to be held liable in negligence? Although *Taylor* may govern cases involving the severely mentally impaired, it is not clear what standard applies to those who suffer less serious impairment. What standard of care should be required of a developmentally handicapped 40-year-old who functions at the age of a 10-year-old?

2. The American Law Institute in the *Restatement of the Law, Second, Torts* (1965), para. 283B provides that: "Unless the actor is a child, his insanity or other mental deficiency does not relieve the actor from liability for conduct which does not conform to the standard of the reasonable man under the circumstances." The position in England appears to be similar. In *Roberts v. Ramsbottom*, [1980] 1 All E.R. 7 (Q.B.), the court held that mental impairment short of automatism would not relieve the defendant from complying with the objective standard of care of a reasonable person. Can you reconcile the American and English positions with the principle of no liability without fault? See generally Picher, "The Tortious Liability of the Insane in Canada . . ." (1975), 13 Osgoode Hall L.J. 1983; Coleman, "Mental Abnormality, Personal Responsibility and Tort Liability" in Brody and Englehardt (eds.), *Mental Illness: Law and Public Policy* (1980), 107; and Splane, "Tort Liability of the Mentally Ill in Negligence Actions" (1983), 93 Yale L.J. 153.

3. The question of who should bear the risks posed by the mentally ill remains a contentious legal and policy issue. In *Hutchings v. Nevin* (1992), 9 O.R. (3d) 776 (Gen. Div.), the defendant, who was having psychotic delusions, caused a car accident injuring his passenger. While acknowledging the general authority of *Buckley*, the plaintiff's counsel argued that Ontario's compulsory automobile insurance legislation had shifted the risk of mentally ill drivers onto the insured. While the judge rejected this argument, the case is under appeal. See *Wenden v. Trikha* (1991), 8 C.C.L.T. 138 (Alta. C.A.).

4. It is well established that the physically handicapped are required to meet only the standard of care of a reasonable person with a similar handicap. This principle is reflected in the case law dealing with the blind. See *Carroll and Carroll v. Chicken Palace Ltd.*, [1955] 3 D.L.R. 681 (Ont. C.A.); *Haley v. London Electric Board*, [1965] A.C. 778 (H.L.); *Crawford v. Halifax* (1977), 81 D.L.R. (3d) 316 (N.S. S.C.); and *Strickland v. St. John's* (1982), 37 Nfld. & P.E.I.R. 208 (Nfld. Dist. Ct.). See also Lowry, "The Blind and the Law of Tort: The Position of a Blind Person as Plaintiff in Negligence"

(1972), 20 Chitty's L.J. 253; and also ten Broek, "The Right to Live in the World: The Disabled in the Law of Torts" (1966), 54 Cal. L. Rev. 841.

5. What standard of care should be expected of automobile drivers who have heart disease or other similar illnesses? What factors should be taken into account to determine whether this standard has been breached? What weight should the court give to the argument that such people should attempt to live as normally as possible? See *Gootson v. R.*, [1948] 4 D.L.R. 33 (S.C.C.) (epileptic seizure); *Boomer v. Penn* (1965), 52 D.L.R. (2d) 673 (Ont. H.C.) (insulin reaction); and *Gordon v. Wallace* (1973), 42 D.L.R. (3d) 342 (Ont. H.C.); and *Dobbs v. Mayer* (1985), 32 C.C.L.T. 191 (Ont. Dist. Ct.) (heart attack). See also Blalock, "Liability of the Unconscious Defendant" (1970), 6(2) Trial 29; and Smith, "Automatism — A Defence to Negligence?", [1980] New L.J. 1111.

6. Can you justify holding the mentally handicapped, but not the physically handicapped, to the objective standard of care of a reasonable person?

(b) THE STANDARD OF CARE EXPECTED OF CHILDREN

JOYAL v. BARSBY

(1965), 55 D.L.R. (2d) 38 (Man. C.A.)

MILLER C.J.M. (dissenting): — ... The real point to be decided in this appeal is whether the infant was guilty of contributory negligence. Negligence on the part of the defendant is not disputed and is not in issue on this appeal.

The action arose out of a motor vehicle accident which occurred around 4 o'clock on the afternoon of July 26, 1963, on P.T.H. No. 75. At the time and place of the accident the road was of hard surface, dry, and the weather clear. The speed limit at the point in question was 60 m.p.h. This highway is one of the main provincial highways and runs between the International Border and the City of Winnipeg, and is the main artery for traffic between the United States and Manitoba.

The infant admittedly ran out onto this busy highway into the side of defendant's motor vehicle and suffered grievous injuries. Her home was between this highway and a railway track, and she and two younger brothers had left their home to cross the highway and enter a park on the opposite side. The infant was aged six years and two months, and both her brothers were younger than she. This is a busy highway and the infant, according to the evidence of the father and the evidence of the infant plaintiff, had been thoroughly instructed in the dangers of crossing this highway and the lesson to "Stop, Look, and Listen" had been thoroughly drilled into her by the father and learned by the infant. There is no question that the evidence established that the infant plaintiff was conscious of the traffic danger inherent on this busy highway.

One of the two younger brothers ran across the highway at a time when it appears to have been dangerous to do so, as a big semi-trailer transport truck was approaching from the north. The truck driver sounded a siren ("fog-horn" as it was called in the evidence) to warn either the boy running across the highway or the children generally. Hearing the "fog-horn", the infant plaintiff and her other brother apparently thought better of following the first venturesome brother across, so they stepped back onto the shoulder of the road and stood there about two feet east of the pavement.

A motorist by the name of Despins was about 100 yards ahead of the defendant's motor vehicle, and, seeing the one boy on the west side of the highway as well as the girl and her other brother on the east side of the highway, he took his foot off the accelerator and by doing so decreased his speed to about 35 m.p.h. He apparently was nervous lest the sister and her other brother should follow the first brother across the highway, but he did not apply his brakes and was satisfied to reduce speed by compression. He saw the girl make a motion to cross the road as he approached and was passing her. Presumably this was just about the time the truck horn sounded, which caused the girl to step back onto the shoulder. She and her brother continued to stand motionless on the shoulder about two feet off the hard surface after Despins had passed. Despins and the defendant were both proceeding north on the east side of the highway. Despins said he first saw the children on the side of the road when he was a considerable distance south, so they must have stood motionless for some little while to let traffic pass. The defendant saw the two children on the east side but concluded — and with some cause — that they had realized traffic was on the highway, were waiting for it to pass, and would stay where they were until he passed them. Apparently he was not close enough to see, or in any event did not see, the one boy run across the highway. Nevertheless, he did as Despins did — took his foot off the accelerator and let the compression decrease his speed from 60 m.p.h. to 38 or 40 m.p.h. When the defendant was less than a car length away from her, the infant plaintiff suddenly started to run across the highway from east to west. She took only four or five steps, and then collided with the rear door of the defendant's vehicle. She was apparently struck by the door handle and sustained severe injuries. I am not going to deal with the matter of injuries because I am holding that the damages awarded should not be changed.

. . .

The defendant's counsel accepted the principle that his client was guilty of some negligence but, as intimated above, conducted his appeal on the ground that the infant was guilty of contributory negligence. This involves first of all the question "Could this six-year old infant be guilty of contributory negligence?"

A binding authority is the decision of the Supreme Court of Canada in *McEllistrum v. Etches*, 6 D.L.R. (2d) 1 at pp. 6-7, [1956] S.C.R. 787, where it is stated:

> It should now be laid down that where the age is not such as to make a discussion of contributory negligence absurd, it is a question for the jury in each case whether the infant exercised the care to be expected from a child of like age, intelligence and experience.

The learned trial Judge had this case before him.

In my opinion this case overrules the remark attributed to Trueman, J.A., in *Eyers v. Gillis & Warren Ltd.*, [1940] 4 D.L.R. 747, 48 Man. R. 164, [1940] 3 W.W.R. 390, to the effect that a young child was incapable of contributory negligence. At p. 6 of the above Supreme Court case it is quite clear that the remarks of Trueman, J.A., were disapproved. It must therefore be concluded that the infant plaintiff, even at her age, could under proper circumstances be deemed guilty of contributory negligence.

The learned trial Judge said she was not more heedless than other children of her age, intelligence and experience, which expression is analogous to the words used in the *Etches* case, *supra*. The sad fact remains that she was heedless, careless, and negligent, despite her training and traffic experience. It appears to me the learned trial Judge found that, as she was no more heedless than other similar children, she could not be guilty of contributory negligence and consequently was not so guilty.

I think the infant plaintiff was partly responsible for this regrettable accident. She was thoroughly trained on the dangers of the highway, had experience with the traffic thereon, and, without first looking, had suddenly left a place of safety for a place of danger. There was still traffic proceeding along the highway, including the defendant's vehicle, which, had she looked, she could not help seeing and have thus avoided the accident. If contributory negligence cannot be found in an instance such as this, against a child with such training and experience, then it would be rare indeed that this doctrine could be invoked against a child.

. . .

On the undisputed facts, I feel justified in holding that the infant plaintiff's negligence contributed to the accident and that she can properly be adjudged liable for contributory negligence to the extent of 40%.

I would allow the appeal and vary the judgment of the learned trial Judge by charging the plaintiffs with 40% liability. The plaintiffs will therefore recover 60% of the damages rather than the 100% awarded by the trial Judge, but will still have their costs in the Court below.

The defendant is entitled to his costs in this Court.

. . .

FREEDMAN J.A., concurs with MONNIN J.A.

MONNIN J.A.: ... The learned trial Judge applied this standard to the case at bar in the manner following. He said:

> The age of the infant plaintiff was six years and two months and she appeared to me not to be of above average intelligence. Living near a fairly busy highway she would know of the danger from passing cars and admitted that her father had warned her of this danger; but she would have had far less experience than a city child of her age. I believe she acted as a normal child of her age and experience could be expected to act. She was momentarily stopped from crossing the highway by the blare of the truck siren, but this terrifying warning completely absorbed her attention. When the truck had passed she did not think of other traffic but darted forward as both Mr. Despins and the defendant anticipated she might do. In doing this she was not more heedless than any other child of her age, intelligence and experience. I do not consider that she was guilty of contributory negligence. The defendant must be held solely responsible.

The learned trial Judge considered the conduct of the child in the context of the situation which confronted her. This, of course, was the proper thing to do, since negligence is always a want of care in the particular circumstances. The learned trial Judge does not say that this child of six years and two months was incapable of being guilty of contributory negligence. He says that her behaviour in the specific situation should not be categorized as contributorily negligent. Faced with the approach of this large truck with its horn blaring, she riveted her attention upon it. That necessarily made her inattentive, for the moment, to traffic approaching from the other direction. But the learned trial Judge finds that the ordinary child of her age, intelligence and experience would have responded to the situation in the same way. Hence he refused to stamp her conduct with the label of negligence. I am not prepared to say he was wrong.

. . .

The appeal is therefore dismissed with costs. The cross-appeal is also dismissed with costs fixed at $50; the costs on the cross-appeal to be set off against the other costs.

NOTES AND QUESTIONS

1. What is the standard of care expected of a child? Is this test objective or subjective? Do you think the plaintiff in *Joyal* was contributorily negligent? In *McEllistrum v. Etches*, [1956] S.C.R. 787, a case referred to by both the majority and dissent, the court indicated that there is an age below which a child cannot be held liable in negligence. Can you suggest an appropriate test of capacity for children?

2. A child involved in a normally adult activity such as driving a car, snowmobiling or hunting, is required to meet the standard of care expected of a reasonable adult. What is the rationale for imposing a higher standard of care in these situations? See *Ryan v. Hickson* (1974), 55 D.L.R. (3d) 196 (Ont. H.C.); *Dellwo v. Pearson* (1961), 107 N.W. (2d) 859 (Minn. S.C.); and *McErlean v. Sarel* (1987), 42 C.C.L.T. 78 (Ont. C.A.). But see *Chaisson v. Hebert* (1986), 187 A.P.R. 105 (N.B. Q.B.).

3. For other examples of the standard of care expected of children see *Ottosen v. Kasper* (1986), 37 C.C.L.T. 270 (B.C. C.A.); *Laviolette v. C.N.R.* (1987), 40 C.C.L.T. 138 (N.B. C.A.); and *Bajkov v. Canil* (1990), 66 D.L.R. (4th) 572 (B.C. C.A.). See also Bohlen, "Liability in Tort of Infants and Insane Persons" (1924), 23 Mich. L. Rev. 9; Dunlop, "Torts Relating to Infants" (1966), 5 U.W.O. L. Rev. 116; and Alexander, "Tort Liability of Children and Their Parents" in Mendes Da Costa (ed.), *Studies In Canadian Family Law* (1975), at 845.

4. Although parents, guardians and others who supervise children are not held vicariously liable when a child commits a tort, they can be held liable if they have negligently failed to monitor or control the child's conduct. The courts have defined the requisite standard of care in terms of a "reasonable parent of ordinary prudence". See *Myers v. Peel County Board of Education*, [1981] 2 S.C.R. 21; and *Thomas v. Hamilton (City) Board of Education* (1994), 20 O.R. (2d) 598 (C.A.). Is it appropriate to use this parental standard in assessing the behaviour of educators, daycare workers and others who are not parents or guardians?

In *LaPlante (Guardian ad litem of) v. LaPlante* (1995), 26 C.C.L.T. (2d) 32 (B.C. C.A.), the defendant father was held liable in negligence for permitting his 16-year-old son, who had recently obtained his licence, to drive in traffic at highway speeds under icy conditions. The court held that a reasonable parent of ordinary prudence would not have let the son drive in those conditions.

(c) THE STANDARD OF CARE EXPECTED OF PROFESSIONALS

At one time only those involved in a limited number of public callings, such as innkeepers and common carriers, were held to a special standard of care. The courts now appear to be developing modified standards of care to govern not only professionals, but also most skilled trades and occupations. The following materials focus on medical cases. Nevertheless, the courts' approach to the special standards of care is similar across professions and trades.

✻ WHITE v. TURNER

(leading in d of c expected of professionals)

(1981), 31 O.R. (2d) 773 (H.C.)

[The defendant plastic surgeon performed a breast reduction operation on the plaintiff. The plaintiff suffered several postoperative complications, and her breasts were scarred and poorly shaped. The plaintiff sued the defendant claiming that he had been negligent both in performing the operation and in not properly disclosing the risks of the surgery. The following excerpt addresses only the first allegations of negligence.]

LINDEN J.: — Needless to say, a mere error in judgment by a professional person is not by itself negligence. The Courts recognize that professionals may make mistakes during the course of their practice, which do not bespeak negligence. Sometimes medical operations do not succeed. Sometimes lawyers lose cases. The mere fact of a poor result does not mean that there has been negligence. In order to succeed in an action against a professional person, a plaintiff must prove, on the balance of probabilities, not only that there has been a bad result, but that this was brought about by negligent conduct.

Before liability can be imposed for the operation itself, therefore, the plaintiff must prove that the defendant performed the surgery in such a way that a reasonable plastic surgeon would consider it to have been less than satisfactory: see generally, *Sylvester v. Crits et al.*, [1956] S.C.R. 991, 5 D.L.R. (2d) 601; affirming [1956] O.R. 132 at p. 143, 1 D.L.R. (2d) 502 at p. 508; *Wilson v. Swanson*, [1956] S.C.R. 804 at p. 811, 5 D.L.R. (2d) 113 at p. 119. See also Picard, *Legal Liability of Doctors and Hospitals in Canada* (1978), at p. 98. In other words, unless it is established on a balance of probabilities that this mammoplasty was done in a substandard way by the defendant, he cannot be held liable in negligence.

Plastic surgery is a specialty that has its own standards — standards which are unique to that specialty. If the work of a plastic surgeon falls below the accepted practices of his colleagues, he will be held civilly liable for any damage resulting. But if his work complies with the custom of his confrères he will normally escape civil liability for his conduct, even where the result of the surgery is less than satisfactory.

There are several aspects of alleged negligence here. The first, which appears to have been abandoned during the course of the trial, was that the Strombeck procedure should not have been utilized on Mrs. White in these circumstances. There was, however, no evidence introduced to the effect that the Strombeck procedure was not appropriate here. Dr. Turner had considerable experience with it and he rightly felt that he could achieve a good result using that method. Dr. John Birch, who testified for the defendant, stated that the Strombeck procedure was commonly used for mammoplasty on medium-sized breasts, which he felt these were. He did some Strombeck operations himself in the mid-1970s, but more recently he has switched to the Robins procedure for these cases, which method evolved in 1976 and thereafter. Dr. Robertson, who testified for the plaintiff, found no fault in the defendant's selection of the Strombeck procedure in this situation. Consequently, there can be no finding of negligence on the basis that an improper procedure was employed by Dr. Turner.

A second basis of negligence that was alleged was that the operation was poorly designed. In other words, it was argued that the advance planning involved in the operation was inadequately done. Even though Dr. Turner agreed that there was an error in the design of the surgery, the evidence does not establish that this was negligence. Neither Dr. Birch nor Dr. Robertson pointed to anything that was done by Dr. Turner in planning this operation that was below the standard of the reasonable plastic surgeon. Both were agreed that it is not customary for plastic surgeons to decide in advance the exact amount of tissue to remove. Rather it is a question of judgment in each case as to the correct amount to remove, which decision is made at the time of closure. . . . Consequently, the quality of the surgical design was not proven to be substandard.

The third area of complaint is with the actual execution of the surgery. Although Dr. Birch testified that a similar result to this could occur without the plastic surgeon being negligent, I find that the evidence, on the whole, supports a finding that the poor result obtained in the mammoplasty performed on Mrs. White was the result of Dr. Turner's negligent execution of the surgery.

The reason for the bad result here was that insufficient tissue was removed by Dr. Turner. . . .

There were two reasons why Dr. Turner did not remove sufficient tissue, both of which I find were negligence in the circumstances: (1) the operation was done too quickly, and (2) the suturing was started before a proper check was made of whether enough tissue had been removed.

As for the length of time taken to perform the operation, the evidence is clear that the usual time required is between two and four hours. Dr. Birch said that the Strombeck procedure took an average of two and a half hours to do. Dr. Robertson testified that more than three hours is required to perform a Strombeck properly. If he has only a junior intern assisting him, he normally requires about four hours to do a Strombeck. If he has an expert assistant, he can do it properly in three and a half hours. He indicated that, when the doctors on his staff at the Toronto General Hospital booked only three hours operating-room time for a Strombeck, they often could not complete the operation in time and other doctors were kept waiting for the operating-room. Dr. Robertson advised his own staff, therefore, to book four hours operating-room time in order to perform a Strombeck.

I have found on the facts here that Dr. Turner did this Strombeck in approximately one hour, 35 minutes. This was described by Dr. Birch as "very fast". He said that the operation was "very rapidly done". Dr. Turner must have seen no "hitches" to go at that speed, he concluded. Dr. Robertson was less charitable than Dr. Birch. He testified that even Dr. Turner's estimate of two and a half to two and three-quarters hours was a "pretty short" time for the Strombeck operation. Dr. Robertson could not imagine that a Strombeck could be properly done in one hour and 35 minutes. To him, it was "almost incredible" that it could. He thought it would take one hour just to close up. A simple mastectomy took one hour and 35 minutes to do. This mammoplasty by Dr. Turner was a "very rapid operation", he opined. "Detail takes time", he said and, consequently, the necessary attention to detail, which required some stepping back, was not done in this case. "When one is in a hurry, expediency rather than art comes into play", he suggested. In such a short time, thought Dr. Robertson, all the considerations could not be taken into account. The more time that is taken, the less likely is an undesirable result, he said. In the time Dr. Turner took to perform this operation, Dr. Robertson testified that he could not look back. Dr. Robertson concluded by saying that, although he hated to talk that way, he felt he had to: the patient was entitled to expect more than she received on this occasion.

I hold, therefore, that Dr. Turner did this operation too quickly. This resulted in his not removing enough tissue, which in turn caused the incisions to open, leading to the substandard result. This was actionable negligence.

As for the failure to make a check of the amount of tissue removed before closing, Dr. Birch testified that it was standard practice, at the conclusion of the cutting, to tack the flaps of skin together with a few sutures and make a judgment about the bulk of the breast. He said that some doctors do not do any actual stitching at this stage, but that all plastic surgeons put the pieces together and take a look before proceeding to close up. I find on the basis of this evidence that this was the standard practice of plastic surgeons.

There is no evidence that Dr. Turner did this standard check. It is not mentioned in his notes of the operation, but this is not controlling, according to Dr. Birch, who said that he did not usually make any notes about doing the check, although he invariably did it. Dr. Turner did not say that he made such a check. He did not even indicate that he was aware that it was standard practice. Actually, even though Dr. Turner did not do this check, he admitted that, when he went to close up, he actually noticed more tension on the flaps than usual, but he did nothing about it. He explained this by observing that there was always "quite a bit of tension". This extra tension should have served as a warning to him that insufficient tissue had been removed. But he was too much in a hurry to do anything about it. Moreover, Dr. Turner's written report stated that he had removed 800 gr., although, in fact, he had taken out only 705 gr. He was fully aware that the removal of only 705 gr. of tissue was less than the usual amount removed in such cases. Dr. Turner agreed that he probably should have taken out an additional 300 gr. of tissue. Dr. Robertson, in correcting the result, removed about 350 gr. (or three-quarter pound), an additional 50% of tissue, which demonstrates that this was no small error. If Dr. Turner had paused to do a proper check, he would have learned that he had removed only 705 gr., that this was less than usual, and that there was too much tension on the flaps. This would have revealed his error to him and permitted him to take the necessary corrective measures before closing. This, in turn, would have avoided the bad result. I find, therefore, that this failure to do the customary check was actionable negligence.

[Affirmed (1982), 12 D.L.R. (3d) 319 (Ont. C.A.)]

NOTES AND QUESTIONS

1. What allegations of negligence were made against the defendant? How did the court define the standard of care expected of the defendant? Summarize the expert evidence adduced by the parties concerning each allegation of negligence. Do you agree with the reasoning in *White*?

2. What is the standard of care that should be imposed on doctors to keep up with new drugs, surgical procedures and treatment programs? See *Dhalla v. Jodrey* (1985), 16 D.L.R. (4th) 732 (N.S. C.A.); *Sigouin (Guardian ad litem of) v. Wong* (1991), 10 C.C.L.T. (2d) 236 (B.C. S.C.); and *ter Neuzen v. Korn* (1995), 127 D.L.R. (4th) 577 (S.C.C.).

3. General practitioners are required to exercise the standard of care of a reasonable, competent general practitioner. This includes knowing their limits and when to refer patients to a specialist. In *Layden v. Cope* (1984), 28 C.C.L.T. 140 (Alta. Q.B.), the plaintiff, who had previously suffered from gout, went to two general practitioners in town. They both concluded that he had gout and prescribed medication. The doctors continued treating him for gout, even though his condition deteriorated and the hospital nurses expressed concern. After nine days, the plaintiff was referred to a specialist, who immediately diagnosed cellulitis with possible secondary infection. The plaintiff's condition deteriorated and his leg had to be amputated. In holding the general practitioners liable, the court stated that the standard of care expected of a general practitioner in a small town is not significantly different from that of general practitioners in a city. They should have considered other diagnoses when the plaintiff's condition did not improve and referred him to a specialist much sooner. See also *Dillon v. LeRoux*, [1994] 6 W.W.R. 280 (B.C. C.A.).

4. The standard of care expected of an intern is that of a reasonably competent intern in the circumstances. Although interns have completed medical school and passed their licensing examinations, they are not qualified to practice on their own. Rather, interns are required to work under the supervision of a fully qualified doctor. Consequently, the standard of care expected of interns is lower than that required of general practitioners. In contrast, residents are fully qualified doctors who seek additional training in a specialty. As a result, even a junior resident would be held to the standard of care expected of a general practitioner. A more senior resident would be expected to have advanced skills in hs or her speciality consistent with a resident of comparable training, but would not be expected to have the skills of a fully qualified specialist. See *Fraser v. Vancouver General Hospital*, [1952] 3 D.L.R. 785 (S.C.C.); *Dale v. Munthali* (1978), 21 O.R. (2d) 554 (C.A.); *Boulay v. Charbonneau* (1988), 46 C.C.L.T. 16 (Que. C.A.); and *Wills v. Saunders*, [1989] 2 W.W.R. 715 (Alta. Q.B.).

5. The growing volunteer movement, the recognition of the value of peer counselling and efforts to reduce costs have resulted in greater use of non-professionals in various health and care situations. Although these individuals would not be expected to meet a professional standard of care, they would be required to have the skills and training necessary to do their assigned tasks competently. They would also be expected to know their own limits and when they should get professional assistance. Agencies that use non-professionals are required to adequately screen, train, place and supervise these workers. For example, an agency might be held liable in negligence for using inadequately trained volunteers to staff a suicide crisis line.

6. Individuals may be held to a professional standard of care if they implicitly or explicitly suggest that they have the skills and training of a professional. By holding themselves out as counsellors or therapists, individuals may be seen as explicitly suggesting that they have professional qualifications and training. Indeed, merely offering to provide a particular service, such as marriage counselling, might reasonably create the impression that one has special training and skills.

7. For additional examples of medical malpractice see: *Lee v. O'Farrell* (1988), 43 C.C.L.T. 269 (B.C. S.C.) and *Davies v. Gabel Estate*, [1995] 2 W.W.R. 35 (Sask. Q.B.) (diagnosis); *Eady v. Tenderenda*, [1975] 2 S.C.R. 599 and *Cherry (Guardian ad litem of) v. Borsman* (1991), 75 D.L.R. (4th) 668 (B.C. S.C.), aff'd. on liability for procedure (1992), 94 D.L.R. (4th) 487 (B.C. C.A.); leave to appeal ref'd. (1993), 99 D.L.R. (4th) vii (S.C.C.) (surgical procedure); *Joseph Brant Memorial Hospital v. Koziol* (1977), 77 D.L.R. (3d) 161 (S.C.C.) and *Pittman Estate v. Bain* (1994), 19 C.C.L.T. (2d) 1 (Ont. Gen. Div.) (post-operative care); and *Champigny v. Ste-Marie* (1993), 19 C.C.L.T. (2d) 307 (Que. S.C.) and *Pierre (Next Friend of) v. Marshall*, [1994] 8 W.W.R. 478 (Alta. Q.B.) (treatment).

8. The current system for resolving allegations of medical mistreatment has been roundly criticized by both patients' rights groups and the medical profession. For a discussion of alternatives to the existing fault-based adversarial approach see Sharpe, "Alternatives to the Court Process for Resolving Medical Malpractice Claims" (1981), 26 McGill L.J. 1036; Mitchell and McDiarmid, "Medical Malpractice: A Challenge to Alternative Dispute Resolution" (1988), 3 Can. L.J. Society 227; Chapman, "Controlling the Costs of Medical Malpractice: An Argument for Strict Hospital Liability'" (1990), 28 Osgoode Hall L.J. 523; and Abraham and Weiler, "Enterprise Medical Liability and the Evolution of the American Health Care System" (1994), 108 Harv. L. Rev. 381.

9. For a discussion of the standard of care expected of lawyers, see *Brumer v. Gunn* (1982), 18 Man. R. (2d) 155 (Q.B.); *Jacks v. Davis* (1982), 141 D.L.R. (3d) 355 (B.C. C.A.); *Pound v. Nakonechny* (1983), 27 C.C.L.T. 146 (Sask. C.A.); and *Central Trust Co. v. Rafuse* (1986), 31 D.L.R. (4th) 481 (S.C.C.). See also Bastedo, "A Note on Lawyers' Malpractice: Legal Boundaries and Judicial Regulations" (1970), 7 Osgoode Hall L.J. 311; and Mahoney, "Lawyers — Negligence — Standard of Care" (1985), 63 Can. Bar Rev. 221.

10. For examples of other special standards of care see: *Dabous v. Zuliani* (1976), 68 D.L.R. (3d) 414 (Ont. C.A.) (architects); *Smith v. B.C. (A.G.)* (1988), 30 B.C.L.R. (2d) 356 (C.A.) (police officers); *Fraser v. Bd. of School Trustees of School District No. 72 (Campbell River)* (1988), 54 D.L.R. (4th) 563 (B.C. C.A.) (teachers); *Hofstrand Farms Ltd. v. B.D.C. Ltd.*, [1986] 1 S.C.R. 228 (common carriers); *Dom. Securities Ames Ltd. v. Deep* (1984), 4 O.A.C. 386 (C.A.) (stockbrokers); *Spiewak v. 251268 Ont. Ltd.* (1987), 61 O.R. (2d) 655 (H.C.) (real estate agents); *Haig v. Bamford*, [1977] 1 S.C.R. 466 (auditors); *Sceptre Resources Ltd. v. Deloitte Haskins & Sells* (1988), 64 Alta. L.R. (2d) 48 (Q.B.) (accountants); *Waldman's Fish Co. v. Anderson Ins. Ltd.* (1979), 25 N.B.R. (2d) 482 (C.A.) (insurance agents); *Graham v. Picot Gorman and A.E.S. Consultants Ltd.* (1985), 66 N.B.R. (2d) 434 (T.D.) (real estate appraiser); *Smith v. Eric S. Bush (a firm)*, [1987] 3 All E.R. 179 (C.A.) (land surveyors); and *R. (L.) v. Nyp* (1995), 25 C.C.L.T. (2d) 309 (Ont. Gen. Div.) (journalists).

11. For the standard of care expected of professionals generally, see Knoppers (ed.), *Professional Liability in Canada* (1988).

6. Degrees of Negligence

The common law basically recognizes one standard of care in negligence — that of a reasonable person. Even the special standards of care focus on what is reasonable to expect of those with recognized disabilities, or unique skills, education or training. There are, however, several statutes which impose liability for only specified degrees of negligence. For example, in some provinces a driver of a non-commercial vehicle will only be held liable to a gratuitous passenger if it is established that he was "grossly negligent". Generally, the courts have been unsympathetic to the policy behind such legislation and have imposed liability for gross negligence in circumstances in which the defendant's conduct appears to have been merely negligent.

NOTES AND QUESTIONS

1. What is the rationale for the guest/passenger legislation? Who are the major beneficiaries of such legislation and what impact has this had on a court's interpretation of the legislation? For an excellent example of the problems of interpreting the guest/passenger legislation see *Engler v. Rossignol* (1975), 10 O.R. (2d) 721 (C.A.). See also *Levesque v. Wedge* (1977), 13 Nfld. & P.E.I.R. 283 (P.E.I. C.A.); *Cheevers v. Van Norden* (1980), 42 N.S.R. (2d) 337 (S.C.); and *McIntyre v. Sawatsky* (1982), 18 Sask. R. 406 (Q.B.).

2. The guest/passenger legislation has been severely criticized. See Gibson, "Let's Abolish Guest Passenger Legislation" (1965), 35 Man. Bar News 274; Univ. of Alta., Institute of Law Research and Reform, *Guest Passenger Legislation* (1979); and Linden, *Canadian Tort Law*, 5th ed. (1993), 162-63.

3. In some provinces a municipality's liability for failing to repair sidewalks and roads, and to keep them clear of snow, is governed by gross negligence legislation. What is the rationale for such legislation? Is it any more or less justifiable than the guest/passenger legislation? See Municipal Act, R.S.O. 1990, c. M.45, s. 284(4); *Dorschell v. Cambridge* (1980), 30 O.R. (2d) 714 (C.A.); and *Mete v. Mississauga* (1984), unreported (Ont. H.C.).

7. Custom

TER NEUZEN v. KORN

(1995), 127 D.L.R. (4th) 577 (S.C.C.)

[The plaintiff contracted HIV as a result of artificial insemination in January 1985. The risk of such infection was not widely known in North America when the procedure was performed. The defendant doctor who performed the procedure was responsible for screening semen donors. Expert evidence established that the physician had adopted standard medical practices in this regard. One of the pivotal issues was whether it was open for the jury to find that the standard practice itself was negligent.]

SOPINKA J.: —

. . .

1. *Standard of care and evidence of standard practice*

It is well-settled that physicians have a duty to conduct their practice in accordance with the conduct of a prudent and diligent doctor in the same circumstances. In the case of a specialist, such as a gynaecologist and obstetrician, the doctor's behaviour must be assessed in light of the conduct of other ordinary specialists, who possess a reasonable level of knowledge, competence and skill expected of professionals in Canada, in that field. A specialist, such as the respondent, who holds himself out as possessing a special degree of skill and knowledge, must exercise the degree of skill of an average specialist in his field.

. . .

It is also particularly important to emphasize, in the context of this case, that the conduct of physicians must be judged in the light of the knowledge that ought to have been reasonably possessed at the time of the alleged act of negligence. As Denning L.J. eloquently stated in *Roe v. Ministry of Health*, [1954] 2 All E.R. 131 (C.A.) at p. 137, "[w]e must not look at the 1947 accident with 1954 spectacles". That is, courts must not, with the benefit of hindsight, judge too harshly doctors who act in accordance with prevailing standards of professional knowledge. This point was also emphasized by this court in *Lapointe, supra*, at p. 14:

> . . . courts should be careful not to rely upon the perfect vision afforded by hindsight. In order to evaluate a particular exercise of judgment fairly, the doctor's limited ability to foresee future events when determining a course of conduct must be borne in mind. Otherwise, the doctor will not be assessed according to the norms of the average doctor of reasonable ability in the same circumstances, but rather will be held accountable for mistakes that are apparent only after the fact.

No issue is taken with this proposition which was applied both in the trial judge's charge to the jury and by the Court of Appeal.

The Court of Appeal, after a thorough review of the evidence, held that it was not possible for a jury acting judicially to have found that, in 1985, the respondent ought to have known of the risk. This is a power to review a jury verdict which a court of appeal clearly possesses: see *Vancouver-Fraser Park District v. Olmstead* (1974), 51 D.L.R. (3d) 416, [1975] 2 S.C.R. 831, 3 N.R. 326. I agree with this finding and can find no basis upon which it can be questioned. Indeed my review of the evidence leads to the same conclusion. The evidence of standard practice on the first aspect of the case was based entirely on the state of knowledge required of the reasonable practitioner in 1985 and it would have been equally impossible for a jury acting judicially to have found that, given the state of knowledge, the reasonable practitioner ought to either have discontinued AI or warned the patients of the risk. It having been admitted that the respondent continued AI and did not warn his patients, there was no issue concerning his conformity with the standard practice.

The appellant, therefore, can only support a favourable finding on this aspect of the case on the basis that the jury was entitled to find that the standard established by the evidence itself departed from that of a prudent and diligent physician and that the respondent, in failing to conform with a higher standard, was guilty of negligence. This raises the issue as to the correctness of the trial judge's charge to the jury to the effect that the jury was so entitled.

With respect to the second aspect of the claim in professional negligence, the Court of Appeal considered that a verdict for the appellant was open to the jury. It is, however, by no means clear the evidence establishes a standard practice with respect to the screening and follow-up of donors. This was a matter for the jury to determine. If the jury found that the evidence fell short of establishing the existence of a standard practice, the question arises as to whether the jury could determine the applicable standard without the aid of expert evidence. This is a legal issue upon which the Court of Appeal did not pronounce but which is closely related to the issue raised by the trial judge's instruction referred to above.

It is generally accepted that when a doctor acts in accordance with a recognized and respectable practice of the profession, he or she will not be found to be negligent. This is because courts do not ordinarily have the expertise to tell professionals that they are not behaving appropriately in their field. In a sense, the medical profession as a whole is assumed to have adopted procedures which are in the best interests of patients and are not inherently negligent. As L'Heureux-Dubé J. stated in *Lapointe*, in the context of the Quebec *Civil Code* (at p. 15):

> Given the number of available methods of treatment from which medical professionals must at times choose, and the distinction between error and fault, *a doctor will not be found liable if the diagnosis and treatment given to a patient correspond to those recognized by medical science at the time, even in the face of competing theories.* As expressed more eloquently by André Nadeau in "La responsabilité médicale" (1946), 6 R. du B. 153 at p. 155:
>
> > "[TRANSLATION] The courts do not have jurisdiction to settle scientific disputes or to choose among divergent opinions of physicians on certain subjects. *They may only make a finding of fault where a violation of universally accepted rules of medicine has occurred. The courts should not involve themselves in controversial questions of assessment having to do with diagnosis or the treatment of preference.*"

(Emphasis added.)

In *The Law of Torts*, 7th ed. (Sydney: Law Book Co., 1987), Professor John G. Fleming observed the following with respect to the role of standard practice, at p. 109:

> *Conformity* with general practice, on the other hand, usually dispels a charge of negligence. It tends to show what others in the same "business" considered sufficient, not that the defendant could not have learnt how to avoid the accident by the example of others, that most probably no other practical precautions could have been taken, and that the impact of an adverse judgment (especially in cases involving industry or a profession) will be industry-wide and thus assume the function of a "test case". *Finally, it underlines the need for caution against passing too cavalierly upon the conduct and decision of experts.*
>
> All the same, even a common practice may itself be condemned as negligent *if fraught with obvious risks.*

(Emphasis added.)

With respect to the medical profession in particular, Professor Fleming noted, at p. 110:

> Common practice plays a conspicuous role in medical negligence actions. Conscious at once of the layman's ignorance of medical science and apprehensive of the impact of jury bias on a peculiarly vulnerable profession, courts have resorted to the safeguard of insisting that negligence in diagnosis and treatment (including disclosure of risks) cannot ordinarily be established without

the aid of expert testimony or in the teeth of conformity with accepted medical practice. However there is no categorical rule. Thus an accepted practice is open to censure by a jury (no expert testimony required) at any rate in matters not involving diagnostic or clinical skills, on which an ordinary person may presume to pass judgment sensibly, like omission to inform the patient of risks, failure to remove a sponge, an explosion set off by an admixture of ether vapour and oxygen or injury to a patient's body outside the area of treatment.

(Emphasis added. Footnotes omitted.)

It is evident from the foregoing passage that while conformity with common practice will generally exonerate physicians of any complaint of negligence, there are certain situations where the standard practice itself may be found to be negligent. However, this will only be where the standard practice is "fraught with obvious risks" such that anyone is capable of finding it negligent, without the necessity of judging matters requiring diagnostic or clinical expertise.

. . .

As was observed in *Lapointe*, courts should not involve themselves in resolving scientific disputes which require the expertise of the profession. Courts and juries do not have the necessary expertise to assess technical matters relating to the diagnosis or treatment of patients. Where a common and accepted course of conduct is adopted based on the specialized and technical expertise of professionals, it is unsatisfactory for a finder of fact to conclude that such a standard was inherently negligent. On the other hand, matters falling within the ordinary common sense of juries can be judged to be negligent. For example, where there are obvious existing alternatives which any reasonable person would utilize in order to avoid risk, one could conclude that the failure to adopt such measures is negligent notwithstanding that it is the prevailing practice among practitioners in that area.

. . .

I conclude from the foregoing that, as a general rule, where a procedure involves difficult or uncertain questions of medical treatment or complex, scientific or highly technical matters that are beyond the ordinary experience and understanding of a judge or jury, it will not be open to find a standard medical practice negligent. On the other hand, as an exception to the general rule, if a standard practice fails to adopt obvious and reasonable precautions which are readily apparent to the ordinary finder of fact, then it is no excuse for a practitioner to claim that he or she was merely conforming to such a negligent common practice.

The question as to whether the trier of fact can find that a standard practice is itself negligent is a question of law to be determined by the trial judge irrespective of the mode of trial. It is, of course, for the jury to determine on the evidence what the standard practice is. If the evidence is conflicting on this issue, the jury will have to resolve the conflict. If, as in this case, the evidence is virtually conclusive, the trial judge should instruct the jury that failure to accept the evidence may very well result in an unreasonable verdict which will be set aside. Moreover, unless the nature of the issue is of a kind to bring it within the exception to the general rule, the jury should be instructed that once they have determined on the evidence what the standard is, the only remaining issue is whether the defendant conformed to the standard. On the other hand, if the case is one coming within the exception so that the jury can fix the standard on the basis of common sense and the ordinary understanding of the jury without the assistance of expert testimony, the trial judge must instruct the jury accordingly.

[The case was sent back to trial on the issue of whether the doctor had been negligent regarding his screening and following up of semen donors for sexually transmitted diseases other than HIV. There may or may not have been a standard practice in 1985 regarding this issue. If there was no such practice, the jury could find that the doctor was negligent without reliance on expert evidence.

However, the issue of the doctor's negligence for failing to screen the semen donor for HIV could not go back to trial. Since the doctor had complied with standard practice concerning HIV, the jury could not find him negligent in the absence of expert evidence or unless that practice was patently unreasonable.]

NOTES AND QUESTIONS

1. The party relying on either compliance with or breach of custom has the burden of proving that such a custom exists. The courts will only accept that an act, approach, or pattern of conduct constitutes a custom if it is a well-established and recognized practice that has been widely accepted in a trade, industry or profession. See generally, *Heeney v. Best* (1979), 11 C.C.L.T. 66 (Ont. C.A.); and *Goodwin v. McCully* (1989), 101 N.B.R. (2d) 289 (T.D.).

2. Prior to *ter Neuzen*, it was generally accepted that compliance with custom provided evidence of reasonableness and breach of custom provided evidence of negligence. How has the decision in *ter Neuzen* changed the impact of compliance with or breach of custom? Is *ter Neuzen* limited to customary practice in highly technical fields?

3. How was the customary practice established in *ter Neuzen*? What was the nature of the dispute over the role of the jury? How did Sopinka J. resolve it? Has Sopinka J. conceded too much authority to professionals to dictate the standards of negligence in their fields?

4. For other judicial discussions of custom see *Vancouver Gen. Hosp. v. McDaniel*, [1934] 4 D.L.R. 593 (P.C.) and *Rothwell v. Raes* (1988), 66 O.R. (2d) 449 (H.C.), aff'd. (1990), 2 O.R. (3d) 332 (C.A.), leave to appeal ref'd. (1991), 2 O.R. (3d) xii (S.C.C.) (doctors); *Moss v. Ferguson* (1979), 35 N.S.R. (2d) 181 (S.C.) and *Lowry v. Cdn. Mountain Holidays Ltd.* (1987), 40 C.C.L.T. 1 (B.C. C.A.) (industrial practices); and *Glivar v. Noble* (1985), 8 O.A.C. 60 (C.A.) (lawyers).

5. For a discussion of custom see Linden, *Canadian Tort Law*, 5th ed. (1993), 169-86; and the American Law Institute, *Restatement of the Law, Second, Torts* (1965), para. 295A.

REVIEW PROBLEMS

1. Dr. Carver, a general practitioner, prescribed a strong buffering agent to Mr. Jones to treat his ulcer, despite the fact that some ulcer patients with certain allergies and two per cent of ulcer patients without these allergies suffer serious reactions to it. There was another drug which was equally effective, but three times more expensive. Since Mr. Jones was poor, Dr. Carver decided to prescribe the buffering agent, and carried out the customary tests used by most general practitioners to verify that Jones had none of the known allergies. Although Dr. Carver had heard of a new study which indicated ways of predicting whether an ulcer patient would react badly to the buffering agent, he had not had time to read it prior to treating Mr. Jones. Had Carver read the new study, he would have realized that there was a 25 per cent chance that Mr. Jones would react badly to the buffering compound.

Unfortunately, Mr. Jones had a severe reaction to the buffering agent which necessitated his hospitalization. He is seeking your advice about suing Dr. Carver in negligence. Your preliminary investigation revealed that Dr. Carver had three years of special training in internal medicine and therefore should have known a great deal more about ulcers than an average general practitioner.

2. Mr. Smith was crossing an intersection on a green light one quiet Sunday morning when he was struck by an ambulance, which was carrying a critically-ill man to the emergency ward of a nearby hospital. Although the intersection was level, Mr. Smith's and the ambulance driver's views

of each other were blocked by a large truck that had stopped in the right hand lane for the red light. The ambulance driver had turned on his flashing beacon and loud siren, and had slowed down from 60 m.p.h. to only 10 m.p.h. when he entered the intersection against the red light. Mr. Smith did not see the ambulance's flashing light because of the truck, and did not hear the siren because he was deaf. Discuss whether the ambulance driver and/or Mr. Smith was negligent.

14

CAUSATION

1. Introduction
2. Determining the Cause-in-Fact
3. Independent Tortfeasors and Multiple Causes
4. Joint Tortfeasors
5. Problems in Assessing the Plaintiff's Loss

1. Introduction

Many of the difficulties that arise in this area stem from a failure to distinguish causation from several related issues. Causation is generally regarded as a factual issue which turns on a determination of whether the defendant's negligent conduct brought about the plaintiff's loss. Proof of causation raises evidentiary questions that are, at least theoretically, independent of legal policy or precedent. If the plaintiff cannot prove on the balance of probabilities that the defendant's negligent act was a cause of her injury, then her claim will fail. As we shall discuss, the causation test varies based on whether there is one, as opposed to several, tortfeasors.

Even if the defendant caused the plaintiff's loss, she will not be held liable if the causal connection between her negligent act and the plaintiff's loss is too tenuous or remote to justify imposing liability. Remoteness of damages is a legal issue and, like duty, it has generated intense academic and legal debate. The distinction between causation and remoteness has been blurred by the courts' use of the term "proximate cause" to refer to both issues. Thus, a proximate cause is a cause which, as a matter of law, is not too remote to justify denying liability. For analytical purposes we have separated these two issues, and will discuss causation in this chapter and remoteness in the next.

2. Determining the Cause-in-Fact

(a) THE BUT-FOR TEST

CORK v. KIRBY MACLEAN LTD.

[1952] 2 All E.R. 402 (C.A.)

[While working as a painter for the defendant, the deceased had an epileptic fit. He fell from a platform 20 feet above the ground and died. The deceased had not informed the defendant that he was an epileptic and that he had been forbidden by his doctor to work at heights. The defendant was in breach of its statutory duty to provide a 34-inch-wide platform with toe-boards and guard-rails.]

DENNING L.J.: — In this case we are again involved in the troublesome question of causation. Nowadays in tort we do not search, as previously, for the effective or predominant cause of the damage. We recognise that there may be many causes of one damage, and we ask: What were the causes of it? What faults were there which caused the damage? Since the Act of 1945 the law says that every person who is guilty of a fault which is one of the causes of the damage must bear his proper share of responsibility for the consequences.

In the present case there were, on the judge's findings, two faults: (i) The employers' fault in not providing a guard-rail or toe-boards in accordance with the regulations; (ii) the man's fault in not telling his employers that he was an epileptic and had been forbidden to work at heights. But the judge has not found that both those faults were causes of the accident. He has found that the employers' fault was a cause of the accident, but the man's fault was not. . . .

Subject to the question of remoteness, causation is, I think, a question of fact. If you can say that the damage would not have happened but for a particular fault, then that fault is in fact a cause of the damage; but if you can say that the damage would have happened just the same, fault or no fault, then the fault is not a cause of the damage. It often happens that each of the parties at fault can truly say to the other: "But for your fault, it would not have happened." In such a case both faults are in fact causes of the damage.

In this case, on the facts, I am clearly of opinion that both faults were causes of the damage. The man's fault (in not telling his employers he was forbidden to work at heights) was clearly one of the causes of his death. But for that fault on his part, he would never have been on this platform at all and would never have fallen. The employers' fault (in not providing a guard-rail or toe-boards) is more doubtful a cause. One cannot say that but for that fault the accident *would* not have happened. All that can be said is that it *might* not have happened. A guard-rail and toe-boards *might* have saved him from falling. If this was a very remote possibility, it could not be said to be a cause at all. But the judge did not so regard it. He thought that it *probably* would have saved him. On that view the employers' fault was also one of the causes of the man's death.

There remains the question of remoteness. Were either of these causes too remote to be regarded by the law as causes of the damage? This is a question of law. The judge has held that the man's fault was too remote to be regarded as a cause, but the employers' fault was not. There is, of course, as the judge said, a distinction between a remote cause and a proximate cause . . . and this distinction is a very real one. But, so far as I know, no one has been able satisfactorily to define the difference. It is, I believe, a question of degree which must be decided according to "the ordinary plain common sense of the business" (*Jones v. Livox Quarries* [[1952] 1 T.L.R. 1377]). All that can be said is that, if the damage might reasonably have been foreseen by the wrongdoer, or if there was no intervening or concurrent cause, then the cause is not too remote. But the converse is not true. A cause does not necessarily become too remote because the damage could not have been foreseen, or because there intervened or concurred the deliberate, or wrongful, or negligent act of another. It is always a matter of seeing whether the particular event was sufficiently powerful a factor in bringing about the result as to be properly regarded by the law as a cause of it: see *Minister of Pensions v. Chennell* [[1946] 2 All E.R. 719].

In this case I think the employers' fault was not too remote a cause. The regulations were intended to guard the workman from the very thing that happened — a fall. The breach, therefore, was a cause of it. It would have been different if he had been injured by something with which the regulations had nothing to do . . .

I take the view also that the man's fault was not too remote a cause. One reason alone is sufficient — the consequences might reasonably have been foreseen by him. He had indeed been warned of the very thing which befell him. In any case, according to ordinary plain common sense, it was one of the causes of his death.

There were, therefore, two faults which caused this man's death — one his own fault; the other his employers' fault. The damages fall to be apportioned according to the causative potency and blameworthiness of the respective faults. I agree that they should be borne half-and-half, and that the appeal should be allowed accordingly.

[Singleton and Romer L.JJ. gave concurring judgments.]

KAUFFMAN v. TORONTO TRANSIT COMM.

(1959), 18 D.L.R. (2d) 204 (Ont. C.A.)

The judgment of the Court was delivered by

MORDEN J.A.: — The defendant appeals from the judgment of McLennan J., dated June 3, 1958, upon the findings of a jury, awarding the plaintiff the sum of $25,000 damages for injuries suffered by her following a fall on an escalator in the defendant's St. Clair Ave. subway station. The defendant's counsel on the appeal argued that the jury's findings were against the evidence, were perverse and did not state any ground of actionable negligence for which the defendant could be held liable.

Late in the evening of February 11, 1955, the plaintiff and a friend, a Mrs. Mathewson, after travelling on a northbound subway train alighted at the St. Clair station. They walked to one of the escalators which was 30 ft. long with 22 steps, each 23-$\frac{3}{8}$ ins. wide and which moves at a speed of 90 ft. per minute. The plaintiff stepped upon the escalator followed by Mrs. Mathewson. Immediately ahead of the plaintiff was a man and ahead of him two youths. The youths began scuffling and fell back against the man who in turn lost his balance and fell back upon the plaintiff. The plaintiff fell upon the escalator steps with these two or three people on top of her. As a result of her fall and of the continuing movement upwards of the escalator, the plaintiff sustained very severe and permanent injuries. The defendant's appeal against the amount of the damages was abandoned at the hearing of the appeal.

. . .

The jury found the defendant negligent specifically as follows:

1. The defendant, in acquiring an escalator of radical departure in hand-rail design, did not sufficiently test or cause to be tested by a qualified expert the coefficient of friction and contour of the Peelle Motor Stair Handrail.

. . .

The theory advanced by the plaintiff's counsel to quote his own words was that

> in the operation of an escalator, particularly in a public transit system where large crowds are to be expected, if a person near the top falls backward (for whatever reason) against the person behind him, each person will fall against the other knocking him down in much the same fashion as a row of dominoes.

But there was a total absence of evidence that the man immediately ahead of the plaintiff or the two reckless and irresponsible youths ahead of him were grasping or attempted to grasp the hand rail before or in the course of the scuffle and consequent falling. Nor was there any evidence that in the circumstances the plaintiff would not have fallen if her hands had been grasping a rubber oval hand rail. In my opinion, there was no evidence to justify a finding that the type of hand rail in use at the St. Clair Ave. station was a contributing cause of the plaintiff's unfortunate and serious accident. It is a fundamental principle that the causal relation between the alleged negligence and the injury must be made out by the evidence and not left to the conjecture of the jury ... The first finding of negligence in view of the evidence in this case does not justify a verdict against the defendant.

. . .

The appeal must be allowed and the action dismissed, both with costs, if demanded.

[Affirmed (1960), 22 D.L.R. (2d) 97 (S.C.C.).]

NOTES AND QUESTIONS

1. Did Lord Denning disagree with the trial judge in *Cork* on the issue of causation, remoteness, or both issues? Explain the difference between a cause and a proximate cause. How does Denning L.J. state the but-for test of causation?

2. Why did the plaintiff's claim fail in *Kauffman*? What kind of evidence should the plaintiff have introduced to convince the court that the defendant's negligence had caused her injury?

3. In *Qualcast (Wolverhampton) Ltd. v. Haynes*, [1959] A.C. 743 (H.L.) the plaintiff, an experienced foundry worker, was injured when a ladle of molten metal slipped and splashed metal on his foot. The defendant company had protective spats which, if worn, would have prevented the injury. However, the company had not ordered the plaintiff to wear the spats, and he had not asked to use them. After recuperating the plaintiff returned to work and still did not wear the spats. The House of Lords held that the defendant was not negligent. Lord Denning stated that in any event the plaintiff's claim would have failed on causation. Do you agree? Would Denning L.J. have reached the same conclusion if the plaintiff had framed the allegation of negligence in terms of the defendant's failure to ensure that he wore spats?

4. In *Richard v. C.N.R.* (1970), 15 D.L.R. (3d) 732 (P.E.I. S.C.), the plaintiff was asleep in his car aboard a ferry when he was awakened by someone shouting: "We're here!" Believing that the statement had been made by the attendant, the plaintiff started his car and backed it off the end of the ferry. Unfortunately, the boat had not yet docked and the car landed in the Gulf of St. Lawrence. The plaintiff sued alleging, among other things, that the defendant had been negligent in untying the nylon rope across the end of the ferry before it docked. The court concluded that the "sole, direct, proximate and effective cause" of the accident was the plaintiff's rash act of backing off the boat, contrary to the warning signs and the crew's attempts to stop him. Do you agree that the removal of the rope was not a cause of the plaintiff's loss? If, as the plaintiff believed, a ferry employee had shouted "We're here!", would his act have been a cause of the plaintiff's loss? Would the result have been the same if the plaintiff had alleged that the defendant was negligent in failing to provide an adequate restraining barrier?

5. For recent Canadian cases on causation, see *Laferrière v. Lawson* (1991), 78 D.L.R. (4th) 609 (S.C.C.); *Arndt v. Smith* (1995), 25 C.C.L.T. (2d) 262 (B.C. C.A.); *Hollis v. Dow Corning Corp.* (1995), 27 C.C.L.T. (2d) 1 (S.C.C.); *Allarie v. Victoria (City)*, [1995] 1 W.W.R. 655 (B.C. S.C.); *Pauluik v. Paraiso* (1994), [1995] 2 W.W.R. 61 (Man. Q.B.), aff'd. (1995), [1996] 2 W.W.R. 57 (Man. C.A.); and *Doern v. Phillips Estate*, [1995] 4 W.W.R. 1 (B.C. S.C.).

6. The but-for test has been subject to considerable academic criticism and comment. For example, in "A Theory of Strict Liability" (1973), 2 J. of Legal Stud. 151 at 161, Epstein states: "Its affinity for absurd hypotheticals should suggest that the 'but-for' test should be abandoned as even a tentative account of the concept of causation". See also Malone, "Ruminations on Cause-In-Fact" (1956-57), 9 Stan. L. Rev. 60; Fraser and Howarth, "More Concern for Cause" (1984), 4 Legal Stud. 131; Pincus, "Progress on the Causal Chain Gang . . ." (1986), 24 Osgoode Hall L.J. 961; Gerecke, "Risk Exposure as Injury: Alleviating the Injustice of Tort Causation Rules" (1990), 35 McGill L.J. 797; and Mirandola, "Lost Chances, Cause-in-Fact and Rationality in Medical Negligence" (1992), 50 U.T. Fac. L. Rev. 258.

(b) CAUSATION AND CORRELATION

Scientific advances have made it possible to establish that certain events and exposures to substances, even 10 to 15 years in the past, increase the risk that a person will develop a disease or disability. Under the but-for test, the increased risk must be such as to make it more probable than not that the defendant's negligent act was a cause of the plaintiff's loss. Traditionally, if the plaintiff could not prove that the increased risk met the but-for test, her claim would fail. Some courts have been willing to abandon the but-for test in certain categories of cases, if the plaintiff can prove that the defendant's negligence significantly increased the risk of a particular kind of injury and that very injury occurred.

In *McGhee v. National Coal Board*, [1972] 3 All E.R. 1008, the majority of the House of Lords held that if the defendant's negligent act significantly increased the risk of a particular kind of injury and that very injury befell the plaintiff, the defendant would be deemed to be a causer. Lord Wilberforce agreed with the result. However, in his view, the burden of proof in causation would shift in such circumstances from the defendant to the plaintiff, and then only if there were good policy reasons for doing so. The House of Lords' broadening of the test of causation should be seen in the factual context of *McGhee* — an industrial illness case in which the defendant employer had a pre-existing duty to the plaintiff employee.

A number of Canadian courts adopted *McGhee*, but focused on Wilberforce L.J.'s minority approach and applied it well beyond the confines of industrial health and safety cases. In *Wilsher v. Essex Area Health Authority*, [1988] A.C. 1074, the House of Lords, in the guise of "re-interpreting" *McGhee*, effectively overturned it. In *Wilsher*, the House of Lords applied the but-for test. In *Snell v. Farrell* (1990), 72 D.L.R. (4th) 289, the Supreme Court of Canada addressed the conflicting House of Lords and Canadian decisions.

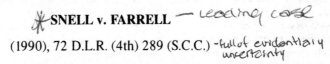

✱ SNELL v. FARRELL — *leading case*

(1990), 72 D.L.R. (4th) 289 (S.C.C.) — *full of evidentiary uncertainty*

[Dr. Farrell performed a cataract operation on Mrs. Snell. After injecting the local anaesthetic into the retrobulbar muscles behind the eyeball, Dr. Farrell noticed a slight discolouration, which he stated on discovery was due to a very small retrobulbar bleed. On further examination, he found no other signs of bleeding. After waiting 30 minutes, he proceeded with the operation. Following the surgery, there was blood in the eye. It cleared nine months later, but the optic nerve had atrophied resulting in blindness in that eye.

The damage to the optic nerve could have occurred naturally or been the result of continuing the operation. Neither expert witness was willing to state with certainty the cause or when the damage occurred. The trial judge accepted the expert testimony that Dr. Farrell was negligent in continuing the operation after noticing the discolouration. Relying on *McGhee v. Nat. Coal Bd.*, [1972] 3 All E.R. 1008 (H.L.), the trial judge concluded that Mrs. Snell had established a *prima facie* case of causation and the burden shifted to Dr. Farrell to disprove causation. Since Dr. Farrell could not discharge this burden, he was held liable. The Court of Appeal dismissed his appeal. He then appealed to the Supreme Court of Canada.]

The judgment of the court was delivered by

SOPINKA J.: — The issue of law in this case is whether the plaintiff in a malpractice suit must prove causation in accordance with traditional principles or whether recent developments in the law justify a finding of liability on the basis of some less onerous standard.

. . .

Causation — Principles

Both the trial judge and the Court of Appeal relied on *McGhee*, which (subject to its reinterpretation in the House of Lords in *Wilsher*) purports to depart from traditional principles in the law of torts that the plaintiff must prove on a balance of probabilities that, but for the tortious conduct of the defendant, the plaintiff would not have sustained the injury complained of. In view of the fact that *McGhee* has been applied by a number of courts in Canada to reverse the ordinary burden of proof with respect to causation, it is important to examine recent developments in the law relating to causation and to determine whether a departure from well-established principles is necessary for the resolution of this appeal.

The traditional approach to causation has come under attack in a number of cases in which there is concern that due to the complexities of proof, the probable victim of tortious conduct will be deprived of relief. This concern is strongest in circumstances in which, on the basis of some percentage of statistical probability, the plaintiff is the likely victim of the combined tortious conduct of a number of defendants, but cannot prove causation against a specific defendant or defendants on the basis of particularized evidence in accordance with traditional principles. The challenge to the traditional approach has manifested itself in cases dealing with non-traumatic injuries such as man-made diseases resulting from the widespread diffusion of chemical products, including product liability cases in which a product which can cause injury is widely manufactured and marketed by a large number of corporations.

. . .

Although, to date, these developments have had little impact in other common law countries, it has long been recognized that the allocation of the burden of proof is not immutable. The legal or ultimate burden of proof is determined by the substantive law "upon broad reasons of experience and fairness": J.H. Wigmore,

Evidence in Trials at Common Law, 4th ed., vol. 9 (Boston: Little, Brown & Co., 1981), s. 2486, at p. 292. In a civil case, the two broad principles are:

1. that the onus is on the party who asserts a proposition, usually the plaintiff;
2. that where the subject-matter of the allegation lies particularly within the knowledge of one party, that party may be required to prove it.

This court has not hesitated to alter the incidence of the ultimate burden of proof when the underlying rationale for its allocation is absent in a particular case: see *National Trust Co. v. Wong Aviation Ltd.* (1969), 3 D.L.R. (3d) 55, [1969] S.C.R. 481. This flexibility extends to the issue of causation. . . .

Proof of causation in medical malpractice cases is often difficult for the patient. The physician is usually in a better position to know the cause of the injury than the patient. On the basis of the second basic principle referred to above, there is an argument that the burden of proof should be allocated to the defendant. . . .

This brings me to the *McGhee* case and its influence on subsequent cases, particularly in the medical malpractice field.

. . .

Two theories of causation emerge from an analysis of the speeches of the Lords in this case. The first, firmly espoused by Lord Wilberforce, is that the plaintiff need only prove that the defendant created a risk of harm and that the injury occurred within the area of the risk. The second is that in these circumstances, an inference of causation was warranted in that there is no practical difference between materially contributing to the risk of harm and materially contributing to the harm itself.

The speeches were subjected to a careful examination and interpretation in *Wilsher v. Essex Area Health Authority*, [1988] 2 W.L.R. 557, by Lord Bridge when some 15 years later, the House of Lords revisited the issue. The plaintiff claimed damages from the defendant health authority for negligence in medical treatment which resulted in a condition of the eyes leading to blindness. A likely cause of the condition, but not a definite one, in the opinion of medical experts, was too much oxygen. The plaintiff proved that for a period of time he was supersaturated with oxygen. A number of different factors other than excessive oxygen could have caused or contributed to the injury. The expert evidence was conflicting. The trial judge applied *McGhee* and held the defendant liable since it had failed to prove that the plaintiff's condition had not resulted from its negligence. The Court of Appeal dismissed the appeal by a majority judgment with the Vice-Chancellor dissenting. The House of Lords allowed the appeal and directed a new trial. Lord Bridge, delivering the unanimous judgment of the Court, reaffirmed the principle that the burden of proving causation rested on the plaintiff. Since the trial judge had not made the relevant finding of fact to sort out the conflicting evidence, a new trial was directed on this basis. Lord Bridge interpreted *McGhee* as espousing no new principle. Instead, *McGhee* was explained as promoting a robust and pragmatic approach to the facts to enable an inference of negligence to be drawn even though medical or scientific expertise cannot arrive at a definitive conclusion.

. . .

where imbalance of knowledge

Lord Bridge concluded with a caution (at p. 571):

> But, whether we like it or not, the law, which only Parliament can change, requires proof of fault causing damage as the basis of liability in tort. We should do society nothing but disservice if we made the forensic process still more unpredictable and hazardous by distorting the law to accommodate the exigencies of what may seem hard cases.

Canadian cases decided after *McGhee*, but before *Wilsher*, tended to follow *McGhee* by adopting either the reversal of onus or the inference interpretation. Which interpretation was adopted made no practical difference, because even when the latter approach was applied, the creation of the risk by the defendant's breach of duty was deemed to have established a *prima facie* case, thus shifting the onus to the defendant ...

Decisions in Canada after *Wilsher* accept its interpretation of *McGhee*. In the circumstances in which *McGhee* had been previously interpreted to support a reversal of the burden of proof, an inference was now permissible to find causation, notwithstanding that causation was not proved by positive evidence ...

The question that this court must decide is whether the traditional approach to causation is no longer satisfactory in that plaintiffs in malpractice cases are being deprived of compensation because they cannot prove causation where it in fact exists.

If I were convinced that defendants who have a substantial connection to the injury were escaping liability because plaintiffs cannot prove causation under currently applied principles, I would not hesitate to adopt one of [the *McGhee*] alternatives. In my opinion, however, properly applied, the principles relating to causation are adequate to the task. Adoption of either of the proposed alternatives would have the effect of compensating plaintiffs where a substantial connection between the injury and the defendant's conduct is absent. Reversing the burden of proof may be justified where two defendants negligently fire in the direction of the plaintiff and then by their tortious conduct destroy the means of proof at his disposal. In such a case it is clear that the injury was not caused by neutral conduct. It is quite a different matter to compensate a plaintiff by reversing the burden of proof for an injury that may very well be due to factors unconnected to the defendant and not the fault of anyone. . . .

[Sopinka J. then discussed how the liberalization of the recovery principles in the United States contributed to their malpractice crises of the 1970's. He noted that a British Royal Commission specifically rejected the proposal to shift the burden of proof in malpractice cases.]

I am of the opinion that the dissatisfaction with the traditional approach to causation stems to a large extent from its too rigid application by the courts in many cases. Causation need not be determined by scientific precision. It is, as stated by Lord Salmon in *Alphacell Ltd. v. Woodward*, [1972] 2 All E.R. 475 (H.L.), at p. 490, ". . . essentially a practical question of fact which can best be answered by ordinary common sense rather than abstract metaphysical theory." Furthermore, as I observed earlier, the allocation of the burden of proof is not immutable. Both the burden and the standard of proof are flexible concepts. In *Blatch v. Archer* (1774), 1 Cowp. 63 at p. 65, 98 E.R. 969 at p. 970, Lord Mansfield stated: "It is certainly a maxim that all evidence is to be weighed according to the proof which it was in the power of one side to have produced, and in the power of the other to have contradicted."

In many malpractice cases, the facts lie particularly within the knowledge of the defendant. In these circumstances, very little affirmative evidence on the part of the plaintiff will justify the drawing of an inference of causation in the absence of evidence to the contrary.

The legal or ultimate burden remains with the plaintiff, but in the absence of evidence to the contrary adduced by the defendant, an inference of causation may be drawn, although positive or scientific proof of causation has not been adduced. If some evidence to the contrary is adduced by the defendant, the trial judge is entitled to take account of Lord Mansfield's famous precept. This is, I believe, what Lord Bridge had in mind in *Wilsher* when he referred to a "robust and pragmatic approach to the ... facts" (p. 569).

It is not, therefore, essential that the medical experts provide a firm opinion supporting the plaintiff's theory of causation. Medical experts ordinarily determine causation in terms of certainties whereas a lesser standard is demanded by the law....

[Sopinka J. stated that part of the problem stems from the reluctance of doctors to express an opinion unless they are 100 per cent certain. The law does not require certainty but rather a balance of probability (i.e. 51 per cent). It is in this sense that the plaintiff's case need not be based on a firm medical opinion.

He then reviewed the evidence, emphasizing that Dr. Farrell was negligent in continuing the operation. While the blindness could have resulted from natural causes, Sopinka J. quoted the expert testimony and it indicated that the continuation of the operation was more likely to have been the cause.]

The appellant was present during the operation and was in a better position to observe what occurred. Furthermore, he was able to interpret from a medical standpoint what he saw. In addition, by continuing the operation which has been found to constitute negligence, he made it impossible for the respondent or anyone else to detect the bleeding which is alleged to have caused the injury. In these circumstances, it was open to the trial judge to draw the inference that the injury was caused by the retrobulbar bleeding. There was no evidence to rebut this inference. The fact that testing the eye for hardness did not disclose bleeding is insufficient for this purpose. If there was any rebutting evidence, it was weak, and it was open to the trial judge to find causation, applying the principles to which I have referred.

I am confident that had the trial judge not stated that "I cannot go beyond this since neither doctor did and I should not speculate", he would have drawn the necessary inference. In stating the above, he failed to appreciate that it is not essential to have a positive medical opinion to support a finding of causation. Furthermore, it is not speculation but the application of common sense to draw such an inference where, as here, the circumstances, other than a positive medical opinion, permit.

While this court does not ordinarily make findings of fact, this course is fully justified in this case. First, I am of the opinion that the trial judge either made the necessary finding or would have but for error of law. Second, it would be a disservice to all to send this case back for a new trial when the evidence is not essentially in conflict. I note that in *Wilsher*, the House of Lords refrained from deciding the case only because the evidence of the experts was seriously in conflict. That is not the case here.

In the result, I would dismiss the appeal with costs.

Appeal dismissed.

NOTES AND QUESTIONS

1. According to Sopinka J., was Mrs. Snell able to prove on the balance of probabilities that Dr. Farrell's negligence was a cause of her loss? What test of causation did Sopinka J. apply?

2. Why did Sopinka J. refuse to shift the burden of proof to Dr. Farrell? Although he suggests that the burden of proof is not "immutable", Sopinka J. then indicates that it would be inappropriate to reverse the burden of proof "for an injury that may very well be due to factors unconnected to the defendant and not the fault of anyone." What are the implications of this statement? Are Sopinka J.'s comments limited to medical malpractice?

3. Assume that the incidence of a particular kind of cancer is 6 per 100,000 a year in a normal population and 10 per 100,000 in a population that is exposed to PCBs. Assume as well, that the plaintiff contracts this type of cancer after the defendant negligently exposes her to PCBs. The scientific evidence establishes that there is no way to distinguish the PCB-induced cancer cases from the naturally occurring cancer cases. How would the causation issue be resolved if a court applied: (a) the but-for test; (b) the *McGhee* alternatives; or (c) Sopinka J.'s approach?

Answer the same question but under the assumption that the normal incidence of cancer is 4 per 100,000 and 10 per 100,000 in those exposed to PCBs.

4. Is the real problem in this area the but-for test or the fact that it creates an all-or-nothing solution? Neither *McGhee* nor *Snell* addresses this latter issue. For a discussion of this problem, see Pardy, "Risk, Cause and Toxic Torts: A Theory for a Standard of Proof" (1989), 10 Advoc. Q. 277; and Fleming, "Probabilistic Causation in Tort Law" (1989), 68 Can. Bar Rev. 661.

5. Prior to *Snell, McGhee* generated considerable confusion and debate. See for example *Nowsco Well Service Ltd. v. Can. Propane Gas & Oil Ltd.* (1981), 122 D.L.R. (3d) 228 (Sask. C.A.); *Letnick v. Metro. Toronto (Mun.)* (1988), 44 C.C.L.T. 69 (Fed. C.A.); *Haag v. Marshall* (1989), 1 C.C.L.T. (2d) 99 (B.C. C.A.); and *Belknap v. Meakes* (1989), 1 C.C.L.T. (2d) 192 (B.C. C.A.). See also Weinrib, "A Step Forward in Factual Causation" (1975), 38 Mod. L. Rev. 518.

6. In *Sindell v. Abbott Laboratories* (1980), 607 P. 2d 924 (Cal. S.C.), the plaintiff was a cancer victim whose mother had taken diethylstilbestrol (DES) during pregnancy. DES was manufactured by approximately 200 pharmaceutical companies, but there were no significant differences in the various products. The drug had been prescribed to prevent miscarriages, but eventually proved ineffective and was found to pose a risk of causing a particular kind of cancer in female children. This cancer was deadly once it manifested itself, but it had a minimum latency period of 10 to 12 years. The plaintiff could prove that her cancer was caused by DES, yet she could not establish which company had produced the DES her mother had taken. The plaintiff sued all of the major manufacturers, arguing that they had been negligent in continuing to market DES when they knew or ought to have known that it was ineffective and highly carcinogenic. The court found the defendant companies negligent and held each company liable in proportion to its share of the DES market, unless it could prove that it had not produced the DES that caused the plaintiff's cancer. The court acknowledged that there was a 10 per cent chance that the DES in question had been manufactured by one of the approximately 195 smaller producers which had not been sued.

As we shall discuss in chapter 19, Proof of Negligence, *Sindell* represents a marked departure from established principles of causation and proof. The case has been introduced at this point because it illustrates the need to re-examine traditional concepts of causation in response to new chemical and environmental hazards, and to the scientific data that is necessary to document their effects. See Strand, "The Inapplicability of Traditional Tort Analysis to Environmental Risks..." (1983), 35 Stan. L. Rev. 575; Black, "Epidemiologic Proof in Toxic Tort Litigation" (1984), 52 Fordham L.R. 732; Legum, "Increased Risk of Cancer as an Actionable Injury" (1984), 18 Ga. L. Rev. 563; Rose-Ackerman, "Market-Share Allocations in Tort Law: Strengths and Weaknesses" (1990), 19 J. Legal Stud. 739; and Stundtner, "Proving Causation in Toxic Tort Cases: T-Cell Studies as Epidemiological and

Particularistic Evidence" (1993), 20 Environmental Affairs 335. See also Brodeur, *Outrageous Misconduct: The Asbestos Industry on Trial* (1985).

7. In *Re "Agent Orange" Product Liability Litigation* (1984), 597 F. Supp. 740 (N.Y. Dist. Ct.), the court approved a settlement on behalf of Vietnamese war veterans who were injured by this potent defoliant. The court found that the manufacturers had failed to warn of the damaging effects of the product, including increased risks of skin and lung diseases and a higher incidence of birth defects. As in *Sindell*, the court found it was impossible to determine which manufacturer's product caused any particular plaintiff's damages. As all the manufacturers were negligent, liability was apportioned by market share. The difference in the *Agent Orange* case was that the plaintiffs could not all be identified.

The *Sindell* and *Agent Orange* cases also illustate some of the issues that arise in what is called "mass tort litigation". Other examples include the asbestos, Dalkon Shield, HIV-positive blood donation, breast-implant, and various toxic waste cases. This litigation typically involves hundreds of potential plaintiffs, multiple corporate defendants, and tens or hundreds of millions of dollars in damages. It has generated widespread bankruptcies in some industries, complicated insurance litigation and very complex settlement packages. See Vairo, "Multi-Tort Cases: Cause for More Darkness on the Subject, or a New Role for Federal Common Law" (1985), 54 Fordham L. Rev. 169; Roe, "Corporate Strategic Reaction to Mass Tort" (1986), 72 Virg. L. Rev. 1; Farber, "Toxic Causation" (1987), 71 Minn. Law Rev. 1219; and Brennan, "Causal Chains and Statistical Links . . ." (1989), 73 Cornell L. Rev. 469.

8. A major mass tort claim may well arise if the Canadian courts find that cigarette manufacturers have been negligent in failing to warn users of the risk inherent in smoking. See Cunningham, "Tobacco Products Liability in Common Law Canada" (1990), 11 Health Law in Canada 43. See also *Hunt v. T & N plc.* (1990), 4 C.C.L.T. (2d) 1 (S.C.C.), which deals with the asbestos industry's potential liability for failing to warn.

3. Independent Tortfeasors and Multiple Causes

The issue of causation becomes more complex when the plaintiff is injured by the negligent acts of two or more independent tortfeasors. In such cases, the court must first determine whether the plaintiff's injuries are divisible. Injuries are considered divisible if they can be divided into distinct losses, and each loss can be attributed to the conduct of a particular tortfeasor. If the plaintiff's injuries are divisible, she will have a separate cause of action against each tortfeasor.

This situation must be distinguished from one in which two or more independent tortfeasors cause a single indivisible harm. In these multiple cause situations each tortfeasor is held jointly and severally liable for all of the plaintiff's losses, regardless of whether she was a major or minor contributor. There are certain multiple cause situations in which the but-for test would prove inappropriate. For example, if two negligent hunters, acting independently, fired potentially fatal shots which simultaneously struck the victim in the head, the but-for test would exculpate both hunters. To avoid this inequity, the courts have developed a modified test of causation.

LAMBTON v. MELLISH

[1894] 3 Ch. 163

The Defendants *Mellish* and *Cox* were rival refreshment contractors who catered for visitors and excursionists to the common, and both the Defendants had merry-go-rounds on their premises, and were in the habit of using organs as an accompaniment to the amusements.

It appeared from the evidence that these organs were for three months or more in the summer continuously being played together from 10 or 11 A.M. till 6 or 7 P.M., and that the noise caused by the two organs was "maddening".

The organs used by *Mellish* had been changed, and it was alleged by him that the organ in use when the motion was made was a small portable hand-organ making comparatively little noise. That used by *Cox* was a much larger one provided with trumpet stops and emitting sounds which could be heard at the distance of one mile.

The Plaintiff now moved against the Defendant in each action for an injunction restraining him from playing any organs so as to cause a nuisance or injury to the Plaintiff or his family, or other occupiers of the Plaintiff's property.

. . .

CHITTY J.: — Notwithstanding the conflict of evidence, I am of opinion that the Plaintiff is entitled to the injunction he asks for as against the Defendant in each action.

A man may tolerate a nuisance for a short period. A passer-by or a by-stander would not find any nuisance in these organs; but the case is very different when the noise has to be continuously endured: under such circumstances it is scarcely an exaggeration to term it "maddening", going on, as it does, hour after hour, day after day, and month after month. I consider that the noise made by each Defendant, taken separately, amounts to a nuisance. But I go further. It was said for the Defendant *Mellish* that two rights cannot make a wrong — by that it was meant that if one man makes a noise not of a kind, duration, or degree sufficient to constitute a nuisance, and another man, not acting in concert with the first, makes a similar noise at the same time, each is responsible only for the noise made by himself, and not also for that made by the other. If the two agreed and acted in combination each would be a wrongdoer. If a man shouts outside a house for most of the day, and another man, who is his rival (for it is to be remembered that these Defendants are rivals), does the same, has the inhabitant of the house no remedy? It is said that that is only so much the worse for the inhabitant. On the ground of common sense it must be the other way. Each of the men is making a noise and each is adding his quantum until the whole constitutes a nuisance. Each hears the other, and is adding to the sum which makes up the nuisance. In my opinion each is separately liable, and I think it would be contrary to good sense, and, indeed, contrary to law, to hold otherwise. It would be contrary to common sense that the inhabitants of the house should be left without remedy at law.

. . .

The Defendants here are both responsible for the noise as a whole so far as it constitutes a nuisance affecting the Plaintiff, and each must be restrained in respect of his own share in making the noise. I therefore grant an interim injunction in both the actions in the terms of the notices of motion.

ARNEIL v. PATERSON

[1931] A.C. 560 (H.L.)

. . .

VISCOUNT HAILSHAM: — My Lords, this is an appeal from a decision of the Court of Session reversing the decision of the Sheriff-Substitute. The point at issue is a very short one, and the facts are not in dispute. It appears that the appellants are farmers who own a flock of black-faced sheep on a farm in Scotland. The respondent is the owner of a dog, and in the early morning of January 21, 1930, the respondent's dog, in company with another dog belonging to the other defender, who has not entered any appearance, attacked the flock of sheep belonging to the appellants. The statement in the condescendence is in these terms:

> On the morning of Tuesday, January 21, 1930, about six o'clock, two dogs, a cross-airedale belonging to the first-named defender and a collie belonging to the second-named defender, trespassed on the pursuers' farm where the said ewes were grazing. The said dogs, acting together, attacked the pursuers' sheep, hunted and chased them, and severely bit, mauled, and worried seventeen of them.

To that condescendence the answer is made:

> For the purpose of this action this defender admits that his dog, along with the other defender's dog, trespassed on the pursuers' farm, and that seventeen sheep were mauled and worried by the said two dogs acting together, and that ten of the sheep have died.

The damages for the total damage done to the sheep were agreed for the purposes of this action at a sum of £60, and at the hearing before the Sheriff-Substitute judgment was given against the present respondent for that amount. On appeal to the Court of Session, the Court of Session held that the respondent was liable only for half of the amount, on the ground that there were two dogs who were jointly concerned in attacking and damaging the sheep, and that in the absence of any evidence as to how much of the damage was done by either of the dogs the damage must be apportioned equally between the two defenders. It is from that decision that this appeal is brought.

. . .

In this, as in any other case, there are two elements which have to be determined: first, the element of liability, and secondly, when liability is established, the element of damage. So far as liability is concerned, it is conceded that the section to which I have just drawn attention imposes on the respondent a liability for the injury done to the sheep by his dog; but it is said that, since his dog was concerned with an other, in the absence of evidence as to how much injury each dog actually did, each must be held responsible only for half the total damage. In my view that is a mistaken construction to be placed upon the statute. I think the statute only alters the common law rule on the question of liability. Once liability is established, then the ordinary measure of damage has to be applied. It has to be ascertained how much injury "that dog" has done to the cattle — in this case to the pursuers' sheep. I think that each of the dogs did in law occasion the whole of the damage which was suffered by the sheep as the result of the action of the two dogs acting together. If that be so, then each of the owners of the two dogs is responsible for the whole of the damage which has been done, and judgment can be obtained against either of them.

[Viscount Dunedin and Lord Atkin gave short concurring speeches. Lords Warrington of Clyffe and Thankerton concurred in the result.]

NOWLAN v. BRUNSWICK CONST. LTEE

(1972), 5 N.B.R. (2d) 529, 34 D.L.R. (3d) 422 (N.B. C.A.)

[The defendant contractor had been negligent in constructing the plaintiff's house, which suffered extensive rot due to leaks in the structure. However, the defendant argued that no damage would have occurred but for the architect's poor design which had not provided for proper ventilation.]

LIMERICK J.A.: ... While structural design particularly in lack of ventilation contributed greatly to the damage occasioned to the building, the poor workmanship of the defendant and poor quality of materials used also contributed.

This is a case of poor design on the part of the architect, as well as poor workmanship and materials contributing to the same damage.

If the design had provided proper ventilation there would have been no dry rot even though leaks occurred due to poor workmanship. Even though the design was poor there would have been no dry rot if the roof had been impervious to water and a proper drain installed and proper vapour barriers and insulation installed and windows had been properly constructed according to the plan.

Where there are concurrent torts, breaches of contract or a breach of contract and a concurrent tort both contributing to the same damage, whether or not the damage would have occurred in the absence of either cause, the liability is a joint and several liability and either party causing or contributing to the damage is liable for the whole damage to the person aggrieved: see *Thompson v. London County Council*, [1899] 1 Q.B. 840 (C.A.), and see Glanville Williams on *Joint Torts and Contributory Negligence* (1951), p. 2.

The defendant is a concurrent wrongdoer and the fact that the damage might not have occurred but for the poor design of the building does not excuse him from the liability arising out of his poor workmanship and inadequate material supplied by him.

The appeal is allowed. The judgment of the trial Judge is set aside. The plaintiffs, appellants shall have judgment against the defendant for the amount of $36,068.48 determined by the trial Judge and costs of trial and appeal.

[Hughes C.J.N.B. concurred with Limerick J.A., and Bugold J.A. wrote a separate concurring judgment. Affirmed (1974), 49 D.L.R. (3d) 93 (S.C.C.).]

NOTES AND QUESTIONS

1. Since the analysis of cases involving independent tortfeasors turns on whether the plaintiff's losses are divisible, this preliminary issue should be resolved before considering the duty of care. The way in which the plaintiff's injuries are characterized may dictate whether they are treated as divisible. For example, assume that two hunters each shoot the plaintiff in the arm, that the bullet wounds are separate and that one cumulative effect of the two wounds is stiffness in the shoulder. Would you characterize the plaintiff's injuries as divisible or indivisible? What criteria would you use in reaching your decision?

2. If the negligent acts of the defendants follow one another closely in time, practical evidentiary problems arise in treating the damages as divisible. For example, if a negligent driver collides with the plaintiff's car and two minutes later a second negligent driver runs into the plaintiff's car, it may not be possible for the court to attribute specific injuries to each defendant. In these circumstances, the court would consider the plaintiff's injuries indivisible and hold both defendants jointly and severally liable for the entire loss. See, for example, *Keith v. Guar. Trust Co. of Can.* (1974), 57 D.L.R. (3d) 475 (Sask. C.A.); and *Spracklin v. O'Flaherty's Estate* (1977), 15 Nfld. & P.E.I.R. 488 (Nfld. S.C.).

3. What does the term, "jointly and severally liable" mean? Is there any advantage to the plaintiff if two independent tortfeasors are held jointly and severally liable for her injuries?

4. At common law there was no contribution among tortfeasors. Thus, a defendant who played a relatively minor role in causing the plaintiff's loss could be held fully liable, and yet have no redress against other tortfeasors who may have been primarily at fault. The provincial Negligence Acts now provide that one tortfeasor may obtain contribution from her fellow tortfeasors, based upon their respective degrees of fault. See, for example, Negligence Act, R.S.O. 1990, c. N.1; and Negligence Act, R.S.B.C. 1979, c. 298, s. 4. See generally Cheifetz, *Apportionment of Fault in Tort* (1981).

5. Why did the court in *Mellish* impose liability on both defendants, even though their individual conduct may not have been tortious? What test of causation did the court apply? Would the result have been the same if the but-for test had been used?

6. In *Arneil*, why were the damages not apportioned on the basis that each owner was liable for 50 per cent of the loss? What test of causation was applied? Would the result have been the same if the but-for test had been used?

7. What test of causation was applied in *Nowlan*?

8. In the United States, the courts use a substantial factor test of causation in both single and multiple causation cases. See Malone, "Ruminations on Cause-In-Fact" (1956-57), 9 Stan. L. Rev. 60 at 88-97; Green, "The Causal Relation Issue" (1962), 60 Mich. L. Rev. 543 at 554; and Wright, "Causation, Responsibility, Risk, Probability, Naked Statistics and Proof:..." (1988), 73 Iowa L. Rev. 1001.

REVIEW PROBLEMS

1. Assume that 20 decibels of noise constitute a nuisance and that noises from different sources have a simple cumulative effect. Based on these assumptions, analyze the liability of the parties in the following situations:
   (a) Allen causes 21 decibels, Barry causes 19 and Carl causes 5;
   (b) Allen and Barry each independently cause 21 decibels;
   (c) Allen causes 10 decibels, Barry causes 9.9 and Carl causes .2; and
   (d) Allen, Barry and Carl each cause 6 decibels and the plaintiff causes 3.

2. Allan and Bob were showing each other their favourite revolvers when they were called upstairs to meet Carol. They left their revolvers on the coffee table and came upstairs. As they talked, Carol's four-year-old son went off to explore the house. He eventually found the revolvers and shot himself with Bob's gun. Allan's gun was also loaded, but the child had not touched it. Carol has sued both Bob and Allan in negligence. Allan has sought your advice regarding his liability.

4. Joint Tortfeasors

It is important to distinguish a situation in which the defendants are independent tortfeasors from one in which they are joint tortfeasors. As discussed above, an independent tortfeasor will only be held liable for the divisible injuries she causes and for the indivisible injuries she has contributed to bringing about. However, a joint tortfeasor is held jointly and severally liable for the torts committed by her fellow joint tortfeasors, even if she has not caused or contributed to the plaintiff's loss in any way. The liability of joint tortfeasors stems from their legal relationship with one another, and not from playing a causal role in the plaintiff's loss.

COOK v. LEWIS

[1951] S.C.R. 830, [1952] 1 D.L.R. 1

[The plaintiff was struck in the face by bird-shot when the defendants fired simultaneously at different birds which had flown in the plaintiff's direction. The jury found that the plaintiff had been shot by one of the two hunters, but was unable to say which one. Yet, it also found that the injuries were not caused by the negligence of either hunter. The Court of Appeal set aside the jury's finding on negligence, because it was perverse and ordered a new trial.

The Supreme Court, with Locke J. dissenting, upheld the Court of Appeal's decision. In the course of its judgment, the Supreme Court dealt with several causation and burden of proof issues. The following excerpt focuses on the plaintiff's argument that the defendants were joint tortfeasors. The other issues raised by *Cook* are discussed in chapter 18.]

The judgment of Estey, Cartwright and Fauteux JJ. was delivered by

CARTWRIGHT J.: — This is an appeal by David Cook, one of the defendants, from a judgment of the Court of Appeal for British Columbia (1) setting aside the judgment pronounced at the trial in favour of the defendants and directing a new trial. The other defendant, Akenhead, does not appeal.

. . .

It is necessary to consider the answer to the 3rd question in which the jury have indicated that they were unable to find which of the two defendants did fire the shot which did the damage.

The general rule is, I think, stated correctly in Starkie on Evidence, 4th Edition, 860, quoted with approval by Patterson J.A. in *Moxley v. The Canada Atlantic Railway Company* [(1887), 14 O.A.R. 309 at 315]:

> Thus in practice, when it is certain that one of two individuals committed the offence charged, but it is uncertain whether the one or the other was the guilty agent, neither of them can be convicted.

This rule, I think, is also applicable to civil actions so that if at the end of the case A has proved that he was negligently injured by either B or C but is unable to establish which of the two caused the injury, his action must fail against both unless there are special circumstances which render the rule inapplicable.

The respondent argues that such circumstances exist in this case. It is said that Akenhead and Cook were joint tortfeasors being engaged in a joint enterprise under such circumstances that each was liable for the acts of the other. Reliance is placed on the fact that they were hunting together and had agreed to divide the bag evenly.

I am unable to find any authority for the proposition that the mere fact that a party of persons are hunting together and have agreed to divide the bag renders each liable for the tortious acts of all the others. The American case of *Summers v. Tice* [(1948), 5 A.L.R. (2nd) 91], relied upon by the respondents is, I think, properly distinguished in the reasons for judgment of Sidney Smith J.A. The decisive finding of fact in that case was that both of the defendants had shot in the direction of the plaintiff when they knew his location. There is no such finding in the case at bar. It is not, I think, necessarily implicit in the jury's findings that one of the two defendants shot the plaintiff but that they can not decide which.

The judgments of the Court of Appeal in *The Koursk* [[1924] P. 140], are of only limited assistance as in that case both the *Clan Chisholm* and the *Koursk* had been found guilty of negligence causing the sinking of the *Itria* and the question was not whether both of them were liable but whether their liability was joint or several. At page 155 Scrutton L.J. says:

> The substantial question in the present case is: What is meant by "joint tortfeasors"? and one way of answering it is: "Is the cause of action against them the same"? Certain classes of persons seem clearly to be "joint tortfeasors": The agent who commits a tort within the scope of his employment for his principal, and the principal; the servant who commits a tort in the course of his employment, and his master; two persons who agree on common action, in the course of, and to further which, one of them commits a tort. These seem clearly joint tortfeasors; there is one tort committed by one of them on behalf of, or in concert with another.

The judgments of Bankes and Sargent, L.JJ. contain similar expressions.

Can it be said that the facts of the case at bar fall within the definition of joint tortfeasors, quoted above, from the judgment of Scrutton L.J. — "two persons who agree on common action in the course of, and to further which, one of them commits a tort"? It is argued that Cook and Akenhead agreed on common action, that is to go out hunting together and to divide the bag, and that it was in the course of this and in furtherance of it that the shot which injured the plaintiff was fired by one or other of them. The difficulty of applying this definition to the facts of the case at bar is pointed out by Sidney Smith J.A. To do so would bring about the result that every member of a party going out together, with a lawful common object, social or sporting, which could be carried out without negligence, would be vicariously liable for the negligence of any member of the party. So far as I have been able to ascertain, such a liability has not been held in any reported case to exist at common law.

There was, I think, no evidence in the case at bar on which it could be found that the relationship of principal and agent or of master and servant or of partners existed between Akenhead and Cook. They were engaged in a lawful pursuit. Neither had any reason to anticipate that the other would act negligently. Neither had in fact either the right or the opportunity to control the other. Neither appears to have assisted or encouraged the other to commit a breach of any duty owed to the plaintiff.

[Appeal Dismissed.]

NOTES AND QUESTIONS

1. The analysis of a case will differ depending on whether the defendants are joint or independent tortfeasors. Therefore, this issue should be addressed before the issue of the duty of care.

2. Identify the three categories of relationships in which individuals have been held to be joint tortfeasors and give an example of each. Why were the defendants in *Cook* not held to be joint tortfeasors? Would they have been joint tortfeasors if it had been shown that: (a) each had acted negligently; or (b) the way in which they agreed to hunt together was negligent?

3. After considerable drinking, three youths broke into the town rink with the intent of stealing whatever they could find. One of the youths negligently caused a fire that resulted in substantial property damage. Although the other two boys were not negligent or even with the boy when he started the fire, all three were held to be joint tortfeasors and equally liable. The court stated that the fire was

caused in pursuit of a common wrongful intention of all three youths. Do you agree? *Newcastle (Town) v. Mattatall* (1987), 37 D.L.R. (4th) 528 (N.B. Q.B.), aff'd. (1988), 52 D.L.R. (4th) 356 (N.B. C.A.).

4. Will the defendants in the following situations be considered joint tortfeasors?

(a) A was driving a truck towing B's disabled van and B was sitting in the driver's seat of the van. When the plaintiff attempted to pass, she was forced off the road by the truck which began to make a left-hand turn. The plaintiff could not see the truck's turn signal and the van's signal was not working. See *Harpe v. Lefebvre* (1976), 1 C.C.L.T. 331 (Alta. Dist. Ct.); and Klar, "Annotation" (1976), 1 C.C.L.T. 331.

(b) A and B each threw a handful of sand at a school bus. Some of the sand hit the plaintiff in the eye, but it was impossible to determine whether that sand had been thrown by A or B. See *Beecham v. Henderson*, [1951] 1 D.L.R. 628 (B.C. S.C.).

(c) A, B and C set out together in a car for a drinking bout. They took turns driving to different bars. All three were impaired, but B was driving when he caused an accident, seriously injuring the plaintiff. See *Hague v. Billings* (1989), 48 C.C.L.T. 192 (Ont. H.C.), varied on apportionment (1993), 13 O.R. (3d) 298 (C.A.). But see *Pizzolon v. Pedrosa* (1988), 46 C.C.L.T. 243 (B.C. S.C.).

5. For other judicial discussions of whether individuals are joint tortfeasors, see *The Koursk*, [1924] P. 140 (C.A.); *Johnston v. Burton* (1970), 16 D.L.R. (3d) 660 (Man. Q.B.); *Bushell v. Hamilton* (1980), 113 D.L.R. (3d) 498 (N.S. C.A.); and *Scarmar Const. Ltd. v. Geddes Contracting Co.* (1989), 61 D.L.R. (4th) 328 (B.C. C.A.), leave to appeal ref'd. (1990), 65 D.L.R. (4th) viii (note) (S.C.C.).

6. Identify a situation where the defendants are: (a) both joint tortfeasors and multiple causers; and (b) joint tortfeasors, but not multiple causers.

7. The provincial negligence acts now permit contribution and apportionment of loss among joint tortfeasors. A potentially important common law principle that remains in effect is that the plaintiff's release of one joint tortfeasor extinguishes her right to sue the other joint tortfeasors. To avoid this problem, the plaintiff may settle with one joint tortfeasor and, rather than releasing her, simply agree not to sue her. The courts do not view this agreement as a release and, therefore, the plaintiff will be free to seek redress from the remaining joint tortfeasors. See *Dixon v. R. in Right of B.C.* (1979), 99 D.L.R. (3d) 652 (B.C. S.C.), aff'd. (1980), 128 D.L.R. (3d) 389 (B.C. C.A.); *Tucker (Public Trustee of) v. Asleson*, [1993] 6 W.W.R. 45 (B.C. C.A.); The University of Alberta, Institute of Law Research and Reform, *Contributory Negligence and Concurrent Wrongdoers* (1979), 27-30; and Ontario Law Reform Commission, *Report on Contribution Among Wrongdoers and Contributory Negligence* (1988).

5. Problems in Assessing the Plaintiff's Loss

(a) DEVALUING THE PLAINTIFF'S LOSS

DILLON v. TWIN STATE GAS AND ELEC. CO.

(1932), 163 A. 111 (New Hampshire S.C.)

· · ·

Action for negligently causing the death of the plaintiff's intestate, a boy of 14. A jury trial resulted in a disagreement.

The defendant maintained wires to carry electric current over a public bridge in Berlin. In the construction of the bridge there were two spans of girders on each side between the roadway and footway. In each span the girders at each end sloped upwards towards each other from the floor of the bridge until connected by horizontal girders about nineteen feet above the floor.

The wires were carried above the framework of the bridge between the two rows of girders. To light the footway of the bridge at its center a lamp was hung from a bracket just outside of one of the horizontal girders and crossing over the end of the girder near its connection with a sloping girder. Wires ran from a post obliquely downward to the lamp and crossed the horizontal girder a foot or more above it. The construction of the wire lines over and upon the bridge is termed aerial. The wires were insulated for weather protection but not against contact.

The decedent and other boys had been accustomed for a number of years to play on the bridge in the daytime, habitually climbing the sloping girders to the horizontal ones, on which they walked and sat and from which they sometimes dived into the river. No current passed through the wires in the daytime except by chance.

The decedent, while sitting on a horizontal girder at a point where the wires from the post to the lamp were in front of him or at his side, and while facing outwards from the side of the bridge, leaned over, lost his balance, instinctively threw out his arm, and took hold of one of the wires with his right hand to save himself from falling. The wires happened to be charged with a high voltage current at the time and he was electrocuted.

. . .

ALLEN J.: — The circumstances of the decedent's death give rise to an unusual issue of its cause. In leaning over from the girder and losing his balance he was entitled to no protection from the defendant to keep from falling. Its only liability was in exposing him to the danger of charged wires. If but for the current in the wires he would have fallen down on the floor of the bridge or into the river, he would without doubt have been either killed or seriously injured. Although he died from electrocution, yet, if by reason of his preceding loss of balance he was bound to fall except for the intervention of the current, he either did not have long to live or was to be maimed. In such an outcome of his loss of balance, the defendant deprived him, not of a life of normal expectancy, but of one too short to be given pecuniary allowance, in one alternative, and not of normal, but of limited, earning capacity, in the other.

If it were found that he would have thus fallen with death probably resulting, the defendant would not be liable, unless for conscious suffering found to have been sustained from the shock. In that situation his life or earning capacity had no value. To constitute actionable negligence there must be damage, and damage is limited to those elements the statute prescribes.

If it should be found that but for the current he would have fallen with serious injury, then the loss of life or earning capacity resulting from the electrocution would be measured by its value in such injured condition. Evidence that he would be crippled would be taken into account in the same manner as though he had already been crippled.

His probable future but for the current thus bears on liability as well as damages. Whether the shock from the current threw him back on the girder or whether he would have recovered his balance, with or without the aid of the wire he took hold of, if it had not been charged, are issues of fact, as to which the evidence as it stands may lead to different conclusions.

Exception overruled.

All concurred.

NOTES AND QUESTIONS

1. What was the cause of the boy's death? How did the court calculate the value of this loss? Is the court's approach consistent with the general principles for assessing damages in tort law?

2. Peaslee and Keeton both state that the plaintiff's loss should only be devalued by a factor which an objective observer would consider certain to cause injury at the time the defendant caused the plaintiff's loss. Thus, in *Dillon*, even if there had been a slight chance that the boy would have fallen into a small, deep pocket of water and escaped injury, the defendant would have been held fully liable for his death. Is it not more appropriate to discount the defendant's liability according to the likelihood of such possibilities? See Peaslee, "Multiple Causation and Damage" (1934), 47 Harv. L. Rev. 1127 at 1138-1141; and Keeton *et al., Prosser and Keeton on The Law of Torts*, 5th ed. (1984), 353-354.

3. Assume that the city had been negligent in permitting children to play on the bridge and the same mishap occurred. What distinguishes this situation from the one in *Dillon*? How would you calculate the value of the loss and who would be responsible for it?

4. Assume that the plaintiff's $100,000 house is situated in the path of a forest fire negligently started by A. Before the flames reach the plaintiff's property, B negligently demolishes the house while cutting down a massive tree. How would you distinguish this case from *Dillon* and the situation in note 3? What is the cause of the plaintiff's loss and how would you calculate it? It is generally agreed that the plaintiff's loss would not be devalued in this situation. What is the rationale for this position?

(b) SUCCESSIVE PARALLEL INJURIES PRIOR TO TRIAL

✳ PENNER v. MITCHELL

(1978), 6 C.C.L.T. 132 (Alta. C.A.)

PROWSE J.A.: — This appeal deals with the effect of successive causes of personal injuries, arising in culpable and non-culpable circumstances, on the assessment of damages of a claim arising in culpable circumstances.

In the present case the trial Judge awarded the respondent special damages for loss of income for a period of thirteen (13) months following the date of the accident which gave rise to the respondent's cause of action. During that 13 month period the respondent would have been unable to work for a period of three months, even if the accident had not occurred, as she suffered from a heart condition which was unrelated to the accident.

The appellant's submission was that the respondent's award of special damages should not have included compensation for loss of wages during that three month period.

. . .

As the respondent relies on obiter dictum in the judgment of Lord Reid, in *Baker v. Willoughby*, [1970] A.C. 467 at 494, [1969] 3 All E.R. 1528 (H.L.), [my italics, infra] I should first consider that case.

There the plaintiff, while crossing a road, sustained injuries to his left leg when he was struck by a motor vehicle operated by the defendant. Shortly before the trial he was shot in the left leg by a robber during the course of robbery. This later injury necessitated the immediate amputation of his left leg. The issue dealt with by Lord Reid was whether the first tortfeasor could call in aid the second tort to reduce the damages he should be made to pay on the ground that the disability the plaintiff suffered in his left leg resulting from the first tort ceased to be an effective cause of further loss after that leg was amputated as a result of the second tort.

In the course of his judgment, Lord Reid stated at p. 492:

"A man is not compensated for the physical injury: he is compensated for the loss which he suffers as a result of that injury. His loss is not in having a stiff leg: it is in his inability to lead a full life, his inability to enjoy those amenities which depend on freedom of movement and his inability to earn as much as he used to earn or could have earned if there had been no accident. In this case the second injury did not diminish any of these. So why should it be regarded as having obliterated or superseded them?"

Then he referred to a number of cases and stated at pp. 493-94:

"It is argued — if a man's death before the trial reduces the damages why do injuries which he has received before the trial not also reduce the damages? I think it depends on the nature and result of the later injuries. Suppose that but for the first injuries the plaintiff could have looked forward to 20 years of working life and that the injuries inflicted by the defendant reduced his earning capacity. Then but for the later injuries the plaintiff would have recovered for loss of earning capacity during 20 years. And then suppose that later injuries were such that at the date of the trial his expectation of life had been reduced to two years. Then he could not claim for 20 years of loss of earning capacity because in fact he will only suffer loss of earning capacity for two years. Thereafter he will be dead and the defendant could not be required to pay for a loss which it is now clear that the plaintiff will in fact never suffer. But that is not this case: here the appellant will continue to suffer from the disabilities caused by the car accident for as long as he would have done if his leg had never been shot and amputated.

"If the later injury suffered before the date of the trial either reduces the disabilities from the injury for which the defendant is liable, or shortens the period during which they will be suffered by the plaintiff, then the defendant will have to pay less damages. But if the later injuries merely become a concurrent cause of the disabilities caused by the injury inflicted by the defendant, then in my view they cannot diminish the damages. *Suppose that the plaintiff has to spend a month in bed before the trial because of some illness unconnected with the original injury, the defendant cannot say that he does not have to pay anything in respect of that month: during that month the original injuries and the new illness are concurrent causes of his inability to work and that does not reduce the damages.*"

It is with some reluctance that I have decided the obiter dictum of Lord Reid should not be applied. I do so because in my view this issue has been resolved by the manner in which the Supreme Court of Canada treated future contingencies in assessing prospective loss of income in *Andrews v. Grand & Toy Alta. Ltd.*, [1978] 1 W.W.R. 577, 3 C.C.L.T. 225, 83 D.L.R. (3d) 452, 8 A.R. 129, 19 N.R. 50, for I am unable to draw any distinction in principle between the relevancy of future contingencies in assessing damages at trial and the relevancy of one of those contingencies when realized before trial.

In the *Baker* case the central issue before the Court was the apportionment of damages from two concurrent causes, that is, the damages which flowed from the combined effect of the tortious acts of the defendant and the robber. Each such cause was a legal cause, as each injury was suffered in culpable circumstances. No difficulty arose in assessing the damages that could be attributed solely to the culpable acts of one of them, such as the loss of wages suffered by the plaintiff before the robbery, as such losses were assessed against the wrongdoer who caused them.

In the present appeal the heart condition was unrelated to the accident and I will refer to such injuries, that is injuries arising in circumstances that do not give rise to a claim against a wrongdoer, as non-culpable injuries.

Turning now to assessment of damages generally, the dominant principle applied is that the injured party should be fully compensated for the pecuniary loss suffered.

. . .

In my view when a Court is faced with the apportionment of damages, which arise from concurrent legal causes, between successive wrongdoers, it should first assess the total damages arising from the concurrent cases. Then, in apportioning those damages the ends of justice will be met if they are apportioned on the basis set out in the *Baker* case, that is, by applying the rule that a wrongdoer takes his victim as he finds him and declining to apply the second rule by not treating the second tortious claim as a relevant factor in assessing damages against the first wrongdoer.

The resolution of the apportionment of the damages between successive tortfeasors arising from concurrent legal causes in the manner set out above affords a claimant compensation for the whole of his loss and further it is a reasonable basis on which to resolve the issue that arises between successive tortfeasors.

The issue on the present appeal is whether the rule applied in the *Baker* case, which resulted in treating the injury arising from the second event as irrelevant in assessing damages against the first tortfeasor, should be applied in the present case when the second event, the heart problem, arose in non-culpable circumstances. Lord Reid in the *Baker* case suggested that it should. In apportioning the damages between the two wrongdoers he was dealing with prospective loss of income arising from concurrent causes in the legal sense. In his obiter dictum, he was dealing with the causes which were concurrent in the physical sense, but not in the legal sense.

In the *Andrews* case, in dealing with prospective loss of income and the effect thereon of contingencies of life, Mr. Justice Dickson stated: "It is a general practice to take account of contingencies which might have affected future earnings such as unemployment, illness, accidents and business depression". [[1978] 1 W.W.R. p. 595] It will be noted that the nature of the contingencies of unemployment, illness, and business depression is such that a person who suffers a loss as a result of their occurrence does not have a cause of action against a wrongdoer as a consequence thereof. If the word "accident" is given its ordinary meaning, then its occurrence also arises in non-culpable circumstances. In my view the contingencies taken into account in assessing prospective loss of income should only include those that occur in non-culpable circumstances, that is, in circumstances that do not give rise to a cause of action. The rule applied in the *Baker* case should be applied only to those contingencies which arise from culpable circumstances.

My reason for concluding that future contingencies arising in culpable circumstances should not be taken into account in assessing damages such as prospective loss of income, is, because if that were done, the plaintiff would receive less than full compensation from the two wrongdoers. This would follow as there would be a deduction from the first loss because of the contingency that the second culpable event might occur and there would be a deduction from the second claim as the first culpable incident had occurred. The result of both deductions would produce a result the *Baker* case sought to avoid. Such a result would infringe the dominant rule applied in assessing damages as the injured person would then receive less than full compensation for the injuries he had sustained.

On the other hand not to take into account future contingencies arising in non-culpable circumstances would result in an injured person being overcompensated. For example not to make some allowance for early retirement which might arise for any number of reasons including health, non-culpable accidents, technological changes, or business depression, would result in the plaintiff being overcompensated in the event such contingency occurred.

The same reasoning applies if the contingency in fact is realized before trial. For example if the claimant was a carpenter and massive unemployment arose before the date of the trial then, to afford him compensation by way of special damages for loss of income, which he could not have earned, would result in him being overcompensated.

. . .

In conclusion, I am of the opinion that the learned trial Judge erred in awarding the respondent damages for the three month period she was disabled as a result of her heart condition. To include in her award damages for that three month period would result in her being overcompensated for the injuries caused by the appellant and the award would then infringe what I have referred to above as the dominant rule in assessment of damages for personal injuries. To include in the award damages for the three month period would have the result of including in the award a sum she would not have earned even if the motor accident had not occurred.

In the result I would set aside the award of special damages in the sum of $12,000 for loss of income and substitute therefor an award of $9,230.

With respect to the appeal against the award of general damages, I am of the view that although it was on the generous side, it was not so high as to warrant this Court disturbing it.

I would allow the appeal set out above and in view of the divided success I would limit the appellant, in taxation of his costs on appeal, to Column 3 of The Rules of Court.

Appeal allowed in
part; damages varied.

NOTES AND QUESTIONS

1. In *Baker*, what injuries did the defendant cause, and were they divisible from those caused by the robbers? For what damages would the robbers have been held liable if they had been caught? Based on *Baker*, state the principles that govern the assessment of damages in cases of successive injuries where: (a) both causes are culpable; and (b) the first cause is culpable and the second is innocent.

2. Did Prowse J.A. in *Penner* agree with the *ratio* in *Baker*? Identify specifically the part of Lord Reid's judgment that Prowse J.A. rejected. What were the bases upon which he disagreed with Lord Reid? Based on *Penner*, state the principles that govern the assessment of damages in cases of successive injuries where: (a) both causes are culpable; and (b) the first cause is culpable and the second is innocent.

3. For recent cases considering *Penner*, see *Paziuk v. Ewbank*, [1987] 2 W.W.R. 317 (Man. Q.B.), aff'd. [1987] 5 W.W.R. 307 (Man. C.A.); and *Sczebel v. Silvertson* (1988), 85 A.R. 293 (Q.B.). See also *Lankenau v. Dutton* (1988), 46 C.C.L.T. 256 (B.C. S.C.), aff'd. (1991), 79 D.L.R. (4th) 705 (B.C. C.A.), leave to appeal ref'd. (1991), 10 C.C.L.T. (2d) 314 (note) (S.C.C.). But see *Sunrise Co. v. The Ship "Lake Winnipeg"*, [1991] 1 S.C.R. 3. In *Sunrise*, the defendant's ship negligently caused the plaintiff's ship to go aground which necessitated 27 days of repairs. In an unrelated incident, the plaintiff's ship sustained damages requiring 14 days of repairs. The repairs were carried out concurrently within the 27-day period. Based solely on shipping cases, the majority found the defendant liable for 27 days of lost earnings. The dissent reasoned on the basis of general negligence principles and found the defendant liable for only 13 days of lost earnings. Which reasoning do you prefer?

4. The British courts have adopted a similar position to *Penner*, at least with regard to non-culpable supervening causes. However, the House of Lords appears to have left open the issue of whether a culpable supervening cause might also be taken into account to reduce the first tortfeasor's liability. See *Jobling v. Associated Dairies Ltd.*, [1981] 2 All E.R. 752 (H.L.).

5. See generally Wagner, "Successive Causes and the Quantum of Damages in Personal Injury Cases" (1972), 10 Osgoode Hall L.J. 368; Newell, "Damages - Supervening Events" (1981), 97 L.Q.R. 210; and Waddams, *The Law of Damages*, 2nd ed. (1991), 13-24 to 13-32.

REVIEW PROBLEMS

1. Jack and Harvey, two friends from Fairview University, were attending a football game at Midwest University. After the game they, along with about 50 other Fairview students, rushed onto the field and attempted to pull down the goal posts. Jack and Harvey were the first students to jump to the crossbar and they urged others to do the same. When the crossbar broke, either Jack or Harvey fell onto Lloyd, a member of the student police who was attempting to protect the goal posts. As Lloyd was clutching his broken arm, Clarkson, another Fairview student who had been hanging from the crossbar, fell onto Lloyd fracturing Lloyd's leg. Discuss Lloyd's potential causes of action against Jack, Harvey and Clarkson.

2. John designed a cottage consisting of three bedrooms, a kitchen, a bathroom, and a living-room. Morris, who had contracted to build the living-room, unwittingly used rotten wooden beams. There was no doubt but that the living-room would collapse within two years and that its collapse would not damage the other rooms. Ralph was the contractor for the bathroom and the three bedrooms. He had noticed that the timbers were rotten, but he decided to take a chance in using them. It is clear that the bathroom and bedrooms would suffer the same fate as the living-room. Ernie, the land-scape contractor, was levelling the grounds after the cottage was completed. While distracted, he drove the bulldozer into the back of the cottage, destroying the bedrooms and the living-room. The next day Desmond, John's neighbour, chopped down a tree which unfortunately landed in the middle of the kitchen. Only the bathroom of John's cottage remained standing.

Ralph, Ernie and Desmond concede that they were negligent, but Morris has been absolved of liability. Discuss the liability of Ralph, Ernie and Desmond.

for sml-grp discussion. → 3. The Cruise Drug Company maintained a research laboratory which was developing a treatment for breast cancer. Lila and the other 47 researchers were required to handle toxic chemicals in the course of their research. Six months after beginning her employment at Cruise, Lila became pregnant. In due course she gave birth to David, who unfortunately was born mentally handicapped. Although he will be able to live in a home setting, David will require special education and full-time adult supervision for the rest of his life. It is agreed that David's total damages are $500,000.

At the time Lila began working for Cruise, the company had known about an American study of a similar research project. That study revealed a greater incidence of birth defects among the children of female employees who worked with such chemicals during pregnancy. The rate of such birth defects is 6 per cent in the general female population, but 9 per cent among female researchers engaged in the American project. Cruise also knew that an elaborate ventilation system would most likely remove the dangerous chemical fumes from the laboratory. The company chose not to install the ventilation system because it found the $80,000 price tag prohibitive. Nor did it bother to inform its employees of the risks because it thought such knowledge would be bad for morale.

Discuss David's cause of action against the Cruise Drug Company.

* risk 50% greater
* standards?

15

REMOTENESS OF DAMAGES

1. Introduction
2. Directness Versus Foreseeability
3. Modifications to the Foreseeability Test
4. Intervening Causes

1. Introduction

As indicated in the preceding chapter, even if the defendant negligently caused the plaintiff's injuries, he will not be held liable for them if they are too remote in law to be recoverable. As the following hypothetical example illustrates, the basic issue raised by remoteness is what limits should be imposed on the extent of the defendant's liability in negligence.

Assume that the defendant carelessly throws his smouldering cigar butt onto a tinder-dry field. The field ignites and the fire spreads to a nearby house where two people asleep in the rear rooms suffer serious smoke inhalation. The firefighters responding to the call make a wrong turn and are delayed five crucial minutes, by which the time the fire has spread to two adjoining commercial establishments. The two businesses have to be closed for a month and $30,000 in profits are lost.

Should the defendant be held liable for all the injurious consequences of his relatively trivial act of negligence? Must he compensate the other parties for the field, house, personal injuries, damages to the adjacent businesses, and loss of commercial profits? How is the defendant's liability affected by the firefighters' mistake, and the resulting delay, that allowed the fire to spread to the commercial establishments? The legal issues raised by such questions are collectively referred to as the "remoteness of damages".

Like the duty of care, remoteness is a legal issue which the courts use to define the scope of liability in negligence. The duty issue concerns the legal relationship between the plaintiff and the defendant. The issue of remoteness concerns the relationship between the defendant's negligent act and the specific damages sought by the plaintiff. There is general agreement among common law judges and academics that the defendant's liability must be limited. Some harms are too far removed from the defendant's negligent act, too remote in space, time or probability, to be justly recoverable from the defendant. However, as the cases in this chapter illustrate, there is less agreement on how these limits should be defined and analyzed.

Remoteness raises difficult legal and policy issues that ultimately focus on the scope of liability in negligence. As in duty, the tests used by the courts have evolved over time. In remoteness, the tests have been constantly reworked and reworded. Unfortunately, reformulating the tests will not make the underlying decisions easier to make. The law has been further complicated by the tendency of some courts to deal with remoteness issues at the duty stage of analysis, particularly in nervous shock and pure economic loss cases.

2. Directness Versus Foreseeability

(a) THE DIRECTNESS TEST

In *Re Polemis and Furness, Withy & Co.*, [1921] 3 K.B. 560, the Court of Appeal established "directness" as the test for remoteness. More specifically, the plaintiff's losses would not be too remote to be recoverable if they were a direct result of the defendant's negligent act. In *Re Polemis*, servants of the defendant negligently dropped a plank into the hold of the plaintiff's ship which contained a cargo of benzine. The plank struck something, causing a spark that ignited the benzine fumes. The plaintiff's ship was destroyed in the ensuing explosion and fire. The court found that the fire was not a foreseeable result of the defendant's negligent act of dropping the plank, but rejected foreseeability as the appropriate test. Rather, it applied the directness test and permitted recovery, because the loss of the ship was a direct result of the defendant's negligence.

NOTES AND QUESTIONS

1. The Canadian courts applied the directness test prior to and after *Re Polemis*. See *Toronto Ry. Co. v. Grinstead* (1895), 24 S.C.R. 570; *Winnipeg Elec. Ry. Co. v. Can. Nor. Ry.* (1919), 59 S.C.R. 352; *Duce v. Rourke; Pearce v. Rourke* (1951), 1 W.W.R. (N.S.) 305 (Alta. S.C.); and *Simms v. Butt* (1975), 8 Nfld. & P.E.I.R. 14 (Nfld. C.A.).

2. The direct consequence test has been criticized as being unworkable, unfair, illogical, too pro-plaintiff, and theoretically unsound. Do you agree? Much of the criticism is based on the fact that the directness test does not relate the degree of the defendant's fault to the extent of his liability. See Seavey, "Mr. Justice Cardozo and the Law of Torts" (1939), 52 Harv. L. Rev. 372 at 381-391; Wright, "The Law of Torts: 1923-1947" (1948), 26 Can. Bar Rev. 46 at 56-58; and Goodhart, "The Imaginary Necktie and the Rule in *Re Polemis*" (1952), 68 L.Q.R. 515.

(b) THE FORESEEABILITY TEST

(knowledge)   The Wagon Mound (No. 1)

OVERSEAS TANKSHIP (U.K.) LTD. v. MORTS DOCK & ENGINEERING CO.

[1961] A.C. 388, [1961] 1 All E.R. 404 (P.C.)

[The appellants, charterers of the Wagon Mound, negligently permitted oil to spill into Sydney Harbour while taking on fuel. The oil, which continued to escape for over a day, was carried by the wind and tide under the respondent's wharf. The respondent's employees were using welding equipment and some molten metal fell, igniting a rag that was floating upon some debris. The burning debris either directly ignited the floating oil or ignited it after first setting the oil-soaked pilings of the wharf ablaze. The respondent's wharf and some of its equipment were severely damaged in the ensuing conflagration.]

. . .

The judgment of their Lordships was delivered by Viscount Simonds, who stated the facts set out above and continued: The trial judge also made the all-important finding, which must be set out in his own words:

> The raison d'être of furnace oil is, of course, that it shall burn, but I find the defendant did not know and could not reasonably be expected to have known that it was capable of being set afire when spread on water.

This finding was reached after a wealth of evidence, which included that of a distinguished scientist, Professor Hunter. It receives strong confirmation from the fact that at the trial the respondents strenuously maintained that the appellants had discharged petrol into the bay on no other ground than that, as the spillage was set alight, it could not be furnace oil. An attempt was made before their Lordships' Board to limit in some way the finding of fact, but it is clear that it was intended to cover precisely the event that happened.

One other finding must be mentioned. The judge held that apart from the damage by fire the respondents had suffered some damage from the spillage of oil in that it had got upon their slipways and congealed upon them and interfered with their use of the slips. He said:

> The evidence of this damage is slight and no claim for compensation is made in respect of it. Nevertheless it does establish some damage, which may be insignificant in comparison with the magnitude of the damage by fire, but which nevertheless is damage which, beyond question, was a direct result of the escape of the oil.

It is upon this footing that their Lordships will consider the question whether the appellants are liable for the fire damage.

. . .

It is inevitable that first consideration should be given to the case of *In re Polemis and Furness Withy & Co. Ltd.* [[1921] All E.R. Rep. 40] which will henceforward be referred to as *Polemis*. For it was avowedly in deference to that decision and to decisions of the Court of Appeal that followed it that the Full Court was constrained to decide the present case in favour of the respondents. In doing so Manning J., after a full examination of that case, said:

> To say that the problems, doubts and difficulties which I have expressed above render it difficult for me to apply the decision in *In re Polemis* with any degree of confidence to a particular set of facts would be a grave understatement. I can only express the hope that, if not in this case, then in some other case in the near future, the subject will be pronounced upon by the House of Lords or the Privy Council in terms which, even if beyond my capacity fully to understand, will facilitate, for those placed as I am, its everyday application to current problems.

This cri de coeur would in any case be irresistible, but in the years that have passed since its decision *Polemis* has been so much discussed and qualified that it cannot claim, as counsel for the respondents urged for it, the status of a decision of such long standing that it should not be reviewed.

Enough has been said to show that the authority of *Polemis* has been severely shaken though lip-service has from time to time been paid to it. In their Lordships' opinion it should no longer be regarded as good law. It is not probable that many cases will for that reason have a different result, though it is hoped that the law will be thereby simplified, and that in some cases, at least, palpable injustice will be avoided. For it does not seem consonant with current ideas of justice or morality that for an act of negligence, however slight or venial, which results in some trivial foreseeable damage the actor should be liable for all consequences however unforeseeable and however grave, so long as they can be said to be "direct". It is a principle of civil liability, subject only to qualifications which have no present relevance, that a man must be considered to be responsible for the probable consequences of his act. To demand more of him is too harsh a rule, to demand less is to ignore that civilised order requires the observance of a minimum standard of behaviour.

This concept applied to the slowly developing law of negligence has led to a great variety of expressions which can, as it appears to their Lordships, be harmonised with little difficulty with the single exception of the so-called rule in *Polemis*. For, if it is asked why a man should be responsible for the natural or necessary or probable consequences of his act (or any other similar description of them) the answer is that it is not because they are natural or necessary or probable, but because, since they have this quality, it is judged by the standard of the reasonable man that he ought to have foreseen them. Thus it is that over and over again it has happened that in different judgments in the same case, and sometimes in a single judgment, liability for a consequence has been imposed on the ground that it was reasonably foreseeable or, alternatively, on the ground that it was natural or necessary or probable. The two grounds have been treated as coterminous, and so they largely are. But, where they are not, the question arises to which the wrong answer was given in *Polemis*. For, if some limitation must be imposed upon the consequences for which the negligent actor is to be held responsible — and all are agreed that some limitation there must be — why should that test (reasonable foreseeability) be rejected which, since he is judged by what the reasonable man ought to foresee, corresponds with the common conscience of mankind, and a test (the "direct" consequence) be substituted which leads to nowhere but the never-ending and insoluble problems of causation. "The lawyer," said Sir Frederick Pollock, "cannot afford to adventure himself with philosophers in the logical and metaphysical controversies that beset the idea of cause." Yet this is just what he has most unfortunately done and must continue to do if the rule in *Polemis* is to prevail.

. . .

Their Lordships conclude this part of the case with some general observations. They have been concerned primarily to displace the proposition that unforeseeability is irrelevant if damage is "direct." In doing so they have inevitably insisted that the essential factor in determining liability is whether the damage is of such a kind as the reasonable man should have foreseen. This accords with the general view thus stated by Lord Atkin in *McAlister (or Donoghue) v. Stevenson* [[1932] All E.R. Rep. 1]:

> The liability for negligence, whether you style it such or treat it as in other systems as a species of "culpa", is no doubt based upon a general public sentiment of moral wrongdoing for which the offender must pay.

It is a departure from this sovereign principle if liability is made to depend solely on the damage being the "direct" or "natural" consequence of the precedent act. Who knows or can be assumed to know all the processes of nature? But if it would be wrong that a man should be held liable for damage unpredictable by a reasonable man because it was "direct" or "natural", equally it would be wrong that he should escape liability, however "indirect" the damage, if he foresaw or could reasonably foresee the intervening events which led to its being done: cf. *Woods v. Duncan* [[1946] 1 All E.R. 420]. Thus foreseeability becomes the effective test. In reasserting this principle their Lordships conceive that they do not depart from, but follow and develop, the law of negligence as laid down by Baron Alderson in *Blyth v. Birmingham Waterworks Co.* [(1856), 156 E.R. 1047].

. . .

Their Lordships will humbly advise Her Majesty that this appeal should be allowed, and the respondents' action so far as it related to damage caused by the negligence of the appellants be dismissed with costs, but that the action so far as it related to damage caused by nuisance should be remitted to the Full Court to be dealt with as that court may think fit. The respondents must pay the costs of the appellants of this appeal and in the courts below.

NOTES AND QUESTIONS

1. Explain the test of remoteness adopted by the court. How does the foreseeability test of remoteness differ from the foreseeability tests applied at the duty of care stage?

2. Why did the court reject the directness test of remoteness? Were the court's criticisms of this test equally applicable to the foreseeability test? Were the arguments in favour of the foreseeability test persuasive?

3. The court proceeded on the basis that the plaintiff's losses were directly caused, but not foreseeable. Do you agree with these factual assumptions?

4. Like *Polemis*, the decision in *Wagon Mound* generated considerable academic debate. See Fleming, "The Passing of Polemis" (1961), 39 Can. Bar Rev. 489; Gibson, "The Wagon Mound in Canadian Courts" (1963), 2 Osgoode Hall L.J. 416; Smith, "Requiem for Polemis" (1964-66), 2 U.B.C.L. Rev. 159; and Davies, "The Road From Morocco: *Polemis* through *Donoghue* to No-Fault" (1982), 45 Mod. L. Rev. 534.

5. It has been argued that neither directness nor foreseeability provides an appropriate test of remoteness. See Green, "Foreseeability in Negligence Law" (1961), 61 Colum. L. Rev. 1401; Smith, "The Mystery of Duty" in Klar (ed.), *Studies in Canadian Tort Law* (1977), 1 at 15; and Rizzo, "The Imputation Theory of Proximate Cause: An Economic Framework" (1980-81), 15 Ga. L. Rev. 1007.

6. It is often difficult to determine which test or tests of remoteness the Canadian courts are applying. For example, in *Richard v. C.N.R.* (1970), 15 D.L.R. (3d) 732 at 739 (P.E.I. S.C.), the judge concluded that the plaintiff was "the sole, direct, proximate and effective cause" of his own injuries. See also *Jones v. Wabigwan* (1969), 8 D.L.R. (3d) 424 (Ont. C.A.); and *Hunter v. Briere* (1989), 49 C.C.L.T. 93 (Man. Q.B.).

Most of the courts in Canada have followed *Wagon Mound*. See McLaren, "Negligence and Remoteness — The Aftermath of Wagon Mound" (1967), 32 Sask. L. Rev. 45; and Linden, *Canadian Tort Law*, 5th ed. (1993), 305-23.

REVIEW PROBLEMS

Analyze the following situations and determine whether the plaintiff's damages are too remote under the directness and foreseeability tests.

(a) The defendant negligently drove into a fire hydrant causing a heavy flow of water which forced open the basement window of the plaintiff's building. The basement was flooded in several feet of water and the plaintiff sued for the damage done to his supplies. See *Weiner v. Zoratti* (1970), 11 D.L.R. (3d) 598 (Man. Q.B.); and *Kennedy v. Hughes Drug (1969) Inc.* (1974), 47 D.L.R. (3d) 277 (P.E.I. S.C.).

(b) The defendant negligently lit his house on fire while using a blowtorch to burn off the paint under the eaves. A fireman suffered burns, despite wearing protective clothing, while attempting to put the fire out. See *Ogwo v. Taylor,* [1987] 3 All E.R. 961 (H.L.).

(c) The defendant negligently drove into the plaintiff's fence causing metal fence staples to be ejected onto the plaintiff's pasture. Several months later, a number of the plaintiff's cattle died as a result of ingesting the staples. The plaintiff sued the defendant for the loss of his cattle. See *Falkenham v. Zwicker* (1978), 93 D.L.R. (3d) 289 (N.S. S.C.).

(d) The defendant took the plaintiff's car without consent and the plaintiff gave chase in another vehicle. As a result of his negligence, the defendant knocked down a hydro pole and ended up in a field. The plaintiff stopped and ran into the field, where he stepped on a downed, live hydro wire. The plaintiff was severely burned and his leg had to be amputated. He sued the defendant for his personal injuries. See *Jones v. Wabigwan* (1969), 8 D.L.R. (3d) 424 (Ont. C.A.).

(e) The defendant negligently polluted the plaintiff's well, which in turn resulted in damage to his crops. The plaintiff claimed damages for developing a new water supply, the loss of his crop and for the heart attack he suffered as a result of the strain caused by the incident. See *Connery v. Gov't. of Man.* (1970), 15 D.L.R. (3d) 303 (Man. Q.B.).

3. Modifications to the Foreseeability Test

(a) THE KIND OF INJURY

HUGHES v. LORD ADVOCATE

[1963] A.C. 837, [1963] 1 All E.R. 705 (H.L.)

LORD REID: — My Lords, I have had an opportunity of reading the speech which my noble and learned friend, Lord Guest, is about to deliver. I agree with him that this appeal should be allowed and I shall only add some general observations. I am satisfied that the Post Office workmen were in fault in leaving this open manhole unattended and it is clear that if they had done as they ought to have done this accident would not have happened. It cannot be said that they owed no duty to the appellant. But it has been held that the appellant cannot recover damages.

It was argued that the appellant cannot recover because the damage which he suffered was of a kind which was not foreseeable. That was not the ground of judgment of the First Division or of the Lord Ordinary and the facts proved do not, in my judgment, support that argument. The appellant's injuries were mainly caused by burns, and it cannot be said that injuries from burns was unforesee-able. As a warning to traffic the workmen had set lighted red lamps around the tent which covered the manhole, and if boys did enter the dark tent it was very likely that they would take one of these lamps with them. If the lamp fell and broke it was not at all unlikely that the boy would be burned and the burns might well be serious. No doubt it was not to be expected that the injuries would be as serious as those which the appellant in fact sustained. But a defender is liable, although the damage may be a good deal greater in extent than was foreseeable.

So we have (first) a duty owed by the workmen, (secondly) the fact that if they had done as they ought to have done there would have been no accident, and (thirdly) the fact that the injuries suffered by the appellant, though perhaps different in degree, did not differ in kind from injuries which might have resulted from an accident of a foreseeable nature. The ground on which this case has been decided against the appellant is that the accident was of an unforeseeable type. Of course, the pursuer has to prove that the defender's fault caused the accident, and there could be a case where the intrusion of a new and unexpected factor could be regarded as the cause of the accident rather than the fault of the defender. But that is not this case. The cause of this accident was a known source of danger, the lamp, but it behaved in an unpredictable way.

The explanation of the accident which has been accepted, and which I would not seek to question, is that, when the lamp fell down the manhole and was broken, some paraffin escaped, and enough was vaporised to create an explosive mixture which was detonated by the naked light of the lamp. The experts agree that no one would have expected that to happen: it was so unlikely as to be unforeseeable. The explosion caused the boy to fall into the manhole: whether his injuries were directly caused by the explosion or aggravated by fire which started in the manhole is not at all clear. The essential step in the respondent's argument is that the explosion was the real cause of the injuries and that the explosion was unforeseeable. He can only escape liability if the damage can be regarded as differing in kind from what was foreseeable.

. . .

This accident was caused by a known source of danger, but caused in a way which could not have been foreseen, and, in my judgment, that affords no defence. I would therefore allow the appeal.

[Lords Jenkins, Morris of Borth-Y-Gest, Guest and Pearce gave concurring speeches, holding that the damage was not too remote.]

NOTES AND QUESTIONS

1. Explain the test of remoteness that was applied in *Hughes*. Do you agree with how the test was applied to the facts?

2. The impact of the test in *Hughes* depends on how broadly or narrowly one characterizes the kind of injury that the plaintiff has suffered. In *Doughty v. Turner Mfg. Co.*, [1964] 1 Q.B. 518 (C.A.), an employee in a metal treatment plant was injured when an asbestos cover slid into the treatment vat. The cover reacted chemically with the contents of the vat causing an eruption of molten liquid that burned the employee. The covers had been used for 20 years, but this chemical reaction had never been observed. The man sued his employer arguing that the injury was foreseeable. The court held for the defendant because it characterized the injury as one caused by a chemical reaction which was not foreseeable. Do you agree? Would it have made a difference if the injury had been characterized as a burn? For a criticism of *Doughty*, see Dworkin, "Risk and Remoteness — Causation Worse Confounded?" (1964), Mod. L. Rev. 344. See also Linden, *Canadian Tort Law*, 5th ed. (1993), 313-40.

3. In *Lauritzan v. Barstead* (1965), 53 D.L.R. (2d) 267 (Alta. S.C.), the defendant's negligence resulted in his car becoming stuck in the snow during a bad storm on a relatively untravelled portion of a rural highway. The plaintiff and defendant were forced by the wind and cold to stay in the vehicle for 36 hours. When the weather broke, the plaintiff went for help. The plaintiff was eventually found by a farmer, but as a result of frost-bite, parts of both his feet had to be amputated. The plaintiff's wife of 26 years apparently left him because she did not want to live with a cripple. While the court held that the plaintiff's physical injuries were not too remote, it held that his claim for loss of *consortium* was not a foreseeable kind of injury and denied this claim. Do you agree with the court's analysis? See also *Antell v. Simons*, [1976] 6 W.W.R. 202 (B.C. S.C.).

4. Should the defendant be held liable for damages that result from the plaintiff's lack of assets? Assume that the defendant negligently damages the plaintiff's car and that the plaintiff cannot afford to repair it for six months or borrow any money to rent a replacement. As a result of his impecuniosity, the plaintiff suffers a far greater loss of income than would otherwise have been the case. Are these additional economic losses too remote in law to be recoverable? Initially, the courts denied such claims, but now will permit recovery if the loss is foreseeable. See *Dredger Liesbosch v. Steamship Edison*,

[1933] A.C. 449 (H.L.); *Dodd Properties Ltd. v. Canterbury City Council*, [1980] 1 W.L.R. 433 (C.A.); and *Kozak v. Gruza* (1989), 63 D.L.R. (4th) 129 (Sask. C.A.). See also Wexler, "The Impecunious Plaintiff: Liesbosch Reconsidered" (1987), 66 Can. Bar Rev. 129.

5. If the plaintiff suffers a "pure" economic loss, that is an economic loss that is not consequent on injury to the plaintiff's person or property, then special principles of duty are applied. These principles are discussed at length in chapter 23. However, if the plaintiff's economic loss results from injuries to his person or property, the issue is dealt with under the remoteness of damages principles.

In *D'Amato v. Badger*, [1994] 10 W.W.R. 141 (B.C. C.A.), the defendant negligently injured the plaintiff in a car accident. In addition to his physical injuries, the plaintiff claimed economic loss due to his inability to perform certain duties for a company that he co-owned. Although the Court of Appeal reduced the amount, it allowed the plaintiff's economic loss claim. See also *Winnipeg Condominium Corp. No. 36 v. Bird Construction Co.* (1995), 23 C.C.L.T. (2d) 1 (S.C.C.).

6. For other judicial discussions of the principle in *Hughes*, see *Williams v. St. John (City)* (1985), 34 C.C.L.T. 299 (N.B. C.A.); *C.N.R. Co. v. Sask. Wheat Pool*, [1986] 4 W.W.R. 371 (Sask. Q.B.); *Smith v. Littlewoods Organisation Ltd.*, [1987] 1 All E.R. 710 (H.L.); and *Belzile v. Dumais* (1986), 69 N.B.R. (2d) 142 (Q.B.).

(b) THE THIN-SKULLED PLAINTIFF RULE

SMITH v. LEECH BRAIN & CO.

[1962] 2 Q.B. 405, [1961] 3 All E.R. 1159

. . .

[The plaintiff's husband was a galvanizer employed by the defendants. The articles to be galvanized were lowered into a tank containing molten metallic zinc and flux. The method used depended on the size of the article. All articles were first dipped in hydrochloric acid and the larger articles were then lowered into the tank, by means of an overhead crane, from a position behind a sheet of corrugated iron. On Aug. 15, 1950, the plaintiff's husband was operating the overhead crane, using the corrugated iron sheet supplied, when a piece of molten metal or flux struck and burned his lower lip. The burn was treated at the time and he thought nothing of it. Some time later, the place where the burn had been began to ulcerate and get larger. He consulted his general practitioner who sent him to hospital where cancer was diagnosed. Treatment destroyed the primary growth but the cancer spread. Despite several operations, the worker died of cancer on October 14, 1953.

Lord Parker, C.J., found that the defendants were negligent, there had been no contributory negligence and that the burn promoted the cancer in tissues which already had a pre-malignant condition as a result of the employee's exposure to tar or tar vapours from 1926 to 1935.

The case is reported only on the question of remoteness of damage.]

LORD PARKER, C.J.: I am confronted with the recent decision of the Privy Council in *Overseas Tankship (U.K.), Ltd. v. Morts Dock & Engineering Co. Ltd.* [[1961] 1 All E.R. 404]. For convenience, that case is always referred to as *The Wagon Mound*. But for *The Wagon Mound*, it seems to me perfectly clear that, assuming negligence proved, assuming that the burn caused in whole or in part the cancer and the death, this plaintiff would be entitled to recover. It is said on the one side by counsel for the defendants, that, although I am not strictly bound by *The Wagon Mound* since it is a Privy Council case, I should treat myself as free, using the arguments to be derived from that case, to say that other cases in the Court of Appeal have been wrongly decided, and, particularly, that *Re Polemis and Furness Withy & Co. Ltd.* [[1921] All E.R. Rep. 40] was wrongly decided, and that a further ground for taking that course is to be found in the various criticisms that have from time to time in the past been made by members of the House of Lords in regard to *Re Polemis*. On the other hand, it is said by counsel for the plaintiff that I should hold that *Re Polemis* was rightly decided and, secondly, that, even if that is not so, I must treat myself as completely bound by it. Thirdly, he said that in any event, whatever the true view is in regard to *Re Polemis, The Wagon Mound* has no relevance at all to this case.

For my part, I am quite satisfied that the Judicial Committee in *The Wagon Mound* did not have what I may call, loosely, the "thin skull" cases in mind. It has always been the law of this country that a tortfeasor takes his victim as he finds him. It is unnecessary to do more than refer to the short passage in the decision of Kennedy, J., in *Dulieu v. White & Sons*, [[1901] 2 K.B. 669], where he said:

> If a man is negligently run over or otherwise negligently injured in his body, it is no answer to the sufferer's claim for damages that he would have suffered less injury, or no injury at all, if he had not an unusually thin skull or an unusually weak heart.

[handwritten margin note: Thin Skull Principle]

To the same effect is a passage in *The Arpad* [[1934] All E.R. Rep. 326]. But quite apart from those two references, as is well known, the work of the courts for years and years has gone on on that basis. There is not a day that goes by where some trial judge does not adopt that principle, that the tortfeasor takes his victim as he finds him. If the Judicial Committee had any intention of making an inroad into that doctrine, I am quite satisfied that they would have said so.

It is true that, if one takes the wording in the advice given by Viscount Simonds in *The Wagon Mound* and applies it strictly to such a case as this, it could be said that they were dealing with this point. But, as I have said, it is, to my mind, quite impossible to conceive that they were, and, indeed, it has been pointed out that they disclose the distinction between such a case as this and the one which they were considering, when they comment on *Smith v. London & South Western Ry. Co.* [(1870], L.R. 6 C.P. 14]. Lord Simonds, in dealing with that case in *The Wagon Mound*, said this:

> Three things may be noted about this case: the first, that, for the sweeping proposition laid down, no authority was cited; the second, that the point to which the court directed its mind was not unforeseeable damage of a different kind from that which was foreseen, but more extensive damage of the same kind . . .

In other words, Lord Simonds is clearly there drawing a distinction between the question whether a man could reasonably anticipate a type of injury, and the question whether a man could reasonably anticipate the extent of injury of the type which could be foreseen. The Judicial Committee were, I think, disagreeing with the decision in *Re Polemis* that a man is no longer liable for the type of damage which he could not reasonably anticipate. The Judicial Committee were not, I think, saying that a man is only liable for the extent of damage which he could anticipate, always assuming the type of injury could have been anticipated. That view is really supported by the way in which cases of this sort have been dealt with in Scotland. Scotland has never, as far as I know, adopted the principle laid down in *Re Polemis*, and yet I am quite satisfied that they have throughout proceeded on the basis that the tortfeasor takes the victim as he finds him.

In those circumstances, it seems to me that this is plainly a case which comes within the old principle. The test is not whether these defendants could reasonably have foreseen that a burn would cause cancer and that Mr. Smith would die. The question is whether these defendants could reasonably foresee the type of injury which he suffered, namely, the burn. What, in the particular case, is the amount of damage which he suffers as a result of that burn, depends on the characteristics and constitution of the victim. Accordingly, I find that the damages which the plaintiff claims are damages for which these defendants are liable.

. . .

[His Lordship awarded £1,500 under the Law Reform (Miscellaneous Provisions) Act, 1934, and £1,564 17s. under the Fatal Accidents Acts, 1846 to 1908.]

MARCONATO v. FRANKLIN

[1974] 6 W.W.R. 676 (B.C. S.C.)

[The female plaintiff suffered relatively minor physical injuries in a car accident caused by the defendant's negligence. Following the accident, she developed symptoms of pain and stiffness for which there was no physical explanation. She became depressed, hostile and anxious. Although the psychiatric evidence indicated that she had paranoid tendencies before the accident, she had been a good wife, mother and housekeeper. The accident triggered a gross personality change and she became moody, depressed and did little around the house.]

AIKINS J.: — I turn to the question of causation. One would not ordinarily anticipate, using reasonable foresight, that a moderate cervical strain with soft tissue damage would give rise to the consequences which followed for Mrs. Marconato. These arose, however, because of her pre-existing personality traits. She had a peculiar susceptibility or vulnerability to suffer much greater consequences from a moderate physical injury than the average person. The consequences for Mrs. Marconato could no more be foreseen than it could be foreseen by a tortfeasor that his victim was thin-skulled and that a minor blow to the head would cause a very serious injury. It is plain enough that the defendant could foresee the probability of physical injury. It is implicit, however, in the principle that a wrongdoer takes his victim as he finds him, that he takes his victim with all the victim's peculiar susceptibilities and vulnerabilities. The consequences of Mrs. Marconato's injuries were unusual but arose involuntarily. Granted her type of personality they arose as night follows day because of the injury and the circumstances in which she found herself because of the injury.

As to the argument that the damage suffered is too remote because not reasonably foreseeable, I refer first to an English case, *Smith v. Leech Brain & Co. Ltd.*, [1962] 2 Q.B. 405, [1961] 3 All E.R. 1159. In this case the plaintiff widow claimed damages for the death of her husband under the Fatal Accidents Acts. The defendant was the deceased's employer. The deceased suffered a burn on his lip; as a result cancer developed at that site, from which the injured man died some three years later. Remoteness on the ground of lack of foreseeability was argued. I cite two passages from the judgment of Lord Parker C.J. The first is at p. 414:

For my part, I am quite satisfied that the Judicial Committee in *Overseas Tankship (U.K.) v. Morts Dock & Engineering Co. (The Wagon Mound)*, [1961] A.C. 388, [1961] 1 All E.R. 404, did not have what I may call, loosely, the thin skull cases in mind. It has always been the law of this country that a tortfeasor takes his victim as he finds him.

. . .

The second passage is at p. 415:

The test is not whether these employers could reasonably have foreseen that a burn would cause cancer and that he would die. The question is whether these employers could reasonably foresee the type of injury he suffered, namely, the burn. What, in the particular case, is the amount of damage which he suffers as a result of that burn, depends upon the characteristics and constitution of the victim.

I also refer to the judgment of McIntyre J. (now J.A.) in *Elloway v. Boomars* (1968), 69 D.L.R. (2d) 605 (B.C.). In *Elloway* the plaintiff developed schizophrenia following injury in a motor accident. At p. 606, McIntyre J. said:

The question of remoteness of damage in such a claim was discussed in *Enge v. Trerise* (1960), 33 W.W.R. 577, 26 D.L.R. (2d) 529 (B.C.C.A.). As I understand the law expressed in that case a schizophrenic condition caused by the wrongful conduct of a defendant may be a basis of compensation as may be schizophrenia caused by the aggravation of a latent condition but always provided that it can be shown that the cause of the condition was the accident.

At p. 607 McIntyre J. said:

I find the plaintiff's present condition was caused by the accident. He suffered from a pre-existing condition which predisposed him to a schizophrenic illness and the accident, operating upon this predisposition, brought about the full schizophrenic illness and it is therefore a proper basis for compensation.

Application

What I have cited might well be transposed in the present case to go as follows: Mrs. Marconato was predisposed by her personality to suffer the consequences which she did suffer as a result of the modest physical injury caused by the accident and it was that predisposition which brought on the unusual consequences of the injury. The defendant must pay damages for all the consequences of her negligence.

. . .

Counsel for Mrs. Marconato stated expressly that he did not invite me to find a permanent disability and, indeed, the evidence does not support such a conclusion. Nevertheless, Mrs. Marconato's problems will not clear up overnight. I need not review evidence further except for one matter which I overlooked. The plaintiffs' intimate married life together virtually came to an end when Mrs. Marconato was injured.

I assess the general damages to be paid to Mrs. Marconato at the sum of $15,000. I assess the general damages to be paid to Mr. Marconato for loss of consortium and servitium at the sum of $2,500.

gender-specific remedy for husband's loss of servitio domestic rinelages

Special damages are agreed. The total comes to $441.85. Of this, $100 was for repair to Mrs. Marconato's automobile. The balance of $341.85 was for taxis and medical services. It appears to me that Mrs. Marconato should have the special damages of $100 and her husband should have the remaining special damages coming to $341.85.

NOTES AND QUESTIONS

1. Explain what is meant by the thin-skulled plaintiff rule. What is the relationship between the foreseeability test of remoteness and the thin-skulled plaintiff rule?

2. What would have been the result in *Smith* had the deceased had no pre-existing susceptability to cancer, but had nevertheless developed cancer at the site of the burn and died of the disease? What would have been the result if the burn had increased the deceased's risk of getting cancer and he developed cancer at the site of the burn and died? See also *Pesonen v. Melnyk* (1993), 17 C.C.L.T. (2d) 66 (B.C. C.A.); *Hunter v. Manning*, [1993] 5 W.W.R. 738 (Sask. Q.B.); *Hooiveld v. Van Biert*, [1994] 4 W.W.R. 143 (B.C. C.A.); and *Buteikis v. Adams*, [1994] 7 W.W.R. 119 (B.C. S.C.).

3. According to *Marconato*, what application does the thin-skulled plaintiff rule have to a plaintiff with an "eggshell" personality? Is the damage award in *Marconato* compatible with the argument that there should be some reasonable relationship between the degree of the defendant's fault and the extent of his liability? See *Price v. Garcha* (1988), 44 C.C.L.T. 1 (B.C. S.C.), aff'd. (1989), 2 C.C.L.T. (2d) 265 (B.C. C.A.). But see *Graham v. Rourke* (1988), 43 C.C.L.T. 119 (Ont. H.C.), varied on damages (1990), 75 O.R. (2d) 622 (C.A.).

4. In *Swami v. Lo*, [1980] 1 W.W.R. 379 (B.C. S.C.), the plaintiff's husband committed suicide 14 months after he had been negligently run over by the defendant. The constant pain forced the husband to give up work and he began to drink heavily. Although the deceased became very depressed, there was no allegation that he was either criminally or civilly insane. The judge concluded that *Smith* did not apply to the facts of the case and dismissed the plaintiff's claim as being too remote. Given the serious physical injuries that the husband suffered in the car accident, was it foreseeable that he would suffer emotional injuries of some kind as a result? If such injuries were foreseeable, should the husband's suicide have been recoverable under the kind-of-injury test in *Hughes v. Lord Advocate*, [1963] A.C. 837 (H.L.)? See also *Wright Estate v. Davidson*, [1992] 3 W.W.R. 611 (B.C. C.A.), leave to appeal ref'd. (1992), 95 D.L.R. (4th) vii (note) (S.C.C.), where the Court of Appeal held that the deceased's suicide following a minor car accident was too remote to be recoverable. Were *Swami* and/or *Wright Estate* rightly decided?

See also *Gray v. Cotic* (1983), 26 C.C.L.T. 163 (S.C.C.), where the plaintiff recovered for her husband's suicide following a car accident, because he had a pre-existing mental health problem. See also *Costello v. Blakeson*, [1993] 2 W.W.R. 562 (B.C. S.C.).

5. As in *Marconato* and *Swami*, a plaintiff may raise the thin-skulled plaintiff rule to establish that an emotional harm stemming from a physical injury is not too remote to be recoverable. These cases must be distinguished from claims for the negligent infliction of nervous shock. As discussed in chapter 12, these latter claims are not consequent on any physical injury to the plaintiff. The negligent infliction of nervous shock is analyzed under special duty of care principles. See *Bechard v. Haliburton Estate* (1991), 10 C.C.L.T. (2d) 156 (Ont. C.A.).

(c) THE POSSIBILITY OF INJURY

The Wagon Mound (No. 2)

OVERSEAS TANKSHIP (U.K.) LTD. v. MILLER STEAMSHIP CO. PTY.

[1967] 1 A.C. 617, [1966] 2 All E.R. 709 (P.C.)

[This case arose out of the same incident as the *Wagon Mound (No. 1)*, [1961] 1 All E.R. 404]. The plaintiffs in this action, however, were the owners of two boats that were damaged in the fire. At trial, the plaintiffs succeeded in nuisance. However, their action in negligence was dismissed because their damages were not reasonably foreseeable and thus too remote to be recoverable. The defendant appealed and the plaintiffs cross-appealed. Only the court's discussion of the negligence issue is reproduced below.]

LORD REID: ... It is now necessary to turn to the respondents' submission that the trial judge was wrong in holding that damage from fire was not reasonably foreseeable. In *Wagon Mound (No. 1)* the finding on which the Board proceeded was that of the trial judge:

> ... [the appellants] did not know and could not reasonably be expected to have known that [the oil] was capable of being set afire when spread on water.

In the present case the evidence led was substantially different from the evidence led in *Wagon Mound (No. 1)* and the findings of Walsh J., are significantly different. That is not due to there having been any failure by the plaintiffs in *Wagon Mound (No. 1)* in preparing and presenting their case. The plaintiffs there were no doubt embarrassed by a difficulty which does not affect the present plaintiffs. The outbreak of the fire was consequent on the act of the manager of the plaintiffs in *Wagon Mound (No. 1)* in resuming oxy-acetylene welding and cutting while the wharf was surrounded by this oil. So if the plaintiffs in the former case had set out to prove that it was foreseeable by the engineers of the Wagon Mound that this oil could be set alight, they might have had difficulty in parrying the reply that then this must also have been foreseeable by their manager. Then there would have been contributory negligence and at that time contributory negligence was a complete defence in New South Wales.

The crucial finding of Walsh, J., in this case is in finding (v): that the damage was "not reasonably foreseeable by those for whose acts the defendant would be responsible." That is not a primary finding of fact but an inference from the other findings, and it is clear from the learned judge's judgment that in drawing this inference he was to a large extent influenced by his view of the law. The vital parts of the findings of fact which have already been set out in full are (i) that the officers of the Wagon Mound "would regard furnace oil as very difficult to ignite on water" — not that they would regard this as impossible: (ii) that their experience would probably have been "that this had very rarely happened" — not that they would never have heard of a case where it had happened, and (iii) that they would have regarded it as a "possibility, but one which could become an actuality only in very exceptional circumstances" — not, as in *Wagon Mound (No. 1)*, that they could not reasonably be expected to have known that this oil was capable of being set afire when spread on water. The question which must now be determined is whether these differences between the findings in the two cases do or do not lead to different results in law.

In *Wagon Mound (No. 1)* the Board were not concerned with degrees of foreseeability because the finding was that the fire was not foreseeable at all. So Viscount Simonds had no cause to amplify the statement that the "essential factor in determining liability is whether the damage is of such a kind as the reasonable man should have foreseen." Here the findings show, however, that some risk of fire would have been present to the mind of a reasonable man in the shoes of the ship's chief engineer. So the first question must be what is the precise meaning to be attached in this context to the words "foreseeable" and "reasonably foreseeable".

Before *Bolton v. Stone* [[1951] 1 All E.R. 1078], the cases had fallen into two classes: (i) those where, before the event, the risk of its happening would have been regarded as unreal either because the event would have been thought to be physically impossible or because the possibility of its happening would have been regarded as so fantastic or far-fetched that no reasonable man would have paid any attention to it — "a mere possibility which would never occur to the mind of a reasonable man" (per Lord Dunedin in *Fardon v. Harcourt-Rivington* [[1932] All E.R. Rep. 81]) — or (ii) those where there was a real and substantial risk or chance that something like the event which happens might occur and then the reasonable man would have taken the steps necessary to eliminate the risk.

Bolton v. Stone posed a new problem. There a member of a visiting team drove a cricket ball out of the ground on to an unfrequented adjacent public road and it struck and severely injured a lady who happened to be standing in the road. That it might happen that a ball would be driven on to this road could not have been said to be a fantastic or far-fetched possibility: according to the evidence it had happened about six times in twenty-eight years. Moreover it could not have been said to be a far-fetched or fantastic possibility that such a ball would strike someone in the road: people did pass along the road from time to time. So it could not have been said that, on any ordinary meaning of the words, the fact that a ball might strike a person in the road was not foreseeable or reasonably foreseeable. It was plainly foreseeable; but the chance of its happening in the foreseeable future was infinitesimal. A mathematician given the data could have worked out that it was only likely to happen once in so many thousand years. The House of Lords held that the risk was so small that in the circumstances a reasonable man would have been justified in disregarding it and taking no steps to eliminate it.

It does not follow that, no matter what the circumstances may be, it is justifiable to neglect a risk of such a small magnitude. A reasonable man would only neglect such a risk if he had some valid reason for doing so: e.g., that it would involve considerable expense to eliminate the risk. He would weigh the risk against the difficulty of eliminating it. If the activity which caused the injury to Miss Stone had been an unlawful activity there can be little doubt but that *Bolton v. Stone* would have been decided differently. In their Lordships' judgment *Bolton v. Stone* did not alter the general principle that a person must be regarded as negligent if he does not take steps to eliminate a risk which he knows or ought to know is a real risk and not a mere possibility which would never influence the mind of a reasonable man. What that decision did was to recognise and give effect to the qualification that it is justifiable not to take steps to eliminate a real risk if it is small and if the circumstances are such that a reasonable man, careful of the safety of his neighbour, would think it right to neglect it.

In the present case there was no justification whatever for discharging the oil into Sydney Harbour. Not only was it an offence to do so, but also it involved considerable loss financially. If the ship's engineer had thought about the matter there could have been no question of balancing the advantages and disadvantages. From every point of view it was both his duty and his interest to stop the discharge immediately.

It follows that in their Lordships' view the only question is whether a reasonable man having the knowledge and experience to be expected of the chief engineer of the Wagon Mound would have known that there was a real risk of the oil on the water catching fire in some way: if it did, serious damage to ships or other property was not only foreseeable but very likely. Their Lordships do not dissent from the view of the trial judge that the possibilities of damage "must be significant enough in a practical sense to require a reasonable man to guard against them", but they think that he may have misdirected himself in saying

> there does seem to be a real practical difficulty, assuming that some risk of fire damage was foreseeable, but not a high one, in making a factual judgment as to whether this risk was sufficient to attract liability if damage should occur.

In this difficult chapter of the law decisions are not infrequently taken to apply to circumstances far removed from the facts which give rise to them, and it would seem that here too much reliance has been placed on some observations in *Bolton v. Stone* and similar observations in other cases.

In their Lordships' view a properly qualified and alert chief engineer would have realised there was a real risk here, and they do not understand Walsh, J., to deny that; but he appears to have held that, if a real risk can properly be described as remote, it must then be held to be not reasonably foreseeable. That is a possible interpretation of some of the authorities; but this is still an open question and on principle their Lordships cannot accept this view. If a real risk is one which would occur to the mind of a reasonable man in the position of the defendant's servant and which he would not brush aside as far-fetched, and if the criterion is to be what that reasonable man would have done in the circumstances, then surely he would not neglect such a risk if action to eliminate it presented no difficulty, involved no disadvantage and required no expense.

In the present case the evidence shows that the discharge of so much oil on to the water must have taken a considerable time, and a vigilant ship's engineer would have noticed the discharge at an early stage. The findings show that he ought to have known that it is possible to ignite this kind of oil on water, and that the ship's engineer probably ought to have known that this had in fact happened before. The most that can be said to justify inaction is that he would have known that this could only happen in very exceptional circumstances; but that does not mean that a reasonable man would dismiss such risk from his mind and do nothing when it was so easy to prevent it. If it is clear that the reasonable man would have realised or foreseen and prevented the risk, then it must follow that the appellants are liable in damages. The learned judge found this a difficult case: he said that this matter is "one on which different minds would come to different conclusions." Taking a rather different view of the law from that of the learned judge, their Lordships must hold that the respondents are entitled to succeed on this issue.

. . .

NOTES AND QUESTIONS

1. How did the court in *Wagon Mound (No. 2)* reach the conclusion that it was foreseeable that the furnace oil would burn, when the court in *Wagon Mound (No. 1)* reached the opposite conclusion? How did the court define foreseeability and what did it mean by the term "real risk"? What did the court mean by the term "justified"? Does *Wagon Mound (No. 2)* apply only to those cases in which the defendant's conduct is without social value? If not, can you distinguish between Lord Reid's test of remoteness and the test used to determine whether the standard of care has been breached?

2. What impact does the rule in *Wagon Mound (No. 2)* have on the scope of recovery in negligence? Glasbeek contends that *Wagon Mound (No. 2)* has, for "all practical purposes", restored the *Re Polemis* test "for surely all direct consequences must be regarded as possible if the ordinary man

is not required to foresee how they are to eventuate." Smith has written that *Wagon Mound (No. 2)* broadened the test of foreseeability of damages from one based upon probability of damages to one based upon a possibility of damages. See respectively "Wagon Mound II — Re Polemis Revived; Nuisance Revised" (1967), 6 U.W.O.L. Rev. 192 at 200; and "The Limits of Tort Liability in Canada: Remoteness, Foreseeability and Proximate Cause" in Linden (ed.), *Studies in Canadian Tort Law* (1968), 88 at 102. Do you agree with Glasbeek's or Smith's assessment of *Wagon Mound (No. 2)*?

ASSINIBOINE SOUTH SCHOOL DIVISION, NO. 3 v. GREATER WINNIPEG GAS CO.

(nothing new: applic. of prev. principles)

[1971] 4 W.W.R. 746 (Man. C.A.)

DICKSON J.A.: — The facts giving rise to this case lie in a compact compass and are not in dispute. At approximately 12:00 noon, 25th February 1968 a Ski Daddler auto toboggan owned by Ephraim Hoffer and operated by his son Michael Hoffer ran out of control at a speed of approximately 30 m.p.h., over a snowbank and across a parking lot, for some 100 yards, and struck a gas-riser pipe servicing Laidlaw School in Tuxedo, Manitoba. The pipe was fractured below the pressure regulator and shut-off valve, with the result that gas under high pressure escaped and, being lighter than air, rose and entered the boiler room of the school through a fresh-air inlet duct situate in the wall of the school immediately above the gas-riser pipe and beneath a wide overhanging eave. In the boiler room the gas reached an explosive mixture and was ignited by the naked flame of the pilot light, or the flames of the gas furnace. An explosion and fire occurred, causing extensive damage to the school. Deniset J., [1971] 1 W.W.R. 1, 16 D.L.R. (3d) 703, allowed damages of $50,739.90 to the School Division of Assiniboine South No. 3, owners of the school, against Ephraim Hoffer and Michael Hoffer as well as against the Greater Winnipeg Gas Company. The Gas Company was responsible for the installation of the gas-riser pipe. The damages were apportioned 50 per cent to Michael Hoffer and Ephraim Hoffer and 50 per cent to the Gas Company. All defendants have appealed.

[Dickson J.A. explained that Ephraim Hoffer had specially altered the machine to allow his 11-year-old son to start it. These changes required the machine to be started in high gear. The father advised his son to put up the kickstand when starting the machine. The son forgot and the machine got away from him. Dickson held that it was probable that a young boy would forget to use the kickstand and "almost inevitable that in such event the machine would get out of control and run away." Dickson J.A. concluded that both the father and son were negligent.]

The second question is whether the damage done by them was reasonably foreseeable and therefore recoverable within the principles stated in *Overseas Tankship (U.K.) Ltd. v. Morts Dock & Engineering Co. Ltd. (The Wagon Mound) (No. 1)*, [1961] A.C. 388, [1961] 1 All E.R. 404. This question is not without difficulty. Denning L.J. said in *King v. Phillips*, [1953] 1 Q.B. 429, [1953] 1 All E.R. 617 at 623: "there can be no doubt since *Hay (Bourhill) v. Young*, [1943] A.C. 92, [1942] 2 All E.R. 396, that the test of *liability for shock* is foreseeability of *injury by shock*". (The italics are mine.) In *The Wagon Mound* (No. 1) Viscount Simonds substituted the word "fire" for "shock" and indorsed this statement of the law. Liability depends upon whether the damage is of such a kind as a reasonable man should have foreseen.

It might well be argued that damage by impact is to be expected when a machine runs amok but not damage by fire and explosion. Their Lordships in *The Wagon Mound* (No. 1) were clearly of the opinion that the Court of Appeal erred in *Re Polemis and Furness, Withy & Co. Ltd.*, [1921] 3 K.B. 560, in allowing recovery in respect of damage from fire and explosion which followed the impact of a plank dropped into the hold of a ship.

In *The Wagon Mound* (No. 1) damage to plaintiffs' wharf by oil fouling was foreseeable when defendants carelessly allowed a large quantity of bunkering oil to spill into Morts Bay but damage by fire was unforeseeable and recovery denied. Vital to the decision was the finding of fact that defendants did not know, and could not reasonably have been expected to know, that furnace oil was capable of being set afire when spread on water.

The force of *The Wagon Mound* (No. 1) was somewhat dissipated by *Hughes v. Lord Advocate*, [1963] A.C. 837, [1963] 1 All E.R. 705, per Lord Jenkins at p. 710:

> "It is true that the duty of care expected in cases of this sort is confined to reasonably foreseeable dangers, but it does not necessarily follow that liability is escaped because the danger actually materialising is not identical with the danger reasonably foreseen and guarded against."

One need not envisage "the precise concatenation of circumstances which led up to the accident": p. 712.

In *Overseas Tankship (U.K.) Ltd. v. Miller Steamship Co. Pty. Ltd. et al. (The Wagon Mound)* (No. 2), [1967] 1 A.C. 617, [1966] 2 All E.R. 709, the Privy Council, on different findings of fact, reached a conclusion different from that in *The Wagon Mound* (No. 1). Lord Reid said at p. 717:

> "The vital parts of the findings of fact which have already been set out in full are (i) that the officers of the Wagon Mound 'would regard furnace oil as very difficult to ignite on water' — not that they would regard this as impossible: (ii) that their experience would probably have been 'that this had very rarely happened' — not that they would never have heard of a case where it had happened, and (iii) that they would have regarded it as a "possibility, but one which could become an actuality only in very exceptional circumstances' — not, as in *Wagon Mound* (No. 1), that they could not reasonably be expected to have known that this oil was capable of being set afire when spread on water".

These words would suggest that recovery may be had, provided the event giving rise to the damage is not regarded as "impossible", and even though it "very rarely happened ... only in very exceptional circumstances". The test of foreseeability of damage becomes a question of what is possible rather than what is probable.

[The Court reviewed recent cases.]

. . .

It is enough to fix liability if one could foresee in a general way the sort of thing that happened. The extent of the damage and its manner of incidence need not be foreseeable if physical damage of the kind which in fact ensues is foreseeable. In the case at bar I would hold that the damage was of the *type* or *kind* which any reasonable person might foresee. Gas-riser pipes on the outside of Tuxedo buildings are common. Damage to such a pipe is not of a kind that no one could anticipate. When one permits a power toboggan to run at large, or when one fires a rifle blindly down a city street, one must not define narrowly the outer limits of reasonable prevision. The ambit of foreseeable damage is indeed broad.

. . .

Counsel for Michael Hoffer concedes that the boy was negligent and that the type of damage that resulted was reasonably foreseeable by him as by any other rational person. Counsel submits, however, that the causation chain, the first link of which was forged by his failure to put the machine on the kick stand before starting it, ended when the riser pipe had been broken and the gas began to escape. I cannot accept this argument. Since *The Wagon Mound* (No. 1) the "scholastic theories of causation and their ugly and barely intelligent jargon", have taken a back place to foreseeability. It is now settled that foresight is the test both for duty and for remoteness. Accepting that the "chain of causation" can be broken by a "nova causa" or "novus actus interveniens", it is clear that the state of affairs created by the Gas Company several years prior to the accident could not be considered a novus actus. Where a state of affairs has already occurred at the time of the wrongful act, that act is regarded as the cause of the damage in the absence of subsequent intervening factors.

It is manifest that Michael's culpable conduct was a causally relevant factor. His failure to exercise due care was the "cause" of the damage in the proper sense of the term. If one applies the "but for" test it is readily apparent that the plaintiff's harm would not have occurred but for Michael's fault. Michael cannot escape liability for the consequences of that fault merely because other causal factors for which he is not responsible also contributed to the damage which resulted. He was *a* cause, though not the *sole* cause of the harm. His fault was a cause-in-fact.

. . .

I agree with the finding of Deniset J. that Ephraim Hoffer and Michael Hoffer are joint tortfeasors.

Liability of Greater Winnipeg Gas Company Limited

I am also of the opinion that Greater Winnipeg Gas Company Limited is liable to the plaintiff on the ground that the installation of the gas service was negligently constructed in the sense that it was constructed in such place and manner as to make likely the type of damage which ensued. The Gas Company was responsible for the construction of the service line leading from the street, the service riser, and attached equipment and meter. It is difficult to conceive of any person, conscious of the explosive properties of natural gas, designing and installing a service so patently dangerous. Gas escaping from any fracture of the pipe below the regulator would assuredly find its way into the boiler room. The Gas Company ought to have reasonably foreseen damage to the gas-riser pipe. It is true that persons are not bound to take extravagant precautions but they must weigh the probability of injury resulting and the probable seriousness of the injury. Although the probability of the gas-riser pipe being struck by an automobile, a motorcyle or an auto toboggan was not great, the pipe being tucked into the corner of the building, the probable seriousness of any injury was very great. Against this must be weighed the cost and difficulty of the precautions which could have been taken. Protective pipes could have been installed at small cost and little difficulty. The duty to take protective measures increases in direct proportion to the risk. In these circumstances, the Gas Company failed to exercise reasonable care where there was a duty to exercise a high degree of care.

. . .

[The appeals were dismissed. Affirmed [1973] 6 W.W.R. 765 (S.C.C.).]

NOTES AND QUESTIONS

1. Do you agree with: (a) Dickson J.A.'s interpretation of the various foreseeability tests; and (b) his application of them to the facts? Does the test in *Hoffer* establish an appropriate relationship between the nature of the defendant's negligent act and the scope of his liability?

2. *Assiniboine* has been widely followed in Canada. See for example *Belzile v. Dumais* (1986), 69 N.B.R. (2d) 142 (Q.B.); and *Monkman v. Singh* (1989), 62 Man. R. (2d) 277 (Q.B.).

3. Critical of the existing law, Linden has suggested that the courts ought to adopt a "new approach" to the issue of the remoteness of damages. In *Canadian Tort Law*, 5th ed. (1993), Linden states at 321:

> It would also be helpful if the courts would approach these remoteness cases with the attitude that a person found to have been negligent should only be relieved of liability if the result of the negligence was truly "freakish", "one in a million", "fantastic or highly improbable." In other words, there should be an assumption of liability unless the court is convinced that it would be too harsh a result in the circumstances.

Will Linden's approach alleviate the difficulties that exist in this area? What new problems, if any, would it create? See also Coval, Smith and Rush, "'Out of the Maze': Towards a 'Clear Understanding' of the Test for Remoteness of Damages in Negligence" (1983), 61 Can. Bar Rev. 561.

4. Should the principles of remoteness be applied in the same way in personal injury and property damage cases? See *Stephenson v. Waite Tileman*, [1973] 1 N.Z.L.R. 152 (C.A.).

4. Intervening Causes

To this point, we have discussed situations in which the defendant's negligent act was the sole cause of the plaintiff's losses. We will now examine cases where the plaintiff's loss is caused by the defendant's negligence and a subsequent intervening cause. Although the courts have not always been consistent in applying the principle, an intervening act is one that causes or contributes to the plaintiff's injury after the original defendant has been negligent. For example, assume that the defendant contractor negligently blocks a sidewalk, forcing pedestrians to walk on the road, and one of the pedestrians is struck by a negligent driver. Both the contractor and the negligent driver are causers of the plaintiff's injuries. However, should the contractor be held liable for the injuries that were caused by the negligent driver?

Traditionally, the original tortfeasor was relieved of liability because the causal link between his negligent act and the plaintiff's loss was seen as being severed by the negligent intervening cause. The issue was framed in various ways — some courts talked about the second act breaking the chain of causation and other courts labelled the act as a *"novus actus interveniens"* (a new intervening act). No matter how it was described, the last human wrongdoer was held solely liable for the plaintiff's loss, even if his conduct was a relatively minor cause of the injury.

As the courts developed more complex analyses of causation, the last human wrongdoer doctrine was replaced. The courts divided intervening acts into three categories based on their nature and moral blameworthiness. The first category, intervening acts that were naturally occurring or non-culpable, were generally held not to break the chain of causation. For example, a contractor will not escape liability because his negligent work only resulted in property damage following an unusually severe storm. The second category, negligent intervening acts, were generally held to break the chain of causation, thereby absolving the original tortfeasor of liability. For example, a negligent driver would not be held liable if the plaintiff he injured died in hospital as a result of being negligently given the wrong drug. The third category of intervening acts, deliberately wrongful or illegal acts, invariably broke the chain of causation, unless the original tortfeasor had a specific duty to prevent the act. Thus, a negligent driver would not be held liable if the wallet of the plaintiff he injured was stolen at the scene of the accident. In contrast, an armed guard who negligently left his truck unlocked would be held liable if a thief walked off with several bags of money.

In turn, this elaborate categorization has, at least in theory, been replaced by a more general principle, namely, the "within the scope of the risk" test. As the following cases illustrate, there is uncertainty as to the test's application. Some courts analyze the issue in terms of whether the plaintiff's *damages* caused by the intervening act were within the scope of the risk created by the original tortfeasor. Other courts ask whether the intervening *act itself* was within the scope of the risk created by the original tortfeasor. Although focusing on the relationship between the plaintiff's specific injuries and the original tortfeasor's negligent act is more consistent with the purpose of the remoteness principles, this issue requires further clarification.

BRADFORD v. KANELLOS

(1973), 40 D.L.R. (3d) 578 (S.C.C.)

MARTLAND J.: — On the morning of April 12, 1967, the appellants, who are husband and wife, were customers in the respondents' restaurant, in the City of Kingston. While seated at the counter in the restaurant, a flash fire occurred in the grill used for cooking purposes. The grill was equipped with an automatic fire extinguisher system, of an approved type, which, when it became operative, discharged carbon dioxide on to the heated area to extinguish the fire.

Shortly after the start of the fire the fire extinguisher was activated, manually, and the fire was extinguished almost immediately. The fire was not a cause of concern to the appellants. No damage was done by the fire because the fire was of very short duration and all that burned was grease that had accumulated in the grill and a rag or rags which had been thrown on the fire when it broke out in an effort to extinguish it.

The fire extinguisher made a hissing or popping noise when it operated. This caused an unidentified patron in the restaurant to shout that gas was escaping and that there was going to be an explosion. The result of these words was to cause a panic in the restaurant. While people ran from the restaurant the appellant wife was pushed or fell from her seat at the counter and sustained injury.

The appellants brought action against the respondents, the appellant wife claiming general damages and the appellant husband claiming special damages for expenses incurred as a result of his wife's injuries.

The trial Judge awarded damages in the amounts of $3,582.43 to the appellant husband and $6,400 to the appellant wife. He found there had been negligence involved in the flash fire because the grill had not been cleaned as efficiently as it should have been, and said: "Therefore while the negligence may be small, it pinpoints this as negligence."

He did not find that the fire, in itself, had caused the panic, but ascribed it to the noise caused by the fire extinguisher. He said:

> As the result of this hissing explosive noise, or whatever it was, some rather foolish people in the restaurant called out that it might explode. For this reason it appears that some consider-able panic ensued and there was a rushing for the door.

trial concl His conclusion was that, while the act of yelling out almost qualified as that of an "idiotic person", the panic could have been foreseen.

By unanimous decision, the Court of Appeal allowed the appeal of the present respondents. Schroeder, J.A., who delivered the judgment of the Court, said [18 D.L.R. (3d) 60 at p. 62, [1971] 2 O.R. 393]:

> The practical and sensible view to be taken of the facts here leads fairly to the conclusion that it should not be held that the person guilty of the original negligence resulting in the flash fire on the grill ought reasonably to have anticipated the subsequent intervening act or acts which were the direct cause of the injuries and damages suffered by the plaintiffs.   *C.A.*

From this judgment the present appeal has, with leave, been brought to this Court.

I agree with the decision of the Court of Appeal. The judgment at trial found the respondents to be liable because there had been negligence in failing to clean the grill efficiently, which resulted in the flash fire. But it was to guard against the consequences of a flash fire that the grill was equipped with a fire extinguisher system. This system was described by the Chief of the Kingston Fire Department, who was called as a witness by the appellants, as, not only an approved installation, but one of the best.

This system, when activated, following the flash fire, fulfilled its function and put out the fire. This was accomplished by the application of carbon dioxide on the fire. In so doing, there was a hissing noise and it was on hearing this that one of the customers exclaimed that gas was escaping and that there was danger of an explosion, following which the panic occurred, the appellant wife was injured.

On these facts it is apparent that her injuries resulted from the hysterical conduct of a customer which occurred when the safety appliance properly fulfilled its function. Was that consequence fairly to be regarded as within the risk created by the respondent's negligence in permitting an undue quantity of grease to accumulate on the grill? The Court of Appeal has found that it was not and I agree with that finding.

In my opinion, the appeal should be dismissed with costs.

Judson and Ritchie, JJ., concur with Martland, J.

SPENCE J. (dissenting): — . . .

I am of the opinion that in the particular circumstances of this case, "the person guilty of the original negligence ought reasonably to have anticipated such subsequent intervening negligence and to have foreseen that if it occurred the result would be that his negligence would lead to loss or damage." Upon the evidence, the owners and proprietors, the respondents here, did anticipate that such negligence as leaving the grill in a dirty and greasy condition would cause a fire and frequently warned the cook of such fact, and requiring the cook not once but on several occasions to clean up the grill. The grill was midway down the length of the restaurant. There was seating for many patrons to the rear of the grill so that the grill intervened between them and the only entrance or exit at the front of the restaurant and the space between the grill and the other restaurant equipment through which the said patrons would have to pass was narrow.

The proprietors knew of the fire extinguisher and its action. Such action was described by the witness Warren Gibson, the Chief of Police of Kingston, as being a very rapid expansion of carbon dioxide that makes a hissing noise which explodes rather rapidly as it expands.

I am of the opinion that any reasonable person knew that a greasy grill might well take fire and that in such event a CO^2 fire extinguisher is put into action either automatically or manually and that such fire extinguisher makes a hissing and popping sound and he could not fail to anticipate that a panic might well result. The panic did result and on the evidence the whole affair from beginning to end was almost instantaneous. The plaintiff Elizabeth Bradford described it variously in the words "no, it was quick": Again, that she had been watching the fire approximately a minute when the man next to her called out "gas" and that thereupon there was an immediate panic.

. . .

I am not of the opinion that the persons who shouted the warning of what they were certain was an impending explosion were negligent. I am, on the other hand, of the opinion that they acted in a very human and usual way and that their actions, as I have said, were utterly foreseeable and were part of the natural consequence of events leading inevitably to the plaintiff's injury. I here quote and adopt Fleming, *Law of Torts*, 4th ed. (1971), at pp. 192-3:

> Nowadays it is no longer open to serious question that the operation of an intervening force will not ordinarily clear a defendant from further responsibility, if it can fairly be considered a not abnormal incident of the risk created by him — if, as sometimes expressed, it is "part of the ordinary course of things." Nor is there room any longer for any categorical distinction in this regard between forces of nature, like rain or ice, on the one hand, and the action of human beings even when consciously controlled, on the other.
>
> Least difficult are instances of just normal and reasonable response to the stimulus of the hazard engendered by the defendant's negligence. . . . A time-honoured illustration is the famous *Squib Case: Scott v. Shepherd* (1773) 2 W.Bl. 892, where a wag threw a lighted fire-work into a market whence it was tossed from one stall to another in order to save the wares until it eventually exploded in the plaintiff's face. Yet it was held that *trespass* lay because "all that was done subsequent to the original throwing was a continuation of the first force and first act and continued until the squib was spent by bursting."

Even if the actions of those who called out "gas" and "it is going to explode" were negligent and, as I have said, I do not think it was, then I am of the opinion that the plaintiffs would still have a right of action against the defendants, here respondents, or against such persons or against both.

. . .

For these reasons, I would allow the appeal and restore the judgment at trial. The appellants are entitled to their costs here and in the Court of Appeal.

Laskin, J., concurs with Spence, J.

NOTES AND QUESTIONS

1. Did Martland and Spence JJ. disagree on the test of remoteness governing the original tort-feasor's liability for intervening causes, or on its application to the specific facts? Which judgment do you find more compelling? Based on *Bradford*, define the test of remoteness governing the original tortfeasor's liability for intervening causes. Should this same test be applied whether the intervening cause is a naturally-occurring phenomenon, the negligent act of a second tortfeasor, a patently reckless act, a deliberate illegal act, or the plaintiff's own contributorily negligent act?

2. In *Oke v. Weide Tpt. Ltd.* (1963), 41 D.L.R. (3d) 53 (Man. C.A.), the defendant knocked down a traffic sign on a gravel strip separating the east and westbound lanes of traffic. The defendant stopped and removed some debris, but was unable to move the sign post which was projecting upwards. Although he informed a garage attendant of the incident, the defendant did not contact the police or highway authorities. The next day a driver, while attempting to pass illegally on the gravel strip, was killed when the post came up through the floor boards and pierced his chest. The majority stated that even if the defendant had been negligent in not reporting the incident, he could not be held liable because the deceased's intervening act of driving on the gravel strip and its consequences could not have been foreseen. The dissent concluded that the defendant had been negligent and that an accident of some kind was a foreseeable consequence of his failure to report the hazardous situation that he had created. Thus, the defendant should be held liable even though the exact way in which the accident occurred and its severity may not have been foreseeable. Do you agree with the dissenting or the majority analysis of remoteness? Would the case have been resolved the same way if the deceased had been pulling over to fix a flat tire?

3. In subsequent cases, the Canadian courts have adopted a broad interpretation of foreseeability. See, for example, *R. v. Cote* (1974), 51 D.L.R. (3d) 244 (S.C.C.); *Hendrick v. De Marsh* (1984), 45 O.R. (2d) 463 (H.C.), aff'd. (1986), 54 O.R. (2d) 185 (C.A.); *Funk v. Clapp* (1986), 68 D.L.R. (4th) 229 (B.C. C.A.); *Smith v. B.C. (A.G.)* (1988), 30 B.C.L.R. (2d) 356 (C.A.); and *Werbeniuk v. Maynard*, [1994] 7 W.W.R. 704 (Man. Q.B.).

PRICE v. MILAWSKI

(1977), 18 O.R. (2d) 113, 82 D.L.R. (3d) 130 (Ont. C.A.)

[The plaintiff injured his right ankle playing soccer and went to the emergency department of a hospital to have it examined. He told the defendant, Dr. M., that he heard his ankle crack and thought it was broken. Dr. M. sent the plaintiff for x-rays but instructed the technicians to x-ray his right foot, not his right ankle. After examining the x-rays, Dr. M. informed the plaintiff that there was no fracture and that his ankle was only sprained. In fact, the ankle was broken.

After a series of visits to his family doctor, the plaintiff was eventually referred to Dr. C., an orthopaedic surgeon, because the ankle remained painful and swollen. Dr. C. telephoned the hospital and discovered that the plaintiff's x-ray results were negative. Despite the plaintiff's complaints, Dr. C. did not order new x-rays even though he had a machine in his office and a technician available to him. He diagnosed the plaintiff's injury as a strained ligament and applied a cast. When the cast was removed four weeks later, the ankle began to swell. Following some further delays, the plaintiff eventually went to another orthopaedic surgeon who took new x-rays and discovered the fractured ankle. As a result of delays in properly treating the fracture, the plaintiff suffered some permanent disabilities.

At trial, both Drs. M. and C. were found liable in negligence and were held equally at fault for the plaintiff's permanent injury. Both defendants appealed the finding of negligence and the quantum of damages.

On appeal Arnup J.A., speaking for the court, affirmed that both defendants had been negligent. Only that portion of his judgment dealing with Dr. M.'s liability for Dr. C.'s intervening act is reproduced below.]

ARNUP J.A.:

. . .

The "foreseeability" argument

As stated in Part III, it was submitted on behalf of Dr. Murray that it was not foreseeable by him that such dire consequences would flow from his initial acts of negligence. Prior to 1961 in England and in Canada it had been accepted that the measure of damages for negligence was that the negligent actor was liable for all of the "direct" or "natural" consequences of his negligent act. The governing case was *Re Polemis et al. and Furness, Withy & Co., Ltd.*, [1921] 3 K.B. 560.

The decision was disapproved in the now famous case of *Overseas Tankship (U.K.) Ltd. v. Morts Dock & Engineering Co. Ltd. (The Wagon Mound)*, [1961] A.C. 388, [1961] 1 All E.R. 404. That case put the basis of liability on foreseeability. If damages were reasonably foreseeable, or were increased by intervening events (including the negligence of others) which were reasonably foreseeable, the negligent defendant was liable, whether the damages were "direct" or not. Conversely, a defendant was not liable for damage not reasonably foreseeable, even though direct. It has been repeatedly observed that in most situations, the result is the same no matter which of the two tests is applied. The observation is probably true of the present case.

The subject has been developed further by the House of Lords in *Hughes v. Lord Advocate*, [1963] A.C. 837, and in several judgments of the English Court of Appeal, and again by the Privy Council in *Overseas Tankship (U.K.) Ltd. v. Miller Steamship Co. Pty. et al.*, [1967] 1 A.C. 617, [1966] 2 All E.R. 709 *sub nom. "Wagon Mound" (No. 2)*, [1966] 3 W.L.R. 498. In the last mentioned case the Privy Council, commenting upon *Bolton et al. v. Stone*, [1951] A.C. 850 (the "cricket ball" case), said that case

> . . . did not alter the general principle that a person must be regarded as negligent if he does not take steps to eliminate a risk which he knows or ought to know is a real risk and not a mere possibility which would never influence the mind of a reasonable man.

(*per* Lord Reid at p. 642).

While there was some initial hesitation on the part of this Court in accepting the principle of *Wagon Mound* (despite the comment of Schroeder, J.A., as to its "deep significance" — see *Foster v. Registrar of Motor Vehicles*, [1961] O.R. 551 at p. 564, 28 D.L.R. (2d) 561 at p. 574), there is no doubt that principle is now part of the common law of Canada: see *Child v. Vancouver General Hospital et al.*, [1970] S.C.R. 477 at p. 488, 10 D.L.R. (3d) 539 at p. 550, 71 W.W.R. 656; *Moran et al. v. Pyle National (Canada) Ltd.*, [1975] 1 S.C.R. 393 at p. 405, 43 D.L.R. (3d) 239 at p. 248, [1974] 2 W.W.R. 586, and *R. v. Cote et al.*, [1976]

1 S.C.R. 595, 51 D.L.R. (3d) 244, 3 N.R. 341, where Dickson, J., discussed "reasonably foreseeable dangers" and said at p. 604 S.C.R., p. 252 D.L.R.:

> It is not necessary that one foresee the "precise concatenation of events"; it is enough to fix liability if one can foresee in a general way the class or character of injury which occurred.

We are concerned here with what one may properly call an intervening act of negligence (*i.e.*, by Dr. Carbin). In *Bradford et al. v. Kanellos et al.*, [1974] 1 S.C.R. 409 at pp. 412-3, 40 D.L.R. (3d) 578 at pp. 578-9, the majority, *per* Martland, J., referring to the hysterical act of a restaurant customer who shouted out "gas!" and that there was going to be an explosion, resulting in a panic which caused injuries to the plaintiff, said:

> Was that consequence fairly to be regarded as within the risk created by the respondents' negligence in permitting an undue quantity of grease to accumulate on the grill [in the restaurant]?

That judgment affirmed a judgment of this Court, written by Schroeder, J.A., [1971] 2 O.R. 393, 18 D.L.R. (3d) 60, which in turn had distinguished *Martin v. McNamara Construction Ltd.*, [1955] O.R. 523, [1955] 3 D.L.R. 51.

A set of facts having some analogy to the present case arose in *Mercer v. Gray*, [1941] O.R. 127, [1941] 3 D.L.R. 564, where it was held that if reasonable care has been used by the plaintiff to employ a competent physician or surgeon to treat personal injuries wrongfully inflicted by a defendant, the results of the treatment are a proper head of damages, even though through an error in treatment, it is unsuccessful.

In *"Wagon Mound" (No. 2)*, *supra*, Lord Reid, referring to cases "based purely on negligence" states at p. 636:

> It has now been established by *The Wagon Mound (No. 1) supra*, and by *Hughes v. Lord Advocate*, *supra*, that in such cases damages can only be recovered if the injury complained of was not only caused by the alleged negligence but was also an injury of a class or character foreseeable as a possible result of it.

Applying these principles to a case in which there are negligent acts by two persons in succession, I would hold that a person doing a negligent act may, in circumstances lending themselves to that conclusion, be held liable for future damages arising in part from the subsequent negligent act of another, and in part from his own negligence, where such subsequent negligence and consequent damage were reasonably foreseeable as a possible result of his own negligence.

It was reasonably foreseeable by Dr. Murray that once the information generated by his negligent error got into the hospital records, other doctors subsequently treating the plaintiff might well rely on the accuracy of that information, *i.e.*, that the x-ray showed no fracture of the ankle. It was also foreseeable that some doctor might do so without checking, even though to do so in the circumstances might itself be a negligent act. The history is always one factor in a subsequent diagnosis and the consequent treatment. Such a possibility was not a risk which a reasonable man (in the position of Dr. Murray) would brush aside as far-fetched — see *"Wagon Mound" (No. 2)*, *supra*, *per* Lord Reid at p. 643 G.

The later negligence of Dr. Carbin compounded the effects of the earlier negligence of Dr. Murray. It did not put a halt to the consequences of the first act and attract liability for all damage from that point forward. In my view the trial Judge was correct in holding that each of the appellants was liable to the plaintiff and that it was not possible to try to apportion the extent to which each was responsible for the plaintiff's subsequent operation and his permanent disability.

NOTES AND QUESTIONS

1. Is there a significant difference between the "foreseeable as possible" test in *Price* and the test in *Bradford*? Had the latter test been applied in *Price*, would the result have been the same?

2. Did Arnup J.A. properly interpret and apply *Wagon Mound (No. 2)*? Can you suggest a way of distinguishing *Wagon Mound (No. 2)* and *Price*?

3. Can you distinguish *Price* from *Mercer v. Gray*, [1941] 3 D.L.R. 564 (Ont. C.A.)? See also *Mercer v. South Eastern & Chatham Ry. Co.'s Managing Committee*, [1922] 2 K.B. 549.

4. In *Papp v. Leclerc* (1977), 16 O.R. (2d) 158 (C.A.), a case decided in the same year as *Price*, Lacourcière J.A., speaking for the court, stated at 161:

> Every tortfeasor causing injury to a person placing him in the position of seeking medical or hospital help, must assume the inherent risks of complications, *bona fide* medical error or misadventure, if they are reasonably foreseeable and not too remote... It is for the defendant to prove that some new act rendering another person liable has broken the chain of causation. This was not done in the present case. I must, therefore, rule against the appellant on this first contention based on lack of foreseeability and *novus actus*.

Is this statement compatible with the decision in *Price*? Is there any reason to treat an intervening act of medical negligence differently than any other negligent intervening act? See also *Thompson v. Toorenburgh* (1973), 50 D.L.R. (3d) 717, aff'd. 50 D.L.R. 717n (S.C.C.); *Robinson v. Post Office*, [1974] 2 All E.R. 737 (C.A.); *David v. Toronto Transit Comm.* (1976), 77 D.L.R. (3d) 717 (Ont. H.C.); and *Katzman v. Yaeck* (1982), 37 O.R. (2d) 500 (C.A.).

5. In what circumstances should the defendant be held liable for injuries that the plaintiff sustains while recovering? In *Block v. Martin*, [1951] 4 D.L.R. 121 (Alta. S.C.), the defendant negligently ran over the plaintiff, causing a slight fracture of his leg. The plaintiff followed his doctor's orders and continued to walk. Six months after the accident, the plaintiff slipped while fishing and completely fractured his leg. It was held that the original injury was a contributing cause of the second fracture and that the plaintiff's conduct in going fishing was not a *novus actus interveniens*. The defendant was held liable for the plaintiff's entire loss. See also *Boss v. Robert Simpson Eastern Ltd.* (1968), 2 D.L.R. (3d) 114 (N.S. S.C.); *Wieland v. Cyril Lord Carpets Ltd.*, [1969] 3 All E.R. 1006 (Q.B.); *Saccardo v. Hamilton* (1971), 18 D.L.R. (3d) 271 (Ont. H.C.); and *Pauluik v. Paraiso*, [1996] 2 W.W.R. 57 (Man. C.A.).

6. Should the original tortfeasor be absolved of liability for an injury the plaintiff sustains while recuperating, if the plaintiff has been contributorily negligent? The courts have apparently answered this question in the affirmative. See *McKew v. Holland*, [1969] 3 All E.R. 1621 (H.L.); *Goldhawke v. Harder* (1976), 74 D.L.R. (3d) 721 (B.C. S.C.); and *Brushett v. Cowan* (1990), 69 D.L.R. (4th) 743 (Nfld. C.A.). Is there any reason to treat the plaintiff's contributory negligence in these cases differently from any other intervening cause? Is this approach consistent with *Bradford* or *Price*?

7. Should the original tortfeasor be held liable for the additional losses a plaintiff suffers as a result of failing to undergo a needed operation? What if the operation posed a small risk of death, was very painful or had only a 70% chance of success? Would it make any difference if the plaintiff had a pre-existing fear of surgery? Is it appropriate to deal with this as a question of remoteness as opposed to an issue of mitigation of loss or contributory negligence? The Supreme Court of Canada addressed these questions in *Janiak v. Ippolito* (1985), 16 D.L.R. (4th) 1. See also *Couillard v. Waschulewski Estate* (1988), 44 C.C.L.T. 113 (Alta. Q.B.); *Tomizza v. Fraser* (1990), 71 O.R. (2d) 705 (H.C.); *Wills v. Doe* (1992), 90 D.L.R. (4th) 164 (B.C. S.C.); and *Engel v. Kam-Ppelle Holdings Ltd.* (1993), 15 C.C.L.T. (2d) 245 (S.C.C.).

8. Should a negligent defendant who causes a car accident be held liable for the additional costs associated with the negligent repair of the plaintiff's car? See *Russell v. Esson (M.F.) & Sons Ltd.* (1986), 72 N.B.R. (2d) 55 (Q.B.).

9. In what circumstances should the original tortfeasor be held liable for the additional damages that result from his victim's suicide? See *Swami v. Lo*, [1980] 1 W.W.R. 379 (B.C. S.C.); *Gray v. Cotic*

(1983), 26 C.C.L.T. 163 (S.C.C.); and *Wright v. Davidson* (1992), 88 D.L.R. (4th) 698 (B.C. C.A.), leave to appeal ref'd. (1992), 95 D.L.R. (4th) vii (note) (S.C.C.).

HEWSON v. RED DEER

[1976] W.W.D. 6, 63 D.L.R. (3d) 168 (Alta. T.D.)

KIRBY J.: . . . The plaintiff claims damages against the City of Red Deer (hereinafter referred to as "the City"), sustained on May 15, 1973, when a tractor owned by the City crashed into the plaintiff's dwelling-house.

The tractor, a "crawler type" weighing approximately 25 tons, was being used to level and stockpile gravel in an open area approximately two and a half city blocks' distance to the south of the Hewson residence. The gravel was brought to the site by trucks from a crushing plant located elsewhere in the City. Loading at the plant was suspended from 12:00 midnight until 1:00 a.m., the last load before this break generally arriving at the stockpile at about 12:15 a.m. The trucks took the loads of gravel up an inclined roadway built for that purpose to the top of the existing pile of gravel which on the day in question had attained a considerable height.

Following the arrival of the last load before the midnight break, Weisenburger, an employee of the City operating the crawler tractor, left the tractor at the top of the stockpile facing in the direction of the inclined roadway and departed from the site in a city truck for coffee and cigarettes. Before leaving, he lowered the blade, adjusted the throttle to idle gear, turned off the ignition but did not remove the key or close and lock the cab to which he had a key.

Weisenburger impressed me as a credible witness and I accept his account as to the precautions he took before leaving the site.

On his return, which he said was about 12:45 a.m. the tractor was gone. He looked for it around the site thinking some fellow employee may have moved it as a joke. Not finding it, he looked for its tracks and found them leading down the inclined roadway and going to the north. In due course he found the tractor crashed into the Hewson residence. The engine was still running and was in high gear. The blade was up. The time at which the crash took place is established by an electric clock in the residence, serviced by wires severed by the tractor. It had stopped at 12:03 a.m.

In the company of police, Weisenburger closely examined the stockpile in the immediate vicinity of where he had left the tractor. Tracks were found indicating that a motor vehicle had turned around on the top of the stockpile. Two footprints consistent with a person having jumped out of the cab of the tractor were found.

I am satisfied and find that the tractor was set in motion by an unknown person, who raised the blade, turned on the ignition and put the engine into high gear causing it to move from the top of the stockpile, down the inclined roadway, across the open space lying to the north, continuing in its course until it crashed into the Hewson residence.

. . .

It is argued, however, that if there was negligence upon the part of Weisenburger or the City, the damages that occurred were too remote to be attributed to them and that the defence of *novus actus interveniens* is applicable.

The principle embodied in this defence is clearly stated by Vaughan Williams, L.J., in *McDowall v. Great Western Railway Co.*, [1903] 2 K.B. 331 at p. 337, 72 L.J.K.B. 652:

> ... in those cases in which part of the cause of the accident was the interference of a stranger or a third person, the defendants are not held responsible unless it is found that that which they do or omit to do — the negligence to perform a particular duty — is itself the effective cause of the accident.

However, the Lord Justice added:

> Bearing that in mind, it seems to me that in every case in which circumstances are such that any one of common sense having the custody of or control over a particular thing would recognise the danger of that happening which would be likely to injure others, it is the duty of the person having such custody or control to take reasonable care to avoid such injury.

In *Hayes v. Harwood*, [1935] 1 K.B. 146 at p. 156, Greer, L.J., said:

> If what is relied upon as novus actus interveniens is the very kind of thing which is likely to happen if the want of care which is alleged takes place, the principle embodied in the maxim is no defence.... It is not necessary to show that this particular accident and this particular damage were probable; it is sufficient if the accident is of a class that might well be anticipated as one of the reasonable and probable results of the wrongful act.

In *Latham v. R. Johnson & Nephew Ltd.*, [1913] 1 K.B. 398 at p. 413, Hamilton, L.J., referred to the general rule laid down in *Scott v. Shepherd* (1773), 3 Wils. K.B. 403, 95 E.R. 1124.

> ... that person who, in neglect of ordinary care, places or leaves his property in a condition which may be dangerous to another may be answerable for the resulting injury, even though but for the intervening act of a third person or of the plaintiff himself ... that injury would not have occurred. Children acting in the wantonness of infancy and adults acting on the impulse of personal peril may be and often are only links in a chain of causation extending from such initial negligence to the subsequent injury. No doubt each intervener is a causa sine qua non, but unless the intervention is a fresh, independent cause, the person guilty of the original negligence will still be the effective cause, if he ought reasonably to have anticipated such interventions and to have foreseen that if they occurred the result would be that his negligence would lead to mischief.

The maxim was not considered applicable by the Supreme Court of Canada in *Booth et al. v. St. Catharines et al.*, [1948] 4 D.L.R. 686, [1948] S.C.R. 564. This case involved an action against the city following an accident which occurred in a city park when a number of boys climbed a flagpole to watch a fireworks exhibit — the pole fell, injuring one plaintiff and killing the daughter of the other plaintiffs. A great deal of the case deals with the question of the duty of care owed by a licensor towards licensees on his property, but the other major issue concerns foreseeability and the *novus actus* doctrine.

Kerwin, J., said at p. 690 D.L.R., p. 569 S.C.R.:

> The maxim *novus actus interveniens* has no application because while the structure was sufficient for its purpose as a flag tower, in view of the great concourse of people and of the fireworks, the presence of boys upon the tower, even though unauthorized, was the very thing that should have been anticipated.

Rand, J., at p. 693 D.L.R., p. 573 S.C.R., observed:

> On the basis of prudent foresight, it must have been anticipated as natural and probable that boys of all ages would climb the tower to get a better view of what was going on.
>
> . . .

In the instant case, however, as has been pointed out, the tractor could be set in motion by any person opening the door of the cab, turning the ignition key and raising the blade. This might have been prevented by taking the elementary precautions of removing the ignition key, engaging the safety lever and locking the cab door, none of which was done.

The stockpile was located in an open field approximately two city blocks from the nearest residential building, two and a half to three city blocks' distance from Red Deer College which was then in session, about 50 ft. from 32nd St. which was surfaced with rough gravel, connecting with a road allowance which in turn intersected with provincial Highway 2.

The stockpile being so located was accessible to persons living in the residences referred to, students and staff at the college and to persons using 32nd St. or the road allowance.

It seems to me that it was reasonably foreseeable that any one of such persons might become aware that the tractor was being left at the stockpile unattended and might be tempted to put it in motion. The elementary precautions referred to above were not taken to prevent this happening. I am of the view, therefore, that the maxim *novus actus interveniens* is not applicable. Accordingly, the plaintiff is entitled to damages against the City.

NOTES AND QUESTIONS

1. Do you agree with Kirby J. that it was reasonably foreseeable that someone would put the bulldozer in motion? Would the result have been the same if: (a) the bulldozer had been parked in a rural, rather than an urban area; (b) the defendant had taken the keys and the intruder started the bulldozer by jumping the wires; and (c) the defendant had left for only five minutes? Do you think that Kirby J. would have reached the same conclusion if the intruder had been caught? See *Wright v. McCrea*, [1965] 1 O.R. 300 (C.A.); and *Moss v. Ferguson* (1979), 35 N.S.R. (2d) 181 (S.C.).

2. Should a driver who leaves the keys in his car be held liable if his car is stolen and the thief negligently causes a car accident? Would the police be able to recover against the driver if they were injured while attempting to catch the car thief? See *Hollett v. Coca-Cola Ltd.* (1980), 37 N.S.R. (2d) 695 (S.C.); *Spagnolo v. Margesson's Sports Ltd.* (1983), 145 D.L.R. (3d) 381 (Ont. C.A.); *Moore v. Fanning* (1987), 60 O.R. (2d) 225 (H.C.); and *Werbeniuk v. Maynard*, [1994] 7 W.W.R. 704 (Man. Q.B.).

3. If a workman leaves without locking the plaintiff's house, should he be held liable for losses caused by theft? See *Stansbie v. Troman*, [1948] 2 K.B. 48 (C.A.); *Thiele v. Rod Service (Ottawa) Ltd.* (1962), 45 D.L.R. (2d) 503 (Ont. C.A.); and *Ward v. Cannock Chase Dist. Council*, [1985] 3 All E.R. 537 (Ch. Div.).

4. Assume that a defendant driver negligently runs over the plaintiff and that during the ensuing commotion someone steals the plaintiff's wallet. Should the defendant be held liable for the theft? See *Brauer v. New York Cent. & H.R.R. Co.* (1918), 103 A. 166 (N.J. C.A.); *Patten v. Silberschein*, [1936] 3 W.W.R. 169 (B.C. S.C.); and *Duce v. Rourke* (1951), 1 W.W.R. (N.S.) 305 (Alta. C.A.).

5. In *Lamb v. London Borough of Camden*, [1981] 2 All E.R. 408 (C.A.), the three judges agreed that the reasonable foreseeability test is not always appropriate for cases involving deliberate intervening acts of third parties. They were concerned that the test would extend the defendant's liability "beyond all reason" and lead to "bizarre and ludicrous" results. However, the judges each adopted a different test to govern these situations. But see *P Perl (Exporters) Ltd. v. Camden London Borough Council*, [1983] 3 All E.R. 161 (C.A.). See also Lee and Merkin, "Human Action as Novus Actus

Interveniens", [1981] New L.J. 965 and Highley, "Comment on *P Perls (Exporters) Ltd. v. Camden London Borough Council*" (1985), 43 U. of T. Fac. L. Rev. 136.

6. Liability may be imposed on those who have a duty to control others despite the illegal act of a third party. See generally Chapter 11.

REVIEW PROBLEM

As a child, Mrs. Adams had been overprotected by her parents. Since they considered bicycles to be dangerous, she had never learned to ride. In an attempt to overcome her fears, Mrs. Adams purchased a bicycle which she rode to and from work. While riding on a quiet street, Mrs. Adams witnessed a car accident right in front of her. Mr. Jones had gone through a stop sign and rammed Mr. King's vehicle. Neither the drivers nor their passengers were hurt. However, the accident startled Mrs. Adams, who veered into the curb and fell, striking her head on the pavement. Her physical injuries were relatively minor and her bike was undamaged, but she became increasingly afraid to leave her house except to go shopping and to work. Her family doctor suggested that she enter therapy to deal with her fear of going out. Through no fault of the therapist, Mrs. Adams had a very unusual and extremely severe reaction to the treatment and has become a complete shut-in. She now refuses to work or to leave the house for any reason. To make matters worse, her husband has left her because he is incapable of dealing with her "paranoia".

After the collision, Mr. King attempted to drive his car to the service station that he usually used. King signalled left at an intersection and stopped for the oncoming traffic. Unfortunately, Mr. King's rear left signal light was no longer working because of the first accident, and his car was struck from behind by Mr. Smith. As a result of this collision, Mr. King's arm was fractured and he had to be taken to hospital in an ambulance. His arm was put in a cast and he was told not to use the arm until the cast came off. Mr. King was still able to run his plumbing store and initially he followed his doctor's orders. However, in a rush to fill a large order for a very important customer, who had already complained about delays, Mr. King tried to assist his shipper. As his doctor feared, in attempting to steady a heavy sink with his broken arm, King refractured the bone. King had to undergo surgery, was hospitalized for four weeks and was prohibited from returning to work for an additional two months.

You have been contacted by Mrs. Adams and Mr. King. She wishes to sue Mr. Jones for all of her physical injuries, the deterioration in her mental health, her financial losses due to her inability to work, and the breakup of her marriage. Mr. King is seeking damages from both Mr. Jones and Mr. Smith. Your initial investigations have established that Mr. King's car sustained $800 damage in the first collision with Jones and an additional $2,200 damage in the collision with Mr. Smith. Mr. King has brought it to your attention that his tool chests worth $500 were stolen at the scene of the second accident.

16

THE ASSESSMENT OF DAMAGES

1. Introduction
2. Damages for Personal Injuries
3. Survival Actions and Dependants' Claims for Wrongful Death or Injury
4. Damages for Property Loss
5. Collateral Benefits

1. Introduction

In this chapter, we introduce the reader to the legal principles governing the assessment of damages in Canada. A number of general principles are referred to in the introduction, and other more specific principles are discussed in the remaining sections. In section two, we examine not only the principles relating to personal injury claims, but also analyze some of the more technical rules governing the assessment of such claims. This detailed discussion is intended to illustrate the complexities of applying the general principles to specific cases. Unfortunately, space limitations do not permit us to provide a similar analysis of other types of damage claims.

(a) THE PURPOSES OF DAMAGE AWARDS IN NEGLIGENCE

As noted in chapter 2, damages may be classified according to the purpose for which they are awarded. In this functional classification system, damages are traditionally divided into three categories — nominal (token), compensatory and punitive (exemplary or vindictive) damages.

Nominal damages are generally awarded to vindicate the plaintiff's rights in situations in which she has suffered no injuries. Since the plaintiff must establish loss or injury as one of the elements of her negligence claim, nominal damages are not available in negligence suits.

With rare exceptions, negligence actions are brought to recover compensatory damages. In negligence, as in intentional torts, the purpose of compensatory damages is to put the plaintiff in the position that she would have been in had the tort not been committed. As will soon become apparent, this principle is easy to understand, but often extremely difficult to apply in even moderately serious property damage or personal injury cases.

Unlike their English counterparts, the Canadian courts have not defined punitive damages narrowly or restricted them to specific categories of cases. Rather, the Canadian courts have held that punitive damages may be awarded in any situation in which the defendant's malicious, outrageous, vicious, high-handed, or otherwise socially unacceptable conduct warrants punishment and/or deterrence. The vast majority of negligence cases involve simple carelessness and thus punitive damages are rarely appropriate. Nevertheless, the Canadian definition of punitive damages encompasses those negligence cases in which the defendant has acted with an arrogant, high-handed or blatant disregard for the plaintiff's safety or other interests. Although the courts have acknowledged this principle in recent years, they have remained reluctant to award punitive damages in negligence.

NOTES AND QUESTIONS

1. For a discussion of nominal damages see *The Mediana*, [1900] A.C. 113 (H.L.); Waddams, *The Law of Damages*, 2nd ed. (1991), 10-1 to 10-5; and Rogers, *Winfield and Jolowicz on Tort*, 14th ed. (1994), 635. In contrast, see Cooper-Stephenson and Saunders, *Personal Injury Damages in Canada*, 2nd ed. (1996), 100, where the authors state "where the plaintiff can provide evidence of quantum but unreasonably omits to do so, the reward may be nominal damages". See also *Fisher v. Knibbe*, [1992] 5 W.W.R. 385 (Alta. C.A.), where the plaintiff was awarded $100 in nominal damages against the defendant solicitor who missed a limitations period. The court awarded nominal damages because the original action would not have succeeded in any event. What purpose would such an award serve?

2. *Robitaille v. Vancouver Hockey Club Ltd.* (1979), 19 B.C.L.R. 158 (S.C.), aff'd. (1981), 124 D.L.R. (3d) 228 (B.C. C.A.) is one of the few negligence cases in which punitive damages have been awarded. The trial judge held that the defendant's medical staff had consciously ignored the plaintiff's complaints about a serious injury. As a result, the plaintiff suffered a permanent disabling injury when he was forced to play in an injured condition. He also got a reputation as a malingerer. The judge characterized the defendant's conduct as "high-handed, arrogant and displaying a reckless disregard for the rights of the plaintiff", and awarded the plaintiff $35,000 in punitive damages. Do you agree with the court's application of punitive damages to the facts? *Robitaille* was approved by the Supreme Court of Canada in *Vorvis v. Ins. Corp. of B.C.*, [1989] 4 W.W.R. 218.

3. In *Kraft v. Oshawa General Hospital* (March 22, 1985) unreported (Ont. H.C.), varied on other grounds (September 4, 1986), Doc. CA196/85 (Ont. C.A.), the plaintiff, a healthy woman, suffered severe brain damage following a cardiac arrest during a relatively safe and simple surgical procedure. The cardiac arrest was precipitated by the failure of the defendant anaesthetist to properly ventilate the plaintiff or monitor her vital signs for a period of at least four minutes. Rather than attending to the plaintiff, the anaesthetist was apparently doing a crossword puzzle that he had clipped onto the plaintiff's chart. In dismissing the plaintiff's claim for punitive damages, the judge stated:

> I am unable to find in the defendant's conduct maliciousness, intent to harm, or that disregard of every principle of decency which is the foundation for an award of punitive damages. It is my view that punitive damages should be awarded only on rare occasions and I am not persuaded that they should be awarded in the circumstances of this case.

Do you agree with the court's statement of the circumstances in which punitive damages may be awarded or the application of this principle to the facts? Is the defendant's conduct in this case any less morally blameworthy than the conduct that gives rise to punitive damages in intentional torts? Can you reconcile *Kraft* and *Robitaille*? See also *Rumsey v. R.*, [1984] 5 W.W.R. 585 (Fed. T.D.).

4. In *Vlchek v. Koshel* (1988), 44 C.C.L.T. 314 (B.C. S.C.), the infant plaintiff, who was a passenger, was seriously injured when she was thrown from an all-terrain vehicle. She sued the manufacturer for failing to recall or redesign the vehicle, despite numerous similar accidents. The court concluded that punitive damages could be awarded even if the defendant's act was not directed toward the plaintiff. Rather, the defendant's conduct must be malicious or reckless enough to indicate a complete indifference to the welfare and safety of others.

Should the same principles apply to a defendant who habitually drives while impaired? In both *Nelson v. Welsh and Snow* (1985), 70 N.S.R. (2d) 422 (S.C.) and *Wilson v. Lind* (1985), 35 C.C.L.T. 95 (Ont. H.C.), punitive damages were denied because the criminal law provides a mechanism for punishing impaired drivers. However, there was no evidence that either driver had been criminally prosecuted. See also Whitehill, "*Taylor v. Superior Court*: Punitive Damages for Nondeliberate Torts: The Drunk Driving Context" (1980), 68 Cal. L. Rev. 911. Can you suggest other types of negligence cases in which punitive damages might be appropriate?

5. A few cases apparently allowed punitive damages for inadvertent negligence. See, for example,

Rowland's Transport Ltd. v. Nasby Sales & Services Ltd. (1978), 16 A.R. 192 (T.D.). The better view is that only advertent negligence, such as in *Robitaille*, will support a punitive award.

6. For cases involving punitive damages in negligence, see *Heighington v. Ontario* (1987), 41 C.C.L.T. 230 (Ont. H.C.); *Coughlin v. Kuntz* (1987), 42 C.C.L.T. 142 (B.C. S.C.), aff'd. (1989), 2 C.C.L.T. (2d) 42 (B.C. C.A.); *MacDonald v. Sebastian* (1987), 42 C.C.L.T. 213 (N.S. S.C.); and *Augustus v. Gosset* (1995), 27 C.C.L.T. (2d) 161 (Que. C.A.).

(b) PRELIMINARY ISSUES

Before turning to the specific principles governing different types of damage claims, there are several preliminary issues that must be addressed. These include the burden and standard of proof in damages, mitigation of damages, the set-off of parallel expenditures, the use of lump-sum payments, and the roles of juries, judges and appellate courts.

The plaintiff has the burden of proving that she has suffered a type of loss that is recognized as being recoverable in tort law. For example, no one doubts that grief and sorrow may be debilitating, but unless they cause nervous shock these are not recognized heads of damage in a common law tort action. The plaintiff also bears the burden of proving the quantum of the damages that she is claiming.

The standard of proof for losses that have occurred prior to trial is relatively straightforward. The plaintiff must prove the existence and quantum of such losses on the balance of probabilities. If the plaintiff meets this standard, she is entitled to recover 100 per cent of the claim, and if she fails to satisfy this test she is denied recovery. The standard of proof for losses that may occur after trial is more complex. In Canada, two conflicting lines of authority appear to have developed. The earlier line of authority supports a balance of probabilities test. If the plaintiff establishes on the balance of probabilities that a future loss will occur, she can recover the entire amount. However, if she cannot meet this test her claim is denied. The second line of cases is based on a reasonable or substantial possibility test. Once the plaintiff establishes that there is a substantial or reasonable possibility of injury, she is entitled to recover for this loss, but subject to the likelihood of it occurring. Pursuant to this second line of cases, a plaintiff who could establish that there was a 35 per cent chance of suffering blindness in the future, would be entitled to 35 per cent of the damages that such blindness would cause her. It appears that this second approach will prevail.

The plaintiff is under an obligation to act reasonably in all of the circumstances of the case to mitigate her loss. The defendant has the burden of proving that the plaintiff failed to do so. McGregor, in *McGregor on Damages*, 15th ed. (1988), at 168-69 outlines three related principles of mitigation: the plaintiff must take all reasonable steps to avoid or minimize her loss; the plaintiff may recover for losses incurred in taking such reasonable steps; and the plaintiff cannot recover for losses that she has successfully avoided, even if she was not required to have avoided them under the first rule. These principles are generally applied more rigorously to claims for property damages and business losses, than to claims for personal injuries. Although relatively easy to state, these principles are often very difficult to apply in specific fact situations.

A defendant is allowed to set-off against the plaintiff's damage claim any parallel expenditures that the plaintiff would have incurred had the tort not been committed. For example, if the plaintiff is claiming the full cost of nursing home care which includes food, the defendant may be permitted to reduce this claim by the amount the plaintiff saved on food during this period. As a general rule, set-off is only permitted if the defendant can establish that the two items in issue are truly parallel in nature, and their values are readily calculable as a matter of practicality.

At common law, damages are awarded in a lump sum to compensate the plaintiff for all the losses she has suffered and will likely suffer in the future. Given the lump-sum payment system, the trier-of-fact is forced to speculate on a range of issues including the future condition of the injured plaintiff, the probable increases in health and nursing costs, and the impact of inflation on the purchasing power of the damage award. If a loss turns out to be far greater or smaller than that calculated at trial, there is no means of re-assessment. As we shall discuss, the inadequacies of this system have been widely criticized by both commentators and judges.

In a jury trial it is the jury's responsibility to assess damages, and the common law does not allow counsel or the judge to provide much assistance. Since special damages must be specifically pleaded and proven, they are not nearly as difficult to calculate as general damages. Counsel cannot mention to the jury the amount of general damages she feels is appropriate. Expert witnesses, while allowed to comment on the extent of the plaintiff's injuries, cannot suggest a monetary value for these losses. A judge may comment on the factual matters in evidence, but even she should not express her opinion on the quantum of damages to the jury.

Neither counsel nor the trial judge is permitted at common law to refer the jury to awards that have been given in similar cases, although counsel may refer to such information on appeal. The problems of inconsistency are further heightened by the general rule that appellate courts are not to interfere with a jury's assessment of damages, unless there is a clear error in law or the amount is so grossly out of line that it must be a "wholly erroneous" estimate of the damages.

NOTES AND QUESTIONS

1. It is often difficult to isolate the issue of the existence of liability from the issue of the extent of liability. The courts often take different approaches to these issues and use different terminology. For example, is it more appropriate to state that there is no duty to avoid causing grief and sorrow, or that grief and sorrow are too remote, or that grief and sorrow are not recognized heads of damage?

2. For cases supporting the balance of probabilities test for future losses see *B.C. Electric Ry. Co. v. Clarke*, [1950] 3 D.L.R. 161 (S.C.C.); *Turenne v. Chung* (1962), 36 D.L.R. (2d) 197 (Man. C.A.); *Corrie v. Gilbert*, [1965] S.C.R. 457; and *Conklin v. Smith* (1978), 5 C.C.L.T. 113 (S.C.C.). For cases supporting the reasonable possibility test see *Davies v. Taylor*, [1972] 3 All E.R. 836 (H.L.); *Schrump v. Koot* (1977), 18 O.R. (2d) 337 (C.A.); *Hearndon v. Rondeau* (1984), 29 C.C.L.T. 149 (B.C. C.A.); *Janiak v. Ippolito* (1985), 31 C.C.L.T. 113 (S.C.C.); and *Steenblok v. Funk*, [1990] 5 W.W.R. 365 (B.C. C.A.), leave to appeal ref'd. (1991), 51 B.C.L.R. (2d) xxxv (note) (S.C.C.).

Although the Canadian courts may now simply follow the reasonable possibility test set out in *Janiak*, this decision did not address the conflicting line of cases. Can you provide an example where the result would be the same regardless of which test was used? Provide an example where the tests would produce different results. Which test is more in keeping with the purpose of compensatory damage awards? For a discussion of these issues see Kirkham, "Proof of Future Loss: Probabilities and Possibilities" (1984), 24 The Advocate 21; Waddams, *The Law of Damages*, 2nd ed. (1991), 13-13 to 13-18; and Cooper-Stephenson and Saunders, *Personal Injury Damages in Canada*, 2nd ed. (1996), 754-61.

3. It may be difficult to determine if the plaintiff's conduct should be raised in remoteness, contributory negligence, mitigation, or in all three issues. Moreover, some courts deal with the question of set-off of parallel expenditures as an issue of mitigation. For a comprehensive review of the principles of mitigation, see Cooper-Stephenson and Saunders, *supra*, 862-92; and Waddams, *supra*, 15-1 to 15-4.1.

4. In *Janiak v. Ippolito* (1985), 31 C.C.L.T. 113 (S.C.C.), the defendant negligently caused the plaintiff's serious back injury. The plaintiff was informed that if he had corrective surgery there was a 70 per cent to 75 per cent chance of complete recovery which would allow him to return to work. The chance of a "poor result" was 10 per cent, including a 1 per cent risk of quadriplegia and a 0.1 per cent risk of death. The plaintiff refused to have the operation. The court had to decide if his refusal constituted an unreasonable failure to mitigate. The Supreme Court held that this issue was to be resolved by the trier-of-fact, and depended upon the risks of surgery, the consequences of refusing surgery and its potential benefits. The Supreme Court concluded that the trial judge was correct in finding that the plaintiff unreasonably failed to mitigate his loss by refusing surgery. Do you agree with this conclusion?

The Supreme Court also stated that a plaintiff's pre-existing fear of surgery do not justify an unreasonable failure to have an operation, unless she suffers a psychological infirmity that precludes rational decision-making. Is this proposition consistent with the general principles governing the thin-skulled plaintiff rule? Should these same principles apply if the surgical procedure violates the plaintiff's religious beliefs? Should the same principles apply to recommended psychiatric treatment, even if participation would stigmatize the plaintiff? See *Brian v. Mador* (1985), 32 C.C.L.T. 157 (Ont. C.A.); *Engel v. Kam-Ppelle Holdings Ltd.* (1993), 15 C.C.L.T. (2d) 245 (S.C.C.); *Gray v. Gill* (1993), 18 C.C.L.T. (2d) 120 (B.C. S.C.); and Kemp, "Mitigation of Damage — Plaintiff's Refusal to Undergo Operation — Onus of Proof" (1983), 99 L.Q.R. 497.

5. For a discussion of mitigation in commercial and property damage situations, see respectively *Hongkong Bank of Canada v. Richardson Greenshields of Canada Ltd.* (1990), 72 D.L.R. (4th) 161 (B.C. C.A.); and *University of Regina v. Pettick* (1991), 77 D.L.R. (4th) 615 (Sask. C.A.).

6. For a discussion of the set-off of parallel expenditures, see *Shearman v. Folland*, [1950] 1 All E.R. 976 (C.A.); *Andrews v. Grand & Toy Alberta Ltd.* (1978), 83 D.L.R. (3d) 452 (S.C.C.); and generally Cooper-Stephenson and Saunders, *supra*, 533-62.

7. For a discussion of the role of the judge and jury see Schroeder, "The Charge to the Jury" in the *Special Lectures of the Law Society of Upper Canada 1959* (1959), 311. In *Howes v. Crosby* (1984), 6 D.L.R. (4th) 698 (Ont. C.A.), the court noted that it would not be an error for a trial judge to inform the jury of the Supreme Court's limits on awards for non-pecuniary loss. However, in *Baurose v. Hart* (1990), 44 C.P.C. (2d) 283 (Ont. Gen. Div.), the court stated that the upper limit should only be mentioned in cases of catastrophic injury. In Ontario, the Courts of Justice Act, R.S.O. 1990, c. C.43, s. 118, now allows the parties and the judge to inform the jury on general damage awards.

8. Although the principles governing an appellate review of a damage award are well-established, it is often difficult to reconcile the cases. For a comprehensive review, see Waddams, *supra*, 13-20 to 13-24.

9. In *Theakston v. Bowley*, [1950] 3 D.L.R. 804, the Ontario Court of Appeal stated that the defendant would have grounds for appeal if any statement was made from which the jury might infer that the defendant was insured. This principle remains in effect in Ontario. What is the rationale for this rule?

10. Do the rules governing judges, juries and appeals make sense given the complexity of the law of damages? Fleming has argued that the inconsistency and apparent arbitrariness of damage awards has led more than anything else to the restricted use of juries in civil actions. "Damages For Non-Material Loss" in *Special Lectures of the Law Society of Upper Canada 1973*, (1973) 1 at 5-10. Should the assessment of damages be left to the judge in jury cases? If not, how would you modify the existing rules?

11. The recovery of pre- and post-trial interest on the plaintiff's losses raises extremely complex issues that are increasingly governed by legislation. See Bowles and Whelan, "The Law of Interest: Dawn of a New Era?" (1986), 64 Can. Bar Rev. 142; and Waddams, *The Law of Damages, supra*, 7-15 to 7-48.

2. Damages for Personal Injuries

(a) INTRODUCTION

Until the late 1970s, the Canadian courts used a "global approach" in assessing damages, which involved selecting a single figure to compensate the plaintiff for all of her injuries. The governing principles were very general, and meaningful appellate review was difficult. Moreover, there was no effective means of curbing the large variations in awards for apparently similar injuries. The global approach resulted in very low damage awards. For example, in *Clarke v. Penny* (1975), 10 Nfld. & P.E.I.R. 220 (Nfld. T.D.) a five-year-old girl who sustained severe brain damage was awarded $180,000 for her loss of earning capacity, future care costs, pain and suffering, and loss of enjoyment of life.

The Supreme Court of Canada fundamentally changed the method of assessing damages in the late 1970s, when it rejected the global approach in concurrent decisions in three serious personal injury cases: *Andrews v. Grand & Toy Alta. Ltd.*, [1978] 2 S.C.R. 299; *Arnold v. Teno*, [1978] 2 S.C.R. 287; and *Thornton v. School Dist. No. 57 Bd. of School Trustees*, [1978] 2 S.C.R. 267. The damage trilogy, as these cases are often referred to, called for the separate assessment of each aspect of the plaintiff's losses based on the available evidence. The trilogy established a framework for quantifying general damages under the following heads:

(1) Pecuniary Loss
    (a) Future Care
    (b) Lost Earning Capacity
    (c) Considerations Relevant to Both Future Care and Lost Earning Capacity
(2) Non-Pecuniary Loss

Perhaps the most striking consequence of the damages trilogy has been the increase in the size of the damage awards. The courts' efforts to rationalize damage assessments have led to inflation adjustments, home care awards, the increasing (grossing up) of the future care costs to offset the impact of taxes, and awards to hire professional financial managers. Million dollar awards, which were unheard of in Canada before the late 1970s, were commonplace by the mid-1980s.

In this section, we will examine the current Canadian framework for assessing personal injury claims, using the relevant portions of Dickson J.'s judgment in *Andrews*. The first excerpt introduces some of the underlying concepts.

ANDREWS v. GRAND & TOY ALTA. LTD.

[1978] 2 S.C.R. 229, 83 D.L.R. (3d) 452 (S.C.C.)

FACTS

DICKSON J.: — This is a negligence action for personal injury involving a young man rendered a quadriplegic in a traffic accident for which the respondent Anderson and his employer, Grand & Toy Alberta Ltd., have been found partially liable. Leave to appeal to this Court was granted on the question whether the Appellate Division of the Supreme Court of Alberta erred in law in the assessment of damages. At trial Mr. Justice Kirby awarded $1,022,477.48 [54 D.L.R. (3d) 85, [1974] 5 W.W.R. 675]: the Appellate Division reduced that sum to $516,544.48 [64 D.L.R. (3d) 663, [1976] 2 W.W.R. 385].

. . .

Let me say in introduction what has been said many times before, that no ~RULE~ appellate Court is justified in substituting a figure of its own for that awarded at trial simply because it would have awarded a different figure if it had tried the case at first instance. It must be satisfied that a wrong principle of law was applied, or that the overall amount is a wholly erroneous estimate of the damage: *Nance v. B.C. Electric R. Co.*, [1951] 3 D.L.R. 705, [1951] A.C. 601, 2 W.W.R. (N.S.) 665.

The method of assessing general damages in separate amounts, as has been *Applic.* done in this case, in my opinion, is a sound one. It is the only way in which any meaningful review of the award is possible on appeal and the only way of affording reasonable guidance in future cases. Equally important, it discloses to the litigants and their advisers the components of the overall award, assuring them thereby that each of the various heads of damage going to make up the claim has been given thoughtful consideration.

The subject of damages for personal injury is an area of the law which cries out for legislative reform. The expenditure of time and money in the determination of fault and of damage is prodigal. The disparity resulting from lack of provision for victims who cannot establish fault must be disturbing. When it is determined that compensation is to be made, it is highly irrational to be tied to a lump-sum system and a once-and-for-all award.

The lump-sum award presents problems of great importance. It is subject to inflation, it is subject to fluctuation on investment, income from it is subject to tax. After judgment new needs of the plaintiff arise and the present needs are extinguished; yet, our law of damages knows nothing of periodic payment. The difficulties are greatest where there is a continuing need for intensive and expen-*Suggestion* sive care and a long-term loss of earning capacity. It should be possible to devise some system whereby payments would be subject to periodic review and variation in the light of the continuing needs of the injured person and the cost of meeting those needs. In making this comment I am not unaware of the negative recommendation of the British Law Commission (Law Com. 56 — *Report on Personal Injury Litigation — Assessment of Damages*) following strong opposition from insurance interests and the plaintiffs' bar.

The apparent reliability of assessments provided by modern actuarial practice is largely illusionary, for actuarial science deals with probabilities, not actualities. This is in no way to denigrate a respected profession, but it is obvious that the validity of the answers given by the actuarial witness, as with a computer, depends upon the soundness of the postulates from which he proceeds. Although a useful aid, and a sharper tool than the "multiplier-multiplicand" approach favoured in some jurisdictions, actuarial evidence speaks in terms of group experience. It cannot, and does not purport to, speak as to the individual sufferer. So long as we are tied to lump-sum awards, however, we are tied also to actuarial calculations as the best available means of determining amount.

In spite of these severe difficulties with the present law of personal injury compensation, the positive administrative machinery required for a system of reviewable periodic payments, and the need to hear all interested parties in order to fashion a more enlightened system, both dictate that the appropriate body to act must be the Legislature, rather than the Courts. Until such time as the Legislature acts, the Courts must proceed on established principles to award damages which compensate accident victims with justice and humanity for the losses they may suffer.

Application

I proceed now to a brief recital of the injuries sustained by the appellant James Andrews in the present case. He suffered a fracture with dislocation of the cervical spine between the fifth and sixth cervical vertebrae, causing functional transection of the spinal cord, but leaving some continuity; compound fracture of the left tibia and left humerus; fracture of the left patella. The left radial nerve was damaged. The lesion of the spinal cord left Andrews with paralysis involving most of the upper limbs, spine and lower limbs. He has lost the use of his legs, his trunk, essentially his left arm and most of his right arm. To add to the misery, he does not have normal bladder, bowel and sex functions. He suffers from spasticity in both upper and lower limbs. He has difficulty turning in bed and must be re-positioned every two hours. He needs regular physiotherapy and should have someone in close association with him at all times, such as a trained male orderly. The only functioning muscles of respiration are those of the diaphragm and shoulders. There is much more in the evidence but it need not be recited. Andrews is severely, if not totally disabled. Dr. Weir, a specialist in neurosurgery, said of Andrews' condition that "there is no hope of functional improvement." For the rest of his life he will be dependent on others for dressing, personal hygiene, feeding, and, indeed, for his very survival. But, of utmost important, he is not a vegetable or a piece of cordwood. He is a man of above average intelligence and his mind is unimpaired. He can see, hear and speak as before. He has partial use of his right arm and hand. With the aid of a wheelchair he is mobile. With a specially designed van he can go out in the evening to visit friends, or to the movies, or to a pub. He is taking driving lessons and proving to be an apt pupil. He wants to live as other human beings live. Since May 31, 1974, he has resided in his own apartment with private attendant care. The medical long-term care required is not at a sophisticated level but rather at a practical care level.

Andrews was 21 years of age and unmarried on the date of the accident. On that date he was an apprentice carman employed by the Canadian National Railways in the City of Edmonton.

I turn now to consider assessment of the damages to which Andrews is entitled.

. . .

NOTES AND QUESTIONS

1. What criticisms did Dickson J. make of: (a) the fault system; and (b) lump-sum awards? Dickson J. elaborated on his concerns about lump-sum awards in the David B. Goodman Memorial Lecture reprinted in (1980), 14 L.S.U.C. Gazette 138.

2. There are two types of periodic payment schemes. In one, the payment schedule is fixed in advance, and, like a lump-sum, cannot be varied later to reflect changes in circumstances as they unfold. In the other, variable periodic payments, the payments may be adjusted as circumstances change. Which type of periodic payment scheme best addresses Dickson J.'s concerns?

3. What extra costs would be incurred with variable periodic payments? Are victims more likely to malinger under such a scheme? Is the case for periodic payments paternalistic? The limited research on how plaintiffs fare after receiving lump-sum damage awards is not encouraging. See Fleming, "Damages: Capital or Rent" (1969), 19 U. of T. L.J. 295 at 300; Keeton and O'Connell, *Basic Protection for the Traffic Victim* (1965), 353-4; Kretzner, "No Fault Comes to Israel" (1976), 11 Israel L. Reports 288 at 306; and Bale, "Encouraging the Hearse Horse Not to Snicker: A Tort Fund Providing

Variable Periodic Payments for Pecuniary Loss", in Steel and Rogers-Magnet (eds.), *Issues in Tort Law* (1983), 91.

4. Periodic payments are a central feature of the increasing number of structured settlements being reached by parties. Typically, a structured settlement includes a sum for expenses already incurred, followed by a series of periodic payments to cover future losses. In most cases, the defendant's insurer purchases an annuity designed to generate periodic payments for the plaintiff's life. The payments may, and usually do, vary over the term of the settlement. For example, cost-of-living increases are built into the schedule and balloon payments may be included to meet projected occasional needs, such as the cost of a child's university education. Thus, a structured settlement may be tailored to the individual plaintiff's needs. Such settlements protect plaintiffs who might otherwise squander or inefficiently manage the lump-sum award. However, the conditions for variation are established at the time of settlement and no adjustment for unanticipated changes in circumstances are possible.

5. The main advantage of a structured settlement is that the periodic payments which are generated are not taxable. Although a lump-sum award is not taxable either, any interest it generates is taxable. This tax savings with structured settlements thus becomes a matter for negotiation, which may be mutually beneficial. The defendant will be able to purchase an annuity for less than the lump sum that would have been awarded, and yet the plaintiff's periodic payments will exceed the after-tax income she would have obtained from the interest on the lump sum. See *Yepremian v. Scarborough Gen. Hosp.* (1981), 120 D.L.R. (3d) 341 (Ont. H.C.), in which a judicially-approved structured settlement is reprinted; Weir, *Structured Settlement* (1984); Holland, "Structured Settlements in Injury and Wrongful Death Cases" (1987), 8 Adv. Q. 185; and Watkin, "The New Method of Structuring Settlement Agreements" (1992), 71 Can. Bar Rev. 27.

6. The tax savings in a structured settlement would also occur in a structured judgment. However, in *Watkins v. Olafson*, [1989] 2 S.C.R. 750, the court held that the courts lacked jurisdiction to impose judgment in a structured form. No Canadian legislation authorized the imposition of structured judgments, although this was recommended by Osborne J., in the *Report of Inquiry into Motor Vehicle Compensation in Ontario* (1988), and by the Law Reform Commission of Saskatchewan, in Proposals for a *Structured Judgments Act* (1993).

7. The Courts of Justice Act, R.S.O. 1990, c. C.43, s. 116, authorizes a court, with the consent of all of the parties, to order the award to be paid periodically and to be subject to periodic re-assessment and adjustment. No such order has apparently been made yet.

In *Wilson v. Martinello* (1995), 23 O.R. (3d) 417, the Court of Appeal stated that s. 116 was badly drafted. According to the Court of Appeal, where a plaintiff seeks a lump sum award including a gross-up, and the defendant proposes a structured award with periodic payments, s. 116 requires the court to impose a structured award unless the plaintiff can prove that it would not be in her best interests.

8. See generally Ontario Law Reform Commission, *Report on Compensation for Personal Injuries and Death* (1987).

(b) PECUNIARY LOSS: FUTURE CARE

ANDREWS v. GRAND & TOY ALTA. LTD.

[1978] 2 S.C.R. 229, 83 D.L.R. (3d) 452 (S.C.C.)

DICKSON J.: —

. . .

In theory a claim for the cost of future care is a pecuniary claim for the amount PRINCIPLE which may reasonably be expected to be expended in putting the injured party in the position he would have been in if he had not sustained the injury. Obviously, a plaintiff who has been gravely and permanently impaired can never be put in the position he would have been in if the tort had not been committed. To this extent, *restitutio in integrum* is not possible. Money is a barren substitute for health and personal happiness, but to the extent, within reason, that money can be used to sustain or improve the mental or physical health of the injured person it may properly form part of a claim.

Contrary to the view expressed in the Appellate Division of Alberta, there is no duty to mitigate, in the sense of being forced to accept less than real loss. There is a duty to be reasonable. There cannot be "complete" or "perfect" compensation. An award must be moderate, and fair to both parties. Clearly, compensation must not be determined on the basis of sympathy, or compassion for the plight of the injured person. What is being sought is compensation not retribution. But, in a case like the present, where both Courts have favoured a home environment, "reasonable" means reasonableness in what is to be provided in that home environment. It does not mean that Andrews must languish in an institution which on all evidence is inappropriate for him.

The reasons for judgment of the Appellate Division embodied three observations which are worthy of brief comment. The first [at p. 699]:

> ... it is the choice of the respondent to live in a home of his own, and from the point of view of advancing a claim for damages, it is a most salutary choice, because it is vastly the most expensive.

I am not entirely certain as to what is meant by this observation. If the import is that the appellant claimed a home life for the sole purpose of inflating his claim, then I think the implication is both unfair and unsupported by evidence. There is no doubt upon the medical and other evidence that a home environment would be salutary to the health of the appellant and productive of good effects. It cannot be unreasonable for a person to want to live in a home of his own.

The next observation [at pp. 699-700]:

> Secondly, it should be observed that in many cases, particularly in Alberta where damages have been awarded, the persons injured were going to live with their families. Here, the evidence (in spite of the fact that the respondent's mother advanced a claim for $237 which represented a towing charge for the motor-cycle and parking, taxis and bus fare expended on visits to her son in the hospital for approximately a nine-month period prior to the issue of the statement of claim) is that the respondent and his mother were not close before the accident, and matters proceeded on the footing that the mother's natural love and affection should have no part in Andrews' future. Again, this situation is the most expensive from the point of view of the respondent.

The evidence showed that the mother of the appellant James Andrews was living alone, in a second-floor apartment and that relations between Andrews and his mother were strained at times. This should have no bearing in minimizing Andrews' damages. Even if his mother had been able to look after Andrews in her own home, there is now ample authority for saying that dedicated wives or mothers who choose to devote their lives to looking after infirm husbands or sons are not expected to do so on a gratuitous basis. The second observation is irrelevant.

The third observation was in these words:

> Thirdly, it should be observed that the learned trial Judge has referred with approval to the English authorities which held that full compensation for pecuniary loss must be given. It does not, however, follow that every conceivable expense which a plaintiff may conjure up is a pecuniary loss. On the evidence, then, should this Court consider that Andrews should live in a home of his own for the next 45 years at the expense of the appellant?

I agree that a plaintiff cannot "conjure up" "every conceivable expense". I do not think that a request for home care falls under that rubric.

Each of the three observations seems to look at the matter solely from the point of view of the respondents and the expense to them. An award must be fair to both parties but the ability of the defendant to pay has never been regarded as a relevant consideration in the assessment of damages at common law. The focus should be on the injuries of the innocent party. Fairness to the other party is achieved by assuring that the claims raised against him are legitimate and justifiable.

. . .

With respect to Andrews' disinclination to live in an institution, the Court commented:

> He might equally say that he would not live in Alberta, as he did not wish to face old friends, or for any other reasons, and that he wished to live in Switzerland or the Bahamas.

Andrews is not asking for a life in Europe or in the Caribbean. He asks that he be permitted to continue to live in Alberta and to see his old friends, but in his own home or apartment, not in an institution.

The Court then expressed the view that the standard accepted by the trial Judge was the equivalent of supplying a private hospital. The phrase "private hospital" is both pejorative and misleading. It suggests an extravagant standard of care. The standard sought by the appellant is simply practical nursing in the home. The amount Andrews is seeking is, without question, very substantial, but essentially it means providing two orderlies and a housekeeper. The amount is large because the victim is young and because life is long. He has 45 years ahead. That is a long time.

In reducing the monthly payment to $1,000 the Appellate Division purported to apply a "final test" which was expressed in terms of the expenses that reasonably-minded people would incur, assuming sufficient means to bear such expense. It seems to me difficult to conceive of any reasonably-minded person of ample means who would not be ready to incur the expense of home care, rather than institutional care, for himself or for someone in the condition of Andrews for whom he was responsible. No other conclusion is open upon the evidence adduced in this case. If the test enunciated by the Appellate Division is simply a plea for moderation then, of course, no one would question it. If the test was intended to suggest that reasonably-minded people would refuse to bear the expense of home care, there is simply no evidence to support that conclusion.

The Appellate Division, seeking to give some meaning to the test, said that it should be open to consider "standards of society as a whole as they presently exist." As instances of such standards the Court selected the daily allowances provided under the *Workmen's Compensation Act* 1973 (Alta.), c. 87, s. 56, and the federal *Pension Act*, R.S.C. 1970, c. P-7, s. 28 [rep. & sub. R.S.C. 1970, c. 22, (2nd Supp.), s. 14(1)]. The standard of care expected in our society in physical injury cases is an elusive concept. What a Legislature sees fit to provide in the cases of veterans and in the cases of injured workers and the elderly is only of marginal assistance. The standard to be applied to Andrews is not merely "provision", but "compensation", *i.e.*, what is the proper compensation for a person who would have been able to care for himself and live in a home environment if he had not been injured? The answer must surely be home care. If there were severe mental impairment, or in the case of an immobile quadriplegic the results might well be different; but, where the victim is mobile and still in full control of his mental faculties, as Andrew is, it cannot be said that institutionalization in an auxiliary hospital represents proper compensation for his loss. Justice requires something better.

. . .

Is it reasonable for Andrews to ask for $4,135 per month for home care? Part of the difficulty of this case is that 24-hour orderly care was not directly challenged. Counsel never really engaged in consideration of whether, assuming home care, such care could be provided at lesser expense. Counsel wants the Court, rather, to choose between home care and auxiliary hospital care. There are unanimous findings below that home care is better. Although home care is expensive, auxiliary hospital care is so utterly unattractive and so utterly in conflict with the principle of proper compensation that this Court is offered no middle ground.

The basic argument, indeed the only argument, against home care is that the social cost is too high. In these days the cost is distributed through insurance premiums. In this respect, I would adopt what was said by Salmon, L.J., in *Fletcher v. Autocare & Transporters, Ltd.*, [1968] 1 All E.R. 726 at 750, where he stated:

> Today, however, virtually all defendants in accident cases are insured. This certainly does not mean compensation should be extravagant, but there is no reason why it should not be realistic ... It might result in some moderate increase in premium rates, which none would relish, but of which no-one, in my view, could justly complain. It would be monstrous to keep down premiums by depressing damages below their proper level, i.e., a level which ordinary men would regard as fair — unprejudiced by its impact on their own pockets.

I do not think the area of future care is one in which the argument of the social burden of the expense should be controlling, particularly in a case like the present, where the consequences of acceding to it would be to fail in large measure to compensate the victim for his loss. Greater weight might be given to this consideration where the choice with respect to future care is not so stark as between home care and an auxiliary hospital. Minimizing the social burden of expense may be a factor influencing a choice between acceptable alternatives. It should never compel the choice of the unacceptable.

(ii) *Life expectancy.* At trial, figures were introduced which showed that the life expectancy of 23-year-old persons in general is 50 years. As Chief Justice McGillivray said in the Appellate Division, it would be more useful to use statistics on the expectation of life of quadriplegics. A statistical average is helpful only if the appropriate group is used. At trial, Dr. Weir and Dr. Gingras testified that possibly five years less than normal would be a reasonable expectation of life for a quadriplegic. The Appellate Division accepted this figure. On the evidence I am willing to accept it.

(iii) *Contingencies of life.* The trial Judge did, however, allow a 20% discount for "contingencies and hazards of life". The Appellate Division allowed a further 10% discount. It characterized the trial Judge's discount as being for "life expectancy" or "duration of life", and said that this ignored the contingency of "duration of expense", *i.e.*, that despite any wishes to the contrary, Andrews in the years to come may be obliged to spend a great deal of time in hospital for medical reasons or because of the difficulty of obtaining help. With respect, the Appellate Division appears to have misunderstood what the trial Judge did. The figure of 20% as a discount for contingencies was arrived at first under the heading of "Prospective Loss of Earnings" and then simply transferred to the calculation of "Costs of Future Care". It was not an allowance for a decreased life expectancy, for this had already been taken into account by reducing the normal 50-year expectancy to 45 years. The "contingencies and hazards of life" in the context of future care are distinct. They relate essentially to duration of expense and are different from those which might affect future earnings, such as unemployment, accident, illness. They are not merely to be added to the latter so as to achieve a cumulative result. Thus, so far as the action taken by the Appellate Division is concerned, in my opinion, it was an error to increase by an extra 10% the contingency allowance of the trial Judge.

This whole question of contingencies is fraught with difficulty, for it is in large measure pure speculation. It is a small element of the illogical practice of awarding lump-sum payments for expenses and losses projected to continue over long periods of time. To vary an award by the value of the chance that certain contingencies may occur is to assure either over-compensation or under-compensation, depending on whether or not the event occurs. In light of the considerations I have mentioned, I think it would be reasonable to allow a discount for contingencies in the amount of 20%, in accordance with the decision of the trial Judge.

· · ·

(v) *Cost of special equipment.* In addition to his anticipated expenses, Andrews requires an initial capital amount for special equipment. Both Courts below held that $14,200 was an appropriate figure for the cost of this equipment. In my opinion, this assessment is correct in principle, and I would therefore accept it.

· · ·

NOTES AND QUESTIONS

1. Why, in Dickson J.'s opinion, is the standard of care provided to injured persons by legislation irrelevant in the case of a tort victim? Do you agree?

2. Do you agree with Dickson J. that the plaintiff should be entitled to be cared for in his own home? What type of evidence must the plaintiff adduce to obtain an award for home care? See *Rayner v. Knickle* (1988), 47 C.C.L.T. 141 (P.E.I. S.C.). The victim's stated preference for home care is not sufficient to justify an award on that basis. See for example *MacDonald v. Alderson* (1982), 20 C.C.L.T. 64 (Man. C.A.).

3. How does the court calculate the duration of the future care period? The insurance industry relies on actuarial tables of "impaired life expectancy" for particular injuries when computing the cost of an annuity for a structured settlement. The courts tend to estimate a longer expectancy period than the tables — another factor which makes structures less expensive than lump-sum awards. Should the courts use the actuarial tables? What are the limitations of applying actuarial evidence to individual cases? See generally Boyle and Murray, "Assessment of Damages: Economic and Actuarial Evidence" (1981), 19 Osgoode Hall L.J. 1; and Anderson, *Actuarial Evidence*, 2nd ed. (1986).

4. What is the purpose of the contingency deduction in future care awards? How was the contingency figure determined in *Andrews*? The court seemed to assume that the contingencies would occur at regular intervals, which is most unlikely. If Andrews were to spend the first 20 per cent of his projected lifespan in an institution, thus using less capital than he would if he was at home, he

would be overcompensated. However, if he was institutionalized for the last 20 per cent of his life, he would have to spend more of his capital early in his projected lifespan and would be undercompensated.

5. The lump-sum award is quantified on the assumption that the plaintiff will invest the sum prudently and that the income from the self-extinguishing fund will be sufficient to meet the projected care costs. Although the lump-sum itself is not taxable, the interest it generates is taxable. Thus, after the trilogy, the Ontario courts increased the future care award by the estimated future tax liability to ensure that the fund would generate sufficient after-tax income to meet the cost of care. This increase is known as the "gross up". The Supreme Court has now confirmed that it is appropriate to gross up the future care award. See *Watkins v. Olafson*, [1989] 2 S.C.R. 750; and *Scarff v. Wilson*, [1989] 2 S.C.R. 776.

6. Although the gross up is sound in principle, it is notoriously difficult and expensive to estimate future taxation in individual cases. The Ontario Law Reform Commission, *Report on Compensation for Personal Injuries and Death* (1987), 139-47, has recommended revisions to the tax laws or standardized assumptions to alleviate these difficulties.

7. The amount for gross up is not insignificant. Gross up in excess of 50 per cent of the future care award has been approved by the courts. See, for example, *Giannone v. Weinberg* (1989), 68 O.R. (2d) 767 (C.A.); *Tronrud v. French* (1991), 84 D.L.R. (4th) 275 (Man. C.A.); and *Macdonald (Guardian ad litem of) v. Neufeld* (1993), 17 C.C.L.T. (2d) 201 (B.C. C.A.). If the gross up is greater than the expected taxes, as some believe is often the case, plaintiffs will not sacrifice the gross up by consenting to a structured judgment. See Feldthusen, "Mandatory Structured Judgments" (1988), 1 Can. Ins. L. Rev. 1.

8. After the trilogy it has been held that the award may include a sum to enable the plaintiff to hire a financial manager "if the plaintiff's level of intelligence is such that he is either unable to manage his affairs or lacks the acumen to invest funds awarded for future care so as to produce the requisite rate of return": *Ins. Corp. of B.C. v. Mandzuk*, [1988] 2 S.C.R. 650. See *Watkins v. Olafson*, [1989] 2 S.C.R. 750. How many people do you think have the necessary acumen?

(c) PECUNIARY LOSS: LOST EARNING CAPACITY

ANDREWS v. GRAND & TOY ALTA. LTD.

[1978] 2 S.C.R. 229, 83 D.L.R. (3d) 452 (S.C.C.)

DICKSON J.: . . . We must now gaze more deeply into the crystal ball. What sort of a career would the accident victim have had? What were his prospects and potential prior to the accident? It is not loss of earnings but, rather, loss of earning capacity for which compensation must be made: *The Queen v. Jennings, supra.* A capital asset has been lost: what was its value?

(i) *Level of earnings.* The trial Judge fixed the projected level of earnings of Andrews at $830 per month, which would have been his earnings on January 1, 1973. The Appellate Division raised this to $1,200 per month, a figure between his present salary and the maximum for his type of work of $1,750 per month. Without doubt the value of Andrews' earning capacity over his working life is higher than his earnings at the time of the accident. Although I am inclined to view even that figure as somewhat conservative, I would affirm the holding of the Appellate Division that $1,200 per month represents a reasonable estimate of Andrews' future average level of earnings.

(ii) *Length of working life.* Counsel for the appellants object to the use of 55 rather than 65 as the projected retirement age for Andrews. It is agreed that he could retire on full pension at 55 if he stayed with his present employer, Canadian National Railways. I think it is reasonable to assume that he would, in fact, retire as soon as it was open for him to do so on full pension.

One must then turn to the mortality tables to determine the working life expec-

tancy for the appellant over the period between the ages of 23 and 55. The controversial question immediately arises whether the capitalization of future earning
capacity should be based on the expected working life span prior to the accident,
or the shortened life expectancy. Does one give credit for the "lost years"? When
viewed as the loss of a capital asset consisting of income-earning capacity rather
than a loss of income, the answer is apparent; it must be the loss of that capacity
which existed prior to the accident. This is the figure which best fulfils the principle
of compensating the plaintiff for what he has lost: see *Mayne and McGregor on
Damages*, 12th ed. (1961), p. 659; Kemp & Kemp, *Quantum of Damages*, 3rd ed.,
vol. 1 (Supp.), c. 3, p. 28; *Skelton v. Collins* (1966), 39 A.L.J.R. 480. In the instant
case, the trial Judge refused to follow the *Oliver et al. v. Ashman*, [1962] 2 Q.B.
210, approach, the manifest injustice of which is demonstrated in the much-
criticized case of *McCann v. Sheppard*, [1973] 1 W.L.R. 540, and in this I think
the judge was right. I would accept his decision that Andrews had a working life
expectancy of 30.81 years.

(iii) *Contingencies.* It is a general practice to take account of contingencies
which might have affected future earnings, such as unemployment, illness, accidents and business depression. In the *Bisson* case, which also concerned a young
quadriplegic, an allowance of 20% was made. There is much support for this view
that such a discount for contingencies should be made; see, *e.g., Warren et al. v.
King*, [1963] 3 All E.R. 521; *McKay et al. v. Board of Govan School Unit No. 29
of Saskatchewan* (1968), 68 D.L.R. (2d) 519, [1968] S.C.R. 589, 64 W.W.R. 301.
There are, however, a number of qualifications which should be made. First, in
many respects, these contingencies implicitly are already contained in an assessment of the projected average level of earnings of the injured person, for one must
assume that this figure is a projection with respect to the real world of work, vicissi-
tudes and all. Second, not all contingencies are adverse, as the above list would
appear to indicate. As is said in *Bresatz v. Przibilla* (1962), 108 C.L.R. 541, in
the Australian High Court, at p. 544: "Why count the possible buffets and ignore
the rewards of fortune?" Finally, in a modern society there are many public and
private schemes which cushion the individual against adverse contingencies.
Clearly, the percentage deduction which is proper will depend on the facts of the
individual case, particularly the nature of the plaintiff's occupation, but generally
it will be small: see J. H. Prevett, "Actuarial Assessment of Damages: The Thalidomide Case — I", 35 Mod. L. Rev. 140 at p. 150 (1973).

In reducing Andrews' award by 20% Mr. Justice Kirby gives no reasons. The
Appellate Division also applied a 20% reduction. It seems to me that actuarial
evidence could be of great help here. Contingencies are susceptible to more exact
calculation than is usually apparent in the cases; see Traversi, "Actuaries and the
Courts", 29 Aust. Law J. 556 (1956). In my view, some degree of specificity, supported by the evidence, ought to be forthcoming at trial.

The figure used to take account of contingencies is obviously an arbitrary
one. The figure of 20% which was used in the lower Courts (and in many other
cases), although not entirely satisfactory, should, I think, be accepted.

. . .

(iv) *Duplication with compensation for loss of future earnings.* It is clear that
a plaintiff cannot recover for the expense of providing for basic necessities as part

of the cost of future care while still recovering fully for prospective loss of earnings. Without the accident, expenses for such items as food, clothing and accommodation would have been paid for out of earnings. They are not an additional type of expense occasioned by the accident.

When calculating the damage award, however, there are two possible methods of proceeding. One method is to give the injured party an award for future care which makes no deduction in respect of the basic necessities for which he would have had to pay in any event. A deduction must then be made for the cost of such basic necessities when computing the award for loss of prospective earnings, i.e., the award is on the basis of net earnings and not gross earnings. The alternative method is the reverse, i.e., to deduct the cost of basic necessities when computing the award for future care and then to compute the earnings award on the basis of gross earnings.

The trial judge took the first approach, reducing loss of future earnings by 53%. The Appellate Division took the second. In my opinion, the approach of the trial Judge is to be preferred. This is in accordance with the principle which I believe should underlie the whole consideration of damages for personal injuries; that proper future care is the paramount goal of such damages. To determine accurately the needs and costs in respect of future care, basic living expenses should be included. The costs of necessaries when in an infirm state may well be different from those when in a state of health. Thus, while the types of expenses would have been incurred in any event, the level of expenses for the victim may be seen as attributable to the accident. In my opinion, the projected cost of necessities should, therefore, be included in calculating the cost of future care, and a percentage attributable to the necessities of a person in a normal state should be reduced from the award for future earnings. For the acceptability of this method of proceeding see the judgment of this Court in *The Queen v. Jennings* (1966), 57 D.L.R. (2d) 644 at pp. 651-2, [1966] S.C.R. 532 at pp. 540-1; affirming 50 D.L.R. (2d) 385 at p. 418, [1965] O.R. 285, *sub nom. Jennings v. Crousberry et al.*, and also *Bisson v. District of Powell River* (1967), 66 D.L.R. (2d) 226 at pp. 239-40, 62 W.W.R. 707 at pp. 720-1.

. . .

NOTES AND QUESTIONS

1. How did Dickson J. determine the base figure that he used to calculate lost earning capacity? How accurate is this approach?

2. In *Arnold v. Teno* (1978), 83 D.L.R. (3d) 609 at 637 (S.C.C.), a case in which a four and one-half year old child was totally disabled, Spence J. arbitrarily selected $7,500 as an "equitable" yearly income for calculating the child's lost earning capacity. He stated that $5,000 was too low because that would relegate the child to poverty and that $10,000, the figure used by the Court of Appeal, was too high. Can such awards be properly made in the absence of actuarial or other expert evidence?

The damages trilogy helped to identify issues, such as future income, that required expert evidence. Lawyers now rely heavily on expert evidence in establishing base figures and contingencies in the calculation of both future care and earning capacity. Unlike *Teno*, the courts are no longer put in the position of having to make such unsubstantiated estimates.

What types of expert evidence would have been useful in *Teno*? Injured children now fare far better than the plaintiff in *Teno*. See *O'Hara v. Belanger*, [1990] 1 W.W.R. 214 (Alta. Q.B.); Bruce, "The Calculation of an Infant's Lost Earnings: *Houle v. Calgary*" (1984), 22 Alta. L. Rev. 291; and Sutherland, "Predicting a Child's Future Wage Loss" (1984), 42 The Advocate 169.

3. Earning capacity is also difficult to estimate when the plaintiff is not a member of the paid labour force, such as in the cases of students and homemakers. How do you think the court would estimate your earning capacity, if you were totally disabled? Many believe that the value of homemaking services, usually provided by women, is grossly undervalued by the courts. How should the lost earning capacity of a woman who has decided to work in the home be calculated? See *Fobel v. Dean* (1991), 9 C.C.L.T. (2d) 87 (Sask. C.A.); *Benstead v. Murphy* (1994), 22 C.C.L.T. (2d) 271 (Alta. C.A.); *Toneguzzo-Norvell (Guardian ad litem of) v. Burnaby Hospital* (1994), 18 C.C.L.T. (2d) 209 (S.C.C.); and *Kroeker v. Jansen* (1995), 24 C.C.L.T. (2d) 113 (B.C. C.A.). See also Cassels, "Damages for Lost Earning Capacity: Women and Children Last!" (1992), 71 Can. Bar Rev. 445; Griffin, "The Value of Women — Avoiding the Prejudices of the Past" (1993), 51 The Advocate 545; and Fast and Munro, "Toward Eliminating Gender Bias in Personal Injury Awards: Contributions from Family Economics" (1994), 32 Alta. L. Rev. 1.

4. If a highly successful lawyer retired at age 40 to pursue a passion for sailing and was then rendered totally unable to work or sail, how should her lost earning capacity be calculated? See generally Reaume, "Rethinking Personal Injury Damages: Compensation For Lost Capacities" (1988), 67 Can. Bar Rev. 82.

5. How does the court estimate the length of time used in calculating the victim's earning capacity? Contrast this to the length of time used to calculate future care awards.

6. What is the purpose of the contingency deduction under lost earning capacity? Distinguish it from the contingency deduction under future care. How did the court arrive at the deduction in *Andrews*? Expert evidence now plays a much greater role and often suggests that positive and negative contingencies tend to cancel one another out. Positive contingencies include private and public plans which cushion the impact of unemployment. See *Fenn v. Peterborough* (1979), 104 D.L.R. (3d) 174 (Ont. C.A.); and *Graham v. Rourke* (1990), 75 O.R. (2d) 622 (C.A.).

7. Explain the problem of potential duplication between the future care and lost earning capacity awards. Outline the two approaches that Dickson J. identifies to address the duplication problem. The *Andrews* approach generally favours the plaintiff, especially when the unadjusted future care award is grossed up. Which approach is more consistent with the basic restitutionary principle of damage quantification? See Feldthusen, "Duplication In Personal Injury Damage Awards" (1987), 66 Can. Bar Rev. 784.

8. The damage trilogy involved catastrophic injuries. In less serious cases, different types of problems may arise, particularly in calculating damages for partial or temporary loss of earning capacity. See, for example, *Lan v. Wu* (1980), 14 C.C.L.T. 282 (B.C. C.A.); *Engel v. Kam-Ppelle Holdings Ltd.* (1993), 15 C.C.L.T. (2d) 245 (S.C.C.); Westcott, "Calculating Loss of Opportunity for Career Advancement: Clearing the Clouds in the Crystal Ball" (1983), 4 Adv. Q. 268; and Wunder, "Compensation for the Plaintiff's Competitive Position on the Labour Market Being Compromised: The Concept and the Law" (1984), 28 C.C.L.T. 117.

(d) CONSIDERATIONS RELEVANT TO BOTH HEADS OF PECUNIARY LOSS

ANDREWS v. GRAND & TOY ALTA. LTD.

[1978] 2 S.C.R. 229, 83 D.L.R. (3d) 452 (S.C.C.)

. . .

DICKSON J.: (i) *Capitalization rate: allowance for inflation and the rate of return on investments.* What rate of return should the Court assume the appellant will be able to obtain on his investment of the award? How should the Court recognize future inflation? Together these considerations will determine the discount rate to use in actuarially calculating the lump-sum award.

The approach at trial was to take as a rate of return the rental value of money which might exist during periods of economic stability, and consequently to ignore inflation. This approach is widely referred to as the Lord Diplock approach, as he lent it his support in *Mallett v. McMonagle*, [1970] A.C. 166. Although this method of proceeding has found favour in several jurisdictions in this country and else-where, it has an air of unreality. Stable, non-inflationary economic conditions do not exist at present, nor did they exist in the recent past, nor are they to be expected in the foreseeable future. In my opinion, it would be better to proceed from what known factors are available rather than to ignore economic reality. Analytically, the alternate approach to assuming a stable economy is to use existing interest rates and then make an allowance for the long-term expected rate of inflation. At trial the expert actuary, Mr. Grindley, testified as follows:

> Yes, as I mentioned yesterday, I was comfortable with that assumption 5% interest because it produces the same result as for example 8% interest and 3% inflation.
>
> . . .
>
> I would be happy to use either of the following two packages of assumption, either an 8% interest rate combined with provision for amounts which would increase 3% in every year in the future or a 5% interest rate and level amount, level amounts, that is no allowance for inflation.

One thing is abundantly clear; present interest rates should not be used with no allowance for future inflation. To do so would be patently unfair to the plain-tiff. It is not, however, the level of inflation in the short term for which allowance must be made, but that predicted over the long term. It is this expectation which is built into present interest rates for long-term investments. It is also this level of inflation which may at present be predicted to operate over the lifetime of the plaintiff to increase the cost of care for him at the level accepted by the Court, and to erode the value of the sum provided for lost earning capacity.

. . .

The approach which I would adopt, therefore, is to use present rates of return on long-term investments and to make some allowance for the effects of future inflation. Once this approach is adopted, the result, in my opinion, is different from the 5% discount figure accepted by the trial Judge. While there was much debate at trial over a difference of a half to one percentage point, I think it is clear from the evidence that high quality long-term investments were available at time of trial at rates of return in excess of 10%. On the other hand, evidence was specific-ally introduced that the former head of the Economic Council of Canada, Dr. Deutsch, had recently forecast a rate of inflation of 3½% over the long-term future. These figures must all be viewed flexibly. In my opinion, they indicate that the appropriate discount rate is approximately 7%. I would adopt that figure. It appears to me to be the correct result of the approach I have adopted, i.e., having regard to present investment market conditions and making an appropriate allowance for future inflation. I would, accordingly, vary to 7% the discount rate to be used in calculating the present value of the awards for future care and loss of earnings in this case. The result in future cases will depend upon the evidence adduced in those cases.

(ii) *Allowance for tax.* In *The Queen v. Jennings, supra,* this Court held that an award for prospective income should be calculated with no deduction for tax which might have been attracted had it been earned over the working life of the plaintiff. This results from the fact that it is earning capacity and not lost earnings which is the subject of compensation. For the same reason, no consideration should be taken of the amount by which the income from the award will be reduced by payment of taxes on the interest, dividends, or capital gain. A capital sum is appropriate to replace the lost capital asset of earning capacity. Tax on income is irrelevant either to decrease the sum for taxes the victim would have paid on income from his job, or to increase it for taxes he will now have to pay on income from the award.

In contrast with the situation in personal injury cases, awards under the *Fatal Accident Act*, R.S.A. 1970, c. 138, should reflect tax considerations, since they are to compensate dependants for the loss of support payments made by the deceased. These support payments could only come out of take-home pay, and the payments from the award will only be received net of taxes: see the contemporaneous decision of this Court in *Keizer v. Hanna et al.* (1978), 82 D.L.R. (3d) 449.

The impact of taxation upon the income from the capital sum for future care is mitigated by the existence of s. 110(1)(*c*)(iv. 1) [enacted 1973-74, c. 14, s. 35] of the *Income Tax Act*, R.S.C. 1952, c. 148 (as amended by 1970-71-72, c. 63), in respect of the deduction of medical expenses, which provides that medical expenses in excess of 3% of the taxpayer's income includes "remuneration for one full-time attendant upon an individual who was a taxpayer ... in a self-contained domestic establishment in which the cared for person lived." This exemption, I should think, permits a deduction for the payment of one full-time attendant for seven days a week, regardless of whether this attendance is provided by several attendants working over 24-hour periods, or one person working 24-hour shifts seven days a week.

The exact tax burden is extremely difficult to predict, as the rate and coverage of taxes swing with the political winds. What concerns us here is whether some allowance must be made to adjust the amount assessed for future care in light of the reduction from taxation. No such allowance was made by the Courts below. Elaborate calculations were provided by the appellant to give an illusion of accuracy to this aspect of the wholly speculative projection of future costs. Because of the provision made in the *Income Tax Act* and because of the position taken in the Alberta Courts, I would make no allowance for that item. The Legislature might well consider a more generous income tax treatment of cases where a fund is established by judicial decision and the sole purpose of the fund is to provide treatment or care of an accident victim.

One subsidiary point should be affirmed with respect to the determination of the present value of the cost of future care. The calculations should provide for a self-extinguishing sum. To allow a residual capital amount would be to overcompensate the injured person by creating an estate for him. This point was accepted by the lower Courts and not challenged by the parties.

. . .

NOTES AND QUESTIONS

1. What is the purpose of the discount or capitalization rate? A 7 per cent rate, as adopted in *Andrews*, means that the lump-sum will be quantified on the assumption that if prudently invested it will generate real earnings of 7 per cent/year net of inflation.

2. The 7 per cent discount rate has been subjected to severe criticism. Experience indicates that in the long run, the gap between the rate of interest and the rate of inflation will be in the vicinity of 2 to 2½ per cent. See Feldthusen and McNair, "General Damages in Personal Injury Suits: The Supreme Court's Trilogy" (1978), 28 U. of T.L.J. 381; Rea, "Inflation and the Law of Contracts and

Torts" (1982), 14 Ottawa L. Rev. 465; and Bale, "Adding Insult to Injury: The Inappropriate Use of Discount Rates to Determine Damage Awards" (1983), 28 McGill L.J. 1015.

3. It is now clear that the calculation of the discount rate is a factual issue to be determined in individual cases. In *Lewis v. Todd* (1980), 115 D.L.R. (3d) 257 (S.C.C.), the court indicated that it lacked the authority to "legislate" a fixed discount rate and that even if it had such authority it was not sufficiently certain of the issues to exercise it.

The costs of litigating the appropriate discount rate on a case-by-case basis are substantial and most Canadian jurisdictions have passed legislation on point. See, for example, the Ontario Rules of Civil Procedure, R. 53.09. Fixed legislative rates are between 2½ per cent and 3 per cent, considerably lower than that used in the trilogy. For a legislative summary and discussion, see The Ontario Law Reform Commission, *Report on Compensation for Personal Injuries and Death* (1987), 218-25.

4. Why does the court not consider the taxes that the plaintiff would have paid in calculating lost earning capacity? This failure to consider taxes would appear to overcompensate the plaintiff. This is offset, albeit not perfectly, by the fact that the plaintiff will pay tax on the investment earnings from the earning capacity award, which is not grossed up.

5. Why should the calculation of the future care award provide for a self-extinguishing sum? Why is the same not true of the earning capacity head?

(e) NON-PECUNIARY LOSS

ANDREWS v. GRAND & TOY ALTA. LTD.

[1978] 2 S.C.R. 229, 83 D.L.R. (3d) 452 (S.C.C.)

. . .

DICKSON J.: Andrews used to be a healthy young man, athletically active and socially congenial. Now he is a cripple, deprived of many of life's pleasures and subjected to pain and disability. For this, he is entitled to compensation. But the problem here is qualitatively different from that of pecuniary losses. There is no medium of exchange for happiness. There is no market for expectation of life. The monetary evaluation of non-pecuniary losses is a philosophical and policy exercise more than a legal or logical one. The award must be fair and reasonable, fairness being gauged by earlier decisions; but the award must also of necessity be arbitrary or conventional. No money can provide true restitution. Money can provide for proper care: this is the reason that I think the paramount concern of the Courts when awarding damages for personal injuries should be to assure that there will be adequate future care.

However, if the principle of the paramountcy of care is accepted, then it follows that there is more room for the consideration of other policy factors in the assessment of damages for non-pecuniary losses. In particular, this is the area where the social burden of large awards deserves considerable weight. The sheer fact is that there is no objective yardstick for translating non-pecuniary losses, such as pain and suffering and loss of amenities, into monetary terms. This area is open to widely extravagant claims. It is in this area that awards in the United States have soared to dramatically high levels in recent years. Statistically, it is the area where the danger of excessive burden of expense is greatest.

It is also the area where there is the clearest justification for moderation. As one English commentator has suggested, there are three theoretical approaches to the problem of non-pecuniary loss (A.J. Ogus, "Damages for Lost Amenities: For a Foot, a Feeling or a Function?", 35 Mod. L. Rev. 1 (1972)). The first, the "conceptual" approach, treats each faculty as a proprietary asset wth an objective value, independent of the individual's own use or enjoyment of it. This was the ancient "bot", or tariff system, which prevailed in the days of King Alfred, when a thumb was worth 30 shillings. Our law has long since thought such a solution unsubtle. The second, the "personal" approach, values the injury in terms of the loss of human happiness by the particular victim. The third, or "functional" approach, accepts the personal premise of the second, but rather than attempting to set a value on lost happiness, it attempts to assess the compensation required to provide the injured person "with reasonable solace for his misfortune." "Solace" in this sense is taken to mean physical arrangements which can make his life more endurable rather than "solace" in the sense of sympathy. To my mind, this last approach has much to commend it, as it provides a rationale as to why money is considered compensation for non-pecuniary losses such as loss of amenities, pain and suffering, and loss of expectation of life. Money is awarded because it will serve a useful function in making up for what has been lost in the only way possible, accepting that what has been lost is incapable of being replaced in any direct way. As Windeyer, J., said in *Skelton v. Collins, supra*, at p. 495:

> . . . he is, I do not doubt, entitled to compensation for what he suffers. Money may be compensation for him if having it can give him pleasure or satisfaction . . . But the money is not then a recompense for a loss of something having a money value. It is given as some consolation or solace for the distress that is the consequence of a loss on which no monetary value can be put.

If damages for non-pecuniary loss are viewed from a functional perspective, it is reasonable that large amounts should not be awarded once a person is properly provided for in terms of future care for his injuries and disabilities. The money for future care is to provide physical arrangements for assistance, equipment and facilities directly related to the injuries. Additional money to make life more endurable should then be seen as providing more general physical arrangements above and beyond those relating directly to the injuries. The result is a coordinated and interlocking basis for compensation, and a more rational justification for non-pecuniary loss compensation.

However one may view such awards in a theoretical perspective, the amounts are still largely arbitrary or conventional. As Lord Denning, M.R., said in *Ward v. James*, [1965] 1 All E.R. 563, there is a great need in this area for assessability, uniformity and predictability. In my opinion, this does not mean that the courts should not have regard to the individual situation of the victim. On the contrary, they must do so to determine what has been lost. For example, the loss of a finger would be a greater loss of amenities for an amateur pianist than for a person not engaged in such an activity. Greater compensation would be required to provide things and activities which would function to make up for this loss. But there should be guidelines for the translation into monetary terms of what has been lost. There must be an exchange rate, albeit conventional. In *Warren v. King, supra*, at p. 528 the following *dictum* of Harman, L.J., appears, which I would adopt, in respect of the assessment of non-pecuniary loss for a living plaintiff:

> It seems to me that the first element in assessing such compensation is not to add up items as loss of pleasures, of earnings, of marriage prospects, of children and so on, but to consider the matter from the other side, what can be done to alleviate the disaster to the victim, what will it cost to enable her to live as tolerably as may be in the circumstances.

Cases like the present enable the Court to establish a rough upper parameter on these awards. It is difficult to conceive of a person of his age losing more than Andrews has lost. Of course, the figures must be viewed flexibly in future cases in recognition of the inevitable differences in injuries, the situation of the victim, and changing economic conditions.

The amounts of such awards should not vary greatly from one part of the country to another. Everyone in Canada, wherever he may reside, is entitled to a more or less equal measure of compensation for similar non-pecuniary loss. Variation should be made for what a particular individual has lost in the way of amenities and enjoyment of life, and for what will function to make up for this loss, but variation should not be made merely for the Province in which he happens to live.

There has been a significant increase in the size of awards under this head in recent years. As Moir, J.A., of the Appellate Division of the Alberta Supreme Court, has warned: "To my mind, damages under the head of loss of amenities will go up and up until they are stabilized by the Supreme Court of Canada": *Hamel et al. v. Prather et al.* (1976), 66 D.L.R. (3d) 109 at p. 127, [1976] 2 W.W.R. 742 at p. 748, In my opinion, this time has come.

It is customary to set only one figure for all non-pecuniary loss, including such factors as pain and suffering, loss of amenities, and loss of expectation of life. This is a sound practice. Although these elements are analytically distinct, they overlap and merge at the edges and in practice. To suffer pain is surely to lose an amenity of a happy life at that time. To lose years of one's expectation of life is to lose all amenities for the lost period, and to cause mental pain and suffering in the contemplation of this prospect. These problems, as well as the fact that these losses have the common trait of irreplaceability, favour a composite award for all non-pecuniary losses.

There is an extensive review of authorities in the Court of Appeal judgment in this case as well as in the *Thornton* and *Teno* cases, *supra*, to which I have referred. I need not review these past authorities. What is important is the general picture. It is clear that until very recently damages for non-pecuniary losses, even from very serious injuries such as quadriplegia, were substantially below $100,000. Recently, though, the figures have increased markedly. In *Jackson v. Millar et al.* (1975), 59 D.L.R. (3d) 246, [1976] 1 S.C.R. 225, this Court affirmed a figure of $150,000 for non-pecuniary loss in an Ontario case of a paraplegic. However, this was done essentially on the principle of non-interference with awards allowed by provincial Courts of Appeal. The need for a general assessment with respect to damages for non-pecuniary loss, which is now apparent, was not as evident at that time. Even in Ontario, prior to these recent cases, general damages allocable for non-pecuniary loss, such as pain and suffering and loss of amenities, were well below $100,000.

In the present case, $150,000 was awarded at trial, but this amount was reduced to $100,000 by the Appellate Division. In *Thornton* and *Teno* $200,000 was awarded in each case, unchanged in the provincial Courts of Appeal.

I would adopt as the appropriate award in the case of a young adult quadriplegic like Andrews the amount of $100,000. Save in exceptional circumstances, this should be regarded as an upper limit of non-pecuniary loss in cases of this nature.

. . .

NOTES AND QUESTIONS

1. What is the purpose of an award for non-pecuniary loss? What are the differences among the three methods of assessing non-pecuniary loss according to the Ogus article, cited in *Andrews*? Which approach do you prefer? See Klar, "The Assessment of Damages for Non-Pecuniary Losses" (1978), 5 C.C.L.T. 262. In *Lindal v. Lindal* (1981), 129 D.L.R. (3d) 263 (S.C.C.), the court affirmed the functional approach, and elaborated on how that approach should be applied. *Lindal* also approved adjusting the $100,000 figure for inflation.

2. The Supreme Court indicated that a plaintiff can recover damages in excess of the upper limit if she can prove exceptional circumstances in which a larger award is necessary to provide solace. Nevertheless, the courts have rarely granted such awards. See *Fenn v. Peterborough*, [1981] 2 S.C.R. 613.

3. By the mid-1990s, the upper limit was approximately $250,000. See *Macdonald (Guardian ad litem of) v. Neufeld* (1993), 17 C.C.L.T. (2d) 201 (B.C. C.A.) — $238,000 non-pecuniary award; *Dube (Litigation Guardian of) v. Penlon Ltd.* (1992), 10 O.R. (3d) 190 (Gen. Div.) — $245,000 non-pecuniary award; and *ter Neuzen v. Korn* (1995), 127 D.L.R. (4th) 577 — where the Supreme Court of Canada held that a non-pecuniary award of $460,000 was inappropriate and ordered that the jury in the new trial be instructed on the upper limit of non-pecuniary awards.

However, in *Hill v. Church of Scientology of Toronto* (1995), 25 C.C.L.T. (2d) 89, the Supreme Court approved a $300,000 general damage award in addition to awards of $500,000 in aggravated and $800,000 in punitive damages. The court said that the cap on non-pecuniary awards does not apply to defamation.

4. In *Andrews*, Dickson J. stated that non-pecuniary loss "is the area where the social burden of large awards deserves considerable weight." Is the justification he provides compelling? Why should this burden fall on the victims of catastrophic personal injuries and not on those who are defamed or those who would otherwise receive punitive damages?

Assume a housewife with no intention of joining the paid workforce is badly burned, and suffers severe ongoing pain and permanent disfigurement. How would her damages be assessed under *Andrews*? Does the so-called functional approach result in an injustice in cases such as these?

5. Prior to *Andrews*, non-pecuniary losses were divided into claims for pain and suffering, loss of amenities, and loss of expectation of life. Traditionally, the award for pain and suffering was assessed on a subjective basis, in terms of the actual pain and suffering the plaintiff experienced. The loss of amenities was assessed objectively in terms of how a reasonable person in the plaintiff's position would have valued the loss of enjoyment of life. Although the courts stated that awards for loss of expectation of life were not simply conventional sums, these awards were limited to several thousand dollars. Waddams indicates that these categories governing non-pecuniary loss may no longer apply, because *Andrews* requires a "functional approach". *The Law of Damages*, 2nd ed. (1991), 3-34 to 3-36.

See *Knutson v. Farr* (1984), 30 C.C.L.T. 8 (B.C. C.A.) which clearly supports Waddams' view. *Knutson* indicated that the functional approach meant that an unconscious plaintiff was not entitled to compensation under this head. See also Mew, "Comment" (1986), 64 Can. Bar Rev. 562; and Waddams, "Compensation for Non-Pecuniary Loss: Is There a Case for Legislative Intervention?" (1985), 63 Can. Bar Rev. 734.

6. Some commentators have argued for the abolition of non-pecuniary damages. See Ontario Law Reform Commission, *Report on Motor Vehicle Accident Compensation* (1973); Woodhouse, *The Report of the National Committee of Inquiry on Compensation and Rehabilitation in Australia* (1974); Pearson, *The Report of the Royal Commission on Civil Liability and Compensation for Personal Injury* (1978); O'Connell and Simon, *Payments for Pain and Suffering: Who Wants What When and Why?* (1972); and Fleming, "Damages for Non-Material Losses", in Law Soc. of Upper Can., *Special Lectures on New Developments in the Law of Torts* (1973), 1. One argument for retaining non-pecuniary damages proceeds from what is called the "*ex ante* insurance perspective", based on the view that rational people would not insure themselves against non-pecuniary loss because money cannot compensate for such loss. See generally The Ontario Law Reform Commission, *Report on Compensation for Personal Injuries and Death* (1987), 79-114, which supports the present law.

*rights vested in estate of deceased's rights (loss)
(to protect deceased's rights*

2 kinds of actions:
→ brought by estate of the deceased (governed by statute)

3. Survival Actions and Dependants' Claims for Wrongful Death or Injury

→ relational claim (for relatives loss)

(a) SURVIVAL ACTIONS

At common law, when an individual died all outstanding or potential causes of action that could have otherwise been brought by or against the deceased were extinguished. Legislation has been enacted in England and all Canadian jurisdictions to nullify this common law rule. Although no two Canadian jurisdictions have identical legislation, the statutes allow the deceased's estate to maintain legal actions that the deceased could have otherwise brought. These statutes also allow others to bring actions against the deceased's estate that they could have otherwise brought against the deceased. The legislation permits the settling of the deceased's affairs and preserves her estate for the benefit of the deceased's beneficiaries.

Typically, the legislation excludes specified causes of action, such as defamation, malicious prosecution, false imprisonment, and adultery. Most jurisdictions also exclude certain types of damages, such as non-pecuniary and punitive damages. The following provisions of the Alberta legislation illustrate some common features of the survival statutes.

Survival of Actions Act,
R.S.A. 1980, c. S-30

DO NOT NEED TO KNOW (ont. Act. in Supp.)

2 A cause of action vested in a person who dies after January 1, 1979 survives for the benefit of his estate.

3 A cause of action existing against a person who dies after January 1, 1979 survives against his estate.

4 If a cause of action for damages suffered by reason of an act or omission would have existed against a person had that person not died at or before the time the damage was suffered, the cause of action is deemed to have existed against the person before his death.

5 If a cause of action survives under section 2, only those damages that resulted in actual financial loss to the deceased or his estate are recoverable and, without restricting the generality of the foregoing, punitive or exemplary damages or damages for loss of expectation of life, pain and suffering, physical disfigurement or loss of amenities are not recoverable.

6 If the death of a person was caused by an act or omission that gives rise to a cause of action, the damages shall be calculated without reference to a loss or gain to his estate as a result of his death, but reasonable expenses of the funeral and the disposal of the body of the deceased may be included in the damages awarded, if the expenses were, or liability for them was, incurred by the estate.

7 A cause of action that survives under this Act and a judgment or order on it or relating to the costs of it is an asset or liability, as the case may be, of the estate to which the cause of action relates.

(b) FATAL ACCIDENTS LEGISLATION

It was established in *Baker v. Bolton* (1808), 1 Camp. 493 (H.L.) that an individual has no common law cause of action for losses that she suffers as a result of the death of another person. This common law rule has been superceded by fatal accidents legislation which is designed to compensate the deceased's dependants for the losses they suffer as a result of the death. Generally, the purpose of this legislation is to put the dependants in the position they would have been in had the victim not been wrongfully killed. Most of the provincial legislation is modelled after the 1846 English legislation, commonly referred to as Lord Campbell's Act. The following Nova Scotia legislation illustrates many of the common features of the provincial statutes. We have also included the Ontario provision, which provides for far broader recovery.

Fatal Injuries Act
R.S.N.S. 1989, c. 163

NOT RESPONSIBLE FOR THIS

Liability

3 Where the death of a person has been caused by such wrongful act, neglect or default of another as would, if death had not ensued, have entitled the person injured to maintain an action and recover damages in respect thereto, in such case, the person who would have been liable if death had not ensued shall be liable to an action of damages, notwithstanding the death of the person injured, and although the death has been caused under such circumstances as amount in law to a crime.

Who may benefit

5 (1) Every action brought under this Act shall be for the benefit of the wife, husband, parent, or child of such deceased person and the jury may give such damages as they think proportioned to the injury resulting from such death to the persons respectively for whose benefit such action was brought, and the amount so recovered, after deducting the costs not recovered, if any, from the defendant, shall be divided among such persons in such shares as the jury by their verdict find and direct.

Damages defined

(2) In subsection (1), "damages" means pecuniary and non-pecuniary damages and, without restricting the generality of this definition, includes

(a) out-of-pocket expenses reasonably incurred for the benefit of the deceased;

(b) a reasonable allowance for travel expenses incurred in visiting the deceased between the time of the injury and the death;

(c) where, as a result of the injury, a person for whose benefit the action is brought provided nursing, housekeeping or other services for the deceased between the time of the injury and the death, a reasonable allowance for loss of income or the value of the services;

(d) an amount to compensate for the loss of guidance, care and companionship that a person for whose benefit the action is brought might reasonably have expected to receive from the deceased if the death had not occurred.

Assessing damage

(3) In assessing the damage in any action there shall not be taken into account any sum paid or payable on the death of the deceased, whether by way of pension or proceeds of insurance, or any future premiums payable under any contract of assurance or insurance.

Funeral expense

(4) In an action brought under this Act where funeral expenses have been incurred by the parties for whose benefit the action is brought, damages may be awarded for reasonable necessary expenses of the burial of the deceased, including transportation and things supplied and services rendered in connection therewith.

Statement of claim

6 In every action the plaintiff on the record shall set forth, in his statement of claim, or deliver therewith to the defendent [*sic*], or his solicitor, full particulars of the person or persons for and on behalf of whom such action was brought and of the nature of the claim in respect to which damages are sought to be recovered.

Apportionment by judge

9 In all cases where for any reason the compensation is not apportioned among the several persons entitled under this Act, a judge may apportion the same and dispose of the costs of the application and inquiry as he thinks just.

Limitation of action

10 Not more than one action shall lie for and in respect to the same subject-matter of complaint and every such action shall be commenced within twelve months after the death of the deceased person.

Family Law Act
R.S.O. 1990, c. F.3.

[handwritten: Responsible for knowing this act]

DEPENDANTS' CLAIM FOR DAMAGES

61. Right of dependants to sue in tort.—(1) If a person is injured or killed by the fault or neglect of another under circumstances where the person is entitled to recover damages, or would have been entitled if not killed, the spouse, *as defined in Part III (Support Obligations),* children, grandchildren, parents, grandparents, brothers and sisters of the person are entitled to recover their pecuniary loss resulting from the injury or death from the person from whom the person injured or killed is entitled to recover or would have been entitled if not killed, and to maintain an action for the purpose in a court of competent jurisdiction.

(2) *Damages in case of injury.*—The damages recoverable in a claim under subsection (1) may include.

[handwritten left margin: (list not exhaust - tive)]

    (*a*) actual expenses reasonably incurred for the benefit of the person injured or killed;

    (*b*) actual funeral expenses reasonably incurred;

    (*c*) a reasonable allowance for travel expenses actually incurred in visiting the person during his or her treatment or recovery;

    (*d*) where, as a result of the injury, the claimant provides nursing, housekeeping or other services for the person, a reasonable allowance for loss of income or the value of the services; and

    (*e*) an amount to compensate for the loss of guidance, care and companionship that the claimant might reasonably have expected to receive from the person if the injury or death had not occurred.

[handwritten left margin: pecuniary]

NOTES AND QUESTIONS

1. What is the rationale for restricting the actions and kinds of damages under the provincial survival legislation? For a discussion of this legislation see Waddams, *The Law of Damages*, 2nd ed. (1991), 12-1 to 12-12; and Cooper-Stephenson and Saunders, *Personal Injury Damages in Canada*, 2nd ed. (1996), 721-46.

2. How does the purpose of the survival legislation differ from that of the fatal accidents legislation? What parties are allowed to recover under each type of legislation? Is there a potential for double recovery because of the overlapping benefits? Generally, the actions are brought together to reduce this problem. See *Balkos v. Cook* (1990), 75 O.R. (2d) 593 (C.A.). For a discussion of how the two types of legislation might be combined see Waddams, "Damages For Wrongful Death: Has Lord Campbell's Act Outlived Its Usefulness?" (1984), 47 Mod. L. Rev. 437.

3. In what specific ways is the scope of the Ontario Family Law Act broader than that of the Nova Scotia Fatal Injuries Act? How do you suppose Nova Scotia deals with these claims in the absence of a statutory right such as that in the Ontario Act? What are the advantages of each approach?

4. Dependants' claims under the Ontario Family Law Act have generated considerable litigation and controversy. One of the interesting issues is the status of claims brought in respect of, or on behalf of, persons who acquire dependency status by subsequent birth or marriage. The authorities are reviewed in *Garland v. Rowsell* (1990), 73 O.R. (2d) 280 (Dist. Ct.). Another interesting issue is the scope of non-pecuniary damages available under s. 61(2)(*e*) [cf. s. 5(2)(*d*) in Nova Scotia, and s. 3(4) Fatal Accidents Act, R.S.M. 1987, c. F50.]. It has been held that a dependant is entitled to damages under s. 61(2)(*e*) for loss of care, guidance and companionship in cases of both death and injury. See generally *Mason v. Peters* (1982), 39 O.R. (2d) 27 (C.A.); *Wessell v. Kinsmen Club of Sault Ste. Marie Ont. Inc.* (1982), 37 O.R. (2d) 481 (H.C.); *Reidy v. McLeod* (1984), 30 C.C.L.T. 183 (Ont. H.C.); *Gervais v.*

Richard (1984), 48 O.R. (2d) 191 (H.C.); *Seede v. Camco Inc.* (1985), 50 O.R. (2d) 218 (S.C.); and *Nielsen v. Kaufmann* (1986), 54 O.R. (2d) 188 (C.A.).

5. Grief and sorrow are not recoverable under s. 61(2)(*e*). However, some other provincial statutes permit a separate award for grief, as opposed to loss of guidance, care and companionship. See, for example, Fatal Accidents Act, R.S.N.B. 1973, c. F-7, s. 3(4).

(i) *The Death of the Family Provider*

KEIZER v. HANNA

[1978] 2 S.C.R. 342, 82 D.L.R. (3d) 449 (S.C.C.)

[Mr. Keizer died as a result of the injuries he sustained in an automobile collision. The defendant admitted that the collision was due solely to his negligence.]

DICKSON J.: — I have had the advantage of reading the reasons for judgment prepared by Mr. Justice Spence and Mr. Justice de Grandpré in this appeal. There are two issues: (i) the deductibility of income tax in arriving at an award of damages; (ii) quantum. Although as a member of the Court, I shared in the decision in *Gehrmann et al. v. Lavoie* (1975), 59 D.L.R. (3d) 634, [1976] 2 S.C.R. 561, [1976] 1 W.W.R. 468, I have concluded, upon reading the reasons for judgment to which I have referred, and upon further reflection, that Mr. Justice de Grandpré is correct in law and that the impact of income tax should be taken into account in assessing a damage award under the *Fatal Accidents Act*, R.S.O. 1970, c. 164.

On point (ii), however, "quantum", I have come to a conclusion other than that arrived at by my brother de Grandpré. I would allow the appeal, and like my brother Spence, award the amount of $100,000 claimed in the statement of claim but deduct therefrom the amount of $6,500 insurance benefits already received by the appellant under the accident and death benefits provision found in Sch. E. of the deceased's insurance policy. In the result, the award of general damages would amount to $93,500.

The accident in which Mr. Keizer was killed occurred on July 16, 1973. At that date he was 33 years of age with a life expectancy of 38.55 years. He was a tool-room foreman for the Town of Renfrew, capable, conscientious, industrious and in good health. He had been married for nine years to the appellant who, at the date of his death was 27 years of age with a life expectancy of 49.60 years. Mr. and Mrs. Keizer had one child, an infant of six months.

The trial Judge projected average earnings of $15,000 for a working expectancy of 31 years. From this figure he deducted $3,200 for income tax, $1,800 for personal use, and $3,000 for personal support leaving disposable income for dependants in the amount of $7,000. The Judge made a deduction for income tax with which the Court of Appeal agreed and which, in my view, was proper. The Court of Appeal did not question the Judge's finding that the deceased would expend $1,800 for his personal use and $3,000 for his personal support. Thus, as a result, $7,000 would be available as disposable income for dependants. The evidence was that he contributed his pay cheque weekly to his family reserving only nominal sums and odd-job earnings for his own use. Having concluded that $7,000 per year would have been available to the appellant and her child each year, the Judge said [55 D.L.R. (3d) 171 at p. 180, 7 O.R. (2d) 327]:

Actuarial tables filed as ex. 1 herein at 9% and 10% compound interest show the present value of $1 to age 65 for the male as $9.9375 and $9.1381 respectively. I believe a more realistic interest rate would be the approximate amount of 6½% which would materially inflate these figures; for example, at 4% the factor is 18.66461. One must consider income tax as a reality of modern life and its depreciating impact along with the contingencies hereinbefore alluded to is reflected in my assessment. Under the provisions of the *Fatal Accidents Act* I award the plaintiff the sum of $120,000, of which sum I apportion $17,500 for the infant Mitchel Stephen.

It is difficult, if not impossible, to know what use, if any, the trial Judge made of actuarial tables to which he was referred. It would seem, however, that he proceeded on an exhausting fund basis, with a discount rate of approximately 6½%. He made an allowance in respect of the income tax which the deceased would have had to pay on his earnings, had he lived, and he further reduced the award by a contingency allowance. He referred to the contingencies which might bear on assessment, as follows [at pp. 177-8]:

(a) Possibility of remarriage;
(b) Possibility of widow's death before expiry of joint expectancy period;
(c) Possibility of deceased's dying under other circumstances prior to expiry of said joint expectancy period;
(d) Possibility of deceased husband's retiring before expiry of joint expectancy period;
(e) Acceleration of inheritance to widow — bearing in mind likelihood of increased inheritance in event death had not occurred;
(f) Possibility the infant child may not be a burden to the father or require additional benefits for the full period of his calculated working life.

On the question of prospects of remarriage, the judge adopted the apt comments of Phillimore J. in *Buckley v. John Allen & Ford (Oxford), Ltd.*, [1967] 1 All E.R. 539, including the statement that Judges should act on evidence rather than guesswork and, there being no evidence of any existing interest or attachment, concluded [at p. 179]: "I therefore accord no material significance to this prospect by way of deduction." He does not say that he is according no weight to the contingency.

As to the possibility of the early demise of either husband or wife, the Judge said:

All of the evidence indicates excellent health prospects and I rule that relatively little real significance can be attached to this contingency by way of reduction.

Again, it is not a question of refusing to consider a particular contingency. The judge considered the contingency, but decided it merited little significance. I do not think he can be faulted on this account.

With respect to the possibility of acceleration of the inheritance to the appellant, the Judge had this to say:

So far as the acceleration of her inheritance is concerned, I am readily satisfied that the same should have no reducing effect as in these circumstances. I am assured it is more than offset by the substantial loss she has suffered in future realization from this source.

Finally, the possibility that the infant child might not be a burden during his father's working life. On this point, the Judge said that he would give this fact material consideration in considering his award. These are his words:

Unquestionably, there is the probability that the child Mitchel Stephen would not have been a burden to his father for anything like the 30 years or so of his working expectancy and I give this fact material consideration in considering this award.

The quantum of the award came before the Court of Appeal for Ontario. In that Court, reference was made by Mr. Justice Arnup, for the Court, to the six contingencies to which the trial Judge referred. Mr. Justice Arnup observed that the trial Judge might have added "possibility of incapacity to earn, occasioned by industrial or other accident, or by illness." He then continued [64 D.L.R. (3d) 193 at p. 200, 10 O.R. (2d) 597]:

> Having listed these contingencies, the trial Judge decided he should make no deduction for any of them. In so doing, he erred. A contingency, in the context of damages under the *Fatal Accidents Act*, is obviously an event that may or may not happen. A defendant is entitled to have contingencies taken into account by way of reduction from the result that would be reached if every contingency turned out favourably to the dependants, although due weight must be given in each case to the probability, or otherwise, of the contingent event actually happening.

I have been unable to find in the trial judgment any statement by the trial Judge that he had decided he should not make any deduction for any of the contingencies. The evidence, as I read it, is to the contrary. It is true that the trial Judge might have considered the possibility of the deceased husband becoming unable to earn, but I do not think it can be said that failure to express himself on this point amounts to reversible error. The award of $120,000 exceeded the amount claimed of $100,000 but that does not preclude an award of $100,000.

In making a gross award of $65,000 the Court of Appeal was content with the following cryptic statement:

> In my view, the appropriate award of general damages in all of the circumstances of this case, as disclosed by the evidence, would have been $65,000.

The judgment does not assist us, or the parties, by explaining why $65,000 should be considered to be the appropriate award. From this amount the Court of Appeal deducted the $6,500 to which I have referred and directed that $10,000 be paid into Court for the infant. In the result, the widow would receive from the defendants for her support and maintenance for the next fifty years the sum of $48,500. This, plus $6,500 already received, totals $55,000.

It is, of course, true that a trial Judge must consider contingencies tending to reduce the ultimate award and give those contingencies more or less weight. It is equally true there are contingencies tending to increase the award to which a Judge must give due weight. At the end of the day the only question of importance is whether, in all the circumstances, the final award is fair and adequate. Past experience should make one realize that if there is to be error in the amount of an award it is likely to be one of inadequacy.

In my opinion, in the circumstances of this case, an award of $55,000 to the appellant can only be described as niggardly. The appellant is entitled to an award of such amount as will assure her the comforts and station in life which she would have enjoyed but for the untimely death of her husband. If one is speaking of contingencies, I think it is not unreasonable to give primary attention to the contingencies, and they are many, the occurrence of which would result in making the award, in the light of events, entirely inadequate. An assessment must be neither punitive nor influenced by sentimentality. It is largely an exercise of business judgment. The question is whether a stated amount of capital will provide, during the period in question, having regard to contingencies tending to increase or decrease the award, a monthly sum at least equal to that which might reasonably have been expected during the continued life of the deceased.

The proper method of calculating the amount of a damage award under the *Fatal Accidents Act* is similar to that used in calculating the amount of an award for loss of future earnings, or for future care, in cases of serious personal injury. In each, the Court is faced with the task of determining the present value of a lump sum which, if invested, would provided payments of the appropriate size over a given number of years in the future, extinguishing the fund in the process. This matter has been discussed in detail in the decisions of this Court in *Andrews v. Grand & Toy Alberta Ltd.; Thornton v. Board of School Trustees of School District No. 57 (Prince George)*; and *Arnold v. Teno*, which are being delivered with the decision in the present case [to be reported].

The object here is to award a sum which will replace present-day payments of $7,000 per year for a future period of 31 years, with some reduction for contingencies. The trial Judge used a discount rate of 6½% without explaining this choice except to say that it was a "more realistic" rate than 9% or 10%. As I have said in *Andrews* and *Thornton*, in my opinion the discount rate should be calculated on the basis of present rates of return on long-term investments with an allowance for the effects of future inflation. Evidence on these matters was not introduced at trial in the present case. However, the 6½% chosen by the Judge can be tested by the fact that present-day investment rates reach about 10½%, and Dr. Deutsch of the Economic Council of Canada forecasted an inflation rate of about 3½% over the long-term future. These two figures suggest that an appropriate discount rate is approximately 7%. This is only marginally different from the rate used by the trial Judge. Ignoring, for the moment, the other factors to be taken into consideration, the sum required to produce $7,000 per year for 31 years, payable monthly, discounted at 6½%, is slightly less than $95,000. The award should be reduced somewhat to account for contingencies although, as I have mentioned, this amount will probably not be large. On the other hand, in order to yield the sum required net of taxes a greater sum would obviously be called for. The resulting amount would not reach the figure of $120,000 which the trial Judge chose. The sum of $100,000, the amount claimed, can be justified, however, with reasonable allowance made for income tax impact and contingency deduction.

I would allow the appeal, set aside the judgment of the Court of Appeal and direct that the appellant recover from the defendants the sum of $93,500. Out of that sum there should be paid to Marilyn E. Keizer the sum of $78,500 and there should be paid into Court to the credit of the infant, Mitchel Stephen Keizer, the sum of $15,000, to be paid out to the said infant when he attains the age of 18 years, or upon further order of a Judge of the County Court of the County of Renfrew. The appellant is also entitled to her award of $1,600 under the provisions of the *Trustee Act*, R.S.O. 1970, c. 470, in respect of funeral expenses and the value of an automobile.

I would allow the appellant her costs at trial against both defendants and her costs in this Court and in the Court of Appeal against the defendant Buch.

[Laskin C.J.C., Martland, Ritchie, Pigeon and Beetz JJ. concurred. Spence J.

dissented in part, holding that income tax should not be taken into account in calculating the value of the deceased's support. De Grandpré J., with whom Judson J. agreed, dissented in part, holding that the Supreme Court of Canada ought not to interfere unless it was convinced the Court of Appeal had erred in principle.]

NOTES AND QUESTIONS

1. What is the basic principle which Dickson J. states should govern the appellant's claim?

2. What is the purpose of reducing the award by the amounts that the deceased would have spent for his own personal use and support? Do these deductions violate the basic principle identified above?

3. What is the "joint expectancy" period and why is it used in fatal accident cases? Is the possibility of the widow's death before the expiry of that period a relevant contingency?

4. What rationale underlies the other contingency deductions in the case? Do you agree with them? Are there other contingencies, positive or negative, which the court should have considered?

5. What adjustment is made in *Keizer* to reflect the income tax the deceased would have paid? Is it appropriate to make such a deduction here, but not in the personal injury cases? See *Lewis v. Todd* (1980), 115 D.L.R. (3d) 257 (S.C.C.). Note that awards for pecuniary loss in fatal accident cases are now "grossed up" for the same purpose and in the same manner as in the personal injury cases. See generally *O'Hara v. Belanger*, [1990] 1 W.W.R. 214 (Alta. Q.B.); *Oleschak Estate v. Wilganowski* (1991), 70 Man. R. (2d) 149 (C.A.); Feldthusen and McNair, "General Damages in Personal Injury Suits: The Supreme Court's Trilogy" (1978), 28 U. of T. L.J. 381 at 401-403; and Rea, "Inflation, Taxation and Damage Assessment" (1980), 58 Can. Bar Rev. 280.

6. Why is evidence about the deceased's former prospects so important in a fatal accident case? What evidence would you adduce on behalf of a dependant on this issue?

7. It is impossible to provide a typical example of a fatal accidents case because quantification depends heavily on the specific attributes of the deceased and the relevant relationships. For a comprehensive review of the case law, see Klar *et al.*, *Damages and Remedies in Tort* (1995), 27-122.28 to 27-146.

(ii) *The Death of a Dependant Spouse and Child*

ALAFFE v. KENNEDY

(1973), 40 D.L.R. (3d) 429 (N.S. T.D.)

[The case arose as a result of a motor vehicle accident in which the plaintiff's wife and four-month-old son were killed. The defendants admitted liability.]

GILLIS J.: —

. . .

While I express my regret and shock at the terrible circumstances that gave rise to the action I am bound to find that the prospect of pecuniary benefit or advantage to flow from the son had he lived, to the father, is at best a speculative possibility. There is nothing, in the evidence, to indicate the probability of pecuniary benefit or advantage, giving rise to disappointment by his death. This part of the plaintiff's claim must be dismissed. Unfortunately, in the case of a baby in arms it appears impossible to demonstrate reasonable expectation of pecuniary benefit.

Finally, I will make assessment of the damages resulting from the death of Lorna Isabel Alaffe.

The *Fatal Injuries Act* provides:

4(1) Every action brought under this Act shall be for the benefit of the wife, husband, parent, or child of such deceased person; and the jury may give such damages as they think proportioned to the injury resulting from such death to the persons respectively for whose benefit such action was brought; and the amount so recovered, after deducting the costs not recovered (if any) from the defendant, shall be divided among such persons, in such shares as the jury by their verdict find and direct.

(2) In assessing the damage in any action there shall not be taken into account any sum paid or payable on the death of the deceased, whether by way of pension or proceeds of insurance, or any future premiums payable under any contract of assurance or insurance.

The measure of damages under the Act is the net pecuniary loss suffered as a result of the death by the claimant entitled thereto. It is the amount of the pecuniary benefit which it is reasonably probable the defendants would have received if the deceased had remained alive.

That general statement brings me to some of the facts to be considered. Lorna Isabel Alaffe is described as, and I accept that she was, in excellent health, a cheerful, ambitious, intelligent girl of a happy nature devoted to her husband and child. It is said that she planned to work at her profession and also looked forward to having a family. By virtue of her education, she was entitled to but had not applied for a T.C.5 teacher's licence with which, had she worked full time in the year of her death, she would have earned $7,225 per annum. There would be increments in succeeding years. It is obvious and I find from the facts that in the school year 1971-72 she did not plan to teach full time. Whether she would in the future, and whether her husband would have gained pecuniary benefit or advantage therefrom, apart from the relief from supporting her, in whole or in part, that he would have had, in the absence of plans or experience shown by the evidence, is a matter of speculative possibility only, in my opinion. While it is likely that she would at some time become a full-time school-teacher, so many contingencies of life are possible of intervention I find it impossible to make the finding of that probability. I do not do so.

She had made some inquiries about substitute teaching and was placed on a list of substitutes kept by one school board. If she had worked as such, which I find was probable in all of the circumstances, for 1971-72 she would have earned a daily rate for each day at work of $7,225 divided by 195, less some deductions. I accept that she would probably accept employment as a substitute teacher, extent unknown, if so called upon, and her husband would have gained some pecuniary benefit or advantage therefrom. I am, however, unable to ascribe any periodic or total sum to this probable benefit. I take it into consideration, however.

However, there is more to be considered favourably to the plaintiff's claim. In *St. Lawrence & Ottawa R. Co. v. Lett* (1885), 11 S.C.R. 422, where by the death of the wife the husband suffered no income or other pecuniary loss, but lost the household services and management given by the wife to himself and their children, Ritchie, C.J., for the majority, at p. 426, said:

I cannot think the injury contemplated by the legislature ought to be confined to a pecuniary interest in a sense so limited as only to embrace loss of money or property, but that, as in the case of a husband in reference to the loss of a wife, so, in the case of children, the loss of a mother may involve many things which may be regarded as of a pecuniary character.

and again at p. 433:

> I think the term injury in the statute means substantial injury as opposed to mere senti-
> mental, and I cannot bring my mind to the conclusion that a husband or infant children may
> not, in the loss of a wife or mother, and did not in this case by such a loss, sustain a substan-
> tial injury and one for which it was the intention of the legislature to indemnify the husband
> and children. I am free to admit that the injury must not be sentimental or the damages a mere
> solatium, but must be capable of a pecuniary estimate; but I cannot think it must necessarily
> be a loss of so many dollars and cents capable of calculation. The injury must be substantial;
> the loss, a loss of a substantial pecuniary benefit, and the damages are not to be given to soothe
> the feelings of the husband or child, but are to be given for the substantial injury. It may be
> impossible to reduce such an injury to an exact pecuniary amount. In estimating the pecuniary
> value of such an injury courts and juries, will, no doubt, be governed by a consideration of the
> relative positions of the parties, such as the relative positions of husband and wife, the ages of
> the children, and the duties discharged by the mother, and in the consideration of all the sur-
> rounding circumstances will give such damages as will afford a reasonable pecuniary compen-
> sation for the substantial injury sustained. No doubt this rule may be somewhat loose and indefi-
> nite, but the rule as to many injuries for which the law gives compensation is not less so.

That the foregoing is the law of Canada today on the question under consideration is confirmed by *Vana v. Tosta et al.* (1968), 66 D.L.R. (2d) 97, [1968] S.C.R.
71: see opinions of Ritchie, J., and Spence, J., particularly the latter, at p. 115.

. . .

The facts for consideration, in the case at bar, are the respective ages of the
husband and wife and the life expectancies of 48.02 and 51.56 years; that there
are no surviving infant children and no household to maintain, no adjustment of
housekeeping arrangements at substantial cost; the deceased's qualifications and
prospects in her profession as already set forth; that the plaintiff, Dwight Alaffe,
is in permanent employment at a satisfactory salary and able to keep himself without
assistance; the possibility of this plaintiff's remarriage. In consideration of the
evidence heard and my observations I find that while this is not yet a prospect,
and I do accept that he has withdrawn from social contacts since the wife's death,
I must find that he is an attractive, intelligent, pleasant young man, from all of
which I accept that there is a good possibility of remarriage.

I find that he has suffered pecuniary loss by the loss of the housekeeping,
management and other services of the wife. I assess the pecuniary loss at $10,000.

From there I refer to the opinions in the House of Lords in *Davies et al. v.
Powell Duffryn Associated Collieries, Ltd.*, [1942] 1 All E.R. 657, [1942] A.C. 601.
There Lord Russell of Killowen said [at p. 658]:

> The general rule which has always prevailed in regard to the assessment of damages under the
> Fatal Accidents Act is well-settled, viz., that any benefit accruing to a dependant by reason of
> the relevant death must be taken into account. Under those Acts, the balance of loss and gain
> to a dependant by the death must be ascertained, the position of each dependant being con-
> sidered separately. It is conceded, and rightly conceded, that the general rule must apply, unless
> some statutory exception to the rule prevents its application.

and Lord Macmillan said [at p. 660]:

> It was common ground that, except where there is express statutory direction to the con-
> trary, the damages to be awarded to a dependant of a deceased person under the Fatal Acci-
> dents Acts must take into account any pecuniary benefit accruing to that dependant in consequence
> of the death of the deceased. It is the net loss on balance which constitutes the measure of damages.

Upon the evidence, I must deduct from the pecuniary loss of the plaintiff, Dwight Alaffe, hereinbefore established, the sum of $2,498.76, being the next result of assets to the value of $3,335.76 which flowed to this plaintiff from the estate of the deceased less the funeral expenses.

I round the figures and assess the damages suffered by the plaintiff, Dwight Alaffe, resulting from the death of his wife, Lorna Isabel Alaffe, at the sum of $7,500.

. . .

NOTES AND QUESTIONS

1. Do you agree that "in the case of a baby in arms it appears impossible to demonstrate reasonable expectation of pecuniary benefit"? Is there any way the plaintiff's lawyer could overcome this difficulty? In cases of this sort, what kind of evidence would you present on behalf of the parent of a deceased child? See Sutherland, "Predicting a Child's Future Wage Loss" (1984), 42 The Advocate 169; and Bruce, "Measure of Damages for the Wrongful Death of a Child" (1987), 66 Can. Bar Rev. 344.

2. In *Mason v. Peters* (1980), 30 O.R. (2d) 409 (H.C.), aff'd. (1982), 39 O.R. (2d) 27 (C.A.), the trial judge awarded the unusually large sum of $45,000 to the disabled, single mother for the death of her 11-year-old son. This exceptional award was the result of the unusually close bond between the mother and her son, and the probability that he would have provided her with emotional and financial support throughout her life.

3. Should the damages awarded for the death of a child be reduced to take into account the parents' expenses in rearing the child? In *Mason v. Peters, supra*, Robins J.A. noted that, save in rare circumstances, the cost of raising and educating children greatly exceeds the pecuniary benefits that they provide to their parents. However, in *Lai v. Gill*, [1980] 1 S.C.R. 431, the court accepted that Chinese traditions encouraging the supporting of one's parents justified a pecuniary award of $25,000 for the parents of a deceased 14-year-old girl. Similar reasoning led to a pecuniary award of $180,000 in *Lian v. Money*, [1994] 8 W.W.R. 463 (B.C. S.C.). However, this award was reversed on appeal, on the grounds that the trial judge failed to consider the contribution that the deceased's older sister would make to the parents' welfare. See [1996] 4 W.W.R. 263 (B.C. C.A.).

4. What factors did the court consider in assessing the pecuniary loss consequent upon the death of Mrs. Alaffe? Do the courts accurately assess the value of the household services performed by spouses who do not work in the labour market? What evidence would you have adduced on behalf of Mr. Alaffe?

In *Nielsen v. Kaufmann* (1984), 28 C.C.L.T. 54 (Ont. H.C.), the value of the deceased's household services was valued in "cold commercial terms" at $8,840 a year. This amount was reduced significantly on appeal, (1986), 54 O.R. (2d) 188 (C.A.). See also *Frawley v. Asselstine* (1990), 73 O.R. (2d) 525 (H.C.); and *Skelding (Guardian ad litem of) v. Skelding*, [1994] 9 W.W.R. 538 (B.C. C.A.), leave to appeal ref'd. [1995] 3 W.W.R. lxiv (note) (S.C.C.). Many people believe that the courts grossly undervalued these services in the past. See Yale, "The Valuation of Household Services in Wrongful Death Actions" (1984), 34 U. of T.L.J. 283; Quah, "Compensation for Loss of Household Services" (1986), 24 Osgoode Hall L.J. 467; and Cooper-Stephenson and Saunders, *Personal Injury Damages in Canada*, 2nd ed. (1996), 319-22.

5. Do you agree that the amount which Mr. Alaffe received from his wife's estate should be deducted from the sum which the court would otherwise have awarded? Does it seem strange that the death of both his wife and child resulted in Mr. Alaffe's damages being reduced below what they would have been had only his wife been killed?

6. How would you assess the damages for dependant children if both parents were killed by a negligent tortfeasor? See *Clement v. Leslies Storage Ltd.* (1979), 97 D.L.R. (3d) 667 (Man. C.A.); *McDermott v. Ramadanovic Estate* (1988), 44 C.C.L.T. 249 (B.C. S.C.); and *Coe Estate v. Tennant* (1990), 46 B.C.L.R. (2d) 62 (C.A.).

7. Damage awards under fatal accidents legislation have generally been limited to pecuniary losses and have excluded claims for grief, mental anguish or solace. See *Vana v. Tosta*, [1968] S.C.R. 71; and *Vale v. R. J. Yohn Const. Co.* (1970), 12 D.L.R. (3d) 465 (Ont. C.A.). However, some legislation specifically allows awards for grief and anguish. For example, the Fatal Accidents Act, R.S.A. 1980,

c. F-5, s. 8(2) allows a claim for "grief and loss of guidance, care and companionship", up to a maximum of $40,000 to a parent or spouse of the deceased and up to $25,000 to a child. The New Brunswick Fatal Accidents Act allows recovery for grief suffered by the parents of a deceased minor. See R.S.N.B. 1973, c. F-7, s. 3(4), (5); and *Nightingale v. Mazerall* (1991), 9 C.C.L.T. (2d) 186 (N.B. C.A.).

8. It is impossible to provide a typical example of a dependant's fatal accident case because quantification depends heavily on the specific attributes of the deceased and the relevant relationships. For a comprehensive review of the case law, see Klar *et al., Damages and Remedies in Tort* (1995), 27-122.28 to 27-146.

4. Damages for Property Loss

The general principles governing the assessment of compensatory damages in personal injury cases apply to claims for damage to, or destruction of, property. For analytical purposes, we have divided our discussion of damages for property loss into three issues: the assessment of the damages to the property itself; the assessment of the economic losses consequent on the damage to the property; and the plaintiff's obligation to mitigate.

(a) THE ASSESSMENT OF THE DAMAGES TO THE PROPERTY ITSELF

As Fleming has stated, "whether the property be damaged or destroyed, the plaintiff is in the first instance entitled to restitution for the loss of its value to him." *The Law of Torts*, 8th ed. (1992), at 250. This principle is often difficult to apply because there are several different ways of assessing the loss in value, including the cost of repair, the cost of replacement and the decrease in the value of the property. The method chosen for assessing the damage may well affect the size of the award.

In most cases of damage to chattels, the cost of repair is the most appropriate measure of damages. However, if a replacement can be readily obtained for less than the cost of repair, then the replacement cost will be awarded. Unless the chattel is unique, the plaintiff will usually be awarded only the decrease in the value of the chattel, if this amount is less than the cost of repair and the cost of replacement. The plaintiff will also be awarded the decrease in the value of the damaged chattel in cases in which it is impossible to adequately repair or replace the object.

In most cases involving damage to real property, the plaintiff will be awarded the lesser of the cost of repair or replacement. As in the case of chattels, the plaintiff will usually be awarded the decrease in the value of the property if this is less than the cost of repair or replacement. However, if the plaintiff owns, possesses and uses the property, the court may award the cost of repair or replacement even if this exceeds the decrease in the value of the property. The plaintiff may also be entitled to the cost of repair or rebuilding on the existing site if the location is essential to her ongoing business. If the defendant's negligent destruction of a building does not decrease the value of the property to the plaintiff, the court will not award damages. This situation would arise if the plaintiff had decided to demolish the building before the incident occurred.

It is not settled whether the defendant's liability should be reduced if the repaired or replaced chattel or property is more valuable than the original. To deny the deduction would place the plaintiff in a better position than she would have been in had the tort not been committed. However, to allow the deduction in effect would force the plaintiff to pay for the unplanned upgrading of her chattel or property. Apparently, the courts will usually allow for a betterment deduction if it is established that the new chattel or property would be worth more to the plaintiff than the original.

(b) THE ASSESSMENT OF THE ECONOMIC LOSSES CONSEQUENT ON THE DAMAGE TO THE PROPERTY

Particularly in the case of business assets, the plaintiff will often suffer economic losses consequent on the damage to her property. The principles governing the recovery of consequential economic loss are basically the same as in personal injury and property loss cases. However, the House of Lords indicated in *Dredger Liesbosch v. S.S. Edison (Owners)*, [1933] A.C. 448 that these principles should be applied more strictly in claims for property loss. In this case, the defendants negligently destroyed the plaintiffs' vessel, which could have been replaced quickly at a reasonable price if the plaintiffs had possessed the necessary funds. Unfortunately, the plaintiffs were in financial difficulties and were forced to incur far greater costs in replacing their vessel. The defendants were absolved of liability for this additional economic loss which was attributable to the plaintiffs' impecuniosity. Although *Liesbosch* has not been directly overruled, it has been frequently criticized and distinguished. See, for example, *Rollinson v. R.* (1994), 20 C.C.L.T. (2d) 92 (Fed. T.D.).

(c) THE PLAINTIFF'S OBLIGATION TO MITIGATE

It is generally accepted that the principles of mitigation are applied more rigorously in claims for property loss than in claims for personal injury. In property loss cases, the courts appear to demand that the plaintiff act reasonably in a business sense. As in so many other areas of damages, the principle is relatively straightforward, but is often difficult to apply in specific cases. For example, it may be reasonable to purchase a replacement machine at an inflated price, if waiting for a damaged chattel to be repaired would generate even greater consequential economic losses.

NOTES AND QUESTIONS

1. In *Darbishire v. Warren*, [1963] 3 All E.R. 310 (C.A.), the defendant negligently damaged the plaintiff's well-maintained used car. Although the car had a market value of only £85, the plaintiff spent £192 repairing it because he felt he could not get a reliable replacement vehicle for less than the cost of repair. The Court of Appeal limited the plaintiff's award to the market value. Harman L.J. stated at 314: "this was not an irreplaceable article, and, therefore, as the cost of repairs greatly exceeded the value, the car should be treated as a constructive total loss and the measure of damages is its value." Pearson L.J. also indicated that the plaintiff had not acted reasonably in mitigating his loss, because he had not made an effort to find a reliable replacement. Although this case is consistent with the general principles, is the result fair to the plaintiff? How much trouble should a plaintiff be put to in mitigating her losses? This case illustrates the problem of assessing damages for certain

kinds of property. See also *Pac. Blasting Ltd. v. D.J. Byrne Const. Ltd.*, [1977] 2 W.W.R. 505 (B.C. S.C.); and *Chappell v. Baratti* (1984), 30 C.C.L.T. 137 (Ont. S.C.).

2. In *N.B. Telephone Co. v. Wright* (1982), 140 D.L.R. (3d) 188 (N.B. Q.B.), the plaintiff was able to replace the vehicle damaged by the defendant with one of its other vehicles which it was not using. Nevertheless, the plaintiff was able to recover the amount it would have cost to rent a replacement. Although this decision is generally accepted as correct, is the result fair to the defendant? Is it consistent with the basic principles of compensatory damages? For other discussions of damages for loss of use see *Pac. Elevators Ltd. v. C.P.R. Co.* (1973), 41 D.L.R. (3d) 608 (S.C.C.); *Municipal Spraying & Contracting Ltd. v. J. Harris & Sons. Ltd.* (1979), 35 N.S.R. (2d) 237 (S.C.); *Hefferman v. Elizabeth Irving Service Centre* (1980), 29 Nfld. & P.E.I.R. 470 (Nfld. T.D.); and *Blair's Plumbing & Heating Ltd. v. McGraw* (1981), 35 N.B.R. (2d) 501 (Q.B.).

3. In *Harbutt's "Plasticine" v. Wayne Tank & Pump Co.*, [1970] 1 All E.R. 225 (C.A.), the plaintiffs could not repair their old premises, and they built a new factory. The issue was whether the plaintiffs were entitled to the cost of replacement even though it exceeded the decrease in the value of the old building. Lord Denning stated at p. 236:

> The destruction of a building is different from the destruction of a chattel. If a secondhand car is destroyed, the owner only gets its value, because he can go into the market and get another secondhand car to replace it. He cannot charge the other party with the cost of replacing it with a new car. But, when this mill was destroyed the plaintiffs had no choice. They were bound to replace it as soon as they could, not only to keep their business going, but also to mitigate the loss of profit (for which they would be able to charge the defendants). They replaced it in the only possible way, without adding any extras. I think they should be allowed the cost of replacement. True it is they got new for old, but I do not think the wrongdoer can diminish the claim on that account. If they had added extra accommodation or made extra improvements, they would have to give credit. But that is not this case.

Did the plaintiffs have to rebuild to mitigate their loss? Could they have mitigated by choosing another business investment? Does the fact that they did rebuild indicate that they thought a new factory was a wise business investment? If so, should the defendant have to bear the full cost? See also *James Street Hardware and Furniture Co. v. Spizziri* (1987), 62 O.R. (2d) 385 (C.A.); and *Nan v. Black Pine Manufacturing Ltd.*, [1991] 5 W.W.R. 172 (B.C. C.A.).

4. In *Waterloo Warehousing & Storage Ltd. v. Swenco Mfg. Ltd.* (1975), 58 D.L.R. (3d) 180 (Ont. H.C.), the plaintiff's building was destroyed in a fire caused by the defendant's negligence. Prior to the fire, the plaintiff had entered into a contract to sell the land and building. Since the purchaser intended to demolish the building and construct an apartment building in its place, the purchase price remained the same after the fire. The Court denied the plaintiff's claim for the amount which it would have cost to replace the building.

In *Jens v. Mannix Co. Ltd.* (1978), 89 D.L.R. (3d) 351 (B.C. S.C.), a house was effectively destroyed because of the defendant's negligence. The property had recently been re-zoned for commercial use, resulting in an increase in its resale value whether or not there were buildings on the property. However, because the plaintiff reasonably planned to keep living there, and had received planning approval to rebuild, he was entitled to recover the cost of replacing his home.

Can you reconcile *Jens* and *Darbishire v. Warren*, [1963] 3 All E.R. 310 (C.A.) which is referred to in note 1? Can you reconcile *Jens* and *Waterloo Warehousing & Storage Ltd.*?

5. For a comprehensive review of the issues raised by *Dredger Liesbosch*, see Phillips, "Compensation For Losses Flowing from an Injured Party's Impecuniosity" (1982), 20 Osgoode Hall L.J. 18; and Wexler, "The Impecunious Plaintiff: Liesbosch Reconsidered" (1987), 66 Can. Bar Rev. 129. *Geld v. Dehavilland Aircraft of Can. Ltd.*, [1983] 6 W.W.R. 229 (B.C. S.C.), *A.G. Ont. v. Fatehi* (1984), 31 C.C.L.T. 1 (S.C.C.); and *Armak Chemicals Ltd. v. Canadian National Railway Co.* (1991), 3 O.R. (3d) 1 (C.A.), leave to appeal ref'd. (1992), 6 O.R. (3d) xiii (note) (S.C.C.), also raise interesting issues relating to economic loss consequent upon damage to property.

6. The principles of contributory negligence and mitigation of loss overlap in some cases. For example, in *Indust. Teletype Electronics Corp. v. Montreal* (1976), 10 N.R. 517 (S.C.C.), the plaintiff considered his flood-damaged inventory to be a total loss and claimed damages for the full replacement cost. The plaintiff offered all of the inventory to the defendant, who declined to take it. Beetz J. stated at 524:

> Finally, according to a defence expert the damages could have been substantially reduced and some new parts still considered as such after the flood, had a cleaning and drying opera-

tion that was simple and inexpensive been diligently carried out. The parts exposed to water remained at the risk of appellants who continued to have custody and ownership of them. If this expert's opinion is accurate, surely the offer made by appellants cannot exempt them from mitigating their damages, as would a reasonable man. Indeed, to allow a plaintiff to rid himself of this obligation by means of such an offer, and allow him the replacement value of the merchandise, would be equivalent to treating as an insurer the perpetrator of the damage. I do not believe that this is the state of our law. This aspect of the case is obviously such as to affect the quantum of the damages, but it goes beyond the question of quantum; it concerns the causal relationship between the fault of the city and the loss sustained by appellants. Thus, the claim of the latter could be reduced to the extent that their own negligence after the flood contributed to increase the damage.

Do you agree with Beetz J. that the plaintiff's conduct should be considered as an issue of contributory negligence, rather than as a question of mitigation? Does it make any difference which approach is adopted? For other illustrations of mitigation of loss see *Can. Western Natural Gas Co. v. Pathfinders Surveys Ltd.* (1980), 21 A.R. 459 (C.A.); *John Maryon Int. Ltd. v. N.B. Telephone Co.* (1982), 24 C.C.L.T. 146 (N.B. C.A.); *Galantiuk v. Regina*, [1984] 6 W.W.R. 262 (Sask. Q.B.); and *Miller Dredging Ltd. v. Dorothy Mackenzie (The)* (1994), 119 D.L.R. (4th) 63 (B.C. C.A.).

5. Collateral Benefits

To this point it has been assumed that the defendant is the plaintiff's sole source of compensation. However, in most cases the plaintiff will also receive compensation in various forms from collateral sources, such as government health insurance, employment benefits or private insurance. There are basically two issues posed by collateral benefits.

First, should the defendant's liability be reduced to reflect the benefit that the plaintiff has received from a collateral source? In the absence of a statutory or contractual provision to the contrary, certain collateral benefits are not taken into account to reduce the defendant's liability. These include: private insurance benefits; charitable, private or benevolent gifts; pension benefits; and public welfare and unemployment benefits. Other collateral benefits, such as those provided by provincial health insurance, workers' compensation and automobile insurance are now largely governed by statute.

As *Cunningham v. Wheeler*, [1994] 1 S.C.R. 359 illustrates, the courts have been divided on the issue of whether the defendant's liability should be reduced by the employment benefits that a disabled or injured employee has received. In *Ratych v. Bloomer* (1990), 3 C.C.L.T. (2d) 1, the majority of the Supreme Court of Canada stated that as a general rule, wage and sick benefits should be taken into account to reduce the defendant's liability. However, if the employee can prove that she made some form of payment directly or indirectly for the benefit, then, analogous to private insurance, a strong argument can be made that the benefit should not be deducted from the award.

Second, if the defendant cannot reduce her liability to reflect the collateral benefit, can the plaintiff keep both the damages and the collateral benefit, or must the plaintiff return the excess to the collateral source? Unless provided otherwise by statute or contract, the plaintiff is entitled to keep both the damage award and the collateral benefit.

(a) THE COLLATERAL SOURCE RULE

CUNNINGHAM v. WHEELER
[1994] 1 S.C.R. 359, 20 C.C.L.T. (2d) 1

CORY J. (Sopinka, Iacobucci and Major JJ. concurring): — On November 14, FACTS 1988, the plaintiff Bradwell Cunningham was injured when he was struck by a car while he was walking across a road. At the time he was 46 years old and had been employed by B.C. Rail, for about 25 years. He was in hospital for 9 days and off work for almost 20 weeks. During this period, pursuant to the provisions of a collective bargaining agreement, he collected disability benefits which amounted to $5,327.15.

No deductions were made from his pay for the disability benefits. However, there was evidence accepted by the trial judge which demonstrated that collateral benefits formed an important aspect of the negotiations between the company and its various unions. A union representative and the company vice-president of human resources explained that if the indemnity coverage was increased, there would be a proportionate decrease in either the hourly wages or the other collateral benefits paid to the employees. Put another way, it was said that under the collective bargaining agreement the employees were entitled to receive an hourly wage package. That package was made up of an hourly rate of pay together with the collateral benefits. If the disability benefits were to be abandoned, then the hourly wage rate would be proportionately higher. The company held the funds for the disability payments and turned them over to the Aetna Group of Canada for management. Mr. Cunningham was not required to repay the weekly disability benefits he recovered from the defendants either to B.C. Rail or to Aetna Group Canada.

. . .

Should the Insurance Exception Apply to the Situation Where Disability Benefits Are Obtained Not Privately But Pursuant to a Collective Bargaining Agreement

The Court of Appeal refused to exempt the disability payments received by the plaintiff because they were obtained as a result of a collective bargaining agreement, rather than by way of a direct deduction from his pay. That, I think, is too narrow an exception. They were bargained for and obtained as a result of a reduction in the hourly rate of pay. These benefits were therefore obtained and paid for by the plaintiff just as much as if he had bought and privately paid for a policy of disability insurance.

The scheme in this case can qualify as an insurance exception on the basis of the reasons of the majority in *Ratych v. Bloomer*, supra. In that case, McLachlin J. writing for the majority specifically limited her comments to benefits which were not in the nature of insurance or gratuitous payments in these words (at p. 983):

> These comments should not be taken as extending to types of collateral benefits other than lost earnings, such as insurance paid for by the plaintiff and gratuitous payments made by third parties.

To say that the exception applies only to private insurance, where actual premiums are paid to the insurance company, would create barriers that are unfair and artificial. It would mean that top management and professionals who could well afford to purchase their own insurance would have the benefit of the insurance exception, while those who made the same provision and made relatively greater financial sacrifices to provide for the disability payments through their collective bargaining agreement would be denied the benefits of the insurance exception. This would be manifestly unfair. There is no basis for such a socially regressive distinction.

Union representation and collective bargaining are recognized as a means for working people to protect their interests. The benefits for which employees have bargained in good faith should not be sacrificed simply because the mode of payment for the disability benefit is different from that in private insurance contracts. Where evidence is adduced that an employee-plaintiff has paid in some manner for his or her benefits under a collective agreement or contract of employment, the insurance exception should apply. It would be unjust to deprive employees of the benefits which, through prudence and thrift, they have provided for themselves.

On the facts of *Ratych v. Bloomer* McLachlin J. found that it could not be established that the plaintiff in that case had paid for the benefits at issue, thus making them in the nature of private insurance. However, she held that if there were evidence that the plaintiff had paid for the benefits, they might not be deductible. At p. 972, she stated:

> I accept that if an employee can establish that he or she has suffered a loss in exchange for obtaining wages during the time he or she could not work, the employee should be compensated for that loss. Thus in *Lavigne v. Doucet* the New Brunswick Court of Appeal quite rightly allowed damages for loss of accumulated sick benefits. I also accept that if an employee can establish that he or she directly paid for a policy in the nature of insurance against unemployment, equivalent to a private insurance, he or she may be able to recover the benefits of that policy, although I would leave resolution of this question for another case.

These are two different exceptions. The first has nothing to do with the insurance exception, but covers a situation where although the employee continues to receive a salary while off work, he or she has to give up something else to receive it. An example of such a loss, provided by McLachlin J., is sick leave. The employee continues to receive wages, but gives up sick days, which he or she could have used at some other time. In such a situation the insurance exception does not arise, because there is in fact no double compensation problem. The employee who uses up his sick leave to get wages while he or she is off work loses the sick benefits, and so should be compensated for them. Or alternatively, the employee could decide not to use his or her sick days, and not get paid. There is also a loss in such a case.

The second exception McLachlin J. describes is an application of the insurance exception. However, she held that proof was required that the employee had paid for the benefit in some way to make it akin to private insurance.

McLachlin J., although recognizing the rule for personal insurance, questioned whether, aside from the evidentiary requirement, there was some substantive reason for there to be deductibility in cases where the benefits arise out of a contract of employment. At pp. 973-74 she wrote:

> The foregoing comments rest primarily on evidentiary considerations. Approaching the problem from a substantive point of view, it may be that there is a valid distinction between

cases where a person has prudently obtained and paid for personal insurance and cases where the benefits flow from the employer/employee relationship. The law has long recognized that in the first situation an exception should be made to the usual rule against double recovery. The existence of such an exception does not mean it should be extended to situations where personal prudence and deprivation are not demonstrated. In the latter case there is little to be weighed in the balance against the general policy of the law against double compensation.

The substantive concern is, I think, inextricably linked with the evidentiary requirement. Once the evidentiary requirement is met, the substantive concern for personal prudence and deprivation will also be satisfied. If the plaintiff can show that he or she has paid for the benefits in the nature of insurance against unemployment akin to private insurance, that same proof will also demonstrate personal prudence and deprivation. Indeed such a deprivation for an employee will often be proportionately very much higher than that of the executive or professional person acquiring personal insurance.

In my view *Ratych v. Bloomer*, supra, simply placed an evidentiary burden upon plaintiffs to establish that they had paid for the provision of disability benefits. I think the manner of payment may be found, for example, in evidence pertaining to the provisions of a collective bargaining agreement just as clearly as in a direct payroll deduction.

Further, the presence or absence of a third party carrier for the insurance will not affect the non-deductibility of the benefits from the wage claim. A requirement of a third-party carrier as a necessary condition for non-deductibility was considered, and in my view properly rejected, by the House of Lords in *Parry v. Cleaver*. At p. 558, Lord Reid asks and answers this question:

Then I ask — why should it make any difference that he insured by arrangement with his employer rather than with an insurance company? In the course of the argument the distinction came down to be as narrow as this: if the employer says nothing or merely advises the man to insure and he does so, then the insurance money will not be deductible; but if the employer makes it a term of the contract of employment that he shall insure himself and he does so, then the insurance money will be deductible. There must be something wrong with an argument that drives us to so unreasonable a conclusion.

It is often more economical for large corporations to self-insure than to purchase insurance from a third party carrier. Risk can be spread among the employees, who are the policy-holders of the self-insurance. The law should not discourage the efficiencies of self-insurance within large corporations or government agencies.

What Proof is Required To Establish Payment for the Disability Benefits by the Plaintiff? In Other Words, What Proof is Necessary To Establish the Insurance Policy Nature of the Disability Benefits?

In *Ratych v. Bloomer*, there was no evidence put forward that the plaintiff had paid for the disability benefits. What type of proof will be required to show that the benefits are in the nature of insurance? It is my opinion that what is required by the *Ratych* decision is that there be evidence adduced by some type of consideration given up by the employee in return for the benefit. The method or means of payment of the consideration is not determinative. Evidence of a contribution to the plan by the employee, whether paid for directly or by a reduced hourly wage reflected in a collective bargaining agreement, will be sufficient.

Generally speaking, any of the following examples, by no means an exhaustive list, provide the sort of evidence that could well be sufficient to establish that the employee paid for the benefit:

(1) Evidence that there were trade-offs in the collective bargaining process, which demonstrate that the employee has foregone higher wages or other benefits in return for the disability benefits. In such a case, the employee has paid for the benefits through wages foregone.

(2) Evidence of some money foregone by the employee in return for the benefits. For example, if the employees gave up the return of a percentage of their Unemployment Insurance Plan premiums in return for the benefits.

(3) Evidence of a direct contribution by the employee, in a form such as payroll deductions, in return for the benefits. Such a contribution need not be 100 percent of the premium.

(4) Evidence of payments by the employer for the benefits made on behalf of the employee which shows that those payments were part of the employee's wages, and thus the employee provided work for the employer in order to have the premium paid. For example, if the employer's contribution is listed on the employee's pay slip or statement of benefits, it can reasonably be inferred that the contribution is part of the employee's wage package.

The application of the insurance exception to benefits received under a contract of employment should not be limited to cases where the plaintiff is a member of a union and bargains collectively. Benefits received under the employment contracts of non-unionized employees will also be non-deductible if proof is provided of payment in some manner by the employee for the benefits. Although there may not be evidence of negotiations for the wage/benefits package which makes up the employee's remuneration, evidence that the employer takes the cost of benefits into account in determining wages would adequately establish that the employee contributed by way of a trade-off against higher wages. Clearly, if the non-union employee contributed to the plan by means of payroll deductions, that would prove the employee's contribution. Again, these suggested methods of proof are not an exhaustive list.

In this appeal, there is evidence that the plaintiff paid for the benefits pursuant to his collective agreements through the trade-off of a reduced hourly wage. For this reason, this case is distinguishable from *Ratych v. Bloomer*, since there is evidence to bring him within the insurance exception.

Disposition of the Cunningham Appeal

In the result, the collateral benefits obtained by Cunningham as a result of his collective bargaining agreement are in the nature of a private policy of insurance. The benefits obtained under the collective agreement, like those obtained under a private policy of insurance, should not be deducted from the claim for lost wages. The order of the Court of Appeal should be amended accordingly. The plaintiff should have his costs throughout.

. . .

Dissent [handwritten]

[McLachlin J., with La Forest and L'Heureux-Dubé JJ. concurring, dissented in part. McLachlin J. was far more concerned than the majority with the prospect of the plaintiff receiving double compensation. She argued that the private insurance exception to the rule against double recovery is very narrow in scope. The anterior facts of the plaintiff's contribution does not address the problem of double recovery. A plaintiff whose loss has been covered by the plan suffers no loss that is recoverable under tort principles. The measure of damages should be what the plaintiff has actually lost, not what the defendant is compelled to pay based on some punitive philosophy.]

(b) THE DOCTRINE OF SUBROGATION

∴ insurance can insure a person against portions unable to be recovered from tortfeasor [handwritten]

The doctrine of subrogation originated in equity, but the right to subrogation may also be created by contract or legislation. At the risk of over-simplification, the effect of subrogation is that a party who has provided an indemnity payment to another is entitled to recover any excess compensation received by that other party for that same loss. For example, assume a fire insurance company pays $25,000 for the loss of a negligently-destroyed home, and the insured then recovers $25,000 from the tortfeasor. Under the doctrine of subrogation, the insured will be required to refund $25,000 to the insurance company. If the insured is awarded $25,000, but only recovers $10,000 from the tortfeasor, she need only refund $10,000 to the insurance company.

Any party who honours a legal obligation to indemnify another has an equitable right to subrogation. Thus, for example, if an employer compensates an injured employee under the provisions of the collective bargaining agreement, the employer can seek recovery from the negligent defendant who caused the injury. However, many employers find it too expensive to pursue subrogated claims and some have abandoned the right in their collective agreements, leaving employees free to attempt to obtain double recovery.

Whenever the right of subrogation is enforced, the collateral source rule becomes a matter of indifference to the plaintiff. Anything the plaintiff recovers from the tortfeasor, for which she has already been indemnified by the collateral source, has to be refunded to the collateral source.

(when will subrogation be enforced?) [handwritten]

NOTES AND QUESTIONS

1. What is the impact of the majority decision in *Cunningham* on the principle established in *Bloomer*? What arguments did the majority in *Cunningham* make in support of its broad interpretation of the private insurance exception? Are these arguments compelling? Based on the facts, did the plaintiff make a sufficient contribution to the benefit to justify not having it deducted from his damage award?

2. Based on McLachlin J.'s position, can you suggest any situation in which an employee, who has received a wage or sick benefit, would be able to recover damages from the defendant? What impact do you think McLachlin J.'s position would have on collective bargaining had she been in the majority?

3. Despite the theoretical justifications provided, does the split in the court simply reflect the justices' pro-plaintiff or pro-defendant leanings? In other words, do the theoretical justifications compel a decision in favour of either position?

4. As McLachlin J. noted in her dissenting judgment, one of the primary justifications for the private insurance exception is that such insurers have a statutory right of subrogation. When the exercises this right, double recovery is avoided. However, as indicated, it may be expensive to e

this subrogation right and it is frequently abandoned. It has been argued that double recovery could be more effectively prevented by making all collateral benefits deductible from the defendant's liability. See Cooper, "A Collateral Benefits Principle" (1971), 49 Can. Bar Rev. 501; and Feldthusen, *Economic Negligence*, 3rd ed. (1994), 253-59. Legislation governing some public benefits has adopted this approach. See for example, the Insurance Act, R.S.O. 1990, c. I.8, s. 267(1); and generally Brown and Menezes, *Insurance Law in Canada*, 2nd ed. (1991), 315-42.

5. For a discussion of Canadian pension and unemployment benefits see *Can. Pac. Ltd. v. Gill*, [1973] S.C.R. 654; *Guy v. Trizec Equities Ltd.*, [1979] 2 S.C.R. 756; and *Jack Cewe Ltd. v. Jorgenson*, [1980] 4 W.W.R. 494 (S.C.C.).

6. The prevailing view is that health benefits received by the plaintiff will not reduce the defendant's liability. For example, in *McLeod v. Palardy* (1981), 124 D.L.R. (3d) 506, the Manitoba Court of Appeal awarded the plaintiff future care costs even though such care was provided free of charge under the provincial health plan. The contrary position was taken in *Wipfli v. Britten* (1984), 29 C.C.L.T. 240 (B.C. C.A.). In reference to cases similar to *McLeod*, Taggart J.A. stated at 270: "I remain unconvinced that they have application to the case of a claimant protected by a universal hospital plan for which he paid nothing in the past (i.e., no premiums or user fee) and is unlikely to be called on to pay anything in the future." Which view is supported by the decision in *Cunningham*?

REVIEW PROBLEMS

1. (a) By all appearances, Helen and Bob were the ideal young couple. Prior to marriage, they carefully made future plans. First, Bob would go to law school while Helen worked and supported him; then Helen would go to law school and Bob would support her. Thereafter, they planned to have two children, one right after the other. Helen would take care of the children until they entered kindergarten. At that time, Helen would join Bob in the law practice.

Things went exactly as planned for the happy young couple until a week before Helen's first year law school exams, when she was seriously injured in a grease fire at a local restaurant. Her face was badly scarred, and even after three painful operations she remained badly disfigured. Moreover, in spite of the doctor's initial optimism, an operation to restore her sight was unsuccessful and it is now clear that Helen will be permanently blind. Not surprisingly, the accident also caused acute personality changes in Helen. She refuses to have anything whatsoever to do with her family or friends, and sits for hours alone in her room playing classical music. After a year of this situation, the marriage was ruined. Although Bob still maintains a home for the two of them and provides for Helen's normal needs, he has lost all interest in the marriage.

Assume Helen has a 50% chance of establishing liability and securing damages from the restaurant's liability insurance company within two years. Prepare Helen's claim for general damages in her tort suit. Organize and itemize the claims, and indicate the type of evidence that you would adduce to secure the greatest possible award for Helen.

(b) What factors would you consider, and what demands would you make, if the insurance company was interested in settling Helen's claim before trial?

2. Albert Sweet was injured when his car was struck by a negligently-driven Ace Transport truck. Liability is admitted by Ace Transport and the sole issue at trial is the quantum of damages. At the time of the accident Albert was 23 years old, and he had just graduated from law school. He was about to start an articling job at an annual salary of $30,000. His pre-accident life expectancy was 52 years but the doctors now estimate he will die within 20 years. Albert suffered brain damage and now has the intellectual capabilities of a 5-year-old child.

Between the time the accident and the trial, Albert and his wife, Miriam, have been supported by her wealthy parents. The proceeds of a small insurance policy have covered all medical expenses and have paid for a nurse for Albert, but these funds are almost exhausted.

You have been contacted by Miriam to assess the possible damage claim that can be brought on behalf of Albert, her parents and herself against Ace Transport.

3. Mr. and Mrs. Troup were an elderly childless couple. Both were actively engaged in the work force throughout their 40-year marriage. Mr. Troup is a famous medical doctor, and Mrs. Troup was a university professor until July 1, 1990. At that time she was compelled to retire from the university and was granted a pension worth 80 per cent of her salary for the remainder of her life. The indi-

vidual income of either Mr. or Mrs. Troup had always been sufficient to meet their joint expenditures, and the Troups had pooled their funds, accumulating a sizeable surplus during their married years.

The only significant quarrel in their lengthy marriage involved Mrs. Troup's nephew. Out of a sense of moral duty to her late sister, Mrs. Troup undertook in 1993 to house and support her nephew for a four-year-period while he attended university. Mr. Troup disliked the nephew, whom he regarded as a leech.

Upon retiring, Mrs. Troup became a famous author of historical novels. Her second novel, allegedly fiction, recounted a story which closely resembled the life of a leading Canadian politician. On July 1, 1995, her home town newspaper, the Press, carried a story announcing that the politician had begun a defamation action based upon the book. National sales of Mrs. Troup's books began to increase dramatically in response to the publicity.

Later that day, Mrs. Troup was shopping in the city when she walked past a construction site. Unfortunately, the cable securing a load of concrete failed. Some of the blocks fell on Mrs. Troup causing her severe injuries. The incident also destroyed the $10,000 gold watch which Mrs. Troup was wearing. Mrs. Troup went into a coma and was taken to the intensive care unit at the hospital. Eighty per cent of her hospital bills were borne by government medical insurance and the remaining 20 per cent was paid by Mrs. Troup's private Blue Cross plan. Mrs. Troup died ten days later, without ever regaining consciousness. She was 67. Mr. Troup was named sole beneficiary and executor under his wife's will. He was also named the sole beneficiary of her $100,000 life insurance policy.

Mr. Troup now seeks your advice with respect to a possible legal action against the construction company that owned and operated the crane. The company has admitted negligence. Based upon the relevant legislation in your province, what damages will flow from the action, to whom will damages be awarded, and how will damages be divided among the possible claimants?

DEFENCES TO NEGLIGENCE LIABILITY

1. Introduction
2. Contributory Negligence
3. Voluntary Assumption of Risk
4. Participation in a Criminal or Immoral Act
5. Inevitable Accident

1. Introduction

Even if the plaintiff proves that the defendant negligently injured him, his claim may be reduced or dismissed if the defendant can establish a defence. The first three defences we discuss — contributory negligence, voluntary assumption of risk, and participation in a criminal or immoral act — deal with blameworthy conduct by the plaintiff that is related to his loss. The defendant must plead and prove each defence separately. Nevertheless, these three defences may overlap and may arise from a single fact situation. Inevitable accident, the fourth defence, is concerned with the factual circumstances surrounding the defendant's conduct and may be viewed as a special denial of negligence.

2. Contributory Negligence

(a) THE DEVELOPMENT OF THE DEFENCE

At common law, the plaintiff was denied recovery if his negligent conduct contributed to his injury. There was no apportionment of loss between the defendant and plaintiff, even if the plaintiff's negligence was a relatively insignificant cause. To avoid this inequity, the courts developed what became known as the "last clear chance" or "last opportunity" rule. This doctrine permitted the plaintiff to recover despite his contributory negligence, if the defendant had the last clear chance to avoid the accident and negligently failed to take it. While the doctrine clearly benefited the plaintiff, it perpetuated the existing all-or-nothing approach by casting the entire loss upon the defendant. With the acceptance of more complex theories of causation and liability, the doctrine came under severe criticism. For example, Fleming, in *The Law of Torts*, 8th ed. (1992), states at 271:

> Over the century of its sway, the last opportunity doctrine developed into a plastic instrument for allocating the loss to either plaintiff or defendant in accordance with the court's view of whose was the disproportionately greater share of responsibility. ... The resulting casuistry tended to make the task of appellate review a veritable farce and eventually prompted a retreat.

Legislation permitting the apportionment of liability was not enacted until well after the turn of this century. By dividing liability according to the parties' relative degrees of fault, the legislation tempered the harshness of the common law's all-or-nothing approach.

NOTES AND QUESTIONS

1. The courts first dealt with contributory negligence as a question of legal causation, rather than as a defence. See *Butterfield v. Forrester* (1809), 103 E.R. 926 (K.B.); and *Davies v. Mann* (1842), 152 E.R. 588 (Exch.). What are the advantages of this approach?

2. Once the courts recognized that there could be more than one legal cause of an accident, was there any justification for continuing to treat contributory negligence as a complete bar to recovery? See Bohlen, "Contributory Negligence" (1908), 21 Harv. L. Rev. 233; Malone, "The Formative Period of Contributory Negligence" (1946), 41 Ill. L. Rev. 151; James, "Contributory Negligence" (1953), 62 Yale L. Rev. 691; and Fleming, "Forward: Comparative Negligence at Last — by Judicial Choice" (1976), 64 Cal. L. Rev. 239.

3. *Davies v. Mann* (1842), 152 E.R. 588 (Exch.) was the first case in which the last clear chance doctrine was clearly articulated. For Canadian applications of the doctrine see *Long v. Toronto Ry. Co.* (1914), 50 S.C.R. 224; *B.C. Elec. Ry. Co. v. Loach*, [1916] 1 A.C. 719 (P.C.); *Boulay v. Rousselle* (1984), 30 C.C.L.T. 149 (N.B. Q.B.); and *Hunter v. Briere* (1989), 49 C.C.L.T. 93 (Man. Q.B.). See also MacIntyre, "The Rationale of Last Clear Chance" (1940), 18 Can. Bar Rev. 665; Williams, *Joint Torts and Contributory Negligence* (1951), 223-55; and Casswell, "Avoiding Last Clear Chance" (1990), 69 Can. Bar Rev. 129.

4. In what circumstances did the last clear chance doctrine work to the defendant's advantage? As we shall later discuss, the apportionment legislation did not eliminate the last clear chance doctrine. Following the enactment of apportionment legislation, in what circumstances would the last clear chance doctrine benefit the defendant?

(b) CONDUCT CONSTITUTING CONTRIBUTORY NEGLIGENCE

WALLS v. MUSSENS LTD.

(1969), 11 D.L.R. (3d) 245 (N.B. C.A.)

HUGHES, J.A.:—

. . .

In the afternoon of January 18, 1968, the defendant Morrison, a serviceman and mechanic in the employ of the defendant Mussens Limited, drove a machine used in logging operations called a timberjack, belonging to one Murdock Hallihan, to the plaintiff's service station premises where he obtained permission to repair the front drive shaft of the timberjack in one of the bays of the service station. Shortly after 6:30 p.m. while Morrison and Hallihan were working on the machine, a propane gas torch being used by Morrison ignited a pool containing gasoline on the floor beneath the machine.

The learned trial Judge found that the gasoline on the floor had leaked from a tube leading from the gas tank to the engine of the timberjack and that the fire was caused by the negligence of Morrison in the use of the propane gas torch while acting in the course of his employment with Mussens Ltd. There is no appeal against these findings.

When the fire started the plaintiff was at home for his evening meal, having left the service station in charge of Terry Hambrook, a 17-year-old high school boy employed by him to tend the gas tanks, change tires and do other such work.

Hambrook, who was in the office talking with two boys, heard someone call out: "Fire — come on out and bring a fire-extinguisher" — but, instead of bringing one of the available extinguishers, Hambrook and others including Morrison, Hallihan and probably the two boys attempted to smother the fire by throwing snow on it. Hallihan says he also tried to extinguish it with water from a hose.

When the plaintiff, who was told of the fire by Hambrook, arrived at the service station the flame was about 18 inches in height and two feet in diameter. The plaintiff joined the others in shovelling snow onto the fire but in the excitement of the emergency the five fire extinguishers which were on the premises were not thought of. Morrison testified that when he realized the snow would not smother the fire he ran out of the building, drove his truck to the door, and tried to tow the timberjack from the building but was unable to do so as his truck was too light to move it. The fire spread quickly and the service station and most of the contents were destroyed.

Alpha D. Curl, an expert in the production, design and use theory of fire prevention equipment, expressed an opinion, which the learned trial Judge accepted, that had the available fire extinguishers been used when the plaintiff arrived at the service station the fire could probably have been extinguished. In their defence the defendants alleged that the damage suffered by the plaintiff was caused wholly by the negligence or breach of duty by the plaintiff, his workmen, licensees, servants and agents. The learned trial Judge carefully considered the evidence and found that the failure of the plaintiff to use the fire extinguishers in the prevailing excitement did not constitute contributory negligence even though his failure to do so may have deprived those present of the chance of minimizing the loss, and he held the negligence of Morrison was the sole cause of the plaintiff's damage.

I have read the evidence with respect to the frantic efforts of all concerned, including the plaintiff, to extinguish the fire, and I agree that the conclusions reached by the learned trial Judge are amply supported by the evidence.

No portion of the responsibility for starting the fire can be attributed to the plaintiff. There was no antecedent negligence on his part and he had no part in the repair work which was carried out by Morrison. The emergency was created solely by the negligence of Morrison for whose acts and omissions Mussens Ltd. is vicariously liable. While it may be unfortunate the plaintiff did not have the presence of mind in the emergency to use the fire extinguishers which were available, and notwithstanding his participation in throwing snow on the fire may have aggravated the situation, I think the plaintiff is entitled to invoke the "agony of the moment" rule as an answer to the allegation of contributory negligence made against him.

. . .

The Law of Torts, 3rd ed., by J.G. Fleming, contains the following statement at p. 247:

On the other hand, a person's conduct, in the face of a sudden emergency, cannot be judged from the standpoint of what would have been reasonable behaviour in the light of hind-knowledge and in a calmer atmosphere conducive to a nice evaluation of alternatives. A certain latitude is allowed when "in the agony of the moment" he seeks to extricate himself from an emergency not created by his own antecedent negligence. The degree of judgment and presence of mind expected of the plaintiff is what would have been reasonable conduct in such a situation, and he will not be adjudged guilty of contributory negligence merely because, as it turns out, he unwittingly took the wrong course.

. . .

The test to be applied in circumstances such as those as in the case at bar is, in my opinion, not whether the plaintiff exercised a careful and prudent judgment in doing what he did, but whether what he did was something an ordinarily prudent man might reasonably have done under the stress of the emergency.

In my opinion it might well have appeared to an ordinarily prudent man in the emergency with which the plaintiff was confronted that shovelling snow on the fire was the most effective way to extinguish it, although in fact it was not, and may actually have tended to spread the fire. It is now apparent that the fire could not have been smothered as it was being fed by gasoline leaking from the fuel line of the timberjack and it is most improbable the plaintiff had any knowledge of that fact until the cause of the fire was investigated. The plaintiff's reaction to the emergency was merely to do what the others were doing and I cannot say that it was something an ordinarily prudent man might not reasonably have done in the circumstances.

In my opinion the appeal on this ground should fail.

NOTES AND QUESTIONS

1. What criteria did the court in *Walls* use in determining whether the plaintiff had breached the standard of care expected of him? Should the four-factor test be applied in exactly the same way in assessing the defendant's negligence and the plaintiff's contributory negligence? See also *Zervobeakos v. Zervobeakos* (1969), 8 D.L.R. (3d) 377 (N.S. C.A.); and *Neufeld v. Landry* (1975), 55 D.L.R. (3d) 296 (Man. C.A.).

2. In *A.G. Ont. v. Keller* (1978), 94 D.L.R. (3d) 632 (Ont. C.A.), the plaintiff, a police officer, was injured in a high-speed chase when his cruiser went out of control and struck a pole. The officer was driving at about 85 miles per hour on icy roads within 100 to 150 feet of the defendant. The court held that the plaintiff was not contributorily negligent because his actions were "no more than was reasonably necessary to carry out his statutory duty." Nevertheless, given the risks involved in high-speed chases, did the officer act reasonably? Should the police officer in *Keller* have been held to a higher standard of care than the average driver? Would the court have found the officer negligent if he had hit a pedestrian? Should it make any difference? See *Priestman v. Colangelo*, [1959] S.C.R. 615; *Roberge v. R.* (1983), 147 D.L.R. (3d) 493 (S.C.C.); *Miller v. Wolbaum* (1986), 47 M.V.R. 162 (Sask. Q.B.); and *Moore v. Fanning* (1987), 41 C.C.L.T. 67 (Ont. H.C.).

3. In *Lewis v. Todd* (1980), 115 D.L.R. (3d) 257 (S.C.C.), a police officer was killed by a driver while investigating a traffic accident. Working alone and ignoring the traffic, Constable Lewis apparently relied on the warnings given by several flashing lights. The Supreme Court of Canada rejected the argument that Lewis was contributorily negligent for not keeping a proper lookout. It stated that his conduct had to be judged according to the standard of care expected of a police officer investigating an accident, and not the standard of an ordinary pedestrian. According to *Lewis* and *Keller*, how would you characterize a police officer's standard of care — is it a higher standard than that of an ordinary citizen, lower or a special standard of care?

4. In *Heeney v. Best* (1979), 108 D.L.R. (3d) 366 (Ont. C.A.), the plaintiff's chickens died of asphyxiation when the defendant negligently cut off the power supply to the plaintiff's barns. An alarm system, that would have warned of a power failure, had inexplicably not been plugged in on the night of the incident. Since only 25% to 50% of local poultry farmers had alarm systems, the plaintiff argued that it was the custom not to have any alarm system. Therefore, the plaintiff contended that he could not be found contributorily negligent for having a non-operating alarm. Nevertheless, the plaintiff was found to have been contributorily negligent for failing to take reasonable care of his own property. Would the court have reached the same conclusion if the plaintiff had not installed any alarm system?

Should compliance with and breach of a custom have the same effect in establishing contributory negligence as it does in negligence?

Heeney raises the issue of the precautions that an individual must take to protect himself from the tortious or illegal conduct of others. Should a homeowner be held contributorily negligent for failing to install a fire alarm if its absence contributed to his fire losses? Would a homeowner be contributorily negligent for failing to replace an existing fire alarm with a more modern and reliable device? Would a homeowner be held contributorily negligent for not purchasing a burglar alarm and other security devices? Would your answers be affected by the costs of the devices? See also the discussion of the duty to control the conduct of others in chapter 11.

5. The standard of care imposed in contributory negligence is affected by the age, disabilities and professional training of the plaintiff. For example, a child is required to meet the standard of care of a reasonable child of a like age, intelligence and experience. See *Myers v. Peel County Bd. of Ed.* (1981), 123 D.L.R. (3d) 1 (S.C.C.); *Laviolette v. C.N.R.* (1987), 40 C.C.L.T. 138 (N.B. C.A.); *Bajkov v. Canil* (1990), 66 D.L.R. (4th) 572 (B.C. C.A.); and *Lee (Guardian ad litem of) v. Barker*, [1992] 5 W.W.R. 256 (B.C. C.A.).

6. By virtue of the doctrine of identification, the common law attributed the negligence of one party to the conduct of another if a special relationship existed between them. For example, at one time the negligence of a child's supervisor or parent was imputed to the child, thereby reducing the child's claim against the negligent defendant. Although this principle has been eliminated in the parent and child relationship, it still applies in certain situations involving a master and servant, and a car owner and driver. See *Ducharme v. Davies*, [1984] 1 W.W.R. 699 (Sask. C.A.); *Alliance & Leicester Building Society v. Edgestop Ltd.*, [1994] 2 All E.R. 38 (Ch.); *Galaske v. O'Donnell* (1994), 166 N.R. 5 (S.C.C.); and Fleming, *The Law of Torts*, 8th ed. (1992), 287-90.

7. As with negligence, the issue of contributory negligence turns on the specific facts of the case. For a discussion of contributory negligence, see *Wells v. Parsons* (1970), 1 Nfld. & P.E.I.R. 513 (Nfld. C.A.); *Comeau v. Laliberte* (1986), 69 N.B.R. (2d) 87 (Q.B.); *Lee v. O'Farrell* (1988), 43 C.C.L.T. 269 (B.C. S.C.); *McEvoy v. Capital Motors* (1992), 88 D.L.R. (4th) 358 (B.C. C.A.); *Findley v. Driver* (1992), 7 O.R. (3d) 48 (C.A.); and *Hutchings v. Nevin* (1992), 12 C.C.L.T. (2d) 259 (Ont. Gen. Div.).

GAGNON v. BEAULIEU

[1977] 1 W.W.R. 702 (B.C. S.C.)

30th December 1976. FULTON J: — The plaintiff was injured in a collision which took place on 31st August 1974 on Highway 401 near Chilliwack, British Columbia, when a 1972 Vega "Hatchback", owned and driven by the defendant Beaulieu and in which the plaintiff was riding as a front seat passenger, ran into the rear end of a pick-up truck which was stopped at a railroad crossing waiting for a train to pass by. Liability of the defendant driver is admitted — the main issue in this connection is whether or not the plaintiff was wearing a seat belt and, if not, whether this constituted negligence contributing to the nature and extent of his injuries.

The plaintiff suffered vertical lacerations of the right forehead and scalp, a deep horizontal laceration running across the right lower eyelid and upper right cheek and into the right temple. The cheek was fractured and crushed, and the right eye was damaged. The injuries are consistent with the plaintiff having been thrown forward by the impact, striking the windshield and/or dashboard of the car with his forehead and face. The defendant maintains that the plaintiff was not wearing a seat belt apparatus provided for the passenger, consisting of a lap belt and shoulder harness, and that if the plaintiff had been wearing this apparatus, he would not have suffered those head and facial injuries.

. . .

For the plaintiff it was contended that failure to wear a seat belt is not per se negligence, and that it is not negligence in any circumstances if the person concerned is not convinced of the efficacy of seat belts and/or believes that the wearing of a seat belt, including particularly the shoulder strap, may in certain circumstances create the hazard of greater injury or damage than if it were not worn — that if, for instance, the car were to overturn, the wearer might be trapped between the seat and the roof. There was evidence that the plaintiff had this opinion.

. . .

The leading case in British Columbia is *Yuan v. Farstad*, supra, a decision of this court.

. . .

What Munro J. [the judge in *Yuan*] seems to me to have clearly said is this: that in the light of modern-day knowledge of the benefits and reduction of danger of injury flowing from the use of seat belts, an occupant of a motor vehicle in which such apparatus is provided for his use who nevertheless fails to wear it is negligent in that he has failed to take reasonable precautions for his own safety. If in those circumstances he is injured in a collision, and if it is established as a fact that in the circumstances of that collision the wearing of the seat belt provided would have prevented or lessened the injuries he sustained, then his negligence in failing to wear it has contributed to the extent of his injuries and becomes contributory negligence. If, of course, it is not shown in connection with the particular circumstances of the accident in question that the wearing of the seat belt would have prevented or lessened the injuries, then the failure to wear it, while negligent in itself, does not constitute negligence contributing to the injuries or to the extent thereof.

. . .

... on the basis of the authorities which I believe to be binding on me, and which, with respect, I believe also to be the logical and sensible application to the situation of facts of which judges, as rational human beings, do have knowledge, I am of opinion that the law in British Columbia on this subject is as follows:

(a) Failure, while travelling in a motor vehicle on a street or highway, to wear a seat belt or any part thereof as provided in a vehicle in accordance with the safety standards from time to time applicable is failure to take a step which a person knows or ought to know to be reasonably necessary for his own safety.

(b) If in such circumstances he suffers injury as the result of the vehicle being involved in an accident, and if it appears from the evidence that if the seat belt had been worn the injuries would have been prevented or the severity thereof lessened, then the failure to wear a seat belt is negligence which has contributed to the nature and extent of those injuries.

(c) In the case of this particular form of contributory negligence, the onus is on the defendant to satisfy the court, in accordance with the usual standard of proof, not only that the seat belt was not worn but also that the injuries would have been prevented or lessened if the seat belt had been worn. The courts should not find the second of these facts merely by inference from the first, even if that has been established.

. . .

Before reviewing the evidence as to the facts of this case to which these propositions apply, I should refer to the argument addressed to me on the basis that people may in fact be unconvinced of the efficacy, or desirability, of wearing seat belts, as was urged on behalf of the plaintiff here. This argument was carefully reviewed by Lord Denning M.R., in the English Court of Appeal, in the recent case of *Froom v. Butcher*, [1975] 3 W.L.R. 379, [1975] 3 All E.R. 520. At p. 526 he said:

> Quite a lot of people, however, think differently about seat belts. Some are like Mr. Froom here. They think that they would be less likely to be injured if they were thrown clear than if they were strapped in. They would be wrong. The chances of injury are four times as great. Yet they believe it honestly and firmly. On this account Nield J. [[1974] 1 W.L.R. 1297, [1974] 3 All E.R. 517 at 520] thought they should not bear any responsibility. He recognized that such persons are in a minority, but he thought that proper respect should be paid to the minority view. He said:
>
> > "... I do not feel that the courts are justified in invading the freedom of choice of the motorist by holding it to be negligence, lack of care or fault to act on an opinion firmly and honestly held and shared by many other sensible people."
>
> I am afraid I do not agree. In determining responsibility, the law eliminates the personal equation. It takes no notice of the views of the particular individual; or of others like him. It requires everyone to exercise all such precautions as a man of ordinary prudence would observe.
>
> . . .

I agree with counsel for the plaintiff that I am not bound by this English case, and need not apply it in the case before me. However, I say at once that I do respectfully agree with the reasoning expressed in that judgment, and consider that it is entirely applicable to the facts established by the evidence before me, which I now review.

The evidence is that the defendant's car was equipped with seat belts consisting of a lap belt and a cross-over shoulder harness on the passenger side, in good working order. The plaintiff does not remember whether he was wearing either part of this equipment: as a result of the blow to his head, his recollection of the circumstances of the accident itself is entirely blank.

. . .

Expert evidence as to the protection afforded by seat belts was given by Mr. A.C. Shiels, director of traffic safety programs for the province of Saskatchewan. Mr. Shiels has done extensive research into the whole question of the protection of occupants of automobiles from injury in accidents, including the measurement of the relative effectiveness of various safety devices and the measurement of the relative severity of collisions and the type and extent of injury which may be expected in collisions of differing degrees of severity as between occupants who wear seat belts with shoulder harnesses and those who do not. His evidence was of considerable help in this regard.

He testified that from the degree of crushing of the front of the car as shown in the photographs Exs. 18 and 19, and from the description of the items in and on the car which were damaged, he rated the severity of the collision as class 2. In a collision of this type he would expect that a passenger in the front seat not wearing any seat belt apparatus would suffer injuries consisting of bumps and bruises, some undetermined degree of head injuries consisting of lacerations, including lacerations to the eyelids and to the face, and possible damage to the eyeball itself. For a passenger wearing properly adjusted seat belt apparatus including the shoulder harness, he said it would be virtually impossible to contact the windshield or dashboard with his head in a collision of this class and that there would probably be minor bruises and tenderness at the points where the restraining harness had taken the load of the body on impact. Here the evidence is that the windshield was struck and shattered; in the opinion of the expert it was struck by a round object such as the head, and the evidence is equally consistent with its having been struck from inside as from outside. The plaintiff received head and facial injuries of the type said to be expected to be incurred in a collision of this type, by a person not wearing a restraining apparatus, and there is no evidence of any marks or bruising on his body such as would be expected if he had been restrained by a lap and/or shoulder belt.

. . .

On the whole of the evidence I am satisfied that the plaintiff knew or ought to have known that the wearing of the seat belt provided, including the shoulder harness, would reduce the possibility of his being injured in a collision, that at the time of this accident he was not wearing the seat belt equipment provided and that, had he been wearing it, and particularly the shoulder harness, his injuries would have been less severe, if not prevented altogether. I consider that the expert, Mr. Shiels, was not merely speculating as to this result, but had a sound basis for his opinion. Applying the law which I have held to be applicable to these circumstances in this province, I find it to have been established that the plaintiff was negligent and that his negligence contributed to the nature and extent of his injuries.

There will be judgment accordingly.

NOTES AND QUESTIONS

1. Why were the plaintiff's beliefs about the safety value of seat belts considered irrelevant? Would the result have been the same if the plaintiff had refused to wear the seat belt because: (a) it was physically uncomfortable for him to do so; or (b) he had a morbid fear of being trapped in a burning vehicle, which made wearing a seat belt emotionally traumatic? See *Froom v. Butcher*, [1975] 3 All E.R. 520 (C.A.); *Davis v. Anderson* (1980), 15 C.C.L.T. 192 (B.C. C.A.); and *Shaw v. Roemer* (1982), 134 D.L.R. (3d) 590 (N.S. C.A.).

2. Based on *Gagnon*, would a driver and owner of a car be negligent for: (a) failing to equip a car with seat belts; (b) failing to make passengers aware of the presence of seat belts; or (c) permitting a passenger to remain in the car without wearing a seat belt? See *Pasternack v. Poulton*, [1973] 2 All E.R. 74 (Q.B.); and *Haley v. Richardson; McCrae v. Richardson* (1975), 60 D.L.R. (3d) 480 (N.B. C.A.). In *Galaske v. O'Donnell* (1994), 166 N.R. 5 (S.C.C.), the Supreme Court of Canada held that the defendant had a duty to ensure that an eight-year-old passenger wore a seat belt. The fact that the boy's father was also a passenger in the car and may have been negligent did not negate the defendant's duty.

3. What evidence did the court in *Gagnon* rely upon in concluding that the plaintiff's failure to wear his seat belt contributed to his losses? Was the court's approach consistent with the general principles that govern causation? See *Lucas v. Antoniak* (1978), 7 C.C.L.T. 209 (B.C. S.C.), aff'd. (1980), 15 C.C.L.T. 195 (B.C. C.A.).

4. Would a passenger in a boat who failed to wear a life jacket, a motorcyclist or bicyclist who failed to wear a crash helmet, an airline passenger who failed to wear a seat belt, or a hockey player who failed to wear a helmet be treated the same way as someone who failed to wear a seat belt while driving? Is there any justification for treating the seat belt cases differently from other contributory negligence cases?

5. All of the provinces have enacted legislation requiring occupants of motor vehicles to wear a seat belt in most situations. See, for example, the Highway Traffic Act, R.S.O. 1990, c. H.8, s. 106. Should the existence of a statutory duty affect the analysis of the seat belt defence? See *Genik v. Ewanylo* (1980), 12 C.C.L.T. 121 (Man. C.A.); and *Shkwarchuk v. Hansen* (1984), 30 C.C.L.T. 121 (Sask. Q.B.). But see *Webber v. Crawford* (1988), 46 C.C.L.T. 1 (B.C. S.C.); and *Wallace v. Berrigan* (1988), 47 D.L.R. (4th) 752 (N.S. C.A.). See also Wakeling, "Seat Belt Legislation: An End to Cruel and Unusual Punishment" (1977-78), 42 Sask. L. Rev. 105.

6. Do you think that the court's recognition of the seat belt defence has significantly affected the patterns of seat belt use? Can you suggest alternative means of inducing people to wear seat belts?

7. For an academic discussion of this issue see Hicks, "Seat Belts and Crash Helmets" (1974), 37 Mod. L. Rev. 308; and Slatter, "Seat Belts and Contributory Negligence" (1977-78), 4 Dalhousie L.J. 96.

(c) APPORTIONMENT OF LOSS

In 1924, Ontario enacted Canada's first apportionment legislation and the remaining common law provinces soon followed suit. Although the form of the legislation varies, there are few substantial differences in the operation of the provincial acts. Basically, the legislation permits the court to divide responsibility for damages between the parties in relationship to their relative degrees of fault.

NEGLIGENCE ACT

R.S.O. 1990, c. N.1

. . .

Extent of liability, remedy over

1. Where damages have been caused or contributed to by the fault or neglect of two or more persons, the court shall determine the degree in which each of such persons is at fault or negligent, and, where two or more persons are found at fault or negligent, they are jointly and severally liable to the person suffering loss or damage for such fault or negligence, but as between themselves, in the absence of any contract express or implied, each is liable to make contribution and indemnify each other in the degree in which they are respectively found to be at fault or negligent.

Recovery as between tort feasors

2. A tortfeasor may recover contribution or indemnity from any other tortfeasor who is, or would if sued have been, liable in respect of the damage to any person suffering damage as a result of a tort by settling with the person suffering such damage, and thereafter commencing or continuing action against such other tortfeasor, in which event the tortfeasor settling the damage shall satisfy the court that the amount of the settlement was reasonable, and in the event that the court finds the amount of the settlement was excessive it may fix the amount at which the claim should have been settled.

Plaintiff guilty of contributory negligence

3. In any action for damages that is founded upon the fault or negligence of the defendant if fault or negligence is found on the part of the plaintiff that contributed to the damages, the court shall apportion the damages in proportion to the degree of fault or negligence found against the parties respectively.

Where parties to be deemed equally at fault

4. If it is not practicable to determine the respective degree of fault or negligence as between any parties to an action, such parties shall be deemed to be equally at fault or negligent.

Adding parties

5. Wherever it appears that a person not already a party to an action is or may be wholly

or partly responsible for the damages claimed, such person may be added as a party defendant to the action upon such terms as are considered just or may be made a third party to the action in the manner prescribed by the rules of court for adding third parties.

Jury to determine degrees of negligence of parties
    6. In any action tried with a jury, the degree of fault or negligence of the respective parties is a question of fact for the jury.

When plaintiff may be liable for costs
    7. Where the damages are occasioned by the fault or negligence of more than one party, the court has power to direct that the plaintiff shall bear some portion of the costs if the circumstances render this just.

NOTES AND QUESTIONS

1. Alberta, Nova Scotia and New Brunswick deal with apportionment between the plaintiff and defendant in one act, and contribution among tortfeasors in another. The other common law provinces deal with both issues in the same legislation. For a comparison see the University of Alberta, Institute of Law Research and Reform, *Contributory Negligence and Concurrent Wrongdoers* (1979), 2-7. See Cheifetz, *Apportionment of Fault in Tort* (1981), who provides a detailed section-by-section analysis of the Ontario legislation, followed by a brief reference to the other provincial acts. See also Law Reform Commission of British Columbia, *Report on Apportionment of Costs and Contributory Negligence: Section 3 of the Negligence Act* (1993).

2. There is an ongoing dispute as to whether the apportionment legislation applies only to negligence actions or to all torts. The Ontario Court of Appeal affirmed a decision which held that "fault" in s. 2 incorporates all intentional wrongdoing "as well as other types of substandard conduct." *Bell Can. v. Cope (Sarnia) Ltd.* (1980), 11 C.C.L.T. 170 (Ont. H.C.), aff'd. 119 D.L.R. (3d) 254 (Ont. C.A.). See also *Anderson v. Stevens*, [1981] 5 W.W.R. 550 (B.C. S.C.); and *Long v. Gardner* (1983), 144 D.L.R. (3d) 73 (Ont. H.C.). See, however, *Chernesky v. Armadale Publishers Ltd.* (1974), 53 D.L.R. (3d) 79 (Sask. C.A.), in which it was held that the comparable Saskatchewan provision applied only to negligence. See also *United Service Funds (Trustees of) v. Richardson Greenshields of Can. Ltd.* (1988), 43 C.C.L.T. 162 (B.C. S.C.).

As a matter of statutory interpretation, which line of analysis do you prefer? In principle, is there any reason to limit contributory negligence and the statutory right to seek contribution to negligence cases? See Kutner, "Contribution Among Tortfeasors: Liability Issues in Contribution Law" (1985), 63 Can. Bar Rev. 1; and Law Reform Commission of British Columbia, *Report on Shared Liability* (1986).

3. It has been suggested that apportionment legislation encompasses not only torts, but other branches of the law as well. See *Giffels Associates Ltd. v. Eastern Const. Co.* (1978), 84 D.L.R. (3d) 344 (S.C.C.); *Can. Western Nat. Gas Co. v. Pathfinder Surveys Ltd.* (1980), 12 C.C.L.T. 211 (Alta. C.A.); and *Tompkins Hardware Ltd. v. North West Flying Services Ltd.* (1982), 139 D.L.R. (3d) 329 (Ont. H.C.). See also Weinrib, "Contribution in a Contractual Setting" (1976), 54 Can. Bar Rev. 338; Klar, "Developments In Tort Law: The 1979-80 Term" (1981), 2 Supreme Ct. L. Rev. 325 at 340-54; and Ontario Law Reform Commission, *Report on Contribution Among Wrongdoers and Contributory Negligence* (1988), 65-83.

4. The apportionment legislation eliminated the rationale for the last clear chance doctrine. Initially, however, most Canadian courts continued to apply the doctrine, while others narrowly interpreted it or avoided the issue. Bowker, "Ten More Years Under Contributory Negligence Acts" (1964-66), 2 U.B.C. L. Rev. 198; and Casswell, "Avoiding Last Clear Chance" (1990), 69 Can. Bar Rev. 129.

The Canadian courts rely on the doctrine far less frequently than in the past, but a uniform approach has yet to emerge. See *Hartman v. Fisette* (1976), 66 D.L.R. (3d) 516 (S.C.C.); *MacKay v. MacLellan* (1976), 1 C.C.L.T. 310 (N.S. C.A.); *Poitras v. Goulet* (1987), 46 Man. R. (2d) 87 (C.A.); *Hunter v. Briere* (1989), 49 C.C.L.T. 93 (Man. Q.B.); and *Fillier v. Whittom*, [1995] N.B.J. No. 592 (C.A.).

The Ontario Act, like the legislation in Nova Scotia, New Brunswick and Manitoba, makes no reference to the doctrine, whereas the British Columbia and Prince Edward Island statutes have specifically abolished it. The remaining common law provinces have attempted to define the doctrine's scope in their apportionment legislation.

MORTIMER v. CAMERON

(1994), 17 O.R. (3d) 1 (C.A.), leave to appeal ref'd. (1994), 19 O.R. (3d) xvi (S.C.C.)

ROBINS J.A.: — On the afternoon of July 17, 1987, following an accounting examination, Stephen Mortimer attended a party at the apartment of a classmate, Sandra Hunt. The apartment was on the second floor of a house owned by Stingray Holdings Limited in the City of London. Those present were drinking and relaxing; no one was boisterous or unruly. By all accounts, the mood was convivial but subdued. At some point late in the afternoon, Mortimer engaged John Cameron, another classmate, in friendly conversation while they were standing at the top of a short stairway in the apartment. They had both been drinking beer and Mortimer was "mildly intoxicated". Neither of them was angry or hostile.

While they were "joking around" with one another, Mortimer made a motion so as to indicate that he was going to pour beer on Cameron. This led to some good-natured horseplay. They began to push each other back and forth and, while doing so, moved down the stairs to the interior landing leading to the front door of the apartment. The door was open at the time. When they reached the interior landing, Mortimer, who was moving backwards, tripped over the raised threshold to the apartment and fell backwards. As he did so, he grabbed Cameron and pulled him towards him. Together, they tumbled onto the exterior landing at the top of the enclosed exterior stairway leading to street level, and came in contact with the exterior wall. Even though they hit the wall with "minimal" or "little" force, it gave way and the two of them plunged to the ground 10 feet below.

Fortunately, Cameron was unhurt. Mortimer, however, suffered a devastating injury. His spinal cord was permanently fractured at the C4-5 or neck level. As a result, Mortimer is a complete quadriplegic without any motor function or sensation below the site of the injury.

The issue here is whether the trial judge erred in holding that the plaintiff's injuries were not proximately caused by his own conduct or by the conduct of the defendant Cameron. The conduct in question is the "horseplay" to which I referred earlier. The city and Stingray contend that, by engaging in this kind of conduct, the plaintiff was guilty of contributory negligence and the defendant Cameron was guilty of negligence. Their negligence, it is contended, contributed in some degree to the loss and should have been taken into account in apportioning liability.

The trial judge described what transpired before the fall as follows (at p. 203):

> After some time, he [Mortimer] extended his left arm toward Cameron. They were still joking with each other. At the time, Mortimer was holding a beer in his left hand. Cameron, quite reasonably, thought that Mortimer was going to pour beer on him and grabbed Mortimer's left forearm with his right hand. He also put his left hand on Mortimer's shoulder and pushed him. Mortimer did not actually pour any beer on Cameron. At this point, Mortimer was standing with one foot at the top of the stairs and the other foot on the first step down from the top. . . .
>
> Mortimer put his hands on Cameron's shoulders and they then began to get down the stairs . . . When they got to the landing at the bottom of the interior stairs, Mortimer and Cameron were still engaged in good-natured shoving back and forth. In the course of this "horseplay", Cameron again pushed Mortimer, who went backwards and hit his heel on the threshold. This caused Mortimer to fall backwards and as he did, he grabbed onto Cameron, pulling Cameron towards him. Mortimer hit the floor of the exterior landing, with Cameron, the taller, on top. The momentum of the fall carried them forward and Cameron's left shoulder hit [the plywood

panel]. Even though he hit it with little force and encountered little resistance from it, [the plywood panel] became dislodged. The slight forward momentum that remained was sufficient to cause them to fall from the landing onto the ground below.

The trial judge specifically found that Cameron breached his duty of care to Mortimer when he pushed Mortimer at the interior landing by the threshold. He also can be taken to have found that Mortimer, in initiating and participating in the horseplay, was in breach of the duty not to harm himself. The trial judge concluded, however, that their conduct did not constitute a proximate cause of Mortimer's injuries and that no liability should attach to them. In his view, the accident was not within the realm of their reasonable foreseeability.

There is no basis for disturbing this conclusion. On the findings made by the trial judge, which are adequately supported by the evidence, the conduct of Mortimer and Cameron cannot be treated as a proximate or effective cause of Mortimer's injuries. It is, of course, true that "but for" the condition created by the horseplay Mortimer and Cameron would not have fallen from the upper landing of the enclosed exterior stairway to the ground below. However, a defendant's negligence is actionable only with respect to harm that is within the scope of the risk that makes the offending conduct actionable. Similarly, a plaintiff's contributory negligence will not limit his recovery unless it is a proximate cause of his injury.

Here, neither Cameron's negligence nor Mortimer's contributory negligence entailed an unreasonable or foreseeable likelihood of the risk or hazard that actually befell Mortimer. It was reasonable for them to assume that what purported and appeared to be a properly constructed wall was in fact a properly constructed wall. In regulating their conduct and having regard for their own safety, they were entitled to rely on the wall providing them reasonable protection. The risk to which they exposed themselves was the risk of being injured by falling down the stairs or onto the exterior landing or by hitting the exterior wall. The risk that materialized was of a different nature. They had no reason to think that the state of the wall was such that it would give way to the modest degree of lateral force that they were found to have applied to it. The risk of falling to the ground through a defectively constructed and unprotected wall was beyond their reasonable contemplation. This risk was not one to which they can be said to have unreasonably exposed themselves or one another: see, generally, Fleming, *The Law of Torts*, 8th ed. (1992), pp. 279-80; Prosser and Keeton, *Torts*, 5th ed. (1984), pp. 457-58; and Linden, *Canadian Tort Law*, 5th ed. (Markham: Butterworths, 1993), pp. 438-39.

These parties were not found to have charged the wall with the force of their combined weight, as the city and Stingray have suggested. Had the wall been properly constructed or a 2 × 4 stud properly installed to eliminate the unprotected gap, and the same sequence of events had occurred, on the findings of the trial judge, the wall could have withstood the minimal force that caused the plywood panel to "pop out". The accident that in fact occurred was, in sum, beyond the reasonable contemplation of these parties; it was not within the scope of the risk created by their horseplay, no matter how imprudent that conduct may be considered.

4. The Apportionment of Liability

The issue here is whether the trial judge erred in apportioning liability as between the city and Stingray at 80 per cent and 20 per cent respectively. In the city's submission, this apportionment is inconsistent with the findings upon which the liability of these parties was based and disproportionate to their relative degrees of culpability.

I agree with this submission. In my respectful opinion, the trial judge reached his findings of relative culpability without proper regard to the facts of this case. In particular, he failed to take into account or give proper weight to the specific findings which he made in holding Stingray liable to the plaintiffs.

The city was held responsible for a far larger proportion of liability than Stingray essentially because the trial judge was of the view that its conduct represented "a marked departure" from the applicable standard of care. The marked departure consisted of its "egregious" failure to comply with the Building Code requirements and good building practice and its having permitted a "particularly insidious condition" to be created by failing to provide the protection to be expected of a wall. In apportioning liability, however, the trial judge did not mention the particulars of Stingray's breach of the duty towards the plaintiff. Nor did he provide any reason why, given his findings, this tortfeasor's negligence was comparatively less egregious or less marked a departure from the applicable standard of care than the city's.

Stingray, it will be recalled, had the "primary burden" for maintaining the stairway in a reasonably safe condition. It was under a legal obligation to take reasonable care to see that persons coming onto the premises were safe while on the premises. In breach of that duty, Stingray failed to conduct a reasonable inspection to determine the soundness of this exterior wooden structure and thus permitted the "particularly insidious condition" to which the trial judge referred to be maintained. It failed to have this inspection notwithstanding the obvious deterioration of the structure. The unsafe condition of the upper landing would have been discovered if a proper inspection had been made, and the plainly foreseeable risk of harm would have been eliminated. Furthermore, Stingray's failure to comply with the building by-law in 1985 resulted in "the continuance of the hazardous condition" that would have been discovered had the required permit been obtained.

In my opinion, a substantially greater degree of fault ought to have been attributed to Stingray for its departures from the standard of care exacted by the law. This company was under an "ongoing duty" to properly inspect these premises. The circumstances were such as to require affirmative action on its part as occupier to see that its premises were reasonably safe for persons in the position of the plaintiff. Its failure to discharge this statutory duty over the many years of its ownership of the property constituted a more proximate or current cause of the accident than did the city's negligence.

Following its final inspection, the city had no reason or opportunity to conduct any further inspection of the premises. The negligence of its inspectors in 1972 when the exterior stairway was constructed, in so far as it was concerned, was undiscoverable. While, as I have said, that negligence remained operative notwithstanding the passage of time, the fact is that had Stingray fulfilled its legal duty the risk created by the city's negligence would have been removed. Stingray cannot, and indeed does not, rely on the inspection made years earlier by the city as an excuse for non-compliance with its primary burden to maintain the safety of the premises. Taking into account Stingray's ongoing breach of the duty of care imposed on it by law, I am of the opinion that the apportionment was disproportionate to the respective degrees of culpability of these parties. Stingray should bear a significantly larger share of responsibility than that fixed by the trial judge.

While I appreciate that an appellate court should rarely interfere with a trial judge's apportionment of liability (*Sparks v. Thompson*, [1975] 1 S.C.R. 618, 46 D.L.R. (3d) 225), I am satisfied that there are sufficiently strong and exceptional circumstances here to warrant doing so. In reaching his conclusion as to relative fault, the trial judge failed to have proper regard to the totality of circumstances and the findings upon which he held Stingray liable. In my opinion, the comparative blameworthiness of these tortfeasors is such that liability for this accident should be apportioned 60 per cent against Stingray and 40 per cent against the city.

NOTES AND QUESTIONS

1. The trial judge held that both Mortimer and Cameron were negligent and that their combined negligence was a cause of Mortimer's devastating injuries. Why was Cameron not held liable to Mortimer and why was Mortimer not found contributorily negligent? Why did the Appeal Court uphold this aspect of the trial judgment? Do you agree with the trial judge's and Appeal Courts' analysis?

2. Would the courts' analysis of these issues have been the same if Cameron had been a well-insured corporate defendant or if Mortimer had suffered only a broken leg and several thousand dollars of economic loss?

3. The Ontario Negligence Act indicates that damages are to be apportioned in relationship to the parties' respective degrees of fault or negligence. Does this test relate to the parties' relative causal contribution or relative blameworthiness? How does the Appeal Court resolve this issue?

4. On what basis did the Appeal Court interfere with the trial judge's apportionment of damages? Do you agree with the Appeal Court's decision to intervene and its apportionment decision? See also *Taylor v. Asody*, [1975] 2 S.C.R. 414; *Rabideau v. Maddocks* (1992), 12 O.R. (3d) 83 (Gen. Div.); and *Hall v. Hebert* (1993), 15 C.C.L.T. (2d) 93 (S.C.C.).

5. In *Chamberland v. Fleming* (1984), 29 C.C.L.T. 213 (Alta. Q.B.), the court suggested that a rough upper limit of 25% should be established for contributory negligence if the plaintiff's negligence did not cause the incident, but merely affected the extent of the loss. Chamberland, a non-swimmer and inexperienced canoeist, drowned when the defendant negligently approached in his motor boat causing a wave to overturn the canoe. The deceased had declined to wear a life jacket that would have saved his life. Do you agree with the court's apportionment of loss in this case? What test did the court use to apportion the loss? Do you think that it is appropriate to establish fixed apportionment ratios for specific kinds of cases? See Irvine, "Annotation" (1984), 29 C.C.L.T. 213.

REVIEW PROBLEM

1. Edward, Ralph and Harry operated a window-washing business in Ontario. Ralph was responsible for checking the equipment and setting up the scaffold. Edward and Harry washed the windows. While the scaffold was at the third storey a frayed rope snapped, tilting the scaffold at a sharp angle. Harry was prevented from falling by his safety line. Edward had forgotten to attach his line and fell onto the roof of Bill's new car.

(a) Edward has sued Ralph in negligence. Ralph concedes that he was negligent, but alleges Edward was contributorily negligent. Discuss Ralph's defence of contributory negligence and the possible apportionment of liability.

(b) Bill has sued both Edward and Ralph in negligence to recover the damages to his car. Advise Edward as to whether he is likely to be held liable to Bill and, if so, to what extent. Assuming that Bill can recover from Edward, what recourse does Edward have against Ralph?

3. Voluntary Assumption of Risk

With the advent of apportionment of loss between a negligent defendant and a contributorily negligent plaintiff, the courts have become increasingly reluctant to apply the defence of voluntary assumption of risk. Although this complete defence remains available, Canadian judges have tended to limit it to narrow circumstances and to special types of cases, such as those involving participation in sports. Even within these categories, the defence has been narrowly applied in some recent cases.

DUBE v. LABAR

(1986), 27 D.L.R. (4th) 653 (S.C.C.)

ESTEY J.: — The appellant (plaintiff) and respondent (defendant), co-workers at a construction site, became acquainted shortly before the car accident giving rise to the action occurred. The night before the accident, the parties had participated in an evening of drinking and partying in Haines Junction, a town close to the construction camp where both lived. The morning of the accident, drinking was resumed early. The parties decided to retrieve the respondent's car, which had become stuck on the way home the night before, and then drive into Haines Junction to retrieve the appellant's eyeglasses and to try to find two young women they had met the previous night. On their arrival in Haines Junction, the appellant and respondent each consumed more alcohol. They left the bar, found the two women, and drove them approximately 50 or 60 miles toward Whitehorse at their request. Having dropped the women off, the parties started back to Haines Junction. The appellant had been driving throughout. The respondent, while a passenger, had apparently been drinking beer in the car. At some point on the return trip, the parties passed two hitchhikers, and decided to stop to pick them up. When the appellant tried to start the car again, he was unable to do so, and the respondent got into the driver's seat and started the car. At about this time, the appellant saw some friends passing in another vehicle, and, when they stopped, went to talk to them. He returned to the car and went to the driver's side, but the respondent was still in the driver's seat. In a short exchange, the respondent said that he was capable of driving. The appellant then got into the car as a passenger.

The accident occurred very shortly thereafter. The respondent, while driving, turned to speak to the hitchhiker sitting in the back seat. As he did so, the car veered to the right. The appellant, according to the testimony of the other hitchhiker who was seated on the front seat between the appellant and the respondent, attempted to grab the wheel and straighten out the car's course. The respondent's attempts at correction resulted, eventually, in the car's overturning on the right-hand embankment, causing personal injuries to the appellant. Samples of the respondent's breath later registered at .25 and .24 in tests administered by the police.

At trial, without objection from the parties, only two defences, *volenti non fit injuria* and contributory negligence, were put to the jury. The trial judge, after summarizing the evidence, charged the jury on the *volenti* defence as follows:

> One of the defences of the defendant in this case is the maxim *volenti non fit injuria*. Translated, that means "to one who is willing no harm no harm is done".
>
> The burden is on the defendant, in each case, to prove that the plaintiff, expressly or by necessary implication, agreed to exempt the defendant from liability for any damage suffered

by the plaintiff, occasioned by the defendant's negligence. In every case, the question is whether the plaintiff gave an express or implied consent to accept or assume the risk without compensation. In other words, did the plaintiff really consent to absolve the defendant from his common-law duty of care, saying or implying, in effect, "I am prepared to take the risk of your negligence and if I am injured you will not be legally responsible for my damages." The question is not simply whether the plaintiff knew of the risk but whether the circumstances were such as necessarily to lead to the conclusion that the whole risk was intentionally incurred by the plaintiff.

. . .

If you find that there is evidence of an initial common design which would, as a matter of common sense, entail the risk of injury, you might think that the appropriate inference may be not that the defendant undertook to exercise due care throughout, but that the plaintiff agreed to take upon himself the obvious risk of harm. The burden lies upon the defendant of proving that the plaintiff, expressly or by necessary implication, agreed to exempt the defendant from liability.

Therefore your test is not simply whether the plaintiff knew of the risk, but whether the circumstances are such as necessarily to lead to the conclusion that the whole risk was voluntarily incurred by the plaintiff.

Immediately after his discussion of the *volenti* defence, the trial judge said:

Having earlier discussed negligence [which was done in an earlier general part of the charge just before *volenti* was discussed], I want to turn to the allied and associated matter of contributory negligence . . . If you are satisfied by a preponderance of evidence that Dube's conduct amounted to a breach of that duty to take reasonable care for his own safety, then you would be justified in ascribing to him a portion of the blame for his injuries . . .

The judge charged the jury that contributory negligence could arise in two ways, "firstly, from the plaintiff's active conduct in grasping the steering wheel . . . secondly, you may find that the plaintiff was negligent about his own safety, when he remained in the vehicle after the defendant took over the driving, knowing what he knew of the defendant's condition at that time".

. . .

[The jury found that the plaintiff was contributorily negligent. However, they held that the plaintiff voluntarily assumed the risk and found for the defendant.]

The plaintiff's appeal to this Court was argued on the basis that the defence of *volenti* is inapplicable to a case involving negligence on the highways. This submission is plainly inconsistent with four decisions of this Court: *Car & General Ins. Corp. Ltd. v. Seymour et al.* (1956), 2 D.L.R. (2d) 369, [1956] S.C.R. 322; *Miller v. Decker* (1957), 9 D.L.R. (2d) 1, [1957] S.C.R. 624; *Lehnert v. Stein* (1962), 36 D.L.R. (2d) 159, [1963] S.C.R. 38, 40 W.W.R. 616, and *Eid v. Dumas; Hatherly v. Dumas* (1969), 5 D.L.R. (3d) 561, [1969] S.C.R. 668, 1 N.B.R. (2d) 445. However, while acknowledging that *volenti* is in principle available to a defendant driver, these cases establish that the defence will only be made out in unusual circumstances. The test has been variously described. . . .

Abbott J., dissenting in the *Miller* case, . . . [stated]:

[F]or a negligent driver to be completely relieved from liability, the plaintiff must have agreed expressly or by implication to exempt the defendant from liability for damages suffered by the plaintiff and occasioned by the negligence of the defendant during the carrying out of the latter's undertaking. In other words, to constitute a defence there must have been an express or implied bargain between the parties whereby the plaintiff gave up his right of action for negligence. As was pointed out by Kellock J. at p. 377 D.L.R., p. 331 S.C.R., the question in each particular case is, in the language of Lindley L.J. in *Yarmouth v. France* (1887), 19 Q.B.D. 647 at p. 660, "'not simply whether the plaintiff knew of the risk but whether the circumstances are such as *necessarily* to lead to the conclusion that the whole risk was voluntarily incurred by the plaintiff'".

Finally, in *Lehnert v. Stein, supra*, Cartwright J. held (at p. 164 D.L.R., p. 43 S.C.R.) that:

[W]here a driver of a motor vehicle invokes the maxim *volenti non fit injuria* as a defence to an action for damages for injuries caused by his negligence to a passenger, the burden lies upon the defendant of proving that the plaintiff, expressly or by necessary implication, agreed to exempt the defendant from liability for any damage suffered by the plaintiff occasioned by that negligence, and that, as stated in *Salmond on Torts*, 13th ed., p. 44:

"The true question in every case is: did the plaintiff give a real consent to the assumption of the risk without compensation; did the consent really absolve the defendant from the duty to take care?"

Thus, *volenti* will arise only where the circumstances are such that it is clear that the plaintiff, knowing of the virtually certain risk of harm, in essence bargained away his right to sue for injuries incurred as a result of any negligence on the defendant's part. The acceptance of risk may be express or may arise by necessary implication from the conduct of the parties, but it will arise, in cases such as the present, only where there can truly be said to be an understanding on the part of both parties that the defendant assumed no responsibility to take due care for the safety of the plaintiff, and that the plaintiff did not expect him to.

Common sense dictates that only rarely will a plaintiff genuinely consent to accept the risk of the defendant's negligence.

. . .

The defence of *volenti* will, furthermore, necessarily be inapplicable in the great majority of drunken driver-willing passenger cases. It requires an awareness of the circumstances and the consequences of action that are rarely present on the facts of such cases at the relevant time.

. . .

Prior to the enactment of legislation allowing for apportionment of damages in cases where the plaintiff's own negligence had contributed to his injuries (here, the *Contributory Negligence Ordinance*, R.O.Y.T. 1971, c. C-14), drawing a distinction between the defences of *volenti* and contributory negligence was unnecessary. Both had the same drastic effect of denying completely compensation to the plaintiff. This is no longer the case. Apportionment permits a sensible distribution of the financial burden of negligent conduct. It is a more flexible and more appropriate response in the great majority of cases in which negligent conduct of the plaintiff is argued to support a *volenti* defence. Thus, it is of great importance to keep the two defences distinct (see *Salmond and Heuston on the Law of Torts*, 18th ed. (1981), at pp. 472-3; Glanville Williams, *supra*, at p. 308).

. . .

The jury's conclusion that the plaintiff consented to bear the legal risk when he entered the car as passenger, knowing of the defendant's state of impairment, is doubtless one that not every jury would have reached. It does not have the character of unreasonableness, however, that must be apparent on the face of a jury verdict before an appellate court can upset it . . .

. . .

I therefore would dismiss the appeal with costs to the respondent.

MCINTYRE and CHOUINARD JJ. concur with ESTEY J.

Wilson J. wrote a concurring judgment.

NOTES AND QUESTIONS

1. How did the court define the elements of voluntary assumption of risk? What policy reasons were given for narrowly interpreting this defence?

2. The courts have been divided on the issue of whether the defence of *volenti* applies at all to willing passengers of drunken drivers. Estey J. states that the defence will be inapplicable in the great majority of cases.

What do you think prompted the jury to conclude that Dube voluntarily assumed the risk? Based on the factual record, do you agree with its conclusion? Given that Estey J. did not agree with the jury, why did he deny the appeal?

3. The courts will also find that the plaintiff voluntarily assumed the risk if he encouraged the defendant to be careless. See *Allen v. Lucas* (1971), 25 D.L.R. (3d) 218 (Sask. C.A.); *Conrad v. Crawford*, [1972] 1 O.R. 134 (H.C.); and *Cherrey v. Steinke* (1980), 13 C.C.L.T. 50 (Man. C.A.). But see *Eid v. Dumas*, [1969] S.C.R. 668; and *Betts v. Sanderson Estate* (1988), 53 D.L.R. (4th) 675 (B.C. C.A.), leave to appeal ref'd. [1989] 3 W.W.R. lxx (note) (S.C.C.).

4. As a matter of policy what principles should govern the legal position of a passenger who accepts a ride from an intoxicated driver? What role does the fact that the driver will most likely be insured have on your analysis? See generally Skene, "Voluntary Assumption of Risk and the Gratuitous Passenger" (1974), 1 Dalhousie L.J. 605; Harpum, "Contributory Negligence Defences for the Drunken Driver" (1977), 40 Mod. L. Rev. 350; and Koressis, "Injured Passenger Actions Against Intoxicated Drivers — Volenti or Contributory Negligence" (1983), 4 Advoc. Q. 297.

5. The debate over the scope of voluntary assumption of risk has also arisen in the context of intoxicated patrons of drinking establishments. See *Jordan House Ltd. v. Menow* (1974), 38 D.L.R. (3d) 105 (S.C.C.); and *Crocker v. Sundance Northwest Resorts Ltd.* (1988), 44 C.C.L.T. 225 (S.C.C.). See text in chapter 11.

6. Is there an age below which children lack the capacity to assess the physical risks of injury and to accept legal responsibility for injuries that may befall them? Should the principles of voluntary assumption of risk be applied the same way in cases involving adults and children? See *Savard v. Urbano* (1977), 85 D.L.R. (3d) 33 (Que. C.A.); *Doiron v. Brideau* (1979), 28 N.B.R. (2d) 520 (C.A.); and *McGinlay v. British Railway Bd.*, [1983] 1 W.L.R. 1427 (H.L.); and *Laviolette v. C.N.R.* (1987), 40 C.C.L.T. 138 (N.B. C.A.).

7. What risks should a participant in a sport be held to have voluntarily assumed? Should it matter whether the participant is experienced or a novice? See *Hanson v. St. John Horticultural Assn.*, [1974] S.C.R. 354; *Delaney v. Cascade River Holidays Ltd.* (1983), 24 C.C.L.T. 6 (B.C. C.A.); *Temple v. Hallem*, [1989] 5 W.W.R. 669 (Man. C.A.); *Potvin v. Stipetic* (1989), 50 C.C.L.T. 233 (Que. C.A.); and *Scurfield v. Cariboo Helicopter Skiing Ltd.*, [1993] 3 W.W.R. 418 (B.C. C.A.), leave to appeal ref'd. [1993] 7 W.W.R. lxviii (S.C.C.). Some Canadian courts have been unwilling to apply voluntary assumption of risk even in the context of violent sports. See *Unruh (Guardian ad litem of) v. Webber* (1994), 112 D.L.R. (4th) 83 (B.C. C.A.), leave to appeal ref'd. [1994] 8 W.W.R. lxvi (S.C.C.); and *Zapf v. Muckalt* (1995), 26 C.C.L.T. (2d) 61 (B.C. S.C.).

8. What risks should a spectator at a sporting event be held to have voluntarily assumed? See *Payne v. Maple Leaf Gardens Ltd.*, [1949] 1 D.L.R. 369 (Ont. C.A.); *White v. Blackmore*, [1972] 2 Q.B. 651 (C.A.); and *Carson v. Thunder Bay* (1985), 52 O.R. (2d) 173 (Dist. Ct.). See generally Kligman, "Tort Liability for Sports Injuries" (1989), 1 C.I.L.R. 153.

9. In the cases discussed to this point, the defence of voluntary assumption of risk has been established by drawing an inference from the plaintiff's conduct. The defence may also be established by express agreement. The meaning and effect given such agreements is essentially governed by the law of contract. See *Dyck v. Man. Snowmobile Assn.* (1985), 58 N.R. 144 (S.C.C.); *ITO — International Terminal Operators Ltd. v. Miida Electronics Inc.* (1986), 28 D.L.R. (4th) 641 (S.C.C.); *Crocker v. Sundance Northwest Resort Ltd.* (1988), 44 C.C.L.T. 225 (S.C.C.); *London Drugs Ltd. v. Kuehne* (1992), 97 D.L.R. (4th) 261 (S.C.C.); *Ocsko v. Cypress Bowl Recreations Ltd.* (1992), 95 D.L.R. (4th) 701 (B.C. C.A.);

and *Greeven v. Blackcomb Skiing Enterprises Ltd.* (1994), 22 C.C.L.T. (2d) 265 (B.C. S.C.). See also Coote, *Exception Clauses* (1964); and Seddon, "Fault Without Liability — Exemption Clauses in Tort" (1981), 55 Aust. L.J. 22.

    10. For a general discussion of voluntary assumption of risk see Hertz, "Violenti Non Fit Injuria: A Guide" in Klar (ed.), *Studies in Canadian Tort Law* (1977), 101 at 119-26; Jaffey, "Volenti Non Fit Injuria" (1985), 44 Cambridge L.J. 87; and Simons, "Assumption of Risk and Consent in the Law of Torts: A Theory of Full Preference" (1987), 67 Boston Univ. L. Rev. 213.

4. Participation in a Criminal or Immoral Act

    The defence of *ex turpi causa non oritur actio* was raised in chapter 6 in relation to intentional torts. The application of the principle is essentially the same in negligence.

HALL v. HEBERT

(1993), 15 C.C.L.T. (2d) 93 (S.C.C.)

[The plaintiff and the defendant got "quite and equally drunk" at a party. While driving home, the defendant stalled his "souped-up muscle" car on a steep, unlit gravel road with a sharp drop-off to one side. At the plaintiff's request, the defendant allowed the plaintiff to drive. They then attempted to get the car going by getting a rolling start. The plaintiff lost control of the vehicle almost immediately and flipped the vehicle in the adjacent gravel pit. The plaintiff was severely injured and sued the defendant for allowing him to drive in his intoxicated condition.

    The major issue on appeal to the Supreme Court was whether the defendant could raise the defence of *ex turpi causa non oritur actio* to negate the plaintiff's cause of action.]

McLachlin J.: —

. . .

    My colleague Cory J. suggests that the defence of ex turpi causa non oritur actio should be eliminated. In its place, he suggests that the courts should be granted the power to disallow a plaintiff's claim, on account of the plaintiff's wrongful conduct, by finding that no duty of care arises. This power is to be exercised under the second branch of the test articulated in *Anns v. Merton London Borough Council*, [1978] A.C. 728, as approved and reformulated in this Court in *Nielsen v. Kamloops (City)*, [1984] 2 S.C.R. 2. On this view, the plaintiff's illegal or immoral conduct may constitute a policy reason for holding that the defendant owed the plaintiff no duty of care.

    A variant of this approach has been adopted in Australia, *Gala v. Preston*, supra, at pp. 251-55, and by the English Court of Appeal, *Pitts v. Hunt*, supra, at pp. 355-56, 358. This view holds that no duty should be postulated where, it is either *impossible* or *improper* for the courts to establish a standard of care to govern the conduct in issue. It is recognized that there is no a priori reason in law why a duty cannot subsist between criminals or wrongdoers. However, some cases raise such "special and exceptional" circumstances that a court cannot, or cannot in good conscience, enquire into the standard of care needed to ground the duty of care in a particular situation. Unlike the view espoused by Cory J., the very possibility of a duty arising is not denied; rather the court declines to enter into the question of whether a duty exists.

With great respect, I am not sure that much is gained by replacing the defence of ex turpi causa non oritur actio with a judicial discretion to negate, or to refuse to consider, the duty of care. Shifting the analysis to the issue of duty provides no new insight into the fundamental question of when the courts should be entitled to deny recovery in tort to a plaintiff on the ground of the plaintiff's immoral or illegal conduct. Moreover, it introduces a series of new problems. In the end I fear that it would prove more problematic than has the defence of ex turpi causa non oritur actio.

I begin by noting that the duty approach, as expressed by Cory J., does not fully capture what we mean when we invoke the principle of ex turpi causa. If what I have said above is correct, the ex turpi causa principle operates most naturally as a defence because its purpose is to frustrate what would be, had ex turpi causa no role, a complete cause of action. Liability for tort arises out of the relationship between the alleged tortfeasor and the injured claimant. The power of the court to deny recovery where it would undermine the coherence of the legal system, on the other hand, represents concerns independent of this relationship. It is important, if only for the purposes of conceptual clarity, that ex turpi causa operate, on those rare occasions where its operation is justified, as a defence to frustrate tort claims which could otherwise be fully made out, because this best expresses what is in fact decided. The courts make it clear that the defendant has acted wrongly in negligently causing harm. They also make it clear that responsibility for this wrong is suspended only because concern for the integrity of the legal system trumps the concern that the defendant be responsible.

Donoghue v. Stevenson, [1932] A.C. 562 (H.L.), the source of our modern law of negligence and of the concept of duty upon which it is founded, requires that a person exercise reasonable care toward all his neighbours. It does not say that the duty is owed only to neighbours who have acted morally and legally. Tort, unlike equity which requires that the plaintiff come with clean hands, does not require a plaintiff to have a certain moral character in order to bring an action before the court. The duty of care is owed to *all* persons who may reasonably be foreseen to be injured by the negligent conduct.

Policy concerns unrelated to the legal rules which govern the relationship between the parties to an action have not generally been considered in determining whether a duty [of] care lies. This follows from the fact that the justice which tort law seeks to accomplish is justice between the parties to the particular action; the court acts at the instance of the wronged party to rectify the damage caused by a particular defendant: see Ernest J. Weinrib, "The Special Morality of Tort Law" (1989) 34 McGill L.J. 403, at p. 408.

The relationship between plaintiff and defendant which gives rise to their respective entitlement and liability arises from a duty predicated on foreseeable consequences of harm. This being the concern, the legality or morality of the plaintiff's conduct is an extrinsic consideration. In the rare cases where concerns for the administration of justice require that the extrinsic consideration of the character of the plaintiff's conduct be considered, it seems to me that this is better done by way of defence than by distorting the notion of the duty of care owed by the defendant to the plaintiff.

It can be argued that the Australian rule avoids these doctrinal problems by recognizing that, while a duty of care might otherwise lie, it cannot be raised because the parties, by their conduct, have made it impossible or improper to consider the claim. In other words, that a duty could arise from the relationship between the parties is not denied — plaintiff is simply barred from relying on it. Thus the Australian High Court formally avoids conflict with the principle it has articulated in earlier judgments: that no person becomes a caput lupinum, or an outlaw, in the eyes of the civil law merely because that person was engaged in some unlawful act: *Henwood v. Municipal Tramways Trust (S.A.)* (1938), 60 C.L.R. 438, at p. 466 (Aust. H.C.). On analysis, however, this notion that the courts cannot, in certain circumstances, consider whether a duty of care arises has the practical effect of denying a duty which would otherwise arise, and hence, in substance, of violating the very principle against making certain parties outlaws to which the court seeks to adhere.

Beyond this, a more practical objection can be raised: why is it necessary to take the rather novel step of positing judicial "inability" to investigate the appropriate standard of care, instead of using the concept by which the law has traditionally recognized considerations that prevent otherwise valid claims from succeeding, that is, the concept of a defence to the action?

The law of tort recognizes many types of defence. Some go to the relationship between the parties; for example, the defence of volenti non fit injuria, the plaintiff's assumption of risk. But others go to matters unrelated to that relationship. Limitation periods, for example, are raised by way of defence. I see no reason to treat ex turpi causa differently. Like a lapsed limitation period, it represents a reason why a cause of action, which might otherwise be fully made out, should not succeed.

The debate is not purely academic. There are practical reasons for finding that it is proper to view ex turpi causa as a defence. I mention three. If the ex turpi causa principle arises in the course of the investigation into whether there exists a duty of care, the onus will lie on the plaintiff to show why he or she should not be disentitled by way of his or her conduct. It is well established that the plaintiff bears the onus of establishing a valid cause of action; if not, the plaintiff faces non-suit. Thus a plaintiff whose conduct is alleged to be immoral or illegal might be bound to disprove the illegality or immorality in order to proceed with her action and avoid non-suit. On the other hand, if the matter is left as a defence, the onus rests on the defendant. As I have indicated, the power to preclude recovery on the basis of the plaintiff's immoral or illegal conduct is an *exceptional* power, operating in derogation of the general principles of tort applicable to all persons in our society. As such, it seems to me appropriate that the onus of establishing the exceptional circumstances should rest with the defendant. The plaintiff should not be required to *disprove* the existence and relevance of his or her illegal or immoral conduct; rather it should be for the defendant to establish it.

Second, the duty of care approach is an all or nothing approach, and cannot be applied selectively to discreet [sic] heads of damage. As discussed above, cases may arise in which a particular damage claim, e.g., for exemplary damages, or for damages for loss of future earnings, might be seen as a claim to profit from an illegal act. Another damage claim in the same action, e.g., one for compensation for personal injuries, could not be so regarded. If the ex turpi causa principle operates as a defence it is possible to distinguish between such claims. If it operates as a factor negating a duty of care, on the other hand, it is not possible to treat an action in the selective manner that justice seems to require.

Finally, consideration of illegal or immoral conduct at the stage of determining the duty of care raises procedural problems. A plaintiff may sue in both tort and contract. If the approach suggested by Cory J. is adopted, in the contract claim, the plaintiff's illegal or immoral conduct would be raised as a defence to the claim; in the tort, the same conduct would be an element of the enquiry into the duty of care. In other words, in contract the onus would be on the defendant to prove the relevance of the plaintiff's conduct; in tort, the onus would be on the plaintiff to disprove the relevance of the conduct. The resulting confusion would unnecessarily complicate the task of the trial judge and the parties.

These considerations lead me to conclude that the important but limited power of the court to prevent tort recovery on the ground of the plaintiff's illegal or immoral conduct is better viewed as a defence than as a factor going to the existence of a duty of care.

II. Application to These Facts

The doctrine of ex turpi causa non oritur actio properly applies in tort where it will be necessary to invoke the doctrine in order to maintain the internal consistency of the law. Most commonly, this concern will arise where a given plaintiff genuinely seeks to profit from his or her illegal conduct, or where the claimed compensation would amount to an evasion of a criminal sanction. This appellant need not be denied recovery since these grounds are not relevant to his claim. The compensation sought by this appellant is for injuries received. This compensation can be reduced to the extent of the appellant's contributory negligence, but cannot be wholly denied by reason of his disreputable or criminal conduct.

[La Forest, L'Heureux-Dubé and Iacobucci JJ. concurred with McLachlin J. Cory J. concurred in the result, but indicated that the defence of *ex turpi causa* should be eliminated. Gonthier J. concurred in the result. While he agreed that *ex turpi causa* had to be limited, he did not accept that it should be limited to the narrow categories that McLachlin J. set out. Sopinka J. agreed that *ex turpi causa* did not apply on the facts, but held that the plaintiff's claim should be dismissed because the defendant did not owe the plaintiff any duty of care.]

NOTES AND QUESTIONS

1. The Canadian courts consistently narrowed *ex turpi causa* in a series of often conflicting cases. While few judges liked the defence, they could not agree on the purpose it should serve. This checkered history is discussed in more detail in chapter 6.

2. McLachlin J. stated in *Hall* that the purpose of the *ex turpi causa* doctrine is to protect "the integrity of the legal system". In her view, the plaintiff's illegal or immoral conduct would only rarely be relevant if the plaintiff was seeking compensation for actual physical injuries or losses. She distinguished these claims from those in which the plaintiff was seeking to profit from his wrongdoing.

Do you agree with McLachlin J. that the doctrine's goal should be to protect the integrity of the legal system? Assuming that this is an appropriate goal, does it follow that the doctrine would only rarely apply to claims for actual physical injuries?

3. McLachlin J. raised three "practical reasons" why *ex turpi causa* should be treated as a defence and not dealt with at the duty stage. Are these reasons compelling?

4. All seven justices appear to agree on the goal of the doctrine, the need to limit it and its inapplicability to the facts in *Hall*. What are the implications of the fact that despite this agreement, there are four judgments?

The complexity of the legal and policy issues generated by the doctrine is reflected by the range of approaches that have been take by other Commonwealth courts. See *Pitts v. Hunt*, [1990] 3 All E.R. 344 (C.A.); *Gala v. Preston* (1991), 172 C.L.R. 243 (H.C. Aust.); and *Brown v. Dunsmuir*, [1994] 3 N.Z.L.R. 485 (Auck. H.C.).

5. For an academic commentary see MacDoughall, "Ex Turpi Causa: Should a Defence Arise from a Base Cause?" (1991), 55 Sask. L. Rev. 1; Klar, "Negligence Defences — . . ." (1993), 72 Can. Bar Rev. 553; and Kostal, "Currents in the Counter-Reformation: Illegality and Duty of Care in Canada and Australia" (1995), 3 Tort L. Rev. 100.

5. Inevitable Accident

RINTOUL v. X-RAY AND RADIUM INDUST. LTD.

[1956] S.C.R. 674 (S.C.C.)

CARTWRIGHT J.: — The facts as deposed to by Ouellette were as follows. On April 13, 1954, at about 8:50 a.m. Ouellette was driving a 1952 Dodge motor vehicle owned by his employer, the respondent X-Ray and Radium Industries Limited, easterly on Wellington Street in the city of Ottawa. He stopped at the intersection of Bayview Avenue for a traffic-light and his service brakes worked properly. From the time that he had left his home up to this point he had applied his service brakes five times and on each occasion they had worked properly. The traffic-light having changed he proceeded across Bayview Avenue and saw that the line of traffic ahead of him was at a standstill. The appellant's car was at the rear of this line of traffic. When Ouellette was about 150 feet away from the appellant's car he took his foot off the accelerator and applied his service brakes. At this moment he was proceeding uphill at a speed of not more than twelve miles per hour; he found that the brakes did not work; the brake pedal went down to the floor of the car without his feeling any braking action; he allowed the pedal to rise and pressed it down again, still without getting any braking action. Thinking that the service brakes had become useless, he applied his hand brakes; at the moment of this application his car was between 50 and 75 feet from that of the appellant. The application of the hand brakes reduced the speed of his car but did not stop it and it was still moving at about 6 miles per hour when it struck the rear of the appellant's vehicle.

. . .

The defence relied on at the trial and before us was pleaded in the Statement of Defence as follows:—

(4) The Defendants allege and the fact is that at the time and place referred to in the Statement of Claim the brakes of the Defendant motor vehicle suddenly and without warning failed and it was in the circumstances impossible for the Defendant driver to avoid the collision.

(5) The Defendants allege and the fact is that they had taken all reasonable and proper

precaution in the care of the brakes on the said motor vehicle and plead that the said collision was an inevitable or an unavoidable accident.

There can be no doubt that, generally speaking, when a car, in broad daylight, runs into the rear of another which is stationary on the highway and which has not come to a sudden stop, the fault is in the driving of the moving car, and the driver of such car must satisfy the Court that the collision did not occur as a result of his negligence. The learned trial judge regarded this principle as applicable to the case at bar but was of the view that the unexpected failure of the service brakes placed Ouellette in a situation of emergency in which he acted without negligence and that the collision was the result of an inevitable accident.

The defence of inevitable accident has been discussed in many decisions. A leading case in Ontario is *McIntosh v. Bell* [[1932] O.R. 179], which was approved by this Court in *Claxton v. Grandy* [[1934] 4 D.L.R. 257 at 263]. At page 187 of the report of *McIntosh v. Bell*, Hodgins J.A. adopts the words of Lord Esher M.R. In *The Schwan* [[1892] P. 419 at 429], as follows:—

> ... In my opinion, a person relying on inevitable accident must shew that something happened over which he had no control, and the effect of which could not have been avoided by the greatest care and skill.

In my view, in the case at bar the respondents have failed to prove two matters both of which were essential to the establishment of the defence of inevitable accident. These matters are (i) that the alleged failure of the service brakes could not have been prevented by the exercise of reasonable care on their part, and (ii) that, assuming that such failure occurred without negligence on the part of the respondents, Ouellette could not, by the exercise of reasonable care, have avoided the collision which he claims was the effect of such failure.

As to the first matter, assuming that the service brakes failed suddenly, the onus resting on the respondents was to show that such failure could not have been prevented by the exercise of reasonable care. In Halsbury, 2nd Edition, Volume 23, page 640, section 901, the learned author says:—

> Driving with defective apparatus if the defect might reasonably have been discovered ... (and other matters) ... are negligent acts which render a defendant liable for injuries of which they are the effective cause.

This passage has been approved by McCardie J. in *Phillips v. Brittania Hygienic Laundry Co.* [[1923] 1 K.B. 539 at 551] and by Hogg J.A. in *Grise v. Rankin et al.* [[1951] O.W.N. 21 at 22], and, in my opinion, correctly states the law.

In the case at bar the respondents have made no attempt to prove that the sudden failure could not have been prevented by reasonable care on their part and particularly by adequate inspection. They called no witness to explain the extraordinary fact that the service brakes which were working properly immediately before and immediately after the accident and passed satisfactorily the test prescribed in the regulations failed momentarily at the time of the accident. Without going so far as to say that such a story appears to be intrinsically impossible, it is clear that its nature was such as to cast upon the defendants the burden of furnishing a clear and satisfactory explanation of so unusual an occurrence.

Furthermore, the respondents have made no attempt to shew that the defect, whatever it was, could not reasonably have been discovered. The evidence is that the respondents' car was a 1952 Dodge. There is no evidence: (*a*) as to when it was purchased, or (*b*) whether it was purchased new or second-hand, or (*c*) how far it had been driven, or (*d*) how often, if ever, the service brakes had been inspected, or (*e*) how often, if ever, the hand brakes had been inspected. The only evidence touching the point at all is Ouellette's statement quoted above that there "was work done on the brakes" the day before the accident. There is nothing to indicate whether the brakes referred to in this statement were the service brakes or the hand brakes although in argument it seemed to be assumed that the reference was to the service brakes. No evidence was given as to what instructions were given to the third party, or as to what work was done by him, or as to what report, if any, was made by the third party when the car was delivered, or as to whether the third party was competent to inspect or repair brakes. The onus resting on the respondents in this regard is not discharged by the bald statement that on the day before the accident there was work (unspecified) done on the brakes.

. . .

In my opinion, on the evidence the respondents have not only failed to show that the alleged failure of the service brakes was inevitable, they have also failed to show that after such failure occurred Ouellette could not by the exercise of reasonable care have avoided the collision. It follows that the appeal of the plaintiff should be allowed.

NOTES AND QUESTIONS

1. What must the defendant establish to invoke the defence of inevitable accident? According to Cartwright J., what standard of care is the defendant required to meet? Is this consistent with Lord Esher's statement in *The Schwan*, which Cartwright J. quotes with approval?

2. What is the effect of the defendant's plea of inevitable accident on the burden of proof? Given its impact in Canada, why would the defendant raise the defence?

3. The Canadian courts have generally applied *Rintoul*. The majority of cases involved sudden mechanical failures and other emergency situations. See *Levesque v. Day & Ross Ltd.* (1976), 15 N.B.R. (2d) 500 (C.A.); *Blackwood v. Butler* (1984), 48 Nfld. & P.E.I.R. 110 (Nfld. C.A.); *Dobbs v. Mayer* (1985), 32 C.C.L.T. 191 (Ont. S.C.); *White v. Sheaves* (1987), 194 A.P.R. 290 (Nfld. S.C.); and *Basra v. Gill*, [1995] 2 W.W.R. 213 (B.C. C.A.), leave to appeal ref'd. [1995] 4 W.W.R. lxviii (S.C.C.).

However, see *Graham v. Hodgkinson* (1983), 40 O.R. (2d) 697 (C.A.); and *Boutcher v. Stewart* (1989), 50 C.C.L.T. 77 (N.B. C.A.) in which it was indicated that inevitable accident was no more than a denial of negligence and that it did not alter either the plaintiff's or the defendant's case.

4. Is there any reason to treat inevitable accident as a defence? See Klar, "Annotation" (1977), 1 C.C.L.T. 273; Smith, "Automatism — A Defence to Negligence?", [1980] New Law Journal 1111; Kligman, "Inevitable Accident and the Infirm Driver: What You Don't Know Can Kill You" (1987), 8 Advoc. Q. 311; and Gilles, "Inevitable Accident in Classical English Tort Law" (1993), 43 Emory L.J. 575.

REVIEW PROBLEM

David Carling and Randy Jones, two 15-year-old students, had several very strong drinks at David's house while his parents were out of town. Randy suggested that they take Mr. Carling's car for a drive and pick up their girlfriends. Although neither Randy nor David had driver's licences, David agreed to the plan despite his parents' explicit prohibition against driving. Carol agreed to accompany them and asked them to bring along some liquor for her. Mary also agreed to go for a ride, but she was unaware that they had been drinking. Carol knew that the boys had taken the car without consent, but Mary did not.

During the drive, they picked up Louise, who was hitchhiking to work. She soon realized that David was drunk and very tired. She twice asked him to slow down. She thought about getting out of the car, but she was late for work. As a result of his speeding and intoxication, David lost control of the car and hit Mr. Crown's parked car. The car was parked illegally, partially blocking the roadway. Had David not panicked, however, he could easily have avoided the car. Both cars were badly damaged and all the occupants of Mr. Carling's vehicle were injured.

Mr. Crown, Louise, Mary, Carol and Randy have sued David in negligence. You have been retained to research the possible defences that David might raise and their impact on his liability.

18

PROOF OF NEGLIGENCE

1. The Burden of Proof in a Negligence Action
2. Exceptions to the General Principles Governing the Burden of Proof
3. *Res Ipsa Loquitur*

1. The Burden of Proof in a Negligence Action

It is important at the outset to distinguish between the legal and evidentiary burdens of proof. The legal burden of proof in a civil action is the burden of proving an issue on the balance of probabilities. In other words, after both sides have been heard, the party who bears the legal burden will lose the issue unless she has convinced the judge or jury to this requisite degree of certainty. Although the balance of probabilities test is clearly less onerous than the criminal standard of beyond a reasonable doubt, it is difficult to define precisely. Fleming, in *The Law of Torts*, 8th ed. (1992), at 314-15 explains the civil standard in the following terms: "[It] requires more than a mere mechanical comparison of probabilities independently of any belief in its reality; the tribunal must feel an actual persuasion based on a preponderance of probability. Thus a merely mathematical or statistical probability of barely 51 per cent is not sufficient because it carries no conviction that the case falls within the 51 rather than the 49." The plaintiff usually bears the legal burden of proving all of the elements of a negligence action, and the defendant has the legal burden of proving any defence.

The evidentiary burden is the legal obligation of a party to adduce evidence in support of her position. A litigant must introduce enough evidence to warrant the judge leaving the issue to the jury or, if the judge is sitting alone, to consider the issue herself. The evidentiary burden of proof usually rests with the party who bears the legal burden. In order to meet this evidentiary burden, the plaintiff in a negligence suit must establish a "prima facie case of negligence". She must adduce evidence which, if believed, would support but not necessarily compel a decision in her favour. If the plaintiff fails to establish a *prima facie* case, the judge will order a nonsuit, because there is no case to go to the jury. Even if the plaintiff discharges her evidentiary burden, she will still lose if she fails to satisfy the legal burden of proof. For example, her evidence may not be believed or it may not be sufficiently persuasive to convince the judge or jury on the balance of probabilities. Alternatively, the defendant's evidence may be equally or more compelling.

Once the plaintiff establishes a *prima facie* case, it is often said that the burden of proof shifts to the defendant. What is usually meant by this statement is that the defendant as a practical matter of good trial tactics should adduce evidence in support of her position, even though she has no legal obligation to do so. In a complicated trial involving contentious issues, this tactical burden may pass back and forth, while the legal burden of proving the case on the balance of probabilities remains with the plaintiff.

WAKELIN v. LONDON & SOUTH WESTERN RY. CO.

wrongful death suit

(1886), 12 App. Cas. 41 (H.L.)

The action was brought by the administratrix of Henry Wakelin on behalf of herself and her children under Lord Campbell's Act, 9 & 10 Vict. c. 93.

The statement of claim alleged that the defendant's line between Chiswick Station and Chiswick Junction crossed a public footway, and that on the 1st of May 1882 the defendants so negligently and unskilfully drove a train on the line across the footpath and so neglected to take precautions in respect of the train and the crossing that the train struck and killed one Henry Wakelin the plaintiff's husband whilst lawfully on the footpath.

The statement of defence admitted that on that day the plaintiff's husband whilst on or near the footpath was struck by a train of the defendants, and so injured that he died, but denied the alleged negligence; did not admit that the deceased was lawfully crossing the line at the time in question; and alleged that his death was caused by his own negligence and that he might by the exercise of reasonable caution have seen the train approaching and avoided the accident.

. . .

Oral evidence was given that from the cottage where the deceased lived it would take about ten minutes to walk to the crossing; that he left his cottage on the evening of the 1st of May after tea, and that he was never seen again till his body was found the same night on the down line near the crossing. There was no evidence as to the circumstances under which he got on to the line. Witnesses for the plaintiff gave evidence (not very intelligible) as to the limited number of yards at which an approaching train could be seen from the crossing, and as to obstructions to the view.

The defendants called no witnesses, and submitted that there was no case. Manisty J. left the case to the jury who returned a verdict for the plaintiff for £800. The Divisional Court (Grove J. Huddleston B. and Hawkins J.) set aside the verdict and entered judgment for the defendants. The Court of Appeal (Brett M.R. Bowen and Fry L.JJ.) on the 16th day of May 1884 affirmed this decision. In the course of his judgment Brett M.R. said that in his opinion the plaintiff in this case was not only bound to give evidence of negligence on the part of the defendants which was a cause of the death of the deceased, but was also bound to give prima facie evidence that the deceased was not guilty of negligence contributing to the accident; and that by reason of the plaintiff having been unable to give any evidence of the circumstances of the accident she had failed in giving evidence of that necessary part of her prima facie case.

From this decision the plaintiff appealed.

. . .

LORD HALSBURY L.C.: — My Lords, it is incumbent upon the plaintiff in this case to establish by proof that her husband's death has been caused by some negligence of the defendants, some negligent act, or some negligent omission, to which the injury complained of in this case, the death of the husband, is attributable. That is the fact to be proved. If that fact is not proved the plaintiff fails, and if in the absence of direct proof the circumstances which are established are equally consistent with the allegation of the plaintiff as with the denial of the defendants, the plaintiff fails, for the very simple reason that the plaintiff is bound to establish the affirmative of the proposition;

. . .

If the simple proposition with which I started is accurate, it is manifest that the plaintiff, who gives evidence of a state of facts which is equally consistent with the wrong of which she complains having been caused by — in this sense that it could not have occurred without — her husband's own negligence as by the negligence of the defendants, does not prove that it was caused by the defendants' negligence. She may indeed establish that the event has occurred through the joint negligence of both, but if that is the state of the evidence the plaintiff fails... It is true that the onus of proof may shift from time to time as matter of evidence, but still the question must ultimately arise whether the person who is bound to prove the affirmative of the issue, i.e., in this case the negligent act done, has discharged herself of that burden. I am of opinion that the plaintiff does not do this unless she proves that the defendants have caused the injury in the sense which I have explained.

In this case I am unable to see any evidence of how this unfortunate calamity occurred. One may surmise, and it is but surmise and not evidence, that the unfortunate man was knocked down by a passing train while on the level crossing; but assuming in the plaintiff's favour that fact to be established, is there anything to shew that the train ran over the man rather than that the man ran against the train?

. . .

Again, is there any legal presumption that people are careful and look before them on crossing a railway, or even when they do see the approach of a train that they never cross when the train is dangerously near? And yet if one of these hypotheses were established the plaintiff must fail, while on the other side it would be extremely difficult to lay down as a matter of law that precautions which the legislature has not enjoined should be observed by a railway company in the ordinary conduct of their traffic. Railway companies are permitted to establish their undertakings for the express purpose of running trains at high speed along their lines. Rightly or wrongly the legislature have permitted the railways to cross roadways on a level, and it must be taken that the legislature, wherever they have given that authority, and without requiring special measures of precaution, have left to the railway company the discretion of using their lines in a reasonable and proper fashion. I can understand that circumstances might exist which might call upon the railway company to take unusual precautions, though not prescribed by statute, but the peculiarity about this case is that no one knows what the circumstances were. The body of the deceased man was found in the neighbourhood of the level crossing on the down line, but neither by direct evidence nor by reasonable inference can any conclusion be arrived at as to the circumstances causing his death.

It has been argued before your Lordships that we must take the facts as found by the jury. I do not know what facts the jury are supposed to have found, nor is it, perhaps, very material to inquire, because if they have found that the defendants' negligence caused the death of the plaintiff's husband, they have found it without a fragment of evidence to justify such a finding.

Under these circumstances, I move that the judgment appealed from be affirmed, and the appeal dismissed.

LORD WATSON: . . . It appears to me that in all such cases the liability of the defendant company must rest upon these facts — in the first place that there was some negligent act or omission on the part of the company or their servants which materially contributed to the injury or death complained of, and, in the second place, that there was no contributory negligence on the part of the injured or deceased person. But it does not, in my opinion, necessarily follow that the whole burden of proof is cast upon the plaintiff. That it lies with the plaintiff to prove the first of these propositions does not admit of dispute. Mere allegation or proof that the company was guilty of negligence is altogether irrelevant; they might be guilty of many negligent acts or omissions, which might possibly have occasioned injury to somebody, but had no connection whatever with the injury for which redress is sought, and therefore the plaintiff must allege and prove, not merely that they were negligent, but that their negligence caused or materially contributed to the injury.

I am of opinion that the onus of proving affirmatively that there was contributory negligence on the part of the person injured rests, in the first instance, upon the defendants, and that in the absence of evidence tending to that conclusion, the plaintiff is not bound to prove the negative in order to entitle her to a verdict in her favour. . . .

The difficulty of dealing with the question of onus in cases like the present arises from the fact that in most cases it is well nigh impossible for the plaintiff to lay his evidence before a jury or the Court without disclosing circumstances which either point to or tend to rebut the conclusion that the injured party was guilty of contributory negligence. If the plaintiff's evidence were sufficient to shew that the negligence of the defendants did materially contribute to the injury, and threw no light upon the question of the injured party's negligence, then I should be of opinion that, in the absence of any counter-evidence from the defendants, it ought to be presumed that, in point of fact, there was no such contributory negligence. Even if the plaintiff's evidence did disclose facts and circumstances bearing upon that question, which were neither sufficient per se to prove such contributory negligence, nor to cast the onus of disproving it on the plaintiff, I should remain of the same opinion. Of course a plaintiff who comes into Court with an unfounded action may have to submit to the inconvenience of having his adversary's defence proved by his own witnesses; but that cannot affect the question upon whom the onus lies in the first instance. . . .

In the present case, I think the appellant must fail, because no attempt has been made to bring evidence in support of her allegations up to the point at which the question of contributory negligence becomes material. The evidence appears to me to shew that the injuries which caused the death of Henry Wakelin were occasioned by contact with an engine or a train belonging to the respondents, and

I am willing to assume, although I am by no means satisfied, that it has also been proved that they were in certain respects negligent. The evidence goes no further. It affords ample materials for conjecturing that the death may possibly have been occasioned by that negligence, but it furnishes no data from which an inference can be reasonably drawn that as a matter of fact it was so occasioned.

I am accordingly of opinion that the order appealed from must be affirmed.

[Lord Blackburn concurred with Lord Watson, and Lord Fitzgerald gave a concurring speech.]

NOTES AND QUESTIONS

1. Should the plaintiff have been nonsuited at trial? If, as Lord Halsbury indicates, there was not a fragment of evidence to justify the jury's finding, what factors induced the jury to find for the plaintiff? Does *Wakelin* add support to those who would abolish civil jury trials? Although civil jury trials are rapidly disappearing in the rest of the Commonwealth, they remain a common and important feature in several Canadian jurisdictions. See Sommers and Firestone, "In Defence of the Civil Jury Trial in Personal Injury Actions" (1986-87), 7 Advoc. Q. 492; and MacIntyre, Manes and McGrenere, "More in Defence of the Civil Jury Trial in Personal Injury Actions" (1987), 8 Advoc. Q. 109.

2. What was the basis upon which Lord Halsbury dismissed the plaintiff's case? What did Lord Halsbury mean by the following statement? "It is true that the onus of proof may shift from time to time as a matter of evidence, but still the question must ultimately arise whether the person who is bound to prove the affirmative of the issue . . . has discharged herself of that burden." For a recent Canadian case on point see *Prinse v. Fraser Valley Foods Ltd.*, [1994] 2 W.W.R. 331 (B.C. C.A.), leave to appeal ref'd. [1994] 1 S.C.R. x.

3. At the time of *Wakelin*, contributory negligence was a complete defence to an action in negligence. What effect did this have on the plaintiff's case? Lord Watson clearly disagrees with Brett M.R. on the issue of who bears the burden of proving contributory negligence. With whom would Lord Halsbury agree?

4. Would the result have been the same if the defendant had the legal and evidentiary burden of disproving negligence?

5. For a discussion of the legal and evidentiary burdens of proof see Klar, *Tort Law* (1991), 347-49; Fleming. *The Law of Torts*, 8th ed. (1992), 308-15; and Tapper, *Cross and Tapper on Evidence*, 8th ed. (1995), 119-75.

2. Exceptions to the General Principles Governing the Burden of Proof

(a) STATUTES AND SHIFTING BURDENS OF PROOF

✸ MACDONALD v. WOODARD

(1974), 43 D.L.R. (3d) 182 (Ont. Co. Ct.)

MATHESON CO. CT. J.: — The plaintiff, a service station proprietor, was struck while standing in front of the automobile of the defendant Donald Woodard just after the plaintiff had given a boost to Woodard's battery from his own station-wagon which had been conveniently positioned nose to nose facing the Woodard automobile.

. . .

What, in the circumstances, does the plaintiff have to establish in order to succeed against the defendant Donald Woodard? Because Angus MacDonald was on his feet, in the process of disengaging the starter cables when the Woodard vehicle crushed him, this is a case where the provisions of s. 133 of the *Highway Traffic Act*, R.S.O. 1970, c. 202, must be considered.

Section 133 reads as follows:

> 133(1) When loss or damage is sustained by any person by reason of a motor vehicle on a highway, the onus of proof that the loss or damage did not arise through the negligence or improper conduct of the owner or driver of the motor vehicle is upon the owner or driver.
>
> (2) This section does not apply in case of a collision between motor vehicles or between motor vehicles and cars of electric or steam railways or other motor vehicles running only on stationary rails on the highway nor to an action brought by a passenger in a motor vehicle in respect of any injuries sustained by him while a passenger.
>
> . . .

This section was enacted in order to overcome difficulties experienced by plaintiffs in obtaining and presenting sufficient evidence of a motorist's negligence to avoid a non-suit at the close of their case. Knowledge of relevant acts and circumstances leading up to an accident might be in the possession only of the defendant and injustice might result if a plaintiff was unable to overcome the initial obstacle of a *prima facie* case and to avoid having his case determined before all the evidence was before the Court. Hence the introduction of a type of statutory *res ipsa loquitur* doctrine under which the owner or driver is *prima facie* liable for damage caused by his motor vehicle unless he satisfied the Court on a preponderance of evidence that he was not in fact negligent.

A plaintiff must therefore show, in order that the section may apply, that his damages were occasioned by the presence of a motor vehicle on the highway.

This does not mean that before the onus begins to operate, the plaintiff must first prove that the effective cause of the collision was the conduct of the driver; he need only show that the collision — not the conduct of the driver — was the cause of the damage: *Stewart v. Ottawa Electric R. Co. and Hollis*, [1945] O.W.N. 639, [1945] 4 D.L.R. 400; affirmed [1948] 2 D.L.R. 800, 62 C.R.T.C. 272; *Mann v. Hilton*, [1953] O.W.N. 908.

The plaintiff has satisfied me that the damage to his knee was occasioned by the presence of the defendant Woodard's motor vehicle on the highway. The onus thus begins to operate. But specifically what is the nature of this statutory onus now upon the defendant Woodard?

The leading authority on the interpretation of this section is *Winnipeg Electric Co. v. Geel*, [1932] 4 D.L.R. 51, [1932] A.C. 690, [1932] 3 W.W.R. 49. In the Supreme Court of Canada, Duff, J., stated ([1931] S.C.R. 443 at p. 446, [1931] 3 D.L.R. 737 at p. 740, 38 C.R.C. 142):

> The statute creates, as against the owners and drivers of motor vehicles . . . a rebuttable presumption of negligence. The onus of disproving negligence remains throughout the proceedings. If, at the conclusion of the evidence, it is too meagre or too evenly balanced to enable the tribunal to determine this issue, as a question of fact, then, by force of the statute, the plaintiff is entitled to succeed.

This statement was approved by the Privy Council where Lord Wright further said at pp. 55-6:

> But the onus which the section places on the defendant is not in law a shifting or transitory onus: it cannot be displaced merely by the defendant giving some evidence that he was not negli-

gent, if that evidence however credible is not sufficient reasonably to satisfy the jury that he was not negligent: the burden remains on the defendant until the very end of the case, when the question must be determined whether or not the defendant has sufficiently shown that he did not in fact cause the accident by his negligence.

It is accordingly upon the whole of the evidence submitted at the trial, including all the circumstances and inferences to be drawn therefrom that the defendant must satisfy the jury that the accident was not in fact caused by his negligence: *Bronson v. Evans and Evans*, [1943] O.R. 248, [1943] 2 D.L.R. 371; *Long v. Registrar of Motor Vehicles*, [1950] 4 D.L.R. 587, [1950] 2 W.W.R. 355. And once the onus is placed on the defendant it will not be discharged unless he satisfied the Court not merely that the damages were in fact sustained without such negligence: *Foster v. Registrar of Motor Vehicles for Province of Ontario*, [1961] O.R. 551, 28 D.L.R. (2d) 561. Thus, it is not necessary to find any specific act of negligence against the defendant in order that liability may attach to him, and if any doubt remains on a consideration of all the evidence as to whether or not the defendant was negligent, the plaintiff is entitled to the verdict.

The plaintiff throughout this trial has remained virtually mute concerning the cause of the accident, allowing the defendants to fight it out between themselves. Indeed with his meagre information he is scarcely in a position to do otherwise.

. . .

In light of the extreme confusion of Donald Woodard's own testimony in so many particulars and areas, and his inability personally or through his witnesses, who gave mechanical evidence, to suggest how this automobile, if properly operated, could "leap" or "lurch" forward at the time in question, I am compelled to find that Woodard has failed to satisfy the onus which s. 133(1) has imposed upon him.

NOTES AND QUESTIONS

1. What must the plaintiff establish in order to invoke s. 133 [now R.S.O. 1990, c. H.8, s. 193(1)]? Explain the effect of s. 133 on the burden of proof in a negligence action.

2. What must the defendant prove to discharge the burden of proof cast upon her by s. 133? See *Angelopoulos v. Machen* (1992), 7 O.R. (3d) 45 (C.A.).

3. In *A.G. Ont. v. Keller* (1978), 94 D.L.R. (3d) 632 (Ont. C.A.), a police officer was seriously injured when his car went out of control and struck a pole during a high-speed chase. The fleeing driver knew he was being pursued and was attempting to escape. At no time did the two vehicles collide. The Court of Appeal held that s. 133 applied to the escaping driver. Do you agree? Would the result have been the same if s. 133 had not been applied? See also *Marks v. Campbell* (1977), 76 D.L.R. (3d) 715 (N.S. S.C.); *De Gurse v. Henry* (1984), 47 O.R. (2d) 172 (H.C.); *Moore v. Fanning* (1987), 60 O.R. (2d) 225 (H.C.); and *Crew v. Nicholson* (1989), 68 O.R. (2d) 232 (C.A.).

4. For a discussion of comparable provisions in other provincial legislation, see *Feener v. McKenzie* (1971), 25 D.L.R. (3d) 283 (S.C.C.); *Horner v. Comeau* (1988), 88 N.S.R. (2d) 295 (S.C.); *Hilderman v. Rattray* (1988), 93 A.R. 217 (Q.B.); *Melnychuk v. Moore* (1989), 57 Man. R. (2d) 174 (C.A.); and *Doern v. Phillips Estate*, [1995] 4 W.W.R. 1 (B.C. S.C.).

(b) DIRECTLY CAUSED INJURY: UNINTENDED TRESPASS

✷ DAHLBERG v. NAYDIUK

(1969), 72 W.W.R. 210, 10 D.L.R. (3d) 319 (Man. C.A.)

[The defendant fired at a deer, but missed. The bullet carried 250 to 300 yards and struck the plaintiff who was working on his farm. The defendant had obtained consent to hunt from the owner of the land on which he was situated, but he had not sought the plaintiff's permission to fire over, or hunt on, the farm.]

DICKSON, J.A.:

. . .

Trespass or negligence

Mr. Dahlberg's action was framed both in negligence and in trespass. This gives rise to one of those strange anomalies of the law. It is this. If Mr. Dahlberg relies on negligence the onus rests upon him to prove Mr. Naydiuk was negligent. This follows the normal evidentiary rule that he who asserts must prove. However, if Mr. Dahlberg relies upon trespass, (i) Mr. Naydiuk is entitled to judgment only "if he satisfies the onus of establishing the absence of both intention and negligence on his part" (*Cook v. Lewis, supra*, p. 15 [D.L.R.]) that is to say the onus rests upon him to disprove negligence, and (ii) the question arises whether such "negligence" means "a negligent (*i.e.*, careless) trespass or something which would give rise to an action on negligence": Street, *The Law of Torts*, 4th ed., p. 14.

As Clyne, J., said in *Walmsley et al. v. Humenick et al.*, [1954] 2 D.L.R. 232 at p. 244:

> It seems to be equally curious that since the passing of the *Judicature Acts* a situation should arise where on the same facts the plaintiffs' action must fail if it is framed in negligence, but might succeed if it is brought in trespass.

Two English cases, decided since *Cook v. Lewis, supra*, might be mentioned. In *Fowler v. Lanning*, [1959] 1 Q.B. 426 (followed in *Beals v. Hayward*, [1960] N.Z.L.R. 131: see also 24 Mod. L.R. 331, and 1959 Cambridge L.J. 33), Diplock, J. (as he then was), in the course of a lengthy judgment, held that the onus of proving negligence, where the trespass is not intentional, lies upon the plaintiff, whether the action be framed in trespass or in negligence. Lord Denning, M.R., took the matter one step further in *Letang v. Cooper*, [1964] 2 All E.R. 929 at p. 932:

> If he does not inflict injury intentionally, but only unintentionally, the plaintiff has no cause of action in trespass. His only cause of action is in negligence, and then only on proof of want of reasonable care.

The late Dean C. A. Wright has referred (Linden, *Studies in Canadian Tort Law*, at p. 44) to "this irrational and unnecessary exception of trespass", expressing the hope that some Canadian Court would "put an end to the possibility of a difference in burden of proof depending solely on the direct or indirect application of the force." If such a change is to be made in the law it must be made by a

Court higher than this. In the present case we, as we must, reached our decision in accord with the dictates of *Cook v. Lewis, supra.*

Finding

It remains to apply the principles enunciated above to the facts before us.

The Judge found that Mr. Naydiuk failed in his duty to take care, and I agree. He failed to prove he was not negligent. In my view of the matter he was negligent in two respects:

 (1) In firing in the direction of farm buildings.

· · ·

 (2) In failing to obtain permission from Mr. Dahlberg before hunting his land or firing across his land.

· · ·

Hunters must recognize that firing over land without permission of the owner constitutes a trespass to land and if injury to person results, trespass to person. A hunter who fires in the direction in which he knows or ought to know farm buildings are located must accept full responsibility for resultant damage to person or property. It is no answer to say he thought the buildings were unoccupied. There are vast areas of western Canada in which deer abound and where no farming activities are carried on. Even in farming areas there are often hills from which one can fire at game in the valley below without risk of injury to others. If a hunter chooses to hunt in a farming area he must do so in full awareness of the paramount right of the farmer to carry on his lawful occupation without risk of injury from stray bullets.

NOTES AND QUESTIONS

1. What must the plaintiff establish to invoke the rule in *Cook*? Had the bullet struck a tree and ricocheted before striking Dahlberg, would the rule in *Cook* have applied?

2. Explain the impact of the rule in *Cook* on the burden of proof. Do you agree with the way in which the rule was applied in *Dahlberg*?

3. Do you agree with Dickson J.A.'s criticism of the rule? If not, can you suggest a rationale for its continued use? See *Bell Canada v. Cope (Sarnia) Ltd.* (1980), 11 C.C.L.T. 170, aff'd. (1981), 119 D.L.R. (3d) 254 (Ont. C.A.). See also Tindale, "The Burden of Proof in Actions for Negligent Trespass in Canada" (1971), 49 Can. Bar Rev. 612; Sharp, "Negligent Trespass in Canada: A Persistent Source of Embarrassment" (1978), 1 Advoc. Q. 311; and Sullivan, "Trespass to the Person in Canada: A Defence of the Traditional Approach" (1987), 19 Ottawa L. Rev. 533.

(c) MULTIPLE NEGLIGENT DEFENDANTS

✳ COOK v. LEWIS (difficult to properly ∴ better to 'state' the rule)

[1951] S.C.R. 830, [1952] 1 D.L.R. 1 (S.C.C.)

[The plaintiff was hit in the face by bird-shot when the defendants fired simultaneously at different birds which had flown in the plaintiff's direction. The jury found that the plaintiff had been shot by one of the two hunters, but was unable to say which one. It also found that the injuries were not caused by the negligence of either. The Court of Appeal set aside the jury's finding on the negligence issue and ordered a new trial. This judgment was upheld by the Supreme Court of Canada, with Locke J. dissenting.]

RAND J.: — I agree with the Court of Appeal [[1950] 4 D.L.R. 136] that the finding of the jury exculpating both defendants from negligence was perverse and it is unnecessary to examine the facts on which that conclusion is based.

There remains the answer that, although shots from one of the two guns struck the respondent, the jury could not determine from which they came. This is open to at least four interpretations:

. . .

Prob.

It will be seen that there is one feature common to the first three: having found that either A or B had been the cause of injury to C, the jury declare that C has not satisfied them which of the two it was. It is then a problem in proof and must be considered from that standpoint.

. . .

What, then, the culpable actor has done by his initial negligent act is, first, to have set in motion a dangerous force which embraces the injured person within the scope of its probable mischief; and next, in conjunction with circumstances which he must be held to contemplate, to have made more difficult if not impossible the means of proving the possible damaging results of his own act or the similar results of the act of another. He has violated not only the victim's substantive right to security, but he has also culpably impaired the latter's remedial right of establishing liability. By confusing his act with environmental conditions, he has, in effect, destroyed the victim's power of proof.

The legal consequence of that is, I should say, that the onus is then shifted to the wrongdoer to exculpate himself; it becomes in fact a question of proof between him and the other and innocent member of the alternatives, the burden of which he must bear. The onus attaches to culpability, and if both acts bear that taint, the onus or prima facie transmission of responsibility attaches to both, and the question of the sole responsibility of one is a matter between them.

. . .

The risks arising from these sporting activities by increased numbers of participants and diminishing opportunity for their safe exercise, as the facts here indicate, require appropriate refinement in foresight. Against the private and public interests at stake, is the privilege of the individual to engage in a sport not inherently objectionable. As yet, certainly, the community is not ready to assume the burden of such a mishap. The question is whether a victim is to be told that such a risk, not only in substantive right but in remedy, is one he must assume. When we have reached the point where, as here, shots are considered spent at a distance of between 150 feet and 200 feet and the woods are "full" of hunters, a somewhat stringent regard to conduct seems to me to be obvious. It would be a strange commentary on its concern toward personal safety, that the law, although forbidding the victim any other mode of redress, was powerless to accord him any in its own form of relief. I am unable to assent to the view that there is any such helplessness.

. . .

Assuming, then, that the jury have found one or both of the defendants here negligent, as on the evidence I think they must have, and at the same time have found that the consequences of the two shots, whether from a confusion in time or in area, cannot be segregated, the onus on the guilty person arises. This is a case where each hunter would know of or expect the shooting by the other and the negligent actor has culpably participated in the proof-destroying fact, the multiple shooting and its consequences. No liability will, in any event attach to an innocent act of shooting, but the culpable actor, as against innocence, must bear the burden of exculpation.

These views of the law were not as adequately presented to the jury as I think they should have been.

I would, therefore, dismiss the appeal with costs. The motion to quash for want of jurisdiction is dismissed with costs.

The judgment of Estey, Cartwright and Fauteux JJ. was delivered by

CARTWRIGHT J. — ... It is argued, however, that *Summers v. Tice* [(1948), 5 A.L.R. (2nd) 91] should be followed and that under the principles stated in that judgment the jury might properly have found both Akenhead and Cook liable for the plaintiff's injury if in their view of the evidence both of them fired in the direction of the clump of trees in which the plaintiff in fact was, under such circumstances that the conduct of each constituted a breach of duty to the plaintiff. I have not been able to find any case in the courts of this country, or of England in which consideration has been given to certain propositions of law laid down in *Summers v. Tice*. The underlying reason for the decision appears to me to be found in the following quotation from the case of *Oliver v. Miles* [(1926), 144 Miss. 852]:

> ... We think that ... each is liable for the resulting injury to the boy, although no one can say definitely who actually shot him. *To hold otherwise would be to exonerate both from liability, although each was negligent, and the injury resulted from such negligence.*

The judgment in *Summers v. Tice* reads in part as follows: —

> ... When we consider the relative position of the parties and the results that would flow if plaintiff was required to pin the injury on one of the defendants only, a requirement that the burden of proof on that subject be shifted to defendants becomes manifest. They are both wrongdoers — both negligent toward plaintiff. They brought about a situation where the negligence of one of them injured the plaintiff, hence, it should rest with them each to absolve himself if he can. The injured party has been placed by defendants in the unfair position of pointing to which defendant caused the harm. If one can escape the other may also and plaintiff is remediless. Ordinarily defendants are in a far better position to offer evidence to determine which one caused the injury. This reasoning has recently found favour in this Court.

I do not think it necessary to decide whether all that was said in *Summers v. Tice* should be accepted as stating the law of British Columbia, but I am of opinion, for the reasons given in that case, that if under the circumstances of the case at bar the jury, having decided that the plaintiff was shot by either Cook or Akenhead, found themselves unable to decide which of the two shot him because in their opinion both shot negligently in his direction, both defendants should have been found liable. I think that the learned trial judge should have sent the jury back to consider the matter further with a direction to the above effect, ...

NOTES AND QUESTIONS

1. According to Rand J., what must the plaintiff establish to shift the burden of proof vis-a-vis causation to the defendants? Is his analysis dependent upon there being more than one defendant? What would the defendants have to establish to discharge the burden of proof cast upon them? Answer these same questions based on Cartwright J.'s judgment.

2. In *Joseph Brant Memorial Hosp. v. Koziol* (1977), 77 D.L.R. (3d) 161 (S.C.C.), a nurse's negligence in failing to maintain adequate records made it impossible to determine the exact circumstances surrounding a patient's death. The Ontario Court of Appeal, quoting from Rand J.'s judgment, held that the burden of disproving causation should be cast upon the nurse. The Supreme Court of Canada rejected this proposition, noting that the "destruction of evidence" rationale had been adopted by only Rand J., and formed no part of the majority judgment. Was Rand J.'s rationale for shifting the burden of proof any less compelling than that of the majority?

3. As in *Koziol*, a patient is often unable to identify the person responsible for a negligent act that occurs during or immediately after surgery. Some courts have aided such plaintiffs by shifting the burden of proof vis-a-vis causation to the defendant doctors. For example, in *Ybarra v. Spangard* (1944), 154 P. (2d) 687 (Cal. S.C.), the court inferred negligence against an entire surgical team of doctors and nurses, even though only one of them may have caused the plaintiff's injury.

Denning L.J. adopted a similar position in *Roe v. Min. of Health*, [1954] 2 All E.R. 131 at 136-37 (C.A.):

> Each of these plaintiffs is entitled to say to the hospital: "While I was in your hands something has been done to me which has wrecked my life. Please explain how it has come to pass" . . .
> I do not think that the hospital authorities and Dr. Graham can both avoid giving an explanation by the simple expedient of each throwing responsibility on the other. If an injured person shows that one or other or both of two persons injured him, but cannot say which of them it was, then he is not defeated altogether. He can call on each of them for an explanation.

Unfortunately, Denning L.J. did not elaborate. Given the majority judgment in *Cook* and the decision in *Koziol*, is Denning L.J.'s approach likely to be followed in Canada?

4. Do the problems of establishing causation in medical malpractice cases warrant the creation of special rules concerning the burden of proof? If so, how would you state these rules? In *Snell v. Farrell* (1990), 72 D.L.R. (4th) 289, the Supreme Court of Canada stated that the burden of proof was not immutable and suggested that where the facts were within the defendant's knowledge and not accessible to the plaintiff, the burden of proof may be shifted. Unfortunately, the court did not elaborate on the issue. The court did not shift the burden of proof in *Snell*, a case in which the plaintiff was left blind in one eye following an operation by the defendant surgeon. See Roth, "Causation and the Burden of Proof: An Age Old Dilemma and a New Age Approach" (1992), 14 Advoc. Q. 70.

5. In *McGhee v. Nat. Coal Bd.*, [1972] 3 All E.R. 1008 (H.L.), Lord Wilberforce stated that the burden of proving causation should shift from the plaintiff to the defendant, if the defendant's negligence materially increased the risk of injury and that very injury befell the plaintiff. Wilberforce L.J. limited his analysis to cases in which it was impossible to determine the cause of the plaintiff's loss and "policy and justice" warranted imposing liability on the defendant as the creator of a risk. In reaching his conclusion, Lord Wilberforce emphasized that this was an industrial disease case involving an employee's suit against his employer. The other four Lords found for the plaintiff without shifting the burden of proof. Nevertheless, *McGhee* would permit a plaintiff to win without having to prove on the balance of probability that the defendant was a cause of her injuries.

6. *McGhee* generated considerable controversy in both Canada and England, and it was subsequently rejected by the House of Lords in *Wilsher v. Essex Area Health Authority*, [1988] 2 W.L.R. 557. In *Snell v. Farrell*, the Supreme Court of Canada rejected *McGhee* in the guise of re-interpreting it. The court held that unless the defendant's conduct increased the risk to the point of establishing cause on the balance of probability, the plaintiff would lose. The burden of proving causation remained on the plaintiff throughout, although it could be satisfied by evidence creating a strong inference. See Pardy, "Risk, Cause and Toxic Torts: A Theory for a Standard of Proof" (1989), 10 Advoc. Q. 277; Fleming, "Probabilistic Causation in Tort Law" (1989), 68 Can. Bar Rev. 661; and Fleming, "Probabilistic Causation in Tort Law: A Postscript" (1991), 70 Can. Bar Rev. 136.

7. The issues posed by cases like *McGhee* are becoming more important. Advances in the medical sciences now make it possible to prove that exposure to toxic chemicals, radiation and other substances may have serious long-term consequences that do not manifest themselves for 20 or 30 years. By

the time the plaintiff becomes ill or disabled, she may not be able to isolate the impact of this exposure from other possible risk factors. The plaintiff's evidence may take the form of extrapolations from animal studies, epidemiological data and other statistical information. In the past, such evidence was often dismissed as being "speculative". *McGhee* suggests that this may no longer be an adequate response, at least in cases where the nature of the defendant's conduct makes it difficult to prove causation. See generally Mulcahy, "Proving Causation in Toxic Tort Litigation" (1983), 11 Hofstra L. Rev. 1299-1326; and Brennan, "Causal Chains and Statistical Links . . ." (1989), 73 Cornell L. Rev. 469.

8. In *Sindell v. Abbott Laboratories* (1980), 607 P. (2d) 924 (Cal. S.C.), the plaintiff was a cancer victim, whose mother had taken diethylstilbestrol (DES) during pregnancy. DES was manufactured by approximately 200 pharmaceutical companies, but there were no significant differences in the products. The drug had been prescribed to prevent miscarriages, but eventually proved ineffective and was found to pose a risk of causing a particular kind of cancer in female children. This cancer was deadly once it manifested itself, but it had a minimum latency period of 10 to 12 years. The plaintiff could prove that her cancer was caused by DES, but she could not establish which company had produced the DES that her mother had taken. The plaintiff sued all of the major manufacturers, arguing that they had been negligent in continuing to market DES when they knew or ought to have known that it was ineffective and carcinogenic. The court found the defendants negligent and held each liable in proportion to its share of the DES market, unless it could prove that it had not produced the DES that caused the plaintiff's cancer. The court acknowledged that there was a 10% chance that the DES in question had been manufactured by one of the approximately 195 smaller producers which had not been sued.

Would the plaintiff have been able to prove causation based on the general principles governing proof in a negligence suit? Would the plaintiff have been able to prove causation based on the multiple negligent defendants rule in *Cook v. Lewis*? Do you agree with the result on the causation issue in *Sindell*? Can you derive a general principle from *Sindell* to deal with similar causation cases?

9. What would have been the result of applying the established principles of apportionment to the defendants in *Sindell*? Do you agree with the court's resolution of the apportionment issue? What changes would have to be made in the apportionment legislation to accommodate the approach in *Sindell*?

See Delgado, "Beyond Sindell: Relaxation of Cause-In-Fact Rules for Indeterminate Plaintiffs" (1982), 70 Cal. L. Rev. 880; Black, "Epidemiological Proof in Toxic Tort Litigation" (1984), 52 Fordham L. Rev. 732; Legum, "Increased Risk of Cancer as an Actionable Injury" (1984), 18 Ga. L. Rev. 563; Farber, "Toxic Causation" (1987), 71 Minn. Law Rev. 1219; Wiechmann, "Standard of Proof for Increased Risk of Disease or Injury" (1994), 61 Defence Counsel J. 59; and Goldberg, "Fungible? New Uses for Sindell" (1992), 78 A.B.A. J. 73.

10. In *Leaman v. Rea*, [1954] 4 D.L.R. 423 (N.B. C.A.) there was a collision between two cars in circumstances in which one or both of the drivers had to have been negligent. The court could not determine which driver had been negligent or whether both drivers had been negligent. Nevertheless, the court held both drivers to be equally at fault and apportioned the losses accordingly, rather than dismissing the actions. What would have been the result if the general principles of proving negligence and causation had been applied? Does this case fit within any of the recognized exceptions to the rules of proof? Would it have made any financial difference to the parties if their claims had been dismissed rather than apportioned equally?

In *Wotta v. Haliburton Oil Well Cementing Co.*, [1955] S.C.R. 377, the Supreme Court specifically rejected the approach adopted in *Leaman* to unexplained collisions. Is there any justification for adopting special rules of proof in cases of unexplained collisions? See also *Bray v. Palmer*, [1953] 2 All E.R. 1449 (C.A.); *Host v. Bassett* (1983), 48 A.L.R. 404 (H.C. Aust.); *Barton v. Weaver* (1981), 36 N.B.R. (2d) 483 (C.A.); and *Stamp v. R. in Right of Ontario* (1984), 47 O.R. (2d) 214 (C.A.).

3. *Res Ipsa Loquitur*

(a) INTRODUCTION

In some cases, the plaintiff must rely upon circumstantial evidence to prove that the defendant was the negligent party who injured her. The term circumstantial evidence is used to refer to evidence from which an inference may be drawn to reach a conclusion. For example, Carol's testimony that she saw Bob shoot Carl is direct evidence that Bob shot Carl. However, Carol's testimony that she found Bob's fingerprints on the murder weapon is circumstantial evidence — it provides a step in the process of logical inference.

The Latin maxim *res ipsa loquitur* (the thing speaks for itself) is used to describe those circumstances in which the occurrence of the accident provides circumstantial evidence from which negligence may be inferred against the defendant. For example, in the classic case of *Byrne v. Boadle* (1863), 159 E.R. 299 (Exch.), the plaintiff was walking on the sidewalk when he was struck on the head by a barrel of flour that had fallen from the defendant's warehouse. The court applied the doctrine of *res ipsa loquitur* to infer that the barrel fell due to the defendant's negligence. Although there is general agreement on the principles governing when the maxim applies, its effect on the burden of proof remains uncertain in some jurisdictions.

(b)   WHEN DOES *RES IPSA LOQUITUR* APPLY?

KIRK v. MCLAUGHLIN COAL & SUPPLIES LTD.

[1968] 1 O.R. 311, 66 D.L.R. (2d) 321 (Ont. C.A.)

EVANS J.A. (orally): — This is an appeal by the plaintiffs from the judgment of W.A.C. Hall, Co. Ct. J., in the 8th Division Court of the County of Ontario on October 25, 1966, dismissing the plaintiffs' action with costs.

The action arises from a claim by the plaintiffs for damages caused to their home in the City of Oshawa as the result of two explosions which occurred in their oil furnace on February 21 and March 6, 1966.

The facts as found by the trial Judge are as follows: The furnace was converted by the installation of an oil burner about 12 years ago and thereafter the defendant supplied oil to the plaintiffs and as part of the arrangement agreed to service the furnace and also clean it annually.

On January 7, 1966, some repairs were made to the furnace by the defendant. On February 21, the first explosion occurred. The furnace was put back in operating order by the defendant and on March 6 the second explosion took place.

The trial Judge accepted the evidence of the plaintiffs that they did not touch the furnace other than the thermostatic control to increase or decrease heat and that no one other than the defendant serviced the furnace.

The plaintiffs could not establish the cause of the explosions and were unable to establish any specific act or negligence which might cast responsibility upon the defendant. It was argued on their behalf that the circumstances surrounding the two accidents were such that the happenings in themselves formed a basis for inferring negligent conduct on the part of the defendant and was a situation where the maxim of *res ipsa loquitur* was applicable. The learned trial Judge rejected this submission, being of the view that exclusive control of the furnace by the defendant was a prerequisite to the application of the doctrine and further that to hold the defendant liable would be to make it an insurer of the plaintiff.

With the greatest respect to the trial Judge, I must disagree. I am of the opinion that all the circumstances surrounding the incidents created a situation where *res ipsa loquitur* comes into operation. It is common knowledge that oil furnaces do not normally explode. The trial Judge accepted the evidence of the plaintiffs that they had done nothing nor had they permitted anything to be done, which might cause the explosions and we are then faced with the problem as to whether the explosions occurred under such circumstances that it is so improbable that they occurred without negligence on the part of the defendant that their occurrences alone immediately give rise to the inference that the defendant was in fact negligent. Having ruled out intervention on the part of the plaintiffs and having accepted the evidence that the defendants alone serviced the furnace, the trial Judge in my opinion was forced to conclude the effective "control" was in the hands of the defendant. I do not consider "control" to mean physical custody or possession. It is sufficient to establish "control" if it is demonstrated that the servicing and repairing of the furnace was the exclusive province of the defendant and that no other agency intervened.

Res ipsa loquitur is no more than a specific instance of circumstantial evidence which may or may not be sufficient to raise an inference. In the present case, I believe that a situation was established where the happening of the explosions in themselves founded a basis from which an inference can be reasonably and properly drawn as a matter of common experience that the explosions resulted from negligence and that the negligence is properly attributed to the defendant.

Whatever procedural advantages the rule may have it does not relieve the plaintiffs of their primary burden of proving their case against the defendant. The defendant may avoid liability if it can meet the inference of negligence by giving an explanation showing the exercise of reasonable care in the maintenance and servicing of the furnace. In my opinion the evidence on behalf of the defendants fails to reach that standard and the inference of negligence raised by the plaintiffs is sufficient to discharge the onus placed on them of proving their case on the balance of probabilities.

I recognize that it is not the function of the defendant to disprove negligence on its part. It is only required to give an explanation that is consistent with the exercise of due care on its part and then the explanation is weighed against the inference arising from the happening of the accident and the liability is determined on the balance of probabilities.

The appeal is allowed with costs fixed at $25. The judgment below is set aside and judgment will issue in favour of the plaintiffs for $394.43 together with costs and a counsel fee of $25.

CLAYTON v. J.N.Z. INVT. LTD.

[1969] 1 O.R. 89, 1 D.L.R. (3d) 440 (Ont. C.A.)

GALE C.J.O.: — This is an appeal from the judgment of I.M. Macdonnell, Co. Ct. J., of the County Court of the County of York allowing damages to the plaintiff in the amount to be assessed. The assessment has not yet taken place.

The action arises by reason of an unfortunate incident which took place on November 22, 1964. The plaintiff moved into an apartment in a large apartment building approximately five and a half months before that date. The building had been completed in February, 1964, and the plumbing therein had been installed by the defendants. On September 15th the heat for the fall term of 1964 was turned on and, inexplicably, one of the lead pipes leading to a radiator in the plaintiff's apartment burst on November 22nd causing damage to some of his furnishings and fixtures.

In the pleadings the plaintiff asserted that his loss had been caused by negligence on the part of the defendants. It is to be noted at once that neither the owners nor those responsible for maintaining the building were made parties to the action.

When the case came on for trial the only fact really proved by the plaintiff was to the effect that the pipe burst on November 22, 1964, at an elbow with a V-shaped fracture and that he did not tamper with the fixture personally. The section of the pipe including the burst was not produced and there was no expert evidence which might have aided the Court as to the cause of the mishap.

The defendants elected to call no evidence.

The learned Judge came to the conclusion that on the evidence which had been adduced he was justified in finding that there was a *prima facie* case of negligence. With great respect we cannot agree with that finding as against these defendants. There was no evidence as to when the installation of the plumbing took place, nor whether the defendants supplied the pipe in question. The Court was not informed as to what happened with respect to the maintenance or condition of the plumbing between the time of the completion of its installation and November 22nd and, in our opinion, we cannot bring ourselves to agree that the mere statement of the plaintiff to the effect that the pipe had burst constitutes evidence of negligence on the part of the defendants. Any number of causes might have been the underlying reason for the failure of the pipe and we do not think it was sufficient in the circumstances for the plaintiff merely to show that the fracture had occurred and that damage had resulted from it.

It might have been otherwise had the owners or those responsible for the maintenance of the apartment also been made parties to the action.

It is our view, therefore, and we are in as good a position as the trial Judge to assess the evidence, that the action ought to have been dismissed. Accordingly, the appeal will be allowed and the action dismissed. Costs here and below, of course, follow the event.

TATARYN v. CO-OP. TRUST CO.

(1975), 65 D.L.R. (3d) 99 (Sask. C.A.)

BROWNRIDGE, J.A., concurs with HALL, J.A.

HALL J.A.: — This is an appeal from Bence, C.J.Q.B., who dismissed the action brought by the appellant Sophie Tataryn under the provisions of the *Fatal Accidents Act*, R.S.S. 1965, c. 109.

Wasyl Tataryn, the husband of the appellant, was killed in an aeroplane crash which occurred near Kuroki, Saskatchewan, on the evening of July 15, 1972. Tataryn was a passenger in the plane. The owner and pilot of the plane, George Prince, and another passenger, Larry Salikin, were also killed in the crash.

The evidence indicates that Prince was a reasonably well-experienced and competent pilot. Neither Tataryn nor Salikin had any training in flying.

The aeroplane was a Cessna 170B, described as having a high wing configuration with conventional landing gear. It had a cruising speed of approximately 120 m.p.h. and a stalling speed of 40 m.p.h. It was also described as a very stable type of aircraft, relatively easy to fly.

A fact which becomes important in the consideration of this case is that the aeroplane was equipped with dual controls which could not be disconnected.

The airstrip or landing strip from which the aeroplane took off was located a few miles north-west of the farm of one Peter Dudey. The landing strip ran in a north-south direction.

Dudey was working in his farmyard at about eight o'clock in the evening when he observed the aeroplane take off from the landing strip. Dudey said that it was a clear, warm, calm day with no wind. The aeroplane flew over the Dudey farmyard at a height of 20 to 40 feet from the ground. Dudey was able to recognize Prince in the left-hand front seat, and Tataryn in the right front. He saw another person in the rear seat but did not know that it was Salikin until he later saw the crash remains. Dudey was acquainted with them as they all lived near Kuroki.

After the aeroplane had passed over the Dudey farm, it proceeded in a south-westerly direction, gaining altitude as it did so. After it had reached a height estimated by Dudey to be 800 to 1,000 feet, it turned and started on a north-easterly course, apparently back towards the landing strip. As it did so, it started a gradual descent. Dudey stated that it sounded to him as though the motor of the aeroplane was not functioning properly. It seemed to be "missing". The aeroplane continued its descent until it crashed at a point approximately one-half mile west of Dudey's buildings and one and a half miles south of the airstrip.

The field in which the crash occurred was a 110-acre field planted to wheat. There was a row of trees along a creek bottom which ran in a north-easterly direction and was located approximately half way between the Dudey buildings and the crash site. Apart from this row of trees the field was an open one and there was a clear path from the crash site to the landing field.

The plaintiff relies upon the principle of *res ipsa loquitur*. This principle has in the past been applied in cases involving aeroplane crashes.

. . .

In the instant case the learned trial Judge held that the maxim was not applicable. In so holding he stated as follows [54 D.L.R. (3d) 154 at pp. 156-7]:

> It is my view and I so hold that the doctrine of *res ipsa loquitur* does not apply to the facts of this case. The law is quoted by Woods, J.A., in *McKay v. Gilchrist et al.* (1962), 35 D.L.R. (2d) 568 at p. 572, 40 W.W.R. 2 at p. 26, when he adopted the statement from *Clerk Lindsell on Torts*, 12th ed., p. 796, which is:
>
> > "'. . . (1) when the thing that inflicted the damage was under the sole management and control of the defendant, or of someone for whom he is responsible or whom he has a right to control; (2) the occurrence is such that it would not have happened without negligence. If these two conditions are satisfied as follows, on a balance of probability, that the defendant, or the person for whom he is responsible, must have been negligent. There is, however, a further negative condition; (3) there must be no evidence as to why or how the occurrence took place. If there is, then appeal to *res ipsa loquitur* is inappropriate, for the question of the defendant's negligence must be determined on that evidence.'"

. . .

The only reasons suggested for excluding the application of the principle of *res ipsa loquitur* to the instant case is that the aircraft was equipped with dual controls. This must have been the reason relied upon by the learned trial Judge although he did not specifically say so.

. . .

I am of the opinion that the existence of dual controls in an aircraft does not, *per se*, exclude the application of the principle of *res ipsa loquitur*. The application must depend upon the facts of each particular case.

In the instant case Prince was a trained and experienced pilot. He was the owner of the aircraft. Neither Tataryn nor Salikin was able to fly the plane. They were in the aircraft as guests of Prince for the purposes of taking a pleasure trip. Neither Tataryn nor Salikin could assume control of the aircraft without the approval and permission of Prince. If the dual controls were not disconnected it was the responsibility of Prince to explain to Salikin and Tataryn the necessity to avoid interference with the flying. Under all of these circumstances it must be said, when considering the maxim of *res ipsa loquitur*, that the aircraft was under the sole control and management of the deceased Prince. The learned trial Judge therefore should have proceeded to consider the other aspects of the maxim.

It is common ground and was so found by the trial Judge that there was no evidence to explain why or how the occurrence took place.

Called at the trial to testify as experts were Laurence Raymond Andrews, the owner and manager of Nipawin Air Services Limited, a qualified engineer for the maintenance of aircraft; and Lloyd Johnson, an experienced pilot and flight instructor. It was not possible for any of the witnesses to tell what had actually happened in the aircraft prior to the time when it crashed. It could be speculated that the aircraft ran out of gasoline or encountered some other form of engine trouble. It appears, however, from the evidence of Andrews and Johnson that the behaviour of the aircraft as described by the witness, Dudey, was equally consistent with a planned and deliberate descent as with engine trouble.

It is clear from the expert testimony of Johnson, that whether the descent was a voluntary one or whether it was one caused by factors beyond the control of the pilot, a pilot of the skill and experience of Prince should have had no difficulty in landing in the field where the crash occurred.

. . .

From all of the evidence it can be said that the happening of the accident is more consistent with negligence on the part of the pilot Prince than with any other cause. Under these circumstances the principle of *res ipsa loquitur* should be applied and Prince should be held negligent unless a reasonable explanation is found to show how the crash may have occurred without such negligence.

. . .

In the instant case the respondent relies upon the suggestion that either Tataryn or Salikin interfered with the controls. In particular the suggestion was put forward that Salikin may have had suicidal tendencies and therefore wanted the aeroplane to crash. The description by Dudey of the manner in which the aircraft descended did not suggest to the witness Johnson that anyone was interfering with the pilot's control of the aircraft. Under these circumstances, in my opinion, the suggestion that one of the passengers interfered with the controls at a crucial moment causing the aircraft to crash is mere speculation or conjecture and can not be considered a reasonable explanation so as to displace the *prima facie* case of negligence established by the appellant. The respondents, therefore, should be held liable to the appellant. The judgment below which dismissed the appellant's action is accordingly set aside.

Because of the view which he took of liability the learned trial Judge did not find it necessary to make an assessment of damages. The action will be returned to him for an assessment of damages.

BAYDA J.A.: — I concur with the judgment of my brother Hall.

May I add that in my respectful view evidence which goes no further than to establish the mere presence of dual controls in an aeroplane is evidence of nothing more than an *opportunity* for some other person to share, with the pilot, management and control of the aeroplane or to interfere with the pilot's sole management and control. There must be some evidence, direct or from which proper inferences may be drawn, of that opportunity being taken before it can be said that the pilot did not have sole management and control. Mere conjecture or speculation is not enough. I have searched the transcript in vain for such evidence.

There is, of course, the evidence of H. L. Hunter and B. J. Schultz, Salikin's neighbour and brother-in-law respectively, of certain utterances, at best ambiguous, made by Salikin, and particularly one in the local beverage-room on the evening in question, from which the Court was invited to draw the inference that Salikin had suicidal tendencies and that they manifested themselves in the aeroplane at a critical time, and that he manipulated the dual controls and thereby interfered with Prince's sole (up to that point) management and control of the aeroplane. Such evidence, wholly devoid, as it is, of any support or foundation, medical or psychiatric, and of expert interpretation or explanation, is completely meaningless and is totally unworthy of forming the basis for the serious inference urged upon the Court by the respondent.

The three conditions mentioned in the statement of law adopted by Woods, J.A., in *McKay v. Gilchrist et al.* (1962), 35 D.L.R. (2d) 568 at p. 572, 40 W.W.R. 22 at p. 26, are satisfied, and the doctrine of *res ipsa loquitur* should apply to this case.

NOTES AND QUESTIONS

1. In *Kirk*, what test did the court use to determine that the explosions provided circumstantial evidence of negligence? What was the basis upon which the court concluded that the mishap raised an inference of negligence against the defendant? Was the defendant in this case in any better position to explain how the mishap occurred than the plaintiff? Should this last factor affect whether the doctrine applies?

2. Why did the court in *Clayton* reject the plaintiff's contention that *res ipsa loquitur* applied? Would the result have been different if the apartment owner and those responsible for maintenance had been joined in the action? What kinds of evidence could the plaintiff have adduced to raise an inference of negligence against the defendant? If the plaintiff had been able to provide such evidence, would he have needed to rely on *res ipsa loquitur*? See *Goguen v. Crowe* (1987), 40 C.C.L.T. 212 (N.S. S.C.); *Franks v. Sanderson* (1988), 44 C.C.L.T. 208 (B.C. C.A.); *Bauman v. Stein* (1991), 78 D.L.R. (4th) 118 (B.C. C.A.); *Penn West Petroleum Ltd. v. Koch Oil Co.*, [1994] 4 W.W.R. 630 (Alta. Q.B.); and *Bhatti v. Insurance Corp. of British Columbia*, [1995] 2 W.W.R. 57 (B.C. C.A.).

3. These and other recent cases indicate that the various courts differ on how readily they will

infer negligence. In *Hunt v. Burgess*, [1993] 4 W.W.R. 1, the Manitoba Court of Appeal concluded that the defendant's smoking caused a smouldering fire in the plaintiff's sofa, resulting in extensive damages. However, the court refused to apply *res ipsa loquitur*, because the plaintiff failed to prove that the defendant had been smoking in a negligent or careless fashion. This case stands in sharp contrast to *Farro v. Nutone Electrical Ltd.* (1990), 72 O.R. (2d) 637 (C.A.), where *res ipsa loquitur* was applied to a fire that was caused by an overheating ceiling fan. The court specifically stated that the plaintiff did not have to show precisely how the fire occurred.

4. Should the doctrine of *res ipsa loquitur* apply in cases where the occurrence of the mishap raises an inference of negligence against one of several defendants, but the plaintiff cannot tell which one? The English courts appear to have been more sympathetic to the plaintiff in these kinds of situations than their Canadian counterparts. See *Bray v. Palmer*, [1953] 2 All E.R. 1449 (C.A.); *Roe v. Min. of Health*, [1954] 2 All E.R. 131 at 136-37 (C.A.); *Wotta v. Haliburton Oil Well Cementing Co. Ltd.*, [1955] S.C.R. 377; *Savoie v. Bouchard* (1983), 26 C.C.L.T. 173 (N.B. C.A.); *Valleyview Hotel Ltd. v. Montreal Trust Co.* (1985), 33 C.C.L.T. 282 (Sask. C.A.); and *Prior v. Hanna* (1987), 43 D.L.R. (4th) 612 (Alta. Q.B.).

Can you suggest a situation in which the occurrence of an accident would raise an inference of negligence against two or more independent tortfeasors? Should the doctrine of *res ipsa loquitur* apply in such cases? See *MacLachlan & Mitchell Homes Ltd. v. Frank's Rentals & Sales Ltd.* (1979), 10 C.C.L.T. 306 (Alta. C.A.); *Goldsworthy v. Catalina Agencies Ltd.* (1982), 142 D.L.R. (3d) 281 (Nfld. T.D.); and *Haverkate v. Toronto Harbour Commissioners* (1986), 30 D.L.R. (4th) 125 (Ont. H.C.), aff'd. (1988), 46 D.L.R. (4th) 767 (Ont. C.A.).

5. Do you agree with the court that the crash in *Tataryn* raised an inference of negligence against the deceased pilot? What standard of care was used to assess the pilot's conduct? Should the court have given more weight to the fact that the pilot was faced with an emergency situation? Would the result have been the same if the plane had simply disappeared with no evidence of a crash? See *Nat. Trust Co. v. Wong Aviation Ltd.*, [1969] S.C.R. 481; and *Cogar Estate v. Central Mountain Air Services Ltd.*, [1992] 3 W.W.R. 729 (B.C. C.A.).

6. Initially, the courts were reluctant to apply the maxim to cases involving a technical activity, because it was thought that juries would have difficulty in determining whether an incident would normally occur without negligence. However, in recent years the courts have applied *res ipsa loquitur* in such cases, provided the plaintiff adduces expert evidence to assist the jury. The evidence is only required to explain the nature of the activity, not the particular incident in question. This change in the court's attitude is perhaps best reflected in the medical malpractice cases. See *Eady v. Tenderenda*, [1975] 2 S.C.R. 599; *Wilcox v. Cavan* (1974), 50 D.L.R. (3d) 687 (S.C.C.); *Hajgato v. London Health Assn.* (1982), 36 O.R. (2d) 669 (H.C.), aff'd. (1983), 44 O.R. (2d) 264 (C.A.); *Ferguson v. Hamilton Civic Hospitals* (1983), 40 O.R. (2d) 577 (H.C.), aff'd. (1985), 18 D.L.R. (4th) 638 (C.A.); *Goguen v. Crowe* (1987), 40 C.C.L.T. 212 (N.S. S.C.); and *Carter v. Higashi*, [1994] 3 W.W.R. 319 (Alta. Q.B.).

7. It should be noted that the courts have applied the maxim to infer gross negligence against a driver. See *Jackson v. Millar*, [1976] 1 S.C.R. 225; *Smith v. Gray* (1979), 100 D.L.R. (3d) 487 (Alta. S.C.); *Morrisey v. Gammon* (1983), 61 N.S.R. (2d) 48 (C.A.); and *Waskul v. Cardinall* (1987), 82 A.R. 161 (Q.B.). But see *Simpson v. Monture* (1967), 3 N.S.R. 792 (C.A.).

8. The trial judge in *Tataryn* cites *Clerk and Lindsell on Torts*, at 796 which provides that "there must be no evidence as to why or how the occurrence took place. If there is, then appeal to *res ipsa loquitur* is inappropriate, for the question of the defendant's negligence must be determined on that evidence.". Would you favour the adoption of this principle? Would its adoption place a plaintiff who had some direct evidence in a worse position than a plaintiff who had only circumstantial evidence?

9. Summarize the principles governing the application of *res ipsa loquitur*.

(c) THE PROCEDURAL EFFECTS OF *RES IPSA LOQUITUR*

MCHUGH v. REYNOLDS EXTRUSION CO.

(1974), 7 O.R. (2d) 336, 55 D.L.R. (3d) 180 (Ont. H.C.)

GOODMAN J.... The plaintiff asserted his claim against the defendant Reynolds on the basis that this was the type of case commonly known as a "products liability case" and that following the decisions of the courts in *M'Alister (or Donoghue) v. Stevenson*, [1932] A.C. 562, and *Grant v. Australian Knitting Mills, Ltd. et al.*, [1936] A.C. 85, if there was negligence on the part of the defendant Reynolds in the design or manufacture of the aluminum ladder, then said defendant was liable to the plaintiff as the ultimate consumer or user of the product, even though there was no contractual relationship between the parties. In so far as establishing such negligence was concerned, the plaintiff took the position that the maxim of *res ipsa loquitur* applied to the facts of this case.

I prefer to deal first with the question of the applicability of the maxim of *res ipsa loquitur*. The evidence of the plaintiff was to the effect that as he lifted his right leg to go over the top rung of the ladder, the ladder suddenly "gave way to the left." As indicated above, he then fell to the driveway on his right side. He stated that he thought one leg of the ladder had gone through the driveway. After he had fallen to the ground, the occupants of the house which he was painting came out from the house to the scene of the accident and brought to his attention the fact that the bottom of the left leg of the ladder was bent. He looked at it and saw its condition within a minute or two after he had fallen to the ground. It is clear from the evidence that prior to the time he commenced to fall and during the course of his fall he was not aware of the fact that the leg of the ladder had bent or crumpled, if, in fact, it had done so.

. . .

At the conclusion of the plaintiff's case, the relevant portions of which I have set forth above, the defendants moved for a nonsuit on the grounds that the plaintiff had failed to establish that the accident occurred as a result of any defect in the ladder or any negligence on the part of any one of the defendants. In considering that motion and in dismissing same I took into consideration the principle that in some circumstances the mere fact that an accident has occurred raises an inference of negligence against the defendant. I also took into consideration the following principles of law, relating to the maxim of *res ipsa loquitur* as set forth in Fleming, *Law of Torts*, 4th ed. (1971), at p. 259:

> *Res ipsa loquitur* is not more than a convenient label to describe situations where, notwithstanding the plaintiff's inability to establish the exact cause of the accident, the fact of the accident by itself is sufficient in the absence of an explanation to justify the conclusion that most probably the defendant was negligent and that his negligence caused the injury.

. . .

In the present case I was satisfied that by the introduction of evidence from the plaintiff of the manner in which he climbed the ladder and of a witness to prove the manner in which he climbed it was a safe manner, the evidence of the plaintiff that the ladder felt "like it was giving way and sinking into the driveway surface", and the subsequent discovery of the bent rail, was *prima facie* proof that he fell as a result of a defect in the ladder and, having once established those facts, the maxim of *res ipsa loquitur* applies in so far as the defendants are concerned and it was not necessary for the plaintiff to negative all or any possible defences.

Counsel for the defendant Reynolds thereupon elected to call evidence.

. . .

In considering the effect in this case of the application of the maxim *res ipsa loquitur* it must be borne in mind that the phrase does not represent a special rule of substantive law but rather represents an evidentiary rule:

> . . . in negligence litigation the "legal" or "ultimate" burden of proving all the facts in issue . . . ordinarily lies on the plaintiff and remains with him throughout the trial in the sense that he must eventually, in order to gain a verdict, persuade the trier of fact that on all the evidence the balance of probability preponderates in his favour.

(Fleming, *Law of Torts*, 4th ed., at p. 266.) In this matter I have already found that at the conclusion of the plaintiff's case he had established sufficient facts, which together with the application of the maxim *res ipsa loquitur*, established a *prima facie* case, *i.e.*, sufficient evidence from which I may infer negligence on the part of either one or both of the defendants. The law applicable to this type of situation is set forth clearly in *Cudney v. Clements Motor Sales Ltd.*, [1969] 2 O.R. 209, 5 D.L.R. (3d) 3, *per* Kelly, J.A., at p. 217 O.R., p. 11 D.L.R.:

> It is unquestionable that, when the facts established by direct evidence or admitted by the defendant are such that, in the light of ordinary common experience, negligence on the part of the defendant may be inferred, the onus of proof passes from the plaintiff to the defendant until it returns to the plaintiff by reason of the defendant putting forward a theory, consistent with the facts, of a way in which the accident may have happened without negligence on his part; when the defendant had done so, the cogency of the facts by themselves disappear and the plaintiff is left as he began in that he must show negligence.

The principle as stated by the learned author of Fleming, *Law of Torts*, 4th ed., at pp. 267-8, is as follows:

> Accordingly, if there are two hypotheses that might account for the accident, one consistent, the other inconsistent with the defendant's negligence, and both are evenly poised, the plaintiff has not discharged the onus incumbent on him of proving the issue on a preponderating balance.

In *United Motors Service, Inc. v. Hutson*, [1937] S.C.R. 294, [1937] 1 D.L.R. 737, 4 I.L.R. 91, Duff, C.J.C., stated at p. 297 S.C.R., p. 738 D.L.R.:

> Broadly speaking, in such cases, where the defendant produces an explanation equally consistent with negligence and no negligence, the burden of establishing negligence still remains with the plaintiff.

After considering all of the evidence in this case I have reached the conclusion that the accident could have occurred in either of two ways. In the first place it could have occurred in the manner in which the plaintiff suggested it happened, namely, that when the plaintiff raised his right leg to climb onto the roof of the house he was painting, the lower part of the left rail of the ladder bent and crumpled under his weight thereby causing it to give way to the left and causing him to fall to the ground. By applying the maxim of *res ipsa loquitur*, the plaintiff says that the bending of the ladder must have been due to the negligence of the defendant Reynolds in the design or manufacture of the ladder or, the negligence of Smith Co. in the handling of the ladder. I am of the opinion that the evidence of the defendant witnesses with respect to the weight-bearing capacity of the damaged ladder in its normal position of use or in a tilted position cast considerable doubt on the plaintiff's theory and, accordingly, on the *prima facie* case which I found he had established. In addition thereto, there is the evidence of the defence witnesses to the effect that if there was a defect in the ladder at the place where it bent, it would have become apparent when the ladder was first used by the plaintiff. It must be remembered that the ladder was used by the plaintiff at the same place, in the same manner and with the same purpose on May 29, 1970, and the ladder did not fail on that occasion. The plaintiff did not call any evidence to rebut this defence evidence. In addition, the theory of the plaintiff is that the ladder commenced to collapse on the left side while both rails were on the ground and the uncontradicted evidence of the defendant is that the ladder in that position was capable of supporting 800 lbs.

The second manner in which the accident could have occurred is the manner in which the defendants suggest the accident happened, namely, that the plaintiff, when he had both feet on the second to last rung of the ladder, raised his right leg over the top rung, thereby losing his balance while standing on one leg only with one hand free to grasp the ladder. This resulted in the ladder falling toward the left and the plaintiff, after briefly grasping the eavestrough with his left hand, fell to the ground striking the steps of the ladder on the way down and causing the tilted left rail to bend with the force of his fall. This theory, in my view, is supported by the statement of the plaintiff that he hit the ground before the ladder and, having regard to the fact that the ladder was between him and the house, it is quite probable that he did strike the lower portion of the ladder on his way to the ground.

In considering the two theories of the manner in which the accident may have occurred, it must be borne in mind that the plaintiff was not expecting to fall; that he did not at any time see the left rail of the ladder bend; that his observations as to the manner in which he fell were made during the agony of an emergency situation, that the giving way or tilting of the ladder to the left as described by him is just as consistent with the theory that the shifting of his weight caused it to go off balance as with the theory that the bending of the rail caused it to tilt. In my opinion, the plaintiff's sensation of the ladder sinking into the driveway surface is just as consistent with the ladder tilting to the left without crumpling as with the crumpling of the rail of the ladder prior to its tilt and fall to the left. Certainly, the act of climbing onto the roof, while holding the handle of a paint can and a brush in the right hand, is consistent with the probability of the plaintiff losing his balance and causing the ladder and himself to fall. I am of the opinion that the evidence of the defence witnesses was such that it renders improbable the allegations to the plaintiff as to the manner in which the accident happened. I believe that the evidence and theory of the defence indicates a way in which the accident might have occurred without negligence on the part of the defendant, and the onus of proof thus shifted back to the plaintiff and remains unsatisfied. On a consideration of all the evidence, I am not satisfied that the plaintiff has proved on the balance of probabilities that the accident and the injuries suffered by the plaintiff were caused by the negligence of the defendants or either one of them.

HOLMES v. BD. OF HOSP. TRUSTEES OF LONDON

(1977), 17 O.R. (2d) 626, 81 D.L.R. (3d) 67 (Ont. H.C.)

ROBINS J.: . . . In medical malpractice actions as in civil actions generally the burden of proof is on the plaintiff; it is for the patient to establish that the doctor fell below the standard of care required of him in the circumstances. The onus is met if on the evidence the plaintiff is able to satisfy the Court not beyond a shadow of a doubt but on the balance of probabilities that the defendant was guilty of negligence. The fact that a medical procedure is unsuccessful does not impose liability; unfavourable consequences are not necessarily synonymous with negligence. Medicine is not an exact science and a doctor does not ensure satisfactory results or a patient's good health; in medical procedures untoward results may occur even when the highest possible degree of skill and care have been applied.

The present case, in so far as the claim against the anaesthetist is concerned, is, it is common ground, one of a class of cases to which the maxim *res ipsa loquitur* applies. "The thing speaks for itself" in this sense: the factual nature of the injurious event of October 28th on the evidence before me is such that in the ordinary course of things it would probably not have occurred if the defendant had acted in accordance with the requisite duty of care; or, put another way, the consequences of the anaesthetic were not such as normally would have followed if the anaesthetist had exercised due care. Because the plaintiff may invoke *res ipsa loquitur* in this case she is assisted in proving her claim — even though she may be unable to demonstrate its precise cause, the happening of the accident in itself, the *res*, is evidence from which negligence on the part of the doctor in control may be reasonably inferred.

It is, as I have said, not questioned that this is a *res ipsa loquitur* situation; but a question has arisen as to the practical procedural effect of *res ipsa loquitur* on the burden of proof. The fact of the happening is, as I view *res ipsa loquitur*, simply a piece of circumstantial evidence justifying an inference of the defendant's negligence. The weight to be given that inference, like that to be given any other circumstantial evidence, will depend on the particular factual circumstances of the case. The strength of the inference may vary: it may be very strong or it may be sufficiently potent only to present a *prima facie* case and prevent the plaintiff from being non-suited; the inference of the accident in Professor Fleming's phrase "may speak in a whisper or cry out aloud." What evidence, if any, the defendant need adduce will depend on the strength of the inference raised against him. The burden of proof remains with the plaintiff throughout; *res ipsa loquitur* does not shift the onus to the defendant or create a legal presumption in favour of the plaintiff which the defendant must disprove before he can escape liability. At the end of the trial the Court must decide whether on all the evidence before it the plaintiff has on the balance of probabilities established the defendant's negligence. If the scales are not tilted in favour of the plaintiff the defendant must be exonerated: see generally, Fleming, *Law of Torts*, 5th ed. (1977), pp. 302-13; see also, Wright, "Res Ipsa Loquitur", Law Society of Upper Canada Special Lectures — *Evidence* (1955), pp. 122-31; for a recent review and compilation of the numerous authorities on the subject, see Schiff "A Res Ipsa Loquitur Nutshell" (1976), 26 U. of T.L.J., p. 451. . . .

NOTES AND QUESTIONS

1. What procedural effects did the court in *McHugh* attribute to the doctrine of *res ipsa loquitur?* Would the defendants have necessarily been held liable if they had chosen to adduce no evidence?

2. As in *McHugh*, the Canadian courts have often held that *res ipsa loquitur* shifts the evidentiary burden of proof to the defendant. The defendant need not prove the actual cause of the accident, but rather he must provide an explanation of the mishap which is equally consistent with no negligence on his part. The defendant's explanation must be based on evidence and not mere speculation. See *Finlay v. Auld* (1973), 43 D.L.R. (3d) 216 (S.C.C.); *Tataryn v. Co-op. Trust Co.* (1975), 65 D.L.R. (3d) 99 (Sask. C.A.); *Hajgato v. London Health Assn.* (1982), 36 O.R. (2d) 669 (H.C.), aff'd. (1983), 44 O.R. (2d) 264 (C.A.); and *Sisters of Charity of the Immaculate Conception v. Fudge (Robert J.) Ltd.* (1988), 87 N.B.R. (2d) 119 (C.A.), leave to appeal ref'd. (1988), 87 N.B.R. (2d) 270 (S.C.C.).

3. What procedural effects did the court in *Holmes* attribute to *res ipsa loquitur?* How does this approach differ from that adopted in *McHugh?* Based on the approach in *Holmes*, is there any reason why the plaintiff would raise *res ipsa loquitur?* See also *Hobson v. Munkley* (1976), 14 O.R. (2d) 575 (H.C.).

4. The doctrine of *res ipsa loquitur* does not apply where two or more parties could have been responsible. See *Haverkate v. Toronto Harbour Commissioners* (1986), 30 D.L.R. (4th) 125 (Ont. H.C.), aff'd. (1988), 46 D.L.R. (4th) 767 (Ont. C.A.).

5. For a discussion of *res ipsa loquitur* see Fleming, *The Law of Torts*, 8th ed. (1992), 320-26; Linden, *Canadian Tort Law*, 5th ed. (1993), 220-29; and Grady, *Res Ipsa Loquitur* (Law and Economics Programme, Faculty of Law, University of Toronto) (1990).

REVIEW PROBLEM

Analyze the following fact situations and discuss the burden of proof and *res ipsa loquitur* as they arise.

(a) Ann went to a race track to photograph racing cars. She found a secluded spot near a sharp curve. As she was photographing one car, she was hit from behind by another car that had left the track and travelled 100 meters. She regained consciousness in the hospital and remembered nothing about the accident. She has sought your legal advice about suing the driver of the car.

(b) Bill set out from his farm at 8 a.m. An hour later, Bill's body was found in a ditch beside his overturned jeep. The road was flat and straight, and the weather was warm and sunny. There were no skid marks, but there were signs that the car veered off the highway on to the gravel shoulder twice, before leaving the road and overturning in the ditch. A mechanical check of the jeep reveals that all four bolts in the steering mechanism were sheared off. A month earlier, a mechanic had replaced the bolts. Bill's wife has contacted you about suing the mechanic. You have found an expert witness who is willing to testify that the bolts could be sheared off in such a manner, if they had been tightened improperly.

(c) Mr. James underwent surgery performed by Drs. Reed and Lang. Dr. Reed, who performed the first part of the operation, had taken longer than anticipated. In order to make up this lost time, the second surgeon, Dr. Lang, took several short-cuts. Both doctors had left the operating room several times to consult with lab technicians and radiologists. During these periods, surgical assistants, operating nurses and medical students explored the incision. When the operation was finished, a nurse indicated that all the sponges were accounted for. Dr. Lang then closed the incision. Mr. James died two days later because a sponge had been left in his abdomen. What legal recourse does the James family have?

STATUTORY PROVISIONS AND TORT LIABILITY

1. Introduction
2. Express Statutory Causes of Action
3. The Use of Statutes in Common Law Negligence
4. The Relationship Between Common Law and Statutory Causes of Action
5. A Note on the Canadian Charter of Rights and Freedoms

1. Introduction

Although tort law remains primarily a common law subject, statutes play an increasingly important role in determining civil liability. There are now two different ways in which Canadian courts may use a statute in a torts suit.

First, the court may interpret a statute as creating an express statutory cause of action. For example, a statute may explicitly create a duty of care and provide a civil remedy in favour of those injured by its breach. This statutory duty may be quite different from the existing common law duty or may govern a situation in which there is no common law duty. The statute may also specify the standard of care and other elements of the action, including the defences. In a statutory cause of action, the court simply interprets and applies the governing legislation.

Second, the courts may refer to a statutory provision in their analysis of a common law negligence action. For example, many regulatory statutes create obligations or prohibit conduct without reference to civil liability, imposing fines and other penalties for any violations. While acknowledging that the legislation does not create a statutory cause of action, the court may consider the provision in deciding whether to recognize a common law duty. Similarly, a safety provision in a statute drafted by experts in the field may be of great assistance to the courts in determining what the common law standard of care ought to be. It is important to emphasize that it is the court, not the legislation, which is defining the common law principles.

NOTES AND QUESTIONS

1. Until 1983 the Canadian courts used statutes in a third way. They attempted to infer from a statute which was silent on the issue whether the legislature intended to create an implied statutory cause of action. There was a body of extremely confusing case law which purported to establish guidelines for making such determinations. In *R. in Right of Can. v. Sask. Wheat Pool* (1983), 143 D.L.R. (3d) 9, the Supreme Court of Canada stated that the courts cannot use statutes to create implied statutory causes of action. See also Linden, *Canadian Tort Law*, 5th ed. (1992), 187-212 and 281-304.

2. Express Statutory Causes of Action

TRESPASS TO PROPERTY ACT

R.S.O. 1990, c. T.21

2.—(1) Every person who is not acting under a right or authority conferred by law and who,

   (*a*) without the express permission of the occupier, the proof of which rests on the defendant,
       (i) enters on premises when entry is prohibited under this Act, or
       (ii) engages in an activity on premises when the activity is prohibited under this Act; or
   (*b*) does not leave the premises immediately after he or she is directed to do so by the occupier of the premises or a person authorized by the occupier,

is guilty of an offence and on conviction is liable to a fine of not more than $2,000.

(2) It is a defence to a charge under subsection (1) in respect of premises that is land that the person charged reasonably believed that he or she had title to or an interest in the land that entitled him or her to do the act complained of.

12.—(1) Where a person is convicted of an offence under section 2, and a person has suffered damage caused by the person convicted during the commission of the offence, the court shall, on the request of the prosecutor and with the consent of the person who suffered the damage, determine the damages and shall make a judgment for damages against the person convicted in favour of the person who suffered the damage, but no judgment shall be for an amount in excess of $1,000.

(2) Where a prosecution under section 2 is conducted by a private prosecutor, and the defendant is convicted, unless the court is of the opinion that the prosecution was not necessary for the protection of the occupier or the occupier's interests, the court shall determine the actual costs reasonably incurred in conducting the prosecution and, despite section 60 of the *Provincial Offences Act*, shall order those costs to be paid by the defendant to the prosecutor.

(3) A judgment for damages under subsection (1), or an award of costs under subsection (2), shall be in addition to any fine that is imposed under this Act.

(4) A judgment for damages under subsection (1) extinguishes the right of the person in whose favour the judgment is made to bring a civil action for damages against the person convicted arising out of the same facts.

(5) The failure to request or refusal to grant a judgment for damages under subsection (1) does not affect a right to bring a civil action for damages arising out of the same facts.

(6) The judgment for damages under subsection (1), and the award for costs under subsection (2), may be filed in the Small Claims Court and shall be deemed to be a judgment or order of that court for the purposes of enforcement.

COMPETITION ACT

R.S.C. 1985, c. C-34

(as amended by R.S.C. 1985, c. 1 (4th Supp.), s. 11(1); c. 19 (2nd Supp.), s. 30(1)

36. (1) Any person who has suffered loss or damage as a result of
   (*a*) conduct that is contrary to any provision of Part VI, or
   (*b*) the failure of any person to comply with an order of the Tribunal or another court under this Act,

may, in any court of competent jurisdiction, sue for and recover from the person who engaged in the conduct or failed to comply with the order an amount equal to the loss or damage proved to have been suffered by him, together with any additional amount that the court may allow not exceeding the full cost to him of any investigation in connection with the matter and of proceedings under this section.

PART VI

OFFENCES IN RELATION TO COMPETITION

45. (1) Every one who conspires, combines, agrees or arranges with another person

(*a*) to limit unduly the facilities for transporting, producing, manufacturing, supplying, storing or dealing in any product,

(*b*) to prevent, limit or lessen, unduly, the manufacture or production of a product or to enhance unreasonably the price thereof,

(*c*) to prevent or lessen, unduly, competition in the production, manufacture, purchase, barter, sale, storage, rental, transportation or supply of a product, or in the price of insurance on persons or property, or

(*d*) to otherwise restrain or injure competition unduly,

is guilty of an indictable offence and liable to imprisonment for a term not exceeding five years or to a fine not exceeding ten million dollars or to both.

NOTES AND QUESTIONS

1. Most violations of section 2(1) of the Trespass to Property Act will also give rise to a common law action for trespass to land. What is the rationale for s. 12? Why is the statutory defence in s. 2(2) broader than the common law defence?

2. One purpose of s. 36 of the Competition Act is to induce private citizens to participate in enforcing the criminal law in this field. Similar provisions in the United States provide treble damages to successful private litigants. See the Clayton Act, 15 U.S.C.A., paragraph 26. What other functions are served by s. 36? Why is private law enforcement necessary or desirable in this field? Is there any reason why the public enforcement agency cannot adequately protect the public interest? Is a private litigant's interest necessarily similar to the public interest?

3. The statutory action pursuant to s. 36 of the Competition Act is similar to the common law tort action for conspiracy. If the plaintiff is unsuccessful under s. 36, should he be able to bring a common law conspiracy action on the same facts?

4. The sections reprinted above are but two of the many statutory provisions which expressly govern civil liability. Such provisions are especially common in statutes concerning governmental and public enterprises. There is no such thing as a typical provision, and care must be taken to search for and interpret relevant legislation on a case-by-case basis.

TRACHSLER v. HALTON

[1955] O.W.N. 909 (Ont. H.C.)

KING J. [orally, after stating the nature of the actions]: ... The duty of a municipality is to keep its highways in such condition that travellers using them with ordinary care may do so in safety. Section 453(1) of The Municipal Act [now R.S.O. c. M.45, s. 284(1)] to which I have referred says:

> Every highway and every bridge shall be kept in repair by the corporation the council of which has jurisdiction over it, or upon which the duty of repairing it is imposed by this Act, and in case of default the corporation shall, subject to the provisions of *The Negligence Act*, be liable for all damages sustained by any person by reason of such default.

It will be noticed that the word used in the subsection, and used twice, is "default" and not merely failure to repair.

The question whether a highway is in repair is a question of fact. The duty to repair a highway may be described generally as a duty to do all things that may be reasonably necessary in the way of repairs to keep it fit for the lawful traffic over it. Notice of need of repair is not an ingredient of the duty to repair, but it may be a controlling factor in the question whether that duty has been performed.

When a highway is put out of repair without any fault of those whose duty it is to repair it, then that duty is reasonably performed if the repair is made within a reasonable time after they are informed, know or should have acquired knowledge of the need of repair.

In *Trueman v. The King; Dewan v. The King*, [1932] O.R. 703 at 708-9, [1932] 4 D.L.R. 676, Riddell J.A. says:

> In cases against a municipality for damages for injury due to a want of repair, the law of this Province has long been settled, and is not disputed. On the occurrence of a want of repair, the municipality is not liable unless, after such occurrence, the municipality has had an opportunity to repair the defect, either by notice or knowledge, or by the lapse of such time as should have enabled it to have discovered the defect.
>
> . . .

The system of inspecting the highways by the defendant County appeared to me to be adequate. No reasonable inspection of the highways could have led to faster action than occurred on this occasion. I do not say, for example, that the police of Trafalgar Township might not have proceeded at once to the place where the upheaval had been reported, but this does not fix any liability upon the defendant County, in my opinion.

It appears to me that by s. 453(1) of The Municipal Act the Legislature aimed at securing for the public reasonably easy and convenient avenues of communication and, as far as might be done by the exercise of corporate diligence, the safety of persons using the highways, but stopped short of providing an accident policy or indemnity against loss without regard to the effort of the corporation to comply with the statute.

On the evidence it appears to me that with respect to any circumstances that might have prevented the accident with which we are concerned, the defendant did all that might be reasonably expected of it in discharge of its duty under The Municipal Act. I believe that the defendant has shown that it was not in default with respect to its obligations imposed by the statute . . .

I do not find, on the evidence, that there is any liability on the defendant municipality.

[King J. dismissed the plaintiffs' actions. A subsequent appeal by one of the plaintiffs was dismissed by the Ontario Court of Appeal, [1955] O.W.N. 912.]

NOTES AND QUESTIONS

1. The terms statutory duty and statutory standard are used inconsistently. The term duty, as used in this chapter, refers to the obligation itself. Thus, in *Trachsler*, the duty was to keep the highway in a state of repair. The term standard refers to the degree of care which the defendant must exercise to meet this duty.

What standard of care did King J. impose? Did he simply adopt the common law standard or did he derive the standard from the statutory language? How should the standard be determined? See also *R. v. Jennings*, [1966] S.C.R. 532; *Allan v. Saskatoon* (1971), 21 D.L.R. (3d) 338 (Sask. C.A.); *R. v. Cote; Millette v. Kalogeropoulos* (1974), 51 D.L.R. (3d) 244 (S.C.C.); *O'Rourke v. Schacht*, [1976] 1 S.C.R. 53; and *Rydzik v. Edwards* (1982), 38 O.R. 486 (H.C.).

2. The current common law obligation of a municipality is similar to the obligation in *Trachsler*. However, at that time, the courts were reluctant to impose affirmative common law duties on statutory

public authorities. Thus, the express statutory duty in the Municipal Act may have been the sole basis for bringing suit in *Trachsler.*

3. Some statutes will specifically define the required standard of care. See for example, the Alberta Municipal Government Act, R.S.A. 1994, c. M-26.1, s. 532. The predecessor to the current section was discussed in *Parkland No. 31 v. Stetar* (1974), 50 D.L.R. (3d) 376 (S.C.C.); and *Berezowski v. Edmonton* (1986), 45 Alta. L.R. (2d) 247 (C.A.).

REVIEW PROBLEM

Answer the following questions based on s. 359 of the Railway Act, R.S.C. 1985, c. R-3.

Breach of Duty under Certain Acts

359. Any company that, or any person who, being a director or officer thereof, or a receiver, trustee, lessee, agent, or otherwise acting for or employed by the company, does, causes or permits to be done, any matter, act or thing contrary to

(a) this Act, the Special Act, the *National Transportation Act, 1987* or the *Railway Safety Act,*

(b) any orders, regulations or directions made under this Act or the *National Transportation Act, 1987*, or

(c) any orders, regulations, emergency directives or rules made under the *Railway Safety Act,* or omits to do any matter, act or thing thereby required to be done on the part of any such company or person, is, in addition to being liable to any penalty elsewhere provided, liable to any person injured by any such act or omission for the full amount of damages sustained thereby, notwithstanding, in the case of the *Railway Safety Act* or any order, regulation, emergency directive or rule made thereunder, any agreement to the contrary with regard to any such person, unless that agreement is authorized by the law of the province in which it is made and by regulation of the Agency, and the damages referred to in this section are not subject to any special limitation except as expressly provided for by this or any other Act.

(a) What statutory duty of care is created by s. 359? On whom is this duty imposed?

(b) What standard of care does this section impose on the railway? Assume the company erected a fence in compliance with the statute and took great care to maintain it. Would the company be held liable in a statutory cause of action if vandals destroyed the fence immediately before the accident?

(c) In *Colonial Coach Lines Ltd. v. Bennett* (1968), 66 D.L.R. (2d) 396 (Ont. C.A.), Laskin J.A. suggested in *obiter* that this statute imposes strict liability. Do you agree with his statement? See also *Paulsen and Paulsen v. C.P.R.* (1963), 40 D.L.R. (2d) 761 (Man. C.A.).

3. The Use of Statutes in Common Law Negligence

R. IN RIGHT OF CAN. v. SASK. WHEAT POOL

(1983), 143 D.L.R. (3d) 9 (S.C.C.)

[The Saskatchewan Wheat Pool delivered infested wheat to the Canadian Wheat Board in violation of s. 86(c) of the Canada Grain Act, S.C. 1970-71-72, c. 7. The Act made no reference to the issue of civil liability for breach of its provisions. The Board made no claim in common law negligence, but rather sought damages based solely on the Pool's breach of s. 86(c).]

The judgment of the court was delivered by

DICKSON J.: — This case raises the difficult issue of the relation of a breach of a statutory duty to a civil cause of action. Where "A" has breached a statutory duty causing injury to "B", does "B" have a civil cause of action against "A"? If so, is "A's" liability absolute, in the sense that it exists independently of fault, or is "A" free from liability if the failure to perform the duty is through no fault of his?

. . .

III

STATUTORY BREACH GIVING RISE TO A CIVIL CAUSE OF ACTION

(a) *General*

The uncertainty and confusion in relation between breach of statute and a civil cause of action for damages arising from the breach is of long standing. The commentators have little but harsh words for the unhappy state of affairs, but arriving at a solution, from the disarray of cases, is extraordinarily difficult. It is doubtful that any general principle or rationale can be found in the authorities to resolve all of the issues or even those which are transcendent.

There does seem to be general agreement that the breach of a statutory provision which causes damage to an individual should in some way be pertinent to recovery of compensation for the damage. Two very different forces, however, have been acting in opposite directions. In the United States the civil consequences of breach of statute have been subsumed in the law of negligence. On the other hand, we have witnessed in England the painful emergence of a new nominate tort of statutory breach. This court was given the opportunity to choose between the two positions in *Sterling Trusts Corp. et al. v. Postma et al.* (1964), 48 D.L.R. (2d) 423, [1965] S.C.R. 324, but did not find it necessary for the determination of that case to attempt the difficult task.... It is now imperative for this court to choose.

(b) *The English position*

In 1948 in the case of *London Passenger Transport Board v. Upson*, [1949] A.C. 155, [1949] 1 All E.R. 60, in the passage quoted above, cited by Cartwright J., the House of Lords affirmed the existence of a tort of statutory breach distinct from any issue of negligence. The statute prescribes the duty owed to the plaintiff who need only show (i) breach of the statute, and (ii) damage caused by the breach.

Legitimacy for this civil action for breach of statute has been sought in the *Statute of Westminster II*, 1285, 9 Edw. I, c. 50, which provided for a private remedy by action on the case to those affected by the breach of statutory duties. However, "old though it may be, the action upon the statute has rarely been the subject of careful scrutiny in English law, and its precise judicial character remains a thing of some obscurity": Fricke, "The Juridical Nature of the Action upon the Statute", 76 L.Q.R. 240 (1960). As the gap widened between "public" and "private" law with the passing centuries this broad general right of action, enigmatic as it was, became hedged. Where a public law penalty was provided for in the statute a private civil cause of action would not automatically arise. The oft-quoted formulation of this principle was found in *Doe d. Rochester v. Bridges* (1831), 1 B. & Ad. 847 at p. 857, 109 E.R. 1001:

> And where an Act creates an obligation, and enforces the performance in a specified manner, we take it to be a general rule that performance cannot be enforced in any other manner.

Although taken out of context, the dictum served the purpose of limiting the multiplication of suits of dubious value. "With the vast increase in legislative activity of modern times, if the old rule were still law it might lead to unjust, not to say absurd, results in creating liabilities wider than the legislature can possibly have intended" (Winfield & Jolowicz, *Tort*, 11th ed. (1979), at p. 154). By the end of the 19th century, however, the civil action on the statute began to revive as a response to industrial safety legislation. The statement of the doctrine propounded in *Doe d. Rochester v. Bridges* did not enjoy a long period of acceptance. *Couch v. Steel* (1854), 3 El. & Bl. 402, 118 E.R. 1193, marked the beginning of a new era of construction. Lord Campbell C.J., relying on statements in Comyn's Digest, concluded that the injured party has a common law right to maintain an action for special damage arising from the breach of a public duty. *Couch v. Steel* was questioned some twenty years later in *Atkinson v. Newcastle & Gateshead Waterworks Co.* (1877), 2 Ex. D. 441. Lord Cairns L.C., dealing with the matter apart from authority, concluded that the private remedy had been excluded. He expressed "grave doubts" whether the authorities cited by Lord Campbell in *Couch v. Steel* justified the broad general rule there laid down. Lord Cockburn C.J. agreed that the correctness of *Couch v. Steel* was "open to grave doubts", while Brett L.J. entertained the "strongest doubt" as to the correctness of the broad general rule enunciated in *Couch v. Steel*.

As Street puts it "The effect of the leading cases in the nineteenth century (which remain important authorities) however, was to make the cause of action rest on proof that the legislature intended that violation of the right or interest conferred by the statute was to be treated as tortious" (Street, *Law of Torts*, 2nd ed., p. 273). Fricke pointed out (76 L.Q.R., at p. 260) that that doctrine leads to many difficulties. In the first place it is not clear what the *prima facie* rule or presumption should be. Some of the cases suggest that *prima facie* an action is given by the statement of a statutory duty, and that it exists unless it can be said to be taken away by any provisions to be found in the Act. Other authorities suggest the *prima facie* rule is that the specific statement of a certain manner of enforcement excluded any other means of enforcement. Sometimes the courts jump one way, sometimes the other. Fricke concludes (pp. 263-4) that as a matter of pure statutory construction the law went wrong with the decision in 1854 in *Couch v. Steel*: "If one is concerned with the intrinsic question of interpreting the legislative will as reflected within the four corners of a document which made express provision of a fine, but makes no mention of a civil remedy, one is compelled to the conclusion that a civil remedy was not intended."

. . .

This fragmentation of approach has given rise to some theoretical, and some not-so-theoretical, difficulties. The pretence of seeking what has been called a "will o' the wisp", a non-existent intention of Parliament to create a civil cause of action, has been harshly criticized. It is capricious and arbitrary, "judicial legislation" at its very worst.

> Not only does it involve an unnecessary fiction, but it may lead to decisions being made on the basis of insignificant details of phraseology instead of matters of substance. If the question whether a person injured by breach of a statutory obligation is to have a right of action for

> damages is in truth a question to be decided by the court, let it be acknowledged as such and
> some useful principles of law developed.

Winfield & Jolowicz, *supra*, at p. 159. It is a "bare faced fiction" at odds with accepted canons of statutory interpretation: "the legislature's silence on the question of civil liability rather points to the conclusion that it either did not have it in mind or deliberately omitted to provide for it" (Fleming, *The Law of Torts*, 5th ed. (1977), at p. 123). Glanville Williams is now of the opinion that the "irresolute course" of the judicial decisions "reflect no credit on our jurisprudence" and with respect, I agree. He writes:

> The failure of the judges to develop a governing attitude means that it is almost impossible to
> predict, outside the decided authorities, when the courts will regard a civil duty as impliedly
> created. In effect the judge can do what he likes, and then select one of the conflicting principles
> stated by his predecessors in order to justify his decision.

"The Effect of Penal Legislation in the Law of Tort", *supra*, at p. 246. Prosser is of the same opinion . . .

The door to a civil cause of action arising from breach of statute had swung closed at the beginning of the 19th century with the proliferation of written legislation and swung open again, for reasons of policy and convenience, to accommodate the rising incidence of industrial accidents at the end of the 19th century. But the proposition that every statutory breach gave rise to a private right of action was still untenable, as it is today. The courts looked for a screening mechanism which would determine the cases to which an action should be limited.

Various presumptions or guidelines sprang up. "Thus, it has often been tediously repeated that the crucial test is whether the duty created by the statute is owed primarily to the State, and only incidentally to the individual, or vice versa" (Fleming, *supra*, at p. 125). A duty to all the public (ratepayers, for example) does not give rise to a private cause of action whereas a duty to an individual (an injured worker, for example) may. The purpose of the statute must be the protection of a certain "class" of individuals of whom the plaintiff is one and the injury suffered must be of a kind which it was the object of the legislation to prevent. Both requirements have, in the past, been fairly narrowly construed and fairly heavily criticized.

Although "[i]t is doubtful, indeed, if any general principle can be found to explain all the cases on the subject" (*Salmond on Torts*, 7th ed. (1977), at p. 243) several justifications are given for the tort of statutory breach. It provides fixed standards of negligence and replaces the judgment of amateurs (the jury) with that of professionals in highly technical areas. In effect, it provides for absolute liability in fields where this has been found desirable such as industrial safety. Laudable as these effects are, the state of the law remains extremely unsatisfactory.

. . .

(c) *The American position*

Professor Fleming prefers the American approach which has assimilated civil responsibility for statutory breach into the general law of negligence (*The Law of Torts, supra*, at p. 124):

> Intellectually more acceptable, because less arcane, is the prevailing American theory which
> frankly disclaims that the civil action is in any sure sense a creature of the statute, for the simple

enough reason that the statute just does not contemplate, much less provide, a civil remedy. Any recovery of damages for injury due to its violation must, therefore, rest on common law principles. But though the penal statute does not create civil liability the court may think it proper to adopt the legislative formulation of a specific standard in place of the unformulated standard of reasonable conduct, in much the same manner as when it rules peremtorily [sic] that certain acts or omissions constitute negligence of the law.

There are, however, differing views of the effect of this assimilation: at one end of the spectrum, breach of a statutory duty may constitute negligence *per se* or, at the other, it may merely be evidence of negligence. This distinction finds its roots in the seminal 1913 article by Professor Thayer, "Public Wrong and Private Action", 27 Harv. L.R. 317 (1913-14), at p. 323:

. . .

The majority view in the United States has been that statutory breach constitutes negligence *per se* — in certain circumstances (Prosser, *The Law of Torts, supra*, at p. 200):

> Once the statute is determined to be applicable — which is to say, once it is interpreted as designed to protect the class of persons in which the plaintiff is included, against the risk of the type of harm which had in fact occurred as a result of its violation — the great majority of the courts hold that an unexcused violation is conclusive on the issue of negligence, and that the court must so direct the jury. The standard of conduct is taken over by the court from that fixed by the legislature, and "jurors have no dispensing power by which to relax it", except in so far as the court may recognize the possibility of a valid excuse for disobedience of the law. This usually is expressed by saying that the unexcused violation is negligence "per se", or in itself. The effect of such a rule is to stamp the defendant's conduct as negligence, with all of the effects of common law negligence, but with no greater effect.

. . .

The American courts have not broken away from a consideration of the purpose or intent of the legislature; the *Restatement, Torts, Second*, sets out the circumstances in which the court may adopt a legislative enactment as embodying the standard of care applicable in the circumstances:

> 286. When Standards of Conduct Defined by Legislation or Regulations Will be Adopted
>
> The court may adopt as the standard of conduct of a reasonable man the requirements of a legislative enactment or an administrative regulation whose purpose is found to be exclusively or in part
>
> (a) to protect a class of persons which includes the one whose interest is invaded, and
> (b) to protect the particular interest which is invaded, and
> (c) to protect that interest against the kind of harm which has resulted, and
> (d) to protect that interest the particular hazard from which the harm results.

The so-called "minority view" in the United States considers breach of a statute to be merely evidence of negligence. There are, however, varying degrees of evidence. Statutory breach may be considered totally irrelevant, merely relevant, or *prima facie* evidence of negligence having the effect of reversing the onus of proof . . .

The major criticism of the negligence *per se* approach has been the inflexible application of the legislature's criminal standard of conduct to a civil case. I agree with this criticism. The defendant in a civil case does not benefit from the technical defences or protection offered by the criminal law; the civil consequences may easily outweigh any penal consequences attaching to the breach of statute; and finally the purposes served by the imposition of criminal as opposed to civil liability are radically different. The compensatory aspect of tort liability has won out over the deterrent and punitive aspect; the perceptible evolution in the use of civil liability as a mechanism of loss shifting to that of loss distribution has only accentuated this change. And so "[t]he doctrine of negligence *per se* is, therefore, not fitted for relentless use, nor is it so used" (Morris, "The Relation of Criminal Statutes to Tort Liability", 46 Harv. L.R. 453 (1932-33), at p. 460). Thus the guidelines in the *Restatement, Torts, Second.*

(d) *The Canadian position*

Professor Linden has said that the "Canadian courts appear to oscillate between the English and American positions without even recognizing this fact": "Comment, *Sterling Trusts Corporation v. Postma*", 45 Can. Bar Rev. 121 (1967), at p. 126. The most widely used approach, however, has been that stated in *Sterling Trusts Corp. v. Postma, supra.* The breach of a statutory provision is "*prima facie* evidence of negligence". There is some difficulty in the terminology used. "*Prima facie* evidence of negligence" in the *Sterling Trusts* case is used seemingly interchangeably with the expression "*prima facie* liable". In a later case in the Ontario Court of Appeal, *Queensway Tank Lines Ltd. v. Moise* (1969), 9 D.L.R. (3d) 30, [1970] 1 O.R. 535, MacKay J.A. assumes *prima facie* evidence of negligence to be a presumption of negligence with concomitant shift in the onus of proof to the defendant.

The use of breach of statute as evidence of negligence as opposed to recognition of a nominate tort of statutory breach is, as Professor Fleming has put it, more intellectually acceptable. It avoids, to a certain extent, the fictitious hunt for legislative intent to create a civil cause of action which has been so criticized in England. It also avoids the inflexible application of the legislature's criminal standard of conduct to a civil case. Glanville Williams is of the opinion, with which I am in agreement, that where there is no duty of care at common law, breach of non-industrial penal legislation should not affect civil liability unless the statute provides for it. As I have indicated above, industrial legislation historically has enjoyed special consideration. Recognition of the doctrine of absolute liability under some industrial statutes does not justify extension of such doctrine to other fields, particularly when one considers the jejune reasoning supporting the juristic invention.

. . .

Tort law itself has undergone a major transformation in this century with nominate torts being eclipsed by negligence, the closest the common law has come to a general theory of civil responsibility. The concept of duty of care, embodied in the neighbour principle has expanded into areas hitherto untouched by tort law.

One of the main reasons for shifting a loss to a defendant is that he has been at fault, that he has done some act which should be discouraged. There is then good reason for taking money from the defendant as well as a reason for giving it to the plaintiff who has suffered from the fault of the defendant. But there seems little in the way of defensible policy for holding a defendant who breached a statutory duty unwittingly to be negligent and obligated to pay even though not at fault.

The legislature has imposed a penalty on a strictly admonitory basis and there seems little justification to add civil liability when such liability would tend to produce liability without fault. The legislature has determined the proper penalty for the defendant's wrong but if tort admonition of liability without fault is to be added, the financial consequences will be measured, not by the amount of the penalty, but by the amount of money which is required to compensate the plaintiff. Minimum fault may subject the defendant to heavy liability. Inconsequential violations should not subject the violator to any civil liability at all but should be left to the criminal courts for enforcement of a fine.

In this case the Board contends that the duty imposed by the Act is absolute, that is to say, the Pool is liable, even in absence of fault, and all that is requisite to prove a breach of duty is to show that the requirements of the statute have not, in fact, been complied with; it is not necessary to show how the failure to comply arose or that the Pool was guilty of any failure to take reasonable care to comply.

The tendency of the law of recent times is to ameliorate the rigours of absolute rules and absolute duty in the sense indicated, as contrary to natural justice. "Sound policy lets losses lie where they fall except where a special reason can be shown for interference": Holmes, *The Common Law*, p. 50. In the case at bar the evidence is that substantially all of the grain entering the terminal of the Pool at Thunder Bay came from agents of the Board. The imposition of heavy financial burden as in this case without fault on the part of the Pool does not incline one to interfere. It is better that the loss lies where it falls, upon the Board.

For all of the above reasons I would be adverse to the recognition in Canada of a nominate tort of statutory breach. Breach of statute, where it has an effect upon civil liability, should be considered in the context of the general law of negligence. Negligence and its common law duty of care have become pervasive enough to serve the purpose invoked for the existence of the action for statutory breach.

It must not be forgotten that the other elements of tortious responsibility equally apply to situations involving statutory breach, *i.e.*, principles of causation and damages. To be relevant at all, the statutory breach must have caused the damage of which the plaintiff complains. Should this be so, the violation of the statute should be evidence of negligence on the part of the defendant.

. . .

In sum I conclude that:

1. Civil consequences of breach of statute should be subsumed in the law of negligence.
2. The notion of a nominate tort of statutory breach giving a right to recovery merely on proof of breach and damages should be rejected, as should the view that unexcused breach constitutes negligence *per se* giving rise to absolute liability.
3. Proof of statutory breach, causative of damages, may be evidence of negligence.
4. The statutory formulation of the duty may afford a specific, and useful, standard of reasonable conduct.
5. In the case at bar negligence is neither pleaded nor proven. The action must fail.

I would dismiss the appeal with costs.

Appeal dismissed.

NOTES AND QUESTIONS

1. What is the English position on the use of statutes in tort actions? What criticisms does Dickson J. make of this case law? Do you agree with his criticisms? For a review of the English law, see Heuston and Buckley, *Salmond and Heuston on the Law of Torts*, 20th ed. (1992), 251-61; and Rogers, *Winfield and Jolowicz on Tort*, 14th ed. (1994), 189-202.

2. What is the majority position in the United States and how has it been modified by the *Restatement of the Law, Torts, Second* (1965), paras. 288B and 286? What is the American minority position? Which position is preferable and which one does Dickson J. favour?

3. Explain the Canadian approach to the use of statutes prior to *Sask. Wheat Pool*. Summarize the principles of law that now govern the use of statutes based on *Sask. Wheat Pool*. Has Dickson J. adequately dealt with the problems in the English, American and prior Canadian positions?

4. Dickson J. indicated that industrial safety statutes have been treated differently than other types of legislation. Can you suggest a rationale for this practice? What principles of law now govern the use of industrial safety statutes in Canadian tort actions?

5. Given the Supreme Court's rejection of implied statutory causes of action, what impact should strict liability in a regulatory statute have on a common law cause of action?

6. For a more detailed discussion of *Sask. Wheat Board*, see Alexander, "Legislation and Civil Liability: Public Policy and 'Equity of the Statute'" (1984), 30 McGill L.J. 1; Fridman, "Civil Liability for Criminal Conduct" (1984), 16 Ottawa L.R. 34; Brudner, "Tort — Civil Liability For Breach of Statutory Duty Abolished" (1984), 62 Can. Bar Rev. 668; and Rogers, "Rusty Beetles in the Elevator", [1984] Cambridge L.J. 23.

HORSLEY v. MACLAREN

[1972] S.C.R. 441, 22 D.L.R. (3d) 545 (S.C.C.)

[One issue the court had to decide was the circumstances in which the operator of a non-commercial passenger boat owed a duty of care to rescue an invited guest, who had fallen overboard through no fault of the operator. A long extract of the case is reproduced in chapter 11. In the following passage Laskin J., dissenting, discusses the relationship between the common law duty of care and the Canada Shipping Act, a statute which governs commercial shipping.]

. . .

LASKIN J.: . . . I do not rest the duty to which I would hold MacLaren in this case on s. 526(1) of the *Canada Shipping Act*, even assuming that its terms are broad enough to embrace the facts herein. That provision, a penal one, is as follows:

> 526(1) The master or person in charge of a vessel shall, so far as he can do so without serious danger to his own vessel, her crew and passengers, if any, render assistance to every person, even if that person be a subject of a foreign state at war with Her Majesty, who is found at sea and in danger of being lost, and if he fails to do so he is liable to a fine not exceeding one thousand dollars.

I do not find it necessary in this case to consider whether s. 526(1), taken alone, entails civil consequences for failure to perform a statutory duty; or, even, whether it fixes a standard of conduct upon which the common law may operate to found liability. There is an independent basis for a common law duty of care in the relationship of carrier to passenger, but the legislative declaration of policy in s. 526(1) is a fortifying element in the recognition of that duty, being in harmony with it in a comparable situation.

. . .

[Ritchie J., who gave the majority judgment, also held that the defendant was under a common law duty to rescue, but he stated that it was "in no way dependent upon the provisions of s. 526(1)." Unlike Laskin J., the majority concluded that the defendant had not breached the common law standard of care.]

NOTES AND QUESTIONS

1. Do you think that Laskin J. would have resolved the duty issue differently in the absence of the statutory duty? See also *Jordan House Ltd. v. Menow*, [1974] S.C.R. 239; and *O'Rourke v. Schacht*, [1976] 1 S.C.R. 53.

2. In *Bhadauria v. Bd. of Governors of Seneca College* (1979), 105 D.L.R. (3d) 707 (Ont. C.A.), Wilson J.A. stated that the Ontario Human Rights Code expressed "the public policy of this Province respecting fundamental human rights." She then referred to *Ashby v. White* (1703), 92 E.R. 126, in support of the proposition that if there was a right there had to be a remedy. It was on this basis that she recognized a new common law tort of discrimination. The Supreme Court of Canada rejected this argument, distinguishing *Ashby* as a case which granted a remedy for a pre-existing right. The court concluded that the Code's remedial provisions were the only remedy available to the plaintiff. (1981), 124 D.L.R. (3d) 193. Is the Supreme Court's decision in *Bhadauria* consistent with its decision in *Sask. Wheat Pool*?

RINTOUL v. X-RAY AND RADIUM INDUST.

[1956] S.C.R. 674 (S.C.C.)

[The case arose out of a motor vehicle collision. The defendant alleged that his foot brake had failed. One of the issues before the court was whether the defendant could have avoided the accident by applying his hand brake. The judgment of the court was delivered by Cartwright J.]

. . .

Accepting the evidence of Ouellette as to the speed and position of his car at the instant he actually applied the hand brakes, it is obvious that if they had been in the state of efficiency prescribed by the regulations he could have stopped his car before the collision occurred, even if the car had not been, as it was, proceeding uphill. It is unnecessary to consider whether the effect of the statute and regulations was to cast an absolute duty on the respondents to have the hand brakes in the prescribed condition, for, at the least, the unexplained failure to comply with the regulation was evidence of a breach of the common law duty to take reasonable care to have the motor vehicle fit for the road. Apart from statute there must obviously be a common law duty on anyone who drives a motor vehicle on a highway to have it equipped with brakes, and the regulations may well be taken as the expression of the Legislature's view as to what constitutes a reasonable braking system.

In my opinion, on the evidence the respondents have not only failed to show that the alleged failure of the service brakes was inevitable, they have also failed to show that after such failure occurred Ouellette could not by the exercise of reasonable care have avoided the collision. It follows that the appeal of the plaintiff should be allowed.

. . .

NOTES AND QUESTIONS

1. How does Cartwright J.'s use of the statute in *Rintoul* differ from Laskin J.'s use of the statute in *Horsley*?

2. What advantage does the legislature have over the court in defining the standard of reasonable care?

4. The Relationship Between Common Law and Statutory Causes of Action

BUX v. SLOUGH METALS LTD.

[1973] 1 W.L.R. 1358, [1974] 1 All E.R. 262 (C.A.)

STEPHENSON L.J.:

. . .

1. The Non-Ferrous Metals (Melting and Founding) Regulations 1962 admittedly applied to the work which the plaintiff was doing when his eyes were injured by molten metal. Therefore, the employers owed him the duty imposed by reg 13(1) to provide and maintain suitable goggles or other suitable eye protection and he was under the duty imposed by reg 13(4) to make full and proper use of the goggles provided for his protection and to report any defect in them without delay.

2. I agree with the judge that the employers provided him with suitable goggles and so performed their statutory duty to comply with reg 13(1). Before his accident they obtained and made available to him on request type 1 'Tough-spec' goggles, and in so doing they provided him with them: *Norris v. Syndic Manufacturing Co. Ltd.* [[1952] 1 All E.R. 935 (C.A.)]. I am unable to accede to counsel for the defendants' argument that all they did was a 'sham providing' or that by Mr. Mantle's failure to reply to the plaintiff's complaint two or three days after the issue of the goggles to him they in some way withdrew or nullified provision of them.

This type of goggles was suitable. They gave the eyes adequate protection and the fact that they misted up did not render them unsuitable: *Daniels v. Ford Motor Co. Ltd.* [[1955] 1 All E.R. 218 (C.A.)]; *Marshall v. Babcock & Wilcox Ltd.* [(1961) S.L.T. 259]. They were recommended to the employers by the British Safety Council as suitable, as I think the judge found, and they were in the opinion of Mr. Bevan, the expert whose evidence impressed the judge, the best that could be obtained, with not much to choose between them and type 4 goggles. Even accepting as the judge did the evidence of Mr. Nirmal Singh, in preference to the evidence of the plaintiff and Mr. Bevan, that they misted up about every 20 minutes and even assuming as I do that it would be most inconvenient for a fast worker on piecework who wore goggles like the plaintiff to have to wipe them so often, there was no evidence that the plaintiff could have been fitted with a pair of type l goggles which misted up less frequently and the judge was entitled to find that they were the most suitable type there was and so suitable though not ideal.

3. I agree also with the judge that the employers owed the plaintiff a duty at common law to take reasonable care for his safety by maintaining a reasonably safe system of work and that that duty, which existed before reg 13 came into force on 30th January 1963, subsisted there after and the regulation did not as a matter of law abrogate or put an end to it. On this point counsel for the defendants' argument appeared to move down from the Olympian height of an irrebuttable presumption that compliance with the statutory code was compliance with the common law duty to a position much closer to reality and to the lowlier view of the learned judge that it was a question of fact and degree.

There is, in my judgment, no presumption that a statutory obligation abrogates or supersedes the employer's common law duty or that it defines or measures his common law duty either by clarifying it or by cutting it down — or indeed by extending it. It is not necessarily exhaustive of that duty or co-extensive with it and I do not, with all due respect to counsel for the defendants' argument, think it possible to lay down conditions in which it is exhaustive or to conclude that it is so in this case. The statutory obligation may exceed the duty at common law or it may fall short of it or it may equal it. The court has always to construe the statute or statutory instrument which imposes the obligation, consider the facts of the particular case and the allegations of negligence in fact made by the particular workman and then decide whether, if the statutory obligation has been performed, any negligence has been proved. In some cases such proof will be difficult or impossible; in others it may be easy. This I take to be the true view supported by such authorities as *Franklin v. Gramophone Co. Ltd.* [[1948] 1 All E.R. 353 (C.A.)]; *Nolan v. Dental Manufacturing Co. Ltd.* [[1958] 2 All E.R. 449]; *Qualcast (Wolverhampton) Ltd. v. Haynes* [[1959] 2 All E.R. 38 (H.L.)]; *Cummings (or McWilliams) v. Sir William Arrol & Co. Ltd.* [[1962] 1 All E.R. 623 (H.L.)], to which the judge referred; *Gill v. Humberstone & Co. Ltd.* [[1963] 3 All E.R. 180 (H.L.)], to which Edmund Davies L.J. referred in the course of the argument; and *Matuszczyk v. National Coal Board* [(1953), S.L.T. 39]; *National Coal Board v. England* [[1954] 1 All E.R. 449]; and *Chipchase v. British Titan Products Co. Ltd.* [[1956] 1 All E.R. 613 (C.A.)]. I see no justification for treating *Wilson v. Tyneside Window Cleaning Co.* [[1965] 1 All E.R. 265 (C.A.)] as supporting a principle that it is only failure to provide protection against insidious disease which can be treated as negligence or as doing more than supplying an illustration of the common sense conclusion that when the risk of injury from not using the safety equipment is obvious the workman will have more difficulty in proving negligence against an employer who fails to provide it or to instruct him to use it.

In imposing statutory duties whose breach may give an injured workman a right of action against his employer, Parliament cannot be presumed to have intended to take from the courts their duty of deciding whether his employer has taken reasonable care of the workman and what the extent of that duty is. In this case, and I venture to think in every case where a plaintiff has alleged a breach of statutory duty, he is entitled to allege negligence at common law and to ask the court to answer the question whether he has proved negligence, irrespective of his having proved a breach of statutory duty. In this case the plaintiff, having failed to prove a breach of statutory duty, can certainly ask the court to decide whether a prudent employer ought to have done more for his safety by way of persuading, instructing or ordering him to wear goggles than his employers did.

. . .

[Stephenson L.J. held that the employer owed a common law duty to encourage his employees to obey the safety laws. The employer breached this duty by acquiescing in the employee's disregard of the regulations. The employee was held 40 per cent at fault because of his own breach of the statutory duty. Edmund Davies and Stamp LL.J. delivered separate concurring judgments.]

NOTES AND QUESTIONS

1. According to *Bux*, what significance does compliance with a statutory provision have in a common law negligence action? The general rule in Canada is the same as that in *Bux*. See, for example, *School Div. of Assiniboine South (No. 3) v. Hoffer* (1971), 21 D.L.R. (3d) 608 (Man. C.A.), aff'd. (1973), 40 D.L.R. (3d) 480 (S.C.C.); and *Rinas v. Regina (City)* (1983), 26 Sask. R. 132 (Q.B.).

2. What impact should the breach of a statutory provision have in a common law action? Could the defendant in *Rintoul* have succeeded by proving that he had a reasonable braking system on his car, despite the fact that the system did not comply with the legislative requirements?

3. In *Varcoe v. Sterling* (1992), 7 O.R. (3d) 204 (Gen. Div.), aff'd. (1992), 10 O.R. (3d) 574 (C.A.), leave to appeal ref'd. (1992), 10 O.R. (3d) xv (S.C.C.), an experienced investor lost a very large amount of money in the highly speculative futures market. The investor, who had not relied on his broker and who made all of his own decisions, sued the broker for his losses. The court held the broker liable in negligence under common law principles, referring at length to the broker's violation of both statutory regulations and industry practice concerning margin calls, trading limits and the transfer of funds between the investor's various stock accounts.

4. Adherence to the common law duty and standard is not a defence to a statutory cause of action. For example, in *London Passenger Tpt. Bd. v. Upson*, [1949] A.C. 155 (H.L.), the defendant bus driver struck a pedestrian in a crosswalk. Lord Porter expressly held that the defendant had taken all reasonable care. Nevertheless, the defendant was liable for breach of a statutory provision which required a driver, who was unable to see if the crosswalk was clear, to proceed at a speed which would enable him to stop before entering it.

5. Some statutes address the relationship between the statutory and common law actions. See, for example, the Trespass To Property Act, R.S.O. 1990, c. T.21, discussed earlier in this chapter. Legislation may also eliminate a common law action and replace it with a statutory cause of action.

5. A Note on the Canadian Charter of Rights and Freedoms

Aside from specific torts statutes, the Charter will probably have as great an impact on civil liability as any other single piece of federal or provincial legislation. There are two ways in which the Charter may affect tort liability. First, an individual whose Charter rights have been violated may have an express statutory cause of action under section 24(1). Second, as part of the supreme law of Canada, the Charter may alter some existing common law causes of action and defences. In this section we set out some of the most relevant Charter provisions and briefly illustrate how they may affect civil liability.

The Canadian Charter of Rights and Freedoms, Constitution Act, 1982

Rights and freedoms in Canada
1. The Canadian Charter of Rights and Freedoms guarantees the rights and freedoms set out in it subject only to such reasonable limits prescribed by law as can be demonstrably justified in a free and democratic society.

Fundamental freedoms

2. Everyone has the following fundamental freedoms:

    (*a*) freedom of conscience and religion;

    (*b*) freedom of thought, belief, opinion and expression, including freedom of the press and other media of communication;

    (*c*) freedom of peaceful assembly; and

    (*d*) freedom of association.

Life, liberty and security of person

7. Everyone has the right to life, liberty and security of the person and the right not to be deprived thereof except in accordance with the principles of fundamental justice.

Search or seizure

8. Everyone has the right to be secure against unreasonable search or seizure.

Detention or imprisonment

9. Everyone has the right not to be arbitrarily detained or imprisoned.

Arrest or detention

10. Everyone has the right on arrest or detention

    (*a*) to be informed promptly of the reasons therefor;

    (*b*) to retain and instruct counsel without delay and to be informed of that right; and

    (*c*) to have the validity of the detention determined by way of *habeas corpus* and to be released if the detention is not lawful.

Equality before and under law and equal protection and benefit of law

15. (1) Every individual is equal before and under the law and has the right to the equal protection and equal benefit of the law without discrimination and, in particular, without discrimination based on race, national or ethnic origin, colour, religion, sex, age or mental or physical disability.

Enforcement

Enforcement of guaranteed rights and freedoms

24. (1) Anyone whose rights or freedoms, as guaranteed by this Charter, have been infringed or denied may apply to a court of competent jurisdiction to obtain such remedy as the court considers appropriate and just in the circumstances.

Application of Charter

32. (1) This Charter applies

    (*a*) to the Parliament and government of Canada in respect of all matters within the authority of Parliament including all matters relating to the Yukon Territory and Northwest Territories; and

    (*b*) to the legislature and government of each province in respect of all matters within the authority of the legislature of each province.

Primacy of Constitution of Canada

52. (1) The Constitution of Canada is the supreme law of Canada, and any law that is inconsistent with the provisions of the Constitution is, to the extent of the inconsistency, of no force or effect.

Section 24(1) creates an express statutory cause of action for individuals whose Charter rights have been violated. However, the plaintiff must first establish that the Charter applies to the situation. By reason of section 32(1), the Charter applies to federal and provincial laws, governments and government agencies. It is equally clear that the Charter does not apply to litigation between private citizens. The Supreme Court of Canada has only recently defined the Charter's application to agencies that operate under legislation or some government control or that receive government funding. This includes organizations such as universities, colleges, professional disciplinary societies, and hospitals.

If the Charter applies, the plaintiff must establish that the defendant violated one of his Charter rights. However, this violation will then be justified or excused under section 1, if the defendant can establish that it is a "reasonable limit prescribed by law that can be demonstrably justified in a free and democratic society." Only unjustified Charter violations give an individual a right to seek a remedy under section 24(1). The court has broad discretion to grant any remedy which it considers appropriate in the circumstances. Although damages, injunctions and prohibitions have been awarded under section 24(1), the plaintiff is not entitled to them as of right.

The Charter may also affect the existing common law causes of action and defences. Section 52 of the Charter provides that the Charter is the supreme law of Canada and renders any law that is inconsistent with it of no force and effect to the extent of the inconsistency. Since the words "any law" include common law torts principles, the Charter may have a significant impact on the existing causes of action. For example, an individual's freedoms of peaceful assembly and association in section 2(c) and (d) may require some modifications in the common law principles governing trespass to Crown land.

The Charter can also be used to negate what would otherwise be a valid common law or statutory defence. For example, assume that a police officer searched the plaintiff at random pursuant to sections 10 and 11 of the Narcotic Control Act, R.S.C. 1985, c. N-1. Assume as well, that the plaintiff sued in battery and that the officer raised the Narcotic Control Act in his defence. If the plaintiff established that this search power violated section 8 of the Charter, which prohibits unreasonable search or seizure, and could not be justified under section 1, then this section would be of no force or effect to the extent that it was inconsistent with section 8. As a result, the officer's search would no longer be authorized by law and his defence of legal authority may fail.

The Charter came into force in 1982, and the Supreme Court of Canada has only begun to define the Charter's impact on civil liability. It may be some time before a full assessment can be made of the Charter's impact on civil liability.

NOTES AND QUESTIONS

1. In *R.W.D.S.U, Local 580 v. Dolphin Delivery Ltd.*, [1986] 2 S.C.R. 573, the Supreme Court held that the Charter does not apply to litigation between private citizens. This generated considerable academic comment. See for example, Belobaba, "The Charter of Rights and Private Litigation: The Dilemma of *Dolphin Delivery*", in Finkelstein and Rogers (eds.), *Charter Issues in Civil Cases* (1988), 29. As to the scope of s. 32(1), see generally Tassé, "Application of the Canadian Charter of Rights and Freedoms", in Beaudoin and Ratushny, (eds.), *The Canadian Charter of Rights and Freedoms*, 2nd ed. (1989), 65; and Hogg, *Constitutional Law of Canada*, 3rd ed., vol. 2 (1992), 34-20.2 to 34-23.

2. A more difficult issue is the application of the Charter to agencies and organizations that operate under some statutory authority or are funded by the government. See *Lavigne v. O.P.S.E.U.*, [1991] 2 S.C.R. 211; and *New Brunswick Broadcasting Co. v. Nova Scotia (Speaker of the House of Assembly)*, [1993] 1 S.C.R. 319. It now appears that the Charter will apply to an agency which is part of government. This determination is based on the form, function, and degree of government control and funding. Moreover, non-government agencies may also be subject to the Charter depending on the degree of government control over the agency. See *McKinney v. University of Guelph* (1990), 76 D.L.R. (4th)

545 (S.C.C.); *Douglas College v. Douglas/Kwantlen Faculty Assoc.*, [1991] 1 W.W.R. 643 (S.C.C.); and *Vancouver General Hospital v. Stoffman*, [1991] 1 W.W.R. 577 (S.C.C.).

3. For a discussion of s. 24(1) and express statutory causes of action, see Pilkington, "Monetary Redress for Charter Infringement", in Sharpe (ed.), *Charter Litigation* (1987), 307; Morgan, "Charter Remedies: The Civil Side After the First Five Years", in Finkelstein and Rogers (eds.), *Charter Issues in Civil Cases* (1988), 47; and Gibson and Gibson, "Enforcement of the Canadian Charter of Rights and Freedoms", in Beaudoin and Ratushny (eds.), *The Canadian Charter of Rights and Freedoms*, 2nd ed. (1989), 781. See also *Poirier v. Canada (Minister of Veterans Affairs)*, [1989] 3 F.C. 233 (C.A.).

4. For a discussion of the Charter's impact on common law causes of action and defences see, in addition to the preceding references, Doody, "Freedom of the Press: The Canadian Charter of Rights and Freedoms, and a New Category of Qualified Privilege" (1983), 61 Can. Bar Rev. 124; Hutchinson and Petter, "Private Rights/Public Wrongs: The Liberal Lie of the Charter" (1988), 38 U.T.L.J. 278; and Gibson, "What Did *Dolphin* Deliver?" in Beaudoin (ed.), *Your Clients and the Charter: Liberty and Equality* (1988), 75. See also *Hill v. Church of Scientology of Toronto*, [1995] 2 S.C.R. 1130.

5. The Charter also applies to procedural matters. Special limitation periods and other procedural rules applying to suits against public authorities have been challenged under the Charter, usually under s. 15. See for example *Colangelo v. Mississauga (City of)* (1988), 53 D.L.R. (4th) 283 (Ont. C.A.), leave to appeal ref'd. (1989), 56 D.L.R. (4th) vii (S.C.C.); *Mirhadizadeh v. Ontario* (1989), 69 O.R. (2d) 422 (C.A.); and *Canadian Assn. of Regulated Importers v. Canada (A.G.)* (1994), 17 Admin. L.R. (2d) 121 (F.C.A.), leave to appeal ref'd. (1994), 21 Admin. L.R. (2d) 159n (S.C.C.).

REVIEW PROBLEMS

1. Assume that section 15(1) of the Charter had been in force at the time of *Bhadauria v. Bd. of Governors of Seneca College* (1981), 124 D.L.R. (3d) 193 (S.C.C.). What would the plaintiff have had to establish in an express statutory cause of action under the Charter? Would the Charter have assisted her claim at common law? See *supra*, chapter 3.

2. Assuming that the Charter had been in force, what impact would it have had on the majority and dissenting judgments in *Harrison v. Carswell*, [1976] 2 S.C.R. 200? See *supra*, chapter 5.

TORT LAW:
THEORIES, CRITICISMS AND ALTERNATIVES

1. Introduction
2. Theoretical Criticism of Tort Law
3. The No-Fault Alternatives

1. Introduction

Academic writing on the theoretical bases of tort law and the role it plays or should play in modern society has been extensive. It is not possible in this book to provide the detailed treatment that these writings warrant. Nevertheless, in section two of the chapter we review some of the more important theories and the issues which they have generated. In section three, we discuss several no-fault insurance plans which have been adopted in some jurisdictions to supplement or replace tort law. The case for adopting such no-fault alternatives depends in large part upon how the goals of tort law are defined.

2. Theoretical Criticism of Tort Law

(a) INTRODUCTION

Theoretical criticism of tort law falls into two general categories: analytical and normative. Analytical criticism is concerned with the basic concepts of tort law. In particular, analytical critics identify and evaluate both the supposed functions of tort law and foundational tort concepts, such as intent, consent, duty of care and fault. The work of analytical critics can be either empirical (i.e., observational investigations of the actual operation of tort systems) or more philosophical (i.e., rigorous investigation of the internal logic of concepts).

The second category of tort criticism involves the use of normative theory. Normative critics engage in the moral evaluation of tort concepts and systems. These critics are interested in the degree to which tort principles and outcomes conform to concepts of "justice". In plainer language, normative critics write about the "rightness" or "wrongness" of tort law. While some normative theorists analyze the morality of particular tort decisions or doctrines in terms of their consequences, others are more interested in the inherent moral qualities and defects of the law.

The first two parts of this section concern the analytical theory of two purported functions of tort law: deterrence and compensation. The third part investigates some recent normative criticisms of tort law.

NOTES AND QUESTIONS

1. See generally Hutchinson and Morgan, "The Canengusian Connection: The Kaleidoscope of Tort Theory" (1984), 22 Osgoode Hall L.J. 69. The authors present a hypothetical tort case followed by a series of judgments, each of which exemplifies a different theoretical approach to the issue. The article also provides a comprehensive bibliography of the theoretical writing on tort law. See also Abel, "A Critique of Torts" (1994), 2 Tort L. Rev. 99.

2. It may be helpful at this stage to review chapter 1, section 6, "The Functions of Tort Law".

(b) DETERRENCE

Many authors suggest that the primary goal of tort law is, or should be, accident deterrence. In this section, we will examine some of the limits on the effectiveness of tort law as a deterrent and the recent contributions that economists have made to deterrence theories.

The object of deterrence is to prevent undesirable conduct in the future. Tort liability may operate as a specific deterrent to the particular defendant and also as a general deterrent to like-minded others. Effective deterrence requires a precise definition of the objectionable conduct and a sanction which discourages such conduct without inhibiting desirable conduct.

There are several inherent limitations on the deterrent impact of tort law. Much of the conduct giving rise to tort liability involves spontaneous, careless behaviour which is not particularly amenable to deterrence. For example, drivers do not contemplate liability when making the complex split-second decisions that are part of driving. The available empirical evidence suggests that individuals who are risk-takers are greatly over-represented in car and other types of accidents and that they are not readily deterrable. The fact that millions of Canadians drink and drive every year despite the risk of death or injury to themselves and others, the risk of criminal prosecution, and the risk of possible civil suits, highlights the limited deterrent impact of tort law on certain conduct and people.

Tort law probably has its greatest impact on planned decision-making in business. For example, profit-maximizing industrial managers would presumably weigh potential liability costs against the costs of safety precautions, and take cost-justified measures of accident avoidance. Posner explains the standard of reasonable care in this manner. However, many legitimate tort claims are not proceeded with, and damage awards rarely reflect all of the personal and social losses. In this sense, tort law may encourage careless conduct.

The deterrent impact of tort law is also affected by an individual's perceptions of both the likelihood of litigation and a finding of liability. The typically long delay between the tortious conduct and the imposition of liability lessens the law's deterrent effect. Finally, the fact that almost all drivers, businesses and industries carry some form of liability insurance also reduces tort law's deterrent impact.

In recent years, legal economists have entered the debate over deterrence theory. They suggest that tort law can operate as an efficient deterrent in two ways. First, tort rules may address the problem of "externalities" by allocating accident costs to the activities that generate them. Second, tort rules can lower the cost of accidents by allocating these costs to the party who is able to avoid them at the lowest possible cost.

The basic premise of economic analysis is that society chooses how much of a good, service or activity its members want through the price system. Other things being equal, demand will fall as prices rise. Provided prices accurately reflect the cost of the activity in question, the price system will produce an efficient allocation of resources. Given the existing distribution of wealth, society is obtaining the optimum mixture of the goods and services that it wants, based on its members' willingness to pay.

Since perfect market conditions rarely exist, our economy does not automatically produce an efficient allocation of resources. One major problem is that prices will not accurately reflect costs if a portion of those costs have been externalized. Economists have recognized that legal rules can be important in preventing the externalization of such costs. For example, if motorists are required to have liability insurance, they must take this cost into account in deciding whether to drive. This law internalizes the cost of accidents and ensures that it is reflected in the price of driving. If the law was changed so that liability insurance was paid for out of general tax revenue, the cost of accidents would be externalized from the activity of driving in two ways. First, some of the costs of accidents would be paid by taxpayers who do not drive. More important, drivers would not have to consider the cost of accidents in deciding whether or not to drive. They would have to pay the tax whether they chose to drive or not. Consequently, some people who would not have driven because of the insurance costs would now choose to drive, thereby increasing the number of cars on the roads and the number of accidents. By externalizing part of the insurance costs of driving, the law would have produced an inefficiently high number of automobile accidents.

Once costs have been internalized, tort law may play a role in determining who should bear them. For example, should the costs of defective brakes be borne by automobile owners or manufacturers? If tort law holds owners liable they would incur the personal and third-party accident costs. In response, they might attempt to reduce their liability by arranging for inspections, repairs or modifications. If manufacturers were held liable, they would either pay damage awards or minimize these costs by designing a safer braking system. An economist would argue that tort law should impose liability on the party who is able to minimize these accidents at the lowest cost and that the law should provide that party with an incentive to adopt the lowest cost solution. Thus, if manufacturers were the cheapest cost-avoiders, liability should be imposed on them. Such a rule would encourage manufacturers to install safe braking systems, rather than to risk incurring liability costs.

In summary, tort law can serve as a deterrent in two ways. First, it can internalize costs which allow the price system to determine the level of accidents for which society is willing to pay. Second, tort law can reduce total accident costs by allocating liability to the cheapest cost-avoider.

NOTES AND QUESTIONS

1. For a helpful discussion of the terms specific and general deterrence in tort law see Brown, "Deterrence and Accident Compensation Schemes" (1978-79), 17 U.W.O.L. Rev. 111; and Williams, "Second Best: The Soft Underbelly of Deterrence Theory in Tort" (1993), 106 Harv. L. Rev. 932.

2. There are many rules of tort law which are not predicated on deterrence. For example, does

the defence of private necessity discourage conduct which society wishes to deter? Can you explain the rules of tort law governing duress in terms of deterrence?

3. For an interesting discussion of the psychology of driving, which apparently insulates drivers from specific and general deterrence, see Netherton, "Highway Safety Under Differing Types of Liability Legislation" (1954), 15 Ohio St. L.J. 110. At page 76 of its *Report on Motor Vehicle Accident Compensation* (1973), the Ontario Law Reform Commission quoted the New York State Insurance Department: "We confront the bizarre conclusion that if the fault insurance system is a deterrent to anything, it is more of a deterrent to becoming a victim than to driving carelessly." See also Brown, "Deterrence in Tort and No-Fault: The New Zealand Experience" (1985), 73 Cal. L. Rev. 976, which strongly suggests that tort liability has a minimal deterrent impact on driving. Little support for the general or specific deterrent function of tort law is found in Ontario, *Inquiry Into Motor Vehicle Accident Compensation in Ontario* (1988), the most extensive recent study on point.

4. Tort law may operate as an educator, reinforcing values and portraying its dramatic lessons with the assistance of the press. Similarly, tort law may act as an ombudsman, serving to apply pressure for social change upon those who wield political and economic power. See Linden, "Reconsidering Tort Law as Ombudsman", in Steel and Rodgers-Magnet (eds.), *Issues in Tort Law* (1983), 1. The Ontario Law Reform Commission, in its 1973 study of automobile accidents, referred to above, concluded that the tort regime could not be justified by its slight educative value, especially compared to alternatives such as mandatory safety education and training.

5. Posner has argued that tort damages are awarded to induce plaintiffs to initiate legal proceedings, thereby maintaining a private system of deterrence. See "A Theory of Negligence" (1972), 1 J. Leg. Studies 29. See also Holmes, *The Common Law* (1881), 95-96; and White, "Risk-Utility Analysis and the Learned Hand Formula: A Hand that Helps or a Hand that Hides?" (1990), 32 Ariz. L. Rev. 77. See also England, "Law and Economics in American Tort Cases: A Critical Assessment of the Theory's Impact on Courts" (1991), 41 U.T.L.J. 359.

The basic idea is that compensatory damages represent the cost of accidents and if a tortfeasor prefers to pay damages rather than to prevent the harm, it is efficient to allow the harm. Assuming the tort system worked perfectly, is this a sound premise? The imperfections in the tort system have led to a call for increasing the role of punitive damages for the purpose of deterrence. See Chapman and Trebilcock, "Punitive Damages: Divergence In Search Of A Rationale" (1989), background paper for the Ontario Law Reform Commission, *Project on Exemplary Damages*.

6. For an explanation of the role of tort law in internalizing the costs of accidents, see Calabresi, *The Cost of Accidents* (1970).

7. In contrast to Calabresi's thesis, the 1967 Report of the Royal Commission of Inquiry on Compensation for Personal Injury in New Zealand expressly rejected efficiency as an appropriate social goal. See generally 177-88. The Commission favoured a general pooling of all risks on the theory that activities are interdependent. Calabresi's analysis suggests that this approach distorts efficient consumption choices, creating more dangerous activities and fewer safe ones than would be the case if costs were assigned properly. Since efficiency is only one social goal, and not necessarily the most important, the Commission's approach may be defended on other grounds.

8. Under perfect market conditions, society would always find the lowest cost solution, regardless of how the law allocated responsibility. For example, assume that the law did not hold a manufacturer liable for injuries caused by defective brakes. If the lowest cost solution was to have manufacturers design and install an improved braking system, owners and accident victims would be better off to pay manufacturers to develop such a system, than to incur the accident costs themselves. However, the transaction costs of getting these people together, allocating a fair share to each driver and enforcing this system, are far too great to make it practical. Thus, in the real world, the proper choice of the liability rule is essential to ensure the lowest cost solution. See Coase, "The Problem of Social Cost" (1960), 3 J. Law and Econ. 1.

(c) COMPENSATION

Accident compensation is widely regarded as one of the most important functions of tort law, particularly in negligence. As noted in chapter 1, compensation serves important social goals and acts as the major motivating factor for individual plaintiffs. However, the present tort system cannot be justified as a rational compensation scheme.

Many potential defendants carry liability insurance, and many potential plaintiffs are eligible for some public and private first party insurance benefits. Most of these collateral compensation systems were created independently of tort law. The overlap among collateral sources and their *ad hoc* development, have created a very complicated system of accident compensation, only tangentially related to tort law. Critics argue that tort law has become largely irrelevant in accident compensation. They favour a comprehensive and rationalized approach to accident compensation, free from the historical fetters of tort law.

There is overwhelming evidence that tort law performs poorly in terms of accident compensation. For example, The Ontario Law Reform Commission stated in its *Report on Motor Vehicle Accident Compensation* (1973), page 48 that:

> All the studies demonstrate that the tort system pays only about one-third of the total pecuniary losses (called "economic losses" in the studies) and further that the money paid out is distributed very unevenly among the victims. Less than half the people who suffer losses receive compensation through the tort regime. More important, perhaps, is the consistent finding in all studies that the more serious the accident, and therefore, generally speaking, the greater the loss, the lower the recovery percentage. Even with non-tort sources added, a large fraction of pecuniary losses remain uncompensated and the pattern of maldistribution does not improve.

It is perhaps unfair to criticize tort law as an accident compensation scheme. Indeed, there is no historical evidence to indicate that tort law was ever intended to operate solely as an accident compensation plan. Rather, it seems more accurate to regard compensation as an important component of the other goals of tort law. Thus, it is not surprising that most countries have found it necessary to supplement tort law with alternative accident compensation programs. As we shall discuss later in this chapter, New Zealand has abolished most of tort law in order to give primary emphasis to compensation and rehabilitation.

NOTES AND QUESTIONS

1. Judicial disagreements on breach of the standard of care often reflect the incompatibility of the goals of deterrence and compensation. To hold a defendant who has taken cost-justified precautions liable in negligence secures compensation for the victim at the expense of discouraging efficient conduct. To encourage efficient safety measures may leave many accident victims impecunious. For example, contrast the views of Spence, J. and de Grandpré, J. on the issue of the mother's negligence in *Arnold v. Teno*, [1978] 2 S.C.R. 287. See also de Grandpré, J. and Laskin, C.J.C. on the liability issue in *Wade v. C.N.R.*, [1978] 1 S.C.R. 1064. This case involved a young child who, as the result of a dare, jumped aboard a moving train. Can you think of other examples? Is it realistic to expect tort law to achieve all of the goals which have been set for it?

2. In the Report of the Royal Commission on Compensation for Personal Injury in New Zealand 1967, 39-41, the Commissioner identified the following as objectives of a compensation scheme: community responsibility, comprehensive entitlement, complete rehabilitation, real compensation, and administrative efficiency. Are these the proper goals of a compensation scheme? Does the present tort system adequately serve these goals?

3. For an examination of the public and private insurance regimes which constitute the hidden reality of the tort system in the field of automobile compensation, see Ontario, *Inquiry Into Motor Vehicle Accident Compensation in Ontario* (1988). The Report was critical of the role of tort law in accident compensation and recommended substantial changes to damage quantification rules and greatly expanded add-on, no-fault benefits. See also Priest, "The Current Insurance Crisis and Modern Tort Law" (1987), 96 Yale L.J. 1521.

4. The New Zealand Royal Commission Report was very critical of tort law's performance in providing accident compensation. Other critical studies include Ison, *The Forensic Lottery* (1967); and O'Connell, *The Injury Industry and the Remedy of No-Fault Insurance* (1971); Ontario, *Ontario Task Force on Insurance, Final Report* (1988); McLaren, "The Theoretical and Policy Challenges in Canadian Compensation Law" (1985), 23 Osgoode Hall L.J. 609; Abel, "A Critique of Torts" (1994), 2 Tort L. Rev. 99; and Dewees and Trebilcock, "The Efficacy of the Tort System and Its Alternatives: A Review of Empirical Evidence" (1992), 30 Osgoode Hall L.J. 57. See also the excellent bibliography in Saunders (ed.), *The Future of Personal Injury Compensation* (1981), 169-77.

5. One of the chief obstacles in the way of an improved understanding of tort systems is the lack of systematic empirical data. See generally, Saks, "Do We Really Know Anything about the Behavior of the Tort Litigation System — and Why Not?" (1992), 140 U. Pa. L. Rev. 1147.

(d) THEORIES OF TORT LAW BASED ON CONCEPTS OF JUSTICE

To this point, we have discussed several goal-based theories of tort law, namely those which focus on deterrence, efficiency and accident compensation. In this subsection, we examine those theories which evaluate the principles of tort according to whether they are right or just. The various concepts of justice which underlie these theories are purportedly derived independently of desirable social consequences. It is important to distinguish these "pure theories" of justice from those which assert that a principle of tort law is just because it promotes a desirable goal, such as accident compensation. The most provocative articles concerning the concepts of justice in tort law have been written in the past 25 years, largely in response to the literature claiming that tort law is based on principles of economic efficiency.

Distributive Justice

Theories of distributive justice are concerned with the appropriateness of the distribution of wealth and entitlements in society. There are many different views, most based on concepts of natural rights or equality. It is generally conceded that tort law plays a relatively minor role in achieving distributive justice. However, some tort rules and decisions have explicit distributional aims, such as those involving the "deep pocket" approach to loss allocation.

Most tort rules have distributional consequences, although these are often subtle and perhaps unintended. For example, it can be demonstrated that, in theory, strict liability and negligence promote precisely the same level of deterrence. By adopting principles of negligence rather than strict liability, society imposes the costs of "unavoidable" injuries on accident victims and not on those who cause the accident. Compensatory damage awards usually protect the pre-existing distribution of wealth. For example, the damages awarded for loss of income to an unemployed labourer will be significantly lower than those awarded to an established accountant. However, the liability insurance premiums paid by the labourer will reflect her potential liability to higher income earners.

Retributive Justice

A tort system based on retributive justice would impose liability on a blameworthy actor to penalize, punish, or nullify her moral fault. A "pure theory" of retribution is solely concerned with ensuring that wrongful acts are appropriately punished as an end in itself. In contrast, retribution could be imposed not because it is just, but rather as a means of appeasing the plaintiff and society by having the wrongdoer's conduct judged and condemned.

There are two criticisms of retributive theories of modern tort law. First, some authors argue that society should not provide an institutionalized vehicle for retribution. Even if retribution is an appropriate social concern, many feel it should be a matter for the criminal law. These concerns are reflected in the debates over punitive damages, the most obvious area of tort law in which concepts of retributive justice arise.

Second, most tort actions, and in particular negligence cases, rarely involve morally reprehensible conduct which would warrant retribution. Thus, it has been argued that modern tort law cannot be explained or justified on the basis of retributive justice. However, retribution is a powerful notion both on an individual and societal level. The belief that tort law serves a retributive purpose may explain much of the support for the present tort system.

Corrective Justice

Most authors indicate that principles of corrective justice best explain modern tort law. The basic premise of corrective justice is that a wrongdoer must provide redress for her wrongful conduct by compensating her victim. Coleman states that corrective justice is concerned with "eliminating undeserved or otherwise unjustifiable gains and losses. Compensation is therefore a matter of justice because it protects a distribution of wealth — resources or entitlements to them — from distortion through unwanted gains and losses. It does so by requiring annulment of both." See "Mental Abnormality, Personal Responsibility, and Tort Liability", in Brody and Engelhardt (eds.), *Mental Illness: Law and Public Policy* (1980), 107 at 123. This definition of corrective justice is procedural rather than substantive, in that it requires an independent definition of what constitutes a wrongful gain or loss. Given the flexibility of the word wrongful, many different values could be incorporated into a theory of corrective justice.

NOTES AND QUESTIONS

1. Posner argues for a theory of distributive justice that would encourage the maximization of social resources by rewarding the wealthy. In contrast, Rawls advances a pure theory of distributive justice which basically seeks to provide the greatest benefits to the least advantaged. See generally Posner, *The Economics of Justice* (1981); and Rawls, *A Theory of Justice* (1971).

2. Some modern authors see an increased role for punitive damages in tort law. For example, England argues that given the deplorable state of public enforcement, the self-initiated private action for punitive damages has an important role to play in achieving society's penal goals. "The System Builders: A Critical Appraisal of Modern American Tort Theory" (1980), 9 J. Legal Stud. 27.

3. For a critical appraisal of retributive justice and related theories in tort law, see England, *ibid.*, at 28, who suggests that "absolute liability in early law was based on an irrational belief in the ubiquity of guilt, which presumed a will behind all causation". See also Ehrenzweig, "A Psychoanalysis of Negligence" (1953), 47 Northwestern U.L. Rev. 855; Fletcher, "Fairness and Utility in Tort Theory" (1972), 85 Harv. L. Rev. 537; Epstein, "A Theory of Strict Liability" (1973), 2 J. Legal Stud. 151; and Coleman, *Risks and Wrongs* (1992).

4. Coleman views corrective justice as secondary to distributive justice — corrective justice operates to prevent wrongful deviations from just patterns of distribution. He argues that tort law is not necessary to achieve corrective justice. For example, wrongful gains could be dealt with under some form of criminal law and wrongful losses under an accident compensation scheme. Others, such as Weinrib and Posner, reject this analysis. They argue that the relationship between the tortfeasor and the victim

is the key to corrective justice. Corrective justice is an end in itself, a means of putting matters right between the two parties. Thus, tort law is the only mode for achieving corrective justice. Do you agree that an element of justice would be sacrificed if suits between the parties were not permitted? See Coleman, "Moral Theories of Torts: Their Scope and Limits: Part II" (1983), 2 J. Law & Phil. 5; Posner, "The Concept of Corrective Justice in Recent Theories of Tort Law" (1981), 10 J. Legal Stud. 187; and Weinrib, "Understanding Tort Law" (1989), 23 Val. U.L. Rev. 1.

5. Studies indicate that accident victims are far more concerned with fair and efficient compensation than with fault-based compensation and the notions of retributive and corrective justice. See, for example, Linden, *Osgoode Hall Study on Compensation for Victims of Automobile Accidents* (1965); and Harris, *Compensation and Support for Illness and Injury* (1984).

(e) DEMOCRATIC RADICAL VIEWS

Shriffrin identifies two general philosophical approaches which dominate American legal theory. The first he describes as ethical liberalism, which underlies the preceding theories of justice. The second approach he describes as democratic radicalism. In "Liberalism, Radicalism and Legal Scholarship" (1983), 30 U.C.L.A. L. Rev. 1103 at 1109, he outlines this second approach:

> What distinguishes this model and unites these authors are the beliefs that liberalism is excessively individualistic, that it cannot be defended by rationalistic premises, that any purported neutrality is a mask for unjustified domination, and that the better course lies in radical politics (that is, supporting alternative structures that are hoped to be more democratic, less competitive, and less individualistic, while retaining commitments to individuality and humane values).

He goes on to contrast the two approaches at 1174, as follows:

> Ethical liberals and democratic radicals both oppose a common ideology. They reject the conception of a civil society in which pleasure-maximizing individuals attempt to advance their materialistic desires by treating others as means rather than as ends. Both reject egoism; both regard property as a social resource; both regard the possibility of individual self-development as a prerequisite in a well-ordered society. Indeed, both believe that society has an affirmative role to play not only in the distribution of property, but also in the shaping of an environment conducive to the flourishing of human personality. How then does democratic radicalism differ from ethical liberalism?
>
> Let us start with this contrast: for the ethical liberal the end of nature is the individual, for the democratic radical the end of nature is political community. The contrast oversimplifies, but in the right direction. Democratic radicals believe that an individual's personality is subverted to the extent he or she exists in a society bereft of shared values and political community. The model of man as a solitary individual cannot furnish a basis for nourishing moral choice. Neither the relativism of the pleasure model nor the abstract formalism of ethical liberalism (viewing man as autonomous moral chooser) captures his or her potential for ethical and fulfilling social life.

NOTES AND QUESTIONS

1. The term democratic radicalism encompasses many different theories, some more radical than others. For example, Abel criticizes tort law for giving priority to compensation rather than safety. He advocates radical social change which would equalize exposure to risk rather than access to compensation. Abel, "A Critique of Torts" (1994), 2 Tort L. Rev. 99.

2. In "The System Builders: A Critical Appraisal of Modern American Tort Theory" (1980), 9 J. Legal Stud. 27, England states at 68:

> The response of modern American scholarship to the crises in tort law consists of an extraordinary effort to fashion an improved general theory of liability. These attempts are doomed to failure because in all their present forms they constitute a desperate scholarly rearguard action

to preserve a traditional system of individualism in a changing world. In Calabresi's and Posner's work the individualistic trait finds expression in its economic form, namely in the idea of free-market deterrence. In Epstein's and Fletcher's analysis classical individualism is articulated by a strict adherence to the conception of corrective justice. Yet the universal trends in accident law point in another direction: ideas of distributive justice have become dominant in a more and more collectivist society.

Do you agree with England's assessment that American tort theory has generated outdated justifications which obscure more promising approaches to accident compensation? What are the implications of his remarks for the future of tort law?

3. For an introduction to feminist criticism of tort law, see generally, Bender, "An Overview of Feminist Torts Scholarship" (1993), 78 Cornell L. Rev. 575.

3. The No-Fault Alternatives

(a) INTRODUCTION

No-fault accident compensation plans are designed to compensate victims of accidents. These schemes are usually a form of first-party insurance under which victims are compensated by their own insurers for their own losses. In contrast, liability insurance covers insured individuals for liability they incur to others. The term "no-fault" indicates only that the victim need not prove fault of another to obtain compensation. Moreover, the victim's compensation does not depend generally on her own conduct having been blameless. No-fault compensation has no impact on the significance of the parties' fault for other purposes. For example, a reckless or impaired driver may still be subject to criminal prosecution.

It is misleading to describe no-fault insurance as an alternative to tort law. Tort law purports to achieve other goals than accident compensation. No-fault is premised on isolating compensation from other goals, such as deterrence or punishment. Typically, the compensatory goals of tort law are different from those under no-fault schemes. The purpose of no-fault is to make compensation more widely and swiftly available to all victims of accidents.

In theory, tort law could co-exist unmodified with no-fault plans, much as it co-exists with other forms of first-party insurance. In practice, the broader coverage of no-fault tends to be funded in part from restrictions on traditional tort rights. This is usually done by restricting the right to sue to the victims of relatively serious injuries and by curtailing the right to recover for non-pecuniary loss.

There is no such thing as a typical no-fault insurance plan. The activities covered by the schemes vary from jurisdiction to jurisdiction. The degree to which they replace the victim's right to maintain a common law tort action also differs. Some are administered by government agencies and others by private insurers. The schemes may be funded by general tax revenue or by levies on the participants in the plan. None of these categories are mutually exclusive.

Comprehensive no-fault plans which provide compensation for all accident losses are relatively rare. Activity-specific compensation plans are far more common, such as those which deal exclusively with employment or automobile accidents.

A "pure" no-fault plan abolishes all tort actions for personal injuries within the scope of the plan. Victims of accidents are paid compensation entirely from the plan. This is the basis upon which most workers' compensation systems operate. It is also an essential feature of Quebec's government-run compensation program for personal injuries caused by automobile accidents.

Many no-fault plans are what O'Connell and Henderson describe in *Tort Law, No-Fault and Beyond* (1975), as either "add-on" or "modified" plans. The add-on plans provide some no-fault coverage without eroding the right to sue in negligence. An injured person is entitled to compensation up to the no-fault policy limit for pecuniary loss, regardless of her own fault or ability to sue another party. The injured person may also sue in tort, subject to provisions to prevent double recovery. In some American states, no-fault automobile insurers have a right to reimbursement if the injured person collects from the defendant. In most Canadian provinces, the no-fault fund is the primary source, in that amounts received through the no-fault scheme are deducted from the tortfeasor's liability.

"Modified" plans are similar, but they impose some limitations upon the victim's right to maintain a tort suit. In some instances, the right to sue for pecuniary damages is retained, while the right to sue for non-pecuniary damages is severely restricted. For example, the right to sue for pain and suffering might be limited to individuals who have suffered at least $1,000 in medical expenses. The point at which this threshold is placed has been a source of concern. It is argued that such fixed criteria provide an incentive to increase medical bills. Thresholds limiting the right to sue to certain types of injuries or to injuries which necessitate missing work for a specified number of days are also common. Other modified plans abolish not only the right to sue for pain and suffering, but also the right to sue for pecuniary losses that are provided for by the no-fault coverage.

These various plans can be administered either by a government agency, or by private insurance companies. Whether public or private, the schemes can be compulsory or voluntary. There are a number of possible funding mechanisms for no-fault plans, and each funding alternative would have different deterrent and loss allocation effects. Although a no-fault scheme can incorporate whatever compensatory principles are desired, most set modest compensatory goals. Proponents of comprehensive no-fault schemes prefer rapid and adequate compensation for all accident victims, rather than "full" compensation for the more limited class of successful plaintiffs.

(b) NO-FAULT ACCIDENT COMPENSATION IN NEW ZEALAND

In 1974, New Zealand abolished all statutory and common law damage claims arising out of accidental death and personal injury. In their place, the government created a comprehensive no-fault accident compensation scheme. The scheme, administered by a Crown Corporation, was designed to provide compensation for all injuries, except those which were deliberately self-inflicted. The legislation is lengthy and complicated and the following is a brief summary.

The scheme was comprehensive, governing all accidental injuries, regardless of how or where the accident occurred. Although the injured party simply applied to the Crown Corporation, for internal purposes the payment was drawn from one of three separate funds. The Earner's Fund covered both employees and self-employed persons, and it was financed by levies against employers and the self-employed. The Motor Vehicle Fund covered all victims of automobile accidents, and was financed by levies on owners and drivers of motor vehicles. The Supplementary Fund, which was financed by general taxation, covered all other cases, such as non-earners injured otherwise than by motor vehicles. The Corporation was empowered to vary the levies against employers or drivers according to the individual's safety record, but this power was seldom used.

Claims were assessed by agents of the Corporation. There were numerous provisions for appeal, first within the Corporation, then to an independent agency, and ultimately to the courts in some cases.

Since its inception in 1974 both the boundaries and the costs of New Zealand's Accident Compensation Scheme have grown steadily. As a consequence, there have been 11 major reviews of the plan. In 1992, the New Zealand government substantially amended the original legislation. The main aim of the reform was to create a more tightly controlled and cost efficient system that respected the objectives of the 1974 plan. This was to be achieved by a combination of measures, including narrower definitions of compensable injury and the elimination of lump sum compensationfor non-economic loss. The 1992 reforms appear to have increased certainty in the scope and cost of the scheme. However, the internal consistency and adequacy of accident compensation, especially for very seriously injured claimants, continues to be debated.

NOTES AND QUESTIONS

1. For an assessment of the New Zealand Accident Compensation Scheme, see Keith, "Compensation in New Zealand 1974-1991", in Wall (ed.), *Proceedings of the Medical Defence Union Conference* (1991); and Palmer, "New Zealand's Accident Compensation Scheme: Twenty Years On" (1994), 44 U.T.L.J. 223. For an earlier assessment of the New Zealand system, see Harris, "Accident Compensation in New Zealand: A Comprehensive Insurance System" (1974), 37 Mod. L. Rev. 86; Palmer, *Compensation for Incapacity* (1979); Klar, "New Zealand's Accident Compensation Scheme: A Tort Lawyer's Perspective" (1983), 33 U. of T. L.J. 80; and Brown, "Deterrence in Tort and No-Fault: The New Zealand Experience" (1985), 73 Cal. L. Rev. 976.

2. O'Connell states in "Elective No-Fault Liability Insurance for All Kinds of Accidents: A Proposal", [1973] Ins. L.J. 495 at 497-98: "Much more than half — 56 cents — of every auto insurance premium dollar is chewed up in administrative and legal costs. This is in contrast to administrative and legal expenses of 3 cents for Social Security, 7 cents for Blue Cross, and 17 cents for Health and Accident plans." The administrative cost of the New Zealand plan is 10% of the total amount paid into it. Can you explain or justify the marked differences in the costs of operating these plans? What are the implications of this data?

3. What was the rationale for the three separate compensation funds in the New Zealand plan? How does this compare to a wholly tax-funded system? Why did the legislature provide for differential levies against certain industries, employers and drivers?

4. What are the advantages and disadvantages of having a fixed schedule and statutory maximums for lost earnings and non-pecuniary damage awards? Which groups benefit the most from the restitutionary principles which govern the common law assessment of damages?

5. The two major differences between the New Zealand plan and the common law are the use of no-fault principles and periodic payments. Which of these features of the New Zealand plan do you think is most important? Should a periodic payment system be incorporated into the present Canadian common law tort system?

6. Liability insurance is compulsory for Canadian automobile owners and is commonly carried by all persons likely to be exposed to negligence liability. Compared to the New Zealand plan, how efficient is liability insurance at spreading losses and ensuring that funds will be available? Would you favour making liability insurance compulsory for activities other than driving? What effect might such compulsory liability insurance and/or comprehensive no-fault accident compensation plan have on the notion of the personal responsibility of individuals?

7. The most common activity-specific schemes are the Workers' Compensation and no-fault automobile insurance plans which are discussed below. Another activity-specific no-fault scheme was recommended for Canadian victims of medical malpractice in Prichard (Chair), *Liability and Compensation in Health Care* (1990). The report stated that over $200 million was paid out each year on direct insurance costs, but that only 250 victims, fewer than 10% of the total number of malpractice victims, received any compensation from the tort system. The report also called for retention of the tort system for the purpose of deterrence.

(c) WORKERS' COMPENSATION

Although no-fault insurance has recently received a great deal of attention, the idea is by no means new. Most jurisdictions had no-fault compensation schemes for work-related injuries by the early twentieth century. Germany was the first country to establish a comprehensive workers' compensation system, including medical treatment and sick benefits. England established a more modest plan in 1897, and all but six American states had workers' compensation systems by 1920.

British Columbia established a compensation scheme based on the English model in 1902, and most of the other provinces followed suit shortly thereafter. In 1914, Ontario introduced the first Canadian workers' compensation scheme administered by an independent government agency. Similar agencies have since been created in every Canadian jurisdiction.

Workers' compensation boards are public bodies created by statute. Employers and employees governed by the scheme are required to participate. As the title suggests, workers' compensation is an activity-specific scheme which provides compensation for personal injuries that occur in the course of employment. Minor injuries are excluded from most schemes by a requirement that the employee must be disabled beyond the day of the accident to make a claim. In part, the Canadian schemes are "pure" no-fault, because the legislation prohibits the employee from suing his employer in tort. However, the employee has the option of claiming from the fund or bringing a tort action against a person other than his employer. Nevertheless, the vast majority of work-related accident claims are dealt with by workers' compensation boards and not courts.

The damages payable under workers' compensation schemes differ significantly from those awarded in negligence. For example, there is no recovery for pain and suffering, or for loss of amenities. The statutes classify the worker's injury as "temporary total disability", "temporary partial disability", "permanent total disability", or "permanent partial disability". Statutory guidelines are provided for assessing compensation in each category. For example, workers with a temporary total disability are entitled to 75 per cent of their average weekly earnings, subject to statutory minimums and maximums.

The legislation provides compensation for other special medical expenses, such as the cost of medical attendants and equipment. The board has discretion to authorize expenditures which it deems necessary for a worker's expedient re-entry into the work force. The schemes also provide for benefits in the case of fatal accidents.

NOTES AND QUESTIONS

1. Risk suggests several reasons why workers' compensation plans were introduced. First, he indi-

cates that litigation was generally regarded as a nuisance. Second, the notion that every accident involved individual responsibility on the part of either the actor or victim was falling into disfavour. Finally, there was increased social concern with the plight of accident victims. He goes on to provide an interesting analysis of why employment injuries were singled out for special treatment. See Risk, "'This Nuisance of Litigation': The Origins of Workers' Compensation in Ontario", in Flaherty (ed.), *Essays in the History of Canadian Law, Volume 2*, (1983), 418.

2. Weiler reports that injured workers in Ontario are compensated on average within 10 days of making their claims. He also estimates that administrative costs account for less than 9% of the total cost of the scheme. In contrast, he notes that the administrative cost of automobile accident compensation amounts to 50% of the total cost. See *Reshaping Workers' Compensation for Ontario* (1980) at 8 and 50.

3. Given the experience with workers' compensation, why have the provinces not introduced comprehensive no-fault insurance programs?

4. Although workers' compensation claims are considered by an administrative tribunal and not a court, both the board and the claimant may have legal representation. It has been suggested that lawyers have thwarted the drafters' intentions by injecting tort principles into the proceedings. See Glasbeek and Hasson, "Fault — The Great Hoax" in Klar (ed.), *Studies in Canadian Tort Law* (1977), 395 at 418. See also Ison, "The Infusion of Private Law in Public Administration" (1976), 17 Les Cahiers Droit 799.

5. The worker may be denied recovery if his injury is attributable solely to his own serious and wilful misconduct. What is the purpose of this rule? Is it consistent with the overall objectives of the legislation? How does it compare to the provisions of New Zealand's plan?

6. See generally Egner, "Personal Injury Awards and Workmen's Compensation" (1980), 18 U.W.O.L. Rev. 269; and Derstine and Nathu, "Workers' Compensation in Ontario: A Decade of Reform" (1990), 48 U. of T. Fac. L.R. 22.

(d) NO-FAULT AUTOMOBILE INSURANCE IN CANADA

Apart from workers' compensation, no-fault insurance has had its greatest impact in Canada in the field of automobile accidents. The majority of academic writing about no-fault insurance has focused on automobile accidents, reflecting the importance of the automobile in our society and the staggering number of deaths and injuries which occur on the nation's highways.

Saskatchewan introduced the first no-fault automobile accident insurance plan in the English-speaking world in 1946. Similar plans have since been adopted in many other jurisdictions. No-fault automobile accident benefits are now available in every Canadian province, but the plans vary considerably. Coverage for no-fault accident benefits is compulsory in most jurisdictions. The maximum amounts and the duration of the payments differ considerably from province to province. These no-fault benefits are provided by private insurers in most provinces. Only Quebec's legislation provides a pure no-fault plan. All the other provinces had add-on plans that gave rise to problems of overlapping compensation. Generally, the no-fault benefits are intended to be the primary source of compensation; a plaintiff can only seek damages in tort if her losses exceed the no-fault benefits.

In 1990, Ontario adopted a modified threshold scheme, administered by private insurers. The threshold is defined in section 266 of The Insurance Act, R.S.O. 1990, c. I.8:

266.—(1) In respect of loss or damage arising directly or indirectly from the use or operation, after this section comes into force, of an automobile and despite any other Act, none of the owner of an automobile, the occupants of an automobile or any person present at the incident are liable in an action in Ontario for loss or damage from bodily injury arising from such use or operation in Canada, the United States of America or any other jurisdiction designated in the *No-Fault Benefits Schedule* involving the automobile unless, as a result of such use or operation, the injured person has died or has sustained,

    (a) permanent serious disfigurement; or

    (b) permanent serious impairment of an important bodily function caused by continuing injury which is physical in nature.

It was estimated that 90-95% of all accident victims would be denied the right to sue, although the interpretation of the threshold has generated considerable litigation. In cases that exceed the threshold, section 267 limits the tortfeasor's liability to losses in excess of the no-fault benefits and abolishes the collateral source rule and related rights of subrogation for other collateral benefits. The insurer need not pay no-fault benefits to anyone who has been compensated under workers' compensation law.

Two auto insurance systems operated in Ontario after the legislation was introduced in 1990. Accidents occurring before June 22, 1990, were governed by the common law tort system, subject to modest statutory no-fault benefits, and accidents after that date were governed by section 266 of the Act. Matters were further complicated when Ontario introduced Bill 164, which amended the Insurance Act as of January 1, 1994. It replaced the right to sue for any economic loss arising from bodily injuries or death in car accidents with stipulated benefits. The right to sue was maintained for non-economic losses in cases of death, serious disfigurement, or serious impairment of important physical, mental or psychological function. The Ontario government has recently proposed changing the no-fault provisions yet again, thereby creating a fourth distinct automobile insurance regime.

NOTES AND QUESTIONS

1. Typical no-fault auto schemes, even fairly extensive ones such as those in Quebec and Ontario, do not deal with property damage on a no-fault basis. Does this make sense?

2. There has been extensive litigation concerning the the thresholds established in s. 266(1) of the Ontario Insurance Act. See *Meyer v. Bright* (1993), 15 O.R. (3d) 129 (C.A.); *Dalgliesh v. Green* (1993), 12 O.R. (3d) 40 (Gen. Div.), aff'd. (March 23, 1993) (Ont. Div. Ct.) [unreported], rev'd. (1993), 15 O.R. (3d) 129 (C.A.) (action combined with *Meyer v. Bright*); and *Leszczynski v. Clark* (1993), 17 O.R. (3d) 447 (Gen. Div.).

3. In 1978, Quebec abolished entirely the right of traffic accident victims to sue for bodily injury damages. Victims are entitled to recover no-fault compensation from the Regie de l'assurance automobile du Quebec, a public carrier. The plan is funded by fees paid by registered owners and drivers of motor vehicles. Benefits are indexed to the consumer price index. Employed workers may recover wage replacement to a maximum gross income of approximately $40,000. There are provisions to address lost earning potential and special provisions for homemakers, the unemployed and students. Limited lump-sum awards for non-pecuniary loss are paid. The Regie operates extensive rehabilitation programs. In 1989, the Act was amended to allow reduced income replacement for victims detained under a judicial process for an indictable offence committed while driving a motor vehicle. See Automobile Insurance Act, R.S.Q. 1989, c. A-25, s. 38.30.

4. When assessing the income replacement provisions of the no-fault plans, keep in mind that they are usually based on gross income and that the no-fault benefits themselves are tax free.

5. Based on the earlier discussion of the different types of no-fault schemes, categorize the no-fault automobile plan in your province.

6. Automobile liability insurance has been common, if not compulsory, throughout Canada for some time. Thus, even before the introduction of no-fault plans, there was more comprehensive accident compensation in this area than in most others.

7. Given that most employment accidents and an increasing number of automobile accidents are

now dealt with by no-fault insurance, what is the rationale for treating other accident victims differently? What is the rationale for treating accident victims differently from victims of serious illness?

8. Although Ontario's no-fault auto scheme will reduce litigation, legal counsel may still be needed given the three concurrently operating auto injury compensation systems, and the disparities in bargaining power between the insurers and injured claimants. See generally Lackman and Firestone, "Ontario Lawyers Still Needed to Negotiate Complex Benefits Web in No-Fault Auto Insurance Scheme", *The Lawyers Weekly* (March 31, 1995) 9.

9. Formal alternative dispute resolution is expected to be used by large numbers of injured claimants as a result of the enhanced benefits introduced on January 1, 1994, under the Statutory Accident Benefits Schedule, O. Reg. 776/93. See generally Sachs, "Dispute Resolution in a Statutory Accident Benefits Compensation Scheme: The Ontario Model" (1994), 16 Advoc. Q. 218.

REVIEW PROBLEM

Iris earns $1,000/week (gross) as a graphic artist. She is extremely talented and much sought after in the industry. She is also independently wealthy and notoriously indifferent to her work. This is her first job in 2 years. Otherwise, she sketches at home, but does not sell her work. She has told co-workers she plans to quit within the year. Her absentee rate is unusually high and she has been cautioned about this by her employer. She was struck by an automobile while crossing the street. It is agreed she will be unable to work for 52 weeks and completely recovered thereafter. Under an employee benefit plan, she is entitled to $400/week in disability benefits to replace lost wages.

Compare how Iris would fare in receiving compensation for loss of income under the no-fault scheme in Ontario and Quebec to how she would fare under the scheme in effect in your province. How do these outcomes compare to how she would fare under the lost earning capacity head under a pure tort system? Make the same assessments of how you would fare if you suffered the same injuries as Iris.

21

INTENTIONAL INTERFERENCE WITH ECONOMIC INTERESTS

1. Introduction
2. Deceit (Fraud)
3. Passing Off
4. Interference with Contractual Relations
5. Intimidation
6. Conspiracy
7. The Innominate Action

1. Introduction

Individuals and corporations sometimes act ruthlessly in pursuit of commercial advantage or profit. In the twentieth century, an increasing number of plaintiffs have attempted to use tort law to gain compensation for injurious economic behaviours. Common law judges, motivated by a variety of ethical and economic concerns, have sometimes responded favourably to these claims. Although in the past 50 years regulation of economic behaviour has largely been usurped by legislative and administrative initiatives, judge-made tort law continues to be important in identifying unacceptable economic conduct and compensating its victims. As chapter 23 will explain, recent developments in the common law of pure economic loss may re-invigorate this highly specialized area of Canadian tort law.

2. Deceit (Fraud)

DERRY v. PEEK

(1889), 14 App. Cas. 337 (H.L.)

[The appellant directors of the company issued a prospectus which stated that the company would make a profit, because it had "the right to use steam or mechanical power instead of horses." The right referred to was not absolute, but rather was conditional on the approval of the Board of Trade. The respondent allegedly relied upon the representations of the absolute right, and invested in the company. The Board subsequently denied general approval for steam or mechanical power, and the company folded. The respondent brought an action in deceit, seeking to recover his lost investment.]

LORD HERSCHELL: . . . My Lords, in the statement of claim in this action the respondent, who is the plaintiff, alleges that the appellants made in a prospectus issued by them certain statements which were untrue, that they well knew that the facts were not as stated in the prospectus, and made the representations fraudulently, and with the view to induce the plaintiff to take shares in the company.

"This action is one which is commonly called an action of deceit, a mere common law action." This is the description of it given by Cotton L.J. in delivering judgment. I think it important that it should be borne in mind that such an action differs essentially from one brought to obtain rescission of a contract on the ground of misrepresentation of a material fact. The principles which govern the two actions differ widely. Where rescission is claimed it is only necessary to prove that there was misrepresentation; then, however honestly it may have been made, however free from blame the person who made it, the contract, having been obtained by misrepresentation, cannot stand. In an action of deceit, on the contrary, it is not enough to establish misrepresentation alone; it is conceded on all hands that something more must be proved to cast liability upon the defendant, though it has been a matter of controversy what additional elements are requisite. I lay stress upon this because observations made by learned judges in actions for rescission have been cited and much relied upon at the bar by counsel for the respondent. Care must obviously be observed in applying the language used in relation to such actions to an action of deceit. Even if the scope of the language used extends beyond the particular action which was being dealt with, it must be remembered that the learned judges were not engaged in determining what is necessary to support an action of deceit, or in discriminating with nicety the elements which enter into it.

There is another class of actions which I must refer to also for the purpose of putting it aside. I mean those cases where a person within whose special province it lay to know a particular fact, has given an erroneous answer to an inquiry made with regard to it by a person desirous of ascertaining the fact for the purpose of determining his course accordingly, and has been held bound to make good the assurance he has given. *Burrowes v. Lock* [10 Ves. 470] may be cited as an example, where a trustee had been asked by an intended lender, upon the security of a trust fund, whether notice of any prior incumbrance upon the fund had been given to him. In cases like this it has been said that the circumstance that the answer was honestly made in the belief that it was true affords no defence to the action. Lord Selborne pointed out in *Brownlie v. Campbell* [5 App. Cas. 935] that these cases were in an altogether different category from actions to recover damages for false representation, such as we are now dealing with.

One other observation I have to make before proceeding to consider the law which has been laid down by the learned judges in the Court of Appeal in the case before your Lordships.

> An action of deceit is a common law action, and must be decided on the same principles, whether it be brought in the Chancery Division or any of the Common Law Divisions, there being, in my opinion, no such thing as an equitable action for deceit.

This was the language of Cotton L.J. in *Arkwright v. Newbould* [17 Ch. D. 320]. It was adopted by Lord Blackburn in *Smith v. Chadwick* [9 App. Cas. 193], and is not, I think, open to dispute.

In the Court below Cotton L.J. said:

> What in my opinion is a correct statement of the law is this, that where a man makes a statement to be acted upon by others which is false, and which is known by him to be false, or is made by him recklessly, or without care whether it is true or false, that is, without any reasonable ground for believing it to be true, he is liable in an action of deceit at the suit of anyone to whom it was addressed or anyone of the class to whom it was addressed and who was materially induced by the misstatement to do an act to his prejudice.

About much that is here stated there cannot, I think, be two opinions. But when the learned Lord Justice speaks of a statement made recklessly or without care whether it is true or false, *that is* without any reasonable ground for believing it to be true, I find myself, with all respect, unable to agree that these are convertible expressions. To make a statement careless whether it be true or false, and therefore without any real belief in its truth, appears to me to be an essentially different thing from making, through want of care, a false statement, which is nevertheless honestly believed to be true. And it is surely conceivable that a man may believe that what he states is the fact, though he has been so wanting in care that the Court may think that there were no sufficient grounds to warrant his belief. I shall have to consider hereafter whether the want of reasonable ground for believing the statement made is sufficient to support an action of deceit. I am only concerned for the moment to point out that it does not follow that it is so, because there is authority for saying that a statement made recklessly, without caring whether it be true or false, affords sufficient foundation for such an action.

. . .

Having now drawn attention, I believe, to all the cases having a material bearing upon the question under consideration, I proceed to state briefly the conclusions to which I have been led. I think the authorities establish the following propositions: First, in order to sustain an action of deceit, there must be proof of fraud, and nothing short of that will suffice. Secondly, fraud is proved when it is shewn that a false representation has been made (1) knowingly, or (2) without belief in its truth, or (3) recklessly, careless whether it be true or false. Although I have treated the second and third as distinct cases, I think the third is but an instance of the second, for one who makes a statement under such circumstances can have no real belief in the truth of what he states. To prevent a false statement being fraudulent, there must, I think, always be an honest belief in its truth. And this probably covers the whole ground, for one who knowingly alleges that which is false, has obviously no such honest belief. Thirdly, if fraud be proved, the motive of the person guilty of it is immaterial. It matters not that there was no intention to cheat or injure the person to whom the statement was made.

. . .

In my opinion making a false statement through want of care falls far short of, and is a very different thing from, fraud, and the same may be said of a false representation honestly believed though on insufficient grounds. Indeed Cotton L.J. himself indicated, in the words I have already quoted, that he should not call it fraud. But the whole current of authorities, with which I have so long detained your Lordships, shews to my mind conclusively that fraud is essential to found an action of deceit, and that it cannot be maintained where the acts proved cannot properly be so termed. And the case of *Taylor v. Ashton* [11 M. & W. 401] appears to me to be in direct conflict with the dictum of Sir George Jessel, and inconsistent with the view taken by the learned judges in the Court below. I observe that Sir Frederick Pollock, in his able work on Torts (p. 243, note), referring, I presume, to the dicta of Cotton L.J. and Sir George Jessel M.R., says that the actual decision in *Taylor v. Ashton* [*supra*] is not consistent with the modern cases on the duty of directors of companies. I think he is right. But for the reasons I have given I am unable to hold that anything less than fraud will render directors or any other persons liable to an action of deceit.

· · ·

[Lord Herschell concluded that the plaintiff had failed to establish deceit. Lords Watson, Halsbury, Bramwell, and Fitzgerald delivered separate concurring judgments.]

NOTES AND QUESTIONS

1. What are the elements of the tort of deceit?

2. Deceit appears to have emerged centuries ago as an independent tort, later becoming associated with contractual warranties. See generally Waddams, *Products Liability*, 3rd ed. (1993), 1-11. This connection was severed by *Pasley v. Freeman* (1789), 100 E.R. 450 (K.B.), which held that the tort remedy in deceit lay against only a party who intentionally induced another to act to his detriment upon a knowingly false statement. Deceit remained the major cause of action for recovery of pure economic losses caused by misrepresentations until the decision in *Hedley Byrne & Co. v. Heller & Partners Ltd.*, [1964] A.C. 465 (H.L.).

3. Although most deceit actions involve pure economic loss, the action also provides redress for physical harm. See, for example, *Graham v. Saville*, [1945] 2 D.L.R. 489 (Ont. C.A.). The defendant, a married man, induced an unmarried woman to believe that he was single and that they had undergone a valid marriage ceremony, when in fact they had not. She subsequently gave birth to a child and sued in battery and deceit. The court found for the plaintiff in deceit, awarding her $4,000, which included compensation for the "physical injury, pain, and suffering in consequence of her pregnancy and the birth of a child." See also *Beaulne v. Ricketts* (1979), 96 D.L.R. (3d) 550 (Alta. S.C.).

4. For a recent discussion of the elements of deceit and how it differs from mere "sharp" or "hardball" business practices, see *Harland v. Fancsati* (1993), 13 O.R. (3d) 103 (Gen. Div), aff'd. (1994), 21 O.R. (3d) 798 (Div. Ct.).

5. In deceit, the tortious misrepresentation is usually based upon a written or oral statement, but it may also be based upon actions designed to mislead. See, for example, *Abel v. McDonald* (1964), 45 D.L.R. (2d) 198 (Ont. C.A.).

6. As a general rule, unless the parties are in a fiduciary relationship, neither silence nor passive failure to disclose the truth is actionable in deceit. See Fleming, *The Law of Torts*, 8th ed. (1992), 630-31, who notes several exceptions to this rule. See also *Sorensen v. Kaye Holdings Ltd.*, [1979] 6 W.W.R. 193 (B.C. C.A.); *C.R.F. Holdings Ltd. v. Fundy Chemical Int. Ltd.* (1981), 19 C.C.L.T. 263 (B.C. C.A.); *Francis v. Dingman* (1983), 43 O.R. (2d) 641 (C.A.); *Rainbow Industrial Caterers Ltd. v. C.N.R.* (1988), 46 C.C.L.T. 112 (B.C. C.A.); and *Canson Enterprises Ltd. v. Boughton & Co.*, [1991] 3 S.C.R. 534.

7. Only factual misrepresentations are actionable in deceit. As discussed in chapter 11, there is no general duty in tort to fulfill gratuitous promises. Provided the defendant made the promise honestly, he can subsequently decide not to fulfill it without incurring liability in deceit. However, if the defendant makes a promise, with no intention of fulfilling it, then his promise may be characterized as a factual misrepresentation of his intentions, and he may be held liable in deceit.

8. For a discussion of damages in deceit, see *West Coast Finance Ltd. v. Gunderson, Stokes, Walton & Co.* (1974), 44 D.L.R. (3d) 232, rev'd. (1975), 56 D.L.R. (3d) 460 (B.C. C.A.); *Siametis v. Trojan Horse (Burlington) Inc.* (1979), 25 O.R. (2d) 120 (H.C.); *C.R.F. Holdings Ltd. v. Fundy Chemical Int. Ltd.* (1981), 19 C.C.L.T. 263 (B.C. C.A.); and *Bitton v. Jakovljevic* (1990), 75 O.R. (2d) 143 (H.C.). See also *Burrows v. Burke* (1982), 36 O.R. (2d) 737 (H.C.); and *Archer v. Brown*, [1984] 2 All E.R. 267 (Q.B.) for a discussion of the circumstances in which the plaintiff is entitled to both rescission

of the contract and damages in deceit. For a recent discussion of Commonwealth case law, see Cumberbatch, "Deceit: The Loss and the Profits" (1992), Aust. Bus. L. Rev. 372.

9. Deceit has become a less important cause of action in recent years, as a result of *Hedley Byrne & Co. v. Heller & Partners Ltd.*, [1964] A.C. 465 (H.L.), which created a broad cause of action for negligent misrepresentation. As well, recent developments in contract law have made it easier to establish that a misrepresentation is part of a contract. See Waddams, *The Law of Contracts*, 3rd ed. (1993), 273-95.

10. Many American courts impose strict liability in tort law against manufacturers and distributors for breach of express and sometimes implied misrepresentations about the quality of a product. See, for example, *Henningsen v. Bloomfield Motors Ltd.* (1960), 161 A. (2d) 69 (N.J. S.C.); *Randy Knitwear Inc. v. Amer. Cyanamid Co.* (1962), 181 N.E. (2d) 389 (N.Y. C.A.); *Seeley v. White Motor Co.* (1965), 403 P. (2d) 245 (Cal. S.C.); and *Santor v. A & M Karagheusian Inc.* (1965), 207 A. (2d) 305 (N.J. S.C.).

3. Passing Off

CIBA-GEIGY CANADA LTD. v. APOTEX INC.

(1992), 95 D.L.R. (4th) 385 (S.C.C.)

[Ciba-Geigy, a pharmaceutical company, sold a drug called "metroprolol" under licence. In 1984, Apotex (legally) began to manufacture and sell the same drug, but in tablets of different size, shape and colour. In 1986, Apotex changed its marketing strategy and started to market the metroprolol drug in a tablet "get-up" nearly identical to that of the plaintiff. This prompted Ciba-Geigy to bring a passing off action against Apotex and another corporate defendant.]

GONTHIER J.: — . . .

A. *Passing-off action*

(1) *General principles developed by the courts*

The concept of passing-off was developed in 1842 in *Perry v. Truefitt* (1842), 6 Beav. 66, 49 E.R. 749, which seems to have been the first case in which the expression "passing-off" appeared: "A man is not to sell his own goods under the pretence that they are the goods of another man" (at p. 73 Beav., p. 752 E.R.). In *Singer Manufacturing Co. v. Loog* (1880), 18 Ch. D. 395 (C.A.) at pp. 412-13; affirmed 8 App. Cas. 15 (H.L.), James L.J. described passing-off and its origins:

> . . . no man is entitled to represent his goods as being the goods of another man; and no man is permitted to use any mark, sign or symbol, device or other means, whereby, without making a direct false misrepresentation himself to a purchaser who purchases from him, he enables such purchaser to tell a lie or to make a false representation to somebody else who is the ultimate customer . . . he must not, as I said, make directly, or through the medium of another person, a false representation that his goods are the goods of another person.

The House of Lords has set out the requirements for a passing-off action on many occasions. In *Erven Warnink B.V. v. J. Townend & Sons (Hull) Ltd.*, [1980] R.P.C. 31, Lord Diplock identified five conditions, at p. 93: there must be (1) misrepresentation (2) by a trader in the course of trade (3) to prospective customers of his or ultimate customers of goods or services supplied by him, (4) which is calculated to injure the business or goodwill of another trader, and (5) which causes actual damage to the business or goodwill of the trader bringing the action.

More recently, in *Reckitt & Colman Products Ltd. v. Borden Inc.*, [1990] 1 All E.R. 873 (H.L.), Lord Oliver reaffirmed, at p. 880:

> The law of passing off can be summarised in one short general proposition, no man may pass off his goods as those of another. More specifically, it may be expressed in terms of the elements which the plaintiff in such an action has to prove in order to succeed. These are three in number. First, he must establish *a goodwill or reputation attached to the goods or services which he supplies* in the mind of the purchasing public *by association with the identifying "get-up"* (whether it consists simply of a brand name or a trade description, or the individual features of labelling or packaging) under which his particular goods or services are offered to the public, such that the get-up is recognised by the public as distinctive specifically of the plaintiff's goods or services. Second, he must demonstrate *a misrepresentation* by the defendant to the public (whether or not intentional) leading or likely to lead the public to believe that goods or services offered by him are the goods or services of the plaintiff . . . Third, he must demonstrate that he suffers or, in a quia timet action, that he is likely to suffer *damage* by reason of the erroneous belief engendered by the defendant's misrepresentation that the source of the defendant's goods or services is the same as the source of those offered by the plaintiff.

(Emphasis added.)

The three necessary components of a passing-off action are thus: the existence of goodwill, deception of the public due to a misrepresentation and actual or potential damage to the plaintiff.

In Canada, the Supreme Court has also had occasion to rule on a passing-off action, in particular in *Oxford Pendaflex Canada Ltd. v. Korr Marketing Ltd.*, *supra*, in which the issue turned primarily on the similar get-up of the parties' products. In that case this court stated that in any passing-off action the plaintiff, in order to succeed, must establish that its product has acquired a secondary meaning.

In *Consumers Distributing Co. v. Seiko Time Canada Ltd.* (1984), 1 C.P.R. (3d) 1 at pp. 15-16, 10 D.L.R. (4th) 161 at p. 175, [1984] 1 S.C.R. 583, this court noted that the requirements of a passing-off action have evolved somewhat in the last 100 years:

> . . . attention should be drawn to the fact that the passing off rule is founded upon the tort of deceit, and while the original requirement of an intent to deceive died out in the mid-1800s there remains the requirement, at the very least, that confusion in the minds of the public be a likely consequence by reason of the sale, or proffering for sale, by the defendant of a product not that of the plaintiff's making, under the guise or implication that it was the plaintiff's product or the equivalent.

A manufacturer must therefore avoid creating confusion in the public mind, whether deliberately or not, by a get-up identical to that of a product which has acquired a secondary meaning by reason of its get-up.

. . .

(2) *Purposes of the passing-off action and target clientele*

In considering those upstream and downstream of the product, two separate aspects must be distinguished. I refer in this regard to the persons who manufacture or market the products, on the one hand ("the manufacturers"), and on the other to those for whom the products are intended, the persons who buy, use or consume them ("the customers").

It is clear that however one looks at the passing-off action, its purpose is to protect all persons affected by the product.

(a) *Protection of manufacturers*

This corresponds to the third point mentioned by Lord Oliver. The right to be protected against the "pirating" of a brand, trade name or the appearance of a product is linked to a kind of "ownership" which the manufacturer has acquired in that name, brand and appearance by using them.

In *Pinard v. Coderre* (1953), 20 C.P.R. 19 at p. 25, [1954] 3 D.L.R. 463 at p. 468, [1953] Que. Q.B. 99, Marchand J.A. of the Quebec Court of Appeal noted (translation): "It would seem that the first occupant of this name or these words acquired a right to use them exclusive of all other persons, comparable in many ways to *a true right of ownership*" (emphasis added).

Accordingly, to begin with, from what might be called the individual or manufacturer's standpoint, the passing-off action is intended to protect a form of ownership.

There is also the concept of ownership, protected by the passing-off action in relation to goodwill, a term which must be understood in a very broad sense, taking in not only people who are customers but also the reputation and drawing power of a given business in its market. In *Consumers Distributing Co. v. Seiko Time Canada Ltd., supra*, Estey J., at p. 13 C.P.R., p. 173 D.L.R., cites *Salmond on the Law of Torts*, by R.F.V. Heuston, 17th ed. (London: Sweet & Maxwell, 1977), at pp. 403-4:

> "The courts have wavered between two conceptions of a passing-off action — as a remedy for the invasion of a quasi-proprietary right in a trade name or trade mark, and as a remedy, analogous to the action on the case for deceit, for invasion of the personal right not to be injured by fraudulent competition. The true basis of the action is that *the passing off injures the right of property in the plaintiff*, that right of property being his right to the goodwill of his business.
>
> . . . . . .
>
> "Indeed, it seems that the essence of the tort lies in the misrepresentation that the goods in question are those of another ...".

(Emphasis added.)

It will then be necessary to look at the relationship between the various merchants or manufacturers, and it is at that point that questions of competition have to be considered. As Chenevard says (*Traité de la concurrence déloyale en matière industrielle et commerciale*, vol. 1 (Paris: L.G.D.J., 1914), at pp. 6-7) (translation) "[c]ompetition is the soul of commerce; it requires unceasing effort and as such is the chief factor in economic progress". Drysdale and Silverleaf, *Passing Off: Law and Practice* (London: Butterworths, 1986), are substantially of the same opinion, at p. 1:

> In countries with a free market system the proper functioning of the economy depends upon competition between rival trading enterprises. It is the mechanism of competition which controls the price, quality and availability of goods and services to the public.
>
> . . .

The purpose of the passing-off action is thus also to prevent unfair competition.

One does not have to be a fanatical moralist to understand how appropriating another person's work, as that is certainly what is involved, is a breach of good faith.

Finally, another more apparent, more palpable aspect, a consequence of the preceding one, must also be mentioned. The "pirated" manufacturer is very likely to experience a reduction in sales volume and therefore in his turnover because of the breaking up of his market. When such a situation occurs in the ordinary course of business between rival manufacturers, that is what one might call one of the rules of the game, but when the rivalry involves the use of dishonest practices, the law must intervene.

(b) *Protection of customers*

In the Anglo-Saxon legal systems (translation), "the person chiefly concerned is the competitor affected by the unfair act": Louis Mermillod, *Essai sur la notion de concurrence déloyale en France et aux États-Unis* (Paris: Pichon & Durand-Auzias, 1954), at p. 176. He is frequently in fact the first party affected by the practice or aware of it.

However, "[i]t should never be overlooked that . . . unfair competition cases are affected with a public interest. A dealer's good will is protected, not merely for his profit, but in order that the purchasing public may not be enticed into buying A.'s product when it wants B.'s product": *General Baking Co. v. Gorman*, 3 F. 2d 891 (1st Cir., 1925). Accordingly (translation), "the power of the court in such cases is exercised, not only to do individual justice, but to safeguard the interests of the public": *Scandinavia Belting Co. v. Asbestos & Rubber Works of America, Inc.*, 257 F. 937 (2d Cir., 1919) at p. 941. The ordinary customer, the consumer, is at the heart of the matter here. According to the civilian lawyer Chenevard, *op. cit.*, at p. 20, in a case of unfair competition it is (translation) "the buyer who is the first to be injured".

The customer expects to receive a given product when he asks for it and should not be deceived. It often happens that products are interchangeable and that a substitution will have little effect. However, the customer may count on having a specific product. There are many reasons for such a choice: habit, satisfaction, another person's recommendation, the desire for change, and so on. I have no hesitation in using the classic saying, taken from popular imagery: "the customer is always right". Merchants must respect his wishes, choices and preferences as far as possible. Where this is simply not possible, no substitution must be made *without his knowledge*. That is the minimum degree of respect which manufacturers and merchants, who we should remember depend on their customers, should show.

There is no shortage of fraudulent or simply misleading practices: one may think, for example, of products having a similar get-up, the use of similar labelling, use of the same trade name, counterfeiting, imitation of packaging. These are all possible ways of attempting, deliberately or otherwise, to mislead the public. The courts and authors have unanimously concluded that the facts must be weighed in relation to an "ordinary" public, "average" customers: ". . . you must deal with the ordinary man and woman who would take ordinary care in purchasing what goods they require, and, if desiring a particular brand, would take ordinary precautions to see that they get it" (Neville J. in *Henry Thorne & Co. v. Sandow* (1912), 29 R.P.C. 440 (Ch. D.) at p. 453.)

The average customer will not be the same for different products, however, and will not have the same attitude at the time of purchase. Moreover, the attention and care taken by the same person may vary depending on the product he is buying: someone will probably not exercise the same care in selecting goods from a supermarket shelf and in choosing a luxury item. In the first case, the misrepresentation is likely to "catch" more readily.

. . .

[Gonthier J. allowed the appeals.]

NOTES AND QUESTIONS

1. What are the elements of the passing off action?
2. What is the purpose of the tort?
3. Passing off is the most frequently litigated of the intentional economic torts. Many of these cases arise in the context of the sports and entertainment industries. For recent exmples, see *Paramount Pictures Corp. v. Howley* (1991), 5 O.R. (3d) 573 (Gen. Div.); *National Hockey League v. Pepsi Cola Ltd.* (1992), 92 D.L.R. (4th) 349 (B.C. S.C.), aff'd. (1995), 122 D.L.R. (4th) 412 (B.C. C.A.); and *Walt Disney Productions v. Triple Five Corp.*, [1994] 6 W.W.R. 385 (Alta. C.A.).
4. As with other intentional economic torts, the courts have been reluctant to extend them beyond the commercial law context in which they were first recognized. See *Polsinelli v. Marzilli* (1987), 42 C.C.L.T. 46 (Ont. H.C.).

4. Interference with Contractual Relations

POSLUNS v. TORONTO STOCK EXCHANGE

[1964] 2 O.R. 547, 46 D.L.R. (2d) 210 (H.C.)

[Employees of firms in the Toronto Stock Exchange required the approval of the Exchange to participate in various trading activities. The Exchange concluded that Mr. Posluns had engaged in these activities without the required approval, and informed Posluns' employer, Daly Co., that it was withdrawing Mr. Posluns' right to act as a shareholder, officer, director, or employee of any member firm. Daly Co. fired Mr. Posluns, and he in turn sued the Exchange for interference with contractual relations and conspiracy. Only the first claim is discussed in the following excerpt.]

GALE J.: . . .

(a) *General Principles*

I propose first to examine the plaintiff's claim against the Exchange for damages for having procured a breach of his contract with the Daly company.

While a contract cannot impose the burden of an obligation on one who is not a party to it, a duty is undoubtedly cast upon any person, although extraneous to the obligation, to refrain from interfering with its due performance unless he has a duty or a right in law to so act. Thus, if a person without lawful justification knowingly and intentionally procures the breach by a party to a contract which is valid and enforceable and thereby causes damage to another party to the contract, the person who has induced the breach commits an actionable wrong. That wrong does not rest upon the fact that the intervenor has acted in order to harm his victim, for a bad motive does not *per se* convert an otherwise lawful act into an unlawful one, but rather because there has been an unlawful invasion of legal relations existing between others.

. . .

To sustain the cause of action now being discussed, and in the circumstances which prevailed, it must be shown that:

1. A valid and enforceable employment contract subsisted between the plaintiff and the Daly company; and
2. The defendant Exchange was or can be assumed to have been aware of the existence of that contract; and
3. A breach of that contract was procured by the Exchange; and
4. Such breach was effected by wrongful interference on the part of the Exchange; and
5. The plaintiff suffered damage as a result thereof. If all of those elements have been proved the plaintiff is entitled to relief.

[Subject to a complication regarding the third point, which need not concern us, Gale J. accepted that the first three points were established and continued.]

(d) *Was there unlawful interference on the part of the Exchange?*

I now pass to the next link in the plaintiff's chain of action. Does he show that the interference, if any, on the part of the Exchange with his contractual rights was such as to sustain his claim, for the law stipulates that to be tortious the interference which is the source of damage to another must be "unlawful" before it will be actionable. It is unnecessary to consider the various kinds of particular interference which have been held to be wrongful; it will suffice to say that to procure a breach of contract by direct intervention is "unlawful", and will give rise to a cause of action to the person who is thereby injured unless it is justifiable. For that proposition I rely, amongst others, upon *D.C. Thomson & Co. Ltd. v. Deakin*, [1952] Ch. 646, where, at pp. 677 and 681 respectively, Lord Evershed, M.R., stated:

> At any rate, it is clear that, when there is such a direct intervention by the intervener [causing a party to break his contract], the intervention itself is thereby considered wrongful.

And:

> Dealing first with individual contractors, it seems to me that the intervener, assuming in all cases that he knows of the contract and acts with the aim and object of procuring its breach to the damage of B, one of the contracting parties, will be liable not only (1) if he directly intervenes by persuading A to break it, but also (2) if he intervenes by the commission of some act wrongful in itself so as to prevent A from in fact performing his contract . . .

In the same case Jenkins, L.J., had this to say at p. 694:

> Direct persuasion or procurement or inducement applied by the third party to the contract breaker, with knowledge of the contract and the intention of bringing about its breach, is clearly

to be regarded as a wrongful act in itself, and where this is shown a case of actionable interference in its primary form is made out: *Lumley v. Gye*, 2 El. & Bl. 216.

I pause here to point out that when considering this tort, care must be taken always to distinguish between a cause of action based upon the procurement of a breach of a contract and one for interference with other civil rights. The House of Lords in England has restricted the scope of the principle which I have just outlined to interference with actual contracts; see *Allen v. Flood*, [1898] A.C. 1 and *Sorrell v. Smith*, [1925] A.C. 700. Thus, some of the observations by Judges in cases such as *Crofter Hand Woven Harris Tweed Co., Ltd. v. Veitch*, [1942] A.C. 435 must be interpreted in the light of the fact that no breach of contract was involved.

Here, there was direct and deliberate interference by the Exchange with the contractual relations between the plaintiff and the Daly company. On the authorities, that interference, unless justifiable, must be deemed to be unlawful action on the part of the Exchange if a breach of those contractual relations was the result. True, it did not act for the purpose of causing damage to Mr. Posluns or with malice or spite, but that is immaterial, for if the Exchange intended to bring an end to the employment contract and such was clearly its purpose, that intention is sufficient and does not have to be accompanied by a wish to do harm.

. . .

In short, therefore, it would seem that the plaintiff is entitled to reparation from the Exchange if the latter by direct, intentional and unjustified intervention through the Daly company, effected a breach of contract of which it was or ought to have been aware.

. . .

(e) *Was the Exchange justified in procuring a breach of contract?*

The limits of the doctrine of justification as it applies to the tort under discussion have never been defined with any degree of precision. Perhaps the only safe guide in the matter is to follow, and try to enlist, the words of Romer, L.J., at p. 574 in the report of the judgments in the Court of Appeal in *Glamorgan Coal Co. Ltd. v. South Wales Miners' Federation*, [1903] 2 K.B. 545, where this appears:

> I will only add that, in analyzing or considering the circumstances, I think that regard might be had to the nature of the contract; the position of the parties to the contract; the grounds for the breach; the means employed to procure the breach; the relation of the person procuring the breach to the person who breaks the contract; and I think also to the object of the person in procuring the breach.

If the act of interference is in itself a lawful one, both as to purpose and means, then no vindication is required unless it was committed in the course of a conspiracy to injure the victim. If, on the other hand, unlawful intervention has been the source of the harm, justification must be shown if the claim is to be avoided. The defence rarely succeeds. Self-interest, alone or with others, or the fulfilment of an undertaking to protect others in the same interest, will not of themselves amount to justification: *South Wales Miners' Federation v. Glamorgan Coal Co. Ltd.*, [1905] A.C. 239: *Pratt et al. v. British Medical Ass'n*, [1919] 1 K.B. 244; nor where there is an honest belief that there is a duty to act: *Camden Nominees, Ltd. v. Forcey*;

nor where a person is induced to break a contract because the other party to it has breached his contract with the intervenor: *Smithies v. National Ass'n of Operative Plasterers*, [1909] 1 K.B. 310. These are but a few of the cases in which it was decided that pleas of justification could not prevail.

On the other hand, in several instances the Courts have sanctioned interference, particularly where it has been promoted by impersonal or disinterested motives. For example, in some of the early cases it was intimated that a defendant might be excused from the consequences of his otherwise illegal act if he was under the influence of some great moral or religious force, reference being made to a father who might induce his impressionable daughter to break a contract for the promise of marriage with a scoundrel. And I suppose if a doctor were to cause a patient to end a contract of service for health reasons, he would likewise be protected. Even in those examples, however, the distinction between inducement and mere advice is significant and should be heeded.

In two instances interference which otherwise would have been illegal was held to be privileged on the ground that it was effected in the public interest. I have in mind *Stott v. Gamble*, [1916] 2 K.B. 504, where a licensing body banned an objectionable film which the plaintiff had arranged to exhibit at another theatre, and *Brimelow v. Casson*, [1924] 1 Ch. 302, where a protective committee was held to be justified in procuring breaches of employment contracts under which chorus girls were so grossly underpaid as to compel them to resort to immorality. In the first case, however, reliance was placed upon a condition attached to the licence, and the second is today of doubtful authority for a contrary view expressed in the *Smithies* case was apparently not considered. Nor has the case been applied, so far as I can find, on any other occasion, and, in fact, was gently criticized by Simonds, J., as he then was, in the *Camden* case. In any event, those cases do not cover the situation before me. The Exchange was not here primarily engaged in upholding the public interest. That certainly was one of the purposes in the minds of the governors but not the predominant one. They were disciplining the Daly firm, Mr. Posluns and, later, Mr. Robb. I am inclined to the view, therefore, that the action of the Exchange, if otherwise illegal, cannot be excused on the theory that it was acting in the public welfare.

Lastly, a person may be justified in encroaching upon another's civil rights because of some statutory or contractual privilege, in which case he can be said to be acting in accordance with a right conferred by contract or a duty imposed upon him by competent authority as distinct from the mere protection of his own interest. Really, this has been already touched upon, for if that person is under such a cloak, he is not deemed to be acting unlawfully. In *Read v. Friendly Society of Operative Stonemasons of England, Ireland & Wales*, [1902] 2 K.B. 88 and 732, for example, Darling, J., stated at p. 95 that a person would be justified in causing the breach of a contract which was incapable of being carried out without infringing his rights under another contract. That appears to be an illustration of a contractual privilege and, in a sense, the *Stott* case exemplifies recourse to a statutory one. Here, the Exchange could not say that it was acting under an explicit statutory licence, but, by reason of its relations with the plaintiff, it enjoyed a very considerable measure of control over him, for he submitted himself to its jurisdiction when he applied to become, and was approved as, a customers' man at Burns. I think it is only reasonable to conclude that he thereby impliedly agreed that so long as he continued under the aegis of the Exchange, he would submit to any control *properly* exerted by it. In this respect, reference might well be made to *Bonsor v. Musicians' Union*, [1956] A.C. 104. A correlative obligation was, however, cast upon the Exchange to act within its own rules and within the realm of natural justice when exerting that control, and unless it did both when dealing with Mr. Posluns, any implied contractual right to interfere was lost.

[Gale J. concluded that the Exchange had fulfilled its correlative obligations, and dismissed the action for inducing breach of contract.]

NOTES AND QUESTIONS

1. Based on *Posluns*, define the tort of intentional interference with contractual relations. How do the elements of this action differ from those of trespass to land or chattels? Why are contractual rights not accorded the same legal protection as tangible property?

2. Do you agree with Gale J. that the defendant's motive should not affect the legality of his conduct? Would the result have been the same if Posluns had proven that the Exchange normally overlooked transgressions such as his and that it had taken action against him out of spite? See also *Gerrard v. Manitoba*, [1993] 1 W.W.R. 182 (Man. C.A.).

3. Gale J. stated that unlawful interference is one of the elements of the tort and then noted that "direct interference" in the contract is *per se* unlawful. Consequently, most cases for direct interference with contractual relations will depend on the issue of justification. Why did Gale J. conclude that the defendant was justified in *Posluns*? For a discussion of the relationship between intent and justification, see *Babcock v. Carr; Babcock v. Archibald* (1981), 34 O.R. (2d) 65 (H.C.); *Thermo King Corp. v. Prov. Bank of Can.* (1981), 130 D.L.R. (3d) 256 (Ont. C.A.); and *Bank of N.S. v. Gaudreau* (1984), 48 O.R. (2d) 478 (H.C.).

4. Heydon, in *Economic Torts*, 2nd ed. (1978) at 46, identifies three different forms of justification:

The possible forms of justification are various, and they are called by a confusing set of names — rights, liberties, interests. But the interests which the defendant claims he is entitled to have protected at the expense of another's contract fall into three groups. The defendant may have some legally enforceable "right" such as a prior contract which gives him a defence against the plaintiff. In effect, two rights to contractual performance clash, and the clash is resolved by giving the defendant a defence. He may rely on some "public interest", which must be important to outweigh the plaintiff's reliance on the public interest in security of contracts, for example, the duty to give medical advice. He may rely on some private interest such as an interest in liberty to trade; this will almost always be outweighed by the plaintiff's contractual rights unless it can be coupled with some public interest, for example, the public interest in complaining about misappropriation of taxation revenue.

5. Several authors recognize two distinct actions for interference with contractual relations: one based on the defendant's direct interference with contractual relations, as in the *Posluns* case; and a second action based on the defendant's indirect interference with contractual relations.

As indicated, Gale J. viewed any direct interference as *per se* unlawful. However, in an action for indirect interference with contractual relations, the plaintiff must prove that the defendant used independently unlawful means to procure the breach. A criminal offence, independently tortious conduct, or a breach of the defendant's own contractual obligations will clearly satisfy this "unlawful means" requirement. As well, a violation of the rules of natural justice or a breach of a regulatory statute may suffice. As with justification, no firm rule has emerged, and the issue has been determined on a case-by-case basis. See Heydon, *Economic Torts*, 2nd ed. (1978), 67. See also *Body v. Murdoch*, [1954] 4 D.L.R. 326 (Ont. C.A.), for an illustration of the difficulty that arises in attempting to balance the conflicting interests involved in this type of case.

6. The most comprehensive Canadian discussion of the action for interference with contractual relations is found in *Garry v. Sherritt Gordon Mines Ltd.* (1987), 42 C.C.L.T. 241 (Sask. C.A.). The two judgments reveal many of the outstanding difficulties in this area and the significance of the action in labour relations disputes.

7. Are the actions for interference with contractual relations necessary? Should the plaintiff be limited to pursuing his contractual remedies against the party who breached the contract? Why are the requirements for indirect interference with contractual relations stricter than those for direct interference?

8. There has been a trend towards expanding tort liability for interference with contractual relations. Several English decisions have extended liability to cases in which the defendant's conduct merely interfered with the plaintiff's contractual relations, but did not result in a breach of contract. *Stratford (J.T.) & Son Ltd. v. Lindley*, [1965] A.C. 269 (H.L.); *Emerald Const. Co. v. Lowthian*, [1966] 1 All E.R. 1013 (C.A.); and *Torquay Hotel Co. v. Cousins*, [1969] 2 Ch. 106 (C.A.). See also *Garry v. Sherritt Gordon Mines Ltd.*, per Bayda C.J.S. For diametrically opposed views of this development and the current Canadian position see Burns, "Tort Injury to Economic Interests: Some Facets of Legal Response" (1980), 58 Can. Bar Rev. 103 at 114-125; and Richardson, "Interference with Contractual Relations: Is *Torquay Hotel* the Law in Canada?" (1983), 41 U.T. Fac. L. Rev. 1. See also Carty, "Unlawful Interference with Trade" (1983), 3 Legal Stud. 193.

As a general rule, interference with contractual relations will only lie in cases in which there is a valid enforceable contract. In *Unident v. DeLong* (1981), 131 D.L.R. (3d) 225 (N.S. T.D.), the plaintiff was awarded damages even though the contract was unenforceable because it violated the Sale of Goods Act, R.S.N.S. 1967, c. 274, s. 6(1). The judge emphasized that the contract was valid in substance and only unenforceable due to a technical defect.

There have been several cases in which damages have been awarded for negligent interference with contractual relations. Regardless of the merits of this development, its wide acceptance would greatly expand liability and largely supersede the actions for intentional interference. See *McLaren v. B.C. Institute of Technology* (1978), 7 C.C.L.T. 192 (B.C. S.C.); *Nicholls v. Township of Richmond* (1983), 24 C.C.L.T. 253 (B.C. C.A.); *Pearl v. Pac. Enercon Inc.* (1985), 19 D.L.R. (4th) 464 (B.C. C.A.); and Danforth, "Tortious Interference with Contract: A Reassertion of Society's Interest in Commercial Stability and Contractual Integrity" (1981), 81 Columbia L. Rev. 1491.

As a matter of policy, are these extensions of liability for interference with contractual relations warranted?

9. A large percentage of these actions arise in the context of labour disputes. See generally, Mandel, "Picketing and the Tort of Inducing Breach of Contract" (1961), 19 Fac. L. Rev. 118; Christie, "Inducing Breach of Contract in Trade Disputes: Development of the Law in England and Canada" (1967), 13 McGill L.J. 101; and Rayner, *The Law of Collective Bargaining* (1995), 20-13 to 20-15.

10. For an interesting contrast between the alleged tortious interference of governmental and private sector actors, see *Cheticamp Fisheries Co-operative Ltd. v. Canada* (1994), 21 C.C.L.T. (2d) 151 (N.S. T.D.), rev'd. (1995), 26 C.C.L.T. (2d) 40 (N.S. C.A.), and *A. & B. Sound Ltd. v. Future Shop Ltd.* (1995), 25 C.C.L.T. (2d) 1 (B.C. S.C.).

5. Intimidation

CENTRAL CAN. POTASH v. GOVT. OF SASK.

[1979] 1 S.C.R. 42, 88 D.L.R. (3d) 609 (S.C.C.)

MARTLAND J.: . . . To summarize, the situation in the present case is this. Pursuant to the *Mineral Resources Act*, a scheme for the control of production of potash in Saskatchewan had been put into effect. The appellant, as a potash producer, was prohibited from producing potash in excess of the amounts prescribed by the licences issued to it. It was required after receiving a licence to submit a production schedule, showing monthly production during the 12-month term of the licence not exceeding the total production authorized.

The appellant, being understandably unhappy with the quota allotted to it, endeavoured to persuade the Minister to increase its allocation, but without success. It sought to compel such an increase by *mandamus*, again without success. It failed to submit a proper production schedule within 30 days of the receipt of its licence for the 1972-73 year. It continued its production upon a scale beyond that which was contemplated by its licence.

This was the situation in which the Deputy Minister wrote the letter of September 20, 1972, calling on the appellant to reduce its production or to face the possibility of a cancellation of its mineral lease. That lease, as has been noted, included a requirement that the appellant, as lessee, would observe, perform and abide by all obligations imposed upon holders of mineral leases by the Act or Regulations thereunder in effect from time to time.

In the present case, the threat by the Deputy Minister was the possible exercise by the Minister of powers which he had reasonable grounds for believing the Minister possessed. In the *Rookes* case the threat was to pursue a course of action which the defendants knew would be a breach of the collective agreement between the union and B.O.A.C.

In the present case, the Deputy Minister sought to induce the appellant to limit the amount of its production to conform with the prorationing scheme which had been established. In the *Rookes* case, the object of the threat was to compel B.O.A.C. to discharge the plaintiff, an action which, except for the pressure, it did not wish to take and which it was under no legal obligation to take.

In the *Rookes* case, the threat was not made to the plaintiff. It was made to a third party, B.O.A.C., with a view to compel it to take a course of action detrimental to the plaintiff. In the present case, the threat was made directly to the appellant and no third party was involved.

I will deal with this distinction now, and will revert to the other distinctions later. It is significant because the plaintiff, in the *Rookes* case, was not in a position to claim a breach of contract by his employer when he was dismissed. The only recourse he could seek was against the defendants who had threatened a breach of the collective agreement between the union and the employer as a means to compel the employer to discharge Rookes. Here the appellant is a party to the contract which it says was threatened to be breached, *i.e.*, the lease, and would have been entitled to pursue its contractual remedies had that contract been illegally breached.

On this point, I am in agreement with the view expressed by the author of *Winfield and Jolowicz on Tort*, 10th ed., p. 458, as follows:

> It is submitted, therefore, that the two-party situation is properly distinguishable from the three-party situation and that it does not necessarily follow from *Rookes v. Barnard* that whenever A threatens B with an unlawful act, including a breach of his contract with B, he thereby commits the tort of intimidation. In fact the balance of advantage seems to lie in holding that where A threatens B with a breach of his contract with B, B should be restricted to his contractual remedies. The law should not encourage B to yield to the threat but should seek to persuade him to resist it. If he suffers damage in consequence he will be adequately compensated by his remedy in damages for breach of contract, as his damage can scarcely be other than financial. Where, however, what is threatened is tort, and especially if the threat is of violence, it is both unrealistic to insist that proceedings for a *quia timet* injunction afford him adequate protection against the consequences of resistance and unreasonable to insist that if violence is actually inflicted upon him he is adequately compensated by an award of damages thereafter. The view is preferred, therefore, that although A commits the tort of intimidation against B where he threatens B with violence or perhaps with any other tort, no independent tort is committed when all that is threatened is a breach of contract.

In my opinion the tort of intimidation is not committed if a party to a contract asserts what he reasonably considers to be his contractual right and that other party, rather than electing to contest that right, follows a course of conduct on the assumption that the assertion of right can be maintained.

I am also of the view that if the course of conduct which the person making the threat seeks to induce is that which the person threatened is obligated to follow, the tort of intimidation does not arise. If, in the *Rookes* case, the collective agreement between the union and B.O.A.C. had contained a closed shop provision so as to require B.O.A.C. to discharge the plaintiff upon his ceasing to be a member of the union, the plaintiff could not have succeeded in his suit because of the threat of a strike, even though the agreement provided that there should be no strikes.

In the present case the *Potash Conservation Regulations, 1969* made under the *Mineral Resources Act* prohibited the appellant from exceeding a specified production of potash. By conforming to the requirements of the Regulations, the appellant would not suffer damage and, therefore, the claim for intimidation is not well founded.

What, then, is the position if, subsequently, it is found that the Regulations were *ultra vires*? Does that finding then mean that there has been intimidation?

In my opinion it does not. The conduct of the Deputy Minister in relation to the tort of intimidation must be considered in relation to the circumstances existing at the time the alleged threat was made. The Deputy Minister was then seeking to induce conformity with the prorationing plan which had been created by legislation which it was his duty to enforce. At the time the threat was made, the legislation stood unchallenged.

. . .

In my opinion it would be unfortunate, in a federal state such as Canada, if it were to be held that a government official, charged with the enforcement of legislation, could be held to be guilty of intimidation because of his enforcement of the statute whenever a statute whose provisions he is under a duty to enforce is subsequently held to be *ultra vires*.

This brings me to the latter portion of the definition of intimidation from Clerk & Lindsell which I have adopted. "The tort is one of intention and the plaintiff, whether it be B or C, must be a person whom A intended to injure." The authority for this statement is found by the authors in the judgments of Lord Devlin and Lord Evershed in the *Rookes* case, and I am in agreement with it. There is no evidence that the Deputy Minister intended to injure the appellant. The correspondence, and particularly the letter of September 20, 1972, make it clear that his purpose was to induce compliance with an existing legislative scheme.

. . .

I would dismiss the appellant's claims for damages.

NOTES AND QUESTIONS

1. As Martland J. noted, the tort of intimidation may involve two or three parties. Two-party intimidation arises if the defendant coerces the plaintiff by means of unlawful threats to do or refrain from doing that which he has a right to do. Three-party intimidation arises if the defendant uses unlawful threats to coerce a third party into committing a specific act which harms the plaintiff. In both situations, the plaintiff must establish that the defendant intended to cause him injury. How does the relation-

ship between the defendant and the plaintiff differ in these two actions, and what impact should this have?

2. Do you agree with Martland J. that the defendant did not intend to injure the plaintiff? Was the injury a necessary consequence? Should the defendant's motive be relevant in intimidation? Is there something special about this case which justifies the concern with motive?

3. The issues of intent, motive and justification are further complicated by Mr. Justice Martland's following statement in *Central Can. Potash*:

> In my opinion the tort of intimidation is not committed if a party to a contract asserts what he reasonably considers to be his contractual right and that other party, rather than electing to contest that right, follows a course of conduct on the assumption that the assertion of the right can be maintained.

According to Martland J., does the defendant's mistaken belief that the threat is lawful preclude liability in intimidation? In the alternative, must both the defendant and the plaintiff mistakenly believe that the threat is lawful? See also *Roehl v. Houlahan* (1990), 74 D.L.R. (4th) 562 (Ont. C.A.), and *Roth v. Roth* (1991), 4 O.R. (3d) 740 (Gen. Div.).

In *J.C. Kerkhoff & Sons Contracting Ltd. v. XL Ironworks Co.* (1983), 26 C.C.L.T. 1 (B.C. S.C.), this principle was applied in a situation involving three-party intimidation. Even though the threat was unlawful, the defendant was absolved of liability because it reasonably believed that the threat was lawful. Should this principle apply in three-party intimidation cases, given the different relationships that exist in the two types of intimidation actions?

4. The threat may be implicit or explicit, and there is no legal distinction between a threat and a warning. It is essential that the threat or warning be unlawful, but this issue is controversial. Clearly, a threat to commit a crime or a tort is considered unlawful. However, in Fleming's words "beyond that, the approach has been casuistic, without any evident rationale related to policy ends, and suffering from some inexplicable inconsistencies." *The Law of Torts*, 8th ed. (1992), 699-700. In *Rookes v. Barnard*, [1964] A.C. 1129, the House of Lords established that, at least in regard to three-party intimidation, a threatened breach of contract is an unlawful threat. This principle has been criticized. Can you suggest why? Should this principle apply to two-party intimidation cases? Heydon suggests that this issue should be resolved in the same manner as the issue of unlawful means in indirect interference with contractual relations. *Economic Torts*, 2nd ed. (1978), 67.

5. Intimidation was elevated to importance as an independent nominate tort in *Rookes v. Barnard*, [1964] A.C. 1129 (H.L.). The defendant trade union threatened to strike in breach of its collective agreement with B.O.A.C., unless B.O.A.C. dismissed the plaintiff. B.O.A.C. dismissed the plaintiff, without committing a breach of contract. The plaintiff successfully recovered damages from the union, based upon the union's threat to breach its collective agreement. For an interesting forerunner to *Rookes*, see *Int. Brotherhood of Teamsters v. Therien*, [1960] S.C.R. 265, in which the same principle was applied without specific reference to the tort of intimidation. See also *J.T. Stratford & Son v. Lindley*, [1965] A.C. 307 (H.L.); *Mintuck v. Valley River Band No. 63A* (1977), 75 D.L.R. (3d) 589 (Man. C.A.); and *Selig v. Mansfield* (1982), 53 N.S.R. (2d) 246 (C.A.). For a general discussion of the tort of intimidation see Fridman, "The Tort of Intimidation" (1963), 113 The Law J. 68; Wedderburn, "Intimidation and the Right to Strike" (1964), 27 Mod. L. Rev. 257; and Burns, "Tort Injury to Economic Interests: Some Facets of Legal Response" (1980), 58 Can. Bar Rev. 103 at 126-140.

6. Conspiracy

POSLUNS v. TORONTO STOCK EXCHANGE

[1964] 2 O.R. 547, 46 D.L.R. (2d) 210 (Ont. H.C.)

GALE J.: . . .

While his counsel did not exhibit much confidence in the plaintiff's alleged cause of action for damages for conspiracy, it was not abandoned and I must therefore give attention to it.

It was pleaded that the defendant George Gardiner along with the other members of the Board who participated in the events of February 28th and March 2nd and the Exchange itself, all combined together to unlawfully injure the plaintiff by sending out the notice, ex. 33, which probably had the result, not only of bringing about his dismissal as an employee and his removal as a director and shareholder, but also of precluding him from obtaining immediate employment with any other member or member corporation of the Exchange, and of damaging his reputation to some extent. Both compensatory and punitive damages were asked for on this branch of the case, and it will be observed, as stated above, that the complaint was not confined to interference with the plaintiff's contract of employment only.

It need hardly be said that a conspiracy consists of an agreement of two or more to do an unlawful act or to do a lawful act by unlawful means. Thus, the tort of conspiracy is committed if a person is damaged by a combination which is formed for the purpose of harming him in his trade, business or other interests, whether or not a breach of contract is the result, or if that damage is caused by an unlawful act on the part of those acting in concert.

. . .

In my opinion, the claim based upon a supposed conspiracy fails for several reasons. To begin with, there was not any agreement to injure the plaintiff or any agreement to do something the doing of which would harm him. All the governors did was to vote in the same way, but, because they had agreed upon nothing before voting, and were not at any time actuated by malice or any other improper motive, they did not merely, by so voting, enter into an agreement, express or implied, to do something which had not yet been done, the requisite of any conspiracy. As Mr. Arnup said, the directors of a corporation do not make an "agreement" in the conspiracy sense by voting the same way. They individually make the same decision. In the popular sense they are "in agreement", but in the sense in which the law of conspiracy uses "agree" they were not. Each simply expressed an individual opinion and the majority opinion prevailed. A contrary view would bring extraordinary consequences. One of its implications would be that each time the majority of a Board of Directors voted to have the corporation pursue a course of action which ultimately turned out to be illegal, those who were in favour of having the corporation act as it did would be conspirators by reason solely of having so voted.

The proposition that the mere taking of a decision by directors or others at a meeting cannot constitute an agreement to conspire unless some of them have entered into a compact in advance of the meeting to induce others to cause the organization on whose behalf they are acting to do something which is wrong, is supported by authority. In *De Jetley Marks v. Greenwood (Lord) et al.*, [1936] 1 All E.R. 863, Porter, J., as he then was, observed at p. 872:

> ...I think it is true that directors in a board meeting could not induce or conspire to induce that meeting to break a contract — at any rate, not without malice.

That language does not substantiate Mr. Williston's suggestion that there is a difference between a vote to have a company break one of its own contracts and a vote to wrongfully procure the breach of a contract between others. I should add that Porter, J., was careful to qualify the quoted statement by pointing out that some or all of the directors could conspire before the meeting to cause the Board to wrongfully break a contract.

. . .

[Gale J. dismissed the action for conspiracy.]

ROMAN CORP. v. HUDSON'S BAY OIL & GAS CO.

[1973] S.C.R. 820, 36 D.L.R. (3d) 413 (S.C.C.)

[Roman Corp. wished to sell its shares in Denison Mines to Hudson's Bay Oil, a foreign-controlled company. Denison Mines was a corporation that was heavily involved in Canadian uranium resources. The agreement was not completed, because two federal cabinet Ministers publicly stated that the government would enact regulations or legislation to prevent any foreign-controlled company from acquiring control of Canadian uranium resources. In view of this, Hudson's Bay Oil refused to complete the contract. Roman Corp. alleged that the Ministers' statements had rendered their Denison shares worthless, and it sued the Ministers for intimidation, conspiracy, and unlawful interference with contractual relations.]

MARTLAND J.: . . .

If valid legislation for that purpose were enacted and it prevented performance of a contract for transfer of such control, there is no doubt that the parties to the agreement would have no cause of action arising out of the enactment of such legislation. A statement of policy made *bona fide* by a Minister of the Crown of the intention of Government to enact such legislation cannot, in my opinion, give rise to a claim in tort for inducing a breach of contract if the parties to the contract elect, in the light of that statement, not to proceed to perform the contract.

The appellants also make a claim in tort for intimidation. In order to succeed under this head, the facts relied upon by the appellants would have to disclose that they had sustained damage by reason of a threat, made by the respondents, of an unlawful act. In my opinion, it cannot be said that a declaration made in good faith by a Minister of the Crown as to Government policy and the intent to implement that policy by appropriate legislation is a threat of an unlawful act. On the contrary, it is part of a Minister's duty to the public to disclose that policy from time to time.

The appellants allege a conspiracy by the respondents to harm the appellants. The leading English authority on the tort of conspiracy is *Crofter Hand Woven Harris Tweed Co., Ltd. v. Veitch*, [1942] A.C. 435. On the assumption that on the facts pleaded it could be said that the respondents combined together, the facts do not establish a combination which would give rise to the tort of conspiracy. I would apply the statement of Lord Simon, L.C., in the above case at pp. 444-5:

> The question to be answered, in determining whether a combination to do an act which damages others is actionable, even though it would not be actionable if done by a single person, is not "did the combiners appreciate, or should they be treated as appreciating, that others would suffer from their action", but "what is the real reason why the combiners did it?" Or, as Lord Cave puts it, "what is the real purpose of the combination?" The test is not what is the natural result to the plaintiffs of such combined action, or what is the resulting damage which the defendants

realize or should realize will follow, but what is in truth the object in the minds of the combiners when they acted as they did.

There is no suggestion in the statement of claim that the actions of the respondents, of which it complains, were taken with a view to injuring the appellants. What they were doing was to enunciate a policy in relation to the control of uranium resources in Canada, the effect of which, if implemented, could prevent the performance of the contract.

The appellants seek a declaration that the respondents committed a tort of unlawful interference with the appellants' economic interest. A claim for such interference, in the circumstances of this case, would have to be brought within the scope of one or more of the three causes of action already discussed.

Counsel for the appellants cited the judgment of this Court in *Roncarelli v. Duplessis* (1959), 16 D.L.R. (2d) 689, [1959] S.C.R. 121. The two cases are hardly analogous. In the *Roncarelli* case the defendant, who was the Prime Minister and the Attorney-General of Quebec, without legal justification and for a wrongful purpose caused the Quebec Liquor Commission to cancel the plaintiff's liquor licence, resulting in substantial damage to his business. He was not acting in the exercise of any of his official powers. In the present case, in my opinion, the respondents, as Ministers of the Crown, were acting in the performance of their public duties in enunciating, in good faith, Government policy.

I would dismiss the appeal with costs.

NOTES AND QUESTIONS

1. The tort of conspiracy can arise in two different kinds of situations. If two individuals make an agreement, the major purpose of which is to harm the plaintiff, they can be held liable in conspiracy. The interesting aspect of this type of conspiracy is that the agreement itself will make the parties liable. An individual who engaged in the same conduct for the same purpose could not be held liable in conspiracy. Indeed, depending on the facts, the individual might be absolved of all liability in tort. *Allen v. Flood*, [1898] A.C. 1 (H.L.). The significance of the agreement has never been satisfactorily explained. Although often criticized, *Allen* has never been overruled. See for example *Sorrell v. Smith*, [1925] All E.R. 1 at 6, 19-21 (H.L.); and Fleming, *The Law of Torts*, 8th ed. (1992), 704-709.

Conspiracy may also be committed if two parties agree to commit an unlawful act and this act causes the plaintiff's loss. In *Can. Cement LaFarge Ltd. v. B.C. Lightweight Aggregate Ltd.; B.C. Lightweight Aggregate Ltd. v. Can. Cement LaFarge Ltd.* (1983), 145 D.L.R. (3d) 385 (S.C.C.), the court held that the plaintiff must prove that the unlawful act was directed against him and that the defendants knew or should have known that he would be injured. In contrast, in England, the courts require proof that the defendant's predominant purpose was to injure the plaintiff.

Which type of conspiracy action was involved in *Posluns* and *Roman*?

2. Why did the conspiracy action fail in *Posluns*? Was Gale J. suggesting that corporate directors could only be liable in conspiracy if they agreed to a course of conduct in advance of a board meeting?

3. Why did the conspiracy action fail in *Roman*? The threatened legislation discussed in *Roman* was never enacted. Is it appropriate for a government to achieve its goals by threatening to enact legislation? Do you agree that the plaintiff failed to establish any intentional economic tort?

4. Conspiracy differs from the other intentional economic torts in that the defendant's purpose or motive is an element of the cause of action. The defendant's motive is also relevant in establishing justification. For a discussion of the difference between conspiracy and interference with contractual relations, see *Garry v. Sherritt Gordon Mines Ltd.* (1987), 42 C.C.L.T. 241 (Sask. C.A.), per Cameron J.A.

5. The defence of justification is unclear. At the risk of oversimplification, conspiracies entered into to advance one's own legitimate interests will likely be justified, whereas those motivated by spite, ill-will or to advance one's prestige will not. For example, in *Mogul S.S. Co. v. McGregor, Gow & Co.*,

[1892] A.C. 25 (H.L.) a conspiracy to cut prices in order to put a competitor out of business was held to be justified as being in the defendant's interest. In *Crofter Hand Woven Harris Tweed Co. v. Vietch*, [1942] 1 All E.R. 142 at 148 (H.L.), the court held that a conspiracy is justified if the parties entering it had the genuine belief that it was serving their "*bona fide* and legitimate interests". Clearly, the concept of justification is defined more broadly in conspiracy than in direct interference with contractual relations. Is this appropriate? Does the justification issue require the courts to make policy decisions in areas in which they lack expertise? See *Hersees Ltd. v. Goldstein* (1963), 38 D.L.R. (2d) 449 (Ont. C.A.); and Heydon, "The Defence of Justification in Cases of Intentionally Caused Economic Loss" (1970), 20 U. of T.L.J. 139.

6. The English common law of conspiracy was re-examined in the 1980s and 1990s by a complicated cycle of litigation initiated by the Lonrho corporation. In 1991, the House of Lords ruled on an interlocutory motion that the tort of conspiracy could be established in two ways: first, by showing that the predominant purpose of the conspirators was an intention to injure the plaintiff in his business; and second, by showing that the conspirators had employed unlawful means to advance otherwise legitimate interests. See *Lonrho plc v. Fayed*, [1991] 3 All E.R. 303 (H.L.). The distinction between a conspiracy to injure business reputation and the tort of defamation was considered in *Lonrho plc v. Fayed (No. 5)*, [1994] 1 All E.R. 188 (C.A.).

7. For additional judicial discussion of conspiracy see *A.G.N.S. v. Christian* (1973), 35 D.L.R. (3d) 692, varied (1975), 9 N.S.R. (2d) 209 (C.A.); *Western Stevedoring Co. v. Pulp, Paper & Woodworkers of Can.* (1975), 61 D.L.R. (3d) 701 (B.C. C.A.); *Maguire v. Calgary* (1983), 25 Alta. L.R. (2d) 249 (C.A.); and *Claiborne Industries Ltd. v. Nat. Bank of Can.* (1989), 69 O.R. (2d) 65 (C.A.). See also *Surrey (District) v. Marall Homes Ltd.* (1988), 48 C.C.L.T. 70 (B.C. S.C.), where the tort of conspiracy was described as an "anachronism" to be restricted to labour and commercial disputes from which it originated. See also Carthy & Miller, "Civil Conspiracy" in L.S.U.C. *Special Lectures: New Developments in the Law of Torts* 1973, 495; Burns, "Civil Conspiracy: An Unwieldy Vessel Rides a Judicial Tempest" (1982), 16 U.B.C.L. Rev. 229; and Sales, "The Tort of Conspiracy and Civil Secondary Liability" (1990), 49 Camb. L.J. 491.

7. The Innominate Action

GERSHMAN v. MAN. VEGETABLE PRODUCERS' MARKETING BD.

[1976] 4 W.W.R. 406, 69 D.L.R. (3d) 114 (Man. C.A.)

The judgment of the Court was delivered by

O'SULLIVAN J.A.: — This is an appeal from a judgment of Solomon, J., of the Court of Queen's Bench awarding to the plaintiff $35,000 and costs in a damage action for the tort of unlawful interference by the defendant with the plaintiff's contractual relationship with Stella Produce Co. Ltd. (hereinafter referred to as Stella Company) and its shareholders.

The defendant is a producers' marketing board established pursuant to the *Natural Products Marketing Act* of Manitoba, R.S.M. 1970, c. N20, and has been given very wide powers, amounting to monopolistic powers, over the marketing of certain vegetables including potatoes and carrots.

The enforcement of regulations made by the producers' board is entrusted to the Manitoba Marketing Board, a separate and distinct entity from the producers' marketing boards.

On August 26, 1974, the defendant adopted the following motion:

Be it resolved that until such time as our account is paid in full, we not [sic] provide credit to any customer of the Board who employs a principal of the Gershman Produce Co. Ltd. in a responsible capacity, but that all sales shall be on a cash or c.o.d. basis.

The minutes of the meeting of the Board on August 26th add to the record of the adoption of this motion the following:

> It was understood that this motion could affect Stella Produce Co. Ltd. and Jobbers' Fruit; also that all shipments would be required to be shipped from the Board warehouse in order to control c.o.d. deliveries.

The resolution of the Board was on the same day communicated by the Board's secretary to Harry Rubenfeld, the principal owner of Stella Company. Rubenfeld disputed that the plaintiff was employed in a responsible capacity since he was warehouse manager and had no control over financial matters; the Board immediately thereupon suspended its normal credit arrangements with the Stella Company which proceeded forthwith to dismiss the plaintiff from his employment and thereafter the Board restored normal credit to the Stella Company.

The learned trial Judge found that the resolution of the Board was passed and implemented not because the Board was concerned about the credit worthiness of the Stella Company, but because it knew that this action would force Stella Company to terminate plaintiff's contractual relationship with it.

In my opinion, the findings of the learned trial Judge are amply justified by the evidence and lead inevitably to his decision that the defendant was liable to the plaintiff for the tort of knowingly procuring a breach by the Stella Company of its contractual relationship with the plaintiff.

The learned trial Judge in his reasons for judgment has reviewed the circumstances which led up to the resolution. It is unnecessary for me to repeat his findings in detail. The plaintiff and his sister were among the principals in a company called Gershman Produce Co. Ltd. which had been active in the wholesale vegetable market in Winnipeg for over 20 years. The Gershman Company had engaged in some litigation disputing on constitutional grounds the validity of the *Natural Products Marketing Act*. It had been subjected to harassment by a number of prosecutions, one of which was dismissed for want of prosecution and one of which was stayed by the Crown after a complaint had been made that it was vexatious.

The Gershman Company had had a fire in March 1974 and subsequently found itself in difficulties. The defendant proceeded on two occasions to petition for its bankruptcy and each time made arrangements to have the petitions dismissed. After the fire, the plaintiff went to work for the Stella Company for $250 per week with an understanding that he would become a part owner through the purchase of the shares of Mr. Rubenfeld, Sr., at a price which had not been fully settled at the time of the defendant's interference.

The learned trial Judge has found, on evidence which clearly supports his findings, that the action of the defendant Board on August 26, 1974, forced the Stella Company to discharge the plaintiff without adequate notice and forced the cancellation of the proven arrangement they had regarding selling shares to the plaintiff.

The plaintiff's sister had gone to work for Jobbers' Fruit; she, too, was the object of the Board's resolution of April 26, 1974, but she is not a plaintiff in these proceedings.

Furthermore, the learned trial Judge has found, on evidence which clearly supports his findings, that there are only seven or eight fruit and vegetable wholesalers in Winnipeg; they are a closely knit group, each member knowing everything about his competitors. He found that the action of the defendant Board not only induced a breach by Stella and its shareholders of their contractual relationship with the plaintiff, but went further and succeeded in ostracizing the plaintiff from a business in which he grew up from childhood with his father. The learned trial Judge found that the secretary of the defendant Board knew that the actions of the Board would force the discharge of the plaintiff from employment and would ostracize the plaintiff from the fruit and vegetable business in Winnipeg.

On these findings, the learned trial Judge followed the principles set out in *Lumley v. Gye*, [1843-60] All E.R. Rep. 208, 2 El. & Bl. 216, 118 E.R. 749. In doing so he said [65 D.L.R. (3d) 181 at p. 189, [1976] 2 W.W.R. 432] that the tort of interfering in contractual relationships covers not only interference with an existing contractual relationship but also interference where "there was an agreement to enter into a contract."

His language suggests that the tort of unlawfully interfering in contractual relationships extends to interference with the formation of such relationships.

The learned trial Judge referred to the dicta of Lord Esher, M.R., in *Temperton v. Russell et al.*, [1893] 1 Q.B. 715 at p. 728:

> It seems rather a fine distinction to say that, where a defendant maliciously induces a person not to carry out a contract already made with the plaintiff and so injures the plaintiff, it is actionable, but where he injures the plaintiff by maliciously preventing a person from entering into a contract with the plaintiff, which he would otherwise have entered into, it is not actionable.

That language has to be assessed in light of the decisions in the subsequent cases of *Allen v. Flood et al.*, [1898] A.C. 1, and the *Crofter's* case, *Crofter Hand Woven Harris Tweed Co., Ltd. et al. v. Veitch et al.*, [1942] A.C. 435. It is said by *Clerk & Lindsell on Torts*, 14th ed. (1975), at p. 395, fn. 10:

> ... the latter decisions make it clear that it is not tortious merely to induce one person not to contract with another. There is a "chasm" between the legality of that action and the unlawfulness of procuring breach of an existing contract.

and at p. 427, para. 808:

> ... it is now recognised to be a "leading heresy" to believe that spiteful interference with another's trade is in itself actionable when no unlawful means have been threatened or employed.

They say that a decision to depart from the principles of *Allen v. Flood et al., supra*, would "put the legality of trade competition completely into the discretion of the judiciary."

It might have been error, in my view, if the learned trial Judge had asserted as a general proposition that the tort of unlawfully interfering in contractual relationship extends to interference with the formation of such relationship. But the language of the learned Judge was geared to the factual situation confronting him and must be so appraised.

On the evidence in this case, there was one relationship with Stella and its shareholders. Here a contractual relationship already existed in respect of the employment. An incident or aspect of that relationship was the likelihood or prospect of the plaintiff acquiring a share interest in the company. What the plaintiff lost by the defendant's wrongful interference was not the opportunity for the formation of a contract but rather the opportunity to extend his already existing contractual relationship of employment into one that would include acquisition of shares. In that respect this case differs from *Allen v. Flood et al.* and the *Crofter's* case, *supra*. The case before us is, therefore, not one in which it is necessary to hold that a defendant is liable for interfering with an agreement to agree.

The judgment is on sound ground in holding that damages for the tort of unlawfully procuring a breach of contract are not limited to those damages which would have been given in an action in contract between the parties to the contract. Counsel for the defendant Board argued that the plaintiff should not have been awarded more than, say two weeks' or a month's pay, even if the defendant Board were liable for procuring a breach of contract, since on the hypothesis that the plaintiff's contract was unlawfully terminated all that an employee can get for lawful termination of employment is wages in lieu of notice.

In my opinion, this submission ignores the fact that damages are given in tort not for the breach of contract but for the wrongful act of procuring its breach, and hence the plaintiff is entitled to be compensated for all the damage that flows from the tortious act.

. . .

It follows, in my opinion, that by reason of its tortious conduct in unlawfully procuring a breach of the contractual relationship between the Stella Company and the plaintiff, the defendant Board was liable for general damages not limited to those which would have been recoverable by the plaintiff in contract but taking into account that as a result of the defendant's tortious conduct the plaintiff lost a valuable position, the plaintiff lost a valuable opportunity to become re-established in the fruit and vegetable-marketing business through the purchase of shares in Stella Company, and the plaintiff lost access to participation in the other companies which ostracized the plaintiff as a result of the Board's attitude and conduct.

Moreover, I think that the findings of the learned trial Judge give rise to liability on other heads besides that of unlawful interference in contractual relationships.

I think that the defendant Board was liable for the tort of intimidation and for the tort of unlawful interference with economic interests.

It is true that the plaintiff's statement of claim is framed with a view to bringing the material facts within the tort of interference with contractual relationships, but it is well settled since the *Judicature Act* reforms that a plaintiff is not to be put out of Court because he has asked for the wrong remedy as long as the material facts which he pleads and proves give rise to some remedy.

It may indeed be that the distinction between the various torts usually discussed under the general heading of "economic torts" is somewhat artificial, although a recognition of the distinctions between them may be helpful.

In any event, it is clear, in my opinion, that *Clerk & Lindsell, op. cit.,* are right when they say at pp. 414-5, para. 802:

> A commits a tort [that of intimidation] if he delivers a threat to B that he will commit an act or use means unlawful as against B, as a result of which B does or refrains from doing some act which he is entitled to do, thereby causing damage either to himself or to C. The tort is one of intention and the plaintiff, whether it be B or C, must be a person whom A intended to injure. Doubts about the existence of this tort were set at rest by *Rookes v. Barnard*, [1964] A.C. 1129 . . .

The editors continue at p. 415, para. 803:

> A threat [for the purpose of this tort] is something which puts pressure, perhaps extreme pressure, on the person to whom it is addressed to take a particular course, something by means of which that person is "improperly coerced." A threat is an "intimation by one to another that unless the latter does or does not do something the former will do something which the latter will not like." The threat must be coercive; it must be of the "or else" kind. Furthermore, the concept is not limited to express threats ...

It is clear that the threatened act must itself be unlawful.

As Lord Wright said in the *Crofter* case, [1942] A.C. 435 at p. 467:

> There is nothing unlawful in giving a warning or intimation that if the party addressed pursues a certain line of conduct, others may act in a manner which he will not like and which will be prejudicial to his interests, so long as nothing unlawful is threatened or done.

. . .

If, therefore, the means proposed by the defendant Board were unlawful, the defendant Board was liable for threatening to commit an unlawful act for the purpose of inducing Stella and its shareholders from continuing their relationship with the plaintiff, whether that relationship was contractual or not.

Furthermore, to quote again from *Clerk & Lindsell, op. cit.*, at p. 425, para. 808:

> There [also] exists a tort of uncertain ambit which consists in one person using unlawful means with the object and effect of causing damage to another. In such cases, the plaintiff is availed of a cause of action which is different from those so far discussed.

This tort was described by Lord Reid in *J.T. Stratford & Son Ltd. v. Lindley et al.*, [1965] A.C. 269 at p. 324:

> In addition to interfering with existing contracts the respondents' action made it practically impossible for the appellants to do any new business with the barge hirers. It was not disputed that such interference with business is tortious if any unlawful means are employed.

In the same case at pp. 328-9, Viscount Radcliffe said: "... the defendants have inflicted injury on the plaintiffs in the conduct of their business and have resorted to unlawful means to bring this about." There were therefore "two sets of tortious ... acts which the plaintiffs can pray in aid against them."

To see if the defendant Board is liable under these heads of tort, in addition to its liability for direct interference with contract, it is necessary to consider the lawfulness of the action threatened by the defendant Board to interfere with the Gershman family.

What the defendant Board did was, to use a colloquial expression, "black-list" the Gershman family.

In my opinion, its action in "black-listing" the Gershman family was illegal and quite beyond the scope of its authority.

The learned trial Judge made findings of fact which clearly show that the Board did not act in good faith. He said [at pp. 191-2]:

> As the hearing progressed and the evidence disclosed more and more acts of vindictiveness by the Board against plaintiff, I found it difficult to believe that this drama was acted out in 1974 in Manitoba and was not from the pages of medieval history. Never in all my 16 years of public life and 18 years on the bench have I come across a more flagrant abuse of power....

In order to demonstrate to plaintiff that his disagreements would not be tolerated, the Board maliciously, with vindictiveness and under pretence that such actions were done to discharge the trust it owed the producers, harassed plaintiff until it drove him out of the wholesale fruit and vegetable business.

. . .

In any event, even if the learned trial Judge went too far in linking the Board's resolution of August 26, 1974, with a course of conduct which he found to be directed at driving the Gershman family out of the wholesale market in Winnipeg (and I do not so find), I do not think that counsel for the defendant Board has shown any justification for the conduct of the defendant Board.

If its intention was to black-list the plaintiff in order to force the plaintiff to see to the payment of the debts of a limited company of which the plaintiff was a shareholder, its conduct was still illegal and wrong.

. . .

[Judgment for the plaintiff.]

NOTES AND QUESTIONS

1. What unlawful means were employed by the defendants in *Gershman*? Can you reconcile Martland J.'s comments on the tort of unlawful interference with economic relations in *Roman*, with the decision in *Gershman*? Is *Gershman* consistent with Gale J.'s observation in *Posluns* that "a bad motive does not *per se* convert an otherwise lawful act into an unlawful one"?

2. If the agreement itself constitutes an unlawful means in conspiracy, then direct interference with contractual relations stands alone as actionable without proof of unlawful means. Can you explain why?

3. As illustrated in *Gershman*, the plaintiff will often succeed in more than one of the intentional economic torts. Similarly, as illustrated in *Roman*, if the plaintiff fails in one of these actions, he will often fail in the others. Is there any reason to retain all of these separate causes of action?

4. In the United States, many of the issues governed by our nominate intentional economic torts are governed by a single *prima facie* tort doctrine. It holds the defendant liable for any deliberate interference with the plaintiff's economic interests, unless he can justify his conduct. See *Tuttle v. Buck* (1909), 119 N.W. 946 (Minn. S.C.); Forkosch, "An Analysis of the *Prima Facie* Tort Cause of Action" (1975), 42 Cornell L.Q. 465; and Shapiro, "The *Prima Facie* Tort Doctrine: Acknowledging the Need for Judicial Scrutiny of Malice" (1983), 63 Boston U.L. Rev. 1101.

The same doctrine might have developed in England. In *Keeble v. Hickeringill* (1706), 103 E.R. 1127 at 1128 (Q.B.), the court stated: ". . . he who hinders another in his trade or livelihood is liable to an action for so injuring him." However, the *prima facie* tort approach was rejected by the House of Lords in *Allen v. Flood*, [1898] A.C. 1, which held that in the absence of a conspiracy, the intentional interference with economic interests by lawful means was not actionable.

The High Court of Australia recognized a principle very similar to the *prima facie* tort doctrine in *Beaudesert Shire Council v. Smith* (1966), 120 C.L.R. 145. The court stated at 215: ". . . independently of trespass, negligence or nuisance but by an action upon the case, a person who suffers harm or loss as the inevitable consequence of the unlawful, intentional and positive acts of another is entitled to damages from that other." This decision has generated considerable criticism and has been largely ignored by other courts. See Dworkin and Harrari, "The *Beaudesert* Decision — Raising the Ghost of the Action on the Case" (1967), 40 Aust. L.J. 296, 347; and Sadler, "Wither *Beaudesert Shire Council v. Smith*?" (1984), 58 Aust. L.J. 38.

In theory, what is the difference between the *prima facie* tort doctrine and the nominate economic torts? How do these principles differ from the principle in *Beaudesert*? In what circumstances would a defendant be held liable under the *prima facie* tort doctrine or *Beaudesert*, but not be held liable under Canadian case law? Which approach is preferable?

5. For other examples of the innominate action see *Int. Brotherhood of Teamsters v. Therien*, [1960] S.C.R. 265; *J.T. Stratford & Son Ltd. v. Lindley*, [1965] A.C. 307 (H.L.); *Volkswagen Can. Ltd. v. Spicer*

(1978), 91 D.L.R. (3d) 42 (N.S. C.A.); and *Can. Safeway Ltd. v. Man. Food & Commercial Workers Local 832* (1983), 22 Man. R. (2d) 12 (C.A.). For a critique of *Canada Safeway* see Vincent, "Everything You Want in a Tort — and a Little Bit More" (1983), 25 C.C.L.T. 10.

REVIEW PROBLEM

Import Company purchased 50 mink coats and contracted to supply them to its best customer, Bridget Furs. The wholesale price of the furs was so low that Bridget advertised them at 25% below the regular price in a brochure that it mailed to 250 preferred customers. They offered to sell the coats to the first 50 customers who presented preferred customers' cards on January 20th.

Retail Union represented the employees of Bridget and was engaged in a lawful strike at the time. The strike was proving ineffective because customers were ignoring the picket lines around the store. Consequently, Retail Union set up "secondary picket" lines around suppliers of Bridget, including Import Company. Secondary picketing is not referred to in any relevant legislation. The employees of Import, members of another union, refused to cross the picket line, thereby preventing the delivery of the mink coats to Bridget.

Steven, an independent trucker, telephoned Import and volunteered to deliver the coats for a fee. Import's management doubted that Steven would be able to do so, but indicated that they would agree if he could enter their premises. Import's guess proved correct as Steven was turned back at the gates by an angry mob of picketers.

Import management then met with Retail Union, which agreed to remove the picket line if Import returned the furs to the American supplier. Import agreed on 19th January. As a result, Bridget was forced to turn away 100 preferred customers, who had lined up at the store on January 20th for the sale.

Discuss the possible economic torts arising from this incident.

22

NEGLIGENT MISREPRESENTATION

1. Introduction
2. Negligent Misrepresentation Causing Pure Economic Loss
3. Negligent Misrepresentation and Contract

1. Introduction

The negligence cases in this chapter differ in two respects from those discussed previously. First, they concern liability for written and oral communications, rather than for physical acts or omissions. Second, many of the cases raise the issue of liability for "pure" economic losses, that is, financial losses which are causally independent of personal injury or property damage.

The typical plaintiff in a negligent misrepresentation action has relied on inaccurate or incomplete advice, written or spoken, and has suffered a pure economic loss as a result. The typical defendant is a professional or quasi-professional advice-giver such as a lawyer, stockbroker, banker, business consultant, or accountant. Such relationships frequently involve contracts, and contractual rights and remedies. Consequently, this chapter will consider the question of "concurrent liability" in contract and tort.

2. Negligent Misrepresentation Causing Pure Economic Loss

(a) WHEN DOES A DUTY OF CARE ARISE?

HEDLEY BYRNE & CO. v. HELLER & PARTNERS LTD.

[1963] 2 All E.R. 575 (H.L.)

LORD REID: — My Lords, this case raises the important question whether and in what circumstances a person can recover damages for loss suffered by reason of his having relied on an innocent but negligent misrepresentation. I cannot do better than adopt the following statement of the case from the judgment of McNair, J.:

> This case raised certain interesting questions of law as to the liability of bankers giving references as to the credit-worthiness of their customers. The [appellants] are a firm of advertising agents. The [respondents] are merchant bankers. In outline, the [appellants'] case against the [respondents] is that, having placed on behalf of a client, Easipower, Ltd., on credit terms substantial orders for advertising time on television programmes and for advertising space in certain newspapers on terms under which they, the [appellants], became personally liable to the television and newspaper companies, they caused inquiries to be made through their own bank of the [respondents] as to the credit-worthiness of Easipower, Ltd. who were customers of the [respon-

dents] and were given by the [respondents] satisfactory references. These references turned out not to be justified, and the [appellants] claim that in reliance on the references, which they had no reason to question, they refrained from cancelling the orders so as to relieve themselves of their current liabilities.

The appellants, becoming doubtful about the financial position of Easipower, Ltd., got their bank to communicate with the respondents who were Easipower, Ltd.'s bankers. This was done by telephone and the following is a contemporaneous note of the conversation which both parties agree is accurate:

> Heller & Partners, Ltd. Minutes of telephone conversation. Call from National Provincial Bank, Ltd., 15, Bishopsgate, E.C.2. 18.8.58. Person called: L. Heller, re Easipower, Ltd. They wanted to know in confidence, and without responsibility on our part, the respectability and standing of Easipower, Ltd., and whether they would be good for an advertising contract for £8,000 to £9,000. I replied the company recently opened an account with us. Believed to be respectably constituted and considered good for its normal business engagements. The company is a subsidiary of Pena Industries, Ltd., which is in liquidation, but we understand that the managing director, Mr. Williams, is endeavouring to buy the shares of Easipower, Ltd., from the liquidator. We believe that the company would not undertake any commitments they are unable to fulfil.

Some months later the appellants sought a further reference and on Nov. 7, 1958, the city office of National Provincial Bank, Ltd. wrote to the respondents in the following terms:

> Dear Sir. We shall be obliged by your opinion in confidence as to the respectability and standing of Easipower, Ltd., 27, Albemarle Street, London, W.I. and by stating whether you consider them trustworthy, in the way of business, to the extent of £100,000 per annum, advertising contract. Yours faithfully, . . .

On Nov. 11, 1958, the respondents replied as follows:

CONFIDENTIAL

> For your private use and without responsibility on the part of the bank or its officials.
> Dear Sir, In reply to your inquiry of 7th instant. We beg to advise: — Re E . . . . Ltd. Respectably constituted company, considered good for its ordinary business engagements. Your figures are larger than we are accustomed to see. Yours faithfully, . . . Per pro. Heller & Partners, Ltd.

National Provincial Bank communicated these replies to their customers, the appellants, and it is not suggested that this was improper or not warranted by modern custom. The appellants relied on these statements and as a result they lost over £17,000 when Easipower, Ltd., went into liquidation.

The appellants now seek to recover this loss from the respondents as damages on the ground that these replies were given negligently and in breach of the respondents' duty to exercise care in giving them.

. . .

Before coming to the main question of law, it may be well to dispose of an argument that there was no sufficiently close relationship between these parties to give rise to any duty. It is said that the respondents did not know the precise purpose of the inquiries and did not even know whether the National Provincial Bank wanted the information for its own use or for the use of a customer: they knew nothing of the appellants. I would reject that argument. They knew that the inquiry was in connection with an advertising contract, and it was at least probable that the information was wanted by the advertising contractors. It seems to me quite immaterial that they did not know who these contractors were: there is no suggestion of any speciality which could have influenced them in deciding whether to give information or in what form to give it. I shall therefore treat this as if it were a case where a negligent misrepresentation is made directly to the person seeking information, opinion or advice, and I shall not attempt to decide what kind or degree of proximity is necessary before there can be a duty owed by the defendant to the plaintiff.

The appellants' first argument was based on *Donoghue v. Stevenson* [[1932] All E.R. Rep. 1]. That is a very important decision, but I do not think that it has any direct bearing on this case. That decision may encourage us to develop existing lines of authority, but it cannot entitle us to disregard them. Apart altogether from authority, I would think that the law must treat negligent words differently from negligent acts. The law ought so far as possible to reflect the standards of the reasonable man, and that is what *Donoghue v. Stevenson* [*supra*] sets out to do. The most obvious difference between negligent words and negligent acts is this. Quite careful people often express definite opinions on social or informal occasions even when they see that others are likely to be influenced by them; and they often do that without taking that care which they would take if asked for their opinion professionally or in a business connection. The appellant agrees that there can be no duty of care on such occasions, and we were referred to American and South African authorities where that is recognised, although their law appears to have gone much further than ours has yet done. But it is at least unusual casually to put into circulation negligently made articles which are dangerous. A man might give a friend a negligently-prepared bottle of homemade wine and his friend's guests might drink it with dire results. But it is by no means clear that those guests would have no action against the negligent manufacturer.

Another obvious difference is that a negligently made article will only cause one accident, and so it is not very difficult to find the necessary degree of proximity or neighbourhood between the negligent manufacturer and the person injured. But words can be broadcast with or without the consent or the foresight of the speaker or writer. It would be one thing to say that the speaker owes a duty to a limited class, but it would be going very far to say that he owes a duty to every ultimate "consumer" who acts on those words to his detriment. It would be no use to say that a speaker or writer owes a duty but can disclaim responsibility if he wants to. He, like the manufacturer, could make it part of a contract that he is not to be liable for his negligence: but that contract would not protect him in a question with a third party, at least if the third party was unaware of it.

So it seems to me that there is good sense behind our present law that in general an innocent but negligent misrepresentation gives no cause of action. There must be something more than the mere misstatement. I therefore turn to the authorities to see what more is required. The most natural requirement would be that expressly or by implication from the circumstances the speaker or writer has undertaken some responsibility, and that appears to me not to conflict with any authority which is binding on this House.

. . .

In *Nocton v. Lord Ashburton* [[1914-15] All E.R. Rep. 45] a solicitor was sued for fraud. Fraud was not proved, but he was held liable for negligence. Viscount Haldane, L.C., dealt with *Derry v. Peek* [(1889), 14 App. Cas. 337] and pointed out that while the relationship of the parties in that case was not enough, the case did not decide

> that where a different sort of relationship ought to be inferred from the circumstances, the case is to be concluded by asking whether an action for deceit will lie . . . There are other obligations besides that of honesty the breach of which may give a right to damages. These obligations depend on principles which the judges have worked out in the fashion that is characteristic of a system where much of the law has always been judge-made and unwritten.

. . .

Lord Haldane gave a further statement of his view in *Robinson v. National Bank of Scotland* [(1916) S.C. (H.L.) 154], a case to which I shall return. Having said that in that case there was no duty excepting the duty of common honesty, he went on to say:

> In saying that I wish emphatically to repeat what I said in advising this House in the case of *Nocton v. Lord Ashburton*, that it is a great mistake to suppose that, because the principle in *Derry v. Peek* clearly covers all cases of the class to which I have referred, therefore the freedom of action of the courts in recognising special duties arising out of other kinds of relationship which they find established by the evidence is in any way affected. I think, as I said in *Nocton's* case, that an exaggerated view was taken by a good many people of the scope of the decision in *Derry v. Peek*. The whole of the doctrine as to fiduciary relationships, as to the duty of care arising from implied as well as express contracts, as to the duty of care arising from other special relationships which the courts may find to exist in particular cases, still remains, and I should be very sorry if any word fell from me which should suggest that the courts are in any way hampered in recognising that the duty of care may be established when such cases really occur.

. . .

Lord Haldane did not think that a duty to take care must be limited to cases of fiduciary relationship in the narrow sense of relationships which had been recognised by the Court of Chancery as being of a fiduciary character. He speaks of other special relationships, and I can see no logical stopping place short of all those relationships where it is plain that the party seeking information or advice was trusting the other to exercise such a degree of care as the circumstances required, where it was reasonable for him to do that, and where the other gave the information or advice when he knew or ought to have known that the inquirer was relying on him. I say "ought to have known" because in questions of negligence we now apply the objective standard of what the reasonable man would have done.

A reasonable man, knowing that he was being trusted or that his skill and judgment were being relied on, would, I think, have three courses open to him. He could keep silent or decline to give the information or advice sought; or he could give an answer with a clear qualification that he accepted no responsibility for it or that it was given without that reflection or inquiry which a careful answer would require; or he could simply answer without any such qualification. If he chooses to adopt the last course he must, I think, be held to have accepted some responsibility for his answer being given carefully, or to have accepted a relationship with the inquirer which requires him to exercise such care as the circumstances require.

If that is right, then it must follow that *Candler v. Crane, Christmas & Co.* [[1951] 1 All E.R. 426] was wrongly decided. There the plaintiff wanted to see the accounts of a company before deciding to invest in it. The defendants were the company's accountants, and they were told by the company to complete the company's accounts as soon as possible because they were to be shown to the plaintiff who was a potential investor in the company. At the company's request the defendants showed the completed accounts to the plaintiff, discussed them with him, and allowed him to take a copy. The accounts had been carelessly prepared and gave a wholly misleading picture. It was obvious to the defendants that the plaintiff was relying on their skill and judgment and on their having exercised that care which by contract they owed to the company, and I think that any reasonable man in the plaintiff's shoes would have relied on that. This seems to me to be a typical case of agreeing to assume a responsibility: they knew why the plaintiff wanted to see the accounts and why their employers, the company, wanted them to be shown to him, and agreed to show them to him without even a suggestion that he should not rely on them.

· · ·

. . . however here the appellants' bank, who were their agents in making the inquiry, began by saying "that they wanted to know in confidence and without responsibility on our part", that is, on the part of the respondents. So I cannot see how the appellants can now be entitled to disregard that and maintain that the respondents did incur a responsibility to them.

The appellants founded on a number of cases in contract where very clear words were required to exclude the duty of care which would otherwise have flowed from the contract. To that argument there are, I think, two answers. In the case of a contract it is necessary to exclude liability for negligence, but in this case the question is whether an undertaking to assume a duty to take care can be inferred: and that is a very different matter. And, secondly, even in cases of contract general words may be sufficient if there was no other kind of liability to be excluded except liability for negligence: the general rule is that a party is not exempted from liability for negligence "unless adequate words are used" — per Scrutton L.J. in *Rutter v. Palmer* [[1922] All E.R. Rep. 367]. It being admitted that there was here a duty to give an honest reply, I do not see what further liability there could be to exclude except liability for negligence: there being no contract there was no question of warranty.

I am therefore of opinion that it is clear that the respondents never undertook any duty to exercise care in giving their replies. The appellants cannot succeed unless there was such a duty and therefore in my judgment this appeal must be dismissed.

LORD MORRIS OF BORTH-Y-GEST: . . . My Lords, I consider that it follows and that it should now be regarded as settled that if someone possessed of a special skill undertakes, quite irrespective of contract, to apply that skill for the assistance of another person who relies upon such skill, a duty of care will arise. The fact that the service is to be given by means of or by the instrumentality of words can make no difference. Furthermore, if in a sphere in which a person is so placed that others could reasonably rely upon his judgment or his skill or upon his ability to make careful inquiry, a person takes it upon himself to give information or advice to, or allows his information or advice to be passed on to, another person who, as he knows or should know, will place reliance upon it, then a duty of care will arise.

. . .

LORD HODSON: . . . Was there then a special relationship here? I cannot exclude from consideration the actual terms in which the reference was given and I cannot see how the appellants can get over the difficulty which these words put in their way. They cannot say that the respondents are seeking to, as it were, contract out of their duty by the use of language which is insufficient for the purpose, if the truth of the matter is that the respondents never assumed a duty of care nor was such a duty imposed on them.

The first question is whether a duty was ever imposed and the language used must be considered before the question can be answered. In the case of a person giving a reference I see no objection in law or morals to the giver of the reference protecting himself by giving it without taking responsibility for anything more than the honesty of his opinion which must involve without taking responsibility for negligence in giving that opinion.

. . .

LORD DEVLIN: — . . . Originally it was thought that the tort of negligence must be confined entirely to deeds and could not extend to words. That was supposed to have been decided by *Derry v. Peek* [*supra*]. I cannot imagine that anyone would now dispute that if this were the law, the law would be gravely defective. The practical proof of this is that the supposed deficiency was in relation to the facts in *Derry v. Peek* [*supra*] immediately made good by Act of Parliament. Today it is unthinkable that the law could permit directors to be as careless as they liked in the statements they made in a prospectus.

. . .

This is why the distinction is now said to depend on whether financial loss is caused through physical injury or whether it is caused directly. The interposition of the physical injury is said to make a difference of principle. I can find neither logic nor common sense in this. If irrespective of contract, a doctor negligently advises a patient that he can safely pursue his occupation and he cannot and the patient's health suffers and he loses his livelihood, the patient has a remedy. But if the doctor negligently advises him that he cannot safely pursue his occupation when in fact he can and he loses his livelihood, there is said to be no remedy. Unless, of course, the patient was a private patient and the doctor accepted half a guinea for his trouble: then the patient can recover all. I am bound to say, my Lords, that I think this to be nonsense. It is not the sort of nonsense that can arise even in the best system of law out of the need to draw nice distinctions between borderline cases. It arises, if it is the law, simply out of a refusal to make sense. The line is not drawn on any intelligible principle. It just happens to be the line which those who have been driven from the extreme assertion that negligent statements in the absence of contractual or fiduciary duty give no cause of action have in the course of their retreat so far reached.

. . .

QUEEN v. COGNOS INC.

[1993] 1 S.C.R. 87

IACOBUCCI J.: —

A. *Introduction*

This appeal involves an action in tort to recover damages caused by alleged negligent misrepresentations made in the course of a hiring interview by an employer (the respondent), through its representative, to a prospective employee (the appellant) with respect to the employer and the nature and existence of the employment opportunity. Though a relatively recent feature of the common law, the tort of negligent misrepresentation relied on by the appellant and first recognized by the House of Lords in *Hedley Byrne, supra*, is now an established principle of Canadian tort law. This court has confirmed on many occasions, sometimes tacitly, that an action in tort may lie, in appropriate circumstances, for damages caused by a misrepresentation made in a negligent manner. . . .

While the doctrine of *Hedley Byrne* is well established in Canada, the exact breadth of its applicability is, like any common law principle, subject to debate and to continuous development. At the time this appeal was heard, there had only been a handful of cases where the tort of negligent misrepresentation was used in a pre-employment context such as the one involved here. . . .

Some have suggested that it is inappropriate to extend the application of *Hedley Byrne, supra*, to representations made by an employer to a prospective employee in the course of an interview because it places a heavy burden on employers. As will be apparent from my reasons herein, I disagree in principle with this view. However, I find it unnecessary for the purposes of this appeal to engage in a general and abstract discussion on the applicability of the tort of negligent misrepresentation to pre-employment representations. The thrust of the respondent's argument before this court is not that the appellant's action is unfounded in law. Rather, the respondent argues that the appellant has not made out a case for compensation based on negligent misrepresentation. Accordingly, this appeal may be disposed of simply by considering whether or not the required elements under the *Hedley Byrne* doctrine are established in the facts of this case. In my view, they are.

. . .

The required elements for a successful *Hedley Byrne*, supra, claim have been stated in many authorities, sometimes in varying forms. The decisions of this court cited above suggest five general requirements: (1) there must be a duty of care based on a "special relationship" between the representor and the representee; (2) the representation in question must be untrue, inaccurate, or misleading; (3) the representor must have acted negligently in making said misrepresentation; (4) the representee must have relied, in a reasonable manner, on said negligent misrepresentation; and (5) the reliance must have been detrimental to the representee in the sense that damages resulted. In the case at bar, the trial judge found that all elements were present and allowed the appellant's claim.

In particular, White J. found, as a fact, that the respondent's representative, Mr. Johnston, had misrepresented the nature and existence of the employment opportunity for which the appellant had applied, and that the appellant had relied to his detriment on those misrepresentations. These findings of fact were undisturbed by the Court of Appeal and, except for a few passing remarks, the respondent does not challenge them before this court. Thus, the second, fourth, and fifth requirements are not in question here.

The only issues before this court deal with the duty of care owed to the appellant in the circumstances of this case and the alleged breach of this duty (i.e., the alleged negligence). The respondent concedes that a "special relationship" existed between itself (through its representative) and the appellant so as to give rise to a duty of care. However, it argues that this duty is negated by a disclaimer contained in the employment contract signed by the appellant more than two weeks after the interview. Furthermore, the respondent argues that any misrepresentations made during the hiring interview were not made in a negligent manner. For reasons that follow, it is my view that both submissions fail.

However, before turning to these issues, I intend to deal with a preliminary matter not directly raised in argument. This appeal was argued before this court in close proximity to the case *BG Checo International Ltd. v. British Columbia Hydro & Power Authority*, S.C.C., Nos. 21939 and 21955, January 21, 1993 [reported 75 B.C.L.R. (2d) 145]. That case involved circumstances somewhat similar to those in the present appeal in that it also dealt with a claim for damages based on an alleged negligent misrepresentation stemming from pre-contractual negotiations. Generally speaking, in *BG Checo* as in the case at bar, it was argued that certain representations made in a pre-contractual setting did not correspond with the post-agreement reality and were made in a negligent manner. In both cases, the defendants relied on the contract signed by the parties subsequent to the alleged negligent misrepresentation in order to bar the plaintiffs' claim in tort. As my conclusion in *BG Checo* is opposite from the one I take herein, I believe it is useful at the outset to explain why this case is clearly distinguishable from *BG Checo*. In doing so, my hope is to clarify some of the confusion which currently exists with respect to pre-contractual negligent misrepresentations.

C. The Duty of Care Owed to the Appellant

The respondent concedes that it itself and its representative, Mr. Johnston, owed a duty of care towards the six job applicants being interviewed, including the appellant, not to make negligent misrepresentations as to Cognos and the nature and permanence of the job being offered. In so doing, it accepts as correct the findings of both the trial judge and the Court of Appeal that there existed between the parties a "special relationship" within the meaning of *Hedley Byrne*, supra.

In my view, this concession is a sensible one. Without a doubt, when all the circumstances of this case are taken into account, the respondent and Mr. Johnston were under an obligation to exercise due diligence throughout the hiring interview with respect to the representations made to the appellant about Cognos and the nature and existence of the employment opportunity.

There is some debate in academic circles, fuelled by various judicial pronounce-ments, about the proper test that should be applied to determine when a "special relationship" exists between the representor and the representee which will give rise to a duty of care. Some have suggested that "foreseeable and reasonable reliance" on the representations is the key element to the analysis, while others speak of "voluntary assumption of responsibility" on the part of the representor. Recently, in *Caparo Industries plc v. Dickman*, [1990] 1 All E.R. 568 (H.L.), a case unlike the present one in that there the whole issue revolved around the existence of a duty of care, the House of Lords suggested that three criteria determine the imposition of a duty of care: foreseeability of damage; proximity of relationship; and the reasonableness or otherwise of imposing a duty.

For my part, I find it unnecessary — and unwise in view of the respondent's concession — to take part in this debate. Regardless of the test applied, the result which the circumstances of this case dictate would be the same. It was foreseeable that the appellant would be relying on the information given during the hiring interview in order to make his career decision. It was reasonable for the appellant to rely on said representations. There is nothing before this court that suggests that the respondent was not, at the time of the interview or shortly thereafter, assuming responsibility for what was being represented to the appellant by Mr. Johnston. As noted by the trial judge, Mr. Johnston discussed the Multiview project in an unqualified manner, without making any relevant caveats. The alleged disclaimers of responsibility are provisions of a contract signed more than two weeks after the interview. For reasons that I give in the last part of this analysis, these provisions are not valid disclaimers. They do not negate the duty of care owed to the appellant or prevent it from arising as in *Hedley Byrne* and *Carman Construction*, supra. It was foreseeable to the respondent and its representative that the appellant would sustain damages should the representations relied on prove to be false and negligently made. There was, undoubtedly, a relationship of proximity between the parties at all material times. Finally, it is not unreasonable to impose a duty of care in all the circumstances of this case; quite the contrary, it would be unreasonable *not* to impose such a duty. In short, therefore, there existed between the parties a "special relationship" at the time of the interview. The respondent and its representative Mr. Johnston were under a duty of care during the pre-employment interview to exercise reasonable care and diligence in making representations as to the employer and the employment opportunity being offered.

. . .

NOTES AND QUESTIONS

1. Why did common law judges hesitate to recognize negligent misrepresentation as an independent cause of action? What factors did their Lordships consider in formulating the special duty of care in *Hedley*? How did *Donoghue* bear on the outcome of *Hedley*? What are the elements of this cause of action?

2. How has the Supreme Court of Canada decision in *Cognos* refined the elements of negligent misrepresentation? Does the approach in *Cognos* differ from that in *Hedley*? On what basis did Mr. Justice Iacobucci find that the appellant was owed a duty of care?

3. The courts will not impose a duty of care in negligent misrepresentation cases unless a "special relationship" exists between the parties. According to *Cognos*, how have the courts defined "special relationship"? Does this concept have clear boundaries? For judicial interpretations of the special relationship concept, see *Central B.C. Planers Ltd. v. Hocker* (1970), 10 D.L.R. (3d) 689 (B.C. C.A.), aff'd. (1971), 16 D.L.R. (3d) 368n (S.C.C.); *Elderkin v. Merrill Lynch, Royal Securities Ltd.* (1977), 80 D.L.R. (3d) 313 (N.S. C.A.); *Sodd Corp. v. Tessis* (1977), 79 D.L.R. (3d) 632 (Ont. C.A.); *V.K. Mason Construction Ltd. v. Bank of Nova Scotia*, [1985] 1 S.C.R. 271; *Gallant v. Central Credit Union Ltd.* (1994), 22 C.C.L.T. 251 (P.E.I. T.D.); and *Hercules Management Ltd. v. Ernst & Young* (1995), 24 C.C.L.T. (2d) 284 (Man. C.A.).

4. A plaintiff in a negligent misrepresentation case might establish duty of care, but fail to prove some other element of the tort. For example, in *Roncato v. Caverly* (1991), 5 O.R. (3d) 714, the Ontario Court of Appeal held that the defendant owed the plaintiff a duty of care and breached the standard of care, but dismissed the action because the plaintiff failed to prove that the misrepresentation had caused his loss. Similarly, in *Auto Concrete Curb Ltd. v. South Nation River Conservation Authority* (1993), 17 C.C.L.T. (2d) 123, the Supreme Court of Canada found that the defendant engineers owed the plaintiff a duty of care, but had not breached the standard of care.

5. Another frequently contentious issue is the reasonableness of the plaintiff's reliance on the defendant's negligent misstatement. See, for example, *Dutton v. Bognor Regis United Building Co.*, [1972] 1 All E.R. 562 (C.A.); *Burman's Beauty Supplies Ltd. v. Kempster* (1974), 48 D.L.R. (3d) 682 (Ont. Co. Ct.); and *Gordelli Management Ltd. v. Turk* (1991), 6 O.R. (3d) 521 (Gen. Div.).

6. Before *Hedley Byrne*, common law judges had recognized that liability could arise when negligent statements caused physical losses. See *Clayton v. Woodman & Son (Builders) Ltd.*, [1961] 3 All E.R. 249 (Q.B.). For post-*Hedley* examples, see *Manitoba Sausage Manufacturing Co. v. Winnipeg (City)* (1976), 1 C.C.L.T. 221 (Man. C.A.); and *Hendrick v. De Marsh* (1984), 45 O.R. (2d) 463 (H.C.). In *T. (a minor) v. Surrey County Council*, [1994] 4 All E.R. 577 (Q.B.), a social welfare agency was held liable for the physical injuries caused by a child-minder that had been negligently recommended by one of its workers. Scott Baker J. ruled that the "plaintiff's position is stronger because he suffered physical rather than mere economic loss". See also, *Spring v. Guardian Assurance plc*, [1994] 3 All E.R. 129, in which the House of Lords found an employer liable for the negligent preparation of a reference.

7. The courts recognize the defence of contributory negligence in negligent representation cases. How can the courts base the duty on reliance, but then apportion the loss because the reliance was negligent? In *Grand Restaurants of Can. Ltd. v. Toronto* (1981), 32 O.R. (2d) 757 (H.C.), aff'd. (1982), 39 O.R. (2d) 752 (C.A.), Trainor J. stated at 775: "there is a distinction at law between reasonable reliance as a necessary prerequisite to ground liability, to constitute the cause of action under *Hedley Bryne*, and reliance in the context of contributory negligence as simply a factor going to the extent of the damage suffered." See generally Roth, "Liability for Loose Lips" (1986/7), 51 Sask. L.R. 317 at 325-26; and Feldthusen, *Economic Negligence*, 3rd ed. (1994), 126-27.

8. A controversial modification to *Hedley Byrne* may have been intended by the Privy Council in *Mutual Life And Citizens' Assur. Co. v. Evatt*, [1971] 1 All E.R. 150 (P.C.). The court reviewed the plaintiff's pleadings in which he alleged that he had received negligent financial advice from the defendant, his own insurance company, about the financial affairs of a subsidiary company of the defendant. The Privy Council held that no valid cause of action had been pleaded. Some courts interpreted this decision to mean that a negligent misrepresentation can only be maintained against defendants who were in the business or profession of giving the relevant advice. The other view was that being in the business was merely the usual manner of holding out that one was undertaking responsibility for such advice, and that the claim in *Evatt* had failed because there was no allegation of any such undertaking in the pleadings. The latter view seems to have prevailed and the once controversial *Evatt* is seldom raised in newer cases. See *Royal Bank of Can. v. Aleman* (1988), 43 C.C.L.T. 245 (Alta. Q.B.).

9. *Hedley Byrne* has been applied against members of various businesses and professions. See, for example, *Chand v. Sabo Bros. Realty Ltd.* (1979), 96 D.L.R. (3d) 445 (Alta. C.A.) (real estate agent); *Fine's Flowers Ltd. v. Gen. Accident Assur. Co.* (1977), 81 D.L.R. (3d) 139 (Ont. C.A.) and *Gen. Motors Accept. Corp. v. Fulton Ins. Agencies Ltd.* (1978), 24 N.S.R. (2d) 114 (C.A.) (insurance agents); *Farish v. Nat. Trust Co.* (1975), 54 D.L.R. (3d) 426 (B.C. S.C.) (trust company); *Elderkin v. Merrill Lynch, Royal Securities Ltd.* (1977), 80 D.L.R. (3d) 313 (N.S. C.A.) (investment dealer); *Central B.C. Planners Ltd. v. Hocker* (1970), 10 D.L.R. (3d) 689 (B.C. C.A.), aff'd. (1971), 16 D.L.R. (3d) 368n (S.C.C.) (security salesman); *Bank of Montreal v. Young*, [1970] S.C.R. 328 (banker); *Haig v. Bamford*, [1977] 1 S.C.R. 466 (accountant); *Tracy v. Atkins* (1979), 105 D.L.R. (3d) 632 (B.C. C.A.) (lawyer); and *Sealand of Pac. Ltd. v. Robert C. McHaffe Ltd.* (1974), 51 D.L.R. (3d) 705 (B.C. C.A.) (architect).

(b) THE PROBLEM OF POTENTIALLY INDETERMINATE LIABILITY

HAIG v. BAMFORD

[1977] 1 S.C.R. 466, 72 D.L.R. (3d) 68 (S.C.C.)

DICKSON J.: — This appeal concerns the liability of an accountant to parties other than his employer for negligent statements. The Court is asked to decide whether there was in the relationship of the parties to the appeal such kind or degree of proximity as to give rise to a duty of care owed by the respondents to the appellant. The damages involved are not large but the question raised is of importance to the accounting profession and to the investing public.

. . .

I come then to the question whether Haig, who received the defective financial statements, and relied on them to his loss, has a right of recovery from the accountants. Mr. Justice MacPherson at trial allowed recovery [32 D.L.R. (3d) 66, [1972] 6 W.W.R. 557]. He held that the accountants knew or ought to have known that the statements would be used by a potential investor in the Company; although Haig was not, in the Judge's words, "in the picture", when the statement was prepared, he must be included in the category of persons who could be foreseen by the accountants as relying on the statement and therefore the accountants owed a duty to Haig. The Judge applied a test of foreseeability.

The majority in the Court of Appeal for Saskatchewan (Hall, J.A., with Maguire, J.A., concurring) came to a different conclusion [53 D.L.R. (3d) 85, [1974] 6 W.W.R. 236]. The majority of the Court were satisfied that the accountants had been informed by Scholler that the statement would be used to induce persons to invest equity capital in the Company. Mr. Justice Hall noted that at that time there was no specific person or group in mind as a prospective investor or investors; Haig was not known to the accountants and they were not aware that he had been shown a copy of the statement or that he had been approached to invest in the Company. The learned Justice of Appeal observed that the financial statement had been given to Haig without the knowledge of Scholler or the Company. With respect, I think this observation is in error as Wiltshire testified that before giving a copy of the statement to Haig he had received Scholler's permission. The point is, however, of no great consequence for if the accountants, at the request of the Company prepared financial statements for distribution, to, *inter alia*, potential investors, and furnished the Company with copies for that purpose, I fail to understand why the Company or anyone on its behalf would be expected to seek permission of the accountants before releasing a copy. The learned Justice of Appeal concluded that the accountants owed Haig the duty to be honest but that they were not liable to him for negligence and, since the misrepresentation contained in the financial statement was the result of an "honest blunder", the appeal should be allowed with costs. The dissenting Judge, Mr. Justice Woods, was of opinion that the accountants knew that the statement was intended for a special purpose, a purpose that would affect the economic interests of those from whom Scholler would attempt to secure funds and that Haig fell within this category. The outcome of this appeal rests, it would seem, on whether, to create a duty of care, it is sufficient that the accountants knew that the information was intended to be disseminated among a specific group or class, as Mr. Justice MacPherson and Mr. Justice Woods would have it, or whether the accountants also needed to be apprised of the plaintiff's identity, as Mr. Justice Hall and Mr. Justice Maguire would have it.

IV

The increasing growth and changing role of corporations in modern society has been attended by a new perception of the societal role of the profession of accounting. The day when the accountant served only the owner-manager of a company and was answerable to him alone has passed. The complexities of modern industry combined with the effects of specialization, the impact of taxation, urbanization, the separation of ownership from management, the rise of professional corporate managers, and a host of other factors, have led to marked changes in the role and responsibilities of the accountant, and in the reliance which the public must place upon his work. The financial statements of the corporations upon which he reports can affect the economic interests of the general public as well as of shareholders and potential shareholders.

With the added prestige and value of his services has come, as the leaders of the profession have recognized, a concomitant and commensurately increased responsibility to the public. It seems unrealistic to be oblivious to these developments. It does not necessarily follow that the doors must be thrown open and recovery permitted whenever someone's economic interest suffers as the result of a negligent act on the part of an accountant. Compensation to the injured party is a relevant consideration but it may not be the only relevant consideration. Fear of unlimited liability for the accountant, "liability in an indeterminate amount for an indeterminate time to an indeterminate class", was considered a relevant factor by Mr. Justice Cardozo in *Ultramares Corp. v. Touche et al.* (1931), 255 N.Y. 170. From the authorities, it appears that several possible tests could be applied to invoke a duty of care on the part of accountants vis-a-vis third parties: (i) foreseeability of the use of the financial statement and the auditor's report thereon by the plaintiff and reliance thereon; (ii) actual knowledge of the limited class that will use and rely on the statement; (iii) actual knowledge of the specific plaintiff who will use and rely on the statement. It is unnecessary for the purposes of the present case to decide whether test (i), the test of foreseeability, is or is not, a proper test to apply in determining the full extent of the duty owed by accountants to third parties. The choice in the present case, it seems to me, is between test (ii) and test (iii), actual knowledge of the limited class or actual knowledge of the specific plaintiff. I have concluded on the authorities that test (iii) is too narrow and that test (ii), actual knowledge of the limited class, is the proper test to apply in this case.

The English authorities

I do not think one can do better than begin with Lord Denning's dissent in *Candler v. Crane, Christmas & Co.*, [1951] 1 All E.R. 426 (C.A.), which later found favour in *Hedley Byrne & Co., Ltd. v. Heller & Partners Ltd.*, [1963] 2 All E.R. 575 (H.L.). After identifying accountants as among those under a duty to use care, Lord Denning, in answer to the question "To whom do these professional people owe this duty?" said, at p. 434:

They owe the duty, of course, to their employer or client, and also, I think, to any third person

> to whom they themselves show the accounts, or to whom they know their employer is going to show the accounts so as to induce him to invest money or take some other action on them. I do not think, however, the duty can be extended still further so as to include strangers of whom they have heard nothing and to whom their employer without their knowledge may choose to show their accounts.

and

> The test of proximity in these cases is: Did the accountants know that the accounts were required for submission to the plaintiff and use by him?

One can find some support in these words for the position taken by the majority in the Saskatchewan Court of Appeal but their effect is tempered by what appears later in the judgment, at p. 435:

> It will be noticed that I have confined the duty to cases where the accountant prepares his accounts and makes his report for the guidance of the very person in the very transaction in question. That is sufficient for the decision of this case. I can well understand that it would be going too far to make an accountant liable to any person in the land who chooses to rely on the accounts in matters of business, for that would expose him, in the words of CARDOZO C.J., in *Ultramares Corp. v. Touche* (174 N.E. 444), to

> " . . . liability in an indeterminate amount for an indeterminate time to an indeterminate class."

> Whether he would be liable if he prepared his accounts for the guidance of a specific class of persons in a specific class of transactions, I do not say. I should have thought he might be, just as the analyst and lift inspector would be liable in the instances I have given earlier.

In the case at bar, the accounts were prepared for the guidance of a "specific class of persons", potential investors, in a "specific class of transactions", the investment of $20,000 of equity capital. The number of potential investors would, of necessity, be limited because the Company, as a private company, was prohibited by s. 3(1)(o)(iii) of the *Companies Act* of Saskatchewan, R.S.S. 1965, c. 131, from extending any invitation to the public to subscribe for shares or debentures of the Company.

One comes then to the *Hedley Byrne* case. The argument was raised in that case that the relationship between the parties was not sufficiently close to give rise to any duty. Lord Reid dealt with that argument in these words, at p. 580:

> It is said that the respondents did not know the precise purpose of the inquiries and did not even know whether National Provincial Bank, Ltd., wanted the information for its own use or for the use of a customer: they knew nothing of the appellants, I would reject that argument. They knew that the inquiry was in connexion with an advertising contract, and it was at least probable that the information was wanted by the advertising contractors. It seems to me quite immaterial that they did not know who these contractors were: there is no suggestion of any speciality which could have influenced them in deciding whether to give information or in what form to give it. I shall therefore treat this as if it were a case where a negligent misrepresentation is made directly to the person seeking information, opinion, or advice, and I shall not attempt to decide what kind or degree of proximity is necessary before there can be a duty owed by the defendant to the plaintiff.

In the present case the accountants knew that the financial statements were being prepared for the very purpose of influencing, in addition to the bank and Sedco, a limited number of potential investors. The names of the potential investors were not material to the accountants. What was important was the nature of the transaction or transactions for which the statements were intended, for that is what delineated the limits of potential liability.

. . .

The American authorities

Judgment in the two leading cases was written by Mr. Justice Cardozo [as he then was]. In *Glanzer et al. v. Shepard et al.* (1922), 233 N.Y. 236, the defendants, public weighers, at the request of a seller of beans, made a return of the weight and furnished the plaintiff buyer with a copy. The buyer paid the seller on the faith of the certificate which turned out to be erroneous. The buyers were entitled to recover from the weighers. The certificate was held to be the very "end and aim" of the transaction and not something issued in the expectation that the seller would use it thereafter in the operations of his business as occasion might require.

The question whether third parties were protected from the negligence of accountants came before the New York Courts in *Ultramares Corp. v. Touche et al.* (1931), 255 N.Y. 170. The breach made in the wall of privity by *Glanzer's* case was narrowed in *Ultramares*. In that case, a company showed a balance sheet prepared by the defendants to a factor who advanced money to the company. The factor was unknown to the defendants, and Cardozo, C.J., held that the defendants owed the factor no duty of care. Although the *Ultramares* decision has been followed widely in the United States, it has also been criticized: see Prosser, *Handbook of The Law of Torts*, 4th ed. (1971), pp. 706-9; Carl S. Hawkins, "Professional Negligence Liability of Public Accountants", 12 *Vand. L. Rev.* 797 (1959); Notes, "Accountants' Liabilities for False and Misleading Financial Statements", 67 *Colum. L. Rev.* 1437 (1967). *Ultramares* has also been distinguished in a case similar to the one at bar, *Rusch Factors, Inc. v. Levin* (1968), 284 F. Supp. 85 (Dist. Ct., R.I.). In *Rusch*, the Court held that the plaintiff investor, who had relied on the financial statement prepared by the defendant, was actually foreseen by the defendant. Pettine, D.J., distinguished *Ultramares* in these words, at p. 91:

> There, the plaintiff was a member of an undefined, unlimited class of remote lenders and potential equity holders not actually foreseen but only foreseeable.

The *Rusch* case was followed by the U.S. Court of Appeals (4th Circuit) in *Rhode Island Hospital Trust National Bank v. Swartz, Bresenoff, Yavner & Jacobs* (1972), 455 F. 2d 847. That case mentions that *Rusch* has been followed in Iowa and Minnesota.

The case before us is closer to *Glanzer* than to *Ultramares*. The very end and aim of the financial statements prepared by the accountants in the present case was to secure additional financing for the Company from Sedco and an equity investor; the statements were required primarily for these third parties and only incidentally for use by the Company. In the *Ultramares* case, Touche would know that the statements were primarily for company use although they might be read in the ordinary course of business by shareholders, investors, banks and countless others.

. . .

In summary, Haig placed justifiable reliance upon a financial statement which the accountants stated presented fairly the financial position of the Company as at March 31, 1965. The accountants prepared such statements for reward in the course of their professional duties. The statements were for benefit and guidance in a business transaction, the nature of which was known to the accountants. The accountants were aware that the Company intended to supply the statements to members of a very limited class. Haig was a member of the class. It is true the accountants did not know his name but, as I have indicated earlier, I do not think that is of importance. I can see no good reason for distinguishing between the case in which a defendant accountant delivers information directly to the plaintiff at the request of his employer (*Candler*'s case and *Glanzer*'s case), and the case in which the information is handed to the employer, who, to the knowledge of the accountant, passes it to members of a limited class (whose identity is unknown to the accountant) in furtherance of a transaction the nature of which is known to the accountant. I would accordingly hold that the accountants owed Haig a duty to use reasonable care in the preparation of the accounts.

I am of the view, however, that Haig cannot recover from the accountants the sum of $2,500 which he advanced to the Company in December, 1965, because by that time he was fully cognizant of the true state of affairs. It cannot be said that the sum was advanced in reliance upon false statements. Haig had the choice of advancing additional money in the hope of saving his original investment. He chose to make a further advance, but the choice was his and not one for which the accountants are liable.

I would allow the appeal, set aside the judgment of the Court of Appeal for Saskatchewan and reinstate the judgment of MacPherson, J., subject only to disallowance of the claim of $2,500, the whole with costs in this Court and in the Courts below.

[Chief Justice Laskin, and Ritchie, Spence, Pigeon and Beetz JJ. concurred in the judgment of Dickson, J. Mr. Justice Martland, with whom Judson and de Grandpré JJ. concurred, gave a separate concurring judgment.]

NOTES AND QUESTIONS

1. What is the difficulty with the foreseeable plaintiff test in a case such as *Haig*? The "very limited class" referred to in *Haig* numbered less than 50 members by virtue of the Companies Act of Saskatchewan. Is a limit of 50 appropriate, or was there some other factor in this case which effectively limited the defendant's potential liability? Can you think of cases in which the rule in *Haig* will not effectively limit recovery?

2. American and Commonwealth courts have used various tests to control the ambit of liability. They have emphasized the defendant's knowledge of the class of potential plaintiffs, knowledge of the contemplated use of the information, or both. However, most of the cases are consistent with a fairly simple rule, derived from *Glanzer v. Shepard* (1922), 135 N.E. 275, at 277 (N.Y.C.A.). In *Glanzer* the court held the defendant liable for losses which he knew or ought to have known were related to the "end and aim" of the transaction giving rise to the misrepresentation. In *Caparo Industries Plc. v. Dickman*, [1990] 2 W.L.R. 358, the House of Lords observed that advice is tendered with a specific purpose in mind and that liability must be restricted to losses incurred in transactions related to that purpose. Is the result in *Haig* consistent with the "end and aim" rule? Given this rule, is there any reason to deny recovery to any foreseeable plaintiff?

3. In *Ultramares*, discussed in *Haig*, Cardozo, C.J. expressed concern that the application of the ordinary rules of negligence law might "expose accountants to liability in an indeterminate amount for an indeterminate time to an indeterminate class." Generally, the courts have shared Cardozo J.'s

concern about the indeterminate amount, and have regarded indeterminate time and class as indirect indicators of this issue. However, each factor may have independent significance.

The issue of potentially indeterminate time was raised in *Williams v. Polgar* (1974), 215 N.W. (2d) 149 (S.C. Mich.). An abstract of a land title was negligently issued in 1926. The defect was not discovered until 1959, when the plaintiffs relied upon the abstract to their detriment. The court held that the defendant's duty ran to any successor in title who relied upon the abstract. Whereas the limitation period in contract had long expired, the tort period had not begun to run until the plaintiffs discovered the negligence. Does this decision violate the policy underlying statutory limitations periods?

The problem of a potentially indeterminate class raises the issue of whether there is a sufficient relationship between the plaintiff and defendant to warrant imposing liability, regardless of the amount of the potential loss. In *Beebe v. Robb* (1977), 81 D.L.R. (3d) 349 (B.C. S.C.), a boat owner commissioned the defendant, a marine surveyor, to evaluate his boat to assist him in obtaining a bank loan. Unknown to the defendant, the owner showed the assessment to the plaintiff, a prospective purchaser, who relied upon it to his detriment. The plaintiff alleged that the defendant had been negligent and sued under the principles in *Hedley Byrne*. Clearly the defendant knew the amount at risk. Nevertheless, the court held that the relationship between the parties was insufficient to justify recognizing a duty of care. A similar result was reached in *Le Lievre v. Gould*, [1893] 1 Q.B. 491 (C.A.). In *Gordon v. Moen*, [1971] N.Z.L.R. 526 (S.C.), a case virtually identical to *Beebe*, the court held the defendant liable. Which line of cases is preferable?

4. In cases subsequent to *Haig*, the Supreme Court has not adopted a single approach to defining the scope of duty. In *Edgeworth Construction Ltd. v. N.D. Lea & Associates Ltd.* (1993), 17 C.C.L.T. (2d) 101, the Supreme Court overruled a lower court's finding that an engineering firm did not owe the plaintiff contractor a duty of care in the preparation of a "tender package". In a single terse paragraph, the majority held that the plaintiff had been within a "definable group" of persons the defendant knew might reasonably rely on their information. This decision is consistent with the current Supreme Court's liberal approach to the duty issue. See also, *Canadian Commercial Bank v. Crawford, Smith & Swallow* (1994), 21 C.C.L.T. (2d) 89, leave to appeal ref'd. (1994), 21 C.C.L.T. (2d) 89n (S.C.C.), in which the Ontario Court of Appeal found that the plaintiff stood outside the class of persons covered by the defendant bank's duty of care.

3. Negligent Misrepresentation and Contract

(a) PRE-CONTRACTUAL MISREPRESENTATIONS

QUEEN v. COGNOS INC

[1993] 1 S.C.R. 87

IACOBUCCI J.: — . . .

As I stated in *BG Checo*, it is now clear that an action in tort for negligent misrepresentation may lie even though the relevant parties to the action (i.e., the representee/plaintiff and the representor/defendant) are in a contractual relationship: see *Esso Petroleum Co. v. Mardon*, [1976] 2 All E.R. 5 (C.A.); *Sodd Corp. v. Tessis* (1977), 17 O.R. (2d) 158 (C.A.); *Kingu v. Walmar Ventures Ltd.* (1986), 38 C.C.L.T. 51 (B.C.C.A.); *Carman Construction*, supra; *V.K. Mason Construction*, supra; *Rainbow Industrial Caterers*, supra; and L.N. Klar, *Tort Law* (1991), at p. 162, n. 89. More particularly, the fact that the alleged negligent misrepresentations are made in a pre-contractual setting, such as during negotiations or in the course of an employment hiring interview, and the fact that a contract is subsequently entered into by the parties do not, in themselves, bar an action in tort for damages caused by said misrepresentations: see, for example, *Esso Petroleum*, supra, and the cases cited above dealing specifically with pre-employment misrepresentation.

This is not to say that the contract in such a case is irrelevant and that a court should dispose of the plaintiff's tort claim independently of the contractual arrangement. On the contrary, depending on the circumstances, the subsequent contract may play a very important role in determining whether or not, and to what extent, a claim for negligent misrepresentation shall succeed. Indeed, as evidenced by my conclusion in *BG Checo*, such a contract can have the effect of negating the action in tort and of confining the plaintiff to whatever remedies are available under the law of contract. On the other hand, even if the tort claim is not barred altogether by the contract, the duty or liability of the defendant with respect to negligent misrepresentations may be limited or excluded by a term of the subsequent contract so as to diminish or extinguish the plaintiff's remedy in tort: see, for example, *Hedley Byrne* (although this case involved mostly post-contractual representations), supra. Equally true, however, is that there are cases where the subsequent contract will have no effect whatsoever on the plaintiff's claim for damages in tort. As will be apparent from these reasons, it is my view that the employment agreement signed by the appellant in March of 1983 is governed by this last proposition.

When considering the effect of the subsequent contract on the representee's tort action, everything revolves around the nature of the contractual obligations assumed by the parties and the nature of the alleged negligent misrepresentation. The first and foremost question should be whether there is a specific contractual duty created by an express term of the contract which is co-extensive with the common law duty of care which the representee alleges the representor has breached. Put another way, did the pre-contractual representation relied on by the plaintiff become an express term of the subsequent contract? If so, absent any overriding considerations arising from the context in which the transaction occurred, the plaintiff cannot bring a concurrent action in tort for negligent misrepresentation and is confined to whatever remedies are available under the law of contract. The authorities supporting this proposition, including the decision of this court in *Central Trust Co. v. Rafuse*, [1986] 2 S.C.R. 147, are fully canvassed in my reasons in *BG Checo*. As alluded to in *BG Checo*, this principle is an exception to the general rule of concurrency espoused by this court in *Central Trust v. Rafuse*, supra.

There lies, in my view, the fundamental difference between the present appeal in *BG Checo*, supra. In the latter case, the alleged pre-contractual misrepresentation had been incorporated verbatim as an express term of the subsequent contract. As such, the common law duty of care relied on by the plaintiff in its tort action was co-extensive with a duty imposed on the defendant in contract by an express term of their agreement. Thus, it was my view that the plaintiff was barred from exercising a concurrent action in tort for the alleged breach of said duty, and this view was reinforced by the commercial context in which the transaction occurred. In the case at bar, however, there is no such concurrency. The employment agreement signed by the appellant in March of 1983 does not contain any express contractual obligation co-extensive with the duty of care the respondent is alleged to have breached. The provisions most relevant to this appeal (clauses 13 and 14) contain contractual duties clearly different from, not co-extensive with, the common law duty invoked by the appellant in his tort action.

Had the appellant's action been based on pre-contractual representations concerning the length of his involvement on the Multiview project or his "job security", as characterized by the Court of Appeal, the concurrency question might be resolved differently in light of the termination and reassignment provisions of the contract. However, it is clear that the appellant's claim was *not* that Mr. Johnston negligently misrepresented the amount of time he would be working on Multiview or the conditions under which his employment could be terminated. In other words, he did not argue that the respondent, through its representative, breached a common law duty of care by negligently misrepresenting his security of employment with Cognos. Rather, the appellant argued that Mr. Johnston negligently misrepresented the nature and existence of the employment opportunity being offered. It is the existence, or reality, of the job being interviewed for, not the extent of the appellant's involvement therein, which is at the heart of this tort action. A close reading of the employment agreement reveals that it contains no express provisions dealing with the respondent's obligations with respect to the nature and existence of the Multiview project. Accordingly, the ratio decidendi of my reasons in *BG Checo* is inapplicable to the present appeal. While both cases involve pre-contractual negligent misrepresentations, only *BG Checo* involved an impermissible concurrent liability in tort and contract; an exception to the general rule of concurrency set out in *Central Trust v. Rafuse*, supra. The case at bar does not involve concurrency at all, let alone an exception thereto.

Having said this, it does not follow that the employment agreement is irrelevant to the disposition of this appeal. As I mentioned earlier, even if the tort claim is not barred altogether by the contract as in *BG Checo*, the duty or liability of the representor in tort may be limited or excluded by a term of the subsequent contract. In this respect, the respondent submits that the Court of Appeal was correct in finding that clauses 13 and 14 of the employment agreement represent a valid disclaimer for the misrepresentations allegedly made during the hiring interview, thereby negating any duty of care. I shall return to this issue in the last part of my reasons. I prefer to deal next with the questions of whether the respondent or its representative owed a duty of care to the appellant during the pre-employment interview and, if so, whether there was a breach of this duty in all the circumstances of this case.

NOTES AND QUESTIONS

1. Can a tort claim be barred by a prior or subsequent contract between the parties? What is the key question in determining the effect of a contract?

2. What was the difference between the contracts in *Cognos* and *BG Checo*? For further detail, see *BG Checo International Ltd.*, which follows in the text.

3. In traditional contract law an innocent misrepresentation which induces a contract might support rescission, but not damages. Alternatively, the court might view the misrepresentation as the basis of a collateral contract, holding that the plaintiff entered into the main contract in return for the promise in the misrepresentation. See *Shanklin Pier Ltd. v. Detel Products Ltd.*, [1951] 2 K.B. 854. Finally, the court may hold that a misrepresentation, which induces a contract, is a term of the contract. See *Mendelssohn v. Normand Ltd.*, [1970] 1 Q.B. 177 (C.A.); and *Esso Petroleum Co. v. Mardon*, [1976] Q.B. 801 (C.A.).

4. A contractual exclusion or limitation clause can operate either to exclude or limit a defendant's liability for a negligent misstatement. For a recent discussion see Iacobucci J.'s dissent in *BG Checo*, which follows in the text.

(b) CONCURRENT LIABILITY IN TORT AND CONTRACT

BG CHECO INTERNATIONAL LTD v. B.C. HYDRO & POWER AUTHORITY

[1993] 1 S.C.R. 12

IACOBUCCI J. (dissenting in part) (SOPINKA J. concurring): — The narrow question raised by this appeal is what remedy should be available for pre-contractual representations made during the tendering process. This question also raises a more general and more important issue. In light of the decision of this Court in *Central & Eastern Trust Co. v. Rafuse*, [1986] 2 S.C.R. 147, can a plaintiff who is in a contractual relationship with the defendant sue the defendant in tort if the duty relied upon by the plaintiff in tort is also made a contractual duty by an express term of the contract?

I. Facts

The appellant and respondent on the cross-appeal, B.C. Hydro and Power Authority, is a British Columbia Crown corporation. The respondent and appellant on the cross-appeal, BG Checo International Ltd., is a large corporation in the business of constructing electrical transmission lines and distribution systems. I will refer to the parties as "Hydro" and "Checo", respectively.

In November of 1982, Hydro called for tenders to erect transmission towers and to string transmission lines. In December, 1982, prior to submitting its tender for the contract, Checo's representative inspected the area by helicopter. He noted that the right-of-way had been partially cleared, and also noted evidence of ongoing clearing activity. The representative assumed that the right-of-way would be further cleared prior to the commencement of Checo's work. On January 2, 1983, Checo submitted its tender, and on February 15, 1983, Hydro accepted Checo's tender and the parties entered into a written contract. Checo contracted to construct 130 towers and install insulators, hardware and conductors over 42 kilometres of right-of-way near Sechelt, British Columbia.

In fact, no further clearing of the right-of-way ever took place. The "dirty" condition of the right-of-way caused Checo a number of difficulties in completing its work. Checo sued Hydro, seeking damages for negligent misrepresentation, or, in the alternative, for breach of contract.

The evidence at trial indicated that Hydro had contracted the clearing out to another company, and that, to Hydro's knowledge, the work was not done adequately. There was no direct discussion between the representatives of Checo and Hydro concerning this issue. There was evidence led at trial that the contract between the parties did not specify clearing standards with the same degree of detail as was present in similar contracts entered into by Hydro.

During the trial, Hydro tendered documents in evidence which Checo had unsuccessfully attempted to discover. These documents indicated that Hydro was aware of the problem with the clearing and of the impact that these problems would have on the successful tenderer. As a result, Checo amended its statement of claim to include a claim in fraud.

The trial judge found that Hydro had acted fraudulently in its dealings with Checo and awarded Checo $2,591,580.56, being "the total loss suffered by [Checo] as a result of being fraudulently induced to enter into this contract." Hydro appealed to the Court of Appeal for British Columbia, which rejected the finding of fraud, but found that there had been a negligent misrepresentation which induced Checo to enter into the contract. The Court of Appeal awarded the sum of $1,087,729.81, for the misrepresentation, and referred the question of breach of contract and damages flowing therefrom to the British Columbia Supreme Court. Checo's cross-appeal for punitive damages and for a higher scale of costs was dismissed.

B. *Concurrent Liability in Tort and Contract*

(1) *Introduction*

It was Hydro's submission on this appeal that it ought to be liable, if at all, in contract and not in tort. For the reasons which I will set out, I agree that in the circumstances of the case, while Hydro may be liable in contract for the representations which Checo complains of, Hydro cannot be liable in tort. Given the importance of the general issue of tort-contract concurrency, I propose to explore it in some detail.

As a general rule, the existence of a contract between two parties does not preclude the existence of a common law duty of care. Subject to the substantive and procedural differences that exist between an action in contract and an action in tort, both the duty of care and the liability may be concurrent in contract and tort. In such circumstances, it is for the plaintiff to select the cause of action most advantageous to him or her. That was the position adopted by Le Dain J. in *Central & Eastern Trust v. Rafuse*, supra. At pp. 204-205 (S.C.C.), Le Dain J. said the following:

> 1. The common law duty of care that is created by a relationship of sufficient proximity, in accordance with the general principles affirmed by Lord Wilberforce in *Anns v. Merton London Borough Council*, is not confined to relationships that arise apart from contract. Although the relationships in *Donoghue v. Stevenson, Hedley Byrne* and *Anns* were all of a non-contractual nature and there was necessarily reference in the judgments to a duty of care that exists apart from or independently of contract, I find nothing in the statements of general principle in those cases to suggest that the principle was intended to be confined to relationships that arise apart from contract . . . the question is whether there is a relationship of sufficient proximity, not how it arose. The principle of tortious liability is for reasons of public policy a general one.

Le Dain J.'s conclusion that a plaintiff is generally entitled to choose, as between contract and tort, the cause of action most favourable to him or her, was supported by a long line of Canadian and English authority, some of which I will consider below. *Central & Eastern Trust v. Rafuse*, supra, has since met with wide acceptance, and has been applied by a number of provincial Courts of Appeal. See *University of Regina v. Pettick* (1991), 90 Sask. R. 241 (C.A.); *Fletcher v. Manitoba Public Insurance Corp.*, 68 O.R. (2d) 193 (C.A.); *Pittman v. Manufacturers Life Insurance Co.* (1990), 76 D.L.R. (4th) 320 (Nfld. C.A.); *Clark v. Naqvi* (1989), 99 N.B.R. (2d) 271 (C.A.), and *Catre Industries Ltd. v. Alberta*, supra.

In *Central & Eastern Trust v. Rafuse*, supra, Le Dain J. recognized two situations in which, notwithstanding what would otherwise be a breach of the duty of care in tort, a plaintiff's ability to sue in tort will be limited by the terms of the contract. In one situation it is the *liability* in tort which is avoided or modified; in the other it is the *duty* in tort which is affected.

Le Dain J. recognized that liability in tort can be limited or excluded by the terms of a contract. A plaintiff will not be permitted to plead in tort in order to circumvent a contractual clause which excludes or limits the defendants liability (at p. 206):

> 3. A concurrent or alternative liability in tort will not be admitted if its effect would be to permit the plaintiff to circumvent or escape a contractual exclusion or limitation of liability for the act or omission that would constitute the tort.

In this case, Hydro argues that the terms of the contract operated to exclude its liability for the conduct of which Checo complains. If Hydro were correct, then Checo would no more be able to recover in tort than in contract. As I will discuss below, I am of the opinion that the contract does not exclude Hydro's liability.

As mentioned, Le Dain J. also recognized that the defendant's duty in tort could be affected by the terms of the contract. If the duty of care alleged in tort is also defined by a specific term of the contract, then the plaintiff will be entitled only to those remedies which may be available pursuant to the contract. The contractual relationship can bring the parties into sufficient proximity to give rise to a duty of care. However, no duty of care in tort can be concurrent with a duty of care created by an express term of the contract. In the words of Le Dain J. (at p. 205):

> 2. What is undertaken by the contract will indicate the nature of the relationship that gives rise to the common law duty of care, but the nature and scope of the duty of care that is asserted as the foundation of the tortious liability must not depend on specific obligations or duties created by the express terms of the contract. It is in that sense that the common law duty of care must be independent of the contract . . . A claim cannot be said to be in tort if it depends for the nature and scope of the asserted duty of care on the manner in which an obligation or duty has been expressly and specifically defined by a contract.
>
> . . .

The facts of this case require me to do what it was not necessary for Le Dain J. to do in *Central & Eastern Trust v. Rafuse*, supra: I must interpret and apply the principles to a contractual relationship in which there are exclusion or limitation of liability clauses which may exclude or limit liability in tort, as well as in contract, and in which there are clauses which may operate to exclude some parts of the duty of care in tort entirely. To interpret and apply the principles in *Central & Eastern Trust v. Rafuse* in the circumstances of this case, it will be necessary for me to review the authorities governing concurrency of obligations in tort and contract. It will also be necessary for me to review the law governing clauses which exclude or limit liability.

(2) *Concurrency of Tort and Contract*

The recent history of concurrency in tort and contract can be characterized as the development of a single regime of concurrency from two sets of rules governing concurrency in distinct circumstances. Until *Esso Petroleum Co. v. Mardon*, [1976] 2 All E.R. 5 (C.A.), there was one set of rules governing obligations in tort and contract for the so-called "status relationships" and another set of rules governing obligations in tort and contract for all other relationships. Since *Esso Petroleum*, supra, these two sets of rules have been assimilated into a single regime governing obligations in tort and contract for all relationships. The principles set out by Le Dain J. in *Central & Eastern Trust v. Rafuse*, supra, are representative of that single regime. To understand better the principles articulated by Le Dain J. in *Central & Eastern Trust v. Rafuse*, it will be helpful to review the process of development which preceded and informed the judgment of Le Dain J.

. . .

(b) *The emergence of a single theory of concurrent liability*

. . .

[T]he trend towards a single theory of concurrent liability in tort and contract was recognized in Canada by La Forest J.A. (as he then was) in *New Brunswick Telephone Co. v. John Maryon International Ltd.* (1982), 43 N.B.R. (2d) 469 (C.A.). After an extensive review of the case law, La Forest J.A. concluded that an architect was concurrently liable in contract and in tort. La Forest J.A. based his conclusion on the concept of a general tort of negligence (at p. 520): "while I could dispose of this case by simply adding the profession of structural engineer to the list of common callings and skilled professions, I prefer to base my judgment on the generalized tort of negligence".

In *Central & Eastern Trust v. Rafuse*, supra, Le Dain J. also rejected any distinction between status relationships and other relationships in determining whether parties to a contract can also recover in tort. Instead, Le Dain J. found that a single rule applied to all relationships (at p. 205): "the question is whether there is a relationship of sufficient proximity, not how it arose." The rule of concurrency which Le Dain J. adopted was a compromise between two strands of authority.

In one strand of authority, that governing the status of relationships, any duty arising in tort had always been concurrent with duties arising under the contract: *Brown v. Boorman*, supra. In the other strand of authority, the duty in tort was only concurrent with the duty in contract if the negligence complained of was unconnected with the performance of the contract: *J. Nunes Diamonds*, supra. The compromise position adopted by Le Dain J. was that any duty arising in tort will be concurrent with duties arising under the contract, *unless the duty which the plaintiff seeks to rely on in tort is also a duty defined by an express term of the contract*. If the duty is defined by an express term of the contract, the plaintiff will be confined to whatever remedies are available in the law of contract (at p. 205):

> [T]he nature and scope of the duty of care that is asserted as the foundation of the tortious liability must not depend on specific obligations or duties created by express terms of the contract. . . . Where the common law duty of care is co-extensive with that which arises as an implied term of the contract it obviously does not depend on the terms of the contract. . . . The same is also true of reliance on a common law duty of care that falls short of a specific obligation or duty imposed by the express terms of a contract.

In my opinion, the compromise struck by Le Dain J. is an appropriate one. If the parties to a contract choose to define a specific duty as an express term of the contract, then the consequences of a breach of that duty ought to be determined by the law of contract, not by tort law. Whether or not an implied term of a contract can define a duty of care in such a way that a plaintiff is confined to a remedy in contract is not at issue in this case. I leave that determination to another day. While the rule articulated by Le Dain J. is a rule of law which does not depend on the presumed or actual intention of the parties, the intention which can be inferred from the fact that the parties have made the duty an express term of the contract provides policy support for the rule. If a duty is an express term of the contract, it can be inferred that the parties wish the law of the contract to govern with respect to that duty. This is of particular significance given that the result of a breach of a contractual duty may be different from that of a breach of a duty in tort. As Wilson J.A. noted in *Dominion Chain Co.*, supra, a plaintiff's substantive rights may be different in contract and in tort (at p. 409):

> His cause of action may arise later in tort resulting in a later expiry of the limitation period. His damage may be greater in quantum and different in kind if he sues in tort. On the other hand his action in contract may survive him or be the subject of a set-off or counterclaim, neither of which would be so if his action were framed in tort.

The fact that damages may be assessed differently in contract from in tort was recently affirmed by this Court in *Rainbow Industrial Caterers Ltd. v. Canadian National Railway Co.*, [1991] 3 S.C.R. 3.

A further policy rationale for the rule advanced by Le Dain J. is that contracts have become, particularly in commercial contexts, increasingly complex. Commercial contracts allocate risks and fix the mutual duties and obligations of the parties. Where there is an express term creating a contractual duty, it is appropriate that the parties be held to the bargain which they have made.

. . .

However, I do not believe that the rule advanced by Le Dain J. that forecloses a claim in tort is absolute in all circumstances. In this respect, I would favour a contextual approach which takes into account the context in which the contract is made, and the position of the parties with respect to one another, in assessing whether a claim in tort is foreclosed by the terms of a contract. The policy reasons in favour of the rule advanced by Le Dain J. are strongest where the contractual context is commercial and the parties are of equal bargaining power. There was no question of unconscionability or inequality of bargaining power in *Central & Eastern Trust v. Rafuse*, supra, as there is no such question in this case. If such issues, or others analogous to them, were to arise, however, a court should be wary not to exclude too rapidly a duty of care in tort on the basis of an express term of the contract, especially if the end result for the plaintiff would be a wrong without a remedy.

LA FOREST and MCLACHLIN JJ. (L'HEUREUX-DUBÉ and GONTHIER JJ. concurring): — We have had the advantage of reading the reasons of our colleague Justice Iacobucci. We agree with his conclusion that Hydro is liable to Checo for breach of contract. We disagree, however, with his conclusion that the contract precludes Checo from suing in tort. In our view, our colleague's approach would have the effect of eliminating much of the rationalizing thrust behind the movement towards concurrency in tort and contract. Rather than attempting to establish new barriers in tort liability in contractual contexts, the law should move towards the elimination of unjustified differences between the remedial rules applicable to the two actions, thereby reducing the significance of the existence of the two different forms of action and allowing a person who has suffered a wrong full access to all relevant legal remedies.

The facts have been fully set out by our colleague and need not be repeated. The tender documents (subsequently incorporated in the contract) stated that clearing of the right-of-way would be done by others and formed no part of the work to be performed by Checo. The tender documents and contract documents also stated that it was Checo's responsibility to inform itself of all aspects of the work and that should any errors appear in the tender documents, or should Checo note any conditions conflicting with the letter or spirit of the tender documents, it was the responsibility of Checo to obtain clarification before submitting its tender. The tender documents also provided that Checo would satisfy itself of all site conditions and the correctness and sufficiency of the tender for the work and the stipulated prices.

Checo argues that the right-of-way was not properly cleared and that the statement in the tender documents and the contract that it had been cleared constituted a breach of contract and negligent misrepresentation.

Hydro argues first that it carried out the clearing required by cl. 6.01.03 of the contract, and second, that in any event it was up to Checo to satisfy itself that the site was adequately cleared before tendering. In other words, if there was ambiguity as to what was meant by "cleared" Checo had assumed the risk of clearing which might not meet its expectations.

The trial judge found Hydro liable for the tort of deceit. The Court of Appeal found that the evidence fell short of supporting that finding, there being no evidence of intention to deceive. That conclusion cannot seriously be contested and Checo's cross-appeal on the issue of fraudulent misrepresentation must accordingly be dismissed. The only issues therefore are whether claims lie in contract and tort and if so, what is the measure of damages.

[Having concluded that Hydro was liable to Checo for breach of contract, the court went on to discuss the claim in tort.]

The Claim in Tort

The Theory of Concurrency

The first question is whether the contract precludes Checo from suing in tort.

Iacobucci J. concludes that a contract between the parties may preclude the possibility of suing in tort for a given wrong where there is an express term in the contract dealing with the matter. We would phrase the applicable principle somewhat more narrowly. As we see it, the right to sue in tort is not taken away by the contract in such a case, although the contract, by limiting the scope of the tort duty or waiving the right to sue in tort, may limit or negate tort liability.

In our view, the general rule emerging from this Court's decision in *Central & Eastern Trust v. Rafuse*, [1986] 2 S.C.R. 147, is that where a given wrong prima facie supports an action in contract and in tort, the party may sue in either or both, except where the contract indicates that the parties intended to limit or negative the right to sue in tort. This limitation on the general rule of concurrency arises because it is always open to parties to limit or waive the duties which the common law would impose on them for negligence. This principle is of great importance in preserving a sphere of individual liberty and commercial flexibility. Thus if a person wishes to engage in a dangerous sport, the person may stipulate in advance that he or she waives any right of action against the person who operates the sport facility: *Dyck v. Manitoba Snowmobile Assn. Inc.*, [1985] 1 S.C.R. 589. Similarly, if two business firms agree that a particular risk should lie on a party who would not ordinarily bear that risk at common law they may do so. So a plaintiff may sue either in contract or tort, subject to any limit the parties themselves have placed on that right by their contract. The mere fact that the parties have dealt with a matter expressly in their contract does not mean that they intended to exclude the right to sue in tort. It all depends on *how* they have dealt with it.

Viewed thus, the only limit on the right to choose one's action is the principle of primacy of private ordering — the right of individuals to arrange their affairs and assume risks in a different way than would be done by the law of tort. It is only to the extent that this private ordering contradicts the tort duty that the tort duty is diminished. The rule is not that one cannot sue concurrently in contract and tort where the contract limits or contradicts the tort duty. It is rather that the tort duty, a general duty imputed by the law in all the relevant circumstances, must yield to the parties' superior right to arrange their rights and duties in a different way. In so far as the tort duty is not contradicted by the contract, it remains intact and may be sued upon. For example, where the contractual limitation on the tort duty is partial, a tort action founded on the modified duty might lie. The tort duty as modified by the contractual agreement between the parties might be raised in a case where the limitation period for an action for breach of contract has expired but the limitation period for a tort action has not. If one says categorically, as we understand Iacobucci J. to say, that where the contract deals with a matter expressly, the right to sue in tort vanishes altogether, then the latter two possibilities vanish.

This is illustrated by consideration of the three situations that may arise when contract and tort are applied to the same wrong. The first class of case arises where the contract stipulates a more stringent obligation than the general law of tort would impose. In that case, the parties are hardly likely to sue in tort, since they could not recover in tort for the higher contractual duty. The vast majority of commercial transactions fall into this class. The right to sue in tort is not extinguished, however, and may remain important, as where suit in contract is barred by expiry of a limitation period.

The second class of case arises where the contract stipulates a lower duty than that which would be presumed by the law of tort in similar circumstances. This occurs when the parties by their contract indicate their intention that the usual liability imposed by the law of tort is not to bind them. The most common means by which such an intention is indicated is the inclusion of a clause of exemption or exclusion of liability in the contract. Generally, the duty imposed by the law of tort can be nullified only by clear terms. We do not rule out, however, the possibility that cases may arise in which merely inconsistent contract terms could negative or limit a duty in tort, an issue that may be left to a case in which it arises. The issue raises difficult policy considerations, viz., an assessment of the circumstances in which contracting parties should be permitted to agree to contractual duties that would subtract from their general obligations under the law of tort. These important questions are best left to a case in which the proper factual foundation is available, so as to provide an appropriate context for the decision. In the second class of case, as in the first, there is usually little point in suing in tort since the duty in tort and consequently any tort liability is limited by the specific limitation to which the parties have agreed. An exception might arise where the contract does not entirely negate tort liability (e.g., the exemption clause applies only above a certain amount) and the plaintiff wishes to sue in tort to avail itself of a more generous limitation period or some other procedural advantage offered by tort.

The third class of case arises where the duty in contract and the common law duty in tort are co-extensive. In this class of case, like the others, the plaintiff may seek to sue concurrently or alternatively in tort to secure some advantage peculiar to the law of tort, such as a more generous limitation period. The contract may expressly provide for a duty that is the same as that imposed by the common law. Or the contractual duty may be implied. The common calling cases, which have long permitted concurrent actions in contract and tort, generally fall into this class. There is a contract. But the obligation under that contract is typically defined by implied terms, i.e., by the courts. Thus there is no issue of private ordering as opposed to publicly imposed liability. Whether the action is styled in contract or tort, its source is an objective expectation, defined by the courts, of the appropriate obligation and the correlative right.

The case at bar, as we see it, falls into this third category of case. The contract, read as we have proposed, did not negate Hydro's common law duty not to negligently misrepresent that it would have the right-of-way cleared by others. Had Checo known the truth, it would have bid for a higher amount. That duty is not excluded by the contract, which confirmed Hydro's obligation to clear the right-of-way. Accordingly, Checo may sue in tort.

We conclude that actions in contract and tort may be concurrently pursued unless the parties by a valid contractual provision indicate that they intended otherwise. This excludes, of course, cases where the contractual limitation is invalid, as by fraud, mistake or unconscionability. Similarly, a contractual limitation may not apply where the tort is independent of the contract in the sense of falling outside the scope of the contract, as the example given in *Elder, Dempster & Co. v. Paterson, Zochonis & Co.*, [1924] A.C. 522 (H.L.), of the captain of a vessel falling asleep and starting a fire in relation to a claim for cargo damage.

The Express-Implied Distinction

Our colleague asserts that where the parties deal with a matter expressly in their contract, all right to sue in tort is lost. We have suggested, with great respect, that this proposition is unnecessarily Draconian. The converse of this proposition is that implied terms of contracts do not oust tort liability.

Although Iacobucci J. states at p. 33 of his reasons [p. 275, post] that he is leaving open the question of "Whether or not an implied term of a contract can define a duty of care in such a way that a plaintiff is confined to a remedy in contract", the distinction between implied and express terms figures in his discussion of the effect of contract terms on tort liability. For example, at p. 32 of his reasons [p. 275, post], our colleague states:

> The compromise position adopted by Le Dain J. was that any duty arising in tort will be concurrent with duties arising under the contract, *unless the duty which the plaintiff seeks to rely on in tort is also a duty defined by an express term of the contract*. [The emphasis is Iacobucci J.'s.]

It would seem to follow from this statement that concurrent duties in contract and tort would lie where the contract duty is defined by an *implied* term of the contract, but not where the term is express. In these circumstances, it is not amiss to consider the utility of the distinction between express and implied terms of the contract as a basis for determining when a contract term may affect tort liability.

In our view, using the express-implied distinction as a basis for determining whether there is a right to sue in tort poses a number of problems. The law has always treated express and implied contract terms as being equivalent in effect. Breach of an implied term is just as serious as breach of an express term. Moreover, it is difficult to distinguish between them in some cases. Implied terms may arise from custom, for example, or from the conduct of the parties. In some cases words and conduct intermingle. Why should parties who were so certain in their obligations that they did not take the trouble to spell them out find themselves able to sue in tort, while parties who put the same matters in writing cannot?

Nor is it evident to us that if parties to a contract choose to include an express term in the contract dealing with a particular duty relevant to the contract, they intended to oust the availability of tort remedies in respect of that duty. In such cases, the intention may more likely be:

(a) To make it clear that the parties understand particular contractual duties to exist as between them, rather than having the more uncertain situation of not knowing whether a court will imply a particular duty under the contract; and/or

(b) To prevent litigation (for breach of contract) in the event of disputes arising — the more certain the parties' respective rights and obligations (as is usually the case when those rights and obligations are set out in express contractual terms), the more likely it will be that disputes between the parties can be settled.

While the tort duty may be limited by the contractual terms so as to be no broader than the contract duty, there is no reason to suppose that merely by stipulating a duty in the contract, the parties intended to negate all possibility of suing in tort.

Indeed, a little further on in his reasons, our colleague appears to concede that the ouster of recourse to tort law must depend on more than the fact the contract has expressly dealt with the matter. He indicates at pp. 34-35 of his reasons [p. 276, post] that whether the parties will be held to have intended to oust tort remedies in favour of contract remedies will depend on the context, including:

(a) whether the contract is commercial or non-commercial;

(b) whether the parties were of equal bargaining power;

(c) whether the court is of the view that to find such an intention will lead to an unjust result in the court action.

Thus the question of whether a concurrent action in tort lies would depend not only on whether the contract expressly deals with the matter, but also on the elastic distinctions between commercial and non-commercial contracts, the court's perception of relative bargaining power, and finally, whether the court sees the result as just or unjust. We do not agree that parties contracting in a commercial context should be presumed to be more desirous of ousting the availability of tort remedies than parties contracting in a non-commercial context. If there are particular commercial relationships in which the parties wish remedies for disputes between them to be in contract only, then they may be expected to indicate this intention by including an express clause in the contract waiving the right to sue in tort. As for equality of bargaining power and the court's view of whether the result would be just or unjust, we fear they would introduce too great a measure of uncertainty. Parties should be able to predict in advance whether their remedies are confined to contract or whether they can sue concurrently in tort and contract. Finally, it seems to us that Iacobucci J.'s test for determining when concurrent liability is precluded will be difficult to apply in situations where the express contractual term does not exactly overlap a tort duty. In the present case, the contractual term was identical to the negligent misrepresentation, but that is not often to be expected.

The Authorities

The authorities, as we read them, do not support the conclusion that the express mention of a matter in the contract, and only its express mention in the contract, ousts any possibility of suing in tort. The opposing schools of thought on the concurrent liability issue have not been divided along such lines. Instead, the issue has been whether there should be concurrent liability where any term of a contract, either express *or* implied, deals with the same duty imposed by tort law. For example, in *Lister v. Romford Ice & Cold Storage Co.*, [1957] A.C. 555 (H.L.), Viscount Simonds noted (at p. 573):

> It is trite law that a single act of negligence may give rise to a claim either in tort or for breach of a term *express or implied* in a contract. [Emphasis added.]

Similarly in *Canadian Indemnity Co. v. Andrews & George Co.*, [1953] 1 S.C.R. 19, Rand J. stated (at p. 26):

> Where a contract *expressly or by implication of fact* provides for a performance with care, as in the case of carriers, the general duty is clearly not displaced and the person injured or damaged in property may sue either in contract or tort. [Emphasis added.]

On the other side of the concurrent liability debate, Wilson J.A. (as she then was), arguing in favour of liability lying in contract only, stated at p. 408 in her dissenting opinion in the Ontario Court of Appeal decision of *Dominion Chain Co. v. Eastern Construction Co.* (1976), 68 D.L.R. (3d) 385, affirmed (sub nom., *Giffels Associates Ltd. v. Eastern Construction Co.*) [1978] 2 S.C.R. 1346:

> The borderline of contract and tort in my opinion exists where a contract *either expressly or impliedly* imposes on A a duty of care vis-à-vis B, the other party to the contract, to do the things undertaken by the contract without negligence and there is also coincidental with, but independent of, the contract of duty of care upon A in tort . . . where the person to whom the duty is owed, the scope of the duty and the standard of care have all been *expressly or impliedly* agreed upon by the parties, it appears to me somewhat artificial to rely upon Lord Atkin's "neighbour" test to determine whether or not the duty is owed to the particular plaintiff and as to the requisite standard of care the defendant must attain. [Emphasis added.]

It is perhaps a source of some confusion that in the course of his judgment in *Central & Eastern Trust v. Rafuse*, supra, Le Dain J. stated (at p. 205):

> Where the common law duty of care is co-extensive with that which arises as an implied term of the contract it obviously does not depend on the terms of the contract, and there is

nothing flowing from contractual intention which should preclude reliance on a concurrent or alternative liability in tort.

In our view, this passage should not be read as predicating the availability of concurrent liability in contract and tort on whether the contractual term is express or implied. Le Dain J. is simply stating that tort liability lies where the contractual term is implied. He does not go on to state that tort liability is always excluded by an express contractual term. This happens only when the express contractual term negates the tort duty. Thus in his summary of the applicable rules, Le Dain J. refers to exclusion clauses — express contract terms that negate general liability — as the kind of contract clause that may oust tort liability.

Our colleague relies on a second passage from *Central & Eastern Trust v. Rafuse*, supra, at p. 205, for the proposition that an express contractual term always ousts tort liability:

> 2. What is undertaken by the contract will indicate the nature of the relationship that gives rise to the common law duty of care, but the nature and scope of the duty of care that is asserted as the foundation of the tortious liability must not depend on specific obligations or duties created by the express terms of the contract. It is in that sense that the common law duty of care must be independent of the contract. . . . A claim cannot be said to be in tort if it depends for the nature and scope of the asserted duty of care on the manner in which an obligation or duty has been expressly and specifically defined by a contract.

Again, with respect, our understanding of the passage is different. In our view, Le Dain J.'s use of the words "created" and "depends" indicates the meaning of this passage is simply that for concurrent tort liability to be available there must be a duty of care in tort that would exist even in the absence of the specific contractual term which created the corresponding contractual obligation.

This interpretation of *Rafuse* accords with the view taken in other cases that concurrent liability in tort and contract is available where the contractual obligation in question arises from an express term of the contract. For example, in *Batty v. Metropolitan Property Realisations Ltd.*, [1978] 1 Q.B. 554, the English Court of Appeal ruled that the plaintiffs were entitled to judgment against the defendant developers in either contract or tort where a house leased to the plaintiffs on a 999-year lease was gradually becoming uninhabitable due to instability of the land on which the house was built. The contractual obligation owed to the plaintiffs by the developers arose from an express warranty in the contract between the plaintiffs and the developers that the house had been built "'in an efficient and workmanlike manner and of proper materials and so as to be fit for habitation . . .'" (p. 563). This contractual obligation in effect corresponded with a tort duty "to examine with reasonable care the land, which in this case would include adjoining land, in order to see whether the site was one on which a house fit for habitation could safely be built" (p. 567).

Nor do we see the reference by Le Dain J. in *Rafuse* to *Jarvis v. Moy, Davies, Smith, Vandervell & Co.*, [1936] 1 K.B. 399 (C.A.), and other related English case law differentiating tort and contract, as supportive of a distinction between express and implied contractual terms. The issue in those cases was one of classifying the causes of action as *either* tort *or* contract for procedural purposes under the successive County Courts Acts. Indeed, they may be seen as resting on the assumption that, apart from statutory prescription, concurrent actions may lie.

Summary

We conclude that neither principle, the authorities nor the needs of contracting parties, support the conclusion that dealing with a matter by an express contract term will, in itself, categorically exclude the right to sue in tort. The parties may by their contract limit the duty one owes to the other or waive the right to sue in tort. But subject to this, the right to sue concurrently in tort and contract remains.

In the case at bar, the contract did not limit the duty of care owed by Hydro to Checo. Nor did Checo waive its common law right to bring such tort actions as might be open to it. It follows that Checo was entitled to claim against Hydro in tort.

NOTES AND QUESTIONS

1. What is meant by the term "concurrency"? Why was it relevant in *BG Checo*?

2. On what point did Justices Iacobucci and Sopinka dissent from the majority? What policy considerations divided the court? Whose reasoning is the most persuasive?

3. Concurrent liability in negligent misrepresentation and contract was recognized in England in *Esso Petroleum Co. v. Mardon*, [1976] 2 All E.R. 5 (C.A.). However, the English courts remain more sympathetic to the contractual approach reflected in Iacobucci and Sopinka JJ.'s dissent in *BG Checo*.

4. For an authoritative discussion of damages in tort and contract, see the majority judgment in *BG Checo*.

5. For further reading on the relationship between tort and contract, see Bloom, "Fictions and Frictions on the Interface Between Tort and Contract", in Burns and Lyon, eds., *Donoghue v. Stevenson and the Modern Law of Negligence* (1991), 139-90.

REVIEW PROBLEM

Alice, a resident of the City of Milbury, suffered a serious heart attack one morning while walking to work. Two nearby pedestrians wrapped Alice in warm clothing, while a third went to call the police on the central emergency number.

The City had just installed a new central switchboard system designed to handle all calls for the police, fire department and ambulance services. Ideally, the calls would be handled by specially trained operators who would rank the emergency and dispatch the appropriate service. The pedestrian tried for over an hour to get through on the central emergency number, but to no avail. When he returned to the scene of the accident, he learned that Alice had just died.

A subsequent investigation indicated that the system's shortcomings were due to inferior equipment supplied by Sonar Corp. Experts in the field indicated that the Sonar equipment was notoriously unreliable, and that all those knowledgeable in this branch of electrical equipment knew it.

The City had hired Panamar Inc. to design the new system, and all parties agree that its design was quite satisfactory. Panamar originally recommended that the equipment be purchased from a Japanese company.

After Panamar completed its contractual obligations and was paid, it kept in touch. Ralph, Panamar's President, had called the appropriate City officials and offered, free of charge, to provide whatever advice he could. The City engineer responsible for implementing the plan took the President up on his gracious offer several times and was favourably impressed by his helpful suggestions.

As a result of labour unrest in Japan, the City fell behind schedule in installing the system. Ralph indicated that the City could get exactly the same equipment immediately for the same price from Sonar Corp. When the City engineer mentioned the rumours about the unreliability of the Sonar equipment, Ralph stated: "I may not be a certified expert, but these rumours are fuelled by foreign competitors playing on Canadians' sense of inferiority." Despite the trade reports to the contrary, Ralph stated that the Sonar equipment was as reliable as any produced in the world. Ralph had used Sonar's products in several jobs 15 years ago, but he had no experience with the new product lines in question and he failed to mention this to the City. The City ultimately took Ralph's advice and purchased $500,000 worth of Sonar equipment for its new system.

The equipment never functioned properly, and complaints began to mount as the system continually broke down. Alice's death was the last straw. The City was forced to take out all the Sonar equipment and replace it at a cost of $600,000.

Discuss Panamar's liability to Alice's estate and to the City of Milbury in negligent misrepresentation.

23

RECOVERY OF PURE ECONOMIC LOSS IN NEGLIGENCE

1. Introduction
2. Product Quality Claims — Tort or Contract?
3. Relational Economic Loss

1. Introduction

As we discussed in chapter 22, a "pure" economic loss is a financial loss which is not directly attributable to a preceding injury to the plaintiff's person or property. In a lawsuit based on pure economic loss, the plaintiff claims compensation solely for the financial damages caused by the defendant's tortious conduct. During the past 20 years, the legal principles governing pure economic loss have undergone significant, divergent, and highly contentious changes in the Commonwealth. These changes are best understood in historical perspective.

By the late 19th century, the English courts had determined that a plaintiff could recover for financial losses that were a direct and foreseeable consequence of the plaintiff's personal injury or damage to property. The same courts also decided that there could be no recovery for pure economic loss. As established in *Cattle v. Stockton Waterworks Co.* (1875), L.R. 10 Q.B. 453, this "exclusionary rule" was justified by the notion that clear boundaries had to be maintained on the scope and extent of recovery in tort. Judges feared that pure economic losses, if compensable, would lead to large and potentially limitless awards of damages. As the American jurist Benjamin Cardozo stated in *Ultramares Corp. v. Touche* (1931), 255 N.Y. 170, at 179 (C.A.), awards for pure economic loss inevitably would lead to "liability in an indeterminate amount for an indeterminate time to an indeterminate class".

The exclusionary rule was not seriously challenged in the Commonwealth countries until *Hedley Byrne & Co. v. Heller & Partners Ltd.*, [1964] A.C. 465 (H.L.) reached the English courts in the early 1960s. In a decision of far-reaching importance, the House of Lords decided to break, at least in part, with the old law. Pure economic losses would be recoverable when they were a direct and foreseeable result of the plaintiff's reliance on the defendant's negligent misrepresentation. Although the House of Lords in *Hedley Byrne* tried to confine recovery for pure economic losses to a narrow class of "reliance" cases, the logic of the decision encouraged further assaults on the exclusionary rule.

By 1990, Canadian common law courts had grafted a number of clear exceptions onto the rule against recovery for pure economic loss. Chapter 22 described these developments in negligent misrepresentation. In *Kamloops (City) v. Nielsen* (1984), 10 D.L.R. (4th) 641, the Supreme Court of Canada established that a plaintiff can recover for pure economic loss from a public authority.

Canadian courts have also established that providers of commercial services can be held liable for the pure economic losses of those within sufficient legal proximity. The leading authority in this area is *B.D.C. Ltd. v. Hofstrand Farms Ltd.* (1986), 26 D.L.R. (4th) 1 (S.C.C.). In *B.D.C.*, the plaintiff instructed the Crown's clerk to courier vital land grant documents to the relevant registry office. The clerk was told that it was essential for the documents to be delivered by a particular date. While the envelope was marked "air express", the clerk did not inform the courier of its contents. The courier failed to deliver the envelope in time and the land deal failed to close. The plaintiff sued the Crown and the courier to recover its financial losses.

Although it dismissed the plaintiff's suit, the Supreme Court used *B.D.C.* to establish general principles governing liability for the careless performance of a service. The crucial factor is the degree of "proximity" between the service-provider and the plaintiff. The assessment of proximity is based on knowledge and reliance. Did the service-provider know of the plaintiff's specific needs or requirements? Did the plaintiff rely on the defendant's performance? If these questions are answered in the affirmative, the plaintiff will be entitled to recover the pure economic losses directly caused by the defendant's negligence.

Two other situations have generated extensive and complex litigation over the recoverability of pure economic losses: the negligent manufacture of goods; and "relational" economic loss claims. The leading cases in both categories are discussed below.

2. Product Quality Claims

RIVTOW MARINE v. WASHINGTON IRON WORKS

[1974] S.C.R. 1189, 40 D.L.R. (3d) 530 (S.C.C.)

RITCHIE J.: ... The appellant was the charterer by demise of a self-loading and unloading log barge the "Rivtow Carrier", fitted with two pintle-type cranes designed and manufactured by the respondent, Washington Iron Works, a company having its head office and chief place of business in the United States of America (which is hereinafter referred to as "Washington"), for which the respondent Walkem Machinery & Equipment Limited (hereinafter referred to as "Walkem"), was at all material times the sole representative and distributor in the Province of British Columbia.

During the month of September, 1966, the logging business in which Rivtow Marine Limited (hereinafter referred to as "Rivtow") was engaged, was passing through the period of coastal operations which was recognized by all concerned as being one of the busiest seasons of the year, and the "Rivtow Carrier" had been sent to Kitimat for the purpose of loading logs when it was ordered back to Vancouver because a crane virtually identical to its own and which had also been designed, manufactured and installed by the respondent Washington on a similar barge called the "Straits Logger", had collapsed, killing its operator. After inspection in Vancouver the appellant found cracks in the mountings of both cranes on the "Rivtow Carrier" and shortly thereafter, on September 20th, the Workmen's Compensation Board of British Columbia issued the following order addressed to Rivtow:

> In view of the recent failure in the mounting of a Pintle type crane, barge mounted, we request that you submit to this office, without delay, a report over the signature of a qualified professional engineer certifying that the lifting and hoisting equipment on your self-loading log barge is structurally sound, is in the same working condition and all competent parts are properly assembled and installed.

Upon closer inspection, very serious structural defects were found in the Rivtow cranes similar to those which were later found to have been the cause of the death of the crane operator when the crane collapsed on the "Straits Logger". These cranes, which had been designed by Washington engineers, had been attached to these barges by Washington Iron Works for Yarrows Limited which had built the barges, and it was agreed by counsel that similar cranes had been installed on three other barges all of which had "suffered cracking in the legs of the pintle masts." In the case of two of these barges, Washington had become aware of the development of identical cracks in the cranes as early as November, 1965, and in January, 1966, an employee of Walkem discovered cracks in the pintle masts of the "Rivtow Carrier" cranes which were the same as those observed in the cranes supplied to the other four barges.

. . .

In the course of his reasons for judgment in the Court of Appeal, Mr. Justice Tysoe added that [26 D.L.R. (3d) 559 at p. 563, [1972] 3 W.W.R. 735]:

> On the hearing of this appeal Washington admitted that the cracking in the "Rivtow Carrier" cranes was due to inadequacies in the design of the pintle cranes and that Washington, through its responsible engineers, had knowledge there was a problem with regard to cracking developing in the legs of the pintle cranes during operation by not later than February, 1966. Washington also admitted that there was carelessness in design; but it denied any liability to Rivtow.

It also emerges from the evidence and from the findings of the Courts below that although Washington and Walkem had both been aware for some time that the pintle-type cranes were subject to cracking due to negligence in design, neither of these companies warned the appellant of the potential danger and accompanying necessity for repair and the appellant was first alerted to the seriousness of the situation after the collapse of the "Straits Logger" crane in September, 1966.

The nature of the appellant's claim is well described in the reasons for judgment of the learned trial Judge which are reproduced in the judgment of the Court of Appeal and are in the following terms [at p. 562]:

> "The plaintiff's action is for special damages for the cost of repairs to cranes on the 'Rivtow Carrier', a self-loading log barge, and for loss of use of the barge during the repair period.
>
> "The claim against the defendant Washington Iron Works, as manufacturer of the cranes, is based on negligent design, failure to warn the plaintiff, as operator, of the dangerous situation created by the serious error in design which was known, or should have been known to Washington, and for making negligent statements in writing, intending them to be relied upon by the plaintiff.
>
> "As against the defendant Walkem, who are distributors and sole representatives of the defendant Washington in the Province of British Columbia, the claim is for failure to warn the plaintiff when Walkem became aware of the serious error in design and in making negligent statements orally and in writing to the plaintiff, intending that such statements be relied upon.
>
> "The action has been discontinued as against Yarrows Ltd."

I think it important to stress the fact that the cranes in question were designed for the express purpose of loading and unloading heavy logs, that the site of the logging operation, *i.e.*, the coastal areas of British Columbia, was well known to both respondents who were in fact aware of the exact task to be required of the cranes by Rivtow. This is not a case of a negligent manufacturer whose defective or dangerous goods have caused damage to some unknown member of the general public into whose hands they have found their way. These respondents knew that the cranes were going to be used by the appellant and the exact use to which they were to be put.

. . .

In its appeal to this Court, the appellant asked for judgment for the cost of repairs to the cranes and for loss of use of the barge and for its actual losses due to the barge's inactivity based on "coastal operations", in accordance with the claim advanced in the statement of claim.

. . .

In my opinion, the knowledge of the danger involved in the continued use of these cranes for the purpose for which they were designed carried with it a duty to warn those to whom the cranes had been supplied and this duty arose at the moment when the respondents or either of them became seized with the knowledge.

In the present case, the respondents not only knew the purpose for which the cranes were to be used, but they had become aware of their inadequacy for that purpose without modification and repair and although there was no contractual relationship between the manufacturer and the appellant, the respondents both knew the appellant as one who was using the cranes for their intended purpose in reliance on their advice, and having regard to their knowledge of the business in which the "Rivtow Carrier" was engaged, they must have known approximately the dates when it would be at the peak of its activities and that by withholding their knowledge of the risk, they were exposing the appellant to the direct consequence of losing the services of the barge for at least a month during one of its busiest seasons.

. . .

In the present case there is no suggestion that liability should be based on negligent misrepresentation and to this extent the *Hedley Byrne* case is of no relevance. I refer to it for the sole purpose of indicating the view of the House of Lords that where liability is based on negligence the recovery is not limited to physical damage but extends also to economic loss. The case was recently distinguished in this Court in *J. Nunes Diamonds Ltd. v. Dominion Electric Protection Co.* (1972), 26 D.L.R. (3d) 699, [1972] S.C.R. 769, where Pigeon, J., speaking for the majority of the Court, said at pp. 727-728:

> Furthermore, the basis of tort liability considered in *Hedley Byrne* is inapplicable to any case where the relationship between the parties is governed by a contract, unless the negligence relied on can properly be considered as "an independent tort" unconnected with the performance of that contract. ... This is specially important in the present case on account of the provisions of the contract with respect to the nature of the obligations assumed and the practical exclusion of responsibility for failure to perform them.

In the present case, however, I am of opinion that the failure to warn was "an independent tort" unconnected with the performance of any contract either express or implied.

In the course of the exhaustive argument which he presented on behalf of the appellant, Mr. Locke referred to a number of recent decisions in the Court of Appeal of England to illustrate the development of the thinking in that Court on the question of recovery for pure economic loss in an action for negligence where no physical damage has been sustained by the plaintiff.

In one such case, *SCM (U.K.) Ltd. v. W.J. Whittall & Son Ltd.*, [1970] 2 All E.R. 245, the Court held that economic loss flowing directly from physical harm was recoverable, but Lord Denning indicated that he would deny recovery for other economic loss except in exceptional circumstances. His reasoning appears to rest on the basis that the damage was too remote although he observed, in the course of his judgment [at p. 251]: "I must not be taken, however, as saying that economic loss is always too remote."

A further lengthy discussion of the same subject is contained in the reasons for judgment of the same learned Judge in *Spartan Steel & Alloys Ltd. v. Martin & Co. (Contractors) Ltd.*, [1972] 3 W.L.R. 502, where he appears to treat the question of remoteness of damage as one to be determined "as a matter of policy" and after referring to the cases of *Cattle v. Stockton Waterworks Co.* and *La Societe Anonyme de Remorquage a Helice v. Bennetts*, he said [at p. 508]:

> On the other hand, in the cases where economic loss by itself has been held to be recoverable, it is plain that there was a duty to the plaintiff and the loss was not too remote.

In the case of *Ministry of Housing and Local Government v. Sharp et al.*, [1970] 2 Q.B. 233 at p. 278, Salmon, L.J., appears to me to have dealt with the question both accurately and succinctly when he said:

> So far, however, as the law of negligence relating to civil actions is concerned, the existence of a duty to take reasonable care no longer depends on whether it is physical injury or financial loss which can reasonably be foreseen as a result of a failure to take such care.

I am conscious of the fact that I have not referred to all relevant authorities relating to recovery for economic loss under such circumstances, but I am satisfied that in the present case there was a proximity of relationship giving rise to a duty to warn and that the damages awarded by the learned trial Judge were recoverable as compensation for the direct and demonstrably foreseeable result of the breach of that duty. This being the case, I do not find it necessary to follow the sometimes winding paths leading to the formulation of a "policy decision".

It will be seen that I prefer the reasoning and conclusion of the trial Judge to those of the Court of Appeal, and for the reasons which I have indicated, I reject the suggestion of Tysoe, J.A., that this conclusion involves an extension of the rule in *M'Alister (or Donoghue) v. Stevenson* where the liability was based on a different ground.

For all these reasons I would set aside the judgment of the Court of Appeal and restore the judgment rendered at trial by Mr. Justice Ruttan.

The appellant will have its costs in this Court and the costs of the respondents' cross-appeal in the Court of Appeal.

LASKIN J. (dissenting in part): — This is the first occasion upon which this

Court has been called upon to determine whether recovery may be had in a negligence action for economic loss which stands alone and is not consequent upon physical injury. The trial Judge awarded damages for the loss of earnings suffered by the appellant for a certain down period required for repairs to the pintle crane, but he denied recovery for the cost of repairs to make the faultily-designed and manufactured crane fit for service. In this view he is sustained in the reasons of my brother Ritchie which I have had an opportunity to read. I agree with the award of damages so far as it goes, but I would enlarge it to include as well the cost of repairs.

I would do this because I do not agree that the liability of the respondents should be rested on the one basis of a failure to warn of the probability of injury by reason of the defective design of the crane. The failure to warn is, of course, the only basis upon which, on the facts herein, liability could be imposed upon Walkem. However, Washington, as the designer and manufacturer of the crane, was under an anterior duty to prevent injury which foreseeably would result from its negligence in the design and manufacture of this piece of equipment. If physical harm had resulted, whether personal injury or damage to property (other than to the crane itself), Washington's liability to the person affected, under its anterior duty as a designer and manufacturer of a negligently-produced crane, would not be open to question. Should it then be any less liable for the direct economic loss to the appellant resulting from the faulty crane merely because the likelihood of physical harm, either by way of personal injury to a third person or property damage to the appellant, was averted by the withdrawal of the crane from service so that it could be repaired?

Two new points are involved in this question. The first is whether Washington's liability for negligence should embrace economic loss when there has been no physical harm in fact, and the second is whether the appellant is a proper plaintiff to recover for economic loss and as well the cost of repairing the defective crane.

A manufacturer's liability in negligence for physical harm extends to ensuing economic loss by the person who has suffered the physical harm: see *British Celanese Ltd. v. A.H. Hunt Ltd.*, [1969] 1 W.L.R. 961; *SCM (U.K.) Ltd. v. W.J. Whittall & Son Ltd.*, [1970] 3 All E.R. 245. There is no doubt that the appellant in the present case was within the ambit of risk of physical harm through the collapse of the defectively-designed and manufactured crane; damage to the barge which it had under charter was a foreseeable consequence of Washington's negligence. It is said, however, that a manufacturer's liability for negligence does not extend to economic loss where no physical harm results, even in a case where physical harm is threatened. It is true that economic interests, ordinarily protected in contract as promised advantages, were for long protected in tort in only limited classes of cases, as for example, cases of intentional torts, such as deceit in interference with contract relations, *per quod* actions by a master for injury to his servant by a defendant's negligence and statutory fatal accidents actions by dependants of a person whose death was caused by negligence of another. To these classes a new member has been admitted; the doctrine of *Hedley Byrne & Co. Ltd. v. Heller & Partners Ltd.*, [1964] A.C. 465, which has been considered in this Court and has been applied in other Courts in Canada, shows that economic or pecuniary loss is not outside the scope of liability for negligence.

The present case is not of the *Hedley Byrne* type, as the reasons of my brother Ritchie show, but recovery for economic loss alone is none the less supported under negligence doctrine. It seems to me that the rationale of manufacturers' liability for negligence should equally support such recovery in the case where, as here, there is a threat of physical harm and the plaintiff is in the class of those who are foreseeably so threatened: see Fleming, *Law of Torts*, 4th ed. (1971), pp. 164-5, 444-5.

. . .

In brief, given the case of a manufacturer who is under a duty not to expose consumers or users of its products to an unreasonable risk of harm (and I would place builders of houses under the same duty), what are the limits on the kind or range of harm for which liability will be imposed if there is a breach of duty? One type of answer has been to invoke the notion of remoteness which may relate to physical harm no less than to economic loss: *cf. Seaway Hotels Ltd. v. Cragg (Canada) Ltd. and Consumers Gas Co.* (1960), 21 D.L.R. (2d) 264, [1959] O.R. 581, and *Spartan Steel Alloys Ltd. v. Martin & Co. (Contractors) Ltd.*, [1972] 3 W.L.R. 502. Another, and more usual answer since *MacPherson v. Buick Motor Co.* (1916), 217 N.Y. 382, and *M'Alister (or Donoghue) v. Stevenson*, [1932] A.C. 562, has been to deny manufacturers' liability unless physical harm has resulted from the breach of duty. Put another way, liability has been denied on the ground that there is no duty to a consumer or user in respect of economic loss alone. It seems to me that this restriction on liability has in it more of a concern to avoid limitless claims for economic loss from any kind of negligence than a concern for the particular basis upon which manufacturers' liability for negligence rests. That liability rests upon a conviction that manufacturers should bear the risk of injury to consumers or users of their products when such products are carelessly manufactured because the manufacturers create the risk in the carrying on of their enterprises, and they will be more likely to safeguard the members of the public to whom their products are marketed if they must stand behind them as safe products to consume or to use. They are better able to insure against such risks, and the cost of insurance, as a business expense, can be spread with less pain among the buying public than would be the case if an injured consumer or user was saddled with the entire loss that befalls him.

This rationale embraces, in my opinion, threatened physical harm from a negligently-designed and manufactured product resulting in economic loss. I need not decide whether it extends to claims for economic loss where there is no threat of physical harm or to claims for damage, without more, to the defective product.

It is foreseeable injury to person or to property which supports recovery for economic loss suffered by a consumer or user who is fortunate enough to avert such injury. If recovery for economic loss is allowed when such injury is suffered, I see no reason to deny it when the threatened injury is forestalled. Washington can be no better off in the latter case than in the former. On the admitted facts, a crane on another person's barge, of similar design to that installed on the appellant's barge, had collapsed, killing its operator. It was when this fact came to its notice that the appellant took its crane out of service. Its crane had the same cracks in it that were found in the collapsed crane, and they were due to the same faulty design in both cases. Here then was a piece of equipment whose use was fraught with danger to person and property because of negligence in its design and manufacture; one death had already resulted from the use of a similar piece of equipment that had been marketed by Washington. I see nothing untoward in holding Washington liable in such circumstances for economic loss resulting from the down time necessary to effect repairs to the crane. The case is not one where a manufactured product proves to be merely defective (in short, where it has not met promised expectations), but rather one where by reason of the defect there is a foreseeable risk of physical harm from its use and where the alert avoidance of such harm gives rise to economic loss. Prevention of threatened harm resulting directly in economic loss should not be treated differently from post-injury cure.

Liability of Washington to make good the appellant's loss of profits being established, it remains to consider its liability for the cost of repairs. It is unnecessary in this case to see this cost as necessarily a foreseeable consequence of the breach of anterior duty resting upon Washington. It can stand on another footing. A plaintiff injured by another's negligence is required to act reasonably to mitigate his damages. If his damages are economic damages only, mitigation may involve him in repairing the defect which brought them about. It may not be open to him to do that because the tortfeasor is in control of the matter that invites repair or correction, as in the *Cragg* and *Spartan Steel* cases already cited. But where the defective product which threatened injury has been in use by the plaintiff, it may be reasonable for him, upon learning of the threat of likely injury from its continued use, to expend money for its repair to make it fit for service. Such an expenditure then becomes part of the economic loss for which Washington must respond. No question was raised in this case about the reasonableness of the appellant's conduct in suspending use of the crane nor about the reasonableness of having it repaired nor of the reasonableness of the cost of repair.

I would, accordingly, allow the appeal, set aside the judgment of the British Columbia Court of Appeal and restore the judgment of Ruttan, J., but would vary it to add the cost of repair of the crane to the amount of economic loss for which he found Washington liable. I agree with the disposition as to costs made by my brother Ritchie.

[Fauteux C.J.C., Abbott, Martland, Judson, Spence, and Pigeon JJ. concurred with Ritchie J. Hall J. concurred with Laskin J.]

NOTES AND QUESTIONS

1. What duty of care did the court impose upon the defendants in *Rivtow Marine*? Would the result have been different if the crane had not been negligently manufactured? Compare this duty to the manufacturer's duty to warn consumers of the risks inherent in the use of their products, discussed in chapter 12.

2. What damage claims did the majority allow and what damage claims did they reject? Is the majority decision consistent with its holding on the duty of care?

3. What additional damages would Laskin J. have awarded? What reason does he give for dissenting from the majority on this point? Why does he distinguish between the claim for lost profits and the claim for repair costs? The majority judgment may be referred to as a "type of harm" approach, whereas the dissent may be referred to as a "type of duty" approach. Explain. Which makes better sense and why?

4. The Canadian courts have also applied *Rivtow* in cases involving building defects. For example, in *Thomas v. Whitehorse* (1979), 95 D.L.R. (3d) 762 (N.B. C.A.), the plaintiffs sued the defendant builder/vendor when cracks and serious flooding occurred in the basement of their home. The court cited

Rivtow in denying the plaintiffs' claim in negligence. See also *McGrath v. MacLean* (1979), 95 D.L.R. (3d) 144 (Ont. C.A.); *Surrey v. Carroll-Hatch & Associates Ltd.* (1979), 101 D.L.R. (3d) 218 (B.C. C.A.); and *Buthmann v. Balzer* (1983), 25 C.C.L.T. 273 (Alta. Q.B.), appeal dismissed (1984), 32 C.C.L.T. xlviii (Alta. C.A.), leave to appeal ref'd. (1985), 32 C.C.L.T. xlviii (S.C.C.). But see *Robert Simpson Co. v. Foundation Co.* (1982), 36 O.R. (2d) 97 at 113-14 (C.A.), which held that *Rivtow* did not preclude an action for substandard construction based upon the defendant's negligent misrepresentations about quality. Should the concern about circumventing the terms of the contract not be as relevant in *Simpson*, as in *Rivtow*? See also *Winnipeg Condominium Corp. No. 36 v. Bird Construction Co.* (1995), 23 C.C.L.T. (2d) 1 (S.C.C.).

5. At first, the English courts followed the dissenting judgment in *Rivtow Marine* and allowed recovery for economic loss provided the product defect posed a risk of physical damage. See *Dutton v. Bognor Regis Urban District Council*, [1972] 1 Q.B. 373 (C.A.); *Anns v. London Borough of Merton*, [1977] 2 All E.R. 492 (H.L.); and *Batty v. Metro. Property Realizations Ltd.*, [1978] Q.B. 554 (C.A.). See also *Junior Books v. Veitchi Co.*, [1982] 3 All E.R. 201 (H.L.), where the court seemed to extend recovery based on proximity alone, even if the defect did not pose a risk of physical damage. While *Junior Books* has been influential in Canadian courts, it has been effectively overruled in England. See, for example, *Muirhead v. Industrial Tank Specialties Ltd.*, [1985] 3 All E.R. 705 (C.A.); and *D & F Estates Ltd. v. Church Commissioners for England*, [1988] 2 All E.R. 992 (H.L.). The House of Lords' decision in *Murphy v. Brentwood District Council*, [1990] 2 All E.R. 908, although it concerned the liability of a public authority, provided an even clearer rejection of more liberal approaches to recovery for pure economic loss. The Supreme Court of Canada's recent rejections of *Murphy* have reinforced the substantial differences between Canadian and English law in this area.

6. In New Zealand, the plaintiff can recover in negligence for defects in real property which pose a risk of physical damage, and perhaps for defects which pose no such risk. In *Bowen v. Paramount Bldrs. (Hamilton) Ltd.*, [1977] 1 N.Z.L.R. 394 (C.A.), the defendant architect designed a house in accordance with his client's specifications. The house was sold to the plaintiff who discovered defects and sued the architect. What impact should the fact that the architect complied with the contract have on his tort liability to the plaintiff? Should it matter if the house contains defects, but poses no dangers to its occupants? See also *Leininger v. Stearns-Rogers Mfg.* (1965), 404 P. (2d) 33 (Utah S.C.).

7. The majority in *Rivtow Marine* cited *Trans World Airlines Inc. v. Curtiss-Wright Corp.* (1955), 148 N.Y.S. 2d 284 (S.C.), in support of its decision to deny repair costs and ordinary lost profits. However, opinion is divided on this issue in the United States. See *Spence v. Three Rivers Bldrs. & Masonry Supply Inc.* (1958), 90 N.W. (2d) 973 (Mich. S.C.) (recovery approved in negligence); *Seely v. White Motor Co.* (1965), 403 P. (2d) 145 (Cal. S.C.) (recovery denied in strict liability); and *Santor v. A. & M. Karagheusian Inc.* (1965), 207 A. (2d) 305 (N.J. S.C.) (recovery approved in strict liability).

The American courts are more likely to impose liability in tort against a manufacturer whose product fails to meet express product quality claims. In addition to *Seely*, see *Randy Knitwear Inc. v. Amer. Cyanamid Co.* (1962), 181 N.E. (2d) 389 (N.Y. C.A.). Why do you think the courts are more receptive to this approach?

8. Claims for economic loss caused by defective products are also governed by legislation in all of the Canadian provinces. Many provinces have warranties of merchantability which cannot be excluded in consumer transactions, and some abolish the privity requirement for suits against the manufacturer. There is also federal and provincial legislation prohibiting false and misleading advertising.

REVIEW PROBLEMS

1. In a construction contract between Owner and Contractor, there is a clause which exculpates Contractor from liability for any losses other than repair costs, should the work or materials provided under contract prove substandard. There is no similar clause in the subcontract between Contractor and SubContractor. Should SubContractor be held directly liable to Owner in negligence for business losses consequent on the subcontractor's installation of faulty materials? Does it matter whether the defect is dangerous or merely shoddy? Would your conclusion change if the exculpatory clause was in the subcontract, but not in the main contract?

2. The plaintiff purchased carpet from the defendant. The carpet began to wear badly after one year. Is the carpet defective? What further information would assist you in your answer? Does this suggest whether negligence or sales law is best suited to deal with claims about shoddy goods?

3. Relational Economic Loss

CANADIAN NATIONAL RAILWAY v. NORSK PACIFIC STEAMSHIP CO.

(1992), 91 D.L.R. (4th) 289 (S.C.C.)

[This decision is the most important precedent in the law of pure economic loss. It is the key case both on pure economic loss generally, and on "relational" economic loss specifically. A "relational" economic loss is an economic loss that is suffered by one party as a result of damage to the property of another. In *Norsk*, CNR sustained a relational economic loss when a tugboat negligently damaged a vital Fraser River railway bridge. Although CNR was the primary user of the bridge, the federal government owned it. CNR's operations and profits were seriously affected by the collision. Lacking a contractual remedy, CNR sued the tugboat operator, Norsk Pacific Steamship Ltd., and Public Works Canada.

The Supreme Court divided 4-3. Justice McLachlin's majority judgment in favour of CNR was supported by Justices L'Heureux-Dubé and Cory. Justice Stevenson wrote a separate concurring judgment. Justice La Forest's lengthy and vigorous dissent was supported by Justices Iacobucci and Sopinka. Together the judgments provide extensive and unreconciled analyses of the relevant law.]

McLachlin J.: —

. . .

A fundamental proposition underlies the law of tort: that a person who by his or her fault causes damage to another may be held responsible. Where the fault is negligence, the duty extends to all those to whom the tortfeasor may foreseeably cause harm: *Donoghue v. Stevenson*, [1932] A.C. 562 (H.L.). This is a proposition of great breadth. It was soon realized that it would be necessary to limit recovery for practical, policy reasons. As Cardozo J. put it in *Ultramares Corp. v. Touche*, 174 N.E. 441 (1931) at p. 444, limits were needed to prevent "liability in an indeterminate amount for an indeterminate time to an indeterminate class".

The search for a principled mechanism of limitation has proved elusive. The law began by limiting recovery to cases where the tortfeasor had caused physical loss or injury to the plaintiff: *Cattle v. Stockton Waterworks Co.* (1875), L.R. 10 Q.B. 453. That case denied recovery of "relational losses" consequent upon the negligent infliction of damage to the property of another person. Only a person whose person or property is damaged can recover in tort. This rule was followed for decades in England and elsewhere in the Commonwealth.

While the criterion of physical damage successfully avoided the spectre of unlimited damages, it suffered from the defect that it arbitrarily, and in some cases, arguably unjustly, deprived deserving plaintiffs of recovery. Why, it was asked, should the right to recover economic loss be dependent on whether physical damage, however minuscule, had been inflicted on the plaintiff's property? Why should a plaintiff who waits for a defective machine to break and cause physical injury or damage be able to recover, while one who prudently repairs the machine before the physical damage or injury occurs be left without remedy? Is there really a generic distinction between the loss resulting from repair of physical damage and loss resulting from loss of use in a commercial situation where the only real loss is one of profit? While it may be argued that physical injury is inherently more deserving than economic loss, particularly where the economic loss is not associated with physical damage (see B. Feldthusen, *Economic Negligence*, 2nd ed. (Toronto: Carswell, 1989), at pp. 8-14), that does not explain why the law should not permit recovery for economic loss where justice so requires nor how damage to property and economic losses can be distinguished in many situations. Someone who invests in a bridge in order to use it, cannot be distinguished from someone who leases a bridge in order to use it. If the bridge is lost they have both lost something of value: the use of the bridge.

Not surprisingly, the courts began to allow recovery of pure economic loss where they thought it was just. However, apart from reliance damages for negligent misrepresentation, the course of the law has been neither uniform nor uncontroversial. This appeal raises anew the issue in the Canadian context.

The answers to the question of recovery of economic loss in negligence are not easy, as the uncertain history of the cases attests. On the one hand, the jurisprudence of the past three decades discloses a resurgent feeling on the part of judges that in some cases beyond physical damage and reliance, economic loss should be recoverable in negligence. On the other hand lies the fear of indiscriminately opening the floodgates of liability.

It is worth stating at the outset certain general propositions which have often been put and may serve as guideposts in our search for the answer to the difficult issue we face.

First, some limits on the potentially unlimited liability which can theoretically flow from negligence are necessary; potential defendants must be able to gauge the extent of the risk they incur and frivolous litigation should be discouraged. The need for a limiting device is recognized in *Rivtow Marine Ltd. v. Washington Iron Works* (1973), 40 D.L.R. (3d) 530, [1974] S.C.R. 1189, [1973] 6 W.W.R. 692, and acknowledged in *Kamloops (City) v. Nielsen* (1984), 10 D.L.R. (4th) 641, [1984] 2 S.C.R. 2, 29 C.C.L.T. 97.

Second, the limits should be relatively clear. Commentators have adverted to the need for certainty such that commercial enterprises have some appreciation of what risk is to be borne by whom: see, for example, J.C. Smith, *Liability in Negligence* (Toronto: Carswell, 1984), at p. 166; *Winfield and Jolowicz on Tort*, 13th ed. (London: Sweet & Maxwell, 1989), at p. 86; and John G. Fleming, *The Law of Torts*, 7th ed. (Sydney: Law Book Co., 1987), at p. 162 ff.

Third, as Lord Denning observed in *Spartan Steel & Alloys Ltd. v. Martin & Co. (Contractors) Ltd.*, [1973] Q.B. 27 (C.A.) at p. 36: "At bottom . . . the question of recovering economic loss is one of policy." The question is not only one of legal doctrine, but of where, from the point of view of individual fairness and economic policy, the loss should ultimately fall.

Finally, a single, simple criterion for recovery in all the disparate circumstances where economic loss is foreseeable and ought to be recoverable is, given the record to date, probably unattainable: see Oliver L.J. in *Leigh & Sillivan Ltd. v. Aliakmon Shipping Co.*, [1985] Q.B. 350 (C.A.), and Wilson J. in *Kamloops v. Nielsen, supra*.

. . .

[At this point, Justice McLachlin discussed the need for clear limits on recovery in pure economic loss. This discussion was followed by a lengthy comparative exposition of the law in various common and civil law jurisdictions. Having concluded that several jurisdictions have permitted some recovery for pure economic loss without generating unlimited liability, Justice McLachlin reviewed recent doctrinal developments in the field. This section concluded with a firm rejection of the House of Lord's decision in *Murphy v. Brentwood District Council*, [1990] 2 All E.R. 908. Justice McLachlin then provided a detailed explanation of the majority judgment.]

In summary, it is my view that the authorities suggest that pure economic loss is prima facie recoverable where, in addition to negligence and foreseeable loss, there is sufficient proximity between the negligent act and the loss. Proximity is the controlling concept which avoids the spectre of unlimited liability. Proximity may be established by a variety of factors, depending on the nature of the case. To date, sufficient proximity has been found in the case of negligent misstatements where there is an undertaking and correlative reliance (*Hedley Byrne*); where there is a duty to warn (*Rivtow*); and where a statute imposes a responsibility on a municipality toward the owners and occupiers of land (*Kamloops*). But the categories are not closed. As more cases are decided, we can expect further definition on what factors give rise to liability for pure economic loss in particular categories of cases. In determining whether liability should be extended to a new situation, courts will have regard to the factors traditionally relevant to proximity, such as the relationship between the parties, physical propinquity, assumed or imposed obligations and close causal connection. And they will insist on sufficient special factors to avoid the imposition of indeterminate and unreasonable liability. The result will be a principled, yet flexible, approach to tort liability for pure economic loss. It will allow recovery where recovery is justified, while excluding indeterminate and inappropriate liability, and it will permit the coherent development of the law in accordance with the approach initiated in England by *Hedley Byrne* and followed in Canada in *Rivtow*, *Kamloops* and *Hofstrand*.

. . .

Are there practical reasons why the recovery of economic loss should be confined to cases where the plaintiff has sustained physical damage or injury or relied on a negligent misrepresentation? Will extension of recovery of economic loss to other situations open the floodgates of liability, prove so uncertain as to be unworkable, or have an adverse economic impact? Such questions are difficult to answer, but some assistance may be gained from looking at what has happened where the rule has been broadened and from examining the merits of the economic arguments urged in support of restricting recovery.

(1) *The comparative evidence*

The comparative historical perspective provides little support for the need for a rule which confines recovery of economic loss to cases where the plaintiff has suffered physical loss or has relied on a negligent misstatement. The civil law in Canada and abroad appears to function adequately without recourse to such a rule. In the common law jurisdictions of Canada, where the availability of damages for pure economic loss has been accepted for a decade and a half, the twin spectres of unlimited recovery and unworkable uncertainty have not materialized. And to the extent that recovery for pure economic loss has been allowed in the United States, it seems not to have provoked adverse consequences but rather to have satisfied the public demand for justice so essential to the maintaining the vitality of the law of negligence.

(2) *Economic theory*

The arguments advanced under this head proceed from the premise that a certain type of loss should not be seen in terms of fault but seen rather as the more or less inevitable by-product of desirable but inherently dangerous (or "risky") activity. Viewing the activity thus, it is argued that it may well be just to distribute its costs among all who benefit from that activity, and conversely unfair to impose it upon individuals who (assuming human error to be the inevitable by-product of human activity) are viewed as the "faultless" instruments causing the loss. This basis for administering losses has been variously described as "collectivisation of losses" or "loss distribution": see Fleming in *The Law of Torts*, supra, at pp. 8-9. It arguably amounts to a rejection or diminution of the concept of personal fault on which our law of tort (and the civil law of delict) is based.

Three arguments are put forward: (a) the insurance argument; (2) the loss spreading argument; and (3) the "contractual allocation of risk" argument. None of them, in my view, establishes that the extension of recovery granted by the courts in this case is unfair or inefficient.

. . .

The plaintiff C.N. suffered economic loss as a result of being deprived of its contractual right to use the bridge damaged by the defendants' negligence. Applying the *Kamloops* approach, its right to recover depends on: (1) whether it can establish sufficient proximity or "closeness", and (2) whether extension of recovery to this type of loss is desirable from a practical point of view.

The first question is whether the evidence in this case establishes the proximity necessary to found liability. The case does not fall within any of the categories where proximity and liability have been hitherto found to exist. So we must consider the matter afresh.

A number of factors have been suggested in support of a finding of the necessary proximity. One might fasten on the fact that damaging the bridge raised the danger of physical injury to C.N.'s property. C.N.'s property — its trains — were frequently on the bridge and stood to be damaged by an accident involving the bridge. Whether they were in fact damaged is immaterial to the question of proximity. What is important is that this danger indicates a measure of closeness which has traditionally been held to establish the proximity necessary to found liability in tort for pure economic loss. However, to found the decision on this criterion would be to affirm the minority position of Laskin and Hall JJ. in *Rivtow* that danger of physical loss is sufficient to found liability. I note that the majority's restriction of recovery of economic loss to the duty to warn has been doubted. Wilson J. in *Kamloops* noted that the problem of concurrent liability in contract and tort may have played a major role in the majority decision in *Rivtow*, and (at p. 681) that "as in the case of *Hedley Byrne*, we will have to await the outcome of a developing jurisprudence around that decision also". MacGuigan J.A. below stated at p. 359: "In my observation, courts will always find sufficient proximity where there is physical danger to the plaintiff's property." However, it is not necessary to address that issue in this case since other factors clearly indicate the necessary proximity.

In addition to focusing upon the relationship between the appellant Norsk and C.N. — a significant indicator of proximity in and of itself — the trial judge based his conclusion that there was sufficient proximity on a number of factors related to C.N.'s connection with the property damaged, the bridge, including the fact that C.N.'s property was in close proximity to the bridge, that C.N.'s property could not be enjoyed without the link of the bridge, which was an integral part of its railway system and that C.N. supplied materials, inspection and consulting services for the bridge, was its preponderant user, and was recognized in the periodic negotiations surrounding the closing of the bridge.

MacGuigan J.A. summarized the trial judge's findings on proximity as follows, at p. 361:

> In effect, the trial judge found that the C.N.R. was so closely assimilated to the position of P.W.C. that it was very much within the reasonable ambit of risk of the appellants at the time of the accident. That, it seems to me, is sufficient proximity: in Deane J.'s language, it is both physical and circumstantial closeness.

Such a characterization brings the situation into the "joint" or "common venture" category under which recovery for purely economic loss has heretofore been recognized in maritime law cases from the United Kingdom (*The "Greystoke Castle", supra*) and the United States (*Amoco Transport, supra*). The reasoning, as I apprehend it, is that where the plaintiff's operations are so closely allied to the operations of the party suffering physical damage and to its property (which — as damaged — causes the plaintiff's loss) that it can be considered a joint venturer with the owner of the property, the plaintiff can recover its economic loss even though the plaintiff has suffered no physical damage to its own property. To deny recovery in such circumstances would be to deny it to a person who for practical purposes is in the same position as if he or she owned the property physically damaged.

The second question is whether extension of recovery to this type of loss is desirable from a practical point of view. Recovery serves the purpose of permitting a plaintiff whose position for practical purposes, vis-à-vis the tortfeasor, is indistinguishable from that of the owner of the damaged property, to recover what the actual owner could have recovered. This is fair and avoids an anomalous result. Nor does the recovery of economic loss in this case open the floodgates to unlimited liability. The category is a limited one. It has been applied in England and the United States without apparent difficulty. It does not embrace casual users of the property or those secondarily and incidentally affected by the damage done to the property. Potential tortfeasors can gauge in advance the scope of their liability. Businesses are not precluded from self-insurance or from contracting for indemnity, nor are they "penalized" for not so doing. Finally, frivolous claims are not encouraged.

I conclude that here, as in *Kamloops*, the necessary duty and proximity are established; that valid purposes are served by permitting recovery; and that recovery will not open the floodgates to unlimited liability. In such circumstances, recovery should be permitted.

In deference to the learned judgments of my colleagues, I add the following comments. With respect to the reasons of my colleague Stevenson J., I, like La Forest J., would not accept, by itself, the "known plaintiff" test or the "ascertained class" test, which, to borrow La Forest J.'s phrase, places a premium on notoriety. With respect to the reasons of La Forest J., we are in agreement that the broad and flexible approach set out in *Anns* governs the right to recover for economic loss in tort. We also agree that the law of tort does not permit recovery for all economic loss. We further agree that where the plaintiff establishes a joint venture with the owner of the damaged property, it should be able to recover economic loss. Where we differ, in the final analysis, is on the test for determining joint venture.

La Forest J. says that the right to recovery in cases such as this depends exclusively on the terms of the formal contract between the plaintiff and the property owner. If the contract creates a possessory interest or a joint venture, or if it provides for indemnification by the property owner, the plaintiff may recover against a tortfeasor who damages the property and causes economic loss. I do not read the authorities which have considered the implications of a joint venture between the plaintiff and the owner of the damaged property as confining themselves to the formal terms of the contract. I prefer a more flexible test which permits the trial judge to consider all factors relevant to their relationship. The terms of the contract are an important consideration in determining whether economic loss is recoverable. But the contract may tell only part of the story between the parties. If the evidence establishes that having regard to the entire relationship between the owner of the damaged property and the plaintiff, the plaintiff must be regarded as standing in the relation of joint or common venturer (or a concept akin thereto) with the property owner with the result that in justice his rights against third parties should be the same as the owner's, then I would not interfere. Here, as elsewhere in the law of tort, the question is where the balance between certainty and flexibility should be struck. It is my conviction, based on the development of the law relating to recovery of economic loss thus far, that the balance must be struck this side of rigid categorization which denies the possibility of recovery in new cases which may not meet the categorical test.

From the point of view of policy, I share La Forest J.'s concern with avoiding recovery which increases the cost of dealing with a given loss and agree with the importance of the considerations he raises as to the contractual allocation of the risk. While important, I do not find these considerations to be exclusively determinative of the issue. For the reasons given earlier, the policy arguments against recovery are not conclusive, particularly when the individual case is considered. In general, the narrower the scope of tort liability, the cheaper liability insurance. But that is not the whole answer. It may be that elimination of all tort liability for accidents would be the best solution from the point of view of economics, given that casualty insurance is cheaper than liability insurance. But for reasons of principle and policy the law rejects such a conclusion.

I agree too that generally people should be able to predict when they can recover economic loss from third parties, so they can determine in advance how to arrange their affairs, *i.e.*, whether to purchase casualty (or accident) insurance or not. I suggest the test I propose permits this in substantial measure, while leaving open the door to future developments in the law; at a minimum if there is no special connection, physical or circumstantial, between the plaintiff's operations and the property damaged, recovery cannot be assumed and casualty insurance should be purchased. I doubt greater predictability in practical terms can be achieved. Is it truly realistic to suggest that a business firm will decide whether or not to purchase insurance on the basis of what a particular contract with the owner of a particular property provides, as La Forest J. suggests? A company such as the C.N.R. has a host of contracts to consider when assessing whether to buy insurance to cover loss resulting from accidents. Some will meet La Forest J.'s criteria; some will not. I suspect that such decisions as to insurance are more likely to be made on the more global basis of asking whether there is any significant risk of loss in the operations which may not be recovered by suing third parties. Moreover, no plaintiff can be sure it will recover its loss, even if the law permits recovery; the party at fault, for example, may be insolvent or uninsured. If there is doubt on any of these questions, the prudent firm will purchase casualty insurance. So predictability is revealed as a more complex matter than looking at a particular contract.

In the end, I conclude that a test for recovery of economic loss outside situations akin to *Hedley Byrne* — whether "contractual relational" economic loss or otherwise — should be flexible enough to meet the complexities of commercial reality and to permit the recognition of new situations in which liability ought, in justice, to lie as such situations arise. With the greatest respect, it seems to me that a test which is confined to the terms of the formal contract between the owner of the property damaged and the person who suffers economic loss as a consequence of that damage, may not fill these objectives.

NOTES AND QUESTIONS

1. In his concurring judgment, Justice Stevenson adopted a different approach to the problem of indeterminate liability in economic loss cases. The key limiting concept, the Justice contended, was that of the "known plaintiff". The relational loss action should only succeed when it is proven that the defendant either foresaw or should have foreseen the plaintiff and his vulnerability to the economic loss. In *Norsk*, CNR proved that the defendants had known both of its dependence on the bridge and the financial implications of serious damage to the bridge. Justice Stevenson concluded that relational "losses should be recoverable wherever the policy concern about indeterminate liability does not apply".

2. Justice La Forest's long and forceful dissent focused on the alleged differences between relational and other types of economic loss cases. In relational loss cases, the third party's recovery cannot be justified on grounds of deterrence. The potential tortfeasor is already deterred by the property owner's right of action in tort. Second, the third-party plaintiff frequently has a contractual remedy against the injured property owner. La Forest J. also stated that it is impossible to consistently apply the rules about who should be compensated for relational losses. He took the view that the plaintiffs in these cases were often sophisticated commercial enterprises in a position to protect themselves by recourse to negotiated contractual protections and insurance. Such parties are in the best position to plan for and bear the risk of economic loss. For these reasons, Justice La Forest, supported by Sopinka and Iacobucci JJ., favoured retaining the traditional exclusionary rule in relational loss cases.

3. In *Winnipeg Condominium Corp. No. 36 v. Bird Construction Co.*, [1995] 1 S.C.R. 85, the defendant was held liable to third party purchasers for the cost of repairing dangerous defects in buildings the defendant had constructed. See Feldthusen and Palmer, "Economic Loss and the Supreme Court of Canada: An Economic Critique of *Norsk Steamship* and *Bird Construction*" (1995), 74 Can. Bar Rev. 427.

4. In *Caltex Oil (Aust.) Property Ltd. v. The Dredge "Willemstad"* (1976), 136 C.L.R. 529, the High Court of Australia held that the plaintiff could recover the costs of alternative transportation incurred when the defendant's dredge negligently damaged the oil refinery pipeline of a third party. For analysis

of this decision, see Hogg, "Relational Loss, the Exclusionary Rule and the High Court of Australia" (1995), 3 Tort L. Rev. 26.

5. Relational economic loss has generated extensive scholarly analysis. See Brindle, "Pure Economic Loss Revisited" (1992), 48 Const. Law Reps. 278; MacTavish, "Tort Recovery for Economic Loss" (1993), 21 Can. Bus. L.J. 395; Fleming, "Comment: Economic Loss in Canada" (1993), 1 Tort L. Rev. 68; and Waddams, "Further Reflections on the Economic Loss: A Canadian Perspective" (1994), 2 Tort L. Rev. 116.

24

OCCUPIERS' LIABILITY

1. Introduction
2. The Common Law Principles of Occupiers' Liability
3. The Provincial Occupiers' Liability Acts

1. Introduction

An occupier's obligation to those who enter her land has been governed by a distinct set of common law principles. Initially, the courts were reluctant to impose an affirmative duty upon occupiers to maintain their property in a safe condition for the benefit of others. An occupier was required merely to refrain from intentionally injuring lawful entrants or from using unnecessary or excessive force in expelling trespassers. Only gradually were positive duties cast upon occupiers to take measures to safeguard those who entered their property. The nature of the duty varied according to the legal status of the entrants, of which there were four major categories — contractual entrants, invitees, licensees, and trespassers.

Urbanization, the decrease in the importance of land as a source of wealth, and the expansion of liability in other branches of negligence led to the ongoing revision of these principles. The boundaries between the categories of entrants, which were never particularly well established, were further complicated by the courts' recognition of the doctrines of allurement and implied licence. The duties themselves were reworded or redefined. An occupier's common law obligations were made increasingly onerous in an attempt to bring this branch of law into line with modern negligence law. Regardless of the merit of this goal, the legal principles that have emerged are confusing and extremely complex. In the words of the Ontario Law Reform Commission, *Report on Occupiers' Liability* (1972), at 6: "In this field, perhaps more than in any other, legal fictions have developed to the extent that the outcome of any particular case now seems almost fortuitous." These concerns have led Alberta, British Columbia, Manitoba, P.E.I., and Ontario to abandon the common law principles in favour of occupiers' liability statutes.

In this chapter, we will first examine the common law principles that govern occupiers' liability. The cases we have selected are intended to illustrate the general operation of the common law rather than to provide a comprehensive review. The chapter ends with a discussion of the British Columbia Occupiers Liability Act, R.S.B.C. 1979, c. 303, as am. S.B.C. 1989, c. 64, s. 31, which provides an example of the statutory alternatives to the existing common law.

2. The Common Law Principles of Occupiers' Liability

(a) WHO IS AN OCCUPIER?

PALMER v. ST. JOHN

(1969), 1 N.B.R. (2d) 311, 3 D.L.R. (3d) 649 (C.A.)

[The female plaintiff was injured when her toboggan went over a hump at the bottom of a hill and flew into the air before landing. A City work crew, in an attempt to make the hill safer, had inadvertently created the hump. The plaintiff sued both the Horticultural Association, which was responsible for maintaining the park, and the City. The trial judge held both defendants liable in occupiers' liability and further indicated that the City was vicariously liable for the negligence of its work crew. The defendants appealed.]

HUGHES J.A.: . . . The defendant, the Saint John Horticultural Assocation, hereinafter referred to as the Assocation, is a statutory corporation incorporated by 1893 (N.B.), c. 83, for the establishment and maintenance of public gardens and the encour-, aging of the cultivation of flowers and planting trees in the City of Saint John. Over a period of many years the Association acquired various parcels of land which now comprise Rockwood Park and has developed the Park for the enjoyment of the public. Near the shore of Lily Lake which is within the Park, the Association has constructed and operates a pavilion. In addition the Association maintains in the Park public gardens, greenhouses and camp sites and has developed recreational facilities for boating, swimming, skating, skiing, coasting and tobogganing.

. . .

The toboggan slide has been used by the public every season since being constructed, without supervision by the Association and without any charge to the public for its use.

The City of Saint John, hereinafter referred to as the City, has for many years made annual grants to the Association to be used to provide recreational facilities in the Park for citizens of the City. From time to time the City also assisted the Association by providing services of City work crews and personnel for maintenance and development of the Park, the cost of which was ordinarily charged by the City against the annual grants. There is no evidence that the City did any work on the slide other than snow plowing after 1934 until the autumn of 1965 when, under the instructions of the City's Commissioner of Works, Albert E. Hanson, and under the direction of the City's Superintendent of Works, Theodore A. Scribner, a City works crew removed outcroppings of rock, cleared bushes and generally smoothened the hill to make it faster and safer for tobogganing and sliding. On the same occasion the crew placed gravel between the bank, which borders the paved roadway near the foot of the slide, and the edge of the Lake for the purpose of flattening out the slope in that area to make it safer for those using the slide. Again in November or December, 1966, works crews of the City under instructions of the Commissioner of Works placed and levelled fill across about three-quarters of the width of the slide at or near the shoreline of the Lake to lessen the severity of the drop from the bank to the edge of the Lake, in an effort to remove a hazardous condition for those using the slide.

. . .

I shall now turn to the question of the liability of the City to the plaintiffs.

The learned trial Judge has found that the City as well as the Association was an occupier of the sliding hill and held the City liable to the plaintiffs in that capacity. The question who is an occupier has been considered in a number of cases. In *Salmond on Torts*, 11th ed., p. 548, the author states:

> . . . The person responsible for the condition of the premises is he who is in actual occupation or possession of them for the time being, whether he is the owner of them or not. For it is he who has the immediate supervision and control and the power of permitting or prohibiting the entry of other persons . . .
>
> . . .

In *Duncan v. Cammell Laird & Co. Ltd.*, [1943] 2 All E.R. 621 at p. 627, Wrottesley, J., said:

> It seems to me that the importance of establishing that the defendant who invites is the occupier of the premises lies in the fact that with occupation goes control. And the importance of control is that it affords the opportunity to know that the plaintiff is coming on to the premises, to know the premises, and to become aware of dangers whether concealed or not, and to remedy them, or at least to warn those that are invited on to the premises.

The evidence establishes that the City and the Association co-operated closely in efforts to provide recreational facilities at Rockwood Park. As previously stated the City made annual grants to the Association and from time to time used City work crews to perform work and services in the Park. Sometimes the work was performed after consultation with the Park's superintendent, but on other occasions work was done by City crews without consultation with the Association. On one occasion at least the City plowed the snow from the slide at the request of a private citizen. The City was not the owner of the Park at the time of the plaintiffs' accident and did not operate the slide or regulate its use. With all due deference to the learned trial Judge I am unable to agree that the evidence justifies a finding that the City was an occupier of the sliding hill so as to subject it to the duty of an occupier.

[However, Hughes J.A. agreed with the trial judge that the City was vicariously liable for the negligence of its work crew, and he dismissed the City's appeal on this basis.]

NOTES AND QUESTIONS

1. What test did the Court of Appeal use to determine if the City was an occupier of the hill? Do you agree with the court's application of this test to the facts? Assuming that both the City and the Association had been occupiers of the hill, would their liability as occupants necessarily have been the same?

2. In *Couch v. McCann; Ferguson v. McCann* (1977), 77 D.L.R. (3d) 387 (Ont. C.A.), the plaintiffs were injured when the barn floor collapsed at an auction they were attending. They sued Fry, the owner of the property, McCann, the person who had use of the barn, and Phifher and Coughlin, the auctioneers who had been hired by McCann to run the auction. At trial, the action against Fry was dismissed, and the remaining defendants were held liable in occupiers' liability. On appeal, the court held that since the auctioneers had invited the public to attend and had conducted the auction in the barn, they were joint occupants of the barn with McCann. Is this decision compatible with *Palmer*? Based on *Couch*, would a singer hired to perform in a concert hall be an occupier of the facility? Would it make any difference if the singer's company was responsible for advertising the event or

if the singer's salary was based on a percentage of the seat sales? See *Haskett v. Univ. of Western Ont.*, [1955] 3 D.L.R. 234 (Ont. H.C.).

3. An occupier is responsible not only for the land and permanent structures, but also for move-able objects that are situated on the land such as aircraft, trains and scaffolding. See Di Castri, *Occupiers' Liability* (1981), 12-14.

4. In the absence of fraud or contract, a landlord was under no common law duty to ensure that unfurnished premises were safe for his tenants and their visitors. What is the rationale for imposing fundamentally different obligations on owners and occupiers? It should be noted that the provincial Landlord and Tenant Acts now impose fairly onerous statutory duties upon landlords to maintain rented premises in a safe and habitable condition. See, for example, the Landlord and Tenant Act, R.S.A. 1980, c. L-6, s. 14; and the Landlord and Tenant Act, R.S.O. 1990, c. L.7, s. 94. See also *Allison v. Rank City Wall Can. Ltd.* (1984), 45 O.R. (2d) 141 (H.C.); and *Day v. Chaleur Developments Ltd.* (1985), 63 N.B.R. (2d) 313 (Q.B.).

Landlords may also have a duty of care to tenants and their invitees under occupiers' liability legislation in certain circumstances. See for example *Stuart v. R. in Right of Can.*, [1988] 6 W.W.R. 211 (Fed. Ct. T.D.); and *Blake v. Kensche* (1990), 3 C.C.L.T. (2d) 189 (B.C. S.C.).

5. Simple ownership of a property will not in itself constitute "occupation" for the purposes of occupier's liability. An "occupier" is a person having direct control or physical possession of particular premises. See *Wiley v. Tymar Management Inc.*, [1995] 3 W.W.R. 684 (B.C. S.C.); and *Murray v. Bitango*, [1995] 1 W.W.R. 79 (Alta. Q.B.).

(b) THE CATEGORIES OF ENTRANTS AND THE CORRESPONDING DUTIES

(i) *Contractual Entrants*

FINIGAN v. CALGARY

(1967), 62 W.W.R. 115, 65 D.L.R. (2d) 626 (Alta. C.A.)

CAIRNS J.A.: . . . The facts are that on May 23, 1966, the appellant accompanied by her husband entered the park and paid an admission fee of 25¢ to view the exhibits there installed. One of the series of exhibits consisted of a group of Indian teepees erected in a grove of trees. There was a pathway about 4 ft. in width cut through the trees to the entrance of one of the teepees. The pathway had been cleared of trees and roots and other debris but there was a root left on the edge of the pathway about 4ft from the entrance to the teepee which protruded about 2 ins. above the surface. Directly in front of the entrance in the middle of the pathway and about one foot from it the stump had been left which protruded about 2 ins. above the surrounding surface. The stump had been cut on a bias and the evidence was that it was difficult to see even if at the time in question, namely, 6:00 p.m., the light was good. In making the pathways the instructions were that all protruding root stumps were to be taken out. It is also a fact that the authorities inspected the grounds continuously and were in the habit of cutting down any obstructions which might be dangerous, but they had not noticed the stump prior to the accident.

The appellant walked down the pathway with the intention of entering the teepee and with her view on the entrance. She tripped on the exposed root and fell forward and was not able to recover her balance until she fell on the stump causing the damage to which I have referred. There is no doubt that it was the stump which caused her injuries.

The learned trial Judge was of the opinion that the case came within the principles governing the liability of an invitor to an invitee as laid down in *Indermaur v. Dames* (1867), L.R. 2 C.P. 311, and subsequent cases to the effect that the invitee using reasonable care for his own safety "'is entitled to expect that the occupier shall on his part use reasonable care to prevent damage from unusual danger of which he knows or ought to know'" [p. 313]. He therefore dismissed the action and must have been of the opinion, although he does not say so, that there was no unusual danger in all the circumstances.

In my view with great deference I think that the learned trial Judge was wrong in arriving at this decision and that even applying the principle he did he could not come to the conclusion that this was not an unusual danger. The facts are perfectly clear. We have a pathway leading to a teepee and in the middle of the entrance was a two-inch stump which was practically invisible and on which the appellant fell. Surely a person entering the teepee could expect not to encounter such an obstruction. There is no evidence that she was in any way negligent. Had the pathway been properly constructed the stump would not have been left there. In any event it should have been noticed by the respondent in one of the many inspections which were made to ensure the safety of the public.

For these reasons I am of the opinion that the respondents created or suffered to exist an unusual danger of which, if damage arose because of it as it did in this case, they are liable even on the principles enunciated in *Indermaur v. Dames*.

However, completely apart from the principles of the invitee cases it is my view that the respondents are liable on the basis of breach of contract.

Here the appellant paid an admission fee to view the exhibits and thereby entered into a contract with the respondents that she might enjoy those privileges provided she exercised prudence herself without risk of danger so far as reasonable care could make the premises safe. This principle was laid down by Rand, J., in *Brown and Brown v. B. & F. Theatres Ltd.*, [1947] 3 D.L.R. 593, [1947] S.C.R. 486, where the learned Judge, in giving the judgment of the Court excepting that of Kellock, J., who came to the same conclusion following *Francis v. Cockrell* (1870), L.R. 5 Q.B. 501, stated at p. 596:

> The case has been treated as raising the ordinary question of the duty owed by a proprietor of premises towards an invitee. I think, however, I should observe that this is not merely a case of such invitation as was present in *Indermaur v. Dames* (1867), L.R. 2 C.P. 311. Here, Mrs. Brown paid a consideration for the privileges of the theatre, including that of making use of the ladies' room. There was a contractual relation between her and the theatre management that exercising prudence herself she might enjoy those privileges without risk of danger so far as reasonable care could make the premises safe. Although the difference in the degree of care called for may not, in the circumstances here, be material, I think it desirable that the distinction between the two bases of responsibility be kept in mind: *Maclenan v. Segar*, [1917] 2 KB. 325 following *Francis v. Cockrell* (1870), L.R. 5 Q.B. [501]. In *Cox. v. Coulson*, [1916] 2 K.B. 177 at p. 181, Swinfen Eady L.J. said: "The defendant must also be taken to have contracted to take due care that the premises should be reasonably safe for persons using them in the customary manner and with reasonable care", citing *Francis v. Cockrell* [(1870), L.R. 5 Q.B. 184].
>
> . . .

The rule in *Francis v. Cockrell* was approved by Cartwright, J. [as he then was] in giving the majority judgment of the Court in *Carriss v. Buxton*, 13 D.L.R. (2d) 689 at pp. 713-4, [1958] S.C.R. 441, where he stated:

The rule in *Francis v. Cockrell* is stated as follows in *Winfield on Tort*, 6th ed., p. 672: "Where

A enters B's structure under a contract entitling him to do so, it is an implied term in the contract that the structure shall be reasonably fit for the purpose for which it is intended; but this does not extend to any unknown defect incapable of being discovered by reasonable means."

There is no doubt therefore that there is a higher duty owed to a person who enters premises under a contract than that which is owed to an invitee under *Indermaur v. Dames*; as Rand, J., stated, *supra*, it is that anyone may enter "without risk of danger so far as reasonable care could make the premises safe" or at least under *Francis v. Cockrell* there is an implied warranty that the place is reasonably fit for the purposes for which it was intended.

In so far as this case is concerned it is immaterial whether there is a slight difference in the rule as to the liability to a contracting party. There is no doubt under either interpretation of the liability that the respondents did not discharge their obligations to see that the property was either "without risk of danger" or "reasonably fit for the purpose" in permitting the stump in question to obstruct the entrance to the teepee, and they are liable to the appellant in damages for such failure.

. . .

McDERMID J.A.: — In *Maclenan v. Segar*, [1917] 2 K.B. 325 at p. 333, McCardie, J., in referring to the warranty implied, stated,

> The principle is basic and applies alike to premises and to vehicles. It matters not whether the subject be a race-stand, a theatre, or an inn; whether it be a taxicab, an omnibus, or a railway carriage. The warranty in each case is the same, and for a breach thereof an action will lie.

As the warranty is contractual I would like to reserve the question as to whether it is the same in respect of a park run for the benefit of the public as it would be in cases where the premises are being run to make a profit for the owner. It does seem odd to me that a public authority who is carrying on a park for the benefit and enjoyment of the public and not for profit has a greater duty than a departmental store which has invited the public onto its premises in order that the store may make a profit; however, such may be the case. In the case at bar the point does not have to be decided, for even if the warranty implied was the same, and I think it could not be less, as the duty imposed in respect of an invitee, there was still a breach of it. Subject to the foregoing comment, I concur in the judgment of my brother Cairns.

ALLEN, J.A., concurs with CAIRNS, J.A.

NOTES AND QUESTIONS

1. What duty of care does an occupier owe to contractual entrants and how does this differ from the duty owed to invitees? Do you agree with the Appeal Court's application of these principles in *Finigan*? See also *Carriere v. Bd. of Gravelbourg School Dist. No. 2244 of Sask.* (1977), 79 D.L.R. (3d) 662 (Sask. C.A.); *Fanjoy v. Gaston* (1981), 127 D.L.R. (3d) 163 (N.B. C.A.); *McGivney v. Rustico Summer Haven* (1986), 197 A.P.R. 358 (P.E.I. C.A.); and *McGinty v. Cook* (1989), 59 D.L.R. (4th) 94 (Ont. H.C.), aff'd. (1991), 79 D.L.R. (4th) 95 (C.A.).

2. Is McDermid J.A. suggesting that the courts should consider the occupier's motive in determining the nature of the implied contractual warranty? What are the advantages and disadvantanges of such an approach? Should the contractual duty owed to a patron who paid $50 for a ticket to a boxing match be higher than that owed to a patron who paid $3?

3. Why was the City of Calgary held to be an occupier of the park in *Finigan*? Can you reconcile this case and *Palmer*?

4. For a more detailed discussion of the duty owed to contractual entrants see Adair, "Occupier's Liability to the Contractual Visitor" (1979), 2 Advoc. Q. 320; and Di Castri, *Occupiers' Liability* (1981), 15-32.

(ii) *Invitees and Licensees*

McERLEAN v. SAREL

(1987), 61 O.R. (2d) 396 (C.A.)

[McErlean, a boy of almost 15 years of age, was severely injured when he collided with Sarel, another trail bike rider. McErlean was racing with another rider on the old roads in the abandoned gravel pit. Sarel was on the wrong side of the road when he collided with McErlean at a sharp corner where there was poor visibility.

The City of Brampton owned the gravel pit and planned to develop it as a park. Although City officials knew that trail bike riders used the pit, they made no attempt to stop or warn them. At trial, the City was held liable as an occupier and found 75% at fault. Sarel was held 15% at fault and McErlean was found 10% contributorily negligent.]

BY THE COURT:—This is an occupier's liability case. The appeal relates both to liability and damages. The occupier of the land at the relevant time was the appellant the Corporation of the City of Brampton. The trial judge found that the respondent Michael McErlean at the time of the accident was a licensee.

. . .

The first question to be asked is whether the respondent, Michael McErlean, was on the appellant's property as a trespasser or a licensee, it being common ground that he was not an invitee. In our opinion, the respondent must be categorized as a licensee and not a trespasser. A license to enter or remain on property may be given by conduct which manifests consent or permission. Here, it is clear that the appellant made no effort to exclude pedestrians, bikers or others from its property by means of signs (except with respect to swimming) warning not to trespass, by the erection of adequate fencing, by supervision or by any other means. Their entry from time to time onto the lands over an appreciable period was readily ascertainable if not actually known. The owner's failure to object to their presence can reasonably be construed as tacit permission to their entry. Persons who, for instance, took short-cuts across this long-vacant piece of property or who came there to walk their dogs or ride their motorcycles or trail bikes cannot be treated as mere trespassers. The owner's inaction, while not amounting to an invitation to use the property, at least manifested a willingness to permit them entry and indicated its toleration of their presence. In these circumstances, the owner so conducted itself that it cannot be heard to say that it did not give permission. This is not a case in which an occupier unsuccessfully sought to prevent people from trespassing on its lands, nor is this a situation in which precautions against their intrusion would be unduly burdensome or expensive or, based on past experience, likely to be futile. Applying the common law approach, this respondent must, in our opinion, be treated as a licensee (albeit, on the authorities, a "bare licensee" or a "licensee without an interest") and the occupier's liability must be determined on the basis of that relationship: see, generally, Prosser and Keeton, *The Law of Torts*, 5th ed. (1984), c. 10; Fleming, *The Law of Torts*, 6th ed. (1983), c. 21; and Linden, *Canadian Tort Law*, 3rd ed. (1982), c. 18.

What then is the duty owed by an occupier of land to a licensee? Traditionally, it has been spoken of as a duty to warn of concealed dangers or traps of which the occupier had actual knowledge: *Hambourg v. T. Eaton Co. Ltd.*, [1935] 3 D.L.R. 305, [1935] S.C.R. 430. This is plainly a less stringent duty than the duty owed to an invitee which has long been expressed as a duty to take reasonable care to prevent damage from unusual danger of which the invitor knew or ought to have known: *Indermaur v. Dames* (1866), L.R. 1 C.P. 274; affirmed L.R. 2 C.P. 311. However, in 1974, the Supreme Court of Canada in *Mitchell et al. v. C.N.R. Co.* (1974), 46 D.L.R. (3d) 363, [1975] 1 S.C.R. 592, 6 N.S.R. (2d) 440, a case involving a nine-year-old infant-licensee, abandoned the traditional requirement that the danger be concealed and held that mere knowledge of likely danger on the part of a licensee falling short of voluntary assumption of risk will not of itself exonerate the occupier. Later that same year, this court in *Bartlett et al. v. Weiche Apartments Ltd.* (1974), 7 O.R. (2d) 263, 55 D.L.R. (3d) 44, a case involving a three-year-old infant-licensee, thoroughly canvassed the then current law as to an occupier's liability to a licensee. Based on an analysis of the judgments of the Supreme Court of Canada in *Mitchell et al. v. C.N.R. Co.*, supra, and in *Hanson et al. v. City of St. John et al.* (1973), 39 D.L.R. (3d) 417, [1974] S.C.R. 354, 6 N.B.R. (2d) 292, Jessup J.A., speaking for the majority of the court at p. 267 O.R., p. 48 D.L.R., restated the general principle governing the liability of an occupier to a licensee in the following terms:

> It is to take reasonable care to avoid foreseeable risk of harm from any unusual danger on the occupier's premises of which the occupier actually has knowledge or of which he ought to have knowledge because he was aware of the circumstances. The licensee's knowledge of the danger goes only to the questions of contributory negligence or *volenti*.

That test has been applied by this court in other licensor-licensee situations: see, *Alaica v. City of Toronto* (1976), 14 O.R. (2d) 697, 74 D.L.R. (3d) 502, 1 C.C.L.T. 212; *Whaling et al. v. Ravenhorst* (1977), 16 O.R. (2d) 61, 77 D.L.R. (3d) 337, 2 C.C.L.T. 114 (C.A.); and *Polnicky et al. v. Queen's Motel et al.* (C.A.), released January 10, 1985, unreported. It represents an accurate statement of the law in effect at the time of this accident, and liability in this case must be determined in accordance with the principles enunciated therein.

Applying this test, an occupier's liability is clearly limited to "unusual dangers" on his property and does not extend to every danger that might be found thereon. Thus, the first and most important question to be asked in this instance is whether at the time and place of the accident there was an "unusual danger" on the occupier's premises which created a foreseeable risk of harm.

Prior to the *Mitchell* case, the term "unusual danger" was applied to the duty owed by an occupier to an invitee, but not to the duty owed a licensee. The latter duty related only to "concealed dangers" or "traps". "Unusual danger" was defined by the House of Lords (*per* Lord Porter) in *London Graving Dock Co. Ltd. v. Horton*, [1951] A.C. 737 at p. 745, as follows:

> I think *"unusual"* is used in an objective sense and means such danger as is not usually found in carrying out the task or fulfilling the function which the invitee has in hand, though what is unusual will, of course, vary with the reasons for which the invitee enters the premises. Indeed, I do not think Phillimore, L.J., in *Norman v. Great Western Railway Co.*, [1915] 1 K.B. 584, 596, is speaking of individuals as individuals but of individuals as members of a type, e.g., that class of persons such as stevedores or seamen who are accustomed to negotiate the difficulties which their occupation presents. A tall chimney is not an unusual difficulty for a steeplejack though it would be for a motor mechanic. But I do not think a lofty chimney presents a danger less unusual for the last-named because he is particularly active or untroubled by dizziness.

(Emphasis added.)

This definition has been generally accepted and was specifically adopted by the Supreme Court of Canada in *Campbell v. Royal Bank of Canada* (1963), 43 D.L.R. (2d) 341, [1964] S.C.R. 85, 46 W.W.R. 49, and in *City of Brandon v. Farley* (1968), 66 D.L.R. (2d) 289, [1968] S.C.R. 150, 63 W.W.R. 116. In light of the fact that *Mitchell* has blurred the distinction between an occupier's duty to an invitee and his or her duty to a licensee, this definition of "unusual danger" can be applied by analogy also to the case of an occupier's duty to a licensee.

An occupier's duty is limited to "unusual dangers" on the theory that he or she is entitled to assume that ordinary reasonable people know and appreciate usual or common dangers and need not, therefore, be warned or otherwise protected against them. No list of dangers that categorically meet this concept of unusualness can be drawn up because, as Fleming points out (*op. cit.*, pp. 432-3), "the quality of unusualness depends not only on the character of the danger itself, but also on the nature of the premises on which it is found and the range of experience with which the [entrant] may fairly be credited". In the final analysis, the issue of what is an unusual danger clearly must, like so many issues in the law of torts, depend on the facts and circumstances of the given case.

. . .

With the negligence of the respondent and Sarel established, the question remaining is whether the owner of the land upon which this unfortunate accident occurred bears any responsibility in law for the occurrence. A licensor is patently not a guarantor of a licensee's safety or an insurer against all injuries which may result from the condition of his or her property. As we have said, a licensor's duty at common law is limited to unusual dangers of which he or she was aware, ought to have known existed with respect to the property. The duty does not extend to usual or common dangers which ordinary reasonable persons can be expected to know and appreciate.

Accepting that the curve could be a danger and that the appellant-landowner should have known that its property was being used in the recreational operation of trail bikes, can it be said that this condition constituted an unusual danger? In our opinion, it cannot be so classified. The requisite quality of unusualness is not present in this case, and the circumstances adverted to by the trial judge in his brief reasons do not elevate the condition into one of unusual danger. We are concerned here with a country-type road on undeveloped private property running between a small lake on one side and dense bush on the other that can only be seen as commonplace and not out of the ordinary in this province. The existence and state of the one curve in this road was open to ordinary observation. It had been there for a long time. When travelled with due care and attention and at an appropriate speed, it was not dangerous. The curve had not been the subject of recent change nor the source of prior mishap. It was not concealed or hidden, nor was it unexpected. It could readily be seen at a considerable distance by persons approaching from either direction.

Appeal allowed

[Liability was apportioned equally between the plaintiff and the defendant, Sarel.]

NOTES AND QUESTIONS

1. How have the courts distinguished between invitees and licensees? Why was the plaintiff not held to be a trespasser? Would the plaintiff have been considered a trespasser if the City had posted signs prohibiting entry and fenced the property?

2. Traditionally, what duty of care did an occupier owe to an invitee? How did the courts define the concept of an "unusual risk"?

3. What duty of care did an occupier owe a licensee? How did the courts define the concept of "concealed danger or trap"?

4. How have *Mitchell* and *McErlean* altered the traditional tests of an occupier's duty to invitees and licensees? Did these cases also change the definition of "unusual danger"?

5. Do you agree with the Court of Appeal's application of the current common law duty to the City's liability?

6. Occupiers also have a duty to protect invitees and licensees from other people who are allowed onto the premises if those entrants pose a foreseeable risk of harm. This issue often arises in taverns where an intoxicated patron becomes unruly or violent. In these situations, the occupier can be found liable under either the common law or occupier's liability legislation for failing to take reasonable steps to eject or restrain the patron. See for example *Duncan v. Braaten* (1980), 21 B.C.L.R. 369 (S.C.); *McGeough v. Don Enterprises Ltd.*, [1984] 1 W.W.R. 256 (Sask. Q.B.); and *McKenna v. Greco (No. 2)* (1985), 52 O.R. (2d) 85 (H.C.), appeal dismissed (1986), 58 O.R. (2d) 63n (C.A.). See also *Rendall v. Ewart*, [1989] 6 W.W.R. 97 (B.C. C.A.).

7. In a controversial decision currently under appeal, an Ontario jury found that occupiers in Ontario are under an affirmative legal duty to prevent intoxicated visitors from placing themselves at risk of personal injury. In *Stringer v. Ashley*, the defendant occupiers were found liable for their failure to prevent an intoxicated guest from diving 2.4 metres off the roof of their home into a backyard pool. The jury found that the defendants' verbal warnings were not adequate to protect the intoxicated plaintiff from his own folly. See Tyler, "Guest who ignored warning ..." *Toronto Star*, 1 Feb. 1994, A.4.

8. The Canadian courts have often taken a broad view of the term "unusual danger". The following have been held to be "unusual dangers": *Houle v. S.S. Kresge Co.* (1974), 55 D.L.R. (3d) 52 (Ont. Dist. Ct.) — potholes in a parking lot; *Pajot v. Commonwealth Holiday Inns of Can. Ltd.* (1978), 86 D.L.R. (3d) 729 (Ont. H.C.) — unmarked glass door; *Lampert v. Simpson Sears Ltd.* (1986), 75 N.B.R. (2d) 128 (C.A.) — water on the floor of a department store; *Sandberg v. Steer Holdings Ltd.* (1987), 45 Man. R. (2d) 264 (Q.B.) — ice in a parking lot; and *Vykysaly v. Jablowski* (1992), 8 O.R. (3d) 181 (Gen. Div.) — open stairwell at back of store. But see *Monteith v. N.B. Command, Royal Can. Legion* (1973), 8 N.B.R. (2d) 438 (Q.B.).

9. In most provinces, occupiers have clear statutory duties to keep their walkways free of slippery substances and hazardous obstructions. The central issue in these cases is not the legal duty, but the standard of care and whether it has been breached in the circumstances. For the purposes of these statutes, the common law distinction between an invitee and a licensee is no longer important. See *Preston v. Canadian Legion of British Empire Service League, Kingsway Branch No. 175* (1981), 123 D.L.R. (3d) 645 (Alta. C.A.); *Yelic v. Gimli (Town)* (1987), 33 D.L.R. (4th) 248 (Man. C.A.), leave to appeal ref'd. (1987), 46 Man. R. (2d) 160n (S.C.C.). Most of the occupiers' liability statutes provide occupiers with the defence of "willingly assumed risk". For a detailed discussion of this defence, see *Waldick v. Malcolm* (1991), 83 D.L.R. (4th) 114 (S.C.C.).

10. An occupier is under a positive duty to carry out periodic inspections of premises in order to maintain a reasonable degree of safety. See *Sauve v. Provost* (1990), 71 O.R. (2d) 774 (H.C.).

(iii) *Trespassers*

VEINOT v. KERR-ADDISON MINES LTD.

[1975] 2 S.C.R. 311, 51 D.L.R. (3d) 533 (S.C.C.)

DICKSON J.: — This is an occupiers' liability case. . . .Whether the entrant is a burglar or wandering child or irreproachable wayfarer, the general principles historically applied were those expressed in *Robert Addie & Sons (Collieries), Ltd. v. Dumbreck*, [1929] A.C. 358, by Lord Hailsham, L.C., at p. 365:

> Towards the trespasser the occupier has no duty to take reasonable care for his protection or even to protect him from concealed danger. The trespasser comes on to the premises at his own risk. An occupier is in such a case liable only where the injury is due to some wilful act involving something more than the absence of reasonable care. There must be some act done with deliberate intention of doing harm to the trespasser, or at least some act done with reckless disregard of the presence of the trespasser.

These rules, of course, perpetuated the traditional 19th century concern for the sanctity of landed property. The general principle was that a landowner could do as he wished with his land. He owed no duty to an intruder, however accidental or inadvertent the intrusion, other than to refrain from shooting him or otherwise recklessly and wantonly doing him harm. The rigour of the rule is exemplified in such cases as *Edwards et al. v. Railway Executive*, [1952] A.C. 737. As could be expected various inventions were employed from time to time to modify and ameliorate the harshness. In some of the cases the landowner's consent was implied or imputed, particularly in "children cases", the status of the intruder being elevated from that of trespasser, which he clearly was, to that of licensee, which he clearly was not. In other cases a generous meaning was given to the phrase "reckless disregard" or a tenuous distinction was drawn between land in a static condition and land upon which an operational activity was being conducted, productive of injury. In time, two distinct, not easy to reconcile, lines of jurisprudence emerged. One perpetuated the letter and spirit of *Addie*'s case *(Com'r for Railways v. Quinlan*, [1964] A.C. 1054, is an example). The other gave effect to changing ideas of social responsibility and imposed upon the owner of land duties well beyond those in contemplation in *Addie*'s case; *Com'r for Railways (N.S.W.) v. Cardy* (1960), 104 C.L.R. 274, and *Videan et al. v. British Transport Com'n*, [1963] 2 Q.B. 650, presaged the change which found expression in the leading case of *British Railways Board v. Herrington*, [1972] A.C. 877.

. . .

In *Herrington*'s case their Lordships exhaustively considered the nature of the duty owed by occupiers to trespassers. Lord Reid applied a subjective test. He said (p. 899):

> So it appears to me that an occupier's duty to trespassers must vary according to his knowledge, ability and resources. It has often been said that trespassers must take the land as they find it. I would rather say that they must take the occupier as they find him.

and later on the same page:

> So the question whether an occupier is liable in respect of an accident to a trespasser on his land would depend on whether a conscientious humane man with his knowledge, skill and resources could reasonably have been expected to have done or refrained from doing before

the accident something which would have avoided it. If he knew before the accident that there was a substantial probability that trespassers would come I think that most people would regard as culpable failure to give any thought to their safety. He might often reasonably think, weighing the seriousness of the danger and the degree of likelihood of trespassers coming against the burden he would have to incur in preventing their entry or making his premises safe, or curtailing his own activities on his land, that he could not fairly be expected to do anything. But if he could at small trouble and expense take some effective action, again I think that most people would think it inhumane and culpable not to do that. If some such principle is adopted there will no longer be any need to strive to imply a fictitious licence.

The test of common humanity was also applied by Lord Morris of Borth-y-Gest (p. 909):

In my view, while it cannot be said that the railways board owed a common duty of care to the young boy in the present case they did owe to him at least the duty of acting with common humanity towards him.

. . .

Herrington's case was considered by the Court of Appeal of England in *Pannett v. McGuinness & Co. Ltd.*, [1972] 3 W.L.R. 387. The following excerpt from Lord Denning's judgment aptly expresses, in my opinion, the more salient points a Judge should have in mind when considering intrusion upon land [at pp. 390-1]:

The long and short of it is that you have to take into account all the circumstances of the case and see then whether the occupier ought to have done more than he did. (1) You must apply your common sense. You must take into account the gravity and likelihood of the probable injury. Ultra-hazardous activities require a man to be ultra-cautious in carrying them out. The more dangerous the activity, the more he should take steps to see that no one is injured by it. (2) You must take into account also the character of the intrusion by the trespasser. A wandering child or a straying adult stands in a different position from a poacher or a burglar. You may expect a child when you may not expect a burglar. (3) You must also have regard to the nature of the place where the trespass occurs. An electrified railway line or a warehouse being demolished may require more precautions to be taken than a private house. (4) You must also take into account the knowledge which the defendant has, or ought to have, of the likelihood of trespassers being present. The more likely they are, the more precautions may have to be taken.

In the very recent case of *Southern Portland Cement Ltd. v. Cooper*, [1974] 1 All E.R. 87, the Privy Council considered the duty owed to a trespasser. Their Lordships rejected the argument that an occupier only comes under a duty to potential trespassers if he estimates or ought to estimate that the arrival of one or more trespassers on his land is "extremely likely". In the course of his speech Lord Reid said: "But in their Lordships' judgment it is now necessary to . . . abandon the limitation of extreme likelihood", and later [at p. 98]:

If the occupier creates the danger when he knows that there is a chance that trespassers will come that way and will not see or realise the danger he may have to do more. There may be difficult cases where the occupier will be hampered in the conduct of his own affairs if he has to take elaborate precautions. But in the present case it would have been easy to prevent the development of the dangerous situation which caused the plaintiff's injuries.

And so we come to the facts of the present case. There is no need to labour them. The plaintiff, 37 years of age, and his wife, on one snowmobile, accompanied by another married couple on another snowmobile, set out from their home for an evening of healthful recreation through woods and across lakes of northern Ontario. They went along well-travelled snowmobile trails, from Larder Lake to Crosby

Lake, along a creek to Beaver Lake, to Bear Lake, to a hydro right of way along which were many ski-doo trails, down an old logging road "which was well ski-doo packed", to a wide, hard-packed, well-ploughed road on which they travelled until the plaintiff, Mr. Veinot, on the leading snowmobile, struck a rusty pipe stretched across the road, at face-height, and sustained very serious injuries. The accident occurred on March 16, 1970. Mr. Veinot had owned snowmobiles since 1966. . . .The jury found that Mr. Veinot did not fail to take reasonable care for his own safety.

The pipe which Mr. Veinot struck was two inches in diameter, supported by unpainted posts located off the road, and invisible at night due to the background of trees. The pipe had been erected some 20 years earlier to prevent the movement of unauthorized vehicular traffic to the defendant company's powder magazine not far from the community of Virginiatown. No point can be made of the fact that the pipe had been there for 20 years without accident for the type of accident which occurred in this case could only have occurred after the advent of snowmobiles.

From the evidence there seems no doubt that during the winter there was a great deal of travel on snowmobiles in and around Virginiatown. . . . The defendant company permitted snowmobile traffic along the road as far as the iron pipe. Such traffic normally then turned to the right and continued north along the right of way until the intersecting east-west hydro right of way was reached which in turn led west to the lakes across which Mr. Veinot and his party had travelled. Generally, as I have indicated, the main ski-doo traffic was east of the iron pipe, but the defendant's security officer conceded that on a very few occasions he had seen ski-doo tracks in the winter of 1969-70 on the powder magazine side of the pipe. He did not report these discoveries to the mine manager and he did nothing about it.

The evidence is undisputed that there were "a lot of snowmobile tracks" on the road leading south from the east-west hydro power line to the ploughed road on which the unfortunate accident occurred. The ploughed road "seemed to be well travelled"; looked like a public road; and had no markings to indicate it was not a public road. Mr. Veinot had no idea he was on private property when he drove along the ploughed road and according to his evidence, which was not challenged, he would not have continued along it if he had known it was private property. Upon all of the evidence and following a charge by the trial Judge to which no objection has been, or could be, taken, the jury made certain findings: (1) That Mr. Veinot on the date of the accident was on the defendant's land with the implied permission of the defendant; (2) That his injuries were caused by a concealed or hidden danger or a trap of which the defendant had knowledge, described by the jury in its answers as "a rusty pipe approximately 2″ in diameter suspended across the travelled portion of the road at a height of approximately 45 inches from the road"; (3) The defendant failed to take reasonable care to avoid injury to persons traversing the area, there being no distinguishing warnings of the location of the pipe across the roadway from either the east or west approach to the pipe or on the pipe itself; (4) The finding to which I have already referred, that plaintiff did not fail to take reasonable care for his own safety. At the close of the evidence presented by the plaintiff a motion was made for a nonsuit. The motion was renewed after the evidence for the defendant had been heard and again after the answers of the jury were received. The trial Judge, Houlden, J., dismissed the motion. He held that the finding of the jury that there was implied permission for the plaintiff to be on the land of the defendant could be substantiated on the evidence.

. . .

Whether or not there was an implied permission was a question of fact for the jury. The jury was properly instructed on the law and brought its finding. I do not think that finding should be disturbed.

. . .

Even if Mr. Veinot is regarded as a trespasser his appeal to this Court should succeed. If he was a trespasser, the inquiry must be as to whether his presence on the ploughed road could reasonably have been anticipated for, if so, the company owed him a duty and that duty was to treat him with ordinary humanity.

Although as a general rule a person is not bound to anticipate the presence of intruders on private property or to guard them from injury, a duty may arise if the owner of land knew of, or from all the surrounding circumstances ought reasonably to have foreseen, the presence of a trespasser. It appears to me that a person of good sense in the position of the defendant company, possessing the knowledge which its responsible officers possessed about snowmobiles and the degree of snowmobile travel in the area, the proclivity for travel by night, the ease by which the ploughed road could be reached by several old roads leading on to it would have been alerted, on a moment's reflection, to the probability of someone reaching the ploughed road as Mr. Veinot did. Stress was laid during argument upon the fact that the plaintiff came in by way of the back door, as it were, and that such avenue of approach could not reasonably have been anticipated. I do not agree. Snowmobiles are ubiquitous. They have an unusual and well-known capacity for travel on and off the beaten path. In an uncharted Canadian wilderness area, of forest, rivers and lakes, one could reasonably expect them to go in almost any direction, at least until such time as they reached *indicia* of private property. If there was a likelihood that someone would come upon the ploughed road on a snowmobile at night, and the evidence in my view supports such a likelihood, then I do not think there can be doubt that the company failed in the duty it owed to Mr. Veinot to treat him with common humanity. The ploughed road gave every appearance of being a public road. Mr. Veinot had good reason to believe that he might freely use it if he wished to do so. Acting on that belief he failed to see or appreciate the abeyant danger of the rusty pipe. The defendant company in my opinion erred in permitting the continuance of what should have been recognized by it as a covert peril, menacing the safety of anyone who came upon the road at night on a snowmobile. And it would have been so easy to have averted the accident, by painting the pipe white or by hanging a cloth or a sign from it.

I would allow the appeal, set aside the judgment of the Court of Appeal and restore the judgment of the trial Judge with costs throughout.

MARTLAND J. (dissenting):

[In his statement of the facts, Martland J. emphasized that the Company had posted several warning signs on the property and had only allowed two people access.]

. . .

The case was tried prior to the judgment of the House of Lords in *British Railways Board v. Herrington*, [1972] A.C. 877. It went to the jury on the basis that the Company's liability was dependent upon Veinot establishing that he was on the Company's land with the implied permission of the Company.

. . .

The Court of Appeal reached the conclusion that there was no evidence of implied licence which could support the finding of the jury on that point.

. . .

The implication of a tacit permission arising from other intrusions upon an owner's land could not be made, under the concept of an implied licence, unless it could be shown that the owner was aware of such intrusions, and, even if he was aware, it had to be shown that he permitted such intrusions on his land and not merely tolerated them.

. . .

As has already been noted, the Company had no knowledge that operators of snowmobiles had used its private road to drive their vehicles from the powder magazine area to the gate, or from the gate to that area. The only tracks seen by the security officer were just to the west of the gate. The persons whose vehicles created those tracks must have been aware of the presence of the gate, the very purpose of which was to indicate resentment of the Company against trespass on its road, and to prevent such intrusion by vehicular traffic.

In my opinion, there was no evidence of implied permission having been given by the Company for the use of its private road by the drivers of snowmobiles.

This conclusion, in itself, does not necessarily involve the failure of this appeal. Counsel for Veinot contends that, even if Veinot was not a licensee, none the less the Company owed a legal duty to him, even as a trespasser, which had, on the facts of this case, been breached. He relied chiefly upon the judgment of the House of Lords in *British Railways Board v. Herrington, supra*.

. . .

The two most recent Privy Council decisions on the matter are *Com'r for Railways v. Quinlan*, [1964] A.C. 1054, and *Southern Portland Cement Ltd. v. Cooper*, [1974] 1 All E.R. 87, both being appeals from Australia.

. . .

The effect of these cases might be summarized as being that an occupier who knows of the existence of a danger upon his land which he has created, or for whose continued existence he is responsible, may owe a duty to persons coming on his land, of whose presence he is not aware, if he knows facts which show a substantial chance that they might come there. This is, in essence, the duty stated by Dixon, C.J., in the *Cardy* case. Such duty, when it exists, is limited, in the case of adults, to a duty to warn. In the case of children somethng more may be required. The existence of a duty will depend on the special circumstances of each case.

I now turn to consider whether or not such a duty existed on the part of the Company towards Veinot.

The only danger which existed upon the Company's land, which is comparable to the live electrical rail in *Herrington*, the electrical cable in *Cooper*, and the beds of hot ash in *Cardy*, was the presence there of high explosives. Warning notices were posted at the powder magazines, and a warning notice was posted by the road inside the gate. The gate itself was put in place as a means of excluding unauthorized access to the private road to the powder magazines and was itself a notice by the Company that entry upon its premises was unauthorized. It had existed, to serve this function, for nearly 20 years prior to Veinot's accident.

It was contended on behalf of Veinot that the Company had created a danger by placing the pipe, unmarked, across its highway. This submission involves the proposition that the existence of something on the Company's land which had been there for some 20 years, during which it was not a danger, became a danger because of the special use made of the Company's land by Veinot in the operation of his snowmobile. In substance, it means that because he elected to make use of the Company's land, not for walking, but to operate a motor driven vehicle, at night, at a speed of some 15 to 20 miles an hour, the Company, because of that fact, permitted the existence of a danger on its land.

. . .

I have dealt with the question of there being a dangerous situation on the premises. Even if such a situation does exist, the duty of the occupier to a trespasser can only arise if he knew the presence of the trespasser upon his land or, to quote Lord Reid in the *Cooper* case (p. 98), "when he knows facts which shew a substantial chance that they [*i.e.*, trespassers] may come there." I have already referred to the absence of any evidence to establish any knowledge by the Company that anyone had operated a snowmobile, as Veinot did, along the private road from the powder magazine area to the gate.

In conclusion, it is my opinion that there is no analogy between the circumstances of this case and those under consideration in *Herrington* and in *Cooper*. The former case involved injuries to a six-year-old boy; the latter involved injuries to a boy of 13. Veinot is an adult.

In *Herrington* the defendant maintained a live electric rail on its railway line running between two public areas where children played. In *Cooper* the defendant had created a situation highly dangerous to human life, *i.e.*, a high tension line in too close proximity to the ground, where the proximate presence of children was to be expected by it. In the present case the Company maintained a pipe, acting as a gate, to protect its premises, which would only prove to be a danger to a person travelling at night, at some speed, in a snowmobile, of whose potential presence there were no facts to warn the Company.

In my opinion, the appeal should be dismissed with costs.

[Laskin C.J.C. and Spence J. concurred with Mr. Justice Dickson. Judson, Ritchie and de Grandpré, JJ. concurred with Mr. Justice Martland. Pigeon J., with whom Beetz J. concurred, agreed with Dickson's conclusion on the basis that there was evidence to support the jury's finding on the implied licence issue. Pigeon J. stated that he was expressing no opinion on the other issues. Note that the order of the judgments has been changed.]

NOTES AND QUESTIONS

1. Do you agree with Martland J. or Dickson J. on the issue of whether the plaintiff was a licensee?

Did they disagree on the test for determining whether there was an implied licence, its application to the facts, or on both issues? In light of *Veinot* and the authorities discussed in it, have the courts rendered the concept of implied licence meaningless?

2. Based on *Herrington*, define the duty of care that an occupier owes to a trespasser. Identify the various factors that a court should consider in determining whether this duty applies in a given fact situation. How does this test of duty differ from that established in *Donoghue v. Stevenson*, [1932] A.C. 562 (H.L.)? How did the decisions in *Pannett* and *Southern Portland Cement* alter the common humanity test established in *Herrington*? Based on these three cases, define an occupier's common law duty of care to a trespasser. What criticisms would you make of this test?

3. Did Martland J. and Dickson J. disagree on the test that governs an occupier's duty to a trespasser, its application to the facts, or on both issues? How were these issues resolved by the other members of the court? What impact did these issues play in the outcome of the case?

4. Traditionally, the courts have distinguished between a passive and an active danger on the defendant's land. An active danger has generally been governed by ordinary principles of negligence, whereas a passive danger, such as that in *Veinot* has usually been governed by occupiers' liability. This distinction, like so many other aspects of occupiers' liability, has generated controversy and confusion. See, for example, *Wade v. C.N.R.*, [1978] 1 S.C.R. 1064; and Gibson, "Torts — Negligence and Occupiers' Liability — Role of Jury — Confusing Words from the Oracle" (1978), 58 Can. Bar Rev. 693.

5. For a further discussion of an occupier's common law duty of care to a trespasser, see Innes, "Recent Developments in the Law of Occupiers' Liability to Trespassers" (1975), 24 U.N.B. L.J. 39; Di Castri, *Occupiers' Liability* (1981), 123-46; and Fleming, *The Law of Torts*, 8th ed. (1992), 40-44.

6. In 1974, Ontario enacted legislation to resolve the conflicts between snowmobile operators and occupiers. See the Motorized Snow Vehicles Act, R.S.O. 1990, c. M.44. See *Cormack v. Mara (Township)* (1989), 59 D.L.R. (4th) 300 (Ont. C.A.), leave to appeal ref'd. (1989), 102 N.R. 399n (S.C.C.).

3. The Provincial Occupiers' Liability Acts

(a) INTRODUCTION

Many of the problems associated with the common law of occupiers' liability are inherent in the conflicting interests at stake. Urbanization, the decline of the relative importance of land, and government regulation of land use and building standards have undermined much of the early common law. In attempting to develop broader and more flexible common law principles, the courts have added to the uncertainty. As the balance has shifted in favour of protecting entrants, the affirmative duty cast on occupiers has become increasingly onerous.

The task of balancing the need to protect entrants and the rights of occupiers has been complicated by the broad range of different types of land, entrants and occupiers. The reform of occupiers' liability law, whether by means of common law evolution or by statute, involves difficult and controversial issues. In the following subsection, we have set out the British Columbia legislation, as an example of how one legislature has attempted to resolve these issues. Alberta, Manitoba, P.E.I. and Ontario have also enacted occupiers' liability statutes, and several other provinces have prepared draft legislation.

(b) THE BRITISH COLUMBIA OCCUPIERS LIABILITY ACT, R.S.B.C. 1979, c. 303, as amended 1989, c. 64, s. 31

Interpretation

1. In this Act

"occupier" means a person who

    (a) is in physical possession of premises; or

    (b) has responsibility for, and control over, the condition of premises, the activities conducted on those premises and the persons allowed to enter those premises,

and, for this Act, there may be more than one occupier of the same premises;

"premises" includes

    (a) land and structures or either of them, excepting portable structures and equipment other than those described in paragraph (c);

    (b) ships and vessels;

    (c) trailers and portable structures designed or used for a residence, business or shelter; and

    (d) railway locomotives, railway cars, vehicles and aircraft while not in operation;

"tenancy" includes a statutory tenancy, an implied tenancy and any contract conferring the right of occupation, and "landlord" shall be construed accordingly.

Application of Act

2. Subject to section 3(4), and sections 4 and 9, this Act determines the care that an occupier is required to show toward persons entering on the premises in respect of dangers to them, or to their property on the premises, or to the property on the premises of persons who have not themselves entered on the premises, that are due to the state of the premises, or to anything done or omitted to be done on the premises, and for which he is by law responsible.

Occupiers' duty of care

3. (1) An occupier of premises owes a duty to take that care that in all the circumstances of the case is reasonable to see that a person, and his property, on the premises, and property on the premises of a person, whether or not that person himself enters on the premises, will be reasonably safe in using the premises.

    (2) The duty of care referred to in subsection (1) applies in relation to the

    (a) condition of the premises;

    (b) activities on the premises; or

    (c) conduct of third parties on the premises.

    (3) Notwithstanding subsection (1), an occupier has no duty of care to a person

    (a) in respect of risks willingly accepted by that person as his own risks, or

    (b) who enters premises that the occupier uses primarily for agricultural purposes and who would be a trespasser under the *Trespass Act,*

other than a duty not to

    (c) create a danger with intent to do harm to the person or damage to his property, or

    (d) act with reckless disregard to the safety of the person or the integrity of his property.

    (4) Nothing in this section relieves an occupier of premises of a duty to exercise, in a particular case, a higher standard of care which, in that case, is incumbent on him by virtue of an enactment or rule of law imposing special standards of care on particular classes of person.

Contracting out

4. (1) Subject to subsections (2), (3) and (4), where an occupier is permitted by law to extend, restrict, modify or exclude his duty of care to any person by express agreement, or by express stipulation or notice, the occupier shall take reasonable steps to bring that extension, restriction, modification or exclusion to the attention of that person.

    (2) An occupier shall not restrict, modify or exclude his duty of care under subsection (1) with respect to a person who is

    (a) not privy to the express agreement; or

    (b) empowered or permitted to enter or use the premises without the consent or permission of the occupier.

(3) Where an occupier is bound by contract to permit persons who are not privy to the contract to enter or use the premises, the duty of care of the occupier to those persons shall, notwithstanding anything to the contrary in that contract, not be restricted, modified or excluded by it.

(4) This section applies to all express contracts.

Independent contractors

5. (1) Nothwithstanding section 3(1), where damage is caused by the negligence of an independent contractor engaged by the occupier, the occupier is not on that account liable under this Act if, in all the circumstances.

> (a) the occupier exercised reasonable care in the selection and supervision of the independent contractor; and
>
> (b) it was reasonable that the work that the independent contractor was engaged to do should have been undertaken.

(2) Subsection (1) shall not be construed as restricting or excluding the liability of an occupier for the negligence of his independent contractor imposed by any other Act.

(3) Where there is damage under the circumstances set out in subsection (1), and there is more than one occupier of the premises, each occupier is entitled to rely on subsection (1).

Tenancy relationship

6. (1) Where premises are occupied or used by virtue of a tenancy under which a landlord is responsible for the maintenance or repair of the premises, it is the duty of the landlord to show toward any person who, or whose property, may be on the premises the same care in respect of risks arising from failure on his part in carrying out his responsibility, as is required by this Act to be shown by an occupier of premises toward persons entering on or using them.

(2) Where premises are occupied by virtue of a subtenancy, subsection (1) applies to a landlord who is responsible for the maintenance or repair of the premises comprised in the subtenancy.

(3) In this section

> (a) a landlord is not in default of his duty under subsection (1) unless his default would be actionable at the suit of the occupier;
>
> (b) nothing relieves a landlord of a duty he may have apart from this section; and
>
> (c) obligations imposed by an enactment in respect of a tenancy are deemed imposed by the tenancy.

(4) This section applies to all tenancies.

Negligence Act

7. The *Negligence Act* applies to this Act.

Crown bound

8. (1) Except as otherwise provided in subsection (2), the Crown and its agencies are bound by this Act.

(2) Notwithstanding subsection (1), this Act does not apply to the Crown in right of the Province or in right of Canada or to a municipality where the Crown or the municipality is the occupier of a public highway or public road or a road under the *Forest Act* or the *Private Roads Act, 1963*, or to an industrial road as defined in the *Highway (Industrial) Act*.

Not to affect certain relationships

9. This Act does not apply to or affect the liability of

> (a) an employer in respect of his duties to his employee;
>
> (b) a person by virtue of a contract for the hire of, or for the carriage for reward of persons or property in, any vehicle, vessel, aircraft or other means of transport;
>
> (c) a person under the *Hotel Keepers Act*; or
>
> (d) a person by virtue of a contract of bailment.

NOTES AND QUESTIONS

1. How does the approach adopted in the B.C. Act differ from that inherent in the common law? Does the B.C. Act require the courts to ignore differences in the resources of occupiers? Can the courts consider the category of entrant in determining an occupier's liability under the Act? Do you think that the Act is significantly easier to interpret and apply than the common law?

2. Like the B.C. Act, both the Manitoba and Ontario Acts define an occupier's duty in terms of taking such care as is reasonable in the circumstances, without formally recognizing different types of occupiers and categories of entrants. See The Occupiers' Liability Act, R.S.M. 1987, c. O8, s. 3(1); and the Occupiers' Liability Act, R.S.O. 1990, c. O.2, s. 3.

The Alberta Act adopts a similar duty for lawful entrants, but provides a much more restricted duty for adult trespassers. The Alberta legislation contains a third set of principles governing an occupier's duty to trespassing children. See Occupiers' Liability Act, R.S.A. 1980, c. O-3, ss. 5, 12, 13.

The Prince Edward Island Act also adopts a reasonable care test for lawful entrants. However, it restricts the duty for trespassers, criminals and those engaging in recreational activities. See Occupiers' Liability Act, R.S.P.E.I. 1988, c. O-2, ss. 3, 4.

3. For a detailed review of the provincial acts see Di Castri, *Occupiers' Liability* (1980), 187-264.

REVIEW PROBLEM

Ms. Nightingale rented part of an old house from Mr. Rafter three weeks before the mishap. Ms. Nightingale had possession of the ground floor and Mr. Rafter kept possession of the basement apartment, which he used for storage and which he kept locked at all times. Neither Nightingale nor Rafter used the stairs connecting the basement to the first floor. Nightingale had no reason or right to enter the basement apartment, and Rafter always used the street entrance to his apartment.

Ms. Nightingale became friends with her neighbour Ms. Lilly Decker, although she disliked Ms. Decker's boyfriend, Hugo. Late one night, Ms. Nightingale heard a commotion at the Decker residence and became fearful for Lilly's safety. Minutes later, Ms. Decker arrived at Ms. Nightingale's front door. Lilly was crying and confided that Hugo was drunk and had threatened her. Suddenly Hugo arrived at her door and, ignoring Nightingale's protests, pushed his way into the house. Lilly ran down the stairs to the basement. Hugo followed her. Unfortunately, two steps were missing and both Lilly and Hugo fell. The missing stairs would have been noticed by anyone who was walking normally. Rafter knew about the missing stairs but he didn't bother to inform Ms. Nightingale, because he thought she would never use them.

Analyze the common law duty of care, if any, that Ms. Nightingale and Rafter owe to Hugo and Lilly. Would they be held liable to Lilly and Hugo under the provisions of the British Columbia Occupiers Liability Act?

STRICT AND VICARIOUS LIABILITY

1. Introduction
2. Liability for Animals
3. Escape of Dangerous Substances — *Rylands v. Fletcher*
4. A Note on *Rylands v. Fletcher*
5. Products' Liability — The American Approach
6. Vicarious Liability

1. Introduction

In the vast majority of tort actions, liability is based on the faulty or blameworthy conduct of the defendant. As we have seen, the two most important theories of fault are wrongful intent and negligence. The purpose of this chapter is to introduce students to four areas of tort law which are governed by non-fault based, or "strict" liability, principles. Although these four bases of strict liability evolved independently, they are unified by the view that some kinds of injurious activities warrant a less onerous threshold of liability than proof of wrongful intent or negligence.

The position of strict liability in tort law has been controversial since the 19th century. Many jurists see strict liability as an unnecessary and unwelcome departure from the fault principle. As we will see, recent decisions in this field reveal deep divisions of opinion among Commonwealth judges. In England and Australia, common law judges appear to have put the common law of strict liability, especially for the escape of dangerous substances from land, on a new footing. Until the Supreme Court of Canada decides another strict liability case, the direction of the Canadian common law in this area will remain uncertain.

2. Liability for Animals

(a) CATTLE TRESPASS

ACKER v. KERR

(1973), 2 O.R. (2d) 270, 42 D.L.R. (3d) 514 (Ont. Co. Ct.)

THOMPSON CO. CT. J.: — This action is brought by the plaintiff as the owner of lot No. 11, Concession 4 in the Township of Proton, in the County of Grey, against the defendant as the owner of adjoining lot No. 12, Concession 4 in the said Township of Proton for damages which the plaintiff alleges were sustained by him as a result of the failure of the defendant to properly confine cattle owned by him and placed by him on his property so that such animals were permitted to stray onto the property of the defendant.

The plaintiff alleges that the straying in question took place in the years 1969, 1970 and 1971 and that as a result of the same, he sustained damages in the sum of $2,650.

Evidence was tendered by both parties which satisfies me that indeed the cattle of the defendant did get onto the property of the plaintiff during the years just mentioned doing some damage to crops of the plaintiff, the extent of which will be more fully referred to later on in my reasons for judgment.

The matter of the liability, if any, of the defendant for the damages in fact sustained by the plaintiff is rather complex and has many ramifications as will be seen.

Counsel for the plaintiff takes the position that once cattle are allowed to stray and damage is done, a trespass has been committed and the injured party is entitled to such damages as he may have sustained regardless of anything done or omitted to be done by such injured party which may have been a contributing factor to the damages so sustained. On the other hand, counsel for the defendant takes the position that the plaintiff was the author of his own misfortune as in essence he failed to keep up and repair a portion of the line fence which existed between the two farms and the cattle were thereby permitted to stray onto his property. Counsel for the plaintiff further contends that whether or not the plaintiff was obliged to maintain the fence and whether or not the fence was in a state of disrepair has nothing whatever to do with the end result and that unless the plaintiff was guilty of some positive act which enabled the defendant's cattle to get onto the plaintiff's land, he could not be held responsible either in whole or in part for the damage resulting from the cattle straying.

. . .

[The judge considered the Line Fences Act, R.S.O. 1970, c. 248, s. 2(1), and concluded that it imposed no affirmative duty on the plaintiff to maintain the fence.]

Counsel for the plaintiff cited innumerable authorities for the proposition that the defendant in circumstances as they exist here is liable to the plaintiff for damages for trespass.

I take it from these cases to be the law that the owner of animals *domitae naturae* is bound to keep them under control and is liable if they escape for such damage as it is ordinarily in their nature to commit. The liability is an absolute liability independent of negligence unless the escape or trespass was involuntary or caused by an Act of God or was due to the act or default of the plaintiff or of a third party for whom the defendant is not in law responsible. No case has been referred to me by counsel for the defendant which in any way detracts from this statement of the law.

The *Pounds Act*, R.S.O. 1970, c. 353, provides in s. 2 as follows:

> 2. The owner or occupant of any land is responsible for any damage caused by any animal under his charge and keeping as though such animal were his own property, and the owner of any animal not permitted to run at large by the by-laws of the municipality is liable for any damage done by such animal, although the fence enclosing the premises of the complaint was not of the height required by such by-laws.

I might say that there was no evidence tendered as to the existence of a by-law permitting animals to run at large so far as this locality is concerned. Clearly the defendant was in breach of the requirements of this particular section but in view of the fact that the section seems simply to set out in statute form the principle enunciated by the common law which principle as I have indicated applies in this case, it is not necessary for me under the circumstances to ascertain whether or not the statute gives a separate cause of action. It would of course be relevant if there had been a by-law passed permitting animals to run at large.

In the cases to which I have made reference there is none which contains exactly the factual situation with which we are confronted here, but none the less I am of the opinion that the principle which I have enunciated is applicable, and on finding as I do, that the escape or trespass was not involuntary or caused by an Act of God or was due to the act or default of the plaintiff or of a third person for whom the defendant is not responsible, liability on the defendant does arise for such escape and subsequent trespass and damages.

As I have indicated, it would be almost impossible to tell just at which part of the fence in question the animals escaped but on the other hand as I have also indicated, it is not necessary for the purposes of my decision to make a finding in that regard because, in my view, it makes no difference whether it was in that portion of the fence which it might be argued was the responsibility of the plaintiff to maintain and repair or that portion of the fence which it might be argued was the responsibility of the defendant to maintain and repair or both. It was the defendant's cattle that escaped and it was the responsibility of the defendant when he put the cattle in the field to see that the fences were kept in such a state of repair as to contain the cattle within such field whether by himself seeing to the necessary work in that connection or by some agreement with the plaintiff which would exonerate the defendant from that responsibility, which agreement I find to be lacking.

. . .

The attitude of the defendant with respect to the matter of the escape and trespass was to say the least somewhat high-handed. He was aware that his cattle were getting onto the plaintiff's property but he chose to adopt the position that they were getting there through a portion of the fence which he considered to be the plaintiff's responsibility to maintain and keep in repair and that it was accordingly the plaintiff's own fault if in his neglect to maintain and repair this portion of the fence, the defendant's cattle got onto his property. This was not the correct position as I find it, in law. Furthermore, the defendant when he ascertained that his cattle were getting into the plaintiff's property apparently on several occasions tied the gate leading from the plaintiff's property to the road in order that the defendant's cattle might thereby be prevented from straying onto the highway from the plaintiff's property and to add insult to injury as it were, he told the plaintiff in effect that he was to keep his, the plaintiff's, gate closed. To say that relations were strained between the parties is I think to put it somewhat mildly.

To sum up therefore so far as the matter of liability is concerned, it is my view that the *Line Fences Act*, the *Pounds Act* and the *Negligence Act* have no application to the circumstances of this particular action and liability falls to be decided according to the common law principle already enunciated by me and with respect to which I find that the defendant is liable to the plaintiff.

NOTES AND QUESTIONS

1. Based on *Acker*, what are the principles governing cattle trespass and its defences? Why was the condition of the plaintiff's fences not considered relevant in determining if there was a defence? In *Singleton v. Williamson* (1861), 158 E.R. 533 (C.A.), the plaintiff's breach of an affirmative obligation to maintain his fence provided the defendant with a defence to cattle trespass. Can you reconcile *Acker* and *Singleton*?

2. The English common law cases provided that an owner of a straying animal was not liable for damages it caused on the highway. *Searle v. Wallbank*, [1947] A.C. 341 (H.L.). In *Fleming v. Atkinson*, [1959] S.C.R. 513, three judges clearly rejected this principle and held that liability in such cases was governed by negligence. The other two judges for the majority did not find it necessary to reject *Searle*, but they did limit its application to narrow circumstances. The two dissenting judges followed *Searle*. Since *Fleming*, the great majority of Canadian courts have held that liability for straying animals on highways is governed by negligence. See, for example, *Crosby v. Curry* (1969), 7 D.L.R. (3d) 188 (N.S. S.C.); *MacKinnon v. Ellis* (1978), 20 Nfld. & P.E.I.R. 297 (P.E.I. S.C.); *Windrem v. Hamill* (1978), 95 D.L.R. (3d) 381 (Sask. C.A.); *Rozon v. Patenaude* (1982), 35 O.R. (2d) 619 (Co. Ct.); and *Ruckheim v. Robinson*, [1995] 4 W.W.R. 284 (B.C. C.A.).

3. At common law, if an animal was lawfully on a highway and then escaped onto the plaintiff's land, the case was governed by negligence. *Goodwyn v. Cheveley* (1859), 157 E.R. 989 (Exch. Ct.). However, if the animal escaped from the defendant's land to the highway and then entered the plaintiff's land, strict liability applied. Should the place from where an animal strays affect the owner's liability? See Williams, *Liability for Animals* (1939), 369-76.

4. Although cattle trespass cases usually involve only property damage, the action can be invoked to recover for personal injuries. See *Wormald v. Cole*, [1954] 1 Q.B. 614 (C.A.).

5. Cattle trespass provides redress for damages caused by any straying animal, even fowl, but not dogs and cats. What is the rationale for this exception? Most provinces have enacted legislation making the owner of a dog liable for injuries to livestock. In some provinces the protection extends to any kind of property damage. See the Sheep Protection and Dog Licensing Act, R.S.S. 1978, c. S-49; and the Dog Act, S. Nfld. 1976, No. 13, s. 9.

6. Most provinces have now enacted legislation to deal with straying animals. In *Acker*, it was held that the Pounds Act, R.S.O. 1970, c. 353 [now R.S.O. 1990, c. P.17] did not alter the common law action for cattle trespass. This is not the case in all provinces. See the Stray Animals Act, R.S.A. 1980, c. S-23, ss. 5-7; and the Livestock Act, S.B.C. 1980, c. 24, s. 10.

7. What was the rationale for imposing strict liability in cattle trespass? Can this principle still be justified? Would you favour the adoption of negligence principles for all cases of straying animals?

8. For a detailed discussion of liability for animals see North, *The Modern Law of Animals* (1972); and Sandys-Winsch, *Animal Law* (1984).

(b) DANGEROUS ANIMALS

RICHARD v. HOBAN

(1970), 3 N.B.R. (2d) 81, 16 D.L.R. (3d) 679 (N.B. C.A.)

BUGOLD, J.A.: — This is an appeal by the defendant from a decision delivered in the Queen's Bench Division whereby the learned trial Judge found in favour of the plaintiffs for a total award of damages in the sum of $2,955.75 and costs to be taxed.

This action is for damages for injuries received by the infant respondent Linda Richard when she was allegedly attacked and bitten by a dog owned, at the time material to the action, by the appellant.

The circumstances of the incident which gave rise to this litigation may be summarized briefly as follows: On or about August 7, 1968, the appellant was the owner of a German Shepherd dog, weighing between 85 to 90 lbs., which he kept confined by means of a chain looped around the bole of a tree in the rear of a trailer which he occupied with his family in the Glenncross Trailer Park at Darlington in the Parish of Dalhousie in the County of Restigouche.

The infant respondent was eight years of age. At approximately 6:30 o'clock in the afternoon of the above mentioned date, she had gone to a canteen located on the trailer park premises and was returning to her home situated outside the trailer park property and somewhat to the west of the Hoban trailer. As she passed the Hoban trailer, she went to the rear of the trailer to see the dog. The latter jumped on her and as a result she sustained head and facial lacerations which necessitated medical treatment and hospitalization.

Paragraph 2 of the respondents' statement of claim alleges, *inter alia*:

> ... The Defendant, Constable Tim Hoban, an R.C.M.P. at all times material to this action was the owner of a German Shepherd dog, whom he knew to be savage and vicious having already bit (sic) several children in the past few months.

Paragraph 3 of the said statement of claim alleges, in part:

> ... she was savagely attacked by a vicious German Shepherd dog owned by Constable Tim Hoban.

The above allegations are denied by the appellant in his defence.

The ownership of the dog is not in issue in this case.

The respondents failed to prove the vital ingredients of the matters complained of, namely, that the appellant knew his dog "to be savage and vicious having already bit (*sic*) several children in the past few months" and that the infant respondent "was savagely attacked".

With the exception of the Appleby incident, which I am about to deal with, I am unable to find any evidence whatsoever on the record to establish that the appellant knew his dog "to be savage and vicious having already bit (*sic*) several children in the past few months."

The photographs showing the nature of the injuries to the head and face of the infant respondent, disclose these injuries would have been caused by the dew-claw of the dog when he jumped up in front of the infant respondent rather than by biting. There is also no evidence to support the allegation of a savage attack by the dog on the infant. The doctor who treated the infant respondent could not voice an opinion as to the cause of the injuries.

At the trial, the respondents adduced evidence relating to an incident which occurred on May 24, 1968, a little over two months prior to the alleged attack on the infant respondent herein. At that time, it is alleged that the dog had attacked and bitten one John Appleby at the rear of the Hoban trailer. Young Appleby was in the vicinity of five years of age.

Immediately following this incident, the appellant personally conducted an investigation into the circumstances which resulted in the alleged injuries to the Appleby boy. During the course of this investigation, the appellant talked with George Appleby, the father of John Appleby, and with the young boy himself. Upon completion of his investigation, the appellant was satisfied that his dog had not bitten John Appleby. Young Appleby's father concurred with the conclusions reached by the appellant.

On the same day of the Appleby incident, the appellant took his dog to a Mr. Thorburn of the S.P.C.A. at Charlo, N.B. The dog showed no signs of rabies, distemper or anything of this nature.

Prior to the Richard incident, the appellant had received no complaints whatever about his dog, with the exception of the Appleby incident. In so far as this latter incident is concerned, the evidence which relates to it is inconclusive to show that the dog bit the Appleby child.

. . .

The present case involves the question of liability for damage as a result of injuries caused by a dog. At common law the dog has been placed in a favoured position, as compared with that of most of the other domestic animals. Like them, the dog did not involve its owner under the strict liability imposed in respect of the keeping of dangerous animals. Liability in respect of a dog, under the strict rule, would only arise if *scienter* were proved.

The common law liability of owners of animals is stated in Halsbury's Laws of England, 3rd. ed., vol. 1, p. 663, para. 1267, in the following words:

> The law assumes that animals which from their nature are harmless, or are rendered so by being domesticated for generations, are not of a dangerous disposition; and the owner of such an animal is not, in the absence of negligence, liable for an act of a vicious or mischievous kind which it is not the animal's nature usually to commit, unless he knows that the animal has that particular vicious or mischievous propensity; proof of this knowledge, or *scienter*, is essential. But where this knowledge exists, the owner keeps such an animal at his peril, and is answerable in damages for any harm done by the animal, even though the immediate cause of the injury is the intervening voluntary act of a third person.

. . .

With regards to proof of *scienter*, Halsbury, *supra*, at p. 665, para. 1268, states:

> The evidence of the *scienter* must be directed to the particular mischievous propensity that caused the damage. In order to recover for the bite of a dog on a human being, it is necessary to show that the owner had notice of the disposition of the dog to bite mankind; it is not enough to show that the dog had previously bitten a goat; but proof of a general savage or ferocious disposition towards mankind, and that it had a habit of rushing at people and attempting to bite them, is sufficient without proof of any actual previous bite.

The essence of liability under the common law is *scienter*, as pointed out by Lord Cranworth in *Fleeming v. Orr* (1855), 2 Macq. 14, 9 S.R.R. 516. This rule has been modified or removed in many jurisdictions. There is no statute in New Brunswick which would remove or modify the common law requirement of *scienter* as it relates to this case.

In the case of *Line v. Taylor* (1862), 3 F. & F. 731 at p. 732, 176 E.R. 335, Erle, C.J. (to the jury), stated:

> The plaintiff, to sustain the action, must satisfy you, not only that he was injured by the dog, but that the dog was fierce and mischievous, and known to be so by the plaintiff. If the plaintiff was really hurt and injured, it does not matter whether it was by the bite of the teeth or merely by a bruise or the effects of a squeeze. And it is not necessary to show that he was used to bite, if he was used to injure people. But if he merely had a habit of bounding upon people in play, even although in so doing he might frighten timid persons or cause some little annoyance, that would not sustain the action.

In the instant case the respondents had to prove three things: (1) that it was the dog in question which inflicted the injury; (2) that the dog had a mischievous propensity to commit the particular act of injury, and (3) that the owner knew of such propensity; in other words, had *scienter*.

There can be no question as to (1). It was the appellant's dog which inflicted the injury.

As to (2), the respondents sought to establish that on a previous occasion the dog had shown a propensity to attack and bite children by introducing the Appleby incident. Since I have already dealt with this incident and since there is no evidence of any other similar incident or incidents prior to the one at bar, I have come to the conclusion that the respondents failed to show any previous bad character of the dog. I find on the evidence — the dog was not "savage and vicious having already bit (*sic*) several children in the past few months."

With regards to (3), the evidence supports an absence of any knowledge or reason for apprehension by the appellant of the likelihood that the dog would attack or bite someone. The appellant, following his investigation of the Appleby incident, had no reason to apprehend any vicious propensity in his dog. The evidence supports the peaceful character of the dog and the ignorance of the appellant of any vicious propensity.

I would allow the appeal and set aside the judgment as directed. The appellant is entitled to costs both here and in the Court below.

BRIDGES C.J.N.B. (dissenting): ... The learned trial Judge made no finding as to whether the injury to the boy was caused by a bite or a bad scratch from a claw. I have no hesitation in believing the cut on the head extending from the top of the skull down to the ear was caused by one of the dog's claws and that his face was bruised when he fell to the ground.

It is my opinion that after the injury to the Appleby boy, the defendant could not but know that he was keeping a dog which, if not vicious, was dangerous for young children to approach, as it was liable to knock them down and cause serious injury. In my opinion, this was sufficient to establish *scienter*.

While the allegations of *scienter* contained in the statement of claim may not be what were proved, I do not think this should make any difference as the defendant was in no way taken by surprise with any evidence. I would allow any amendment that may be necessary.

I would dismiss the appeal with costs.

[Limerick J.A. concurred with Bujold J.A. Appeal allowed.]

NOTES AND QUESTIONS

1. As indicated by *Richard*, the common law distinguishes between animals which by nature of their species are ordinarily ferocious (*ferae naturae*), and animals which as a species or by virtue of long domestication are not usually dangerous (*mansuetae naturae*). A keeper is held strictly liable for injuries caused by *ferae naturae*, but is only held strictly liable for injuries caused by *mansuetae naturae* if he had *scienter*.

What is the *scienter* requirement? How does it differ from proof of negligence? Is it accurate to state that actions requiring proof of *scienter* involve strict liability?

2. The English courts have held that a keeper is strictly liable for any injury caused by a *ferae naturae*, even if the injury is unrelated to the animal's ferocity. However, a keeper is only held strictly liable for injuries attributable to the dangerous propensity of a *mansuetae naturae*. See *Behrens v. Bertram Mills Circus*, [1957] 1 All E.R. 583 (Q.B.); and *Glanville v. Sutton*, [1928] 1 K.B. 571.

3. Traditionally, a keeper was held strictly liable in these actions even if the animal was on his land and was restrained when it caused the injury. See Fleming, *The Law of Torts*, 8th ed. (1992), 357-59; and *McNeill v. Frankenfield* (1963), 44 D.L.R. (2d) 132 (B.C. C.A.). However, two cases indi-

cate that strict liability applies only if the keeper loses control or custody of the animal. See *Maynes v. Galicz*, [1976] 1 W.W.R. 557 (B.C. S.C.); *Lewis v. Oeming* (1983), 24 C.C.L.T. 81 (Alta. Q.B.); and Irvine, "Annotation" (1983), 24 C.C.L.T. 82.

4. Voluntary assumption of risk is the only generally recognized defence to actions involving dangerous animals. It is not clear whether the defendant can raise the plaintiff's contributory negligence, and it is doubtful whether "acts of God" or "acts of a stranger" are applicable defences. See Fleming, *The Law of Torts*, 8th ed. (1992), 346-47. See also *McNeill v. Frankenfield* (1963), 44 D.L.R. (2d) 132 (B.C. C.A.); *Lewis v. Oeming* (1983), 24 C.C.L.T. 81 (Alta. Q.B.); and *Witman v. Johnson* (1990), 5 C.C.L.T. (2d) 102 (Man. Q.B.).

5. The plaintiff has the option of suing in both strict liability and negligence. See *Fleming v. Atkinson*, [1959] S.C.R. 513; *Morris v. Baily* (1970), 13 D.L.R. (3d) 150 (Ont. C.A.); *Maynes v. Galicz*, [1976] 1 W.W.R. 557 (B.C. S.C.); and *Moffett v. Downing; Downing v. Moffett* (1981), 16 C.C.L.T. 313 (Ont. C.A.).

6. Many provinces have enacted legislation governing liability for dangerous animals. Some of the statutes simply embody the common law rules, but other legislation imposes significantly different principles. For example, Ontario, Manitoba and Newfoundland impose liability on dog owners for the personal injuries caused by their pets without proof of *scienter*. See the Dog Owner's Liability Act, R.S.O. 1990, c. D.16, s. 2. While the Ontario legislation is based on strict liability, it also provides that damages shall be adjusted in proportion to the defendant's degree of fault. See *Strom (Litigation Guardian of) v. White* (1994), 21 O.R. (3d) 205 (Gen. Div.); the Animal Husbandry Act, R.S.M. 1987, c. A90, s. 26; and the Dog Act, S. Nfld. 1990, c. D-26, s. 8. See *Whitehorse (City) v. Domingue* (1988), 3 Yukon R. 273 (Terr. Ct.).

7. Many actions resulting from animal attacks are brought under the common or statutory law of occupier's liability, as discussed in chapter 24. What are the advantages and disadvantages of this approach? See *Taller (Guardian ad litem of) v. Goldenshtein*, [1994] 3 W.W.R. 557 (B.C. C.A.).

3. Escape of Dangerous Substances — *Rylands v. Fletcher*

(a) INTRODUCTION

RYLANDS v. FLETCHER

(1868), L.R. 3 H.L. 330 (H.L.)

THE LORD CHANCELLOR (Lord Cairns): — My Lords, in this case the plaintiff (I may use the description of the parties in the action) is the occupier of a mine and works under a close of land. The defendants are the owners of a mill in his neighbourhood; and they proposed to make a reservoir for the purpose of keeping and storing water to be used about their mill upon another close of land, which, for the purposes of this case, may be taken as being adjoining to the close of the plaintiff, although in point of fact some intervening land lay between the two. Underneath the close of land of the defendants on which they proposed to construct their reservoir there were certain old and disused mining passages and works. There were five vertical shafts, and some horizontal shafts communicating with them. The vertical shafts had been filled up with soil and rubbish; and, it does not appear that any person was aware of the existence either of the vertical shafts or of the horizontal works communicating with them. In the course of the working by the plaintiff of his mine, he had gradually worked through the seams of coal underneath the close, and had come into contact with the old and disused works underneath the close of the defendants. In that state of things the reservoir of the defendants was constructed. It was constructed by them through the agency and inspection of an engineer and contractor. Personally the defendants appear to have taken no part in the works, nor to have been aware of any want of security connected with them. As regards the engineer and the contractor, we must take it from the case that they did not exercise, as far as they were concerned, that reasonable care and caution which they might have exercised, taking notice, as they appear to have taken notice, of the vertical shafts filled up in the manner which I have mentioned. However, my Lords, when the reservoir was constructed and filled, or partly filled, with water, the weight of the water, bearing upon the imperfectly filled-up and disused vertical shafts, broke through those shafts. The water passed down them and into the horizontal workings and from the horizontal workings under the close of the defendants, it passed on into the workings under the close of the plaintiff and flooded his mine, causing considerable damage, for which this action was brought. The Court of Exchequer, when the special case stating the facts to which I have referred was argued before them, were of opinion that the plaintiff had established no cause of action. The Court of Exchequer Chamber, before whom an appeal from their judgment was argued, were of a contrary opinion, and unanimously arrived at the conclusion that there was a cause of action, and that the plaintiff was entitled to damages. My Lords, the principles on which this case must be determined appear to me to be extremely simple. The defendants, treating them as owners or occupiers of the close on which the reservoir was constructed, might lawfully have used that close for any purpose for which it might, in the ordinary course of the enjoyment of land, be used; and if in what I may term the natural user of that land there had been any accumulation of water, either on the surface or underground, and if by the operation of the laws of nature that accumulation of water had passed off into the close occupied by the plaintiff, the plaintiff could not have complained that that result had taken place. If he had desired to guard himself against it, it would have lain on him to have done so by leaving or by interposing some barrier between his close and the close of the defendants in order to have prevented that operation of the laws of nature. As an illustration of that principle, I may refer to a case which was cited in the argument before your Lordships, the case of *Smith v. Kendrick* in the Court of Common Pleas, reported 7 C.B. 564. On the other hand, if the defendants, not stopping at the natural use of their close, had desired to use it for any purpose which I may term a non-natural use, for the purpose of introducing into the close that which, in its natural condition, was not in or upon it — for the purpose of introducing water, either above or below ground, in quantities and in a manner not the result of any work or operation on or under the land; and if in consequence of their doing so, or in consequence of any imperfection in the mode of their doing so, the water came to escape and to pass off into the close of the plaintiff, then it appears to me that that which the defendants were doing they were doing at their own peril; and if in the course of their doing it the evil arose to which I have referred — the evil, namely, of the escape of the water, and its passing away to the close of the plaintiff and injuring the plaintiff — then for the consequence of that, in my opinion, the defendants would be liable. As the case of *Smith v. Kendrick* is an illustration of the first principle to which I have referred, so also the second principle to which I have referred is well illustrated by another case in the same court, the case of *Baird v. Williamson*, which was also cited in the argument at the Bar, and is reported in 15 C.B., N.S., 376. My Lords, these simple principles, if they are well founded, as it appears to me they are, really dispose of this case. The same result is arrived at on the principles referred to by Blackburn, J. in his judgment in the Court of Exchequer Chamber, where he states the opinion of that court as to the law in these words:

> We think that the true rule of law is that the person who, for his own purposes, brings on his land and collects and keeps there anything likely to do mischief, if it escapes must keep it in at his peril, and if he does not do so is *prima facie* answerable for all the damage which is the natural consequence of its escape. He can excuse himself by showing that the escape was owing to the plaintiff's default, or, perhaps, that the escape was the consequence of *vis major* or of the act of God; but, as nothing of this sort exists here, it is unnecessary to inquire what excuse would be sufficient. The general rule as above stated seems on principle just. The person whose grass or corn is eaten down by the escaping cattle of his neighbour, or whose mine is flooded by the water from his neighbour's reservoir, or whose cellar is invaded by the filth of his neighbour's privy, or whose habitation is made unhealthy by the fumes and noisome vapours of his neighbour's alkali works, is damnified without any fault of his own; and it seems but reasonable and just that the neighbour who has brought something on his own property (which was not naturally there), harmless to others so long as it is confined to his own property, but which he knows will be mischievous if it gets on his neighbour's, should be obliged to make good the damage which ensues if he does not succeed in confining it to his own property. But for his act in bringing it there no mischief could have accrued, and it seems but just that he should at his peril keep it there so that no mischief may accrue, or answer for the natural and antici- pated consequence. And upon authority this, we think, is established to be the law, whether the things so brought be beasts, or water, or filth, or stenches.

My Lords, in that opinion, I must say, I entirely concur. Therefore I have to move your Lordships that the judgment of the Court of Exchequer Chamber be affirmed, and that the present appeal be dismissed with costs.

LORD CRANWORTH. — My Lords, I concur with my noble and learned friend in thinking that the rule of law was correctly stated by Mr. Justice Blackburn in delivering the opinion of the Exchequer Chamber. If a person brings or accumu- lates on his land anything which, if it should escape, may cause damage to his neighbour, he does so at his peril. If it does escape and cause damage, he is respon- sible, however careful he may have been, and whatever precautions he may have taken to prevent the damage. In considering whether a defendant is liable to a plaintiff for damage which the plaintiff may have sustained, the question in general is, not whether the defendant has acted with due care and caution, but whether his acts have occasioned the damage. This is all well explained in the old case of *Lambert v. Bessey*, reported by Sir Thomas Raymond, p. 421. And the doctrine is founded on good sense. For when one person in managing his own affairs causes, however innocently, damage to another, it is obviously only just that he should be the party to suffer. He is bound *sic uti suo ut non loedat alienum*.

. . .

NOTES AND QUESTIONS

1. What are the elements of an action under the rule in *Rylands*?
2. In the court below (1866), L.R. 1 Exch. 265, Blackburn J. stated at 282:

   there does not appear to be any difference in principle, between the extent of the duty cast on him who brings cattle on his land to keep them in, and the extent of the duty imposed on him who brings on his land water, filth, or stenches, or any other thing which will, if it escape, naturally do damage.

Should these two instances of strict liability be governed by the same principle? See *Read v. J. Lyons & Co.*, [1947] A.C. 156 at 166-67 (H.L.), per Viscount Simon.

3. Aside from Lord Macmillan's *obiter* in *Read v. J. Lyons & Co.*, [1947] A.C. 156 at 173 (H.L.), the authorities indicate that *Rylands* also applies to personal injuries. See *Shiffman v. Order of St. John*, [1936] 1 All E.R. 557 (K.B.); *Schubert v. Sterling Trust Corp.*, [1943] 4 D.L.R. 584 (Ont. H.C.); *Aldridge and O'Brien v. Van Patten*, [1952] 4 D.L.R. 93 (Ont. H.C.); *Perry v. Kendricks Transport Ltd.*, [1956] 1 All E.R. 154 (C.A.); and *Gertsen v. Municipality of Metro. Toronto* (1973), 41 D.L.R. (3d) 646 (Ont. H.C.).

4. The rule in *Rylands* has been the topic of considerable academic attention. See, for example, Morris, "Absolute Liability for Dangerous Things" (1948), 61 Harv. L. Rev. 515; Prosser, "The Principle of *Rylands v. Fletcher*", in *Selected Topics on the Law of Tort* (1953), 136; Fridman, "The Rise and Fall of *Rylands v. Fletcher*" (1956), 34 Can. Bar Rev. 810; Linden, "Whatever Happened to *Rylands v. Fletcher*?", in Klar (ed.), *Studies in Canadian Tort Law* (1977), 325; Fleming, "Comment: The Fall of a Crippled Giant" (1995), 3 T.L.R. 56; and Husak, "Varieties of Strict Liability" (1995), 8 C.J.L.J. 189; and Pardy, "Fault and Cause: Rethinking the Role of Negligent Conduct" (1995), 3 Tort L. R. 143.

5. The rule in *Rylands* has found acceptance among proponents of enterprise liability. Although enterprise liability can be supported on several loss distribution principles, it is most closely associated with market deterrence. The essential feature of enterprise liability was summarized by Lang in "The Activity-Risk Theory of Tort: Risk, Insurance and Insolvency" (1961), 39 Can. Bar Rev. 530 at 530: "The basic proposition and starting point is that activity should bear the risks of harm that it produces. Unless the act is sufficiently worthwhile to pay for the increase in risks that accompany it, the act should not be done at all." See generally Calabresi, *The Cost of Accidents* (1970); and Cane, *Atiyah's Accidents, Compensation and the Law*, 5th ed. (1993).

6. One of the most interesting criticisms of enterprise liability is implicit in the work of Coase, "The Problem of Social Cost" (1960), 3 J. L. Econ. 1. The author suggests that it is difficult to determine which party should be assigned the cost of a particular activity. For example, in *Rylands* is the damage a cost which ought to be attributed to constructing the reservoir or to maintaining the mine? Presumably the defendant's conduct would have been harmless if the plaintiffs had not been engaged in an equally "unnatural" use of their land. What significance do you attach to the fact that the defendant was the active party? Since no trespass was committed, should it matter that the water escaped from the defendant's land to the plaintiffs'? Why should the plaintiffs' interest be preferred to that of the defendant, particularly when both are major commercial enterprises? See also Morris, "Hazardous Enterprises and Risk-Bearing Capacity" (1951), 61 Yale L.J. 1172; Calabresi, *supra*; Fletcher, "Fairness and Utility in Tort Theory" (1972), 85 Harv. L. Rev. 537; Coleman, "The Morality of Strict Tort Liability" (1976), 18 Will. & Mary L. Rev. 259; and Schwartz, "The Vitality of Negligence and the Ethics of Strict Liability" (1981), 15 Georgia L. Rev. 963.

(b) ESCAPE

READ v. J. LYONS & CO.

[1947] A.C. 156, [1946] 2 All E.R. 471 (H.L.)

VISCOUNT SIMON L.C.: My Lords, in fulfilment of an agreement dated Jan. 26, 1942, and made between the Ministry of Supply and the respondents, the latter undertook the operation, management and control of the Elstow Ordnance Factory as agents for the Ministry. The respondents carried on in the factory the business of filling shell cases with high explosives. The appellant was an employee of the Ministry, with the duty of inspecting this filling of shell cases, and her work required her (although she would have preferred and had applied for other employment) to be present in the shell filling shop. On Aug. 31, 1942, while the appellant was lawfully in the shell filling shop in discharge of her duty, an explosion occurred which killed a man and injured the appellant and others. No negligence was averred or proved against the respondents. The plea of *volenti non fit injuria*, for whatever it might be worth, has been expressly withdrawn before this House by the Attorney-General on behalf of the respondents, and thus the simple question for decision is whether in these circumstances the respondents are liable, without any proof or inference that they were negligent, to the appellant in damages, which have been assessed at £575 2s. 8d, for her injuries.

. . .

Now, the strict liability recognized by this House to exist in *Rylands v. Fletcher* [(1868), L.R. 3 H.L. 330] is conditioned by two elements which I may call the condition of "escape" from the land of something likely to do mischief if it escapes, and the condition of "non-natural use" of the land. This second condition has in some later cases, which did not reach this House, been otherwise expressed, *e.g.*, as "exceptional" user, when such user is not regarded as "natural" and at the same time is likely to produce mischief if there is an "escape". Dr. Stallybrass, in a learned article in 3 Cambridge Law Review, p. 376, has collected the large variety of epithets that have been judicially employed in this connection. The American Restatement of the Law of Torts, III, s. 519, speaks of "ultra-hazardous activity," but attaches qualifications which would appear in the present instance to exonerate the respondents. It is not necessary to analyse the second condition on the present occasion, for in the case now before us the first essential condition of "escape" does not seem to me to be present at all. "Escape", for the purpose of applying the proposition in *Rylands v. Fletcher* [*supra*] means escape from a place which the defendant has occupation of, or control over to a place which is outside his occupation or control. Blackburn J., several times refers to the defendant's duty as being the duty of "keeping a thing in" at the defendant's peril and by "keeping in" he means, not preventing an explosive substance from exploding, but preventing a thing which may inflict mischief from escaping from the area which the defendant occupies or controls. In two well-known cases the same principle of strict liability for escape was applied to defendants who held a franchise to lay pipes under a highway and to conduct water (or gas) under pressure through them: *Charing Cross Electric Co. v. Hydraulic Power Co.* [[1914] 3 K.B. 772]; *Northwestern Utilities, Ltd. v. London Guarantee, etc., Co.* [[1936] A.C. 108].

In *Howard v. Furness Houlder Argentine Lines, Ltd.* [[1936] 2 All E.R. 781] Lewis, J., had before him a case of injury caused by an escape of steam on board a ship where the plaintiff was working. The judge was, I think, right in refusing to apply the doctrine of *Rylands v. Fletcher* [*supra*] on the ground that the injuries were caused on the premises of the defendants. Apart altogether from the judge's doubt (which I share) whether the owners of the steamship by generating steam therein are making a non-natural use of their steamship, the other condition on which the proposition in *Rylands v. Fletcher* [*supra*] depends was not present, any more than it is in the case with which we have now to deal. Here there is no escape of the relevant kind at all and the appellant's action fails on that ground.

In these circumstances it becomes unnecessary to consider other objections that have been raised, such as the question of whether the doctrine of *Rylands v. Fletcher* [*supra*] applies where the claim is for damages for personal injury as distinguished from damages to property. It may be noted, in passing, that Blackburn, J., himself when referring to the doctrine of *Rylands v. Fletcher* [*supra*] in the later case of *Castle v. Stockton Waterworks* [(1875), L.R. 10 Q.B. 453] leaves this undealt with. He treats damages under the *Rylands v. Fletcher* [*supra*] principle as covering damages to property, such as workmen's clothes or tools, but says nothing about liability for personal injuries.

On the much litigated question of what amounts to "non-natural" use of land, the discussion of which is also unnecessary in the present appeal, ...

. . .

LORD MACMILLAN: ... The doctrine of *Rylands v. Fletcher* [*supra*], as I understand it, derives from a conception of the mutual duties of adjoining or neighbouring landowners and its congeners are trespass and nuisance. If its foundation is to be found in the injunction *sic utere tuo ut alienum non laedas*, then it is manifest that it has nothing to do with personal injuries. The duty is to refrain from injuring not *alium* but *alienum*. The two prerequisites of the doctrine are that there must be the escape of something from one man's close to another man's close and that that which escapes must have been brought on the land from which it escapes in consequence of some non-natural use of that land whatever precisely that may mean. Neither of these features exists in the present case. I have already pointed out that nothing escaped from the defendants' premises, and, were it necessary to decide the point, I should hesitate to hold that in these days and in an industrial community it was a non-natural use of land to build a factory on it and conduct there the manufacture of explosives. I could conceive it being said that to carry on the manufacture of explosives in a crowded urban area was evidence of negligence, but there is no such case here and I offer no opinion on the point.

It is noteworthy in *Rylands v. Fletcher* [*supra*] that all the counts in the declaration alleged negligence and that on the same page of the report on which his famous *dictum* is recorded (L.R. 1 Exch. 265, at p. 279), Blackburn J., states that:

> the plaintiff ... must bear the loss, unless he can establish that it was the consequence of some default for which the defendants are responsible.

His decision for the plaintiff would thus logically seem to imply that he found some default on the part of the defendants in bringing on their land and failing to confine there an exceptional quantity of water. Notwithstanding the width of some of the pronouncements, particularly on the part of Lord Cranworth, I think that the doctrine of *Rylands v. Fletcher* [*supra*], when studied in its setting, is truly a case on the mutual obligations of the owners or occupiers of neighbouring closes and is entirely inapplicable to the present case, which is quite outside its ambit.

. . .

LORD SIMONDS: ... My Lords, in this branch of the law it is inevitable that reference should be made to what Blackburn, J., said in *Fletcher v. Rylands* [(1866), L.R. 1 Exch. 265] and what Lord Cairns said in *Rylands v. Fletcher* [*supra*]. In doing so I think it is of great importance to remember that the subject-matter of that action was the rights of adjoining landowners and, though the doctrine of strict liability there enforced was illustrated by reference to the responsibility of the man who keeps beasts, yet the defendant was held liable only because he allowed, or did not prevent, the escape from his land onto the land of the plaintiff of something which he had brought onto his own land and which he knew or should have known was liable to do mischief if it escaped from it. I agree with the late Mackinnon, L.J., that this and nothing else is the basis of the celebrated judgment of Blackburn J., and I think it no less the basis of Lord Cairns' opinion. For it is significant that he emphasises that, if the accumulation of water (the very thing which by its escape in that case caused the actionable damage) had arisen by the natural user of the defendant's land, the adjoining owner could not have complained. The decision itself does not justify the broad proposition which the appellant seeks to establish, and I would venture to say that the word "escape" which is used so often in the judgment of Blackburn, J., meant to him escape from the defendant's premises and nothing else. It has been urged that escape means escape from control and that it is irrelevant where damage takes place if there has been such an escape, but, though it is arguable that that ought to be the law, I see no logical necessity for it and much less any judicial authority. For as I have said, somewhere the line must be drawn unless full rein be given to the doctrine that a man acts always at his peril, that "coarse and impolitic idea" as O.W. Holmes somewhere calls it. I speak with all deference of modern American text books and judicial decisions, but I think little guidance can be obtained from the way in which this part of the common law has developed on the other side of the ocean, and I would reject the idea that, if a man carries on a so-called ultra-hazardous activity on his premises, the line must be drawn so as to bring him within the limit of strict liability for its consequences to all men everywhere. On the contrary, I would say that his obligation to those lawfully on his premises is to be ultra-cautious in carrying on his ultra-hazardous activity, but that it will still be the task of the injured person to show that the defendant owed to him a duty of care and did not fulfil it. It may well be that in the discharge of that task he will sometimes be able to call in aid the maxim *res ipsa loquitur.*

My Lords, I have stated a general proposition and indicated that there are exceptions to it. It is clear, for instance, that, if a man brings and keeps a wild beast on his land or a beast known to him to be ferocious of a species generally *mansuetae naturae,* he may be liable for any damage occurring within or without his premises without proof of negligence. Such an exception will serve to illustrate the proposition that the law of torts has grown up historically in separate compartments, and that beasts have travelled in a compartment of their own. So, also, it may be that in regard to certain chattels a similar liability may arise though I accept and would quote with respect to what Lord Macmillan said in *Donoghue v. Stevenson* [[1932] A.C. 562 at p. 611]:

> I rather regard this type of case as a special instance of negligence where the law exacts a degree of diligence so stringent as to amount practically to a guarantee of safety.

There may be other exceptions. Professor Winfield, to whose "Textbook of the Law of Tort," 3rd edn., 1946, I would acknowledge my indebtedness, is inclined to include certain "dangerous structures" within the rule of strict liability. This may be so. It is sufficient for my purpose to say that, unless a plaintiff can point to a specific rule of law in relation to a specific subject-matter he cannot, in my opinion, bring himself within the exceptions to the general rule that I have stated. I have already expressed my view that there is no rule which imposes on him who carries on the business of making explosives, though the activity may be "ultra-hazardous" and an explosive "a dangerous thing," a strict liability to those who are lawfully on his premises.

. . .

[Lords Porter and Uthwatt delivered separate concurring speeches.]

NOTES AND QUESTIONS

1. What must the plaintiff establish to meet the "escape requirement" in *Read*? What is the rationale for this requirement? In *Deyo v. Kingston Speedway Ltd.*, [1954] 2 D.L.R. 419, aff'd. [1955] 1 D.L.R. 718 (S.C.C.), two spectators at a stock car race were injured by a racing car that went out of control. The claim based on *Rylands* was dismissed because there had been no escape. In *Aldridge v. Van Patter*, [1952] 4 D.L.R. 93 (Ont. H.C.), a stock car went out of control, crashed through a fence and injured the plaintiff, who was in an adjoining park. One of the bases upon which liability was imposed was the rule in *Rylands*. Can you justify the results in these two cases?

2. Linden is very critical of the escape requirement and cites a number of cases in which it has been loosely interpreted or ignored. *Canadian Tort Law*, 5th ed. (1993), 488-89.

3. What are the advantages and disadvantages of dealing with injuries suffered on the defendant's land under the principles of occupiers' liability? Under what circumstances will these principles produce different results than the rule in *Rylands*?

4. In *Dokuchia v. Domansch*, [1945] 1 D.L.R. 757 (Ont. C.A.), the plaintiff was injured while pouring the defendant's gasoline into the defendant's truck, which was on a highway. *Rylands* was applied, notwithstanding that there was no connection with either party's land, let alone an escape. Do you agree with this application of *Rylands*? Can you justify a rule which makes the owner of dangerous substances strictly liable for any injuries they cause?

(c) NON-NATURAL USE

GERTSEN v. METRO. TORONTO

(1973), 2 O.R. (2d) 1, 41 D.L.R. (3d) 646 (Ont. H.C.)

[Two municipalities, Toronto and York, reached an agreement whereby Toronto dumped putrescible organic waste into a land-fill site in York. Eventually methane gas seeped from the site, some of which accumulated in the plaintiff's garage and exploded when he started his car. The plaintiff sued both municipalities in nuisance, negligence and strict liability. The following excerpt is limited to the court's discussion of strict liability.]

LERNER J.: ... Blackburn, J., in *Fletcher v. Rylands et al.* (1866), L.R. 1 Ex. 265 at p. 279; affirmed L.R. 3 H.L. 330, stated the rule which has been sometimes distinguished and sometimes restricted in its application:

> We think that the true rule of law is, that the person who for his own purposes brings on his lands and collects and keeps there anything likely to do mischief if it escapes, must keep it in at his peril, and, if he does not do so, is prima facie answerable for all the damage which is the natural consequences of its escape.

This rule, if applicable on the facts of the case, makes liability absolute. The defendants by joint agreement brought putrescible organic matter on the lands of York as a means of disposing of same. This organic matter generated methane gas, admittedly a dangerous substance in itself. The gas escaped onto the plaintiffs' land and caused them damage. *Prima facie* the defendants should be liable without proof of negligence: *Clerk and Lindsell on Torts*, 13th ed. (1969), p. 1481, *Read v. J. Lyons & Co. Ltd.*, [1947] A.C. 156 at p. 166. However, there are sometimes other considerations brought to bear which, if applicable, somewhat restrict the rule.

York argued that the work was under the control of Metro which would relieve it from liability. It has, however, been held that a defendant (York) cannot avail itself of the absence of negligence on its part and even of those over whom it has control. The owner (York) is charged with keeping a dangerous substance at its peril: *Dunn et al. v. Birmingham Canal Co.* (1872), L.R. 7 Q.B. 244 at p. 259.

Another submission of York is that waste disposal was a natural user of these lands. If the owner uses his land in the exercise of his ordinary rights, he incurs no liability under the rule if he injures his neighbour: *Rylands v. Fletcher, per* Lord Cairns, pp. 338-9.

In *Rickards v. Lothian*, [1913] A.C. 263, the Privy Council withdrew a wide range of activities from the ambit of strict liability under this rule on the basis that it applied only to damage due to non-natural use of land. As an incident thereof, since the non-natural user thereof is an essential element of liability, the burden of proving it rests on the plaintiff: *Pett v. Sims Paving & Road Construction Co. Pty. Ltd.*, [1928] V.L.R. 247 at p. 255.

When the use of the element or thing which the law regards as the potential source of mischief is an accepted incident of some ordinary purpose to which land is reasonably applied by the occupier, the *prima facie* rule of absolute responsibility for the consequences of its escape must give way. In applying this qualification, the Courts have looked not only to the thing or activity in isolation, but also to the place and manner in which it is maintained and its relation to its surroundings. Time, place and circumstance, not excluding purpose, are most material. The distinction between natural and non-natural user is both relative and capable of adjustment to the changing patterns of social existence: Fleming, *Law of Torts*, 4th ed. (1971), p. 283.

> The distinction between natural and non-natural user has served the function principally of lending the rule in *Rylands v. Fletcher* a desirable degree of flexibility by enabling the courts to infuse notions of social and economic needs prevailing at a given time and place ... Yet caution should be observed lest the qualification be pushed too far. There is no merit, for example, in occasional suggestions to exempt all activities redounding to the "general benefit of the community", such as nationalized industries or even the manufacture of munitions in time of war. Not only is there no warrant in principle for prejudicing private rights by the facile pleas of overriding public welfare, at least in the absence of statutory authorization, but many are the decisions which have attached strict liability to enterprises engaged in community services such as public utilities and the like.

Fleming, p. 284.

I must now decide whether this garbage-fill project was natural or non-natural user of the land. I am emboldened by the statement of Lord Porter in *Read v. J. Lyons & Co., Ltd.*, at p. 176, where he states:

> Possibly a further requisite is that to bring the thing to the position in which it is found is to make a non-natural use of that place ... Manifestly these requirements must give rise to difficulty in applying the rule in individual cases and necessitate at least a decision as to what can be dangerous and what is a non-natural use ... For the present I need only say that each seems to be a question of fact subject to a ruling of the judge as to whether the particular object can be dangerous or the particular use can be non-natural, and in deciding this question I think that all the circumstances of the time and place and practice of mankind must be taken into consideration so that what might be regarded as dangerous or non-natural may vary according to those circumstances.

In the same case Viscount Simon stated at pp. 169-70:

> I think it not improper to put on record, with all due regard to the admission and dicta in that case, that if the question had hereafter to be decided whether the making of munitions in a factory at the Government's request in time of war for the purpose of helping to defeat the enemy is a "non-natural" use of land, adopted by the occupier "for his own purposes", it would *not seem to me* that the House would be bound by this authority to say that it was.

(The italics are mine.) That statement seems to have been provoked by the opinion of Lord Buckmaster in *Rainham Chemical Works, Ltd. (in Liquidation) et al. v. Belvedere Fish Guano Co., Ltd.*, [1921] 2 A.C. 465 at p. 471. Injuries had been sustained by the inspector in the factory of the defendants who were making munitions when an explosion occurred. Lord Buckmaster stated that the making of munitions was certainly not "the common and ordinary use of the land."

I take judicial notice, supported by the exhibits and all testimony, that this was a relatively small ravine surrounded by heavily populated urban areas. It was originally subdivided apparently for occupation by the citizenry but because of its difficult contours and a stream in the lower areas, it appears to me that it was not practicable for such use. This does not, however, in my view, alter the case and the fact that Metro was seeking garbage and waste disposal areas does not change the situation either. I find that the primary purpose for filling this ravine in this manner was a selfish and self-serving opportunity for Metro who held out a "carrot" to York that if this were permitted York would end up with a level area instead of an "eyesore" and also gain attractive facilities, at no expense. This, in my view, having regard to its location together with the known temporary and permanent problems caused by such a garbage-fill project, cannot be said to be supported by the "overriding public welfare" theory. The initial benefits were to Metro which was responsible for disposing of garbage, etc. and not to the general benefit of the community directly affected by this use, *i.e.*, the owners and occupiers of the surrounding land. They were the community that I must consider. Applying the propositions of time, place and circumstances and not excluding purpose, I find that this was a non-natural user of the land and, therefore, that exception to the rule of strict liability also fails.

. . .

[Both defendants were held liable under the rule in *Rylands*, as well as in nuisance and negligence.]

NOTES AND QUESTIONS

1. In *Rylands*, Lord Cairns suggested that a non-natural use of land involved the introduction of "that which in its natural condition was not in or upon it". Why was mining considered any less natural a use than milling? In *Rickards v. Lothian*, [1913] A.C. 263 at 280 (P.C.), the court said: "There must be some special use bringing with it increased danger to others ... not merely the ordinary use of the land or such a use as is proper for the general benefit of the community." This latter interpretation of non-natural use was adopted in both *Read* and *Gertsen*. How has the definition of non-natural use changed, and what is the significance of this change? Which interpretation is preferable?

2. For a criticism of the restrictive definition of non-natural use see Linden, *Canadian Tort Law*, 5th ed. (1993), 483-89. See also Newark, "Non-Natural User and *Rylands v. Fletcher* (1961), 24 Mod. L. Rev. 557; and Williams, "Non-Natural Use of Land" (1973), 32 Cambridge L.J. 310.

3. The escaping object or substance must be likely to cause harm, or in other words be a "dangerous thing". This may include both objects which are dangerous in themselves and objects which are likely

to escape and thereby pose risks to others. It is difficult to determine which objects and substances would be considered "dangerous things" without resort to the case law. *Rylands* has been applied to water, gas, electricity, sparks from a steam locomotive, strips of metal foil, caravan dwellers, and a car with a full gas tank in a garage.

4. For Canadian cases interpreting the related concepts of non-natural use and dangerous things see *Heintzman & Co. v. Hashman Const. Ltd.* (1973), 32 D.L.R. (3d) 622 (Alta. S.C.); *Schenck v. R.; Rokeby v. R.* (1981), 34 O.R. (2d) 595 (H.C.); *Quondam v. Francis Belliveau Excavations Ltd.* (1983), 46 N.B.R. (2d) 352 (C.A.); *Palma v. Stora Kopparbergs Berslags Aktiebolag* (1983), 26 C.C.L.T. 22 (N.S. T.D.); *Beaudry v. Tollman*, [1983] 6 W.W.R. 660 (Alta. Q.B.); *Chu v. Dawson* (1984), 31 C.C.L.T. 146 (B.C. C.A.); and *Tock v. St. John's Metropolitan Area Board* (1989), 1 C.C.L.T. (2d) 113 (S.C.C.). See also Stallybrass, "Dangerous Things and the Non-Natural User of Land" (1929), 3 Cambridge L.J. 376.

5. The early common law held an occupier strictly liable if a fire in his control escaped and caused damage to another's property. This common law rule has been supplanted by legislation in all the Canadian provinces, eliminating strict liability for accidental fires. However, it has been held that these statutes do not affect the rule in *Rylands*. Therefore, the escape of a "non-natural fire", such as that used in an industrial setting, may give rise to strict liability. For examples of fires that constitute a non-natural use see *A.G. Can. v. Diamond Waterproofing Ltd; Pillar Const. v. Defence Const. (1951) Ltd.* (1974), 48 D.L.R. (3d) 353 (Ont. C.A.) (storing highly flammable material near a heater); and *Hudson v. Riverdale Colony of Hutterian Brethren* (1980), 114 D.L.R. (3d) 352 (Man. C.A.) (grass fire started to contain larger fire). For examples of fires that constitute a natural use see *O'Neill v. Esquire Hotels Ltd.* (1972), 30 D.L.R. (3d) 589 (N.B. C.A.) (propane gas used for cooking); *Lickoch v. Madu; Oscar v. Lickoch* (1973), 34 D.L.R. (3d) 569 (Alta. C.A.) (farmer burning trash); *Dudeck v. Brown* (1980), 33 O.R. (2d) 460 (H.C.) (homeowner using wood-burning stove); and *Dahler v. Bruvold*, [1981] 5 W.W.R. 706 (B.C. S.C.) (logger starting fire to clear land pursuant to a provincial permit). But see *Smith v. Widdicombe* (1987), 39 C.C.L.T. 98 (Man. Q.B.), where the court held that a fire used to burn stubble prior to cultivation was a natural use. See also Ogus, "Vagaries in Liability for the Escape of Fire" (1969), 27 Cambridge L.J. 104.

(d) DEFENCES TO THE RULE IN *RYLANDS v. FLETCHER*

As we have seen, the courts have narrowly interpreted and applied *Rylands*. They have further limited its impact by recognizing six defences — consent, common benefit, default of the plaintiff, act of God, act of stranger, and statutory authority. This situation has led Fleming in *The Law of Torts*, 8th ed. (1992), to state at page 343: "The aggregate effect of these exceptions makes it doubtful whether there is much left of the rationale of strict liability as originally contemplated in 1866."

(i) *Consent*

If the defendant can establish that the plaintiff implicitly or explicitly consented to the presence of the danger, he will have a complete defence to a claim under *Rylands*. The courts may imply consent from the nature of the legal relationship between the parties or from the physical circumstances. For example, a tenant in a lower floor is taken to implicitly consent to the presence of water pipes in the upper floors and cannot invoke *Rylands* if water seeps into his premises causing damage. The tenant's remedy, if any, would lie in negligence. See generally, *Peters v. Prince of Wales Theatre (Birmingham) Ltd.*, [1943] 1 K.B. (C.A.); *Holinaty v. Hawkins* (1965), 52 D.L.R. (2d) 289 (Ont. C.A.); *Federic v. Perpetual Invt. Ltd.* (1968), 2 D.L.R. (3d) 50 (Ont. H.C.); *Elfassy v. Sylben Invts. Ltd.* (1978), 21 O.R. (2d)

609 (H.C.); and *Pattison v. Prince Edward Region Conservation Authority* (1984), 30 C.C.L.T. 305 (Ont. H.C.).

(ii) *Common Benefit*

If the source of the danger is maintained for the common benefit of both the plaintiff and the defendant, the defendant cannot be held liable under *Rylands*. In the classic case of *Carstairs v. Taylor* (1871), L.R. 6 Exch. 217, rain water was collected in a special box on the roof and flowed through the drains. When a rat made a hole in the box, water flowed into the plaintiff's ground floor premises, damaging his property. The plaintiff's action under *Rylands* was dismissed, because the water was collected for the mutual benefit of both the defendant and the plaintiff. Since the defendant had not been careless, the plaintiff's claim also failed in negligence. Some authors now treat the common benefit defence as a form of implied consent. See generally *Danku v. Town of Fort Frances* (1976), 73 D.L.R. (3d) 377 (Ont. Dist. Ct.); and *Gilson v. Kerrier District Council*, [1976] 3 All E.R. 343 (C.A.).

(iii) *Default of the Plaintiff*

The plaintiff cannot recover under *Rylands* if he voluntarily and unreasonably encounters a known danger. Recovery will be denied if the plaintiff's wanton, wilful or reckless misconduct materially increased the probability of injury. Nor will the defendant be held liable for damages which are caused by the abnormal sensitivity of the plaintiff's property. See *Dunn v. Birmingham Canal Co.* (1872), L.R. 8 Q.B. 42 (Ex. Ch.); *Ponting v. Noakes*, [1894] 2 Q.B. 281; and *Hoare v. McAlpine*, [1923] 1 Ch. 167.

(iv) *Act of God*

An act of God is a force of nature that arises without human intervention. To provide a defence, the natural force must be so unexpected that it could not have been reasonably foreseen, and thus its effects could not have been prevented. See *Nichols v. Marsland* (1875), L.R. 10 Exch. 255, aff'd. (1876), 2 Ex. D. 1 (C.A.); *Greenock Corp. v. Caledonia Ry. Co.*, [1917] A.C. 556 (H.L.); *Smith v. Ont. & Minnesota Power Co.* (1918), 45 D.L.R. 266 (Ont. C.A.); and *Goldman v. Hargrave*, [1967] 1 A.C. 645 (P.C.).

(v) *Act of a Stranger*

If the defendant can prove that the escape of the dangerous thing was due to a deliberate unforeseeable act of a stranger, he will be absolved of liability under *Rylands*. The onus is on the defendant to show that he could not have prevented the escape even with the exercise of reasonable care. The owner of a dangerous thing remains strictly liable for foreseeable harm caused by third parties. It is not always clear whether an intermeddler will be considered a stranger, as opposed to a person for whom the defendant will be held accountable. An occupier is held responsible for the conduct of his servants acting within the scope of their employment, independent contractors, invitees, and probably licensees and even family members acting under his control. The defence of an act of a stranger introduces into this area concepts commonly associated with negligence. See *Rickards v. Lothian*, [1913] A.C. 263 (P.C.); *Northwestern Utilities Ltd. v. London Guarantee & Accident Co.*, [1936] A.C. 108 (P.C.); and *Hale v. Jennings Brothers*, [1938] 1 All E.R. 579 (C.A.). For a discussion of people who are considered to be strangers see *Schubert v. Sterling Trusts Corp.*, [1943] 4 D.L.R. 584 (Ont. H.C.); *Holinaty v. Hawkins* (1965), 52 D.L.R. (2d) 289 (Ont. C.A.); *Saccardo v. Hamilton* (1970), 18 D.L.R. (3d) 271 (Ont. H.C.); *Smith v. Scott*, [1973] Ch. 314; and *Holderness v. Goslin*, [1975] 2 N.Z.L.R. 46 (S.C.).

(vi) *Statutory Authority*

Activities which may involve the escape of dangerous substances, such as gas, water, electricity, and sewage are now generally under the management of public utilities operating under statutory authority. If the defendant can prove that his conduct giving rise to the action was authorized by statute, he will have a defence to a claim under *Rylands*. Legislation seldom expressly addresses the issue of tort liability, and the scope of this defence is often a matter of statutory intepretation. If the statutory language is mandatory, that is, it imposes an obligation on the defendant to supply the service, then the defendant will not be held liable for acts done pursuant to that obligation in the absence of negligence. However, if the statutory language is permissive, the courts will not usually interpret it as authorizing the defendant to violate the rule in *Rylands*. See *Benning v. Wong* (1969), 43 A.L.J.R. 467 (Aust. H.C.); *Himmelman v. Nova Const. Co.* (1969), 5 D.L.R. (3d) 56 (N.S. S.C.); *Gertsen v. Municipality of Metropolitan Toronto* (1973), 41 D.L.R. (3d) 646 (Ont. H.C.); *Schenck v. R.; Rokeby v. R.* (1981), 34 O.R. (2d) 595 (H.C.); and *Lyon v. Village of Shelburne* (1981), 130 D.L.R. (3d) 307 (Ont. Co. Ct.). See also Linden, "Strict Liability, Nuisance, and Legislative Authorization" (1966), 4 Osgoode Hall L.J. 196.

REVIEW PROBLEMS

1. Summarize the elements of the original cause of action in *Rylands*. How have the courts altered the action? What is the impact of these changes, and can they be justified on policy grounds?

2. Summarize the defences that were originally available in *Rylands*. How have the courts altered the defences to actions based on *Rylands*? What is the impact of these changes, and can they be justified on policy grounds?

3. In light of the changes that have been made to the rule in *Rylands*, does this doctrine serve a useful purpose in modern tort law?

4. A Note on *Rylands v. Fletcher*

Like all other common law cases, the decision in *Rylands v. Fletcher* was the product of particular legal and historical circumstances. Three factors appear to have been especially important to the outcome. First, as an English landowner who had innocently suffered serious damage to his property, Rylands made an ideal plaintiff in the Victorian era. Second, Rylands was a deserving plaintiff with no obvious legal remedy. When it became clear that Rylands could not establish a case in negligence, sympathetic Law Lords had no choice but to identify some alternative theory of liability. Third, the research of legal historian A. Simpson has revealed that the *Rylands* case had been preceded by a number of notorious burst-reservoir disasters. The judges who posited the strict liability rule appear to have been motivated, in part, by the desire to deter future calamities of this kind. See Simpson, "Legal Liability for Bursting Reservoirs: The Historical Context of the Rule in *Rylands* v. *Fletcher*" (1984), 13 J. Leg. St. 209.

Whatever its historical origins, modern common law judges have never been entirely at ease with the doctrine of strict liability. At least two aspects of *Rylands* are problematic. The first is the imprecision of the decision's key terms. Phrases such as "dangerous substance" and "non-natural use" have resisted consistent interpretation and application. This difficulty aside, many judges have also had fundamental misgivings about the fairness of strict liability, and about its anomalous position in relation to the predominant tort principles of negligent and intentional fault. In recent years, a number of leading Commonwealth jurists have concluded that *Rylands* is a doctrinal anachronism, a legal principle that has outlived whatever rationale or usefulness that might once have justified its existence. In the 1990s this view has hardened, especially among the appellate judges of England and Australia.

Two recent cases are particularly important examples of mounting judicial hostility toward the line of cases that began with *Rylands*. The first is the House of Lords decision in *Cambridge Water Co. v. Eastern Counties Leather plc*, [1994] 1 All E.R. 53. The defendant was a leather manufacturer and the plaintiff its distant neighbour. Over a 20-year period, 1,000 gallons of chemical solvent seeped from the defendant's property into the plaintiff's well. When the contamination was discovered and traced, the plaintiff sued in negligence, nuisance, and on the principles established in *Rylands v. Fletcher*. The first two pleas failed for lack of reasonable foreseeability. With regard to strict liability, the Law Lords unanimously decided that "knowledge, or at least foreseeability of the risk" is a precondition even of so-called "strict" liability. Since the plaintiff had been unable to prove that the seepage of solvents into his distant well had been foreseeable, the defendant was not liable under the rule of *Rylands*.

According to some commentators, the House of Lords' explicit pronouncement that reasonable foreseeability of harm is an element of strict liability has all but submerged the doctrine in the tort of negligence. See Fleming, "The Fall of a Crippled Giant" (1995), 3 T.L.R. 56. However, in *Cambridge Water* both the English Court of Appeal and House of Lords deliberately stopped short of overruling *Rylands*.

In *Burnie Port Authority v. General Jones Ltd.* (1994), 120 A.L.R. 42, the Australian High Court has been bolder. The case involved a fire that had spread from part of a building owned by the defendant, to part of the same building that the plaintiff rented for cold storage. Prior to the fire, the defendant had brought a large quantity of a highly flammable substance into its property. The defendant did this with the knowledge that welding would take place in close proximity. After the ensuing fire, the plaintiff sued on theories of both strict and negligence liability.

Writing for five of seven judges, Mason C.J. criticized the notorious "obscurity" and "quite unacceptable uncertainty" of strict liability principles. The Chief Justice further noted that in the hundred years since *Rylands* there had been a crucially important legal development, namely the "emergence of a coherent law of negligence to dominate the territory of tortious liability for unintentional injury". Mason C.J. concluded that in Australia the rule in *Rylands* had been "absorbed by the principles of ordinary negligence". The defendant in *Burnie Port Authority* was found liable in negligence for failing to take reasonable care in storing a highly flammable substance, but not liable in strict liability. In summary, *Burnie Port Authority* appears to have expunged strict liability from the common law of Australia.

Canada's highest appellate courts still have not undertaken a careful review of the line of cases that began with *Rylands*. For this reason, the myriad of cases on "dangerous substances" and "natural use", as well as the common law defences to allegations of strict liability, remain relevant to Canadian lawyers.

5. Products' Liability — The American Approach

As indicated in chapter 1, liability rules are not immutable. Students should question whether the existing categories of strict liability ought to be maintained and whether new categories should be recognized. The difficulties consumers encounter in recovering for injuries caused by defective products have prompted calls for reform in several countries. Almost all of the jurisdictions in the United States have responded by imposing strict liability on manufacturers for defective consumer goods. Although the Canadian courts have not followed suit, the American experience warrants brief consideration for two reasons. First, products' liability is an important branch of tort law, and the American reliance on strict liability should be contrasted with the Canadian courts' continued use of negligence principles in this field. Second, the American experience illustrates the process of judicial reform of the liability rules. The fact that some courts have adopted special principles of causation and proof in medical malpractice, toxic torts, environmental torts, and industrial accident cases suggests that this process of judicial reform is continuing. It is equally apparent that many of these common law innovations are controversial, and might be overridden by state and federal legislators intent on "tort reform".

NOTES AND QUESTIONS

1. Many torts books have a separate chapter on products' liability. We have not followed this practice, in part out of concern with limiting the length of our book. Moreover, many important products' liability cases, such as *Donoghue v. Stevenson*, [1932] A.C. 562 (H.L.) and *Rivtow Marine v. Washington Iron Works*, [1974] S.C.R. 1189, have general application to all negligence law. In our view several features of Canadian products' liability law should be discussed in the context of related issues. For example, in chapter 12 we included a section on a manufacturer's and supplier's duty to warn in a chapter dealing with other special duties of care.

2. The Canadian courts have not adopted the doctrine of strict liability for injuries caused by defective products. However, there is provincial and federal legislation, especially in the consumer sales field, which does impose strict liability in certain circumstances for defective products. The legislation varies considerably from jurisdiction to jurisdiction. For a detailed description of the legislation see CCH Canadian Ltd., *Canadian Commercial Law Guide* (1990), chapters 15 and 20.

HENNINGSEN v. BLOOMFIELD MOTORS INC.

(1960), 161 A. (2d) 69 (N.J. S.C.)

[The Henningsens purchased a new car on May 9th, 1955, and initially drove it without incident. Ten days later, Mrs. Henningsen heard a loud noise while driving, the steering wheel spun in her hand and the car veered off the highway into a brick wall. The vehicle, which had only 460 miles on the odometer, was a total loss. The Henningsens sued the car's manufacturer, seeking damages for Mrs. Henningsen's injuries and the loss of the car. The plaintiffs were unable to establish that the manufacturer had been negligent. They also sued in contract, alleging a breach of an implied warranty of merchantability.]

FRANCIS J.: ... Chrysler points out that an implied warranty of merchantability is an incident of a contract of sale. It concedes, of course, the making of the original sale to Bloomfield Motors, Inc., but maintains that this transaction marked the terminal point of its contractual connection with the car. Then Chrysler urges that since it was not a party to the sale by the dealer to Henningsen, there is no privity of contract between it and the plaintiffs, and the absence of this privity eliminates any such implied warranty.

There is no doubt that under early common-law concepts of contractual liability only those persons who were parties to the bargain could sue for a breach of it. In more recent times a noticeable disposition has appeared in a number of jurisdictions to break through the narrow barrier of privity when dealing with sales of goods in order to give realistic recognition to a universally accepted fact. The fact is that the dealer and the ordinary buyer do not, and are not expected to, buy goods, whether they be foodstuffs or automobiles, exclusively for their own consumption or use. Makers and manufacturers know this and advertise and market their products on that assumption; witness, the "family" car, the baby foods, etc. The limitations of privity in contracts for the sale of goods developed their place in the law when marketing conditions were simple, when maker and buyer frequently met face to face on an equal bargaining plane and when many of the products were relatively uncomplicated and conducive to inspection by a buyer competent to evaluate their quality. See, Freezer, "Manufacturer's Liability for Injuries Caused by His Products," 37 Mich. L. Rev. 1 (1938). With the advent of mass marketing, the manufacturer became remote from the purchase, sales were accomplished through intermediaries, and the demand for the product was created by advertising media. In such an economy it became obvious that the consumer was the person being cultivated. Manifestly, the connotation of "consumer" was broader than that of "buyer". He signified such a person who, in the reasonable contemplation of the parties to the sale, might be expected to use the product. Thus, where the commodities sold are such that if defectively manufactured they will be dangerous to life or limb, then society's interests can only be protected by eliminating the requirement of privity between the maker and his dealers and the reasonably expected ultimate consumer. In that way the burden of losses consequent upon use of defective articles is borne by those who are in a position to either control the danger or make an equitable distribution of the losses when they do occur. As Harper & James put it, "The interest in consumer protection calls for warranties by the maker that *do* run with the goods, to reach all who are likely to be hurt by the use of the unfit commodity for a purpose ordinarily to be expected."

. . .

Although only a minority of jurisdictions have thus far departed from the requirement of privity, the movement in that direction is most certainly gathering momentum. Liability to the ultimate consumer in the absence of direct contractual connection has been predicated upon a variety of theories. Some courts hold that the warranty runs with the article like a covenant running with land; others recognized a third-party beneficiary thesis; still others rest their decision on the ground that public policy requires recognition of a warranty made directly to the consumer.

. . .

We see no rational doctrinal basis for differentiating between a fly in a bottle of beverage and a defective automobile. The unwholesome beverage may bring illness to one person, the defective car, with its great potentiality for harm to the driver, occupants, and others, demands even less adherence to the narrow barrier of privity.

. . .

Under modern conditions the ordinary layman, on responding to the importuning of colorful advertising, has neither the opportunity nor the capacity to inspect or to determine the fitness of an automobile for use; he must rely on the manufacturer who has control of its construction, and to some degree on the dealer who, to the limited extent called for by the manufacturer's instructions, inspects and services it before delivery. In such a marketing milieu his remedies and those of persons who properly claim through him should not depend "upon the intricacies of the law of sales. The obligation of the manufacturer should not be based alone on privity of contract. It should rest, as was once said, upon 'the demands of social justice'." *Mazetti v. Armour & Co.*, 75 Wash. 622, 135 P. 633, 635, 48 L.R.A., N.S., 213 (Sup. Ct. 1913). "If privity of contract is required," then, under the circumstances of modern merchandising, "privity of contract exists in the consciousness and understanding of all right-thinking persons." *Madouros v. Kansas City Coca-Cola Bottling Co., supra*, 90 S.W. 2d at page 450.

Accordingly, we hold that under modern marketing conditions, when a manufacturer puts a new automobile in the stream of trade and promotes its purchase by the public, an implied warranty that it is reasonably suitable for use as such accompanies it into the hands of the ultimate purchaser. Absence of agency between the manufacturer and the dealer who makes the ultimate sale is immaterial.

II.

The Effect of the Disclaimer and Limitation of Liability Clauses on the Implied Warranty of Merchantability.

Judicial notice may be taken of the fact that automobile manufacturers, including Chrysler Corporation, undertake large scale advertising programs over television, radio, in newspapers, magazines and all media of communication in order to persuade the public to buy their products. As has been observed above, a number of jurisdictions, conscious of modern marketing practices, have declared that when a manufacturer engages in advertising in order to bring his goods and their quality to the attention of the public and thus to create consumer demand, the representations made constitute an express warranty running directly to a buyer who purchases in reliance thereon. The fact that the sale is consummated with an independent dealer does not obviate that warranty. *Mannsz v. Macwhyte Co., supra; Bahlman v. Hudson Motor Car Co., supra; Rogers v. Toni Home Permanent Co., supra; Meyer v. Packard Cleveland Motor Co.*, 106 Ohio St. 328, 140 N.E. 118, 28 A.L.R. 986 (1922); *Baxter v. Ford Motor Co., supra*; 1 Williston, Sales, *supra* § 244a.

In view of cases in various jurisdictions suggesting the conclusion which we have now reached with respect to the implied warranty of merchantability, it becomes apparent that manufacturers who enter into promotional activities to stimulate consumer buying may incur warranty obligations of either or both the express or implied character. These developments in the law inevitably suggest the inference that the form of express warranty made part of the Henningsen purchase contract was devised for general use in the automobile industry as a possible means of avoiding the consequences of the growing judicial acceptance of the thesis that the described express or implied warranties run directly to the consumer.

In the light of these matters, what effect should be given to the express warranty in question which seeks to limit the manufacturer's liability to replacement of defective parts, and which disclaims all other warranties, express or implied? In assessing its significance we must keep in mind the general principle that, in the absence of fraud, one who does not choose to read a contract before signing it, cannot later relieve himself of its burdens. *Fivey v. Pennsylvania R. R. Co.*, 67 N.J.L. 627, 52 A. 472, (E. & A. 1902). And in applying that principle, the basic tenet of freedom of competent parties to contract is a factor of importance. But in the framework of modern commercial life and business practices, such rules cannot be applied on a strict, doctrinal basis. The conflicting interests of the buyer and seller must be evaluated realistically and justly, giving due weight to the social policy evinced by the Uniform Sales Act, the progressive decisions of the courts engaged in administering it, the mass production methods of manufacture and distribution to the public, and the bargaining position occupied by the ordinary consumer in such an economy. This history of the law shows that legal doctrines, as first expounded, often prove to be inadequate under the impact of later experience. In such cases, the need for justice has stimulated the necessary qualifications or adjustments.

. . .

The traditional contract is the result of free bargaining of parties who are brought together by the play of the market, and who meet each other on a footing of approximate economic equality. In such a society there is no danger that freedom of contract will be a threat to the social order as a whole. But in present-day commercial life the standardized mass contract has appeared. It is used primarily by enterprises with strong bargaining power and position.

> The weaker party, in need of the goods or services, is frequently not in a position to shop around for better terms, either because the author of the standard contract has a monopoly (natural

or artificial) or because all competitors use the same clauses. His contractual intention is but a subjection more or less voluntary to terms dictated by the stronger party, terms whose consequences are often understood in a vague way, if at all.

Kessler, "Contracts of Adhesion — Some Thoughts About Freedom of Contract," 43 Colum. L. Rev. 629, 632 (1943); Ehrenzweig, "Adhesion Contracts in the Conflict of Laws," 53 Colum. L. Rev. 1072, 1075, 1089 (1953). Such standardized contracts have been described as those in which one predominant party will dictate its law to an undetermined multiple rather than to an individual. They are said to resemble a law rather than a meeting of the minds. *Seigelman v. Cunard White Star,* 221 F. 2d 189, 206 (2 Cir. 1955).

Vold, in the recent revision of his Law of Sales (2d ed. 1959) at page 447, wrote of this type of contract and its effect upon the ordinary buyer:

> In recent times the marketing process has been getting more highly organized than ever before. Business units have been expanding on a scale never before known. The standardized contract with its broad disclaimer clauses is drawn by legal advisers of sellers widely organized in trade associations. It is encountered on every hand. Extreme inequality of bargaining between buyer and seller in this respect is now often conspicuous. Many buyers no longer have any real choice in the matter. They must often accept what they can get though accompanied by broad disclaimers. The terms of these disclaimers deprive them of all substantial protection with regard to the quality of the goods. In effect, this is by force of contract between very unequal parties. It throws the risk of defective articles on the most dependent party. He has the least individual power to avoid the presence of defects. He also has the least individual ability to bear their disastrous consequences.

The warranty before us is a standardized form designed for mass use. It is imposed upon the automobile consumer. He takes it or leaves it, and he must take it to buy an automobile. No bargaining is engaged in with respect to it. In fact, the dealer through whom it comes to the buyer is without authority to alter it; his function is ministerial — simply to deliver it. The form warranty is not only standard with Chrysler but, as mentioned above, it is the uniform warranty of the Automobile Manufacturers Association. Members of the Association are: General Motors, Inc., Ford, Chrysler, Studebaker-Packard, American Motors, (Rambler), Willys Motors, Checker Motors Corp., and International Harvester Company. Automobile Facts and Figures (1958 Ed., Automobile Manufacturers Association) 69. Of these companies, the "Big Three" (General Motors, Ford and Chrysler) represented 93.5% of the passenger-car production for 1958 and the independents 6.5%. Standard & Poor (Industrial Surveys, Autos, Basic Analysis, June 25, 1959) 4109. And for the same year the "Big Three" had 86.72% of the total passenger vehicle registrations. Automotive News, 1959 Almanac (Slocum Publishing Co., Inc.) p. 25.

The gross inequality of bargaining position occupied by the consumer in the automobile industry is thus apparent. There is no competition among the car makers in the area of the express warranty. Where can the buyer go to negotiate for better protection? Such control and limitation of his remedies are inimical to the public welfare and, at the very least, call for great care by the courts to avoid injustice through application of strict common-law principles of freedom of contract. Because there is no competition among the motor vehicle manufacturers with respect to the scope of protection guaranteed to the buyer, there is no incentive on their part to stimulate good will in that field of public relations. Thus, there is lacking a factor existing in more competitive fields, one which tends to guarantee the safe construction of the article sold. Since all competitors operate in the same way, the urge to be careful is not so pressing. See "Warranties of Kind and Quality," 57 Yale L.J. 1389, 1400 (1948).

Although the courts, with few exceptions, have been most sensitive to problems presented by contracts resulting from gross disparity in buyer-seller bargaining positions, they have not articulated a general principle condemning, as opposed to public policy, the imposition on the buyer of a skeleton warranty as a means of limiting the responsibility of the manufacturer. They have endeavoured thus far to avoid a drastic departure from age-old tenets of freedom of contract by adopting doctrines of strict construction, and notice and knowledgeable assent by the buyer to the attempted exculpation of the seller. 1 Corbin, *supra*, 337; 2 Harper & James, *supra*, 1590; Prosser, "Warranty of Merchantable Quality," 27 Minn. L. Rev. 117, 159 (1932).

. . .

VI.

Plaintiffs contend on cross-appeal that the negligence claim against the defendants should not have been dismissed. Their position is that on the facts developed, the issue should have been submitted to the jury for determination. The result we have reached on the other aspects of the case makes it unnecessary to consider the problem. For that reason we express no opinion thereon.

All other grounds of appeal raised by both parties have been examined and we find no reversible error in any of them.

VII.

Under all of the circumstances outlined above, the judgments in favor of the plaintiffs and against the defendants are affirmed. . .

GREENMAN v. YUBA POWER PRODUCTS INC.

(1962), 377 P. (2d) 897 (Cal. S.C.)

TRAYNOR J.: . . . Plaintiff brought this action for damages against the retailer and the manufacturer of a Shopsmith, a combination power tool that could be used as a saw, drill, and wood lathe. He saw a Shopsmith demonstrated by the retailer and studied a brochure prepared by the manufacturer. He decided he wanted a Shopsmith for his home workshop, and his wife bought and gave him one for Christmas in 1955. In 1957 he bought the necessary attachments to use the Shopsmith as a lathe for turning a large piece of wood he wished to make into a chalice. After he had worked on the piece of wood several times without difficulty, it suddenly flew out of the machine and struck him on the forehead, inflicting serious injuries. About ten and a half months later, he gave the retailer and manufacturer written notice of claimed breaches of warranties and filed a complaint against them alleging such breaches and negligence.

After a trial before a jury, the court held that there was no evidence that the

retailer was negligent or had breached an express warranty and that the manufacturer was not liable for the breach of any implied warranty. Accordingly, it
submitted to the jury only the cause of action alleging breach of implied warranties against the retailer and the causes of action alleging negligence and breach
of express warranties against the manufacturer. The jury returned a verdict for
the retailer against the plaintiff and for plaintiff against the manufacturer in the
amount of $65,000. The trial court denied the manufacturer's motion for a new
trial and entered judgment on the verdict. The manufacturer and plaintiff appeal.
Plaintiff seeks a reversal of the part of the judgment in favour of the retailer, however, only in the event that the part of the judgment against the manufacturer
is reversed.

. . .

Moreover, to impose strict liability on the manufacturer under the circumstances of this case, it was not necessary for plaintiff to establish an express warranty as defined in section 1732 of the Civil Code. A manufacturer is strictly liable
in tort when an article he places on the market, knowing that it is to be used
without inspection for defects, proves to have a defect that causes injury to a human
being. Recognized first in the case of unwholesome food products, such liability
has now been extended to a variety of other products that create as great or greater
hazards if defective.

[3] Although in these cases strict liability has usually been based on the theory
of an express or implied warranty running from the manufacturer to the plaintiff, the abandonment of the requirement of a contract between them, the recognition that the *liability is not assumed by agreement* but *imposed by law* (see e.g.,
Graham v. Bottenfield's, Inc., 176 Kan. 68, 269 P. 2d 413, 418; *Rogers v. Toni Home
Permanent Co.*, 167 Ohio St. 244, 147 N.E. 2d 612, 614, 75 A.L.R. 2d 103; *Decker
& Sons, Inc. v. Capps*, 139 Tex, 609, 617, 164 S.W. 2d 828, 142 A.L.R. 1479),
and the refusal to permit the manufacturer to define the scope of its own responsibility for defective products (*Henningsen v. Bloomfield Motors, Inc.*, 32 N.J. 358,
161 A. 2d 69, 84-96; *General Motors Corp. v. Dodson*, 47 Tenn. App. 438, 338
S.W. 2d 655, 658-661; *State Farm Mut. Auto. Ins. Co. v. Anderson-Weber, Inc.*, 252
Iowa 1289, 110 N.W. 2d 449, 455-456; *Pabon v. Hackensack Auto Sales, Inc.*, 63
N.J. Super. 476, 164 A. 2d 773, 778; *Linn v. Radio Center Delicatessen*, 169 Misc.
879, 9 N.Y.S. 2d 110, 112) make clear that the liability is not one governed by
the law of contract warranties but by the law of strict liability in tort. Accordingly, rules defining and governing warranties that were developed to meet the
needs of commercial transactions cannot properly be invoked to govern the manufacturer's liability to those injured by their defective products unless those rules
also serve the purposes for which such liability is imposed.

[4] We need not recanvass the reasons for imposing strict liability on the manufacturer. They have been fully articulated in the cases cited above. (See also 2
Harper and James, Torts, §§28.15-28.16, pp. 1569-1574; Prosser, Strict Liability
to the Consumer, 69 Yale L.J. 1099; *Escola v. Coca-Cola Bottling Co.*, 24 Cal.
2d 453, 461, 150 P. 2d 436, concurring opinion.) The purpose of such liability
is to insure that the costs of injuries resulting from defective products are borne
by the manufacturers that put such products on the market rather than by the injured
persons who are powerless to protect themselves. Sales warranties serve this purpose

fitfully at best. (See Prosser, Strict Liability to the Consumer, 69 Yale L.J. 1099, 1124-1134.) In the present case, for example, plaintiff was able to plead and prove an express warranty only because he read and relied on the representations of the Shopsmith's ruggedness contained in the manufacturer's brochure. Implicit in the machine's presence on the market, however, was a representation that it would safely do the jobs for which it was built. Under these circumstances, it should not be controlling whether plaintiff selected the machine because of the statements in the brochure, or because of the machine's own appearance of excellence that belied the defect lurking beneath the surface, or because he merely assumed that it would safely do the jobs it was built to do. It should not be controlling whether the details of the sales from manufacturer to retailer and from retailer to plaintiff's wife were such that one or more of the implied warranties of the sales act arose. (Civ. Code, §1735.) "The remedies of injured consumers ought not to be made to depend upon the intricacies of the law of sales." (*Ketterer v. Armour & Co.*, D.C., 200 F. 322, 323; *Klein v. Duchess Sandwich Co.*, 14 Cal. 2d 272, 282, 93 P. 2d 799.) To establish the manufacturer's liability it was sufficient that plaintiff proved that he was injured while using the Shopsmith in a way it was intended to be used as a result of a defect in design and manufacture of which plaintiff was not aware that made the Shopsmith unsafe for its intended use.

. . .

The judgment is affirmed.

GIBSON C.J., and SCHAUER, MCCOMB, PETERS, TOBRINER and PEEK JJ., concur.

NOTES AND QUESTIONS

1. *Henningsen* is an excellent example of creative decision-making which has led to the adoption of a new principle of law. Do you agree with Francis J. that the historical rationales for the doctrine of privity and for the law governing disclaimers are inapplicable to modern mass marketing?

2. What were the social goals that Francis J. hoped his new liability principle would achieve? Are they consistent with one another? Do you believe his principle will achieve these goals?

3. It is not clear if *Henningsen* created a new doctrine of contract law or a new category of strict liability. Although some courts interpreted *Henningsen* in terms of an express warranty in contract, most viewed it as creating strict liability in tort. Why did Traynor J. in *Greenman* adopt this latter view of *Henningsen*? Does it matter if *Henningsen* is classified as a rule of contract law, rather than as a rule of tort law?

4. What is the difference between a case governed by *Henningsen* and one governed by negligence? How significant is this difference? The plaintiff's major difficulty in both cases will probably be in proving that the product was defective. See *Phillips v. Ford Motor Co. of Can.* (1971), 18 D.L.R. (3d) 641 (Ont. C.A.). Is it likely that a Canadian manufacturer would be absolved of liability in negligence if the plaintiff proved that the product was defective?

5. In *Gen. Motors Products of Can. Ltd. v. Kravitz* (1979), 93 D.L.R. (3d) 481 the Supreme Court of Canada, relying on the Quebec Civil Code, in effect held a manufacturer strictly liable to the purchaser of a defective car. See Schwartz, "The Manufacturer's Liability to the Purchaser of a 'Lemon' . . ." (1979), Ottawa L. Rev. 583; and Waddams, "*General Motors v. Kravitz* — Implications for the Common Law" (1980), 1 Sup. Crt. L. Rev. 417.

6. For a review of the development of Canadian products' liability law see Stradiotto, "Products Liability in Tort", in *Law Society of Upper Canada, Special Lectures 1973, New Developments in the Law of Torts* (1973), 189; and Mueller, "Products' Liability in Tort", in *Law Society of Upper Canada, Special Lectures 1983, Torts in the 80s* (1983), 83. See also Waddams, *Products Liability*, 3rd ed. (1993). In addition to discussing the Canadian law, Waddams includes many helpful references to the Ameri-

can authorities. For an introduction to American products' liability law, see Keeton *et al., Prosser and Keeton on Torts*, 5th ed. (1984), 677-724.

6. Vicarious Liability

(a) THE RATIONALE FOR VICARIOUS LIABILITY

T. G. BRIGHT & CO. v. KERR

[1939] S.C.R. 63, [1939] 1 D.L.R. 193 (S.C.C.)

[The court considered whether the defendant wine dealer was vicariously liable for the negligence of its motorcycle deliveryman. Although the deliveryman was held to be the defendant's agent, the majority concluded that he was not the defendant's servant because the defendant had no control over the precise manner in which the task was performed. The following excerpt from Duff C.J.C.'s dissenting judgment is limited to the issue of vicarious liability.]

DUFF C.J.C. (dissenting).: ... It would appear to be necessary to make some reference to the ground upon which the responsibility of a principal for the acts of his agent rests.

Respondant superior is a rule which does not rest upon any notion of imputed guilt or fault. The fallacy that it does was responsible for the difficulty that great lawyers of the last century felt (Bramwell, B., for example) in admitting the liability of a corporation for the fraud of its agents. In *Hern v. Nichols*, 1 Salk. 289, 91 E.R. 256, the point in issue was the responsibility of a merchant for the deceit of his factor beyond the sea. Holt, C.J., states the broad ground of responsibility thus: —

> ... for seeing somebody must be a loser by this deceit, it is more reason that he that employs and puts a trust and confidence in the deceiver should be a loser, than a stranger ...

In *Hall v. Smith*, 2 Bing. 156, at p. 160, 130 E.R. 265, Best, C.J., says: —

> The maxim of *respondeat superior* is bottomed on this principle, that he who expects to derive advantage from an act which is done by another for him, must answer for any injury which a third person may sustain from it.

The principal having the power of choice has selected the agent to perform in his place a class or classes of acts, and, to adapt the language of Collins, M.R., in *Hamlyn v. Houston & Co.*, [1903] 1 K.B. 81, at pp. 85-6, it is not unjust that he who has selected him and will have the benefit of his services if efficiently performed should bear the risk of his negligence in "matters incidental to the doing of the acts the performance of which has been delegated to him."

The rule has been precisely explained in the House of Lords in two modern cases in which Story's statement of it has been adopted. In *Percy v. Glasgow Corp.*, [1922] 2 A.C. 299, at pp. 306-7, Viscount Haldane said: —

> As was laid down by Story in a passage adopted in an earlier case by Blackburn J. and approved in this House in *Lloyd v. Grace, Smith & Co.* [[1912] A.C. 716, 737] "the principal is liable to third persons in a civil suit 'for the frauds, deceits, concealments, misrepresentations, torts, negligences, and other malfeasances or misfeasances, and omissions of duty of his agent *in the course of his employment*, although the principal did not authorise, or justify, or partici-

pate in, or indeed know of such misconduct, or even if he forbade the acts, or disapproved of them. The limitation is that 'the tort or negligence occurs in the course of the agency. For the principal is not liable for the torts or negligences of his agent in any matters beyond the scope of the agency, unless he has expressly authorised them to be done, or he has subsequently adopted them for his own use and benefit.' "

(b) MASTER-SERVANT RELATIONSHIPS

ARMSTRONG v. MAC'S MILK LTD.

(1975), 7 O.R. (2d) 478, 55 D.L.R. (3d) 510 (Ont. H.C.)

HOLLAND J.: . . . It is crucial to the liability of Mac's Milk to decide whether the arrangement between it and Mikecz was that of master and servant or principal and independent contractor.

Mikecz came to Canada in 1965. He was first employed by Mac's Milk in 1966 as a painter and then at the sign shop. He was with the company for a year-and-a-half to two years and was then laid off because of a shortage of work. He was called back on one or two occasions and was trained in installing window signs or decals in 1970. At this time he was an hourly-rated employee. In November of 1970, he was again laid off due to a shortage of work and was recalled in January of 1971. At this time a new arrangement was entered into: he was to do exactly the same work but at a fixed price per store. Mikecz was advised of the store locations. He could work in his own time and provided his own transportation for stores both in and out of Toronto. His equipment, consisting of a tray and squeegee, was supplied by Mac's Milk. There was no written contract.

The conventional test for distinguishing a servant from an independent contractor is the "control" test. MacKinnon, L.J., in *Hewitt v. Bonvin et al.*, [1940] 1 K.B. 188 at p. 191, said:

> I think the definition of a servant in Salmond on Torts can hardly be bettered: "A servant may be defined as any person employed by another to do work for him on the terms that he, the servant, is to be subject to the control and directions of his employer in respect of the manner in which his work is to be done."

As pointed out in *Fleming, Law of Torts*, 4th ed. (1971), at p. 316, changes in the structure of modern business have made it increasingly difficult to apply the control test as a meaningful working rule to many situations characteristic of modern conditions. Another test that has been applied is the "organization" test. Lord Denning, in *Stevenson Jordan and Harrison, Ltd. v. Macdonald and Evans*, [1952] 1 T.L.R. 101 at p. 111, said:

> It is often easy to recognize a contract of service when you see it, but difficult to say wherein the difference lies. A ship's master, a chauffeur, and a reporter on the staff of a newspaper are all employed under a contract of service; but a ship's pilot, a taxi-man, and a newspaper contributer are employed under a contract for services. One feature which seems to run through the instances is that, under a contract of service, a man is employed as part of the business, and his work is done as an integral part of the business; whereas, under a contract for services, his work, although done for the business, is not integrated into it but is only accessory to it.

Applying either of these tests it seems to me that Mikecz was a servant of Mac's Milk at the time. He had been trained by Mac's Milk and was doing exactly the same work as he had done for Mac's Milk when an hourly-rated employee:

the only difference being that he was paid on a "per store" basis and could choose his own time to do the work. He was certainly under the control of Mac's Milk as to where the work should be done and as to how it should be done and his work was done as an integral part of the business of Mac's Milk.

As indicated above, I am of the opinion that Mikecz was negligent in spilling water on the sloping area and not warning Pollard. This negligence occurred in the course of his employment. In my view it is not necessary to attempt to apply any special or artificial rules dealing with the liability of an occupier. The duty of Mac's Milk, as an occupier, was augmented by a general duty of care in the performance, in this case, of the installation of signs. Mikecz was in breach of this general duty and Mac's Milk is vicariously liable for any damages flowing from his negligence.

(c) IN THE COURSE OF EMPLOYMENT

C.P.R. v. LOCKHART

[1942] 2 All E.R. 464, [1942] 3 D.L.R. 529 (P.C.)

[Stinson, an employee of the Canadian Pacific Railway Company, was directed by his foreman to travel from West Toronto to North Toronto. Stinson ignored available C.P.R. transportation and drove his own car, negligently injuring the plaintiff en route. Although nothing had been said about transportation for the specific assignment, C.P.R. had issued standing orders prohibiting employees from exposing it to liability by driving uninsured vehicles while on company business. C.P.R. argued that under those circumstances it should not be held vicariously liable for Stinson's tort.]

LORD THANKERTON: ... Their Lordships agree with the decision of the Supreme Court, and, in particular with the reasons given by Crocket J., as also with the reasoning of McTague J.A. in his dissenting judgment in the Court of Appeal, in the passages already quoted. There is little dispute as to the facts, but their Lordships prefer to proceed on the statement of the learned trial Judge that there was no evidence on which it could be found that the Company had winked at the non-observance of their prohibition, rather than on the view expressed by some of the learned Judges of the Supreme Court to a contrary effect.

The general principles ruling a case of this type are well known, but ultimately, each case will depend for decision on its own facts. As regards the principles their Lordships agree with the statement in Salmond on Torts (9th ed.), p. 95, viz.:

> It is clear that the master is responsible for acts actually authorised by him: for liability would exist in this case, even if the relation between the parties was merely one of agency, and not one of service at all. But a master, as opposed to the employer of an independent contractor, is liable even for acts which he has not authorised, provided they are so connected with acts that he has authorised that they may rightly be regarded as modes — although improper modes — of doing them. In other words, a master is responsible not merely for what he authorises his servant to do, but also for the way in which he does it ... On the other hand, if the unauthorised and wrongful act of the servant is not so connected with the authorised act as to be a mode of doing it, but is an independent act, the master is not responsible; for in such a case the servant is not acting in the course of his employment, but has gone outside of it.

The well-known dictum of Lord Dunedin in *Plumb v. Cobden Flour Mills Co.*, [1914] A.C. 62 at p. 67, that "there are prohibitions which limit the sphere of employment, and prohibitions which only deal with conduct within the sphere of employment," may be referred to. Their Lordships may also quote passages from the judgment of this Board in *Goh Choon Seng v. Lee Kim Soo*, [1925] A.C. 550, which was delivered by Lord Phillimore, at p. 554:

> The principle is well laid down in some of the cases cited by the Chief Justice, which decide that "when a servant does an act which he is authorized by his employment to do under certain circumstances and under certain conditions, and he does them under circumstances or in a manner which are unauthorized and improper, in such cases the employer is liable for the wrongful act . . ."
>
> As regards all the cases which were brought to their Lordships' notice in the course of the argument this observation may be made. They fall under one of three heads: (1) The servant was using his master's time or his master's place or his master's horses, vehicles, machinery or tools for his own purposes: then the master is not responsible. Cases which fall under this head are easy to discover upon analysis. There is more difficulty in separating cases under heads (2) and (3). Under head (2) are to be ranged the cases where the servant is employed only to do a particular work or a particular class of work, and he does something out of the scope of his employment. Again, the master is not responsible for any mischief which he may do to a third party. Under head (3) come cases like the present, where the servant is doing some work which he is appointed to do, but does it in a way which his master has not authorised and would not have authorised had he known of it. In these cases the master is, nevertheless, responsible.

In *Goh Choon Seng's* case the appellant's servants had been employed by him to burn vegetable rubbish collected on his land, and they burnt some of it by lighting fires on Crown land left waste and uncultivated, which was wedged in between the appellant's land and that of the respondent, with the result that the fires spread to the respondent's land and caused damage to his property. The appellant was held liable to the respondent.

In the opinion of their Lordships, the present case does not fall under the first head of Lord Phillimore's classification. That the use of his own motor car for the journey might be a more convenient means of transport for Stinson does not alter the fact that he was performing the journey for the purpose of, and as a means of execution of, the work which he was employed to do. In these cases the first consideration is the ascertainment of what the servant was employed to do. The existence of prohibitions may, or may not, be evidence of the limits of the employment. In the present case Stinson was employed to work as a carpenter and general handy-man and for that purpose he was required to go from his headquarters at West Toronto Station to other railway buildings of the Company throughout Toronto and district. The means of transport used by him on these occasions was clearly incidental to the execution of that which he was employed to do. He was not employed to drive a motor car, but it is clear that he was entitled to use that means of transport as incidental to the execution of that which he was employed to do, provided the motor car was insured against third-party risks. If the prohibition had absolutely forbidden the servant to drive his motor car in the course of his employment, it might well have been maintained that he was employed to do carpentry work and not to drive a motor car, and that, therefore, the driving of a motor car was outside the scope of his employment, but it was not the acting as driver that was prohibited, but the non-insurance of the motor car, if used as a means incidental to the execution of the work which he was employed to do. It follows that the prohibition merely limited the way in which or by means of which the servant was to execute the work which he was employed to do, and that breach of the prohibition did not exclude the liability of the master to third parties.

Their Lordships are therefore of the opinion that the appeal fails and they will humbly advise His Majesty that the appeal should be dismissed with costs as between solicitor and client and that the judgment of the Supreme Court of Canada should be affirmed.

GRIGGS v. SOUTHSIDE HOTEL CO.

[1947] O.R. 674, [1947] 4 D.L.R. 49 (Ont. C.A.)

Hogg J.A.: — This is an appeal from a judgment of LeBel J. of May 16, 1946, [[1946] 4 D.L.R. 73], awarding damages in the sum of $1,500 to the plaintiff against the defendant German, and dismissing the action against the respondent hotel company. The appellant claims that the hotel company should have been held liable and that the sum of $1,500 is inadequate in view of the nature of the injury sustained by the plaintiff.

. . .

The trial Judge stated that the chief defence relied upon by the respondent hotel company was that when German struck the plaintiff he was not acting in the course of his employment, and the trial Judge came to the conclusion that the plaintiff's injury was caused by an act on the part of German which was an independent act " 'not so connected with the authorised act as to be a mode of doing it' " [[1946] 4 D.L.R. at p. 77]. He was of the opinion that the striking was more consistent with the view that it was done solely because of a sudden provocation than with the view that it was done in an attempt to force the appellant to leave the premises.

. . .

The question, therefore, is whether German was acting in the course of his employment, or whether it was an independent act at the time the appellant was hit and injured. In *Bayley v. Manchester, Sheffield & Lincolnshire R. Co.* (1873), L.R. 8 C.P. 148 at p. 154, Blackburn J. said that

> where a servant, acting within the scope of his employment, does an act negligently, or with excessive violence, the master is responsible for the consequences,

and he referred to the case of *Seymour v. Greenwood* (1861), 6 H. & N. 359, 158 E.R. 148, where there was a

> very great excess of violence used by the servant, and yet the master was held responsible because the servant was acting within the scope of the employment, however outrageous and improper the manner in which he did it might be.

It was within the course of German's employment, who, as was found by the learned trial Judge, was at the time in charge of the beverage-room, to see that order was maintained, and to ask persons who were conducting themselves in a manner contrary to the statute or the regulations to leave the premises, and, if necessary, to remove such persons forcibly. German had already requested the appellant to leave the beverage-room, which he did not do at the time. Subsequently, after a short interval had elapsed, the discussion to which reference has been made took place between the appellant and German while German was standing at the bar. This discussion again related to the subject of the appellant being under obligation to leave the premises if asked to do so. This seems to have been the sole topic of this particular conversation. The appellant became angry at being told he could be put out, used very insulting language towards German, and the latter at once struck at him with a beer bottle and injured him. Immediately before the assault was committed, German was acting in the course of his employment in informing the appellant that he might be put off the premises. The matter had not reached the stage where German had made any attempt to remove the appellant forcibly from the room, and the act of German in striking the appellant was, therefore, not connected in any manner with the appellant's forcible removal. There was not an excess of violence used by the servant while attempting to remove a person from the beverage-room, and, therefore, while the servant was acting within the scope of his employment, "however outrageous and improper the manner in which he did it might be," as was said by Blackburn J. in the *Bayley v. Manchester etc. R. Co.* case. In the present instance the wrongful act committed by German was not, in my opinion, connected with the act of removing the appellant from the beverage-room, so as to be a mode of doing such act, but it was an independent act which had no relation to the business of the employer at the time it was done and for which, for the reasons I have stated, I have concluded the respondent hotel company is not liable.

Although the amount of damages awarded by the learned trial Judge is less than I think I might have seen fit to give, I see no error in principle with respect to his decision, and I do not think this Court would be warranted in finding the amount of damages unreasonably small: *Barrette v. Fox* (1923), 23 O.W.N. 577.

The appeal should be dismissed with costs.

[Henderson J.A., with whom Aylesworth J.A. agreed, delivered a separate judgment dismissing the appeal.]

NOTES AND QUESTIONS

1. In what circumstances will an employer be held vicariously liable for the torts of his employees?

2. According to Duff C.J.C. in *T.G. Bright & Co.*, what is the rationale for the principle of *respondeat superior*? Compare his view with the rationale underlying enterprise liability. In your view what was the purpose of vicarious liability? Is your answer affected by the fact that at common law an employer who was held vicariously liable could seek recovery from his employee? See *Lister v. Romford Ice & Cold Storage Co.*, [1957] A.C. 555 (H.L.).

3. How do the "master-servant" and "in the course of employment" requirements relate to the goals of strict liability? More specifically, do these requirements suggest that vicarious liability serves a deterrent function?

4. Does it make sense to hold an employer liable, as in *C.P.R.*, when the employee violates orders? How can an employer avoid being held liable in such cases?

5. Do you agree with the decision in *Griggs*? What are its implications for servers and patrons of taverns? Is *Griggs* consistent with *C.P.R.*? See also *Downey v. 502377 Ont. Ltd.* (Jan. 28, 1991), O.J. No. 468 (Gen. Div.).

6. There are several interesting issues that arise concerning a hospital's vicarious liability for the torts committed by doctors, nurses and other hospital personnel. At one time, doctors were considered employees of the patient, and not the hospital. In recent years, there has been a trend to extend the scope of a hospital's vicarious liability for doctors as well as other staff. See Magnet, "Liability of

a Hospital for the Negligent Acts of Professionals" (1977), 3 C.C.L.T. 135; and Picard, *Legal Liability of Doctors and Hospitals in Canada*, 2nd ed. (1984), 313-28.

7. In recent years there has been extensive litigation on the vicarious liability of employers for the physical, sexual and verbal misconduct of employees. For example, in *Boothman v. R.* (1993), 49 C.C.E.L. 109 (F.C. T.D.), a Crown employer was found liable for its office supervisor's verbal harassment of a co-worker. In *B. (P.A.) v. Curry* (1995), 25 C.C.L.T. (2d) 302 (B.C. S.C.), the judge ruled that the defendant employer, a charitable foundation operating a home for troubled children, was vicariously liable for sexual batteries of one of its counsellors. These cases represent an important break from the traditional reluctance of courts to find employers liable for the intentional wrongdoing of their employees.

8. The provincial highway traffic legislation holds an owner of a motor vehicle vicariously liable for torts committed by any person who is driving with the owner's consent. These apparently straightfoward statutory provisions have generated a great deal of controversy. See, for example, *MacDonald v. Mitchell* (1969), 10 D.L.R. (3d) 240 (N.B. C.A.); *Deakins v. Aarsen* (1970), 17 D.L.R. (3d) 494 (S.C.C.); *Hayduk v. Pidoborozny* (1971), 19 D.L.R. (3d) 160 (Alta. C.A.); *Daigle v. Theo Couturier Ltd.* (1973), 43 D.L.R. (3d) 151 (N.B. C.A.); *Honan v. Gerhold* (1974), 50 D.L.R. (3d) 582 (S.C.C.); *Schroth v. Innes* (1976), 71 D.L.R. (3d) 647 (B.C. C.A.); *Mader v. MacPhee* (1978), 84 D.L.R. (3d) 761 (N.S. C.A.); and *Lajeunesse v. Janssens* (1983), 3 D.L.R. (4th) 163 (Ont. H.C.). See also Lattin, "Vicarious Liability and the Family Automobile" (1928), 26 Mich. L. Rev. 796; and Fridman, "The Doctrine of the 'Family Car': A Study in Contrasts" (1976), 8 Tex. Tech. L. Rev. 323. See also *Pawlak v. Doucette*, [1985] 2 W.W.R. 588 (B.C. S.C.), where the test of vicarious liability in motor vehicle cases was applied to the owner of a boat.

9. For a discussion of vicarious liability in Canada see Schmidt *et al.*, "Vicarious Liability in Tort" (1966), 5 Alta. L. Rev. 74; Magnet, "Vicarious Liability and the Professional Employee" (1979), 6 C.C.L.T. 208; and Fridman, "Vicarious Liability in Torts — New Approaches", in *Law Society of Upper Canada, Special Lectures* 1983, *Torts in the 80s* (1983), 305. See also Atiyah, *Vicarious Liability in the Law of Torts* (1967); and Rose, "Liability for an Employee's Assaults" (1977), 40 Mich. L. Rev. 420.

26

NUISANCE

1. Introduction
2. Private Nuisance
3. Public Nuisance
4. Remedies

1. Introduction

In chapter 5, we briefly compared the actions for private nuisance and trespass to land. In this chapter, we consider private nuisance in more detail and also examine the private action for public nuisance.

The common law tort action for private nuisance has a long history that can be traced to the late 12th century. It may be helpful to view trespass to land and private nuisance as corollary actions. Trespass to land protects the plaintiff's possessory interest in land from direct, physical intrusions, whereas private nuisance protects the plaintiff's beneficial interest in land from unreasonable interferences of any kind. The focus in nuisance is not on the nature of the defendant's conduct, but rather on whether it results in an unreasonable interference with the plaintiff's use and enjoyment of her land. Private nuisance encompasses a broad range of interferences, including overhanging branches, seeping sewage, foul odours, barking dogs, bright lights, vibrations from explosions, machinery or traffic, industrial pollutants, subsidence of supporting soil, obstruction of sunlight or a view, and even unwanted telephone calls. However, the law cannot provide a remedy for every minor or transitory interference with other people's use and enjoyment of their land, and hence the courts' main task is to determine which interferences are sufficiently disruptive or harmful to warrant redress.

The common law tort action for public nuisance has its origins in the criminal law which made it an offence to create a "common or public nuisance". In addition to being prosecuted, the defendant could be held civilly liable to compensate the state and those members of the public that had suffered some special damage. The tort of public nuisance is based upon an unreasonable interference with a public interest, such as the right of passage on a public highway or waterway, the unimpeded flow of streams and rivers, or the general public interest in unpolluted air and drinking water.

2. Private Nuisance

340909 ONT. LTD. v. HURON STEEL PRODUCTS (WINDSOR) LTD.

(1990), 73 O.R. (2d) 641 (H.C.)

[The plaintiff built an apartment building immediately to the northeast of the defendant's stamping plant in 1977. The plant had been in operation since 1947. In 1979, the defendant purchased an 880-tonne press and installed it across the street from the plaintiff's apartment building. The plaintiff complained of noise and vibrations. Although a second such press was installed in 1983, successful efforts were made to reduce noise and vibrations. Thus, the second press met Ministry of the Environment guidelines. The plaintiff brought an action for nuisance claiming loss of rental income and loss of the value of the building.]

POTTS J:— ...

DOES THE PLAINTIFF HAVE A CAUSE OF ACTION IN NUISANCE?

Private nuisance can be defined as an unreasonable interference with the use and enjoyment of land. J.G. Fleming, in *The Law of Torts*, 4th ed. (Sydney: Law Book Co., 1971), states at p. 346 that the court goes through a balancing process to determine whether a nuisance exists or not:

> The paramount problem in the law of nuisance is, therefore, to strike a tolerable balance between conflicting claims of landowners, each invoking the privilege to exploit the resources and enjoy the amenities of his property without undue subordination to the reciprocal interests of the other. Reconciliation has to be achieved by compromise, and the basis for adjustment is reasonable user. Legal intervention is warranted only when an excessive use of property causes inconvenience beyond what other occupiers in the vicinity can be expected to bear, having regard to the prevailing standard of comfort of the time and place. Reasonableness in this context is a two-sided affair. It is viewed not only from the standpoint of the defendant's convenience, but must also take into account the interest of the surrounding occupiers. It is not enough to ask: Is the defendant using his property in what would be a reasonable manner if he had no neighbour? The question is, Is he using it reasonably, having regard to the fact that he has a neighbour?

Furthermore, each case must be considered in light of the particular facts in question. In *Oakley v. Webb* (1916), 33 D.L.R. 35, 38 O.L.R. 151 (C.A.), Hodgins J.A. stated at p. 158 O.L.R.:

> I think the rule stated by Middleton, J., in *Appleby v. Erie Tobacco Co.*, 22 O.L.R. 533, at p. 536, and adopted by Sutherland, J., in *Beamish v. Glen*, 36 O.L.R. 10, as correct, is the proper test to be applied in this case. It is that "an arbitrary standard cannot be set up which is applicable to all localities. There is a local standard applicable in each particular district, but, though the local standard may be higher in some districts than in others, yet the question in each case ultimately reduces itself to the fact of nuisance or no nuisance, having regard to all the surrounding circumstances.

"Unreasonableness" in nuisance law is when the interference in question would not be tolerated by the ordinary occupier. What constitutes "unreasonable" interference is determined by considering a number of factors:

(1) the severity of the interference, having regard to its nature and duration and effect;

(2) the character of the locale;

(3) the utility of the defendant's conduct;

(4) the sensitivity of the use interfered with.

It is not necessary to deal with the sensitivity of the use interfered with, since the plaintiff's use of its property is not an unusually sensitive one. The remaining three factors will be discussed below.

(1) *The severity of the interference, having regard to its nature, duration and effect*

(a) *Nature of the interference*

The interference must be considered from the plaintiff company's point of view. However, the noise and vibration are allegedly disrupting the use and enjoyment by the tenants. This will ultimately affect the plaintiff as landlord, since the interference could be one reason why a tenant moves out. Therefore, the interference from the tenants' points of view is relevant, since it is *part of* the interference from the plaintiff's point of view.

. . .

Three expert witnesses testified in the area of sound and vibration assessment. I accept the proposition that was put forward in *Halsey v. Esso Petroleum Co.*, [1961] 2 All E.R. 145, that such evidence is helpful to confirm or disprove the evidence of other witnesses.

. . .

Kende made observations and took sound readings of the Huron Steel plant operations in December 1980. He testified that the #1 press was clearly audible and easily identifiable inside and outside the plant. The sound "was not a residential neighbourhood noise" and he "would not want to live with it".

. . .

He recorded an equivalent sound level (leq) of 69 dBA (not impulse) which exceeded the traffic level of 59 dBA and was in violation of the other guidelines the Ministry of the Environment uses.

. . .

Lightstone and Coulter both took impulse and sound and vibration measurements of Huron Steel plant operations. They agree that the impulse sound level at the apartment building is from 70-73 dBAI, with the Prince Road doors closed. Coulter also took indoor readings at the apartment with the window open and recorded about 60 dBAI. The *E.P.A.* guidelines are not meant for indoor readings. However, Lightstone agreed that this reading appears consistent with what he would expect, *i.e.*, 13-14 dBAI lower indoors. It should be mentioned that on cross-examination, Lightstone agreed that impulsive sounds are more intrusive than continuous ones.

Coulter and Lightstone agree that the #1 press is the source of the problem, although other sounds come from the plant as well. The press sound would be more noticeable at night, especially with the windows open, because the ambient levels are lower. Lightstone emphasizes the fact that many of the apartments facing the plant are equipped with air conditioners. The air conditioners, when running, would supposedly negate much of the sound from Huron Steel.

. . .

(b) *Duration*

The Huron Steel plant has been in operation since 1947. According to Mr. Andy Paonessa, who worked at Huron Steel from 1955 to 1978 and as plant manager from 1972, stamping occurred at the plant when he was there.

The number of shifts varied over the years. In 1974 or 1975, it was a three-shift operation, at which time it went to a one-shift, but when Morrison purchased the plant in 1977, it went to three shifts in three months. This continued after the #1 press was installed in 1979.

The major sound and vibration problems seem to occur when the #1 press is blanking heavy gauge material. This presumably would occur when orders had to be filled. Witnesses testified that, although the problem was not continuous, it was fairly regular. The press often operated during the night and on weekends, although there were periods of time when it did not run at all. The situation has continued since 1979, *i.e.*, ten years.

(c) *Effect*

To be successful, the plaintiff must show that the alleged nuisance has caused it damage. As discussed above, at least one of the plaintiff's tenants, Sbrocca, testified that he moved out primarily because of the noise and vibration coming from Huron Steel. Kenney testified that he received other tenant complaints about Huron Steel and that rents had not been increased and standards had been lowered in order to keep the vacancy rate down. Other property owners in the area testified as to the disruption they had experienced from the Huron Steel operations.

Mr. F.R. Jordan was put forward by the plaintiff as an expert in the value of real estate. He testified that he had examined the rent rolls of the plaintiff's apartment building for 1979-1987, in comparison with Canada Mortgage and Housing Corporation (C.M.H.C.) statistics. Based on a capitalized income approach, he concluded that the building lost revenue because of the comparatively high vacancy rate. Jordan stated that there was something abnormal about the property that caused the high vacancy rate and in his report he pointed to the disruptive Huron Steel operations as a probable cause. Jordan also concluded that there had been a loss in value of the building of about $71,000.

The defendant called two expert witnesses to discuss the effect the alleged nuisance had on the plaintiff. Mr. Glen Ladouceur is a business valuator. He examined Jordan's report and did his own study and concluded that the apartment as an income-producing asset did better than three similar buildings, worse than three and the same as one. He testified that he could not conclude that there was any loss in value based on these comparisons.

Mr. D. Rostant is an expert in chartered accountancy. He examined Jordan's report and the rent rolls. He concluded that it was not clear that the plaintiff suffered any loss of rental income over 1979-1988 because of Huron Steel operations.

I accept that the effect of the Huron Steel operations has been such as to cause some damage to the plaintiff.

(2) *Character of the locale*

Counsel for the plaintiff contends that technological advances have weakened the application of this type of "defence". Defendant's counsel places much greater emphasis on this aspect. Relatively recent cases continue to hold that this is an important factor and I accept it as such: In *Walker, supra,* Morden J. stated at p. 38 O.R.:

> The law makes it clear that the character of the locality is of importance in determining the standard of comfort which may reasonably be claimed by an occupier of land. "What would be a nuisance in *Belgrave Square* would not necessarily be so in *Bermondsey*": *Sturges v. Bridgman* (1879), 11 Ch.D 852 at p. 865.

The Huron Steel plant is bordered by Sandwich Street to the north (approximately), Peter Street to the south, Hill Avenue to the west and Prince Road to the east.

. . .

I find that the character of the locale is one of "mixed use". The area contains apartment buildings, houses, at least one school, and one church, commercial establishments, and factories.

The standard of comfort to be expected varies from area to area, depending on the character of the locale in question. According to Linden, *Canadian Tort Law,* p. 505, the standard to be expected in a predominantly residential area differs from that of an industrial or commercial one. However, "[t]he process of determining the proper standard becomes more difficult when the area is one of mixed or changing use".

. . .

First of all, it is well established that it is no defence to a nuisance action that the plaintiff moved to the nuisance: Linden, *Canadian Tort Law,* pp. 506-07). Secondly, many of the witnesses testifed that although there was some noise coming from the Huron Steel plant prior to 1979, the problems with noise and vibration began when the #1 press was installed. *Rushmer v. Polsue & Afieri Ltd.,* [1906] 1 Ch. 234 (C.A.); affd [1907] A.C. 121, [1904-7] All E.R. Rep. 586 (H.L.), stands for the proposition that the addition of a fresh noise may give rise to a nuisance no matter what the character of the locale. In the Court of Appeal decision, Cozens-Hardy L.J. stated at pp. 250-51:

> A resident in such a neighbourhood must put up with a certain amount of noise. The standard of comfort differs according to the situation of the property and the class of people who inhabit it . . . But whatever the standard of comfort in a particular district may be, I think the addition of a fresh noise caused by the defendant's works may be so substantial as to create a legal nuisance. It does not follow that because I live, say, in the manufacturing part of Sheffield I cannot complain if a steam-hammer is introduced next door, and so worked as to render sleep at night almost impossible, although previously to its introduction my house was a reasonably comfortable abode, having regard to the local standard; and it would be no answer to say that the steam-hammer is of the most modern approved pattern and is reasonably worked. In short . . . it is no answer to say that the neighbourhood is noisy, and that the defendant's machinery is of first-class character.

(3) *The utility of the defendant's conduct*

The importance of the defendant's enterprise and its value to the community is a factor in determining if the defendant's conduct is unreasonable. However, this tends to go to the leniency of the remedy, rather than liability itself. Furthermore, the question whether the defendant took all reasonable precautions is relevant as to whether the interference is unreasonable.

Morrison and defendant's counsel mentioned that the Huron Steel plant is important to the community, since it employs about 200 people. Supposedly these jobs would be at risk if Huron Steel were required to make extensive structural changes to the plant to cut the noise and vibration from the #1 press.

. . .

I accept Mr. Morrison's contention that a lot of thought and effort went into the planning, purchase and installation of the #1 press. I also appreciate that the defendant has taken what it considers to be all reasonable and economically practical steps to alleviate the noise and vibration problem. However, the expert evidence indicates that improvements could be made to the building envelope that would ameliorate the situation.

. . .

CONCLUSION ON LIABILITY

The evidence indicates that the defendant's Huron Steel plant operations have caused and continue to cause an unreasonable interference with the plaintiff's use and enjoyment of its property.

. . .

Although this case has certainly not been clear cut, after considering all of the circumstances and factors set out above, I find that on balance of probabilities, the defendant's operations, and the #1 press in particular, do constitute an actionable nuisance.

[The plaintiff was awarded $14,927 for lost rental revenue and $56,500 for the reduction in value of the apartment building. The parties agreed to a remedial course of action and an injunction was granted incorporating the terms of the agreement.]

NOTES AND QUESTIONS

1. What were the plaintiff's allegations of nuisance? The judge considered four criteria in determining whether a nuisance had been committed. Explain in your own words the matters to be considered under each criteria. What evidence did the judge consider in assessing each criteria? Do you agree with the judge's application of the facts to the criteria?

2. Do you think the judge gave equal weight to all four criteria? Should he have done so?

3. Do you think the judge would have resolved this case the same way if:

(a) the #1 press was operating when the apartment building was constructed;

(b) the #1 press operated just within Ministry guidelines with occasional violations;

(c) there was another factory on the other side of the apartment building which produced noise and vibrations equal to the #1 press; or

(d) the defendant employed 1,000 workers and was the largest single employer in Windsor?

4. In *Kent v. Dom. Steel & Coal Corp. Ltd.* (1965), 49 D.L.R. (2d) 241 at 246 (Nfld. S.C.), the court stated:

If I can adopt some other manner in the use of my land to achieve the same effect then it becomes all the more evident that I am using my land in an unreasonable way. To apply this to this case; Dosco could haul its ore across its land in such a way as to avoid the creation of a dust nuisance if it prepared its road of non-dust producing materials; if for example it paved the road, or if it did earlier what it did later, apply suitable dressing to the surface so as to eliminate the dust; or even more simply if it caused its trucks to drive at a slow rate of speed. It is clear that Dosco was unwilling to expend the money which paving would cost and perhaps the chemical dressing was not industriously sought by them; and as to moving the loads of ore at a low speed this would have reduced the rate of production at the mines and added to their costs. From its point of view these reasons — if in fact they were the reasons, for on this point I can only speculate — would have seemed reasonable to Dosco. But they would not provide much consolation to the plaintiff, nor could they be deemed reasonable to him. It would seem to me, though I am making no substantive finding on the point, that Dosco could have used its land in a way which would not have given the plaintiff any cause for complaint. But it did not do so, and I have no hesitation in rejecting Mr. Lewis' submission on this point.

Do you agree with the court? If it is cheaper for the plaintiff to avoid the harm than it is for the defendant to adopt an available alternative, is the defendant using his land in a reasonable way? See also *Renken v. Harvey Aluminum Inc.* (1963), 266 F. Supp. 169 (Ore. D.); and *Cambridge Water Co. v. Eastern Counties Leather plc*, [1994] 1 All E.R. 53 (H.L.).

5. Some courts have made a distinction between nuisances that cause material damage and those that merely interfere with the use and enjoyment of land. Generally, an interference that falls short of causing material damage must be continuous before it will constitute a nuisance. See *Andrews v. R. A. Douglas* (1977), 19 A.P.R. 181 (N.S. C.A.); and *Chu v. Dawson* (1984), 31 C.C.L.T. 146 (B.C. C.A.). See also Fleming, *The Law of Torts*, 8th ed. (1992), 412-14; and Keeton *et al.*, *Prosser and Keeton on Torts*, 5th ed. (1984), 627-30.

6. It is often difficult to predict which interferences will be held to be nuisances, and which will not. For example, in what circumstances should nuisance protect a landowner's interest in aesthetic scenery? See Noel, "Unaesthetics Sights as Nuisance" (1939), 25 Cornell L. Rev. 1. See also *Muirhead v. Timber Bros. Sand & Gravel Ltd.* (1977), 3 C.C.L.T. 1 (Ont. H.C.); *St. Pierre v. Ont.* (1987), 40 C.C.L.T. 200 (S.C.C.); and *Zbarsky v. Lukashuk*, [1992] 1 W.W.R. 690 (B.C. C.A.).

7. The categories of interests protected by nuisance have expanded to address new uses of property made possible by modern technology. For example, in *Nor-Video Services Ltd. v. Ont. Hydro* (1978), 84 D.L.R. (3d) 221 (Ont. H.C.), the defendant's interference with the plaintiff's television reception was held to be an actionable nuisance. See *Bridlington Relay Ltd. v. Yorkshire Electricity Bd.*, [1965] 1 All E.R. 264 (Ch.). See also *Motherwell v. Motherwell* (1976), 73 D.L.R. (3d) 62 (Alta. C.A.), a case in which repeated harassing telephone calls were held to constitute a nuisance. See also, *Khorasandjian v. Bush*, [1993] 3 All E.R. 669 (U.K. C.A.); and Cooke, "A Development in the Tort of Private Nuisance" (1994), 57 Mod. L. Rev. 289.

8. Increasingly, sophisticated scientific techniques reveal that substances once thought to be merely annoying are in fact damaging to health and property. As discussed in chapters 14 and 18, the courts have modified the general tests of causation and proof in cases involving toxic chemicals, radiation and industrial pollutants. Should similar exceptions be recognized in nuisance? In addition to chapters 14 and 18, see *Palmer v. N.S. Forest Industries* (1983), 2 D.L.R. (4th) 397 (N.S. S.C.).

9. An occupier may be held liable in nuisance if she knows or ought to know that a third party has created a hazard on her property and she fails to take reasonable steps to abate the risk to the nearby properties. See *Turner v. Delta Shelf Co.* (1995), 24 C.C.L.T. (2d) 107 (B.C. S.C.).

10. Although the provincial limitations acts generally provide that actions expire six years after the cause of action arises, in nuisance a new cause of action arises each day the nuisance continues. See *Kerlenmar Holdings Ltd. v. Matsqui (District)* (1991), 81 D.L.R. (4th) 334 (B.C. C.A.).

11. For a discussion of the history of nuisance see Winfield, "Nuisance as a Tort" (1930-32), 4 Cambridge L.J. 189; Loengard, "The Assize of Nuisance: Origins of an Action at Common Law" (1978), 37 Cambridge L.J. 144; McLaren, "Nuisance Law and the Industrial Revolution — Some Lessons from Social History" (1983), 3 Oxford Legal Stud. 155; and Lewin, "Compensated Injunctions and the Evolution of Nuisance Law" (1986), 71 Iowa L. Rev. 775. For a review of contemporary developments, see Cross, "Does Only the Careless Polluter Pay? A Fresh Examination of the Nature of Private Nuisance" (1995), 111 L.Q.R. 445.

HOLLYWOOD SILVER FOX FARM LTD. v. EMMETT

[1936] 2 K.B. 468, [1936] 1 All E.R. 825

[The plaintiff was a breeder of silver foxes. The sign that he had erected to advertise his business annoyed the defendant, who alleged that it was detrimental to his development of a building estate. When the plaintiff refused to move the sign, the defendant threatened to discharge guns near the fox pens during their breeding season, in order to interfere with their whelping. When the defendant carried through with this threat, the plaintiff sued in nuisance.]

MACNAGHTEN J.: . . .

Mr. Roche, who put the case for the defendant extremely well, argued that if the defendant had sent his son to shoot at the boundary of his land for the purpose of injuring the plaintiff and that if his conduct was malicious because he wanted to harm the plaintiff, nevertheless he had not committed any actionable wrong. The defendant was entitled to shoot on his own land. He might shoot there to keep down rabbits, or he might shoot for his own pleasure and if it pleased him to annoy his neighbour, although his conduct might be considered unneighbourly, he was entitled at law to do so. In the course of his argument, Mr. Roche relied upon the decision of the House of Lords in the case of *Bradford Corpn. v. Pickles* [[1895] A.C. 587]. In that case the Corporation of Bradford sought an injunction to restrain the defendant from sinking a shaft on land which belonged to him because, according to their view, his object in sinking the shaft was to draw away water which would otherwise become the property of the Corporation. Pickles was acting maliciously. His sole object in digging was to do harm to the Corporation. The House of Lords decided, once and for all, that in such a case the motive of the defendant is immaterial. In *Allen v. Flood* [[1898] A.C. 1], Lord Herschell, commenting on *Bradford Corpn. v. Pickles* [above], said this, at page 124:

> It has recently been held in this House, in the case of *Bradford Corpn. v. Pickles*, that acts by the defendant upon his own land were not actionable when they were within his legal rights, even though his motive were to prejudice his neighbour. The language of the noble and learned Lords was distinct. The Lord Chancellor said "This is not a case where the state of mind of the person doing the act can affect the right. If it was a lawful act, however ill the motive might be, he had a right to do it. If it was an unlawful act, however good the motive might be, he would have no right to do it." The statement was confined to the class of cases then before the House; but I apprehend that what was said is not applicable only to rights of property, but is equally applicable to the exercise by an individual of his other rights.

In the same case Lord Watson, at page 101, discussing the duck-decoying case of *Keeble v. Hickeringill* [(1706), 11 East. 574], said this:

> No proprietor has an absolute right to create noises upon his own land, because any right which the law gives him is qualified by the condition that it must not be exercised to the nuisance of his neighbours or of the public. If he violates that condition he commits a legal wrong, and if he does so intentionally, he is guilty of a malicious wrong, in its strict legal sense.

Mr. Roche contended that in this case the defendant had committed no nuisance at all in the legal sense of this case and he referred to *Robinson v. Kilvert* [(1889), 41 Ch. D. 88]. In that case complaint was made by the appellant that the brown paper which he kept on the ground floor of his premises suffered some damage from heat in the basement below, and it was held by the Court of Appeal that no actionable wrong was being committed by the defendant in that the heating was not of such a character as would interfere with the ordinary use of the rest of the house. He supplemented the argument, based on the consideration of that case, with the observations of Lord Robertson in *Eastern & South African Telegraph*

Co. v. Cape Town Tramways Cos., [[1902] A.C. 381], where Lord Robertson, delivering the judgment of the Privy Council, said, at page 393:

> A man cannot increase the liabilities of his neighbour by applying his own property to special uses, whether for business or pleasure.

It was argued that the keeping of a silver fox farm was not an ordinary use of land in the county of Kent, and what the defendant had done in discharging the bird-scaring cartridges would cause no alarm to the sheep or cattle which are usually to be found on Kentish farms. It was only because Captain Chalmers had brought these highly nervous animals — not natural to this country — that had caused the plaintiffs any loss and if silver foxes were brought to the county of Kent, one could not thereby restrict their neighbours in the matter of shooting. I am not satisfied that there is any substance in that argument. It is a perfectly lawful thing to keep a silver fox farm and I think the fact that the shooting took place intentionally for the purpose of injuring the plaintiffs made it actionable.

The authority for the view that in cases of alleged nuisance by noise, the intention of the person making the noise is not to be disregarded is to be found in the case of *Gaunt v. Fynney* [(1872), 8 Ch. App. 8]. Lord Selborne, L.C., delivered the judgment of the court, and he was dealing there with the question of nuisances, and he said this, at page 12:

> A nuisance by noise (supposing malice to be out of the question) is emphatically a question of degree.

It has been observed by high authority that Lord Selborne was always extremely careful in the use of language and that parenthetical statement "supposing malice to be out of the question" clearly indicates what his Lordship thought in the case of alleged nuisance by noise, where the noise was made maliciously. Different considerations would apply to cases where that ingredient was absent. Indeed, the matter is put beyond doubt by the decision of North, J., in *Christie v. Davey* [[1893] 1 Ch. 316]. The plaintiff and the defendant lived side by side in semi-detached houses in Brixton. The plaintiff was a teacher of music and he had a musical family. The result was that throughout clouds of music pervaded his house and were heard in the house of his neighbour. His neighbour did not like music to be heard and after writing rather an unfortunate letter of protest, he took to making noises himself by beating trays and rapping on the wall, and thereupon the music teacher brought an action for an injunction. The action came before North, J., and he delivered judgment in favour of the plaintiff and granted an injunction restraining the defendant from permitting any sounds or noises in his house so as to annoy the plaintiff or the occupiers of his house, and in the course of his judgment he said, at page 326:

> The result is that I think I am bound to interfere for the protection of the plaintiffs. In my opinion the noises which were made in the defendant's house were not of a legitimate kind. They were what, to use the language of Lord Selborne in *Gaunt v. Fynney* [above] "ought to be regarded as excessive and unreasonable." I am satisfied that they were made deliberately and maliciously for the purpose of annoying the plaintiffs. If what has taken place had occurred between two sets of persons, both perfectly innocent, I should have taken an entirely different view of the case. But I am persuaded that what was done by the defendant was done only for the purpose of annoyance, and in my opinion it was not a legitimate use of the defendant's house to use it for the purpose of vexing and annoying his neighbours.

. . .

In my opinion, the authorities to which I have referred support the view that a person who shoots on his own land, or makes other noises on his own land, for the purpose of annoying or injuring his neighbour, does, by the common law, commit the actionable wrong of nuisance for which he is liable in damages at common law and was liable to be restrained by an injunction in a court of equity before the Judicature Act. I think that the plaintiff is entitled to maintain this action and he has established the cause of action which he alleged.

. . .

[The plaintiff was awarded £250 in damages and granted an injunction which was limited to the breeding season.]

NOTES AND QUESTIONS

1. What is the relationship between the defendant's motive and the elements of a nuisance action? How did the court deal with this issue? See *A.G. Man. v. Campbell* (1985), 32 C.C.L.T. 57 (Man. C.A.).

2. Does a landowner have a duty to protect her neighbours from damages resulting from a natural use of her property, if such damages are foreseeable? See *270233 Ontario Ltd. v. Weall & Cullen Nurseries Ltd.* (1993), 17 C.C.L.T. (2d) 176 (Ont. Gen. Div.), a case in which natural drainage channels on the defendant's sloping land emptied mud and silt onto the plaintiff's golf course, thereby causing damage.

3. In *Hollywood*, would the shooting have constituted a nuisance if it had been carried out for a legitimate purpose, such as destroying rodents on the defendant's land? See *Rattray v. Daniels* (1959), 17 D.L.R. (2d) 134 (Alta. C.A.).

4. How did the court in *Hollywood* deal with the defendant's contention that it could not be held liable due to the principles established in *Bradford Corp. v. Pickles*, [1895] A.C. 587 (H.L.)? Can you reconcile the decisions in *Hollywood* and *Bradford*? For conflicting interpretations of these two cases see Fleming, *The Law of Torts*, 8th ed. (1992), 424-25; and Heuston and Buckley, *Salmond and Heuston on the Law of Torts*, 20th ed. (1992), 66-67.

5. It is generally accepted that an individual's ordinarily innocuous conduct will not constitute nuisance simply because the plaintiff is abnormally sensitive to that conduct. The defendant in *Hollywood* argued that the plaintiff only suffered loss because he had put his land to an extraordinary use that made him abnormally vulnerable to the sound of gun shots. How did the court address this argument, and do you agree with its analysis? For a criticism of the court's analysis see Heuston and Buckley, *Salmond and Heuston on the Law of Torts*, 20th ed. (1992), 67. See also *Nor-Video Services Ltd. v. Ont. Hydro* (1978), 84 D.L.R. (3d) 221 (Ont. H.C.); *Devon Lumber Co. v. MacNeil* (1987), 42 C.C.L.T. 192 (N.B. C.A.); and *Ward v. Magna International Inc.* (1994), 21 C.C.L.T. (2d) 178 (Ont. Gen. Div.).

TOCK v. ST. JOHN'S METROPOLITAN AREA BOARD

[1989] 2 S.C.R. 1181

LA FOREST J. (Dickson C.J. concurring):—In the early afternoon of October 10, 1981, a day of exceptionally heavy rainfall, the Tocks discovered that a large amount of water had entered their basement. They immediately notified the Board and attempted, in vain, to pump the water out themselves. Two employees of the Board came to inspect the storm sewer in the vicinity and determined that the sewer was blocked. A crew was summoned and by early evening it had located and removed the blockage. Within ten to fifteen minutes of the removal, the water drained from the basement which had, by this time, incurred substantial damage.

. . .

The trial judge, Adams C.J. Dist. Ct., held that the flooding was caused by the blockage and not by the exceptionally heavy rainfall. He went on to dismiss the claim in negligence, holding that the Board had not been negligent in the construction, maintenance or operation of the storm sewer. He did, however, hold that the escape of the water into the Tock's residence constituted a serious interference with their right of enjoyment of their property and, in consequence, allowed the claim in nuisance. In his opinion, the collection and drainage of water from rain or other sources constituted a non-natural user of land within the meaning of the rule in *Rylands v. Fletcher*. In the result, the trial judge awarded the Tocks a total of $13,456.11 in damages.

The Newfoundland Court of Appeal reversed this judgment. Gushue J.A., writing for a unanimous court, held that the rule in *Rylands v. Fletcher* had no application. In his view, the provisioning of an indispensable service such as a water and sewer system could not be held to constitute a non-natural user of land within the meaning of the rule.

On the question of nuisance, Gushue J.A. expressed the view that a claim in nuisance would not lie against a municipal corporation for damage resulting from a service provided under statutory authority if that body could establish that the occurrence complained of was inevitable in the sense that it could not have been avoided by the exercise of all reasonable and available expertise and care in the design, construction and operation of the service. On the facts, he concluded that the Board had satisfied the onus of demonstrating that it had done everything that could reasonably be expected to avoid the occurrence.

. . .

Turning to the question of inevitability, it seems to me that, in strict logic, most nuisances stemming from activities authorized by statute *are* in fact inevitable. Certainly, if one is to judge from the frequency with which storm drain and sewer cases occur in the reports, it would seem a safe conclusion that blockage of such systems is inevitable if one accepts this to mean that it is demonstrably impossible to operate these systems without such occurrences. But what escapes me is why any particular importance should be accorded this fact when weighing a nuisance claim against a statutory authority. The fact that the operation of a given system will inevitably visit random damage on certain unfortunate individuals among the pool of users of the system does not tell us why those individuals should be responsible for paying for that damage.

. . .

I would allow the appeal, set aside the judgment of the Court of Appeal and restore the judgment of the trial judge. The appellants are entitled to their costs throughout.

The judgment of Lamer, Wilson and L'Heureux-Dubé JJ. was delivered by

WILSON J.—I have had the benefit of reading the reasons for judgment of my colleague, Justice La Forest, and, while I agree with his proposed disposition of the appeal, I have reservations about his approach to the law of nuisance as it applies to public bodies acting under statutory authority. The facts are set out in detail by my colleague and I need not repeat them here.

I agree with my colleague's conclusion that the rule in *Rylands v. Fletcher*

(1868), L.R. 3 H.L. 330, has no application to this case but that the appellants are entitled to recover from the respondent in nuisance. I agree with him also that the Court of Appeal erred in concluding that if the respondent could show that it had not been negligent, then it could not be liable in nuisance.

I do not, however, share La Forest J.'s view that this Court should, or indeed can, on this appeal virtually abolish the defence of statutory authority for policy reasons and treat municipalities exercising statutory authority in the same way as private individuals. Such a major departure from the current state of the law would, it seems to me, require the intervention of the legislature.

Moreover, I do not favour replacing the existing law in this area with a general test of whether it is reasonable or unreasonable in the circumstances of the case to award compensation. This test may, because of the high degree of judicial subjectivity involved in its application, make life easier for the judges but, in my respectful view, it will do nothing to assist public bodies to make a realistic assessment of their exposure in carrying out their statutory mandate. Nor will it provide much guidance to litigants in deciding whether or not to sue. It is altogether too uncertain. Nor can I, with respect, accept the proposition that a single individual suffering damage from an isolated nuisance should be dealt with differently from a group of people suffering damage from an ongoing nuisance. This seems to me to be quite incompatible with the concept of principled decision-making. Accordingly, while I agree with my colleague in the result he has reached in this case, I prefer to write my own concurring reasons.

I agree that the flooding of the appellants' basement constituted an unreasonable interference with the appellants' use and enjoyment of the property and that, had the parties been two private individuals, it clearly would have been an actionable nuisance. However, since the respondent is a municipality, the law dictates that different considerations apply. The crucial question is whether or not the respondent is able to rely on the defence of statutory authority in the circumstances of this case.

Since the availability of the defence of statutory authority depends on the language of the statute I set out the relevant provisions of *The Municipalities Act*, S.N. 1979, c. 33, on which the respondent must rely:

> 154. (1) The council may, subject to the provisions of *The Department of Consumer Affairs and Environment Act, 1973* and regulations made thereunder, construct, acquire, establish, own and operate
>> (a) a public water supply system for the distribution of water within or, with the approval of the Minister, outside of the town,
>> (b) a public sewerage system, either independently of or in conjunction with a public water supply system, for the collection and disposal of sewerage within or, with the approval of the Minister, outside of the town, and
>> (c) a storm drainage system within or, with the approval of the Minister, outside of the town.
>
> (2) For the purposes of subsection (1) the council may
>> (a) acquire any waters required for the purpose of providing a sufficient supply of water for the town, and
>> (b) acquire by purchase or expropriation any lands adjacent to such waters to prevent pollution of those waters.
>
> (3) For the purpose of exercising its powers under subsection (1) the council may lay out,

excavate, dig, make, build, maintain, repair, and improve all such drains, sewers, and water supply pipes as the council deems necessary.

There is no doubt that these provisions authorize the respondent to construct and continue to operate and maintain the sewage system in question. They are, however, permissive as opposed to mandatory. They confer a power; they do not impose a duty. Is this distinction relevant to the question of the respondent's liability in nuisance? To answer this it is necessary to review some of the leading authorities on the subject.

. . .

The principles to be derived from the foregoing authorities would seem to be as follows:

(a) if the legislation imposes a duty and the nuisance is the inevitable consequence of discharging that duty, then the nuisance is itself authorized and there is no recovery in the absence of negligence;

(b) if the legislation, although it merely confers an authority, is specific as to the manner or location of doing the thing authorized and the nuisance is the inevitable consequence of doing the thing authorized in that way or in that location, then likewise the nuisance is itself authorized and there is no recovery absent negligence.

However:

(c) if the legislation confers an authority and also gives the public body a discretion, not only whether to do the thing authorized or not, but how to do it and in what location, then if it does decide to do the thing authorized, it must do it in a manner and at a location which will avoid the creation of a nuisance. If it does it in a way or at a location which gives rise to a nuisance, it will be liable therefor, whether there is negligence or not.

In other words, in the situations described in (a) and (b) above the inevitability doctrine is a good defence to the public body absent negligence. In situation (c) it is no defence at all and it is unnecessary for the plaintiff to prove negligence in order to recover.

In my view, these principles make a great deal of sense. The inevitability doctrine represents a happy judicial compromise between letting no one who has suffered damage as a consequence of the statutorily authorized activities of public bodies recover and letting everyone so suffering damage recover. Recovery will be allowed unless it is shown that the interference with the plaintiff's rights was permitted by either:

(1) express language in the statute such as a provision specifying that no action for nuisance may be brought for any damage caused: see, for example, the decision of this Court in *District of North Vancouver v. McKenzie Barge & Marine Ways Ltd.*, [1965] S.C.R. 377; or

(2) by necessary implication from the language of the statute coupled with a factual finding that the damage was the inevitable consequence of what the statute ordered or authorized the public body to do.

. . .

In my view, to the extent that some of the more recent cases are inconsistent with the early principles, they should not be followed. I find no acceptable rationale for the extension of the inevitable consequences doctrine to cases where the public body was perfectly free to exercise its statutory authority without violating private rights. It is only in cases where the public body has no choice as to the way in which or the place where it engages in the nuisance-causing activity that the inevitable consequences doctrine protects it. For only in such cases can it be said that the legislature has authorized any nuisance which is the inevitable consequence of the public body's carrying out its mandate.

. . .

The legislation in this case was purely permissive within the meaning of these cases. It authorized a sewage system to be constructed but did not specify how or where it was to be done. The respondent was accordingly obliged to construct and operate the system in strict conformity with private rights. It did not do so. The defence of statutory authority is not available to it and the appellants are entitled to recover. The case calls for a straightforward application of *Metropolitan Asylum District v. Hill.*

For these reasons I would allow the appeal, set aside the judgment of the Court of Appeal, and restore the judgment of the trial judge. The appellants are entitled to their costs both here and in the courts below.

SOPINKA J.

. . .

The burden of proof with respect to the defence of statutory authority is on the party advancing the defence. It is not an easy one. The courts strain against a conclusion that private rights are intended to be sacrificed for the common good. The defendant must negative that there are alternate methods of carrying out the work. The mere fact that one is considerably less expensive will not avail. If only one method is practically feasible, it must be established that it was practically impossible to avoid the nuisance. It is insufficient for the defendant to negative negligence. The standard is a higher one. While the defence gives rise to some factual difficulties, in view of the allocation of the burden of proof they will be resolved against the defendant.

If we are to depart from this state of the law, so recently confirmed by two decisions of this Court, there should be very strong ground for so doing. Moreover, there should be substantial unanimity. It is apparent from the reasons in this appeal that there is little unanimity as to whether we should retrench, advance or stay the same.

The change proposed by La Forest J. subsumes the defence of statutory authority within the test as to when it is reasonable to compensate the plaintiff. Trial judges will still have to grapple with the elements of the defence of statutory authority but in the context of a test of reasonableness. This will simply add uncertainty to any uncertainty which is said to exist.

Nor do I agree that it is logical or practical to distinguish between public works that are required and those that are permitted. While it was fashionable to require such works in the railway building age, mandatory public works are a feature of a by-gone era.

The disagreement with the result reached in the Court of Appeal is not because the law is defective but because it was incorrectly applied. As La Forest J. points out, the Court of Appeal exonerated the respondent from liability in nuisance on the basis that there was an absence of negligence. In my opinion, the heavier onus which must be discharged was not met in this case. The trial judge so found. I therefore would dispose of the appeal as proposed by my colleagues.

Appeal allowed with costs.

NOTES AND QUESTIONS

1. What is the major premise in each of the three judgments? With which do you agree?

2. In *Tock*, all of the judges agreed that the fact that the defendant acted reasonably is no defence in nuisance. A defendant will not be held liable if she unintentionally and without negligence, physically injures a plaintiff in a public place. Why should the defendant be treated differently when she accidentally interferes with the plaintiff's use and enjoyment of her land? For an application of *Tock*, see *Ratko v. Woodstock (City) Public Utility Commission* (1994), 17 O.R. (3d) 427 (Div. Ct.).

3. *Tock* is a major departure from many recent cases on the defence of statutory authority, and the Supreme Court may have to provide further clarification. For a review of the previous authorities see the judgment of Wilson J. For a review of the effect of *Tock* see Klar, "The Supreme Court of Canada: Extending the Tort Liability of Public Authorities" (1990), 28 Alta. L.R. 648. See also *Canada (Attorney General) v. Ottawa-Carleton (Regional Municipality)* (1991), 8 C.C.L.T. (2d) 256 (Ont. C.A.); and chapter 27.

4. Can you explain why the balancing of interests in nuisance could lead to liability, whereas the balancing of interests in negligence could lead to absolving the defendant?

The courts' attempts to distinguish between the two torts has not always been helpful. See, for example, *Overseas Tankship (U.K.) Ltd. v. Miller S.S. Co. Pty.*, [1967] 1 A.C. 617 per Lord Reid at 639-40 (P.C.). See also Newark, "The Boundaries of Nuisance" (1949), 65 L.Q.R. 480; Rogers, *Winfield and Jolowicz on Tort*, 14th ed. (1994), 414-18; and Fleming, *The Law of Torts*, 8th ed. (1992), 409-11 and 424-26.

5. The fact that the defendant exercised care and skill, acted in the public benefit or was simply one of several causers of the nuisance provides no defence. It would also appear that the defendant can invoke the defences of consent and contributory negligence in certain limited circumstances, although this is controversial. See Rogers and Fleming, *supra*.

6. The defendant can also raise as a defence to private nuisance that she has a right to commit the tort by prescription. After an uninterrupted period of 20 years, the defendant's conduct becomes, in Fleming's words, "retrospectively legalized as if it had been authorized by a grant from the owner of the servient land". *The Law of Torts*, 8th ed. (1992), 441. This defence can only be invoked if the nature of the nuisance remains the same over the period, and the plaintiff was aware of the nuisance. See *Sturges v. Bridgman* (1879), 11 Ch. D. 852 (C.A.); *Pilliterri v. Nor. Const. Co.* (1930), 66 O.L.R. 128 (T.D.); *Russell Tpt. Ltd. v. Ont. Malleable Iron Co.*, [1952] 4 D.L.R. 719 (Ont. H.C.); and *Schenck v. The Queen* (1981), 34 O.R. (2d) 595 (H.C.), aff'd., [1987] 2 S.C.R. 289.

7. As the preceding cases and notes illustrate, the law of nuisance is frequently used to resolve conflicts between two lawful and socially useful activities. Traditionally, the courts have assumed that the active party has caused the harm. Although the active party's interest in the use of her land is considered, the law favours the passive user. This view was challenged by Coase in an influential article entitled, "The Problem of Social Cost" (1960), 3 J. Law and Econ. 1. He argues that nuisance raises the issue of reciprocity. Any court decision which precludes the active party from harming the passive will necessarily harm the active party by preventing her from making lawful use of her land. Coase argues that unless the law has a more important reason for favouring one party over another, it should resolve the issue in a manner which maximizes scarce social resources. Thus, liability should be imposed on the "cheapest cost avoider"; that is, the party that can avoid the harm at the lowest cost. This may favour the passive user in some cases and the active user in others.

Can the Coase approach adequately take into account variables such as peace and quiet, clean air, and unpolluted water that have no easily ascertainable economic value? Do the courts have the ability or sufficient evidence to make determinations about the "cheapest cost avoider"? For a critique of Coase's analysis see Fletcher, "Fairness and Utility in Tort Theory" (1972), 85 Harv. L. Rev. 537; Epstein, "A Theory of Strict Liability" (1973), 2 J. Legal Stud. 151; Gjerdingen, "The Coase Theorem and the Psychology of Common-Law Thought" (1983), 56 S. Cal. L. Rev. 711; and White, "Risk-Utility Analysis and the Learned Hand Formula: A Hand that Helps or a Hand that Hides?" (1990), 32 Ariz. L. Rev. 77.

3. Public Nuisance

A public nuisance is one that affects the general community, not merely one or two individuals. Although a public nuisance may interfere with the use and enjoyment of privately held land, as in a case involving noxious factory fumes that permeate an entire neighbourhood, the action is not limited to such interferences. A public nuisance can also be committed by interfering with the general public's interest in passable highways, clean waterways or other public resources.

Ordinarily, public nuisances are governed by public law. If the defendant's conduct constitutes a criminal offence, the government may prosecute. In any event, the Attorney-General, as the representative of the public, may sue the defendant seeking damages and an injunction. The Attorney-General may consent to a relator action which enables a private citizen to seek injunctive relief in the Attorney-General's name. The Attorney-General has virtually unfettered discretion in deciding whether to prosecute, sue civilly or consent to a relator action.

Originally, a private citizen injured as a result of a public nuisance could not recover damages. When the courts recognized such claims they limited recovery to cases in which the private citizen had suffered some kind of special injury above and beyond that borne by other members of the public. The development of this private action for public nuisance has been the source of controversy and confusion.

In the following section, we address two main issues. First, how do the courts distinguish between private and public nuisance? Second, how do the courts determine which plaintiffs will be permitted to maintain private actions for public nuisance?

A.-G. ONT. v. ORANGE PRODUCTIONS LTD.

[1971] 3 O.R. 585, 21 D.L.R. (3d) 257 (H.C.)

[The Attorney-General sought an interim injunction to restrain the defendants from holding an outdoor rock concert, alleging that it would constitute a public nuisance. Evidence was given that there had been acts of trespass to private property, public sexual intercourse, and public consumption of alcohol and illicit drugs at one of the defendant's previous concerts.]

WELLS C.J.H.C.: — The law relating to public nuisance had its flowering in the late 18th Century and the early 19th Century. However, in 1957, a case, *A.-G. v. P.Y.A. Quarries, Ltd.*, [1957] 1 All E.R. 894, arising from the operation of a quarry in Wales, came before the Court of Appeal in England. A very strong Court consisting of Lord Justice Denning (as he then was), Lord Justice Parker (as he then was) and Lord Justice Romer considered the matter at some length. The principal judgment is that of Romer L.J. He went into the matter in great detail taking into account the various historical definitions of public nuisance over at last two centuries. I do not propose to set out this very detailed review he made but he went back to cases in the middle and late 18th Century and came down from the 19th Century up to the time he gave his judgment. This review is found at pp. 900-2. I do not propose to quote it. But it is of great assistance in dealing with the problem before me. His conclusions are found at p. 902 and are briefly set out as follows:

> The expression "the neighbourhood" has been regarded as sufficiently defining the area affected by a public nuisance in other cases also (see, for example, *A.-G. v. Stone* (1895), 60 J.P. 168; *A.-G. v. Cole & Son*, [1901] 1 Ch. 205; and *A.-G. v. Corke*, [1933] Ch. 89).
>
> I do not propose to attempt a more precise definition of public nuisance than those which emerge from the textbooks and authorities to which I have referred. It is, however, clear, in my opinion, that any nuisance is "public" which materially affects the reasonable comfort and convenience of life of a class of Her Majesty's subjects. The sphere of nuisance may be described generally as "the neighbourhood"; but the question whether the local community within that sphere comprises a sufficient number of persons to constitute a class of the public is a question of fact in every case. It is not necessary, in my judgment, to prove that every member of the class has been injuriously affected; it is sufficient to show that a representative cross-section of the class has been so affected for an injunction to issue.

. . .

It was, of course, argued by the defendant quarry that this was in effect a private nuisance and that the action should not have been brought by the Attorney-General on behalf of the public generally, and at p. 906 Romer, L.J., made the following pertinent observations:

> Some public nuisances (for example, the pollution of rivers) can often be established without the necessity of calling a number of individual complainants as witnesses. In general, however, a public nuisance is proved by the cumulative effect which it is shown to have had on the people living within its sphere of influence. In other words, a normal and legitimate way of proving a public nuisance is to prove a sufficiently large collection of private nuisances. I am therefore of opinion that there was nothing improper or irregular in the statement of claim as originally delivered, or in the reception at the trial of evidence of the local residents' experiences.

It was also evident that, despite the strongly expressed public discontent with the operation of the quarry, the defendants had paid scant attention to the local residents or the representations of the local authorities and that they were slow to adopt the improvements suggested with reference to the escape of dust which was reasonable to the people living around the quarry. All these matters are found in the present case before me.

Before I part with the case I think I should deal with some of the observations of Lord Justice Denning (as he then was). At p. 908 he dealt with the question as to the distinction between public and private nuisance and he expressed himself as follows:

> The classic statement of the difference is that a public nuisance affects Her Majesty's subjects generally, whereas a private nuisance only affects particular individuals. But this does not help much. The question: when do a number of individuals become Her Majesty's subjects generally? is as difficult to answer as the question: when does a group of people become a crowd? Everyone has his own views. Even the answer "Two's company, three's a crowd" will not command the assent of those present unless they first agree on "which two". So here I decline to answer the question how many people are necessary to make up Her Majesty's subjects generally. I prefer to look to the reason of the thing and to say that a public nuisance is a nuisance which is so widespread in its range or so indiscriminate in its effect that it would not be reasonable to expect one person to take proceedings on his own responsibility to put a stop to it, but that it should be taken on the responsibility of the community at large. Take the blocking up of a public highway or the non-repair of it; it

may be a footpath very little used except by one or two householders; nevertheless the obstruction affects everyone indiscriminately who may wish to walk along it. Take next a landowner who collects pestilential rubbish near a village or permits gypsies with filthy habits to encamp on the edge of a residential neighbourhood. The householders nearest to it suffer the most, but everyone in the neighbourhood suffers too. In such cases the Attorney-General can take proceedings for an injunction to restrain the nuisance: and when he does so he acts in defence of the public right, not for any sectional interest: see *A.-G. v. Bastow*, [1957] 1 All E.R. 497. When, however, the nuisance is so concentrated that only two or three property owners are affected by it, such as the three attornies in Clifford's Inn, then they ought to take proceedings on their own account to stop it and not expect the community to do it for them; see *R. v. Lloyd* ((1802), 4 Esp. 200) and the precedent in *3 Chitty on Criminal Law* (1826), pp. 664, 665. Applying this test, I am clearly of opinion that the nuisance by stones, vibration and dust in this case was at the date of the writ so widespread in its range and so indiscriminate in its effect that it was a public nuisance.

. . .

In my opinion, the whole festival with the weight of numbers and the noise and dust, was a painful and troublesome experience for all those living in the neighbourhood and was, in fact, a social disaster to those who normally live there. Until proper sanitation has been installed in the park and some limitation put on the numbers attending, I do not think the festival should take place. It is unfair to the neighbourhood. It is actually unfair to those who attend it and it is operated at considerable risk as to health and well-being both of the guests of the park and those who live in the neighbourhood and who are entitled to quiet enjoyment of their property. The pressure on the neighbourhood when these festivals are held is, in my opinion, grossly excessive and is something that should be restrained.

[Interim injunction granted.]

HICKEY v. ELEC. REDUCTION CO.

(1970), 2 Nfld. & P.E.I.R. 246, 21 D.L.R. (3d) 368 (Nfld. S.C.)

FURLONG C.J.: . . . The defendants by the discharge of poisonous waste from its phosphorus plant at Long Harbour, Placentia Bay, destroyed the fish life of the adjacent waters, and the plaintiffs, as all other fishermen in the area suffered in their livelihood. I have said "all other fishermen", but the resulting pollution created a nuisance to all persons — "all Her Majesty's subjects" — to use Stephen's phrase. It was not a nuisance peculiar to the plaintiffs, nor confined to their use of the waters of Placentia Bay. It was a nuisance committed against the public.

A somewhat similar occurrence happened at a fishing settlement in Labrador, at Little Grady Island, in 1927, when a whaling company erected a factory at Watering Cove on Big Grady Island and polluted the waters adjacent to the premises of a fishing establishment on the former island. In the event an action was taken by the fishery owners against the whaling company. The case was heard in this Court in 1929 by Kent, J., and his judgment has remained unchallenged. He found that amongst other things, that there was serious pollution of the fishing waters from the waste materials of the whale factory. The case is *McRae v. British Norwegian Whaling Co. Ltd.*, [1927-31] Nfld. L.R. 274. After declaring at p. 282 that:

It is an established principle that the right to fish in the sea and public navigable waters is free and open to all. It is a public right that may be exercised by any of the King's subjects, and for any interference with it the usual remedies to vindicate a public right must be employed.

He proceeded to apply the principle to the facts before him at pp. 283-4:

> The plaintiffs in the present action must, therefore, in order to succeed on this cause of complaint, show that the injury inflicted upon them by the acts of the defendants, insofar as they affect the right of fishing in the public navigable waters in the vicinity of Little Grady Island, is, in regard to them, particular direct and substantial, over and above the injury thereby inflicted upon the public in general. It is not enough for the plaintiffs to show that their business is interrupted or interfered with, by the public nuisance, to enable them to maintain a private action against the defendants in respect thereof, for such interruption or interference is not a direct but merely a consequential damage resulting to them from the nuisance. Neither is it an injury peculiar to the plaintiffs themselves, but is suffered by them in common with everyone else whose right to fish in these public waters is affected by the nuisance. The plaintiff's right, as one of the public, to fish may be affected to a greater extent than that of others, but they have no ground of complaint different from anyone else who fishes or intends to fish in these waters. If the nuisance took the form of obstructing the right of the plaintiffs as adjacent land owners, of access from their land to the public navigable waters, the injury would be peculiar to themselves, not because it interrupted their right to fish in common with others in the public waters, but because it interrupted their right of access to these waters, which is an incident to the occupation of property adjacent to the sea and would therefore be an interference with a right peculiar to themselves and distinct from their right as one of the public to fish in the public waters. For these reasons I have come to the conclusion that the plaintiffs have failed to establish their right to maintain a private action in respect of the pollution by the defendants of these public navigable waters.

A somewhat similar situation arose in New Brunswick in 1934 in *Fillion v. New Brunswick International Paper Co.*, [1934] 3 D.L.R. 22, 8 M.P.R. 89. The waste from a paper mill into the Restigouche River in that Province polluted the waters of a bay where the plaintiff, with others, carried on smelt fishing. An action was taken in nuisance against the owners of the paper-mill and that part of the case was dismissed, Baxter, J., saying at p. 26:

> Assuming then, that the defendant's act constituted a public nuisance, and if it is wrongful I do not see how it can be anything else, the plaintiff has suffered differently from the rest of the public only in degree. That is not enough to entitle him to recover. Nearly all of the cases in which this principle has been invoked concern the obstruction of a highway, but *Ashby v. White*, 2 Ld. Raym. 938, at p. 955, 92 E.R. 126, *per* Holt, C.J., and the case of *Williams* in 5 Co. Rep. 72(b), 77 E.R. 163, show that the *ratio decidendi* is that it is inexpedient that there should be multiplicity of actions and that where a nuisance or injury is common to the whole public the remedy is by indictment but that no private right of action exists unless there is a special or particular injury to the plaintiff.

    . . . .

I think it is clear that the facts, as we have them, can only support the view that there has been pollution of the waters of this area of Placentia Bay which amounts to a public nuisance. If I am right in this view then the law is clear that a private action by the plaintiffs is not sustainable.

Counsel for the plaintiffs, Mr. Robert Wells, argued that when a public nuisance has been created anyone who suffers special damage, that is direct damage has a right of action. I am unable to agree to this rather wide application of Salmond's view that a public nuisance may become a tortious act. I think the right view is that any person who suffers peculiar damage has a right of action, but where the damage is common to all persons of the same class, then a personal right of action is not maintainable. Mr. Wells suggests that the plaintiff's right to outfit for the fishery and their right to fish is a particular right and this right having been interfered with they have a cause of action. This right which they enjoy is a right in common with all Her Majesty's subjects, an interference with which is the whole test of a public nuisance; a right which can only be vindicated by the appropriate means, which is an action by the Attorney-General, either with or without a relator, in the common interest of the public.

Rose et al. v. Miles, [1814-23] All E.R. Rep. 580, which has been cited is not in point, as the judgment of Lord Ellenborough, C.J., clearly shows [at p. 581], "This is something substantially more injurious to this person, than to the public at large," and Dampier, J., said "The present case admits of this distinction from most other cases, that here the plaintiff was interrupted in the actual enjoyment of the highway." With great respect I hold that view that that judgment was applicable only to the particular facts of that case, and can only support the general proposition that a peculiar and particular damage, distinct from that of the general public, is necessary to sustain an action.

. . .

[Action dismissed.]

NOTES AND QUESTIONS

1. How do Denning L.J.'s and Romer L.J.'s tests of public nuisance, that are cited in *A.G. Ontario*, differ? Which test is more useful?

2. What is the rationale for the restrictive standing rule in public nuisance? In *Thorson v. A.G. Can.* (1974), 43 D.L.R. (3d) 1 at 10 (S.C.C.), Laskin J. stated that this rule was justified because "there is a clear way in which the public interest can be guarded through the intervention of the Attorney-General who would be sensitive to public complaints about the interference with public rights." Do you agree? See *Rosenburg v. Grand River Conservation Authority* (1975), 69 D.L.R. (3d) 384 (Ont. C.A.); and Estey, "Public Nuisance and Standing to Sue" (1972), 10 Osgoode Hall L.J. 563.

3. Had the Attorney-General not acted or consented to a relator action in *A.G. Ont. v. Orange Productions*, would the individuals in the vicinity have succeeded in private nuisance or in a private action for public nuisance?

4. In *A.G. N.S. v. Beaver* (1984), 31 C.C.L.T. 54 (N.S. S.C.), aff'd. (1985), 32 C.C.L.T. 170 (N.S. C.A.), the plaintiff sought an injunction in public nuisance to prohibit prostitutes from soliciting. The trial judge dismissed the application. He stated that equitable remedies such as injunctions should not be used to suppress criminal conduct, thereby undermining the important procedural safeguards of criminal law. However, a similar action in *A.G. B.C. v. Couillard* (1984), 31 C.C.L.T. 26 (B.C. S.C.) succeeded. Apparently, this injunction resulted in the prostitutes moving to an adjacent area. The Attorney-General of B.C. declined to bring a subsequent action at the request of this adjacent neighbourhood. When these individuals brought a private action, the court dismissed their claim on the basis that the annoyance amounted to a public nuisance and they had no standing to sue. *Stein v. Gonzales* (1984), 31 C.C.L.T. 19 (B.C. S.C.).

These cases and the academic comments about them demonstrate the difficulties of defining the tort of public nuisance and making sense of the muddled case law that the tort has generated. See Klar, "Recent Developments in Canadian Tort Law" (1985), 17 Ottawa L. Rev. 325 at 386-88; and Cassels, "Prostitution and Public Nuisance: Desperate Measures and the Limits of Civil Adjudication" (1985), 63 Can. Bar Rev. 764.

5. The court in *Hickey* concluded that to succeed the plaintiffs had to suffer damages that were different in kind from those suffered by other members of the public. It was not enough that the damages were different in degree. Do you agree with the way the court applied this test to the facts? See also *A.G. Man. v. Adventure Flights Centre Ltd.* (1983), 25 C.C.L.T. 295 (Man. Q.B.); and *Bolton v. Forest Pest Management Institute* (1985), 21 D.L.R. (4th) 242 (B.C. C.A.)

There is considerable authority for the view that a plaintiff in a private action for public nuisance need only suffer damages that are different in degree. See, for example, Linden, *Canadian Tort Law*, 5th ed. (1993), 505-6; and Fleming, *The Law of Torts*, 8th ed. (1992), 411-12.

6. Probably the largest single category of private actions for public nuisance involves plaintiffs injured on public sidewalks, highways or waterways. Newark has identified this development as the major reason for the blurring of the boundaries of nuisance — a subject which is so "intractable to definition and analysis that it immediately betrays its mongrel origins". "The Boundaries of Nuisance" (1949), 65 L.Q.R. 480. Fleming is equally critical, stating that these cases have "saddled the law with a series of capricious distinctions which are difficult to justify on any rational basis". *The Law of Torts*, 8th ed. (1992), 412. See also Laskin, "Torts — Nuisance or Negligence — Collisions On Highways With Standing Truck" (1944), 22 Can. Bar Rev. 468.

The Canadian case law reflects these difficulties. See, for example, *Lickoch v. Madu* (1973), 34 D.L.R. (3d) 569 (Alta. C.A.); *Goodwin v. Pine Point Park* (1974), 54 D.L.R. (3d) 498 (Ont. C.A.); and *Chessie v. J.D. Irvine Ltd.* (1982), 140 D.L.R. (3d) 501 (N.B. C.A.).

7. For a discussion of nuisance in the context of environmental concerns see Silverman and Evans, "Aeronautical Noise in Canada" (1972), 10 Osgoode Hall L.J. 607; McLaren, "The Common Law Nuisance Actions And The Environmental Battle — Well Tempered Swords or Broken Reeds" (1972), 10 Osgoode Hall L.J. 505; McLaren, "The Law of Torts and Pollution" in L.S.U.C., Special Lectures 1973, *New Developments in the Law of Torts*, 309; Jeffery, "Environmental Enforcement and Regulation in the 1980's . . ." (1984), 10 Queen's L.J. 43; and Cross, "Does Only the Careless Polluter Pay? A Fresh Look at the Nature of Private Nuisance" (1995), 111 L.Q.R. 445.

4. Remedies

MENDEZ v. PALAZZI

(1976), 68 D.L.R. 582 (Ont. Co. Ct.)

HOLLINGWORTH CO. CT. J.: . . . The nub of this action is that roots from the poplar trees have allegedly ruined the plaintiffs' lawn, rock-garden and patio, and are allegedly threatening the septic tank, weeping tiles, and indeed the foundation of the plaintiffs' home and have gravely interfered with the enjoyment of their property.

. . .

What are the plaintiffs' remedies? It is necessary to decide whether damages are a proper remedy or whether a mandatory injunction shall issue or perhaps at the very least a *quia timet* injunction. The governing principles are set forth in the judgment of A.L. Smith, L.J., in *Shelfer v. London Electric Lighting Co.*, [1895] 1 Ch. 287 at pp. 322-3:

> (1.) If the injury to the plaintiff's legal rights is small,
> (2.) And is one which is capable of being estimated in money,
> (3.) And is one which can be adequately compensated by a small money payment,
> (4.) And the case is one in which it would be oppressive to the defendant to grant an injunction:--

. . .

These principles have been followed in Ontario by Middleton, J.A., in *Duchman v. Oakland Dairy Co. Ltd.* (1928), 63 O.L.R. 111 at p. 134, [1929] 1 D.L.R. 9 at p. 16, and by Morden J., in *Walker et al. v. Pioneer Construction Co. (1967) Ltd.* (1975), 8 O.R. (2d) 35 at p. 51, 56 D.L.R. (3d) 677 at p. 693. I would hold in this case that paras. (2), (3) and (4) of A.L. Smith, L.J.'s dicta would be apposite. Is an injunction justified?

A careful review of the Canadian case law reveals no Canadian case in point.

There are, however, English and Commonwealth authorities which are pertinent. In *Middleton v. Humphries* (1912), 47 I.L.T. 160, an Irish case before Ross, J., damage was caused to the plaintiff by the roots of a tree. The trial Judge had no trouble granting an injunction restraining the defendants from continuing to permit the injury and also awarded damages. Similarly, in *Butler v. Standard Telephones & Cables, Ltd.*, [1940] 1 K.B. 399, the plaintiff's house was damaged by Lombardy poplar roots burrowing under the house. Damages were awarded as apparently an injunction, although pleaded, was not asked for at trial.

In *McCombe v. Read et al.*, [1955] 2 All E.R. 458, again poplar roots damaged a house. Harman, J., granted damages and an injunction. In *Davey v. Harrow Corp.*, [1957] 2 All E.R. 305, the plaintiff obtained damages and an injunction when the roots "caused subsidence so that his house has been extensively damaged". Finally, in *Morgan v. Khyatt*, [1964] 1 W.L.R. 475, the Board, on Appeal from the Supreme Court of New Zealand, affirmed that Court's decision in granting damages and an injunction when the roots from four pohutukawa trees damaged a concrete wall and drains.

In order for an injunction to issue, as I read the cases, there must be two conditions precedent. First, there must be actual damage; second, that damage must be substantial. In the case at bar there is actual damage to the lawn, as I have found as a fact, but not that degree of substantial damage, for example, damage to the house foundation or the tile beds, to merit issuing a mandatory injunction. To order here a mandatory injunction would, in the words of A.L. Smith, L.J., be "oppressive to the defendant" but should a *quia timet* injunction issue? The principles governing the *quia timet* injunction have been cited by Pearson, J., in the case of *Fletcher v. Bealey* (1884), 28 Ch. D. 688. At p. 698 the learned Judge laid down the two necessary ingredients:

> [1] There must, if no actual damage is proved, be proof of *imminent danger*, and [2] there must also be proof that the apprehended damage will, if it comes, be very substantial.

[Emphasis added.] I would say it must be proved damage will be irreparable; if the danger is not proved to be so imminent that no one can doubt that if the remedy is delayed the damage will be suffered, I think it must be shown that, if the damage does occur at any time, it will come in such a way and under such circumstances, that it will be impossible for the plaintiffs to protect themselves against it if relief is denied to them in a *quia timet* injunction.

Here, there was no evidence at all that the roots had reached the tile bed. Although one root shoot was found near the house, there is no probative evidence before me that the basement has settled or has been damaged as a result of root action. Finally, although plaintiffs' counsel argued for a *quia timet* injunction, his pleadings are silent on this matter.

Therefore, a *quia timet* injunction shall not issue.

. . .

[The judge found damages to be the appropriate remedy and awarded the plaintiffs $500 special and general damages.]

NOTES AND QUESTIONS

1. A *quia timet* injunction is sought to prevent future threatened harm. A mandatory injunction is one which compels the party to do or refrain from doing a certain thing. Although the case does not make this clear, it appears the plaintiff was seeking a mandatory *quia timet* injunction.

2. Should the court have refused the injunction? What difference did it make to the plaintiff?

3. *Fletcher*, a case relied upon in *Mendez*, was reinterpreted in *Hooper v. Rogers*, [1975] Ch. 43 (C.A.). In *Hooper*, the court said that the requirement of "imminent danger" merely raised the issue of whether the plaintiff's request for an injunction was premature. Would *Mendez* have been decided differently using this approach?

4. For additional Canadian cases involving the granting of injunctions see *Palmer v. N.S. Forest Indust.* (1983), 2 D.L.R. (4th) 397 (N.S. S.C.); *Bolton v. Forest Pest Management Institute* (1985), 21 D.L.R. (4th) 242 (B.C. C.A.); *Banfai v. Formula Fun Centre Inc.* (1984), 34 C.C.L.T. 171 (Ont. H.C.); *A.G. N.S. v. Beaver* (1985), 32 C.C.L.T. 170 (N.S. C.A.); and *Hynes v. Hynes* (1989), 3 R.P.R. (2d) 142 (Nfld. C.A.); *Nippa v. C.H. Lewis (Lucan) Ltd.* (1991), 82 D.L.R. (4th) 417 (Ont. Gen. Div.); and *Ward v. Magna International Inc.* (1994), 21 C.C.L.T. (2d) 178 (Ont. Gen. Div.).

MILLER v. JACKSON

[1977] Q.B. 966, [1977] 3 All E.R. 338 (C.A.)

[The plaintiffs bought a house in a new subdivision which was adjacent to a small well-established cricket club. They sued the club in nuisance and negligence after a number of balls had been hit onto their property, causing minor damage to their house and garden. In an effort to prevent injury to the plaintiffs, the club had erected a high fence and instructed batsmen to keep their shots down. The club also offered to place a net over the plaintiffs' garden whenever there was a game, to install unbreakable window glass, to provide shutters and to pay for any damage. The plaintiffs rejected these offers and sought damages and an injunction. At trial, the plaintiffs succeeded in both nuisance and negligence, and were awarded damages and granted an injunction. The defendant appealed.

A lengthy excerpt of this case was included in chapter 13. It may be helpful to read that excerpt before reading the following extract, which is limited to the issue of nuisance and the appropriate remedy.]

LORD DENNING M.R.:

. . . In our present case, too, nuisance was pleaded as an alternative to negligence. The tort of nuisance in many cases overlaps the tort of negligence. The boundary lines were discussed in two adjoining cases in the Privy Council: *The Wagon Mound (No. 2)* and *Goldman v. Hargrave*. But there is at any rate one important distinction between them. It lies in the nature of the remedy sought. Is it damages? Or an injunction? If the plaintiff seeks a remedy in damages for injury done to him or his property, he can lay his claim either in *negligence* or *nuisance*. But, if he seeks an injunction to stop the playing of cricket altogether, I think he must make his claim in nuisance. The books are full of cases where an injunction has been granted to restrain the continuance of a nuisance. But there is no case, so far as I know, where it has been granted so as to stop a man being negligent. At any rate in a case of this kind, where an occupier of a house or land seeks to restrain his neighbour from doing something on his own land, the only appropriate cause of action, on which to base the remedy of an injunction is nuisance: see the report of the Law Commission. It is the very essence of a private nuisance that it is the unreasonable use by a man of his land to the detriment of his neighbour. He must have been guilty of the fault, not necessarily of negligence, but of the unreasonable use of the land: see *The Wagon Mound (No. 2)* by Lord Reid.

It has often been said in nuisance cases that the rule is sic utere tuo ut alienum non laedas. But that is a most misleading maxim. Lord Wright put it in its proper place in *Sedleigh-Denfield v. O'Callaghan:*

> [It] is not only lacking in definiteness but is also inaccurate. An occupier may make in many ways a use of his land which causes damage to the neighbouring landowners, yet be free from liability . . . a useful test is perhaps what is reasonable according to the ordinary usages of mankind living in society, or, more correctly, in a particular society.

I would, therefore, adopt this test: is the use by the cricket club of this ground for playing cricket a reasonable use of it. To my mind it is a most reasonable use. Just consider the circumstances. For over 70 years the game of cricket has been played on this ground to the great benefit of the community as a whole, and to the injury of none. No one could suggest that it was a nuisance to the neighbouring owners simply because an enthusiastic batsman occasionally hit a ball out of the ground for six to the approval of the admiring onlookers. Then I would ask: does it suddenly become a nuisance because one of the neighbours chooses to build a house on the very edge of the ground, in such a position that it may well be struck by the ball on the rare occasion when there is a hit for six? To my mind the answer is plainly No. The building of the house does not convert the playing of cricket into a nuisance when it was not so before. If and insofar as any damage is caused to the house or anyone in it, it is because of the position in which it was built.

. . .

In this case it is our task to balance the right of the cricket club to continue playing on their cricket ground, as against the right of the householder not to be interfered with. On taking the balance, I would give priority to the right of the cricket club to continue playing cricket on the ground, as they have done for the last 70 years. It takes precedence over the right of the newcomer to sit in his garden undisturbed. After all he bought the house four years ago in mid-summer when the cricket season was at its height. He might have guessed that there was a risk that a hit might possibly land on his property. If he finds that he does not like it, he ought, when cricket is played, to sit in the other side of the house or in the front garden, or go out; or take advantage of the offers the club have made to him of fitting unbreakable glass, and so forth. Or, if he does not like that, he ought to sell his house and move elsewhere. I expect there are many who would gladly buy it in order to be near the cricket field and open space. At any rate he ought not to be allowed to stop cricket being played on this ground.

This case is new. It should be approached on principles applicable to modern conditions. There is a contest here between the interests of the public at large and the interest of a private individual. The *public* interest lies in protecting the environment by preserving our playing fields in the face of mounting development, and by enabling our youth to enjoy all the benefits of outdoor games, such as cricket and football. The *private* interest lies in securing the privacy of his home and garden without intrusion or interference by anyone. In deciding between these two conflicting interests, it must be remembered that it is not a question of damages. If by a million to one chance a cricket ball does go out of the ground and cause damage, the cricket club will pay. There is no difficulty on that score. No, it is a question of an injunction. And in our law you will find it repeatedly affirmed that an injunction is a discretionary remedy. In a new situation like this, we have to think afresh as to how discretion should be exercised. On the one hand, Mrs. Miller is a very sensitive lady who has worked herself up into such a state that she exclaimed to the judge:

> I just want to be allowed to live in peace. Have we got to wait until someone is killed before anything can be done?

If she feels like that about it, it is quite plain that, for peace in the future, one or other has to move. Either the cricket club have to move, but goodness knows where. I do not suppose for a moment there is any field in Lintz to which they could move. Or Mrs. Miller must move elsewhere. As between their conflicting interests, I am of opinion that the public interest should prevail over the private interest. The cricket club should not be driven out. In my opinion the right exercise of discretion is to refuse an injunction; and, of course, to refuse damages in lieu of an injunction. Likewise as to the claim for past damages. The club were entitled to use this ground for cricket in the accustomed way. It was not a nuisance, nor was it negligence of them so to run it. Nor was the batsman negligent when he hit the ball for six. All were doing simply what they were entitled to do. So if the club had put it to the test, I would have dismissed the claim for damages also. But as the club very fairly say that they are willing to pay for any damage, I am content that there should be an award of £400 to cover any past or future damage.

. . .

I would allow the appeal, accordingly.

. . .

GEOFFREY LANE L.J. . . . The only question is whether it is unreasonable. It is a truism to say that this is a matter of degree. What that means is this. A balance has to be maintained between on the one hand the rights of the individual to enjoy his house and garden without the threat of damage and on the other hand the rights of the public in general or a neighbour to engage in lawful pastimes. Difficult questions may sometimes arise when the defendants' activities are offensive to the senses, for example by way of noise. Where, as here, the damage or potential damage is physical the answer is more simple. There is, subject to what appears hereafter, no excuse I can see which exonerates the defendants from liability in nuisance for what they have done and what they threaten to do. It is true no one has yet been physically injured. That is probably due to a great extent to the fact that the householders in Brackenridge desert their gardens whilst cricket is in progress. The danger of injury is obvious and is not slight enough to be disregarded. There is here a real risk of serious injury.

There is, however, one obviously strong point in the defendants' favour. They or their predecessors have been playing cricket on this ground (and no doubt hitting sixes out of it) for 70 years or so. Can someone by building a house on the edge of the field in circumstances where it must have been obvious that balls might be hit over the fence, effectively stop cricket being played? Precedent apart, justice would seem to demand that the plaintiffs should be left to make the most of the site they have elected to occupy with all its obvious advantages and all its equally obvious disadvantages. It is pleasant to have an open space over which to look from your bedroom and sitting room windows, so far as it is possible to see over the concrete wall. Why should you complain of the obvious disadvantages which arise from the particular purpose to which the open space is being put? Put briefly, can the defendants take advantage of the fact that the plaintiffs have put themselves in such a position by coming to occupy a house on the edge of a small cricket field, with the result that what was not a nuisance in the past now becomes a nuisance? If the matter were res integra, I confess I should be inclined to find for the defendants. It does not seem just that a long-established activity, in itself innocuous, should be brought to an end because someone chooses to build a house nearby and so turn an innocent pastime into an actionable nuisance. Unfortunately, however, the question is not open. In *Sturges v. Bridgman* this very problem arose. The defendant had carried on a confectionery shop with a noisy pestle and mortar for more than 20 years. Although it was noisy, it was far enough away from neighbouring premises not to cause trouble to anyone, until the plaintiff, who was a physician, built a consulting-room on his own land but immediately adjoining the confectionery shop. The noise and vibrations seriously interfered with the consulting-room and became a nuisance to the physician. The defendant contended that he had acquired the right either at common law or under the Prescription Act 1832 by uninterrupted use for more than 20 years to impose the inconvenience. It was held by the Court of Appeal, affirming the judgment of Jessel MR, that use such as this which was, prior to the construction of the consulting-room, neither preventible nor actionable, could not found a prescriptive right. That decision involved the assumption, which so far as one can discover has never been questioned, that it is no answer to a claim in nuisance for the defendant to show that the plaintiff brought the trouble on his own head by building or coming to live in a house so close to the defendant's premises that he would inevitably be affected by the defendant's activities, where no one had been affected previously. See also *Bliss v. Hall*. It may be that this rule works injustice, it may be that one would decide the matter differently in the absence of authority. But we are bound by the decision in *Sturges v. Bridgman* and it is not for this court as I see it to alter a rule which has stood for so long.

Injunction

Given that the defendants are guilty of both negligence and nuisance, is it a case where the court should in its discretion give relief, or should the plaintiffs be left to their remedy in damages? There is no doubt that if cricket is played damage will be done to the plaintiffs' tiles or windows or both. There is not inconsiderable danger that if they or their son or their guests spend any time in the garden during the weekend afternoons in the summer they may be hit by a cricket ball. So long as this situation exists it seems to be that damages cannot be said to provide an adequate form of relief. Indeed, quite apart from the risk of physical injury, I can see no valid reason why the plaintiffs should have to submit to the inevitable breakage of tiles and/or windows, even though the defendants have expressed their willingness to carry out any repairs at no cost to the plaintiffs. I would accordingly uphold the grant of the injunction to restrain the defendants from committing nuisance. However, I would postpone the operation of the injunction for 12 months to enable the defendants to look elsewhere for an alternative pitch.

. . .

CUMMING-BRUCE L.J.:

So on the facts of this case a court of equity must seek to strike a fair balance between the right of the plaintiffs to have quiet enjoyment of their house and garden without exposure to cricket balls occasionally falling like thunderbolts from the heavens, and the opportunity of the inhabitants of the village in which they live to continue to enjoy the manly sport which constitutes a summer recreation for adults and young persons, including one would hope and I expect the plaintiff's son. It is a relevant circumstance which a court of equity should take into account that the plaintiffs decided to buy a house which in June 1972 when completion took place was obviously on the boundary of a quite small cricket ground where cricket was played at weekends and sometimes on evenings during the working week. They selected a house with the benefit of an open space beside it. In February, when they first saw it, they did not think about the use of this open space. But before completion they must have realized it was the village cricket ground, and that balls would sometimes be knocked from the wicket into their garden, or even against the fabric of the house. If they did not realize it, they should have done. As it turns out, the female plaintiff has developed a somewhat obsessive attitude to the proximity of the cricket field and the cricketers who visit her to seek to recover their balls. The evidence discloses a hostility which goes beyond what is reasonable, although as the learned judge found she is reasonable in her fear that if the family use the garden while a match is in progress they will run the risk of serious injury if a great hit happens to drive a ball up to the skies and down into their garden. It is reasonable to decide that during matches the family must keep out of the garden. The risk of damage to the house can be dealt with in other ways, and is not such as to fortify significantly the case for an injunction stopping play on this ground.

With all respect, in my view the learned judge did not have regard sufficiently to these considerations. He does not appear to have had regard sufficiently to these considerations. He does not appear to have had regard to the interest of the inhabitants of the village as a whole. Had he done so he would in my view have been led to the conclusion that the plaintiffs having accepted the benefit of the open space marching with their land should accept the restrictions on enjoyment of their garden which they may reasonably think necessary. That is the burden which they have to bear in order that the inhabitants of the village may not be deprived of their facilities for an innocent recreation which they have so long enjoyed on this ground. There are here special circumstances which should inhibit a court of equity from granting the injunction claimed.

. . .

[Appeal allowed. Past and future damages assessed at £400.]

SPUR INDUST. INC. v. DEL E. WEBB DEV. CO.

(1972), 494 P. (2d) 700 (Ariz. S.C.)

[The appellant operated a cattle feedlot. For many years the area had been exclusively agricultural. In 1959, the respondent began to plan a new city. To this end, 20,000 acres of farmland were purchased at a price considerably lower than that in nearby Phoenix. As the city expanded, the respondent found that the smells generated by the appellant's business made it impossible to sell his lots. Proceedings were then issued by the respondent, alleging that the feedlot was a nuisance because of the flies and odours that it generated.]

CAMERON VICE CHIEF JUSTICE. From a judgment permanently enjoining the defendant, Spur Industries, Inc. from operating a cattle feedlot near the plaintiff Del E. Webb Development Company's Sun City, Spur appeals. Webb cross-appeals. Although numerous issues are raised, we feel that it is necessary to answer only two questions. They are:

1. Where the operation of a business, such as a cattle feedlot is lawful in the first instance, but becomes a nuisance by reason of a nearby residential area, may the feedlot operation be enjoined in an action brought by the developer of the residential area?
2. Assuming that the nuisance may be enjoined, may the developer of a completely new town or urban area in a previously agricultural area be required to indemnify the operator of the feedlot who must move or cease operation because of the presence of the residential area created by the developer?

MAY SPUR BE ENJOINED?

[1.2] The difference between a private nuisance and a public nuisance is generally one of degree. A private nuisance is one affecting a single individual or a definite small number of persons in the enjoyment of private rights not common to the public, while a public nuisance is one affecting the rights enjoyed by citizens as a part of the public. To constitute a public nuisance, the nuisance must affect a considerable number of people or an entire community or neighbourhood. City of Phoenix v. Johnson, 51 Ariz. 115, 75 P. 2d 30 (1938).

[3] Where the injury is slight, the remedy for minor inconveniences lies in an action for damages rather than in one for an injunction. Kubby v. Hammond, 68 Ariz. 17, 198 P. 2d 134 (1948). Moreover, some courts have held, in the "balancing of inconveniences" cases, that damages may be the sole remedy. See Boomer v. Atlantic Cement Co. 26 N.Y. 2d 219, 309 N.Y.S. 2d 312, 257 N.E. 2d 870, 40 A.L.R. 3d 590 (1970), and annotation comments, 40 A.L.R. 3d 601.

Thus, it would appear from the admittedly incomplete record as developed in the trial court, that, at most, residents of Youngtown would be entitled to damages rather than injunctive relief.

We have no difficulty, however, in agreeing with the conclusion of the trial court that Spur's operation was an enjoinable public nuisance as far as the people in the southern portion of Del Webb's Sun City were concerned.

. . .

Del Webb, having shown a special injury in the loss of sales, had a standing to bring suit to enjoin the nuisance. Engle v. Clark, 53 Ariz. 472, 90 P. 2d 994 (1939); City of Phoenix v. Johnson, supra. The judgment of the trial court permanently enjoining the operation of the feedlot is affirmed.

MUST DEL WEBB INDEMNIFY SPUR?

A suit to enjoin a nuisance sounds in equity and the courts have long recognized a special responsibility to the public when acting as a court of equity.

In addition to protecting the public interest, however, courts of equity are concerned with protecting the operator of a lawfully, albeit noxious, business from the result of a knowing and wilful encroachment by others near his business.

In the so-called "coming to the nuisance" cases, the courts have held that the residential landowner may not have relief if he knowingly came into a neighbourhood reserved for industrial or agricultural endeavours and has been damaged thereby:

> Plaintiff chose to live in an area uncontrolled by zoning laws or restrictive covenants and remote from urban development. In such an area plaintiffs cannot complain that legitimate agricultural pursuits are being carried on in the vicinity, nor can plaintiffs, having chosen to build in an agricultural area, complain that the agricultural pursuits carried on in the area depreciate the value of their homes. The area being *primarily agricultural* any opinion reflecting the value of such property must take this factor into account. The standards affecting the value of residence property in an urban setting, subject to zoning controls and controlled planning techniques, cannot be the standards by which agricultural properties are judged.
>
> People employed in a city who build their homes in suburban areas of the county beyond the limits of a city and zoning regulations do so for a reason. Some do so to avoid the high taxation rate imposed by cities, or to avoid special assessments for street, sewer and water projects. They usually build on improved or hard surface highways, which have been built either at state or county expense and thereby avoid special assessments for these improvements. It may be that they desire to get away from the congestion of traffic, smoke, noise, foul air and the many other annoyances of city life. But with all these advantages in going beyond the area which is zoned and restricted to protect them in their homes, they must be prepared to take the disadvantages.

Dill v. Excel Packing Company, 183 Kan. 513, 525, 526, 331 P. 2d 539, 548, 549 (1958). See also East St. Johns Shingle Co. v. City of Portland, 195 Or. 505, 246 P. 2d 554, 560-562 (1952).

And:

> ... a party cannot justly call upon the law to make that place suitable for his residence which was not so when he selected it ...

Gilbert v. Showerman, 23 Mich. 448, 455, 2 Brown 158 (1871).

Were Webb the only party injured, we would feel justified in holding that the doctrine of "coming to the nuisance" would have been a bar to the relief asked by Webb, and, on the other hand, had Spur located the feedlot near the outskirts of a city and had the city grown toward the feedlot, Spur would have to suffer the cost of abating the nuisance as to those people locating within the growth pattern of the expanding city:

> The case affords, perhaps, an example where a business established at a place remote from population is gradually surrounded and becomes part of a populous center, so that a business which formerly was not an interference with the rights of others has become so by the encroachment of the population. ...

City of Ft. Smith v. Western Hide & Fur Co., 153 Ark. 99, 103, 239 S.W. 724, 726 (1922).

We agree, however, with the Massachusetts court that:

> The law of nuisance affords no rigid rule to be applied in all instances. It is elastic. It undertakes to require only that which is fair and reasonable under all the circumstances. In a commonwealth like this, which depends for its material prosperity so largely on the continued growth and enlargement of manufacturing of diverse varieties, "extreme rights" cannot be enforced . . .

Stevens v. Rockport Granite Co., 216 Mass. 486, 488, 104 N.E. 371, 373 (1914).

[7] There was no indication in the instant case at the time Spur and its predecessors located in Western Maricopa County that a new city would spring up, full-blown, alongside the feeding operation and that the developer of that city would ask the court to order Spur to move because of the new city. Spur is required to move not because of any wrongdoing on the part of Spur, but because of a proper and legitimate regard of the courts for the rights and interests of the public.

Del Webb, on the other hand, is entitled to the relief prayed for (a permanent injunction), not because Webb is blameless, but because of the damage to the people who have been encouraged to purchase homes in Sun City. It does not equitably or legally follow, however, that Webb, being entitled to the injunction, is then free of any liability to Spur if Webb has in fact been the cause of the damage Spur has sustained. It does not seem harsh to require a developer, who has taken advantage of the lesser land values in a rural area as well as the availability of large tracts of land on which to build and develop a new town or city in the area, to indemnify those who are forced to leave as a result.

Having brought people to the nuisance to the foreseeable detriment of Spur, Webb must indemnify Spur for a reasonable amount of the cost of moving or shutting down. It should be noted that this relief to Spur is limited to a case wherein a developer has, with foreseeability, brought into a previously agricultural or industrial area the population which makes necessary the granting of an injunction against a lawful business and for which the business has no adequate relief.

It is therefore the decision of this court that the matter be remanded to the trial court for a hearing upon the damages sustained by the defendant Spur as a reasonable and direct result of the granting of the permanent injunction. Since the result of the appeal may appear novel and both sides have obtained a measure of relief, it is ordered that each side will bear its own costs.

NOTES AND QUESTIONS

1. Given that Lord Denning would have denied relief even if the defendants had refused to pay damages, which of the three suggested outcomes in *Miller* is preferable? Which approach maximizes social resources? What other factors should the court consider? Is *Miller* an appropriate case for the unusual remedy adopted in *Spur*?

2. Generally, an individual is viewed as having merely an interest, rather than a right, in the reasonable use and enjoyment of her land. This stands in contrast to the situation in trespass which protects an individual's right to the uninterrupted possession of her land. This feature of nuisance explains Denning M.R.'s and Cumming-Bruce L.J.'s balancing of interests approach in *Miller*. However, if there is a physical interference, particularly if it is repeated, the courts will usually hold that it constitutes a nuisance and will grant an injunction. In effect, the courts are treating these types of physical interferences as an invasion of the plaintiff's property rights. This was the approach of Geoffrey Lane L.J. in *Miller*, which was approved in *Kennaway v. Thompson*, [1980] 3 All E.R. 329 (C.A.). Does

the fact that the interference is physical and repeated justify the granting of an injunction, virtually as a matter of right? See generally Sharpe, *Injunctions and Specific Performance*, 2nd ed. (1992), 4-1 to 4-37.

3. Do you agree with the result in *Spur*? What factors should be considered in adopting this solution in other cases? What would have been the result in *Spur* if the court had found for the defendant?

4. The court in *Spur* gave considerable weight to the position of the individuals who had bought property in the plaintiff's development. Assume the defendant had established that it could not have relocated in the same area and that many of its present staff would have lost their jobs if an injunction were granted. Should this be relevant to the court's decision? See *Bottom v. Ont. Leaf Tobacco Co.*, [1935] O.R. 205 (C.A.). See generally Hawkins, "In and Of Itself: Some Thoughts on the Assignment of Property Rights in Nuisance Cases" (1978), 36 U. of T. Fac. L. Rev. 209; and Ogus and Richardson, "Economics and the Environment: A Study of Private Nuisance", [1977] Cambridge L.J. 284. Should the same principles be applied in granting remedies in public and private nuisance? See *Boomer v. Atl. Cement Co.* (1970), 257 N.E. (2d) 870 (N.Y. C.A.).

5. What role did the doctrine of "coming to the nuisance" play in the judge's analysis in *Spur*? The majority of the American cases do not recognize the fact that the plaintiff "came to the nuisance" as a defence, provided the plaintiff bought the land in good faith and not for the purpose of bringing a lawsuit. Despite Lord Denning's view, the English authorities also support this principle. See Heuston and Buckley, *Salmond and Heuston on the Law of Torts*, 20th ed. (1992), 78-79; Rogers, *Winfield and Jolowicz on Tort*, 14th ed. (1994), 429-30; and Keeton *et al.*, *Prosser and also Keeton on Torts*, 5th ed. (1984), 634-36.

6. Calabresi and Melamed provide an interesting analysis of nuisance remedies in "Property Rules, Liability Rules and Inalienability: One View of the Cathedral" (1972), 85 Harv. L. Rev. 1089. The authors suggest that the courts must first decide which party "to entitle" in a nuisance action, and then must decide whether to grant the entitled party "property rule protection" or "liability rule protection". The authors distinguish between the rules in the following manner at 1092:

> An entitlement is protected by a property rule to the extent that someone who wishes to remove the entitlement from its holder must buy it from him in a voluntary transaction in which the value of the entitlement is agreed upon by the seller. It is the form of entitlement which gives rise to the least amount of state intervention: once the original entitlement is decided upon, the state does not try to decide its value. It lets each of the parties say how much the entitlement is worth to him . . .

> Whenever someone may destroy the initial entitlement if he is willing to pay an objectively determined value for it, an entitlement is protected by a liability rule. This value may be what it is thought the original holder of the entitlement would have sold it for. But the holder's complaint that he would have demanded more will not avail him once the objectively determined value is set. Obviously, liability rules involve an additional stage of state intervention: not only are entitlements protected, but their transfer or destruction is allowed on the basis of a value determined by some organ of the state rather than by the parties themselves.

For example, if the court had granted the Millers an injunction, that would have amounted to entitling them with property rule protection. If the cricket club wished to continue, it would have had to reach an agreement with the Millers, perhaps by compensating them or purchasing their home. If the club violated the injunction it could have been held in contempt. By refusing to award an injunction, the court entitled the Millers with liability rule protection. The club would be liable in damages for any interference with the Millers' property. In this case, it is the court and not the parties that determine the amount of compensation. The following chart illustrates the authors' approach in reference to *Miller*.

	Entitle the Homeowner	*Entitle the Cricket Club*
Property Rule	Injunction to enjoin club	Neither injunction nor damages
Liability Rule	Damages for future interference, but no injunction.	Allow injunction, but the plaintiff must pay to relocate the club.

How do you think the authors would have resolved *Miller* and *Spur*? Can you suggest circumstances in which the property rule would be preferable to the liability rule and vice versa? Will the authors' approach likely produce different results than those produced by the existing doctrine?

See Note, "Injunction Negotiations: An Economic, Moral and Legal Analysis" (1975), 27 Stan. L. Rev. 1563; Polinsky, "Resolving Nuisance Disputes: The Simple Economics of Injunctive and Damage Remedies" (1980), 32 Stan. L. Rev. 1075; and Prichard, "An Economic Analysis of *Miller v. Jackson*" (1985), Cambridge Lect. 171.

7. A common law alternative to seeking damages and an injunction is the remedy of abatement of nuisance. Like the other self-help remedies, abatement can be traced to the early years of the common law. It provided an expedient, informal and inexpensive alternative to legal proceedings. However, it also entailed a potential for violence if the person against whom it was invoked chose to resist. This limitation, common to all self-help remedies, explains the recent trend toward restricting abatement. The case law is quite complex, particularly in regard to rights of entry. Wactor has provided a useful summary of the major principles governing abatement. He lists several factors the courts consider in upholding the defence of abatement, including: does the nuisance regularly manifest itself and require an immediate remedy; will the benefit of abatement be lost by waiting for a judicial remedy; and can the abatement be effected without a breach of the peace or unnecessary damage? The defendant may be held civilly, and even criminally, liable if she breaches the peace, causes damage or trespasses without notice. See Wactor, "Self-Help: A Viable Remedy for Nuisance: A Guide for the Common Man's Lawyer" (1982), 24 Arizona L. Rev. 83 at 98. See also Heuston and Buckley, *Salmond and Heuston on Tort*, 20th ed. (1992), 585-87; and Keeton *et. al.*, *Prosser and Keeton on Torts*, 5th ed. (1984), 641-43.

REVIEW PROBLEM

Jonathan Bognor is the owner of a farm on which he had raised dairy cattle. When he purchased the farm in 1959, a steel mill owned by the National Steel Corporation, a company 50 per cent owned by the federal government, was already operating on federal land about one mile from the farm's nearest boundary. The steel mill is and was a visible source of air pollution because its relies on tall chimneys as a method of dispersing pollutants. This was a common approach to air pollution problems in 1959, but it is one that is no longer used in new plants. Technologies such as electrostatic precipitators now represent the state of the art in stationary source pollution control.

The price that Bognor paid for the farm was several thousand dollars less than the price of comparable properties situated further away from the mill. In the past, however, the pollutants had never had any serious discernible effect on Bognor's farm. The only possible apparent effect had been a slight browning of some grass, and Bognor had never been sure whether this was caused by the mill.

In 1978, dairy prices fell drastically. Foreseeing a difficult period ahead for dairy farmers, Bognor decided to diversify his farming activities in order to obtain greater security against future market fluctuations. After making extensive inquiries, he decided to grow blueberries, strawberries and other fruits.

The results of his first season's crop were disastrous. Most of the fruit was covered with brown speckles. A consultant advised Bognor that the brown speckles had been caused by sulphuric acid, which in turn was caused by the emissions from the steel mill. The consultant also said that this acid caused the browning of the grass and that Bognor's new crops were much more sensitive to the acid. The consultant's report noted that it had not been known when the steel mill was established that sulphur from the coal fuel could mix with moisture in the atmosphere and produce sulphuric acid. In recent years, however, this connection had been clearly established and had been much discussed in the scientific literature.

Bognor is the only farmer in the area suffering such damage because he is the only one who has switched from dairy farming. It is also clear that the operators at the steel mill have no idea that they are harming Bognor's farming operations.

The steel mill was established by a federal statute which stated that the Corporation was author-ized to erect a steel mill and to use the federal land for this purpose.

Bognor now wishes to sue the Corporation for both damages and an injunction. Advise him.

THE TORT LIABILITY OF PUBLIC
AUTHORITIES

1. Introduction
2. Judicial Review
3. Special Immunity Rules
4. The Tort Liability of Administrative Authorities

1. Introduction

Many of the day-to-day functions of government are delegated by legislation to public authorities. Typically, the legislation creates a statutory agency or office and defines the jurisdiction within which it is empowered to operate. In Canada, an extremely broad range of public functions is performed by various public authorities. These include marketing, licensing and professional boards, regulatory agencies, investigatory commissions, prison administrations, police forces, labour arbitrators, and municipal governments. The legal remedies available against a public authority that misuses its power vary depending largely upon the nature of its enabling legislation.

For the purposes of both tort and administrative law, it is important to classify public authorities according to the specific functions which they perform. Some public authorities are empowered to enact rules or regulations, and when doing so they are performing a legislative function. Thus, a municipal government generally performs a legislative function when it passes municipal by-laws. Other public authorities perform quasi-judicial functions, resolving disputes within a limited jurisdiction. In some of these situations the authority hears submissions by counsel, receives evidence under oath and in other respects closely resembles a court of law. In other quasi-judicial settings, the proceedings are far less formal. A statutory labour arbitrator performs a quasi-judicial function when interpreting the labour relations legislation governing a union-management dispute. More commonly, however, statutory public authorities perform administrative functions. Generally, they do not adjudicate claims between adversarial parties, but rather establish and apply policy which affects the public. For example, a liquor licence board would be performing an administrative function when deciding that no alcoholic beverages are to be sold at professional sporting events.

It is important for analytical purposes to classify the function at issue, rather than the public authority which is performing it, because a public authority may perform several different functions. For example, if a liquor licence board meets to evaluate complaints about a tavern owner's conduct and decides to revoke the tavern's licence for breaching the act, the board is performing a quasi-judicial function.

The chapter begins with a brief discussion of judicial review, which is the main means of challenging the actions of public authorities. Although the administrative law remedy of judicial review is substantively and procedurally distinct from the tort remedy, it is difficult to understand the tort principles without an appreciation of the fundamental concepts of judicial review. Next, we discuss the special immunity rules that protect public authorities from tort liability when performing legislative and quasi-judicial functions. Finally, we consider the special difficulties that arise when suing an administrative public authority in tort.

2. Judicial Review

At common law, superior courts exercised control over inferior courts through prerogative writs. These writs have been expanded and may now be used to control virtually any statutory public authority. Several provinces have incorporated the old prerogative writs into new statutory remedies, but the character of the available remedies has not greatly changed.

In theory, judicial review is an entirely different remedy from an appeal. In an application for judicial review, the court is not concerned with the merits of the decision, but rather with its lawfulness. The enabling statute that creates the public authority specifies the area of competence within which the public authority is authorized or directed to act. For example, a municipal building inspector might be empowered by statute to inspect and supervise new residential housing construction within the municipality. If the inspector purports to deal with commercial buildings or with residential buildings outside of the municipality, he is obviously acting *ultra vires*, that is, outside his statutory mandate. An aggrieved individual could apply for judicial review, seeking an order prohibiting the inspector from continuing to act in an *ultra vires* manner and an order quashing any *ultra vires* decisions that the inspector has already made.

If, however, the inspector makes a decision that is within his statutory mandate, that determination should not be reconsidered by the reviewing court. Thus, even if the court concludes that the inspector erred in applying the building code to a residential building within the municipality, it should not interfere. In the absence of a statutory right of appeal, the court assumes that the legislature intended the public authority to have the final say on any issue within its jurisdiction. An aggrieved individual is left to pursue complaints about the merits of an *intra vires* decision through the political process.

The basic issue in the remainder of this chapter is whether the plaintiff can successfully sue the public authority in tort law, in addition to or in lieu of pursuing these administrative law remedies.

3. Special Immunity Rules

(a) MEMBERS OF PARLIAMENT AND THE LEGISLATURES

Members of the federal and provincial legislatures enjoy a wide range of legal privileges and immunities. These evolved during the British Parliament's struggle for power and independence, and they cannot be fully understood without a detailed knowledge of parliamentary history. Of particular interest is the immunity that members enjoy for torts committed during proceedings in, or necessarily incidental to, parliament. Members are not thereby placed above the law. Rather, it is the responsibility of the legislature, not the courts, to sanction improper conduct arising from parliamentary proceedings.

(b) JUDICIAL OFFICERS

BRADLEY v. FISHER

(1872), 80 U.S. 646 (S.C.)

[The plaintiff was a member of the Bar of the Supreme Court in the District of Columbia, and the defendant was a judge of the Criminal Court in that jurisdiction. As a result of the plaintiff's contemptuous language and conduct, the defendant directed an order striking the plaintiff's name from the roll of attorneys practicing in the Criminal Court. This was subsequently interpreted as also striking the plaintiff from the rolls of the Supreme Court. A judge of the Criminal Court had no jurisdiction to strike an attorney from the rolls of the Supreme Court, and the plaintiff sued to recover damages suffered because he was unable to practice in the Supreme Court. The United States Supreme Court held that the defendant was not responsible for that error. The Court then went on to consider the defendant's plea of judicial immunity. The judgment of the majority was delivered by Field J.]

. . .

FIELD J.: — For it is a general principle of the highest importance to the proper administration of justice that a judicial officer, in exercising the authority vested in him, shall be free to act upon his own convictions, without apprehension of personal consequence to himself. Liability to answer to everyone who might feel himself aggrieved by the action of the judge, would be inconsistent with the possession of this freedom, and would destroy that independence without which no judiciary can be either respectable or useful. As observed by a distinguished English judge, it would establish the weakness of the judicial authority in a degrading responsibility. *Taaffe v. Downes*, 3 Moore, P.C. 41, n.

The principle, therefore, which exempts judges of courts of superior or general authority from liability in a civil action for acts done by them in the exercise of their judicial functions, obtains in all countries where there is any well-ordered system of jurisprudence. It has been the settled doctrine of the English courts for many centuries, and has never been denied, that we are aware of, in the courts of this country.

It has, as Chancellor Kent observes, "a deep root in the common law." *Yates v. Lansing*, 5 Johns, 291.

Nor can this exemption of the judges from civil liability be affected by the motives with which their judicial acts are performed. The purity of their motives cannot in this way be the subject of judicial inquiry. This was adjudged in the case of *Floyd and Barker*, reported by Coke, in 1608 (12 Coke, 25) where it was laid down that the judges of the realm could not be drawn in question for any supposed corruption impeaching the verity of their records, except before the King himself, and it was observed that if they were required to answer otherwise, it would "tend to the scandal and subversion of all justice, and those who are the most sincere, would not be free from continual calumniations."

The truth of this latter observation is manifest to all persons having much experience with judicial proceedings in the superior courts. Controversies involving not merely great pecuniary interests, but the liberty and character of the parties and, consequently, exciting deepest feelings, are being constantly determined in those courts, in which there is a great conflict in the evidence and great doubt as to the law which should govern their decision. It is this class of cases which imposes upon the judge the severest labor, and often creates in his mind a painful sense of responsibility. Yet it is precisely in this class of cases that the losing party feels most keenly the decision against him, and most readily accepts anything but the soundness of the decision in explanation of the action of the judge. Just in proportion to the strength of his convictions of the correctness of his own view of the case is he apt to complain of the judgment against him, and from complaints of the judgment to pass to the ascription of improper motives to the judge. When the controversy involves questions affecting large amounts of property or relates to a matter of general public concern, or touches the interests of numerous parties, the disappointment occasioned by an adverse decision, often finds vent in imputations of this character, and from the imperfection of human nature this is hardly a subject of wonder. If civil actions could be maintained in such cases against the judge, because the losing party should see fit to allege in his complaint that the acts of the judge were done with partiality, or maliciously or corruptly, the protection essential to judicial independence would be entirely swept away. Few persons sufficiently irritated to institute an action against a judge for his judicial acts would hesitate to ascribe any character to the acts which would be essential to the maintenance of the action.

If upon such allegations a judge could be compelled to answer in a civil action for his judicial acts, not only would his office be degraded and his usefulness destroyed, but he would be subjected for his protection to the necessity of preserving a complete record of all the evidence produced before him in every litigated case, and of the authorities cited and arguments presented, in order that he might be able to show to the judge before whom he might be summoned by the losing party — and that judge perhaps one of an inferior jurisdiction — that he had decided as he did with judicial integrity; and the second judge would be subjected to a similar burden, as he in his turn might also be held amenable by the losing party.

. . .

[Davis and Clifford JJ. dissented, holding that the plaintiff was entitled to sue if he alleged both an error of jurisdiction, and a malicious or corrupt act by the judge. Appeal disallowed; rulings of the court below affirmed.]

NOTES AND QUESTIONS

1. The privileges of legislators are at least partially governed by statutes in all Canadian jurisdictions. See, for example, Parliament of Canada Act, R.S.C. 1985, c. P-1, s. 4. See also *Roman Corp.*

v. Hudson's Bay Oil & Gas Co. (1973), 36 D.L.R. (3d) 413 (S.C.C.); May, *Parliamentary Practice*, 19th ed. (1976), 67-115; and Chisholm, "Cautionary tales for actions against Cabinet", Ont. Lawyers Weekly, Nov. 8, 1985, 1.

2. There are relatively few actions brought against judicial officers. The older case law is very complex. See generally Thompson, "Judicial Immunity and the Protection of Justices" (1958), 21 Mod. L. Rev. 517; Rubenstein, "Liability in Tort of Judicial Officers" (1964), 15 U. of T L.J. 317; Brazier, "Judicial Immunity and the Independence of the Judiciary", [1976] Pub. Law 397; Sadler, "Judicial and Quasi-Judicial Immunities: A Remedy Denied" (1982), 13 Melb. U. L. Rev. 508; and Rosenberg, "Whatever Happened to Absolute Judicial Immunity?" (1984), 21 Hous. L. Rev. 875.

3. There has been a longstanding debate as to whether judicial immunity should be limited to judges of superior courts, extended to judges of courts of record, or applied to all judges and even justices. It would now appear that immunity extends to any court of record. In *Sirros v. Moore*, [1974] 3 All E.R. 776 (C.A.), Lord Denning indicated that the immunity rule ought to cover all judges and justices. However, he failed to consider the Justices Protection Act, 1848 (11 & 12 Vict.), c. 44 which governs the liability of justices of the peace. See *McC v. Mullan*, [1984] 3 All E.R. 908 (H.L.). There is similar legislation in the common law jurisdictions of Canada. Generally, the legislation distinguishes between judicial acts done within jurisdiction and errors committed without or in excess of jurisdiction. A justice acting within his jurisdiction can only be held liable in tort if the plaintiff can establish that the justice acted maliciously and without reasonable and probable grounds. See *Foran v. Tatangello* (1976), 73 D.L.R. (3d) 126 (Ont. H.C.); and Feldthusen, "Judicial Immunity: In Search of an Appropriate Limiting Formula" (1980), 29 U.N.B.L.J. 73, at 80. Do you agree with Denning L.J. that the immunity granted judges should not vary according to the level of court? See also *Morier v. Rivard*, [1985] 2 S.C.R. 716.

4. There is federal and provincial legislation which permits a reviewing court upon quashing a conviction to issue an order protecting the original judge from tort liability. See, for example, the Criminal Code, R.S.C. 1985, c. C-46, s. 783; and the Justices and Judges Protection Act, R.S.N. 1989, c. 243, s. 14(1). No clear governing principles appear to have emerged in this area. See generally, *Re Royal Can. Legion Branch 177* (1964), 48 D.L.R. (2d) 164 (B.C. S.C.); *Re Yoner* (1969), 7 D.L.R. (3d) 185 (B.C. S.C.); and Johnson, "Tort Liability: . . ." (1971), 4 Ottawa L. Rev. 627.

5. In *Nelles v. Ont.* (1989), 60 D.L.R. (4th) 609 (S.C.C.), the court held that the Crown was protected by statute from civil suits based on how it discharged its judicial responsibilities. However, it denied immunity to the Attorney-General and Crown Attorneys personally. L'Heureux-Dubé J., dissenting in part, objected to personal liability for acts done in the furtherance of public functions. The court reviewed the rationale and authority for judicial as well as prosecutorial immunity. See also, *MacAlpine v. H. (T.)* (1991), 7 C.C.L.T. (2d) 113 (B.C. C.A.); *Prete v. Ontario* (1993), 16 O.R. (3d) 161 (C.A.), leave to appeal ref'd. (1994), 17 O.R. (3d) xvi (note) (S.C.C.); and *Milgaard v. Kujawa*, [1994] 1 W.W.R. 338 (Sask. Q.B.), aff'd. [1994] 9 W.W.R. 305 (Sask. C.A.), leave to appeal ref'd. [1995] 2 W.W.R. lxiv (note) (S.C.C.).

6. In *MacKeigan v. Hickman*, [1989] 2 S.C.R. 796, the court affirmed judicial immunity from being compelled to testify about the decision-making process or composition of the court in a particular case. This immunity principle is grounded in constitutional theory about the independence of the judiciary from legislative control. The decision summarized much of the relevant background to the Donald Marshall Inquiry in Nova Scotia.

7. The courts have extended judicial immunity to public authorities other than judges who perform quasi-judicial functions. However, no clear position has emerged to determine which boards, tribunals and officials will be granted immunity and which will not. See *Everett v. Griffiths*, [1921] 1 A.C. 631 (H.L.); *Calvert v. Law Soc. of Upper Can.* (1981), 121 D.L.R. (3d) 169 (Ont. H.C.); *Howarth v. The Queen* (1984), 29 C.C.L.T. 157 (Fed. Ct.), aff'd. (1985), 13 Admin. L.R. 189 (Fed. C.A.); and *Lonrho plc. v. Tebbit*, [1991] 4 All E.R. 973 (Ch.). See also Rubinstein, "Liability in Tort of Judicial Officers" (1964), 15 U. of T. L.J. 317; Brazier, "Judicial Immunity and the Independence of the Judiciary", [1976] Pub. Law 397; and Sadler, "Judicial and Quasi-Judicial Immunities: A Remedy Denied" (1982), 4 Melb. U.L. Rev. 508.

8. Are the arguments in favour of limiting the liability of judicial officers compelling? Which types of judicial decisions should be immune to liability and which types should not? Answer these same questions in relation to Attorneys General, crown counsel, and quasi-judicial decision makers.

4. The Tort Liability of Administrative Authorities

(a) PRELIMINARY ISSUES

In addition to the substantive difficulties which arise when suing a public authority, there are a number of procedural issues which must be addressed.

Special limitation periods apply to actions brought against most public authorities. Invariably, these limitation periods are shorter than the general tort limitation periods. These special limitation periods may be found not only in the enabling legislation, but also in general legislation governing Crown agencies and public authorities. In addition, there may be other limiting provisions, such as a requirement that the public authority be notified prior to issuing the writ.

It must also be determined whether the public authority is capable of being sued. For example, a marketing board is neither a natural person nor a private corporation, and it may not have a legal status which enables it to sue or be sued. Occasionally, the enabling legislation will address this issue, but more frequently the legislation is silent and the courts must resolve this point. No conclusive guidelines have yet emerged.

Finally, difficulties may arise if the public authority is a Crown agent. Not all public authorities are Crown agencies — only those over which the Crown has a significant degree of actual or potential control are characterized as such. The problem is that at common law the Crown cannot be sanctioned by the courts. Consequently, the Crown is only liable to the extent that it voluntarily assumes liability by statute. In most jurisdictions, the Crown has assumed vicarious liability for the torts of its servants and agents. However, the specific provisions of the legislation are often complicated.

NOTES AND QUESTIONS

1. For examples of legislation imposing special limitation periods or other special procedural rules, see the Justices and Judges Protection Act, R.S.N. 1989, c. 243; and the Protection of Persons Acting Under Statute Act, R.S.N.B. 1973, c. P-20. Special limitation periods and other procedural rules applying to suits against public authorities have been challenged under the Charter, usually under s. 15, with varying outcomes. See for example, *Colangelo v. Mississauga (City)* (1988), 53 D.L.R. (4th) 145 (Ont. C.A.), in which the relevant case law is reviewed; and *Miradizadeh v. Ont.* (1989), 66 O.R. (2d) 422 (C.A.). See also, *Prete v. Ontario* (1993), 16 O.R. (3d) 161 (C.A.), leave to appeal ref'd. (1994), 17 O.R. (3d) xvi (note) (S.C.C.).

2. On the issue of whether a public authority is capable of being sued, see *MacLean v. Liquor Licence Bd. of Ont.* (1975), 51 D.L.R. (3d) 64, rev'd. in part (1975), 61 D.L.R. (3d) 237 (Div. Ct.). *MacLean* also dealt with the issue of whether the Board was an agent of the Crown.

3. For an excellent discussion of the Ontario legislation which deals with suing the Crown, see Goldenberg, "Tort Actions Against the Crown in Ontario", in *Law Society of Upper Canada, Special Lectures* (1973), 341-412. The other common law provinces have similar legislation.

(b) INTENTIONAL TORTS AND NUISANCE

Citizens enjoy rights against intentional interference with their person or property. The relevant actions are usually derived from the writ of trespass *vi et armis*. These actions may be enforced against a public authority in the same manner as a private defendant. However, the otherwise tortious interference may be expressly, or by necessary implication, authorized by statute. To rely on the defence of statutory authority, the defendant must prove its actions were *intra vires* of its statutory jurisdiction. Public authorities may exceed jurisdiction in a number of ways, including failing to obey statutory conditions, breaching the implied rules of procedural justice, or acting for a purpose knowingly foreign to the object of administration. Liability in trespass, for example, based on the *ultra vires* conduct of a public authority is strict and relatively straightforward.

Although actions in nuisance protect a plaintiff's interests in land use, not freedom from interference, the Supreme Court of Canada has decided to treat the defence of statutory authority in nuisance much as it would be treated in trespass.

Purely economic interests have never enjoyed the relatively strict protection granted to interests in land. Actions against public authorities under the intentional economic torts tend to require proof of bad faith such as deliberate abuse of statutory authority.

RONCARELLI v. DUPLESSIS

[1959] S.C.R. 121, 16 D.L.R. (2d) 689

[The plaintiff was the proprietor of a first class restaurant in Montreal which had held a liquor licence for 34 years. He was also a member of the Witnesses of Jehovah, a religious sect whose printed works had been provoking considerable social unrest in the primarily Roman Catholic province of Quebec. Starting in 1945, the provincial authorities had arrested large numbers of the Witnesses of Jehovah in an effort to end what they considered to be the group's insulting and offensive conduct. The plaintiff had provided bail for approximately 380 Jehovah's Witnesses. Beyond that, the plaintiff had not engaged in behaviour which the provincial government found objectionable.

Mr. Archambault, the Liquor Commissioner, notified Mr. Duplessis, the Attorney General and Premier of Quebec, of the plaintiff's conduct. Duplessis, feeling that his position in the provincial government required him to do so, directed Mr. Archambault to refuse to renew the plaintiff's liquor licence. The plaintiff sued Mr. Duplessis for his loss of profits, stemming from the government's refusal to renew the restaurant's liquor licence.

The relevant legislation gave Mr. Archambault the sole authority to grant or cancel liquor licences, and specified that the "Commission may cancel any permit at its discretion".

In a 6-to-3 judgment, the defendant was held liable, and the plaintiff was awarded approximately $33,000. Mr. Justice Martland, with whom Kerwin C.J. and Locke J. agreed, gave one majority judgment. Mr. Justice Rand, with whom Judson J. agreed, gave another, and Abbott J. gave a third. Justices Taschereau, Cartwright and Fauteaux gave separate dissenting judgments. Only a brief excerpt of Rand J.'s judgment is reprinted below.]

RAND J.: . . . At the same time the issue of permits has a complementary interest in those so catering to the public. The continuance of the permit over the years, as in this case, not only recognizes its virtual necessity to a superior class restaurant but also its identification with the business carried on. The provisions for assignment of the permit are to this most pertinent and they were exemplified in the continuity of the business here. As its exercise continues, the economic life of the holder becomes progressively more deeply implicated with the privilege while at the same time his vocation becomes correspondingly dependent on it.

The field of licensed occupations and businesses of this nature is steadily becoming of greater concern to citizens generally. It is a matter of vital importance that a public administration that can refuse to allow a person to enter or continue a calling which, in the absence of regulation, would be free and legitimate, should be conducted with complete impartiality and integrity; and that the grounds for refusing or cancelling a permit should unquestionably be such and such only as are incompatible with the purposes envisaged by the statute: the duty of a Commission is to serve those purposes and those only. A decision to deny or cancel such a privilege lies within the "discretion" of the Commission; but that means that decision is to be based upon a weighing of considerations pertinent to the object of the administration.

In public regulation of this sort there is no such thing as absolute and untrammelled "discretion", that is that action can be taken on any ground or for any reason that can be suggested to the mind of the administrator; no legislative Act can, without express language, be taken to contemplate an unlimited arbitrary power, exercisable for any purpose, however capricious or irrelevant, regardless of the nature or purpose of the statute. Fraud and corruption in the Commission may not be mentioned in such statutes but they are always implied as exceptions. "Discretion" necessarily implies good faith in discharging public duty; there is always a perspective within which a statute is intended to operate; and any clear departure from its lines or objects is just as objectionable as fraud or corruption. Could an applicant be refused a permit because he had been born in another Province, or because of the colour of his hair? The ordinary language of the Legislature cannot be so distorted.

To deny or revoke a permit because a citizen exercises an unchallengeable right totally irrelevant to the sale of liquor in a restaurant is equally beyond the scope of the discretion conferred. There was here not only revocation of the existing permit but a declaration of a future, definitive disqualification of the appellant to obtain one: it was to be "forever". This purports to divest his citizenship status of its incident of membership in the class of those of the public to whom such a privilege could be extended. Under the statutory language here, that is not competent to the Commission and *a fortiori* to the Government or the respondent: *McGillivray v. Kimber* (1915), 26 D.L.R. 164, 52 S.C.R. 146. There is here an administrative tribunal which, in certain respects, is to act in a judicial manner; and even on the view of the dissenting Justices in *McGillivray*, there is liability: what could be more malicious than to punish this licensee for having done what he had an absolute right to do in a matter utterly irrelevant to the *Alcoholic Liquor Act*? Malice in the proper sense is simply acting for a reason or purpose knowingly foreign to the administration, to which was added here the element of intentional punishment by what was virtually vocation outlawry.

It may be difficult if not impossible in cases generally to demonstrate a breach of this public duty in the illegal purpose served; there may be no means, even if proceedings against the Commission were permitted by the Attorney-General, as here they were refused, of compelling the Commission to justify a refusal or revocation or to give reasons for its actions; on these questions I make no observation; but in the case before us that difficulty is not present: the reasons are openly avowed.

The act of the respondent through the instrumentality of the Commission brought about a breach of an implied public statutory duty toward the appellant; it was a gross abuse of legal power expressly intended to punish him for an act wholly irrelevant to the statute, a punishment which inflicted on him, as it was intended to do, the destruction of his economic life as a restaurant keeper within the Province. Whatever may be the immunity of the Commission or its member from an action for damages, there is none in the respondent. He was under no duty in relation to the appellant and his act was an intrusion upon the functions of a statutory body. The injury done by him was a fault engaging liability within the principles of the underlying public law of Quebec: *Mostyn v. Fabrigas* (1774), 1 Cowp. 161, 98 E.R. 1021, and under art. 1053 of the *Civil Code*. That, in the presence of expanding administrative regulation of economic activities, such a step and its consequences are to be suffered by the victim without recourse or remedy, that an administration according to law is to be superseded by action dictated by and according to the arbitrary likes, dislikes and irrelevant purposes of public officers acting beyond their duty, would signalize the beginning of disintegration of the rule of law as a fundamental postulate of our constitutional structure. An administration of licences on the highest level of fair and impartial treatment to all may be forced to follow the practice of "first come, first served", which makes the strictest observance of equal responsibility to all of even greater importance; at this stage of developing government it would be a danger of high consequence to tolerate such a departure from good faith in executing the legislative purpose. It should be added, however, that that principle is not, by this language, intended to be extended to ordinary governmental employment: with that we are not here concerned.

It was urged by Mr. Beaulieu that the respondent, as the incumbent of an office of state, so long as he was proceeding in "good faith", was free to act in a matter of this kind virtually as he pleased. The office of Attorney-General traditionally and by statute carries duties that relate to advising the Executive, including here, administrative bodies, enforcing the public law and directing the administration of justice. In any decision of the statutory body in this case, he had no part to play beyond giving advice on legal questions arising. In that role this action should have been limited to advice on the validity of a revocation for such a reason or purpose and what that advice should have been does not seem to me to admit of any doubt. To pass from this limited scope of action to that of bringing about a step by the Commission beyond the bounds prescribed by the Legislature for its exclusive action converted what was done into his personal act.

"Good faith" in this context, applicable both to the respondent and the General Manager, means carrying out the statute according to its intent and for its purpose; it means good faith in acting with a rational appreciation of that intent and purpose and not with an improper intent or for an alien purpose; it does not mean for the purposes of punishing a person for exercising an unchallengeable right; it does not mean arbitrarily and illegally attempting to divest a citizen of an incident of his civil status.

NOTES AND QUESTIONS

1. *Roncarelli* was an action brought under article 1053 of the Quebec Civil Code. How would you have framed this case if it had been brought in a common law jurisdiction? Would the result have been different if the case had been brought in a common law court? Would any of the common law legislative immunity rules have protected Duplessis?

2. How does Rand J. define malice and good faith??

3. What is the basis for Rand J.'s finding of liability? Is liability predicated on intentional excess of jurisdiction, excess of jurisdiction independent of any intent, improper purpose, or a combination of these factors?

4. Fauteaux and Taschereau JJ. dissented on the basis that Roncarelli had failed to give Duplessis adequate notice in breach of article 88 of the Code of Civil Procedure, which reads: "No public officer or other person fulfilling any public function or duty can be sued for damages by reason of any act done by him in the exercise of his functions. ... unless notice of such action has been given him at least one month before the issue of the writ of summons..." How do you think the majority avoided the effect of this section?

5. Cartwright J. gave a separate dissenting judgment in *Roncarelli*. He held that the defendant was exercising an administrative discretion which should not be reviewed by the courts. Alternatively, if the defendant was exercising a quasi-judicial function, Cartwright J. argued that he should be protected by judicial immunity. Do you agree that judicial immunity should be extended to those performing quasi-judicial functions? Even if the principles of judicial immunity applied, would they have protected Duplessis given the facts of the case? Is there any justification for absolving public authorities of liability if they abuse their powers?

6. There is some authority for the existence of a tort which might be characterized as malfeasance in public office. For example, *Smith v. East Elloe Rural Dist. Council*, [1956] 1 All E.R. 855 (H.L.) and *David v. Abdul Cader*, [1963] 3 All E.R. 579 (P.C.) appear to support a cause of action for malicious abuse of power. See also *Farrington v. Thomson*, [1959] V.R. 286 (Vict. S.C.), a case in which the court imposed liability for a deliberate and knowing excess of jurisdiction. See *Sirros v. Moore*, [1974] 3 All E.R. 776 (C.A.); and *MacKenzie v. MacLachlin*, [1979] 1 N.Z.L.R. 670 (S.C.). But see *Shaw v. Trudel* (1988), 44 C.C.L.T. 194 (Man. Q.B.), which held that abuse of power *per se* is not a cause of action.

7. The concepts of *ultra vires* or jurisdictional error are extremely complex, and are beyond the scope of this chapter. For present purposes the brief explanation in section 2 will suffice.

8. Even in trespass cases, it is not always clear whether a public authority's bad faith influenced the court to hold it liable. See *Cooper v. Wandsworth Bd. Of Works* (1863), 143 E.R. 414 (C.P.); and *Sulisz v. Flin Flon* (1979), 9 C.C.L.T. 89 (Man. Q.B.).

9. The defence of statutory authority in nuisance is outlined in *Tock v. St. John's Metro. Area Bd.*, [1989] 2 S.C.R. 1181, excerpted in chapter 26. See Klar, "The Supreme Court of Canada: Extending the Tort Liability of Public Authorities" (1990), 28 Alta. L. Rev. 648. See also, *Canada (Attorney General) v. Ottawa-Carleton (Regional Municipality)* (1991), 5 O.R. (3d) 11 (C.A.).

10. For an example of the application of the intentional economic torts to public authorities, see *Gershman v. Man. Vegetable Producers' Marketing Bd.* (1976), 69 D.L.R. (3d) 114 (Man. C.A.), excerpted in chapter 21.

(c) NEGLIGENCE LIABILITY

Absent express statutory language to the contrary, a public authority, just as any private employer, may be held vicariously liable for torts committed by its employees. More problematic is the independent liability of the authority for alleged negligence in its own policy-making and implementation spheres.

For analytical purposes, it is important to first establish whether the public authority is vested with a statutory duty or power. If the enabling legislation requires the public authority to take a particular course of action, the authority is exercising a statutory duty. If the authority has discretion, it is exercising a statutory power. Although a public authority may be held liable in negligence in both cases, the governing principles differ.

As indicated earlier, a public authority will not be held liable for doing what it is required to do by statute. However, a public authority can be held liable for negligently performing its statutory duty. Moreover, the authority's failure to fulfill its statutory duty may be considered by the court in determining whether to recognize a common law cause of action. A public authority exercising a statutory duty has no discretion, and the courts need not be concerned with usurping the statutory mandate that the legislature has given the authority.

The courts have been more cautious about holding a public authority liable in negligence when it exercises a statutory power. In these situations, the legislature has expressly given the public authority discretion in making decisions. Consequently, the courts have been concerned that by imposing liability in negligence, they would be substituting their assessment of what constitutes reasonable conduct for that of the public authority.

JUST v. B.C.

[1989] 2 S.C.R. 1228

The judgment of Dickson C.J. and Wilson, La Forest, L'Heureux-Dubé, Gonthier and Cory JJ. was delivered by

CORY J. — This appeal puts in issue the approach that should be taken by courts when considering the liability of government agencies in tort actions.

Factual Background

On the morning of January 16, 1982, the appellant and his daughter set out, undoubtedly with high hopes and great expectations, for a day of skiing at Whistler Mountain. As a result of a heavy snow fall they were forced to stop in the northbound line of traffic on Highway 99. While they were waiting for the traffic to move forward a great boulder weighing more than a ton somehow worked loose from the wooded slopes above the highway and came crashing down upon the appellant's car. The impact killed the appellant's daughter and caused him very serious injuries. He then brought this action against the respondent contending that it had negligently failed to maintain the highway properly.

Highway 99 is a major commuter road between Vancouver and the major ski resorts located at Whistler Mountain. The appellant alleged that there had been earlier rock falls near the scene of the tragedy. As well it was said that the climatic conditions of freezing and thawing, coupled with a heavy build-up of snow in the trees and resulting tree damage created a great risk of rock falls. Trees were said to be a well-known factor in levering rocks loose. It was contended that inadequate attention had been given to all these factors by the respondent and that a reasonable inspection would have demonstrated that the rock constituted a danger to users of the highway.

At the time of the accident the Department of Highways had set up a system for inspection and remedial work upon rock slopes particularly along Highway 99. At the apex of the organization was a Mr. Eastman, the regional geotechnical material engineer. He is a specialist in rock slope maintenance and together with another engineer was responsible for inspecting rock slopes and making recommendations regarding their stability.

. . .

Was the Decision of the Rockwork Section as to the Quantity and Quality of Inspections a "Policy" Decision Exempting the Respondent from Liability?

The respondent placed great reliance on the decision of this Court in *Barratt v. District of North Vancouver*, [1980] 2 S.C.R. 418. In the *Barratt* case injury occurred as a result of a pothole on the road. It was established that the City of North Vancouver had a policy of inspecting its roads for potholes every two weeks. Indeed it had inspected the road where the accident occurred one week earlier and found no pothole. It was found that the inspection policy established by the municipality was a reasonable and proper one. However, Justice Martland in giving the reasons for this Court went on to express an opinion that the municipality could not be held negligent for formulating one inspection policy rather than another. He put it this way at pp. 427-28:

> In essence, he [the trial judge] is finding that the Municipality should have instituted a system of continuous inspection to ensure that no possible damage could occur and holds that, in the absence of such a system, if damage occurs, the Municipality must be held liable.
>
> In my opinion, no such duty existed. The Municipality, a public authority, exercised its power to maintain Marine Drive. It was under no statutory duty to do so. Its method of exercising its power was a matter of policy to be determined by the Municipality itself. If, in the implementation of its policy its servants acted negligently, causing damage, liability could arise, but the Municipality cannot be held to be negligent because it formulated one policy of operation rather than another.

This statement was not necessary to the decision as it had already been determined that the system of inspection established by the municipality was eminently reasonable. Neither was there any serious question raised that there had been any negligence in carrying out the system of inspection. The finding that a reasonable system of inspection had been established and carried out without negligence constituted the basis for the conclusion reached by the Court in that case. With the greatest respect, I am of the view that the portion of the reasons relied on by the respondent went farther than was necessary to the decision or appropriate as a statement of principle. For example, the Court would not have approved as "policy" a system that called for the inspection of the roads in a large urban municipality once every five years. Once a policy to inspect is established then it must be open to a litigant to attack the system as not having been adopted in a *bona fide* exercise of discretion and to demonstrate that in all the circumstances, including budgetary restraints, it is appropriate for a court to make a finding on the issue.

The functions of government and government agencies have multiplied enormously in this century. Often government agencies were and continue to be the best suited entities and indeed the only organizations which could protect the public in the diverse and difficult situations arising in so many fields. They may encompass such matters as the manufacture and distribution of food and drug products, energy production, environmental protection, transportation and tourism, fire prevention and building developments. The increasing complexities of life involve agencies of government in almost every aspect of daily living. Over the passage of time the increased government activities gave rise to incidents that would have led to tortious liability if they had occurred between private citizens. The early governmental immunity from tortious liability became intolerable. This led to the enactment of legislation which in general imposed liability on the Crown for its acts as though it were a person. However, the Crown is not a person and must be free to govern and make true policy decisions without becoming subject to tort liability as a result of those decisions. On the other hand, complete Crown immunity should not be restored by having every government decision designated as one of "policy". Thus the dilemma giving rise to the continuing judicial struggle to differentiate between "policy" and "operation". Particularly difficult decisions will arise in situations where governmental inspections may be expected.

The dividing line between "policy" and "operation" is difficult to fix, yet it is essential that it be done. The need for drawing the line was expressed with great clarity by Becker J. of the United States District Court, in *Blessing v. United States*, 447 F.S. 1160. The case required him to deal with a claim under the *Federal Tort Claims Act*, 28 U.S.C. § 2680 which provides:

> The provisions of this chapter and section 1346(b) of this title shall not apply to —
> (a) Any claim based upon an act or omission of an employee of the Government, exercising due care, in the execution of a statute or regulation, whether or not such statute or regulation be valid, or based upon the exercise or performance or the failure to exercise or perform a discretionary function or duty on the part of a federal agency or an employee of the Government, whether or not the discretion involved be abused.

He wrote at p. 1170:

> Read as a whole and with an eye to discerning a policy behind this provision, it seems to us only to articulate a policy of preventing tort actions from becoming a vehicle for judicial interference with decisionmaking that is properly exercised by other branches of the government and of protecting "the Government from liability that would seriously handicap efficient government operations," *United States v. Muniz*, 374 U.S. 150, 163, 83 S.Ct. 1850, 1858, 10 L.Ed.2d 805 (1963). Statutes, regulations, and discretionary functions, the subject matter of § 2680(a), are, as a rule, manifestations of policy judgments made by the political branches. In our tripartite governmental structure, the courts generally have no substantive part to play in such decisions. Rather, the judiciary confines itself — or, under laws such as the FTCA's discretionary function exception, is confined — to adjudication of facts based on discernible objective standards of law. In the context of tort actions, with which we are here concerned, these objective standards are notably lacking when the question is not negligence but social wisdom, not due care but political practicability, not reasonableness but economic expediency. Tort law simply furnishes an inadequate crucible for testing the merits of social, political or economic decisions.
>
> . . .

The duty of care should apply to a public authority unless there is a valid basis for its exclusion. A true policy decision undertaken by a government agency constitutes such a valid basis for exclusion. What constitutes a policy decision may vary infinitely and may be made at different levels although usually at a high level.

The decisions in *Anns v. Merton London Borough Council* and *City of Kamloops v. Nielsen, supra,* indicate that a government agency in reaching a decision pertaining to inspection must act in a reasonable manner which constitutes a *bona fide* exercise of discretion. To do so they must specifically consider whether to inspect and if so, the system of inspection must be a reasonable one in all the circumstances.

For example, at a high level there may be a policy decision made concerning the inspection of lighthouses. If the policy decision is made that there is such a pressing need to maintain air safety by the construction of additional airport facilities with the result that no funds can be made available for lighthouse inspection, then this would constitute a *bona fide* exercise of discretion that would be unassailable. Should then a lighthouse beacon be extinguished as a result of the lack of inspection and a shipwreck ensue no liability can be placed upon the government agency. The result would be the same if a policy decision were made to increase the funds for job retraining and reduce the funds for lighthouse inspection so that a beacon could only be inspected every second year and as a result the light was extinguished. Once again this would constitute the *bona fide* exercise of discretion. Thus a decision either not to inspect at all or to reduce the number of inspections may be an unassailable policy decision. This is so provided it constitutes a reasonable exercise of *bona fide* discretion based, for example, upon the availability of funds.

On the other hand, if a decision is made to inspect lighthouse facilities the system of inspections must be reasonable and they must be made properly. See *Indian Towing Co.*, 350 U.S. 61 (1955). Thus once the policy decision to inspect has been made, the Court may review the scheme of inspection to ensure it is reasonable and has been reasonably carried out in light of all the circumstances, including the availability of funds, to determine whether the government agency has met the requisite standard of care.

At a lower level, government aircraft inspectors checking on the quality of manufactured aircraft parts at a factory may make a policy decision to make a spot check of manufactured items throughout the day as opposed to checking every item manufactured in the course of one hour of the day. Such a choice as to how the inspection was to be undertaken could well be necessitated by the lack of both trained personnel and funds to provide such inspection personnel. In those circumstances the policy decision that a spot check inspection would be made could not be attacked (See *United States v. S.A. Empresa De Viacao Aerea Rio Grandense (Varig Airlines)*, 467 U.S. 797 (1984).)

Thus a true policy decision may be made at a lower level provided that the government agency establishes that it was a reasonable decision in light of the surrounding circumstances.

The consideration of the duty of care that may be owed must be kept separate and distinct from the consideration of the standard of care that should be maintained by the government agency involved.

Let us assume a case where a duty of care is clearly owed by a governmental agency to an individual that is not exempted either by a statutory provision or because it was a true policy decision. In those circumstances the duty of care owed by the government agency would be the same as that owed by one person to another. Nevertheless the standard of care imposed upon the Crown may not be the same as that owed by an individual. An individual is expected to maintain his or her sidewalk or driveway reasonably, while a government agency such as the respondent may be responsible for the maintenance of hundreds of miles of highway. The frequency and the nature of inspection required of the individual may well be different from that required of the Crown. In each case the frequency and method must be reasonable in light of all the surrounding circumstances. The governmental agency should be entitled to demonstrate that balanced against the nature and quantity of the risk involved, its system of inspection was reasonable in light of all the circumstances including budgetary limits, the personnel and equipment available to it and that it had met the standard duty of care imposed upon it.

It may be convenient at this stage to summarize what I consider to be the principles applicable and the manner of proceeding in cases of this kind. As a general rule, the traditional tort law duty of care will apply to a government agency in the same way that it will apply to an individual. In determining whether a duty of care exists the first question to be resolved is whether the parties are in a relationship of sufficient proximity to warrant the imposition of such a duty. In the case of a government agency, exemption from this imposition of duty may occur as a result of an explicit statutory exemption. Alternatively, the exemption may arise as a result of the nature of the decision made by the government agency. That is, a government agency will be exempt from the imposition of a duty of care in situations which arise from its pure policy decisions.

In determining what constitutes such a policy decision, it should be borne in mind that such decisions are generally made by persons of a high level of authority in the agency, but may also properly be made by persons of a lower level of authority. The characterization of such a decision rests on the nature of the decision and not on the identity of the actors. As a general rule, decisions concerning budgetary allotments for departments or government agencies will be classified as policy decisions. Further, it must be recalled that a policy decision is open to challenge on the basis that it is not made in the *bona fide* exercise of discretion. If after due consideration it is found that a duty of care is owed by the government agency and no exemption by way of statute or policy decision-making is found to exist, a traditional torts analysis ensues and the issue of standard of care required of the government agency must next be considered.

The manner and quality of an inspection system is clearly part of the operational aspect of a governmental activity and falls to be assessed in the consideration of the standard of care issue. At this stage, the requisite standard of care to be applied to the particular operation must be assessed in light of all the surrounding circumstances including, for example, budgetary restraints and the availability of qualified personnel and equipment.

Turning to the case at bar it is now appropriate to apply the principles set forth by Mason J. in *Sutherland Shire Council v. Heyman, supra,* to determine whether the decision or decisions of the government agency were policy decisions exempting the province from liability. Here what was challenged was the manner in which the inspections were carried out, their frequency or infrequency and how and when trees above the rock cut should have been inspected, and the manner in which the cutting and scaling operations should have been carried out. In short, the public authority had settled on a plan which called upon it to inspect all slopes visually and then conduct further inspections of those slopes where the taking of additional safety measures was warranted. Those matters are all part and parcel of what Mason J. described as "the product of administrative direction, expert or professional opinion, technical standards or general standards of care". They were not decisions that could be designated as policy decisions. Rather they were manifestations of the implementation of the policy decision to inspect and were operational in nature. As such, they were subject to review by the Court to determine whether the respondent had been negligent or had satisfied the appropriate standard of care.

At trial the conclusion was reached that the number and frequency of inspections, of scaling and other remedial measures were matters of policy; as a result no findings of fact were made on the issues bearing on the standard of care.

Since the matter was one of operation the respondent was not immune from suit and the negligence issue had to be canvassed in its entirety. The appellant was therefore entitled to a finding of fact on these questions and a new trial should be directed to accomplish this.

. . .

SOPINKA J. (dissenting) — My colleague's reasons are based essentially on an attack on the policy of the respondent with respect to the extent and manner of the inspection program. In my opinion, absent evidence that a policy was adopted for some ulterior motive and not for a municipal purpose, it is *not* open to a litigant to attack it, nor is it appropriate for a court to pass upon it. As stated by Lord du Parcq in *Kent v. East Suffolk Rivers Catchment Board*, [1940] 1 K.B. 319, at p. 338:

> . . . it must be remembered that when Parliament has left it to a public authority to decide which of its powers it shall exercise, and when and to what extent it shall exercise them, there would be some inconvenience in submitting to the subsequent decision of a jury, or judge of fact, the question whether the authority had acted reasonably, a question involving the consideration of matters of policy and sometimes the striking of a just balance between the rival claims of efficiency and thrift.

This statement was approved by Lord Wilberforce in *Anns v. Merton London Borough Council*, [1978] A.C. 728, at p. 754.

If a court assumes the power to review a policy decision which is made in accordance with the statute, this amounts to a usurpation by the court of a power committed by statute to the designated body. As pointed out by Wilson J. in *City of Kamloops v. Nielsen, supra*, at pp. 9-10:

> It is for the local authority to decide what resources it should make available to carry out its role in supervising and controlling the activities of builders. For example, budgetary considerations may dictate how many inspectors should be hired for this purpose, what their qualifications should be, and how often inspections should be made. He approved the statement of du Parcq L.J. in *Kent v. East Suffolk Rivers Catchment Board* . . . that public authorities have to strike a balance between the claims of efficiency and thrift and whether they get the right balance can only be decided through the ballot box and not in the courts.

In *Anns v. Merton London Borough Council, supra*, Lord Wilberforce was of the opinion that although the exercise by a public authority of discretionary power was not entirely immune from attack, it was open to challenge only if no consideration was given to whether to exercise the power which, there as here, was whether to inspect and the manner of the inspection, *supra*, at p. 755. He did not elaborate as to whether such a challenge could be by way of a claim for damages by a person injured by the failure to inspect. Lord Salmon, however, was of the view that an improper exercise of discretion could only be corrected by *certiorari* or mandamus, and did not give rise to an action for damages, *supra*, at p. 762.

In the following passage, at p. 755, Lord Wilberforce makes it clear that a decision to inspect, and the time, manner and techniques of inspection, may all be within the discretionary power:

> There may be a discretionary element in its exercise — discretionary as to the time and manner of inspection, and the techniques to be used. A plaintiff complaining of negligence must prove, the burden being on him, that action taken was not within the limits of a discretion bona fide exercised, before he can begin to rely upon a common law duty of care. But if he can do this, he should, in principle, be able to sue.

If, as here, the statute creates no duty to inspect at all, but simply confers a power to do so, it follows logically that a decision to inspect and the extent and manner thereof are all discretionary powers of the authority.

It is not suggested here that the respondent failed to consider whether to inspect or the manner of inspections. The trial judge and the Court of Appeal found that a policy decision was made that inspections would be carried out by a crew of men called the Rockwork Section. In view of the fact that the crew had responsibility for the inspection of the slopes of all highways, the extent and manner of the inspection was delegated to the Rockwork Section. While it might be suggested that guidelines for inspection should have been laid down for the guidance of the crew, this would be second guessing the policy decision and not a matter for the Court. The appellant's attack on the conduct of the respondent and its employees is an attack on the manner in which they carried out the inspection and scaling of the mountain. The Rockwork Section had decided it could not closely monitor all slopes at all times. Some slopes would only be visually inspected from the highway. The appellant contended that the slopes above manmade cuts should have been closely inspected and that the trees should have been removed within ten feet of a cut slope. The trial judge made the following important findings concerning the decision of the respondent as to the extent and manner of the inspection program:

> The question in the case at bar is thus whether the failure of the Crown to take the steps which the plaintiff says it should have taken to prevent the rock fall was a matter of policy or operational. In order to answer it, it is necessary to consider the nature of the decisions here in question. The Crown had never established as a matter of policy that all slopes above highways must be inspected for potential rock fall. Nor had it laid out specific guidelines for dealing with problems if danger was perceived. What it had done was to establish a small crew of men (the rock scaling crew) to deal with problems arising on cliff faces throughout the Province. This crew responded to specific requests from various highway districts for inspection and scaling. For the most part, however, it developed and followed its own program. Given that it was responsible for inspection of slopes and appropriate remedial measures for all the highways in the Province, it could not closely monitor all slopes at all times. The slope here in question was visually inspected from the highway on a number of occasions. However, there had never been scaling or close inspection of the area above the cut because the rock scaling crew did not deem that work to be a priority.

In stating that the authority "must specifically consider whether to inspect and if so the system must be a reasonable one in all the circumstances", my colleague is extending liability beyond what was decided in *Anns v. Merton London Borough Council, Barratt v. District of North Vancouver,* and *City of Kamloops v. Nielsen, supra.* The system would include the time, manner and technique of inspection. On this analysis it is difficult to determine what aspect of a policy decision would be immune from review. All that is left is the decision to inspect. It can hardly be suggested that all the learning that has been expended on the difference between policy and operational was expended to immunize the decision of a public body that something will be done but not the content of what will be done. It seems to me that a decision to inspect rather than not inspect hardly needs protection from review. The concern that has resulted in extending immunity from review in respect of policy decisions is that those entrusted with the exercise of the statutory powers make the decision to expend public resources. It is not engaged by a decision simply to do something. It is the decision as to what is to be done that will entail the taxation of the public purse. Lord Wilberforce underscores this concern when he states, at p. 754:

> Let us examine the Public Health Act 1936 in the light of this. Undoubtedly it lays out a wide area of policy. It is for the local authority, a public and elected body, to decide upon the scale of resources which it can make available in order to carry out its functions under Part II of the Act — how many inspectors, with what expert qualifications, it should recruit, how often inspections are to be made, what tests are to be carried out, must be for its decision. It is no accident that the Act is drafted in terms of functions and powers rather than in terms of positive duty. As was well said, public authorities have to strike a balance between the claims of efficiency and thrift (du Parcq L.J. in *Kent v. East Suffolk Rivers Catchment Board* [1940] 1 K.B. 319, 338): whether they get the balance right can only be decided through the ballot box, not in the courts.

In this case, the extent of the inspection program was delegated to the Rockwork Section. The respondent acted within its statutory discretion in making that decision. It was a decision that inspections should be done and the manner in which they should be done. In order for a private duty to arise, it would have to be shown that the Rockwork Section acted outside its delegated discretion to determine whether to inspect and the manner in which the inspection is to be made.

NOTES AND QUESTIONS

1. What is the purpose of immunizing policy decisions? Do you agree? Why is this purpose not relevant in the operational sphere? Which definition of the operational sphere in *Just* makes better sense, if one accepts the purpose of policy immunity?

2. What special consideration does Cory J. extend to public authorities on the question of the standard of care? Why is the standard not the same as for private defendants? At this point, are the courts not usurping the public authorities' decision on how to allocate their budgets? Are courts institutionally competent to make such determinations?

3. Smillie has argued that public authorities should be under a duty of care whenever the same conduct would attract a duty if the defendant were a private citizen. See "Liability of Public Authorities For Negligence" (1985), 23 U.W.O. L. Rev. 213. Can a meaningful analogy be drawn to private conduct leading to a duty of care in *Just*? In contrast, Cohen and Smith emphasize the unique public authority aspects of cases such as *Just*, where the plaintiff's claim rests on her failure to obtain a public benefit. See "Entitlement and the Body Politic: Rethinking Negligence in Public Law" (1986), 64 Can. Bar Rev. 1. See also, Reynolds and Hicks, "New Directions for the Civil Liability of Public Authorities in Canada" (1992), 71 Can. Bar Rev. 1.

4. The negligence liability of police departments is particularly contentious. See generally, chapter 11; and McLure, "Duty to All and Duty to None: *Jane Doe v. Board of Commissioners of Police for the Municipality of Metropolitan Toronto*" (1991), 48 U.T. Fac. L. Rev. 168.

5. The policy/operational distinction was first articulated in *Anns*. It built upon the decision in *Dorset Yacht Co. v. Home Office*, [1970] A.C. 1004 (H.L.). There are many similarities between *Anns* and the decision in *Welbridge Holdings Ltd. v. Greater Winnipeg*, [1971] S.C.R. 957, where the court immunized legislative functions of municipal governments from negligence liability. See also, *Comeau's Sea Foods Ltd. v. Canada (Minister of Fisheries & Oceans)* (1992), 11 C.C.L.T. (2d) 241 (F.C. T.D.).

6. The policy/operational distinction has been endorsed throughout the Commonwealth, but there is considerable divergence in how it is interpreted within and among the different jurisdictions. The differences in the two judgments in *Just* are typical of these differences. Although Sopinka J. stood alone in *Just*, his opinion seems more in line with *Anns* itself and earlier decisions of the Supreme Court, including *Barratt v. North Vancouver* (1980), 14 C.C.L.T. 169 and *Welbridge Holdings*. In England, contrast *Dennis v. Charnwood Borough Council*, [1983] Q.B. 409 (C.A.); and *Fellowes v. Rother District Council*, [1983] 1 All E.R. 513 (Q.B.).

7. Prior to *Just*, the leading Canadian authority on the negligence liability of public authorities was *Kamloops v. Nielsen*, [1984] 2 S.C.R. 2. As in *Just*, the majority and minority disagreed on the

boundary between the policy and operational spheres. See Irvine, "Case Comment: *Kamloops v. Nielsen*" (1985), 29 C.C.L.T. 185; Gibson, "Tort Law" (1985), 7 Sup. Ct. L. Rev. 387, at 400-18; and Feldthusen, "*City of Kamloops v. Nielsen*: A Comment on the Supreme Court's Modest Clarification of Colonial Tort Law" (1985), 30 McGill L.J. 539.

8. For recent judicial applications of *Just* and *Kamloops*, see *Brown v. British Columbia (Minister of Transportation & Highways)* (1992), 10 C.C.L.T. 188 (B.C. C.A.), aff'd. [1994] 4 W.W.R. 194 (S.C.C.); *Swinamer v. Nova Scotia (Attorney General)* (1992), 10 C.C.L.T. (2d) 207 (N.S. C.A.), rev'd. (1994), 19 C.C.L.T. (2d) 233 (S.C.C.); *Mero v. Waterloo (Regional Municipality)* (1992), 10 C.C.L.T. (2d) 197 (Ont. C.A.), leave to appeal ref'd. (1992), 92 D.L.R. (4th) vi (note) (S.C.C.); *Arsenault v. Charlottetown (City)* (1992), 90 D.L.R. (4th) 379 (P.E.I. T.D.), leave to appeal ref'd. (1992), 95 D.L.R. (4th) vii (note) (S.C.C.); and *Lewis (Guardian ad litem of) v. British Columbia*, [1994] 6 W.W.R. 737 (B.C. S.C.), rev'd. [1996] 1 W.W.R. 489 (B.C. C.A.).

9. For recent discussions of the negligence liability of public authorities, see generally, Klar, "The Supreme Court of Canada: Extending the Tort Liability of Public Authorities" (1990), 28 Alta. L. Rev. 648; Woodall, "Private Law Liability of Public Authorities for Negligent Inspection and Regulation" (1992), 37 McGill L.J. 83; Cohen, "Government Liability for Economic Losses: The Case of Regulatory Failure" (1992), 20 Can. Bus. L.J. 215; Cohen and Finkle, "Crown Liability in Canada: Developing Compensation Policies for Regulatory Failure" (1994), 37 Can. Pub. Admin. 79; and Perell, "Negligence Claims Against Public Authorities" (1994), 16 Advoc. Q. 48.

10. *Anns* was overruled in *Murphy v. Brentwood District Council*, [1990] 3 W.L.R. 414 (H.L.). Specifically, it was held that *Anns* was wrongly decided in so far as it had allowed recovery for the cost of remedying structural defects after the defects had become manifest. This issue is discussed in chapter 23. The public authority immunity approach was not considered, probably because the case involved breach of a public duty rather than a challenge to statutory discretion. However, most of the speeches in *Murphy* express general reservations about the common law liability of public authorities. The House of Lords appears to favour extensive immunity, even in the case of breach of statutory public duties. If so, the law in Canada and England will diverge significantly. For a recent discussion of *Murphy* and its implications, see Hayes, "After *Murphy*: Building on the Consumer Protection Principle" (1992), 12 Ox. J. L. S. 112.

REVIEW PROBLEM

Harold is a fruit farmer who owns a number of peach and apple orchards in the Niagara peninsula. His orchards are next to a major provincial highway which receives the highest level of winter maintenance from the Works Department. As part of the maintenance program, the Department spreads large quantities of road salt on the highway whenever conditions are icy. The Department does not use sand for this purpose.

Harold can prove that when the Department's trucks pass his orchard applying road salt, some of the salt bounces onto his land. In addition, when the Department plows the roads, additional quantities of salt mixed with snow are pushed onto his orchards. However, the majority of the salt on his orchards is carried by water when the roadside snowbanks melt.

Over the years, a sufficient quantity of salt has accumulated on Harold's orchards to render a 30-foot strip of his land adjoining the highway useless for fruit production. The peach trees in this strip have withered and died, and the apple trees produce virtually no fruit.

The pertinent legislation is the Highway Maintenance Act. There is only one relevant section which reads: "The Provincial Works Department shall maintain all public highways and take all reasonable steps to ensure that motorists may obtain safe passage thereon at any time."

Is Harold likely to succeed in a tort suit against the Department in: (a) trespass; (b) negligence; (c) nuisance; or (d) under the rule in *Rylands v. Fletcher*? First, analyze these issues assuming that the Department is not a Crown agency. Second, analyze these issues assuming that the Department is a Crown agency, governed by the relevant legislation in your province. This probem is based on the case of *R. in Right of Ont. v. Schenck; R. in Right of Ont. v. Rokeby* (1984), 15 D.L.R. (4th) 320 (Ont. C.A.), aff'd. [1987] 2 S.C.R. 289.